THE 1980-81 EDITION OF AMERICA'S
MOST POPULAR MONEY-SAVING GUIDE

EUROPE
ON $15 A DAY

by ARTHUR FROMMER

with sightseeing commentaries by HOPE ARTHUR

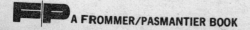
A FROMMER/PASMANTIER BOOK

Copyright © 1957, 1959, 1960, 1961, 1962, 1963, 1964, 1965, 1966, 1967, 1968, 1969, 1970, 1971, 1972, 1973, 1974, 1975, 1976, 1977, 1978, 1979, 1980

Published by The Frommer/Pasmantier Publishing Corporation
A Simon and Schuster Division of
Gulf & Western Corporation
380 Madison Avenue
New York, New York 10017

ISBN 0-671-25522-3
Library of Congress Catalog Card Number: 80-65209

Manufactured in the United States of America

Cover design by Lew Holloway

*KLM Royal Dutch Airlines has exercised no
editorial control over the choice of
establishments appearing in this book, or in
the comments made about them; the views of
the author are his alone.*

*Although every effort was made to insure the accuracy
of price information appearing in this book,
it should be kept in mind that prices
can and do fluctuate in the course of time.*

PREFACE TO
THE TWENTY-THIRD
YEARLY EDITION OF
EUROPE ON $15 A DAY

TWENTY-THREE YEARS AGO, under its earlier title, this book made its first appearance on the travel shelves of the nation's bookstores—and provoked something close to a minor riot. "Impossible!" cried one class of readers, as they spotted its name. *"Europe on $5 a Day?"*

"Is he crazy?" countered another. "I did it on $2 a day."

Now controversy was expected when this book appeared. But no one—not even my most Bohemian advisers—anticipated complaints that I had *over* priced the cost of a European vacation. And yet there came such letters: gentle, chiding letters, suggesting that the guide to a really low-cost vacation was yet to be written; regretful letters, stating it was such a shame I had missed that cute little hotel in Madrid where a room-plus-three-meals cost—at that time— $4.10 a day.

Among the hundreds of letters that readers have written, letters of the disappointed variety were happily few in number. But I mention the minority reaction to *Europe on $15 a Day* to prove a point. Fifteen dollars a day is no miracle budget for life in Europe. There is nothing fantastical about this book, or about the recommendations it contains. Mention its title to a European—or to an experienced American tourist—and they will ask what all the fuss is about.

Do you still doubt it? Do you wonder that travel on a strange continent can cost a fraction of the amount you'd spend in the United States? Thousands of Americans have come, seen, and been convinced. For an opening bit of proof, try the following letter from an Army captain and his wife, who were equally doubtful:

"Frankly, we took a rather jaundiced view of your book because of the sharp contrasts it offered to American vacation prices. Nevertheless, we took it with us on our first trip to Paris, which we regarded as the supreme test. We bought $400 in francs here in Nuremberg prior to departure, drove to Paris and back in our own car, stayed seven days, followed your book almost completely, and returned with $90 in francs . . . Our room at the Hotel Voltaire on the Left Bank cost $12 a night for the two of us, and while it was three flights up, it was a charming place with a little balcony that opened onto the Seine. We have a friend who is studying at the Sorbonne, and as we walked with him to lunch one day, we passed a sidestreet on which we recognized the Restaurant St. Michel from your book. We ate for $3.50 apiece among students and artists, and we had a wonderful time. Our friend, who has been in Paris for over a year, was amazed as to how we could have discovered such a true Parisian hangout . . . There were superb meals at the other restaurants you mentioned—meals that couldn't be found in the U.S. at three times the price—so as far as we're concerned, they can keep the Tour d'Argent and Maxim's."

The mail was literally filled with such experiences. There was, for instance, the middle-aged lady from Portland, Oregon, who found that she could stay near her beloved Tate Gallery in London, in a quaint and comfortable board-inghouse-hotel packed with other art enthusiasts, for only $9 a night. There were the honeymooners from Atlanta, Georgia, who had breakfast in bed for 10 francs ($2.30) in Nice. There was the co-ed from Radcliffe who was able to purchase a full-course meal in the price paradise of Madrid for less than she'd pay for an ice cream sundae at home.

To me, communications like these convey the best travel news of the year. They are evidence that after a decade of fear and bewilderment, Americans are finally and forcefully "wising up" about Europe.

In the years that followed the war, a legend spread about the cost of a European vacation. The story went that a heavy curtain had descended over the continent—a curtain composed of crisp, green travelers' checks. These checks came in wads thick as your fist, and they were said to peel away like the leaves of Fall. Believing the tale, Americans trudged without protest to the most expensive hotels and restaurants in Europe, reacted in horror and disgust when the bills came in, and created bad vacations for themselves and bad impressions for our nation overseas.

Well, it just wasn't so. While all the travel books advised American tourists to budget $50 a day for their trips in Europe, the average European tourist—the Frenchman, the Englishman, the Swiss—was enjoying a far better vacation at the rates and standards prescribed in this book. Fifty dollars a day for life in Europe? Why, some Europeans at that time considered themselves lucky to earn $50 a week!

But the most pitiful part of the average American vacation was not its price. By the mere act of overpaying, Americans robbed themselves of all the thrill and flavor of Europe. Invariably, they bought themselves into the most dreary hotels and restaurants—the most elegant bores—the most gold-plated clip joints—that Europe had to offer.

Who needs it? Who needs suffer the pink-and-porcelain "recreation lounges" of a de luxe class European hotel? Who needs the waltz competitions and the planned picnics of a Biarritz resort? Who but an ancient Victorian would prefer the cathedral quiet of the Restaurant Ritz to the briskness of a sidewalk Paris bistro? It is the tourist who lives inexpensively on his European vacation, who lives relaxed, who seeks out the European side of European life—it's that man who enjoys his European trip.

An ever-growing number of Americans have caught on to this secret of European travel. You'll spot them at the airports and on the homecoming Atlantic liners, as they eagerly swap stories of the exciting low-cost finds of their European tour. They engage in no endless monologues about an unending succession of overcharges and cheats. For them Europe was a fulfilling experience, because they dared to live as the Europeans do, and in return, encountered warmth and friendship wherever they went. The size of this group is reflected by the success of the first twenty-two editions of *Europe on $15 a Day,* and by the fact that it has now eclipsed in sales a better-known guidebook whose author believes that the best way to belittle a European hotel is to say that it "reeks of local color."

I've tried to keep faith with the readers of *Europe on $15 a Day* in this twenty-third edition. Europe has again been revisited, hotels reviewed, meals re-eaten, and at least four pairs of my shoes worn out. The result is a completely revised, expanded and up-to-date version of a book that has now carved out its own established niche in the world of travel, and will be issued, similarly revised, in every year to come. For aiding me to do this, my thanks go out to the tens of thousands of persons who gave such an eager, exciting reception to the earlier editions of *Europe on $15 a Day*. In their disdain for ostentation and their love of people, they are the truest diplomats our country has, and they have my everlasting admiration and affection.

I hope the readers of this new edition will enjoy the book as much as I've enjoyed researching and writing it. Travel, after all, is a marvelous thing. It's a time of your life when all the habits and obligations of daily existence are hurled aside, and the scope of your needs becomes no bigger than a suitcase. You emerge from familiar routine into a world where everything is unexpected, where even your language can no longer serve as a handy crutch. In that kind of setting, all the minutiae of life can fall away, an individual can finally know what he or she is all about—and find freedom.

To the discovery of that spirit of freedom, this book hopes to contribute. Have a good trip!

Arthur Frommer

New York, N.Y.
January, 1980

A FINAL NOTE FROM A.F.: I could not send this 1980-81 edition to press without acknowledging the indefatigable efforts of my associate, Nickolaus Lorey, in reviewing the accuracy of each factual assertion in this book. His contributions to this revision—in discovering new establishments worthy of recommendation, in commenting on current operations of existing recommended establishments, and his dogged, punctilious attention to detail and precision, the hallmark of this book—have been absolutely invaluable to me.

Europe on $15 a Day

The title of this book refers to a self-imposed allowance of $15 a day for basic living costs in Europe—that is, room and all three meals. That limit is normally maintained by spending no more than $6.50 per person for a double-occupancy room, $1.50 for breakfast, $2.50 for lunch, $3.50 or $4 for dinner. In countries where a free breakfast is provided with the room charge (England and Holland), the allocation for hotels can rise to $9-or-so for a single room, $16 to $17 for a double.

The cost of transportation within Europe, of sightseeing and entertainment, is not included in the $15 figure. Because of that, this book is not a guide to mere subsistence-level living, but deals instead with clean and comfortable accommodations that can be used with safety by persons of all ages and by both sexes.

A Modest Proposal

Numerous readers have written in to complain that this book, in its successive yearly expansions, has become too bulky for easy use in Europe. Some have suggested that I print it on perforated pages, or issue the book in three-ringed, loose leaf binder form, or simply split it into three or more separate volumes. Adoption of any of these proposals would necessarily require a substantial increase in the retail price of "Europe on $15 a Day," which is to me inconsistent with its theme and philosophy.

May I suggest the following? Each of our chapters begins on a right-hand page, and ends on a left-hand page. If you will carefully bend back the pages at the opening and end of a chapter, you will find that you can easily tear out that chapter intact, and then stuff it into pocket or purse for use in the city it covers. Although this may seem a somewhat mercenary suggestion on my part (because it results in the systematic destruction of this book), it is, I submit, a better idea than to adopt a format costing $10.95 or more per copy.

A Note to Readers

In the last edition of this book, I wrote that *Europe on $15 a Day* hoped to become "a clearing-house for the low-cost hotel and restaurant finds of its readers." As the pages of this edition indicate, hundreds of readers were delighted to take the hint. Their cost-saving choices and schemes make up the sections entitled "Readers' Selections" now found in each chapter.

In part, this book will continue to be a joint enterprise. If you've discovered an establishment which belongs on these pages, then write a letter about it to Arthur Frommer, 380 Madison Avenue, New York, New York 10017. Free copies of the next edition will be sent to all persons whose recommendations are printed as a "Readers' Selection."

A Small Disclaimer

Many thousands of hours of research are each year directed to insuring the accuracy of prices appearing in this book, and for the most part, we believe that we've succeeded in obtaining reliable up-to-date data. Nevertheless, prices do change in the course of time, and proprietors of establishments sometimes do change price policies in the course of a travel season. Therefore, it's fairly obvious that we cannot guarantee that each and every such price will remain unchanged during the lifetime of this edition.

CONTENTS

MAPS

To
my beloved
HOPE

Introduction

EUROPE ON $15 A DAY

The Reason Why

THIS IS A BOOK for American tourists who
a) own no oil wells in Texas
b) are unrelated to the Aga Khan
c) have never struck it rich in Las Vegas
and who *still* want to enjoy a wonderful European vacation.

This is also a book for Americans who would like, on their overseas trip, to see Europe and Europeans, and not simply other Americans.

Rarely has a travel book contained such information. For proof, let's examine a few.

I have one of the better-known European guidebooks before me as I write. This tome states that one really can't consider staying in Paris at hotels other than the Ritz, the Crillon or the Plaza Athenée (at $105 for room and bath). It recommends the elegant Tour d'Argent and Maxim's for your evening meal. It shudders at any form of European train transportation other than First Class. It maps out, in other words, the short quick road to insolvency that most American tourists have been traveling for years.

But money and economy are not the only areas in which the normal sources of travel information fall short. More often than not, the high-priced hotels and restaurants they recommend are the least-European, least-interesting and most-disappointing accommodations available to you.

Across the street from Terminal Station in Rome, for instance, stand five great continental hotels. These are the "name" establishments to which all the travel books and vacation pamphlets direct the American tourist. They attract no one else. Walk into one of these spots on a summer night in Rome, and you might just as well have never left home. English fills the air. Bridge games go on in the lobby. For $60 a day in the Eternal City, you have bought the equivalent of a Legion convention in Detroit.

Three blocks away, of course, are a host of smaller Italian hotels and pensions—uncrowded, quiet and inexpensive. These are the lodgings patronized by European tourists, who find rooms within them, clean and comfortable rooms, for prices ranging around $8 per person per night. Americans never hear of them. Because most guidebooks assume that every American carries with him gunny sacks of gold, Americans continue to crowd into the least satisfying hotels in Rome, while Europeans vacation comfortably, at one-fourth the price, just three blocks away.

Contrasts such as these, repeated all across the continent of Europe, have convinced me that there is a crying need for one American guidebook devoted to the inexpensive hotels, the inexpensive restaurants, the inexpensive methods of touring Europe. Such a book would collect, in one volume, all the "finds" of the continent: a Left Bank restaurant in Paris where a superb three-course dinner costs $3.45; a hotel in Florence, fronting the Arno River, where sunny and spacious rooms rent for $7.50 per person.

These finds exist, in abundance, in nearly every city of Europe. They exist because of the hard, unalterable fact that prices, wages and costs in many European countries are at least a third below those of the United States. It is a fact—check it if you will—that an experienced secretary in London can earn less than $160 a week. A young architect in Italy earns $190 a week. Yet these people travel, and travel well. They are able to vacation on limited costs because they know the rules of European living, and they know where to stay and where to eat.

The smart American can do the same. *I say that most of the major cities of Europe can still be traveled, adequately and well, for living costs per person (that is, room and board) of no more than $15 a day. I say that the same budget vacations which once thrilled the pre-war tourist are still available to the American who is willing to think and plan for himself.*

The items to be had for these cut-rate costs are surprising in their quality. Fifteen dollars a day is no mere survival budget: no one expects you to eat picnic lunches or sleep in a tent. The recommendations set forth in this book are designed for normal vacation living: tasty and filling restaurant meals, clean and comfortable hotel beds.

An inexpensive European vacation requires more, though, than lists of restaurants and hotels. You'll need transportation information, currency tips, menu translations, entertainment advice—a flock of other suggestions and aids. Here's how *Europe on $15 a Day* intends to set forth that information:

■ **Chapter 1,** immediately ahead, deals with the problem of getting to Europe. All the best price-cutting schemes are discussed—standby seats and "budget" fares, "apex," "super-apex," and the "public charter." The chapter then ends with a fast look at the cost of sea transportation.

■ **Chapter 2** expounds on the general theories of budget living in Europe —the broad rules and principles to be followed wherever you go. This chapter sets the stage for the more detailed information on specific cities which follows. It must be read in advance of those later chapters, because it explains the terminology that will be used and the assumptions that will be made.

■ **Chapters 3 through 19** are devoted to the major tourist centers of Europe: London, Paris, Brussels, Copenhagen, Stockholm, Oslo, Amsterdam, Munich, Vienna, Venice, Florence, Rome, Nice, Zurich, Berlin, Athens and Madrid. For each of these 17 cities, *Europe on $15 a Day* provides specific data on best buys in restaurants, hotels and entertainment. The book also tells you how to reach the establishments recommended. The city chapters are accompanied by maps showing the exact location of the hotels, restaurants and night spots described in the main body of the text.

■ **Chapter 20**—"A Tale of Many Cities"—fulfills a long-time ambition of mine to expand *Europe on $15 a Day* into a comprehensive, self-sufficient guide that need not be supplemented by another travel book. Here, we briefly survey sleeping and eating accommodations in more than one hundred smaller or more remote European cities, setting forth our recommendations of the best budget hotels and restaurants in each. The inclusion of this chapter is an interim step toward the day—next year, I hope—when many of these cities will be the subjects of individual chapters in this book.

■ **Chapter 21** provides capsule vocabularies in seven European languages —short lists of the words and phrases you'll need to make yourself understood, plus phonetic pronunciations of the same.

■ **Chapter 22** offers translations of the menus you'll encounter in seven European countries. Enough said.

■ **Chapter 23** contains a concise railway timetable of the major European expresses, giving their hours of departure and arrival in every major European city. The chapter also includes some hints on the science of European train travel—which you'll discover is quite an art.

■ **Chapter 24** tells you how and where to change your dollars into foreign currency. It ends with a set of tables showing current rates of exchange.

■ **Chapter 25** offers my wife Hope's advice on the articles of clothing that ought to be packed for a low-cost trip to Europe. You would not think that the contents of a suitcase can affect your expenses—but they do, vitally. Read Chapter 25 and learn why.

■ **Chapter 26** discusses a topic in which (judging from their letters) more and more of the readers of this book are showing interest—auto rentals. We'll discuss the cheapest methods of traveling by car in Europe, and all the other ramifications of this complex, tricky subject.

■ **Chapter 27** consists of a bargain shopping guide, disclosing the where-to-find-it details on my idea of the finest low-cost purchases—from Danish candlesticks to Italian gloves—available in Europe. Our main focus will be on items costing $6 and less.

■ And, finally, **Chapter 28** is for our higher-spending readers—luxury-oriented types willing to spend $25-or-so for a double room, up to $5 and $6 for meals. In this chapter, called "Europe on $20 a Day," we deal with higher-priced budget establishments in several major European cities.

Nearly all of the foregoing information was gathered in a basic, firsthand manner—on foot—by walking and searching, notebook in hand, through most of the urban centers of Europe.

I first came to Europe as a G.I., and took my three-day passes and leaves on a lot less than $15 a day. Many times since, I've returned as a civilian, with a little more cash on hand, but with the same aversion to clip joints, padded bills and other classic tourist traps. Europe has never lost its thrill for me, and I have never found that a bulging wallet is the key to an enjoyable European vacation.

On the contrary, the Europe I love is chiefly unavailable to the tourist who does overspend. Whenever I've strayed from the budget formula, and gone to a grand hotel or eaten in a Maxim's-type restaurant, I have soon discovered that my vacation had become self-conscious, fettered, and really quite dull. These high-priced establishments—created for the unthinking tourist—they are not "my" Europe, and they are not the Europe of all those Americans whose trip was a profound, living experience, rather than an unvarying series of guided tours and snapshots. If these comments seem insufferably dogmatic (and they certainly are!), then I simply hope that you will put me to my proof, and discover for yourself that traveling on a budget is not only done out of necessity, but—more important—because it is desirable.

One last word before we begin. You will find very little in this book about the sights of Europe you've come to see. That doesn't mean that your author looks upon a European vacation as consisting of nothing but hotels and restaurants. It is precisely because I believe that the daily mechanics of European living should take second place to the art and culture of that continent, that this book tries so hard to render those mechanical details as effortless as possible. That's a full-time task. Though occasionally I may break loose from the crass financial details, I make no effort to duplicate the more descriptive guidebooks of which the bookstores are so full.

And now we start. The first problem of a European vacation is getting there. For suggestions, see Chapter 1.

Chapter I

GETTING THERE

Go-Now Pay-Later and Assorted Gimmicks

MY VERY FIRST TRIP to Europe was made in the aluminum bucket-seat of an Army transport plane, filled with dank canvas knapsacks. Yet even under those unpromising conditions, the sight of the coast of Europe—which I had longed for years to see—was one of the great thrills of my life. Suddenly to be passing over tiny squares of manicured fields, above farm villages with ancient church steeples, and then to see the familiar landmarks of large cities, was like re-living a thousand novels and picture books.

Since that first Atlantic flight, I've repeated the process on many occasions and under radically-changed circumstances—the last time in a sleek four-engine jet, attended by blonde stewardesses who kept shoving plates of hot hors d'oeuvres at me. And yet, even as the supposedly blasé many-time traveler, I felt the same surge of excitement as the loudspeaker said that that line of surf in the distance was the coast of Europe. To leave one's job and one's cares behind, to step on a plane and hurtle overnight to an entirely different way of life, is an experience that never goes stale.

You've probably gathered from the above that I greatly enjoy the act of flying to Europe, and still become thrilled over the prospect of a trans-Atlantic flight. But how do the costs work out, and what are the best fares? That's a more sobering subject. The price of flying to Europe has never been cheaper in real terms, but never more difficult to comprehend and compute.

PLANE ECONOMICS: Time was when this chapter on transportation to Europe could consist of a few simple charts setting forth standard rates to various European capitals. Prior to 1980, all major airlines—other than tiny Icelandair and upstart Laker—belonged to the International Air Transport Association

("I.A.T.A."), which prescribed fares and periodically revised them, on a uniform basis for all its members. As a result, all I.A.T.A. airlines charged the same fares to the same cities.

Then came along a new U.S. President and his appointee to head the Civil Aeronautics Board, Dr. Alfred Kahn, and "deregulation" of international air fares began on a cataclysmic scale. Today, I.A.T.A. no longer prescribes uniform fares for international flights, and the setting of fares is either a matter for individual airline decision (in the case of Holland and the Benelux countries) or for bilateral negotiations between the U.S. and various European governments, country by country (in the case of most other European nations). To many destinations, an airline now proposes a fare structure. Another airline then files a competing and different fare structure. A process of jockeying occurs, which may, or may not, result in a uniform price structure for all airlines flying to that particular country. It all adds up to chaos—but often *beneficial* chaos for the alert traveller willing to study the various alternative plans and fares available to differing European nations.

To bring order out of confusion requires that we examine these air fares country by country, as we'll now proceed to do: please keep in mind, throughout, that none of the fares I'll quote is immutably fixed. They can be changed at will, and some may already have been changed by the time you read this chapter.

We're not citing all of the fares available to particular destinations, but only those of interest to the most cost-conscious of holiday travellers. Normal first class or economy fares, even normal excursion fares, are now of a level that should be avoided at all cost! The budget traveller will want to seek out low cost, promotional fares—and the key to finding them is usually the concept of "advance booking"—a willingness to make your travel plans, and to purchase your tickets, as far ahead as possible. More than half of the low cost trans-Atlantic fares are available only if purchased from 21 to 30 days in advance of departure. Moreover, since the number of seats allocated to low cost, "advance purchase" fares is severely limited (sometimes less than 25% of the capacity of a particular plane), it will often be the early bird who obtains the low cost seat, although this may not always be the case.

In any event, and hopefully without adding further confusion, here are the current, low cost air fare possibilities, as of the day and hour that this discussion is being dictated (4:20 p.m., December 27, 1979), and prior to a probable 7% increase that everyone expects in the first days of 1980!

Fares to Amsterdam

"The Air Ocean unites all Peoples." So said the late Albert Plesman, founder of **KLM Royal Dutch Airlines,** and with that declaration Holland became the first nation to endorse a policy of "freedom of the skies". For decades, the liberal Dutch followed the most liberal of aviation policies in allowing other airlines to land in Amsterdam, and in early 1979, they became the first European nation to permit U.S. air carriers to fly virtually at will to their home city, charging whatever rates they wished! In 1980, no fewer than four American airlines—**T.I.A., National, Braniff, World**—will be competing with KLM to Amsterdam in a free marketplace of transportation.

KLM itself will be fighting back with two particularly inexpensive individual air fares from New York (and similar ones from Chicago, Houston and Los Angeles): First, a "Dutch treat" fare, round-trip between New York and Amsterdam, of $445 in "basic season", $545 in "peak season" (eastbound, May 15 through September 14). With hardly any restrictions at all (tickets may be bought up to 24 hours ahead of departure), "Dutch Treat" will be confined to a limited number of seats per flight, sold on a first-come, first-served basis. More heavily available will be a bargain-priced "apex" (advance purchase excursion) fare, which must be booked at least 30 days in advance: $430 round-trip between New York and Amsterdam in "basic season", $500 in "peak".

National Airlines, which flies to Amsterdam from both New York and Miami, has matched the KLM excursion rate of $445 and $545, round-trip between New York and Amsterdam, but again for only a limited number of seats per flight. **Transamerica Airlines** has scheduled three flights a week from New York to Amsterdam, on Mondays, Wednesdays and Fridays, on which occasions every seat in the three planes (all being 254-seat-DC-8s) will be priced at $449, round-trip, in winter; $499 until mid-June; $549 thereafter, again round-trip. Starting May of 1980, a similar service to Amsterdam will be offered from Los Angeles, at yet-to-be determined rates.

From Boston and Dallas/Fort Worth, Braniff will be flying stand-by passengers to Amsterdam at rates, round-trip at "off-peak" times, of $344 (Boston) and $440 (Dallas/Fort Worth); simultaneously, it will offer "apex" fares, to be purchased 21 days in advance of departure, of $416 (Boston) and $599 (Dallas/Fort Worth), again, during the non-peak time of Sept. 15 to May 14; peak period Braniff rates are still to be determined as we write these lines. World Airways, another major contender, has not yet announced its air fares to Amsterdam as we go to press.

To Athens

On its flights from New York to Athens, **Olympic Airways** has set aside exactly 110 seats every Tuesday and Wednesday, except from June 16 to July 31 eastbound and August 16 to September 30 westbound, at a remarkable price of only $599, round-trip. On peak season summer dates, or on any dates when those $599 wonders are sold out, your next best bet will be an Apex ticket that must be purchased 21 days in advance. These will be priced, round-trip, at $685 basic season, $785 peak season. If you can't book that far in advance, or if all apex seats have been sold out, you'll simply have to purchase an excursion ticket (permitting 6-to-90-day stays) for $725 round-trip in basic season, $825 in peak season. **TWA,** America's flag carrier servicing Athens, has matched the Olympic air fare structure—including its $599 mid-week fare—in every respect.

To Brussels

To the capital of Belgium, **Capitol International Airways**—once purely a charter carrier, now also a scheduled carrier—offers a spectacular "Skysaver" fare of only $409, round-trip between New York and Brussels from late March through May, $459 from June the first onwards. That's for every seat of a DC-8 flying five times a week. No advance booking requirement, no minimum required stay. **Sabena,** the flag carrier of Belgium, which flies to Brussels from both New York and Atlanta, Georgia, has responded with a "Super Budget" air fare applicable to a portion of the seats on its flights: $401, round-trip between New York and Brussels in "basic" season, $458 in peak season (essentially, June, July and August). The same round-trips are $460 and $516, respectively, between Atlanta and Brussels. "Super Budget" seats must be purchased at least 15 days in advance of departure, and are subject to a 20% cancellation charge.

To Dublin

Aer Lingus (Irish International Airlines), matched by **TWA,** offers a "super apex" fare (to be purchased at least 21 days in advance), good for stays of 7 to 60 days. For a round-trip flight between New York and Shannon, the cost is presently $412 in "basic" season, $492 in the "peak" summer season; add $14 in summer if you're staying on to Dublin. There are flights, as well, from Boston (deduct $5 from all prices) and Chicago (add around $60).

To Frankfurt, Munich, Cologne, Hamburg

Lufthansa, Pan Am, Delta and **Braniff** provide the direct service from U.S. cities, and the key fare for cost-conscious travellers is Lufthansa's "Holiday Fare" (matched fairly closely by Pan Am) of $425 "low season", $491 "high season", round-trip between New York and Frankfurt, Hamburg or Cologne; $451 and $526, respectively, round-trip between New York and Munich. Ticket must be purchased at least 30 days before departure, the stay abroad can be from 14 to 60 days. A fairly-similar "apex" fare costs approximately $60 more in "low season", $95-or-so more in "high season"—the latter from May 14 to September 14.

Braniff flies to Germany from Dallas/Fort Worth and from Boston, and its major focus is on a "Budget Fare" (choose your week of departure three weeks in advance, learn the date of departure 7 to 14 days in advance): $450 winter, around $500 summer, round-trip between Dallas/Ft. Worth and Frankfurt; $354 winter, $426 summer, round-trip between Boston and Frankfurt. Alternatively, and for greater certainty of departure dates, Braniff's round-trip "Apex" fare is $609 off-season, as yet undetermined for summer, between Dallas/Ft. Worth and Frankfurt; $426 off season, around $550 summer, between Boston and Frankfurt. And finally, Braniff also offers stand-by possibilities to Germany for fares identical to its "Budget" rates. As for Delta, it services Frankfurt from Atlanta, at rates that are lowest on a standby basis: $370 and $426, basic and peak season respectively, between Atlanta and Germany's commercial capital.

To Geneva, Zurich

Swissair and **TWA** are the two major carriers flying direct, and "super-apex" air fares—purchased at least 21 days in advance, valid for stays of 14 to 60 days—are the way to go: $438 and $562, basic and peak seasons, respectively, round-trip between New York and Zurich or Geneva; $433 and $557 between Boston and the Swiss cities, $535 and $659 between Chicago and those cities. These rates are approximately $200 less than the next lowest-priced excursion fares to Switzerland.

To Lisbon

The "apex" air fare, which must be purchased at least 21 days in advance of departure, is $409 in "basic" season (November 1 to March 31), $442 "shoulder" season (April through mid-June, mid-August through October), $482 "peak" season, round-trip between New York/Boston and Lisbon. **TAP Portuguese Airways** and **TWA** are the carriers flying direct from U. S. cities.

To London

It's never been cheaper—and more complicated—to fly to London! We'll try to bring order out of confusion by classifying the fares according to their basic function:

Stand-by fares (total uncertainty)

First, every airline flying to London offers "stand-by" fares sold at the airport on the day of departure, and subject to availability. You simply take a chance, and run the risk of waiting for hours to be told if you're confirmed, and of being "stranded" for one to several days on the return leg of your trip.

If you're emotionally ready to hazard those risks, and your school or job schedule permits you to do so, then you'll fly to Europe at the lowest rates imaginable. **British Airways, Air India, Pan Am, TWA,** and **Iran Air** offer stand-by seats between New York and London at a round-trip price of $343 in basic season, $370 peak season (June through August). The same stand-by opportunities to London are available on **Delta** from Atlanta, Georgia, for $448 round-trip in peak season; on **Braniff** from Dallas for $400 round-trip in non-peak months; on **British Caledonian Airlines** from Houston for $440 round-trip in peak season; and on **National Airlines** from Miami for $518 round-trip in peak season.

Cheapest of the stand-by offerings is of course the New York-to-London **"Skytrain"** of Sir Freddie Laker, which started the entire trend. Here, a large number of seats are sold on a stand-by basis (on one DC-10 a day, supplemented by a second plane in summer) at a round-trip price of $299 between New York and London, approximately $409 between Los Angeles and London.

Budget fares (semi-uncertainty)

Introduced by **Pan Am,** and matched by **Air India, TWA, Delta** and **Braniff,** these can be less expensive—from some cities—than even a stand-by fare. And what you do is simply designate, at least 21 days in advance, the week when you wish to travel to London. At least 7 to 10 days in advance, the airline will then assign you to a particular date and flight within that week. You later repeat the process in England, for your return flight. Round-trip budget fares are as follows, low and high season respectively, between the following sample U.S. cities and London: New York, $343 and $370 (via Pan Am, Air India, TWA); Dallas, $400 and $530 (via Braniff); Atlanta, $366 and $448 (via Delta).

Super-apex fares (certainty)

Most heavily used fare to London is the "super-apex," known also (by British Airways) as the "Dollar Stretcher." It's valid for a stay abroad of from 7 to 180 days, must be purchased at least 21 days in advance of your outbound flight to London, and, with slight variations among airlines, is priced from New York, round-trip to London, at $417 in winter, $442 in "shoulder season" (generally, the months of May and September), at $528 in "peak" (June, July and August). The same fares are $10 less from Boston, $30 to $40 more from Chicago. What if all "super apex" seats are sold out (their capacity being limited)? You then ask for just-plain "apex", priced at from $40 to $50 above "super apex" levels; apart from price, their terms and conditions are identical. Super apex rates in peak season from still other cities: $551 round-trip between Miami and London (National Airlines), a still-to-be-determined rate of around $599 round-trip between Dallas and London (Braniff).

To Luxembourg

This one's easy: only **Icelandair** flies there direct (and sometimes non-stop) from the U.S. at a uniform price through May 16 of $230, one-way between New York and Luxembourg; $394 round-trip. Thereafter, round-trip rates increase to $475 in late May and September, to $575 at the height of the summer season. There are no restrictions or conditions whatever; every seat sells for the same price; and flights are also available from Baltimore and Chicago for only $20 to $34 more than from New York.

To Madrid

Iberia Airlines and **TWA** fly there directly from the U.S., and both offer "apex" (advance purchase excursion) air fares that must be purchased at least 21 days in advance of departure, for a stay in Spain (or Europe) of at least 7 to 60 days. Meet those requirements, and you'll pay $413 in "basic season" (November through March), $449 in "shoulder season" (April 1 through June 14, and August 15 through October 31), $490 in "peak season" (June 15 through August 14, eastbound), round-trip between New York and Madrid. Add $15 in shoulder and peak season for Iberia's flights from Miami to Madrid; add $20 each way for weekend flights. Normal excursion fares—the kind that don't require advance purchase—are approximately $200 more, round-trip.

To Paris

A spectacular new travel concept known as "Vacances" and offered by **Air France,** has revolutionized trans-Atlantic travel between New York and Paris. Quite simply, Air France has set aside four jumbo jet flights a week (Monday, Thursday, Friday, Saturday) for all-economy operation, with limited food service and other amenities, but with rates of only $398 round-trip between New York and Paris, probably increasing by about $100 in summer of 1980 (the decision hasn't been reached yet). Every seat in each of the three planes is sold at that price, and there are no advance booking or minimum stay requirements of any sort; it's simply "first come, first served"—but there are stiff penalties if you cancel or change the flight. "Vacances" flights are now available throughout the year; to match the rates they provide, **TWA** has set aside blocs of seats on several of its narrow-bodied 707s to Paris, at the same price of $398, round-trip, and again without booking restrictions. You simply phone up, and if there's still a seat at that price, you get it, on a non-refundable basis.

If "Vacances" seats, or Vacances-type seats, have been sold out by the time of your own decision (and obviously, they're selling fast), then your next best bet is to seek a "mid-week" fare on Air France's services from Chicago, Houston or Los Angeles to Paris; these operate on a somewhat similar basis to "Vacances" (no advance booking), but they're available only from those three cities, and only on Wednesdays and Thursdays. And if these are sold out, then you'll need to seek an "Apex" fare offered by all the airlines flying to France. These must be purchased at least 30 days in advance, for trips of 7 to 60 days' duration, and cost $460, round-trip between New York and Paris, in "basic season"; $520 peak season. And if those "Apex" seats are sold out, you'll then have to make do with a normal excursion air fare (minimum stay of 14 days, maximum of 45 days) costing $691 in basic season (approximately September through May), $801 in peak season (June, July and August).

Those are the fares from New York. From Boston, **Braniff** offers a "stand-by" air fare or "budget air fare" to Paris of $359 (basic season) and $525 (peak season); and from Dallas/Ft. Worth of $439 (basic season) and $610 peak season. On a non-standby, non-budget, and completely confirmed basis, you can purchase an "Apex" ticket from Braniff (30 days in advance) costing $380 (basic season) or $484 (peak season), round-trip between Boston and Paris; $495 and $629, respectively, between Dallas/Ft. Worth and Paris.

To Rome, Milan

Alitalia offers an "apex" fare, too: $567 in "basic season", $655 "peak", round-trip between New York and Rome, provided that the booking is made at least 21 days in advance of departure, for a trip lasting at least 7 days. But as we go to press, Alitalia is also reported to be considering a special mid-week fare, good for Tuesday, Wednesday and Thursday flights, and for a maximum of only 100 seats per flight, without advance booking requirements. Tentatively titled the "Flight Fantastic", it will cost $469 round-trip New York-Rome from April 1 to May 14, and from September 15 through October 31, rising to $588 round-trip between May 15 and September 14; but travel on the special fare will not be permitted from June 20 to July 10. If you can't book either the "apex" or "Flight Fantastic", you'll need to settle for a normal 14-to-90-day excursion fare costing $579, round-trip between New York and Rome in "basic season", $740 in peak season. Similar fares to Milan are generally about $40 less than to Rome. Expect to find **Pan Am** and **TWA,** which compete to Italy, matching the very same price concepts and fares.

To Scandinavia

SAS relies on a concept known as "Mini Fares", which work exactly the same as "Budget Fares": you choose the week of your departure at least 21 days in advance, and are then advised by SAS between 7 to 10 days before that week of your exact departure date and flight. You repeat the same process in the other direction. Round-trip "Mini Fares" between New York and all major Scandinavian gateways—Copenhagen, Oslo, Gothenburg, Stockholm—are exactly the same, regardless of the city to which you fly: $370 in "basic season" (September 15 to May 14), $438 in "peak season" (May 15 to September 14). A round-trip, 14-to-45-day "apex fare" of $500 (basic season), $634 (peak season), to be purchased 30 days in advance, provides your next best alternative. **Northwest Orient Airlines,** which flies to Copenhagen and Stockholm from Minneapolis/St. Paul, Detroit and New York, offers identical super-apex air fares and conditions from New York, which then cost $46 more from Detroit, $154 more from Minneapolis/St. Paul.

To Yugoslavia

Yugoslav Airlines, popularly known as "JAT", is the airline that flies direct from New York, using big, 376-passenger DC-10s. They depart Mondays and Fridays to Zagreb and Belgrade, Wednesdays to Ljubljana and Belgrade, and—rumor has it—they'll be introducing a non-stop service to Dubrovnik on another day of the week, shortly before the start of the summer, 1980 season.

All year around, JAT offers a round-trip "Budget Fare" of $532 between New York and Zagreb or Ljubljana, $575 between New York and Belgrade: you select the week when you want to travel at least three weeks in advance, purchase the seat, and are then informed by JAT at least 7 to 10 days in advance of departure of the exact date and flight they've assigned to you.

If you can't live with that kind of uncertainty, then you select a simple "excursion fare". These can be booked down to the day of departure and cost, round-trip, $540 to $570 in "winter" (Sept. 15 to May 14), $660 to $699 in "summer" (May 15 to Sept. 14). Trips must be of at least 14 days' duration, but no longer than 45 days in winter, 60 days in summer. Children and infants receive sharp reductions on "excursion fares", but not on "budget fares".

CHARTERS TO EUROPE: Though greatly diminished by "super-apex" competition, charters will be operated to most major European cities in the summer of 1980, at prices from $60 to $100 per person less than most super-apex rates. Travel agents are the source of information as to their dates of operation and availability. Since many observers believe that super apex seats will be sold out on numerous key dates, the charter alternative remains very much alive for the budget tourist.

GATEWAY: With the money question under control, you'll now want to plan the schedule of your trip and your travel itinerary. The scheduling part is easy. By far the great majority of trans-Atlantic flights leave in the evening, arrive in Europe the next morning, after you've had a night's sleep.

As for your itinerary, most trips to Europe are planned around a key "gateway"—a major city at which you'll either arrive, or from which you'll later depart on the return trip. It used to be that travel counselors advised choosing London, as the gateway, on the theory that the lack of a language barrier would ease you into European life by gradual degrees. But that ancient advice has little relevance to the travel conditions of modern-day Europe—particularly in such countries as Holland, where English is virtually a second language. Far more important than the number of persons who speak English is *how* they speak it—whether they do so with sincerity and warmth, thus enabling you to begin your trip in a pleasant and enjoyable manner. On that score, the Dutch rank high as one of the warmest, most outgoing people in Europe.

In choosing a gateway, it's obviously far better to rely on practical considerations, not clichés. You'll want, first, to begin your trip in a city that is conveniently located for a tour of the continent. For that purpose, I usually choose Amsterdam, which stands at the very entrance to the heartland of Europe—with Paris, Brussels and London just an hour away by plane, Frankfurt and Copenhagen less than an hour and a half away, Rome just two hours and ten minutes distant.

There are, in addition, several budget considerations that usually point to Amsterdam as your most advantageous gateway. For one thing, auto rental rates in Holland are generally acknowledged to be among the lowest in Europe. If, therefore, you've planned a trip by car through Europe, you can achieve substantial savings (sometimes as much as $70 on a 30-day trip) by picking up the car in Amsterdam. You can, in addition, purchase a European car, tax-free, at the famous "Ship-Side Showroom" located on the very grounds of Amsterdam International Airport. This unique auto agency will complete the arrangements for you in less than an hour after you've stepped off the plane—the purchase itself, issuance of all necessary papers, delivery of the car.

Finally, in choosing a departure point for your return trip to the U.S. or Canada, Amsterdam is probably once again your best bet. For, by common acknowledgment, its airport possesses the largest and cheapest Tax-Free Shopping Center on the continent. That means that just prior to flight time, you can stock up on a vast array of low-priced perfume, liquor, cameras, watches, jewelry and the like, and carry them not across the continent, but simply into

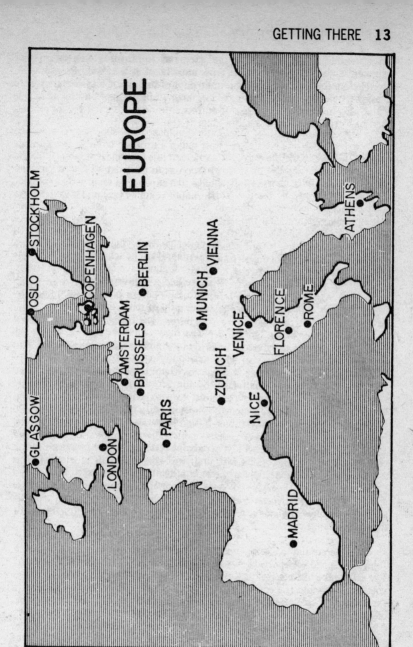

the plane!

TIPS ON SHIPS: So much for planes; we come now to the subject of sea transportation to Europe. But that form of travel, sad to say, must quickly be dismissed for budget-minded travellers. Even before the cost of oil caused heavy "fuel surcharges" to be added to the price, the charge for a one-way summer crossing in the most basic of sea accommodations had already topped $400. Even before the fuel crisis, shipline after shipline had announced that they were ceasing to operate trans-Atlantic. Thus, a memorable form of travel is no longer a realistic one for budget tourists to Europe, although it remains a "once-in-a-lifetime" experience for our more affluent readers.

FREIGHTERS: And for the most part, you can forget about these, too. With the exception of occasional ships leaving from Norfolk or Newport News, Virginia, the average freighter charges only about $35 less than a normal passenger liner for the one-way trip across the North Atlantic. Indeed, some freighters offer such luxurious accommodations to their eight or ten passengers that they actually charge *more* than the passenger liners. But even when you can save $35, you'll nearly double your travel time (most freighters take from 8 to 10 days to cross the Atlantic) and you'll also place yourself at the mercy of erratic and sporadic sailing schedules (some passengers wait a week in New York for their freighter to finally leave).

This is not to say that a freighter-crossing isn't a unique and satisfying experience. As a passenger, you'll receive unparalleled service, you'll have the run of the ship, and you'll form a fast camaraderie with the entire crew. If you have unlimited time, and want a relaxed, informal crossing, you might do well to take a freighter berth. One reader wrote me:

"For those few of us who are making the trip on money saved just prior to resignation from a job, and who, therefore, are limited only by monetary considerations, to spend the fourteen days required to move from New York to Copenhagen on a small Danish ship is to arrive in Europe partially Europeanized and completely exhausted from the daily social life that Danish crews and passengers seem to consider normal. More practically, for $370 you will receive accommodations that no passenger ship can furnish in even their luxury berths, and a completely personalized treatment from crew and agent. Of course no one who is subject to seasickness should attempt such a voyage, but for any others with unlimited time I heartily recommend this means of travel—especially if the ship is Danish."

Now you have the pros and cons. My own opinion remains as before, that if you are the normal vacationer, who wants to leave and return on a set date, and take only five or six days for the trip, you'd best pass up the freighters, for their financial advantages are slight.

We'll continue to assume you're going by plane. Logical starting point is John F. Kennedy Airport, New York. Want to start living like a $15-a-day'er? The 40-minute airlines bus to Kennedy charges a stiff $4 per person, to which you must also add the cost of getting to the air terminal (on 37th Street and 1st Avenue) to pick up the bus. A taxi from Manhattan to Kennedy Airport costs a minimum of $15, plus tip. To beat the system, take the IND subway ("E" or "F" train) to the Union Turnpike Station (50¢); then change, at the subway exit, to a Q-10 bus (50¢), which wanders through the borough of Queens for half an hour, but then shoots straight to the international departure area at Kennedy Airport in ten more minutes. Total cost is $1 and total elapsed time is 1 hour and 15 minutes, as compared with the 40 minutes you'd be in an airlines bus or taxi.

How to spend that time? By boning up on the General Theory of Inexpensive European Travel—expounded in the next chapter.

Chapter II

RULES OF THE GAME

The Basic Theory

THERE ARE RULES to traveling inexpensively in Europe. There are subtle ways of conducting yourself which should never vary, regardless of the particular European country in which you happen to be. Even such common habits as your attitude towards baths and breakfast can mean the difference between a budget vacation and a bankrupt one.

Sounds silly? Let's test the statement by examining an unheard of travel topic—the theory of baths—which can cut your costs by amazing amounts on every day of your European trip.

BATHS IN EUROPE: When an American registers at a European hotel and is asked if he wants a private bath with his room, his normal reaction is to answer, "Of course." By so doing, he immediately increases the cost of his hotel by more than 50%, and yet obtains essentially the same bath he could have had by answering "No." The reason is as follows:

Few Europeans regard a bath or shower as a daily necessity. The usual practice overseas is to start the day with a simple splash in the sink. Because of this, very few rooms in the lower-priced European hotels are equipped with private bath; and consequently, the rental charge for those rare rooms with bath is unusually high. I know of a large six-story hotel in high-priced Munich with over a hundred rooms, of which only nine have private baths. The rooms without bath in this hotel cost a reasonable $10 a night per person; the few rooms with bath cost $18 and up. The story is the same all over Europe—baths cost money. And moreover, insistence on a private bath will often make it impossible for you to stay in some of Europe's most delightful, and least expensive, budget lodgings—guesthouses and pensions, particularly—that sometimes have no rooms at all equipped with private bath.

This doesn't mean, however, that you must forego baths to travel inexpensively in Europe; you need only know where to take them. Virtually every hotel or other lodging in Europe maintains a room per floor solely as a private bath. To use that room, you ring for the chambermaid. She draws the bath, piles out large towels for your use, and you then pad across the hall in robe and slippers and splash away. In Germany, this costs one mark fifty (82¢). In Italy it costs about 60¢. By adding this charge to your hotel bill, you can have a room *and* bath for $7.60 per person, instead of a room *with* bath for $12. The room is the same in either case. The saving results from the simple act of walking across the hall.

Rule 1 of your European travels is, therefore, never to ask for a private bath with your hotel room. It is impossible to travel cheaply in Europe otherwise. The prices listed for hotel rooms in later chapters of this book are all for rooms without baths, but all in hotels or pensions where baths are available for a slight supplemental charge.

BREAKFASTS: Where and how you eat breakfast in Europe is another key to successful budget living. We start with these facts:

Outside of England and Holland, Europeans confine their morning meal to the so-called "continental breakfast," which consists of nothing but coffee and pastry or rolls. Poverty is not the reason. To a European, gorging on eggs, bacon and oatmeal at this hour would be nothing short of barbaric.

This will have an important effect upon your costs. Because European restaurants aren't geared to provide large breakfasts, the American-style meal of eggs-plus-all-the-trimmings will cost a small fortune. The same restaurant that serves a reasonably-priced lunch or dinner, will charge an outrageous sum for breakfast.

On the other hand, because the continental breakfast is so standardized and mass-consumed, it costs very little—provided you eat it in the right place. In France, for instance, nearly every cafe, bar or pastry shop sets up a coffee machine and a box of croissants (delicious, moon-shaped rolls) in the morning hours. This breakfast is identical to the one you'd be served in a restaurant or hotel dining room. The difference is that the coffee-and-croissants purchased in a Paris bar will cost about 80¢, while precisely the same meal will run to $2.25 in a hotel or restaurant. A similar price paradox exists in the rest of Europe, too.

All this adds up to the following tips. First, never enter a restaurant for breakfast in Europe. You'll find the same small continental breakfast available elsewhere (in bars and cafes) at one-third the price. Second, if you must have a large breakfast, try filling up on two or three continental breakfasts in place of the eggs and bacon. The latter will wreck your budget. If you can't stand that much coffee and that many rolls, try obtaining the additional foods at places other than restaurants. On my own trips to Italy, I usually take the continental breakfast in a bar or cafe, then stroll over to a market place for fruit and cheese—all for a few pennies. Try any of these alternatives. But whatever you eat, and however you do it, don't go to a restaurant for breakfast.

Disregard this advice in Holland and England, though. There, breakfast should always be eaten in the dining room of one's hotel, because the price of a Dutch or English hotel room always includes a *free* breakfast—and it's a whopper. For no extra price, you can have your fill of eggs, bacon, porridge, kippers, toast, jam and tea. More about this subject in our chapters on Amsterdam and London.

RESTAURANTS: Although succeeding chapters of this book provide specific names and addresses of good, inexpensive restaurants, there will still be times and occasions when you yourself must find a place to dine. Certain general restaurant tips are thus in order. Remember, first, never to patronize an establishment which doesn't display a menu in its window. That way, you can't possibly be overcharged once inside, or be handed a menu whose prices differ from those quoted to local residents.

Try, in addition, to discover restaurants which offer fixed price meals—that is, several courses for one lump sum, as opposed to the "à la carte" meal where you pay a separate sum for each individual dish. The cost of the fixed price dinner is considerably lower. Ask your waiter whether his restaurant serves a fixed price (in France, the "prix fixe," in Italy, the "prezzo fisso") dinner, for in many restaurants the fixed price menu will not automatically be handed to you. Search the menu for a possible cover charge. Particularly in France, you may find that the cover has catapulted the price on what had seemed to be a reasonable meal.

And finally, give thought to occasionally dispensing with a restaurant visit altogether, in favor of a do-it-yourself meal purchased from a grocery and eaten in a park or your hotel room. The delicatessen and food counters of Europe not only offer a means for saving money, but a chance to sample exotic and unforgettable foods. Indeed, once you've seen the colorful display cases of a French "charcuterie" (delicatessen), or the Chianti-selling-for-pennies in an Italian wine shop, you'll realize that picnic meals in Europe can be a supreme, but budget-priced, adventure.

FINDING A HOTEL: This, of course, is the make-or-break task of every one of your stops; the right choice, at the right price, can make the difference between your hating a city and loving it. Therefore, don't leap to find a hotel. However tired you may be from the trip, it is vitally important that you make a careful and deliberate study of several hotels before alighting at one. An hour spent at this job can result in several full days of pleasant consequences.

For the major cities of Europe, we've tried to eliminate most of the work by providing you with specific hotel descriptions and recommendations. For other cities not yet included in this book, the following is our "standard operating procedure":

Don't embark on the search laden with luggage. Either check your bags at the airport terminal or train station, or else leave them (and your travelmate) at a restaurant or cafe while you go out to look. Obviously, you need mobility and ease to make a proper selection.

Never rent a room sight unseen. On approaching each hotel, ask to see the rooms, and then check the bath and toilet facilities on each floor. Show a healthy regard for price. Let it be known that you are willing to proceed down the street if rooms are unavailable in your price range.

Naturally, you needn't become a disagreeable horse-trader in these dealings, or regard every hotel as an enemy to be out-foxed. Remember only that

in renting a room, you are making a purchase which, multiplied by the days of your stay, can amount to a hefty sum. The choice should receive the same thoughtful care that any equivalent purchase would get. By analogy, no self-respecting British tourist would step to a hotel counter, learn that a room is available, and then immediately sign the register, as so many American tourists are quick to do.

Check, too, to determine whether any extra charges are to be added to the basic room rent. Are taxes included? Is breakfast included? Is breakfast at the hotel obligatory? If breakfast at the hotel is not taken, is a penalty charge added to the hotel bill? (This amazing practice is actually far more prevalent at de luxe hotels than at budget ones.) If any difficulty in communication exists between you and the hotel clerk, have him write the price of your room on a piece of paper, and keep the notation for later proof.

Properly and courteously done, these requests will not even slightly offend a European hotel management. Instead, they will evoke a measure of respect similar to that which the champions of budget travel—the British—have been receiving for years.

NEVER JUDGE A HOTEL BY ITS COVER: One final note about judging a budget hotel: never be deterred by the exterior appearance of the hotel or by its lack of all those streetside touches that mark most American hotels—i.e., marquees, ground-floor lobbies, smartly-designed entrances. Many excellent European hotels just aren't built that way—and to prove my point, let me use an analogy.

There are millionaires in Italy, who live in buildings that resemble, from the outside, an 18th century warehouse; their walls are crumbling, ancient, peeling, cracked. Yet walk inside and you'll discover elegance unheard of—for Europeans value the architecture of the past and would never think of remodeling the exterior of a genuine period building.

The same with hotels. One particular budget choice of ours in Florence occupies the second floor of a loggia-enclosed building, constructed in the 18th century. Peer into the entrance and all you'll see is a dark, stone staircase, without decoration or amenities of any sort. But walk upstairs, and suddenly you'll be in a perfectly clean, charming and sunny hotel, whose rooms are as comfortable as any in Italy. You simply can not judge a European hotel by its exterior.

Then, too, some European hotels and pensions are located on the second and third floors of business buildings. The excellent Hotel Hemmet in Stockholm, for instance, looks—from the outside—like a collection of lofts, housing fly-by-night offices. But once again, walk upstairs and you'll find chintz curtains and a cozy lounge and rooms that would satisfy a D.A.R. member.

Always reserve judgment until you have actually seen the rooms. Get used to inspecting hotels that carry no outside markings other than a small plaque. Remember that you are in the Old World, whose surroundings and outlook are different from ours—and rejoice in that fact!

HOTEL RESERVATIONS: Do you need them? That depends on your own personal inclinations and travel habits, and upon a balancing of advantages against disadvantages.

The advantages of advance reservations are obvious. You arrive in a European city and immediately check into a hotel without fuss or bother. In some cities, at certain periods of the year, that can save a lot of hotel searching.

The disadvantages are equally obvious. By making advance reservations (which often require deposits), you necessarily must accept a fixed and unalterable schedule for your travels in Europe. You cannot, mid-trip, decide to lengthen or shorten your stay in a particular city without affecting the reservations you've made in other towns. And, of course, you must go through the process of writing ahead to many hotels, some of which may answer that they're fully booked.

For those who do want the certainty of a room at a particular hotel, there are several general rules to follow. First, remember that these are budget hotels, and that the cost of conducting an air-mail correspondence over reservations is a relatively heavy one for them. You must accompany your reservation request with at least 40¢ in "International Postal Response Coupons" available at any U.S. Post Office. Do not send American stamps, which are useless to a European hotel owner. Second, you must state an exact date of arrival and departure, and not simply an "on or about" estimate. And finally, be prepared to pay an advance deposit on your reservation, to be forfeited if you don't show up on the exact date you've stated (a hotel may hold your room vacant on that date, and thus lose the chance for other business).

For those readers who'd prefer to follow a looser schedule and itinerary, without reservations, I've tried to ease the task in the formulation of our hotel recommendations. In seeking hotels for this book, I seek clusters of hotels, so that if one hotel is full, readers may simply walk to another hotel, a few feet away. Although, in that manner, you may not end up in your preferred choice, you'll usually find a suitable budget hotel without too much difficulty, depending on the city and the time of year.

The $15-a-Day Plan

There is still a third alternative available to you—and that is to let someone else (an airline or travel agent) make reservations for you. But that, too, involves advantages and disadvantages.

Up until recently, few airlines or travel agents either wanted or were able to plan the trip of a budget tourist. The difficulty of handling budget business, and of dealing with low-cost European hotels, measured against the return, simply didn't warrant the effort.

Then along came KLM Royal Dutch Airlines with its now-famous "$15-a-Day Program" (which was inspired, I'm proud to say, by this book, and which is operated by Arthur Frommer International, Inc., of which I am owner). It constituted the first attempt by the organized travel industry to service the needs of true budget tourists, at costs that are almost—but not quite—as inexpensive as those prescribed in this book.

The KLM program is quite simple. All you need do is to stop in at any KLM office in the U.S. or Canada or at the office of a KLM-authorized travel agent, and tell them which European cities you plan to visit, and the number of days you plan to spend in each city. Then depending on your choice of cities or categories, you pay them $15 for every day of your stay. The $15 plan is available in 22 major European cities.

All the rest is done for you. In exchange for your $15-a-day payment, you'll receive confirmed reservations (for double-occupancy rooms without private bath) at budget-class European hotels or pensions similar to those recommended in this book. You'll also receive vouchers entitling you to bed and breakfast for every day that you spend at those hotels, and also entitling you to an introductory sightseeing tour in each of the cities on your itinerary in which your stay amounts to at least three nights. When you arrive in Europe, you simply hand the vouchers to the desk clerks at the hotels or pensions in which you've been booked—and that constitutes payment for your room and breakfast throughout your entire stay. No money of any kind need pass between you and the hotel—no service charges, no taxes, nothing. You also hand the vouchers to the city sightseeing companies in the cities on your itinerary, and that constitutes payment for the tours you receive from them.

Please note, however, that a KLM $15-a-day program does not always involve as inexpensive a method of traveling through Europe as that prescribed in this book. We seek to show you how to obtain your hotel room and all three meals for $15 a day. In contrast, the KLM program provides you only with room, breakfast and sightseeing in each city for $15 a day. Obviously, a part of the $15 payment you make to KLM goes to cover the cost of making advance reservations and of operating the program. It does not, therefore, constitute the least expensive way to travel through Europe, although it is undoubtedly the least expensive *pre-arranged* method of traveling through Europe. And in exchange for this slightly higher cost, you receive the convenience of having reservations and of being able to prepay your hotel, breakfast and sightseeing expenses. Supplement for a single room on the $15-a-day plan: $5 per day.

To sign on for a KLM "$15-a-day" tour, simply go to any KLM office or to a KLM travel agent, or—if you live in the East—to Arthur Frommer International, Inc., 380 Madison Avenue, New York 10017, which operates the program for KLM. If you'd like further details relating to the plan, write to KLM Royal Dutch Airlines, 437 Madison Avenue, New York, New York 10022, and they'll send you a free illustrated brochure. And obviously, if you'd like to keep your costs down to $15 a day for room and all three meals, do it yourself, using this book, either by making your own reservations, or by going without any reservations at all.

HOW TO USE THIS BOOK: We move from these general rules to specific details in the upcoming pages of this book. It's important that you know the form in which these facts will be presented.

Your housing needs come first. In those cities where the $15 budget is most easily adhered to, we'll provide names and addresses of hotels, pensions or guest houses where double rooms are available for from $13 to $15 without breakfast, for slightly more with. And we'll list establishments, too, offering single rooms at budget rates. In each case, the prices listed are for rooms without private baths. Except in Spain and Greece, where prices are so low that even the other variety is available at our level, insistence on a private bath will destroy the utility of this book.

Most city chapters also contain a list of at least a dozen good, but inexpensive, restaurants—the type charging (depending on the city) from $2.50 to $4 for an adequate meal. The aim, remember, is Europe on $15 a day, which means hotel for from $6.50 to $7 per person (using double occupancy rooms), breakfast for $1.50, lunch for $2.50, dinner for $3.50 or $4. But every city chapter will also sneak in a section entitled "Starvation Budget," showing you how to make it on a lot less. For comic relief, there'll be an occasional paragraph called "The Big Splurge," revealing the whereabouts of "luxury" meals that may run as high as $5 or $6.

Finally, this twenty-third edition of *Europe on $15 a Day* contains many hundreds of "Readers' Selections"—a term which refers to hotel and restaurant recommendations mailed in by readers. I have no doubt but that these choices may provide some of the most satisfying meals and rooms of your trip. At the same time, I cannot personally vouch for any of them, because the establishments listed as "Readers' Selections" are only those which I've been unable to see and try for myself. Rather than postpone their mention for a subsequent edition, I've included them now, untested except by the reader making the choice. But that's no small recommendation. Take it from me that the readers of this book are the most interesting, discerning and elite travelers of all who cross the Atlantic.

How much do the prices in this book change in the period before revised editions are issued? Not much at all. The point, you see, is to recommend hotels and restaurants which cater mainly to European tourists. These people simply won't tolerate sharp revisions in price, and their number is still far greater than the number of Americans who come overseas. In those few instances where European establishments have over-reacted to their mention in this book, they have been mercilessly yanked from this edition. That Parisian restaurant which put a copy of the book in its window, doubled its prices, and printed a separate menu in English, just won't be found in these newly revised pages.

THE $15-A-DAY TRAVEL CLUB: In just a few paragraphs you'll begin your explorations of the low-cost attractions of Europe. But before you do, you may want to learn about a device for saving money and determining value on *all* your trips. We refer, of course, to the now widely known **$15-a-Day Travel Club,** which has gone into its 16th successful year of operation. The Club was formed at the urging of numerous readers of the $$$-a-Day and Dollarwise Guides, who felt that such an organization could provide continuing travel information and a sense of community to budget-minded travelers in all parts of the world. And so it does!

In keeping with the budget concept, the membership fee is low and is immediately exceeded by the value of your benefits. Upon receipt of $10 (U.S. residents), $12 (Canadian and Mexican residents), or $14 (other foreign residents) in U.S. currency to cover one year's membership, we shall send all new members, by return mail (book rate), the following items:

(1) The latest edition of *any two* of the following books (please designate in your letter which two you wish to receive):

Europe on $15 a Day
Australia on $20 a Day
England and Scotland on $20 a Day
Greece and Yugoslavia on $15 & $20 a Day
Hawaii on $25 a Day
Ireland on $15 a Day
Israel on $15 & $20 a Day
Mexico and Guatemala on $10 & $15 a Day
New Zealand on $15 & $20 a Day
Scandinavia on $20 a Day
South America on $15 a Day
Spain and Morocco (plus the Canary Is.) on $10 & $15 a Day
Turkey on $10 & $15 a Day
Washington, D.C. on $25 a Day

Dollarwise Guide to the Caribbean (including Bermuda and the Bahamas)
Dollarwise Guide to Canada
Dollarwise Guide to Egypt
Dollarwise Guide to England and Scotland

Dollarwise Guide to France
Dollarwise Guide to Germany
Dollarwise Guide to Italy
Dollarwise Guide to Portugal (plus Madeira and the Azores)
Dollarwise Guide to California and Las Vegas
Dollarwise Guide to New England
Dollarwise Guide to the Southeast and New Orleans
(Dollarwise Guides discuss accommodations and facilities in all price ranges, with emphasis on the medium-priced.)

The Caribbean Bargain Book
(A one-of-a-kind guide to the "off-season" Caribbean—mid-April to mid-December—and the fabulous resorts that slash their rates from 20% to 60%; includes almost every island group in the Caribbean, and covers the Bahamas too.)

Where to Stay USA
(By the Council on International Educational Exchange, this extraordinary guide is the first to list accommodations in all 50 states that cost anywhere from $3 to $20 per night.)

(2) A copy of **Arthur Frommer's Guide to New York,** a newly revised pocket-size guide to hotels, restaurants, night spots, and sightseeing attractions in all price ranges throughout the New York area.

(3) A one-year subscription to the quarterly Club newsletter—**The Wonderful World of Budget Travel** (about which more below)—which keeps members up-to-date on fast-breaking developments in low-cost travel to all areas of the world.

(4) A voucher entitling you to a $5 discount on any Arthur Frommer International, Inc. tour booked by you through travel agents in the United States and Canada.

(5) Your personal membership card, which, once received, entitles you to purchase through the Club all Arthur Frommer Publications for a third to a half off their regular retail prices during the term of your membership.

Those are the immediate and definite benefits which can assure to members of the Club at this time. Further benefits, which it has been our continuing aim to achieve for members, are announced to members in *The Wonderful World of Budget Travel (WWBT)*. An eight-page, full-size newspaper, *WWBT* carries such continuing features as "The Traveler's Directory" (a list of members all over the world who are willing to provide hospitality to other members as they pass through their home cities) and "Share-a-Trip" (offers and requests from members for travel companions who can share costs); worldwide travel news and feature stories by our acclaimed expert travel writers; plus tips and articles on specific plans and methods for travel savings.

If you would like to join this hardy band of international budgeteers and participate in its exchange of travel information and hospitality, simply send your name and address, together with your membership fee of $10 (U.S. residents), $12 (Canadian and Mexican residents), or $14 (other foreign residents) in U.S. currency to: $15-a-Day Travel Club, Inc., 380 Madison Avenue, New York, NY 10017. And please remember to specify which *two* of the books in section (1) above you wish to receive in your initial package of members' benefits. Or, if you prefer, use the last page of this book, simply checking off the two books you select and enclosing $10, $12, or $14 in U.S. currency.

By this time, your plane has touched down at an airport in Europe. Customs clearance takes but a short while. Soon you'll emerge from the terminal exit, to a staging area where an airport bus (usual fare: about $3) waits to take you to the heart of your first city. You are now ready to start touring Europe—on $15 a day.

Chapter III

AMSTERDAM

The Surprising City

AS I STEPPED OUT of the airport bus, on my very first trip to Amsterdam, I expected to see a rather sleepy city, populated by plump, red-cheeked people who spent their time strolling along quaint canals.

What a surprise I had in store!

■ In no more than a few hours, I had passed restaurant after restaurant where dark-skinned, turbaned waiters were serving exotic dishes of the East Indies to residents and tourists alike.

■ I had walked through a massive amusement area—the famous "Rembrandtsplein"—where literally scores of cafes and cabarets were offering the kind of entertainment you expect to find only in Paris—but available here for one-third the price!

■ I had sat at sidewalk cafes in the student section where bearded young scholars were arguing the merits of op art and underground films.

■ I had seen the shops of chic couturiers standing side-by-side with open-air herring stands, at which lovely Dutch girls, in the most modern hairdos, were dipping chunks of raw fish into bowls of chopped-up onions and chomping away!

■ I had quaffed beer in a cafe on the 13th floor of a futuristic skyscraper overlooking the port of Amsterdam, and then descended in an elevator to an area, several square miles in size, where scarcely a building had changed since the 17th and 18th Centuries!

Amsterdam—as you've undoubtedly grasped from the above exposition—is a city of fantastic surprises, a place crammed with sights and activities that seem to bear not the slightest resemblance to the picture of tulips, cheese, and wooden shoes that most visitors expect to find.

That's not to say, of course, that the famed quaintness of Amsterdam doesn't still exist. There will be times when you round a corner to come upon one of the city's 50 canals, and to view one of its 500 bridges, and as you gaze upon the vista of quiet waters that flow between an unbroken line of trees and gabled old mansions, you will catch your breath at the sheer beauty of it all. And indeed, the massive central section of Amsterdam, whose architecture has been maintained unaltered for centuries, has been called "the largest open-air museum in the world."

But the predominant impression of Amsterdam is that of an active, throbbing, cosmopolitan city. It is, of course, one of the chief trading ports on the continent to which dozens of ships each month, from Indonesia, Dutch Guiana and other exotic lands, wend their way, through the North Sea Canal and then into the harbor at the heart of the city. These, together with all of the trains and planes that every day pour into Amsterdam, in staggering numbers, make it a true crossroads city—a Europe in miniature—and therefore an unbelievably exciting place.

A QUICK ORIENTATION: Amsterdam, in its physical aspect, is almost entirely a product of the so-called "Golden Age" of the Netherlands—that period in the 17th century when Holland surged to the near-pinnacle of world power, after its victory over Spain in the brutal Eighty Years War. It was during this period that the merchants of Amsterdam—then the dominant element in the city—laid out a pattern of gently-curving, concentric canals that occupy the central section of Amsterdam and constitute the city's particular glory today.

The canals run in a fairly regular pattern that makes it quite easy to orient yourself. Starting at the Central Station, the first of the canals is the **Singel**. Then comes the **Herengracht** ("Gentlemen's Canal"), then the **Keizersgracht** ("Emperor's Canal"), and finally the **Prinsengracht** ("Prince's Canal"). Along these canals the merchants of 17th-century Amsterdam constructed what seem today like endless lines of gilded, patrician mansions and homes. These have, in recent years, been occupied by business firms, but their façades are absolutely untouched—and it is in this most beautiful centuries-old setting that you'll want to spend most of your time in Amsterdam.

Crossing through this pattern of parallel, concentric canals, like the spokes of a wheel, are avenues, the most important of which is the **Damrak,** which starts at the **Central Station** and heads straight to the **Dam Square,** site of the Royal Palace, the Nieuwe Kerk (New Church), and National Monument. From the Dam Square, this street becomes the **Rokin,** and veers a bit as it heads to the **Mint Square** (Muntplein), where the famous old Mint Tower of Amsterdam stands, and where the Amstel River begins. Near the Mint Square is the **Rembrandtsplein** (Rembrandt's Square), one of the two major entertainment areas of Amsterdam; a bit further out, and to the west, is the **Leidseplein** (Leidse Square), the other entertainment section of Amsterdam, and site of the Stadsschouwburg (Municipal Theatre). And beyond this central area is a slightly more modern section where you'll find the three great art museums of Amsterdam—the renowned **Rijksmuseum,** the **Vincent van Gogh,** and **Stedelijk Museum**—as well as the famous home of its much-acclaimed orchestra, the **Concertgebouw.**

The trolleys of Amsterdam

In traversing this area, be sure to make use of the fabulous trolleys of Amsterdam, which race through the town at surprisingly short intervals, and offer unusual transfer privileges at no extra charge.

The Amsterdam streetcars are modern vehicles, each consisting of three connected cars which you enter at the back. They are virtually soundless in their operation, and comfortable to ride. The fare per trip is either 1.15, 1.35 or 1.60 Dutch guilders (58, 68 or 80 U.S. cents), depending on distance travelled, which includes the right to unlimited transfers or return trips within a one-to-two hour period, but few Amsterdammers buy single fares and neither should you; rather, you pay four guilders ($2) to the streetcar driver for a one-day ticket allowing you unlimited travel on the streetcars, buses or metro of Amsterdam for that length of time, or else you pay 6.25 or 7.50 guilders ($3.13 or $3.75) for a two-day or three-day ticket at the public transport information kiosk in front of the train station—tram drivers don't sell the longer-duration variety.

Every tram bears a number which indicates the route it follows. There are, in all, 15 such routes (and therefore 15 numbers), 10 of which travel to and from the Central Station.

Trams #1 and 2 start at the Central Station, go down the Nieuwe Zijds Voorburgwal over to the Spui, then turn down the Leidsestraat and travel the entire distance of that street to the Leidseplein; they cross the Leidseplein, but then take different routes: tram #1 goes down the Overtoom, while tram #2 heads in the direction of the Rijksmuseum, via the 1e C. Huygenstraat, then turns into the Willemsparkweg, goes along that street to Koninginneweg, and then proceeds the entire length of that street. Both trams also make the same trips in the opposite direction. To summarize their key stops: take either tram #1 or #2 to go to the **Leidseplein**; take tram #2 to go to a location near (but not at) the **Rijksmuseum**; take either tram to go to the **Centraal Station.**

Trams #5, 16, 24 and 25 also start at the Centraal Station, but travel down the Damrak and the Rokin to the Mint Square. At this point, they proceed straight down the entire length of the Vijzelstraat, cross the Singelgracht, and then take different routes. Tram #16 goes past the Van Moppes diamond factory, then over near the KLM bus terminal in the Museumplein, and then down the entire length of De Lairessestraat, passing near the Amsterdam Hilton Hotel. Trams #5 and #24 turn into Beethovenstraat, and afterwards go to the Zuid (south) Station of the Schiphol Airport railway line (#25), and along the Stadionweg to the Olympic Stadium (#5). Tram #25 heads down Ferdinand Bolstraat into Churchill Laan, and then down that lovely residential street. All three trams, of course, make the same trips in the opposite directions. Key points to remember: to get near the **KLM Bus Terminal**, take tram #16; to get from the KLM terminal to the inner and old city, take tram #16; to get to and from the **Hilton Hotel** (few budget-minded travelers will want to), take tram #16 to Corn. Schuytstraat.

Trams #4 and 9 also start at the Centraal Station, and travel down the length of the Damrak and Rokin into the Mint Square. At this point, both turn down the Reguliers Breestraat into the Rembrandtsplein, but then take different routes: tram #4 turns down the Utrechtsestraat to the Frederiksplein and the Congress Centre; tram #9 heads across the Amstel River past the Waterlooplein, then turns and travels in the direction of the Artis Zoo. **Tram #7** (which you can pick up on the Leidseplein) heads straight to the Amstel Railroad Station (which is not to be confused with the Centraal Station). All trolleys make the same trip in the other direction. To sum up the highlights:

take tram #4 or 9 to reach the **Rembrandtsplein;** take tram #4 for the **Frederiksplein;** take tram #9 for the **Artis Zoo;** take tram #7 for the **Amstel Station.**

Finally, **trams 13 and 17** start at the Centraal Station, travel along the N.Z. Voorburgwaal until they pass the Raadhuisstraat, turn into the Raadhuisstraat, ride past the Westerkerk (West Church), near which the Anne Frank house is located, and then continue on the Rozengracht out into the modern Western sector of the city. Then they make the return trip. Point to remember: to reach the Anne Frank house from the Centraal Station, take tram #13 or 17.

With these routes in mind, you can now find a room for your stay, in some of the most delightful lodgings that Europe offers:

CANAL-HOUSE HOTELS: The budget hotels of Amsterdam are like no others on earth. Located chiefly in canal houses of 17th and 18th century construction, they go up, not out. So narrow are these buildings that their stairways are like a ship's—thin little ledges that require a banister for support. On the outside of each house, you'll see an iron beam with pulley that juts over the roof. That's for hauling furniture and other heavy items—which simply can't be carried up the steep stairs!

But don't let the stairway situation discourage you; older tourists are always placed on the ground or lower floors, and younger or more vigorous ones will look upon the stairs as a sightseeing attraction!

Some other features of the budget hotels in Amsterdam: each of them serves a gigantic, free breakfast—just as the British hotels do—except that here the emphasis is not on bacon and eggs, but on cheese, ham, several different kinds of Dutch bread, butter, and milk. Always remember that every quoted hotel price, at a budget hotel in Amsterdam, includes a whopping big morning meal. And that price is often quoted as a per person rate—rather than for single or double rooms. A hotel in Amsterdam will often charge either twenty-three guilders per person, or twenty-five or twenty-eight, regardless of whether you occupy a single or double room.

We've grouped our hotel choices in Amsterdam according to price, beginning with the more expensive "big splurge" hotels, and then proceeding downwards, guilder-by-guilder. Obviously, our lowest-priced categories are composed of the very oldest canal houses, with the steepest stairs; but as we ascend in price, the stairs will flatten out (a little), the rooms will grow in size, and you'll discover that Amsterdam offers some of the best hotel values in Europe.

25 to 35 guilders ($12.50 to $17.50) per person, breakfast and service included

On the canals: We begin our search along the great, concentric canals that form the inner portion of Amsterdam: the Singel, Herengracht ("Gentlemen's Canal"), Keizersgracht ("Emperor's Canal"), Prinsengracht ("Prince's Canal"), and Stadhouderskade. Loveliest and most elegant of these (and with the most consistent 17th Century architecture) is the patrician Herengracht, on which a former recommendation of ours—the stylish **Hotel Ambassade,** 341 Herengracht (phone 26-23-33)—has sadly departed the budget scene through embellishments, refurbishing and price increases that now render most of its rooms just a touch too high for our budget. But on that same elegant canal, and quite charming with its potted plants and other authentic touches, is the

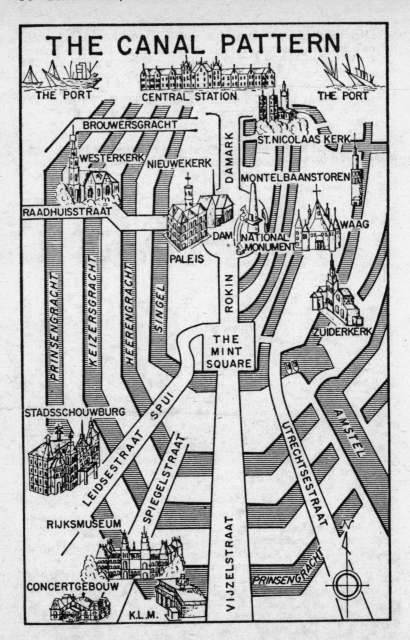

THE CANAL PATTERN

superbly-located but pricey **Hotel Hegra,** 269 Herengracht (phone 23-53-48), built in 1656, no less, with 11 rooms, of which three bathless ones rent for 36 guilders per person, with breakfast and service included, 42 guilders for the nine rooms with private shower. This, again, is on an awesomely beautiful water-way, and bears numerous features of traditional Dutch decor and architecture. If the Hegra can't take you, then, on the almost-as-lovely Prinsengracht, near-by, you'll find a very adequate and less costly substitute in the **Hotel Prinsen-hof**, 810 Prinsengracht (phone 23-17-72), with its beautiful, big, old rooms with beamed ceilings and wall-to-wall carpets. The price here is 27.50 guilders ($13.75) per person in double rooms, 35 guilders single, and the breakfast features four kinds of bread, a boiled egg, cheese and jam. No rooms with private bath or shower, but of course you can't expect that in a 17th Century merchant's house. And don't hesitate to stay in the cozy, top-floor rooms, to which your luggage will be transported via pulley!

On the quiet Leidsegracht (the "Leidse Canal"), a short walk from the important Leidseplein ("Leidse Square", one of the two major entertainment areas of Amsterdam), you should be well-pleased with the **Hotel De Leydsche Hof**, 14 Leidsegracht (tel: 23-21-48), where most rooms rent for 28 to 30 guilders per person (with nearby baths and showers always available at no extra charge), including an all-you-can-eat buffet breakfast, service charge and tax. A beautiful oak staircase here, unusually large wood-paneled rooms, and baby cots available for children (with special prices for children, too). Highly recom-mended. Nearby, the **Hotel Brabant**, 111 Leidsegracht (tel: 23-26-83), is an alternative choice, if the De Leydsche Hof is full. The price per person here can be as low as (but can be higher than) 30 to 35 guilders, including—as in all these hotels—breakfast and service charge.

Ranking close to the Brabant is the **Hotel Beekhof-de la Haye**, at 114 Leidsegracht (tel: 24-40-44), on the same lovely canal just off the important Leidseplein, where the Opera House and many cafes of Amsterdam are to be found. This is a solid, family-style establishment, with sparkling clean accom-modations, delicious breakfasts, a proprietress who sometimes puts fresh flow-ers in your room—and rates of 30 guilders per person, breakfast, service and tax included. A short, three blocks away, **Het Witte Huis Hotel**, at 382 Marnixstraat (phone 25-07-77), offers 24 far less expensive rooms (16 singles and 8 doubles) at 30 guilders ($15) single, 25 guilders ($12.50) per person double or twin, including a remarkable breakfast of coffee, tea or milk, an egg, cheese, ham, sausage, marmelade, chocolate-spread and four types of bread (2 slices of white, 1 each of brown and biscuit bread). Owner is Mr. Klaassen, speaking excellent English, and a supplement of only 12 guilders ($6) is charged for a third bed in a twin room.

There are other canalside establishments that compete quite closely, begin-ning with several on that stretch of the broad canal that encircles the inner city of Amsterdam and is called the Stadhouderskade; on it, near the Heineken Brewery but almost equally near to the Rijksmuseum, is a solid old home with stained glass doors, a marble entrance, and red Persian carpets, all housing the once-elegant, now moderately-priced, **Hotel Linda**, 131 Stadhouderskade (phone 72-56-68), where 30 guilders per person brings you the works including service charge (but without private bath), in rooms that are, if anything, over-furnished. If the Linda is full, as it often is, try the barely less expensive (28 guilders per person) **Hotel l'Esperance** at 49 Stadhouderskade (phone 71-40-49), whose managers, Mr. and Mrs. DeZeeuw, have been unusually cordial to readers, and provide large, carpeted, cheery rooms. For both hotels, take tram #16 or 24 from the Centraal Station.

One of the tiniest of the city's canal houses, but full of warmth and fellowship, is the **Hotel van Hulssen**, 108 Bloemgracht (phone 26-58-01), a few steps away from several earlier recommendations. While the van Hulssen hasn't the style of the higher-priced houses, the charm of its proprietor—Mr.

Loak van Onna, a consummate Dutchman—makes up for much—and Mr. van Onna's charge is only 28 guilders per person, including breakfast, service and tax. A few doors away, Mr. van Onna's second hostelry, the 25-bed **Hotel van Onna,** at 102 Bloemgracht (phone 26-58-01), reflects some of the same intimate warmth of this ancient section of Amsterdam (it also offers central heating), charges the same 28 guilders per person in singles, doubles or triples, all included. Take trams numbers 13 or 17, four stops (and three minutes) from the central railroad station.

Again on the Prinsengracht, but this time at no. 328, fairly close to the Central Station and the Anne Frank House, is the 38-room (that's large for a canal house) **Hotel Wiechmann** (tel: 22-54-10), whose American owner, Ted Boddy (from Oklahoma), has somehow taught his Dutch wife to speak English with an absolutely authentic U.S. accent! His charge for bed, breakfast and service in most rooms is 30 guilders per person (but there are some smaller rooms for 25 guilders, some with private shower for 37.50 guilders), and his breakfast is one of the best in Amsterdam: Dutch currant bread, white bread, wheat bread, a rusk, honey cake, a soft-boiled egg, a slice of breakfast cheese, coffee or tea, and of course plenty of butter, jam or marmalade. The establishment, as you'd expect, is quite popular, and you'd be advised to reserve more than three weeks in advance, although a phone call on the day before your arrival can also sometimes turn the trick.

A somewhat similar canal house, cleverly called **"Het (The) Canal House"**, has recently been installed in a 17th century home at 148 Keizersgracht (phone 22-51-82), and rooms in it will rent in 1980 for 35 guilders per person, including breakfast and service, no bath; I wandered through just before its opening, and was favorably impressed with the manner in which this well-located waterside mansion was being converted into a hotel: beamed ceilings remain in several guest rooms, the ballroom has become a breakfast room-lounge, a pleasant garden is available for sunning and strolls; and owner is a congenial American-turned-Amsterdammer, Len Irwin, who has made a career of operating pleasant budget hotels in Holland.

Off the Canals: The land-locked choices, in this price category, begin (in order of preference) in the area of the Concertgebouw and KLM Air Terminal, where the quiet and rather intimate guesthouse of **Mrs. Bakker-Stoit** (it's called "Huize Bakker-Stoit," and puts on all sorts of cordial services for guests), 81 Nic. Maesstraat (phone 79-89-09), is a top choice at this price: exactly 25 guilders per person in double rooms, 27.50 in singles, including breakfast and service. There's a small garden out back, balconies for sitting, babysitting available.

Another major cluster of $12.50-to-$15-a-night hotels is found on the Damrak, just a few steps from the Centraal Station. I particularly like the **Hotel van Gelder,** up a seemingly-endless flight of near-perpendicular stairs at 34 Damrak (tel: 24-78-79); you'll be surprised at how nice the hotel is, once you've reached its upstairs lobby. Per person rate is 30 guilders ($15) a night, including breakfast, service and tax, in all months other than the winter ones. Several other budget hotels are a few doors in either direction.

In a quiet, residential neighborhood beyond the Rijksmuseum, the 23-bed **Hotel Casa Cara** at 24 Emmastraat (phone 72-31-35) receives high marks for cleanliness, rates and careful management by a charming, young couple, Mr. and Mrs. Kerkhof. They charge 33 guilders ($16.50) single, 52 guilders ($26) for a double, 90 guilders ($45), including a hearty Dutch breakfast and free showers. Take tram 2 or 16 from the center, to the Emmastraat stop.

Finally, an entire group of 25 to 35 guilder hotels is found in a string of Victorian-looking, apartment-house-type buildings on the Jan Luykenstraat, which runs along the side of the Rijksmuseum, and is a perfect location for tourists wishing to spend a good deal of time at that institution. The **Hotel Acro**, 42 Jan Luykenstraat (tel: 72-55-38), is one of the best of these, with heavily-furnished, large rooms (most with radios) and a dining hall in "Old Dutch style." Most rooms here rent for slightly under 30 guilders per person, double, and there are four-bedded dorms costing only 28 guilders per person, eight-bedded dorms renting at only 19 guilders per bed, with breakfast and all else included. Astonishingly, too, there's an elevator. Highest recommendation. Alternatively, try the **Hotel Museumzicht**, 22 Jan Luykenstraat (tel: 71-29-54), which charges 24 guilders per adult (all included) for some of its rooms; or the nice **Hotel Aalders**, 15 Jan Luykenstraat (tel: 72-01-16), whose much costlier rooms (several are quite large) are generally 35 guilders per person, breakfast included. Other hotels on the same street offer rates that hover about the 25 to 28 guilder mark, and all these hotels can be reached via the #2 tram from the Centraal Station.

22.50 to 25 guilders ($11.25 to $12.50) per person, breakfast and service included

A canal house somewhat more basic than others we've named, but with exceptionally friendly proprietors (Mr. and Mrs. Peter de Vries), is the **Hotel Keizershof**, 630 Keizersgracht (between Leidsestraat and Vijzelstraat, tel: 22-28-55), with charges of 25 to 28 guilders per person per night (double occupancy), breakfast service, and free showers included. Again the hotel is in a 17th Century building, this time furnished with piano, tv, soft leather chairs—and with a peaceful, little beflowered backyard—particularly suitable for older tourists.

The **Hotel Fantasia,** at 16 Nieuwe Keizersgracht (phone 23-82-59), is still another large canal house, as canal houses go, located only 50 yards from the most broad and beautiful portion of the Amstel River, near the famous "Skinny Bridge" ("de Magere Brug"). It has 20 rooms that can accommodate up to 40 or 45 persons, and most of them rent for 25 guilders per person, including breakfast, service, and tax. This is an excellent hotel for *groups*.

In the area of the Central Station, and also near the Dam Square, **Hotel Beursstraat,** at #9 Beursstraat, occupies an excellent location, provides showers for free, throws in a soft-boiled egg when serving continental breakfast (always included in the price of rooms), and charges an extremely reasonable 15 guilders ($7.50) per person for a very large room with seven beds, 20 guilders ($10) per person in triples, 22.50 guilders ($11.25) in doubles; it also rents six small "apartments" housing four to six persons apiece (and thus ideal for large families and groups), containing kitchenettes and the like, four rooms per apartment, for 20 guilders ($10) per person, this time not including breakfast. The linguistic Mr. Jaromir Panyrek (six languages, each with total, accentless fluency) is the friendly, competent manager.

Much further out, in a pleasant and quiet residential area near the Zoo, the **Hotel Olszewski** at 87 Plantage Muidergracht (phone 23-62-41), is owned and managed by a friendly but somewhat strict retired police officer of Polish descent, Viktor Olszewski, who rents bathless rooms (showers are free) at 30 guilders ($15) per single, 25 guilders ($12.50) per person double, 27.50 guilders ($13.75) per person for twin beds, all in well-furnished and impeccably clean rooms—but ones in which you can't hold a noisy party at night (you'll be asked to leave the next day)! There's also a 1:15 a.m. curfew. And downstairs, the lounge and bar is decorated with flags, badges and postcards from fellow police officers all over the world. Here's one for readers seeking order and security in a turbulent world.

22 to 24 guilders ($11 to $12) per person, breakfast and service included

An entire collection of extremely cheap hotels (again with near-perpendicular stairs, but satisfactory rooms) is found in an almost unbroken line, comprising half a dozen establishments, on the Raadhuisstraat—which is a three-minute walk from the Dam Square, between the Herengracht and the Keizersgracht. My favorite here is the **Hotel Westertoren**, 35B Raadhuisstraat (tel: 24-46-39), owned by a young Dutch-American couple (he's from Boston), Alan and Sigrid Grusd, both excellent hosts who make a point of explaining the history and layout of the city to their guests. Their charge per person is 22 guilders per night; and their hotel is best for use in the off-season, when the central heating and the Dutch TV are both on full blast, and Alan and Sigrid can give you their full attention and advice. The several other hotels on this street charge, with some exceptions, slightly more—as, for example, the **Hotel Galerij,** 43 Raadhuisstraat (tel: 24-88-51) (27.50 guilders per person for bed and breakfast); the **Hotel Ronnie,** 41 Raadhuisstraat (tel: 24-28-21) (22.50 guilders for bed, breakfast, service and tax); the **Hotel Pax,** 37c Raadhuisstraat (phone 24-97-35; English speaking owners, and similar in price—22 guilders per person—to the others).

15 to 21 guilders ($7.50 to $10.50) per person, breakfast (some times) and service included

Now the price is again lower, but the location is the lovely Herengracht, where the **Hotel Groot,** an old canal house at 137 Herengracht (phone 24-70-51), charges only 20 guilders ($10) per person, and provides reasonably acceptable rooms, as well as central heating and a family atmosphere. Recently, the Groot's new management sent me an inch-thick batch of xeroxed pages from their guestbook, recording poems and paeans of praise: "It's Great at the Groot." "We had a few Hoots . . . At the Hotel Groots." "We got quite a fright . . . When we saw the first flight . . . But . . ." So, with fingers crossed, I've restored the inexpensive Groot to these pages, in the hope that previously grumpy attitudes by the management have improved.

Again in the heart of the city, but for young tourists mainly, the magnificently-located and much better **Hotel de Beurs,** at 7 Beursstraat (one block from American Express, just off the Damrak), phone 22-07-41, with 80 beds, is primarily a 20-guilder-per-person establishment (including free showers, but without breakfast). Beds here are cots (but with good, innerspring mattresses), and most are arranged four or five to a room; but the hotel is light and cheerful, the proprietress is a motherly woman who maintains a color TV set in the lounge of the hotel, downstairs; and the location (just a short walk from the Central Station) is a marvelous one, even though not on a canal.

Hotel Rambler, at 27 Roemer Visscherstraat (phone 18-84-79), in the area of the museums and near the Vondelpark, was built for a rich family in 1892, then converted into a budget hotel without alterations to the facade. Rooms are simple, but clean and cheap: 18.50 to 24 guilders ($9.25 to $12) per person, depending on whether you occupy a six-to-eight bedded dorm (18.50 guilders), a four-bedded room (22 guilders) or a twin-bedded double (24 guilders per person); there are no singles. Highly recommended for the value it provides, especially since the price includes breakfast, served in a basement canteen/

lounge where a two-course, 6-guilder ($3) dinner is offered at other times of the day.

For reservations at the Rambler, phone or visit when you arrive in Amsterdam; the hotel does not have the facilities to respond to reservation letters. And if the Rambler is full, then try the little **Hotel Brian** at 69 Singel (phone 24-46-61), which charges 21 guilders per person for top floor rooms, with bacon-and-egg breakfast included, no less. Here, there's only cold running water in the rooms, but unlimited hot water in the bathrooms, and the hotel itself is as much a scene as a hotel: Bob Marley posters in the lobby, rock music playing, and hip young owners—Jopsie Colle and Bob Brimicombe—in *High Times* t-shirts. Also simple, but really quite pleasant, is the **Hotel Venix** at 27 Singel (phone 23-75-60), at 12 guilders—that's right, 12 guilders—no breakfast. A last possibility on the same stretch of the Singel: **Hotel J. Kuit,** at 15 Singel (phone 26-31-08), 15 guilders per person without breakfast (optional, at 4.50 guilders more), and some rooms with lace curtains on windows with flower boxes, overlooking the canal.

Bed and breakfast for 12 guilders ($6) per person

Almost directly on the waterfront, near the Centraal Station, the 450-bed **Hotel Schreierstoren,** 10 Geldersekade (phone 22-43-70), bills itself as a youth hotel, and is heavily patronized by students, but not strictly limited to them—there is, in particular, no official student status to the establishment. These are, however, primarily dormitory accommodations using double-decker iron beds (8 to 14 persons per room), all in a fairly institutional, barracks-like setting of fluorescent lighting and the like; and there's a curfew of 2:30 a.m. every night including Saturday. The breakfast (three guilders extra) is a good one (bread-meat-cheese-egg-jam), there's a bar-discotheque where you can dance, and you can't beat the 12-guilder price. Just don't expect the Ritz!

The Specialty Hotels

There remain to be considered the "specialty" hotels of Amsterdam:

(1) A hotel for ministers

The **Hospice San Luchesio,** 9 Waldeck Pyrmontlaan (tel: 71-68-61), which can be reached by taking tram #2 to the Amstelveenseweg stop, is a modernistic, big-windowed building built in 1961 by the Third Order of Saint Francis for the accommodation of both Roman Catholic and Protestant clergymen (and their families), as well as members of religious orders. It has 31 rooms (20 singles, 11 doubles), each with private shower, a recreation room—and seven altars for daily Mass! The cost per person, including breakfast: 27.50 guilders ($13.75).

(2) Hotels for students

There are many of these, for Amsterdam ranks with Paris in the variety and number of its student housing facilities—indeed, no other city in Europe touches these two in that regard. And leading the list is the recently-renovated (and therefore relatively expensive—24 guilders per person for triple or 4-bedded rooms with "semi-private" shower) **Hans Brinker Stutel** at 136 Kerkstraat (phone 220-687), which surely must rank among the continent's finest student lodgings. Ingeniously re-created out of a former in-city monastery, in a marvelously central location just a 5-minute walk from the Leidseplein, the

"Stutel" has a capacity of 250 beds, in a configuration that places one private shower between every two rooms. If you're concerned about such things, you'll have to carefully lock the door to the adjoining room before stripping to the buff! There's a large garden with a terrace, a restaurant, a late night student bar, two dormitory rooms in which rates descend to 20 guilders and less, and a large student travel office across the street. Rates include breakfast, service and tax.

The largest of the student lodgings (second in preference only to the Hans Brinker "Stutel") is the **Hotel Cok,** 30 Koninginneweg (tel: 72-80-95), which is not to be confused with several other hotels bearing the name Cok—this one is an imposing mansion on grounds of its own, 15 minutes by trolley from the Centraal Station (take tram #2 from the station, which passes directly in front of the door and stops a block away). Inside, the rooms are not nearly as imposing—they are almost all dormitories in style—but there are 180 beds available, which rent in 1980 for as little as 22 guilders ($11) per person in 7 to 8 bedded rooms, including breakfast, service and all taxes. Next door is a spectacular new annex (the self-styled "Young Budget Hotel," brightly decorated) with 200 additional beds renting for the same price, but with considerably upgraded, modern comforts. In both buildings lunch is 7.50 guilders, dinner 11.50. Bar, restaurant, and laundry facilities are available. A similar and cheaper dormitory-type establishment is the comfortable **Hotel Adolesce,** 26 Nieuwe Keizersgracht (tel: 26-39-59), where students pay 16 guilders ($8) a night for one of 130 available bunks, breakfast and service included; 21 guilders ($10.50) for normal rooms.

Much of the overflow from these three major establishments goes to the generally-less-expensive **Kabul Budget Hotel** at 42 Warmoesstraat (phone 23-71-58), only 100 yards from the front of the central railroad station, in a far more congested area of Amsterdam, and on a narrow, narrow street. Here, multi-bedded rooms are 15 to 19 guilders a night (depending on the number of beds in them), breakfast is 5 guilders extra, and there's a pleasant self-service restaurant and recreation room. Only if the Kabul is full should you try two less-attractive student hangouts in the same area: first, the quaint **Last Waterhole** in the midst of the red-light district, near the station at 12 Oude Zijds Armsteeg, charging 12 guilders for dormitory beds (some dorms are co-ed), in rooms with 18 beds, 4 guilders for key to a private locker, rates including showers. A bar/disco on the main floor has live rock, much of it punk, and occasionally folk or bluegrass. Then, return to the narrow Warmoesstraat, which runs between the station and the Dam Square, and at #91 (phone 24-14-06), over a dark, atmospheric bar where the sounds of rock blend with the din of countless pinball machines, you'll find the 10-guilder-a-night ($5) **Parima Hotel** offering dorms at that unusually low price, but without breakfast. . . . For additional student hotels (and there are more), consult the V.V.V. . . . A final, pleasant surprise: the student hotels of Amsterdam require no special student international identification card or other student credentials: if you look like a student, you get in!

ROOMS IN PRIVATE HOMES: As you've seen from our earlier discussion, scattered hotels in Amsterdam offer rooms with breakfast for less—sometimes considerably less—than 22 guilders ($11) per person, but the great majority charge from three to seven guilders more. Therefore, to keep your costs in an acceptable budget range, your next alternative is to seek a room in a private home. Those in central city tend to charge 20 guilders for bed-and-breakfast, those further out tend to drop the price somewhat (see our "Readers' Selections" for several such examples).

Thus, in her well-located canal house, **Mrs. Huser,** at 2 E Kostverlorenkade, first floor, phone 16-92-56, provides you with your own private entrance, and also includes showers in her price of 20 guilders ($10) per person. Take streetcar 13 from the Central Station. . . . Care for a house-boat? **Mr. H. J. Steens,** at Ark Oase, opposite Da Costakade 216, phone 16-76-14, rents one of the rooms of his spacious boat, on a canal in the center of town, at 20 guilders ($10) per person, and the floating room has three beds. . . . **Mrs. P. Van Buren,** Saaftingestraat 15 ND, phone 19-74-92, rents a guest room in her quiet home (nicely furnished) for 20 guilders per person ($10): it has two beds, and breakfast and free showers are included in the price. . . . For a room overlooking a windmill, phone **Mrs. Sloof,** at 84-11-66. She lives with her husband at Willem de Zwijgerlaan 353, reached in 20 minutes by boarding Bus No. 21 at the Central Station. Rate per person, breakfast included, is 22 guilders ($11). . . . Closer to the center of town, five minutes from the Leidseplein and museum areas, at Helmerstraat 55 HS, phone 12-61-76, **Mrs. Kriegenbergh** can accept from one to four guests in her private home, at 20 guilders ($10) per bed per night. . . . Families may find it convenient to stay with **Mrs. Kraak,** Scheldestraat 81, third floor, phone 64-22-98, who offers two spacious rooms with 4 to 5 beds and a good breakfast for 22.50 guilders ($11.25) per person, including free showers; this one is near the city Congress Hall. . . . Near the Anne Frank house and Westerchurch, at Elandsstraat 13, phone 24-84-07, **Mrs. A. Herfurt** rents a single room for 21 guilders ($10.50), a double room for 20 guilders ($10) per person. You'll like the typical Dutch setting, in the heart of the popular "Jordaan" area. . . . The **Smits Family,** at Derkinderenstraatt 85, phone 13-05-01, charge 23 guilders ($11.50) per person for one of their quiet rooms with garden view, in which they can also place additional cots for children. Take bus No. 18 from the Central Station, and get off at the Postjesweg stop, 20 minutes later. . . . **Mr. and Mrs. Sabeel,** an elderly retired couple residing at Geulstraat 6 HS (HS means ground floor), phone 64-07-57, will proudly display letters received from satisfied American guests ("staying with you was the nicest part of our 3-month trip", etc.). They charge 22.50 guilders ($11.25) per person for a double room, inclusive of a generous Dutch breakfast. Take tram No. 4 or 25 from the Central Station. . . . And finally, the **Schouten Family,** 4 Plataanstraat, (phone 95-35-63), nice people who like children, rent two of their rooms (doubles, with extra cots for children) for 19 guilders ($9.50) per person in a double, 25 guilders if rented as a single; and they will reduce these rates for children, depending on their age. Location is in the Duivendrecht area, half an hour by yellow bus no. 26 from the Central Station—a member of the Schouten family will await you at the bus stop and escort you to the house, if you phone ahead.

READERS' HOTEL SELECTIONS (13.50 Guilders): "At the **Hotel Schröder,** 48 B. Haarlemmerdijk (phone 266272), a few minutes' ride via bus #22 from the Central Station, we received our best room in two months of traveling in Europe. And the price of 13.50 guilders per person included the huge breakfast one expects in Amsterdam. The establishment is run by a wonderful couple who are only too happy to help you plan your day in their wonderful city" (Robert Rothenhaus, Long Island City, New York; note by AF: the Schröder, in a letter confirming the 13.50 guilder rate for 1980, says it hopes to become the "least expensive hotel in Amsterdam").

READERS' HOTEL SELECTIONS (17.50 Guilders): "At the **My Home Hotel,** 82 Haarlemmerstraat (phone 242-320), a ten-minute walk from the central station, the 17.50 guilder per person charge for room and a large breakfast is well worth it and very reasonable for

Amsterdam. Atmosphere is provided by a spirited grandma who prefers to be called 'Mums' and speaks English with an affectionate Brooklyn accent!" (Joe and Pat Barile, Belmont, California).

READERS' HOTEL SELECTIONS (25 Guilders): "At the **Hotel Schirmann,** 23 Prins Hendrik-kade (phone 241-942), rooms are simple but clean, hot and cold running water, no breakfast, 25 guilders per person. A two-minute walk from the railroad station" (Donald Lamont, Downsview, Ontario, Canada). . . . "Inexpensive but entirely proper is the **Klein Astoria,** 15 Martelaarsgracht, phone 24-71-80, located just across the bridge from the train station, where we had a double room, with hot water in the room and a shower on every floor, plus a huge breakfast of ham and eggs and all the coffee we could drink, for $12.50 each (25 guilders per person, service included). The owners, Mr. and Mrs. Mulder, are two of the nicest people we met during five months of European travel, and both speak excellent English; they're happy to advise budget-minded travelers about inexpensive restaurants" (Mr. & Mrs. Robert L. Klawier, Washington, D.C.).

READERS' HOTEL SELECTIONS (27.50 to 37.50 Guilders): "For young and adventurous people, we loved the **Hotel California,** (121 Nieuwendijk), which is two blocks from either the railroad station or American Express, and two steps from the shopping district. The cost is 30 guilders per person; and if it is not too late at night, you may call the hotel (24-44-97) and the owner will pick you up in his car so that you can get an early start on the nightspots" (Charles Meyers, Louisville, Kentucky; consistently good recommendations from other readers as well; the hotel will not, however, make advance reservations) . . . "On two visits I have enjoyed staying at the **Hotel Smit,** phone no. 76-63-43, P. C. Hoofstraat, next door to the Museum Hotel. For 65 guilders ($32.50) we had a double room with bath plus lavish breakfast, including egg and orange juice" (Mrs. Frances Vogel, Glenview, Illinois). . . . "We discovered a fantastic budget hotel near the Leidseplein Square—the **Hotel Koning,** 2e Helmersstraat (tel: 020-187132). It's a ten-minute walk from both the Heineken Brewery and the Rijksmuseum, easily accessible from the train station by taking tram #1. English-speaking owner Mr. J. Middelberg, charges $13.75 per person in a double room, breakfast included" (Patti Largen/Caren Schrier, Summit, New Jersey"). . . . "I recommend the **Old Nickel Hotel,** Nieuwe Brugsteeg 11; telephone 24-1912; it's a two-minute walk from the Central Station if you walk up the left side of Damrak, turn left at the second bridge, cross the canal and the street, then look on the left side, where the Old Nickel is a few doors from the corner. Price for bed and breakfast is 27.50 guilders year-round and a bath is free; if you walk 50 yards too far down the street, you're at the beginning of the red-light district, but the Old Nickel is quite respectable; 90% of its guests are English, which speaks for itself" (L. K., Santa Cruz, California; seconding recommendation from Dr. Robert L. Wolk, Brooklyn, New York). . . . "I spent five nights at the **King Hotel,** Leidsekade 85, phone 24-96-03, where a single room cost me 36.50 guilders a night, including breakfast and service charge; doubles are 29.75 guilders per person. This included an ample breakfast brought to my room. The hotel is about a 3-minute walk from the Leidseplein, where you'll find the American Hotel, Opera House, restaurants and shops, and it's about a 10-minute walk from the Rijksmuseum. My single room was very small, but it was comfortable, and the doubles I saw were large and tastefully furnished. Stairs here were *very steep,* but the climb was made completely worthwhile by the cordiality of the host and his wife" (Grace Ewing, Jamaica, New York; note by AF: several other readers' endorsements were received for the King Hotel; for a moderately-priced, but larger, hotel nearby, try the **Hotel de Rijk,** 91 Leidsekade (phone 23-38-68), which charges 35 guilders for bed and breakfast, service included). . . . "We are staying at the **Hotel Impala,** Leidsekade 77 (phone 23-47-06), 30 guilders per person all year round, including service, breakfast and free showers. The breakfast is magnificent—an egg, cheese, bread, jam, butter and many cups of coffee. The hotel is run by an amiable young couple, and the place is immaculate. Our room has a fabulous bay window, plus another huge window, and would be perfect for a family. Our windows overlook the junction of two canals, around the corner from the Leidseplein" (Philip W. Sultz, Amsterdam, Netherlands; note by AF: other hotels on the Leidsekade, all in the 40-guilders-per-person range, include the **Hotel Kooyk,** 82 Leidsekade (where Messrs. Monen and Bosch are particularly sweet and helpful to "lost sheep" Americans; their dining room is decorated with photographs of film stars of the 30's; phone 23-02-95); this is just around the corner from the big American Hotel and the action and color of the Leidseplein). . . . "**Hotel De Ijtunnel,** at 145 Prins Hendrikkade (phone 230-430), is extremely well located near the railroad station, has numerous rooms for which it charges 30 guilders per person, including a large and delicious breakfast, possesses an annex a few doors away, and is capably operated by Mr. and Mrs. Grishaver; a wonderful place, well heated in winter" (Pauline Hadley, New York City). . . . "We had such a pleasant stay at the **Hotel Belga,** 8 Hartenstraat (phone 24-90-80), Amsterdam, we feel we should recommend it to other travelers. We were there in summer, when a double room without private bath cost 37.50 guilders per person, including breakfast and free use of the shower. The owners, Mr. and Mrs. Letteboer, speak English very well and are eager to advise on sightseeing and to provide helpful tips on the best places to shop. There are about ten cheerful rooms, always filled with fresh flowers from Mr. Letteboer's rooftop garden, and unpretentiously but comfortably furnished. Of course the famous Dutch breakfast is served, and to greet you in the morning there are the Letteboers' two finches and canary, who keep you company from their perches on the wall. The location, although only a few minutes' walk from the Dam or the Anne Frank House, is quiet, and you can hear the wonderful bells of Amsterdam chime through the day" (Mr. and Mrs. Robert L. Feldman, Alexandria, Virginia).

PRIVATE HOMES THAT READERS HAVE LIKED: "The home of **Eugene Heuvel,** 147 Nieuwe Kerkstraat (phone 22-79-14), offers private rooms for 16.50 guilders per person. This is the best buy in town and Eugene vows it will remain that way. The rooms are clean, cozy, carpeted and comfortable. We had at no extra charge, a large Dutch breakfast, complete with eggs, ham, tomato, bread, jam, peanut butter and a bottomless pot of tea. The nicest part was Eugene's warmth, his knowledge of Holland and our feeling of being at home. Great location, too. Take tram # 9 from Central Station to the first zoo ('Artis' in Dutch) stop" (Glenn Kesselhaut and Brian Coven, West Orange, New Jersey). . . . "Centrally located just two minutes from the K.L.M. Air Terminal and near major museums, the **Family Home Willemsen,** 95 Willems Parkway (tel: 020-760564), offers all the comforts of home and warm hospitality to their guests. Rooms cost 27 guilders per person a night, including a huge breakfast and shower. Tram # 2 is in walking distance" (Vera Massaro, Cleveland, Ohio; Brenda Nisbet, Hermosa Beach, California; Richard Burton, Gloucester, Massachusetts). . . . "I would like to recommend the **Pension La Petite,** 114 Marco Polo Str. (tel: 129502), the homey domain of the Hulscher family. Rooms are without bath, but showers are free, and guests are always welcome for TV and conversation in the Hulscher's living room. Rates of 27 guilders per person per night include an enormous breakfast" (David A. Campbell, Omaha, Nebraska). . . . "We stayed with **Mr. and Mrs. C. P. Riphagen** in their private home at 27 Nich. Japiksestraat, and fell in love with this family who speak English, offer a delicious breakfast, hot shower, and treat you like one of the family. All for 16 guilders per person. Call 151520 or take Tram #1 to Johan Huizingalaan (the tram driver will be glad to tell you when to get off). Walk down a flight of stairs, turn left, and go past the Algemene Bank. Continue past Peter's Snackbar (which is, by the way, a very good place to eat) and the Laundry Mat until you reach Nich. Japiksestraat; you will see a Texaco Service Station across the street. Turn right and walk up this street to No. 27 (the name C. P. Riphagen is on the door). You will be glad you did!" (Woodrow and Letress Berryhill, Phoenix, Arizona; subsequent seconding recommendation from C. W. Page, Bethany Beach, Delaware, and Paul Trinkkeller, Pacific Palisades, California). . . . "I was directed to the home of **Mrs. Meijer,** 2e Helmerstraat, 9 (a short distance past the Leidseplein—take tram #1 from the Central Station to Overtoom), phone 171-752, where for 17.50 guilders per night, I had a cozy little room and a large, tasty breakfast. The greatest discovery, however, was my hostess herself. When I arrived from the station shortly after midnight, she served me coffee instead of complaining that I had awakened her. The next day she was most helpful in telling me—in fluent English—how to reach various museums. Throughout my stay she and her family offered me helpful advice on travel throughout Holland, good food, and friendly conversation; she even offered to wash my clothes" (Carol Jones, Wilmington, Delaware). . . . "I had the good fortune of staying at the fine home of **Mr. and Mrs. B. Bruinsma,** 63 Akerwateringstraat, Amsterdam-Osdorp (phone 194-411), 20 minutes by tram no. 1 from train station, and thus away from the turmoil of downtown. They were the perfect hosts, and for 25 guilders per person, we received a double room, shower, and gigantic breakfast" (Kenneth E. Beasley, Alameda, California; similar recommendation from Mr. and Mrs. Wayne DuBose, Colorado City, Texas). . . . "Do contact **Mr. and Mrs. J.P. van Oosterhout,** 68 Jekerstraat (phone 73-82-99), for rooms in the 20-guilders-per-night category. These wonderful people have several large airy rooms they can rent. Take the #25 tram for a short 10 minute ride from the Central Station. Get off at

Churchill-Laan and Maasstraat. Jekerstraat is one block south of the Churchill-Laan. If the world had more people like the van Oosterhouts, it would have a lot less trouble" (Mrs. A. L. Dolmatz, San Carlos, California; rave reports from other readers as well). . . . "We were most fortunate and we believe your readers should be aware of our almost unbelievable find at the home of **Mrs. H. A. Van Horssen,** Bonairestraat 95, phone 169-907, where we had a spotless double room on the ground floor, with a shower and double doors leading on to a private flower garden. The house is practically in the heart of Amsterdam and only ten minutes from the Central Station via Tram #17. Mrs. Van Horssen is pleasant, courteous and helpful, and her charge is only 27.50 guilders per person, including breakfast and service" (Mr. and Mrs. Walter T. Carroll, Huntington, New York). . . . "**Mrs. Charlotte Wormer** runs a congenial and pleasant pension at 91 Marco Polostraat (phone 12-64-82), just 10 minutes by tram #7 or 13 from the Central Station, charges 25 guilders per person, and provides a phenomenal breakfast of bacon, eggs, cheese, tomatoes, cucumbers, ham, toast and coffee" (Cecilia Ruvalo, Hialeah, Florida; Molly Gerkin and three other co-eds from Oklahoma State University). . . . " **Dick and Maria Dykstra,** their three daughters, teenage son and dog, are a delightful family possessing a plesant home at 10 Wierdestraat (phone 190-138), Osdorp, Amsterdam; take tram #1 to the end of the line, about 20 minutes from the Central Station. Our stay there, costing only 17 guilders per person, was a highlight of our trip" (Walter, Sylvia and Cherisse Killick, Edmonton, Alberta, Canada; similar comments from Herb Wendroff, Princeton, New Jersey: ". . . There you will stop traveling for a moment and find a place where you feel home is not so remote"). . . . "**Mrs. Lucken,** 72 Jekerstraat (phone 71-49-89), can accommodate 5 or 6 persons in her two rooms (both large and airy) and her breakfast is outstanding. 19 guilders per person" (Judith Phillips, APO, New York).

READERS' SELECTIONS JUST OUTSIDE AMSTERDAM "In nearby Hoofddorp, reached by bus from the central railway station in Amsterdam, we stayed for only 20 guilders per person per night in the home of D. G. v. d. Breggen, **"Huize Ingrid,"** 12 Beemsterstraat (phone 02503-16762), enjoying accommodations that were immaculate, homey and warm, and a breakfast of eggs, bread, cheese, meat, coffee, tea, rolls, and chocolate sprinkles!" (Nadine Krueger, New York, New York). . . . "The **Herman van Empels** are not only the best 'bargain' (19 guilders per person, including breakfast, service, and tax) we have found in our travels, but also the best hosts. The address is Mathijs Sterklaan 13, Halfweg-Zwanenburg, tel. 02907-5235, 15 minutes by bus (#85, on the road to Haarlem) from the center of Amsterdam. Not only are the beds comfortable and breakfast plentiful, but the personal attention they give their guests is noteworthy, and the fresh-ground, fresh-brewed coffee is the best by far we encountered on the continent. Many of our friends go there and are as enthusiastic as we are, particularly as the van Empels go 'All Out' for their guests, especially Americans, and it is fun to meet people of all nationalities in their homey living and dining rooms. They are very generous with outstanding TV programs and often will show color slides, and help plan scenic days of interest. They have even picked up and returned guests to the airport, and there is a bus nearby to Amsterdam" (Mrs. Thorburn S. McGowan, Storrs, Connecticut; also D. S. Rintoul, Hong Kong; William E. Brewer, Indianapolis, Indiana; Florence Stark, Desert Hot Springs, California; note by AF: Mr. van Empel has confirmed that he will continue to charge only 19 guilders in 1980, and points out that his house is only 10 km. from the center of Amsterdam, and thus particularly suitable for readers with cars). . . . "Only two doors away from the incomparable van Empels, same street, was another family who also had a pension. They are **Katherine and Gees Prins,** 7 Mathijs Sterklaan, Halfweg-Zwanenburg, phone 02907-4825. We spent three memorable days with the Prinses and their teenage son, Alexander. The room and house were immaculate and attractive, with bathroom shared with family, plus a small basin in the room. The price was 17.50 guilders ($8.75) per person with a bountiful breakfast. They are fine people and we will long remember the chats, Gees' piano playing (American pieces like *Beautiful Dreamer,* for our benefit) and sharing coffee with whipped cream in the evening. We felt very much at home" (Mr. and Mrs. R. G. Keister, Scott Depot, West Virginia). . . . "Our first choices in hotels in Amsterdam were filled due to a busy Easter and tulip-time week-end. At that point a man, who had approached us before, reappeared and offered rooms at his private home near Volendam. We were wary of this tactic, but, in desperation, said we'd take a look. The quaint lakeside community of Volendam delighted us, as did our stay with the perfectly charming family of **H. Rikkers,** Iepenlaan 16, Volendam (N.H.), tel. 02993-63933. He speaks English, his wife makes an excellent try. She also serves a huge

Holland breakfast and on our arrival—too late for restaurants—she made an appetizing dinner for us. In the evenings we were served coffee or drinks in the family living room, were helped with our plans for excursions within the Netherlands. This family was certainly worth getting to know and I highly recommend their home to readers who want to be part of the community life of this warm village. I almost forgot: the price for 1980 is only sixteen guilders per person" (Sue Ann Allen, Flint, Michigan). . . . "We were lucky enough to find accommodation in another private home in Volendam, at **Mr. Klaas Kes,** 11 Populierenlaan (phone 02993-64688); proprietors are friendly and helpful; their home is spotlessly clean; and bed and breakfast costs only 19 guilders per person. They can accommodate as many as 10 persons, in two three-bedded rooms, two doubles" (Marianne Klepfisz, London, England). . . . "**Mr. and Mrs. Klaas de Boer,** 20 Gladiolenstraat in Volendam (phone 02993-64770), are among the nicest people we've met. Their charming and immaculate little 3-story house accommodates as many as 11 guests in rooms on the second floor; their breakfasts were extraordinary; the beds very comfortable; and the price for four of us was only 19 guilders per person" (S. Earl Saxton, El Cerrito, California). . . . "I chose to arrive in Holland on the weekend of the Queen's birthday -(a big, big mistake) and was forced to stay an hour from Amsterdam at the **Familiehotel Berg en Bos** at 58 Aquamarijnstraat (phone 055-25-23-52); but it was a blessing in disguise. For 25 guilders ($12.50), I had a single room with breakfast at the hotel find of the century, operated by lovely people. From there, I never had to travel more than two hours to any of the country's key attractions—tulips, windmills, canals" (George Ziebell, Oakland, California).

We'll now assume that you're ensconced in an Amsterdam hotel and are ready to eat—an activity that, in this town, can involve some gratifying surprises.

RESTAURANTS AND MEALS: To begin with, the restaurants deal in the most exotic cuisine of Europe. There are, for instance, Indonesian restaurants here, by the dozen, where you'll see residents at work on a *twenty*-dish dinner called "rijsttafel"; there are just as many Chinese-Indonesian restaurants where secretaries and office boys dart in for a normal lunch of "nasi goreng," with a "loempia" on the side! In even the most elegant restaurants, smoked eel pops up as one of the most popular opening courses, and for snacks throughout the day, you'll discover the ubiquitous but unique sandwich shops ("broodjeswinkels") of Amsterdam, serving ground raw meat on a soft bun! There are so many of these food surprises in Amsterdam—including a cocktail drink called "Advokaat" which you eat with a spoon!—that there's scarcely time for a three- or four-day visitor to sample them all.

How to organize this information? In preparing a recent guide to Amsterdam, I ate my way through more than 100 of the city's restaurants and peered over the shoulders of diners in about 30 more. I've concluded that the only coherent plan for presenting my restaurant suggestions is to group them according to the meal of the day in which they specialize. And thus, we'll deal first with breakfast, then with lunch, then with snacks, and then with dinner, concentrating always on establishments that offer budget-priced meals.

Breakfast in Amsterdam

The first meal of the day presents no problem in Amsterdam—it is always served in your hotel, is nearly always included free in the cost of your hotel room, and is always the most incredibly-large morning feast you've encountered: several sorts of Dutch breads and rolls, huge hunks of butter, marmalade, slices of luscious Dutch cheese, at least one slice of meat, sometimes a boiled egg, followed of course by tea or coffee. This is the "typical Dutch breakfast," and most tourists are unable to eat again until evening. I'm told that even larger breakfasts are served in the south of Holland, but I for one find that hard to believe!

Lunch

What do the Dutch eat for lunch? Well, most of them eat a *second* breakfast! By that, I refer to the famous institution of the "Hollandsche Koffietafel" (Dutch "coffee table"), and although it may be unfair to refer to it as a "breakfast," it is essentially an expanded version of what you've had upon arising: several different kinds of bread, slices of cheese, butter, slices of meat—usually supplemented, this time, by a single small hot dish, such as a hot meat croquette or a bowl of soup, followed by either milk or coffee or tea. For that percentage of traditionally-minded Dutch who lunch on a "koffietafel," the custom is to put off a big hot meal until evening. And if that seems strange, then let it be known that the Dutch have the highest longevity rate in the world, which many attribute to their eating habits. Nor will the custom seem so strange if you will remember that many people in other countries—most particularly, the citizens of the United States, England and Scandinavia—also have a cold meal at lunch—consisting usually of sandwiches.

Restaurants serving the Hollandsche Koffietafel

A large percentage of the restaurants in Amsterdam include a "koffietafel" on their lunch-time menu, even when they specialize in hot meals. It's rarely difficult, therefore, to find a "koffietafel," and it's also good to remember that a koffietafel is an inexpensive lunch to have. Typical of what you'll receive and pay is the koffietafel served at the moderately-priced **Koffiehaus Herenmarkt,** 64 Haarlemmerstraat, a short walk from the Central Station (west of it), which charges 7.50 guilders ($3.75), all in, for an enormous koffietafel lunch that includes a hot meat croquette and milk or coffee. In other restaurants throughout the city, the koffietafel is occasionally referred to by its alternate name, a "twaalfuurje" (a 12 o'clock bread-lunch), costs 7 guilders (including service charge), and consists of a thick slice of bread with ham, an equally thick slice of bread with roast beef, Russian salad, and a choice of coffee, tea or milk. Try **Snackbar Pierre,** corner of Herengracht and Oude Leliestraat, or **Mini Leeuw,** 229 Nieuwendijk (50 yards from the Dam Square), for precisely such a meal. Still other establishments serve a "Brabantse koffietafel" for 7 guilders (exactly $3.50, including service), which includes most of the above items plus an egg, an extra slice of bread, and a second glass of coffee or milk.

Sandwich shops (broodjeswinkels)

Even more prevalent than the restaurants serving koffietafels, are the unusual sandwich shops of Amsterdam ("broodjeswinkels"), where again a large percentage of the population—perhaps a third—take their cold lunches, consisting usually of two or three "broodjes" (sandwiches) and a glass of milk. And if that sounds rather unexciting, then you haven't tasted a Dutch sandwich! Prepared on a buttered soft roll, liberally sprinkled with salt, its ingredients consist of a full half-inch to an inch of thinly-sliced (and therefore unusually tender) meat, including some of the most delicious rare roast beef in the world. Or you can have a "broodje tartare"—ground raw hamburger on a soft bun—or a "broodje warm vlees," which is a hot meat sandwich, covered with a heavy, brown gravy and eaten on a plate with a fork and knife. The variety of ingredients spread out before you is enormous and appealing, but the most significant aspect of a Dutch sandwich lunch is its cheapness: many of the broodjes cost only 2 guilders ($1), and only the unusual varieties, or those involving hot meats, rise to more than 2.50 ($1.25). Two broodjes and a glass of milk make an excellent, quickly-served lunch—perfect for a fast-moving tourist—and that repast should rarely cost more than 5 guilders—$2.50. Warning: order only one or two broodjes at a time: you'll be surprised to discover how filling they are. The greatest danger, and worst temptation, to tourists in Amsterdam is overeating!

Where do you find broodjeswinkels? Everywhere—you can scarcely walk for a block without passing the invitation to enjoy "belege broodjes" (diverse sandwiches). The most numerous chain of shops is that operated by the brilliantly-named **Broodje van Kooje** (try pronouncing it), most of whose broodjes (sandwiches) cost 2 or 2.30 guilders, including service and tax, and whose shops are located at 12 Rembrandtsplein, 20 Leidseplein, and 28 Spui. Here, if you'll order a big, hot meat croquette on a buttered roll (1.90 guilders), and a glass of milk (1.25 guilders), the total—including service—will be 3.15 guilders ($1.57), and who can eat more than that? The largest of the broodjeswinkels is **Van Dobben** at 5 Korte Reguliersdwarsstraat (just ten yards off the Rembrandtsplein), but the one with the largest and most attractive selection of ingredients is—to my mind—the **Plein 24**, at 24 Leidseplein, but with slightly higher prices (2 to 2.50 guilders for most broodjes) than the rest. Another unusually good sandwich shop—where you will always find hot meat sandwiches with gravy, along with other varieties—is a place that is actually called (in English) the **"Sandwich Corner,"** and which stands at # 1 Kromme Elleboogsteeg, a tiny alley that runs off the Rokin, near the Dam Square. (It's closed on Sundays.) Here, the broodjes range from 1.60 to 3 guilders. A typical Frommer feast, that leaves me perfectly well filled: one broodje croquette (1.80 guilders), plus 2 glasses of milk (2.80 guilders). Total, including service charge: 4.60 guilders ($2.30). Never overeat!

At any broodjeswinkel, the best buy, bar none, is the hot meat croquette ("kroket") broodje selling for never more than 1.80 guilders (90¢). It's phenomenal in taste. And incidentally, the price for milk ("melk") or coffee ("koffie") at most broodjeswinkels is 1.40 guilders (70 U.S. cents). You'd be well advised to drink the superb Dutch milk, which is consumed in staggering quantities in Holland—perhaps another explanation for the long life spans of the Dutch.

Uitsmijters

Another item offered at most sandwich shops and restaurants—and which many Amsterdammers consume for lunch—is an "uitsmijter" (pronounced "out-smay-ter," it means "bouncer"), a plate consisting of two buttered slices of bread, topped with either ham or roast beef, atop which is then a fried egg or two! You'll learn very quickly that it is unusually filling (consumed with a glass of milk)—and relatively cheap (usually no more than 4.50 to 6.50 guilders ($2.50 to $3.25). Places serving uitsmijters: virtually every sandwich shop in town, plus the well-located **Honeds' Bakhuisje**, 39 Kerkstraat, off the Leidsestraat; the large cafe-restaurant of the **American Hotel**, 28 Leidseplein (ham or cheese uitsmijter for 6.50 guilders, meat or cheese croquettes for 3); the **Sandwich Corner**, 1 Kromme Elleboogsteeg (see above; uitsmijters for as little as 4.50 guilders).

Bami Goreng, Nasi Goreng

And now, lest we leave the impression that everyone in Amsterdam eats a cold lunch, we'll turn to an especially popular, noontime warm dish. Although many Amsterdammers have a normal meat-and-potatoes meal for lunch, several thousands of them head instead for an Indonesian or Chinese-

Indonesian restaurant and order a heaping plate of "bami-goreng" or "nasi goreng." While these items are available for dinner, too, they carry a much lower price tag at lunch, when they are consumed in great quantity. Indeed, in nearly a dozen restaurants, you can have a three-course bami goreng or nasi goreng meal (starting first with chicken soup—"kippensoep"; then an eggroll—"loempia"; then the bami goreng or nasi goreng) for about $2.50 to $3.

And what are these strangely-named concoctions? In their purest Indonesian state, "bami goreng" is a heaping plate of buttered noodles mixed with little strips of meat, while "nasi goreng" is a plate of rice with meat. But the Dutch have added other embellishments: a fried egg atop the pile, a slice of ham or pork underneath, some crisper noodles along the side, the whole garnished with lettuce and pickles. It tastes better than it sounds, it provides a whopping big meal that you won't be able to finish, and it is—as we noted—unusually cheap.

Every Indonesian and Chinese-Indonesian, and even a few Dutch, restaurants serve an inexpensive bami goreng or nasi goreng meal at lunch, and we'll list a few, categorized according to the area of town in which they're found.

On the tourist-heavy **Damrak**, leading up from the Centraal Station, you'll discover the **Wah Nam Restaurant**, at 32 Damrak, serving kippen-soep (chicken soup), eggroll, nasi or bami goreng, and coffee, all for a relatively high (for Amsterdam) 6.75 guilders at lunch (a more elaborate nasi or bami goreng dinner in the evening costs 12 guilders).

But on the less expensive **Nieuwendijk**, a shopping street that runs parallel to the Damrak, the **Chinese Canton Restaurant**, 65 Nieuwendijk, charges only 7 guilders (including service) for a four-course nasi or bami goreng lunch, as do one or two other establishments (the **Lin Fa** at # 149 Nieuwendijk, for example: 5 guilders) on that stretch of the Nieuwendijk that is closer to the station.

Again running parallel to the Damrak, but on the other side, the narrow Warmoesstraat is the site of several restaurants serving 3-course nasi goreng meals for as little as 4.75 guilders, and I'd particularly invite you to try the rather basic **Tsuan Sheng**, at 83 Warmoesstraat (only 5 guilders for lunch), whose prices at night are also remarkably cheap: 5 guilders for a "nassi rames," 6 guilders for a "nassi rames special"—an abbreviated rijsttafel—highly recommended.

On the **Damstraat**, which runs off the Dam Square, the place to visit is the **Insulinde Restaurant**, 18 Damstraat, where the lunchtime meal (served only from noon to 3) consists of kippensoep, bami or nasi goreng, coffee or tea, and costs exactly 5.50 guilders.

On the **Rembrandtsplein**, the **Indrapoera**, 40 Rembrandtsplein, serves bami or nasi goreng à la carte at lunch for 5.50 guilders. But just 75 yards from the Rembrandtsplein, the tiny **Restaurant Madoera**, at 86 Reguliersdwarsstraat, charges only 5.75 guilders for a three-course bami or nasi lunch of unusually high quality—and all served by a particularly exotic crew of waiters with Indonesian headbands.

In the area of the **Stedelijk Museum**, the **Restaurant De Orient**, 21 Van Baerlestraat, a fairly expensive place, nevertheless charges only 6.50 guilders ($3.25) for a fairly elegant, two-course nasi or bami goreng dinner. Open daily from 4:30 to 11:30 p.m.

On the **Oude Zijds Voorburgwal**, a short walk up from the station, the **Restaurant Tai Pang**, 47 O.Z. Voorburgwal, charges 7 guilders for a three-course b-or-n goreng lunch (including soup, eggroll and coffee), charges 12.50 guilders for four courses at night.

And finally, for your most numerous collection of restaurants serving this inexpensive specialty, head for the **Binnen Bantammerstraat,** fairly near to the railroad station, which forms the heart of Amsterdam's district of Chinese restaurants. There you'll find at least four restaurants (including the **Ling Nam,** 3 Binnen Bantammerstraat; the **Azie,** 9 Binnen Bantammerstraat) serving a three-course lunch of this sort for 7.50 guilders, including service and tax.

Afternoon Snacks

Around four hours after lunch, you'll be ready for the favorite afternoon snack of the Amsterdammers—a raw herring, eaten with a toothpick, from the counter of an open-air stand! While other European cities specialize in hot sausage stands, scattered around town, Amsterdam offers herring stands instead—and after eating your first raw Dutch herring, covered with chopped onions, you'll understand why. I don't care how many other species of herring you've had—marinated, creamed, pickled, salted—there's nothing so good as a raw Dutch herring, for which the charge is usually 3.50 guilders ($1.75) at the famous open-air herring stands of Amsterdam.

There are, quite literally, at least a score of herring stands in the central part of Amsterdam, never far from where you may be (ask a resident to point one out). If you're lucky, you'll arrive at the stand while a true Dutchman is imbibing the succulent fish. Notice how he grabs it daintily by the tail, holding it high above his mouth, and then devours from the bottom up. For your, the owner of the stand will cut the skinned and gutted fish into four pieces, give you a wooden pick with which to pick the pieces up, and a bowl of diced onions into which to dip the fish. The best time for herring is late April or May, when the first catch of "nieuwe haring" comes in. The quality remains high throughout the end of September but begins to disappear as the winter months set in. Whatever your normal attitude is towards herring, don't miss an opportunity to taste the Dutch variety—it's incomparable, a major surprise of amazing Amsterdam.

Dinner

But now we arrive at the normal, hot-meal-serving restaurants of Amsterdam, to which most people go at night (although they can obviously patronize them at lunchtime, as well). These include restaurants of every nationality and kind—Dutch, French, Spanish, Italian, you name it—but the most unusual, and the ones for which Amsterdam is particularly famed, are the Indonesian and Chinese-Indonesian restaurants serving "rijsttafel." You can't pass through Amsterdam without sampling this glorious meal at least once!

Rijsttafel Restaurants

Rijsttafel (literally, "rice table") is a meal the Dutch discovered during the days of their empire in the Dutch East Indies (now Indonesia); it consists of a central, large dish of rice, surrounded by as many as twenty (that's right, twenty) other small dishes, each including a serving of unusually-prepared and often fairly spicy, meat or vegetables. One or two at a time, you transfer the contents of the little dishes onto the big pile of rice, eat the rice and its condiments together, and then cool your red-hot throat with big draughts of cold Dutch beer. Not all the dishes are as spicy as I may have implied, however, and the more cautious eaters can put together a rijsttafel meal that is memorable and unique—even though not spicy.

What's in the little dishes that surround your main bowl of rice? To describe them best, I should describe the best-known of Amsterdam's rijsttafel restaurants, which is the famed but expensive **Bali**, 95 Leidsestraat (two short blocks below the Leidseplein). It charges exactly 37.50 guilders ($18.75) per person, including service and tax, for a 22-dish rijsttafel consisting of rice, soup, pork in soya sauce, meat in madura sauce, steamed meat, liver in a special sauce, eggs in sauce, sweet potatoes, bean sprouts, roast pork on sticks, fried bananas, stuffed omelet, bamboo shoots, shrimp bread, mushrooms, java sauce, soybean cakes, vegetables in peanut sauce, cucumber in sour sauce, mixed sour vegetables, fruit in a sweet and sour sauce, and fried grated coconut. And now you know what a rijsttafel is!

No budget tourist, however, need pay as much as the Bali asks, because other restaurants in town—particularly those on the famous **Binnen Bantammerstraat**—offer a nearly-equivalent rijsttafel for far less money. Simply ask a resident for the location of the Binnen Bantammerstraat, which is a street in the area to the southeast of the railroad station. There you'll discover, in one block, no fewer than six restaurants serving rijsttafel. Try, in particular, the **Kong Hing**, 11 Binnen Bantammerstraat (9.50 guilders for a 14-item rijsttafel); or the **Ling Nam**, 3 Binnen Bantammerstraat (10 guilders for 14 items). I should prefer one, but after having eaten at each at least twice, can't decide which I like best! Friendly, unpretentious atmosphere—and good rijsttafel—at both.

Abbreviated rijsttafels? The tiny **Restaurant Madoera**, 86 Reguliersdwarsstraat (just 75 yards off the Rembrandtsplein), serves 12 items for 12.50 guilders, while the swankier **Restaurant Indrapoera**, directly on the Rembrandtsplein, at # 40, serves 19 items ("Rijsttafel Populair") for 17.50 guilders ($8.75).

A slightly-more-expensive version of these multi-item dinners can be had at the tiny, but well-located, **Kow Loon**, 498 Singel, on the street of the Amsterdam flower market, just 50 yards away from the Nieuw England Department Store and the beginning of the Leidsestraat. Here, a 13-item rijsttafel is only 14 guilders, 20 items sell for 18.50 guilders, and the same 20 items can be served for two persons for only 30 guilders (which comes to approximately $7.50 apiece). An important budget bonus: from noon to 4 p.m. and again at night from 9:30 to 10:30 p.m., the Kow Loon serves a still different abbreviated, but filling, version of a rijsttafel, called "Nasi Ramas," for only 7 guilders ($3.50); a stick of barbecued pork next to a mountain of rice, over which are poured a number of rijsttafel ingredients.

(Incidentally, this "Nasi Ramas" or "Nasi Ramas Speciaal" is offered by nearly all the Chinese restaurants of Amsterdam, and is, as we've mentioned, a stripped-down version of a rijsttafel—poured directly onto a vast mound of rice, and lacking the excitement of the 15-or-so separate dishes in which a normal rijsttafel comes. It also consists of not more than six items. Still, it's a cheap alternative or follow-up to the standard rijsttafel.)

Finally, on the Nieuwendijk (that shopping street that parallels the Damrak), you can have a 14-dish rijsttafel for 11 guilders at the somewhat plain, but utterly authentic, **Lin Fa Restaurant**, 149 Nieuwendijk; a 10-dish rijsttafel for 10 guilders at the **Fong Won Restaurant**, 85 Warmoesstraat (also running parallel to the Damrak); and a 9-item rijsttafel, at dinner only, for 13.50 guilders, at the **Restaurant de Orient**, 21 Van Baerlestraat (near the Concertgebouw and the Stedelijk Museum; open daily); all including service and tax, but plus the cost of your beverage, of course.

The Normal Meals

Now we move into the less exotic areas of Dutch cuisine. And because we've listed a great many lunchtime spots where you can eat well for $2.50 to $3.50 (the restaurants serving Hollandsche Koffietafels, for instance; the sandwich shops; the Chinese-Indonesian restaurants with their bami goreng and nasi goreng), we can now afford to splurge a bit—surveying, first, the restaurants offering full lunches and dinners for about $8, including tax and service, returning then to the more normal budget-type establishment where dinner is $4 and under.

CURRENCY RATES: As we go to press the Dutch guilder is valued at approximately 2 to the dollar, which makes each guilder worth about 50 U.S. cents. Although you should recheck these rates at the time of your own trip to Holland, they shouldn't vary too greatly from the 2 to 1 ration that presently exists.

SUPER-SPLURGE—FOR$8.75: First a lunchtime splurge, then an evening selection. Having already discussed the Dutch "koffietafel", we'll now refer to an establishment where this typical Dutch meal has gotten so big, varied, and out-of-hand, that it more nearly resembles a full scale Smorgasbord, but at a remarkably low price. In the charming, Old Dutch style restaurant of the **Hotel Trianon**, just behind the Concertgebouw, at 3 J.W. Brouwersstraat, you'll walk into a Dutch atmosphere of blue-and-white tiles, beams on the ceiling and gaily-flowered red chairs; and then glimpse a buffet table groaning with, of all things, a Scandinavian-type assortment of mussels and shrimps, gooseliver pâtés, rollmop herrings, tuna and salmon salads, roast beef and pork, vegetables, salads, meat pies, and nearly a dozen other pastries and vegetable ingredients for an unprecedented feast. For a flat price, including service charge and tax, of 17.50 guilders (about $8.75), you'll first take your choice of five hot soups, then make as many trips as you wish to the buffet table, and try to finish up with coffee, tea or milk, and fruit. The Trianon's restaurant serves this epic repast from noon to 2, daily including Sundays; then serves a normal dinner from 5:30 to 9 p.m. (for 20 guilders).

For an interesting evening meal costing around $8, you might next try the picturesque **Holland's Glorie Restaurant,** 220 Kerkstraat (right off Vijzelstraat), which I call the "poor man's Five Flies." The reference is to Amsterdam's expensive and famous "Five Flies" restaurant, which has one of the most authentic 17th Century interiors in Holland. This budget counterpart—Holland's Glorie—bears a startling resemblance to its wealthier brother, with stained glass windows, mahogany walls, pewter mugs, and all the other accoutrements of 17th-century life—an exciting atmosphere, to which you might even take someone you're trying to impress! You might order a delicious beefsteak "Grand Mère" (with mushrooms, ham, onions and sauce) for 15 guilders. Soup of the day is 3 guilders ($1.50) and desserts are 3 and 4 guilders. It's easy to eat well for a flat $8.50 (and sometimes less) in one of the most stunningly-decorated dining rooms in all of surprising Amsterdam.

For $7.50

A cheaper splurge? **Honed's Bakhuisje,** 39 Kerkstraat (just off the Leidsestraat, near the Leidseplein), our top recommendation in this category, is an ornately decorated little place (stained glass windows and Delft china on the walls) where there's always one three-course dinner for 15 guilders ($7.50), including service charge: soup, meatballs, potatoes, vegetable, pudding. The daily, blue-plate specials ("dagschotels") are 10 to 13 guilders, and are piled with food four inches high; there's nothing dainty about these longshoreman's type dinners, but they'll fill you for hours. Closed Sundays except during summer.

(Incidentally, most main plates at Honed's—as at most other restaurants in Amsterdam—carry huge portions of meat, gravy, potatoes, and are almost impossible to finish. Therefore, unless you're famished, it's wise to skip the appetizers and soup at this and other restaurants in Amsterdam—a practice that will considerably reduce the cost of your meals.)

MEALS FOR $4-AND-LESS: The more typical, and lower-priced, restaurants include some exciting finds, among which are the following:

(1) The cafeteria of the **Hema Department Store** (second floor), 174 Nieuwendijk (near the Demrak), cheapest self-service restaurant in town, where you can stuff yourself for $2.50, and yet a beautiful, modern and clean room that provides for fairly pleasant, although strictly utilitarian, dining. Prices are almost unprecedented by Amsterdam standards: only 80 Dutch cents for milk, 1.10 guilders for coffee, only 5 guilders ($2.50) for plates such as calves liver with potatoes and applesauce, or for other daily special platters, 3.90 guilders ($1.95) for two luscious meat croquettes with french fries, 3 guilders for platters of hard boiled eggs, tuna fish, and potato salad (large enough for two to share). Here's an institution that's always reliably cheap for reasonably-well-prepared food, but is open—quite obviously—only until 6 p.m., and is closed Sundays.

(2) **Keuken van 1870,** 4 Spuistraat (a short walk up from the central station), is probably the cheapest of Amsterdam's *sit-down* restaurants, and is therefore also described in our "starvation budget" section, a few pages on. Patronized by more and more tourists each year, it is nevertheless only for occasions when you're plainly dressed, and desirous of heaping portions of plain but nourishing food selling for 5.50 guilders ($2.75) per big platter. Picturesque interior and atmosphere, picturesque location, thoroughly Dutch, and (along with the Hema Cafeteria, above), an Amsterdam standout. But closed weekends.

(3) The **Studenten-Eethuisje Cantharel,** 377 Kerkstraat (20 yards from Utrechtsestraat), which is open from 5 to 9:30 p.m., charges 6.75 to 13 guilders ($3.37 to $6.50) for most of its vast meat plates with potatoes and vegetables, and gives a discount to students of 20 Dutch cents per plate. Even if you're not a student, you can enjoy a bountiful meal of liver, vegetables and potatoes for 8.50 guilders. Plastic tablecloths, of course, but with gaily-muraled walls. Closed Sundays.

(4) The small **Mothersmilk Restaurant** (10 tables) at 10 Korte Koningsstraat, in the old city area, is a favorite hangout for students. Open Tuesday through Sunday from 5:30 to 9:30 p.m. (closed Monday), it specializes in macrobiotic dishes (wheat, vegetables, nuts and fish, no meat), and offers large daily platters for 8 guilders ($4), soup for 2 guilders, dessert 2, grape juice 1. Chopsticks available in great profusion, presumably because so many Indonesian students eat here.

(5) **In De Oude Goliath,** at Kalverstraat 92, directly on the pedestrians-only shopping street, is actually the restaurant of the Historical Museum, but open to the general public; it's named after the enormous, 20-foot statue of Goliath carved out of a tree, with a tiny David next to him, both built in the 17th century for a Dutch amusement park. Daily dishes and salad bowls are 8.50 guilders ($4.25), various soups (with a roll) 4.25 guilders ($2.12), pancakes 6 ($3), and a choice of 12 different teas (china melange, yunnan, orange pekoe, yasmin, darjeeling, mate, peppermint, rum, lemon, sweet orange, earl grey, and old Dutch "slemp," which is tea with anis), served between 2:30 and 4:30 p.m., at 1.50 guilders (75¢) for a large cup. Open Monday to Saturday from 9:30 a.m. to 5 p.m., Sunday from 1 to 5 p.m.

(6) **Moeders Pot,** 119 Vinkenstraat, in the Haarlemmer Square area, serves giant daily platters for 8.50 guilders ($4.25), and provides a mixed salad with each platter for no extra charge. Opens at 5 p.m., closed Monday, a small place with an intimate and pleasant atmosphere.

(7) **Cocky's Coffeebar,** at Raadhusstraat 10, corner Singel, near the Dam Square, is a self-service cafeteria, four steps down from the street, serving hot dishes for 8 guilders ($4), hot dogs for 2 guilders ($1), a large assortment of sandwiches priced from 1.50 to 3 guilders, expresso for 1.25 guilders. Handy, if you're in the immediate area. But open only until 6 p.m., and closed on the weekends.

(8) **De Lantaarn,** 64 Tweede Const. Hugyensstraat (just 10 yards off the Overtoom), another typical little "eethuisje" (eating house), with very good food, for which the charge averages 6.50 guilders a plate; soup is 2.25 guilders. Within walking distance (just barely) of the Leidseplein; you'll notice it by the little green lantern that hangs outside, but don't confuse De Lantaarn with De Groene Lanteerne in the area of the Central Station. Closed weekends. Highly recommended.

Finally, for a meal that will cost about $3.25, walk over at lunchtime to the **Valkenburgerstraat** near the Waterlooplein (the daily flea market of Amsterdam) where you'll find stands selling a cup of filling, hot erwten soep (pea soup) for 2 guilders, a bag of french fried potatoes for 1.50 guilders, and a portion of raw herring for 3 guilders. Delicious!

READERS' RESTAURANT SELECTIONS: "For a change of pace, try the Israeli specialties at **Negbah,** Kerkstraat 245 (phone 020-231823), where one can have a complete meal for 14.50 guilders ($7.25), or enjoy less expensive à la carte dishes—falafel, eggplant salad, shish kebab, shashlik, etc. Open Sunday through Thursday from noon to 10 p.m., Friday till 4 p.m., and Saturday from 6 p.m." (Jim Castelluzzo, New York, New York). . . . **"Pomplemouse,** N.Z. Voorburgwal 161, is a cozy French restaurant with a bistro-cum-coffee shop ambience. Snacks and light meals are served (a cheese omelette is 5 guilders, soup 3.50 guilders), and the 'daily menu' is priced at 13 guilders ($6.50)" (Aida Turturro, New York, New York).

DRINKING IN AMSTERDAM: All the normal soft and hard drinks are of course available in Holland, including the incomparable, world-famous Dutch beers. But you'll want to try the Dutchman's favorite aperitif, a gin drink called *genever*—which all the world knows as "Dutch gin." It packs a wallop, it needs a little time to get accustomed to, but it grows upon you! And it's cheap; normally about $1 per shot; in a nightclub therefore, you'd be well advised to keep ordering only genever (chased, perhaps, by beer).

Genever, by the way, is available as either "jonge genever" (young genever) or "oude genever" (old genever); the young kind has less of the distinctive perfumed taste of the other, and is usually more palatable to tourists trying this drink for the first time. Lady tourists, for whom genever may be too strong an item, can try another unusual drink called "Advokaat"—a heavy, spiked, egg-nog-type substance which you eat with a spoon. Prior to World War II, I'm told, Advokaat was about the only drink a proper lady would be caught imbibing; during the war, however, the ladies switched to genever and drink it today in about the same quantity that U.S. ladies devour dry martinis.

THOSE INCOMPARABLE CROQUETTES: This, now, is our final food tip: when in doubt in Amsterdam, order meat croquettes ("croquetten"). Breaded and crisp outside, creamy and smooth inside, and served with a plate of french fried potatoes covered with a tangy, tartar-type sauce, they are a Dutch classic—and they are always cheap, even at the most expensive of restaurants (expect to spend a maximum of 6 guilders for two croquettes, french fries and sauce). At restaurants up and down the Kalverstraat (the walking street), just off the Dam Square, 2 meat croquettes with bread are 4.50 guilders; with french fries as well—5.50 guilders; go to the swank counter-restaurant of Amsterdam's new Schiphol Airport, and you'll pay scarely more than 50 Dutch cents extra. And at the **Sandwich Corner,** 1 Kromme Elleboogsteeg, that amazing little snack-bar on the alley that runs off the Rokin, a croquette sandwich can be had for only 1.85 guilders without french fries, for 3 guilders with. At least for a snack, and even for a meal, have a Dutch croquette!

AMSTERDAM'S STUDENT FACILITIES: We've already reviewed the student hotels of Amsterdam, in our general section on housing. For student meals, another large group of institutions exists for your benefit but the best of them is the modern **Mensa Happetap,** at 3 Damstraat just off the Dam Square. No student card is required, and you can eat for exactly 5.50 guilders (around $2.75) at dinner (served from 5 to 7 only, Monday through Saturday.) For a change of pace, head for the less attractive (and slightly more expensive) **Studenten Eethuisje Cantharel,** 377 Kerkstraat (20 yards from the Utrechtsestraat), which serves a low-cost evening meal only (weekdays only) for less than $3.50.

STARVATION BUDGET: For dormitory accommodations in Amsterdam, see again our section on specialty hotels, which discusses student hotels that are not strictly limited to students; and add to that list the **Christian Youth Hostel "Eben Haëzer",** 179 Bloemstraat, tel. 24-47-17, which offers dormitory accommodations for just 9 guilders a night (8 guilders if you bring your own sleeping bag). Breakfast is 2.50 guilders extra, dinner 3 to 5 guilders.

Male travelers living on a starvation budget, and utterly intrepid female ones (although I doubt that most ladies would feel comfortable in this next place), will like the plain but tasty food at the **Keuken van 1870** ("Kitchen of 1870"), 4 Spuistraat, where the most expensive meat plate with vegetables and potatoes (enough to feed a horse) is only 5.50 guilders ($2.75), and most other items come for even less. A large restaurant, patronized by somewhat indigent but utterly respectable workingmen, it will do fine—provided you leave your better clothes at the hotel. Open noon to 7, closed weekends, and currently enjoying a trendy reputation that attracts more and more tourists and fewer residents.

Budget Alley

It might be noted that "Keuken van 1870" (see above) is located on a stretch of downtown thoroughfare (near the Station and the waterfront) which I call "Budget Alley", and which is packed with starvation budget-type places for both food and accommodations. Beginning at the station, the street is called Martelaarsgracht; as it passes the Nieuwendijk, it veers to the right and is called Hekeleveld and then Spuistraat. As you walk along, you pass the famous **Quick Snackbar** (see "Sub-Starvation Budget," below), then the aforementioned Keuken van 1870.

French Fried Potatoes Street

Then there's the **Nieuwe Nieuwestraat,** a little alley off the Nieuwendijk (which itself parallels the Damrak), where you'll find shops selling large paper cones of freshly-made french fries covered with a mayonnaise-like sauce, for 1.75 guilders (87 U.S. cents). Combine a cone with a huge Dutch meat ball or meat croquette for another 1.20 guilders (60 U.S. cents), and you have a filling $1.47 lunch.

READERS-ON-THE-STARVATION BUDGET: "We stayed at the Christian youth hostel called "The Shelter" at 21 Barndesteeg (phone 25-32-30), right smack in the heart of the Red Light District! Our accommodations were in segregated dormitories (according to sex), for which we paid 9.50 guilders per person, plus 3.25 guilders for breakfast. Very clean; good showers; youth hostel card not necessary; strict curfew rules (midnight); no mixing of men and women; and a pervasive but utterly non-pressured religious attitude, with Bible-study groups offered, gifts of prayer books, etc. There's also an excellent and inexpensive restaurant here serving delicious home-made vegetable soup for one guilder, daily platters for 5.50 guilders, many more tasty foods. All within 10 minutes' walk of the railroad station" (Mrs. Gregory Brandis, Danbury, Connecticut).

SUB-STARVATION BUDGET: A meal for $1.50? All over Holland, you'll encounter automat-type stores (they're called "automatieks") selling hot food items individually displayed in little glass cases that you open by inserting a coin. Amsterdam has the largest—and most astonishing—of these in its **Quick Snackbar,** which is located at 50 Nieuwendijk, corner of Martelaarsgracht, in the area near the Central Station (the Nieuwendijk, as you'll remember, is that inexpensive shopping and jukebox street that runs parallel to the important Damrak). One entire side of the Quick is a wall of glass display cases containing literally scores of different sandwiches, hors d'oeuvres, various hot meat croquettes and the like, all priced at a guilder (50¢) per item. Three items—which should always include one of those creamy breaded Dutch croquettes—cost a total of $1.50, and make an entirely filling meal! Open six days a week from 6:30 a.m. to midnight; closed Wednesdays.

Other automatieks with similar prices but not so large a selection: at 102 Leidsestraat, just off the Leidseplein; nearby at 47 Kerkstraat, just off the Leidsestraat; at 332 Spuistraat, just off the Spui.

ALTERNATIVE AMSTERDAM: Thus far, our recommendations in this chapter have been of fairly traditional tourist facilities. But there's another type of tourism here. As every savvy traveler knows, Amsterdam has become the world's capital for young people pursuing an alternative life style—and if you're among them, hats off to you! For the group variously known as "hippies," "flower people," "freaks," Amsterdam offers special lodgings, special restaurants, special nightspots and markets—even special advice centers for when things go wrong.

Public Sleep-Ins

At the bottom of the scale (and it's quite a bottom indeed) are the emergency "Sleep-Ins"—old and dilapidated warehouses fitted out with cattle-like pens, in which young people are invited to lay their sleeping bags on metal bunks with foam rubber mattresses, six or twelve to a pen, boys and girls indiscriminately. If the Nativity Scene comes to mind, that's exactly the image. "What if you want some privacy?" I asked one long-haired couple. "You get in the same sleeping bag," came the calm reply.

In the summer of 1979, Amsterdam maintained a 700-bed **"Sleep-In"** costing 7 guilders ($3.50) a night at Rozengracht 168-180 (open July 1 to August 31) in the Jordaan area, and it is probable that the very same structure will open on the very same schedule, and for the very same 7-guilder rate, in 1980 (phone 23-58-71 to learn). The extremely basic "Sleep-In" should not be confused with the better multi-bedded dorms of the Kabul Student Hotel mentioned earlier in this chapter and offered as a less expensive (20 guilders) alternative to the Hans Brinker Stutel.

Far superior to the Sleep-Ins is the 9-guilder-a-night **Christian Youth Hostel "Eben Haezer"** at 179 Bloemstraat (phone 24-47-17), mentioned earlier in this chapter, or the attractive **Stadsdoelen** youth hostel at 97 Kloveniersburgwal (phone 24-68-32), the latter charging 13.25 guilders ($6.62) per person, breakfast included, in its 25-bedded dorms. A mellow place, with good vibes and attractive rooms, a non-institutional ambience, the Stadsdoelen requires a youth hostel card, unfortunately, which they'll sell on the spot for 24 guilders ($12). A last hostel, not quite as attractive, is the **Jengdhotel Waldeck** at 27 Groenburgwal (phone 24-84-29), charging 15 guilders per night for a dormitory bed, breakfast included, and offering dinner for 7 guilders. . . . Frankly, why endure a Sleep-In when such places as the Eben Haezer are available for $1.50 more?

Sleeping in the Vondel Park near the Leidseplein is no longer permitted, although Amsterdam's hippie groups continue to gather there by day.

Privately-owned "Sleep-Ins"

For a still-reasonable 12 guilders ($6) a night, you should like the 16 dorms, 75 double-decker beds, and 15 free showers of the typical, three-story canal house called **Fat City Hostel** at 157 O.Z. Voorburgwal (phone 22-67-05); that's in the very heart of the red light district, but there's no cause for concern: owner/manager Zev Alony, a wiry, young Israeli, is strict about keeping the hostel free of unsavory elements. The 12-guilder price includes breakfast, and the large, ground floor bar overlooks the town's cheapest discotheque, to which guests of the hostel are admitted free. An incidental note: toilets here are the cleanest I've seen in any hotel in Amsterdam. From the Dam Square, turn into Damstraat and, crossing the first bridge, you'll see Fat City.

Again in the heart of the inner city near the train station, **Bob's Youth Hostel** at 92 N.Z. Voorburgwal (phone 23-00-63), contains 100 double decker beds on four floors, for which the charge is 12.50 guilders ($6.25) per bed, with breakfast, sheets and showers included. Opened in late 1978 by a man from Morocco named Bob El-Moutamid (his English is perfect), it quickly became popular for three reasons: central location, new mattresses, a friendly staff. It's less than five minutes on foot from the station.

Eat-Ins

Amsterdam's alternate food? It's macrobiotic, vegetarian, organic—macrobiotic at the **Kosmos,** 142 Prins Hendrikkade near the train station (but for members only; see below) and at **The Garden,** a macrobiotic restaurant and tea house serving healthful meals from 10 a.m. to 10 p.m. There's a book and herb shop upstairs. At each of these, 7.50 guilders should result in vast platters of grains, vegetables, fruits.

Be-Ins

The really mind-boggling features of Amsterdam's youth scene are, however, its unique, mind-stretching nightspots, famous—or infamous—throughout the world. Two names lead the list: the immense **Paradiso** at 6 Weteringschans, two blocks from the Leidseplein (open Tuesday, Wednesday, Thursday, Friday and Saturday from 8 p.m. to 1 a.m., 3 to 7.50 guilders admission), which features far-out rock, and all the pharmacology associated with lightsshows and far-out rock; and **Kosmos,** the "Center of Meditation," at 142 Prins Hendrikkade (phone 267477 or 230686), near the train station, open Monday through Friday from 6 p.m. to midnight, 6 guilders entrance, (less for members), where the purists pursue various forms of transcendental experience: both Western and Eastern yoga, astrology, herbs, tarot, magic, a co-ed sauna, and kabbala. Downstairs, in a basement restaurant, you can balance your yin and yang with a macrobiotic meal (lentil soup, a rice-bean-soya-seaweed-lettuce-cabbage-nuts-raisin dish, then an apple, for 7 guilders ($3.50), and if you only want the meal, without the other activities, you'll be refunded your entrance charge). Several other competing establishments run the leaders a hard race, of which the most important is **Melkweg** ("Milky Way"), at 234a Lijnbaansgracht, behind the Opera House, off the Leidseplein (experimental theater, live music, films, and workshops); it's housed in an old milk factory and open Wednesday and Thursday from 6 p.m. to 1 a.m. (entrance 4 guilders) and Friday through Sunday from 6 p.m. to 2 a.m. (entrance 5 guilders), when its offerings consist of folk, rock, jazz, classical and dance concerts, as well as theater, and a market of little shops. A restaurant on the premises serves light meals and snacks.

And help

And to round out the institutions, there's a **Youth Advisory Center** ("Jongeren Advies Centrum") at 30 Amstel, tel. 242-949, around the corner from the Rembrandtsplein, for legal, financial and spiritual scrapes; a number of public bathhouses for the unwashed (200 Da Costakade, 5 Marnixplein, 3 Fronemanstraat); a "free-market" on the Leidsebosje off the Leidseplein, daily except Sunday from 9 a.m. to 7 p.m., where anyone at all can sell handicrafts and art. Whatta scene!

DAYTIME SIGHTSEEING: Both day and night, there's far too much to see and do here. To provide you with even a minimum list requires that we describe two basic tours and fifteen indispensable sights, of which about ten can be packed into a three-day stay.

(1) A Canal Boat Ride

The very first thing to do in Amsterdam? Why, that's to take a ride along the canals and into the harbor of Amsterdam, in one of the many glass-sided

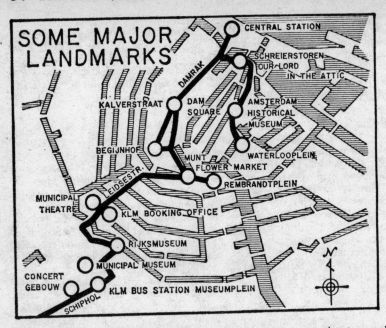

SOME MAJOR LANDMARKS

CENTRAL STATION

SCHREIERSTOREN
OUR LORD
IN THE ATTIC

DAMRAK

KALVERSTRAAT

DAM SQUARE

AMSTERDAM HISTORICAL MUSEUM

BEGIJNHOF

MUNT
FLOWER MARKET

WATERLOOPLEIN

LEIDSESTR.

REMBRANDTPLEIN

MUNICIPAL THEATRE

KLM BOOKING OFFICE

RIJKSMUSEUM

MUNICIPAL MUSEUM

CONCERT GEBOUW

SCHIPHOL

KLM BUS STATION MUSEUMPLEIN

canal boats that operate throughout the year. No better way exists to see all the essential features of the city, and to see them in only an hour and a quarter of time. The boats pass alongside the façades of old patrician homes on the Herengracht and other canals; they show you the picturesque "Skinny Bridge" (Magere Brug) on the Amstel, and the furniture hooks on top of the canal houses; they pass dozens of other important sites; and finally, they sail out into the vast harbor of Amsterdam, past freighters from exotic lands, and past drydocks where gigantic ships have been lifted from the waters for cleaning and repairs. Throughout, the pretty-and-witty girl guides (or the learned male guides) keep up a running commentary on the attractions you pass along the way. How much for this entire tour? Exactly 6 guilders ($3) per person.

The departure docks of the several companies that run these tours can be spotted by a sign reading "Rondvaart" (round-trip), which you'll see displayed at several waterside locations in town. All charge the same 6-guilder price; all offer departures throughout the day, generally at half-hour intervals; all run essentially the same tour; and all of the following companies can be counted on for an excellent hour ride: **Holland International,** whose boats leave from the bottom tip of the Damrak, just opposite the Centraal Station, and which offers departures almost every ten minutes in summer; **Reederij Plas,** also on the Damrak, a bit further up from the Station; **P. Kooij,** on the Rokin, near the Spui, and just a block away from the Mint Tower (here they take snapshots of you as you enter the boat, and have the finished photos ready for your inspection—and possible purchase—at the end of the one-hour trip); **Nord-Zuid,** 25 Stadhouderskade, opposite the Adda Park Hotel; several other similar companies. In the summer, beginning around June 15, the "rondvaart" companies run nighttime canal tours as well, so that you can see the city's 17th Century canal houses in their illuminated state—one of the great sights of Europe.

(2) A Motorcoach Tour of the City

Other aspects of Amsterdam can best be seen by bus. For a traditional tour of the city, lasting 2½ hours, there are motorcoach departures every day of the week at 10 a.m., from a number of tour offices located up and down the Damrak. These begin by edging their way through the narrow streets of the original city, passing the Montelbaan Tower, Rembrandt's House, the Waag and the Nieuwmarkt, the Portuguese Synagogue, and a score of other famous sites (many of which are described later in this chapter); they then pass into the plush residential sections of Amsterdam near the Hilton Hotel, drive through the Leidseplein and the Rembrandtsplein, stop for a visit to a diamond cutter, where you're shown the polishing and shaping of stones, and then end with a lengthy guided tour of the Rijksmuseum. The price for all this is a standard 25 guilders ($12.50), including all entrance fees, and among the companies offering these trips, I particularly like **Holland International Travel Bureau,** 26 Damrak (10 a.m. and 2:30 p.m. departures, 25 guilders) and **Wagons-Lits/Cook,** 19 Dam (10 a.m. and 2:30 p.m. departures, 25 guilders).

AMSTERDAM BY BIKE: One reason why Holland suffers only slightly from the energy shortage is that virtually every Dutchman and Dutchwoman (from age 5 to 80) travels and commutes by bicycle along the country's absolutely level terrain. So why not do the same? An easy-to-find bicycle rental firm is housed in a red-and-yellow hut using an old bike as signpost, at 33 Stationsplein, to the left of the central railroad station (as you face it). Open six days a week from 5:30 a.m. to 6:30 p.m., it's called **Rent-a-Bike,** and it charges only 6 guilders ($3) a day, 30 guilders ($15) per week, after you've made a refundable 50-guilder ($25) deposit.

A more organized form of bicycle touring, **Ena's Bike Tours,** in Delft (tel: .015-143797), is the creation of an enthusiastic group of young people (Ena Govers is their senior tour leader) who purport to "show you Holland by bike," along carefully selected scenic country lanes through farmland and quaint Dutch villages. En route, visits are made to a working windmill that dates to 1741, a farm where cheese is still produced by hand (a refreshing treat that gives you energy for the rest of the ride), and a lake with excellent swimming facilities (a boat ride is part of the tour). You can bring a picnic lunch or dine at a restaurant by the lake. Tours leave daily at 10 a.m. from various points in Amsterdam and return at 5:30 p.m. Total cost: 24 guilders ($12), which includes the bike, the cheese farm visit, and the boat ride. Call for reservations, and you'll enjoy a delightful experience.

(3) The Rembrandthuis (the Home of Rembrandt)

Now we start the visits that you'll make on your own. One of the important ones is to the home of Amsterdam's most celebrated citizen, Rembrandt Harmenszoon van Rijn, who first came here as a young art apprentice in 1623, and spent the remaining 46 years of his life in this very city, where he created nearly 500 paintings, 287 etchings, and 1,400 ink and pencil sketches—all with such genius that he is now ranked with El Greco, Raphael and Velasquez as the greatest artist of all time. A few remarks about the early fame of Rembrandt will help set the scene for a visit to his home.

Rembrandt had established himself, at the age of 26, as one of the city's most successful painters. Commissioned by a Professor Tulp to paint a group of surgeons attending a dissection, he succeeded so well in his "The Anatomy Lesson of Dr. Tulp" (now hung in The Mauritshuis in The Hague) that other portrait commissions poured in by the dozens. Around the same time, he met and married a plump, pretty blonde from Friesland named Saskia van Uylenburgh, whose dowry amounted to 40,000 florins (guilders); there followed eight years of extravagant living which culminated on the day that Rembrandt saw and fell in love with a magnificent three-story home on the Jodenbreestraat, of a splendor that few artists could normally aspire to. He purchased it on credit, incurring a heavy and continuing debt, and several years later discovered that the citizens of Amsterdam were no longer purchasing his paintings!

Part of the reason for Rembrandt's economic decline was his own increasing mastery, which made him increasingly unwilling to follow the art fashions of the time. In 1642, for instance, he was commissioned by a certain Captain Banning Cocq to do a group portrait of a company of the Civil Guard of Amsterdam—a "corporate" portrait for which each person portrayed in the painting would contribute a portion of the artist's fee. Normally, these paintings gave equal prominence to each contributor, and showed them standing or sitting in one or two uniform lines. But Rembrandt had a greater vision, and portrayed the men in a moment of action, as they assembled for a parade upon the visit of Maria de Medici (the widowed queen of France) to Amsterdam. The resulting painting—the Rijksmuseum's great "Night Watch," which some acclaim as the greatest painting of all time—portrayed a number of these civilian-soldiers in shadows, obscured others entirely, cut off the bottom of one face with an outflung arm. The men of Captain Banning Cocq's troop were furious, and their enraged outcries caused all Amsterdam to look upon the portrait as a failure. From that moment, paintings by Rembrandt were no longer in favor, the fortunes of the artist declined, and crushing interest payments on his expensive house soon placed him in bankruptcy. Rembrandt moved from the Jodenbreestraat to the poorer Rozengracht, and for the rest of his life was forced to evade his creditors by working as the employee of an art firm formed by his son, Titus, and his mistress (Saskia having died), Hendrickje Stoffels.

Knowing all this, I think you'll experience both a chill and a thrill to visit the magnificent **Rembrandthuis**, at 4 Jodenbreestraat, whose interior is an almost exact reproduction of the style of the 17th century. The visiting hours are from 10 to 5 on weekdays and Saturdays, from 1 to 5 on Sundays, and the admission is only 1.50 guilders (75¢) for adults, 50 Dutch cents (25 U.S. cents) for children; you can reach the house by taking bus no. 22, 55, or 56 or tram no. 9 at various points in town, or simply by walking for 10 minutes from the Dam Square (head down the Damstraat, which then becomes Doelenstraat, then Hoogstraat; as you pass the Zuiderkerk—South Church—you'll encounter St. Antoniesbreestraat, which you follow for 1½ blocks to the Rembrandthuis; it stands almost on the corner of the Zwanenburgwal canal). Inside are displayed more than 200 of Rembrandt's etchings (one of the largest collections of them in the world), numerous of his sketches, and his etchings press. But for paintings by this awesome genius, you must now turn to the Rijksmuseum, for which the Rembrandthuis serves to whet the appetite!

(4) The Rijksmuseum

This is certainly one of the greatest (if not the greatest) art museums in the world. It was originally housed on the upper floors of the Royal Palace on the Dam Square, was then transferred to the Trippenhuis on the Kloveniersburgwal in 1818, but then, in 1885, acquired its own home in this massive building at 42 Stadhouderskade, which was designed by P. J. H. Cuypers. He also designed the Centraal Station in Amsterdam, and you'll notice similarities between the two buildings.

The hours of the Rijksmuseum (that means "National Museum") are from 10 to 5 on weekdays and Saturdays, from 1 to 5 on Sundays, and admission is totally free on Wednesdays, three guilders on all other weekdays, only 1.50 guilders (75 U.S. cents) on Saturdays and Sundays, with children under 18 and senior citizens (over 65) admitted for one guilder. Immediately upon entering, go straight to the second floor, where you'll see signs directing you on an itinerary of rooms that eventually leads to the large gallery housing the "Night Watch." Initially, as you walk through these rooms, you'll encounter Dutch art of the 16th Century; later the breathtaking 17th Century begins, represented by such marvels as Frans Hals' "The Merry Toper," Ruysdael's "The Mill at Wijk bij Duurstede," the witty paintings of Jan Steen, countless others. Then, four rooms before the "Night Watch," there appear paintings by the "school of Rembrandt," beginning first with several works by his most famous students and apprentices—Gerard Dou, Ferdinand Bol, Govert Flinck, Nicolaes Maes —and followed then by three glorious rooms of paintings (any museum in the world would be lucky to have one) by the master himself: "Samson and Delilah"; a famous Self Portrait; a portrait of his mother; and of Saskia; Titus; "The Oriental Potentate," "The Jewish Bride" (done in tones of gold and red that seldom are even barely captured in reproductions, and slathered on with blobs of paint a quarter of an inch thick); and finally, "The Syndics of the Drapers' Guild" (more popularly known as the "Staalmasters"), another famous regents' piece (or corporate painting) done by Rembrandt late in his life, and designed to be hung in the old Cloth Hall of Amsterdam. The chief reputation of the Cloth Guild, by the way, was for honesty—an attribute reflected in a stern refusal ever to let a flawed bolt of cloth be shipped out of Amsterdam. Notice how Rembrandt captures this quality in his painting, which depicts the Staalmasters at a meeting, as they gaze out at a questioner from the floor.

Now, in the next and larger hall, there finally appears: the "Night Watch," in which Captain Banning Cocq and Lieutenant van Ruytenburgh (the latter clad in a brilliant yellow jerkin with gold braid) go striding forth eternally into the fame that Rembrandt's masterpiece alone brought them. Keep in mind that the painting has been considerably cut down from the original; if you'll examine a small 17th Century copy displayed at one side of the room, you'll see how the original first looked. It is thought, too, that the painting is not of a night scene at all, but that successive layers of protective varnish—now removed— once darkened the canvas much beyond Rembrandt's intention; the purists argue that "Night Watch" is a misnomer, and simply call the painting "The Company of Captain Frans Banning Cocq and Lieutenant Willem van Ruytenburgh." To appreciate the leap in art that "Night Watch" represents, look at the dull, uniformly-lighted regents painting by van der Helst, which is hung to the left of the "Night Watch" itself.

When you have seen the "Night Watch," don't prepare to leave the Museum, because something equally good is still to come. That's found at the opposite end of the room from the "Night Watch," where a short half-flight of stairs leads to several further rooms in which the small, cameo-like masterpieces of the great Jan Vermeer (together with several lesser, but excellent, small paintings of Pieter de Hooch and Gerard ter Borch) are hung: "A Street in Delft," "A Maidservant Pouring Milk," "Woman Reading a Letter," "The Love Letter"; only 36 paintings remain of the work of Vermeer, and these four are among the greatest of them. Contrast their silent, exquisitely-composed style with the slashing, strong emotion that flows from Rembrandt's portraits; the results, in any event, are enthralling, and you'll surely want to pick up reproductions of the paintings (10 guilders for a one foot by 8-inch plasterboard) at the sales desk of the Rijksmuseum, also on the second floor.

After you've returned to the room that houses the "Night Watch," you can walk down a long "Gallery of Honor" where works of great foreign artists—Goya, Tintoretto, Veronese, among them—are hung. Downstairs, on the ground floor, are prints, etchings and watercolors of several different periods, together with a good deal of 18th and 19th Century art—but none of it comparable to the magnificent oils upstairs. The Rijksmuseum also houses a Department of Sculpture and Applied Art (furniture, Delftware, engraved glass, etc.), a print room of graphic art, a museum of Asiatic art (in the basement), and an art library. Schedule at least two hours for this remarkable institution, and be prepared to return time and again.

(5) The Stedelijk (Municipal) Museum

Within easy walking distance of the Rijksmuseum is the second great gallery of Amsterdam, which occupies a position in modern art that is akin to the status of the Rijksmuseum in classic art; indeed, with the possible exception of the Museum of Modern Art in New York, I know of no other museum of modern art that even remotely compares to the Stedelijk in Amsterdam.

In summer, the Stedelijk displays its entire permanent collection: a priceless, almost unequalled array of Chagalls, Picassos, Monets, Cezannes, Matisses and Mondrians, mixed and matched with the post-1945 output of the current reigning modernists: Appel, De Kooning, Dubuffet, and some unusually far-out local examples of Pop Art, Nouveau Réalisme, and Colorfield painting. In winter, much of the permanent collection is sent into storage, and the space is devoted to sculpture, as well as graphic and applied art. In either season, the items on display are a provocative reflection of the modern world, that enlarge and uplift your spirit. All this is found at 13 Paulus Potterstraat, weekdays from 9:30 a.m. to 5, Saturdays from 9:30 a.m. to 5 p.m., Sundays and public holidays from 1 to 5 p.m., for an admission of 2 guilders ($1) adults, free for escorted children 10 and under, 1 guilder for kids ages 11 to 16. The combined cost of $2.50 for visiting both the Rijksmuseum and the Stedelijk is probably the finest art bargain in the world!

Until recently, the paintings at the Stedelijk that caught most visitors by surprise were an incredibly numerous collection of Van Goghs on the second floor—more than 200 individual paintings and sketches by the great Dutch impressionist. Now these 200 works have been supplemented by 500 more and all moved next door into a remarkable new museum that has quickly become the city's third major attraction and one of the world's greatest galleries:

(6) The Rijksmuseum Vincent van Gogh (next door to the Stedelijk Museum)

It was completed in the 70s, a cubistic structure open to daylight—because Van Gogh painted in daylight—containing 200 paintings, 500 drawings, by the tortured Dutchman who became a giant of modern art. Van Gogh was born in the Dutch province of Noord-Brabant in 1853, received his upbringing and later his art education in Holland, and died by his own hand in 1890, in Auvers-sur-Oise, France, at the age of 37. It was perhaps inevitable that the Dutch would construct this superb museum and acquire for it nearly half of everything he painted. Here are the incomparable originals of scenes you've seen in reproduction all your life: "Portrait of My Room at Arles," "Sunflowers," "The Zouave," "Cornfield with Crows," "The Armchair," "Boats on the Strand"—and that bitter indictment from Van Gogh's earlier period, "The Potato Eaters" (De Aardappeleters). There are so many that they nearly overwhelm the senses. And here, too, is a library of literature on Van Gogh, a bookshop, a cafe, an atelier in which visitors are encouraged to pick up a brush and themselves attempt a painting. Admission is three guilders ($1.50) on all days other than Wednesdays (when it's free), and the National Museum Vincent Van Gogh, at 7 Paulus Potterstraat, is open Monday through Saturday from 10 to 5, Sundays from 1 to 5 p.m. Take tram #2 or 16 from the Central Station.

(7) A Visit to a Brewery

Next: a free tour on which you'll receive food and drink—and one that you should take. For, while the citizens of such countries as Germany or Denmark will argue loud and long over whether Holland produces the world's best beer, no one will dispute that Amsterdam offers the best free brewery tours in Europe! In other cities, the breweries take you through their premises, and then give you free beer. But in Amsterdam, they give you free beer, cheese and "nibb-its" crackers! Typical of what's offered is the free visit to the great **Heineken's Brewery**, 78 Stadhouderskade (a short walk over from the Rijksmuseum), which you can make by appearing at Heineken's weekdays only, at either 9 a.m. or 11 a.m. in June, July and August, and at 10 a.m. all other months. You'll receive an informative guided stroll through all areas of the huge plant (including the fascinating, clanking bottling works) and then be led into a richly-furnished beerhall where tables have been set with beer (generous servings, within reason, can be had), cheese, toothpicks for the cheese, and those savory "nibb-its." It's all unusually convial and pleasant.

Incidentally, although the brewery itself receives no admission charge, a one guilder (50¢) contribution to UNICEF (the United Nations Childrens Fund) is currently requested.

(8) A Visit to a Diamond Cutter

Diamond cutting is another major industry of Amsterdam, and here no one disputes that the Dutch are the most skilled diamond cutters in the world. They're also the most friendly, and offer free tours of their diamond cutting factories, regardless of whether you plan to purchase a diamond at the end of the tour. Although you'll need invitations to visit some of the city's diamond works, these are readily available at most hotels, and can always be picked up—in a last resort—at the main office of the V.V.V., at 5 Rokin.

The largest of the diamond cutting factories is **A. Van Moppes & Zoon**, 2 Albert Cuypstraat, corner of Ruysdaelkade (a short walk from Heineken's Brewery, an only slightly longer walk from the Rijksmuseum), which conducts thousands of visitors each year on a thoughtfully-planned-out tour of all phases of diamond cutting, shaping and polishing; they also display the world's smallest diamond, along with replicas of the world's most famous diamonds—the "Hope Diamond," the "Shah of Persia," the "Jubilee." Visits can be made from 9 to 5 daily; closed Sundays in winter. Among the many other companies offering free diamond exhibitions are **Cordes Slijper**, 4 Weesperplein (4th floor, room 105-107), whose visiting hours are from 9 to 5 on weekdays; **Bernard Schipper**, 38 Kalverstraat (this being a jewelry store primarily, but with a small diamond cutting room in back); **Gassan Diamond House**, 17-23 Nieuwe Achtergracht (weekdays, 9 to 5; Saturdays and Sundays, 10 to 5; a major establishment located near the Weesperplein, and reached by bus 5 or 55); and **Holshuysen-Stoeltie**, 13 Wagenstraat (from the Rembrandtsplein, walk a few feet down Amstelstraat, then turn left into Wagenstraat; this last-named spot is unusually pleasant and patient in explaining the entire process; weekdays and Saturdays 9 to 5, Sundays in summer from 10 to 5). None of Amsterdam's diamond cutters will coerce you actually to buy a diamond, but you'll enjoy the world's lowest prices for diamonds if you do.

And now, a different—and most important—sort of Amsterdam experience:

(9) The Home of Anne Frank

"In spite of everything, I still believe that people are really good at heart. If I look up into the heavens, I think that it will all come right, that this cruelty too will end, and that peace and tranquility will return again."   —From *The Diary of Anne Frank*

Those words were written in Amsterdam by a 14-year-old girl who had just spent two years hiding in the secret annex of a building at 263 Prinsengracht. With her were her parents, an older sister, two family friends—the Van Daans—and their teen-age son, Peter, and a dentist named Dussel. On August 4, 1944, the Gestapo broke into their secret hiding place, and sent the entire group, along with other Dutch Jews, to extermination camps at Auschwitz and Bergen-Belsen. Only Otto Frank, Anne's father, survived. When he returned to Amsterdam after the war, he found a diary that Anne had maintained throughout the two years of the family's concealment. It is one of the classic volumes of literature produced in this century, and it has made a shrine out of the building at 263 Prinsengracht (around the corner from the West Church —the "Westerkerk", where a tenderly tiny memorial statue of Anne by Mari Andriessen was unveiled by her father in March, 1977, at the Raadhuisstraat side of the church, near Prinsengracht) to which thousands of tourists now pay visits of tribute each year. None of us should ever pass through Amsterdam without making a similar pilgrimage—both to recall the terrible events of World War II, and also to gain inspiration from Anne's immortal and unflagging spirit.

The building is open weekdays from 9 to 5, Sundays from 10 to 5, for an admission fee of 3 guilders (1.50 guilders for children under 16). Inside, you walk behind a bookcase that conceals a stairway to the clandestine upstairs apartment, then into the now-bare rooms where the family lived, and along the wall, protected by glass, you'll see the yellowing clippings which teen-age Anne pasted there—a photo of Deanna Durbin, a news item about the little princesses—Elizabeth and Margaret—of England. The effect is searing, heartbreaking, infuriating beyond belief. Downstairs, regularly changing exhibitions deal with present-day racism and political repression. The Anne Frank House can be reached by trolleys #13 and #17. You'll want to support the Foundation's work by signing on as a member; but in any event, you'll want to visit the Anne Frank House on your stay in Amsterdam.

(10) Our Lord in the Attic

This is the world's most unusual church, a product of that Reformation period in the 1600s when Catholic worship was in disfavor in Amsterdam, but still tolerated and connived at by the civic authorities. The compromise they reached was a semi-clandestine form of Catholic services, conducted at times in the attics of normal houses! This particular attic church, which actually occupies the top floor of the three adjoining buildings at 40 Oude Zijds Voorburgwal, represents the highest form of this covert church architecture: a miniature-sized and quite beautifully furnished cathedral, capable of accommodating as many as 200 worshipers, all concealed within three very typical, 17th-Century houses. Because the downstairs portion of the canal house has also been perfectly preserved, with its original furnishings and paintings, the entire establishment is known technically as the "Museum Amstelkring," but all the world knows of its upstairs church as "Our Lord in the Attic" ("Ons' Lieve Heer op Solder"). You can visit weekdays from 10 until 5, on Sundays from 1 to 5, for an admission charge of 1.50 guilders (75 U.S. cents); and you should, because the oddness of this situation, combined with the ornateness all around, provides a fascinating glimpse into the spirit of the Dutch "Golden Age."

(11) Canal Mansions

Ever cared to know what one of those 17th-Century canal mansions looks like on the inside? Most of them are today operated as offices, but two have been turned into museums whose chief interest is the glimpse they give you into 17th-Century life.

The first, **The Toneelmuseum** (Theatre Museum), 168 Herengracht, houses such stage items as old props, busts of famous Dutch performers, and sketches and models of early stage scenery. But it is chiefly fascinating for its interior, which is that of a sumptuously-decorated merchant's home, with marble floors and walls, frescoes, and little plaster figures decorating the ceiling. Open weekdays from 10 to 5, on Sundays from 1 to 5, with admission of 1.50 guilders (75 U.S. cents); half price for children 14 and under.

The second of these establishments, the **Willet-Holthuysen Museum**, 605 Herengracht, is simply devoted to displaying the contents of the very typical patrician mansion that it is. This one provides a perfect introduction to the mood of elegant, old Amsterdam: the interior is more sedate, less flamboyant than that of the Theatre Museum, and the household exhibits include glassware, china, tapestries and paintings, some lovely items in gold, silver and ivory, even an old sea chest. Open daily from 9:30 a.m. to 5, except on Sundays, when it opens at 1 p.m.; the admission is 1.25 guilders (63¢), 75 Dutch cents for kids 16 and under. To get here, take trolleys #4 or #9. Something on the same order is the **Museum van Loon**, 672 Keizersgracht, a patrician mansion built in 1671 and now completely restored to its late 18th century state. Open daily except Wednesdays from 10 to noon and 1 to 4, for a 3-guilder admission charge.

(12) The Begijnhof

The most enthralling spot in Amsterdam? Without hesitation, I say the **Begijnhof** (Beguine Court), an oasis of beauty that 90% of all tourists miss because it's located behind unmarked and closed (but usually unlocked) doors and walls just twenty yards away from the bustling Kalverstraat, the main shopping street of Amsterdam! (If they are locked, simply turn the corner to the other entrance on the Spui.) Walk down the Kalverstraat until you pass a tiny side street (the Begijnensteeg) between numbers 130 and 132 on the Kalverstraat; then walk to the end of Begijnensteeg, and enter the gate at the bottom, at which point you'll gasp in surprise as you suddenly find yourself in the quiet 18th Century, in a perfectly-preserved grass-covered quadrangle that is flanked on all sides by 18th Century dwellings inhabited today by elderly lady pensioners. The Begijnhof is the best-known of the many "hofjes" scattered through Amsterdam—a "hofje" being a little plaza of homes built by socially-conscious, wealthy families of the 1600s and 1700s, as "housing developments" for the poor of Amsterdam. In a courtyard are an English Presbyterian, and a Roman Catholic, church, both of which merit a visit; but most important, simply stand silently in the quadrangle and drink in the view. Wouldn't it make a marvelous movie set?

(13) The Waag

Not everything in Amsterdam was built in the 17th Century! Smack in the center of the Nieuwmarkt Square is the 15th Century **Waag** (a weighing house for merchandise), whose circular interior, with surprising nooks and crannies, is as delightful as its circular, turreted exterior would indicate. Since 1926, the building has housed the **Jewish Historical Museum** (ceremonial religious objects of great splendor, owned by Amsterdam's once-large Jewish population) on its ground and first floors, the **Historical Medical-Pharmaceutical Museum** (a 17th Century "anatomy theatre," an 18th Century chemist's shop, and like items) on the second floor. A fee of 1.25 guilders (63¢)—75 Dutch cents for kids—admits you to both museums, which are open on weekdays from 9:30 a.m. to 5, on Sundays from 1 to 5.

(14) The House of Mr. Tripp's Coachman

Don't go out of your way to see this next spot, but if you happen to be near #26 Kloveniersburgwal, take a look at the narrowest house in Amsterdam. It was built by a wealthy 17th Century merchant named Tripp, whose coachman had been overheard to say: "I'd be happy if I had a house as wide as your front door." So, Mr. Tripp built him a house as wide as Mr. Tripp's front door!

(15) Walks Around Town

In the last analysis, the most interesting way to see Amsterdam is on your own two feet, by merely wandering at random through a city whose every streetcorner seems to hold a surprise. And what if you get lost? Well, first, it's almost impossible to get lost in Amsterdam—because you can always simply ask a bystander (in English) to tell you where you are. And if you still get lost, you simply hop aboard any trolley marked "Centraal Station" and thus return to the center of town.

To aid you in your wanderings, however, we'll set forth two suggested walking tours—one of the oldest sections of the city, one of a relatively newer area. Neither tour should take more than three hours, and each can be done in considerably less. Both start from the **Dam Square,** at the side of which is the **Royal Palace** built in 1648.

A foot tour of the oldest sections

From the **Dam Square,** walk to the **Damstraat,** at the side of the Krasnapolsky Hotel, and then start walking down the Damstraat, gazing at the old canals you'll pass along the way. One block down, the Damstraat becomes the **Oude Doelenstraat,** then the **Oude Hoogstraat;** three blocks along you'll cross the **Kloveniersburgwal** canal. Turn down that canal for one block into the **Nieuwmarkt Square,** where you'll be able to visit the **Waag** (Weighing House). Then, from the Nieuwmarkt, walk along the **Sint Antonies Breestraat,** which leads you eventually to the **Rembrandthuis** (Rembrandt's House) on the **Jodenbreestraat.** Now you'll be in the center of the old Jewish section of Amsterdam; from here (after visiting the Rembrandthuis) walk three further blocks down the Jodenbreestraat, and then down **Lazarus Straat** to the **Portuguese Synagogue,** which is only one block from the **Waterlooplein**—a big, old square that used to be the setting for Amsterdam's daily-except-Sunday flea market (a sight you can still see on the Valkenburgerstraat, reached via a tunnel entrance from the Waterlooplein). From the Waterlooplein, across the **Amstel Bridge,** and then walk along the banks of the Amstel (where ships are passing and gulls are circling overhead) to the **Mint Tower.** And from the Mint Tower, walk down the **Rokin** back to the Dam Square.

A foot tour of "modern" Amsterdam

From the Dam Square, walk down the famous **Kalverstraat**—which is Amsterdam's main shopping street, and which winds all the way to the **Mint Tower.** At the tower, detour one block down the **Reguliersbreestraat** to the **Rembrandtsplein,** circle that entertainment area, then return to the tower. And then, from the Mint Tower, walk along the flower market on the banks of the **Singel,** which in one block leads to the **Koningsplein.** From the Koningsplein, walk one block to the **Leidsestraat,** and next walk the entire length of the Leidsestraat (passing the **Herengracht, Keizersgracht** and **Prinsengracht**) to the **Leidseplein.** At the **Leidseplein,** cross the bridge at the end of the square, and then walk down the **Stadhouderskade** to the **Rijksmuseum.** After visiting the Rijksmuseum, end your tour by walking over to the colorful **Albert Cuypstraat** street market—a fascinating and indispensable last stop.

NIGHTTIME ENTERTAINMENT: The most surprising aspect of Amsterdam is its night life. No other capital of Europe has so high a per person ratio of cafes featuring variety acts, exotic dances, jazz, and other after-dark divertissements —and it's all so unexpected! Somehow, nothing you have ever read about "quaint" Amsterdam quite prepares you for the sight of the dozens of sophisticated cafes on the Rembrandtsplein, or the bright lights of the Leidseplein, or the frenetic action on the Zeedijk.

And the best thing about the nightlife of Amsterdam is that it is unusually cheap. On weekday nights—and in some establishments, even on weekends— there is seldom a need to pay more than the price of a single inexpensive drink for the right to dance or view a nightclub show. Because of that, the citizens of Amsterdam don't go to just one nightspot on their evenings out—they skip from one to another! So, if you've ever wanted to play the part of a nightclub-crawling playboy, this is your chance!

Of course, in addition to the cafes and cabarets, all the more sedate forms of evening entertainment are on hand as well. We'll deal first with the normal theatres and presentations, and then turn to the delights of the Rembrandtsplein, Leidseplein and Zeedijk.

(1) The Concertgebouw

The crowning glory of Amsterdam's evening cultural life is the great **Concertgebouw** orchestra, which you may have encountered on one of its innumerable concert tours throughout the world. But to hear this orchestra in its own hall (the Concertgebouw building, on the Museumplein), which is one of the most acoustically-perfect in the world, is a major opportunity that shouldn't be passed up. The orchestra's performances are concentrated in its mid-September-through-May season, but there will be other weeks—particularly during the time of the yearly "Holland Festival" (in 1980, from June 1 to June 23)—when you will also see its performances advertised; when that

AMSTERDAM AT A GLANCE

happens, run, do not walk, to get tickets. These cost a maximum of 30 guilders ($15) at the height of the Festival fervor, and can be had for as little as 15 guilders ($7.50) on other occasions.

(2) The Stadsschouwburg

The opera house of Amsterdam is the **Stadsschouwburg** (Municipal Theatre) on the Leidseplein, where various national theatre groups and ballet companies (the "Haagse Comedie," the "Nieuw Rotterdams Toneel," the "National Ballet") alternate with the important "Nederlandse Operastichting"; unfortunately, the theatrical performances are in Dutch, but you will definitely want to attend the operas, which are almost always presented in the French, German or Italian of their original composition. I won't pretend that the "Nederlandse Operastichting" is one of the greatest of the world's opera troupes, but it puts on a lusty show, whose enjoyment is heightened for me by the relatively intimate size of the opera house itself. Compare a performance of "Faust" or "Rigoletto" here with one presented in the cavernous Metropolitan Opera House in New York—and see which you like best! Compare the prices, too, and you'll receive a gratifying surprise: the most expensive orchestra seats are 24 guilders ($12), there are excellent loge and front balcony locations for 13 to 18 guilders ($6.50 to $9), and seats in the second gallery go for only 10 guilders— the latter price being exactly $5. Ballet performances are much less. Performances, which begin at 8 p.m., are well advertised in the papers and in "This Week in Amsterdam" (which you'll find at newsstands all over town), in addition to being prominently displayed on posters in front of the opera house itself (a building you'll pass on the trolley at least several times a day); generally, the box office is open for seven days before each performance, from 10 a.m. to 3 p.m.

(3) The Theatres

Elsewhere in town are numerous, excellent theatres—the **Nieuwe de la Mar**, the **Kleine Komedie**, the **Bellevue Theatre, De Brakke Grond** (this latter being a playhouse for the avant garde), many others—but as their performances are usually in Dutch, they aren't of special interest to tourist. One, however— the colossal **Theatre Carré**, on the Amstel River, a single long block from the Amstel Hotel—specializes in musical revues that will entertain you as much as they will any resident of Amsterdam. Here you'll be able to see—among others—the top stars of the Dutch music-hall and variety theatre (Toon Hermans, Herman van Veen, in particular) in a lengthy succession of dances, sketches and songs that require a knowledge of the language only at times. Weekday performances, which start at 8 p.m., cost only 7.50 guilders for the gallery, 12 to 14 guilders for the balcony, 17.50 to 25 guilders for the better orchestra locations, but balcony seats are perfectly adequate in the vast, unobstructed, horseshoe-shaped hall.

(4) The Movie Theatres

Here, now, is an area of evening entertainment in which you'll have no language problem. For, unlike the movies presented in France, Italy and Germany, where voices are dubbed into the local languages, all films shown in the Netherlands are presented in their original languages, with written Dutch sub-titles superimposed. On every night of your stay, you'll be able to choose from more than a score of mid-town movie houses showing American, British, and French films. Like other entertainment in Amsterdam, the admission prices are moderate (from 6 to 9 guilders in the most expensive movie theatres, but generally averaging about 6 guilders in the neighborhood locations); and the shows go on at 2:30, 6:45 and 9:30 p.m. on weekdays, at 1:30, 3:45, 7 and 9:30 p.m. on Saturdays and Sundays (although these times vary a bit with individual theatres). The big **Tuschinski** theatre, on the Reguliersbreestraat (just off the Rembrandtsplein), occasionally throws in a stage show, too, as does the elegant **City Theatre** on the Kleine Gartmanplantsoen (just off the Leidseplein). A movie theatre which generally shows English language films: the **Cineac Damrak** on the Damrak (next door to American Express), which charges 6 guilders ($3) for its showings at 2:30 p.m.; and 9 guilders after that time.

(5) Nightclubs and Cabarets

Now comes the action. The nightclub industry in Amsterdam is one of the most unusual in the world, in that it is intended to provide—and is priced to provide—entertainment at not much greater cost than you would incur in a bar or tavern. On Mondays, Tuesdays, Wednesdays and Thursdays, there is scarcely ever an admission charge to any Amsterdam nightclub, and even on the weekends, the normal entrance fee is only four or five guilders ($2 to $2.50)—provided that a fee is charged at all. After that, your only expense is for drinks, which can cost as little as 4 guilders (if you order genevers or beers), and rarely goes higher than 10 guilders or so for brandy or highballs. On that price per person per drink, you can dance—and see an entire show.

The bright lights

There are three basic nightclub-and-cafe areas in Amsterdam: the **Leidseplein**; the **Rembrandtsplein** (with its adjoining **Thorbeckeplein**); and the so-called "sailor's district" around and along the Zeedijk (which we'll discuss later, in a separate section). Of the first two, the Leidseplein houses the slightly more sedate establishments, while the spots on the Rembrandtsplein (and particularly on the Thorbeckeplein) go in heavily for those Dutch "ecdysiasts" (ladies who sinuously doff their clothing) that you may have heard about. With respect to all the establishments in these areas, it's important to know their exact hours of operation (which we'll set forth); some open late and close late, others open early and close early, others operate in the mid-evening, from 8 to 2 a.m.

Student nightclubs

The youngsters of Amsterdam—those in their late teens and early 20s—patronize one particular spot for dancing: The **Lucky Star,** 28 Korte Leidsedwarsstraat (just off the Leidseplein), is packed on weekend nights with its younger clients, then attracts a barely-older group (mid 20s) on the weekdays. There's action here on two midget floors to recorded rock and other music, and a bar observation post which allows spectators to view both floors at once. Admission: the Dutch equivalent of 75 U.S. cents for women, about $1.50 for men, with beer or genever for 2.50 guilders.

Amsterdam's famous **Paradiso** and **Kosmos,** two other immensely popular nightspots, are so very different from the traditional discotheque that we've discussed them in a separate section—"Alternative Amsterdam"—appearing earlier in this chapter.

Bars with entertainment

For losing your inhibitions, ridding yourself of aggressions, and generally immersing yourself in noise and music, there are two outstanding bars among the scores of bars that Amsterdam offers.

The one that can always guarantee the above results is the celebrated **Bamboo Bar,** 64 Lange Leidsedwarsstraat (two short blocks from the Leidseplein), a crowded, smoky room with African masks displayed on the walls, a pianist (who bears a strong resemblance to Mao Tse-tung) in one corner, two mariachi players alongside the pianist, and a crowd of somewhat tipsy Amsterdammers (20s, 30s and up) ranged in front of the painist, usually singing at the top of their lungs. There's no room to dance, and scarcely enough space to consume the very inexpensive drinks (2.50 guilders for genever and most other potions); the only remaining alternative is to join in the fun and meet the Dutch! Not a place for shy people. Less crowded is the **Carrousel,** 20 Thorbeckeplein (off the Rembrandtsplein), where drinks are 6 to 10 guilders, and the entertainment consists of a live orchestra, not to mention topless lady bartenders. Here, scenes such as those which always erupt at the Bamboo Bar, *sometimes* occur —and that, in the last analysis, is up to you and your fellow patrons.

(6) Sidewalk Cafe Sitting

This next evening activity (which can also be practiced during the day) is a major occupation in Amsterdam—and a cheap and pleasant one, too. No sidewalk cafe will ever require that you take more than a single cup of coffee, over which you're then permitted to linger the entire evening as you watch the passing parade in Amsterdam's two major entertainment squares: the Rembrandtsplein and the Leidseplein.

Of the two, the Rembrandtsplein possesses a bit more activity, and here the cafes, with their sidewalk table areas, are lined almost solidly along two sides of the square. On the Leidseplein, the major outdoor cafes are those operated by the American Hotel and the Cafe Moderne, but the three most exciting ones are the **Hoopman Bodega,** the **Cafe Reynders,** and the **Cafe Eylders,** all three on the Korte Leidsedwarsstraat, just off the Leidseplein, alongside (but across another small square from) the Opera. Of these, the **Cafe Reynders** is the outstanding student cafe of Amsterdam, heavily patronized by Amsterdam's version of the hippie, along with their surprisingly pretty, hair-to-the-waist companions. Obviously, there's no minimum, no cover charge, and drinks average 2 guilders ($1), for which you can sit and meet people all evening. The Cafe Eylders is a slightly more polished version of the Reynders, and the Hoopman Bodega is a somewhat more elegant bar, patronized by some fairly elegant older people; its prices are about 20 Dutch cents higher than those charged at the Reynders and Eylders for jonge genever (2.10 guilders) and beer (2 guilders). During the winter, all three establishments continue full blast, but without the sidewalk tables.

(7) The Sailors' Quarter

One final nightlife area deserves consideration, because it represents a phenomenon that is fast disappearing from Europe, and that continues to exist in its classic form only in Amsterdam, Hamburg, and a few other cities: a full-fledged, rip-roaring, wide-open sailors' entertainment area, which in Amsterdam comprises the district on and near the winding **Zeedijk.** Here there are not merely dozens of bars, but scores of them—sporting such names as "Casa Blanca," "City Lights," "Sailor's Place," "Salon Mexico," "Skip O Hoy Bar"—and it's a highlight of your European trip to stroll alongside them, peering into the taverns, and then walking along the equally bawdy streets nearby (particularly, the Oude Zijds Achterburgwal and the Oude Zijds Voorburgwal). For those of you who would like to do this area in an organized manner, I suggest the follwoing evening foot tour:

From the Krasnapolsky Hotel on the Dam Square, walk down the narrow Warmoesstraat until you come to the bottom of the Zeedijk, near the Centraal Station. Then walk up the entire length of the Zeedijk, until you reach the Nieuwmarkt. From the Nieuwmarkt, walk across the Barndesteeg to the Oude Zijds Achterburgwal, and walk down the Oude Zijds Achterburgwal to its end, near the station; then cross over to the parallel Oude Zijds Voorburgwal and walk up that canal until you reach the Damstraat, where you can turn in again to the Dam Square. Did you ever expect to find *this* in Amsterdam?

EXCURSIONS OUTSIDE AMSTERDAM: After you've spent three-or-so days in the city, you'll want to tack on some extra time for all the many one-day excursions that can be made to places near Amsterdam—to **The Hague** and **Rotterdam,** for instance, or to the tulip fields of Keukenhof, or to Leiden, Haarlem, Arnhem, Delft—or to a dozen other spots. If I had time, however, for only one excursion from Amsterdam, I'd make it to a site associated with the former Zuiderzee—either to the stupendous **Enclosure Dike** (Afsluitdijk) that transformed the Zuiderzee into a peaceful lake (the Ijsselmeer), or to **Marken** and **Volendam**—two picturesque fishing villages on the Zuiderzee—or to the newly-built, planned cities that now stand on "polders" carved out from that body of water. It's fascinating to contrast these new towns, created from the sea, with the centuries-old ports of the Zuiderzee, now deprived of their former importance as major shipping centers. In some of these—primarily on the island of **Marken** and in the village of **Volendam,** both of them less than 40 minutes from Amsterdam—the inhabitants still wear the traditional ancient clothing of The Netherlands: the men in black, bell-bottom trousers, tight black jackets, and tight visored caps; the women in broad aproned dresses reaching to their feet, with white lace caps, and curls that hang down straight on both sides of their faces. And all, of course, in wooden shoes!

Marken was once an island in the Zuiderzee, inundated at least once a year; many of its houses are therefore on stilts that enabled them to ride out the floods. Volendam is an equally picturesque fishing village whose residents wear costumes and carry on traditions that differ in subtle ways from those prevailing on Marken. Although Marken is still almost entirely surrounded by water, a dike—atop which is a highway—now connects it to the mainland; and sadly, the construction of the Markerwaard Polder will soon make it a normal, landlocked town. Try and see it now, in its glorious island state!

Visiting the sites on the Zuiderzee

To visit these sites inexpensively, you can use several alternative forms of transport.

First, you can make these excursions on your own, by car. From Amsterdam to Marken and Volendam is a half-hour's ride, once you've crossed the Ij by ferry. And if you're a good driver, you can reach **"Den Oever,"** one of the terminal points of the Afsluitdijk (Enclosure Dike), in less than an hour more. Crossing the dike takes about 30 minutes (but allow a 20-minute stop at the tower monument, for a birdseye view of the entire phenomenon), and you can then spend three-hours-or-so driving south along the other side of the Zuiderzee (now the Ijsselmeer), visiting the planned city of Emmeloord, and viewing the most recently-drained polders. This entire circular tour of the Zuiderzee can quite easily be made in a day. Or, if you prefer to go directly to the polders from Amsterdam, you can drive east along the bottom of the Zuiderzee and then head north toward Emmeloord. A glance at a good highway map will make the routes instantly clear to you.

If you do not have a car, you can still make the trip to Marken and Volendam on your own by taking one of the fabulous **"NZH"** bus rides there for a round-trip price of exactly 11 guilders ($5.50). The ride starts from a point on the Prins Hendrikkade near the Victoria Hotel, almost directly in front of the Centraal Station, with departures at 30-minute intervals throughout the day, starting at 9:30 a.m., daily from April 1 to September 27. From there, you'll be taken by bus through a tunnel under the Ij River, and then through actual polderland to the quaint, old town of Monnickendam, from which you take a boat to Marken. From Marken, when you're ready to return, you take another boat to Volendam, and then—after strolling about for as long as you wish—you catch another bus back to Amsterdam. All for 11 guilders.

Guided tours to Marken, Volendam, and the Enclosure Dike

If you'd prefer to make these trips in a group, and with a guide, then simply visit the offices of any of the tour operators in Amsterdam, for whom the Marken excursion is a major business item. **Holland International Travel Service,** 7-10 Damrak (phone 22-25-50 or 25-30-35), and **General Travel Bureau,** 41 Damrak (tel: 24-97-02), operate tours to Marken twice a day, at 10 a.m. and 2:30 p.m., and charge 32.50 guilders ($16.25) per person. Both tours last a total of four hours, go first to Monnickendam, then proceed to Marken, and stop at a cheese factory in the village of Broek in Waterland on the return trip to Amsterdam.

Most of the Amsterdam tour companies also operate guilded tours to the Enclosure Dike, but only three times a week (the days vary) from April through September; the all-day excursion costs 45 guilders ($22.50), not including lunch. These tours visit another major point of interest along the way—the Friday morning cheese market in the town of **Alkmaar.** You may, however, want to consider the trip to Alkmaar on your own, via the next surprising method of transport: a Cheese Express (see below):

The Kaasexpres (Cheese-Express) to Alkmaar

Alkmaar, where a world-famous cheese market is held on Friday mornings in summer, less than an hour from Amsterdam, is a picturesque Dutch town replete with canals, lovely old houses, and a major square in which the cheese market takes place. On Friday mornings, from May through September, the square erupts into a frenzy of color and activity, as white-suited cheese porters, each wearing a red, blue or yellow hat according to the guild to which he belongs, go trotting across the square carrying sleds of stacked cheeses. Ranged around the square are literally thousands of tourists, for whom the Netherlands Railways has arranged unusually inexpensive transportation, via a special **"Cheese Express"** (the "Kaasexpres"). It leaves Amsterdam's Centraal Station at 9:27 a.m. on Fridays from mid-June through early September, arrives in Alkmaar at 10 a.m., and costs only 10.40 guilders ($5.20) round-trip, second class. Aboard the train, volunteer ladies in traditional costumes pass out free cheese.

If you can't be in Amsterdam on a Friday, but do happen to be there on a Thursday from mid-June to mid-August, you can take advantage of a similar deal—the **"Schagermarkt-Expres"**—to visit the West Frisian Market in the town of Schagen. Farmers and their wives from miles around, in traditional

West Frisian dress, come here to make purchases and to participate in or watch exhibitions of West Frisian folk dancing. The special train to Schagen leaves the Amsterdam Centraal Station at 9:31 a.m. on Thursdays from June 17 to August 19, arrives in Schagen at 10:24 a.m., and costs 15.90 guilders ($7.95), round-trip, second class.

Care for a Wednesday tour? On that day from June 11 to August 13, a train leaves the Amsterdam Station at 8:37 a.m., arrives in the 600-year-old town of Hoorn at 9:12 a.m., depositing you at a market of clog makers, net menders, potters and other quaint folk, who set up a profusion of stalls and sell their wares and services while groups of folk dancers and musicians perform. This one costs 11.10 guilders ($5.50) round-trip, and the return can be made via almost hourly trains to Amsterdam throughout the day.

The Other Towns

Unfortunately, we haven't the space to go into detail about the many other Dutch towns within one-day excursion range of Amsterdam. But you may be interested in the transportation procedures for getting to two of them—The Hague and Rotterdam.

To reach The Hague from Amsterdam, you can—as a first alternative—simply take the train: they depart at least every hour (and sometimes more often) from the Centraal Station, take slightly under an hour for the trip, and cost 16.60 guilders ($8.30), round-trip second class. For only 2.40 guilders more (a total of 19 guilders) you can also take a Netherlands Railways' "Day Excursion" from Amsterdam to The Hague and Scheveningen, on a ticket that not only includes your round-trip transportation to and within The Hague, but also covers admission to Madurodam and the Pier at Scheveningen. Pick up your ticket for this trip at the Centraal Station.

There are, in addition, a number of full-day escorted bus tours to Rotterdam, The Hague and Delft, and half-day tours simply to The Hague and Delft, which all the major tour operators in Amsterdam (their offices are located up and down the Damrak) offer for approximately the same price: 45 guilders ($22.50) for the full-day version, 32.50 guilders ($16.25) for half a day. The former invariably begin at 10 a.m., drive first to Aalsmeer (where you visit the flower auctions, several hot-houses, and a wooden-shoe-making factory), and then head to The Hague, where stops and visits are made at the Peace Palace, the Binnenhof, the Royal Palace, and the Huis ter Bosch ("House in the Woods," a summer residence of the Queen), Madurodam, and Scheveningen. After lunch, the bus then proceeds to the beautiful canal city of **Delft** (one of the best preserved of the old Dutch towns), where you pay a visit to the Royal Delft Ware Factory "De Porceleyne Fles," that famous manufacturer of Delft Blue China (since 1653). And some of the tours, on the return trip to Amsterdam, even manage a stop in **Leiden** and **Haarlem** (in which latter city they visit the renowned Frans Hals Museum).

From Amsterdam to Rotterdam, excellent superhighways permit a good driver to make the trip in just slightly more than 75 minutes; by train from Amsterdam's Centraal Station, the second-class, round-trip fare is around $10.10 (20.20 guilders), and there are hourly departures. On a Netherlands Railways "Day Excursion" from Amsterdam to Rotterdam (operated daily from April 1 to September 30), the price is 28.50 guilders, and that includes a "Spido" boat trip through the harbor area, and admission to the Blijdorp Zoo.

Cities nearer to Amsterdam? Hope likes Haarlem, and here's her report:

HOPE IN HAARLEM: "The easiest half-day excursion you can make is to the evocative old city of Haarlem, chartered in the 13th Century, and now best known to tourists for its **Frans Hals Museum.** Trains leave Amsterdam's Centraal Station every 15 minutes, take 15 minutes for the trip, cost 5.60 guilders ($2.80) for the round-trip, and provide some bonus pastoral scenes of grazing cows along the way. Once there, allow ample wandering time for savoring the atmosphere, which is especially heady in the immediate vicinity of the museum: an area of narrow old cobble-stoned streets with rows and rows of gabled houses, interspersed with charming antique shops. If the historic beauty of the street of Groot Heiligland (the Frans Hals is at #62) doesn't make you dizzy with the sensation that you've stepped into a 17th Century etching, then the 'Grote Markt,' the city square, is sure to get to you. On it, you'll find the City Hall, a part of which was originally begun in the 13th Century as a palace for Dutch nobility (if you arrive before 2 p.m., and if you're lucky enough to be in Haarlem on a day when no marriages are being performed, you may get a chance to see the 14th-century 'Gravenzaal'—Hall of the Counts, among many points of interest *inside* the Hall); St. Bavo Church (the 'Grote Kerk'), an enormous, imposing, dark stone, medieval structure (15th and 16th Centuries—Frans Hals, and other dignitaries, are buried here), with a famous 18th Century organ (open weekdays 9 to 5, entrance fee 1 guilder, 50 Dutch cents for children); and 'De Hallen,' an affiliate museum of the Frans Hals, with temporary exhibitions of both old and new art. (Not far from the Grote Markt, at Spaarne 16, is **The Teylers Museum,** the oldest in Holland, with a very varied and interesting collection of fabulous fossils, gems and minerals, bones and skeletons, pre-historic-looking insects or lizards with monstrous jaws and teeth, historical scientific instruments—and, just for good measure, a couple of rooms of paintings and drawings, including some by Rembrandt, Raphael, Michelangelo and Claude Lorrain. Open daily, March through September, Tuesday through Saturday from 10 to 5, winters till 4, and the first Sunday of every month from 1 to 5, for an admission of 2 guilders, 75 Dutch cents for children.)

"But the key visit is to the 'Frans Halsmuseum'; immediately upon stepping off the train, cross the street in front of the station, look for the stop marked 'Perron D', board Bus #2 or #70—direction Schalwijk (fare is 1 guilder), and ask the driver to let you off at the proper stop and point you in the direction of the museum: 62 Groot Heiligland, open weekdays from 10 to 5, Sundays from 1 to 5, admission of 1.85 guilders from March through October, free from November through February. (If you need further help, you'll find a V.V.V. office to the right as you exit from the station.)

"You may agree with me that the Frans Hals is a strangely moving experience. For here one enjoys that all too rare combination, the perfect marriage between setting and subject matter. The building, which opened its doors as an Old Men's Home, is an almost perfectly preserved, early 17th century mansion, with a beautiful formal garden in its inner courtyard. The structure itself stirs the imagination, with its rooms so reminiscent of the very scenes that inspired the School of Haarlem painters during the 17th Century (Frans Hals not the least among them). Of course, all of these gentlemen (Jan Mostaert, Jacob van Ruysdael, Adriaen van Ostade, Jan Steen, Adrien Brouwer, Cornelis Dusart, among others) are represented here, along with Dutch and Flemish artists who were not of the Haarlem school. Also on display are rooms of period furniture, china and silver, coins and medals, a replica of an ancient pharmacy, and a cunning antique doll house with tiny dogs, dishes on the table, and the most minuscule playing cards imaginable.

"The star attraction remains Hals himself, and two particular master-pieces: 'Governors of the Old Men's Home at Haarlem' and 'Lady Regents of the Old Men's Home at Haarlem', which I would travel a lot further than the distance between Amsterdam and Haarlem to see! Both were done in 1664, when the artist was over 80! In his last years, after a successful career, Hals found himself alone and impoverished (the art histories tell us he was fond of the good life, and incurred too many debts), and relegated to living on a subsidy from the town: 200 guilders a year, and three cartloads of peat! For these paintings, his last commission, the governors of the home must have reckoned something like this: 'Let old Frans Hals earn his keep by painting our picture', and the rather sardonic results are now before you—the women with their dry, monkey-like faces, the men younger but ineffectual looking. One of the older guards tells me that Manet came to the Frans Halsmuseum when *he* was a very old man, and sat for hours in the room of The Governors.

Further afield

"A much longer trip is to the **Kröller-Müller Museum** in Otterlo, which sophisticated museum devotees acclaim as one of the world's best; but reaching the museum is exhausting, and totally impractical in winter, unless you have a car: 1¼ hours by train first to Arnhem (21.60 guilders round-trip), then another 40 minutes by bus to Otterlo (take the bus marked 'Hoge Veluwe' in front of the railway station, 9.50 guilders round trip including admission to Hoge Veluwe Park—buses leave on the hour, *almost* every hour, check the posted schedule). (But warning: this direct bus operates only from June to August; other months one must bus to Otterlo, then taxi or hike for about 20 minutes to the museum.) Take only an 'Intercity' train to Arnhem leaving Amsterdam's Centraal Station every hour at 17 minutes past and 13 minutes to the hour, or an international 'D' train bound for Germany and leaving Amsterdam at 8:18 a.m.; all other trains to Arnhem are locals or take an indirect and interminably long route.

"Still, if you've got the stamina and time, you'll find here an exquisite collection amassed, for the most part, and donated to the public by Mrs. Kröller-Müller, who spent a good deal of her time musing on the possibilities of interplay between architecture, art and nature. It is the juxtaposition of these elements which make this one of the world's outstanding musuems: a quiet forest surrounds you, inside the museum the paintings are displayed with good taste and good lighting, and the 'Sculpture Garden' (late 19th century to the present, including Henry Moore, Barbara Hepworth and Dubuffet), which covers eleven acres of ground with nature as a backdrop, is unbelievably moving and beautiful. (Incidentally, white bicycles are provided free of charge by the museum, so you can pedal around the collection or through the woods comfortably for as long as you wish.) As if all this were not enough, the Kröller-Müller also happens to have a large collection of priceless Van Goghs. To be exact (according to their catalogue), there are 89 paintings and 187 drawings here—many famous and familiar, but also some little-known, and extremely off-beat, early work. Since it was Mrs. Kröller-Müller's intention to assemble a collection that would illustrate the development of painting from the 19th century on (though there are early Dutch and Flemish masters here, too, and Lucas Cranach), the Impressionists are quite well represented. Required viewing for museum builders and curators, the Rijksmuseum Kröller-Müller charges no admission (but there *is* a charge to enter the Park: 4.50 guilders for adults, 4.50 guilders extra for a car, 2 guilders for children 16 and under, no charge for bicycles or motorcycles though; on the bus your admission fee is included in the fare) and is open on weekdays from 10 to 5 (Sculpture Park closes at 4:30, and is closed completely in winter), and Sundays from 1 to 5 (Summers from 11; Sculpture Park from 11 to 4:30)."

A READER'S WHIRLWIND EXCURSION: "If you are rushed for time, our suggestion is not to take the separate day excursions to The Hague and Rotterdam respectively, but simply to purchase a round-trip train ticket from Amsterdam to Rotterdam. Go direct to Rotterdam, get a city map at the Information Desk, and walk out of the station 200 yards straight downtown, then turn left into the famous shopping boulevard where no cars are allowed. After this, proceed to the Euromast and then return to Rotterdam Station, where you take the train to Amsterdam via The Hague. At The Hague, stop off and proceed with Tram No. 8 outside the station to the Peace Palace. Stop off here for one of the organized tours (1.50 guilders), then again take the No. 8 Tram to Scheveningen, and walk around the sea-side resort for about a half-hour. Then take Tram No. 9 to the miniature town of Madurodam, stop there for an hour, then take Tram No. 9 back to the train station, and return to Amsterdam—all on one ticket at a third of the price of the two excursion trips. But to do it all in one day, you must leave at 8:30 a.m. and move fairly fast" (Lenard G. Lever and Ben-Zion Surdut, Cape Town, South Africa). . . . "Upon arriving in The Hague, take tram #9 opposite the train station to the Mauritshuis —one of the best small museums in Europe, with mouthwatering Rembrandts and Vermeers. Continue on tram #9 to Madurodam; we spent nearly an hour and a half there, but you could do it in less; continue on tram #9 to Scheveningen, and walk to the end of the Pier. If it's a warm day, there will be thousands on the beach—a colorful scene—and you can swim or lie on the beach too, if you like. Then return on tram #8, which passes the Peace Palace. Continue on tram #8 to the central station, and take a train that stops in Haarlem (they run about every 15 minutes). Follow Hope Frommer's instructions for reaching the Frans Hals Museum, which we found most rewarding. Then return to Amsterdam. We did this entire trip without hurrying or feeling rushed, and were back in Amsterdam shortly after 5 o'clock" (Mr. and Mrs. Paul Redin, Oklahoma City, Oklahoma; note by AF: at windows #13 of the train station in Amsterdam, buy a 'day excursion' to The Hague for this trip (19 guilders), which includes round-trip transportation for the day to The Hague, stopovers on the way, unlimited tram transportation in The Hague, and admission to Madurodam and to the Pier at Scheveningen. Trains to The Hague run every few minutes, with one particular express leaving Amsterdam at 8:59 a.m., arriving The Hague at 9:26 a.m.)

READERS ON BIKES: "The high point of my entire journey was a bicycle trip through the Dutch countryside, near Leiden, leaving from the Hans Brinker Stutel (student hotel) in Amsterdam. We went by car to Leiden and then spent about three or four hours bicycling through some very charming countryside, including windmills, canals, etc. We also stopped for lunch (sandwiches) and ate in a field. If readers are interested in this, I suggest they contact in Amsterdam Miss Anja Nort, a totally charming and informative guide. Her address is 11 Brouwersgracht, phone 252-014" (Ronald Merkin, Brooklyn, New York). . . . "At the **Waterlooplein Flea Market,** you can purchase bicycles for as little as 75 guilders. The dealer who sold me a bike for that sum promised to buy it back for 50 guilders. After riding around the canals for a week, I returned the bike and the total cost was only 25 guilders, compared with the daily rental of 5.50 guilders!" (Kerry Pattison, Westwood, California).

FINDING A SELF-SERVICE LAUNDRY: Look for the sign "Wasserette" or sometimes even "Launderette." They charge around 6 guilders ($3) for the washing and drying of one machine-load of laundry, and generally maintain hours of from 8 a.m. to 8 p.m. on weekdays. Four centrally-located "wasserettes": at #12 Oude Doelenstraat (best in town), a continuation of the Damstraat, about 1½ blocks from the Dam Square; at 9 Ferdinand Bolstraat (near the Heineken's Brewery); at 375 Kerkstraat (near Utrechtsestraat); at 59 Elandsgracht (near the Leidseplein).

SOME FINAL FACTS ABOUT AMSTERDAM: It's hard to believe that you'll want to better the 5.50 guilders ($2.75) fare charged by the **KLM** bus that goes from the Museumplein out to the Airport of Amsterdam (Schiphol). Still, if you're really strapped for funds, go to the back of the Centraal Station where you'll see a sign from which a commercial bus company runs trips to Schiphol for only 2 guilders ($1). Alternatively, and for the same price, you can take a Central Nederland bus (line CN5, 25 or 45) from 134 Prins Hendrikkade in front of the Centraal Station (and just a few steps from the large Victoria Hotel). These leave daily, every twenty minutes, from 6:25 a.m. until midnight, and also service the towns of Hoofddorp, Haarlem, Leiden, Amstelveen, others. Take the bus marked Schiphol-Centrum, *not* Schiphol-Oost. . . . The famous "Get in Touch with the Dutch" program, operated by the **V.V.V.** (Amsterdam's Tourist Association) from its main office at 5 Rokin (tel: 22-10-16, ext. 135 or 117), will give you the name and address of a Dutch family (if you wish, someone who shares your business, profession, or other interests) to whose home you can drop over for a visit. Contact the V.V.V. in advance of, or on the day of, your arrival in Amsterdam, as these meetings take a day or so to arrange; in either event, you'll have to appear in person at the V.V.V. office to make the final arrangements. . . . Amsterdam's student activities? They're operated by the **N.B.B.S.** (Netherlands Office for Foreign Student Relations) out of an office at Dam Square 17 (phone 23-76-86), open 9:30 a.m. to 5 p.m. weekdays, 10 a.m. to 2 p.m. Saturdays. Here's where you'll learn about student discounts on sightseeing tours, restaurants, student charter flights, student trains. . . . Bicycle rentals? Since Holland is almost entirely flat, it's the perfect land for cyclists (who can even make an excursion to Marken and Volendam from Amsterdam). For motorbikes, the chief supplier is **Heja Rijwiel-en Brom-fietsbedrijf,** 39 Bestevaerstraat (phone 129-211), which charges between 16.50 and 19.50 guilders a day (depending on the model), between 99 and 117 guilders per week; it also rents bicycles for 6 guilders per day, 27.50 guilders per week. From the station, take tram #13, or bus #33, to reach Heja's showroom. . . . In case you've been wondering, the population of Amsterdam is between 800,000 and 900,000, while the bicycles owned by that population exceed 300,000! I'm told that a used bike can be bought at the Amsterdam flea market (on the Waterlooplein) for the equivalent of $25. . . . For cheap indoor swimming in Amsterdam (3 guilders), the address is 19 Heiligeweg ("the **Zwembad Heiligeweg"),** just off the solely-for-pedestrians shopping street called Kalver-straat. . . . The city has over 50 different canals, between 500 and 600 bridges (and that makes Venice "the Amsterdam of the South")! The population of the Netherlands itself exceeds 14,000,000. . . . Restaurant tipping: A service charge —usually 15%—is automatically included in your bill (as is tax), and there is no obligation to leave anything other than the very small change which you'll receive back (i.e., a few 10-Dutch-cents-pieces). Most Dutchmen don't even do that!

On the normal multi-stopover plan, you can fly from Amsterdam to London for no extra charge. That's what we'll now do, as we head to our second city on this $15-a-day tour.

Chapter IV

LONDON

Breakfast is Included

LONDON, to some, is an imposing place, to be respected rather than enjoyed. To me, this city is as unpretentious as the smallest country hamlet. When London is known and absorbed, it remains in the mind not as a memory of monuments and museums, but of utterly simple and sympathetic sights: the galleries at Covent Garden filled with students rapt upon a Frederick Ashton ballet; the calm and smoky innards of a corner pub; the clusters of children in Kensington Park; the cheese-and-ale parties in the one-room skylight flats of Chelsea.

All you've heard to the contrary, Londoners are among the friendliest people of Europe, and London itself is an inviting town. It has charm and a politeness of attitude, in such abundance, that few travelers fail to extend their stay, once they've arrived. Can you live in London on $15 a day? To answer that question, let's examine some human statistics.

PRICES AND WAGES: I have a friend in London who is a graduate of the Old Vic Company, and a recognized, steadily-employed actor in the theatres of the West End. His salary averages to barely more than 80 pounds ($176) a week, less tax. On that sum, he maintains not merely a proper standard of living, but a constant round of entertaining and much-too-frequent pub-crawling. I know a woman reporter who works for one of Britain's top weekly magazines. She averages 90 pounds a week ($198). She dresses well, has a comfortable flat near Marble Arch, and is considered in England to be quite adequately paid. For these two people, a ten-dollar bill has the purchasing power of nearly fifteen dollars over here, and neither of them would be shocked, surprised or in any way nonplussed by the standards prescribed in this book.

You would expect one of the oldest democracies on earth to possess a price structure with a broad, mass appeal—and it does. Despite the surface elegance of England, the entertainment, eating and housing facilities of that nation are actually far more concentrated in the middle and lower-class areas than in the United States. Low-cost chain restaurants, moderate hotels and inexpensive night-spots are astonishingly abundant, at prices that would shame their American counterparts, because they are geared to the low (for America) wages of the overwhelming bulk of the British population. Because of that, the tourist who can't find a satisfying meal for $3, or a satisfying room with breakfast for as little as ten dollars per person, just isn't half-trying.

You'd like proof? Read on.

HOTELS: These can be obtained for less than half of what you'd pay in an American city. And that outlay results not only in a room, but in breakfast as well! The first thing to know about budget-priced British hotels is that most of them include a free, enormous morning meal in their room charges. Served each day at stated hours in the hotel's dining room, it costs nothing and it's a whopper—the kind that would be priced at least at $3 in the U.S. And so, when a London hotel owner quotes you a nightly rate of, say, $10 per person, he means that room *and* breakfast will come to $10 per person—an exceptional value.

Consequently, to stay on a budget in London, you can go as high as $12 per person in your room charges ($24 for a double), because that price includes a large breakfast (usually with unlimited servings). But $12 is stretching it a bit, and we've scoured the city for rooms costing even less. Here are the results:

Russell Square (£6 to £8.50)

In any but the high-season months, you needn't hesitate in your search for a moderately-priced London hotel. Head immediately for the nearest "tube" station (the subway), and take the first train you see to the **Russell Square** stop. Russell Square, a lovely little park, forms the heart of a district of budget hotels, all of them incredibly well-located within walking distance of the theatre section, the Soho area, the University of London and the British Museum. While the hotels here are often higher-priced than some we'll recommend in other sections of London, they provide amazing value for the extra pound-or-so they'll charge. Keep in mind, though, that they are almost always jammed from May through October, when you'd do best to try one of the other hotel areas discussed in this chapter, or else phone first to determine whether vacancies exist. Keep in mind, too, that the per person rates we quote are, unless otherwise stated, for double or twin-bedded rooms.

Bernard Street

Emerging from the Russell Square station, you'll be on **Bernard Street (1)**, which juts off from the Square and which consists (on one side of the street) of virtually nothing other than a solid row of British guest houses—homey, little brownstones with charges as low as six pounds ($13.20) per person for bed-and-breakfast. These little buildings have no elevators—they are homes that have been converted into hotels. They have living room-lounges with family-type "tellies" (tv sets); they have breakfast rooms with sideboards, from which the big morning feast is served; some of them permit you to use washing machines, outdoor lines and ironing boards; and all of them are patronized by the average middle-class Englishman from out of town. Nothing could be more

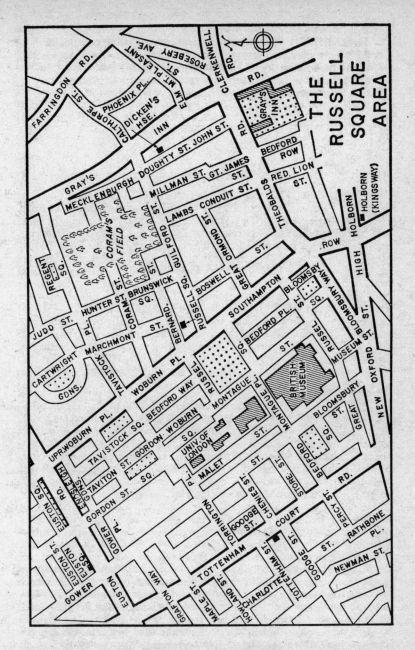

THE RUSSELL SQUARE AREA

British or more typically representative of English life.

On Bernard Street, you'll find at least six recommended choices within a 100-yard walk. My favorites are, in order of preference, the newly-refurbished

THE BRITISH POUND ("£"), presently worth approximately $2.20, is divided into 100 pence ("p") worth 2.2¢ apiece. £1.50 means one pound and 50 pence; £10 are ten pounds, 10p are 10 pence. To calculate the rough value of English prices, simply double the figure, and you'll be only slightly off.

Tudor House Hotel, 17-18 Bernard Street (phone 837-1691), whose 34 rooms (of which 17 are singles) rent for £6.65 ($14.63) per person, double or triple, from £7.47 single, and which lets you hang your drip-n-dry wash in the backyard and iron it downstairs (an exceptionally friendly, happy establishment); and the **Edinburgh House,** 23 Bernard Street, phone 837-6263 (from £6 to £9 for b-and-b; unusually pleasant proprietors who promise to "burn the bacon" for American guests). Enclose reply postage (in the form of an international postal response coupon) with your reservation requests to both of these popular establishments, whose postal zone number is London W.C.1. Elsewhere on the street, the **Garden House Hotel,** 19 Bernard Street (837-5176), £6.75 ($14.85) for b-and-b, per person in a double room, £7 single; has also been checked out, and is clean and suitable. All of these, you'll note, are found on the south side of Bernard Street; the north side is currently being upgraded with considerable new construction.

The Incomparable Cartwright Gardens

Now, if you'll walk from Bernard Street to the end of Marchmont Street (see our map), you'll encounter the most attractive and pleasant street of budget hotels in this area, which faces a tree-lined, dead-end square on which are spotted tennis courts of the University of London. That's the famous **Cartwright Gardens,** on which there's a two-block crescent of handsome Nineteenth Century town houses (they feature cut-glass windows and chandeliers, red-carpeted entrance hallways), every one of which is today a top-notch budget hotel. The roomiest of these is the **Harlingford** (phone 387-1551) at 61 Cartwright Gardens, which has both a tv-lounge and a lounge-without-tv for people who prefer conversation, and which charges £7.70 to £9.90 ($16.94 to $21.78) per person for bed and breakfast; while nearby are three other favorites of frequent visitors to London: **The Avalon,** at 46 Cartwright Gardens (phone 387-2366, £8.50 to £10 ($18.70 to $22) per person—including breakfast and V.A.T., and whose proprietors, Mr. and Mrs. Taylor, not only provide showers at no extra charge, but will direct you to nearby tennis courts costing 50 pence an hour); the **Mentone Hotel,** at 54 Cartwright Gardens (phone 387-3927), whose 30 rooms rent for £8 per person double, £9 single; and **Jenkins Hotel,** the latter at 45 Cartwright Gardens (phone 387-2067), charging from £8 ($17.60) per person, including V.A.T., for b-and-b, in double rooms. Especial kudos go to the **Mentone Hotel,** now undoubtedly the best on Cartwright Gardens, with its new furniture, brightly colored walls, bedspreads, carpets and unusually pleasant owners (an English couple). A private tennis court across the way can be used by guests for only 30 pence (66¢) an hour. Additional praise for the **Jenkins Hotel,** which can turn a pleasant London stay into a memorable one; two budget-minded members of Parliament, including a Privy Councillor, live here during sessions, and the air crackles with intellectual debate; then, too, Mr. and Mrs. Williams—who manage the Jenkins—are superb hotel proprietors. A uniform £7.50 ($16.50) per person for b & b is charged by the rather stylish **Crescent Hotel,** 49 Cartwright Gardens (phone 387-1515); singles are £9 ($19.80), all prices including breakfast, service and tax). And a fractionally higher rate is asked by the **George Hotel,** 60 Cartwright Gardens (387-1528), £7.50 to £8.50 per person for bed and breakfast, with central heating in winter and reduced rates for children. To reach this street, turn right on Bernard Street, as you emerge from the Russell Square subway exit, walk half-a-block to Marchmont Street, then straight up Marchmont Street for 3 blocks. At this point, Marchmont Street curves half-left and changes its name to Cartwright Gardens.

Bloomsbury and Gower Streets

A cluster of cheaper hotels, in almost as pleasant a setting, is found at the far side of the Square (an easy walk from the Russell Square tube exit) on the famous **Bloomsbury Street (2),** which bears that designation for about a hundred yards, and then becomes **Gower Street (3).** Both names are identified with a brilliant period of pre-World War I British intellectual history (Sidney and Beatrice Webb, George Bernard Shaw, Virginia Woolf), and you'll find book-publishers, university buildings, philanthropic societies and schools all along the length of the street.

The higher-priced budget hotels are on Bloomsbury Street (for which the nearest underground stop is Tottenham Court Road), in an exquisite series of Georgian town houses. One of these, the **Gresham Hotel,** 36-38 Bloomsbury Street (phone 636-1067), built in 1880, charges from £7.50 to £9 ($16.50 to $19.80) per person, depending on the size of the room, is directly around the corner from the British Museum. The **Morgan Hotel,** at 24 Bloomsbury Street (636-3735), charges £8 ($17.60) for the same deal, is highly recommended, as is the **Regent House Hotel** at 28 Bloomsbury Street (636-4888), with roughly similar rates per person in double rooms. All three hotels are located just next to tiny Bedford Square, a well-known publishing center which intersects Bloomsbury Street and Gower Street.

On the other side of Bedford Square, Bloomsbury Street becomes Gower Street, and the hotel prices descend as you move deeper into the area of the University of London. The exceedingly friendly **Arran House Hotel,** 77 Gower Street (636-2186), is my choice here, because of its colorful, ex-British Army-officer-proprietor (Maj. W. J. Richards), who puts you at ease, and charges £6.75 ($14.85) per person, tax included, for a broad variety of rooms. Numerous readers have liked the rose garden out back, the military etchings and other touches in the breakfast room. Try, also, the 23-room **Staunton Hotel,** 13-15 Gower Street (phone 636-5583), in a 200-year-old building with interesting winding staircases and outgoing, almost effervescent in attitude proprietors, Mr. and Mrs. Morgan (£7 per person in twin rooms, including full English breakfast); the **Ridgemount Private Hotel,** 65 Gower Street (636-1141), £7 ($15.40) per person for bed-and-breakfast, tax included, in a centrally-heated establishment operated by a warm-hearted Welsh lady, Mrs. Rees; the **Jesmond Hotel,** 63 Gower Street (636-3199), £6.50 per person in a double, £6 in triple or 4-bedded rooms for b & b; **Langland Hotel,** 29 Gower Street (636-5801), whose proprietors, Mr. and Mrs. Thomas, enjoy the loyalty of a worldwide clientele, have rear rooms overlooking a peaceful little garden, and ask £6.25.

per person in twins, £8 single; **Maree Hotel,** 25 Gower Street (636-4868), £ 5 to 7 per person; and **Gower House,** 57 Gower Street, £6.25 in a double room, £5 per person in a 4-bedded room, including breakfast served by the proprietors themselves. At the last of these Gower Street hotels, you'll be directly across the street from the Royal Academy of Dramatic Art ("R.A.D.A."), where the greats of the British Stage, from John Gielgud to Albert Finney, have trained. The Borg brothers and their respective wives operate Gower House, and offer washing and ironing on the premises; phone 636-4685 to learn about vacancies.

By the way, a station called "Goodge Street" is the closest underground stop to the Gower Street hotels.

V.A.T.: Like other nations in the European Common Market, England assesses a "Value Added Tax" ("V.A.T."), currently 15%, on hotel rates. Unlike the hotels in those European nations, however, English hotels don't always quote their hotel charges with Value Added Tax included. Some do, some don't. Unless specifically stated to the contrary, most of the hotel rates quoted in this chapter include the 15% tax, as do restaurant prices listed later on.

Bedford Place (Big Splurge Only)

A far more elegant street running off Russell Square is a solid row of white Georgian town houses, with Bloomsbury Square (a park) at one end, Russell Square at the other. Unfortunately, only one hotel here—the relatively-plain **Thanet,** at 8 Bedford Place (636-2869)—is within our budget range, with bed-and-continental-breakfast rates throughout the year of £7.50 ($16.50) per person (in double rooms), including tax. The proprietors here are tourists themselves, having used our guide, "England on $5 & $10 a Day," on their honeymoon early in 1965! Four other quite lovely hotels—the **Wansbeck,** 5 Bedford Place, phone 636-6232 (8.50 pounds per person in twin rooms); the **Bedford House,** 1 Bloomsbury Place, phone 636-0577 (£8 for b-and-b, service and tax included); the **Haddon Hall,** 40 Bedford Place, phone 636-0026 (£8.50 per person twin, £9.50 single, a Georgian gentleman's townhouse, now offering reduced rates for children, and babysitters on request); and the large **St. Margaret's Hotel,** 26 Bedford Place, 636-4277 (£8.75 ($19.25) per person b & b, all included)—are beyond our usual limits, but might be tried in an emergency. The nearest underground stop for all four hotels is: Holborn.

Sussex Gardens (£4.50 to £8.50)

A second, major hotel area in London is a single, but many-blocks-long, avenue called **Sussex Gardens (8),** which is almost continuously lined with bed-and-breakfast houses charging somewhat less than the going rate around Russell Square. The hotels here are so numerous, that it's hard to imagine you won't find a vacancy, even at the peak of the summer season when Russell Square will very definitely present difficulties. Side streets off Sussex Gardens—particularly the guesthouse-crammed **Norfolk Square** near Paddington Station

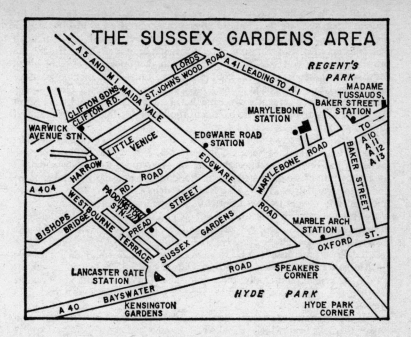

THE SUSSEX GARDENS AREA

—offer further possibilities and even cheaper rates.

Sussex Gardens lies just off Edgware Road, and Edgware Road leads, in a short walk, to Marble Arch and Hyde Park. The best tube stops are Paddington Station (for reaching the buildings on Sussex Gardens numbered 100 or higher) or the Edgware Road station of the Metropolitan line (for the numbers under 100), from which any passerby will point the way to Sussex Gardens. A particular advantage of Sussex Gardens, for readers with cars, is that it has an inner parallel road on which there's unrestricted parking.

The most numerous Sussex Gardens hotels are those closest to Edgware Road, these normally charging £6.50 ($14.30) to £7 ($15.40) per person for bed-and-breakfast. They include the **Red Court Hotel** (14 Sussex Gardens, phone 723-6378; £7.50 per person plus Value Added Tax; manager is a Maltese/Australian named John Louis Bayada); **Cameron Hotel,** 10 Sussex Gardens (£8 for room and breakfast; phone 262-1538); **Devon Court Hotel,** 24 Sussex Gardens (phone 723-5268), £6.50 per person in high season; **Winrose Guest House,** 26 Sussex Gardens (phone 723-5656, £7.50 single, £7 per person double, inclusive of V.A.T. and breakfast); **Cambridge House,** #36 (phone 723-9936), £7.50 per person, double; the exceptionally friendly **Haven Hotel,** #8 (phone 723-2195; £7.50 per person), whose wonderfully friendly and gregarious landlady, Bridget Giles, likes receiving families with children; **Orchard House,** #88 (723-0370), £7.50, children welcome; **Stuart House,** 30 Sussex Gardens (723-2486), £7.50 to £8 per person; and **Nayland Hotel,** 134 Sussex Gardens (phone 723-3380), charging £6.50 to £7.50 ($14.30 to $16.50) per person, including a big English breakfast, and operated for the past 25 years by various members of the Naylor family, whose experience is evident in the personal attention and service they provide.

But the best Sussex Gardens hotels (nearly always £6.50 to £8 a night for bed-and-breakfast) are the group of houses that bear #'s 120 to 148. They're located along a particularly nice stretch of the avenue, and most of them welcome families with children. Try, for instance, the **Tyburn Hotel,** 148 Sussex Gardens, phone 723-5096 (in a slightly higher price category, but which promises to charge from £8 ($17.60) to readers of this book, including service and tax, and will cook bacon in the American style—"burned"). One proprietress along this block recently wrote me that she has "come to know and respect American likes and dislikes: no basement rooms, no top floor, showers, lots of towels, scrambled eggs, burnt bacon!"

Further along the street, the prices dip a bit, and our choices include: **Lyndon House Hotel,** 84 Sussex Gardens (262-2387), £8 ($17.60) per person, including full English breakfast and tax, long recommended in this guide and long a favorite of students studying in London; the unusually well-decorated and attractive **Milrex Hotel,** 86 Sussex Gardens (723-5787; £7 per person), until recently owned by the proprietors of Lyndon House, "Iris and Lyn," whose photo—with their distinctive poodle and cat—adorns the mantelpieces at home of hundreds of former guests; and two doors away, **Cornwall House,** 82 Sussex Gardens (phone 262-2941), £7 per person ($15.40) for b-and-b. Try, too, the **Gresham House Hotel,** 118 Sussex Gardens (723-3323), £8 per person; the **Margam Private Hotel,** 120 Sussex Gardens, 723-0528, bed-and-breakfast for £8 per person; and finally, the comfortable **Berkeley Court** at 94 Sussex Gardens (723-4801), charging £8 for singles, £7 per person double, including breakfast.

If these, however, are full, then you still have at least 30 other hotels on Sussex Gardens from which to make your choice; and consequently, if you've arrived in London in June, July or August, you might save quite a bit of time by simply heading for this hotel-packed area, sans further ado. Especially because:

Nearby Norfolk Square

The pickings are even larger, and cheaper, on nearby **Norfolk Square,** a block from Sussex Gardens and a block, in the other direction, from Paddington Station. Its greatest recommendation is that most of the hotels here sport multi-consonant Welsh names or are owned by Welshmen, characteristically warm and hospitable. Why so many Welshmen? "If we ever get homesick," one proprietor explained to me, "we can hop a direct day-trip to Wales from Paddington Station." Try: the yellow-trimmed **Ty-Melyn Hotel** (which means yellow house in Welsh), 48 Norfolk Square (phone 262-6318 or 723-3050), charging £7 ($15.40) per person and operated by Mrs. Delvaux, who spent six years in Long Beach, California; the pink-and-grey **Camelot Hotel,** 45 Norfolk Square (phone 262-1980), £7 per person for bathless double rooms, less for multi-bedded rooms (highest recommendation, especially for families); the 38-room **Falcon Hotel,** 11 Norfolk Square, phone 723-8603, charges £7.50 per person in a double, £8 single (its owner, Mr. Rees, one of those outgoing Welshmen, has installed showers and a color tv set in every room); the **Border Hotel,** 14 Norfolk Square, phone 723-2968, charging £8.50 per person in double rooms (Mrs. Davies, who hails from Port Talbot, is proprietress); the unusually comfortable (large rooms, soft carpeting) but reasonably priced **St. George Hotel,** 46 Norfolk Square (723-3560), charging only £6.50 per person in double rooms, including V.A.T. and full English breakfast, only £7 single; and the **Tudor Court Hotel,** at 10 Norfolk Square, phone 723-6553, charging £8 per person, and featuring full central heating.

Cheapest of the Norfolk Square establishments is the **Bristol Hotel/ Hostel,** 38 Norfolk Square (phone 723-0114), which sometimes calls itself a youth hostel, but actually caters to all age groups. Unusually attractive for a hostel, it charges £4 ($8.80) per person in a crisply new blue and white dorm-style room, £4.50 ($9.90) per person in a double, always including a cooked breakfast and use of kitchen facilities. Manager David Ardener and his wife Lee also operate the similarly-priced **Avon Hotel,** three doors away at 50 Norfolk Square (phone 723-49-21), where weekly rates are as little as £21 ($46.20) per person in a double-decker bunk. Capacity is about 100 beds in all at the exciting Bristol and Avon.

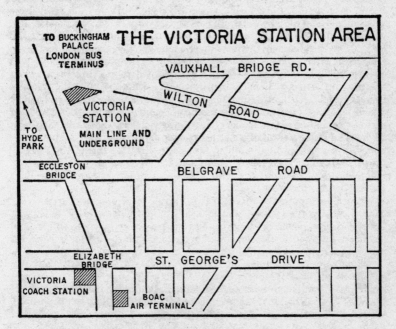

Victoria Station—Belgrave Road (£6 to £8.50)

Another solid line of bed-and-breakfast houses—less crowded in summer than those around Russell Square or Sussex Gardens—is found on Belgrave Road, just a hundred yards behind Victoria Station (which is itself behind Buckingham Palace and relatively near to Westminster Abbey and the houses of Parliament). Because of their location, and not because the street itself, or the houses, are more attractive than others we've named, most of the Belgrave Road establishments charge a bit more per person than do their counterparts on Sussex Gardens or around Russell Square. At the same time, it's hard to deny that the location is good; you're only a few short blocks from Victoria Coach Station (the city's major bus terminal, from which tours depart for outlying areas of England), a 3-minute walk from Victoria Rail Station, a 10-minute walk from the Air Terminal.

Probably your best bet here for finding rooms is at the big (150 beds) **Easton Hotel,** 36 Belgrave Road (834-5938), which consists of three tan-and-white town houses joined together as one hotel, and where the charge is £7 ($15.40), bed and breakfast per person, in double rooms, £8 in singles. Another collection of Belgrave Road houses operates as the **Leicester Hotel Group,** 24 Belgrave Road (834-4296), a name that includes a house at 44 Belgrave Road, two on Eccleston Square, and three others on nearby Gillingham Street. The establishment at 24 Belgrave Road is too dear for our purposes, but the management there can book you into their five other hotels, some of whose double rooms range in price from £7 ($15.40) per person, with still other annexes going for £8 ($17.60). All hotels in this chain are among the best in their category, and are highly recommended.

Dozens of other quite similar hotels inhabit Belgrave Road, including the homey and highly-recommended **Corona Hotel** at 87 Belgrave Road (phone 828-9279, £7.10 ($15.62) per person for b & b, including V.A.T., in a twin room with hot and cold running water, well managed by Mrs. E.M. Nunn and family, who also offer several "family rooms", such as one with four beds, at £5.50 ($12.10) per person; and **Central House Hotel,** 37 Belgrave Road (corner of Gloucester Street), phone 828-0644, owned by the helpful Mr. Rachim, who charges £7.50 ($16.50) per person in twin-bedded rooms. But those of our readers who arrive in London in winter will particularly like the **Victoria Private Hotel,** 23 Belgrave Road (834-0907), which is one of the several budget establishments around here to have central heating! The charge is £8.50 per person, bed-and-breakfast; manageress is a Scottish lady who scrubs and shines all day; and staff here will organize babysitting services (around one pound per hour) for parents wishing to attend the theatre. In this same (£7.50 to £8.50 per person) category, the newly-redecorated **Hobbs Hotel** at 86 Belgrave Road (phone 828-8661), a series of townhouses, offers rather slick accommodations and good value for money.

Overflow digs in the Belgrave Road area? Walk one block over to the parallel **St. George's Drive,** and look in at **St. George's Hotel** at 107 St. George's Drive, phone 834-0210 (spotless, pastel-colored doubles with central heating, a lovely little chandelier and good English breakfast for only £6 per person in a number of rooms).

Finally, some new hotels on nearby Warwick Way: the aptly named **Bed and Breakfast,** 104 Warwick Way (834-0082), charging £7.50 ($16.50) per person in a twin room with full English breakfast; the **Surtees Hotel,** 94 Warwick Way (834-7163), and the **Brindle House Hotel,** just off Warwick Way at 1 Warwick Place North (828-0057), also £7.50 per.

Ebury Street—The Big Splurge (£7.10 to £8.50)

The London area known as "Belgravia," wedged between Sloane Square and Victoria, is a plush precinct of film stars, politicians, and socialites that nevertheless possesses a moderately-priced street of guesthouses—Ebury Street (underground stop is Victoria)—marvelously convenient to Buckingham Palace, Victoria Station and the British Airways terminal. Every morning at around 11:15 a.m., the Queen's Own Regiment approaches Buckingham Palace for the Changing of the Guard by parading down Ebury Street—right under your bedroom window if you choose one of the guesthouses below. You'll get the flavor when you walk into **Alison House Hotel,** 82 Ebury Street (phone 730-9529), and are handed a welcoming glass of sherry by proprietors Frank and Alison Haggis; they may even walk you around the corner to Chester Square to point out the homes of neighbors Julie Andrews and Tony Curtis! The charge is £7 to £8 ($15.40 to $17.60), plus V.A.T., per person for a twin-bedded room with a "burster" of an English breakfast. **Lewis House,** at 111 Ebury Street (phone 730-2094), charges the very same for bathless bed-and-breakfast, and here you're in the former residence of Noel Coward, possibly

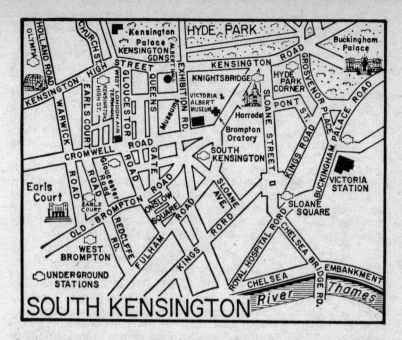

sleeping in his very bedroom. Mr. and Mrs. Lewis are warmhearted and extremely capable guesthouse managers. Alternatives include **Harcourt House,** 50 Ebury Street (phone 730-2722), and **Ebury House,** 102 Ebury Street (phone 730-1350), both charging £8.50 ($18.70), plus V.A.T., per person per night, and **Markus House Hotel,** 92 Ebury Street (phone 730-6776), at £9 per person, all inclusive.

Near King's Cross Station (£5 to £7)

And now, a last hotel district, where you'll find the city's largest collection of low-cost bed-and-breakfast houses, but in one of the less-interesting areas of London. Its main virtue is that it's largely undiscovered by overseas tourists, and patronized—thus far—almost entirely by English visitors.

Several blocks to the north of Russell Square, on Euston Road, are two major railroad stations of London—St. Pancras and King's Cross—and in front of the King's Cross station are three more-or-less parallel and somewhat shabby streets—Birkenhead, Crestfield, and Argyle—that lead in a short walk to the far more attractive Argyle Square. It is on these three streets and square that more than 50 budget-type guesthouses can be found, in less than a two-minute walk from the King's Cross/St. Pancras tube exit. Though, once again, this area can't compare in attractiveness or location with Russell Square, Sussex Gardens or Belgrave Road, it is one of the few such sections where single persons traveling alone in summer can fairly easily find single rooms—a commodity virtually unobtainable at that time in the other establishments we've named.

Undoubtedly one of the best of the budget spots here is the centrally-heated **Alambra Hotel,** 17 Argyle Street, King's Cross, London W.C. 1 (837-9575), whose 1980 price of £6 ($13.20) a night reduces to only £5 ($11) if you stay for 2 or more nights, and includes breakfast. Singles are a uniform £8 ($17.60), without discount for longer stays. The owner of this 30-room hotel, Mrs. Gina Filliez, has long been recommended in this book, partly because of her consistently fine attitude towards U.S. and Canadian tourists. Slightly higher in price (£7 to £9 per person, double or single) is the **Ferndale Hotel,** 21 Argyle Square (837-4974), whose proprietors, Mr. and Mrs. Castle, offer several large family rooms (one double bed and two singles) overlooking a garden. Breakfast here starts with cornflakes or juice, then goes on to bacon and eggs, tomatoes, sausages or "fried bread" (try it), with plenty of tea, toast, butter and assorted jams on the side. Or try: **Helen's Hotel,** 34 Argyle Street (837-9627), charging a standard £6 per person double, £8.50 single, including breakfast and tax.

Bed-and-breakfast in twin rooms for £5 to £6 per night: **Myrtle House Hotel,** 20 Argyle Square (837-5759), with pleasant Scottish owners, in their late 30's; numerous other hotels on Argyle Street, where the prices are lower and the vacancies more frequent than on the square itself. For students only, the **Rees Hotel,** 22 Argyle Street (phone 837-6200), charges only £4.25 per night in dormitory-style accommodations, including breakfast and V.A.T.

Elsewhere in London
(£5, £6.50 and £7 per person)

Thus far, we've focused on areas in the city where budget hotels are clustered. There are, of course, numerous budget hotels that stand alone. Since many of these are particular stars, they call for careful consideration. But remember that you must phone first to determine whether rooms are available; for as to the selections that follow, you can't always count on finding other hotels in the same block.

In **West London** (which is near Hyde Park, Kensington Gardens, the Victoria and Albert Museum), and in **West Central London** (which is near the theatres, the British Museum, and Russell Square), phone the following:

First, the **Y.W.C.A. Central Club,** 16 Great Russell Street (636-7512), less than 100 yards from the Tottenham Court Road underground station, near the British Museum. In a lovely neo-Georgian building with an excellent central location, it charges £6.90 ($15.18) per person for bed and breakfast in a double room, slightly less than that in several multi-bedded rooms, £8 ($17.60) in a single, the latter being much in demand and usually requiring advance reservations. This Y.W.C.A. has a self-service restaurant, a library, swimming pool, laundry facilities, hair-dressing salon, and many other valuable features. Women only.

Helen Graham House (another Y.W.C.A.), at 57 Great Russell Street (phone 405-5892), directly opposite the British Museum, is not quite as new as the Y.W.C.A. Central Club, further up the block, but has wonderfully-low prices: £4.20 per person in a triple room (breakfast included), £5.50 per person in a double room, £7 for a single room. Girls from all nations (they're required to stay at least four days) are the guests.

The Queensway Court Hotel, 36 Queensway (229-5184), caters to a young crowd. Newly decorated and spotless rooms cost £7 to £8 ($15.40 to $17.60) single, £6.50 to £7.50 ($14.30 to $16.50) per person double, and £6 to £7 ($13.20 to $15.40) per person triple. Weekly rates are lower. The nearest tube station is Queensway. If Queensway Court is full, manager Timothy Kemp will accommodate you at his other establishment at 33 Cranley Gardens (same prices).

The Sutherland, 90 Sutherland Avenue, Maida Vale (289-3858), was converted from a spacious townhouse to a guesthouse in 1976, and all the appointments within are spanking new. Room charges are £5.50 ($12.10) per person in triple or four-bedded rooms, £6.50 ($14.30) in twins, £8 single. To get there, take the tube to Warwick Avenue, walk north for about three blocks, and make a left into Sutherland Avenue.

The London Musical Club, 21 Holland Park (727-4440), is a rare find, but only for stays of at least a week, when room (with piano!) and full board can be had for £5 ($11), and less, a day. Opportunity to engage in chambermusic and ensemble-playing; concerts; recitals; conversation with other music lovers in a comfortable lounge. The underground stop is Holland Park; the founding president of the club was Sir John Barbirolli, now succeeded by his widow, Lady Barbirolli.

An unusually large establishment (with a total of 200 rooms) catering almost exclusively to young people and students, is **The Camborne and Leinster Hotels,** 7/11 Leinster Square (229-7232), a short walk from the Bayswater Tube station; it consists of several houses around Leinster Square (reception offices are at #8 and #62 on the Square) with both a central dining room and reception office at the above address. Bed and breakfast are a uniform £5.50 in double or triple rooms, £7 single. If the Camborne can't take you, then try the **Armitage Hotel,** 58 Leinster Square (727-0387), where the charge, including breakfast, service and tax, is £6.50 per person in a double, £8 single.

In **Southwest London** (near Buckingham Palace) there are two establishments you might try:

Hotel "167", 167 Old Brompton Road (373-0672), a family-run hotel whose proprietors have visited the United States, and know the problems of the American tourist. Bed and continental breakfast are £8 per person, double occupancy. Bus #30 passes in front of the door, nearest underground stop is South Kensington.

Elizabeth House Y.W.C.A., 118 Warwick Way (834-0313), even closer to Victoria Station, disposes of nearly sixty beds, for which the bed-and-breakfast charge, in rooms housing three persons, can be as little as £3.50 ($7.70) per person per night; families with children over 8 years of age are also accepted at the same rate; and there are some doubles for £5 ($11) per person, singles for £6 ($13.20).

And finally in **South London:**

The International Language Club, 13 Addiscombe Grove, East Croydon, London (phone 688-2634), is an odd, but exciting, "hotel," consisting of 17 adjacent town houses on a single square, all serviced by a central building where meals are served, table tennis and chess are played, and residents of the 16 other buildings—who usually represent over 30 different countries—congregate to practice speaking with one another in foreign tongues. Had Henry Higgins really existed, this is where he would have chosen to stay! Priority, of course, is given to permanent or one-week residents (for whom the charge is 30 pounds a week, including *two* meals a day, only 28 pounds if you share a room). Mr. T. Driscoll is the man who began this unique experiment in international living 44 years ago; he has since accommodated over 50,000 persons, including 96 from Malaya, 30 from Sri Lanka, 1,500 from India, 500 from France, 47 from Singapore, and 1 from the Seychelle Islands. The location is in a suburb of London, but only 20 minutes by underground to Victoria or Charing Cross; take the train to the East Croydon Station, then walk up Addiscombe Road on the right for two blocks; but phone first: 688-2634.

Some years ago, and again in south London, Mr. Driscoll of the International Language Club (see above) purchased the old Ada Lewis Hostel and

converted it into the for-women-only **Ladies Hotel,** 172 New Kent Road, S.E.
1 (phone 703-4175), where the charge is again 30 pounds a week for a single
room, with two meals a day included and all meals on weekends! There's a color
television lounge here, library, piano room, sewing room, and 200 single guest
rooms. Elephant and Castle is the nearest tube stop. While long-term residents
are obviously given priority, tourists with only one or two weeks to spend in
London are occasionally accepted. All hail Mr. Driscoll.

Last Resort

If you can't find a room at any of the hotels we've listed (which is highly
unlikely), then there are two old-standby establishments in London which you
might try. Both of them are relatively large and usually have vacancies, neither
charges more than £6.50 per person for bed-and-breakfast, including V.A.T.,
and neither is as highly recommended as the hotels listed above (but for reasons
of location only). They are, with addresses and phone numbers: the 60-room
Ladbroke Gardens Hotel, 28 Ladbroke Gardens, off Kensington Park Road
(727-8569), London W.11 (largish rooms furnished with old-fashioned charm,
dining room overlooking a garden, proprietors—the Muller family—who serve
a traditional afternoon tea for 60p); the 86-bed **Hotel Northumberland,** 9-11
Euston Road (837-5675), London N.W. 1 (opposite King's Cross Station).
. . . And if these final listings don't work, then apply for aid, first, to the **London
Tourist Board** in the arrival hall of Victoria Station opposite platform 15—
that's the official city tourist organization (whose main headquarters is at 26
Grosvenor Gardens, phone 730-0791); or else go to the privately-owned **Hotel
Bookings International, Ltd.,** either at their desks in Heathrow Airport, or by
phoning 459-1212. Usually, however, no such searching is necessary; merely
head for Sussex Gardens, Norfolk Square, King's Cross or Victoria in the
spring and summer months, or for Russell Square in off-season.

A last observation, in which I go way out on a limb: generally speaking,
I think you'll find that English hotels, in all price ranges, are not as good as
those on the continent, and—except for their phenomenal free breakfasts—fail
to offer values comparable to those found in Holland, Germany, Scandinavia—
even Italy and France. But the important point to remember is that the inexpensive English guesthouses share these defects to no greater an extent than do
most First Class English hotels.

Some readers, for instance, have complained that their guesthouse rooms
had a Dickensian gloom about them, with heavy mahogany fixtures, and brown
woolen drapes. Other readers have written in that their breakfast bacon was
underdone, and the eggs greasy. Fact: the hotels in the elegant Mayfair section
serve underdone bacon and greasy eggs.

When in London, expect these things, and revel in them. For England
would not be England if the interiors of hotels were decorated in Scandinavian-
type pastels. And what would the stories of Sherlock Holmes be like—if it
weren't for the fog!

One thing of which you can be sure in England: that if, in dealing with
hotel personnel, you comport yourself with the dignity and restraint that
Englishmen expect, you'll get back an unprecedented quantum of politeness,
amiability and warmth, that will more than make up for the ancient fixtures
and decorations of most budget-priced London hotels.

ECONOMY BUDGET: Now we turn to an even less costly form of housing—to the numerous homes and small hotels that offer single rooms with breakfast for $7.15 to $10, doubles for $11 to $18 (including two vast English breakfasts). And have no fear: in these intimate, 20-guest communities, you will experience European life more intensely—and enjoyably—than the higher-living tourists could ever dream of doing. Here are names and addresses, with phone numbers for checking on whether vacancies exist.

In **West and West Central London:** a guest house at 12 Gunterstone Road (603-9835), long recommended in this guide when it was owned by Mrs. P. MacNamara (who would sometimes take her guests pub-crawling!), has now—upon the retirement of Mrs. MacNamara—been taken over by a Mrs. Bedford, who promises that she will continue the old price policies: £5 ($11) per person for bed and breakfast, in either *single,* double, twin or triple rooms. Mr. and Mrs. Rattenbury are the new managers of the house which, for want of a name, should probably simply be called "Mrs. Bedford's Guest House." There's an annex to this establishment (same £5 price) at 39 Gunterstone Road (phone 603-3551), for which the nearest subway stop is West-Kensington.

In **South and South West London:** Here you'll want to try the popular lodgings of Lancashire-born Mrs. Alice Coleman (**Abbeville Guest House**), at 89 Abbeville Road, Clapham Common (tel: 622-5360), whose per person charge is only £4 to £4.50 ($8.80 to $9.90) per night, bed and breakfast. Take the underground to Clapham Common. Or seek out the home of **Mrs. Mary Ward,** 98 Hambalt Road, Clapham Common (phone 673-1077), £3.25 ($7.15) per person, including English breakfast, and free use of the bathtub. The kindly Mrs. Ward offers six simple but comfortable and spotlessly clean rooms.

Elsewhere in town, Mr. K. R. Frerichs, proprietor of the widely-known **"Hunter's Lodge,"** at 20 & 38 Trebovir Road (370-2529), near West London Air Terminal in the Earl's Court area, is an exceptionally pleasant host who charges only £6.50 for singles, £4.50 to £5 ($9.90 to $11) per person for doubles, including full English breakfast and Value Added Tax. His guest house has lots of stairs, but he attempts to put young people as high as possible, and reserves the ground and lower floors for elderly and middle-aged clients. Short walk from the Earls Court Station.

The highly recommended lodgings of **Mrs. J. Purcell,** 26 Dartmouth Park Avenue (485-5903), offer "bed-sitter" (temporary apartment) accommodations for periods of at least a week or more, at the rate of only £35 per week for a double room—that's £17.50 per person. Renters pay the gas bill (there are cooking facilities) but hot water and cleaning of rooms once a week are included.

G. I. Housing

American G.I.'s can stay at the British Army's **Union Jack Club,** on Sandell Street (phone 928-6401), one minute from Waterloo Station, where bed-and-breakfast is £5.60 ($12.32) in singles, £5.20 ($11.44) per person in double rooms.

Starvation budget

Now for the dorms, which we'll review in very quick fashion: **Gayfere Hostel,** 8 Gayfere Street, S.W.1 (phone 222-6894), provides dormitory accommodations for students only (both sexes), charges £3.75 ($8.25) per night, £25 ($55) per week in high season, including tax and linen, but does not provide breakfast; it is well-located on a quiet Georgian street behind Westminster

Abbey (and therefore enforces a strict midnight curfew); take the underground to Westminster, turn right, walk toward Millbank, and again turn right in Great Peter Street to Gayfere. The 190-bed **King George VI Memorial Youth Hostel** (phone 937-0791), a tree-shaded complex of buildings in historic Holland Park, is open only to members of the Youth Hostel Association, charges £2.35 per person in dormitory-style accommodations, 80 pence for a full English breakfast, £1 for a three-course evening meal. Nearest underground is Holland Park.

Starvation budget

In the basement of St. Peter's Church on plush Eaton Square (of "Upstairs/Downstairs" fame), the appropriately-named **Last Resort** (phone 743-5708) houses both male and female backpackers of any age from July 1 to September 30 only, on 100 mattresses laid on parquet-patterned floors; these are without blankets or sheets, and the per night charge, appropriately enough, is only one pound ($2.20). Next morning, until around 9 a.m., breakfast food is sold over a window-type counter: 25 pence for cornflakes or a müsli, same price for a buttered roll with jam, 15 pence for coffee, 10 for tea. All this is but a five minute walk from Victoria Station.

READERS' HOTEL SELECTIONS (SUSSEX GARDENS AREA): "Our **Tregaron Hotel,** 17 Norfolk Square, W.2 (phone 723-3375) will charge £6.35 per person in 1980 for bed, breakfast and Value Added Tax. We shall be most pleased to accommodate your readers and shall do all in our power to help them and make them comfortable" (W. George, London, England; note by AF: the **Ashley Hotel,** next door to the Tregaron at 15 Norfolk Square (phone 723-3375), is under the same management, charges the same rates). . . . "If you have difficulties finding hotel vacancies in Sussex Gardens at the height of the season, then try the similar hotels on Norfolk Square, which lies between Sussex Gardens and Paddington Station. The **Belvedere Hotel,** 52 Norfolk Square (phone 723-8848), charges £7 per person for large, clean and pleasant rooms, breakfast included. Take the underground (Circle Line) to Paddington Station" (Mr. and Mrs. Wm. E. Scott, Seabrook, Maryland).

READERS' HOTEL SELECTIONS (KING'S CROSS STATION): "My 'reader's selection,' is the **Wardonia Hotel** at 48 Argyle Street (phone 837-7747), just two short blocks from the King's Cross underground station. Here we spent a most enjoyable 18 days with Mr. and Mrs. Abomnes and their young son. Our double room with breakfasts of eggs, sausages and bacon, juice, buttered toast with orange marmalade, and coffee (milk for my son), cost us only £12 ($26.40) a day. Baths were free; we could wash out our clothes and hang them outside to dry; later we could use Mrs. Abomnes' iron to press these same clothes! The hotel is kept spotlessly clean; breakfast is served in a bright and cheerful dining room. Single rooms are £7 ($15.40)" (Elizabeth Apetz, New York City) . . . "The new owners of the **Albion House Hotel,** 29 Argyle Square, phone 837-4373, are friendly and helpful people; their hotel is freshly decorated, service is perfect, and the charge is £5.50 per person per night, including an excellent breakfast" (Mr. and Mrs. Alan Shusterman, Durham, North Carolina; note by AF: readers requesting reservations at the Albion House Hotel must send International Postal Response Coupons with their requests). . . . "At the **Violet House Hotel,** 54 Birkenhead Street, near King's Cross Station (phone 837-4935), the charge is £7 ($15.40) per person, including Value Added Tax and the best breakfast we've had in all our travels" (Maxine Knowles, Miami, Florida).

READERS' HOTEL SELECTIONS (RUSSELL SQUARE): "The **St. Athan's Hotel,** 20 Tavistock Place (837-9140), is a charming old brownstone in the Russell Square area of London. We had a cozy attic room overlooking an old English street where milk wagons rolled by in the morning. Breakfasts were delicious, consisting of juice, eggs, bacon, coffee and toast served in a charming dining room. Our fellow guests included a group of French school boys and their masters, and a charming Irish priest who was attending the races at Ascot. The price for two was £15 ($33), including breakfast" (Mr. and Mrs. R. S. Zimmerman,

New York, N.Y.; note by AF: this is one of the few hotels on Tavistock Place that charge as little as £7.50 for bed-and-breakfast, including V.A.T.).

READERS' HOTEL SELECTIONS (VICTORIA STATION AREA): "We were fortunate to find a super new bed-and-breakfast establishment in the Pimlico area, called **Rosemary Kraemer's,** 122 Lupus Street (phone 834-2155). Just off the embankment between Dolphin Square and Chelsea Bridge, it is on the bus line to Trafalgar Square, five minutes from the Pimlico tube station, and a 10-minute walk from Victoria Station. Recent prices were £ 8 ($17.60) single, £15 ($33) double, including a large, delicious breakfast, hot baths and luggage storage" (Mr. and Mrs. Bob Simson, Victoria, B.C., Canada). . . . "Only six blocks from the Victoria Airport Terminal, we stayed at the small **Douglas Hotel,** 84 Warwick Way, paying $30 for a clean double room with sink, plus a good English breakfast. Mr. and Mrs. Reginald Bizzell are the most helpful and nice proprietors" (Mr. and Mrs. Harry Liddicote, Santa Barbara, California).

READERS' HOTEL SELECTIONS (KENSINGTON): Note by AF—Kensington is an area that surrounds the West London Air Terminal, south of Hyde Park; readers' finds are as follows: "**Sloane Rooms Hotel,** 30 Lower Sloane Street, London SW1S 8BP (tel: 01-730-3217), just a minute away from the Sloane Square underground stop, and convenient to Chelsea and South Kensington, offers clean, quiet, well-heated rooms. There's a dining room on the premises, and the management is efficient and friendly. The price is £7.50 per night for a single, including VAT, service and an English breakfast" (Ann Cagan, Brooklyn, New York). . . . "**Western House Hotel,** 8 Holland Road, Kensington (tel. 603-3099), charges £4.50 to £6.50 per person for bed and breakfast, and is within walking distance of the underground station, Kensington High Street. I think it's more interesting to take the bus into the center of town, however, and both #73 and #9 stop close by. The owners must spend a little more for the food they serve, because the breakfast was excellent and very appetizing. They will burn the bacon if you ask them to" (Edward Pietraszek, Chicago, Illinois; seconding recommendations from Steve and Mary Aujmuth, Niles, Illinois, who report that "the couple who run the Western House are an enjoyable pair who carry on a lively repartee while serving breakfast"). . . . "By chance, I hit upon the **Vicarage Private Hotel,** 10 Vicarage Gate, Kensington (tel: 229-4030). I'm in my second month here now, and I like the place more and more. Unlike many London hotels, the Vicarage has many single rooms (approximately £7.50 a day). The ample breakfast will carry you through a full day of sightseeing, and the B.E.A. Terminal is just a £1 taxi fare away. The location is superb—Kensington Gardens is just a block away—and the Circle, Central and District Underground stations are just 5 minutes away. A two-minute walk will get you to a couple of large shopping areas, where you'll find two laundromats—a Godsend for the weary traveler with a suitcase of dirty clothes" (C.J. Kennedy, San Francisco, California; enthusiastic seconding recommendations from Mrs. Ursula Duffy, Suitland, Maryland, who reports rates of £6.20 per person in double rooms). . . . "We spent over one month, on and off, at the **Meyer Guest House,** 21 Redcliffe Street, SW 10 (phone 370-2822), where we paid £4.75 per person per night, breakfast and bath included. The proprietor, Mr. Meyer, could not have been kinder or more helpful, even storing our numerous pieces of luggage when we left London for short trips. This is close to the Earls Court station, and within walking distance of Kensington and Chelsea" (Allison Reed, Pukekone, New Zealand). . . . "For younger followers of your book, I strongly recommend **Karen's Guest House,** 34 Rockley Road. The location is good: there are many buses (including a rare London night bus), and it is about a block from the Central Line's Shepherd's Bush stop. The rate of £6 a day, with continental breakfast, is hard to beat in inflation-hit London. But the real pleasure of Karen's Guest House is its owner. She is a surrogate mother to everyone. One Finnish lad had a cold, so she isolated him in the sunroom and watched over him until his sniffles left. I had to leave about 6 a.m. to catch a train, so she got up before me to make sure I got up on time, and prepared breakfast for me, because, 'No one should have to face the world without his morning tea' " (Gary F. Suggans, Baltimore, Maryland).

READERS' HOTEL SELECTIONS (FURTHER OUT): The rates decrease in locations a few minutes by tube beyond the ones we've discussed, as witness: "I discovered **Mario's Guesthouse** at 69 St. Georges Avenue (Northern Line—Tufnell Park stop; phone 607-6386), London N7, where there are seven rooms, some with three and four beds apiece. Mario charges only £4.50 per person including a large and delicious breakfast, a cup of tea whenever you come in, and great conversation. This is no hotel—it is a home, and you truly feel a part of it" (Carol Boss, Far Rockaway, New York). . . . "Our find makes some of your cheaper places look expensive. The house is in an outer London suburb, Hendon, about 30 minutes from Leicester Square by tube on the Northern Line. It's Mrs. L.M. Tyler's **"Solana"**, at 18 Golders Rise, Hendon NW4, phone 202-53-21. £8 ($17.60) a night acquired a warm double room with comfortable beds and adjacent toilet and bathroom. Breakfast is included. Smokers, however, are apparently not welcome, as the many signs in the house emphasize" (Dr. J. Szer, East Bentleigh, Victoria, Australia). . . . "The private home of **Mr. and Mrs. W. F. Beasleigh**, at 93 Thurlstone Road, London SE 27, tel: 670-2495, provides attractive, clean rooms in a nice residential area. Full bath privileges and a great cooked-to-order breakfast are included in the price of £4.50 ($9.90) per person; the Beasleighs are warm and friendly people; and good public transportation is available" (Abraham Freed, New York, N.Y.).

READERS-ON-THE-STARVATION-BUDGET: "A clean and proper place to stay, yet for only £3 a night per person, is **O'Callaghan's Nightly Tourist Accommodation** at 205 Earl's Court Road (phone 370-3000), across from the tube station" (Linda Rorke, Montreal, Quebec; note from AF: in addition to several approving letters from readers, a note from Mr. O'Callaghan himself confirms the rate, and states that "young people are very welcome"). . . . "Please do your readers the favor of including **Mr. and Mrs. Dennis Ward**, 98 Hambalt Road, Clapham Common (phone 673-1077), near the corner of Abbeyville and Hambalt Roads, who charge only £3.50 ($7.70) per person for bed and breakfast" (Jane McAlonan, Uppsala, Sweden). . . . "Anyone under the age of 28 is advised to try the **Saney Guruji Hostel**, 18a Holland Villas Road, W.14 (phone 603-3704), which offers dormitory style accommodations to both men and women for exactly £2.15 ($4.73) per night, not including breakfast or added value tax. Cooking facilities are available, and you can get a key giving you a chance to come in as late as you wish. Terrific, friendly atmosphere" (Stuart Lewis, Albany, New York; note by AF: Saney Guruji is operated by "International Co-operative and Socialist Youth Hostels, Ltd."; nearest tube station is Holland Park, on the Central Line). . . . "Scouters, Scouts and Cubs can now find accommodations at **B. P. (Baden-Powell) House**, Queen's Gate, South Kensington, S.W.7 (phone 584-7030); and I think that it may be possible for women and girls to stay there, too. There is a good cafeteria as well, and this is quite certainly open to qualified persons and their guests, of either sex. I stayed there for about a week, and found it quite a good place—though the noise of traffic in Cromwell Road, below my bedroom windows, was rather troublesome. The rate per person per night, including breakfast and V.A.T., is £4.85 ($10.67) in a multi-bedded room, £7 ($15.40) in a twin, and £8.50 ($18.70) in a single room (with ladies and married couples undoubtedly being placed in the single and twins). B.P. House is quite near the Gloucester Road Underground station" (C. P. Wright, Ottawa, Ontario, Canada; note by AF: Baden-Powell House is open only to members of the Scouting movement, although in the case of couples, only one spouse need be in order for both to stay there).

READERS-ON-THE-SUB-STARVATION-BUDGET: "One very nice place that should be in your book is **Helix Lodge**, 51 Bonham Road, London S.W.2 (phone 274-7166), which charges only £2.50 a night per person! They have six small, one-room apartment-like set-ups. There is a gas coin-operated stove and, in the bathroom, a coin-operated hot water meter. I learned that four pence was more than enough for a bath for one person, as opposed to the five pennies that other guests advised were necessary" (Judith Boss, Grand Junction, Colorado, enthusiastically seconded by Mildred and Carl K. Frost, Vancouver; note by AF: in response to a follow-up from me, the owners of Helix Lodge have confirmed the £2.50 per person rate for 1980, and added the following details: their guest house has six double apartments, every apartment has fully self-contained facilities for preparing meals, the house is "attractively decorated and clean," they require stays of at least five nights, and location is in the Brixton section of London (tube stop is: Brixton), five minutes by train from Victoria Station, a few minutes from the center of London by frequent buses (#59, 159 or 50). . . . "**Office of the Youth Hostels Association**, which will accommodate you throughout England and Wales for about $3 a night, average, is at 14 Southampton Street, London W.C.2, phone 836-8541" (Rosemary Jordan, Oxford, England). . . . "I suppose that most of your readers go to more expensive places than our tented hostel, but we must have had thousands of Americans enjoying the atmosphere of our place last summer. **Tent City**, Old Oak Common Lane, London W3 (phone 743-5708); underground train to East Acton, open from June through late August, consists of 16 large tents (men's, women's and mixed) in which there are 500 beds; you use your own sleeping bag or hire our bedding; come at any time to leave your baggage and sleep; pay only £1.30 ($2.86) a night; and reach the hotel from Heathrow Airport by taking direct bus number 105 to East Acton. We don't always mention our official name in literature because we aren't churchy Christians, and we fear the word will put people off" (Barnaby Martin, **Christian Action,** 2 Amen Court, London EC4).

HOTELS AND GUESTHOUSES SEEKING MENTION: "Our terms in 1980 are from £4 per person per night, and we give a large and varied English breakfast which is included in the price. A homely atmosphere," (Mr. and Mrs. D. Powell, **Edward's Guest House,** 91 Abbeville Road, Clapham Common, London S.W.4, phone 622-6347). . . . **"Our Don Ludwig Student House,** at 372 Grays Inn Road, almost opposite King's Cross Station (phone 837-6543), is designed for young people up to the age of 30, and charges only £3 per person per night, including linen and tax, in fully carpeted dormitories. We offer, in addition, a television lounge, newspapers and journals, washing, ironing and cooking facilities, but we do not serve breakfast" (The Warden, Don Ludwig House, International Students and Youth Centre). . . . "Our **Venus Hotel,** 163 Westbourne Grove (phone 229-2862), is managed by young people for young people, and there is a very pleasant atmosphere here. Most rooms are large, with four/five beds, but they have their own private shower, and yet the price is only £4 per person, bed and continental breakfast, depending on the type of room" (Andrew Chris, Manager, Venus Hotel). . . . "At the **Jill Doldrina Student House,** 285 Pentonville Road (phone 278-5385), the charge will be £3.50 ($7.70) per person per night, bed only, including bed linen and Value Added Tax. Accommodation is provided in small dormitories with a maximum of 5 people in a room; nearest Underground station is King's Cross" (Warden, Jill Doldrina Student House). . . . "We are the same sisters as are located at Via del Gianicolo 4A in Rome, listed in your book. Could our London hostel be listed? We are located in the beautiful residential district of Hampstead, three minutes from a tube stop, in a home surrounded by a large garden; and we take individuals and groups the year around, for a charge of £6, bed and breakfast" (Sister June Sadler, **Sisters of Saint Dorothy International Hostel,** 99 Frognal, Hampstead, London, phone 794-6893 or 794-8095). . . . "I am a sister of Mrs. Ward at 98 Hambolt Road, who is in your book, and I am quite familiar with the likes and dislikes of your readers. At my guesthouse we only charge £3.75 for bed, bath and full breakfast. We intend to keep the price down to the minimum. I am sure I won't let the required standard down" (**Mrs. Nancy Swain,** 84 Abbeville Road, Clapham Common, London S.W.4, phone 622-7589). . . . "I run a newly-opened students and tourists' accommodations house. We have 50 rooms, each with two or more bunkbeds for sharing. Each room has hot and cold water; there are cooking facilities, tv, showers, free parking, own keys, no curfew, use of the canteen for relaxation. The charge is £2 per night, £12 per week" (**Student Hostel,** 23 Cross Street, Islington, London N. 1., phone 359-6549 or 359-5191).

LONDON ROOMS FOR LENGTHY STAYS: Apart from renting your own apartment or one-room flat ("bedsitters," the Londoners call the latter), the most pleasant and often the cheapest way to stay in London for several weeks is with a private family, whose names are available from the **London Tourist Board Office** located near Platform 15 at Victoria Station; they'll provide you with a mimeographed list of at least 15 "self-catering accommodation offices" to be phoned from a nearby telephone booth. And the latter will then confirm an accommodation (for minimum stays of a week) at rents of around £35 a week, breakfast included, in the inner London areas, around £30 in the suburbs. The Victoria Station office is open from 9 a.m. to 9 p.m., seven days a week.

Or, you can find a low-cost room or flat, for weekly rental, by purchasing a copy of the *London Weekly Advertiser,* sold for 12 pence on all major newsstands in London, which contains numerous listings of "Furnished Flats to Let," mainly in the 30 to 35-pound-a-week category. Need a roommate? Call **Share-a-Flat Ltd.,** Empire House, 175 Piccadilly (phone 493-1265), which will seek to match you up with someone of similar age and background; their rates average 25 pounds a week outside the center, 35 pounds in central London. For a much cheaper room or flat, consult the bulletin boards you'll find outside some London subway stations, where local residents often list their rooms—a description of one such notice area appears in our "readers' selections" section below.

A multi-room apartment in London, for temporary rental? Try the housing firm of **James and Jacobs,** 94 Jermyn Street, St. James's, London S.W.1 (phone 930-0261), which maintains a long fresh list of furnished flats for rent. Minimum period of rental is three months; rents start at about 60 pounds per week for one-bedroom flats.

READERS' SELECTIONS AND OFFERS FOR LENGTHY STAYS: "We occupy a large Victorian-period terraced house in the West London 'bed-sitter' area, and accommodate both bona fide students and under-thirties-on-tour, who would prefer to look after themselves. Rooms are furnished with all facilities, including a gas cooker. The charge is $26 per person per week, for a minimum stay of four weeks, and about twenty rooms are available" (F. Stuart Webb, **Barons Court Rooms,** 5 Fairholme Road, West Kensington, phone 385-6785).... **"Sacred Heart House,** at 119 Cedars Road, Clapham Common, near Battersea Park (phone 622-0466 and take the underground to the Clapham Common Station), is a Catholic hostel for priests and male students, with a chapel, daily masses, central heating. Rates average £35 per person per week during your first 2 weeks, £21 per week thereafter, all during the summer months" (Joao Luis Leitao, Lisbon, Portugal).... "The best bargain accommodation, available all-year-round, is a private room in which you stay on a weekly basis. Even in fashionable Hampstead, NW3, it should not cost more than £19 per week. How to find them? Take the Underground to the Earl's Court Road stop. When you get out, look in the shop windows around the station; you will find plenty of addresses, but take only those with inner London telephone numbers to make sure you get a room in the right area. Generally speaking, you will find addresses on the boards of any London suburban sweet or grocery shop" (Ditmar Grünewald, Mainz, Germany; note by AF: the largest and best known of the bulletin boards offering rooms is a vast one at 214 Earl's Court Road (near the Earl's Court Road subway station, entree to the area sometimes known as "London's bedroom"), in a tiny arcade leading to a stationery store; it also carries ads of items for sale, rides to be shared, jobs to be had at one pound an hour).... **"London Tourist Holiday Flatlets** are perfect for readers who plan to stay in London for several weeks. They are at 4 Cornwall Mews, London S.W.7., and are operated by a Mr. Wiggins. He charges 20 pounds a week for a nicely furnished single with full kitchen, and doubles are also available for £35. Phone 937-1011" (Robert Johnson, Sacramento, California).... "I supply twin-bed accommodation with breakfast in my own home, at the daily rate of £5.50 ($12.10) per person for any length of stay from one night to six months. I provide fresh bed linen and clean the rooms and there are bathroom and toilet facilities not used by the family. We have bus services and Chiswick Park underground nearby. **Rose Sutton,** private home with breakfast, 33 Fairlawn Avenue, Chiswick, London W. 4, phone 995-8506".

With a room acquired, we turn now to the question of meals—a tricky subject, but not from the standpoint of cost:

RESTAURANTS: London is unlike the other capitals of Europe in its attitude towards food. Outside of England, meals are occasions, and cooking is an art. The restaurants in Rome and Vienna and Paris are restaurants—and not mass-production, plate-lunch joints. In London, on the other hand, chain restaurants abound, standardized places, serving fast meals, cheap.

With great despair, this book recommends that you eat in these inexpensive chains, while in London, and save your money for the better meals available in France and Italy. Cooking is a lost art in Great Britain. Your meat-pie-with-cabbage will turn out to be just as tasteless for $2.50 in a chain restaurant as it will for $7 in a posh London hotel. At least for one meal a day, stop in at any of the major British chains—the **"Jolyons,"** the **Chicken Inns,**

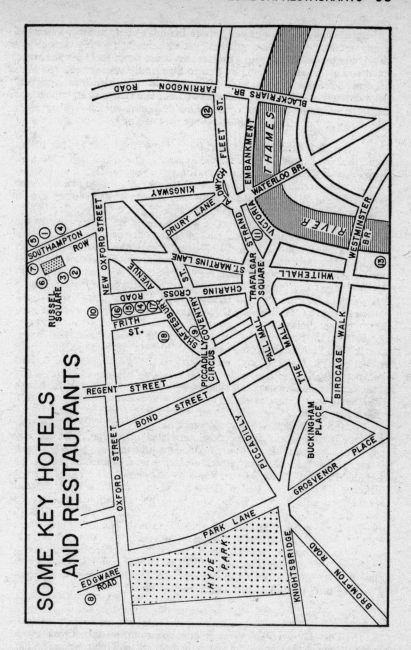

the **Model Inns**, and **Express Dairies**, the **A.B.C.'s**, **Stewarts**, **Fullers**—they're scattered all across the city, and you needn't spend more than $3.50 at any of them.

The "Pots"

But though the major chains provide London's cheapest food, a string of trendy restaurants with the word "Pot" in their titles (and don't go getting any ideas) offer budget dining with a flair, at only a few pence more per plate than you'd pay at the chains. Catering also to a generally younger clientele than frequent the chains, the Pots avoid that air of defeatism that sometimes pervades the chains—and throw in touches of decor like plaited straw lamps, pine panelling, and peach-rose plastic tables. Don't expect too much—these are still very, very low-budget establishments—but they can make an occasion out of the cheapest meal.

Best located of the "Pots" is **The Stockpot** at 40 Panton Street, two blocks from Piccadilly Circus, two blocks from Leicester Square, only half-a-block off Haymarket. It serves a thick minestrone for only 35 pence (77¢), four thoughtful main courses (like "ham and chicken fricassee" or "stuffed pimento") for £1 ($2.20) to £1.50 ($3.30), omelettes for less, desserts for 35 to 40 pence, milk for 20, and warns that "the minimum charge is 75 pence"! So popular, in fact, is this "Stockpot" that it's spawned a worthy competitor directly across the street: the **"Three Lanterns"** at 5 Panton Street, offering seven daily specials for only £1 to £1.60 ($2.20 to $3.52)—and they include no less than beef stroganoff with three vegetables, chicken and mushrooms vol au vent, roast beef and Yorkshire pudding (with three vegetables). Quiet atmosphere, quick service, and one of London's best values—causing **Panton Street** to join **Rupert Street** (Indian restaurants) and **Denman Street** (fish and chips—see our discussion further on) as Piccadilly Circus' key locations for pre-theatre or post-theatre budget dining.

Sister to the Panton Street "Stockpot" is **The Stockpot** at 6 Basil Street, a block from famous Harrod's Department Store (a sightseeing attraction in its own right) in Knightsbridge. Same decor as the first, same menu. A third **Stockpot** at 98 King's Road, and also known as the "Chelsea Kitchen," caters to the trendy young crowd and shop owners of the boutiques lining King's Road. Same approximate rates and offerings as at the other "Pots": 90 p to £1 for main courses, 25 pence for coffee, 40 pence for "sweets" (desserts).

The three "Stockpots," as you'd guess, are part of a chain; another slew of "Pots" under totally independent, unrelated ownership, have recently sprouted along and off Earls Court Road. This time they're variously known as the **"Hotpot"** (on Kenway Road, a block from Earls Court Road), the **"Original Pot"** (at 322 Earls Court Road, serving omelettes for 75 pence, roast chicken for 95 pence), and best of all, the just plain **"Pot"** at 5A Hogarth Road (again a short walk from the Earls Court Road tube station), where soup is 28 pence, steak and mushroom casserole 85 pence, salad 60 pence, sweets 40 pence, coffee 25 pence, tea or milk 20 pence. Despite the competing titles, these "Pots" also promote a common theme: traditional English dishes in a fresh, country-like atmosphere without tablecloths or linen napkins, but with young continental girls as waitresses and prices that permit you with care to stay below £1.50 ($3.30) for an attractive, tasty meal. This is Economy with Dignity, and we bless the unknown founder of the "Pots."

The Spaghetti Houses

The Pots, however, enjoy hot competition from the only-slightly-more-expensive "Spaghetti Houses," of which there are presently thirteen in London. Italian residents flock here in numbers because the pasta dishes, with their thick sauces, are as good as in Italy, and radically different from the sorts normally found in the U.S. and England. At a typical **Spaghetti House**, 77 Knightsbridge, two short blocks from the Hyde Park Hotel, four blocks from Harrod's Department Store, various large pasta plates with superb sauces, enough for a meal, are only £1 ($2.20), and a side cup of tea is 25 pence, while large and attractive "salad platters" (with meat) start at £1.90. But these prices are available only downstairs, in the self-service "tavola calda" portion of the "Spaghetti House". A second "Spaghetti House", the **Ristorante Da Sandro,** is found near the end of Southampton Row, just off Vernon Place, two blocks from the Holborn underground station; and here the cheap area is on the ground floor. Closed Sundays. Slightly more expensive is the original **Spaghetti House** at 15 Goodge Street, off Tottenham Court Road, just behind the University of London, where the decor is so fanciful—fake Italian farmhouse style, in green and red—that you might even schedule a stop for a special night out. Here, you can spend as little as $4.50 for an excellent meal, in contrast to other Spaghetti Houses where careful à la carte ordering can keep the check to $3.50.

Two final Spaghetti House selections: at **10 Blenheim Street** near the Bond Street Tube Station (minestrone for 55 pence, various pasta dishes for £1.20 to £1.40), and at **30 St. Martin's Lane** near Leicester Square (spaghetti Napoli or Bolognese for only £1, stuffed peppers for 80 pence).

The Fish 'n Chips spots

Fast disappearing from London's food scene, because of the rising cost of fish and competition from new fast-food outlets, the fish 'n chips stores can still provide you with a quality meal for $2.75, tea included. At the popular **Friar Tuck,** 113 Lupus Street near the Pimlico tube station, people queue up outside during "frying times", which are weekdays from 11:30 to 2:30 and from 5 to 10 p.m., Saturdays from 11:30 to 2:30 only, and what results are: cod for 50 pence, plaice for 65, haddock for 51, chips for 18 pence, fish cakes (delicious) for 22, soup for 22 pence, steak and kidney pie for 33 pence. Tuck is my own personal favorite for fish 'n chips in London. Alternatively, try the larger and slightly costlier **Kings Cross Fish Bar** at 290 Pentonville Road, a short walk from the Kings Cross underground station, charging 20 pence for chips, 70 for haddock, one pound for "skate", only 28 pence for a portion of cod roe. And remember: fish 'n chips shops are fading fast; enjoy them while you may!

The Non-Chain Budget Restaurants

Another type of budget eatery in London is more difficult to describe. They have no distinguishing characteristics, except for the fact that they are individually-owned, extremely plain and simple, tiny in size, serve English food only, and are refreshingly cheap. But the only way to find these budget havens is to have their addresses, which are now set forth.

Near **Piccadilly,** the prime examples of these midget-type eateries are found on **Denman Street,** just off the bottom of Shaftesbury Avenue, a few feet from Piccadilly Circus. All the standard plates are available at moderate cost at the **New Piccadilly Restaurant,** 8 Denman Street, which charges £1.35 ($2.97) and under for most meat plates with two vegetables, and is open seven days a week. The straightforward **"Cafe-Restaurant"** (that's its name), nearby at 3 Denman Street, offers similar rates (£1.50 for most meat plates with vegetables, 50 pence for desserts, 50 pence for soup) and is an always-reliable, eat-it-on-the-run, Piccadilly Circus dinery.

Opposite the exit of the **Earls Court Road** subway station, at 183 Earls Court Road, is an **ABC Self-Service Cafeteria** with lunchtime prices (28 pence for soup, 80 pence for steak pie and vegetables, 25 pence for tea, 30 pence and up for desserts) that can't top $2.50 for two courses. Try also the several eateries on Hogarth Road, almost directly opposite the Earls Court Road tube station, and on Kenway Road, a block away.

Sidoli's Buttery, corner of Alfred Place and Store Street, is a favorite haunt of London University students who like the thick sandwiches priced at 40 pence. For 70 pence ($1.54) you can order a chicken cutlet platter with chips and peas, or Vienna steak with fried potatoes and baked beans. Apple tart and custard for dessert is 30 pence (66¢).

Near **Victoria Station,** the **Green Cafe** at 16 Eccleston Street, managed by a hard-working Italian family, is one of the best value-for-your-money choices in this area. At seven small tables in a corridor-like room, it serves a daily "plat du jour" (actually, a two-course meal, like roast lamb preceded by soup) for £1.25 ($2.75), a club sandwich with a cup of tea for 80 pence ($1.76), spaghetti bolognaise for 80 pence.

Across the street from the **British Airways Victoria Terminal, The Well** at 2 Eccleston Place, proclaims that "all the food served is prepared on the premises on the same day." Luncheon—the quick type—is usually under one pound ($2.20) in price—an example is steak and kidney pie with a vegetable salad. But it's at supper time that the talents, activities and fantasies of jolly Mr. Savage (the owner, who is also the cook) move into high gear. That's when you find a delicious onion soup for 25 pence, a leg of lamb (of Dorchester quality) for £2.25, various "sweets" (desserts), of the sort rarely found in a budget location, for 60 pence, a "nice cup of tea" for 15 pence. Ordering the lamb, you'll feast for about $6, tip included, but you can easily limit the check to $4. Atmosphere and excellent food—on a budget. Closed Saturday and Sunday evenings.

Off **The Strand** at 49 Bedford Street, a side-street of that famous thoroughfare, the **Strand Cafe** serves up tomato soup for only 20 pence, roast lamb with vegetables for only 90 pence, fish 'n chips for 75 pence, steak pie with two vegetables for 60 pence, a big cheese-and-ham omelette with chips for 78 pence, coffee for 15, milk for 12. Plain and strictly matter-of-fact in setting and mood, it still provides the best inexpensive food in this relatively expensive part of London.

Near the **Bond Street tube station,** the **Widow Applebaum** at 46 New Milton Street is recommended here only for its take-away sandwiches, which cost considerably more if you eat them on the premises. This is where celebrity guests of nearby Claridges Hotel buy their pastrami sandwiches for £1.10, salt beef (akin to our "corned beef") sandwiches for 85 pence, various salads for 40 pence apiece.

In the **Russell Square** area, two other proprietary restaurants of this sort are clustered on Southampton Row, just below the Square. The better one is the somewhat pricey **Trattoria Verdi,** at 110 Southampton Row, which can be visited on a budget basis only for lunch (when soup is 65 pence, main courses £1.75), and somewhat less expensive is the nearby **Green Parrot,** at 146 Southampton Row, where a set, three-course lunch (soup, meat with two vegetables, a sweet and coffee) is two pounds, exactly.

The **Central YWCA** (whose restaurant is one of the top budget values in all of London), on Great Russell Street, just down the block from The British Museum, serves high quality meals for £1.15 ($2.53), and is open to the public at large, of both genders and all ages, who flock to this address and wait in a fast-moving line. On weekends, only lunch is served. Don't confuse this establishment with the Helen Graham YWCA, on the same street, where the restaurant is for members only.

An inexpensive eatery in the posh **Knightsbridge area,** immensely popular, is the **Upstairs Restaurant** on Basil Street, a country-style dining room with wood tables, whitewashed walls and leaded windows. You can help yourself to all you can eat from the "Salad Bowl"—an array of meat salads, rice molds, egg dishes, cold casseroles, etc.—for £2.25 ($4.95), including a sweet from the trolley. Or you can make your selections (once again, all you want) from the "Copper Hot Plate," where the likes of creamed chicken, beef Stroganoff, vegetables, and potatoes are the featured fare. Including dessert, the latter meal costs £2.60 ($5.72). You can cut that cost to £1.43 ($3.14) by simply choosing a salad for 90p, toast and butter for 25p, a pot of tea for 28p. Open for lunch noon to 3, closed Sundays.

Finally, **Queensway Street** offers a veritable bazaar of ethnic budget eateries, among them: **Pizzaland** (#77) charging 90 pence ($1.98) for a large, filling, cheese and tomato pie; the Czechoslovakian **Moravia** (#62), where typical fare such as knockwurst with sauerkraut and sauteed potatoes costs £1.60 ($3.52); and **Delphi Taverna** (#98) for a Greek meal including an appetizer and entree of moussaka for £2.20 ($4.84).

Indian Restaurants

For a budget-minded traveller, the best change-of-pace from English cooking is provided by the many inexpensive Indian restaurants that have sprouted all over London; many of them offer hot curry dishes for as little as 90 pence to £1.10 (and that one plate is all you'll be able to finish); add rice, a beverage and tip, and you'll generally spend $3.50-or-so for a memorable, spicy meal that brings tears of satisfaction (both physically and symbolically). To spend even less, order a half portion of curry, or one plate of curry and two plates of rice for two persons—which is still more than you'll be able to finish.

Here's where you'll find them:

In the **Sussex Gardens** area, a really excellent Indian restaurant is the **Golden Shalimar** at 7 Spring Street, just off Sussex Gardens near Paddington Station. Open daily including Sundays from noon to midnight, with normal low prices for Indian food (except for your opening course of soup, for which they inexplicably charge 45 pence—it's a top of 40 pence elsewhere), courteous Indian waiters, and the right to order half-portions of some menu items, for half the menu price—an opportunity that should be seized whenever you eat in an Indian restaurant. Nearby, and with slightly lower prices, is the **Taqdir Indian Restaurant** at 8 Norfolk Place (near Praed Street), to which you might want to alternate visits; Taqdir is open seven days a week, and serves a complete, three-course Indian lunch (soup, meat or chicken curry, dessert) for only £2 on weekdays.

In the **Russell Square area,** an exceptionally cheap Indian restaurant is the **New Madras,** at 51 Marchmont Street, where a spicy, thick mulligatawny soup (which you ought always to choose for openers in an Indian restaurant) is 50p ($1.10), a full order of meat curry is £1.50 ($3.30), a vast side plate of rice is 50p ($1.10), and mango chutney is 25 pence. It might be wise, again, to order half portions of the beef or lamb curry at the New Madras, 80p ($1.76), since you can always order more if they fail to fill you (unlikely). On **Tavistock Place** in the Russell Square area, the slightly more attractive **New Shahbhag Restaurant,** at 52 Tavistock Place, charges a bit less (£1 for the beef curry), and actually encourages the ordering of half portions (50 pence).

Around **Earls Court Road,** the curry king is **Sri Hatta,** at #10 Hogarth Road, the street opposite the Earls Court Road subway station (£1.40 for most beef curries, £1 for chicken curry, 40 pence for mulligatawny soup).

And finally, near Piccadilly Circus, the moderately-priced curry restaurants cluster on **Rupert Street** (from the Eros Statue, walk down Coventry Street for two short blocks and turn left on Rupert), where the **Koh-I-Noor,** the **West End Curry Centre,** and the **New Curry Centre,** all offer inexpensive and filling plates, though at higher plate prices than elsewhere in London. At all of them, vegetable curry is only 90 pence, meat curry £1.50, chicken curry £1.65, and mulligatawny soup ranges from 40 pence at the New Curry Center (#18 Rupert Street) and Golden Curry (#34 Rupert Street) to 50 pence at Koh-I-Noor (#29 Rupert Street). Order tea, not coffee, to conclude, and keep Rupert Street in mind for pre-theatre dinner.

Of course, don't assume that all Indian restaurants are inexpensive; some of the slicker ones charge substantially more than the 90 pence to £1 you'll want to pay for curry. And don't hesitate to ask Londoners for their own Indian recommendations in other sections.

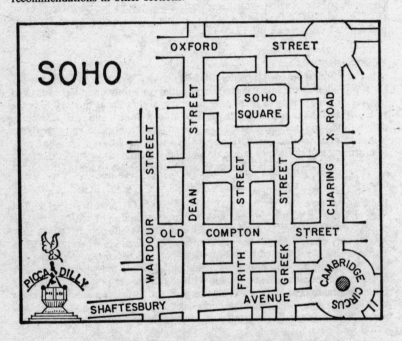

Soho—for Higher-Priced Eating

At some point, now, you'll want to vary the English fare with still other instances of foreign cooking, and for that, the area to visit is fabulous **Soho**—a jumble of foreign restaurants, dives and bars, resembling a cross between New York's Greenwich Village and San Francisco's Fisherman's Wharf. Soho is located just north of the theatre section, within an easy walk from Piccadilly. Although its prices are somewhat higher than those we've been considering, it's still hard to spend more than $5 here, and quite easy to spend much less.

The main thoroughfare of Soho is Frith Street, on which you'll find a score of international restaurants. I like, in particular: **The Asia Indian** (formerly known as the Pakistan) **(14),** 44 Frith Street (chicken curry with rice and chutney for $4); and the **Trattoria Piemonte (15),** 48 Frith Street, £2.30 ($5.06) for an excellent, three-course Italian dinner (an especially good value), the same for lunch, plus 20 pence for bread and butter, and 12½% for service.

Soho is also the site of London's largest Chinese restaurant, **Choy's (17),** at 45 Frith Street. For Sunday dining particularly, when many other London restaurants are closed, Choy's is the place for a big and tasty meal, at moderate, around $6-per-person costs—even less if you are 3, 4 or 5 persons dining together and can take advantage of family dinner selections. Four persons, for instance, can order chicken with mushrooms and spices, stewed pork, sweet and sour pork, chicken chop suey, and fried rice (Dinner #H), for a total cost of $20.80—or $5.20 apiece. If you're dining alone, order half-portions of every-thing, because the full servings are gargantuan in size.

PUB LUNCHES: One other meal-time subject requires special attention, because it involves the most popular lunch-time restaurant of the average Englishman —the pubs. Nearly every pub in London serves either hot or cold food at lunchtime, some of them elaborately, others by merely placing a serving bowl, containing a single food item—hot macaroni and cheese, for instance—onto the bar.

The food at pubs is surprisingly tasty and consists of the best British specialties—such items as "Scotch eggs" (a hard-boiled egg surrounded by ham and veal, and enclosed in a dough crust), a veal pie (a cutaway chunk of bread, with a hard-boiled egg and veal inside it), or meat "salad" (roast beef with a touch of greens, tomatoes and cole slaw), and all accompanied by a pint of beer (mild or bitter or "half-n-half"). None of these items should run to more than 90 pence at a pub, and an entire pub lunch shouldn't exceed £1.50. If you'll eat standing up (the sit-down meals in a pub are always more expensive), and are prepared to gain your acceptance in the pub by being quiet and unobtrusive, you'll partake of a wonderful English experience, and you'll have some of the best meals available in London. Where are the pubs? They're everywhere—and they carry quaint names like **"The Lamb & Flag,"** or **"The King's Head,"** or **"The Museum Tavern,"** the latter being opposite the British Museum and one of the best in town (lunch only, however, from noon to 2:30). Some pubs tip you off to the existence of their hot plates by displaying cryptic references to "hot pork and platter dishes," as does **The Salisbury Buffet,** a pub on St. Martin's Lane, corner of St. Martin's Court, in the heart of the theatre district. A pub in the Sussex Gardens area? Try the **Fountains Abbey,** at #109 Praed Street, a block from Paddington Station, where a homemade steak-and-kidney-pie with mashed potatoes cost 95 pence ($2.09) in 1979. A luncheon-serving pub on Earls Court Road? Try the **Bolton Pub,** 326 Earls Court Road (corner of Old Brompton Road). More pubs? On the Strand, next door to #408, is the **Nell Gwynne Tavern,** a pub with cold luncheon counter. Behind Victoria Station, near our hotel choices on Belgrave Road, is **St. George's Tavern,** 14 Belgrave Road (corner of Hugh Street), where homemade steak and kidney pie is 40 pence, a Scotch egg costs 35 pence (77¢), and portions of potato salad, cole slaw or baked beans are 35 pence (77¢).

A typical pub meal? Hope usually has a Scotch egg, potato salad, and tomato juice; I have a slice of meat pie with mustard, and a glass of lager. Total cost for both of us: £2, or $4.40.

A last food tip:

WHEN IN DOUBT: Order steak-and-kidney pie in London, which invariably comes with two vegetables, rarely costs more than 95 pence, often costs less. It's a tasty and inexpensive dish, even in the higher-priced restaurants.

READERS' INDIAN RESTAURANTS: "Indian food enthusiasts should head for the area around Paddington Station, where two good (and cheap) Indian restaurants are located. Probably the best is the **Taqdir Restaurant** at 8 Norfolk Place, between Praed Street and Sussex Gardens, where an order of beef curry, rice, and a pitcher of water cost only £1.65 ($3.63), and vegetable curry can be had for 90 pence. The other is the **Golden Shalimar,** 6 Spring Street," (S. C. Gruber, Hunting Beach, California). . . . "The **Agra Restaurant,** 137 Whitfield Street, near the Warren Street Tube Station, is renowned for its Tandoori meal, which is Punjabi food cooked in the Sikh community. For £2, one receives an ample half chicken which is first marinated in spices, then cooked in a special oven, which is rather like a clay hole in the ground. With it you eat 'nan'—a puffy soft bread for about 40 pence." (Helen Kilick, London, England).

READERS' RESTAURANT SELECTIONS (NEAR SIGHTSEEING ATTRACTIONS): "The cafeteria (not the restaurant) at the **Victoria and Albert Museum** is a good place for a very cheap meal. You would have trouble spending over 80 pence for a meal without wine or beer" (D. L. Goldwater, Swarthmore, Pennsylvania). . . . "It is often difficult to find a restaurant for a snack on a Sunday in the vicinity of Trafalgar Square, and I would like to recommend the very quiet and restful **buffet inside the National Gallery,** where one can sit as long as one likes over a 25-pence cup of tea and a sandwich. It's open most days between 10 a.m. and 5 p.m. and open between 2:30 and 5 on Sundays" (Miss R. E. Seaton, Bath, Somerset, England). . . . "It's still possible to go into a restaurant in London and spend only about $3.50 and yet order à la carte. **Perdoni's Restaurant,** 8-10 Kennington Road, SE 1, is where to head, near **Waterloo Station** (tube station Lambeth North), the **Imperial War Museum** and the **Old Vic National Theater.** Here's what I had: roast beef with Yorkshire pudding and two vegetables, 90 pence; minestrone soup 28 pence; apple pie 25 pence; and tea 25 pence. All for approximately $3.70" (Edward T. Pietraszek, Chicago, Illinois). . . . "I hope you will allow a mere Englishman to make a recommendation in regard to his own country. During a recent rare visit to London, I was struck by your lack of budget food opportunities in the neighborhood of the Tower of London. By a happy chance my wife and I came across the small budget establishment of Mr. Novani, at the **Minories Restaurant,** under the railway arches about one hundred and fifty yards north of the Tower. There, at 105A The Minories, we had a splendid 3-course meal with coffee for £1.50 ($3.30) a head, of British home cooking of a standard rarely met with these days, in an atmosphere much more redolent of homely Amsterdam than of over-developed London. Although we were obviously not big spenders, we were welcomed by the owner and made to feel we had known him for years" (M. G. Habberley, Powys, Wales).

A READERS' HIGH TEA SELECTION: "Everyone visiting London should have a proper **English tea** some afternoon, and our favourite place for tea is **Harrod's Department Store** (underground stop: Knightsbridge). Every day, from 3:30 p.m. to store-closing, there is a fantastic tea served in the fourth floor **restaurant.** The waiters brings you tea and milk, and you help yourself from a huge table covered with every conceivable kind of cakes, pastries, lovely scones with Devonshire cream as thick as butter, and strawberry jam. You can eat all you like, and you might not want dinner that night. All this for £2.10 ($4.62)" (David Finkel, Lewisburg, Pennsylvania).

READERS' FISH-AND-CHIPS: "In London's Cartwright Gardens area, the **North Sea Fish Bar and Restaurant** is excellent for fish. Cod and chips, £1.30, and cod only is 65p. The food is steaming hot and good. That's at 8 Leigh Street, intersection of Leigh and Sandwich Streets, just off Marchmont" (Marie J. Moreau, Lakeside, California). . . . "Since many people in England earn 45 pounds ($99) or less during a week, you know there must be economical places to eat. Just a short block or so from Victoria Station, at 83 Wilton Road, one should try the **Seafresh Restaurant.** Haddock and chips - £1.30," (John L. Gatfield, Napa, California); enthusiastic seconding recommendation from Don and Shirley Ward of Unionville, Ontario, Canada, who hail "the tastiest fish eaten in all our travels through Britian").

READERS' PUB COMMENTS: "A note on pubbing: most English pubs are divided into first and second class. The first section, with appropriate clientele and higher prices, is called 'Saloon Bar' or 'Lounge Bar'; the second class section, also with appropriate clientele and lower prices, is called 'Public Bar' or just plain 'Bar.' The cheapest beer, and I think the best, is 'ordinary bitter.' The pub is a superb institution, steeped in tradition as a congenial neighborhood retreat. Go to one, talk to the customers, converse with the barkeep—this is the way to see and know the British. Warning: all pubs close at 11 p.m. One pub with an attractive gimmick is **The Sherlock Holmes**, at 10 Northumberland Avenue, on the left-hand side, and one block toward the Thames from Trafalgar Square; it has a Holmes tableau and much memorabilia. Another pub that the English tourists (that is, the country people who come to visit the big city) all go to see is **The Prospect of Whitby**, in the dock section, alongside the Thames; it displays a colorful nautical exhibit. That's a half hour from the West End, however; take the Underground to Whitechapel, and change there for Wapping. Or you might try asking any Englishman where a good pub can be found; he'll be most happy to tell you" (John H.M. Austin, New Haven, Connecticut).

THE TOP SIGHTS: We turn now to the real reasons for your trip to London. To see everything of interest in this vast, sprawling capital would take a decade. To make even a more-or-less thorough tour of the more important buildings and museums—will take two weeks. For readers with less time available, there is a basic minimum of four indispensable sights, that must be seen.

The Tower of London

For this, the most profound experience of your London stay, schedule an entire weekday afternoon—and never, never go on Sunday, when it's badly crowded. Rather, immediately after a weekday lunch, enter the London Underground and take a train of the Inner Circle or District lines to the Tower Hill Station, from which, a two-minute walk away, is the fabled **Tower of London**, on the banks of the Thames. Admission to the grounds in summer is £1 for adults (but only 50 pence from October through March), 50 pence for children, and there's an extra 50 pence charge for entrance to the underground building which houses the Crown Jewels. That $3.30 will plunge you into the turbulent, bloody world of British history, which surrounds you with intense reality as you wander into the stone apartments of Sir Walter Raleigh, his place of imprisonment for twelve years; and see the room in which the Little Princes were smothered; the scaffold site of the execution of kings and queens; and finally, the "Armories" in the important White Tower, in the very center of the tower complex, where the armor of King Henry VIII is mounted atop a white horse. In the grounds, wander the famous "Beefeaters" (they've heard the gag about the gin hundreds of times) and the ravens with clipped wings, who are symbols of the tower. Don't allow yourself to be shortchanged for time, and don't—again—go on Sunday.

The British Museum

In this massive building on Great Russell Street (the nearest tube stations are Holborn and Tottenham Court Road), Britain preserves and displays its most awesome State documents and manuscripts: the original Magna Carta, the log-book of Admiral Nelson and his half-finished letter to Lady Hamilton, written just before he died; the first draft of the dream-inspired "Xanadu" by Samuel Coleridge; a deed to William Shakespeare; a host of other papers that will send chills up your spine. And here, too, is kept the plunder of Britain's Imperial era: the famous Rosetta stone, the small Sphinxes of Egypt, the stunning Elgin Marbles from the front of the Parthenon. There is no admission charge, and there are, in addition, free lecture tours conducted Monday through Saturday at 1:15 p.m., as well as gallery talks presented at 3 p.m., Monday through Saturday, by a staff that sometimes includes ex-university dons, who each day deal with a different subject: "Everyday Life in Assyrian Sculpture," "Karl Marx in England," "The Boer War". Don't miss a visit to the museum, and to start things off, ask the guards to direct you to the "manuscript rooms" and the "Elgin Marbles." The building is open from 10 to 5, Monday through Saturday, and from 2:30 to 6 p.m. on Sundays.

Madame Tussaud's

And next, to see frighteningly-lifelike wax statues of the men whose lives are reflected in the British Museum, go to the celebrated waxworks of **Madame Tussaud** (on Marylebone Road, near the Baker Street tube station), where figures of the world's most famous personages, past and present (they have astronaut Neil Armstrong, John F. Kennedy, Marilyn Monroe, too) are grouped into amusing and fascinating tableaux—all so real that when you stare into the face of Pablo Picasso or Winston Churchill, you'll think that he's staring back and about to open his mouth! All quite eerie, not to be missed, and the admission charge is £1.70 ($3.74) for adults, 85 pence ($1.87) for children, which includes the right to visit "the Chamber of Horrors." Open daily *including* Sundays, from 10 a.m. to 6:30 p.m., except in winter, when closing hours are at 5:30 p.m.

Parliament

Finally, Hope and I make it a point, on each of our visits to London, to attend a session of the House of Commons, in the great Palace of Westminster; because the ritual, the pageantry and the brilliant debate of this most famous of legislative bodies is an inspiring experience, that reinforces one's belief in democracy.

To gain entrance without standing in line, you'll need a ticket from the American Embassy—but that's really too much of a chore to consider. Except for debates of exceptional importance, you'll rarely have to wait more than an hour for admission, and you can spend this time sitting on a cushioned ledge in the hall that leads to the visitors' galleries.

Sessions of the House of Commons begin at 2:30 p.m. from Monday to Thursday, at 11 a.m. on Friday, and often last late into the evening (except on Fridays, when they usually end at 4:30 p.m.; August and September are usually, but not always, the months of recess). Visitors who do not possess tickets from their Embassy or from an M.P. are admitted to the galleries beginning at around 4:15 p.m., at 11:30 a.m. on Fridays. (On Saturdays, when the House is not in session, and on public days during recess, you'll be admitted to wander around between 10 a.m. and 4:30 p.m.) Keep in mind, as you watch the session, that amplifiers are ingeniously concealed in the woodwork at your shoulders. Therefore, if you lean back slightly, rather than lean forward, you'll be able to hear perfectly.

Best time for avoiding a wait in line to enter Parliament? Around 6 p.m., when the crowd thins out—the only disadvantage being that the more important opening speeches of debates are usually concluded by that time. The tube station for Parliament is Westminster.

Incidentally, it is usually a bit easier to attend sessions of the House of Lords, where the ritual and pageantry are decidedly more impressive than in

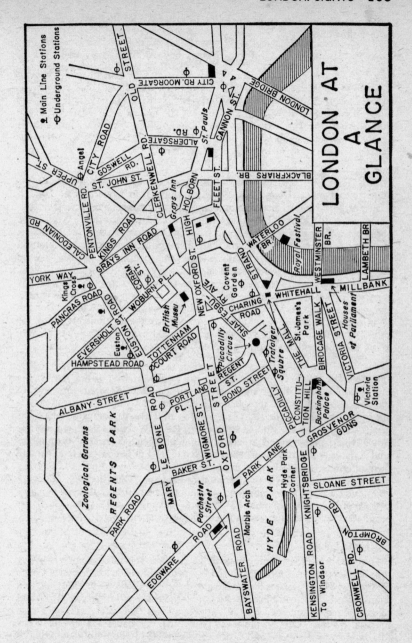

the Commons, as is the chamber itself. Sessions of the Lords begin at 2:30 p.m.
Monday to Wednesday and 3 p.m. on Thursday (the Lords take a long, long
weekend) and end about 8 p.m. Visitors are admitted from the beginning of the

sitting; go to the same entrance as for Commons, and then ask a guard for further directions.

The Other Six

The Tower of London, the British Museum, Parliament, and Madame Tussaud's—those are among the 10 top sights of London we think you'll want to see. The other six: Westminster Abbey; the National Gallery (and Trafalgar Square); Buckingham Palace (Changing of the Guard), The Mall and Hyde Park Corner; the Tate Museum; The Victoria and Albert Museum, with its across-the-street neighbor, the Science Museum; and St. Paul's Cathedral. Details, and methods of touring, are now coming up:

TOURS: The most fabulous value in all European city tours is the $4.40, two hour, twenty-mile **"Round London Sightseeing Tour"** offered by "London Transport," the official city bus company. The tours leave from both the south side of Piccadilly Circus (you'll see a special stand), from Marble Arch (near Speaker's Corner in Park Lane), and from Buckingham Palace Road, about a block-and-a-half south of Victoria Station: take the underground to Victoria Station, then walk up Buckingham Palace Road towards the British Airways Air Terminal; you'll soon find the departure point for the bright-red buses. They leave every day of the week throughout the year except on Christmas day, every hour on the hour from 10 a.m. to 5 p.m. in summer, until 4 p.m. in winter, charge £2 for adults, £1.50 pence for children, pass by every major London sight, and sometimes (but not always) provide a running commentary—all for a third of what you'd pay to a commercial tour company. An incomparable way to see the city, which should be one of your first activities in London.

The Standard Tours

If you'd prefer, however, to take a normal, escorted sightseeing tour of London and vicinity, you'll probably receive the most value for your money at one of the branches of the 100-year-old **Charles Rickards** company, which has departure points in the Russell Square area (at 17 Woburn Place, opposite the Royal Hotel), in the Grand Arcade at Trafalgar Square, corner of Northumberland Avenue, and from the Charles Dickens Hotel in Lancaster Gate. Among their offerings for 1980 are a morning tour of the West End (£4.20, every morning except Sunday), an afternoon tour of the "Old City" (£5.50, every afternoon), a Sunday morning tour of London for £3.50, an unusually inexpensive evening tour of London (2½ hours, starting at 7:15 p.m.; £3.50 per person), many other tours which you can learn about by phoning 493-3181.

Outside of London

For the cheapest tours outside of London (operated summers—May through September—only), go to the "Information Office" at **Victoria Coach Station,** 164 Buckingham Palace Road (phone 730-0202), just a short walk up from Victoria Railroad Station, and you'll find racks of brochures, plus ticket sales counters maintained by the tour companies that cater to local, *British* tourists. As one example, the tours offered by **"National Travel"** include a full-day trip to Blenheim and Oxford for £5.60 ($12.32), a full-day outing to Woburn Abbey for £5.30 ($11.66), and more than a dozen half-day tours, such as one to the Costwolds for £4.20 ($9.24), to Warwick Castle for £4.20 ($9.24), and along the Kentish coast for £4.20 ($9.24). Compare those prices with those of the tours offered to Americans in the American-oriented, large hotels, and you'll get quite a shock. After choosing your tours from the pamphlets (an especially good one is National Travel's "Day and Half-Day Tours and Excursions from London," which can also be obtained by writing to National Travel, Victoria Coach Station, 164 Buckingham Palace Road, London S.W. 1), you can then make your reservations (if possible, a day or so in advance) at the ticket windows. Most tours leave early in the morning (often as early as 8 a.m.) from the bus-loading bays at Victoria Coach Station, and at the peak of the summer season, there are several leaving every day. Prices generally do not include meals eaten along the way.

MUSEUMS: None of the leading museums of London charges admission, and five of them are exceedingly important institutions, to which you ought to schedule a visit: the **Tate Gallery,** on Millbank (modern art primarily, but don't miss the room of watercolors by William Blake, in the downstairs gallery; 10 to 6 on weekdays, 2 to 6 on Sundays, take the tube to Pimlico, or bus #88 or #77; pastries and tea served in the basement for $1); the **National Gallery** on Trafalgar Square (housing the classic paintings; 10 to 6 on weekdays, 2 to 6 on Sundays; take the tube to Trafalgar Square); the **Wallace Collection,** on Manchester Square (17th- and 18th-century French and other paintings; miniatures, sculpture, ceramics, furniture and armor; 10 to 5 on weekdays (but closed Fridays), 2:30 to 5:50 p.m. Sundays; tube to Bond Street); the **Victoria and Albert Museum,** corner of Cromwell and Exhibition Roads (sculpture and applied arts, a magnificent assortment; 10 to 5:50 weekdays, except Fridays; 2:30 to 5:50 Sundays; take the underground to South Kensington, and walk several blocks north); the **Science Museum,** on Exhibition Road (across from the Victoria and Albert, 10 to 6 on weekdays and Saturdays, 2:30 to 6 on Sundays). There are, of course, many, many others; if you've time for only two, make them the National Gallery and the Tate; but go to the British Museum ahead of all.

FREE SIGHTS: "Speaker's Corner" at Hyde Park (near Marble Arch) is a Sunday must. Soapbox orators of every variety: Communists, violent racists, vegetarians. They undergo the finest heckling in the world, a vicious repartee, by professionals who've known the speaker for years and vice-versa. Take the underground to Marble Arch. . . . **Old Bailey,** the famous criminal courts building of London, opens its public galleries at 10:15 a.m. and 1:45 p.m. on weekdays. Leave your camera at the hotel (they're not permitted here), take the underground to St. Paul's and look for the public gallery entrance on Newgate Street. Lesser crimes are tried at the **Bow Street Magistrate's Court,** 10 a.m. to 5 p.m., for which the underground stop is Covent Garden. . . . Civil law courts open their public galleries from 10 to 4 on weekdays, when court is in session; tube stop is Temple. . . . Changing of the guard? It takes place daily at 11 a.m. in front of **Buckingham Palace;** and to reach the palace, take the underground (Circle, District or Victoria Line) to Victoria, the Piccadilly Line to Hyde Park Corner, or the Piccadilly or Victoria Lines to Green Park. . . . The **London Stock Exchange,** Old Broad Street, maintains a free visitors' gallery, 10 a.m. to 3:15 p.m., weekdays, and provides girl guides, plus explanatory movies. Nearest underground station is "Bank." . . . Finally, you needn't be reminded to visit **Westminster Abbey,** where all but two of England's sovereigns were crowned; see Hope's description below (and take the underground to "Westminster"). . . . And, while the crypt at **St. Paul's Cathedral** (take the underground to "St. Paul's") charges 35p admission and shouldn't appear in this section, nevertheless, it's here that you'll see the famous ornate funeral carriage of the Duke of Wellington, and memorials to many other British greats, all of which exercise a strange fascination, and shouldn't be missed.

SOME ORDER TO YOUR TOURING: The vastness of London makes this a large task; perhaps the best course is to choose one particular feature of London life, and thereafter concentrate on either "Royal London" (Buckingham Palace, The Mall, The Tower, The Horse Guards, Changing of the Guard), "Literary London" (Dickens' House, Carlyle's House, Sherlock Holmes' Baker Street, The Cheshire Cheese, The Old Curiosity Shop), "Legal and Financial London" (The City, Inns of Court, The Stock Exchange, the Guildhall), "Residential London" (Belgravia and Mayfair), or any of a dozen other aspects of this phenomenon of cities—you won't run out of "aspects" to see. "When a man is tired of London," said Samuel Johnson, "he is tired of life; for there is in London all that life can afford."

My wife Hope has tried her hand at suggesting methods of touring London that deal with attractions other than those I've described before. We'll turn to her discussion now, and then go on to excursions outside of London.

HOPE'S LONDON: "During World War II when bombs fell on the city, there was discovered in the rubble a little red flower that had not been seen since London's Great Fire in 1666: the people named it 'London Pride' and Noel Coward wrote a song about it. In the section that follows, we'll try to discover the sources of 'London Pride.'

A Proud and Royal Tour

"After visiting Parliament as Arthur suggests (subway stop is Westminster), cross the street to **Westminster Abbey,** which is the nation's most impressive example of early English Gothic architecture and the most awesome burial place you are ever likely to see. Everyone Who Was Anyone in England either has a memorial or is actually entombed here, from Chaucer to Churchill. Most English kings and queens are buried here, too, and since 1066, when William the Conqueror was crowned King of England within these walls, the Abbey has provided the setting for practically every coronation. The building itself, which was polished and re-gilded for its 900th birthday in December, 1965, is a spectacle of gold leaf, stone and stained glass. Definitely pay the 60p admission price ($1.32; free on Wednesdays from 6 to 8 p.m.) to see the Royal Chapels (not open to view on Sunday) and Tombs, the Coronation Chair (with the famous Stone of Scone under the seat), and Henry VII's Chapel, a magnificent sixteenth century fane with filigreed, fan-vaulted ceiling and banners of Knights of the Bath. I think you'll find especially thrilling the Tombs of Queen Elizabeth I, the Little Princes who were killed in the Tower (Edward V and Richard, Duke of York), and Mary Queen of Scots (her monument is decorated with Scottish thistles). The Abbey is open daily from 8 a.m. to 6 p.m. (Wednesdays till 8; except when a service is being conducted) and admission to the nave is free. *Extra:* a favorite secret spot of mine—peaceful and atmospheric—is the Cloisters behind the Abbey, which also include the Chapter House and the Abbey Treasures Museum. For details see Readers' Selections.

"Now, head north (back in the direction of Westminster Tube Station) toward Trafalgar Square for a walk along **Whitehall,** which used to be the site of Whitehall Palace but is now famous as the street of British Government

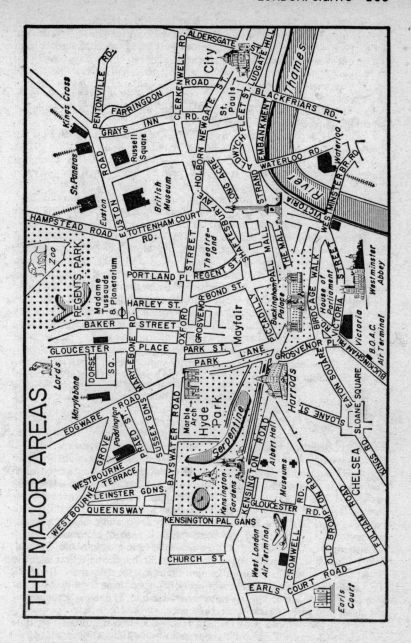

Offices. Make a short detour to your left, near the Cenotaph, to have a look at **No. 10 Downing Street,** a modest little three-story brick building with only two solitary "Bobbies" keeping watch in front, which serves as residence for the English Prime Minister. Compare it to our White House!

"A little further on, also on your left, is the colorful **Horse Guards;** you can't miss it—two men in splendid uniforms on horseback, stationed in front of a quaint looking tower. If you arrive at 11 a.m. (10 on Sundays), you'll see a Changing of the Horse Guard, which takes place half an hour before the equally elaborate ceremony at Buckingham Palace. A shorter, simpler "inspection" takes place at 4 every day. If you like, you can walk through the Archway and see the **Horse Guard Parade,** a wide open yard used for the 'trooping of the colors' on the Queen's official birthday.

"Directly across the street from the Horse Guards is the **Banqueting House,** all that is left of the old Whitehall Palace, and now open from 10 to 5 on weekdays, from 2 to 5 on Sundays, closed Mondays, for an admission charge of 20p (children 10p). It was designed by Inigo Jones, completed in 1622, and has a ceiling of nine panels painted by Rubens. Here King Charles I stepped through a second floor window onto a scaffolding to have his head cut off; William and Mary accepted the Crown of England; and many other events of historical interest occurred on the site.

"Now, continue on your walk to **Trafalgar Square** where you'll see, directly across the Square, the **National Gallery** already described by Arthur; if you're curious to know how London looked a century ago, the trip to Trafalgar Square and the National Gallery (gaze at the top of the Square) will give you an idea. Arriving at this spot also provides the opportunity to nip into the **National Portrait Gallery** located directly behind the National Gallery on St. Martin's Place and Charing Cross Road. Admission is free, and the gallery is open from 10 to 5 on weekdays, Saturdays till 6, and from 2 to 6 on Sundays. I recommend the National Portrait Gallery to you as a kind of picture book history. There are paintings of everyone from the fifteenth century onwards, and while the paintings themselves are for the most part not worth mentioning (notable exceptions: Holbein's Henry VIII, the Rubens' sketches of the Earl of Arundel, superb self-portraits by Gainsborough and Reynolds, the portrait of the Bronte sisters by their brother Branwell), they are bound to appeal to the gossip in you.

A Group of Historical Walks

"You might next like to see a session of the **Royal Courts of Justice** (tube stops are Temple or Aldwych) from the Visitors' Gallery, which is open when Courts are in session on weekdays from 10 to 4. Directly across the street are two of the Inns of Court called "The Temple," which contain the **Middle Temple Hall,** and **Temple Church.** The former was built in 1570 by Elizabeth I and is a glorious Tudor Hall with crests everywhere and ornamental armor and guns; it is believed that the Shakespeare Company performed *Twelfth Night* here in 1601, and the hall does have the feeling of jolly old England. Admission is free; hours are 10 to 12 and 3 to 4:30 (but the hall is occasionally closed to the public when in use). Temple Church, open daily from 10 to 4:30, is a gabled Gothic building that was badly damaged during the War but has been faithfully restored. The nave was completed in 1185 and has stone effigies of knights and earls (Crusaders) on the floor.

"From The Temple, walk through Inner Temple Gate; directly opposite the Gate is Chancery Lane; walk about half way up the first block and you'll find on your right the **Public Record Office** with its small museum, admission free and open Monday to Friday from 1 p.m. to 4 p.m. This is a history student's dream, for here you can see the famous Domesday Book (William the Conqueror's list of all the property in his new realm, drafted for him in 1086), a copy of the final version of the Magna Carta, Royal Autographs, letters of Ben Jonson, Bacon, Milton, and many others too numerous to mention.

Now turn back to **Fleet Street,** turn left and walk up the street about two blocks, because you ought now to pay a visit to **Dr. Johnson's House,** at 17 Gough Square (watch for a sign on your left pointing the way); admission 40 pence (20p for students and children), open from 11 to 5:30, 5 in winter, closed Sundays. It was in this house that most of the work on his magnum opus was done, and you can actually see a copy of the first edition of Dr. Johnson's famous Dictionary here (visit the Dictionary Garret where Johnson's copyists worked), along with portraits of most of the people connected with Johnson, and all manner of Johnson memorabilia.

"After your visit to St. Paul's (tube stop: St. Paul's), make a short detour to the **Church of Saint Bartholomew the Great,** open daily till dusk and located near Smithfield Market (from the tube station find a street called Little Britain and walk along nearly to the end; there are two entrances to the church, one on Little Britain itself, or turn right into a street called Cloth Fair). This lovely Norman structure, built in 1123, is the oldest parish church in all of London. Next, walk back toward the tube station and ask for Wood Street, which leads into Gresham St., and at the junction of Gresham and King Streets you'll find **The Guildhall,** built in 1425, admission free, open Monday through Saturday from 10 to 5. The Guildhall is the Civic Hall of the City of London, and while a very correct English friend of mine tells me it's been restored and is therefore not strictly authentic, I find here a wonderful sense of the way London must have been five hundred years ago. In any event, part of the interior of the porch, part of the hall, and the crypts are genuine 15th century, and the hall itself is wonderfully stone-Gothic with stained glass windows, and includes a statue of Winston Churchill, Gog and Magog, and the official standards of lengths.

The Houses of Some Men to be Proud Of

"For 60p (50 pence for students, 25p for children), you can visit **The Dickens House, Library and Museum** at 48 Doughty St. (subway stop: Russell Square, then walk three blocks up Guilford Street, away from Russell Square, or Buses 19 or 38 to John Street), open daily except Sundays and bank holidays from 10 to 5. Charles Dickens lived here from 1837 to 1839, during which time he wrote most of *The Pickwick Papers, Oliver Twist,* and *Nicholas Nickleby,* and thus became a very famous and celebrated man while still in his mid-twenties. The house is just the kind of place you'd expect Dickens to live in, and is filled with personal mementos, family portraits, photographs, the desk and chair used during the last years of his life, and pictures and crockery celebrating famous Dickens characters.

"Real Dickens enthusiasts will also want to pay a visit to **The Old Curiosity Shop,** 13-14 Portsmouth Street (tube stop—Holborn; come out on Kingsway, turn left and walk about three blocks to Sardinia St., turn left again and Portsmouth is the first street in on your right), open every day of the year, except Christmas, from 9:30 to 5:30. Lovers of Little Nell and her Grandfather will remember this tiny old Tudor shop, built in 1567, from the graphic pages of Dickens' novel *The Old Curiosity Shop.*

"Next, you might go to Apsley House, townhouse of the first Duke of Wellington, now known as **The Wellington Museum,** 149 Piccadilly, near the entrance to Hyde Park (tube is Hyde Park Corner; open every weekday except Monday and Friday from 10 to 6 and Sundays from 2:30 to 6, admission free). It contains many priceless paintings, relics and honors collected by the Duke, conqueror of Napoleon—in the vestibule, for instance, stands Canova's gigantic nude statue of Napoleon, a rather sardonic touch. The dining table and chairs in the Waterloo Gallery were used by the Duke at his annual victory celebrations or Waterloo Banquets, as he called them, and the ornate silver and gilt centerpiece was given to him by the Prince Regent of Portugal. There are some highly interesting political cartoons in the basement.

"If you plan to take a walk around **Chelsea** (London's former Bohemia-land), and I heartily recommend that you *do* if you have the time, then at 24 Cheyne Row (located off Cheyne Walk between Albert Bridge and Battersea Bridge) you'll find the charming old **House of Thomas Carlyle,** open daily, except Mondays and Tuesdays, from April 1 to October 31, from 11 a.m. to 5 p.m., Sundays from 2 to 5 p.m., and charging an 80 pence admission fee to adults, 40p to children. Carlyle lived here for nearly 50 years, from 1834 to 1881, and left a strong imprint on the place; all the furnishings and decorations are just as he and his wife placed them; you can feel his presence. You'll see photos, drawings, and paintings of Mr. and Mrs. Carlyle, as well as letters, books, pens, pipes and spectacles, the attic room in which he worked, his desk, and a very touching letter from Disraeli. The surrounding neighborhood is delightful, too, with its lovely old Georgian and Victorian houses and many famous landmarks, such as **The Chelsea Old Church** and **The Chelsea Royal Hospital.** As you walk through Chelsea (which ignores the seasons, and somehow always looks green), keep your eyes peeled for those little round blue disks identifying famous London sites, because for a couple of hundred years there were more famous and illustrious writers and painters living (and dying) in Chelsea than anywhere else in London. (Nearest tube stop: Sloane Square, then a fairly long walk; or from the West End, take buses 11, 19 or 22 to Chelsea Town Hall—which puts you closer to the heart of the neighborhood; to get to Carlyle's House from here, take the first street on your left, Oakley Street, then the first street on your right, Upper Cheyne Row, to Cheyne Row, first street on your left.)

Some Extras

"Be sure to save time for **Covent Garden** (tube stop is Strand), where the historic wholesale marketplace has now been replaced by a modern retail **'Jubilee Market,'** open weekdays from 9 to 5, of 100 Cockney-manned stalls selling fresh farm produce, clothing, confectionery, homemade sweets. (The building itself is currently closed for cleaning and restoration, but one can still see how beautifully romantic a structure it is.) And have a look at **St. Paul's Covent Garden** (enter from King St.), a small church designed by Inigo Jones, where Ellen Terry and many other notables are buried, and whose portico provided the setting for the opening scene of the film of G. B. Shaw's *Pygmalion.* . . . Archaeology Pros and Amateurs: there are 'digs' in London! All along the Thames-front, from near and around London Bridge to Blackfriars, archaeologists have been uncovering ancient artifacts (from as far back as Roman London), and considerably dating (with clear signs and maps) the revealed structures for the curious. Volunteers are welcome, and on-site workers are extremely friendly and knowledgeable. This summer, when I visited the Mermaid site where I saw Medieval ruins from the 13th and 14th centuries (now covered up), I was told by the chief archaeologist that the current excavations were the largest and most important of their type in the country. They have provided a uniquely detailed picture of the development and quality of London waterfront life. Digging will continue for the next ten years. Highly recommended by a London newspaper are sites at Trig Lane near the river front, and a large GPO site in Newgate Street. For current information on how to locate sites, call the British Tourist Information Center. . . . London's magnificent **Harrod's Department Store** in Knightsbridge, especially its ground floor, is a sightseeing attraction in its own right and shouldn't be missed. . . . A worthwhile purchase by tourists remaining in England long enough to justify it is an **'Open to View'** ticket, which costs $12, is valid for 30 days from the first day of use, and admits the bearer to over 400 varied attractions—all under the jurisdiction of the British National Trust. In London: Banqueting House; Carlyle's House; the Tower of London; and Westminster Abbey. Outside London: Hampton Court Palace; Kew Palace; Stonehenge; Windsor Castle; Harvard House and Shakespeare's Birthplace in Stratford-upon-Avon; Woburn Abbey; Edinburgh Castle and Palace of Holyrood House in Edinburgh; and Scone Palace. If interested, mail a check or money order to Britrail Travel International, 270 Madison Avenue, New York, N.Y. 10016, and you'll receive an 'O.V.' ticket, along with a booklet describing the attractions at which it can be used.

"**Flash for Feminists:** The vast library, data, and memorabilia collections of **The Fawcett Society,** documenting the fight for women's rights over the past 200 or more years, has recently found a permanent home in "Calcutta House" on Old Castle Street, a five-minute walk from Petticoat Lane, ten minutes from the Tower. Among many items of interest in their collection is a first edition of Mary Wollstonecraft's 'A Vindication of the Rights of Women,' published in 1792. Believe it or not, the current head librarian is Rita Pankhurst, daughter-in-law of Sylvia Pankhurst, whose mother was Emmiline Pankhurst, the courageous, militant suffragette (and *their* letters are here too). Telephone the Fawcett Society for viewing hours and details (283-1030, extension 570); they've just moved in, but I am hoping to be able to check out their treasure trove this summer."

READERS' SIGHTSEEING TIPS: "One of the oldest rituals in London, the **Ceremony of the Keys,** takes place at 9:40 p.m. at the Tower of London. It's free, and very impressive, but only a limited number of people can watch it. You must write in advance to the Resident Governor, HM Tower of London, EC3N4AB Endorsing SAE," giving a preferred date and an alternate date, and specifying the number of people in your party" (Janet Zimmerman, Pittsburgh, Pennsylvania). . . . "We would like to highly recommend the **London Walks** offered by the Tourist Office. The topics of the walks are numerous, among them 'Ghosts of the West End' and 'Dickens' London.' The price is 80 pence for a 2- to 2½-hour walk with a very knowledgeable guide" (Steve & Dolores Bartholomew, Warsaw, Poland; note by AF: there are more than 40 London walks, among them "Jack the Ripper," "In the footsteps of Sherlock Holmes," "London and the Monarchy"; phone 882-2763 for current information) . . . "The best collection of French Impressionists and post-Impressionists outside of France, is to be found at **The Courtauld Institute Galleries,** which are part of London University (located in the Warburg Building, on Woburn Square at the corner of Torrington Place—Tube: Goodge Street, Russell Square or Euston Square; admission is free weekdays from 10 to 5, Sundays from 2 to 5). If you include a stop here on your itinerary, I assure you, you're in for some thrilling surprises" (Robert Rogers, New York, New York). . . . "We spent a delightful day exploring **Kensington Gardens**—the Round Pond, Broad Walk, Sunken Garden, Orangery, etc. Our excursion gave us the chance to visit the *State Apartments* in Kensington Palace, where we were most taken by Queen Victoria's bedroom (where she first learned she was to be Queen), and the Ante-Room which contains Victoria's doll house and other toys. Open weekdays from 10 to 6, and Sundays from 2 to 6 (except in winter, when the closing time is 4 p.m.), admission 30 pence—tube stops are Queensway, Bayswater or Kensington High Street" (Mathew Marshall, New York, New York). . . . "Brass-rubbing enthusiasts needn't travel miles to deserted and desolate country churchyards. Just go to the **London Brass Rubbing Centre** at St. James Church, Piccadilly, where you will be given all the materials you need to make brass rubbings from their exhibition brasses of medieval knights, ladies, merchants and priests. A staff member will show you how if you've never done a rubbing before, and charges start at 45p and go to £5, depending on the size of the rubbing. The London Brass Rubbing Centre is open Monday to Saturday, 10 a.m. to 6 p.m., and on Sundays from noon to 6 p.m. After you've done your brass rubbing, you should pay a visit to St. James Church itself. Set back from the hustle and bustle of Piccadilly, and behind its own courtyard with gardens and a fountain, this famous Wren church includes some of the finest work of the British master woodcarver, Grinling Gibbons. . . . ("Speaking of Brass Rubbing, there's another Centre at **St. Margaret's Church,** open daily, except Sundays, for rubbing enthusiasts, from 10:30 to 6:30, and with some fine examples of the art displayed in the north entrance hall. I don't think there's any charge, and also don't know if materials are provided. St. Margaret's Church itself is 'sandwiched' between The Abbey and The Houses of Parliament, I *was* amazed and delighted here to re-discover that any and every corner of London is alive with evocative material of historical significance. Beginnings are somewhat shrouded in the fog of time; it is known that the site was inhabited as long ago as the Roman Era, because a Roman sarcophagus was found in the Church Yard (it's currently on view at the entrance to The Abbey's Chapter House). St. Margaret's is (since 1614) the parish church of the House of Commons. It was here that Thanksgiving services were held at the endings of World Wars I and II; here that Sir Winston and Lady Churchill were married in 1908. Also, Sir Walter Raleigh was executed (1618) right outside the church, and his remains are buried underneath the high altar—with the exception of his head, which his widow took charge of (the West Window inside the church is a memorial to Raleigh). Famous parishioners at St. Margaret's have included Oliver Cromwell, Chaucer, Samuel Pepys, John Milton (who delivered sermons here; he also has a window memorial with an inscription by John Greenleaf Whittier), and William Caxton, who was recently honored in London for having introduced printing in England (he's commemorated by a brass memorial). Another real curiosity is the East Window, originally made in Flanders on the occasion of the marriage of Catherine of Aragon in 1501 (at age 15) to Arthur, the Prince of Wales. Five months after the wedding Arthur died and the lovely but unlucky Catherine married his brother, Henry VIII; the rest, as they say, is history" (Laib Belle, Evanston, Illinois). . . . "Hope, don't short-change **Westminster Abbey!** Your readers should know about **The Cloisters** behind The Abbey, with its charming inner courtyard garden. And **The Chapter House,** one of the oldest remaining sections of The Abbey and the first meeting hall for The House of Commons (open daily, except Sundays, from 10:30 to 6:30, winters closing at 4, admission is around 15p). And what about **The Westminster Abbey Treasures** containing a fascinating collection of funeral effigies, Henry V's sword and saddle, and the ring Elizabeth I gave to Essex? The Treasures are open daily from April through September from 9:15 a.m. to 5 p.m., closed on Sundays throughout the rest of the year. Admission is 15 pence for adults, 5 pence for children under 16" (Corky Rissman, Chicago, Illinois). . . . "Those in the mood for the grisly and the ghoulish might try London's newest 'experience': **The London Dungeon,** at 34 Tooley Street, in an old vaulted warehouse beneath London Bridge Station (take the Northern Line on the underground to London Bridge stop). Note that a cob-web covered board suspended from the shadows lists the fates of those who have gone before you—69 fainted, 12 are semi-mad, four totally insane—and the management "accepts no responsibilities for subsequent nightmares." Featured are realistic tableaux of Great Britain's criminal and horrific past from the Dark Ages to the end of the 17th century, including Morgan le Fay, Merlin, a murdered Thomas à Becket and Charles I at his beheading. As you pass through the shadowy, candlelit halls, you hear from the darkness the sound of witches' chants and bats, a lone menacing drum beat, a sword being sharpened. Definitely not for the nervous or for very young children. For other daring souls, The London Dungeon is open daily from 10 to 6, with an admission of £1.40 for adults, 75p for children" (Kathy Pasmantier, London, England). . . . "If you find yourself in the area of Lincoln's Inn Fields, near the Old Curiosity Shop, be sure to drop in at #13, **Sir John Soane's Museum,** open Tuesday through Saturday from 10 to 5, with free admission. Soane was an architect (he did the Bank of England) and collector extraordinaire; and he designed and lived in this house for 25 years, till his death in 1837. Soane was an innovative and imaginative classicist, and architects visit the museum in droves—but even if you're not an architect, the house is so bizarre and amusing (with its Monk's Parlour, Crypt, decorated hallways, mirrored domes, etc.), it's worth a visit. And the collections are fascinating, including an Egyptian Sarcophagus; Greek and Roman architectural fragments and vases; busts and statuary (and plaster casts); ceramics, architectural models; William Hogarth's series of paintings, 'The Election' and 'The Rake's Progress'; landscapes by Turner; drawings by Piranesi; and all manner of the collector's mania—too numerous to mention, but lots of fun to look at" (Mrs. Lou Levy, Augusta, Georgia). . . . "The **Imperial War Museum,** across the river in Lambeth Road (tube is Lambeth North or Elephant and Castle), contains a wealth of memorabilia on the two World Wars; the new display on the origins of World War I is superb. Hours are: 10 to 6, Mondays through Saturdays, 2 to 6 on Sundays, and admission is free. The new **National Army Museum**, on Royal Hospital Road in Chelsea, is an excellent presentation of the evolution of British military tactics, leadership, uniforms and equipment, keyed to specific wars, campaigns and opponents" (Harry Roach, Willow Grove, Pennsylvania; note by AF: the Imperial War Museum's latest 1979 acquisitions are the campaign caravans of Field Marshal Montgomery). . . . "A visit to the **RAF Museum** at Hendon (underground to Colindale and a short walk—turn left out of station and follow signs) provides a fascinating account of aviation history and the Battle of Britain" (John and Mary Banbury, Breckenridge, Colorado).

EXCURSIONS OUTSIDE LONDON:

EXCURSIONS OUTSIDE LONDON: At least once during your stay, you'll want to venture outside the city boundaries to one of the following, major sights of England—most of them no more than an hour-or-so away:

(1) **Hampton Court Palace:** This, to me, is the most interesting of all England's "stately homes." Built by Cardinal Wolsey over 400 years ago, and then "presented" by him to King Henry VIII, it is the most mammoth Tudor structure ever built, and contains such eye-openers as an indoor kitchen where an entire ox could be roasted whole. The State Apartments here are open from 9:30 a.m. to 5 p.m., the grounds until 9 p.m., and a single admission of £1 ($2.20) in summer, 50p ($1.10) in winter, admits you to virtually everything. Either take the train from Waterloo Station in London to Hampton Court, or else a #718 Green Line Coach (bus) from Victoria Station to Hampton Court; the trip takes 40 minutes and passes through Chelsea, Putney, and Kingston-upon-Thames.

(2) **Windsor Castle:** The largest inhabited palace in the world, which is open to visitors even when the Queen is in residence there; it stands in an 1,800 acre park. Open 10:30 a.m. to 5 p.m. (from 1:30 p.m. to 5 p.m. on Sundays) for a 60p admission charge; you reach it either by train from Waterloo or Paddington Station, by Green Line Coach buses 704 or 705 from Hyde Park Corner, or by Green Line bus 718 from alongside Victoria Station. The school of Eton, incidentally, is a short walk from the Castle, and is usually combined with a visit to it.

(3) **Brighton:** This invigorating seaside resort, on the English channel, is only an hour by train (and £3.46 for a single day round-trip excursion) from London's Victoria Station. Or, you can take a bus from Victoria Coach Station (2 hours, because of many stops).

(4) **Greenwich:** The famous Thames River port of London, where "Greenwich Mean Time" is fixed, it houses the impressive Royal Naval College (which you can visit free), the National Maritime Museum (again free), and the clipper ship "Cutty Sark" (30 pence). Take a train there from Charing Cross Station, on The Strand; round trip fare is only 65p ($1.43). Or better yet, take a Thames river boat (phone 730-4812 for information) in summer from Charing Cross Pier to Greenwich; they leave every 20 minutes from 10:20 a.m. to dusk, take 50 minutes each way, and charge £1.40 round-trip.

(5) **Kew Gardens:** Site of the Royal Botanic Gardens (admission one pence), it can be reached simply by taking the subway (District Line, Richmond train) to Kew Gardens.

(6) **Cambridge:** It's only 56 miles from London, and can best be reached by train (from Liverpool Street or King's Cross Stations) in about 1½ hours. Round-trip day excursion: £4.

(7) **Oxford:** Nearly 64 miles from London, and again easily accessible (about 1½ hours) by train from Paddington Station. One-way fare is £3.72, round-trip day excursion only £3.78, total.

(8) And, of course, **Stratford-on-Avon,** 121 miles and two hours by train from London's Paddington Station, for a round-trip day excursion fare of £6.70.

READERS' EXCURSION RECOMMENDATIONS: "We did not have time for more than a one-day excursion out of the London area. We decided to go to **Salisbury.** British Railways runs day excursions to just about anywhere in England, out of any London railway station. You can take any train, at any time, with a few rare exceptions. As long as you leave London and arrive back on the *same day,* you can ask for an excursion fare ticket and save plenty. Example: it costs only £5.25 round-trip to Salisbury on the day excursion, compared to an ordinary one-way price of £4. If you don't ask for the excursion, of course, you are stuck" (Barbara and Bob Budnitz, Cambridge, Mass.; note by AF: the British Railways hand out a red-colored pamphlet that describes scores of "day excursions" (the British call them "cheap-day returns") offered by them; it's often pleasant, early on a summer morning, simply to go to Waterloo or Charing Cross stations and choose your destination and excursion on the spot; especially recommended is the one-hour journey to Brighton, which costs only £3.46, round-trip, second class, on a "day excursion"). . . . "Visitors to London can get to **Stonehenge** easily, quickly and cheaply by catching the 1 p.m. train to Salisbury from Waterloo Station. A Hants & Dorset bus will meet you at the Salisbury station at 2:38, take you to the ruins, and get you back to the station in time for the 4:40 train which gets to London at 6:14. Railroad, bus fares, and Stonehenge admission came to £6.25 (£2.85 for children). The same British Rail Excursion Ticket includes a trip to Old Sarum (the Norman castle and cathedral ruins) and Salisbury Cathedral if you can get to Waterloo Station at 9:05 a.m." (Josephine Blair, No. Babylon, New York). . . . "We highly recommend the hour-long boat ride down the Thames River to **Greenwich** (£1 one way, £1.50 round-trip), during which the boat captain calls out points of interest, and which allows you to walk around Greenwich to see the Clipper Ship 'Cutty Sark' and the naval museum" (Walter J. Dwyer, Woodside, New York; note by AF: in summer, there are departures every 30 minutes from Westminster pier to Kew (site of the Royal Botanic Gardens and Kew Palace, round-trip fare of £1.80), to Greenwich and the "Cutty Sark" (round trip one pound), and—at less frequent intervals—to Hampton Court Palace (home, first, of Cardinal Wolsey, and then of Henry VIII, round-trip for £3.10); phone **Thames Launches,** operator of the cruises, at 930-8294). . . . "A cheap-day return ticket (that's a round trip ticket in English lingo) to **Brighton** costs exactly £3.46 ($7.61), with trains leaving from Victoria Station at 9, 10, 11 a.m. and 12 and 1 p.m., arriving there in 55 minutes. Return trains to London leaving in the afternoon and evening are as follows: 3:45, 4:45, 5:45, 6:45, 7:45 and 8:45 p.m. Brighton is so close to London that I personally would recommend it only as a one-day excursion and not for an overnight stay. An interesting note about Brighton is that many plays, before arriving on the London theater scene, try out there. Perhaps some of your readers will be lucky enough to catch one. . . . The cheap day return ticket to **Oxford** costs exactly £3.78, and the trip takes one hour and five minutes. Trains leave from Paddington Station 15 minutes after the hour starting at 8 a.m. Trains from Oxford leave at 2:25 p.m., 3:35, 4:15, 6:35 & 8:41 p.m. Oxford is such a small college town that all the major sights and colleges can be seen and enjoyed on your own with a map that you can get at the railroad station. The Enquiry Office will give you a free map which outlines a two hour walking tour and, believe me, this is really going at it leisurely. . . . A cheap day return ticket to **Cambridge** costs only £4. Trains depart from Kings Cross station at 9:05 a.m. and 11:35 and return from Cambridge at 3:40 and 5:40 p.m. Departures from Liverpool Station are 8:36 a.m., 9:36, 10:36 and 12:36 p.m. and return to the same station at 2:40 p.m., 3:55, 4:40 & 6:40 p.m. from Cambridge. A walking tour of the college at Cambridge can be made in about two hours. Heading back to the railroad station after seeing all the colleges in Cambridge, you'll find on either Hill or Stationroads, the fabulously cheap restaurant in the **Great Northern Pub,** where three-course luncheons cost around £1.30 ($2.86). It was a perfect way to wind up the trip. . . . There are very frequent trains leaving for **Greenwich** each day and the cheap day return tickets cost only 65 pence ($1.43) and leave from Charing Cross station. An afternoon trip here is better than one in morning because, of the three major sights, the Royal Naval College does not open its doors until 2:30 p.m." (Edward H. Pietraszek, Chicago, Illinois). . . . "An easy way to go to **Stonehenge** is to take the train from Waterloo Station to Salisbury, a bus from Salisbury to Amesbury, and then a little bus going to Shrewton, which drops you about a mile from Stonehenge, to which you have a beautiful walk on a 'Public

Footpath.' It costs about a third as much as taking a tour from London" (Dorothy Gamble, Glendale, California).

EVENING ENTERTAINMENT—THE THEATRE: London offers playgoing in its most exciting, comfortable and inexpensive form. At least 40 plays or musicals are always running and all but the top two or three hits have available seats up to five minutes of curtain time, which is 8 or 8:30 p.m. in most London theaters, 7:30 p.m. in a few. The highest-priced orchestra seats (here they're called "stalls") in the best theaters, rarely cost more than £5 ($11), but you needn't pay more than $3 or $4 in the "upper circle" (first balcony); and you can do it for less. "Slip seats" (side circle) for performances at the new National Theatre on the South Bank can be had for as little as £1. My idea of a London vacation is to see a play-a-night. They're the city's top attraction, and they can be managed on the tightest budget.

In fact, if you are extreme theatre buffs, as Hope and I are, you can hustle to as many as three plays in one day in London. That's because on certain matinee days, some London theatres schedule their afternoon performances for 2 p.m., others for 5 p.m. On one memorable Saturday in London, we saw Alec Guinness in "Ross" at 2 p.m., Ralph Richardson in "The Complacent Lover" at 5 p.m., and Sir John Gielgud in "The Ages of Man" at 8 p.m. We did it by eating sandwiches at numerous intermissions throughout the day and evening (sandwiches & tea are sold in most London theatres), and by then taxi-ing to the next theatre in the five-or-so minutes between performances. I certainly don't recommend this tiring fanaticism, but merely set it forth, as an example of the attraction that London theatre can have. . . . Try to avoid buying your tickets at brokers. Since nearly all theatres have available seats, there's no need to incur the added commissions.

London theatres with especially cheap seats: the **Globe Theatre,** with upper circle seats for £3 ($6.60); the **Apollo Theatre,** charging the same; the 101-year-old **Criterion Theatre,** again the same; the **Theatre Royal Haymarket,** with gallery seats for £2.50 ($5.50); the renowned **Aldwych Theatre** (home of the Royal Shakespeare Co.), with "top circle" seats for £2, less at matinees; the **Comedy Theatre,** balcony for £2.50 ($5.50); the **Shaftesbury,** balcony for £2.50; the **Wyndham Theatre,** £3 ($6.60) for balcony seats; more than a dozen other theatres (the Queens,-the Phoenix, among them) which offer good first balcony or upper circle seats for £2.50 ($5.50).

Note from HA: Student Rush Tickets—If you can produce a bona fide Student I.D. card half an hour before performance time, you'll be able to get a Special Stand-By Rate (discounts of 50% or more) at selected London theatres. Theatres offering discounted tickets to students identify themselves with a circled 'S' in their ads and at the theatres themselves.

A READER'S COMMENT: "Any bright tourist should take advantage of the British theatres—every night! You can appear 10 or 15 minutes before curtain time at any theater of your choice and you can always find a 'single' priced at just about $5 and often less" (Anne Fomin, Dearborn Heights, Michigan).

DISCOTHEQUES AND DANCING: London's inexpensive night life is centered in a number of rock clubs which sprout and die much too rapidly for this once-a-year book to keep up with them. They're listed, though, in a weekly magazine called *The Melody Maker,* to be picked up at any London newsstand. . . . For disco dancing, you ought definitely to make at least one visit to the phenomenal **Empire Ballroom** on Leicester Square (get off at the Leicester Square tube stop), a gigantic dance hall and legitimate pick-up spot for London's unmarried young people. This is one of the top tourist attractions of London: hundreds and hundreds of single men and women (on a Saturday night), flashing colored lights, a famous revolving globe of light-reflecting mirrors, continuous bands on a revolving stage. The action extends from 8 p.m. to 2 a.m., Monday through Wednesday; (when admission is £1.90 before 9 p.m., £2.50 thereafter), from 8 p.m. to 3 a.m. on Thursdays (prices same as above), and again from 8 p.m. to 3 a.m. on Fridays and Saturdays (admission of £2.50 before 10 p.m., £2.80 thereafter), as well as on Sundays (when admission is £2 before 10 p.m., £2.50 thereafter). You're under no obligation to pay a single thing more, after you've purchased your entrance. A somewhat older crowd patronizes the once-renowned **Lyceum** on Wellington Street, off The Strand, which has been somewhat pushed into the shadows by the new Empire Ballroom. At the Lyceum, Edwardian "music hall variety" is currently featured on Tuesday and Sunday (£1.50), "international discotheque" on Monday and Saturday (with admission of £1 Mondays, £1.75 on Saturdays). Smaller, more intimate in atmosphere, the disco **Le Kilt** at 60 Greek Street in Soho (nearest underground station is Tottenham Court Road), is visited primarily by student-age Londoners, charges £3 per admission to non-members, and is open seven days a week from 8:30 p.m. to 3 a.m.

READERS' ENTERTAINMENT TIPS: "For real, down-to-earth nakedness, there are a dozen or more strip shows in the Soho area, where admission is generally £1; the best of these (for those interested in this particular art form) are on and about Dean Street" (Henry S. Sloan, New York, New York; note by AF: though admission to some strips is only £1, an additional "membership" fee of 50 pence is often assessed once you're inside; the shows themselves—which normally consist of motionless posing by the girls—are not up to Jersey City or Baltimore standards). . . . "The best concert buy I know anywhere is for the **'Proms' at The Royal Albert Hall**. This is a series of daily concerts in July, August and September, featuring superb soloists and orchestras in a gigantic oval auditorium that alone is worth the price of admission (£1). Find out the time of the concert in 'What's On In London,' then take the Underground to South Kensington, arriving 90 minutes in advance, ask the way to the Royal Albert Hall (about 3 blocks), and join the queue for the 'Arena.' On the way, stop at a bakery and pick up some food, because everyone takes his supper and eats it while waiting in line. Once in the auditorium, you will discover that the 'Arena' is the bottom of the hall, a flat area with no seats and a Fountain in the middle. This is where the orchestra seats would be if they had any—which means that if you are willing to stand, you can get within six feet of the conductor, or if you wish to sit you'll still be only some twenty-five feet away. The arena audience is young, intense, and often informally dressed. 'Doing the Prom' is a wonderful experience; count it high among the attractions of London" (John H. M. Austin, New Haven, Connecticut). . . . "Ballet Tip: If you're eager to see a ballet or opera at Covent Garden and are told 'All sold out,' don't despair. Just drop by the theater about 45 minutes before curtain time and join the discreet line forming to the left of the main entrance. Presided over by the charming and capable Sergeant-at-Arms, Sgt. Martin, this line snaps right along as cancellations to the performance are phoned in. Everything from boxes to standing room are offered, strictly fairly, to the first man in line and then so on down the line if he decides to wait and see what else comes up. We never failed to get in, even when Nureyev and Fonteyn were dancing" (Dr. and Mrs. Kenneth Korven, Susanville, California; note by AF: the Royal Opera House at Covent Garden is usually closed in August).

OFF-BEAT LONDON: Every night throughout the year, London sees a succession of protest meetings, forums and fests by society's dissenters. If you'll buy a copy of the weekly *New Statesman* (25 pence), and turn to the back page, you'll find advertisements of free lectures, films and discussions, ranging in subject from politics to vegetarianism, and sponsored by organizations running the gamut from the Bertrand Russell Foundation and the Fabian Society, on the left, to the "Empire Loyalists" on the right; non-political meetings deal with spiritualism, theosophy, what-have-you. These events provide a marvelous opportunity for meeting interesting Englishmen and women, and the setting is somehow conducive to easy introductions and quick friendships. . . . Roulette, anyone? London, amazingly enough, has become one of the world's major gambling capitals, as you may have deduced from the casino scenes in James Bond movies. While all the casinos are run as clubs for members only, all offer temporary membership to visitors from overseas who register at the clubs at least 48 hours before they plan to play, and the cheapest of the clubs—**Charlie Chester's Casino,** 12 Archer Street (near Piccadilly Circus)—charges a fee of only £1 to sporting bloods from abroad for the temporary right to try its roulette, black jack, and Las Vegas dice. Open daily including Sundays until 4 a.m. . . . Most sophisticated movie theatres in London, attracting a dedicated audience of movie buffs: the **Academy Cinemas,** 165 Oxford Street (phone 437-2981 or 437-5129); these are three adjoining auditoriums, of which one is reserved for club members only; the other two play unusual films, such as Kon Ichikawa's "Tokyo Olympiad."

A READER'S SUGGESTION: "An interesting way to put in an evening and meet the Londoners is to visit the **Centurions' Arms Club** at 7:30 p.m. on Wednesday (except in August) at St. Martin-in-the-Fields Church, near Trafalgar Square. Tea is served and a program follows. In April, when I was there, they presented a travel film; in October, they had a program from the musical conservatory—excerpts from the 'Marriage of Figaro' sung in English. Visitors are welcome" (J. Y. Guinter, Chicago, Illinois; note by AF: a Saturday afternoon event at St. Martin-in-the-Fields, called the **International Club,** caters more specifically to overseas visitors, meets from 4 to 6 p.m. (except in August), and charges entrance of 20 pence, which includes refreshments; the Saturday activity is far more suitable for readers than the Wednesday evening gathering of 'Centurions').

TRANSPORTATION: For those who have played the sardine in New York's subway, the London "underground" is a revelation. Quiet, clean, comfortable; the normal fare ranges from 20 pence to 50 pence (44¢ to $1.10), depending on the length of the ride, but your average trip should cost no more than around 88¢ (40 pence). Hold on to your ticket, which must be presented upon exiting. Incidentally, so good is the London subway system that it really doesn't matter where you stay in London; you're never more than 15 comfortable minutes away from any major location.

Free subway map: available at the **London Transport Enquiry Office** in the underground stations of Piccadilly Circus, St. James's Park, Oxford Circus, King's Cross or Eccleston Bridge (Victoria).

READERS' TRANSPORTATION TIPS: "If you plan to be in London for six days or more, you ought to purchase a **Go As You Please** ticket for £13.70 ($30.14), only £5.40 for children. It is good for a week, allows you to ride on the underground (subway to us!), as well as on all the red buses, and saves all that standing in line for tube tickets when you're in a hurry. Furthermore, you can get to Hampton Court and Windsor Castle without spending an extra penny. To get to Hampton Court, take the Piccadilly line to Hammersmith, then take bus #267. To reach Windsor Castle, take the tube to Uxbridge, then a country bus to Windsor" (Sue Coffman, Fort Worth, Texas; note by AF: "Go as You Please" tickets of four days' duration for £9.90 ($21.78) adults, £3.90 ($8.50) for children, of 3 days' duration for £7.90 ($17.38), £2.90 for children, are also available and can be purchased at any London Transport "Travel Enquiry Office" located in major subway stations—such as the one in Piccadilly Circus). . . . "One soon finds that bus travel in the British Isles is simple, efficient, and often 40% less than travel by rail. For example, from the Victoria Coach Station on Buckingham Palace Road, across from the BOAC terminal, London to Edinburgh is £9.50 ($20.90), leaving day and night. To Dublin,

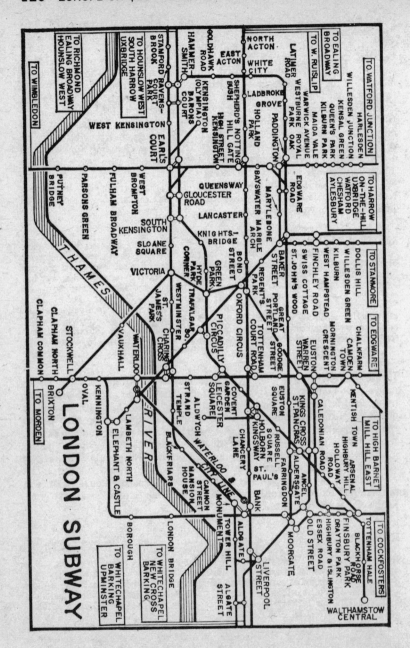

coach to Liverpool is £7.50 ($16.50), steamer from there to Dublin £19.50 ($42.90). To Dover, where you get a steamer for the continent, the ride is £3.30 ($7.26). Compare these rates with fares asked by British Railways" (Thomas A. Giltner, Dallas, Texas).

BICYCLE RENTAL: Savile's Stores, 97 Battersea Rise, Battersea (phone 228-4279), charges £5.85 the first week, 55 pence per day thereafter; and also sells used cycles under a guaranteed re-purchase plan. Closed Wednesdays and Sundays; bring your passport if you plan to rent. Alternately, but at a higher price, try **Rent-a-Bike Limited** in the Kensington Student Centre on Kensington Church Street (phone 937-6089), charging £1.80 a day, £8.50 a week, £14 for two weeks, £18 for three weeks, only £21 for a month; that's for a three-speed, small wheel foldaway. Care for a moped instead? With helmet, basket in front, security lock and insurance coverage? **M and D Rent-a-Ped Ltd.,** 29 Orde Hall Street (near Russell Square, no phone), will provide, at £5 ($11) per day, plus a refundable deposit of $50. Included are 50 miles of free petrol. And if you hire for a week, two days are free.

TIPS: Buy a copy of *"What's On In London"* (25 pence), or *"Time Out"* (30 pence), available at all newsstands, the moment you arrive. This weekly pamphlet provides details on every current entertainment attraction in London. . . . If you feel like a movie in London, then consider one of the several **"Classic Repertory Theatres"** (addresses are listed in "What's On In London"). The "Classics" play nothing but the best of the old films—the Greta Garbo epics, masterworks like "The Informer"—and charge only one pound ($2.20) for admission, less if you go in before 3 p.m. . . . Need a druggist after 6 p.m.? **"Boots,"** on Piccadilly Circus, is the most conveniently located late-night chemist in London. . . . Nicest walk in London: down the Mall, from Trafalgar Square to Buckingham Palace. . . . A swimming pool in chilly London? The best one is the indoor **Oasis,** corner of High Holborn and Endell Streets, directly across from the Shaftesbury Theatre. Open daily, with both swimming (43 pence on weekdays, plus 11 pence for the rent of the towel) and hot baths (20 pence for the baths, including use of a towel, 5 pence for soap). And there's an inexpensive cafeteria in the same building. To get here, take the underground to the Holborn or Tottenham Court Road stations. . . . Best advance reading for London: Dickens, any novel he ever wrote. . . . Always order tea in London. It's incomparable. . . . Used, pre-1968 London taxicabs are available from **London Cab Co.,** 1 Brixton Road (phone 735-7777), from 900 pounds up. . . . Computer dating: **Dateline,** 23 Abingdon Road, London W.8, phone 937-6503.. . . London with children: phone 246-8007 for a recorded message on special London events and attractions for children. And for a memorable children's visit, try **Pollock's Toy Museum** at the corner of Scala and Whitfield Streets, next to Tottenham Court Road. Open daily except Sundays from 10 a.m. to 5 p.m.; 10 pence for children, 25 pence for you. "If you love art, folly, or the bright eyes of children, speed to Pollock's," wrote Robert Louis Stevenson. . . . In addition to the lectures we've described at the British Museum, talks are offered at 1 p.m. on Wednesdays and Thursdays at the **National Gallery,** Trafalgar Square; Tuesdays, Wednesdays, Thursdays and Saturdays, at 3 p.m., at the **Natural History Museum;** Tuesdays and Wednesdays at 1:15 p.m., and Saturdays at 3 p.m. at the **Victoria and Albert Museum.**

READERS' TIPS: "The best bargain I came across in London were the free haircutting clinics at the **Vidal Sassoon** salons. There are several shops around the city, and all hold free cutting sessions on Mondays, Tuesdays and Wednesdays, starting at 6 p.m. Students at the salons give you a wash and a very good cut for absolutely nothing, and you can have whatever style you want. Men, women, and even children can go. Call the shop nearest you for an appointment" (Abby Biggs, Fort Washington, Pennsylvania) . . . "The privately owned Turkish baths of London can be quite expensive, as at the Savoy, but this need not be so. The city of London operates many municipal baths and charges as little as £4.25 (which includes what they call a soap shampoo in which an attendant will soap you from neck to foot) for use of the steam and dry rooms and 'plunge pool.' In the Bayswater area of London there is the **Porchester Hall Turkish Baths,** Porchester Road (U-Royal Oak), phone 229-3226, open from 9 a.m. until 7 p.m. for men, Monday, Wednesday and Saturday, and alternate days (except Sunday, the closed day) for women" (Edward H. Pietraszek, Chicago, Illinois).

STUDENT TRAVEL: The Travel Department of the **National Union of Students,** at 117 Euston Road (phone 388-7051, open Monday to Friday from 9:30 a.m. to 5:30 p.m., Saturdays from 10 a.m. to 12:30 p.m.), is a fully-accredited travel agency that sells air, rail and sea tickets to most destinations on the continent. Although they grant no student discount, they nevertheless specialize in the low-cost excursion fares and arrangements that students like (including cut-rate student charter flights), and you'd be well advised—provided you have irrefutable student identification credentials, a requirement for their services—to stop in for a visit at some point in your stay. The same department will provide details on reduced-price student admissions to the theaters and museums of London. A competing specialist in student charter flights, chartered student trains, and the like, is **British Student Travel Centre,** 329 Putney Bridge Road (across the Thames from Hammersmith; tube: Putney Bridge), phone 788-3587, which publishes an unusually comprehensive brochure of charter departures and prices.

Transalpino Youth Travel Office

For young people planning rail travel throughout Britain, or from London to the continent, or within the continent, the name "Transalpino"—Europe's largest youth rail operator—is an important word to be treasured. In London, its offices are at 71-75 Buckingham Palace Road (phone 834-9656), across the street from the main entrance to Victoria Station, and they're visited each day in summer by literally thousands of customers, who receive attention from nearly 20 bilingual clerks. Provided only that you're under the age of 27, and regardless of whether you're a student, you'll receive discounts of from 40% to 60% on European rail tickets purchased from Transalpino, whose hours are weekdays from 9 to 7, Saturdays from 9:30 to 5 (with shorter opening times in winter). Although we've scattered the Transalpino addresses throughout other chapters of this book, it's helpful to look them up in whatever major European city you're visiting. John McCarthy is the American sales manager of the London office.

FLEA MARKET!: On weekends in London, the city's big open-air markets roar into operation, and if you're an indefatigable shopper, with a fair amount of endurance, you'll return with unusual values.

The Saturday market is held on **Portobello Road,** in the Notting Hill section (take the underground to Notting Hill Gate), but is limited mainly to antiques, silver, metal bric-a-brac of every kind. The larger and more varied market takes place Sunday morning (but continuing till about 1 p.m.) on **Petticoat Lane,** which is known as Middlesex Street the rest of the week. This time, take the underground to either Liverpool Street, Aldgate or Aldgate East, and be prepared to encounter huge, jostling crowds, plus everything you can name in the way of cheap or second-hand articles for sale.

THE LAUNDERETTES OF LONDON: They're fast becoming available in great profusion. In the **Russell Square** area, try "Red and White Laundries," 78 Marchmont Street (see our map), open daily including Sundays from 8 a.m. to 10 p.m.: 50 pence for the machine, 10 pence for the dryer, 15p for soap. In the **Earls Court Road** area, near the West London Air Terminal, there's a similar-ly-priced serve-yourself laundry at 5 Kenway Road, another at 4 Hogarth Place (directly opposite the entrance to the Earls Court Road tube station). Near **Paddington Station,** you'll find the **Wash Inn Self Service Laundry** at #14 Craven Road, half a block from the station and open 7 days a week.

READERS' DEPARTURE SUGGESTIONS: "**Dan-Air Services** runs flights from London to Paris for approximately £24 ($52.80), one way. Buses leave from Victoria Coach Station, right in the heart of London, and drive to Lydd Airport. Turbo-props fly across the Channel to Beauvais, France, where buses take passengers into central Paris. The advantages are numerous; inexpensive fares, courteous service, short ride (five hours city-to-city), no shuttles needed out to airport, and convenient running times" (Susan Nagler, Phila-delphia, Pennsylvania). . . . "**Dan-Air Services,** 33 Elizabeth Street (680-1011), provides a round-trip from London to Paris for as little as £37 ($81.40). This is surely the cheapest thing around! You go by bus from Victoria Coach Station to Lydd Airport (2 hours ride through lovely Kentish countryside). Then a 45-minute flight over the channel in a jet prop lands you in Beauvais, and another 90 minutes by bus takes you to Paris. Total time: 4 hours, 15 minutes. There are two advantages: 1) Price is almost as cheap as the railroad, and the flight is quick over the channel. The bus rides through the countryside were beautiful on both ends. 2) Courtesy. These people are the most courteous people we found in Europe! We were flying from Copenhagen to Paris, and then had a quick connection to get onto the Dan-Air Services bus. We missed that connection because our plane from Copenhagen was late arriving in Orly, and we telephoned Dan-Air Services in their Paris office (phone 203-4600). They arranged for us to go directly from Orly airport to the Beauvais airport by train (we had missed the regular Dan-Air Services bus), and we arrived in time to catch the Dan-Air Services airplane. Their courtesy in handling our dilemma was great! Our problem was that we had to get to London that day, because we had a charter flight from London to Boston to catch. If we had missed Dan-Air Services, we would have had to pay $101 (£45.90) to fly by regular airlines to London. They handled our arrival smoothly, and when we were 5 minutes late for the airplane takeoff in Beauvais, they held the plane for us. We had telephoned and asked them to do so, but we were really impressed. We recommend Dan-Air Services to all, for price and service" (Barbara and Bob Budnitz, Cambridge, Mass.; note by AF: Dan-Air Ser-vices' office, as noted above, is Victoria Coach Station, whose precise address is 33 Elizabeth St., London S.W.1. For reservations, phone 680-1011. . . . The cheapest round-trip price quoted (£37) is available if you book for a three-night stay in Paris. Dan-Air Services also operates cheap flights (Rolls Royce prop jets) three times a week in summer to Clermont-Ferrand, Perpignan and Montpellier in France, to Bergen, Berne and Newcastle). . . . "We took a 'stand-by' flight from London to Edinburgh, which allowed us 1/3 reduction on the normal fare. This was in August, right before the Edinburgh Music Festival—we wouldn't recommend it during the Festival" (Ed and Nan Storke, Wheaton, Illinois).

A FINAL AID: The staff of my own **Arthur Frommer International, Inc.,** upstairs in the Dolcis House Building at 87 New Bond Street (corner of Oxford Street) in the heart of London (nearest tube stops are Oxford Circus or Bond Street, phone 493-6271), are willing to assist readers in purchasing tours and tickets (including some theatre tickets sold at reduced price), arranging two-night and three-night trips to Paris, Amsterdam or Scotland, performing any number of other travel functions. Manager Hans Kortekaas is supported by a fair-sized staff here. Open weekdays from 9:30 to 5:30, Saturdays from 9:30 to one.

LEAVING LONDON: Simply descend into any subway station of the Piccadilly Line and take the first train (they run every 10 minutes) to the end of the line—Heathrow Airport, 40 minutes and £1.20 away. The airport buses get there just as quick, but charge £1.70 and leave only from the British Airways' Victoria Terminal. To Gatwick Airport, from which most charter flights leave, you can take a direct train from Victoria Station for £1.85, second class.

LONDON ON A BUDGET: You've seen it can be done. Bed and breakfast for $9, luncheon for $2.50, dinner for $3.50, with subway rides at 44¢, and a $5 theatre seat in the evening.

And now the stop is Paris, land of Giscard d'Estaing, Truffaut and the "prix fixe" meal, where prices are high, but "finds" are everywhere—important, low-cost finds that can enable you to keep room-and-meals costs to $15 a day.

The trip from London to Paris is most pleasantly made by plane, which costs little more than the same trip by train and channel steamer. The planes leave London Airport every hour, arrive an hour later at Paris' futuristic Charles de Gaulle Airport, from which a bus to the city costs $3.95. Just a short while after leaving London, you're in the place of which you've always dreamed —the City of Light—Paris.

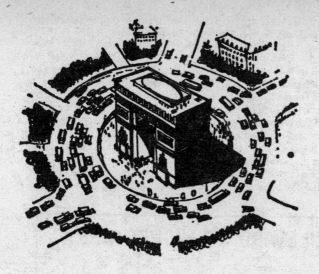

Chapter V

PARIS

Life in the Latin Quarter

THE PRICES OF PARIS are perhaps the most talked-about topic of European travel. Let's put the matter in a little perspective. Been to New York lately? At their very worst, Parisian prices are no higher than those of New York, even for the most luxurious of purchases. A meal at New York's "21," La Grenouille, or Quo Vadis costs just as much as the world-renowned repasts to be had at Paris' Maxim's, Fouquet's, or Tour d'Argent.

Let's move a step further. In the middle-class area, Parisian prices are much lower than their New York counterparts. The highest-priced seat at Paris' thrilling Comédie Française costs 55 francs (approximately $12.79). Compare that with the $20 you'd pay for a Broadway show.

And now for the comparison most pertinent to this book: the prices paid by the average Parisian for his basic, low-cost needs, are so much lower than those in New York that they would set eyes to blinking. The level of those prices permits even a low-salaried Frenchman to live in a most enjoyable French manner. He eats and imbibes regally, because he avoids the glitter of the Champs Elysées, just as you'd avoid Park Avenue. Scattered throughout Paris are incredible values for the tourist on a budget.

Don't, therefore, be fazed by the legend—illogical as well as untrue—that the cost of visiting Paris is simply beyond human means, and that Paris has lost all its charm, as a result. This is still the haven for the adventurous, the resourceful, and the young in heart—the capital of Europe—a city of breathtaking beauty, pervaded throughout with an exciting intellectual atmosphere. It can't be missed, and it needn't be. Can you live enjoyably in Paris on $15 a day? With care, with a proper approach, and with a sort of pinpoint accuracy in choosing your hotel and restaurants, you can. Here's how.

HOTELS: Paris is cut in half by the River Seine, and that's the most important fact from which you begin. On the Left Bank of the Seine ("La Rive Gauche") are generally located the inexpensive areas of the city—the students' and artists' quarters, the markets, the small hotels and cafes. On the Right Bank ("La Rive Droite"), you'll find the broad avenues, the establishments of Messrs. Givenchy and Dior, and the screaming prices. This isn't always so: Montmartre and Pigalle are on the Right Bank, the swank Quai D'Orsay area is on the Left. But in general, go to the Left Bank for inexpensive meals and accommodations. Go there also for a real taste of Paris; it's the Champs Elysées which has become commercial and hard; the Latin Quarter, on the Left Bank, retains its honesty.

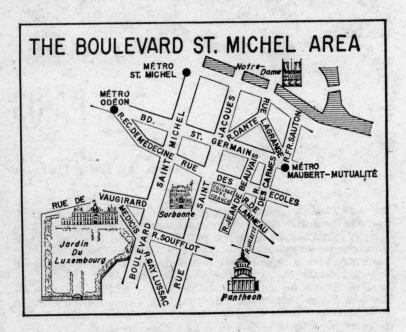

THE BOULEVARD ST. MICHEL AREA

The Sorbonne Area

If, in particular, you're a young and/or adventurous tourist, and want to live in a section jammed with the student population of Paris, then take the "metro" (Paris' subway system) to the **St. Michel Station (1).** Go up the steps and you're on the Boulevard St. Michel—heart of Paris' university area. The Sorbonne and the Ecole des Beaux Arts are all within walking distance. The Boulevard St. Michel, itself, is a broad avenue lined with bookstores and sidewalk cafes. Walk up the Boulevard as it goes uphill. Three blocks along, you'll find the Rue des Ecoles. Turn left. This, to me, is one of the great hotel streets of Paris. It has some of the cleanest and most comfortable budget accommodations in the city—priced, true, at splurge-type levels in the section closest to the Boulevard, but descending in price as you stroll along and particularly as you head down the sidestreets to the parallel Rue du Sommerard or Rue Monge.

The very best hotel on the street (although it's also by far the most expensive) is a big splurge selection called the **Hotel Claude Bernard (2)**, at 43 Rue des Ecoles (phone 326-32-52), which offers neatly arranged singles without bath for an overly high 90 francs ($20.93) a night, and several beautiful double rooms for 140 francs ($32.55), and those prices include *breakfast,* taxes, and all service charges. Often, the Claude Bernard charges less for rooms on its top floor ("au sixième étage"), yet here, you'll have tall French windows, which open onto a small balcony, and provide a view of the entire Latin Quarter. Primarily, the hotel is typically French and family run; sneak a look behind the counter, and you'll see a living room where the owners dine at night.

Directly across the street from the Claude Bernard, the larger and less costly **Hotel California (3)**, at 32 Rue des Ecoles (phone 634-12-90), charges 85 francs ($19.76) for a bathless double with breakfast, taxes and service charge included, 75 francs ($17.44) for a single, but the hotel doesn't compare with the quality available across the street. Next door to the Claude Bernard, the **Hotel St. Jacques (4)**, 35 Rue des Ecoles (tel: 326-82-53), is, to me, a far more attractive hotel, even though its official rating is a bit lower than the California's. The St. Jacques offers double and twin rooms without bath, but with breakfast, for 85 francs ($19.76), taxes and service included; singles for 50 and 55 francs ($11.62 to $12.79). Similar rates are charged by the **Hotel des Carmes,** a block away at 5 Rue des Carmes (tel: 329-78-40), which formerly was under the same management as the St. Jacques, but is not as good a buy at 103 francs single, 112 francs ($26.04) double or twin, breakfast and service included (for indifferent rooms). Four single rooms on the sixth floor, however, rent for only 52 francs!

The first major avenue you'll cross is the Rue St. Jacques, where half a block downhill at #73 you'll find the **Hotel Diana** (phone 354-92-55), a fine budget choice where you'll pay 44 francs ($10.23) for a bathless single, 63 francs ($14.65) double, breakfast, service, and taxes included. The lack of an elevator in this clean and well-kept six-floor hotel, explains the low rates.

As you continue walking down the Rue des Ecoles, you'll pass many other hotels with prices in the St. Jacques' range—and lower. The **Grand Hotel Moderne (5)**, for instance, at 33 Rue des Ecoles (phone 354-37-78), has bathless double rooms for 47 francs ($10.93) per person, breakfast, service and taxes included. Next door, at 31 Rue des Ecoles, the **Hotel Sully,** whose former proprietor resembled the late Henri Matisse, has left the budget range with his departure. But one door along, the rates again diminish at the **Hotel des Nations** (354-62-14), 29 Rue des Ecoles, where the lobby has a newly-refurbished look, and rooms are clean, and a few of them newly and brightly repapered. Eighty-two francs ($19.06) for a double, 110 francs for a double with shower, breakfast and all else included.

A few steps on, you'll pass the Rue de la Montagne, which leads uphill, in about a hundred yards, to a truly medieval section of Paris that remains, even today, a quarter for impoverished writers and artists—the poet Verlaine wrote his famous "Il pleure dans mon coeur . . ." in one of these very buildings. But keep walking along the Rue des Ecoles. In another twenty yards, you'll pass, on the left, the tiny Rue des Bernardins. It's here that the linguistic (he spoke 5 languages) Mr. René Corre was forced to transfer his Hotel du Square Monge (formerly recommended in this guide, and later confiscated by the French government). The new and elevator-equipped hotel at #42 on the street, is called the **Hotel du Square Monge (7)**, phone 634-13-00, and during a recent visit, its new owner, Mr. René Baur, showed me every room. They are perhaps too small for families, but they are utterly clean and well-maintained, they contain bidets and outlets for both American and European electric razors (a touch of thoughtfulness you'll appreciate when you travel through other towns), and they rent for 89 francs ($20.69) double, 75 francs ($17.44) single, with breakfast, service and taxes included. The hotel receives the same high recommendation that the late M. Corre had in the past. Across the Rue des Ecoles from the Hotel Square Monge et Bernardins, the newly renovated and refurbished **Hotel Plaisant,** at 50 Rue des Bernardins (phone 354-74-57), charges 80 francs ($18.60) for a bathless double room, breakfast, service and tax included. It has nice proprietors, and perfectly acceptable rooms, some with balconies that look onto a little square. . . . If you're willing to walk farther down the Rue des Ecoles, you'll come to the somewhat basic, but friendly, **Hotel Minerve,** 13 Rue des Ecoles (phone 326-81-89; 78 francs double or twin), and next door, the **Hotel Familia** (phone 354-55-27; 80 francs double, 45 francs single, a good choice), but by this point, you'll probably feel that you're too far from the exciting Boulevard St. Michel.

The cheaper Rue du Sommerard

A less expensive hotel street in the same neighborhood, yet one with even a bit more charm, is the Rue du Sommerard, which runs parallel to the Rue des Ecoles, between the Boulevard St. Germain and Rue des Ecoles. To reach it, again walk uphill on the Boulevard St. Michel until you pass the Rue du Sommerard on your left, one block before the Rue des Ecoles. Or else simply take the métro to the Maubert-Mutualité stop, which is also the closest subway station to the great majority of Rue des Ecoles hotels.

The star attraction here is the sprightly, little **Hotel Marignan,** 13 Rue du Sommerard (phone 634-20-90), whose multilingual owners provide babysitters on request, make washing and ironing facilities available to the customers, send cables for you, and maintain a good library of tourist information. The cost for all this is 74 francs ($17.20) for a double or twin-bedded room (breakfast and service included), 115 francs for a triple, 52 francs for a single—again with breakfast and service included in all those charges.

Down the block, a close runner-up (and it's a large hotel) is the **Hotel Wetter,** 9 Rue du Sommerard (phone 326-81-05), which charges far too much for singles, but only 86 francs ($20) double, 129 francs triple, all prices including breakfast and taxes. The Wetter's owners, M. and Mme. Lacroix, speak only a bit of English, but their daughter is fluent; a high recommendation for this friendly hotel, whose prices are moderate for rooms of fair quality. If the Wetter is full, walk in the other direction to the much cheaper, and equally popular (mainly among students), **Hotel "At Home",** just around the corner from the Rue du Sommerard, at 7 Rue Thenard (phone 326-78-36), which charges a standard 35 francs single, 46 francs double, service but not breakfast included; or else make do with the starvation budget lodgings of the big **Grand Hotel de la Loire** at 20 Rue du Sommerard, whose English-speaking proprietors—M. and Mme. Victor—receive high praise in a number of recent letters to me. They charge 33 francs single, 43 francs (only $10) double, 61 francs triple, not including breakfast. Phone 354-97-60.

Off and on the Boulevard St. Michel

Only a few steps from the "St. Mich'," on the tiny Rue Champollion, which runs off the Rue des Ecoles, the **Hotel Central des Ecoles (8),** 3 Rue Champollion (phone 634-14-20), has English-speaking proprietors (M. and

Mme. Handaye) who for years have been busily engaged in both modernizing and "humanizing" their hotel. A lounge, a reading room and a new elevator are among the latest additions to this simple but pleasant house, where room prices are 81 francs ($18.83) for a double, breakfast included, 61 francs ($14.18) for most singles, again with breakfast. A high recommendation.

If you'd prefer to stay closer to the Seine, at the base of the Boulevard St. Michel, and are willing to spend a bit more, then, as you leave the St. Michel metro exit, look to the left and you'll see two tiny streets: Rue de la Harpe and Rue de la Huchette. At # 1 Rue de la Harpe, the **Hotel d'Albe** (phone 634-09-70) charges a top of 95 francs ($22.09) for breakfast for two, service charge, and a bathless double room (elevator-building, telephones in all the spanking-clean rooms), and is the hotel par excellence for readers who like to be surrounded by color and excitement; while the **Hotel du Mont Blanc,** 28 Rue de la Huchette (phone 033-49-44), in the same bustling neighborhood, is another superb second class choice, half of whose rooms come with private bath or shower; the rate is 140 francs ($32.50) for a double with bath, including breakfast, service and tax, 110 francs ($25.58) for the bathless variety, 80 francs ($18.60) for a bathless single, again with breakfast and all else included.

Still another cluster of inexpensive hotels in the $15 range are found on the **Rue Cujas** (two blocks past the Rue des Ecoles, on the left off the "Boul' Mich") and around the corner on the **Rue Victor Cousin.**

Top choice here is the **Hotel de la Sorbonne,** 6 Rue Victor Cousin (354-58-08), where a nicely decorated double with phone but no bath is 58 francs ($13.48), breakfast, service, and taxes included. Also highly recommended is the attractive **Hotel Cujas,** 18 Rue Cujas (354-58-10), offering bathless singles for 28 francs ($6.44), doubles and twins for 42 francs ($9.66). All rooms at the **Hotel Saint-Michel,** 19 Rue Cujas (354-47-98) have bath or shower. Rates, *sans* breakfast, are 76 francs ($17.67) single, 94 francs ($21.86) for doubles or twins with complete private bath. If the above are full you might try the **Hotel de Flandres,** 16 Rue Cujas (354-67-30), a simple but comfortable establishment with bathless doubles for 55 francs ($12.79), bathless singles for 46 francs ($10.69), breakfast, service, and taxes included.

The Panthéon

If you'd like to live cheaper (or if the hotels on Rue des Ecoles or Rue du Sommerard are packed), then keep walking up the Boulevard St. Michel for two more blocks until you hit the Rue Soufflot, and again turn left. 100 yards ahead stands the **Panthéon,** a shrine to France's most illustrious public figures (entombed here are Voltaire, Rousseau, Zola, Victor Hugo, among others). At the right of the Panthéon, accommodating starry-eyed visitors to Paris for seemingly eons, is the somewhat shabby but stolid and substantial **Hotel du Panthéon** at 19 Place du Panthéon **(11),** phone 354-32-95. Recommended mainly to the young, its rates are a refreshing 45 francs ($10.46) single, 63 francs ($14.65) double, including breakfast, service and tax. And you'll be excited by its setting, in this central university quarter with a very special flavor. To reach the Panthéon area, take bus #38 from the Gare de l'Est, or bus #21 or 27 from the Gare St. Lazare, to the Luxembourg stop, or go by subway to St. Michel and walk the long distance uphill.

St. Germain des Prés

Although the Sorbonne area has more moderately-priced hotels than any other district in Paris (and thus provides you with the optimum chance of

THE ST. GERMAIN DES PRES AREA

finding a budget room in the summer months), nevertheless, the district can't compare in color and charm with the bustling area around the Ecole des Beaux Arts, near the Seine. How would you now like to live la vie Bohème, and plunge into a world of art galleries and studios, palettes and beards? Walk down the Boulevard St. Germain to the breathtakingly-beautiful **Eglise** (church) **St. Germain des Prés,** and turn right on the Rue Bonaparte, to the Seine. As you approach the river, you'll pass the Rue Jacob. And if you turn right on the Rue Jacob, you'll come to the Rue de Seine. These are the three blocks for budget hotels in this area: The Rue Bonaparte, the Rue Jacob, and the Rue de Seine. The metro stop for all three is called: St. Germain, and as you consider stopping there, keep in mind that the hotels in this district (the 6th arrondissement, around the St. Germain des Prés church) are of a slightly higher quality and price than those in the preceding section (the 5th arrondissement, around the student-packed Boulevard St. Michel); they also cater to a somewhat older age level than do the hotels near the Boulevard St. Michel.

Several hotels on these blocks offer especial values for their rooms with private bath. On the Rue Jacob, for instance, the redecorated, now-stylish, and elevator-equipped **Hotel des Deux Continents** at #25 (phone 326-72-46), offers doubles with private shower for 125 to 140 francs ($29.06 to $32.55), doubles with bath for 175 francs ($40.69), inclusive of breakfast and all else.

A few doors away at 21 Rue Jacob, the **Hotel des Marronniers** (354-91-66) rents bathless doubles for a much cheaper 71 francs ($16.51), 122 francs ($28.37) with private shower. Most rooms look out over a charming, terraced garden where breakfast (included in rates) is served. On the Rue Bonaparte, but this time on the other side of Boulevard St. Germain, the **Hotel Bonaparte** (tel: 326-97-37), 61 Rue Bonaparte, is a turn-of-the-century-type establishment, with elegance, chic, and enormous rooms, and average room charges of $36 for a double with bath, two breakfasts included, $33 single. Many ladies stay here and love it; don't be discouraged by the small and incongruous service station on one side of the street—around the corner is a lovely little square. A scant block from the church, and right near the famed Café Flore, the **Hotel Montana,** 28 Rue St. Benoit (548-62-15), rents bathless doubles for 58 francs ($13.48), doubles with private shower for 86 francs ($20), those rates not including breakfast. If all these hotels are filled, then walk down the Boulevard St. Germain (or the parallel Rue Jacob) to the Rue Saint Pères, where a longtime favorite of students, the well-appointed **Hotel de l'Academie,** at #32 Rue Saint Pères (phone 548-36-22), has single rooms without bath for 58 francs ($13.48), singles with shower for 80 to 100 francs, including breakfast and service, and has its own little restaurant off the lobby. However, it is closed late July and August.

Throughout this section, inexpensive restaurants abound, and there are markets, cafes, theatres—much life. Jean-Paul Sartre lives one block from the St. Germain metro stop.

The Luxembourg Gardens

For families traveling with children, the top hotel section in Paris is just below the beautiful Luxembourg Gardens (still on the Left Bank), where there are enclosed playing areas, with attendants, and an atmosphere of peace and charm. And on a quiet street called Rue Madame, which runs just parallel to the gardens, there are three quite suitable budget hotels to which families have flocked for many years, with good results.

I'd rate them in the following order: first, **Regent's Hotel** at 44 Rue Madame (phone 548-02-81), in a completely new building, modern and sparkling clean, and with elevator; then, further up the block, the older **Hotel de l'Avenir** at 65 Rue Madame (phone 548-84-54; it also has an elevator); and finally the much more basic **Hotel Perreyve,** 63 Rue Madame (phone 548-35-01), which lacks an elevator. The latter two are only 50 yards from an entrance gate to the lovely gardens. At Regent's, you'll pay 100 francs ($23.25) for a bathless double, two breakfasts included. At the more expensive l'Avenir, you'll pay 86 francs ($20) for same, plus $6.50 for an extra bed and breakfast; and at the elevator-lacking—but still relatively adequate, turn-of-the-century—Perreyve, the rate is only 48 francs ($11.16) single, including breakfast and service, only 58 francs ($13.48) double, without bath but including two breakfasts!

To reach any hotel in this area, take the metro to the St. Sulpice or St. Placide stop. You'll find that you're only a short walk away from the bustling St. Germain des Prés, and yet in a calm residential section.

THE FRENCH FRANC: At the present time the French franc is exchanged at the rate of 4.30 French francs to the dollar. That makes the franc worth about 23 U.S. cents, which is the basis for all dollar prices appearing in this chapter.

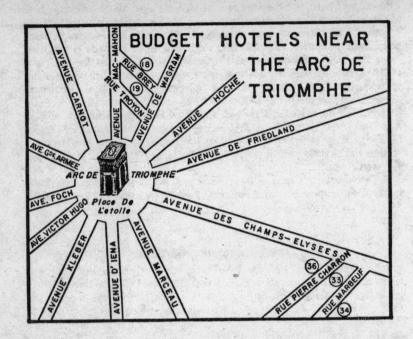

BUDGET HOTELS NEAR THE ARC DE TRIOMPHE

Place de l'Odéon

As our last Left Bank hotel area, we've chosen a locale for older readers who'd like to be near the excitement of the Left Bank, but who wish to stay in quiet, and relatively dignified surroundings. That prescription is filled by the stately Odéon, a square dominated by the marble Théâtre de France, which is one of the three state-run theaters in Paris. Only three blocks away is the Boulevard St. Michel; but here it's a different world.

On one side of the square, the **Michelet Odéon**, 6 Place de l'Odéon (phone 634-27-80), is a beautiful budget hotel, but one in which nearly every room is now with shower or bath, for which the charge ranges from 138 to 160 francs ($32.09 to $37.00) double, including breakfast, service and tax. Get one in the lower bracket, and you'll be well-pleased. On the streets that run off from the Odéon, several other fine hotels include the **Hotel Racine**, at 23 Rue Racine (phone 326-00-60 or 325-89-26), with a number of especially posh rooms with private bath, for which the charge is 89 francs ($20.69) single, 140 to 160 francs ($32.55 to $37.20) double, breakfast included. There are red carpets on the stairs and a bust of Racine in the lobby. The cheaper hotels are on the Rue Casimir-Delavigne, where three generally lower-cost choices, all close to the square, are excellent for older tourists: the **Hotel des Balcons**, 3 Rue Casimir-Delavigne, phone 634-78-50 (doubles with breakfast for 60 francs, $13.80, and every room possessing a balcony); the excitingly low-cost and highly recommended **Hotel Delavigne**, 1 Rue Casimir-Delavigne (phone 326-45-43) (doubles for 60 francs—$13.95); and the **Hotel St. Sulpice**, 7 Rue Casimir-Delavigne, phone 326-92-44 (doubles for 84 francs—$19.32—including breakfast and service). At 20 Rue Monsieur-le-Prince (the street that intersects the

Rue Racine) is the **Hotel Majory** (634-26-40), where an impeccably clean double, breakfast for two, taxes, and service amount to 65 francs ($15.11), doubles with private shower are 112 francs ($26.04), all inclusive; bathless singles, 53 francs ($12.32). Downhill, at the base of Rue Monsieur-le-Prince, is the little **Hotel Novelty**, Rue Dupuytren (354-89-72). Bathless singles are 40 francs ($9.30), doubles 62 francs ($14.41), triples 86 francs ($20), breakfast, taxes, and service included. Just behind the Théâtre de France, is the **Hotel de Lisbonne**, 4 rue de Vaugirard (326-95-47), which boasts a lobby recently furnished *à la méditerranée*, and bathless doubles costing a low 77 francs ($17.90), including breakfast. Less expensive: the nearby **Grand Hotel de France**, 10 Rue de Vaugirard (326-08-83), where large, spotless doubles rent for 56 francs ($13.02), twins for 73 francs ($16.97), with breakfast an additional 10 francs per person. The metro stop for all the above choices is, of course, Odéon.

Champs Elysées—Arc de Triomphe

Most of the older readers of this book, however, will probably prefer to live in an area closer to the shopping districts of the Right Bank, and less infused with students. While the Odéon and Ecole des Beaux Arts area on the Left Bank will appeal to some, there are several different Right Bank sections—the Arc de Triomphe area, the streets near the Palais Royal and the Louvre, the area of the Opera, and others—which should suit these wants with precision.

The most plentiful cluster of budget hotels on the Right Bank is found—surprisingly enough—in a small area just two and three short blocks from the Arc de Triomphe. If you want to be sure that you'll find an available room on the Right Bank without much searching, then this is the section to visit.

Walk up the Champs Elysées to the Arc de Triomphe. That monument stands on a plaza now formally named the "Place Charles de Gaulle," but popularly known as L'Etoile—so called because it forms the axle of twelve broad avenues, which radiate out like the spokes of a wheel. The inexpensive hotels are to be found at the right of the Arc de Triomphe, as you face it from the Champs Elysées, and they are mainly on the side streets which intersect the spoke-like avenues.

Rue Brey

Walk away from the Arc de Triomphe down the Avenue de Wagram. After three blocks, you'll see the **Rue Brey (18)** on your left. This little street is lined with budget hotels in a $12-a-night per person (and under, without breakfast) category: the **Hotel Neva**, 14 Rue Brey, phone 380-28-26 (especially recommended, but only for couples; the single rooms are high; very clean; very friendly staff; 95 francs ($22.09) for bathless doubles but 2 breakfasts are included; most rooms are now with private bath and rent for 152 francs, double or twin, all included); the greatly improved **Hotel Tilsitt**, 23 Rue Brey, phone 380-39-71 (77 francs for a bathless double, including breakfast); and the **Hotel Wagram** at 3 Rue Brey (phone 380-15-52; recently refurbished throughout and now my top choice on the street—105 francs ($24.41), all included, for bathless doubles). You'll find, as you search, that the manager of the Neva is especially cordial and helpful to readers of this guide, and he will undoubtedly manage to place you elsewhere on the Rue Brey (or on the nearby Rue Troyon, which has still other hotels), if his own establishment is full.

Downhill on the Champs Elysées

Other hotel-bearing streets jut off from the Champs Elysées itself, a few hundred yards before you reach the Arc de Triomphe. The side streets to the left of the Champs, as you approach the Arch, house the expensive ones. The narrower and more bustling shopping streets to the right of the Champs have a few good budget choices. On the Rue du Colisée, for instance, just twenty yards from the Champs Elysées, the **Hotel du Colisée**, at 6 Rue du Colisée (phone 359-95-25), has clean, but compact, double rooms without bath for 107 francs ($24.88) a night; while across the street, the **Hotel Royal**, at 7 Rue de Colisée (phone 359-32-40), is still another alternate choice, but higher in price. Though both hotels are on the busiest little side street you can imagine, their location is a superb one, just a few feet from a metro exit on the Champs Elysées (which I believe is the Franklin Roosevelt stop).

Off the Tuileries

Even more attractive in appearance than the Right Bank streets we've thus far described, is the charming Rue St. Roch, which runs off the breathtaking Tuileries Gardens, several hundred yards in front of the Louvre. And here, in quick succession, you'll find two favorites of lady travelers to Paris; they are—in ascending order of price: the **Hotel Saint Romain**, 5 Rue St. Roch (phone 260-3170), charging 94 francs ($21.86) for a double without bath (of which there are only a few), two breakfasts and service included, the same for a twin; and the recently refurbished **Hotel St. Roch**, 25 Rue St. Roch (phone 260-17-91), with splurge rates of 135 francs ($32.90) for a double with shower, including breakfast, service and tax. Staying here, you'll be only steps away from the fashionable shops of the Rue St. Honoré, and always you'll be in sight of gardens, a tiny stroll from the chic Place de la Concorde at your right, the massive Louvre to the left.

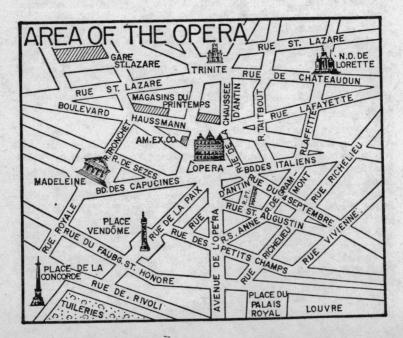

Area of l'Opéra

And next, for another area superb in location, the streets around the centrally-located **Place de l'Opéra,** near American Express, contain several good budget finds for either older or younger tourists seeking the less exotic life of Paris' Right Bank—as, for example, on the Rue du Helder, between the Blvd. des Italiens and the Boulevard Haussmann, east of the Opéra (metro is Opéra or Chaussée d'Antin). Our first choice here would be the **Hotel du Nil,** 10 Rue du Helder (phone 770-80-88), charging 89 francs ($20.69) for a small, bathless double, with breakfast and service included; followed closely by the **Hotel du Helder,** 4 Rue du Helder (phone 770-70-67), which charges the same. This is a pleasant, well-located street, with two good budget hotels.

In Pigalle

Near the heart of this sometimes raucous area, whose reputation is worse than the reality of it, and on a quiet and rather charming sidestreet that suggests the middle-class character of the neighborhood in former times, stands the **Hotel de Navarin et d'Angleterre,** 8 Rue Navarin (phone 878-3180), whose proprietress—Mme. Ginette Maylin—is unusually cordial to visiting Englishmen and Americans. As summer of 1980 approaches, Mme. Ginette is busily "redoing" rooms and lobby, which is a pity, because the current impression of the hotel is like that of visiting a French family: entrance consists of a glass-enclosed "office," an old-fashioned sitting room, a typically French family dining room, all leading to a garden with two immense acacia trees, a waterfall and tables for breakfasting. Guests in rooms on the garden are awakened by singing birds. There are old-fashioned guest rooms, no elevator. For this you'll pay only 60 francs ($13.95), double or twin, breakfast included, only 96 francs ($22.32) for a double with private shower. Metro stop is St. Georges or Pigalle. Almost next door, the **Hotel Royal Navarin,** 7 Rue de Navarin (phone 878-5173), is good for the overflow, at 50 francs ($11.62) single, 62 francs ($14.41) double, 66 francs twin, breakfast included, in a structure now bearing a few welcome Oriental touches by its new Vietnamese owner. If they're full too, try the nearby **Paris Hotel,** 23 Rue Henri-Monnier (phone 878-2874), whose interior is far better than its facade would lead you to believe. Operated by the son of the owner of the Grand Hotel des Ecoles (see below), the hotel charges 55 francs ($12.79), breakfast included, for a room with a big double bed, 65 francs ($15.11) for a twin.

Seven Scattered Choices
(with doubles for $10 to $16,
some including breakfast)

Finally, because a high percentage of the foregoing choices charge as much as $12 single, $18 for a bathless double (but scan the text carefully for the lower-priced selections), we've sought out and briefly described a number of always-reliable budget hotels whose rates have remained, for 1980, at $10 to $16 for a bathless double, including breakfast, service and tax.

Left Bank

Hotel de l'Avenir, 52 Rue Gay Lussac (phone 354-7660): Forty-eight rooms in a typical iron-balconied building. The rooms are small, simple, with old furniture, but the wallpaper and paint are new, some rooms have fireplaces, all are carpeted, impeccably clean and neat. Singles with breakfast 38 francs ($8.83), doubles 55 francs ($12.79), doubles with bath 78 francs ($18.13).

Hotel de Nevers, at 3 Rue de l'Abbé-de-l'Epée (phone 326-8183), around the corner from the Hotel l'Avenir, has simple but clean rooms, all with working fireplaces, and hospitable proprietors—Monsieur and Madame Allanic—whose son is fluent in English. Bathless singles 45 francs ($10.46), bathless doubles 58 francs ($13.34), including breakfast, service and tax.

Hotel des Grandes Ecoles, 75 Rue du Cardinal-Lemoine (phone 326-7923), has unusual character, and an unusual location in a lovely garden off the street: one enters through high wooden gates and then passes along a cobbled lane to the garden. Simple but practical rooms, new beds, nice proprietors, nice relaxed clientele; you'll need advance reservations for this one. Bathless doubles are 42 to 50 francs ($9.76 to $11.62), triples 66 francs ($15.34), singles aren't available.

Hotel du Centre, 24 bis Rue Cler (phone 705-5233; metro: Ecole Militaire), is located above one of the colorful food shops that line the Rue Cler, itself one of the major market streets of the 7th arrondissement. Once you've climbed to the upstairs reception area, you'll find a gaily-decorated lounge that more resembles the foyer to a private apartment than to a hotel. There are 28 rooms here, small but clean, and renting for 43 francs ($10) single, 58 francs ($13.48) double, including breakfast.

Hotel du Cirque, 21 Rue Duvivier (phone 705-0163), same metro as for the Hotel du Centre, above, is around the corner from the fascinating Rue Cler, and operated by a lady who's fiercely proud of the immaculate condition of her hotel. Rooms are quite large, and with period French furniture, all spotlessly clean, and range in cost from 37 francs single, 42 francs double to 51 francs triple, plus 10 francs for breakfast. No reservations accepted without a deposit, but if you phone and there's a room available, rush right over!

Right Bank

New Hotel, 40 Rue de Saint Quentin (phone 878-0483), directly across from the Gare du Nord. Squeezed between two cafes, its entrance is little more than a hallway, but the motel-style rooms are efficient, clean, practical, and done with a bit of taste. Bathless doubles, breakfast included, for 70 francs ($16.27), doubles with shower for 99 francs ($23.02).

Hotel Victoria, 17 Avenue Victoria (phone 233-5424), is a curious glass-fronted building across from the metro and bus stops of Chatelet. Operated by an elderly couple who speak no English; the high-ceilinged rooms suggest past elegance but carry low rates: 86 francs ($20) for a bathless double with breakfast, 102 francs ($23.72) for four in a room with two large beds and four breakfasts. Singles, surprisingly, are a high 60 francs.

PARISIAN PENSIONS: Readers who plan a fairly lengthy visit to Paris may want to consider staying in a family-operated pension, where they can take meals along with their room. Among the establishments offering those arrangements are the well-recommended: **Pension Familiale "Littré,"** 42 Rue d'Assas (phone LIT 89-72), operated by the incomparable Bermond family (they like Americans) and charging weekly rates of 438 francs ($101) per person for room and two meals, with wine included; it's within view of the Luxembourg Gardens; **Pension Pedron,** 78 Rue d'Assas, phone 633-08-14 (in the St. Germain des Prés area; metro stop is Vavin); about $13.95 per person for demi-pension, minimum required stay of 10 days, tourists accepted only from June 15 to

October 1, children accepted; **Pension Ladagnous,** 78 Rue d'Assas (phone 326-7932), 60 francs or $13.95 per person for room and demi-pension; **Les Marronniers,** 78 Rue d'Assas (326-37-71), offers accommodations to tourists and short-term, demi-pension boarders for 68 francs ($15.81) per day; vegetarian cuisine can be arranged; **Residence LaFayette,** 24 Rue Buffault, phone 878-73-57 (metro Cadet), with charming, sunny rooms, charges 55 francs ($12.79) per person, demi-pension—monthly stays are asked; **Residence Ralph,** 4 Rue du Cardinal Mercier, phone 874-1616 (in the area of the Place Clichy, near raucous Pigalle), offering rooms with two meals for 1600 francs per person per month (and Scott Fitzgerald lived here in the '20s); and **Pension de Famille,** 5 Rue H. Chevalier (phone 548-94-35), 68 francs per person full pension, 65 francs demi-pension, in single rooms, less in doubles, metro is St. Sulpice.

STARVATION BUDGET HOTELS: And now we descend in price.

Cleanliness fetishists among our starvation budgeteers will like the big **Hotels des Bains,** 33 Rue Delambre (which runs directly off the broad Boulevard Montparnasse, near the intersection of the Blvd. Raspail, metro: Vavin, 10 yards away), phone 320-85-27, which happens to be a public baths building as well as a hotel. There is no end to the hot showers (8 francs) available here! Actually, the very clean, very proper hotel is physically separate from the baths, and the rooms—all of which are doubles—resemble what you'd find in the ordinary species of hotel. Twenty of the rooms rent for 40 francs ($9.30) that's for *two* people, remember!—while 10 larger ones go for 60 francs ($13.95), service and tax included. A single drawback for shy people is that none of the rooms has twin beds, but are equipped instead with what the French call "un lit (bed) matrimoniale" (a large one).

Perhaps the largest cluster of cheap-but-decent hotels in Paris ($4.50 to $5 per person, per night) are found on the romantic **Ile St. Louis**—that little island in the Seine that seems to be annexed to the larger Ile de la Cité, on which Notre Dame stands. On the adjoining Ile de la Cité, the **Hotel Henry IV,** 25 Place Dauphine (phone 354-44-53), charges 35 francs for singles, 45 francs double, 54 francs twin, 60 francs triple, 74 francs for four, including breakfast and service. M. Balitrand is the English-speaking owner; he requires a $10 deposit for reservations, and has more rooms in August than in July.

Near the Saint Germain des Prés, I like the hotels on the Rue Ancienne Comédie and Rue de l'Echaudé, which are a block away from all the existentialist activity, and which include the **Hotel Molière,** at 11 Rue Ancienne Comédie (phone 326-85-79), (37 francs double), and the almost-as-cheap **Hotel Providence** at 11 Rue de l'Echaudé (phone 326-09-51). If you recall the hotel room in which Jeanne Seberg and Jean-Paul Belmondo trysted in the movie "Breathless," then you'll know what the interiors of these places look like: they're for young couples or adventurous males only.

Students' starvation budget

The **Association des Etudiants Protestants de Paris,** 46 Rue de Vaugirard (phone 354-31-49), metro stop is St. Sulpice or Odeon (in the Sorbonne area), accepts foreign students of both sexes throughout the year, charges only 28 francs ($6.51) in five-bedded dorms, 31 francs in a double, 34 francs in a single, breakfast and free showers included. Minimum stay of 5 days; office closed on Sundays. On the right bank, near the Louvre (metro stop is Palais Royal), the **Foyer Jacques de Rufz de Lavison,** 18 Rue J. J. Rousseau (phone 508-02-10), takes student-age foreigners of both sexes, from June 1 to September 30, for

32 francs per person, including breakfast, in either single, double, triple or quadruple rooms. This one sports a courtyard garden, and is beautifully located, just off the Rue de Rivoli. Sharing this superb location, and accepting students *all* year round, is the **Centre International de Paris**, 20 rue Jean-Jacques Rousseau (236-88-18). Students are accepted on demi-pension at 52 francs ($12.09) per day, or full pension at 58 francs ($13.48). There are three to six beds per room. Management is top-notch, and the mix of nationalities makes for a polyglot's paradise.

STUDENTS IN PARIS: The most exalted citizens of France are students—and that's a category applied as easily to a sophomore from Rutgers as to an existentialist from the Sorbonne. Any student, whether French or foreign, studying in Paris or simply there on vacation, can take advantage of literally dozens of government-operated, or government-subsidized, student hotels, and of more than 30 student restaurants, in Paris, whose prices (about $8 for bed and breakfast, around $2.80 for meals) are among the best values in Europe. Generally (but not always), you'll need proof of full-time student status, best obtained by requesting an International Student Identity Card (which costs $3.50) from the **Council on International Educational Exchange**, 777 U.N. Plaza, New York, New York (phone 661-0310), or 49 Rue Pierre Charron, Paris 8e (phone 359-2369). Write first for the application form which, properly filled out and submitted with payment, will later result in your receiving the all-important card. With one, you can then proceed to obtain your housing and meals in Paris by following any one of three courses of action:

By writing to the O.T.U.

First, and best of all, is to write to the **Organisation pour le Tourisme Universitaire**, 137 Boulevard St. Michel, Paris, whose function, among others, is to book students in summer into centrally-located student hotels in Paris, provide them with access to student restaurants, French-language courses, and all the rest. Given enough advance notice, they'll book you for a minimum stay of 3 days in a student residence (from July 1st till September 1st) where the charge for room and breakfast can go as low as $7 a night. They'll also provide you with a brochure on other O.T.U. services, advise you on special student transport within Europe, student resorts, many other items.

A timely letter to the O.T.U., accompanied by at least $1 in international postal response coupons, can obviously prove of aid. But if you have neglected to do this in advance of your trip, you can try again, in person, at the Paris office of the O.T.U. (137 Boulevard St. Michel—the nearest metro stop is Port-Royal—phone 329-12-88) upon your arrival in the city. This time, the student-age personnel who man the office will attempt to place you in a student hotel or residence—provided you plan a stay in Paris of at least a week. Even if you don't, you should drop in to pick up their list of student restaurants serving meals for $2.80 (hors d'oeuvres, entree, dessert and beverage) and to obtain current information on where student meal tickets can be gotten (one student restaurant at which these are always available is the big **Mabillon**, at 3 Rue Mabillon, Paris 6; others, more likely to be open in August and September, include the **Censier**, 5 Rue Censier; the **Cuvier**, 8 bis Rue Cuvier). There's also a bulletin board here that simultaneously offers car rides and the like, and also portrays the hijinks of Parisian studentdom: "Jeune étudiant Canadien cherche une jeune fille qui veut faire l'auto-stop en Suède."

If you write to O.T.U. for the purpose of making a definite booking, enclose $7 in international postal response coupons; they'll apply $5 of this as a deposit.

Cité Universitaire

Contrary to a popular impression, the O.T.U. will not book you into any of the buildings of Paris' famous **Cité Universitaire**—that vast complex of 37 student residences situated at the side of the Parc Montsouris, 10 minutes out from the Latin Quarter. Rather, O.T.U. utilizes centrally-located and scattered student hotels, in the heart of the central city.

If you'd prefer to live in this total student community—whose 37 buildings, each surrounded by gardens, are nothing less than the "city" their title proclaims—then write to the **Fondation Nationale de la Cité Universitaire,** 19 Boulevard Jourdan, Paris XIV, which accepts foreign students and teachers during the period from July 15 to September 30 (minimum stay, one week). Specify your dates of arrival and departure in Paris, and whether you require a single room or will agree to share a twin-bedded room. They'll house you in one of the 37 "Maisons" of the Cité (if you write at least a month in advance), and charge you only 25 francs per person per day in a double room, 30 francs in a single; meals generally run around 13 francs ($3). The Cité possesses over 4,300 rooms (of which 600 are reserved for girls), and its major congregating spot during the summer is "La Maison Internationale," with its game room and lounges, restaurants, gymnasium and tennis courts; this was built by John D. Rockefeller, Jr., and is a sister institution to the "international houses" he founded at Berkeley, Chicago and Columbia Universities; mammoth cafeteria inside, where meals are 11 francs. An alternate name for the institution you'll be visiting: "Cité Internationale de l'Université de Paris"; I've heard of students appearing on the spot for accommodations, without reservations (metro stop is "Cité Universitaire"), but that's tricky: phone 589-68-52, first.

Accueil des Jeunes en France

A final, room-finding, student-helping organization, **Accueil des Jeunes en France,** 270 Rue St. Jacques (325-06-20), operates a 24-hour service during the summer months. They will find you accommodations in one of their many newly refurbished student hotels for 30 francs ($6.97) a night, including breakfast, and, if a car is available, even transport you from their Rue St. Jacques headquarters (metro: Port Royale) to the hotel at no extra charge. Although these are "student accommodations" with several beds to a room, there is no age restriction or requirement of student status.

Other student facilities

Not to be compared with the Cité Universitaire, but still a cut above the quality of most other student accommodations, in central Paris, is **l'Association pour l'Accueil des Etudiants Etrangers,** at 13 Rue de Vaugirard (phone 326-50-78), 20 yards from the Blvd. St. Michel, for males only. Thirty-five francs ($8.13) per person in 4-bedded rooms, breakfast included. On a recent visit to this Left Bank hospice, several tenants mentioned that they prefer to take their meals, however, on the Right Bank, in the vicinity of the Folies Bergere: specifically, at Paris' YMCA **("U.C.J.G.")** located at 14 Rue de Trevise (phone 246-65-50) and charging only 14 francs ($3.25) for an evening repast of hors d'oeuvres, meat with vegetable and potatoes, cheese and dessert, bread. If you're planning a visit to that shrine of topless showgirls, keep the "Y" in mind.

READERS' HOTEL SELECTIONS (BLVD. ST. MICHEL AREA), LEFT BNK: "You have overlooked one of the nicest small hotels in Paris, the **Grand Hotel de Lima** at 46 Blvd. St. Germain (at the corner of Rue des Bernardins), phone 634-02-12. It is immaculate, always warm, and there is always an abundance of hot water. The breakfast coffee is superb, and you get three grand cups of it! Notre Dame Cathedral is a block away, and it's conveniently close to all of the attractions in the student quarter. I lived at the hotel for an entire winter, spring and early summer while I was writing travel stories for the *Houston Post,* and I cannot recommend it enough. The manager, M. Massot, speaks English and has lots of opinions on various matters and an appealing frankness in discussing them with you; his wife is helpful and considerate, and the small staff of maids is efficient. A small single room (with lavatory and bidet) costs 60 francs; doubles cost 75 francs; and doubles with showers are 110 francs. The prices include all service and taxes, and it's only 10 francs more for a good breakfast of rolls, jam, butter, and coffee, which is served either in your room or in a cheerful dining room" (Mary Anne Haynes, New York, New York). . . . "We spent 3 days in Paris at the **Hotel Studia,** 51 Boulevard St. Germain (Sorbonne area near the métro stop Maubert-Mutualité, phone 326-81-00), in a large, clean double with breakfast but without bath, overlooking the boulevard, for 80 francs (with bath, 145 francs). There is a TV available to guests in a lounge off the hotel lobby, and the friendly proprietors and relaxed atmosphere made it a genuine pleasure to stay there. One added nicety were the buckets of fresh flowers that greeted us daily in the lobby" (Lorraine Stalberg, Los Angeles, California). . . . "At the **Hotel Cluny Square,** 21 Blvd. St. Michel (metro stop St. Michel), phone 354-21-39, you will find clean, well-kept rooms, with hot water and access to a bath. The landlady reminisces sadly about her short stay in England, where she picked up the little English needed for understanding, and the understanding goes so far as to give the price of 35 francs per person for a double with breakfast, 45 francs single. The location was about a 2 minute walk to Notre Dame, a minute from the Seine, a few blocks from the Luxembourg Gardens, and right in the heart of the student center. With a self service right around the corner and the handy Metro, I could live like a king on a $15 budget!" (Stephen Z. Smith, Harrisburg, Pa.). . . . "**Hotel de France** at 108 Rue Monge, phone 707-19-04 (metro: Censier-Daubenton), in the St. Michel area, was the most pleasant stop of our trip, as everyone there went out of their way to make our stay enjoyable. A double room with delicious French 'petit dejeuner' cost 50 francs ($11.62) per person" (Carol Siegal and Mimi Flicop, Cambridge, Mass.).

READERS' HOTEL SELECTIONS (AREA OF THE ODEON), LEFT BANK: " At the **Hotel du Grand Condé,** 2 Rue Saint-Sulpice (phone 326-03-40), near the Odeon, we had a small but lovely room on the second floor for 68 francs ($15.81), double; singles, we learned, are 35 francs, including breakfast. The hotel is run by a young, charming French-American couple who are most helpful in answering questions about the city" (Wendy and Edward Friedman, Peekskill, New York). . . . "A lovely pension near the Place de l'Odeon is the **Hotel des Ecoles,** 19 Rue Monsieur-le-Prince, operated by the delightful Mme. Arends. We had a room for two for 75 francs ($17.44), including a fantastic free breakfast of baguettes and croissants" (Dr. and Mrs. John Dabel, Dover, Delaware). . . . "At the **Grand Hotel des Etrangers,** 2 Rue Racine (phone 634-26-50), just off the Boulevard St. Michel a block from its intersection with the Boulevard St. Germain, a clean, bathless double, large, cost 79 francs a night, including breakfast. Fluent English spoken by the management" (Richard and Jean Hjorth, Cherry Hill, New Jersey).

READERS' HOTEL SELECTIONS (MONTPARNASSE): "Besides being located in the middle of the most famous section of Montparnasse (La Coupole is a three-minute walk), the **Hotel du Danemark,** 21 rue Vavin (phone 326-93-78), is right up the street from the Luxembourg Gardens and is also near two extremely convenient métro stops: Vavin and Notre Dame des Champs. Doubles are only 51 francs ($11.86), twins 62 francs ($14.41), with breakfast an additional 12 francs per person. For a hotel with these prices, I don't think it can beaten: the water is always steaming hot, the beds comfortable, the rooms well lit, and I cannot imagine more sympathetic service than that given by M. Nurit and his wife" (Royal S. Brown, City University of New York; seconding recommendations from G. Moldovanu, Quebec City, Canada, and Sue and Frank Bundy, Omaha, Nebraska).

READERS' HOTEL SELECTIONS (THE MARAIS, RIGHT BANK): "A jewel among Parisian hotels is the **Hotel des Celestins,** 1 Rue Charles V (phone 887-87-04). Near metro stop Bastille, this modest hotel is clean, quiet and well run. Attractive rooms for two cost 90 francs with private bath, 47 francs without bath" (Mrs. L.D. Eykelboom, Meridian, Mississippi). . . . "Although you have a subsection entitled 'Don't Miss the Marais,' you neglect to point out that there are some marvelous, cheap hotels and restaurants in this area. One of the nicest rooms my husband and I stayed in while we were in Paris was in the **Hotel Stella,** 14 rue Neuve St. Pierre (phone 272-23-66). This hotel is near the Bastille metro stop, off the Rue de St. Antoine. For a charming double room, we paid 46 francs. Baths were 12 francs extra, per person. And the Rue de St. Antoine is loaded with pastry, wine, cheese, and meat shops. For very satisfying meals, we would buy the component parts at these stores—often supplemented by deliciously fresh fruits from one of the many street vendors who lined both sides of the street. Near the Marais (within walking distance), we found another great hotel, the **Grand Hotel des Arts et Métiers,** on the Rue Borda (phone 887-73-89). The best way to reach this quaint hotel is to get off at either the Arts & Métiers metro stop or the Republic metro stop. We had a delightful room, with small balcony, for 76 francs—which included breakfast in bed! Baths were 10 francs extra, per person" (Gale Glazer, Cambridge, Mass.).

READERS' HOTEL SELECTIONS (NEAR AIR TERMINAL INVALIDES, LEFT BANK): "I was searching for a hotel near the 'Aerogare,' the Paris Air Terminal (behind Les Invalides), from where I could later on take my return trip to New York. Five hundred yards away, I hit upon the **Comète Hotel,** tel: 705-0853. As I inquired, the most friendly and helpful proprietress said she charges 52 francs ($12.09) for a single room, including breakfast. This price seemed very satisfactory, as other hotels around the Gare du Nord (where I had to stay first) charged 60 francs. This happened in the first week of July. And when I returned to Paris at the end of August and took a room at the Comète, to my surprise I was charged only 50 francs for the single room with breakfast. Friends of mine to whom I recommended the hotel occupied a large double room with shower and toilet for 108 francs; seemingly because the tourist season was regarded as over" (Peter N. Abbott, New York, New York).

READERS' HOTEL SELECTIONS (RIGHT BANK): "Within easy walking distance of the Arc de Triomphe, and only a block off the Champs Elysées, the **Hotel D'Artois,** 94 Rue de la Boetie (tel: 225-76-65), gave us a double room with bidet and toilet for $25 a night. Included were tax, services and continental breakfast" (Robert Shannon, Hayward, California). . . . "My wife and I were delighted with our stay at the **Hotel Britannique,** 20 Avenue Victoria, near Boulevard de Sebastopol (phone 233-74-59). It was run by a most helpful and engaging English family. We had a huge, light, comfortable room for three with a double bed and a single bed for 120 francs a night, including breakfast. The hotel is conveniently located, quite near the Chatelet metro stop (a junction of four metro lines), on the Right Bank, a half-block from the Seine" (Sayre P. Schatz, New York, New York; note by AF: I have seen photographs of the handsome Hotel Britannique, which has been owned by the Perret-Baxter family since 1860; all rooms are now with private bath, yet rent for only 100 francs ($23.25) double, 80 francs ($18.60) single, breakfast included).

READERS' HOTEL SELECTIONS (NEAR RAILROAD STATIONS, RIGHT BANK): "Right opposite the Gare de l'Est and about 20 feet from the metro station, **Hotel de Champagne et de Mulhouse,** 87 Boulevard de Strasbourg (tel: 607-51-26) is a fine choice for the middle-bracket visitor. Rates for a room with shower and w.c., breakfast included, are 80 francs single, only 90 francs double, and everything is very clean" (Tino Christofilis, Nassau, Bahamas). . . . "An easy walk from the Gare de l'Est, **Hotel du Jura,** 6 Rue Jarry (tel: 770-06-66), is clean, friendly and quiet. A double room cost us 65 francs, breakfast included" (W.C. & Karen P. Prewitt, APO New York). . . . "Turn right after leaving the Gare du Nord and continue until you come to Boulevard Magenta. There you will see an entire block of hotels. The best of these is the newly rebuilt and decorated **Hotel de Londres et d'Anvers** at #133 (878-24-35), where doubles without private bath or breakfast are 60 francs. Breakfast will be a steep 12 francs each, but the rooms can be rented without breakfast. Cheaper in price at 129 Bd. Magenta (878-03-65), is the nearby **Grand Hotel Magenta,** 66 francs, including breakfast" (James and Yvonne Bunting, Woonsocket, Rhode Island). . . . "I traveled by train from Amsterdam to Paris, and arrived at the Gare du Nord extremely tired and with *Europe on $15 a Day* tucked away in my luggage. Not wishing to disarrange my suitcase on the station floor, I went to the Gendarmerie and asked for the name of a good cheap hotel ('un bon hotel à bon marché'). The officer pointed across the street and muttered in sleepy French: 'La, à gauche.' And 'la à gauche,' there were seven hotels. Eliminating one which looked expensive (it had balconies), I played eenie-meenie and chose the **Hotel Apollo**, at 11 Rue de Dunkerque (phone 878-04-98). I couldn't have been happier. I received room #41 on the top floor, which had a magnificient view; and the charge was only $12 per person (double), including breakfast" (Burton Wolfson, New York City; note by AF: mixed reactions to this hotel in recent letters). . . . "A well-located hotel—the **Little Regina Hotel**, 89 Blvd. de Strasbourg (phone 607-86-73), Paris 10e, right opposite the Gare de l'Est—offers a small single room without bath—wonderful comfortable bed—for 60 francs ($13.95), breakfast, service and tax included. M. Corbel, who speaks English, owns this with his charming mother" (Mrs. Christine Mead, London, England). . . . "We arrived on a rainy night at the Gare de l'Est, and—walking several blocks to the Gare du Nord—found a very pleasant hotel. **Hotel Paris Nord Est** was its name and it is across the street and around the corner (at 133 Rue du Faubourg St. Denis; phone 607-40-20) from the station. For a charming room *with* private bath, our double with two breakfasts came to only 86 francs" (Mr. and Mrs. Richard L. Dabney, Birmingham, Alabama). . . . "My family and I found the rooms to be well-furnished, clean, and very moderately priced (95 francs for a double without shower, 130 francs for a double with shower) at the **Helvetia Hotel**, 28 bis Boulevard Diderot (phone 343-25-19), only 1½ blocks from the Gare de Lyon. And breakfast is included in the rates" (Andrew Hickerson, age 10, Kowloon, Hong Kong). . . . "Eighty-five francs is the total charge for a double room at **Hotel Paradis**, 9 Rue du Paradis, near the Gare du Nord . . . and it's a classy place, with tapestry bedspreads, an old armoire in our room, shops selling Limoges and Baccarat on the street downstairs. Also: tres tranquille all night long. The night staff (university students) were particularly helpful, actively offering assistance. They enjoyed working their English as much as we enjoyed using our bit of French" (Roberta Kehret, Palo Alto, California).

READERS' HOTEL SELECTIONS (SINGLE ROOMS): "One block northwest of the St. Lazare Station at #12 Rue Stockholm is the **Hotel President Wilson**, (phone 522-10-85), a slightly shabby but respectable (American Methodist ministers were staying there) hotel, whose proprietress speaks perfect English and where single rooms go for 51 francs ($11.86) a night, including breakfast. A post office is across the road and bakeries, dairies, and epiceries abound in the area for a quick put-together lunch. President Wilson is one-star" (Bill Gazer, Guelph, Ontario, Canada). . . . "A charming family-run establishment in the Quarter Latin, clean, with plenty of hot water, daily service (cleaning rooms, etc.), and a number of single rooms for 44 francs, breakfast and all else included, is the **Hotel du Globe**, 71 rue Monge, Paris 5; tel. 331-2564, Metro: Place Monge" (Richard Kadulski, North Vancouver, B.C., Canada, and numerous others).

READERS' PENSION SELECTIONS: "There is a quaint little pension at #7 Rue de Navarin, Montmartre (phone 878-51-73), quite aptly named the **Hotel Royal Navarin,** presided over by a Vietnamese 'famille,' with tiny lobby and 'petit' breakfasting area with TV and charming 'serveuse' to pop in and out with fresh rolls and croissants (from the corner patisserie if you are in a still bigger rush) and with steaming pots of delicious tea or coffee as you may prefer. Breakfast, of course, as well as service and taxes, are all included in the nominal rates, as follows: For our own family of 5, including 3 teenagers, we reserved 2 rooms at the front of the hotel, on the 4th floor (there are 5 floors) which was reached via the lift (only 3 persons per trip, please). One room, housing the 2 male members, had twin beds, window overlooking the street and bath (100 francs); the other room, for the 3 gals, boasted double beds, 2 casement windows on the front, with bathroom facilities and shower with heated towel racks (also phone in rooms), 115 francs. This is a grand total, per day, of about $50 for 5 persons, or about $10 each, with private bath. It is 3 short blocks up the hill to Pigalle and another 3 or 4 to Sacre Coeur and the artists' Montmartre, home of Toulouse-Lautrec and as colorful, or more so, than the Latin Quarter. You can go anywhere in the city via the Pigalle metro (up the hill from your hotel) or St. Georges, which is down the hill. Walking to the Moulin Rouge or Folies Bergère and the wonderful cafeteria Montmartre and smart boutiques is a breeze, and from the top of the hill, Sacre Coeur, can be seen all the true beauty below of the whole of Paris, which at night is a breathtaking spectacle and all for free" (Mrs. A. M. Monaco, Miami, Fla.; note by AF: The Royal Navarin has bathless rooms as well, for which the charge, including breakfast, is 65 francs double, 72 francs twin). . . . "Men traveling alone can stay at **Les Pères Maristes** (the Maristes Fathers), 104 Rue de Vaugirard, phone 222-3104, for 60 francs ($13.80) a day for room and all three meals; closed in August" (Mrs. Robert Nadeau, Quebec, P.Q., Canada).

READERS' SELECTIONS (STARVATION BUDGET): "For the hard-pressed student or family, the **Hotel du Commerce**, 14 Rue de la Montagne Saint Genevieve (phone 033-8969), metro: Maubert, charges only 50 francs ($11.62) per double room, without breakfast. It is not in the best of shape, nor is it that well looked after, but you also receive a human alarm clock in the form of a little old lady who knocks at the door every morning at 9, asking 'Vous restez ou vous partez?' "(John Vanderlaan, Cambridge, Ontario, Canada). . . . "A double room at the small, one star hotel, the **Grand Hotel du Loriet**, 8 Rue des Mauvais Garçons (phone 887-77-00), near the Hotel de Ville (city hall), will be only 42 francs ($9.76) in 1980, not including an optional breakfast at 18 francs ($4.18) for two" (John Nemeth, Madrid, Spain). . . . "A high recommendation for the student dormitory (**"Foyer d'Etudiants"**) at 18 Jean Jacques Rousseau (phone 508-02-10), just a 5-minute walk from the Louvre metro stop. Rooms have between two and four beds in them; showers are free, and plentiful; price is only 35 francs ($8.13) per person, breakfast included. The location is excellent for sightseeing at the Louvre and visiting the Comédie Française" (Mark G. Simkin, University of California, Berkeley; note by AF: open from June 15 to September 30 only, minimum stay of 3 days). . . . "Le Foyer International des Etudiantes, 93 Blvd. St. Michel, phone 354-49-63, houses girl tourists during Christmas, Easter and summer vacation periods (male students in summer only) for 35 francs per person a night, breakfast extra, in twin-bedded rooms, for a minimum stay of 5 nights. That's in the heart of the Latin Quarter, near the Luxembourg Gardens, and the accommodations are neat and comfortable, with shower" (Jeannine Beaudoin, Paris, France). . . . "I suggest for the young and impecunious **La Maison Internationale des Jeunes**, 4 Rue Titon (phone 371-99-21; metro stop is Faidherbe-Chaligny or Nation), where the accommodation is 2 to 6 beds to a room, but only 32 francs ($7.44) per bed, breakfast included, in a building that is open all year. It is a good place to meet people, and does not require a hostel card, because it is independent" (Dana Green, Atlanta, Georgia).

RESTAURANTS: Finding an inexpensive restaurant in Paris is much harder than finding an inexpensive hotel. The French place much more emphasis on food than we do, and devote much more of their budget to it. There will be times in Paris when you will wonder where the non-millionaires could possibly eat.

But there are inexpensive restaurants in Paris, and the quality of their cuisine, at the prices they charge, makes for an astonishing value. If you'll follow our street directions, and plan to be in certain locations at mealtimes, you'll experience what can only be described as miracles in budget eating. They fall into three price categories: the unbelievable finds serving three-course meals for $4.18 to $5.58; the numerous cafeterias where three courses and beverage can be had for about $3.50 to $5 (and individual plates for less); the "bistros" (little family-operated restaurants) where you can receive full meals for $4 to $6.

(1) The 12 Best Budget Restaurants: Full Meals for $4 to $5.50

There are, I can say with foot-weary certainty, precisely 11 of these little wonders (for I've searched, oh how I've searched). And since their prices and typical French cuisine are all fairly similar, I'll devote—in most instances—more space to describing where they are than what they're like.

On and off the "Grands Boulevards" (Right Bank)

(1) **Le Drouot**, 103 Rue de Richelieu (metro stop is Richelieu-Drouot): To find this first "little wonder", you should know that the term "Grands

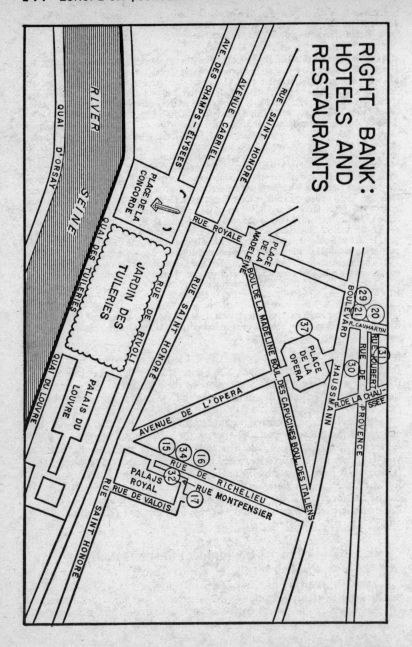

Boulevards" refers to the single avenue that starts out at the Opera as the "Boulevard des Italiens", then changes its name successively into the "Boulevard Montmartre", "Boulevard Poissoniere", "Boulevard Bonne Nouvelle",

"Boulevard St. Denis", "Boulevard St. Martin." It's a broad, bustling thoroughfare, lined with movie theatres, variety music halls, stores and shops, that progressively gets poorer, and therefore more interesting, as you stroll along it—and to stroll along it is the advice of a famous Yves Montand recording, in which he tells you there are 'tant de choses à voir' (so many things to see) here, including, I might add, Communist Party headquarters, decked out with red flags. If, from the Opera, you'll walk for five minutes down the Boulevard des Italiens, to that point where the avenue veers right and becomes the Boulevard Montmartre, you'll find the famous Le Drouot, upstairs, at the corner of Boulevard des Italiens and Rue de Richelieu (it's 20 yards down on the Rue de Richelieu; revolving doors, a small green sign, and a blackboard listing plates of the day, are all you'll see). Upstairs, you'll emerge into a large room decorated in 1920s modern, where hundreds of non-tourist Parisians dine on appetizers priced at 4 francs, on main courses with vegetables ("Cassoulet Parisien", "Rognons sauté aux Champignons", many others) that average 10 francs, and on cheese or other desserts—many of which are priced between 3 and 3.50 francs. $5 meals, which include a 12% service charge, are easily possible. Open from 11 a.m. to 3 p.m., from 6 to 9:30 p.m., every day of the week throughout the year, and much less crowded at night than it is at lunch.

(2) **Restaurant Chartier,** 7 Rue du Faubourg Montmartre: Walk one block further along the "Grands Boulevards" (here, the Boulevard Montmartre) until you come to the Rue du Faubourg Montmartre; turn left and in 30 yards, on a colorful open market street, you'll see a courtyard, at the end of which is a mammoth, wood-paneled former library (you can still see the index card files) housing the Restaurant Chartier. Here, if you can imagine it, the charges are even lower than at Le Drouot and the setting more picturesque. And thus, if you'll have pâté de campagne (3 francs) or a tomato salad (3.50 francs) to begin, then a plate like langue de boeuf sauce piquante (beef tongue in a spicy sauce, with potatoes, 10 francs) and yogurt ("yaourt") for dessert (2.50 francs), you'll pay a total of about 20 francs including wine, but plus a 12% service charge. Open every day of the week, for both meals.

Near the Comédie Française (Right Bank)

(3) **Ma Normandie,** 11 Rue Rameau, decorated and furnished in "Normandie" style, serves a 3-course prix-fixe menu for 21 francs ($4.88), this time including wine (red, white or rosé) served in brown pitchers, or a bottle of cider—a typical product of Normandy. The available choices are listed on a blackboard hanging on a wall opposite the entrance, and provide as many as five selections for your appetizer, as many as eight main plates (including coq au vin, choucroute, and other mouth-watering French specialties). From the Comédie Française, walk up the Rue Richelieu until you find the Rue Raméau on your left, four short blocks up. Open Monday to Friday only, from 11 a.m. to 2:30 p.m.

In Montparnasse (Left Bank)

(4) **Le Texel,** at 11 Rue Texel (Métro: Gaité), is operated by two young Tunisians who offer a 3-course, prix-fixe menu for only 22 francs ($5.11). It includes 5 choices of appetizer (such as sardines in olive oil), a choice among six main plates (e.g., beef steak, cheese omelet, cous-cous), a choice among four desserts (fruit, yogurt, ice cream or coffee). Wine is included, and everyone ordering the 22 francs menu is offered a free apertif. Open 7 days a week from 10 to 3 and from 6 p.m. to midnight.

Near the Eiffel Tower (Left Bank)

(5) **Restaurant le Commerce,** 51 Rue du Commerce: In the general area of the Eiffel Tower, but a bit too far to be reached on foot (it's really closer to the back of the Parc du Champ de Mars, behind the tower; closest metro to the restaurant is Emile Zola; the station called Commerce is also nearby), this is another of those large miracle restaurants, where appetizers or hors d'oeuvres are 3 to 4 francs, main courses are 10 francs (in most cases), desserts are 3.50 to 4.50 francs. My last visit, I had celeri remoulade (4 francs) to begin, petit salé aux lentilles (a marvelous cheap Parisian dish, found everywhere—corned beef with lentils, in sauce; here, 10 francs), then a mousse au chocolat for dessert (4.50 francs) for a total of exactly 18.50 francs plus 12% service. Location is on another of those colorful market streets, appropriately enough called "Rue Commerce," and the restaurant is open every day of the year.

On and off the Boulevard St. Michel (Left Bank)

(6) **Restaurant St. Michel,** 10 Boulevard St. Michel (metro: St. Michel): In the student and university area of Paris (the "Latin Quarter"), the budget restaurants are apt to be plainer than those we've found elsewhere, but they offer values just as remarkable—as, for example, directly on the Boulevard St. Michel, at no. 10, where the Grand Restaurant St. Michel serves three courses, bread, and service charge, for a prix fixe total of 23 francs ($5.34). I won't pretend that the furnishings here are terribly dainty or relaxing (paper table cloths, packed-together tables). But for a total of $10.68, Hope and I had two plates of fresh tomatoes in olive oil for an opener, two plates of boeuf à la bourguignonne with carrots and potatoes, one yogurt, one ice cream, one beer and one Coke—and tipping is forbidden ("pourboire interdit"). The upstairs dining room is the more pleasant spot to eat. Open every day.

Near St. Germain des Prés (Left Bank)

(7) **Restaurant Jean,** 132 Boulevard Saint Germain: This, and the restaurant that follows (La Petite Source), just barely make the list, and are not to be compared with our earlier three selections—Restaurant Chartier, Le Drouot and the Le Commerce—which, in that order, are the finest budget restaurants of Paris. Indeed, the least prepossessing of all our choices, and a bit sinister in appearance until you relax in it, is the Restaurant Jean, two short blocks from the St. Germain des Prés Church and the famous existentialist gathering points —the Cafe aux Deux Magots and Cafe de Flore. The Jean is an entirely proper, and very popular establishment nevertheless, and even prints an English menu for its tourist visitors, although I'd advise you to use the more-frequently-changing French one. You walk through an arcade-like tunnel ("le Passage du Commerce") at the above address to find it; inside, in bare and very un-intimate surroundings, you're charged 4.50 francs for most hors d'oeuvre choices, 11 to 15 francs for most main courses (but there are several other main dishes—like mutton couscous, 12 francs—for less); 3 francs for yogurt; 24 francs for a set three-course meal, including wine and service. Plain food, naturally, but very French; and if you walk past the restaurant, you'll suddenly be in the rarely-seen and quite beautiful Square du Studio Rohan, where Marat published his newspaper and the guillotine was first constructed. Closed Mondays.

(8) **La Petite Source,** 130 Boulevard St. Germain: Totally lacking the character of some of our earlier selections, this is a slick, plastic-covered cafe that would not appear out of place in Newark; but its prices are strictly Left Bank Parisian. It specializes in quickly-served snacks and meals, and serves up

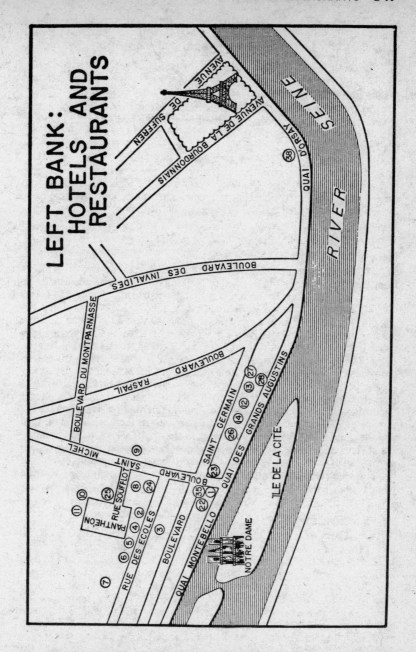

vast quantities of its "salads de tomates" (4.50 francs), followed by the French
student favorite of "bifteck avec pommes frites" (13 francs); or the equally
popular plates of sausages ("saucisse") and french fries ("pomme frites") for

only 10 francs. Wine is 3 francs, draft beer 3.50 fr., and you can have quite a good omelette for only 7 francs. Located next door to the passageway for the Restaurant Jean, La Petite Source stays open until midnight, is closed Sundays and the month of August.

Off the Boulevard St. Germain (Left Bank)

(9) Owned and managed with great dedication by Jean Padilla, an author of several French cook books, **Auberge Inn** at 34 Rue du Cardinal Lemoine, is a very special vegetarian restaurant where there's always one plat du jour (daily special) selling for 18 francs ($4.18—an example is polenta with vegetables) and always one three-course prix fixe menu priced at 25 francs ($5.81)— as, for example, soup, then cooked rice with fresh green peas, then white cheese and a glass of carrot juice. Smoking is not allowed. Monsieur Padilla, who speaks English well, will be happy to answer questions about cuisine or to discuss his unique methods for the organic cultivation of vegetables. Learn while you eat.

In the area of "Les Halles" (Right Bank)

(10) **Le Restaurant du Grand Cerf,** 145 Rue Saint Denis, two-or-so blocks from the Rue Reaumur and reached by walking through an arcade called "Le Passage du Grand Cerf," offers a prix fixe, three-course meal for only 18 francs ($4.18), including wine and service, and charges 3.50 francs for most appetizers, 8 to 11 francs for most main courses, on its 40-item à la carte menu, only 3 francs for dessert, 2.50 francs for a quarter liter of red wine. Crowded at lunch (noon to 2 p.m.), less so at dinner (7 to 9 p.m.), closed Sundays and in August.

(11) **Chez Dédé,** 5 Rue Mandar, just off the Rue Montmartre, is always crowded with employees of the area seeking out its 24 franc ($5.58), three-course, prix fixe meal, served daily except Sunday; there is no à la carte menu. Rather, you choose from no fewer than 18 hors d'oeuvres, from 10 different "plats du jour," then choose either cheese or dessert, and receive a small bottle of wine or mineral water thrown in. You eat best in the upstairs room, then pay the standard 24 francs as you leave, to the "patron" behind the counter. It's obvious that the main courses here—boeuf bourguignon, pepper steak, pot au feu, calves liver, tripe—are the kind rarely found on the prix fixe menus of low-cost establishments, and that quite obviously accounts for the immense popularity of Chez Dédé.

Near the Champs Elyseés

(12) **Chez Melanie** at 27 Rue du Colisée, near the Franklin D. Roosevelt métro stop, is probably the finest value in this entire high-priced district, a small, family-run restaurant on the fourth floor of an apartment house less than a minute from the Champs Elysées. It's worth the inconvenience to be squeezed onto 50 seats in two small dining rooms, because the food is well-prepared, quickly-served, and costs only 23 francs ($5.34) for a three-course prix fixe starting with hors d'oeuvres, followed by a "plat garni" (example: roast veal with green beans), then cheese or dessert, wine, and "pain à volonté" (as much bread as you wish). And service is included. Entering the house at no. 27, you step into a tiny courtyard, then ascend 60 steps of a narrow staircase to the Melanie.

And there you have the 12 wonder restaurants of Paris. Have I missed any?

(2) The Cafeterias of Paris: Full Meals for $3.50 to $5

We now move upward (but only a bit) in price.

Much to the horror of the super-gourmets, Paris has begun to sprout with cafeterias—that's right, cafeterias in Paris, but cafeterias with a special French flavor, like little flasks of wine (60¢) at the end of the serving line. The food served in these cafeterias is like no cafeteria fare you've ever encountered—it's tasty, attractive to look at, and well-planned—for even when the French aren't trying, they do awfully well. Best yet, the cafeteria food is marvelously low-priced; you can see what you're buying and you can easily put together a meal for about $3.50. Finally, you can eat quickly, instead of dawdling for an eternity in the typical Parisian bistro. For your basic meals in Paris—the ones priced at the above levels—go to a cafeteria. They're scattered all over the city, rarely more than five minutes from any major location.

Not all the cafeterias, however, are similarly priced; they range from a number of wonderfully cheap (and generally independent) establishments charging 9 to 12 francs for main plates, to the generally higher-priced chain of Jacques Borel cafeterias, which can usually be recognized by the words "Auberge Express" in their titles. We've sought out only the cheaper cafeterias, and we'll now attempt a geographical rundown of them:

In the **Sorbonne** district, a typical choice is the **Latin-Cluny Self-Service (35)**, 98 Boulevard Saint Germain, corner of Boulevard St. Michel, where I recently stuffed on hors d'hoeuvres (3.50 francs), followed by a casserole dish of roast chicken, surrounded by parsley, potatoes, mushrooms and a delicious sauce (all for 12 francs). Total with wine: only slightly more than $4.15. No cover charge; no tipping. Other typical dishes: a small steak with french fries (11 francs), Frankfurt sausages with ham and sauerkraut (2.50 francs), cheese for 3.80 francs, a little jar of yogurt for 2.50 francs. And those are fairly representative prices, which you can expect to prevail in the lower-cost category of Parisian cafeterias.

Further up the Boulevard St. Michel, the cafeteria **La Source,** at 35 Boulevard St. Michel (just above the Rue des Ecoles), is a particular favorite of the students in this neighborhood, with prices a shade lower than those at the Latin-Cluny. Always look, here, for the "plat du jour" costing 9 to 12 francs ($2.07 to $2.76).

In the area of the **Arc de Triomphe** (100 yards away) the cafeteria **Le Self-Service Monte Carlo,** at 9 Avenue Wagram, is conveniently located, moderate—but not cheap—in price. Hors d'oeuvres for 3.50 to 4 francs, main courses from 13 to 19 francs, desserts for 3.50 to 4.50.

Behind the major **department stores,** upstairs at #73 Rue de Provence (near the corner of the Rue de la Chaussée d'Antin), **La Biella** is a bit more expensive than its cafeteria colleagues on the Left Bank: hors d'oeuvres range from 3 to 9 francs; a number of main courses are priced at 13 to 18 francs (although some are a franc or more higher). Closed Sundays.

On a sidestreet midway along the **Champs Elysées,** and only a few steps in from it, the **Self Elysées (36),** 67 Rue Pierre Charon, specializes in chicken, but has other dishes available; and offers typical-to-higher self-service prices (15 francs for "steak frites," 8 francs for an omelette, 12 to 19 francs for most other main plates). The very best of the Champs Elysées cafeterias is, however, located near the bottom (down-hill) end of the Champs Elysées, at the back of the arcade (and upstairs) at 34 Champs Elysées. Bearing the simple title **"Self-Service Restaurant",** it offers hors d'oeuvres for only 2.50 to 5 francs, main plates for only 8 to 15 francs, omelettes for 8 francs, coffee for 2.80 francs; a large meal for under $5 is quite easily possible. And the clear way in which food items are displayed should be a model for every self-service. Open seven days a week, from 11 a.m. to 9:30 a.m.

In the **American Express** area, the **Self-Service Rallye-Opera,** on the second floor of 35 Boulevard des Capucines, exactly one block up the Rue Scribe from American Express itself, serves a complete meal at lunch—hors d'oeuvres, entree, cheese or dessert, and bread—for 21 francs ($4.88). It's given a hard race by the **Restaurant Self-Service Caumartin** at 33 Rue Caumartin. To reach the Rallye-Opera, walk down the Rue Scribe from Am Ex to Boulevard Capucines, and don't confuse the cafeteria with the more expensive Restaurant Rallye, around the corner at Rue Daunou.

One block from the **Folies Bergère,** the super choice is the **Super Self Service Montmartre,** 16 Faubourg Montmartre (subway stop is Rue Montmartre); moderate prices, including an immense twin beefsteak with french fries for 14.50 francs, other main plates for less, and a full, three-course, prix fixe meal for only 20 francs ($4.65). This is one of the largest and best of the cafeterias.

In the area of the **Louvre,** almost directly opposite the Tuileries metro stop, the **Self-Service des Tuileries,** 206 Rue de Rivoli, between the Rue du 29 Juillet and Rue St. Roch, is another excellent cafeteria, but with prices a trifle higher than those in similar spots (main courses with vegetables for 10 to 14 francs).

And finally, in the basement of the **Galeries Lafayette** department store, the "Self-Service Bar Rapide" will serve your meal-time needs, but only at stand-up tables.

There are many others you'll discover in other areas. At all of them, you can eat for the same $3.50 to $5 price.

(3) The Bistros of Paris:
Full Meals for $4.80 to $7.60

But now, for your more leisurely meals, priced in the $4 to $6 range, we'll take up the subject of the Paris "bistro"—those little restaurants scattered around the city, where the art of French cuisine is often as well-practiced as on the Champs Elysées. The best finds for a budget vacation are the bistros serving "prix fixe" meals—a set three- or four-course meal for one lump sum. Since these restaurants concentrate on the dishes they've included in the "prix fixe" the cooking is apt to be very good, often better than the quality you'd find in a more expensive à la carte house. No self-respecting artist, student or other cost-conscious Parisian would eat in any but a restaurant offering prix fixe meals. I've scoured Paris for them, and have come up with the following finds:

Boulevard St. Michel area—Left Bank

We start in the same area recommended for your best hotel buys: the Sorbonne district, near Boulevard St. Michel. Get out at Metro stop St. Michel. Look to your left and you'll notice the small **Rue de la Harpe (22).** At 35 Rue de la Harpe (also near the Cluny metro stop) stands **La Petite Hostellerie,** a typically-tiny and inexpensive bistro, with good food and a friendly-to-American staff. Its budget prix fixe meal consists of three delicious courses and costs 33 francs ($7.67). Wine is 2.50 francs (58¢) extra. Open daily except Sunday, throughout the year.

For a somewhat more exotic meal, proceed up the Boulevard St. Michel, to Rue des Ecoles (our street for hotels), turn left, and in another block, you'll find the tiny Rue Champollion. The **Restaurant Champollion (24),** at 3 Rue Champollion, is also a tiny place, but the quality and moderate cost of its

French-Russian food have begun to attract persons from all over the Sorbonne area. The chef is the son of the Russian emigré who founded it in 1930; his three-course prix fixe meal is 32 francs ($7.44), including service charge; and his borscht (which you can order on the prix fixe) is a soup specialty that tastes like nectar. By the way, don't be scared away by the line of people that almost always blocks the door; the line is composed of Sorbonne students trying to get into the cheap movie theatre *next* door.

And now, if you're confident enough to attempt an à la carte restaurant, which has no prix fixe but remarkably cheap rates, then your destination should again be the Rue de la Harpe (that little street that runs off the Boulevard St. Michel, near the Seine), where you'll find **Les Balkans**, at 3 Rue de la Harpe, another enormously popular Left Bank establishment charging 10 to 13 francs ($2.32 to $3.02) for most main courses with vegetables. Generally, your meal here—carefully chosen—will run to less than $5; and if you're lucky, you can have the meal at a sidewalk table. You can also try another (and less crowded) branch of the **Restaurant Les Balkans** at 33 Rue Jacques (corner of Boulevard St. Germain). It may be my imagination, but I've always enjoyed the food at the St. Jacques branch of Les Balkans more than at the Rue de la Harpe location, even though the menus and prices are identical.

St. Germain des Prés—Left Bank

In another Left Bank section—near the Ecole des Beaux Arts—you'll find several budget restaurants of a particularly wonderful flavor. The **Restaurant des Beaux Arts (27)**, 11 Rue Bonaparte, across the street from the school, is anyone's conception of how a French restaurant should look: open kitchen in view of the diners, buxom waitresses, an intense, disputatious clientele. And a three-course, prix fixe dinner, including wine and service, for 24 francs ($5.58 see upper right hand corner of menu); à la carte prices totaling about $6.50 for a complete gourmet meal of excellent food.

On the other side of the Boulevard St. Germain, near the 17th-century church of St. Sulpice, is the restaurant **Lou Pescadou**, 16 Rue Mabillon, serving two prix-fixe menus at 21 and 26 francs ($4.88 and $6.04), wine and service included. In good weather you can dine al fresco under a bright red awning, savoring the typical sidewalk bistro atmosphere that abounds here.

A lighter, and cheaper meal, in the area of the St. Germain des Prés church, can be had at **A la Bonne Crêpes**, 11 Rue Gregoire des Tours (the little alleyway that leads into the Rue de Buci from the Boulevard St. Germain), where 14-or-so francs brings a prix fixe dinner that always includes "crêpes" (thin pancakes surrounding an inner ingredient of various sorts) as the main course. The meal comes with a bowl of cider, of all things, and the prix fixe total includes service charge. Heavily crowded with young people. Closed Sundays for lunch. . . . Nearby, **Au Vieux Casque**, 19 Rue Bonaparte, typically Rive Gauche, charges 25 francs ($5.81), for a three-course prix fixe, including wine and service.

Near the Palais Royal—Right Bank

If you're art minded and want to camp near the Louvre, you'll find a surprising number of good restaurants nearby. Walk the short distance from the Louvre to the Palais Royal. Alongside the Palais Royal runs the little Rue Montpensier, and next to it, runs the Rue Richelieu—two narrow little streets. At 23 Rue Montpensier, there's a narrow little restaurant which calls itself the Unbelievable—**Restaurant L'Incroyable (32)**—where a prix fixe meal of hors

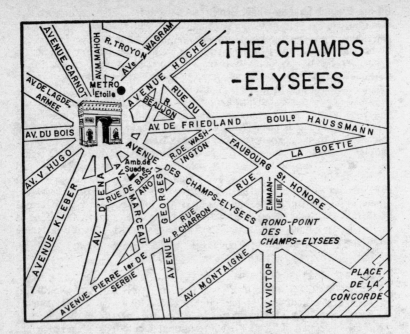

THE CHAMPS
-ELYSEES

d'oeuvres, meat, vegetables, cheese, fruit or dessert, wine and bread, costs 26 francs ($6.04), service included. There's another entrance to L'Incroyable, by the way, through a small arcade at 26 Rue Richelieu. Serves only from noon to 2:30 and from 6:30 to 9; closed Sundays, and the month of August. In the same general area, near the Tuileries Gardens, both **Pizza Pizzo,** at 12 Rue du Mont Thabor, and **Le Grand Directoire,** 2 Rue Cambon, charge a similar price for the same kind of meal.

Near the Arc de Triomphe—Right Bank

And amazingly enough, this next elegant section is the site of some of Paris' best restaurant values.

In the very shadows of the Arc de Triomphe, an exciting budget bistro (discovered for me by the then 12-year-old Josh Friedman, son of novelist Bruce Jay Friedman) is **A L'Etoile Verte,** 13 Rue Brey (just off the Avenue de Wagram, three blocks from the Arch itself), a bigger-than-usual cafe, with astonishing à la carte prices for an astonishing range of dishes: 5 francs for a dozen different appetizers, 15 to 18 francs for most main courses with potatoes, two francs for camembert or yogurt, 3.50 francs for soup, only 22 francs for a prix fixe menu, wine included. And all prepared with care and élan. Open daily throughout the year, except for three weeks in August.

A similarly inexpensive à la carte restaurant, in the same area, is **Au Rendez-vous des Chauffeurs,** 14 Avenue de Wagram, a block-and-a-half from the Etoile, and also convenient to our budget hotel selections on Rue Brey and Rue Troyon. Appetizers or soup for 3.50 to 5 francs, main courses for 11 to 14 francs, in all but a few instances. Closed Sundays.

Off the Champs Elysées—Right Bank

Can you eat cheaply near the Champs Elysées? You can, with a sort of pinpoint accuracy in choosing your restaurants.

Walk downhill on the Champs Elysées to the Rond-Point, and turn into the Rue Jean-Mermoz. At No. 19 Rue Jean-Mermoz, the restaurant **Chez Germain** serves a three-course menu for 28 francs ($6.57), with wine an extra 3 francs (69¢) per quarter liter. . . . Or, walking downhill on the Champs Elysées from the Arc de Triomphe, turn left on the third side street down, Rue Washington, to No. 13 Rue Washington. There, the tiny **Chateaubriand** serves a three-course menu ("le menu conseillé") for only 24 francs ($5.73), but without wine. Your best chance for finding a seat is at dinner time, not at lunch. Closed weekends.

STARVATION BUDGET—A RIDICULOUSLY CHEAP RESTAURANT ODDITY: Appropriate fanfare should now be heard for the astonishing **Restaurant Casa Miguel,** 48 Rue Saint-Georges (which runs off the Rue St. Lazare near the Gare St. Lazare, on the Right Bank; metro: St. Georges): Cheapest restaurant in all of France, that's what this next one is—a curiosity for whose continued prosperity (and survival) I pray each night. Open seven days a week throughout the year, from noon to 2 and 7 to 9, it charges only 5.50 francs for a three-course meal with wine, but then shyly adds that: "service non compris". For a total of six francs ($1.39), including the service, you choose from five different appetizers, but from a single main course, and select either cheese or fruit at the end. And you enjoy all this in a pleasant little room of eight tables covered with pink-checked oilcloths, under a sign reading: "Mangez mieux, mangez plus, Economisez." Is it a stage setting? A Russian plot? The work of a saint returned to earth?

But let me, in the manner of our former President, make one thing perfectly clear: Restaurant Casa Miguel is not of the quality of our "little wonder" restaurants earlier described; those are for tourists of every station, offering superb local color and ample food for the price. At Casa Miguel, portions are small (but you can order second helpings of anything for from 1.50 to 2 francs), and main courses consist of couscous au mouton (Algerian rice with lamb) on Sundays, Mondays, Wednesdays and Thursdays, of lamb with green beans or roast pork sausage ("saucisse de Toulouse") on Tuesdays, of maccaroni bolognaise on Fridays, and of lentils with lamb or pork sausage on Saturdays. But if all you have is 6 francs ($1.39), what a find!

A CHANGE OF PACE—COUSCOUS: Way back when, in the days of my first trips to Paris, "couscous" were a relatively rare food item, served only one or two days a week in tense Algerian restaurants, catering to an almost exclusively Algerian clientele. One evening, on my once-a-week visit to eat couscous, I arrived at one of these spots just minutes after the chef had been machine-gunned by fellow Algerian nationalists for some political misdeed.

Today, couscous—a sort of grainy Algerian rice, over which are poured meat and various sauces—are served daily all over Paris, and—with the advent of an enlightened French policy toward rebellious colonies—eating them isn't dangerous at all. The largest cluster of good, cheap couscous restaurants is found on the Left Bank, on the **Rue Xavier Privas,** a tiny street running off the Rue St. Severin, which itself runs off the Rue de la Harpe, near that point where the Boulevard St. Michel meets the Seine. Ask a gendarme.

The Rue Xavier Privas—"couscous street," to me—houses six different couscous restaurants charging 5 to 7.50 francs for appetizers (a tomato salad is good for openers) and from 15 to 22 francs for couscous and meat—enough for a sumptuous meal. These are, in ascending order of price, **Au Meilleur Couscous** at #10 Rue Xavier Privas (only 5 francs for tomato salad, 19 francs for couscous); **Le Latin** at #22 Rue Xavier Privas (4 and 15 francs for same); **La Belle Etoile** at #15 Rue Xavier Privas (20 francs for couscous, a tiny place); **Privas** at #9, **Au Village** at #14, and (most expensive of all) **Au Bon Couscous** at #7. One couscous is more than enough for two—no one ever finishes it alone—and with the couscous, you drink—you guessed it—Algerian wine.

THE WEE HOURS: When the sidewalk cafe starts to take in its chairs, and it's 1 a.m. and you don't want to sleep, walk down the Boulevard St. Germain towards the Eglise (church) St. Germain. A block before the church, you'll pass the little Rue Echaudé. Turn right, and you'll find the tiny **Restaurant Echaudé** —open till 3 a.m. It's the nearest you'll come to the life of Hemingway's *The Sun Also Rises*—you'll see what I mean. Prices in this jolly place: too high for a full meal (pieds de veau at 19 francs is the cheapest entree), but fine for a middle-of-the-night snack—desserts for 10 to 12 francs, a good coffee for 5 francs, a liter of wine for 16. L'Echaudé is closed Sundays and in August.

CHARCUTERIES: A final way to eat cheaply but well in Paris is to purchase picnic ingredients for do-it-yourself meals (consumed in your hotel room or in a park) at a Parisian charcuterie (delicatessen). But to call a charcuterie a delicatessen is to do this unique institution a severe injustice. They are more properly gourmet appetizer shops, selling subtly-favored pâtés, salads, cheese, pickled snack items, and the like, and they're heavily patronized by French housewives, who demand reasonable prices. Some addresses of typical charcuteries? The city's best, in my opinion, is the **Pou,** at 16 Avenue de Ternes, two short blocks down from the Avenue Wagram, and therefore only a short walk from the Arc de Triomphe. Closed Mondays. Runner-up, in the area near the Tuileries Gardens, is the immense **Gargantua** at 284 Rue St. Honoré, off the Rue des Pyramides. Nearer the Palais Royal and the Au Louvre department store, there's a typical charcuterie at 136 Rue St. Honoré, and another at 41 Rue Richelieu. Again on the right bank, at 1 Rue Montmartre, next to Les Halles, the **Bruneau** opens daily at an astonishing 4 a.m., closes at 7 p.m. Monday through Friday, 6 p.m. Saturday and 11:30 a.m. Sundays. And on the left bank, near the Panthéon, you'll find charcuteries all up and down the Rue St. Jacques, the best being at 198 Rue St. Jacques.

SOME FINAL FOOD TIPS: Wherever you eat in Paris, several rules of thumb will keep your costs down: (1) Order soup as your opening course; it's invariably priced at 3 francs, unfailingly good. (2) When in doubt, choose an omelette as your main course; French chefs coax marvelous results out of just-plain-eggs, and rarely charge more than 8 francs ($1.85), often as little as 6.50 francs, for the omelette of your life. (3) Alternatively, keep in mind that old standby, "steak frites," a small, thin steak with a mound of french fries made only as they do here, and invariably priced between 11 and 13 francs. It is always available in every restaurant and cafeteria, although it must often be specifically requested and individually prepared for you in cafeterias. (4) Eating in an à la carte restaurant, never order a separate vegetable ("legume") with your main course unless you're utterly famished; even though the menu may not mention it, your main course will already be "garni" (accompanied by vegetable or potatoes), and the order of a separate dish will simply result in an uneaten portion. (5) Try ordering yogurt ("yaourt") as your dessert, just as the French do. It costs only 2.50 francs, it clears the palate, and is, as Commander Whitehead would say, "curiously refreshing." (6) Finally, never let your eyes overeat in a cafeteria. Skip the appetizer, and order only a main course and dessert— usually, in Paris, that will be as much as you'll want or are able to finish.

READERS' RESTAURANT SELECTIONS (BIG SPLURGE VARIETY): "I heartily recommend the **Restaurant du Dragon**, 14 Rue du Dragon, Paris VI, metro stop Saint-Germain des Prés. This is truly a Frenchman's restaurant, with 'natives' lining up to dine before it opens for dinner at 7 p.m. Service was unusually attentive. For 27 francs, a full dinner included a ¼ bottle of wine, appetizer, several main dish choices and dessert. It is one block from the 'Drugstore' on St. Germain des Prés" (Henrietta Rothaizer, Kew Gardens Hills, New York; note by AF: The Dragon's 27 franc prix fixe menu, which includes wine and service, appears on the back of its hectographed and rather expensive à la carte menu; the restaurant is closed weekends and from August 10 to September 15). . . . "No visitor to Paris should miss a meal at the **Café Procope**. A special menu meal at lunchtime comes to 24 francs, though the dinner menu is a steep 55 francs, including service charge. The 24 francs buys the best food available in Paris, and the restaurant is atmosphere plus. The plaque at the door tells the reader that the 'café' was founded in 1686, and has been frequented by such diverse Parisians as Napoleon I, Voltaire, Benjamin Franklin, and Diderot. It is located at 13 rue de l'Ancienne Comédie, a tiny street near the metro Odéon—be sure to eat upstairs" (Robert M. Gill, Blacksburg, Virginia; note by AF: Many letters have come in praising Procope; it is closed the month of July). . . . "Just a few steps down from Le Drouot at 99 Rue Richeleiu, I enjoyed several of the biggest and best meals I have ever had, at the restaurant **Le Grand Richelieu**, also called **Chez Kadoussi**. For an incredibly low 28 francs ($6.51), you can eat *"à volonté"* (as much as you want). To begin, there is an hors d'oeuvres table consisting of an extensive display of patés and saucissons, salads, pickles, fresh and prepared vegetables, hard-boiled eggs, lentils, tuna, etc., etc., etc.!!! The mayonnaise is home-made and fresh. Next, you choose from a selection of 12 main courses. The menu usually includes several beef dishes, veal, couscous-brochette, duck à l'orange, steaks. Next, there is a large and varied selection of cheeses, followed by an amazing dessert table. The choice and the quality are staggering. Wine, bread and service are included. I still have trouble convincing myself that this place actually consists, although I ate there several times. I hope you will recommend it to others" (Elaine Goldberg, Brighton, Massachusetts). . . . "A perfect splurge is the restaurant **Monsieur H** at 65 Rue du Faubourg Montmartre, Paris 9, closed weekends and Monday evenings. For 37 francs ($8.60), you can eat all the hors d'oeuvres you want, pour your own unlimited wine from a wooden cask. After that, I had steak à la vodka, fruits and vegetables, choice of ice cream or pastry, cheese dish, and unlimited bread. The atmosphere is very nice; the price includes service" (Armand J. Boulay, Berkeley, California).

READERS' BUDGET RESTAURANT SELECTIONS: "We would like to recommend the **Self-Service Restaurant Capoulade**, 63 Boulevard St. Michel, up a flight of stairs just across from the Jardin du Luxembourg. We got a very ample serving of roast chicken and pommes frites for 10 francs, steak pommes frites for 12.50 francs. There's also a filling plat du jour for just 15 francs" (Rev. Earl Peterson, Paris, France). . . . "We found the very modestly priced **Restaurant de Bourgogne**, 172 Avenue de Clichy (metro stop Brochant). Three of us had couscous, brochette, wine and coffee for 90 francs, and the service and food were excellent" (John Nellis, Cincinnati, Ohio).

READERS' EATING TIPS: "My money-saving trick in Paris was to shop for my lunch in the little food shops where the Parisians go. A baguette of crisp, hot bread, a cheese or bit of pâté, some of those superlative strawberries, and demi-bottle of wine, and lunch was eaten in my room at a total cost of about $2.40 (American). To do this, *one must* speak at least basic French, but I feel one should try this anyway. If one does, the people seem more helpful and friendly and their smiles are warmer, even though they may be smiling at one's bad French. This trip was, without a doubt, one of the most marvelous things in the life of a fifty-ish grandmother, which I am, and I am planning to return next year, God willing" (Mildred H. Devlin, San Francisco, California). . . . "Tell your readers always to seek out the *marchés,* or open air markets appearing regularly once or twice a week at the same spot in Paris. (*e.g.,* there is one on Av. Pres. Wilson in front of the Musée d'Art Moderne every Wed. and Sat. morning). Besides being colorful and fun, they offer absolutely the best bargains and freshest foods: fruits, vegetables, cheeses, etc., all offered in a hurly-burly atmosphere, a tradition that goes back to the dawn of the first city and shows no sign of dying in Paris. Here your readers can get everything they need for a fabulous picnic except the wine and the bread. And you can also buy thread, underwear, flowers and 'bas-collants' (panty hose). The original one-stop shopping center! One warning: bring your own shopping bags" (Susan DeSimone, Paris, France). . . . "One good way to save money, or to permit yourself to afford a splurge, is to eat lunch in your hotel room. The basis, of course, is the wonderful French bread, which should be picked up fresh. The names, weights and prices of the various loaves are as follows: Gros Pain, 1 kilogram 5.75 Fr; Baguette Longue, 250 gr. 1.55 Fr; Parisien, 500 gr. 2.30 Fr; Petit Parisien (vulgarly called Bâtard), 250 gr. 1.55 Fr; Ficelle (small and round, nearly all crust), 100 gr. 1.20 Fr; Petit Pain, a 2½-oz. size that is ordinarily enough for one person, a complete small crusty loaf, 70 gr. 0.75 Fr; and a section of a longer loaf, about 60 gr. cut off a longer one, 0.40 Fr. . . . If one prefers a dark bread, it may be obtained (of a very fine quality) from a number of health food stores; if wrapped in a moist towel, will keep for almost a week, quite fresh. . . . Then, as a pièce de résistance, one should eat cheese. I began with one variety at a time, eating it until I got tired, first Brie, then Camembert, then taking up the smelly 'classic' cheeses, Pont l'Eveque and Livarot, and so on. A French cheese store presents an almost innumerable variety. Finally, after six months of cheese every day for lunch, I finally got tired of all cheese and took up cold cuts. A fine place is **Charcuterie du Seine** at 81 rue du Seine 6°; that store has a fine assortment at fair prices, for that is where the penny-conscious French housewives shop. . . . As for wine, one can easily afford a quality above the vin ordinaire; for 8 or 9 francs one can get wine with the words, 'Appellation Controlée' ('Registered Label') on the label; that was as good a quality as I could appreciate. With cheese one should drink white wine. If a novice, one may wish a somewhat sweet wine such as Montbazillac, or Entre Deux Mèrs" (Pauline Hadley Maud, New York City). . . . "What we usually do is buy our own food and eat right here in our hotel room for *less* than half the price we'd pay in restaurants. *And no service charge!* The food itself is nine times out of ten of better quality, as well. In Paris, the delicatessens are of a standard 'par excellence' and plentiful. Let me give you just one example of a typical 'homemade' meal: half a hot chicken costing 9 francs for two big double portions. A good French 'vin ordinaire' costs 6 francs per bottle, which is enough for two meals. Half a French bread costs about 65 centimes. Instead of chicken, you may have sausages or wonderful French meat loaves, all of which are beautifully and tastefully prepared. The above portions are big and can obviously be cut down considerably, but they are what we consider a good meal" (R.A. Dyker, Johannesburg, South Africa). . . . "Throughout our trip, we had no difficulty in finding nice, clean and inexpensive eating places. We also like to buy the good breads they have over there and have our evening snack in our room—with cheese, fruit, etc.; what could be better!" (Woodrow and Letress Berryhill, Phoenix, Arizona). . . . "A 'Croque Monsieur', consisting of ham and melted cheese on toasted bread, is a typically Parisian snack, and is available for 4 francs at cafes and street vendor carts. There is also a 'Croque Madame', which adds a fried egg on top, but is rarely seen" (Martha Brooks, Bryrup, Denmark).

DAYTIME IN PARIS—THE TOP TEN SIGHTS: The very best way to sightsee in Paris is simply at random, wandering wherever your fancy takes you, witnessing the colorful day-to-day life of the Parisians, and savoring the unexpected scenes and delights that every quarter of the city holds in abundance. But if you're determined to do it in an organized fashion, you'll need a quick checklist of the more important sights. We'd rate them as follows: (1) First, the Arc de Triomphe and the Champs Elysées (metro station for the Arc is Etoile, for the Champs Elysées go to Franklin D. Roosevelt); (2) Then, Notre Dame (metro is Cité); (3) Sainte Chapelle (Cité); (4) The Louvre and the Jeu de Paume (metro is Palais Royal for the Louvre, Concorde or Tuileries for the Jeu de Paume); (5) Invalides, the Tomb of Napoleon, and the Army Museum (metro is Invalides); (6) The Eiffel Tower (metro is Bir-Hakeim or Trocadéro); (7) Sacre Coeur and Montmartre (metro is Abbesses); (8) Versailles (metro to Pont de Sèvres, then bus 171); (9) The galleries and studios of the area of St. Germain des Prés—from here, walk down the Rue Bonaparte toward the Seine; and (10) the Pantheon and the Latin Quarter (metro is St. Michel, then a walk). Here's how to tour them:

ESCORTED SIGHTSEEING: Commercial sightseeing is expensive in Paris and readers will note that I've set forth numerous suggestions for do-it-yourself touring. Still, if you'd like a preliminary, escorted ride through the city, then you'll want to know that the wildest and most comprehensive tour of Paris is run by a company called **"Cityrama,"** which owns a fleet of double-decker buses almost entirely covered in glass—each is an apparition straight from a Jacques Tati movie. The customers sit in easychair-type seats, to which are attached ear-phones hooked up to a magnetic tape recorder, carrying a tour commentary in seven different languages. You dial your own language—just like at the U.N.—and then hear a canned commentary as the bus travels a pre-arranged route. The tour lasts three hours, costs 75 francs ($17.44), and leaves at 9:30 and 10 a.m., and then every hour until 4 p.m. (except at noon) from #2 Rue du 29 Juillet, which is off the Rue de Rivoli, near the Louvre, directly opposite the Tuileries metro stop. While **American Express (37)** and other tour companies offer slightly shorter, slightly cheaper (56 francs-$13.02) half-day tours of the city, theirs cover only one aspect of Paris per half day— either "modern" or "historical"—and aren't nearly as jazzy as the Cityrama. . . . During your visit, you ought not to miss a boat tour of Paris, along the Seine, which costs less than the bus does. The **"Bateaux Mouches,"** the tour boats, leave every half-hour between 10 and noon, 2 and 6 p.m., and 9 and 10:30 p.m., from a dock on the Right Bank, next to the Pont de l'Alma (metro stop is Alma Marceau), on a 1¼ hour cruise costing 15 francs ($3.48) per person, 7.50 francs for children under 12. This offers fantastic opportunities for camera addicts (the gargoyles of Notre Dame, the bridges of the Seine), and you'll be left with a striking impression of how awesomely beautiful Paris really is.

TIPS FOR INDEPENDENT SIGHTSEEING: Virtually all the museums and monuments of Paris (including the Louvre and Fontainebleau) are closed on Tuesdays, when you ought to take that trip to Versailles or Chartres. For consistent money-saving, schedule your visit to the Louvre for Sunday, when no admission is charged. . . . You can sit all day at a sidewalk cafe in Paris for the price of a cup of coffee; it's considered bad form for a waiter to ask you to move on. Watching the passing parade on the Champs Elysées in this manner is about the best form of entertainment in Paris—and it's free. . . . For a view of the Paris babes with a little less on, schedule an afternoon at the **Piscine Deligny**— a swimming area in the **Seine River,** Left Bank, next to the **Pont de la Concorde.** Two francs to check belongings, 11.50 francs to swim. . . . Most thrilling sights of Paris? The **Jeu de Paume,** a small museum on the grounds of the Tuileries Gardens, Place de la Concorde, housing the most famous impressionist paintings of the 19th century, which still aren't permitted in the Louvre. Closed Tuesdays; admission 6 francs, half-price on Sundays, free to young people under 18; don't miss the upstairs Van Goghs. . . . The **Eiffel Tower,** of course. Subway stop is Trocadéro, and the cheapest ascent (to the tower's first level) is 5 francs by elevator, three francs on foot. . . . The **Tomb of Napoleon** (an indispensable visit). . . . The **Musée de l'Armée,** behind the

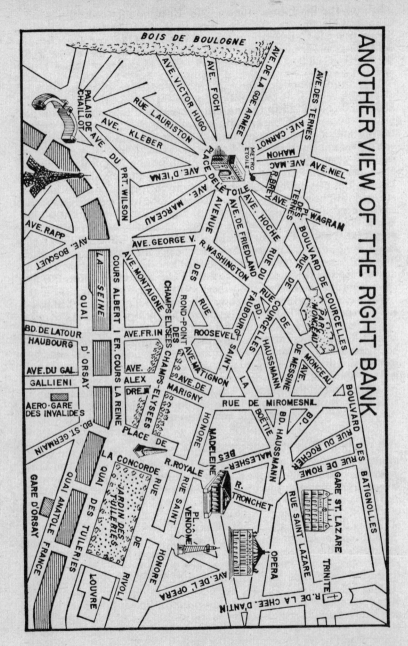

tomb (10 to 6 daily; closed Jan. 1, May 1, Nov. 1, and Dec. 25; 6 francs).
... **Montmartre,** at dusk. ... The **Rodin Museum** (6 francs admission, 3 francs
on Sundays), on the Left Bank, 77 Rue de Varenne (metro stop: Varenne), filled

with works by the greatest sculptor since Michelangelo. Closed Tuesdays.

SOME SIGHTSEEING MISCELLANY: The two-franc visit to the **Sewers of Paris** ("Les Egouts de Paris") is the continent's weirdest tour, on which you'll not only view a 200-meter section of the famous Paris sewer (shades of Jean Valjean!) but also peruse an actual midget museum devoted to the history of the Paris sewer system (only in France). Entrance is from a stairway on the southeast sidewalk of the Alma Bridge (Pont de l'Alma) across the Seine, at the corner of the Quai d'Orsay on the Left Bank. Take the metro to Alma-Marceau, then cross the bridge to the Place de la Résistance. In 1979, visits were permitted between 2 and 5 p.m. every Monday, Wednesday, and the last Saturday of every month; closed on public holidays and the day before and after the holiday. I'm hoping that, with Gallic logic, the schedule remains unchanged in 1980. . . . The open-air food markets of Paris, open every morning except Monday, are a fascinating sight as well as a valuable source of inexpensive picnic lunches and eat-them-in-your-room snacks. Try those on the Rue Mouffetard (Left Bank, metro is Censier-Daubenton), the Rue de Buci (Left Bank, metro is Odéon), the Cité Retiro (Right Bank, metro is Madeleine), or the Rue Lepic (Right Bank, metro is Blanche). . . . A "Do-it-Yourself" trip to **Versailles** costs a fraction of what the commercial tours charge. Simply take the subway (metro) to the Pont de Sèvres exit (it's marked "Coté Pont de Sèvres"), where you'll find the waiting place for municipal bus #171 (it's almost always there as you emerge from the subway). The bus takes 15 minutes for the ride to Versailles, charges 7.50 francs (but you can pay with three metro tickets taken from your carnet of 10, and thus spend only 4.50 francs). While you can also take a 3.80 franc train from the Gare Montparnasse to Versailles, that leaves at scheduled times only and goes not to the gates of the palace (as bus #171 does) but to the railroad station in Versailles, where you'll have to take another bus to the palace grounds. Bring a picnic lunch for a meal on the unbelievably magnificent grounds, and then—for the touring portions of your outing—simply attach yourself to any of the large groups being taken around. When the tour is over, don't fail to visit also the Petit Trianon and the Bergerie —the latter being a simulated farm where Marie Antoinette and her court cavorted as shepherds, herders, and the like.

VERSAILLES VIA EURAILPASS: "By far the best way for Eurailpass holders to get to **Versailles** is as follows: there is a commuter line to Versailles which has a train leaving every 15 minutes from a small station directly connected to the Invalides Metro station. It's a local line, but run by the S.N.C.F. (the French railways) and therefore free to Eurailpassers. One debarks at the Versailles-Rive Gauche station, turns right on coming out of the station, and proceeds along the street. Turn left at the first main street, and you will see the palace just ahead. This route is much faster than bus #171 and costs not a centime" (Mr. and Mrs. Roger Beare, Ottawa, Ont., Canada). . . . "Cheaper and faster than the bus to Versailles is the commuter railroad which goes along the left bank of the Seine. It looks exactly like the Metro and costs 3.80 francs. Changes from ordinary Metro to commuter system are at the Metro stations: **Invalides** and **Javel,** just follow the signs: 'S.N.C.F.—Versailles-Rive Gauche.' This commuter train ends up just 200 yards in front of the palace. Please do not confuse it with ordinary trains which stop miles from the castle!" (Matthias Risch, Munich, Germany). . . . "A tip we thought you might want to pass on to Eurailpass holders. By taking the Metro to the **Invalides** station, one can take a train there for free (with Eurailpass) to Versailles. It is then a five-minute walk to the Chateau" (Steve Alvo and Howie Ende, Flushing, New York). . . . "Chartres and Versailles can both be visited the *same* day if train departure is made from the Montparnasse station. This should be good news for those traveling by train and pressed for traveling time! Of course Eurailpasses are valid. The train destined for Chartres makes a scheduled stop at Versailles. We suggest going to Chartres first and stopping at Versailles on the return trip. (When leaving Versailles to return to Paris, a choice by train is available either via the SNCF Versailles station, from which the train goes to the Paris Montparnasse station, or via the Versailles SNCF Rive Gauche station whose train goes to the Paris Invalides station.) We saved additional time by returning via Invalides station. However, check the train schedule for your particular plans" (C. W. Page, Bethany Beach, Delaware). . . . "On the way to or from Versailles, one may get off the bus or métro at Pond de Sèvres and visit the Sèvres factory and museum for five francs. They also operate an outlet store for their fine chinaware products" (Douglas King, West Germany). . . . "Trips to Chartres and Fontainebleau can also be made by train, free of charge, by Eurailpass holders" (C. W. Page, Bethany Beach, Delaware).

THROUGH MEDIEVAL PARIS WITH HOPE: To gain the best appreciation of Paris, a study of its origins and medieval history is most important. My wife Hope has come up with a description of some fascinating sights, which follows now:

"The city was originally a village on the Ile de la Cité, in the middle of the Seine, where Notre Dame now stands. As an introduction to its mood, wander through the old section of the Ile between the Cathedral and the Quai Aux Fleurs, which used to be the Old Cloister and School area of Notre Dame, and where you'll see markings of the old Roman wall, the site of the home (on the Quai) of philosophy's most torrid, tragic lovers, Heloise and Abelard, wonderful medieval-looking alleys and homes, and the charming flower market of Paris.

Notre Dame

"**Notre Dame** itself, that grey stone Gothic marvel, begun in 1163 and now the very soul of Paris, is most often associated with Maurice de Sully, Bishop of Paris, under whose aegis it was begun, and Violett-le-Duc, who did a major restoration job on the Cathedral in the 19th century—unfortunately the original architect remains an anonymous genius. In touring it, don't hit and run. Notre Dame is beautiful from every angle and it's worthwhile and satisfying to walk all around her taking a good long look—sit for a moment in the small park in back to get the best view of the awesome flying buttresses of the Apse.

"Note especially the magnificent carved portals (almost the beginning of sculpture) and the famous Gothic Rose Window (begun in 1230), which became models for so much that was to come. As you face the Cathedral, the central portal is known as 'The Last Judgment'; on your right is 'St. Ann's Portal'; and on your left, the only door with a gable, 'The Portal of The Blessed Virgin Mary'—all intricately and cunningly carved. Inside Notre Dame (open every day from 8 a.m. to 7 p.m.), you'll want to see those two vivid Rose Windows at the intersection of the transept; both date from the 13th century but the rose-toned window has been greatly restored, while the predominantly blue-toned glass opposite, on your left, is almost totally intact. Also in the transept on the right side is the 14th century statue, The Virgin of Notre-Dame de Paris. And all around the Chancel is a quaint and lovely series of 14th century haut-reliefs, done in stone with gold, depicting scenes from the life of Christ. Unless you're very religious, skip The Treasury, which is not very interesting, is closed on Sundays, and also requires a 3 franc entrance fee. But if you can make it, it's quite a thrilling view from **The Tower of Notre Dame** (252 steps to the Grand Gallerie, another 90 or so more up to the South Tower), and worth the 4 franc ticket (half price on Sunday); open every day except Tuesday from 10 to 6, entrance around the left on Rue Cloitre-Notre-Dame, inside an iron fence (look for a sign reading 'Tours' which means 'Towers' in French).

"After your visit to the Cathedral, don't fail to spend a few extra minutes at the nearby Conciergerie, 1 Quai de l'Horloge, near the Pont au Change, and then at the Sainte Chapelle (in the Palais de Justice), both on the Ile (Metro stop for the Ile is Cité). Both of them charge five francs (2.50 francs on Sundays, and every day for students), and both are open every day except Tuesday. Hours to visit the Conciergerie are from 10 to 2 and 1:30 to 4 in winter (9:30 to 12 and 1 to 6 in summer); Sainte Chapelle's winter hours are 10 to 11:45 and 1:30 to 4:45 (10 to 11:45 and 1:30 to 5:45 in summer). The Conciergerie closes on Fridays in winter only.

The Conciergerie

"Once part of a medieval palace, the Conciergerie later became a prison to which most of the famous victims of the French revolution—Marie Antoinette, Robespierre, Danton and Madame du Barry—were sent to await their executions. A guided tour (French only) leaves every twenty minutes (no extra charge for this, but tip the guide), and as you wait in the dark, damp and very forbidding Gothic foyer, you'll be able to imagine how it must have felt to be led away from here to the Guillotine. You'll then be taken through the Salle St. Louis (or Salle Des Gens D'Armes), an enormous and impressive Gothic stone chamber, where you'll see the dining room and kitchen of the old palace, and the shaving room for prisoners who were about to be executed—and finally, you'll see cells that housed some of the personages named above.

Sainte Chapelle

"Just around the corner from the Conciergerie is the Sainte Chapelle (chapel), a stained-glass flower of the Middle Ages, with windows as alive and shimmering as a rainbow—an infinity of Biblical scenes, and a lovely rose window too. This was built in the 13th Century by St. Louis (King Louis IX, the Crusader King, who was later canonized) to house the Crown of Thorns and a piece of the Cross that Louis purchased in Constantinople. Surprisingly, for those like me who have always looked upon the Middle Ages as a dark and brooding time, the chapel is made almost entirely of glass, and inside (on the upper floor) it is so light and airy that you almost have the feeling of being in the open air.

The Pont Neuf and the Square du Vert Galant

"From here, you can rest awhile in the Square du Vert Galant, a charming tiny green park that is a ten-minute stroll away from Sainte Chapelle. Simply walk to the tip of the Ile (at the opposite end of the island from Notre Dame) until you find the equestrian statue of Henry IV (the Vert Galant himself—a fond nickname of the people for a king who was a noted ladies' man). Go down the stairs behind the statue, and you'll find the park, which is shaped like the 'prow' of the Ile, underneath the Pont Neuf. The Pont Neuf itself is the oldest bridge in Paris, and has a row of cunning heads carved along it; bearded and very hairy heads they are, too, some with the most comical expressions.

The Musée de Cluny

"From the Ile de la Cité, proceed now to the Left Bank, where you'll be able to visit the outstanding medieval museum of Paris: the Musée de Cluny at 24 Rue du Sommerard or 6 Place Paul-Painlevé (metro stop is Odéon or St. Michel)—a magnificently fanciful 15th century Gothic structure which houses a display of medieval painting, sculpture (including original pieces from the facades of Notre Dame and Sainte Chapelle), jewelry, religious and ecclesiastical relics, enamels, furniture, tools and household articles from the middle ages, as well as its most famous exhibit, the 'Lady and the Unicorn' tapestries. And as if all this were not reason enough to visit the Cluny, the 'cherry on the top' is the ruins of old Roman baths, located in the basement (where the exhibits have been expanding to include columns and sculpture from the Gallo-Roman era). Open daily except Tuesdays from 9:45 to 12:30 and from 2 to 5:15; a top sight but with a stiff 6-franc admission fee to visitors other than students, so go only on Sundays when you can get in for 3 francs.

"Now we move to the Right Bank, for a visit to the Marais.

Don't Miss The Marais

"Marais (or marsh-lands), supposedly the second oldest inhabited area of Paris (populated after the people outgrew the Ile), is now a workingman's living quarter with a large Jewish section (look for the colorful Rue des Rosiers), and is one of the most fascinating places in which to wander—not only because of its rather exotic present character, but also because it is dominated by the spirit of beloved King Henry IV, and has some of the finest old mansions in Paris. A good plan is to start with the **Place de la Bastille** (metro stop: Bastille), walk from there to the **Place des Vosges** and its **Victor Hugo Museum** (making a small detour to look at the **Hotel Sully** before entering the Place), and then on to the **Museum Carnavalet,** and the **Palais Rohan-Soubise.**

(1) Place de la Bastille (metro: Bastille)

"Prepare, first, for a surprise; what you will see as you emerge from the Metro is a cheery, busy, carnival-like, enormous traffic circle—a miniature Place de la Concorde—with nothing left to remind you of the grim prison except some tracings along the pavement that outline where the Bastille used to stand. In the center of the vast plaza stands the airy, delicate-looking, monumental **July Column,** which the adventurous tourist used to be able to climb, being rewarded at the top with splendid views of Paris. Now, alas, the structure is permanently closed to the public.

(2) Place des Vosges

"You used to be able to see the **Place des Vosges** (a genuine 17th century square, built by Henry IV) from the top of the July Column; now to get there, you take your life in your hands again and cross the traffic circle opposite the little stone ticket building of the July Column, to the Rue St. Antoine, walk away from the Column for four blocks, turning right on Rue de Birague (to reach the **Hotel Sully,** described below, continue a bit further along the Rue St. Antoine), and a few feet ahead you'll spot the entrance to the Place des Vosges. Inside is a large square and a strolling arcade and a very active kiddies' park in its center. The buildings today are all dulled oranges and yellows and crumbling, but the lush Renaissance spirit of Henry IV's pet project shines through nevertheless. The King was assassinated before the Place was completed but still it had its share of distinguished tenants; among them were Richelieu (#21), Corneille, Descartes, Pascal and Molière.

(3) Maison de Victor Hugo

"Not the least distinguished resident of the square was the genius, Victor Hugo, who lived at 6 Place des Vosges, now **The Victor Hugo Museum** (open from 10 to 5:40 every day except Monday; entrance fee is 3 francs, half price for students, free on Sunday), housing a collection of 19th century illustrations for Hugo's novels (you'll recognize those from *The Hunchback of Notre Dame*), a few Daumiers (caricatures on the staircase), a virtual gallery of drawings by Victor Hugo himself (350 to be exact: landscapes, castles, portraits); and costumes-pictures-manuscripts of many of his plays. But for me, the most personal and therefore the most interesting part of the 'Maison' is the third floor—the apartment occupied by the writer from 1832 to 1848, where you get a keen sense of the flamboyant spirit of the artist and the fantastic range of his talents: you'll see the incredible 'Chinese' dining room decorated and furnished by Hugo himself, and the intricately carved wooden bench (and two sideboards) that he personally designed. And, in addition to his writing desk, there's the usual death mask of the man of the house in his bedroom.

(4) Musée Carnavalet

"The Musée Carnavalet, nearby at 23 Rue de Sévigné (open every day except Monday and Tuesday from 10 to 5:40; entrance, sad to report, has escalated to five francs, but is still half price to students), is just a hop, skip and a jump from the Place des Vosges (or take the metro to Saint-Paul); to walk there, head diagonally across the Square from the Victor Hugo Museum to the Rue des Francs-Bourgeois, which leads to the Rue de Sévigné. The Museum is devoted to the history of Paris commencing at the end of the 16th century (antique street decorations, artists, famous people, events of Paris—especially rich material on the Revolution), and contains too many interesting relics to look at, let alone list. The mansion itself is also worth a visit: built in 1545 and decorated by the famous sculptor Jean Goujon (note the elegant sculptures on the façade and in the cour d'honneur), then touched up in 1655 by the celebrated François Mansart, it's a graceful stone building with a fastidiously manicured inner courtyard whose focal point is a statue of Louis XIV (a petit Versailles). Madame de Sévigné lived here from 1677 to 1696; she's the lady who wrote to her daughter and you can see some of her letters in the museum. Also inside, don't miss the model of the Old Bastille (on the ground floor); numerous mementos of Marie Antoinette and Louis XVI (locks of their hair, his shaving articles, games used by their children in prison, and some of the furniture from their cell at Temple); the palette of Daumier; Napoleon's field kit; and an astonishingly tiny glove worn by the Emperor (small hand, large ambition?).

(5) Hotel de Sully

"If you had the fortitude *not* to turn right at Rue de Birague (for the Place des Vosges), but continued along the Rue St. Antoine, you'll be rewarded at number 62 with the **Hotel de Sully**, recently cleaned and restored and wedding-cake lovely. Sully, as you know, was Henry IV's brilliant Minister of Finance who spent most of his days living in spartan simplicity until he retired and broke out into the kind of splendor you'll see in his 'Hotel.' This petit palais opens its doors to the public on Wednesday, Saturday and Sunday at 3 p.m. for a one hour guided visit (but only with French spoken), and the price is rather high: 10 francs for adults, 8 for children. If you are lucky enough to be in Paris during a Festival du Marais (in June, but not every year), you may see a concert here. Students or 'specialists' may be interested to know that the Hotel de Sully is the information center for all Historic Monuments of France. Programs of daily activities (which include listings of all cultural events: sound and light shows, festivals of dance, music and poetry, etc.), information on guided visits (tariff usually runs around 10 francs, in French—guided 2 hour walking tours available daily at 3; lower rates for groups and 30% off for students), maps, etc., available on request. During the tourist season (sometimes from mid-June to mid-July only), they also sponsor nightly visits of the illuminated Marais, with rendezvous usually at 9:30 in front of the metro station 'St. Paul' or from the Eglise Saint Gervaise—a two hour walking tour for 13 francs (11 francs for students). Still, it costs nothing to view the Hotel and its lovely courtyard from the outside, and it's worth making the side-trip to see it.

(6) National Archives in the Palais Rohan-Soubise

"The Palais Rohan-Soubise, home of the National Archives since the days of Napoleon and now also housing The Musée de l'Histoire de France, is a *short* five-block walk from the Musée Carnavalet, and located at #60 Rue des Francs-Bourgeois (at the intersection of Rue des Archives—nearest Metro is Hotel de Ville or Rambuteau). The Palais Soubise itself is worth seeing—a delightful, cream-colored, stone manor house flanked by classic porticos forming a long cobblestone courtyard (with old garret windows peeping over the wall) which invites you into the early 18th century building housing the Museum of the History of France. (Incidentally, the architect had the good taste to include the turreted door of the 14th century Clisson Mansion in his design for this palace—you can see it around the corner on Rue des Archives.) The Museum, open every day except Tuesday from 2 to 5 for a two-franc entrance fee (one franc on Sunday), displays original documents (letters from such as Henry IV, Richelieu, Marie Antoinette, Napoleon, etc.), and rare objects illustrating the history of France from earliest times on. But the most intriguing parts of the museum (and reason enough to visit here) are the two 18th-century rococo suites of the Princess Rohan-Soubise: the 'Chambre de Parade,' with its royally-outfitted red-canopied bed, gilded walls and crystal chandelier; and the even more impressive (and perfect in its way) 'Salon Ovale,' which is absolutely filled with gold—little gilded cherubs, inset wall paintings, mirrored and decorated to the teeth, but most pleasing. The surrounding neighborhood is fascinating, too, and full of history. If you have enjoyed what you've seen of The Marais and would like to know more about it or see more of it, pick up the excellent little brochure (with a marked map) called 'Le Marais' from the above-mentioned information center at the Hotel de Sully, or from The French National Tourist Office at 127 Champs Elysées, in the department called 'France-Accueil.'

Centre National d'Art et de Culture G. Pompidou

"This brand new, controversial Cultural Center, located on Rue Beaubourg, and often referred to casually as The Beaubourg (Métro: Hotel de Ville, Rambuteau or Chatelet), has fast become the most popular attraction in Paris, a bee-hive of activity that exudes gayety and a freshness of spirit, an audacious poem to technology, with all the "guts" of the building on the outside. One rides up to the exhibition floors on an escalator encased in an outside futuristic see-through tube, and the view of the city from the top terrace is spectacular.

But the fun starts even before you enter the building, in the outdoor square filled with all manner of street entertainers (dog acts, jugglers, magicians, snake-charmers, etc.), somewhat like a circus (and in fact, when I was last here, there *was* a circus encamped in the square, which may or may not be a permanent fixture). Inside, the scope of activities is broad and ambitious, almost as active as the happenings outdoors, and one can wander and see a lot before an admission ticket becomes necessary. There's a Library (including the latest in Audio-Visual), an Industrial Design Center, Children's Workshops (and a huge climbing nest for the kids outside), Music Center, Cinema, concerts, film, plays, and special exhibitions. And, of course, this is the new headquarters for the **Museum of Modern Art,** whose collection—in greater space—looks much better than before. Open daily, except Tuesdays, from noon to 10 p.m., and Saturdays and Sundays from 10 a.m. to 10 p.m. You can buy a 14 franc "Discovery Ticket" valid for the entire day and admitting you to everything.

Le Forum des Halles

"Built on the site of the now-demolished, once-celebrated, early-morning food market of Paris, **Le Forum des Halles**—a gigantic and partially-underground shopping center—has become the latest sightseeing attraction of Paris, following its opening in late 1979. Two hundred shops and boutiques, sixteen restaurants purveying everything from french fries to lobsters, one dozen movie theatres, a wax museum, banks and hair dressers, create a crazy melange, and the architectural style is a mixture of marble and neon, the engine-and boiler-room of a trans-Atlantic liner, the plexiglass gangways of Aeroport Charles de Gaulle, the sculpture of Niki St. Phalle, all connected by escalators and elevators, stairways and streets. On weekends, an estimated 200,000 Parisians and tourists go window-shopping here, sometimes shouting "merveilleux" or "horrible" as they glimpse a particular display. The rather expensive Le Forum is not recommended for shopping—at least not to readers of this book—but it's a must for students of modern society, an urban experiment that stirs the senses. Take the metro Les Halles or Chatelet.

More beauty marks of Paris

"Don't, of course, miss the gardens of the **Palais Royal** (built by Cardinal Richelieu), with their lovely shops and apartments (metro stop is Palais Royal, directly opposite The Louvre). The French Revolution was ignited here by Camille Desmoulins at the now-demolished Cafe Foy.... And schedule a stroll through the **Luxembourg Gardens** (metro stop is Odéon or St. Sulpice), which is like walking through a Seurat painting.... Attention all Interior Decorators, Designers, Scenery Designers, and Antique Collectors: you will love the **Musée des Arts Decoratifs,** 107 (and be sure you *enter at 107*) rue de Rivoli (metro: Palais Royal); entrance a too-high 6 francs (free to all students with valid I.D.'s); open from 10 to 12 and 2 to 5 weekdays except Mondays and Tuesdays, which has rooms full of furniture and trappings tracing the history of decoration not only in France, but in Europe and the Orient as well (also watch for exciting, very "*Now*" *S*pecial *E*xhibitions, which usually are worth the 8 franc admission).... **The Petit Palais,** Avenue Alexandre III or Avenue Winston Churchill (metro: Champs Elysées—Clemenceau, directly across the bridge from Invalides), has an interesting collection of antiques, mostly 'objets d'art' of the 13th to 19th centuries (including stamps, books, dishware, 18th century furniture), some sculpture, a small Flemish collection, some drawings by Rembrandt and Van Dyck, several Monets, Renoirs, Degas, Cezannes, Rodins,

Daumiers, Bonnards, Vuillards, and a whole roomful of Courbets. The inner circle of the museum contains the picture gallery, the outer one houses everything else, and there's a nice garden in the center in which one can rest. Tariff is 5 francs; free on Sundays; students can always get in for half price; hours are from 10 to 5:40 every day except Monday. (Warning: the Petit Palais plays host to many 'Special Exhibitions' and then remains open on Monday, but prices soar from 6 to 10 francs). . . . **The Galleries Nationales of the Grand Palais,** directly across the street, are used for temporary exhibitions of national character. Open daily, except Tuesday from 11 a.m. on—closing hours and fees vary depending on the show (and range from 5 to 15 francs, half price for students). This is not to be confused with the **Palais de la Découverte,** housed in another section of the Grand Palais, and described below.

For the kids

"The junior tourists will like the **Palais de Chaillot** (metro: Trocadéro), with its cafes and park fronting on the Eiffel Tower, and most important for its complex of museums, which are open from 10 to 5 (summers till 6) every day except Tuesdays, for charges averaging 6 francs (some offer half-price tickets on Sundays). Among the institutions clustered here are the **Musée de la Marine** (a maritime exhibition); the Musée de L'Homme (anthropology); the Musée des Monuments Français (historical survey in plaster casts and models of large French monuments; hours here are 9:45 to 12:30 and 2 to 5:15). And for the children who like fish, there's the **Aquarium of the Trocadéro Gardens** (facing the Tour Eiffel, go down the stairs to your left, signs will point the way) housed in a cold, dark grotto, open from 10 to 5:30 (6:30 in the summer) for a 2.70 franc admission fee (half price for children under 10, and special family rates). All the while, parents will undoubtedly enjoy themselves more at the nearby **Museum of Modern Art of the City of Paris,** (11 Avenue du President Wilson), which has a permanent exhibit of paintings and sculpture belonging to the city (not quite up to the standard of *the* Modern, but good—some Matisses, Dufys, Modiglianis, Utrillos, Picassos, Legers, Braques and Gris): it's also used for changing shows of very interesting 'now' painters. Admission 5 francs, half price for children and students (free on Sundays), and open every day except Tuesday from 10 to 5:45. . . . Directly across the way at #13, in the premises formerly occupied by the Museum of Modern Art, is the **Palais de Tokyo** (sometimes called the Palais de l'Alma), displaying an attractive collection of *Post* Impressionists, along with some works that were left behind when The Modern moved to Beaubourg. Here you'll see paintings by Seurat, Pissaro, Signac, Bernard, Maillol, Bonnard, and some wonderful Vuillard, among others—a collection that not only fills an historic gap, but creates a pleasant ambiance all its own. Open every day, except Tuesday, from 10 to 5:45, it charges 8 francs to see everything, 5 francs for just the Post Impressionists, half price for children and students, and half price for everybody on Sunday. . . . Elsewhere, the **Palais de la Découverte,** Avenue Franklin Delano Roosevelt (metro: F. D. Roosevelt), open every day except Monday from 10 to 6, charging 6 francs for admission (children under 3 admitted free, older kids pay 3 francs), is an Institute with working demonstrations in various branches of science (including space problems, computers and energy). All done with great flair, very much in the French manner. There is also a Planetarium here, for which you'll have to pay an additional entrance charge of 3.50 francs.

Some final thoughts on top sights

"First a warning: Ladies in spiked heels will not be admitted to ancient buildings or museums. . . . Now I'd like to set down, for easier touring, some extra data on a few must-see sights already mentioned by Arthur.

"The **Hotel des Invalides** (metro: Invalides), built in 1670–74 by Louis XIV as a home for pensioned soldiers—and now housing both the grand Musée de L'Armée (open every day from 10 to 6 except on Jan. 1, May 1, Nov. 1, and Dec. 25.), the Eglise St. Louis (the Army Church, decorated with banners captured from France's enemies, and containing mementos from Napoleon's tomb at St. Helena, as well as the funeral carriage which transported his remains to Paris), and the Eglise du Dome (an elegant, classical structure by Mansart, whose golden dome is a Parisian landmark)—is considered one of the finest buildings in the city. But the main reason why visitors flock here is that the Church of the Dome contains **Napoleon's Tomb** (open every day except Tuesday from 10 to 6, for an entrance fee of 6 francs, which also admits you to the Army Museum). Nineteen years after his death, Napoleon's wish to return to Paris was finally carried out (note the following words inscribed over the entrance to his tomb: 'Je désire que mes cendres reposent sur les bords de la Seine, au milieu de ce Peuple Français que j'ai tant aimé'), and he was buried with great pomp and ceremony along the banks of the Seine in this magnificent grey and white stone church. His tomb is sunken (one floor below, to get there use the staircases on either side of the rococo gold altar—you'll spot it as you enter), but is dead center in the middle of the building directly under the cupola, and has a balustrade around it permitting you to gaze down on the gigantic rust colored porphyry tomb (inside Napoleon is encased in six caskets!). Around the Tomb are twelve enormous, almost identical stone maidens, holding laurels or keys commemorating Napoleon's most famous battles. On the main floor, sharing the glory, are Napoleon's relatives and generals (to your left, as you enter, the most ornate gilded chapel is a memorial to Napoleon's son, the King of Rome, whose actual remains were lowered in 1969 and placed in a crypt at the foot of a statue of Napoleon in holy robes, facing the Emperor's tomb), and a few chosen heroes of France, such as World War I's Marechal Foch. Don't overlook the adjacent **Army Museum,** probably the best of its kinds in the world; its collections evoke the military and political history of France and all nations, from the Paleolithic era through World War II. Armor, weapons, cannon, flags, banners and uniforms through the ages, all very colorfully displayed and quite fascinating. Also, coming directly from his tomb, with Napoleon in the forefront of the mind, you'll find some astonishing exhibits on him: on the ground floor (in the building to your right, when approached from the Dome Church) is the standard flag room; but upstairs on the first floor you'll find Napoleon's tent, his death mask, his portable battle library, his sword, famous hat and greatcoat (now crumbling a bit, but very recognizable), and a number of personal objects used by him on Elba and St. Helena—including his death bed, and one of the Emperor's favorite horses, stuffed and decorated with his Parade Saddle. But skip the old Musée des Plans-Reliefs, which can be of interest only to the most technical military strategists.

"**The Rodin Museum** (metro stop: Varenne), at 77 Varenne, is located directly across from the side of Invalides (you will exit from the Dome Church to Avenue de Tourville, make a left to the Boulevard des Invalides, left again and cross the street; Varenne is the first street on your right), and is open every day except Tuesday from 10 to 5 (summers till 6) for a ghastly admission price of 6 francs; try to go on Sunday for only 3 francs. (Young people under 18 enter free, and students 18–25 pay half-price). The museum is housed in the enchanting dark grey stone Hotel Biron, a mansion surrounded by grounds which grow into a small park behind the house, providing a luxuriant background for Rodin's sculptures. To your right, as you enter the cobblestoned inner courtyard, is Rodin's most famous work 'The Thinker,' to your left the intriguing composition 'Les Bourgeois de Calais,' and the fantastic unfinished work 'The Gate of Hell' (of which 'The Thinker' is a central figure), which was partly inspired by Dante's *Inferno* and is a stunning depiction of the agonies of mankind. Rodin is usually regarded as a poet of romantic or sexual love (i.e., 'The Kiss' or 'The Eternal Spring'), but when you look around this museum, which once was his home and has originals or replicas of nearly everything he did, you begin to sense another side—a brooding imagination concerned with tragic thought as well (note, for example, the evocative 'Obsession' or 'Main Sortant de la Tombe,' 'The Good Genie' and 'The Bad Genie,' as well as 'The Gate of Hell'). Two of my favorites (both on the second floor) are the nude study of Balzac rising from a tree-trunk (which caused a furor when it was first shown); and the tender, young, striving wholly upward-moving 'L'Enfant Prodigue.'

"The **Jeu de Paume** (Place de la Concorde, open every day except Tuesday from 9:45 to 5:15—tickets on sale till 4:45; admission is 6 francs (2.50 francs on Sunday, always free to young people under 18), already mentioned by Arthur, is devoted to impressionist paintings (Manet's famous 'The Picnic,' Degas, Renoir, Van Goghs, Monet, Cezanne, Gauguin) and is not, on any account, to be missed. But directly behind the Jeu de Paume, and often overlooked, is the little **Museum of the Orangerie** (also part of The Louvre, it is used mostly for special exhibitions), which gave me a surprise and thrill on a trip or two ago to Paris. I had come to see a special showing of the works of Vuillard, and wandered unaware into two large oval rooms on the ground floor which contained Claude Monet's painfully beautiful, absolutely other-worldly, shimmering 'Les Nymphéas' (right, the famous 'Water Lilies')! This is a rare experience; beg or borrow, but see it if you can. The Museum is open every day, except Tuesday, from 10 to 8 p.m. (Wednesdays till 10 p.m.), but admission is a sad 10 francs, 6 francs on Saturday, for students, and 3 francs for children. But if you're not particularly interested in this month's 'Orangerie Special', you can see only the 'Salles de Nymphéas' for 5 francs on weekdays (half-price on Saturday), from 10 to 5:15 (of course, your general admission ticket to The Orangerie *includes* admission to 'Les Nymphéas,' even with an evening purchase; save the ticket and come back with it the following day): there's a separate entrance on the Seine side—inquire at the main desk.

"Still another 'must' for art lovers is the now quite celebrated **Marmottan Museum,** which was transformed from a seldom visited collection of Renaissance and Empire furnishings (and a few Monets) to a major attraction by the acquisition in 1971 (through a bequest by his son) of 65 of Claude Monet's paintings. The exhibit, in a specially built wing of the museum, entitled 'Monet and His Friends', includes the work of other famous impressionists (portraits of Monet by Renoir, works by Pissarro, Sisley, Delacroix, others), and is probably the largest collection of Monet anywhere in the world—the impact is stunning. Downstairs, the large canvases are breathtaking: there are some renowned oils as well as the famous world of blue and purple Water Lilies, casting a mysterious spell of infinity caught; and several unfinished paintings which look surprisingly avant-garde. Unfortunately, the Marmottan, at 2 rue Louis-Boilly (just off the Bois de Boulogne), is not very centrally located—best take the Metro to La Muette; it's a pleasant walk from the station and signs will point the way. The Museum is open from 10 to 6 every day except Monday, for a 10 franc admission fee, while students pay half-price.

"Just a word about **The Louvre** (it'd be rather pretentious to try to say more), open every day except Tuesday from 9:45 to 5:15, for a 6 franc admission, half price (3 francs) for persons under 25 or over 65, and free to all on Sundays (metro stops are Palais Royal or Louvre). This may be the world's greatest museum, but it surely is one of the world's hardest museums to see. You can't possibly cover all of it, but the more time you have, the greater will be your reward. I have never recommended this before, but for the Louvre, it might not be a bad idea to invest 7 additional francs in one of the guided tours the museum provides (in English and French, duration 1 hour, 15 minutes) every day except Tuesday and Sunday at 10:30 and 3 (or the Bureau of Information will give you explanations, in French, of what you are seeing in the painting galleries). Of course everyone knows about and wants to see the 'Venus de Milo,' 'Winged Victory,' and Da Vinci's masterwork, the 'Mona Lisa,' but there is much more here—over 125 works classified 'masterpieces'! The Greek and Roman Antiquities present a stunning collection (watch for fragments and pieces from The Parthenon); there is so much in the department of Paintings and Drawings I can't even begin to talk about it (but please try to see the Rembrandts—four of his great self-portraits and 'Bathsheba', among others). In the room of 'The Mona Lisa' are more excellent Da Vinci's near the door, Veronese's stunning 'Marriage at Cana,' Giorgione's haunting 'The Concert,' and Titan's 'Man with the Glove.' To the right of the 'Winged Victory' are famous Botticelli frescoes from The Villa Lemmi; there are unusually complete collections of Egyptian and Oriental Antiquities; Sculpture; and Objets d'art (including the 'Galerie Apollon' with 'The Crown Jewels', Napoleon's Crown, Louis XV's Crown, and a ring of St. Louis). Bon Appetit! And make it a long feast."

A READER'S EXCURSION TO MALMAISON: "Anyone interested in Napoleon (and Josephine) can easily make the short excursion to **Malmaison,** the 'relax-away' home that General Bonaparte and his wife bought a few years after they were married. Located in Rueil-Malmaison, about 10 miles outside Paris: take the new R.E.R. subway line from Auber or L'Etoile to the La Defense station (and *not* to Rueil-Malmaison, too far from the chateau), then take Bus #158A to Chateau Malmaison, which is a short walk from the bus stop. (When you exit from the Metro, the bus stop is right there, just *be sure* you are waiting in the correct place for #158A—the bus ride costs 5 francs and takes about 15 minutes.) Malmaison, which incidentally was built on the grounds of what used to be a leper colony (hence, the name), is open every day except Tuesdays and legal holidays from 10 to 12 and 1:30 to 5:30 (winters they close one hour earlier), and the price of admission is 6 francs, and half-price for everyone on Sundays. This small charming gray stone Chateau, with a manicured garden in front and sizeable park in the rear, is full of history—many important institutions and documents were created here; it was to Malmaison that Josephine retired after her divorce, and here she died; it was to this home that Napoleon returned from Waterloo, etc. And since the home contains the possessions of Napoleon and Josephine and most of the original furnishings, the spirit of this famous couple lingers evocatively about the place—especially Josephine's. Of the more formal rooms on the ground floor (the classical vestibule, drawing rooms, elegant dining room with golden state serving dishes, music room, Napoleon's library), probably the most striking is the Council Chamber, which is decorated like a military tent (the one where Cassius met Brutus flashed across my mind). Upstairs, among many important mementos (fancy dress clothes worn by the Emperor, including his Coronation Robe, a table made to commemorate the victory at Austerlitz, the well-known painting 'Bonaparte Crossing the Alps' by David, dishware, etc.), most interesting to me was Josephine's sumptuous red-draped bedroom, with her ornate Empire bed (golden swans form the sides of the head-board), and filled with personal objects such as her slippers, hats, shawls, sewing table and her portable 'toilette.' You also see her bathroom (a plumbing feat, I guess, in its day). A guide is included in your entrance fee and you must wait for him to take the tour (French speaking only); a small tip is expected" (Pauline Rissman, Chicago, Illinois). . . . Note by HA: "Avid Napoleon enthusiasts will also want to make an excursion to the famous **Fontainebleau,** so intimately associated with the Emperor: he made his famous 'Farewell to the troops' in the grand 'White Horse' courtyard here; signed his first abdication from the Fontainebleau study (you'll also see his bedroom, Josephine's bedroom, and much more). And of course, the grounds and the Chateau (dating back to St. Louis in the 13th century, and added to helter-skelter by succeeding monarchs) are gorgeous. Here one finds not only exciting historical associations, but also many rooms of sumptuous art-work—of special note, the 'Salle de Bal' and 'Gallery of Francis I'. Trains for Fontainebleau leave from the Gare de Lyon (early a.m. departures, late p.m. returns—check the train schedules); roundtrip fare is 34 francs for a 2nd class ticket. When you arrive at the town of Fontainebleau, you'll find buses to your left as you exit from the station; they leave every 15 minutes for the Chateau and cost one franc; Entrance to the Palace, which is open daily except Tuesday from 10 to 12:30 and 2 to 5, costs 5 francs, half-price on Sunday."

READER'S SIGHTSEEING SUGGESTIONS: "You'll have to add the **Catacombs of Paris** ('Les Catacombes de Paris,' 2 bis Place Denfert-Rochereau, Paris XIV; 6F admission) to your list of weird tours. From October 16 through June 30, the catacombs are opened at 2 P.M. on the 1st and 3rd Saturday of each month (every Saturday from July 1 through October 15). Arrive with your boots on about thirty minutes early and be prepared for a macabre one-hour hike through subterranean tunnels. The tomb entrance bears the inscription 'Arrête, c'est ici l'empire de la mort.' As you pass below this admonition, you will view the remains of literally millions of Parisians, whose bones were placed here when certain cemeteries were needed for other purposes. Begun as a tomb near the end of the 18th century, the catacombs became the final resting place for many of the victims of the French Revolution" (A. Emerson Smith, Columbia, South Carolina). . . . "The **Catacombs,** for me, were among the highlights of my trip. (Metro: Denfert-Rochereau; Saturdays only.) The cost is 6 francs to enter. Upon entering you descend a dark, narrow, winding stairway. Then you walk down dark, damp passageways until you come to the first room of bones stacked in symmetrical designs. Every so often you will come across a sign which gives the date and the name of the cemetery from which the bones were dug up. (Dates begin in the 18th century and continue into the 19th century). Don't be shocked by the long line. Everyone will be admitted with little waiting once the doors open" (Joyce C. Swenson, Encino, California). . . . "At Pont D'Austerlitz on the Seine, you'll find the **Jardin des Plantes** (Place Valhubert, Paris V), one of the oldest public gardens and zoos in Paris. In the park itself, there are experimental flower gardens, a huge tropical hot house (afternoon tours available), a zoological museum and plenty of benches for enjoying this beautiful little uncrowded oasis in the heart of Paris. The excellent **Menagerie** (5F adult admission) is full of exotic animals and is maintained as part of the science center of the University of Paris. This zoo is smaller and not as crowded as the much larger, more publicized zoo at the Bois de Vincennes, Avenue de Saint Maurice, Paris XII" (A. Emerson Smith, Columbia, South Carolina). . . . "Terrific fun for kids: the **Jardin d'Acclimatation,** the Children's Amusement Park in the Bois de Boulogne, which charges a 3 franc entrance fee to all over the age of 3, and is open from 9 to 6 (metro is Les Sablons). Nearby, and fun for you (kids might enjoy it, too) is the new **Musée National des Arts et Traditions Populaires,** open daily except Tuesday from 10 to 5. Six francs to enter, free for kids under 18, and half price for everyone on Sunday: entrance is around the corner from the Jardin, on Route du Mahatma Gandhi" (Mrs. Lou Levy, Springfield, Illinois). . . . "It's an easy and worthwhile excursion from Paris to see the historic **Basilica at St. Denis** (legend has it that St. Denis was buried here, and the present church had its early beginnings in 475); take the metro to St. Lazare, then change to metro line #13 to Carrefour Pleyel (watch the light-up signs on the platform, do not go to Clichy), it's the last stop on the line; then, just at the metro exit, take bus #153 or #142 to the church. This is not only the first great Gothic Church, and therefore the model for much that was to follow (e.g., Chartres, etc.), but it was also the burial place of all the kings and queens of France (from Dagobert on). Unfortunately, most of the bodies were exhumed during the French Revolution, but the tomb sculptures were saved—and they are fascinating, because from the time of Phillippe III (late 13th century) the royal likenesses were done from actual death masks. Also, the Romanesque Crypt does contain the tomb of the Bourbons, where the bodies of Louis XVI, Marie-Antoinette and Louis XVIII are buried. You must wait for a guide to take you through and the cost is 4 francs—open for visiting from 10 to 6 (winters till 5) daily, except Tuesdays or when a religious service is in progress" (Pauline Rissman, Miami, Florida). . . . "The best panoramic view of Paris is to be had—free—from the roof garden of the **Samaritaine Department Store** at the Pont Neuf. Go to the #2 store, take the elevator to the 9th floor, and walk up one additional flight; you'll find the railing decorated with illustrated maps indicating landmarks, and the use of a telescope will cost 25¢ to 30¢—depending on the scope. An inexpensive outdoor cafe on the roof itself makes this a good mid-afternoon stop-off. And Samaritaine is one of the city's biggest and most complete department stores" (Mr. and Mrs. Arthur Lake, Paris, France). . . . "An afternoon's entertainment that no female in Paris should miss is the high fashion couturier showings. They start every afternoon at 3 p.m. at all the houses. Many of the smaller houses require no reservation or appointment—just appear at 3 o'clock. Each house presents its line in its own way, and each is a fascinating experience, all for the price of a little ingenuity—if you don't give in to expensive temptation!" (Ann Fomin, Dearborn Heights, Michigan). . . . "**Pigalle Street** is filled with clip joints; readers should be advised against going to see any of the Parisian Striptease shows on or near Pigalle. But it does offer perhaps the most interesting free entertainment in Paris. Merely wander up and down the streets and alleys and *look*" (Nathanial R. Risenberg, Madison, Wisconsin). . . . "The **Marché aux Puces** (flea market) at the Porte de Clignancourt is open on Saturdays, Sundays and Mondays, and advertises itself as the biggest in the world; everything is to be had there at varying prices, from carrousel horses of the 19th century to sandals, Chinese vases, books, old coins, clothing, campaign supplies, chickens, and hours of free entertainment watching people try to think of a practical use for the old brass thingamajig they've got their hearts set on buying" (Victoria Rippere, Paris, France). . . . "The most impressive new sight in Paris is the **Monument to the Two Hundred Thousand Who Died in the Concentration Camps.** It is reached by crossing the Pont de l'Archevêché, directly behind Notre Dame—the monument is located in the Square de l'Ile de France. There is a flight of stairs at the tip of the square which leads down to the major part of the edifice, and the sculpture inside the crypt-like building and the poetry on its walls are an experience I shall not forget. Nor will I forget the inscription you read as you leave: 'Pardonne, Mais N'Oublie Pas' " (Mrs. Henrietta Rothaizer, Flushing, New York). . . . "I would advise others to steer clear of the Place de l'Opéra area if they're looking for local atmosphere. One of my favorite devices was to plan to be near the 'Galeries Lafayette' or 'Au Printemps' department stores around lunch time and have a tasty and inexpensive light lunch in one of the innumerable small restaurants in that vicinity. Camembert on a baguette with white wine is delicious, followed by a fresh fruit and black coffee" (G. LaPorte, Brooklyn, New York).

EXCURSIONS INTO THE ILE DE FRANCE: "A visit to Paris is incomplete without a visit to at least one of the towns or chateaux of the Ile de France, some of which rival those of the Loire Valley itself. Such points may be reached quite conveniently by frequent trains from Paris. Among the sites available to you are the following: **Fontainebleau**—round-trip rail fare is 34 francs, and a bus marked 'au château' will take you to the door of the famous palace for an additional two francs. The bus leaves from the square in front of the station. Another excellent day excursion takes you to the chateau of **Rambouillet,** a favorite residence of General De Gaulle; **Maintenon,** the exquisite home of Mme. de Maintenon; and the cathedral of **Chartres**—in that order, and all for 48 francs. Maintenon is my favorite of the French chateaux (and I saw some 20 in the Loire Valley alone)—and a walk through the little town provides a charming rural French vista. But an early start is necessary to see all three sights. My advice is to forget Rambouillet and to visit simply Maintenon and Chartres. Another excursion would be to the race track, chateau, and museum of **Chantilly.** And from Chantilly one can take a bus to **Senlis,** a gem of a French town with cathedral, chateau, and ancient Roman ruins. Anyone wanting to spend a night in rural France would do well to do it in Senlis. Total cost of a ticket to both towns is only 27 francs round trip. A final fascinating rural town is **Provins,** an ancient walled city famous for its roses, which was once more important than Paris itself. Rail fare is 51 francs round trip" (Robert M. Gill, Blacksburg, Virginia). . . . "Consider an excursion to the village and chateau of **Chantilly,** about 26 miles from Paris. Take the metro to the Gare du Nord, stop and hop on one of the frequent trains to Chantilly. If you're feeling energetic, you can walk from the train station to the chateau (about 20 minutes); otherwise, take the bus marked Chantilly-Senlis, which leaves the station every hour or so. If time permits, have a meal at the **Lion D'Or** on the road to the chateau. Fixed price menu for 22 francs, including regional specialties such as rabbit. And be sure to try some of the famous Chantilly cream" (Mr. and Mrs. Dennis Halloran, Madison, Wisconsin). . . . "**Chartres Cathedral** is a must! Trains run hourly from the Montparnasse Station at 24 francs each way" (Steven and Linda Cades, Edison, New Jersey). Note from HA: Trains leave almost every two hours (check R.R. schedule; take the Metro to

Montparnasse) and a fast train will reach Chartres in one hour. This Romanesque-Gothic cathedral, with its differing spires, flying-buttresses, and magnificent sculpture around the entire edifice, is awe-inspiring and not to be missed. The Treasury and the Towers are open from 10 to 11:30 and 2 to 6 weekdays; Sundays 2 to 6 for the Treasury, but the Towers are closed. Inside, you will be able to see the Crypt (the oldest part of the Cathedral) and muse upon the 167 windows: each tells a story, and most are different from one another. Some look like glittering celestial postage stamps: all are gorgeous). . . . "Do-it-yourself trips to **Fontainebleau** can easily be made by train from the Gare de Lyon, for a round-trip cost of 34 francs" (Isaac Barry, Chicago, Illinois). . . . "A worthwhile side-trip, via Eurailpass, is to **Mont St. Michel.** Trains leave fairly frequently from the Montparnasse station bound for Avranches, where you can catch a train for the town nearest to the Mont. From here, it is about five minutes by bus, on an inexpensive ticket" (John Kuehnle, Painted Post, New York).

EVENING MISCHIEF: The nightlife of Paris is available to you in infinite variety, but it's most cheaply pursued by simply sidewalk cafe-sitting, as the world and demi-monde passes by before you. Spend one evening on the Champs-Elysées, another at one of the congregating points on the Left Bank (St. Germain des Prés, Boulevard St. Michel), but avoid three of the more expensive sidewalk cafes of Paris: the Cafe de la Paix near the Opera, the Cafe des Deux Magots and the Cafe de Flore near St. Germain des Prés. Contrasting with them in price is the huge cafe **La Coupole** on the Boulevard Montparnasse (Left Bank, metro is Vavin), where coffee costs 6 francs and can suffice for an entire evening of cafe sitting (closed in August).

Variety Music Halls

And then try an evening of French vaudeville, liberally sprinkled with topless showgirls. The **Theatre Mayol,** 10 Rue de l'Echiquier (metro stop is either Strasbourg-St. Denis or Bonne Nouvelle), specializes in such strippers, presents two shows (4:15 and 9:15 p.m.) every day except Wednesday, has some back orchestra seats for 58 francs, balcony locations for 40 francs, standing room for 25 francs. Its counterpart on the Left Bank, the **Bobino Music Hall** in Montparnasse, 20 Rue de la Gaité (metro stop is Gaité or Edgar Quinet), places a greater emphasis on musical acts, including Beatles-type quartets, girl singers, and the like. Here, standing room is again only 25 francs, balcony is 50, and the show begins at 8:30 p.m. on all nights other than Monday, when the theatre is closed (Sunday matinee at 5). The big pop stars, and occasional musical extravaganzas, appear at the large **Olympia Music Hall** on the Blvd. des Capucines, near the Madeleine, where some seats sell for 35 to 55 francs.

The Theatre and Nightclubs

Three, in particular, are musts for your Paris stay. The renowned **Comédie Française,** first, for its stylized productions of the French classics—Molière, Racine, Corneille. Most of its performances start late—at 8:30 or 8:45 p.m.—and side gallery seats can be had for as little, believe it or not, as 12 francs, while the gallery de face and second balcony have excellent views for 25 and 35 francs. To purhcase the cheapest seats, go to the little sidewalk ticket office ("au petit bureau") located not at the front of the theatre, but alongside it, on the Rue Montpensier. It opens half an hour before each performance and dispenses third and fourth gallery seats for 11 francs, amphitheatre seats for only slightly more. Located on the Place du Théâtre Française, next to the Palais Royal, the metro stop for the Comédie Française is Palais-Royal. . . . Next, the Paris **Opéra** which, unfortunately, is closed from July 20 to September 15. Orchestra seats sell for a maximum of 200 francs ($46.51); but descend rapidly from there, and are available for as little as 20 francs in the upper locations; a surprising number of seats can often be picked up the day of the performance (during boxoffice hours, from 11 a.m. to 6 p.m.). Metro is, of course, Opéra. If tickets are unavailable, try the lighter operas *(Marriage of Figaro, Madame Butterfly, La Bohème)* at the **Opéra Studio de Paris** (formerly the Opéra Comique, closed in summer), 5 Rue Favart (off the Grands Boulevards; metro is Richelieu-Drouot), where the maximum price is 60 francs ($13.80), and numerous good seats can be picked up for between 20 and 30 francs.

I don't recommend that you see the **Folies Bergère**, because I think you'll find the production has become sloppy and the nudity de-emphasized. But knowing that no one will take this advice, I do at least recommend that you get the cheapest admission possible, which is a seat in the second gallery ("fauteuils galeries deuxieme série") for 57 francs ($13.25), as compared with the 152 francs ($35.34) charged for top orchestra locations. The Folies, with those elaborately plumed and costumed beauties parading before lavish stage sets, are located at 32 Rue Richer (metro stop is Cadet), and there's a show every evening except Monday at 8:45 p.m.

LES CAVES: These are the smoky basement nightclubs in which the impecunious of Paris nurse a single drink for hours on end. The youngest students go to the **Caveau de la Huchette,** 5 Rue de la Huchette, for a 20 franc entrance fee, which includes the right to buy the first drink inside for only 6 francs, or to **Le Chat Qui Pêche,** 25 francs entrance, including the first drink. The latter is also on the Rue de la Huchette, off the Place St. Michel. . . . Serious, and older, jazz addicts like the **Trois Mailletz,** 56 Rue Galande, which is off the Rue St. Jacques, a block from the Blvd. St. Michel, near the Seine, 5 francs entrance, 20 francs per drink at the bar; top, avant garde bands; closed Mondays and late July and August. Don't go unless one of the big names (Memphis Slim, Bill Coleman, Don Byas, Slide Hampton) is playing. . . . The older folks (or even young, tired ones) will enjoy the **Caveau des Oubliettes,** a few steps from the Trois Mailletz (go to #11 Rue St. Julien le Pauvre, in the courtyard of the 12th Century Church of St. Julien le Pauvre, you'll see signs), where there's a homey show of French folk-singing, and reasonable admission and drink prices. It's great fun and your only charge is a 35 franc drink, which allows you to see the show, presented from 9 p.m. to 2 a.m. Afterwards, a guide takes you further into the depths to see chastity belts, instruments of torture, and the holes ("oubliettes") through which medieval prisoners were once dropped into the Seine. . . . In the area of the Ecole des Beaux Arts (near the St. Germain des Prés), the top student "cave" is **"Le Riverbop,"** 67 Rue St. Andre des Arts (18 francs weekend entrance, drinks from 10 francs, mostly jazz and little dancing; closed Sundays, Mondays, and the month of August), followed by the more expensive and elegant **"Le Caméléon,"** 57 Rue St. Andre des Arts (dancing downstairs, where the first drink is 18 francs on weekdays, 25 francs on weekends; magnificent jazz band; no dancing upstairs where the drinks are 10 francs. Closed on Sundays all year, open Friday and Saturday nights only in August. . . . And finally, there's now a Right Bank "cave," the **"Slow Club,"** 130 Rue de Rivoli (near the Louvre), where entrance is 30 francs, but drinks are only 5. Teenagers and students in their early 20s are the clientele; many, many singles of both sexes. The action begins at 9:30 p.m., closed Sunday and Monday. . . . Remember, all these spots are the basements of ordinary-looking cafes; the excitement doesn't begin until you walk downstairs.

Just plain ballroom dancing, for older tourists? That takes place daily at the big **La Coupole,** 102 Boulevard du Montparnasse (downstairs), on the Left

Bank, from 4:30 to 7 p.m. and from 9:30 to 2 a.m. Drinks at night are 30 francs, service included, but that's all you'll need to pay for a full evening of dancing to a live band, among couples and stags in their 30s and 40s. Take the metro to Vavin.

SOUND AND LIGHT: Finally, an impressive evening show that for years has been presented only for a French-speaking audience. Now, in 1980, the illuminations, music and dramatic commentaries ("Sound and Light") in the courtyard of **Les Invalides** (metro is La Tour Maubourg or Invalides) are available in an English language version at 9 and 11 p.m. from Easter to November (but only at 11 p.m. in June, July and August). The charge is 17 francs ($3.95) per person, 12 francs for children under 12, the show is called "Shades of Glory", and the "shades" are those of Louis XIV, Napoleon, L'Aiglon, and Rouget de l'Ile, whose words you'll hear as lights play upon different sections of the historic structure built by the architect of Versailles. It's a special sort of evening entertainment for a visit to Paris, and about the cheapest evening show you'll find in the city.

THE METRO: Once you get the hang of it, the Paris subway system will become one of your best touring aids, inexpensive and efficient. There are 14 subway lines, all criss-crossing each other like the grids on a map. To reach your destination, you must usually make at least one change ("correspondance"): you go up one line and then across another, or across one and then up another. This seems complicated, but the task is eased by a lighted board on the wall next to the ticket booth in most Paris metro stations. You press a button opposite the name of the station to which you want to go. Immeidately, the board lights up, showing the two lines you must take to reach your destination. It becomes clear instantly. Paris subway fare (second class) is 2.50 francs (about 58¢) to any point in the city; but a book ("carnet") of ten subway tickets is only 15 francs, reducing the cost of each such ticket to only 1.50 francs (34¢)—always buy the book of ten tickets.

A FINAL NOTE: Readers staying in Paris for at least a month will want to take French language lessons at the renowned **Alliance Française,** 101 Blvd. Raspail (nearest metro is Notre Dame des Champs or Saint Placide), phone 544-38-28, where you can enroll any week throughout the year, and where the fee is only 280 francs ($65.11) a month for a daily, two hour course. The school also operates an 11-franc restaurant and numerous social events, and is one of the best places around for "meeting people" in Paris. . . . Tired of those interminable waits to cash travelers' checks at American Express? A French money-changer, across the street and then a few doors up at Rue Scribe #9, has no line—and sometimes gives a better exchange rate, to boot! . . . A long thin loaf of that wonderful French bread costs only 1.30 francs at any neighborhood bakery. Buy sandwich ingredients at a nearby "charcuterie," and you've beaten the high cost of living in Paris. . . . And ordering wine in any French restaurant, ask for a "rouge ordinaire" or a "blanc ordinaire"; all of them carry ordinary table wine, which you'll find to be surprisingly tasty and cheap. . . . In fact: "Three things in Paris are cheap," goes the saying. "Bread, wine and the métro." In any Paris cafeteria, a long loaf of crusty French bread is 60 centimes, a small bottle of red wine is 3 to 3.50 francs, and a big slab of luscious country pâté, pickle on the side, is about 5 francs. Spread the pâté on the bread, slice and arrange the pickle, imbibe it all with the wine, and you have an ever-satisfying 6.85 franc ($1.58) meal. . . . In Parisian groceries, the price affixed to meats and vegetables is the price per kilo (2.2 pounds), and that's usually more than you'll want. 200 grams ("deux cent grammes, s'il vous plaît") of lunch meat or pâté will usually suffice for two or three persons, 150 grams for two.

OTHER $$$-A-DAY-BOOKS: Europe on $15 a Day has now been supplemented by six other $$$-a-day guides dealing with individual European countries or areas: **Ireland on $15 a Day, Greece and Yugoslavia on $15 & $20 a Day, Spain and Morocco (plus the Canary Islands) on $10 & $15 a Day, England and Scotland on $20 a Day, Scandinavia on $20 a Day,** and **Turkey on $10 & $15 a Day.** In contrast with the book you are now reading, which deals primarily with 17 major European cities, each of the above guides treats in depth one particular country or area, and sets forth hotel, restaurant and sightseeing suggestions for literally scores of individual cities and tourist destinations in that country or area. The $$$-a-Day Books can be obtained at most bookstores, or by mailing the appropriate amount (refer to the last page in this guide) for each book to: Frommer/Pasmantier Publishing Corporation, 380 Madison Avenue, New York, New York 10017.

READERS' TIPS: "The **Alliance Française** (101 Blvd. Raspail) can be one of the most frustrating places to walk into. Here is information on where to go and what to do. When you arrive, with a view to enrolling in a course, proceed through the main entrance doors (opposite the newsstand) and go up the stairs to the first floor (French first floor, that is), turn right and go to Room #11. In this room behind the desk are the only officials who speak English here. Here you will be given a test and some forms to fill out. (Don't be afraid of the test. It's the only basis they have for placing you.) The test is used primarily for the grammar courses so if you want conversation also or instead, please make this known. Further, they will require your passport and two photos. Near the school on Boulevard Raspail, there are photo machines which charge three francs for the necessary pix. These pictures will be used when you pay, which is done after registration, on the main floor. Before you know it, you're a student in Paris. If all the commotion disturbs you when you arrive and you're frustrated because you can't speak to anyone and don't understand the signs, wait for someone carrying the **Herald Tribune.** He or she will have been through it all and will have the answers" (Ken Caunce, Ontario, Canada). . . . "Readers should be aware that enrollment at **Alliance Française** entitles them to student discounts at theatres, cinemas, parks and museums in Paris. If you have your student card from Alliance Française (or an International Student ID card), be sure to ask 'Avez-vous un rabais pour les étudiants?' ('Do you have any student discounts?') whenever an admission fee is charged. Many establishments do not openly advertise these student discounts; so, always present your card and ask for a discount. Discounts at parks and museums run about 30% and at the cinema (except those on the infamous Champs-Elysées) about 20 to 30%. Show up at the box office of many theatres about 45 minutes before a performance and receive about 30% off on any seat not sold by that time" (A. Emerson Smith, Columbia, South Carolina). . . . "It was in Sweden that I heard about the **Accueil Franco-Nordique,** 66 Rue St. Lazare (phone 280-30-27), which specializes in placing Scandinavian girls in French homes. Girls have their choice of working 2 hours for room, or 4 hours for room and board, or five hours for room and board and pocket money. The work usually consists of simple housework and child care which enables the girl to practice her French while living as a member of a French family. This agency will now accept American girls who wish to live in Paris to study the language and the French way of living. They would be grateful if girls would include international reply stamps with their letters, though, as this is a non-profit organization which cannot pay high mailing costs (later there is a $30 fee). There is also a club the agency sponsors to promote activities between the au-pair girls and the French young people. The agency is willing to help girls with any problems that might arise, and in my case definitely helped me to adjust to a different environment" (Janice Frederickson, Glenview, Illinois).

THE OTHER WAY TO ORLY: "At Orly, walk past the Air France buses, and just after you'll find buses operated by the city of Paris, whose fare is only three subway tickets (4.50 francs) OR 7.50 francs cash. The buses leave every ten to fifteen minutes and take you to Place Denfert Rochereau (Metro: Denfert Rochereau). From there, you can take the Metro to wherever you like. (The Hotel des Bains and Grand Hotel des Écoles are within walking distance.) Service begins at about 6 a.m. and lasts until late at night. Transportation can be acquired in any direction (from Orly to Rochereau or vice versa). Besides, you'll be glad to see that you're mingling with stewardesses and Parisiens, and not simply other tourists" (Alan Minz, Montreal, Que., Canada). . . . "The S.N.C.F. (French National Railway) now has a cheap and convenient rail connection between Orly Airport and the S.N.C.F.-Pont St. Michel Metro stop. A bus called 'S.N.C.F. Aerogare' departs from Orly Airport about every 20 minutes. It connects with a train which runs to the Pont St. Michel Metro stop (which is quite central). Eurailpasses are accepted. From Pont St. Michel, one can then make Metro connections to almost anywhere in Paris. This rail route is much cheaper and more convenient that the Air France bus service" (John Albin Broyer, Edwardsville, Illinois; note from AF: for cheap (5 metro tickets), rapid, city bus transportation to **Le Bourget** or **Charles de Gaulle Airports,** take bus #350 from the Gare de l'Est (which is also a métro station), or (to Charles de Gaulle only) bus #351 from Place de la Nation (also a métro). For Orly, as outlined above, take bus #215 from Place Denfert-Rochereau).

PARIS ON $15 A DAY: With continental breakfasts for $1.50, hotels for $8 per person, and meals prix fixe, you can easily keep basic costs to a reasonable figure. Since all these items can be found, with a little effort, for lesser sums, there's room for leeway in your travel budget—even in high-priced Paris.

Brussels is next. Trains leave from the Gare du Nord several times a day, take three hours for the trip.

Chapter VI

BRUSSELS

The Triumph of Miniver Cheevy

THERE IS A SQUARE in the heart of Brussels, called La Grand' Place, which instantly reveals the character of this city. It's a spectacular sight: I know of none other in Europe to equal it—neither Princes Street in Edinburgh, nor the Duomo in Milan, nor the Place de la Concorde. This is a square whose only buildings are the ancient and untouched Guild Halls of the Middle Ages. Each is festooned with a brilliantly-colored medieval flag, and the cornices of the buildings are covered in pure gold leaf. Stand in this square, and you will be thrillingly transported to the world of Breughel and Van Eyck, of Rubens and Bosch. But—

You can be bored silly in Brussels—bored, that is, unless you approach this town with either the proper background or inclination for it. Ever hear of the old adage that Europe brings to you only what you bring to it? That's Brussels. If you're a medievalist at heart, or have a fairly substantial desire to study that age, then you'll love Brussels. If not, stay far, far away, for this city is all history, and little else. It has neither the fleshpots of Paris, nor the grandeur of Rome, nor the boisterousness of Munich. It does offer a unique introduction to the culture that is Flemish—that strange amalgam of the French and Dutch—which occupies such a vital place in the art and events of Western Europe.

You'll want to see: the **Muséc de l'Art Ancien,** Rue de la Regence, housing the most magnificent collection of Flemish art in the world (open daily except Monday from 10 a.m. to 5 p.m.; admission 17¢); the **Palais de Justice,** on the Place Poelart, an incredibly massive stone structure, whose courtyard affords a panoramic view of Brussels below (admission is free); the **Hotel de Ville,** on the Grand' Place, a superb example of Gothic architecture with only one flaw:

an off-center door in the main tower (an apocryphal legend, almost certainly untrue, has it that the architect committed suicide when he discovered his mistake); the battlefield of **Waterloo,** just outside the city (take bus "W" from Place Rouppe to Waterloo, the last stop); and finally, the statue which all the ladies from Dubuque deplore: the **Manneken-Pis,** which isn't vulgar at all in its Brussels setting (just behind the Hotel de Ville, off the Grand' Place). Other spots of interest are listed in a booklet which you can obtain from the Brussels Tourist Office at 61 Rue Marché-aux-Herbes (phone 513-89-40), just off the Grand' Place.

First, though, you'll need a hotel, of which Brussels has many moderately-priced specimens, but of a somewhat lower quality than you'll find for the same price in other European cities. That's because this is one of the continent's most expensive cities. Thus forewarned, be assured that you can still live on a budget in Brussels, as follows:

HOTELS: Nearly everyone travelling to Brussels wants to stay near the **Grand' Place (9),** close to the colorful restaurants and medieval atmosphere of the narrow streets that jut off the main square. But there's only one, budget-priced establishment in the streets immediately adjacent to the square: that's the highly-recommended **Hotel aux Arcades (10),** on the narrow, medieval Rue des Bouchers #36 (phone 511-28-76), occupying a superb Flemish structure built in 1696, and far more attractive inside than its ancient façade would indicate. It's also pleasantly and cheerfully operated by an English-speaking staff (who play classical records in a breakfast room beautifully decorated with murals of scenes from the life of Till Eulenspiegel), and therefore worth a splurgey rate of 700 francs ($23.33) double, 820 francs ($27.33) twin, including breakfast, service and tax for two. Just a bit further away, directly in front of the Central Station (which is not to be confused with the Gare du Midi), the nearly-as-well located **Hotel Elysée,** 4 Rue de la Montagne (phone 511-96-82), is a tiny place which unhappily asks a high 900 francs ($30) for a bathless double, breakfasts, taxes and service included (singles are far too high for this book). Less expensive and a true budget find for Brussels—but around 250 yards from the Grand' Place and 100 yards from the Bourse: the **Hotel Ruche-Bourse,** #1 Rue Gretry (phone 218-58-87). Another small place, with 16 rooms and 22 beds, it charges 550 francs ($18.33) single, 660-700 francs ($22-$23.33) double or twin, 825 francs ($27.50) triple, always including continental breakfast served in the tiny ground-floor restaurant. In that same restaurant, between noon and 2 p.m. only, a hearty two-course meal—such as vegetable soup, followed by steak tartare with Belgian french fries and salad—is offered for 130 francs ($4.33) by the English-speaking owner (and cook), Mr. Verhoest. An alternate address for the Ruche-Bourse: 23 Rue des Halles.

Off the Place Rogier

If you've been to Brussels before, you'll recall that the area of the most plentiful budget hotels was once the **Place Rogier (1),** which stands at the head of the garish Boulevard Adolphe Max, the main street of Brussels and—in the words of the cab drivers—"un petit Broadway." Except for the magnificent "Grand' Place," the Boulevard Adolphe Max contains virtually all the city's nightlife—the movies, theatres, cafes. Therefore, the Place Rogier district is for those who like action and excitement, neon signs and bustling sidewalk cafes. Unfortunately, so much construction of new office buildings and department

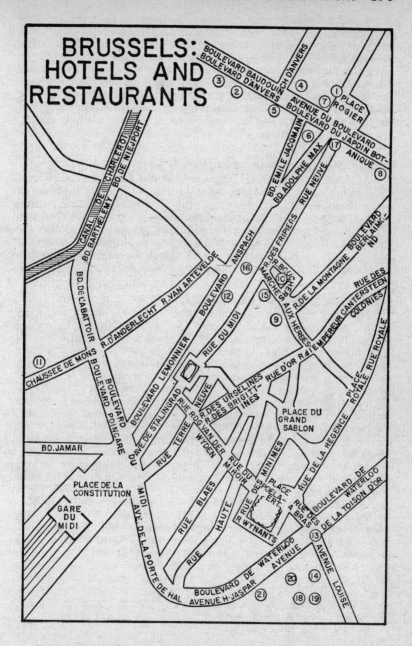

stores is currently in progress around the "Place," that only one, suitable, budget hotel remains undemolished. To find it, seek out the broad boulevard bearing different names—"Boulevard d'Anvers," "Avenue du Boulevard,"

"Boulevard du Jardin Botanique"—which runs perpendicular to the Boulevard Adolphe Max, just below the Place Rogier. Then, from the big square, walk for about 200 yards down this wide avenue to the **Hotel Avia**, 10 Boulevard d'Anvers (phone 217-55-88 or 217-02-65), and ascend the stairs to a walk-up lobby decorated with postcards mailed in by satisfied customers from around the world. Rates are currently 400 francs ($13.33) per person for a bathless double room, including breakfast and all else, only 500 francs ($16.66) per person for a room with private bath or shower. And while the surroundings outside are rather dingy, the hotel itself is proper, pleasant, relatively modern, and within walking distance of the Gare du Nord.

Cheaper Hotels on the Boulevard du Jardin Botanique

A fairly basic budget hotel is located a few blocks from the Place Rogier, uphill on the Boulevard du Jardin Botanique. That's the 60-bed **Residence du Jardin Botanique (8)** at 171 Rue Royale (tel: 217-82-20), just off the Avenue, which directly overlooks the beautiful gardens, enjoying one of the best sites in Brussels, and yet offers rooms for as little as 300 francs ($10) single, 550 francs ($18.33) double, 250 francs ($8.33) per person in triples and four-bedded rooms, including breakfast, service and tax. (Much recent renovation has considerably improved this elevator-equipped establishment).

Near the Gare du Midi (and less expensive)

Now walk out of the Gare du Midi (South Station) one block to your right, and you'll be on a square (Place Bara), off which runs the Avenue Clemenceau; this is at the end of the long main street of Brussels known successively as the Blvd. Adolphe Max, Blvd. Anspach and Blvd. M. Lemmonier, and therefore away from the bright lights and activity that converge near the Place Rogier; but the area is easily accessible to that action by direct street car. We mention it because, at 1 Avenue Clemenceau, the **Residence Clemenceau** (phone 521-45-38) is a particularly appealing, homey, and comfortably-furnished guesthouse that prices its rooms at 350 francs ($11.66) per person in a double room, 400 francs ($13.33) per person in a twin, breakfast, service and tax included. While there is no elevator at the Clemenceau (and there are five floors), there are radios in every room, a little lounge, and paintings everywhere. Highly recommended. Its only disadvantage is an 11:30 p.m. curfew, which owners Mr. and Mrs. Nollomont justify as permitting them to dispense with the cost of a night porter. If you can't live with that curfew, then head for the **Hotel du Merlo** at 2 Avenue Fonsny (phone 538-15-69), next to the station, where bathless singles are 280 to 335 francs ($9.33 to $11.16), doubles 380 to 520 Belgian francs ($12.66 to $17.33), triples 590 to 750 francs ($19.66 to $25), the higher rates in each range being for rooms on the first three floors, the lower prices for rooms on the fourth floor. And if you'll agree to climb to the fifth floor (there is no elevator), you'll enjoy the romantic atmosphere of rooms looking out "sur les toits de Bruxelles" for only 170 Belgian francs ($5.66) per person in a double, 215 francs ($7.16) single. For all guests, an optional breakfast is served in the ground-floor cafe, next to the three billiards tables, for 65 francs ($2.16) per person. A simple, but entirely clean and proper, place.

Three old standbys

Finally, a large second class hotel (90 rooms, 160 beds), which usually has room available when the others are filled, is the **Van Belle (11)**, 39 Chaussée de Mons, phone 521-35-16 or 521-35-40. This hotel throws in a free breakfast with its all-inclusive rates of 430 francs ($14.33) per person (but only to persons who show them this book on registering) for a double room sans bath; it's located three trolley stops (take tram # 101) from the Gare du Midi, and is the always reliable budget hotel of Brussels: each room is attractive and unique; windows sparkle and floors are waxed to a high gloss; and a semi-American breakfast—orange juice, cornflakes, cheese, rolls, coffee or hot chocolate—is served in a pleasant dining salon with adjacent bar. Single rooms with breakfast: 585 francs ($19.50), again reflecting a 5% discount given to readers of this book. . . . More conveniently placed, but more heavily booked, is the large **Hotel du Rhin**, only steps off the Place Rogier at 90 Rue St. Lazare (phone 217-06-86). This is the classic group hotel of Brussels, and rates reflect that function: 384 francs ($12.84) per person in a triple room, 343 francs ($11.43) per person quad, 398 francs ($13.26) per person in a bathless double, 468 francs ($15.60) per person twin, 605 francs ($20.16) single, always with breakfast included, and all for tastefully furnished accommodations, some of them enhanced by oil paintings done by the owner's talented Japanese son-in-law, Mr. Shimohara. These are specially reduced rates for readers of this book. . . . Elsewhere, in the "upper" section of Brussels known (to me) as "Little America", near the Brussels Hilton and the chic shops of the Avenue de la Toison d'Or, the 30-room **Hotel les Chevaliers**, at 68 Rue de Stassart (phone 513-34-60), is a cheaper standby—but solid, reliable, even a bit bourgeois, at 465 francs single, 810 francs ($27) double, 900 francs twin, breakfast and all else included. A restaurant and bar on the premises provide three-course prix fixe meals for 210 francs, as well as a decorous pool table whose use is free to guests.

And incidentally, all of the hotels just named are considerably superior in surroundings to the hotels earlier named, although none of them approaches the low rates of the latter.

PEACE AND QUIET: For older tourists, the most elegant section of Brussels is the **"Porte Louise" (13)**, where you'll find the quiet Rue de Suisse, just two blocks off the Avenue Louise. Here, a superb pension charging 475 francs ($15.83) single, 600 francs ($20) for a double room, breakfast included, is the **Pension Les Bluets**, 24 Rue de Suisse (tel: 538-44-28), with garden and large, old-fashioned rooms, perfect for readers seeking restful accommodations. "Bluets" is the name of a blue prairie flower, and owner Madame Mente grows lovely lilacs in the garden. An alternate in the same area, if les Bluets is full: the **Residence Osborne** at 67 Rue Bosquet (phone 537-92-51), charging 430 francs ($14.33) single, 610 francs ($20.33) double. To maintain those low rates at the immaculate and well-furnished Osborne, English-speaking owner Vladimir Jansen asks guests to make their own beds, though rooms are otherwise cleaned by maids. . . . Nearby, the even more exciting and much larger **Hotel-Pension Astor**, 9 Rue Capitaine Crespel (tel: 511-60-86), a beautifully-furnished townhouse closer to the activity of the Porte Louise, is also recommended—particularly for families (to whom it offers 3- and 4-bedded rooms). Room and breakfast at the Astor, for two persons, totals 660 francs ($22), including breakfast, service and tax. . . . To reach les Bluets from the Porte Louise, walk down the Avenue Louise to the Rue Jean Stas, and follow that street to Rue Suisse. To reach the Osborne, walk one block from les Bluets. To reach the Astor (one of the best of the lodgings recommended in this chapter), simply head for the new Brussels Hilton on the swank Avenue de la Toison d'Or, only 50 yards away; then, from the Hilton, look for the little Rue des Drapiers which curves into the Rue Capitaine Crespel.

Three other recommendable Porte Louise choices begin with the **Richmond House Hotel,** 21 Rue de la Concorde (tel: 512-62-59), elevator-equipped and with pine-paneled dining room and elegant reception room with carved and gilded ceiling, marble fireplace and crystal chandeliers. Rooms have an assortment of furnishings with an emphasis on rattan and bamboo. Rates for bathless doubles, including breakfast and free showers, are 650 to 700 francs ($21.66 to $23.33); tiny singles begin at 425 francs, and larger singles are 450 to 500 francs. Next, the attractive **Concorde Louise** at 59 Rue de la Concorde (tel: 512-86-10), which has 12 bathless rooms for which a special rate is offered if you display this book: singles for 548 francs, doubles 744 francs, triples 1,088 francs, breakfast, service and tax included. Finally, the **Residence Berckmans,** 12 Rue Berckmans (tel: 537-89-48), offers spotlessly maintained rooms furnished in an assortment of flea market-type antiques. Bathless singles are 330 to 480 ($11 to $16), doubles 550 to 685 francs ($18.33 to $22.83), triples 710 to 870 francs ($23.66 to $29), breakfast 75 francs extra. Lower rates are for the rooms on the higher floors, and a 10% discount is given to readers of this book, starting with the second day of their stay.

STARVATION BUDGET ROOMS: Despite their title, the **"Student Homes"** of the Free University of Brussels, available to visitors from July 15 to September 30 each year, are rented to students and non-students alike, of any age, and offer one of the great values in European lodgings: individual rooms with complete bathrooms, assembled around a common living room with refrigerator, for only 200 francs ($6.66) per person per day, including breakfast, for persons under the age of 26 staying for more than 3 days; for 220 francs ($7.33) per person, including breakfast, for under-26ers staying less than 3 days; for 440 francs ($14.66), however, for persons over the age of 26 (although I'm told the age and price distinctions aren't too strictly observed). The nearby "mensa" (no age limits there) serves a filling, three-course meal (soup, main dish, dessert) for just 100 francs ($3.33). But all this is fairly far out at the Oefenplein campus, or specifically at "Studentenwijk Oefenplein," 1 Triomflaan (phone 648-55-40, extension 183). . . . From the Central Station, take the new subway to the Pétillon stop (7 minutes, 20 francs) and you'll soon spot the campus buildings.

Of the traditional commercial hotels in this low-priced category, you'll find a cluster priced at starvation budget levels (double rooms for $14 and $15, all included) on the rather raucous Rue du Marché, which runs between the Rue des Croisades and the Avenue du Boulevard, just steps away from the Place Rogier and the Gare du Nord. The top choice here (and there are numerous hotels to choose from) was once the elevator-equipped **Hotel L'Aigle d'Or,** 15 Rue du Marché (tel: 217-79-92), but there the rates have risen, for 1980, to 700 francs ($23.33) for a double, including two breakfasts, 490 francs single, again all included; close behind that, however, comes the shabby but proper **Hotel des Touristes,** 11 Rue du Marché (tel: 217-64-37), which charges only 300 francs ($10) single, 380 francs ($12.66) double, 450 francs ($15) triple, only 560 francs for a room with four single beds, service and tax included. A 70-franc optional eggs-with-bacon breakfast at the Touristes is an especially good one, and proprietors M. and Mme. Huart are quite accommodating. Highly recommended is this exciting find that draws numerous approving letters each year. And don't be frightened by its exterior appearance.

ROOMS FOR THE "BIG SPLURGE": Feeling flush? On the well-located Rue des Croisades, just off the Place Rogier, you'll see a number of large establishments

—the Hotel Siru, the Hotel des Colonies, others. Most suitable for us is the 180-bed **Hotel des Colonies,** at 8 Rue des Croisades (tel: 217-00-94), a large and rather ancient building that's seen better days, decorated in Andalusian style, with rates considerably less than those of other large Brussels hotels, for its bathless rooms ($33, double, including breakfast, service charge and tax). Up the street, the far-better-maintained, cheerier **Hotel Siru,** with a Place Rogier address (phone 217-75-80), is only pennies more expensive, (1,015 francs, $33.83, for a double with breakfast) and might be used when you're really flush.

READERS' HOTEL SELECTIONS: "The 17-room **Hotel George V,** 23 Rue 't'Kint (phone 513-50-93), offers a friendly, relaxed, home-like ambience, and a delightful proprietor who is colloquially fluent in both English and French. Bathless singles are 500 francs, doubles 630 francs, with breakfast included" (Lloyd Seaver, Oakland, California). . . . "**Hotel à la Grand' Cloche,** 11 Place Rouppe (phone 512-61-40), a short walk from the Grand' Place, is highly recommended, safe, quiet, and endowed with a most friendly and helpful manager, Christian Michelle. It also charges, in 1980, only 800 francs ($26.66) for a double, 550 francs ($18.33) single, inclusive of continental breakfast served in the delightful restaurant attached to the hotel, downstairs" (Marty and Joan Maynard, New York, New York).

HOTELS SEEKING MENTION: "My **Pension Universel,** 176 Rue de la Poste (phone 215-58-86), is especially suitable for young people visiting Brussels, with its rates of only 280 francs ($9.33) per person for bed and breakfast, 360 francs for half-board" (Mireille DeReyser, Brussels, Belgium).

READERS-ON-THE-STARVATION-BUDGET: "The **International Youth Home,** 21 Rue du Congres (phone 218-48-53), offers housing for 150 francs ($5) per person, including breakfast. An ideal place for the girl alone" (Mrs. Thomas L. Ferrier, Virginia Beach, Virginia; note by AF: these are dormitory accommodations, for both boys and girls; 53-year-old Jacques Sokay, a veteran of more than 30 years of youth hotel work in the United States, is now the new manager, and he does not require youth hostel membership).

EATING IN BRUSSELS: Although it's one of the most expensive cities of Europe, the town nevertheless enjoys a substantial number of budget eating places where you'll dine magnificently, at reasonable cost (for the Belgians love to eat). We'll deal first with the normal, sit-and-be-served restaurants where you can eat for $4.50 to $5.50, then with the self-service restaurants that charge slightly less, and then with the slightly better restaurants where you can try the food specialties of Brussels—particularly, mussels ("moules") and "carbonades flamandes"—for from $6.50 to $7.50 (appetizer and dessert included).

(1) $4.50 to $5.50 Restaurants

To bring order into this first category, we'll group our choices geographically.

Around the Grand' Place

Both on and off the awesome Grand' Place are at least two little bistros where fixed-price, two-course meals cost 150 or 165 Belgian francs ($5 to $5.50)—with individual plates for less. To orient yourself in the "Place," note that the City Hall is on one side, the Maison du Roi on the opposite side; and that of the other two sides, one has a higher elevation than the other—this we'll refer to as the "top side" of the Grand' Place. Directly on the Grand' Place, at the "top side", is a quaintly-decorated cellar restaurant which you'll scarcely be able to find until you nearly fall into it. **Au Caveau d'Egmont et de Horne,** 14 Grand' Place (named after two martyred noblemen of medieval Brussels, but better known as "Au Caveau") is one of the premier budget restaurants of the city, serving generously-portioned, two-course meals for either 145, 150 or 165 francs ($4.83, $5, or $5.50), depending on their ingredients, offering an omelette with ham for only 85 francs ($2.83), a beefsteak with french fries for 150 francs ($5), and that outstanding specialty of Brussels: "moules/frites" (a huge serving of mussels with french fries) for 190 francs ($6.33). Closed Mondays and Tuesdays.

Less crowded in summer, but simply because it's a block (about 50 yards) from the famous square, is the **Snack Les Deux Cloches**, 25 Rue des Eperonniers, on a narrow street that also runs off the Grand' Place. Here, in a short, narrow room attended by uniformed waiters with epaulets on their shoulders, two course meals cost 170 francs ($5.66), but lower-priced entrees include a "plat du jour" for 150 francs ($5), omelettes of various sorts for 80 francs, and a popular, filling, salad bowl (chicken, corn, lettuce, cucumber, carrots, tomatoes and bacon) for 130 francs ($4.33). A surprisingly comfortable restaurant for such moderate (in Brussels) rates. Closed Sundays.

Near the Place Louise

In this area, which is a bit more elegant than other parts of Brussels, the always-reliable eatery is the **Restaurant La Fringale,** at 5 Rue Jourdan, just off the Avenue Louise; from the Place Louise, walk down the Avenue Louise for only one short block and then turn right. Here, in fairly slick, bar-restaurant surroundings, there are excellent and filling plates (meat courses with salad and french fries for 170 francs) priced within the range we seek, and usually one two-course meal (soup, plate of the day) for 180 francs. Recently, the "patron" got married, and that may even further improve the quality of the cooking! Open weekdays only, from noon to 9 p.m.

(2) Self-Service Meals for $3.50 to $4.50

But the truly outstanding food values of Brussels are to be found in its many self-service restaurants, which fight it out with Paris for supremacy in the serve-yourself league. And typical of these is the large, 4th floor restaurant of Brussels' major department store—**Au Bon Marché (17)**—on the corner of Boulevard du Jardin Botanique and Rue Neuve (entrance to the restaurant is on the boulevard), just opposite the Place Rogier. The 4th floor here is one vast restaurant, but be sure to head only to the self-service portion of it, where 400,000 people ate in 1979! The hot plates are huge and garnished with many vegetables, moderate in price by the high price standards of Brussels (vol au vent for 90 francs, quarter of a chicken with french fries for 115 francs, a daily special—such as paupiette de boeuf, farcie forestiere, with new potatoes—for 135 francs), and extraordinarily tasty. Soup is 22 francs, hors d'oeuvres start at 50 francs, and the check carries no service charge.

Saturday is an especially good day to visit the cafeteria here: for it's an occasion on which large numbers of the burghers of Brussels turn out in their distinctive pork pie hats, shepherding flocks of children to the Au Bon Marché's big self-service lunch (served from 11 a.m. to 3 p.m.). Au Bon Marché is open from 9 to 8 on weekdays and Saturdays, from 9 to 9 on Fridays, and is closed on Sundays.

Cheaper, better

In recent years, cafeterias of the **Innovation** and **Sarma** department stores, both on the Rue Neuve leading to the Place de la Monnaie, have forged ahead

> **A CURRENCY NOTE:** Prices in this chapter have been convert-
> ed into dollars at the rate of 30 Belgian francs to one dollar. If
> that rate should change by the time of your arrival in Brussels,
> then dollar equivalencies in this chapter may be slightly off, al-
> though prices set forth in francs will remain the same.

of Bon Marché in both value and variety. Innovation's third-floor cafeteria is
now larger in size, and offers a one-course meal for 120 francs ($4), cold dishes
from 45 to 150 francs. The even less expensive Sarma cafeteria (upstairs at the
end of the building, and open daily including Sunday), charges 110 francs
($3.66) for its daily special, less than 100 francs for various other platters, only
18 francs for soup.

Self-service on the Avenue de la Toison d'Or

"Upper" Brussels—the area along the elegant, modern Avenue de la
Toison d'Or and Avenue Louise overlooking the older parts of the city—is
scarcely where you'd expect to find a budget cafeteria, yet there's one here that
vies with the department stores as a low-cost leader. **Mister G.B.** at the Porte
de Namur, in the arcade of the big AG Building skyscraper standing at the
Porte de Namur, is an ultra-modern, tastefully-decorated cafeteria whose
prices belie its luxurious interior: as little as 120 francs for several main courses,
22 francs for soup, 35 francs for dessert, all permitting—through careful selection of daily specials—a $5 to $5.50 meal. Other "Mister GB's" are located in
residential shopping centers elsewhere in Brussels, but this one was obviously
meant to be the showplace of the chain. A high recommendation, for an eatery
open seven days a week, from 8 a.m. to 9 p.m.

Self-Service on the Blvd. Adolphe Max, near the Place Rogier

Not to be compared with Mister GB (above)—nor, for that matter, with
the cafeterias in Paris—the aging **Restaurant Colmar** at 144 Boulevard Adolphe Max is still a reliable source for a quickly-eaten, filling and moderately-
priced meal, taken self-service in a stolid Brussels atmosphere. Soup for 30
francs, main courses for 100 and 150 francs, a big plate of spaghetti for 99
francs.

(3) The $6.50 to $7.50 Restaurants

And now, for your extra special culinary treats, return to the Grand' Place
and search out the tiny Rue Chair et Pain, which runs off the Place, just at the
side of the Maison du Roi (which is itself opposite the City Hall). A short walk
along the Rue Chair et Pain, crossing the Rue Marché aux Herbes, and the
street changes into the famous, colorful, and bustling **Petite Rue des Bouchers,**
which then runs into the diagonal **Rue des Bouchers.** These two medieval-like
streets, both less than 50 yards-or-so from the Grand' Place, are almost uninter-
ruptedly lined with picturesque Belgian restaurants, in virtually every price

range. Indeed, as you initially walk down the Petite Rue des Bouchers, you'll pass at least five of them—Le Bigorneau, La Flibuste Joyeuse, Le Moufon d'Or, the expensive Aux Armes de Bruxelles—where you can eat, with care, for from $9 to $10. But if you proceed to the intersecting Rue des Bouchers, you'll find—immediately ahead of you—my favorite $6.50 to $7.50 restaurants in Brussels—**Chez Leon,** 18 Rue des Bouchers, and **Leon 2,** 24 Rue des Bouchers, both serving that incomparable food specialty of Brussels which, fittingly enough, is mussels!

Steamed mussels—a dish that is variously called "moules marinieres" or "moules casserole," and which consists of mussels steamed in a vegetable broth—are available in any period other than May through mid-July. They can be ordered in Brussels simply by asking for "un speciale." Upon uttering those words, you'll receive an iron pot full of mussels and broth, with a side dish of french fried potatoes—all of which is a complete meal in itself, and is so considered in Belgium. Indeed, the serving is so large that it's always advisable to order one "speciale" for two persons.

"Un speciale" will cost exactly 200 francs ($6.66), with beer 30 francs ($1), and service (16%) extra, at either Chez Leon (which happens to be my favorite among the joints serving mussels in Brussels), or at Leon 2 (where you should look for a section of the menu with the heading, "Les Moules sont Notre Specialité"); Leon 2 also serves a filling stew called "Cassoulet Toulousain" for 180 francs. It comes in a big metal pot—enough for two persons, although served to one!—and consists of beef, potatoes, and white beans, all in a brown sauce. A tomato salad (40 francs) makes a good accompanying dish, and brings the entire meal to around $7.50, with tip. Try, if you can, however, to have a mussels dish, in those months when mussels are served.

And now let's repeat an important budget tip, for use at either Chez Leon or Leon 2: order one speciale for two persons (and a smaller dish for the second person), or else moules casserole for one of you, and the less expensive moules provençales—moules with a tomato and cheese sauce—for the other.

You can, of course, have mussels with french fries for 200 francs or less at other restaurants, such as **Au Caveau d'Egmont** (previously mentioned, 190 francs for moules and frites), but Chez Leon and Leon 2 are by far the giants in the field—in 1979, Chez Leon consumed more than 200,000 kilos of mussels! (Both Leons are closed in June).

A similarly-priced meal on a street just off the Grand' Place? At **La Coquille d'Or,** 7 Rue de la Colline, amid oilcloth tablecloths, lace-curtained windows, comfortable oak and leather chairs, a three-course prix fixe—potage; plat du jôur, roast chicken with french fries and salad or **goulash**; and dessert— is just 180 francs ($6). . . . And for a $6.66 meal served directly on the Grand' Place, you'll like the comfortable **Restaurant Le Chêne,** 37 Grand' Place, where three courses cost a prix fixe total of exactly 200 francs. It's wise to select the three-courser that includes "carbonades flamandes" (braised beef cooked in beer)—an item which ranks second only to mussels as a favorite of the citizens of Brussels. The dishes are prepared by the wife of the owner, and you enjoy them on upholstered banquettes.

STARVATION BUDGET: In the United States, as readers of *New York on $20 a Day,* and *Washington D.C. on $25 a Day,* have discovered, a sub-starvation-budgeteer can usually walk into a Chinese restaurant, order a bowl of rice for 75¢, and then flavor the rice with the free Soya Sauce found on every table. In Brussels, the trick is to have french fries (the Belgians make the world's best french fries) with béarnaise sauce—a meal in itself for as little as 30 francs ($1).

In the cafeteria of the Au Bon Marché department store, for instance: if you'll take a plate of french fries (30 francs), then specifically request the béarnaise sauce ("une portion de sauce béarnaise, s'il vous plaît"—they'll give you a small portion for 5 francs, 16¢), and precede it all with soup (25 francs), you'll have quite a passable, if starchy, meal for about $2.

Free mayonnaise with your French fries

Even smarter, though, is to head for the spots that provide free Belgian-style mayonnaise (almost a sauce béarnaise, and almost as tasty) with your incomparably delicious, Belgian french fries. The restaurant of the **Sarma Department Store,** which charges 30 francs for french fries and unlimited free mayonnaise (taken from pots at the side of the dining room), is one such place; as is the **Self-Service Colmar** (see the offerings at the end of the serving line), diagonally across from the Sarma at the end of the Rue Neuve; as is **Mr. G. B.** at the Porte de Namur. And if you think I'm balmy about the prospects of a meal from french fries with Belgian mayonnaise, try it—just once!

The perfectly acceptable practice of eating with the "Army"

Finally, an excellent three-course meal is available for only 80 francs ($2.66), both at lunch and supper, at the no-frills dining room of the **Armée du Salut** (Salvation Army), 27 Rue Bodeghem, where the setting and atmosphere are definitely not à la Ritz, but where it is perfectly safe and acceptable to eat (and that advice applies to both sexes). At least a dozen normally-dressed, middle-income residents appear here each meal. This is on a small side street near the Place Anneessens, a few minutes on foot from the Grand' Place. Open seven days a week, from noon to 1:30 p.m. and again from 6:30 to 8:00 p.m., the method of operation is self-service, and a typical three-course meal might consist of soup, then a quarter of a roast chicken with vegetable, followed by a dessert such as chocolate cream or fruit. Plastic table tops, of course.

THE BIG SPLURGE: If you're now in the mood for a $12 dinner, you'll do well at the **Restaurant au Coq au Vin,** 62 Rue Marché au Charbon, four blocks from the Grand' Place, which charges exactly 380 Belgian francs for soup, a magnificent wagon laden with hors d'oeuvres, main course and dessert (but that price does not include the 16% service charge or wine—a bottle of a good "Vin du Patron", enough for four people, will cost $8.50). It's a thoroughly native-type restaurant, perfect for a big splurge in Brussels, but always packed with Belgians, and usually requiring a reservation—phone 513-23-68. Closed Sundays and the month of August.

READERS' RESTAURANT SELECTIONS: "Just 10 minutes by foot from the Grand' Place, I stumbled into **La Tartinette,** at 126 Rue du Midi, operated by an English-speaking Vietnamese who serves you through a round window that looks like a ship's porthole. Here, one can have the dish of the day, usually served with rice or potatoes, for only 100 francs; a filling soup for 24 francs; sandwiches or omelettes for 30 francs. But this is open weekdays only" (L. D. Lacson, New York, New York).

YOUTH HOSTELS AND YOUTH RESTAURANTS: The city offers five lodgings of this type, each with restaurant, and at two of them the definition of that vague concept, "youth", includes travellers into their early 30s.

The traditional youth hostels are the **Auberge Jeunesse** at 91 Rue de la Poste (phone 217-86-55), and **Centreurop** at 124 Rue Verte (phone 217-45-59),

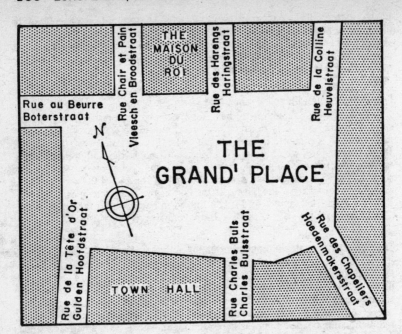

both within a block of each other in an area to the side of the North Station but a fairly long walk from it. The first, whose name in the Flemish version is "Vlaamse Jeugdherberg," occupies an old church; can lodge up to 240 young people in 16-bedded dorms; charges only 120 francs ($4) for bunk and breakfast; and serves a hearty 100-franc ($3.33) supper in its 140-seat restaurant. Manager is Marcel van Geem, a bearded Charles Laughton lookalike. Centreurop, managed by young Patrice Begaux and his English-speaking wife, contains seven large dormitories for both men and women, charges 150 francs ($5) per night, including breakfast, and maintains a large cafeteria on the premises where 110 francs ($3.66) brings you soup, meat with french fries and vegetables, then fruit or a sweet. At both the Auberge Jeunesse and Centreurop, showers are free, curfew is at 11:45 p.m., and youth hostel cards (which you can buy on the spot for 345 francs, $11.50) are required for persons staying more than one night.

A third hostel of Brussels, and one that does not require a hostel card, is the **Auberge Marais** (also known as the "Sleep-Well"), at 27 Rue de la Blanchisserie (phone 218-13-13), only a few steps from the central Place Rogier; unfortunately, it's open only in the months of July and August. Here, 40 available beds are placed in two single rooms (240 francs, $8), eight twin rooms (140 francs, $5, per person), two 5-bedded dorms for girls, and one dorm with 10 beds for boys (100 francs, $3.33, per person). Breakfast (rolls, butter, coffee), use of showers, a reading room, TV lounge, bar and canteen, are included in these rates. Not so central, but open all year, is the **Maison Internationale des Etudiants,** 205 Chaussée de Wavre (phone 648-85-29), renting 25 *single rooms* for 250 francs ($8.33) a night to persons possessing student identity cards, for 280 francs ($9.33) to person without, including breakfast and free showers. A monastery until 1970, the Maison is reached from the Gare du Nord by bus no. 38 (to the Chaussée de Wavre stop) or from the Gare du Midi by bus no. 20 or 21 (to the Quartier Leopold stop).

Finally, there's **CHAB** (which stands for "Centre d'Hebergement de L'Agglomération de Bruxelles"), at 6 Rue Traversière (phone 219-47-50), in the Botanical Gardens area—another of the "youth hotels" of Brussels (officially, the age limit here is 30 years, but nobody checks), charging 150 francs ($5) for beds in the dorm, 280 francs ($9.33) per person in 3-to-5-bedded rooms, 330 francs ($11) per person in doubles, 400 francs ($13.66) in singles, always including breakfast, without any requirement of membership in the youth hostel organization. Across the street, at no. 13, CHAB operates a very far-out youth-type restaurant called "École Buissonière," featuring a three-course menu, including wine, for 160 francs ($5.33).

If you're travelling onwards from Brussels to other Belgian cities, you'll want to check out the ingenious "free bicycle rental" offered by the bearded young manager—Patrice Begaux—of Centreurop. You simply pay him a deposit, pedal to the next city, and leave the bike with the youth hostel there, which will reimburse your deposit!

Picnic meals in Brussels? Go to the open-air market in the **Place St. Catherine,** in the vicinity of the Bourse; or, if you're more fastidious try the self-service grocery on the 3rd floor of the **Bon Marché** department store.

STUDENT HOUSING, STUDENT FLIGHTS: Acotra, at 38 Rue de la Montagne (phone 513-44-80 for lodgings, 512-55-40 for travel), upstairs, near the Grand' Place, is where students are sent for student lodgings in Brussels, and for student flights and trains; you might as well head directly there, weekdays from 9 to 5, Saturdays from 9 to noon. Among the better student hostels (because it offers individual rooms, not dorms): **Hotel des Jeunes,** 14 Rue des Etudiants (phone 539-07-25), charging 250 francs ($8.33) a night for a single room with bed and sink, breakfast included; closed during winter months.

DAYTIME SIGHTSEEING: Apart from the Grand' Place and Waterloo, the one indispensable visit in Brussels is to the great **Musée de l'Art Ancien** (the Classical Art Museum), at 3 Rue de la Regence, about 30 yards from the Place Royale, which opens every day except Monday from 10 to 5, charges the amazing admission of only 5 francs (17¢) all times other than Wednesdays and weekends (when it's free), and houses probably the most breathtaking collection of Flemish art in the world. The paintings are on the second floor, where you should patiently wend your way to the rooms housing the surrealistic masterpieces, centuries ahead of their time, of Hieronymus Bosch (1450 to 1516); they actually depict men bombing villages from flying-fish-airplanes! Nearby, you'll see the renowned "Kermesse Flamand" of P. Breughel, his equally-famous "De Kindermoord" (Murder of the Innocents), and at least a dozen "Temptations of St. Anthony" done by both Breughel the elder and younger, by Van der Heck and others. Mainly, you'll want to concentrate on Breughel's scenes of Flemish village life, in which literally scores of individually-drawn peasants enliven each canvas; but there are as well in this stupefying museum a number of Van Dycks and Rubens (including a Van Dyck portrait of the sculptor who created the Manneken Pis)—and even a few Dutch painters (Rembrandt, Hals, Steen), too. . . . Up the street, at 1 Place Royale, is the **Museum of Modern Art** (open 10 to 1 and 2 to 5, closed Mondays, admission free), which houses a few, and fairly second-rate, Belgian expressionists of the current day, and can be passed up if you lack the time. But don't miss the Musée de l'Art Ancien.

HOPE IN BRUSSELS: While I traipse through the hotels and restaurants of Brussels, my wife Hope likes to stick to the Grand' Place. Here's her report on the specific sights to be seen, both here and in other areas of town:

Around the Grand' Place

"This magnificent square, described earlier by Arthur, began its life as a market place, and is still used for that purpose to this very day—come early in the morning and you'll see the stands. But the most thrilling time to visit the square is at night, particularly when the town puts on its own free 'Sound and Light' show by flashing colored beams across the Hotel de Ville and playing Bach or Beethoven over concealed loudspeakers. You can catch these enchanting performances on Wednesday, Friday and weekend evenings during summer —check with the local tourist bureau for exact times. Adults pay 100 francs, children under 12, 80.

"Wherever you go in Brussels, you'll be drawn back to the Grand' Place like a magnet, and the feeling is not to be resisted, because there are three major attractions in the area: the Hotel de Ville, the Maison du Roi, and the old Church of Gudule, nearby. Skip the Brewery Museum, located on the square, which is heavily advertised and is a heavy disappointment.

Hotel de Ville

"The **Hotel de Ville**, or Town Hall, is the oldest (begun in 1402), largest, and most imposing structure on the Grand' Place, and also one of the finest examples of Gothic architecture in Europe. It's open to visitors from 9 to 4:30 weekdays, and 10 to noon weekends the year round; but try to avoid arriving around lunchtime, as the guides may be out. (The tower, which affords an excellent view of Brussels, is temporarily closed for repairs.) For 10 francs admission (33¢) you'll be taken on a guided tour of the interior, which includes the splendid, red-and-gold Council Room, the Mayor's room filled with paintings of old Brussels, the 'Salle Gothique' festooned with tapestries of the Guilds, and the beamed-ceilinged Marriage Chamber with its old tile floor and shields of the Guilds. While all of these are immensely impressive, I get a particular thrill from reading the two framed posters on either side of the door to the main lobby, which contain defiant proclamations of the two wartime Mayors (Bourgermasters) of Brussels—Adolphe Max and F. J. van de Meulebroeck—during the occupation of the city by German troops in World War I and II. Both counsel the citizens to remain calm and give no aid to the enemy—especially to any puppet government official who might be appointed by occupying forces. And one ends with the ringing words: "Je suis, je reste, et je resterai le seul bourgmestre legitime de Bruxelles."

Maison du Roi

"Located directly opposite the Hotel de Ville is the **Maison du Roi**, constructed in the sixteenth century, restored faithfully to the original in the nineteenth century, and now the historical Municipal Museum of Brussels (open from 10 to 12 and 1 to 4, summers til 5, on weekdays; Saturdays and Sundays from 10 to 12, with admission free on Sundays, otherwise 20 francs). Apart from its historical and archaeological relics relating to the city (altarpieces, ceramics, porcelain, tapestries, and, most interesting to me, sculptures and pieces of sculpture from the Hotel de Ville, the Maison, and the Churches of N. D. du Sablon, N. D. de la Chapelle, and St. Michel Cathedral), it displays paintings (a Breughel on the first floor) and puppets, and an amusing exhibit on the third floor (to the right of the staircase) of some of the costumes, decorations, and honors that have been bestowed upon the Manneken Pis! There are scores of models here of that symbol of "l'esprit ironique" of Brussels, all costumed in different uniforms, including one of the Foreign Legion, into which he was inducted with the following words:

> 'Petit bonhomme légendaire
> Illustration de la cité
> Te voici donc incorporé
> Dans la Legion Etrangère.'

St. Michel Cathedral

"The official cathedral of Brussels, **St. Michel Church** (still called **St. Gudule** by the natives, although in 1962 it was discovered that St. Gudule never existed), is only a short walk from the Maison du Roi. The church, begun in the ninth century, is a large grey stone cathedral with twin towers that took over 300 years to build (from the 14th to the 17th century). Its impressive main entrance is opened only on State occasions (the doors being too old and delicate for constant use) like the marriage of King Baudouin and Queen Fabiola, or last year's Brussels International Festival—but a visit through the side door will be more than worth your time; note the Baroque wooden pulpit, which was carved from a single tree trunk; and more important, the exquisite stained glass windows which experts in church architecture say are among the finest in the world.

The Sablon

"The charming and fashionable district of Sablon, located off the Place Royale, near the Museum of Ancient Art (2 blocks down, and cross the street), has as its centerpiece the gardens of the **Place du Petit Sablon** (right off Rue de la Régence), created to honor two victims of the long arm of the Spanish Crown, the Counts Egmont and de Hornes, whose statues are the focal points of the park. (The 'Place,' a small green square, is enclosed by a charming wrought iron fence which is decorated with Gothic-looking pillars, each one supporting a different statuette, representing the ancient Guilds—a closer look will reveal which Guild you're looking at. And the surrounding neighborhood has some restored houses dating back as far as the early 16th century.) . . . Music-makers or music-lovers might like to drop in at **The Brussels Museum of Musical Instruments,** on a corner of the square at 17 Place du Petit Sablon, open Tuesday, Thursday and Saturday from 2:30 to 4:30, Wednesday from 5 to 7, Sunday from 10:30 to 12:30. There's free admission on all days of operation, and guided tours can be arranged; both European and non-European musical instruments are displayed. . . . Afterwards, you can cross the Rue de la Régence to the Place du Grand Sablon where you can see the interesting, flamboyant Gothic church **Notre-Dame du Sablon** (very romantic looking at night when it's lit up), whose interior has vaulted stone ceilings, but is nevertheless decorated in the rococo manner. On Sundays, some very elegant antique stalls set up shop in front of the church—and the surrounding neighborhood is filled with antique shops, too. . . . While in the neighborhood, do have a look at the King's "office", **The Royal Palace** (once a royal residence, but the present

King lives elsewhere), a grand Louis XVI style building filled with marble, shimmering chandeliers, Goya tapestries, Royal family portraits, silver, china, and a most interesting special exhibition on Albert I. Open daily, except Monday, from 10 to 4 (from July 26 through September 10); admission free.

Marolles

"Below the Palais de Justice, off and around the Rue Haute, is the rougher, more medieval, Breughel-like section of Brussels (matter of fact, Breughel the Elder lived at # 132). Turn off at Rue du Renard or Rue de la Rasière to get to the quaint cobblestoned Place du Jeu de Balle—and go particularly on Sunday mornings when the Place becomes the lively **Flea Market of Brussels** (good bargains too, amid piles of junk: a pair of antique wooden bellows for $12!). . . . After you finish exploring the neighborhood, you can walk up the Rue Haute toward the center of town where, in about five blocks, you'll come to the lovely Romanesque-Gothic **Church of La Chapelle** (which is actually closer to Notre-Dame au Sablon); begun in the 12th century, the sides of the Church are especially beautiful, and Peter Breughel is buried in one of the chapels.

Small Excursions

Royal Museum for Central Africa

"**The Royal Museum for Central Africa,** 11 Leuvensesteenweg, Tervuren (open daily from 9 to 5:30, 10 to 4:30 in the winter, free admission), is located on the outskirts of Brussels in Tervuren Park (an exquisitely sylvan retreat), and is a 30-minute, 20 franc (66¢) ride from the center of town (take the metro at Gare Centrale to Montgomery, ask for a "ticket de transit" and use it to board tram No. 44 at Montgomery, then get off at the end of the line, and signs will point the way). You'll find it an interesting trip, through some of the most elegant residential districts of Brussels, then the forest; and the Museum itself offers some of the best African art to be seen anywhere. It's a large and unusually comprehensive collection, encompassing everything to do with the life and culture of Central Africa. You start, of course, with zoological and agronomical exhibits, then go on to a fine collection of minerals, and a gallery on the prehistory of Africa; but more interesting are the vast sections devoted to crafts and customs (especially the ceramics and woven goods of great beauty), and to African art, revealing the surprising diversity of the various Central African cultures: a wealth of material. There are also two galleries dealing with the opening up of Central Africa (including personal artifacts of Stanley and Livingstone) and (probably a bit of nostalgia for local residents) the history of the Belgians in Africa.

The Home of Erasmus

"A last visit, for students of the early Renaissance, is to the House of Desiderius Erasmus—the great humanist and Latin scholar—which is located a fair distance (20 minutes) from the center of town, at 31 Rue du Chapitre, Anderlecht (take bus # 76 from the Place de Brouckère or tram # 103 from the Gare du Midi). The interior of this substantial home has been maintained in its original state, is filled with carefully preserved Bibles translated and annotated by the famous philosopher, and has numerous other relics of the time. Admission is 20 francs; hours are from 10 to 12 and 2 to 5, every day except Tuesday and Friday.

"*Tip:* Unless you have considerable time in Brussels, you can safely skip **The National Art and History Museum,** and the much-touted **Antoine Wiertz Museum-Gallery** (both of some interest, but out-of-the-way places and not worth the effort); you'll do better to spend that extra time in those two unforgettable Belgian cities—Bruges and Ghent."

TOURS: Sightseeing buses leave from any number of tour companies located up and down the Boulevard Adolphe Max (a typical one is **Cobeltour,** at # 119) on a comprehensive series of tours, including two daily sightseeing trips through the city proper, each costing 350 francs ($11.66). The morning tour departs at 10 a.m., covers the best-known attractions; the afternoon tour goes at 3 p.m., and highlights the more modern aspects of the city, including the site of the 1958 World's Fair. For 390 francs ($13), you can take a lengthier tour (departing daily at 3 p.m.) into the outskirts of Brussels, visiting the Museum of Central Africa in the park of Tervueren, then stopping at Waterloo to see the famous "Lion's Mound" (where the popular Prince of Orange was wounded in that famous battle), then to the World's Fair Site, and back along all the sights of the city itself. And finally, for Joyce Kilmer fans, the 680 francs ($22.66), all-day tour, leaving daily at 9 a.m., takes you through Flanders Field, and then to the medieval towns of Ghent and Bruges (swans, lace and Van Eyck).

READERS' SELECTIONS: "Instead of taking an expensive guided excursion to Bruges, I went to the railroad station and bought a ticket for 'un beau jour à Bruges et au littoral.' This included, for $7.40, round-trip fare from Brussels to the seashore via Bruges, a ticket of entry to the city museum in Bruges, and a ticket for a ride on the canals of the little city. I was in Bruges the whole day until about 4:30 p.m.; then I took the train to Blankenberg, swam, ate an enormous pile of 'moules'; returned to Bruges, where I walked around for an hour looking at the lit-up monuments; and finally took the train back to Brussels. Such 'Beau Jours' are available for many other excursions and a list of them is available in any railroad station" (Peter J. Feibelman, New York, New York; note by AF: ask specifically, at the ticket window, for "Une journée à la mer" (a day at the seashore), which permits you during the summer months only (July to mid-October) to buy a round-trip, one-day ticket to any seaside location in Belgium, for the one-way fare there—an average of 222 francs, $7.40).

A READER'S TIP: "Instead of taking the airport train to the North Station at a cost of 160 F for the 4 of us (2 adults and 2 children), we caught a city bus which, after very few stops, dropped us within a block of the hotel and the driver told us when to get off. It cost us a total of 116 F, or 29 F each fare, and no need to transfer. Gare du Nord is the label on the front. For the return trip, the buses leave the corner of the Rue Royale and the Boulevard du Jardin Botanique about every 20 minutes and are designated BZ. The driver will tell you which ones go all the way to the airport" (John and Gini Mitchem, San Jose, California).

READERS-ON-AN-EXCURSION: "No one should leave Belgium without making a trip to **Antwerp,** but don't plan your trip for a Monday, when many of the main attractions are closed. This is a marvelous city, where you may even want to spend several days. There is so much to see. The train for Antwerp leaves from the Gare Centrale every 30 minutes. If you take the express train, the trip is only 30 minutes. The local train can take as much as an hour to get there so it is worth waiting ten minutes for the express, on which a round trip ticket is about 182 BF ($6.06). You can also drive to Antwerp easily, passing the World Fair Grounds and then the Royal Residences. Coming into Antwerp you will see the first tank to come into the city for the liberation from the Germans during World War II. Follow the signs to the Central Station and park your car there. Everything is in walking distance.

"On the back of the map you'll receive at the Tourist Office, you'll find a list of things to see in the city. The following are musts: **Rubens House** (Rubens was one of the few artists of the time who was recognized as a great during his lifetime. Consequently, he lived like a rich man of the time. His house is fascinating, and the admission is free)! **Open Market** (The open market place is right down the street from Rubens House; it is where the produce market is held on Saturdays. This is really fascinating to see, and a great place to meet the people. If you want some fresh fruit to munch on, what better place can you find to buy it?); **Groet Market** (This is the Grand' Place of Antwerp. It is not as grand as the one in Brussels, but a must to see. It typifies the city. The statue and fountain in the center of the square is of Brabo, the hero of an old legend. According to the story, the site of Antwerp was inhabited by the giant Antigoon. He extracted a tribute from all who navigated the river and cut off the hand of those who refused to pay. The giant was finally killed by the Roman soldier Brabo, who cut off the giant's hand and threw it in the river. And thus the name of the city 'Ant', from the word hand and 'Werpen,' from the verb to throw. The throwing of the hand is portrayed here); **The Steen** (This old turreted castle now houses the Navigation Museum. It also provides a good view of the harbor—the second largest on the North Sea. If you have the time, you can take a boat tour of the harbor, which is operated by the Flandria Line and leaves from just to the left of the Steen. And if you are ready for a snack, the frites stand at the foot of the ramp to the Steen sells excellent french fries. The section between the Steen and the Cathedral is also an excellent area to try the local specialty, mussels); **The Cathedral** (You should plan your visit to the Cathedral for after lunch. The famous triptychs by Rubens are closed in the morning to protect them from the strong sunlight which shines on them); **Plantin-Moretus Museum** (This museum houses a complete antique press and engraving plant. In the 16th century, it was the finest printing and engraving shop in Antwerp. Plantin's work was carried on by his son-in-law Moretus and his heirs for three centuries); **The Zoo** (The zoo is beside the Central Station. It is reputed to be one of the finest in Europe). And if you are looking for nightlife, try the places on the side streets off the Groet Market, or the Koningin Astrid Plein by the Station" (Judy Nesbit, Kohlenweg, Germany).

"**Bruges** (Brugge) is a city of the past living in the present. By train it's about an hour from the Gare Centrale in Brussels. From the station walk to the Market Square on the other side of town; the little old streets are delightful. Then walk to the adjoining Burg Square, which is surrounded by four buildings representing four different centuries. One of them is the **Chapel of the Holy Blood**, the most famous building in Bruges, housing the relic which was brought from the Holy Land in the 12th century (it is displayed on Friday mornings). On Ascension Day you can see the Procession of the Holy Blood, a spectacular sight which attracts people from all over the world. . . . Next I would suggest that you take a canal tour of the city. There are several departure spots. After the tour, head toward **Notre Dame Church.** Charles the Bold and Mary of Burgundy are both buried here and there is a beautiful marble Madonna by Michelangelo. By this time, it should be about lunch time. There is a picturesque little restaurant across the street where, for about $3.50, you can have, for example, an omelette, french fries and a Coke, or 'tomates crevette' (tomatoes stuffed with little shrimp—a really typical Belgian dish worth trying) and a Coke. Around the corner is the **Memlinc Museum.** From here continue on to the **Beguinage.** Inside, to the left of the gate, is the Beguinage house which is open to visitors. . . . In your walk through the city you should see ladies sitting out in old costumes making lace. This is a fascinating art, you can't leave Belgium without a piece of this world famous lace. The shops near the Beguinage are good ones. From here you are not too far from the railroad station. There are maps posted all over the city, so you should have no trouble finding your way around" (Judy Nesbit, Kohlenweg, Germany).

"Another must is a stop at **Ghent.** This can be done on the way back from Bruges if you get an early start. From the railroad station take the train to the center of town, where you should be sure to see the famous polyptych, The Adoration of the Mystic Lamb, by van Eyck, in a chapel of the **Cathedral of St. Bavon.** The guard will supply an explanation in English. He will also close it so that you can see the outside panels. You should see the rest of this Cathedral, the 12th Century Castle of the Count of Flanders, and the views from St. Michael's Bridge and from the Belfrey" (Judy Nesbit, Kohlenweg, Germany; note by AF: trains for Bruges and Ghent leave the North Station (Gare du Nord) nearly every 40 minutes throughout the day, at a charge of 378 francs— $12.60—round-trip).

"Some of your readers may enjoy the university town of Louvin (Leuven), 20 minutes from the Nord Station in Brussels. It features an entirely new and architecturally-interesting university a few kilometers outside the 'old' Louvin; the loveliest town hall in Europe (say I), a few minutes' walk from the station; and a worthwhile cathedral. Eat nearby at the New Garden Indonesian restaurant for 200 Belgian francs" (J. Auth, Toledo, Ohio).

THE INDISPENSABLE ONE-DAY EXCURSION: To Bruges, approximately one hour away by train costing 378 francs, round-trip. And don't even dream of also stopping in Ghent; Bruges has enough to occupy you for a week. A fully-developed, almost fully-preserved 14th and 15th century Flemish city, perhaps the most beautiful on earth, reflecting the vigor and taste of a long-ago time, it will change all your opinions about those supposedly dark days of the Middle Ages.

EVENING ENTERTAINMENT: The only always-satisfying means of evening entertainment in Brussels is to grab a chair at a sidewalk cafe in the Grand' Place and drink in the beauty of the floodlight-illuminated, golden buildings that ring the square. It's amazing how much one can discover about these buildings by staring at them for hours on end, and that—strangely enough—is a pleasant and moving task. A coffee on the Grand' Place is 45 francs, plus 5 francs service charge, but for that you can sit forever.

The outstanding cafe of the Grand' Place is called, appropriately enough, the **Cafe de la Grand' Place.** It's located at the bottom side of the Place (corner of Rue au Beurre), has no identifying number, but can be spotted by the gilded head of a Cardinal out front or by the unbelievably picturesque decor inside— which is that of a typical, 15th century Belgian inn. That means that there are posts and timbers, and rough-hewn walls of wood, a center fireplace with a roaring fire, leather bladders suspended from the beams, and a stuffed, full-size horse at the stairway leading to the "estaminet" (old tavern) on the second floor. Don't fail to roam throughout the entire establishment, including the smoky "bier kelder" downstairs; to do all of this requires the purchase of as little as a single beer (30 francs), a glass of wine (45 francs) or a coffee or tea (45 francs); in particularly cold weather, you can spend a wonderfully dreamy evening by the fire, sustained by a "vin chaud" (heated wine) for 65 francs.
. . . Brussels' historic puppet playhouse, the **Theatre Toone,** is found at the end of a tiny blind alley called the Impasse Schuddevelde, next to # 21 Petite Rue des Bouchers (the colorful restaurant street near the Grand' Place). "Spectacles" nightly except Sunday at 8:30 p.m., 125 to 250 francs for seats, dialogue in French with a distinct Brussels accent. "Toone" is named after Antoine, founder of the theatre in 1830. . . . After absorbing the beauty of the Grand' Place, you'll want to walk to the **Manneken-Pis.** Simply head behind the City Hall straight down the Rue Charles Buls for two short blocks.

Blues in Brussels? **Moustache,** at 14 Borgwalstraat, was once a popular banjo parlor, has now switched to a blues-and-jazz format presented starting at 9 p.m. every Wednesday, Friday, Saturday and Sunday. Admission to hear is 50 francs. . . . Again just for listening, with no dancing, is the jazz tavern called **Pol's Bierodrome,** at 21 Place Fernand Cocq, this time in the uptown ("haut de la ville") area of the Brussels Hilton, up the Avenue d'Ixelles from the Porte de Namur. Officially designated as Chapter 1152 of the organization called "Friends of Jazz," Pols features live jazz combos, in a dark and smoky college-beerhall-type setting whose walls are covered with college pennants and photos of jazz greats. I've never been there at night, but the charwoman who showed me through one afternoon assured me it was "pas cher, monsieur"— 150 francs admission for non-members, 80 francs for drinks. . . .The younger

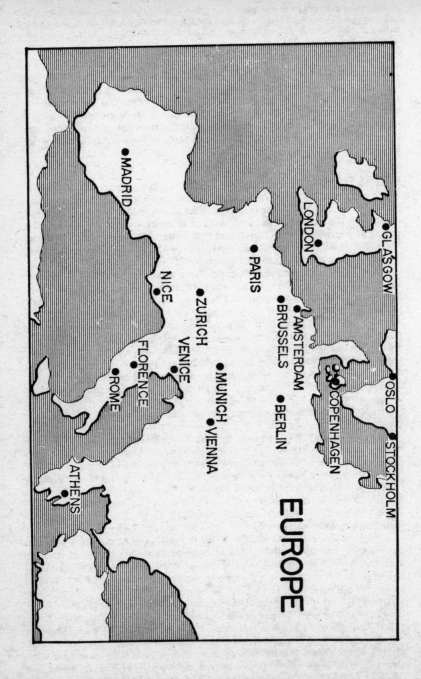

teenagers dance in Brussels at the Y.W.C.A. on Saturday nights (see our starvation budget section for addresses and directions). . . . And the Belgians in their 40s and 50s dance to the live band of a large cafe-restaurant called **Old Brussels** at # 5 Boulevard du Jardin Botanique, between the Boulevard Emile Jacqmain and the Boulevard Adolphe Max, where there's no admission charge and only normal drink prices (50 francs) in a French-style "Hofbrauhaus" setting. There are also meeting possibilities here—but only if you speak French.

One last, and relatively unexpected, form of evening entertainment is provided by Brussels' **Musée du Cinema** (Cinema Museum), in the Palais des Beaux-Arts, 9 Rue Baron Horta (phone 513-41-55), which shows "classic" films in their original languages (René Clair, John Ford, David Lean, Billy Wilder) every evening at 6:15, 8:15, and 10:15, and charges only 30 francs ($1) per showing.

BRUSSELS MISCELLANY: An easy-to-find laundromat is the **Self-Service Lav-O-Net,** at 23 Rue du Marché, just around the corner from the Rue des Croisades (off the Place Rogier). For 80 francs ($2.66) you can do 5 kilograms of laundry. . . . The old-time tradition of non-stop, daytime vaudeville is what's practiced at **La Gaité Theatre,** 18 Rue Fossé aux Loups (next door to the expensive Chez Paul au Gaîté nightclub, off the Place de Brouckère), which actually presents a continuous, 8-hour live show—Ed Sullivan-type variety acts, in French—from 3 p.m. to 11 p.m. Balcony seats range from 200 to 300 francs ($6.66 to $10), and you'd be well advised to buy the cheapest variety. . . . Arriving in Brussels, you'll want to disembark at the Gare du Midi for hotels in the Porte Louise area, at the Gare du Nord for hotels around the Place Rogier, at the Gare Centrale for hotels near the Grand' Place. . . . And change your travellers' checks into Belgian currency *before* arriving in Belgium, or change them only *once* in Belgium for enough cash to last your entire stay: there's a dastardly charge of 89 Belgian francs ($2.96) every time you cash travellers' checks in Belgium, regardless of the number or amount that are cashed.

WATERLOO!: Suddenly, as you drive out of Brussels on the road to Charleroi, signs begin appearing that bear crossed sabres accompanied by the numerals, "1815". They contain, and need, no identifying words. June 18, 1815, was the date of Waterloo, the battle that decided the destiny of Europe; and the signs point to the village of Waterloo in the suburbs of Brussels, beyond which is the still untouched plain—several square miles in size—that witnessed the brutal clash between the forces of Napoleon and the armies of the Allies, under the Duke of Wellington.

I can't anticipate what your reaction to these farmlands will be, but my own visits there have been among the more soul-stirring occasions of my life—an idiosyncrasy that may date back to the days when I played with tin soldiers who wore uniforms like those of Napoleon's troops. Today, there exists little on the battleground except the gigantic, pyramid-like "Lion's Mound," from the top of which you gaze out upon the fields and plains where once these armies clashed. Below are a number of garish carnival-like "museums" that play nickelodeon-type films of the event (admission: 35 francs; the soundtrack is in French, but you won't mind), as well as the genuinely-interesting circular building that houses a panoramic painting of a scene at the height of the battle.

That—and a few scattered monuments and ruined farmhouses—is all there is. And yet, so help me, I can't approach this vast and silent place without feeling a subtle tremor and without hearing the imagined sounds of a cavalry charge, and the shouted orders of Marshals Ney and Blucher, or the crackling muskets of a square of English infantry. Read a history of Waterloo—there are several books sold on the site—and perhaps you too will share the sentiments of Victor Hugo, who lived near here (in the Hotel des Colonnes) to gather battle data for scenes in his *Les Miserables,* and then wrote:

> 'Quarante ans sont passés, et ce coin de la terre,
> Waterloo, ce plateau funèbre et solitaire,
> Ce champ sinistre . . .
> Tremble encore d'avoir vu la fuite des géants!'

> (Forty years have passed, and this corner of earth,
> Waterloo, this solitary and funebral plain,
> This sinister field—
> Still trembles from having seen the fall of giants!)

To get to Waterloo on your own, take Bus "W" from the Place Rouppe (leaving every half hour, for a one-way charge of 40 francs), but stay on past the village itself until you reach Mont St. Jean and the "Lion's Mound"— center of the battlefield. Best, of course, is to drive there; and next best course is to take a tour.

Time now to pep it up with the happiest people of Europe—the Danes. A flight from Brussels to Copenhagen takes 1½ hours. The smiles on the faces are the first thing you'll see.

Chapter VII

COPENHAGEN

Where the Budget "Hotels"
Are Private Homes

AFTER COPENHAGEN, Europe can become a footnote. For this city has everything: a populace with friendship in their very souls; an astonishing variety of sights and activities; the gaiety and charm of a continuing festival.

Want an example of some of these qualities? On the outskirts of Copenhagen, in a small wooded park, is a country-style nightclub and dance-hall of gigantic size. Over 300 Danes gather here each night to dance, to eat, and to witness a floor show that brims with the vitality and good-humor of Denmark. I first came here on a first date in Copenhagen, during my penny-pinched years as a G.I. overseas.

Like almost every other establishment in Copenhagen, there was no cover charge, no minimum, no glares, no pressures—only merriment and warmth. We danced the entire evening; I had a beer, she had an orange squash. When the bill was presented, it came to 4 kroner 50 öre—at that time, 63¢—including service charge. I left 6 kroner on the table.

"You don't understand," said the waiter. "The service charge is already included." "Well," I stuttered, "I thought I'd leave a little more." "In that case," he answered, "thank you very much." He smiled broadly, shook my hand, escorted us to the door, and said he hoped we'd return.

That's Copenhagen—a near perfect civilization.

A BUDGET SURVEY: But now for the depressing part. In the wave of inflation that has battered the cities of northernmost Europe, Copenhagen has surfaced well near the top. It's less expensive than Stockholm, more expensive than Oslo, and more on a par with prices in American cities than with those we've learned to expect in the rest of Europe.

But can you combat the high cost of Copenhagen? You most definitely can, if you acquire the know-how. The main job is to avoid the fantastic surcharges that pile up on almost every penny you spend in Denmark. Years ago, the Danish government was one of the first in Europe to levy an "added value tax" of 10%, called "Moms" (it's pronounced "mumps" and is every bit as painful), on almost every item sold and service rendered in the country. As new governments were successively ushered in, "Moms" went up to 20%. That means that when you rent a room or buy a meal in Copenhagen, you pay the price of the room or meal, plus 15% service charge, plus 20% government tax, and thereby up your total outlay by 35%.

Certain places, however, are exempt from these surcharges, and it is *these* you should frequent. Private citizens, for instance, who rent out rooms in their homes, do not charge either service or tax. Self-service restaurants (which are popping up all over the country) don't add a service charge. And if you should purchase something expensive in one of Copenhagen's superb shops, and have it shipped from the shop—even if it's only to the next country on your itinerary —you'll save the tax.

If you can't completely avoid the surcharges, you can at least be sure of what you're paying. When you check into a hotel, make the desk clerk (even if you have to twist his arm) quote you the full price of the room, *with* service and tax included. When reading a menu prior to deciding on a restaurant, look for the line "Alle priser incl. Moms," meaning "all prices include tax." By now, virtually every price quoted to you in restaurants and hotels should be an all-inclusive one: that is, it will include service charge and tax.

In working out your basic expenses in Copenhagen, you should, of course, figure on spending more than you would in Southern European cities. In the following pages, we've compiled a list of rooms in private homes renting from $13.50 to $18 for two persons, of rooms in pensions and budget hotels for $21 to $36, double, and of restaurants where hot meals cost from $4.50 to $5. Picnic places and dormitories are included for our rock-bottom budget travellers, but regular tourists should count on paying a minimum of $17 to $19 a day for the bed-and-three-meals basics.

Once you've got the basics squared away, though, you're "home free." Because there's lots to do and see in Copenhagen that costs hardly a cent. There's free entertainment all evening at Tivoli, free drinks at the breweries, free admission to most of the museums and sights, and simply a freedom in the air that makes you want to stroll through the lanes and squares smiling back at all the Danes who are smiling—so freely—at you.

ORIENTATION: Let's first find where we are. The most important geographical fact is that nearly everything of interest to tourists is conveniently grouped in the center of town. The two major downtown streets are H. C. Andersens Boulevard and Vesterbrogade. These intersect at one corner of the **Raadhus-pladsen**—the Town Hall Square. Walking away from the Town Hall along Vesterbrogade, you first come to **Tivoli** on your left (Copenhagen's famous summer amusement center) and then the **Central Station.** And at the Central Station, you'll find the tourist information office; the hotel-booking service; the main terminal of the **S-Tog** (S-Train), Copenhagen's local rail service; and

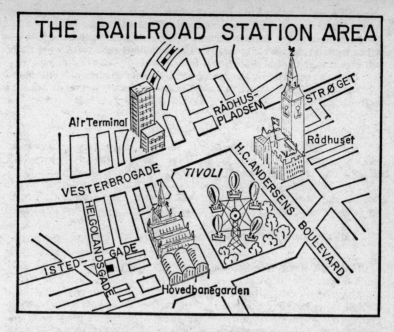

THE RAILROAD STATION AREA

finally, the **S.A.S. Air Terminal,** to which the airport bus delivers arriving air passengers. In the streets that run alongside the Central Station are the majority of our recommended budget hotels, while along the Vesterbrogade is an excellent selection of budget restaurants.

Buses, trams and sight-seeing coaches all leave from the vicinity of, or pass through, the Town Hall Square ("Radhuspladsen"). On the opposite side of the square from Vesterbrogade, is the start of the **Strøget,** a fascinating mile-long shopping street maintained for pedestrians only—and which is a "must see" sight for tourists. The Strøget winds through **"Old Copenhagen";** on either side are tiny lanes, antique buildings, churches and museums. It ends at **Kongens Nytorv,** the "King's Square," where the Royal Theatre stands and where **Nyhavn,** the rowdy sailors' district, begins. There are parks, museums and sights in various parts of the city, but for a taste of Denmark, old and new, the sector from the Town Hall to the King's Square, along the Strøget, affords the most concentrated variety.

TRANSPORTATION: The bus ride from the airport to the center of town will cost you 10 kroner ($1.90), if you go by airport coach. If you travel instead by local bus #32, which leaves from the Arrival Terminal every 20 minutes, and deposits you on the Town Hall Square, you'll pay only 3 kroner (66¢) and your ticket will entitle you to transfer to any in-town bus within one hour after the time of purchase. Within the city, you can get around by an easily-navigated system of buses, most of which leave from the vicinity of Town Hall. Tickets cost 3 kroner (66¢) and you can transfer freely within one hour after purchase. Better yet, buy nine "Mermaid Tokens" for 20 kroner ($3.80), which give you the same transfer privileges and save you about 20% of the fare. They're available from all bus and streetcar conductors. An inexpensive way to do your own sightseeing is by bus and tram; ask at the Tourist Board, beside the railway station, for a free transportation map and helpful sightseeing folder.

Copenhagen also has an efficient electric train network—the S-Tog—which runs through the city and out to the various suburbs. All the trains converge on the Central Station and fare depends on your destination.

Taxis can be hailed on the streets, and charge a minimum of 8 kroner and 4.75 for each kilometer which includes the service charge; you're not expected to tip an extra cent!

Cycling

But to really get around town during your stay, why not try a bike or small motorbike? That's what most of the Danes do—and the city is a cyclist's paradise, as a result. **København's Cyklebørs,** 157 Gothersgade (phone 14-07-17), near the parade grounds of Rosenborg Castle, is the cheapest of the bicycle firms. It rents standard, smooth-riding bikes for only 15 kroner a day, 25 kroner for two days and 65 kroner for a week, with a 50 kroner deposit. Closed Sundays.

And now, back to the task of finding a room.

ACCOMMODATIONS: Whether you arrive in Copenhagen by plane or train, you'll ultimately be deposited near the railroad station **(1).** Inside the station are a number of booths bearing alphabetical signs. Walk over to the booth ("Kiosk") marked "P," which is operated by the Copenhagen tourist association. This remarkable organization maintains a register of every hotel and guesthouse in or near Copenhagen, as well as the names of nearly 300 guest-accepting private homes; but more important, the organization stays in daily contact with these establishments to learn whether vacancies exist. As visitors approach the kiosk, they're given a form to complete, in which they designate the price range of the rooms they seek. Kiosk P then makes a few fast phone calls, and soon provides you with name, address and bus instructions to an establishment willing to take you at that price. Their booking fee? Only 10 kroner ($1.90) per person.

Rooms in Private Homes

During months other than June, July and August, Kiosk P will usually be able to find rooms in normal hotels or guesthouses for budget-minded tourists who check off the least expensive price category on the application form they're given. That's the category which prescribes a *maximum* room rent of 100 kroner ($19.04) per person, including breakfast, service and tax. And since such vacancies usually exist in the non-summer months, Kiosk P will usually be unwilling in those periods to book you into less expensive lodgings in a private home. These latter rooms normally rent for either 42 or 50 kroner ($8 or $9.52) per person, including service and tax but not breakfast, which is often available for 16 kroner ($3.04) extra. If such should be the case, then try placing your own phone calls to the private homes we've listed at the end of this section. Their names and phone numbers result from a visit to Copenhagen in late 1979, and the accommodations and prices they offer provide the sure way—sometimes the only way in relatively-high-priced Copenhagen—to live within a low, low budget.

In June, July and August, however, the attendants at Kiosk P make heavy use of their private home listings and will be happy to send you to such a residence. For then, if you check the least expensive category on the application form, you'll quite often find that all hotel rooms are booked. At that point, after first suggesting a higher priced category, these attendants will capitulate quite readily and phone a private home. Thus, you're back to living on a budget!

Amazingly enough, during certain short periods of the year, you may have no choice between a hotel in any price range and a private home. Copenhagen has become so popular that its hotel accommodations are occasionally overwhelmed by the tourist rush (sounds incredible, but it's true). In the last week-or-so in July, and the first week in August, travelers arriving late in the day may be told by the attendants at "Kiosk P"—as I once was—that there simply isn't a vacant hotel room in all of Copenhagen.

That bit of news may turn out to be your greatest fortune. On the occasion just mentioned, Hope and I were given the address of a private home just ten minutes by bus from the heart of town. We arrived at a near-palatial estate, surrounded by grounds and flower gardens, and were greeted at the door by a gracious Danish lady who had patriotically responded to a broadcast appeal for additional private rooms. Our room cost $11 a night for the two of us. We were accorded the utmost privacy. We had breakfast at a neighborhood cafe, and then waited at the bus stop to go into town with Danes who were going to work. It was an experience that the $50-a-day tourists never know, and one we would not have missed.

On one recent crisis occasion, the Prime Minister of Denmark took foreign tourists into his home!

But let me not raise your expectations too high. The private room you rent will usually be simple (but clean and homey) and your hostess non-eminent (but just brimming with Danish good cheer and a warm-hearted concern for your comfort). Here's the list we promised, for so-it-yourself'ers seeking inexpensive lodgings in private homes:

Rooms in Private Homes—from $6.66 to $9.04 per Person

Mrs. Viola Iversen and **Mr.** and **Mrs. Arthur and Minna Allin,** 49 Gammel Kongvej (phone 246-315 for Mrs. Iversen, 249-562 for Mr. and Mrs. Allin), occupy two adjoining apartments at the most centrally-located of our selections, but five flights (and 70 steps) up; that's less than 15 minutes on foot from the central railway station, or a 10-kroner taxi ride. There they rent two single, and six double, rooms, all very simply furnished, for 35 kroner ($6.66) per person double, 45 kroner ($8.57) single, plus 14 kroner per continental breakfast (18 kroner with egg and bacon); showers are free. Mr. Allin and his green parrot, speak English.

Mrs. Dahl-Nielsen, 53 Roskildevej (phone 30-62-16), sixth floor (there's an elevator), rents a cozy, carpeted room with panoramic view, which can be used either as a double (advisable only for small people!) for 90 kroner ($17.14), or as a single for 50 kroner ($9.52) per night. Take bus no. 28 or 41 from the station, and get off one stop after the zoo.

Mrs. Ellen Lund, 1 Langogade (phone 200-183), is a charming, English-speaking, 75-year-old widow who rents two single rooms at 45 kroner ($8.57) per bed, plus 14 kroner for breakfast-with-an egg, in an apartment filled ("overloaded" is the better word) with furniture, bric-a-brac, and pendulum clocks on every wall other than those of the bathroom. As you arrive, Mrs. Lund will give you a handwritten information sheet, decorated with red hearts, listing museum hours and bus schedules. Take bus no. 6 from the central station.

Mrs. Carla Lynnerup, 40 Eschrichtsvej, 2500 Valby (phone 176-930), speaks very little English, but compensates by serving a remarkable, 18-kroner breakfast that includes four types of cold meats and sausages, an egg, tomatoes and cheese; she also rents one double room for 40 kroner ($7.61) per bed. From the central station, take the S-train to Valby, and walk five minutes from there.

Mrs. Kathy Andersen, 53 Sobyholmsvej, 2500 Valby (phone 714-599), is a widow in her sixties who years ago worked in the Chrysler Building in New York, and of course her English is perfect. She rents three rooms on the second floor of her grey house, at 60 kroner ($11.42) for a single, 95 kroner ($18.09) double, 145 kroner ($27.61) triple, plus 15 kroner for an optional breakfast. The double room, with two corner windows, is especially attractive; the furniture antique (in a positive sense); the walls decorated with oil paintings and old weapons (such as swords); the floors covered with oriental rugs; and baths are free. Take bus no. one from its stop directly across from the main railroad station (on Vesterbrogade), show the address to the driver, and he'll stop there after a 15-minute ride.

Mrs. Rigmor Hansen, 87 Fuglebakkevej (phone 346-677), whose home is perfect for travelling families, rents only one very large room for up to four guests, at 40 kroner ($7.61) per bed for the first two beds, 30 kroner ($5.71) each for the third and fourth, with continental breakfast at 15 kroner per person. English-speaking and always smiling, Mrs. Hansen (who wears horn-rimmed glasses) maintains a stock of children's furniture (small tables and chairs), which she'll place in your room at no extra charge. Take bus no. 8 or 13 to the Fuglebakken stop.

Mr. and Mrs. Viggo and Gurli Hannibal, 2 Lighedsvej (Frederiksberg) (phone 861-310), both charming people, live in a small, spotlessly-clean house in a quiet, residential section ten minutes by bus no. 1 from the central station. All they rent is one room with two single beds, at 45 kroner ($8.57) per bed, into which they can also place a third bed at a 30-kroner ($5.71) supplement. Breakfast, optional at 15 kroner, is a feast of cheese, a boiled egg, warm Danish pastry, juice, coffee or tea, marmalade and more. You'll find the Hannibals extremely anxious to please as witness a small library of English-language books in your room, everything from "90 Minutes at Entebbe" to "The Brothers Karamazov"—and you'll especially like the garden with well-kept lawn, weeping willow, roses, rhododendrons, and (the Hannibals' pride) Chinese water pine tree.

Mrs. Daphne Paladini, 20 Dyrehavevej, 2930 Klampenborg (phone 64-07-44), who comes from Ireland and is fluent in six languages, rents two large double rooms and one small single, all of them furnished in superb, cultivated taste, on the first floor of her white brick bungalow; and all at a 1980 rate of only 44 kroner ($8.38) per bed in the two doubles, 42 kroner ($8) single, with breakfast for 18 kroner, and baths and showers for free. On your way to the free beach only three minutes away, you may meet a roaming reindeer in the nearby forest. From the central station, there are S-trains making the 15-minute trip to Klampenborg every 20 minutes or so, for four kroner, and from the Klampenborg station it's less than a five-minute walk to the refined atmosphere of Mrs. Paladini's lovely home.

Mr. Gregoire Sandler, 16 Laurids Bings Allee, 2000 Frederiksberg (phone 864-332), inhabits a former bishop's residence, a small "palais" of a house located in the midst of a beautiful park where, with the aid of his still-energetic, 83-year-old mother, he rents the entire second floor consisting of two double and three twin-bedded rooms, all exquisitely furnished and with green wall-to-wall carpeting, for 45 kroner ($8.57) per bed, with free showers and baths. No breakfast is served, but a large kitchen, amply equipped with pots and pans, cutlery and the like, is made available for your use. To reach this embassy-type address, take the S-train to Peter Bangsvej station (from which it's a one-minute walk), or take bus no. 1 to Bangsvej, about seven stops from the central station.

Mrs. Lillian Pretzsch, at 36 Christiansvej (phone 63-51-48), in the suburb of Charlottenlund, speaks English perfectly, likes receiving families with children (who can play in the garden with two Alsatians and a cat), and offers two doubles and a single renting for 88 kroner ($16.76) double, 50 kroner ($9.52) single, 38 kroner ($7.23) for a supplementary bed in the double rooms. Easily reached by A-train from the Central Station to Charlottenlund.

And finally, Mrs. Gerda Oslev, 62 Bronshojvej, 2700 Bronshoj (phone 287-456), rents a single room (48 kroner) furnished like a ship's cabin, a double room (80 kroner for two) with balcony overlooking a garden, and charges 18 kroner for breakfast—all this in a charming, red brick house in a quiet residential location. And baths are free.

Please bear in mind that these 12 private homes possess a total of about 49 beds only, the capacity of one small pension, and some may be fully booked during the dates of your stay. Always *phone* before boarding taxi, bus or S-train!

PRIVATE-HOMES-THAT-READERS-HAVE-LIKED: "Stay with a Danish family—ours was wonderful! At the home of **Mrs. Robert Hansen,** Ellemosevej 57 (phone 65-81-78), we paid 75 kroner ($14.28) a night for a large, extra-clean, double room; a bath-shower is also there for your use" (Marilyn and Mitchell Shapiro, New Orleans, Louisiana). . . . "We stayed at the house of **Meta Jensen,** Dronningensvej 19 (tel: 87-35-40), 25 kroner each per night in a triple room, 30 kroner per person double, 35 kroner single, and Mrs. Jensen was most friendly and spoke English a little" (Malcolm Cothran, Timmonsville, South Carolina; note by AF: Mrs. Jensen's home, which has four rooms, is 10 to 15 minutes from center Copenhagen, by bus 1 or 14). . . . "Try a call to **Mrs. Sonja Sprogoe,** 7A Langkaervej, Vanløse (phone 716-029), who speaks perfect English and has a modern home, reached by taking bus # 1 to Alstrupvej (K. B. Hallen) or bus # 14 to Vanløse, 70 kroner ($13.33) for a huge double room; 50 kroner for a smaller one; an extremely interesting family" (James A. Tortorella, Silver Spring, Maryland). . . . "A private home, with garden (which we were urged to use), quiet and clean, and only one block from the main street and bus line, is our recommendation. One double with our own toilet and basin for only 100 kroner ($19.04). Owner: **Mrs. Else Skovborg,** who speaks excellent English. Address: Jyllandsvej 29 (phone 462572)" (Mr. and Mrs. Michael Fleming, New York, New York). . . . "We stayed in the private home of **Mrs. Sorensen,** Ceresvej 18 (phone 31-68-14), a 15-minute walk from the station, where a large double room for the two of us cost 90 kroner ($17.14). Plenty of hot baths were available for nothing extra. Her home, which also has a triple room for rent, is situated in a lovely residential area of Copenhagen, very country-like. We were sorry to leave after only 4 nights" (Linda G. Lasker, Brooklyn, New York; strong seconding recommendation from Tom and Sheila Jones, Belmont, California, who received a "large and richly-furnished room" in the "warm and casual home" of Mrs. Sorensen). . . . "We were sent to the residence of **Mr. Kurt Dahl,** Hoejdedraget 30, 2500 Valby, phone 306090, who has been redecorating his house with unusual original ideas using delightful colors. He spoke excellent English and was a charming host, even bringing us fresh strawberries from his garden. Bus number 6 or 41 will deliver you almost to his doorstep. The room per persón was 40 kroner ($7.61)" (Mrs. L. I. Patterson, Indianapolis, Indiana; enthusiastic second from Walter Dotts, Richmond, Virginia). . . . "A really delightful double room was made available to us in nearby Virum for 85 kroner, which included breakfast and baths, at the home of **Faye and Gyde Sorensen,** Malmmosevej 97, 2830 Virum-Copenhagen (phone 02-85-2347). Faye is an American residing there for 20 years and is extremely helpful" (M. McCormick, Seattle, Washington). . . . "A good example of that wonderful Danish hospitality which you mention in your book (although at a higher rate than that charged in many other private homes) can be found at the home of **Mrs. Kate Riise,** Norrevoldgade 27, tel: 13-1846. Mrs. Riise is a retired movie actress who speaks five languages. She has four rooms, including one that can be a triple. Average price is 50 kroner per person. Typical Danish breakfast can be had for 14 kroner in a cafeteria across the street, where you meet everyone, and Mrs. Riise answers all questions about Copenhagen" (James Young, Lake Worth, Florida: note by AF: Mrs. Riise's flat is in the center of Copenhagen, but on the 4th floor of a stairs-only building). . . . "At the home of **Meta Jensen,** 19 Dronningsvej (phone FA-3540), where I stayed last summer, the charge will be 100 kroner ($19.40) for a double room in 1980, not including breakfast—which you'll want to obtain in the form of incredible Danish pastries at several shops down the block. This is only 10 minutes by bus from the center, in a nice residential district near the zoo and Frederiksberg Castle. Mrs. J. let us use her laundry and clothes line, and if you'll ring her up, she'll tell you which bus to catch" (Michele Travers, Melbourne, Australia). . . . "We stayed with **Gregers and Mary Hansen** at 29 Ellemosevej (phone 69-14-29), who provided us with a lovely room, a breakfast of delightful breads, pastries, cheeses, sausages, ham, all served in what they call their winter room, a glassed-in solarium. It was a touch of heaven, and the Hansens delightful people. Ninety kroner ($17.14) per night for a double room, 40 kroner ($7.61) for an extra bed, 15 kroner ($2.85) for breakfast" (Doris C. Robinson, Portland, Oregon). . . . "We must mention the hospitality and warmth of **Else Rathje**, Jyllandsvej 5, phone 86-45-02, in wonderful *(wonderful)* København, where we were accommodated in the most pleasant of situations, near the very beautiful Frederiksberg Have. Others we have spoken with have found their stay here equally 'godt'. It must be partially attributed to the Rathjes' very Danish ability of making complete strangers feel comfortable in their home. And the double room amounted to only 75 kroner ($14.28) per night" (B.V. Vanberg and J. Fleming, Minneapolis, Minnesota; warmly seconded by W. R. Greer, St. Paul, Minnesota). . . . "**Mrs. Stella Holm**, Kronprinsensvej 5, 2000F, Copenhagen, phone GO 7548, is a charming lady who has traveled all over the world. She rents rooms in her home for 45 kroner single, 90 kroner double" (John and Mary Banbury, Breckenridge, Colorado).

PRIVATE FAMILIES FURTHER OUT: "The best place we stayed anywhere in Europe was the home of **Nina Gertz** and family at 172 Lundevej (phone 531-028), Dragor, a 500-year old fishing village only a short bus ride from Copenhagen. Not only do they make you a part of their warm and hospitable Danish family, but their village is a vacation in itself. In short, our stay with them was a rest within a vacation. Rates are 100 kroner ($19.04) per double room and for another 20 kroner each you get a breakfast which is delicious and enormous" (Mr. and Mrs. Richard Wein, Boston, Massachusetts). . . . "Best place to stay in the suburbs is at the private home of **Anna and Tage Petersen**, 7 Gentoftegade, 2820 Gentofte, phone 65-82-71, easily reached by S-train in 15 minutes, followed by a 5-minute walk from the Gentofte Station. We stayed there for a week, at $15 a day, including two wonderful breakfasts. The Petersens are reasonably fluent in English, and are exceedingly helpful; there are also excellent, inexpensive food and laundromat facilities nearby" (Laurie Robas, Phoenix, Arizona). . . . "We have bought a home in Virum, northwest of the center of Copenhagen, in beautiful surroundings near a lake and not far from the Open Air Museum. Our guestroom is priced at only 70 kroner per night" (**Lise Fuhrimann**, 135A Malmmosevej, phone 02-85-93-43).

The Budget Hotel Area

Back to the more standard beds and buildings. In Copenhagen, the most efficient way to rent a low-cost hotel room is through Kiosk P, of course. But if you'd rather avoid the booking fee or if you prefer to see what you're buying before putting up your cash, you'll want to consult our own recommendations below.

The majority of Copenhagen's cheaper hotels are ranged handily along two streets—the **Colbjornsensgade** and the **Helgolandsgade**—that run off Vesterbrogade, parallel to the side of the railroad station. They are all within a five-minute walk of the station, the airline bus terminal, Tivoli, and many of the best budget restaurants discussed further on. Their prices, however, are mixed, ranging anywhere from a pension renting a bathless double for 125 kroner ($23.80), service and taxes included, to a hotel renting a bathless double for a top 220 kroner ($41.90), inclusive. Instead of listing them by price, we've arranged the entire lot in the order in which you'd pass them walking along each street.

ALONG THE COLBJORNSENSGADE: Hotel Cosmopole (formerly the Hotel "Cuba"), 9 Colbjornsensgade (phone 21-33-33), a 56-room hotel spread over five floors, and with no elevator, caters to a great many European tourists, and

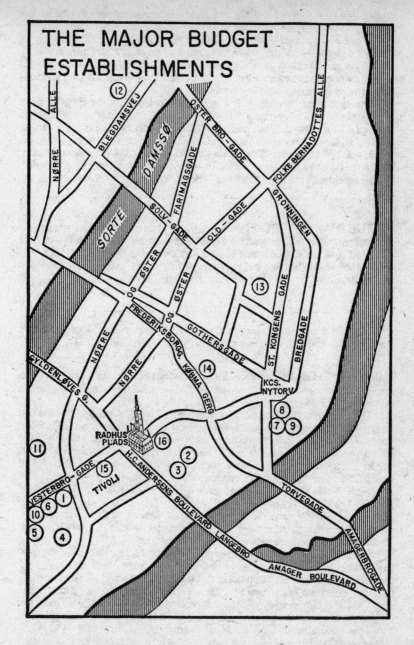

even gets some in the businessmen's bracket, to whom it offers small but comfortable rooms, many of which are completely equipped with new furniture. Room rates for 1980: 140 kroner ($26.66) single, 230 kroner ($43.80) double, 260 kroner ($49.52) triple, including continental breakfast, 15% service charge and 20% government tax.

Hotel Union, next door at 7 Colbjornsensgade (phone 22-44-33), is an elevator-equipped structure whose 50 rooms all have new furniture and wall-to-wall carpets. Its rates are identical to the Cosmopole's, and both hotels are indeed owned and managed by Mr. Niels Pedersen, a gentleman extremely helpful to readers on numerous occasions.

Our best-recommended choice on Colbjornsensgade, is the **Saga Hotel** at No. 20 (phone 24-45-59), managed by Mrs. Ruth Bredwig and her son, Torben, who speaks excellent English and even accepts credit cards. Both try hard to create a friendly atmosphere. Rates in 1980, for rooms located on the upper floors, will be 110 kroner ($20.95) single, 195 kroner ($37.14) double or twin, 95 kroner ($18.09) for an extra bed. Breakfast and free showers are included, but the reception area in this elevator-lacking, four-story hotel is one flight up.

THE DANISH "CROWN": $1 currently buys 5.25 Danish kroner, making each krone worth a little less than 19 U.S. cents. We've used that figure to convert kroner into dollars in this chapter, but should warn that the exchange rate fluctuates in Denmark and might differ by the time of your own trip there.

Elsewhere on Colbjornsensgade, you'll find the excellent **Missionshotellet Ansgar** at number 29, which is described under "Mission Hotels."

ALONG THE HELGOLANDSGADE: This, now, is the next parallel block over from the Colbjornsensgade. Note, first, the two Missionhotels facing each other at numbers 3 and 4.

Hotel Triton, 7 Helgolandsgade (phone 31-32-66), is a big (275 beds) and lovely establishment with exceptionally good rooms, all with polished-wood floors and first-class hotel furnishings—but with big splurge prices only, even for its rooms without private bath. The latter rent for 135 kroner ($25.71) single, 230 kroner ($43.80) double, including breakfast, service and tax. Add nearly 75 kroner per room for private shower and toilet.

Hotel Selandia, 12 Helgolandsgade (phone 31-46-10), is slightly less expensive: 130 kroner ($24.76) single, 210 kroner ($40) for a double, 270 kroner ($51.42) for a triple room, including breakfast, service and free showers. Although the entrance to this five-floor hotel is rather dark, it's a new place, with elevator, wall-to-wall carpets and modern furniture.

Hotel Absalon, 19 Helgolandsgade (phone 24-22-11), with 100 rooms, 10 bathrooms, hot and cold running water in each room, and no charge for showers, is the classic budget hotel in this area, and is my highest recommendation. Four floors, a brand-new elevator, cheerful breakfast room, little "coffee shop" off the entrance way, rooms furnished in Danish modern, hallways floored in simple, well-scrubbed linoleum, and exceptionally friendly proprietors—the young, much-travelled Nedergaard brothers. Rates for 1980: 85 to 100 kroner ($16.19 to $19.04) per person, which includes bed, an all-you-can-eat breakfast, service and tax. Although a bit beyond our limits, this is one of the best deals around. (Across the street at #16, the Absalon recently opened a cellar restaurant called the **Kaelder,** very convenient for budget meals).

We do not recommend the **Hotel Peters, Astor** or **Noblessa**, also on the Helgolandsgade. We do suggest that if all Helgolandsgade establishments are full, you walk to the end of the street, and then turn right on Halmtorvet, which soon becomes the Sonder Boulevard. There, at #53, Mr. Emanuel Jensen operates the 60-bed **Hotel Rosendal** (phone 21-0651) on the fourth and fifth floors of the building, elevator-equipped, and charges 130 kroner single, 165 kroner ($31.42) double, inclusive of continental breakfast and free showers down the hall. A nice atmosphere. For quickest access, take bus #10 from the rear of the station and get off at the third stop.

Mission Hotels

For some of the finest values, try the chain of **"Mission Hotels"**—there are four of them in Copenhagen—and don't be frightened away by the name—these aren't for vagrants, but for ordinary tourists. Owned and operated by the Temperance Societies in Copenhagen, their main function is to foster the good life, which means that liquor isn't served on the premises and room rates are considerably lower than they would be in hotels of similar quality. Furthermore, their floors are so clean they shine and the linens as fresh as from a family wash. While some of the Missions are somewhat austere in appearance, who's going to quibble when the saving is that great?

The largest of the chain, the 275-bed **Missionshotellet (2)** at 27 Longang-straede (phone 12-65-70), has now equipped every single room with private bath, and is therefore outside our range (doubles with private bath, and breakfast for two, about $55 per room). But bathless, budget-worthy rooms are found in abundance at the **Missionshotellet Nebo (4)**, 6 Istedgade (phone 21-12-17), next to the side entrance of the railroad station, which is another big (90 rooms), white-fronted hotel kept meticulously clean by an army of maids (most of them from Ireland) and well-managed by an efficient staff. Rates in 1980, including breakfast: 95 to 110 kroner ($18.09 to $20.95) single, 190 to 210 kroner ($36.19 to $40) double, 70 kroner ($13.33) for an extra bed in the room—and showers for free.

Missionshotellet Hebron (5), 4 Helgolandsgade (phone 31-69-06), two blocks from the railroad station and across the street from the Missionshotellet Westend, has 155 beds and, again, well-maintained, updated facilities. Rates for 1980, *breakfast,* service and taxes included, will be 110 to 140 kroner ($20.95 to $26.66) single, 185 to 230 kroner ($35.23 to $43.80) double, for bathless rooms, of course.

Some Scattered Budget Choices

And then there are the scattered choices—places renting double rooms for an average of 120 kroner ($22.85), service and taxes included.

Among the best of these is the **Hotel Ry**, 14 Ryesgade (phone 376-961), a cheerful, 35-room, four-story hotel with no elevator, located in a busy residential area. With shiny parquet floors, flower boxes at the windows, worn—but very clean—furnishings, it has a helpful, English-speaking clerk and is popular with students. 1980 rates (including service and tax) are: 70 kroner ($13.33) single, 110 kroner ($20.95) double, 145 kroner ($27.61) triple. Breakfast is an extra 18 kroner. Tram #16 comes up from the Town Hall Square in ten minutes and stops a block away.

Pension Nielsens, at Vesterbrogade 33 (phone 24-13-10), only a few blocks from the Central Railway Station, occupies four floors of what was previously an apartment building. Mrs. Nielsens, a kind old lady, charges 80 kroner

($15.23) single, 110 kroner ($20.95) for a double room, but usually rents only to persons staying for at least seven nights.

The Y.M.C.A.-sponsored **K.F.U.M. Soldiers' Home,** 115 Gothersgade (phone 15-40-44), gives priority to military guests, but always has a few available rooms for civilian tourists at a charge of 75 kroner ($14.28) single, 125 kroner ($23.80) double, only 22 kroner ($4.19) per bed in a 6-bedded dorm. Clean, proper and sedate (as witness its 1 a.m. curfew).

This time near the Osterport, the **Pension Centria,** Lipkesgade 5 (phone TRIA 8004), has elevator and comfortable modern rooms with TV and radio. Although rooms normally rent only by the week (singles 511 kroner, doubles 500 kroner per person per week), they're occasionally available on a daily basis, when singles are 90 kroner (17.14), double or twin rooms 150 kroner ($28.57), including breakfast and free showers. Owner Egon Christiansen, who speaks perfect English, suggests you take Bus No. 40 to the Lipkesgade stop.

As a final resort, the 50-room, 70-bed **Soemannshjemmet Bethel,** at 22 Nyhavn (phone 13-0370), is a merchant-marine-sailors'-mission-hotel primarily, but is open to all, and charges 85 kroner ($16.19) for one of its 32 single rooms, 150 kroner ($28.57) for doubles, with breakfast (optional) at 15 kroner. Take bus 1, 6, 28 or 48 from the Central Station and get off at the "Bethel" stop.

Big Splurge Hotels

Finally, we consider the more expensive—and exotic—brand of Copenhagen hostelry: good-quality hotels that nevertheless possess some moderately-priced-rooms. Among them, in a central portion of town, two blocks from the Kongens Nytorv, is a five-story modernistic structure maintained primarily for seamen and their families, which nevertheless manages to accommodate a great many tourists each summer. This is the hard-to-pronounce **Hotel Søfolkens Minde (9),** 19 Peder Skramsgade (phone 13-4882), whose prices for 1980 (including service and tax) will be 110 kroner ($20.95) single, 180 kroner ($34.28) double, 230 kroner ($43.80) triple. Breakfast is served in the inexpensive cafeteria downstairs, which also offers hot plates from 10 to 19 kroner and a daily special of two courses for 24 kroner. The ferry to Sweden leaves from the docks one block away. Proper, quite respectable, and an excellent find—if you can get one of those few tourist openings.

The **Hotel Sibertsen,** at Rosenornsalle 43 (phone 35-12-71), offers 40 beds, for which it charges 95 kroner ($18.09) single, 170 kroner ($32.38) double, including breakfast and showers. Easily reached from Town Hall Square via Bus No. 2, which stops right in front of the hotel, it's in quiet surroundings, ideal for light sleepers.

Five final splurge possibilities:

The recently-built **Hotel Sonne,** 33 Egilsgade (phone 54-44-44), modern, neat and laundromat-equipped. 120 kroner ($22.85) single, 185 kroner ($35.23) double, including breakfast and free showers. Take bus #40 from the central station to Njalsgade, second stop after the bridge.

The 15-room, elevator-equipped **Hotel Sankt Joergen** (that means St. George), centrally located at 22 Julius Thomsensgade (phone 35-5471), and owned and managed by the friendly Mr. Max Muller. Shiny brass door knobs, wall-to-wall carpets in all rooms, which rent for 100 kroner ($19.04) single, 180 kroner ($34.28) double, breakfast and free showers included. Take bus #2, 8 or 19 from Town Hall Square, two stops away.

The much larger (five-story, 160-bed) **Hotel City** at 24 Peder Skramsgade (phone 13-06-66), around the corner from the hydrofoil to Malmö, Sweden (take bus #41 from the Central Station). Singles (there are 26 of them) rent for 125 kroner ($23.80), doubles for 170-210 kroner ($32.38 to $40, depending on size), again including breakfast and free showers.

Hotel Ibsen, 25 Vendersgade (phone 13-1913), a typical, old-fashioned family hotel where children are welcomed, and well-managed by Mrs. Bertram and her daughter, who both try hard to please their guests. 105 kroner single, 180 to 200 kroner double, 70 kroner extra for a third or fourth bed, always including breakfast and free showers. Take bus 16 from the station.

Last of all, but equally well-recommended, the 27-bed **Hotel Windsor,** 30 Frederiksborggade (phone 11-08-30), conveniently located near the Norreport Station, is managed by a stern-looking lady with a heart of gold, who charges 95 kroner ($18.09) single, 175 kroner ($33.33) double, inclusive of breakfast and free showers. That's for bathless rooms, of course, and in an apartment building with no elevator.

Student Hostels and Dorms

Copenhagen's major youth hostel is the **Bellahoj Vandrerhjem,** 8 Herbergvejen (phone 28-9715), which is open all year except from December 21 to January 6, has 344 beds, and requires international youth hostel membership. Price per bed in 8-bedded dorms, including breakfast, is 35 kroner ($6.66). Two minor drawbacks: the hostel is closed between 9:30 a.m. and noon for cleaning (but guests can use a "common room" during those hours), and curfew is a strict 1:30 a.m. Take bus #2 from Town Hall Square for about 20 minutes (and 3 kroner) to Fuglsang Allé. Even if you're not staying here, you might consider using its large, 200-seat cafeteria for which no youth hostel card is needed and where unlimited second helpings are permitted for every food item except the meat. Lunch and supper are each 22 kroner ($4.19) and consist of three courses apiece. And there's an open-air swimming pool (admission, with locker, 4 kroner) only 500 yards away.

The remainder of Copenhagen's hostels and dorms do not require either student identification or youth hostel membership. While they appeal mainly to young people, presumably anybody of any age who wishes can book into them.

The best-located of them all is the **Vesterbro Ungdomsgard,** a large, white bungalow-type building set in a garden only a few blocks down the Vesterbrogade from the station at 8 Absalonsgade (phone 31-20-70). It is open from May 5 through September 1, offers 160 beds in separate dormitory rooms for men and women, imposes no curfew at night, and in 1980 will charge 48 kroner ($9.14) for bed-and-breakfast. Sheets are required and can be rented for 12 kroner, for the entire duration of your stay. Take buses 6, 28 or 41 if you don't care to walk from the station.

By far the least expensive of the hostels is the **Active University Hostel** at 40 Olfert Fishersgade (phone 15-61-75), near the Osterport Station, charging only 18 kroner ($3.42) per night, plus 5 kroner-one time only-for a blanket. Open all year and managed by a dignified Indian national, Mr. Dipak Das, it takes up to 116 guests, male and female, in 10 dorms with double-decker bunks, provides free showers and a free sauna (mixed), but closes the rooms from 12:30 to 5 for cleaning, and imposes a 1 a.m. curfew. Either take bus no. 10 to Kronprinsessegade, or the S-train to Osterport Station, and look for a red-brick church topped by a spire looking like an inverted ice cream cone; the three-story hostel is nearby.

THE MAJOR AVENUES

SUB-STARVATION BUDGET: In an effort to cope with the yearly, summer invasion by masses of international young people, the city has converted a former industrial fair ground into a huge **Sleep-In,** at 85 Hulgardsvej, admittedly on the outskirts of town, but easily reached (10 minutes) from the center by bus #8, 63 or 68, or by taking the S-train to the Fuglebakken stop. Open in July and August only, it can accommodate up to 800 guests in cavernous, 25-to-75-bedded dorms, for only 28 kroner ($5.33) per person, including breakfast and free showers. But while there's no curfew, the dorms are closed from noon to 6 p.m. for cleaning. If you're in the mood for such comforts and conviviality, you can book space by phoning 19-49-91, or by visiting the offices of **Use-It,** at 14 Magstraede (phone 15-65-18), open daily from 10 a.m. to 8 p.m., and less than 5 minutes on foot from Town Hall Square. Needless to say, Use-It offices are also congregating centers for young people (they need not be students) seeking other forms of assistance and facilities in Copenhagen. Use it.

Consistent with a 25 kroner bed is a 15 kroner meal, which, in Denmark, is had in the form of "lobescowes"—a potato stew that, in my experience, consists 90% of potatoes, 7% of water, and 3% of shredded beef—it resembles a similar item available in Hungary, and is surprisingly tasty. In the summer of 1979, lobescowes sold for only 15 kroner ($2.85) at a smoky basement student beer-drinking restaurant called **Skindbuksen** ("Leather Pants"), on the Lille Kongensgade, #4, one street over from the Stroget, opposite the Magasin du Nord department store. Other items there—for example, potatoes topped with two fried eggs for 16 kroner—are also quite cheap. Hours are 11 a.m. to 1 p.m.; and you should come early for the lobescowes.

And now to the open sandwiches, the superb beer, and the gravy-doused food:

MEALS: Eating inexpensively in Copenhagen can take some doing—but let me assure you that the game is worth the flame. Denmark is much like France in the pride its people take in their cuisine. It's hard to find a really bad restaurant in Denmark, regardless of the price range, and often the tinier and less expensive the spot, the more care is lavished on the cookery. Most Danish restaurants post their menu outside the door and you can feel safe venturing into any one of them—after, of course, you've checked the prices.

Denmark's most distinguished delicacy is *smørrebrod,* which means literally "butter and bread." These are what we call Danish open-faced sandwiches; they are based on a simple slab of bread spread with butter, but the artistry comes in the construction of the super-structure, which can consist of anything from a single slice of cheese to a mass of tiny, pink shrimp to steak tartare (raw beef) topped with a raw egg yolk. Most restaurants have long lists of their special smørrebrod. The waitresses will bring you the list and you check with a pencil how many of each sandwich you want for your party. The Danes eat smørrebrod for lunch, for snacks, for appetizers and just for fun. And since one of the best budget travel rules is "When in a country eat what the natives eat," we trust you'll be piling into plates of smørrebrod yourself. These "sandwiches," by the way, are never picked up in the hand, but always eaten on the plate with a fork and knife.

Here, now, are some general tips on sticking to your food budget and the specific places that we like best. The categories and the establishments are set forth in generally *ascending* order of cost:

1. Do-it-yourself picnics

Very soon in your stay, you'll discover that Copenhagen is much like one enormous smorgasbord, with all the national delicacies laid out for your choice in pastry shop windows, smørrebrod stores and the most modern of magnifi-cently-stocked supermarkets. Choosing a meal from among all these tempting assortments can be the most delightful—and least expensive—way to eat in this city. On warm, sunny days, make it a picnic in Tivoli or alongside one of the mid-city canals or in the park on the harbor where the Little Mermaid sits. On chilly days or at night, take the food back to your hotel room. Your menu might consist of several open sandwiches, a side salad, a pastry and something to drink. Go to a supermarket—the **Irma** chain is one of the best—for the salad and beverage. Mixed salads packed into plastic containers cost around 4 kron-er; ½ liter of milk will cost 2 kroner; a bottle of Danish beer in a grocery shop will cost only 5 kroner, in contrast to the 9 kroner and more charged for the same beer in a restaurant. Pastries will cost from 3 to 3.50 kroner in one of the many pastry shops spotted about the city; and these shops also usually sell milk. Danish smørrebrod varies in price from 3 kroner to about 5 kroner, in the stores, depending on the ingredients. You can buy pre-wrapped picnic packs very cheaply from the white wagons on the Town Hall Square in the summer. After the smørrebrod shops have closed for the night, they often place their leftover sandwiches in vending machines outside the shops—insert 3 kroner and out pops a sandwich, just like in the Automat. One of the best shops in the city for smørrebrod—and one that stays open 24 hours a day—is **Favori-ten's**, just opposite the Central Station at 6 Vesterbrogade. The variety is extensive, and prices range from 10 to 15 kroner (choose the cheaper ones, such as salami and onion, or cheese), and all are immediately well-wrapped "to go." For a "walk-away" snack, purchase a "polser," the Danish version of the hot dog, from one of the many mobile hot dog stands for 3.50 kroner, and follow that up with a rich "soft ice" for 3 kroner.

2. Chinese (Kinesisk) Cafeterias

Apart from the "do-it-yourself" method, the next least expensive means of eating well in Copenhagen is to patronize an absolutely unique collection of institutions known as "Chinese" (Kinesisk, in Danish) "Cafeterias". They are Chinese—but only in the sense that they're operated by Chinese residents—the food itself is Danish workingmen's variety, served with rice or noodles; and they are cafeterias, but only in the sense that you walk to a counter, order your dish, and carry it to be consumed at another counter or table. Totally nonde-script in appearance, and less than dainty in their offerings of fried or roasted food items, the "Chinese cafeterias" undercut the prices of most other Danish restaurants by several kroner per dish, probably because an entire Chinese family usually works long hours in each "cafeteria." Like the Chinese laundries at home, they provide exciting value.

The cheapest and most easily located of the Chinese cafeterias is probably the **Mandarin Grill** at #1 Istedgade, immediately at the side of the railroad station, in the interesting (and perfectly safe) Copenhagen area of porno shops and budget hotels. Open until 2 a.m., 7 days a week, the Mandarin has a staff of white-clad Chinese waiters and waitresses who serve you with amazing speed from a posted, English-language menu that lists all sorts of meat, rice and vegetable plates for only 10 to 16 kroner (extremely cheap for Copenhagen), and even less costly servings of "frikadeller" (hot meat balls) with cold potato salad for 10.50 kroner, hamburgers for 4 kroner, french fries for 3.50 kroner. You can combine a smaller individual serving of meat balls (1 krone) with french fries (3.50 kroner) for a perfectly adequate 4.50 kroner snack. . . . Further down the Istedgade, at No. 23, near Viktoriagade, the higher quality but tiny **Kinesisk Grill Hus** charges 11 kroner for fillet of plaice with french fries and mayonnaise, 17 kroner for soya pork with bamboo shoots, 18 kroner for chicken and shrimps with fried rice or noodles, 18 kroner for chicken curry and rice, 5.75 kroner for "lys pilsner" (light, local beer—always the cheapest).

In other parts of Copenhagen, you might try the **Kina Grill** at 100 Norre-brogade (soup for 7.50 kroner, fried cod fillet with curry rice for 14.50 kroner; closed Sundays), or the much larger **Mandarin Cafeteria** at 74 Osterbrogade, open every day of the week and with prices almost as low as those at the Mandarin Grill of Istedgade, described above.

Largest of all the Chinese cafeterias is the **Kinesisk Cafeteria** at 30 Dronningens Tvaergade, where a simple Scandinavian decor is accented by dragon-trimmed plates. Here the Danish specialties are varied with curries, spaghetti and chop suey, and you can order sharkfin soup (7 kroner) with your Danish frikadeller (meat balls) at 9 kroner. Or else a quarter of a roast chicken with rice for 13.50 kroner ($2.57). . . . And then there's the **China Garden Grill** at Vaernedamsvej 20 (a small side-street off Gammel Kongevej, near Vesterbros Torv), a combination delicatessen and self-service restaurant open daily from noon to midnight, where various sandwiches go for 6 to 8 kroner, a hot dog for 4 kroner, and a quarter of a roast chicken with french fries for 9.50 kroner. And thus those industrious Chinese do battle with inflation.

3. Cafeteria meals

Serve yourself and save the service charge—it's as simple as that. Cafeteria dining is popular with the practical Danes and there are good cafeterias in every sector of the city. But the budget champ of them all—a veritable samaritan to low-cost travelers—is the **Vista Self-Service Restaurant**, upstairs at 40 Vesterbrogade, a five-minute walk from the station.

The Vista serves the largest food portions I have ever seen in preparing this book. On a recent summer evening there, while Hope, daughter Pauline and I were vainly trying to finish two plates we had ordered for the three of us, a trio of British rock-and-roll types ordered one plate of fried potatoes with fried eggs on top (16 kroner), picked up the unlimited servings of fresh Danish bread that the Vista offers free, split the mound (it looked a foot high) among them, and still weren't able to finish their meal. Of the 28 vast platters offered on the menu, 14 are priced at from 14.75 kroner ($2.80) to 22.75 kroner ($4.33), and the top price—for veal steak with grilled ham and fried egg—is 48.50 kroner ($9.23). And the amazing thing is that each order is cooked especially for you! You walk to the serving counter, ask for the English-language menu (it's printed on yellow paper), place your order, receive a number, and then wait at a table until a loudspeaker announces (also in English) that the chefs have completed making your huge Danish repast. If you don't want to wait, you can choose from four immediately-ready two-course dinners-of-the-day, which are priced from 16.75 to 26.50 kroner. Be prepared, of course, to encounter large, lively crowds—including every itinerant hippie and aspiring Rolling Stone from across the continent, who seem drawn to the Vista by some ultrasonic homing device, and whose presence adds to the fun. The restaurant opens at 9 a.m. and closes punctually at 8 p.m.; get there early for dinner.

Other cafeterias? The increasingly popular vegetarian cafeteria, **"City Helsecenter"**, at 6 Vendersgade, sells filling daily platters for 25 kroner ($4.76) that might consist of red peppers stuffed with rice and bean sprouts. On a recent Sunday afternoon, I ordered a second portion of the cooked rice with almonds and cherry sauce, only $1.85. Open Sunday to Thursday until 8 p.m., Fridays until only 6:30 p.m., closed on Saturdays. . . . Cheaper is the cafeteria in Copenhagen's cheapest department store—**Daell's Varehus**—where 25 varieties of open sandwiches sell for 7 kroner each, and a pair of sausages with bread are 2.80 kroner. That's a 300-seat room on the 6th (top) floor of the bustling **Daell's,** on the Nørregade, down the "walking street" from Town Hall Square. . . . Though most other department store cafeterias are considerably more expensive, you might also try the relatively moderate **Anva Cafeteria** at 2E Vesterbrogade, across from Tivoli. . . . In the "student quarter" of Copenhagen, those busy streets near the university, the **Expresso Cafeteria,** 94 Norre Voldgade, is remarkably good for the price. Excellent smørrebrod start at 8.75 kroner; hot plates average 24 kroner for tasty "biksemad" (chopped meat) dishes or "frikadeller" (meat balls); hours are 7:30 a.m. to 10 p.m.; and there's a colorful outdoor cafe in summer, photo murals of the marching Royal Guard on the walls, and a cheerful, student-crowded atmosphere. . . . Next door to the Expresso, the small **Bodega** at 96 Norre Voldgade, a popular hangout for students, offers three open sandwiches for a total of 16 kroner ($3.04), which you accompany with a beer for 8 kroner ($1.52).

4. Stocking up for the day on smorgasbord

Danish smorgasbord is a huge, all-you-can-eat, buffet, where all the national specialties are trotted out for your enjoyment. Served traditionally at lunchtime only, it consists of multiple varieties of fish, salads, meats, usually a hot dish or two, cheese and fruits. There is a method to eating smorgasbord and it's not the pile-it-on-and-dig-in-to-your-elbows technique of the Western chuckwagon that has possibly done more to alienate Danes from American tourists than any breach in international policy could ever do.

The rules are very simple. When you enter the restaurant, the buffet table will be in the center and all the tables around will be set up with plates and silverware. Sit down and wait for a waiter to approach you. Give him your beverage order. It is customary to drink "snaps" with the first course of herring and to follow that up with beer. But since both these drinks are rather expensive, don't be embarrassed to order an apple cider or a soft drink. After he has your order for drinks, pick up the plate before you, go over to the table and fill it up with as much herring and fish as you wish. The fish is always the first course and you never mix it with anything else. Go back to your table, eat the herring, then—leaving your plate behind you (the waiter will clear it off)—go back to the table, pick up a new plate and fill it up with any of the salad and meat dishes you want. One never uses the same plate for fish and meat. You can go back to the table as often as you wish and you can take a new plate each time if you prefer. You will notice that on all the large platters on the buffet table, the main dish is surrounded by such accessories as pickles and sauces. Let this be your guide as to what to eat with what (e.g., the steak tartare will be accompanied by horseradish, pickles, cucumber salad and raw egg yolk). Now, unlike the Swedish smorgasbord, the Danish dishes are not necessarily meant to be eaten as is, but are supposed to be laid out on slices of bread, sm ørrebrod style, and eaten as open sandwiches. To this end, you will be provided with a basket of bread at your table. If you find your appetite failing, however, feel free to dispense with the bread as you work along. After attacking all the cold dishes, you follow up with the hot ones (of which there are seldom more than one or two) and then turn to the last course of fruit and cheese. At this point the waiter will approach you again and take your order for coffee.

Smorgasbord, eaten properly, can take the better part of an afternoon and it can certainly render you unwilling to eat again for hours. Thus, though it is usually "big splurge" in price, it is an excellent investment in both quantity and enjoyment.

Largest, "cheapest" (by Copenhagen standards) and most conveniently found of the smorgasbord restaurants is the large **Bistro Buffet** in Copenhagen's main railroad station ("Hovedbanegaard"). Here, in attractive surroundings, you can make your choice among 187(!) different dishes for the all-inclusive price of 49.50 kroner ($9.42), plus beverage. This is the only place in the city that serves smorgasbord every day from 11:30 a.m. to 2:30 p.m., and from 5:30 to 9:30 p.m. Do try it at least once.

(And incidentally, the same railroad station offers an all-you-can-eat *breakfast* smorgasbord from 7 a.m. to 10 a.m., this time for 24 kroner ($4.57), including beverages; both meals are among the top values of Copenhagen. Look for the "Restaurant" sign at the head of the corridor leading to the Bistro Buffet, and don't confuse the Bistro with the large snackbar restaurant, alongside).

Working up through the ranks of higher-priced smorgasbords, the **Hotel Osterport** on Oslo Plads (just opposite the S-Tog station at Osterport), offers a 40-item smorgasbord from noon to 3 p.m. and charges 64 kroner ($12.19) for all-you-can-eat. The restaurant is downstairs and its soaring windows look out on the railroad tracks; it's interesting to note how the straight parallel lines of the tracks seem to merge with the straight lines of the Danish decor inside. The charming **Captain's Grill,** off the lobby of the **Hotel Penta,** 50 H.C. Andersens Blvd., serves a similar selection daily from noon to 2:30 p.m. for 79 kroner ($15.04). All these prices include tax and service, but beverage is always extra.

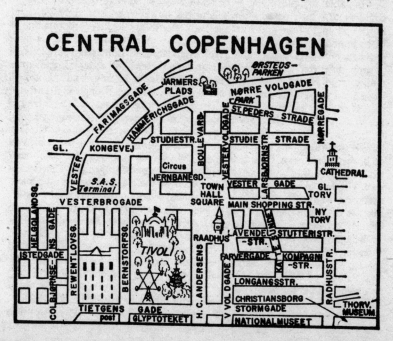

5. The best of the budget restaurants

Practically unknown to tourists, but wildly popular among local residents, is **Morten Larsens Middagsroekken,** where the price is only 18 to 22 kroner ($3.42 to $4.19) for exceptionally large portions of a hearty, three-course meal —example: soup, fish filet or real beefsteak with vegetables and potatoes, with as many second helpings of potatoes as you want, plus a "sweet" (dessert) such as a pudding, or bread. And drinks are reasonable, too: milk or coffee for 3 kroner, a small Pilsner beer 3.75 kroner. You won't be able to remember the name, let alone pronounce it; simply look for the flag-sign "Spisesalon" above the door at #4 Sorgenfrigade, a sidestreet off Nørrebrogade, reached by bus #5 or 16 from Town Hall Square. The 15-table establishment is open Monday through Friday only, from noon to 7 p.m., and cuts the price by half for children.

Raadhuskroen at 12 Longangstraede charges a uniform 25 kroner for each of its many large plate meals, each sufficient for many hours of hard touring.
. . . **Axelborg Bodega,** Axelborg 1, next to the airline terminal, is an old "Vinstue" cafe that's a popular downtown eating place for Danes (in contrast to just tourists), who imbibe great platterloads of its Danish frikadeller and potato salad for 20 kroner, "biksemad" (see description below) for 21 kroner, a serving of three colorful open sandwiches for 15 kroner.

6. Eating out in Tivoli

Inside the Tivoli Gardens (later described), the restaurants are almost all expensive—probably the most expensive in Copenhagen. And it hurts terribly to recommend that you stay away from them, because they are so flower-filled and breathtakingly-lovely as to be reminiscent of another age—Renoir alone could capture their pastel hues. The prices, however, are positively 20th century. You might try—and I am perfectly serious about this—ordering one of their dinners, for two people, with extra plates. When Hope and I stopped in recently for a late "snack" at a Tivoli establishment, I ordered a simple bowl of soup, only to watch the waitress cart out a tureen large enough for an entire family. And Hope's "plate" of chicken livers, onion rings and cucumbers turned out to be a two-foot-long silver tray, again large enough to feed three.

There are, however, two moderately-priced restaurants in Tivoli, where the atmosphere isn't as elegant but neither are the prices. **Groften** (immediately to the right of the Peacock Theatre, as you face it) serves a 27 kroner "tourist's table d'hote dinner" of two courses, as well as individual plates for as little as 16 kroner (sausages with fried potatoes); but service and food have been somewhat disappointing on my latest visits there. **Paafuglen** (meaning Peacock), a spot with lots of outdoor seating, is owned by the management of a far more expensive downtown restaurant, and offers a large "turisplatte" of herring, salad, roastbeef, salami, liverpaste and other items (you spread them all on bread) for 45 kroner. A nice touch here is the Børneplatte (children's plate) for 25, which consists of four small open sandwiches—flat and easy for the children to handle. Finally and fortunately for us, there is one cafeteria in Tivoli called the **Bix'en Self-Service Restaurant,** to the rear of the gardens near the rides (it's to one side of "Det Mystiske Hus"), which is probably the cheapest sit-down place in the area; it is basically utilitarian, but there are tables under the trees outside, and colorfully-lit arches around the tables. Hot plates include such items as roast beef or fish, but don't go above 30 kroner ($5.71) in price, and average 25 kroner for the plainer dishes (fiskefilet, biksemad, frikadeller).

7. Some final food and drink tips

Go easy on the beer. Amazingly enough, those beer-loving Danes have loaded the sale of beer in restaurants and bars with so many taxes that it gets surprisingly expensive—as much as 12 kroner per bottle, as opposed to the 5 kroner you'd pay for the same bottle in a grocery store. To order draft beer, which is both better and cheaper, order "fadøl." If you must have it bottled, ask for "Pilsner," not "Export," which costs only 10 kroner in most restaurants and is closer in taste to draft. Cheapest of all is the "Lys Pilsner," which has a low alcohol content and costs only 8 kroner in restaurants. . . . Milk is actually the least costly beverage to have with your meal, at a price considerably under the cost of tea, coffee or beer. . . . When in doubt over a Danish menu, ask for "biksemad," or point out the word to your waiter, if you find it hard to pronounce. "Biksemad" is chopped meat fried with onion and potatoes, with a fried egg on top. It's always filling, always tasty, and always cheap. . . . Other reliables: "smorstegte hakkeboffer" (hamburger beefsteak), "sprodstegte fiskefiletter" (fried filet of fish). . . . What's the most popular open sandwich sold in Denmark? It's "leverpostej"—liver-paste and pickled cucumber, with a small chunk of meat jelly. . . . The real oddity: Danish pastry in Denmark is called "Wienerbrod," and must be ordered as such or you won't get it. . . . The best breakfasts in Copenhagen are the ones you can purchase in a bakery ("Konditori" or "Bageri"). They'll serve you half a liter of milk, plus two luscious Danish pastries (Wienerbrod), for 5 kroner. . . . At least once, order the famous, unpronounceable Danish dessert—"rødgrød med fløde" (most K.A.R. restaurants serve it in summer)—whose taste is as delightful as the way it sounds (ask your waitress to speak the words aloud). . . . And finally, in reading Danish menus, don't confuse the abbreviation "kr" with "kl". The first stands for kroner, the second for the hour of the day. And thus, when a menu is headed with the words "Fra Kl. 12", it does *not* mean, as some non-Danish-speaking readers have supposed, that the meals cost 12 kroner, but instead that they are served starting at 12 noon.

THINGS TO DO, PLACES TO SEE: Good news, there's lots that's worth doing in Copenhagen that never costs a cent. You can prowl through the antique lanes of the old city. Tour a brewery and have a free beer. Stroll along the harbor and strike up a nodding acquaintance with Hans Christian Andersen's Little Mermaid. Visit the National Museum, where there is never any admission charge, or the other museums on special "free" days. Explore the museum-like shops on the Strøget. Take a canal cruise to a small cluster of harbor-side shops and historic showplaces. And—above all—get to know personally some of the wonderful people that make up this "Wonderful Copenhagen."

Tours

First we'll consider the free tours, then one for 57¢, and finally an assortment of bus tours that start at $7.23 and climb from there.

For Free

The stellar free attractions of Copenhagen are the tours of the city's famous big breweries, which produce what some people consider to be the world's greatest beer. You can visit either the **Carlsberg Breweries** (whose tours begin punctually at 9 a.m., 11 a.m. and 2:30 p.m. weekdays), or the **Tuborg Breweries** (which runs them continuously from 8:30 a.m. to 2:30 p.m., again weekdays only), and you ought to do it, first, because the beer-making procedure is a fascinating art—and second, because there's free beer for you to drink at the end of each visit. More interesting of the two is probably the Carlsberg visit because of the astonishing art gallery and photograph collection that adjoins its beer-drinking hall; but on the other hand, Tuborg seems to provide a more intimate tour. The guides at both plants deliver humorous and pun-laden spiels, which you should vastly enjoy. Take either the S-Tog to Enghave Station, or bus No. 6 to reach Carlsberg (whose address is 140 Ny Carlsbergvej); and take Bus #1 from the center of town or Bus #21 (ringline) to get to Tuborg (at 54 Strandvejen).

For 57¢

Summers only, you can ride out to the "Langelinie," where the famous Copenhagen mermaid sits pensively on a rock, via special Bus #50," whose round-trip fare is only 3 kroner (57¢) if you return within an hour. The city transport company operates this whimsical ride from the "bus port" at 12 Vesterbrogade near City Hall Square in front of the Kong Frederik Hotel, at 10:30 a.m. and then at half-hour intervals until 5:30 p.m. Look for the yellow sign: "Mermaid No. 50," from which the bus sets off on its 10-minute ride. It then lingers at the statue for 10 minutes-or-so of picture taking, before returning to City Hall Square. Alternatively, you can make the same trip by sea (weather permitting) for 12 kroner ($2.28), round-trip, by boarding the Langelinie Boat Service at the Gammel Strand, across from Thorwaldsen's Museum. It departs every hour from 10 a.m. to 5 p.m., daily, and provides an especially pleasant experience. .

For $7.23

The normal city tours are run by the organization called **Copenhagen Excursions,** whose buses leave from the statue of the Lure Horn Blowers **(16)** —two men blowing curved horns—on the Town Hall Square. Best for openers is the **City Tour With a Visit to a Brewery,** which consists of a 1½-hour bus tour around all the most famed spots and concludes with a stop-off at one of the two Copenhagen breweries. These leave on the hour from 9 a.m. to 2 p.m. in summertime and cost 38 kroner ($7.23). The same city tour, without the brewery, is given on the hour from 3 to 5 p.m., at the same price; go early and you'll save yourself the trouble of getting to the breweries on your own. (No brewery tours are ever included, however, on Saturdays or Sundays).

And Up

A more unique **Sociological** tour costs 60 kroner ($11.42), leaves at 9:15 a.m., weekdays only, lasts 2¾ hours, and visits the far-advanced social institutions of Copenhagen: day nurseries for children of working mothers; low-cost apartment projects for old people; centers of special education; a typical Danish high school; and so on. This latter tour is really quite a unique experience, which Hope and I regard as one of the high spots of our European trips. If you'll pardon a political note, this view of sunny, active, comfortable old folks' homes, where elderly Danes live in dignity, and of nurseries to which working mothers can bring their children for $15 a week, should make us ashamed. There simply is no reason why the richest country on earth can not provide as well.

After "life-seeing," you might consider the **Industrial Art Tour,** which leaves at 1 p.m., weekdays only, and costs 60 kroner for an inspection trip through the silver workshops of Georg Jensen and A. Michelsen, the famous porcelain and ceramics factories of Denmark, the shops and studios of other renowned producers of decorative products; also the comprehensive 2¾-hour "Royal Tour" of the city for 70 kroner (10 a.m.).

Tivoli

Step one foot inside, and you'll want to camp there for life. A vast amusement park in the heart of Copenhagen (between the Central Station and the Town Hall Square), this is one of Europe's top attractions—the lightest, loveliest, most refreshing area in the world, brimming with both goodhearted fun and culture! Go during the day to sit in the sunshine and have a picnic of smørrebrod in company with Danish mothers and their towheaded offspring, pretty secretaries and office-workers from the downtown firms. Go at night, when colored lights bathe the park in a fairytale glow and the entertainment schedule is packed. Admission before one p.m. is only 7 kroner. After one p.m., that rises to 8 kroner, but children are always admitted at half price.

If you'll arrive just slightly before 7 p.m., you'll be exactly in time for the action. **At 7 p.m.:** Danish variety acts (tight-rope walkers, trained seals) on the open-air stage in the center of the gardens; free. **7:30 and 9:30 p.m.:** top-name international stars entertain at the Varieteen Theater, where the cheapest tickets are 12 kroner and every seat in the house is good. **7:45 p.m.:** pantomime in the traditional Commedia dell'Arte style (Harlequin, Columbine, and all your friends) on the Peacock Stage to the left of the main entrance; free. **9 p.m.:** the Tivoli Symphony, in the concert hall; usually free. **9:45 p.m.:** modern ballet on the Peacock Stage; free. **Midnight:** fireworks, three times a week, on Wednesday, Saturday and Sunday.

Then there's dancing everywhere, vivacious blondes everywhere, fun houses and rides, and colorful parades of the Tivoli Boy Guards, every Saturday and Sunday at 6:30 and 8:30 p.m. (the Boy Guards consist of 85 youngsters from 6 to 16 years, who assemble before parading, near the Chinese Tower—the best spot to watch).

Tivoli stays open from May 1 to mid-September. I don't want to appear blunt, but if you come to Copenhagen and miss this place, you are simply off your rocker!

Bakken

And there's another, even vaster, amusement park on the outskirts of Copenhagen—**Bakken**—which is supposed to be the oldest amusement park extant in the world. This is a far earthier place—very popular among the young Danes for dancing—with rides, restaurants and good-hearted, apple-cheeked Danish strip shows. There's no admission charge. Take the S-Tog marked "Klampenborg" from the Central Station at 14, 34 and 54 minutes past the hour. Round-trip fare is 12 kroner; the park is usually open from mid-April till the end of August, starting at 3 p.m.

Seeing the Shops

The Danes, so famed for their interior design, arts and crafts, give to their shops such a museum-like quality that a few very pleasant hours can be spent poking through them, whether or not you intend to buy the wares. Take at least one long walk along the pedestrian street, Strøget (pronounced "Stroyet"), that runs from the Town Hall Square to Kongens Nytorv, where **Georg Jensen** peddles its silver, **Royal Copenhagen** their porcelain, and **Birger Christensen** his mink. Don't miss a tour of the famous **Illums Bolighus** or of **Illum's** department store, a brilliant showcase for the best in Danish furniture and household accessories. Another—and the most important—showcase to visit: **Den Permanente** (The Permanent Exhibition), two blocks from the central railroad station, on Vesterbrogade, but on the other side of the street (and also in a smaller annex that recently opened on Town Hall Square). Here on show (and for sale) are the highest-quality arts and crafts items in all Denmark, chosen for their merit by a special committee.

Museums and Castles

To my mind, there are three which shouldn't be missed: the **Frihedsmuseet** (Museum of the Danish Resistance Movement, 1940-45), the important **National Museum** (Danish history is the subject matter), and the **Ny Carlsberg Glyptotek,** for modern art and sculpture. Then you'll want to take one of the hourly tours of the Royal Reception Rooms at **Christiansborg Palace.** For the details on these and many more interesting places, here's my Copenhagen-loving wife, Hope:

THROUGH ROYAL COPENHAGEN WITH HOPE: "An independent and fascinating aspect of Copenhagen is the one associated with its royal history, and found today in the areas around its three major palaces: Amalienborg, Christiansborg and Rosenborg.

Amalienborg Palace

"To the first of the three, you'll want to make only the briefest of visits. For, while the Queen of Denmark presently lives in one of the four palaces on Amalienborg Square, all you can see there is the Changing of the Guard (daily at 12 noon, but most colorful when the Queen is in residence). Far more interesting, in my opinion, is the place where her predecessors lived, the great—

Christiansborg Palace

"Christiansborg Slot—on the Slotsholmen (the small island where the city began—was the official residence of the Danish kings until 1794, and with its spacious, cobblestoned courtyards and darkish grey buildings, it's a most impressive palace, which now houses the Royal Reception Rooms, the Danish Parliament, the Supreme Court and Ministry of Foreign Affairs—and a whole host of museums. You can take a 3-kroner conducted tour (departing daily in summer, daily except Saturdays at all other times, from a small office near the main gate from 10 a.m. to 4 p.m.) of the basement ruins of Absalon's Castle (he being the famous Archbishop who founded Copenhagen).

"Now, look for signs that lead you to the Royal Reception Rooms, where you can take another tour—for 8 kroner, this time—departing at 2 and 4 p.m., daily except Mondays in summer, and at 2 p.m. only, daily except Mondays and Saturdays in winter. Your guide will be a good-humored Dane who has quite a spiel prepared for your trip through the richly-decorated rooms, including the famous quip about King Christian IX being the "father-in-law" of Europe (one of his daughters became Queen of England, another the Czarina of Russia, his son King George I of Greece). Another element of fun on the tours is provided by the soft overshoes you'll be asked to wear upon entering the Palace. You'll fairly skate through the rooms—helping to polish the floors!

The Theatre Museum

"One of the grandest sights of Christiansborg Palace—but open only on Sundays and Wednesdays (Fridays too, June thru September) from 2 to 4 p.m.—is the Theatre Museum, at 18 Christiansborg Ridebane, in the Palace's own Royal Court Theatre (from 1766). It's an old baroque court theatre, wood, gold and red velvet, in the style of 19th-century Old Europe, but still aristocratic and regal. You'll be able to wander through and on the orchestra, the loges, the steeply-raked stage, the 200-year-old dressing rooms (each left with the trappings of a famous Danish actor), leisurely taking in the pictures and displays (which trace the development of almost three centuries of Danish Theatre); two costumes and ballet shoes of Anna Pavlova's, drawings of Sarah Bernhardt (who played in Denmark in 1880 and 1904), "Armida," a ballet program, listing Hans Christian Andersen as an extra, a model of the Globe Theatre. Admission of only 3 kroner; don't miss it!

The Royal Danish Arsenal

"Not far from the Theatre Museum at Tøjhusgade 3, is the admission-free Arsenal Museum (Tøjhusmuseet) located in one of the longest halls in all of Europe. Ordinarily, I am not a great one for arsenals, but this one is really quite interesting, with airplanes suspended from the ceiling and tanks in the middle of the floor, as well as the expected historical displays of cannons, cannon balls and the like. Even the guards in their colorful red, gold and black uniforms seem part of the exhibition. Open in summer from 1 to 4 p.m. on weekdays, from 10 to 4 p.m. on Sunday; in other seasons, until only 3 p.m., Sundays 11 to 4; don't fail to go upstairs, as well, to see the several thousand firearms of the Armory Hall.

The National Museum

"If you'll now walk from the Palace courtyard in the direction of the City Hall, you'll cross a romantic little grey stone bridge which brings you to The National Museum, at 12 Frederiksholms Kanal—once the palace of the Crown Prince, now a gigantic museum housing what its own guidebook describes as a 'picture book of the cultural history of man.' The emphasis, of course, is on Danish history—with one of the most important items being the Bronze Age 'Sun Chariot from Trundholm,' Denmark's most famous find—but the exhibits deal with other cultures as well (an exposed Egyptian mummy, for instance), and the collection consists, in the main, not of mere paintings but of actual artifacts from bygone days—primitive tools, coins, structures, all else you can name. Admission is free, and the museum is open every day in summer from 10 a.m. to 4 p.m., and generally from 11 to 3 in other months. Skip Tuesdays, when only two departments are open.

Rosenborg Castle

"Finally, the castles of Copenhagen include an ornate Renaissance palace —Rosenborg—which stands in the Kongens Have (King's Garden) at 4a Ø stervoldgade (from the Central Station, take the S-Tog to the Nørreport Station, from which the Castle is only a short walk away). Built in 1606 by King Christian IV (a hard-drinking, hard-swearing, wenching young man who became one of Denmark's great improvers and builders, a man of culture and good taste), it now houses a chronological collection of the treasures of the Danish Royal Family, not the least of which are the Crown Jewels. You'll see the spectacular saddle and riding outfit of Christian IV, all studded with sapphires, diamonds, and pearls; the Crown Jewels in the Treasury in the cellar; the mirror room on the second floor; the 'Knights' Hall' on the third floor. Hours at the Castle (whose name means "Castle of the Roses") are from 11 to 3, daily, from May 1 to October 21; on Sundays, Tuesdays and Fridays from 11 a.m. to 1 p.m. in other months; and admission is 8 kroner for adults, 1 krone for children.

The Royal Museum of Fine Arts

"Within walking distance of Rosenborg Castle (or take bus #40) is the vast **State Art Museum** ("Statens Museum for Kunst") housing the world's largest collection of Danish art, as well as a small, but representative sampling of masterworks from other nations. Admission is free, and the museum is open daily, except Monday, from 10 to 5; on Wednesday evenings until 8 p.m. Engrossed as you may be in its collection of paintings, don't miss the Print Room and Library, where you will find more Albrecht Dürers than in any city other than Munich, many Rembrandts, Hogarths, Daumiers, Titians and Tintorettos. On my last visit, the guard mentioned that the day before, the King of Sweden had spent an hour in the Royal Print Room.

Royal Gifts from the Beer Kings

"Now we turn to another type of royalty. Denmark owes a large debt of gratitude to J. C. Jacobsen and his son Carl Jacobsen who, in addition to brewing a most delicious beer, in 1876 established the Carlsberg Foundation, which uses brewery profits for the advancement of art, science and Danish culture. Through their generosity, Copenhagen is graced with **The Ny Carlsberg Glyptotek** and **The Kunstindustrimuseet** or Museum of Applied Art (among other donations too numerous to mention here).

The Ny Carlsberg Glyptotek

"Located on Dantes Plads, off H.C. Andersens Blvd., the Glyptotek is directly across the street from the back entrance of the Tivoli Gardens, and is open May through September from 10 to 4 daily except Mondays, October through April from noon to 3 p.m. on weekdays (except Mondays) and from 10 to 4 Sundays, charging admission of 5 kroner, but none on Wednesdays and Sundays. The museum contains a vast collection of ancient art (Egyptian, Mesopotamian, Etruscan, Greek and Roman works), a large assortment of French painting and sculpture including numerous Impressionists, and finally a major selection of modern Danish artists: all displayed in a rambling stone building with a lovely winter garden in its center courtyard. Two recognized treasures of the Egyptian collection are the black stone "Head of a King" (circa 400 B.C.) and the 5,000-year-old miniature "Hippopotamus" (in Room 3); be sure to see, as well, "Gebu" or "Lord Privy Seal," whose image reaches out over the ages as the timeless incorruptible politician, and the ever-fascinating "Anubis" the Keeper of the Dead, with his dog's head on a human body. And don't miss Room #2, which contains a small but enthralling collection for mummy fanciers like me. One interesting sidelight of the French collection is the opportunity it affords to see some pre-Tahitian Gauguins: from them, you'll learn how Tahiti vivified and actually defined Gauguin as an artist.

Kunstindustrimuseet

"The 'Kunstindustrimuseet,' or Museum of Decorative Art, located between Amalienborg Palace and The Esplanaden at Bredgade 68 (if in doubt, start from Kongens Nytorv where Bredgade begins), charges no admission except on Sundays and holidays (when 5 kroner are asked), and is open daily except Mondays from 1 to 4. Housed in a graceful grey stone building with a small courtyard in front, this museum has large and pleasantly displayed collections of furniture, textiles, tapestries (the most famous being the Flemish Tournai from the 15th century), and all forms of decorative art; as well as a lovely large library which is open to the public weekdays (except Mondays) from 10 to 4. Modern design is not stinted: you'll see Matisse tapestries, as well as pieces from Georg Jensen, the Royal Porcelain Factory, recent Danish furniture, design, etc.

Royal and Non-Royal Extras

"For a good panoramic view of the city, try the old **Round Tower,** built in 1642, by our all-time Danish favorite Christian IV as an observatory; it's located on Kobmagergade (not too far from the 'Strøget'), is open in summer on weekdays from 10 to 5, Sundays and holidays from noon to 4. On weekdays you'll be charged 3 kroner to climb the long circular ramp to the top. . . . And if you have time, do try to see that marvelous antique in the midst of the city, the **Nyboder** section, which was also built by Christian IV. Only a short walk from The Esplanaden or The Resistance Museum: head for Gernersgade or Store Kongensgade, where you'll find a series of streets made up of tiny low-roofed orange doll houses, with short doors, small rooms, gas lamps on the streets: everything (except the cars parked out front) conspiring to transport you back 300 years. . . . **The Copenhagen Bymuseum** or City Museum, Vesterbrogade 59, contains objects and paintings illustrating the history of the city, done in typically charming Danish fashion. There's a large model of Copenhagen in 1550 on the grass in front of the building (complete with water in the canals), peepshows inside, city models that light up, a huge model brewery, another model honoring the development of the Fire Brigade, and also a special room devoted to personal objects of Soren Kierkegaard. You can have all this, and more, for free; the museum's open daily, April to October, from 10 to 4, November to March from 1 to 4 (except Mondays, when it's closed), and all Tuesdays from 7 to 9 p.m. . . . **Thorvaldsen's Museum,** located near Christiansborg Castle (look for the most classy classical-looking building in the neighborhood, complete with friezes), open every day from 10 to 4 in summer, until 3 in the winter, (when it closes on Tuesdays), with free admission, is a monument to Denmark's foremost sculptor, Bertel Thorvaldsen (1770-1844), and contains his statues and works, models and sketches for works in progress, his own private art collection (all of which he bequeathed to the City of Copenhagen), and his grave (he's buried in the courtyard). I find his work a bit schmaltzy and too conventionalized in the classic tradition for my tastes, but go and judge for yourself. . . . Last, but certainly not least, do visit **Denmark's Fight for Freedom Museum** ("Frihedsmuseet"), in Churchill Park, open daily except Monday in summer from 10 to 4 (Sunday til 5), in winter from 11 to 3 (Sunday 11 to 4—closed Monday), which displays a chronological and graphic record of the German occupation of Denmark, and then shows you how the Danish resistance was set up (with illegal presses and radios, homemade rifles) and how the Germans reacted, with grisly exhibits of Nazi tortures, cases of material relating to the flight of Danish Jews to Sweden. Buy the 4 kroner guide book in English (or ask for an automatic guide-tour) so that you can follow this inspiring exhibition of the courage, daring and determination of the Danish people to be free."

OFFER FROM A SIGHTSEEING GUIDE: "I intend to quit my summer job as a guide on the ordinary bus tours, not only for the week-ends like this year, but all the time next year. I am tired of having to speak 2, 3 or 4 languages on the same bus—which of course is completely unsatisfactory to the tourists, too—and of rushing by everything of interest in a hurry. The best way to see a city is definitely by foot. From June 25 to September 5, 1980, I therefore plan the following program:

"**Sunday at 4 p.m. and Wednesday at 5:30 p.m.:** A guided walking tour thru the heart of the old city. We meet at the Dragon & Bull Fountain in front of the Town Hall.

"**Monday and Thursday at 5:30 p.m.:** A guided walking tour to the old canals and the 'Castle Island'. Meeting point: same as above.

"**Saturday at 2 p.m.:** Meeting at the ramp of the Stock Exchange (Borsen), we'll go to Christianshavn ('Little Amsterdam').

"**Sunday at 10:30 a.m.:** We meet at the corner of Gothersgade and Øster Voldgade to walk through the Botanical Gardens and visit the Royal Museum of Fine Arts.

"**Tuesday at 10:30 a.m.:** Meeting point: Entrance of the Botanical Gardens, as above. A guided tour through 'The King's Garden' and the Rosenborg Castle (crown jewels, etc.) Entrance fee is 8 kr., students 4 kr.

"**Monday and Thursday at 10:30 a.m.:** A guided visit to the prehistorical section of the National Museum. Meet in the hall, entrance from canal side.

"My charge will be 10 kr. per person per tour, but young people aged 14-25 pay 7 kr., children under 14 are free. Duration of each tour: 1½-2 hours. Language: English exclusively. Hope to see you!" (Mr. Helge Seidelin Jacobsen, **"The Guide Ring,"** 91 Kongelundsvej, 2300 Copenhagen, phone 51-25-90).

NIGHT-TIME ENTERTAINMENT: In addition to what you'll find at the Tivoli, Copenhagen enjoys a 24-hour night life, that roars on till morning in jazz clubs and dance halls, coffee houses and nightowl restaurants. Things don't start swinging until around 10 p.m., though. While the streets of Copenhagen may look absolutely deserted at that time, you'll be surprised at all the activity that's going on inside.

Jazz

The city's major jazz club (music and dancing) is **Daddy's,** at Axeltorv 9, near the Royal Hotel Air Terminal, which looks like a white castle; you can't miss it. Entrance costs 10 to 20 kroner ($1.90 to $3.80), and festivities continue, unabated, until 5 a.m.

The slightly cheaper **Vingaarden,** at Sct. Nikolajplads 21, is another jazz spot, with dancing this time, that features live Dixieland and swing combos—young bands and a young clientele (it is, in fact, jammed with cute, blonde nymphets and college kids). There's an admission of 10 kroner ($1.90), per person here on weeknights, which rises to 15 kroner on Fridays and Saturdays. Beer is 7 and soda 8, and there is no minimum. Very lively, with an ultra-friendly crowd, it's owned by a fellow called "Bamse," who operates the wildly surrealistic bar at the rear.

Finally, **Vognporten,** Magstrade 14, specializes in traditional jazz and swing music. Admission is 10 to 20 kroner ($1.90 to $3.80), depending on the day of the week and whether you are a club member. Open daily from 9 p.m. to 1 a.m.

Dancing

This is a highly-developed sport in Copenhagen, seriously pursued. And since most Danes speak English, the prospects for a lonely single American tourist—male or female—are just great.

The choice of a dance hall is best made according to age-group. For those in the 18-to-30 range, **Taverna** inside Tivoli, is usually crowded to capacity, bright and noisy; it charges no admission except on Friday and Saturday nights (10 kroner). . . . Danish students (18 to 26), and thus far very few tourists, are presently flocking to the **Pussy Cat,** an attractive discotheque at Gothersgade 15. Here there's admission of 15 kroner (depending on the night), a low-lit warm and dark wooden-walled setting, and two floors-full of blondes in both sexes. The same age group also frequents **Vingaarden,** mentioned above. . . . People of all ages—in couples or stag—head for **Den Røde Pimpernel** ("The Scarlet Pimpernel") at Hans Christian Andersen Boulevard 7, where you knock on a mysterious-looking red door until an eye peeps out at you, the door swings open, and you are ushered into a large, lively club where a live orchestra plays all the usual dance tunes. There's a Friday and Saturday admission charge of 15 kroner (all other days, there's none), a one-drink minimum; drinks start at 8 kroner for snaps or akvavit, 10 kroner for a Cherry Heering, but it is perfectly permissible to sit and sip a coffee or Coke all night. This is an especially good place for women who are travelling alone, and it is open seven days a week from 8 p.m. to 2 a.m.

Beer Halls

Our older and heartier readers will enjoy **Vin & Ølgod,** 45 Skindergade, a Danish beer hall where guests are presented with printed song pages and everybody joins in singing international rousers. A brass band keeps the crowd singing and swilling; the result is very-Hofbrauhaus, and admission (after 8 p.m.) is 15 kroner (with women admitted free on Tuesday and Thursday nights). Closed Sundays.

Inside Tivoli, there's another such place and it's possibly the most popular summertime drinking-spot in all Copenhagen, for the Danes. Its name is **Faergekroen,** and it's a pink-painted wooden building on the Town Hall side of the lake. Everybody who can, squeezes around the tables inside where a man at a piano belts out Danish, American, English and German beer-drinking songs and whole benches of strangers link arms, singing and swaying, while pouring down mugs of beer at 15 kroner each. Those who can't fit are relegated to being mournful onlookers from the outdoor tables by the lake. There's no admission charge, but you'll want to drink.

Nyhavn

Now you're in the Greenwich Village of Copenhagen, a rowdy street of bars and cafes that parallels an often-pictured canal, located—amazingly enough—just a few steps from the plush Hotel d'Angleterre, near the big square called Kongens Nytorv. It's a rough-hewn, raucous area, but not dangerous (although women will be more comfortable with escorts), much frequented by Swedish sailors in search of the brew they can't purchase so easily across the sea. A hop from bar to bar makes for a modest "walk on the wild side." At **Cap Horn,** Nyhavn 21, you'll find Dixieland jazz, a topless, female disc jockey, and topless waitresses; **#41 Nyhavn** features pop bands alternating with a free jukebox; **Sailor's Inn** at 17 Nyhavn collects an authentic crowd of old sea-dogs and their mates, all telling tales and acting frisky, often to the background strains of an accordion; the **Sailor's Inn** at #25 Nyhavn is much the same. At none of the clubs will you pay an entrance fee, although beer costs a stiff 11 to 14 kroner. All the clubs close down promptly at 2 a.m., in an obvious attempt to keep the lid on, and things aren't really roaring till about 11 p.m. It's an experience that shouldn't be missed. Items to note: the huge anchor at the head of the canal, a memorial to Danish sailors who lost their lives in World War II; the small, white house at #67, where Hans Christian Andersen lived from 1845 to 1867; the 200-year-old Danish courtyard—a picture postcard sight—at #53 (walk in); the top of #11 Ny Havn, where you'll see the lit-up face of an astronomical clock, such as sailors use; and several real-life tattoo parlors, of which the main specimens are **Tattoo Ole and Arno** at no. 17, and **Tattoo Jack, Jorgen and Bimbo** between nos. 37 and 39. Here you'll be adorned with up to 5,000 different motifs, ranging from a blue swallow or seagull for your bicep (for 60 to 100 kroner) to a butterfly or rose for your chest (for around 150 kroner). And if you have a month to spend in Copenhagen, plus a few thousand kroner, you can order a full-body job, including the Manhattan skyline, all known birds, animals and flowers, hearts, anchors, ships, and the Monster of Loch Ness.

Copenhagen's Garden Restaurants

For more than 125 years, Danes have been flocking to eat, drink, sing and dance until 1:30 a.m. at the eight wooden huts and buildings, surrounded by gaily-colored lamps, benches and trees, that make up **Krogers Have** ("have" meaning garden) at 18 Pileallee—Copenhagen's largest outdoor restaurant outside of Tivoli. A dance floor with continually-playing band, strolling accordionists, and strategically-situated pianists, completes the picture, and there's food in all price categories: 25 varieties of smorrebrod from 10 to 24 kroner, beer for 10 kroner, coffee for 8. If you can't find a vacancy among the 1,500 seats, then walk down the street to two similar but smaller establishments at #10 ("Hansens Gamle Familiehave") or #16 ("Petersens Familiehave"), all of which are best reached by bus no. 28. Less ambitious than the Tivoli, the garden restaurants provide Danish families, and their friends, with simple, wholesome relaxation on warm summer days or nights, which may suit your own mood at the time of your visit.

The Circus

And lastly, schedule a performance at the **Cirkus Benneweis** on the Axeltorv, one block from Town Hall Square. One of our readers says, "This is the number one circus in all of Europe; the Benneweis horses are second only to those of the Spanish Riding School." We heartily concur, and add that this is probably the most exciting circus-going experience a big-city person will ever have! The theatre is small, and the performances are therefore closer and more real than they would be at, say, Madison Square Garden—if an aerialist were to fall, chances are good he might fall on you! There are matinees here on Wednesdays, Saturdays and Sundays at 4 p.m., evening performances every night of the week at 8 p.m., and prices range from 15 to 55 kroner. April through mid-October is the season.

STUDENT IN COPENHAGEN: As we noted earlier, the co-ordinator of youth activities in Copenhagen is an organization called **"Use-It"**, which publishes a summer newspaper of the same name, and operates out of a fascinating old building at 14 Magstraede (phone 15-65-18), open daily from 10 a.m. to 8 p.m.

From the Town Hall Square, stroll down the Walking Street ("Strøget") to Gammel Torv, then turn right along Radhusstraede, and use the entrance at 14 Magstraede. "Use-It" will help you with housing through the virtually unlimited beds they control at various campsites, "sleep-ins," dormitories, hostels and private homes, and provide you with nearly every other form of assistance except in the field of student transportation; for the latter, go to the offices of D.I.S. on the Skindergade (see below).

After you've visited the "Use-It" reception area at 14 Magstraede, you'll also soon discover an upstairs cinema showing high-quality films, the wildly-active jazz center called Vognporten on the ground floor mentioned above, a youth-style restaurant known as "Spisehuset", a cafe named after socialist revolutionary Rosa Luxemburg (entrance from Radhusstraede), and many other constantly changing facilities and activities. Obviously, this is a key center for young people arriving in Copenhagen. . . . For the price of a beer, you can meet fellow students at any of several other gathering spots in the city. At **Pilegaarden** on Pilestrade, just squeeze in wherever you can make a space and you'll be involved in conversation in no time. Crowded, noisy and candlelit, Pilegaarden is strictly for swilling and philosophizing. **Lille Apotek,** 15 Store Kannikestraede, has a bistro aura about it (it was originally an 18th-century pharmacy), as does **Laurits Betjent,** Ved Stranden 16 (the sign reads "Royal" in green neon), is for the serious talkers, although there's an occasional small combo and dancing. Located across the canal from the Royal Palace, this place pulls them in daily from 10 p.m. to 5 a.m., and charges an admission of 10 kroner. **Hviids Vinstue,** a remarkable cellar cafe—dark, smoky and dating atmospherically back to 1723—captures not just the students but theater folk from the Royal Theater across the square and a cross-section of Copenhagen's intelligentsia. Tradition makes this "the" spot for a before-dinner drink and for its famous hot, mulled wine served all day long during the Christmas season. . . . For information on student charter flights from Copenhagen to other European cities, stop at the modern offices of the **D.I.S.** (Danish International Student Committee), 28 Skindergade (phone 11-00-44), which offers breathtaking possibilities. Student railway fares? They're even cheaper. Check at the same D.I.S. office, which is best reached by walking up the Strøget (the walking street) from Town Hall Square, half a block past the Gammel Torv, then passing through "Jorck's Passage" to Skindergade.

MISCELLANY: The Danes are great gagsters. Cartoon translated from a Danish newspaper shows one waiter yelling to another, "Hey, Povl, your Danish is better than mine. You'd better serve this Dane." Another depicts a tourist at Elsinore, asking: "If Hamlet never existed, then why did you build this castle?" . . . The one all-night pharmacy in town is the **Steno Apotek,** at 6C Vesterbrogade, opposite the train station. . . . For a laundromat in the budget hotel area at the side of the Central Station, try the large **Quick Vask** at 45 Istedgade (corner of Absalonsgade), six short blocks from the station; a machine-load (6 kilos) costs 12 kroner, and the attendants are there until 6 p.m. on weekdays. . . . Readers staying in the vicinity of the Kongens Nytorv can use instead the **Vesketeria** laundromat at 2 Borgergade, which is open from 6 a.m. to 11 p.m. seven days a week, and charges 15 kroner for 9 kilos of wash. Directly across the street, **Rekord Rens** at 18 Borgerade, does same-day cleaning at reasonable rates. . . . Cheapest department store in Copenhagen, for that vital odd item: **Daells Varehus,** 12 Nørregade. . . . A genuine, open-air flea market? One operates every Saturday from 9 a.m. to 2 p.m. on Israel Plads, a block west of the Norreport Station, on Frederiksborggade. And even though it's in dignified

Scandinavia, you bargain. . . . Need a youth hostel card? You can buy one for 60 kroner (good all throughout Europe) at **Herbergsringen,** 35 Vesterbrogade. . . . A budget steam bath? The extremely pleasant, community-owned **Kø benhavns Bad,** Borgergade 12, offers "vapour" (steam) baths for 10 kroner, sunbaths for from 8 to 11.50 kroner. . . . Readers who will be driving to Copenhagen from the mainland of Europe should remember to buy a *round-trip* ticket on the auto ferry going there, which brings you a 30% savings over the cost of two one-way tickets; the round-trip reduction is applicable even if you are returning to the mainland by a different ferry than the one you took going over. . . . Want to return to England by boat? Or go to Oslo by boat? **D.F.D.S.** is the steamship line to consult at their offices ("D.F.D.S. Travel Bureau") at 4A Vesterbrogade (phone 15-63-41), Copenhagen. And if you're in England, and want to come to Copenhagen by boat (via Harwich or Newcastle in England and Esbjerg in Denmark), consult **D.F.D.S. Seaways,** Mariner House, Pepys Street (phone 481-3211), London. There are daily summer departures in both directions. Cost of the one-way trip is as little as $67, not including meals on ship. . . . Inexpensive babysitters? Try **University Students Babysitters Minerva,** 20 Akrogen, Glostrup (phone 02-450-90-45), 17 to 27 kroner an hour.

READERS-ON-EXCURSIONS: "An all-day trip by train from Copenhagen to **Odense** is fascinating, very easy, and can be done for less than half the cost of the conducted bus tour. The day before, provide yourself with a map of Odense at the Tourist Bureau in Copenhagen beside the Central Station, and buy a round-trip 2nd class rail ticket for 148 kroner ($28.19). Take the early morning Lyntog (lightning Train) from the Central Station at 7:15 a.m. The entire train is put on the ferry from Korsør to Nyborg (a delightful 55-minute trip) and arrival in Odense is at 9:51 a.m. With your map of Odense, you will have no difficulty walking from the station through the park and the town to Hans Christian Andersen's house and museum on Hans Jensensstraede—it isn't far. Tours stay only a few minutes; we spent more than an hour here and enjoyed it thoroughly. There is also a delightful gift shop (Klods-Hans Kunsthaandvaerk) across the street, with superb and inexpensive Christmas items, among other delectable tidbits. Then go back one block to the bus stop on the 6-lane highway and, for 1 krone, take local bus #2 going south, to "Den Fenske Landsby", or "The Funen Village"—the driver will let you off at the right place. This is a remarkable reconstruction of an Old Danish village, with farmhouses, a windmill, an inn, etc. Lunch at the Sortebro Kro (inn) here will cost $4 to $4.50 (best bet is an omelet); it's a picturesque place with low beamed ceilings, rustic furniture, old pewter, candle molds, etc. Take the bus back to the center of town and have a look at the Town Hall. Then, if you have to wait for a train, spend the time by the pond in the beautiful park opposite the station. There are trains back to Copenhagen approximately every hour. We took the one at 4:16 p.m., arriving Copenhagen 7:13 p.m. It was the best excursion of our whole trip" (Mr. and Mrs. Paul Redin, Oklahoma City, Oklahoma). . . . "Anyone who visits the charming little town of **Dragør,** 8 miles southeast of Copenhagen, will want to stay several hours, taking pictures all of the time. Simply board bus #33 from the Bus Terminal in Copenhagen (across the street from the City Hall), and in 20 minutes you will be in Dragør, using your city bus-transfer as part of the fare. Buses run every 20 minutes back and forth from Copenhagen. You might also like to take the ferry to Sweden from Dragør, which will land you at Limhamn, not far south of Malmö. You can then come back to Copenhagen via ferry or hydrofoil" (Mrs. Calvin Smith, Clinton, Michigan). . . . "As wonderful as Copenhagen is, Denmark is really fun to visit, and about an hour away by train is **Køge,** a small old harbor town that, like almost every place we visited, had its own tourist office which could provide friendly and informative assistance. The Saturday morning open air market is an especial treat" (Craig Nauman, Madison, Wisconsin). . . . "A must for those who visit Copenhagen is a trip to **Hillerød,** the home of Frederiksborg Slot. This was one of the most spectacular palaces in Europe (and we tried to see them all) and is virtually unknown to most tourists. Take the S-train from the Central Station (free to Eurail) and ask for directions to Frederiksborg Castle at the Hillerød station. It is located about 20 minutes' walk from the station. Admission is 8kr, or 4kr for students and 2 kr for children" (John and Mary Banbury, Breckenridge, Colorado). . . . "The **Danish Open Air Museum**

("Frilandsmuseet") situated on 90 acres in Lyngby, about 10 miles from downtown Copenhagen, consists of 50 authentic rural structures, completely unchanged, including several farms in simulated working condition, with horses, cows and chickens. Use your Eurailpass for the S-train to Sorgenfri, or take bus #84. Admission is 3 kroner and hours are from 10 to 5, Tuesday through Sunday, but only May through September" (Jeffrey Stanton, Marina del Rey, California; reminder from AF: since the Eurailpass is honored on all state railways, and since the subways and suburban railways (S-trains) in Copenhagen are state facilities, Eurailpass holders can travel free to many of the attractions listed above).

READERS-ON-BIKES: "I rode to the **Louisiana Museum** at Humlebaeck, 22 miles up the coast from Copenhagen. It's a beautiful ride—with Sweden right across the water. The suburbs north of Copenhagen are probably the most beautiful in the world; Arne Jacobsen's hand is everywhere. The Louisiana itself is a museum of contemporary art with a few pieces from the 30s, but almost all from the 50s and 60s including abstract, Pop-Op—the whole thing. It is also a beautiful building with fine sculpture around it and a view of the water. Hours are 10 a.m. to 5 p.m., daily, admission of 10 kroner. Four miles beyond is Helsingor, which translates as Elsinore, Hamlet's home. I did not have the strength to go there, but it might be worthwhile" (B.L. Wendell, Baltimore, Maryland). . . . "We took a very enjoyable trip in one day from Copenhagen to **Elsinore**—an hour's train ride away. At the Elsinore Train Station, we then rented bikes (it's best to reserve them ahead of time) and pedaled to Kronberg Castle, where we had lunch. Afterward, we biked six kilometers to 'Louisiana,' the most beautiful modern art museum in all of Europe. It overlooks the sea and is worth visiting for its architecture alone! The entire trip—including train fares and bicycles for two persons—cost only $9" (Deirdre Henderson and Mark Koplik, New Haven, Connecticut).

A FAST BOAT TO SWEDEN: "An experience no one should miss is the hydrofoil or "Flying Boat", from Copenhagen to **Malmö**, Sweden. It leaves every hour, on the hour, from the corner of Nyhavn Canal and Havnegade (take bus #41 from Town Hall Square to end of line on Havnegade, or take any bus that goes to Kongens Nytorv and walk to the end of the Nyhavn Canal). Cost is 31 kr. ($5.90) one way, and no reduction for round-trip, but you can go over on the hydrofoil (35 minutes) and come back on the ferry (1½ hrs.) for 48kr. ($9.14), round-trip. There is a good restaurant and bar on the ferry; frequent departures, about one every hour. Malmö itself is an interesting city, and one of the things not to be missed is its modern Municipal Theater, and the fountain on its grounds" (Mr. and Mrs. Paul Redin, Oklahoma City, Oklahoma). . . . "Travelers staying in Copenhagen would do well to take the early boat to **Malmö**, Sweden, look around for an hour, and then take the train to **Lund** ($2.20, I believe) to see a beautiful Gothic university town, very sophisticated, with quaint shops. Then one would do well to have lunch at **Staket** (I'm not sure of the spelling, but the railroad has a tourist booth that will help you), which is the oldest building in the city and a favorite mealtime gathering place of the students. (Dinner with over a pint of milk was $4). Lund is a beautiful city. I think anyone will be enchanted with its beautiful parks and buildings. You can still return to Copenhagen by a late ferry in time for the ballet/opera. We did!" (Karl Davis, New York, New York; note by AF: one-way on the ferry (not the hydrofoil) to Malmö is 19 Danish kroner, round-trip is 38; the trip takes about 1½ hours each way, and you can board the boat free with a Eurailpass; boats leave and tickets are sold from the Oresund Company pier on Havnegade, just at the end of Nyhavn, and departures are almost hourly during the summer). . . . "We strongly recommend going to **Elsinore** by train, and then to **Helsingborg**, Sweden, by ferry, where you can have a walk around, and then return to Copenhagen by direct steamer" (Bruce Marschak, Chicago, Illinois).

READERS' SUGGESTIONS: "If you come to Denmark via the Puttgarden-Rodby ferry, then, no matter what the hour, go to one of the ship's restaurants and have the 'Kolde Bord'—cold table—all you can eat from a fabulous table of both hot and cold Scandinavian specialties—$6. The variety and attractiveness—and tastiness—of the dishes is almost overwhelming" (Jess and Alice Brewis, Taylor, Michigan). . . . "On the **Tuborg** tour, I was lucky enough to draw the public relations man as a guide, and there were only five of us on his tour. He treated us to some very interesting tales and some of the strong beer, which is rated 20% over here. It made my bike ride thru rush hour quite thrilling, to say the least. At the opera and ballet, I had seats in the gallery for $1.50; and I saw Rubinstein at the Tivoli Concert Hall for only $2" (Richard D. Gold, Los Altos, California). . . . "We left Copenhagen for Oslo by the overnight DFDS 'ferry', which was cheaper than airfare and much cleverer than by train since, for slightly more, we got an overnight 'hotel' room included in the deal. The second class cabin had running water, two berths and a porthole (a necessity for travelling since the ship got rather warm)" (Dr. and Mrs. S. M. Marcus, Keflavik, Iceland). . . . "There's free admission to the **Deer Park** next to Bakken, a beautiful, wild area where many deer wander unfenced. You can rent bikes at the train station for 15 kroner a day, and burn up some calories in the most wonderful way" (Bob and Chelley Gutin, Hartsdale, New York). . . . "Eurailpass owners should note that their passes are valid on the municipal S-Tog ('S-Train'), which is actually owned by the national railways" (Anthony Miller, Freehold, New Jersey). . . . "In the large central hall of the **Copenhagen Town Hall,** open to the public, stand four impressive statues, and although this is a public building, none are of political figures. Two of the four are of special interest to foreign visitors: Niels Bohr, the famous physicist who helped to give man so much physical power, and Hans Christian Andersen, whose wonderful stories may help to give us a little of the wisdom needed to use this power for good instead of harm. Perhaps this is a little beyond your subject of *Europe on $15 a Day,* but the combination of Bohr and Andersen seemed impressive to me in the same way as the World War II plaque which you wrote about seeing on the Ponte Vecchio in Florence—and perhaps worthy of mention for the same reason" (Richard A. Givens, New York, New York).

Scandinavia only begins with Copenhagen, and a taste of this northern city should whet your appetite for more. The logical next stop is a quick flight to Stockholm.

Chapter VIII

STOCKHOLM

Under 3 Crowns

STOCKHOLM, very simply stated, is like no other city you have ever seen. At times, it resembles a Camelot, all surrounded by forests, laced with spires and turrets, very stately in its aspect, and seemingly as conservative as the John Birch Society. To think that this is the birthplace of cradle-to-grave security, and of experimental marriage, is a shock that often takes a few hours to overcome.

Physically, the city is one of the loveliest of capitals. It spreads over 14 separate islands, each connected by vaulting bridges, under which the waters of Lake Mälaren—which flow into the Baltic Sea—are often covered with sailboats, cruising deep into the city. Some of the islands rise on steep cliffs from the water, and on these cliffs, high above, are the stern, dignified buildings of Sweden, untouched by the ravages of war for nearly two hundred years. Best yet, the city is surrounded by woodland and farms, never more than 10 minutes away from any point in town.

Viewed from another aspect, the city is one of the most sophisticated in Europe, not only in the attainments of its art and culture, but in the social relationships of its citizens. There is no public graft in Sweden, no discernible poverty. If you'll probe deep enough, you'll be constantly surprised by the projects and ideas erupting about you: the futuristic suburbs, all built within the past twenty years; the ingenious efforts to make life pleasant and full, within a framework of democracy. It may be a minor example, but it's typical of

Sweden, that old-age pensioners are permitted to buy tickets on the Swedish Railways at half price.

For the tourist, there's an endless variety of sights and activities: the unique open air "museums," the Archipelago of Stockholm, the brilliant Royal Dramatic Theatre, the Milles Sculptures, the mysterious Flagship Wasa. When Hope and I last had to depart this city, we felt we were being dragged away.

But how much, you now ask, does all of this cost?

A BUDGET SURVEY: Well, despite all of Stockholm's very notable attractions, it has—by this book's standards—one major problem: it is Europe's most expensive city. Even the Stockholm tourist office, publishing a pamphlet of hints for penny-pinching tourists, had the grace to title it "See Stockholm at a MODERATE Price," instead of "See Stockholm Cheaply." "Moderate" is the accurate word. You will find meals in Stockholm selling at $4.50 to $5, but most likely you'll put out $5.50 to $6.50 for the average dinner. You can get a bed in a hostel for $6 or a room in a private home for $16, double, but if you plan to stay in a pension or a hotel, you will have to pay from $22 to $26 for a bathless double, including service charge.

As in our Copenhagen chapter, we'd suggest that you don't stay away— not by any means—Stockholm is far too fascinating to miss. But that you budget a little more for the daily necessities—about $18 or so—and consider Stockholm a "Big Splurge" city. With meals and lodgings under control, you'll find that low-cost sightseeing and entertainment abound, and much of it is covered in the pages to come.

Here, now, is how I'd organize a first visit:

ORIENTATION: The very first thing to do upon arriving in Stockholm is to go to the hotel accommodations bureau **("Hotellcentralen")** in the Central Station and obtain a room (details appear in our section on accommodations, below). Then, after depositing your bags, the very next thing to do is to take the subway ("Tunnelbana") to the "Slussen" stop, where you'll find the great **Katarina Elevator** (one krona per person), which rises in an open lift to the roof of a tall building, from which you can see all the way to the Baltic and to the beginning of the Stockholm Archipelago. The city is spread out below you: the boats that go to Finland are on your left, the ships to nearby Russia are directly ahead.

From this vantage point, you'll first begin to understand the arrangement of the 14 islands that make up the city of Stockholm. But only five of them need concern you: Norrmalm, Södermalm, Gamla Stan, Kungsholmen and Djurgarden (the Deer Park).

The big northern island, which contains the shopping areas, the office buildings, the railroad station, air terminal, and almost all the hotels we'll recommend, is the **Norrmalm.** The major squares in the Norrmalm are the Norrmalmstorg, the Stureplan, and the Gustav Adolfs Torg (where the Opera is located).

Directly below the Norrmalm, and almost touching upon it, is the tiny island of **Gamla Stan**—the Old City—where the Royal Palace stands, and where the streets are narrow, twisting, and incredibly picturesque. Although there are some cheap hotels here, they're mainly in centuries-old and some-what-damp-feeling buildings, and we've recommended few of them. The Gamla Stan does have some of the best restaurants and nightspots of Stockholm, together with several bustling shopping streets, so narrow that cars are exclud-

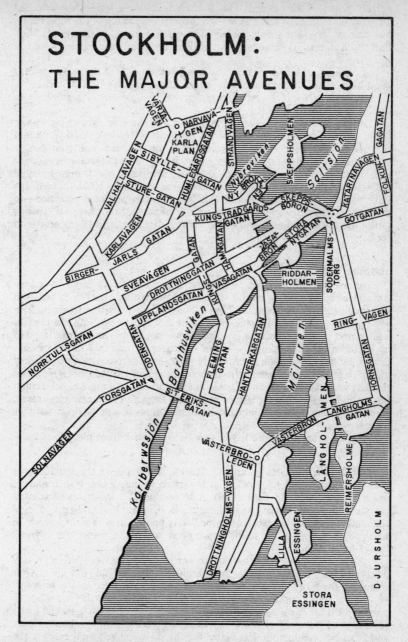

ed. It can't be missed.

Directly below the Gamla Stan is **Södermalm**—the Brooklyn of Stockholm—where the residents speak with a special argot all their own, and are fiercely proud of their island. This is almost entirely a residential area, and virtually no tourists—including us—go there. It's at the top of the Södermalm, however, at the point where the island nearly touches upon the Gamla Stan, that the Katarina Elevator stands, and there are two recommended hotels in this area.

To the left of Gamla Stan is the **Kungsholmen,** site of the major government buildings of this capital of Sweden, including the City Hall of Stockholm. Except for the City Hall—which you definitely should visit—there's little to attract you to Kungsholmen.

But to the right of the Gamla Stan (after first skipping over an even tinier island—the **Skeppsholmen**—site of the Museum of Modern Art), you'll find the magnificent **Djurgarden** ("Deer Park"), pronounced yoor-gohr-dun, a breathtaking, wooded fairyland, on whose lands the royalty of Sweden once rode to the hounds and let graze their pet deer, and which even today is maintained solely as a park, with few residential or business buildings on it. It's to Djurgarden that the people of Stockholm go for their summer recreation—to the fascinating open air museum and park of **Skansen,** to the carnival grounds of the **Tivoli Gröna Lund,** and to the various dance halls scattered near both spots.

The other tower

As a slightly-more-expensive alternative to the Katarina Elevator, and for a "farther-reaching" view and introduction to the city, take the No. 69 bus from Norrmalmstorg to the **Kaknäs Tower,** Stockholm's television tower built in 1967 and the tallest building (508 feet high) in Scandinavia. Note first the two wall murals in the entrance hall, which incorporate shapes and metals inspired by teletechnics. Then take the elevator (3 kronor for adults, 1 krona for children) up to the observation room, where you can walk from window to window identifying the various islands from the colored and labeled photographs set into the base of each window. If you want to scan any spot more closely, climb up one flight to the open-air terrace and view it through a telescope (one krona). Open daily from 9 a.m. to midnight in summer, from 10 a.m. to 7 p.m. in other seasons.

Having oriented yourself, you now need to move from place to place:

TRANSPORTATION: Getting around Stockholm by public transportation is both cheap and efficient. Stockholm boasts an extensive bus system and an underground called the Tunnelbana. A large blue "T" designates all subway entrances. Taxis are expensive, walking can be tiring, so it's best to get yourself acquainted with public transport immediately upon arrival. You can purchase a subway/bus map at the tourist office or at any of the many "Pressbyran" kiosks for 8 kronor.

All buses and subways charge 3 kronor per ticket for rides within the city limits and you can use the ticket for unlimited transfers within one hour. After midnight, the fare doubles and the transfer time is extended to 1½ hours. If you expect to do considerable commuting, it might be worth your while to purchase a set of 20 coupons, good for 10 single rides within the inner city limits (2 coupons-1 ticket), for 20 kronor. These are available at Pressbyran kiosks and from bus conductors. Far better for the do-it-yourself sightseer, are the Tourist Cards which provide you with unlimited transportation for the time purchased. A one-day card costs 10 kronor for the inner city, 15 kronor for city including suburbs; a three-day card is 33 kroner and is valid for city and suburbs. The 15 and 33 kronor pass takes you out to such places as Drottning-holm Palace without extra outlay on your part. Both are available throughout the year and can be picked up at any tourist office.

The airline bus from Arlanda Airport, charging 17 kronor one-way, goes to the new airline terminal next to the Central Station. It's in the station that you'll find "Hotellcentralen," where you can request a room at a budget price (see our "Accommodations" section below for particulars and fees) or else seek directions to a hotel or pension you've chosen from this book. Finding accommodations is, of course, your major task:

ACCOMMODATIONS: Just as in Copenhagen, the hotels of Stockholm are heavily booked in the summer months. That, however, doesn't mean that the city is crawling with tourists—as Venice, for example, is—but simply that no overwhelming number of hotels exist for the tourists who arrive in summer.

But just as in Copenhagen, the city guarantees that it will eventually find you a room. To pick up their offer, go to the Central Railroad Station, where you'll find an office called **"Hotellcentralen"** on the station's lower level. Staffed with English-speaking aides, it maintains contact with a large and approved assortment of hotels and guesthouses (although not with every such establishment in Stockholm), and stays open every day of the week from 8 a.m. to 11:30 a.m. and 12:30 p.m. to 11:30 p.m. (winter, 8 a.m. to 5 p.m.) to obtain a room for you. Charge for the service is 10 kronor ($2.38), for which you get a confirmed reservation, together with travel instructions to the hotel you choose.

Rooms in Private Homes

The hotel price level of Stockholm is such, however, that true budget tourists will want to obtain rooms in less expensive private homes (although there are some hostels and Ys within our budget range). But Hotellcentralen can often get a bit sticky about sending you to a private home if vacancies exist in higher-priced hotels. So what do *you* do if they refuse to give you the name of a private home? You walk out and walk over to the office of a commercial and slightly more expensive private-room-finding service, of which a prime example is found within a short walk of the Central Railroad Station.

Room Rental Agencies

As you leave the station, turn left on Vasagatan and proceed to **Hotel Tjanst**, 38 Vasagatan (phone 10-44-37 or 10-44-57), whose plain and rather starkly-lit office is on the second floor of an elderly building. Here you'll find Mr. Gustavsson, the owner and only employee of this one-man organization, who speaks fluent English and will, at your request, book you into a private home whose charges start at 60 kronor single, 80 kronor, double, including booking fee. That converts to $14.28 and $16.66, single and double, which is reasonable for Stockholm. Hotel Tjanst is open from 9 to noon and 1 to 5, but from Monday to Friday only.

Six actual private homes, charging 37.50 to 47.50 kronor per person ($8.92 to $11.30), including breakfast

If you'd rather go directly to one of my own recommendations, try:

Mrs. Eva Gisslar, 49 B Skeppargatan, second floor (phone 634-957)—she's a blonde, English-speaking lady in her 30s who rents a spotlessly-clean room with French double bed, parquet floor and green carpet for 90 kronor ($21.42) per night, including free showers. Notice the original Miros in the living room. Centrally-located, Mrs. Gisslar's is best reached via the T-bana to Östermalms, emerging from the Sybillegatan exit (from which the house is a five-minute walk).

Mr. Harold Jonasson, a friendly and always smiling, English-speaking gentleman, lives alone in a large apartment at 78 Asögatan (phone 847-008), in the Östermalm district of central Stockholm, where he rents three relatively small but adequately furnished rooms for 70 kronor ($16.66) per room (for two), including free use of the modern kitchen for preparing breakfast or other meals (the laundromat is 6 kronor extra). And there's a bathroom and separate WC. Take the T-Bana to Skanstull, a short walk away.

Mrs. Lidia Sallström, at 2 Stadshagsplan (phone 500-549), via elevator to the third floor, occupies a book-lined apartment in which she rents two double rooms, each with a balcony and parquet floor, for 95 kronor ($22.61) per room, breakfast included. Take the T-Bana to Stadshagen, in the Kungsholm district.

On the outskirts of Stockholm:

Mrs. Kristina Brolin, at 16 Mariehällsvagen, 13147 Nacka (phone 716-3170), is known as much for her cooking as for the bungalow in which she rents two tastefully-furnished rooms; on request, she'll prepare a superb supper for 22 kronor per guest. 55 kronor ($13.09) for a single room, 80 kronor ($19.04) for a double, including breakfast for all, and if you're travelling with children, Mrs. Brolin may offer two additional beds in the small garden cottage (where there's no running water—the kids will love it anyway).

Young **Mrs. Britt Aslund,** 15 Skandiavagen (north of Djursholm), phone 755-7113, lives in a home made of large red sandstone bricks which stands in the midst of a beautiful park with towering, old trees. There she rents two rooms at 50 kronor ($11.90) single, 75 kronor ($17.85) double, including breakfast which you prepare yourself, using ingredients (coffee, bread, marmalade) found in the large kitchen. Showers are free, and rooms are unusually spacious, with modern furniture and wall-to-wall carpeting. Take the T-bana to Mörby Centrum, then bus 616 to Framnäsviken, and walk five minutes from there.

And finally, **Mrs. Peggy Huss** and her two charming teenage daughters, Kristina and Jeanette (all three speak perfect English), rent a large, well-furnished, upstairs room, whose chintz-curtained windows overlook the garden, for 80 kronor ($19.04), double, breakfast for two included. Down the hall is a separate bathroom with the largest tub I've ever seen. All this is at 6 Enevägen, 16359 Spänga, phone 368-200, and if the number doesn't answer, phone Mrs. Huss' office number, which is 366-158. Then take the T-bana to Brommaplan (a 15-minute trip), then a #117 bus for five minutes more—it's the yellow house with the red chimney.

As you'll note from the above, private homes in Stockholm charge as much as 50% less than budget hotels, a refreshing differential that isn't found in such cities as Vienna or Amsterdam. But don't expect to find vacancies all the time, and always phone first.

Budget Pensions and Hotels

For a few dollars more (anywhere from $22 to $29 for a double room), you can stay in a hotel or pension. I've set forth my choices here, and it might be wise—especially if you are traveling in the peak of the summer—to write ahead for reservations, making certain to enclose an international postal response coupon. The following suggestions are arranged by location, rather than by price, with $22 pensions next to $29 hotels, so you might read through the lot before picking those that appeal. Some of the best over-all values for summer visitors are to be found at the summer "dorms" referred to below, where double rooms with full private showers rent for $31 to $34, including service charge. And if you're looking for the cheapest digs, turn now to our section on "Hostels" at the very end.

Near the Railroad Station

The railroad station area, as you'd expect, has the greatest cluster of budget hotels and pensions. The street running directly in front of the station is Vasagatan, and along it are office-type buildings often housing as many as three pensions apiece. Best of these is the elevator-equipped building at 40 Vasagatan, where I'd first seek a room at the **Hotel Wasa,** fifth floor (phone 23-16-00), whose rooms and lobby, with its sheetglass front, are light and airy. 28 rooms, singles priced at 91 kronor ($21.66), doubles at 130 kronor ($30.95), triples at 160 kronor ($38.09), plus 12 kronor for breakfast.

The very same rates are had at the **Hotel Brunkeberg,** first and second floors (phone 20-14-31), a cheerful, homey pension with high-ceilinged rooms and walls splashed in pastel colors.

SWEDISH KRONOR: As we go to press, the Swedish krona sells at a rate of 4.20 to the dollar, making each krona worth, in our terms, about 24¢. That 4.20 conversion is the basis for dollar figures used in this chapter.

The **Hotel Linde,** on the fourth floor (phone 21-48-94), has 18 rooms, all with old-fashioned furnishings and brightly-flowered quilts. Singles are 75 to 90 kronor ($17.85 to $21.42), doubles 110 to 140 kronor ($26.19 to $33.33), triples 180 kronor ($42.85), including service charge and tax, and breakfast, if you want it, is an additional 9 kronor per person.

Now walk a block further up Vasagatan to Bryggargatan, and turn right. Top find here is the **Hotel Ansgar,** 10 Bryggargatan (phone 23-04-70), a neat and spotless, 32-room mission hotel, where every room is equipped with hot-and-cold water and telephones, and 1980 prices will average 95 kronor ($22.61) single, 140 kronor ($33.33) double, 175 kronor ($41.66) triple, including service charge.

Costlier, and therefore only for emergencies, is the **Hotel Savoy,** 12b Bryggargatan (phone 22-12-80), which caters to Swedish businessmen and prices its rooms at 125 kronor ($29.76) single, 180 kronor ($42.85) double, service and breakfast included.

Keep in mind that, though Bryggargatan may not be the most prepossessing of streets in appearance, the hotels on it are patronized by normally well-off Swedish tourists who like its central location, just two minutes by foot from the station and all the important department stores in the heart of Stockholm.

Returning now to Vasagatan and proceeding a few blocks further up, you'll see a brown-and-green building with two towers and a clock; if you'll turn right before reaching this landmark, you'll be on Barnhusgatan where, at No. 4, young, English-speaking Tommy Berglund manages the cheapish **Hotel**

Callmar, third floor (phone 212-175). Six double rooms (and they can hold more), of which three are with running water, three without, and each room has a stove reaching to the ceiling. For all this adventure, the charge is 110 kronor ($26.19) per double room, 50 kronor ($11.90) for a third or fourth bed, 12 kronor for a breakfast that includes cheese. Quiet location.

A final railroad-station-area choice: the 40-bed **Hotel Sana,** 6B Upplandsgatan (phone 203-982), managed by an English-speaking former law student named Uvenbeck. He charges bargain rates (for Stockholm) of 80 to 90 kronor ($19.04 to $21.42) single, 110 to 125 kronor ($26.19 to $29.76) double, 45 kronor for a supplemental bed, 8 kronor for breakfast, nothing for showers, and places a free tv set in the majority of rooms. Upplandsgatan is a continuation of Vasagatan, and the address is less than a five-minute walk from the station.

Near the Norrmalmstorg

Another center of activity, close to the Kungsträdgården, a central-city park where international travelers rendezvous throughout the summer, is the Norrmalmstorg. And near here my favorite is the **Hotel Christina,** 8-10 Norrlandsgatan (phone 20-92-57), once for ladies only, now open to all: a calm and dignified establishment, tending however to be a trifle expensive. The hotel has an elevator and lounge, very attractive rooms, three charming, enthusiastic and English-speaking lady proprietors—Anita, Karin and Ulla, and can be reached from the Central Station in five minutes by taking bus #47. Singles are 100 kronor ($23.80), doubles 120 kronor ($28.57), triples 140 kronor ($33.33), and breakfast is 12 kronor ($2.85), all with service included.

Near the Stureplan

Smiths Hotellpensionat, Linnegatan 9 (phone 61-11-08), 4th floor, is another home-atmosphere-category hotel, charging 85 kronor ($20.23) single, 130 kronor ($30.95) double, including service, for large, high-ceilinged rooms, and it's quite well located, only two blocks from the Stureplan, a starting point for many of the city's trams and buses (from the Central Station, take the subway —T-Bana—one stop away to the "Ostermalmstorg," and get out at the Nybrogatan exit). The famous steam baths of Stockholm are also nearby. Mrs. Smith herself runs the hotel, and looks zealously after the welfare of her tourist guests. Highest recommendation.

Near the Hötorget

In the area of Stockholm's big skyscraper center (the Hötorget), we have three splurge-priced selections:

Fralsningsarmen Hotel City, at 66 Drottninggatan (phone 22-22-40), is the largest Salvation Army hotel in Scandinavia—with 85 singles, 67 doubles—but it's a normal commercial hotel—something like the mission hotels in Denmark—and definitely not a flophouse. Entirely pleasant and cheerful, with bathless singles priced at 105 kronor ($25), bathless doubles 155 kronor ($36.90), including tax and service charge, and with a moderately-priced restaurant and cafeteria (breakfast for 17 kronor) on its ground floor.

Slightly cheaper in the same area: the 36-bed **Hotel Regent,** 10 Drottninggatan (phone 20-90-04), charging 80 kronor single, but only 135 kronor double, 165 kronor triple. Somewhat costlier, nearby: the recently-modernized **Hotel Queen,** 71A Drottninggatan (phone 20-08-89), whose rates include a large, Scandinavian-style breakfast, and are 110 kronor ($26.19) single, 180 kronor ($42.85) double, 240 kronor ($57.14) triple, all for features and decor that make this surely among the most attractive of our Stockholm selections; and owners Christer Dahlberg (a graduate of Cornell) and Kenneth Theorin speak English fluently.

Near Radmansgatan

In the area between Odenplan and the Hötorget, at 38 Odengatan, third floor (phone 306-349), a kindly gentleman named Chiffa, who immigrated here from India many years ago, rents spotlessly clean rooms for 75 kronor ($17.85) single, 95 kronor ($22.61) double, 45 kronor ($10.71) per additional bed, in his **Pensionat Oden,** where showers are free. Since breakfast isn't served, guests are allowed use of the kitchen to prepare their own.

Not far away, at 31 Wallingatan (phone 111-076), a bearded Finnish artist named Anssi Aro owns and operates the **Pension Danielson** primarily for Finns (his reception room is covered with their photographs bearing effusive dedications), but is happy to accept North Americans as well; his English is excellent. Rates are 78 kronor ($18.57) for a single without running water, 90 kronor ($21.42) with, 120 kronor ($28.57) for doubles, all of which are with running water. Showers are free, rooms spacious and well furnished, and one (room no. 8) comes with three big windows.

Two short blocks from the Radmansgatan T-Bana stop, the **Pensionat Svinhufud** at 51 Doebelnsgatan (phone 32-07-54), is ideal for small groups or large families, to whom owner Anita Dorff (perfect English) offers special rates if they are readers of this book: 160 kronor ($38.09) for a room for four, 200 kronor ($47.60) for two connecting rooms with six beds. She'll also house backpackers possessing their own sleeping bags, space available, at the special rate (again for readers of this book only) of 30 kronor ($7.14) per night. What's the catch? There is none. And these are not dorm-style rooms, cots lined up as in a barracks, but comfortably-furnished, airy and attractive bed chambers, whose rental will also entitle you to free additional cots for small children, free showers, free use of the semi-automatic washing machine, and free use of kitchen facilities (with large freezer). Mrs. Dorff is one of those remarkable European hostesses who, time permitting, will drive you free in her own private car, to the Milles Garden, City Hall and Drottningholm Court Theater, provided that you pay the cost of gasoline for the 30-mile trip. Why? Because, she explains, these three attractions are not properly covered on the standard sightseeing tours. Wait until you hear her expertly-delivered descriptions!

On Gamla Stan (Old Town)

There are only two establishments we consider suitable for tourists in the ancient buildings of the Old City, and one is the very fine, 52-room Salvation Army hotel: **Fralsningsarmen Hotell Gamla Stan,** 25 Lilla Nygatan (phone 24-44-50), most of whose rooms have been recently painted and are fresh and cheerful, if filled with a mixed bag of furnishings. Singles are priced from 75 to 80 kronor ($17.85 to $19.04), doubles from 120 to 130 kronor ($28.57 to $30.95). Breakfast is 18 extra. And the subway stop is, of course, Gamla Stan. . . . A close runner-up is **Hotell Mälarstrand,** 23 Tyska Brinken (phone: 10-16-93), operated by a charming lady, Inger Rudman, who offers 20 beds in three nicely-furnished singles and seven doubles (some of which have a third bed). Her price is 85 kronor ($20.23) single, 135 kronor ($32.14) for a double, 17 kronor for an optional breakfast. And the sole drawback is a flight of 54 red steps to reach the lobby.

On Södermalm

Just south of Gamla Stan on the island of Södermalm (where stands the Katarina Elevator), you'll find an increasingly popular Stockholm choice, highly suitable for people who don't mind staying a bit out of the center for considerable savings in price. The relatively-new, 42-room **KFUM Hotel**, Mariagränd 3 (phone 42-68-60), opened in 1968, consists of two buildings dating back to the 17th century, which have been completely renovated. Rooms are small and simple, with yellow walls and orange drapes. The hotel itself sits inconspicuously back in an alleyway off Götgatan. There are shower rooms, cafeteria and TV-room, and although the hotel is under the auspices of the YMCA, it is open to visitors of both sexes. Singles cost 93 to 116 kronor ($22.14 to $27.61), doubles 128 to 156 kronor ($30.47 to $37.14), triples 180 kronor ($42.85), four-in-a-room dormitory accommodations are 48 kronor ($11.42) per person, and subway stop is Slussen. No curfew.

And Elsewhere

Hotel Hospits Elim at 25 Gamla Brog (off Vasagatan), about a five-minute walk from the Central Station (phone: 11-29-36), is a 27-room pension with interiors in Scandinavian decor with lots of colorful rugs and potted plants—a homey, spotless lodging where singles are 85 kronor ($20.23), doubles 115 kronor ($27.38), breakfast 14 kronor, and showers are free.

Pensjonat Stjernströms, on the second floor of 90 Odengatan (phone 32-46-49), is an extremely simple but perfectly clean and proper eight rooms renting for 130 kronor ($30.95) double, 170 kronor ($40.47) triple, 190 kronor ($45.23) quad, with breakfast optional at 13 kronor more, and showers for free.

Two final pensions are located in the same building at 9 Kommendörsgatan, within walking distance of the Östermalmstorg subway station. The cheaper is **Östermalms Gästhem** (phone 62-57-81), on the second floor, an 8-room pension with nice big homey rooms, decorated with lace curtains, old-fashioned desks and pleated lampshades. The large, elegant sitting-room is worth visiting to see, with its huge candle-equipped chandelier. Not all the rooms have running water, but there are sink closets in the halls. Singles are 85 kronor ($20.23), doubles 130 kronor ($30.95), service and tax included. Upstairs on the fourth floor, is **Bergenstrahle** (phone 60-21-00), which has 10 rooms, prettily done with chintz spreads and some lovely antique furnishings. Here, too, there are sinks in some rooms, sink closets outside others. Singles are 100 kronor ($23.80), doubles 145 kronor ($34.52), and continental breakfast—embellished with cheese and caviar!—is 20 kroner. The building has an elevator. And owner Mrs. Lindahl also offers more rooms around the corner at 50 Grev Turegatan, where you'll find the reception office for both properites. Highest recommendation for the Bergenstrahle, Ostermalms, and Elim.

The "Deluxe" Dorms

In summer only, you can also consider staying at one of the modern, new student hotels maintained by the University of Stockholm, which are open in summer to tourists of all ages. These are, of course, "dormitories"—but only in the sense that they are maintained on university grounds. They offer beautiful, modern, private rooms, not bunks; and all the rooms are equipped with private toilet and most with shower, which makes them a trifle expensive, but still within reasonable limits. Each "dormitory" is also endowed with huge lounges and breakfast rooms, and each becomes a sort of international community in summer months.

Largest of these is the **Hotel Jerum,** Studentbacken 21 (phone 63-53-80), whose top rates for Summer, 1980, will be 107 kronor ($25.47) for a single with private shower, 154 kronor ($36.66) for a similarly-equipped double, breakfast included. It's open from the 1st of June until August 31 and is operated by hard-working students, who provide Waldorf-like service. To reach the hotel, simply take the subway to the Gärdet station, four minutes from center city. And to make advance reservations, write to **S.S.R.S.-Hotelservice,** Box 5903, Stockholm 11489.

The second of the student hotels—again accepting tourists of all ages—is the equally modernistic **Domus,** 1 Körbärsvägen (phone 15-50-90), open from June through August. Rates here are slightly higher: 110 kronor ($26.19) for singles with private bath, 145 kronor ($34.52) for doubles with private bath, 170 kronor ($40.47) triple, with breakfast for 11 kronor more. Bus #53 links you to the heart of town. Beginning in the fall of 1980, a few (but a very few) of the Domus' rooms will be rented to tourists all year around—and not simply in the summer.

Hostels and Dorms

The hostel situation in Stockholm has its pluses and minuses. On the plus side, all hostels in the city are open to people of all ages and to families, and no hostel cards are required at any of them. On the minus side, many hostels— like the amazing hostel-ship **Af Chapman**—are booked out months in advance and it's chancy to wait until you reach the city to do something about getting hostel space. The following prices are for ordinary tourists—members of youth hostel organizations are sometimes charged less.

The amazing Af Chapman

For life in Stockholm on a starvation budget, let us first introduce you to the **"Af Chapman,"** a three-masted sailing ship, and the most unusual youth hostel in the world. Years ago, "Af Chapman" was a training ship for officer candidates of the Swedish navy. When the navy tired of the "Af Chapman" and announced it would scrap it, an idea came to the brilliant chief of the Stockholm Tourist Office. He bought the "Af Chapman" for exactly 5,000 kronor, moored it to a dock on the centrally-located island of Skeppsholmen, and turned it into a youth hostel. There it has remained ever since—a fixture of the city to such an extent that all the maps of Stockholm now contain little drawings of the "Af Chapman."

You can spot the "Af Chapman" from the verandah of the plush Grand Hotel (what a contrast!), and you can also easily walk to the dock from the Grand. There you'll board a real-life massive sailing ship—straight from an Errol Flynn movie—with crow's nests, portholes, towering masts, and sea gulls circling above. It's open from mid-March till the end of October, charges exactly 28 kronor ($6.90) for a bunk (23 kronor if you're a card-carrying Youth Hostel member), and is so popular that it imposes a maximum stay of five nights. It has a phone number too: 10-37-15 or 20-57-05.

Incidentally, members of the public can visit the Af Chapman, even if they don't plan to stay there. Hope and I recently did. And as we strolled on the weather-beaten deck, the ship's bells sounded!

The modest Mälaren

There's still another. Originally used as living quarters for Swedish engineers working on various projects in the Archipelago, the brightly-red-colored

Mälaren at Söder Mälarstrand, Dock No. 6 (phone 444-385), is yet a second Stockholm ship that's been transformed into a youth hostel housing 32 guests in 16 double-decker cabins (price for a bunk is 25 kronor ($5.95 per night). Owner-manager is Jill Martenson, who also operates a cheap snack bar on board that's popular even with young people not staying on the Mälaren. That's a 10-minute walk over the Central Bridge from the main railroad station.

Hostels of the "Y"s

And then there's the **KFUM** (YMCA), whose hostels in Stockholm are open to all ages and both sexes. Easily the best of these is the **Columbus Student and Youth Hostel** at 11 Tjärhovsgatan (phone 44-70-72), open from May 1 to September 30, and charging 25 kroner ($5.95) per person, plus 10 kronor (one time only) for the rental of bedding if you have no sleeping bag, in 3 to 7-bedded dorms. Non-dorm rooms, for men and women, rent for 90 kronor double, 105 triple, 120 kronor quad, with no need to pay extra for bedding. And there's no curfew. But warning: as this edition goes to press in January of 1980, owners of the Columbus are reportedly agonizing over whether to sell the establishment. If the phone at 44-70-72 doesn't answer, phone the KFUM at 42-68-60 for information on the Columbus; and if you do find it's been closed (a terrible blow to the Cause), you can consider alternative, but higher-priced, accommodations at the unusual **Zinken** at 2 Pipmakargränd (phone: 68-57-86). Seven yellow-painted bungalow-type houses make up this 115-room youth and student hotel called "Zinken", where single and double rooms (no dorms) cost 40 kronor ($9.52) per person per night, plus 10 kronor for bedding and linens, while breakfast is 11 kronor extra, and showers, cooking facilities and use of the washing machine, are free. (Off-season, rates are considerably lower in this congenial spot where guests seem to mingle and have a good time). Take subway 13, 14 or 15 to Hornstull, the fifth stop after the Central Railway Station and four stops after Gamla Stan. Leave at the exit marked Högalidsparken, cross the street, enter the pedestrian tunnel on the opposite end, go down the stairs on your right to Drakenbergsgatan. Then take the street to the left, walk to the end, go through the passage, turn to the right (where the rocks are), and you're at the Zinken.

Sub-starvation budget

A last resort. Although their facility is officialy available only to persons travelling with car and tent, the management of the **Sätra,** an unusually scenic and well-equipped camping site located 7 miles south-west of Stockholm, will occasionally accept up to six backpacker-type tourists, whom they permit to sleep in the locker room of the sauna for only 8 kronor ($1.90) per person. You also get to use the sauna. Considering the high costs of Stockholm and the fact that summer days occur when every Stockholm hostel and ship is completely booked, I mention the possibility, but with some trepidation. From the central station, take subway 13 or 15 to the Bredäng stop (6 kronor, 20 minutes) and walk 15 minutes up the marked road to the camping entrance; nearby is one of the free sand beaches of Lake Mälaren. But always phone—97-70-71—first; they speak fluent English.

READERS' ROOM SELECTIONS: "We strongly recommend the **Bema Hotel,** Upplandsgatan 13, phone 102381, whose proprietor speaks excellent English, helped with maps, etc. The charge for a double with hot and cold water in the room and a hall bath was $20. That is not at all bad by Swedish standards. Spotlessly clean, quiet and convenient to downtown and buses" (John G. Sindorf, Palmer, Alaska; note by AF: in 1980, the Bema will charge 80 kronor ($19.27) single, 115 kronor ($27.38) double, 12 kronor per person for breakfast, nothing for showers; take bus #59 from the Central Station and get off at the third stop called Tengnerlunden).

MEALS: Eating out in this city can be costly indeed. Count on a minimum of $4.50 for a light meal, $6.50 for a full dinner, and $11 for the "Big Splurge." To keep within the bounds of even these generous allowances, study each menu carefully and try to choose from the least expensive main dishes offered, adding a non-alcoholic beverage and a low-cost dessert. As in many other European countries, it is often cheaper to have your main meal at lunchtime, when many restaurants offer an inexpensive price-fixed menu, and eat a lighter supper at night. Take that in a self-service restaurant where you'll save the service charge. But having warned you, don't let us scare you. It is not necessary, when in Stockholm, to go either hungry or broke. Rather, you can keep your food costs cut to the bare minimum by reading and following these few simple tips.

1. Eat in the "spaghetti houses"

Italian immigrants to Sweden provide the city's tastiest, least expensive meals. Reason: they tend to work in family units, all members waiting on tables, washing the dishes, toiling long hours, and thus keeping costs down. A prime example is the 15-table **Spaghetti House** (also called the "Spaghetteria"), at 12 Nybrogatan adjoining the Nybroplan-Square, where the particular bargain is a 17 kronor ($4.04, service included) "snabblunch" served from 10:30 a.m. to 4:30 p.m., weekdays. It consists of a daily changing menu (such as tuna salad as an appetizer, followed by beef cutlet with boiled potato or risotto con carne), accompanied by bread, butter, milk, coffee or beer—all included in the 17 kronor price! Weekends, the emphasis shifts to costlier spaghetti dishes—12 different varieties—costing 19 kronor apiece, ladled onto your plate from huge, steaming, copper pots; and while the value isn't quite the same as the phenomenal "snabblunch," it's nevertheless quite a value for Stockholm.

Other recommended "spaghetti houses": **Pizza Bella Napoli** at 41 Odengatan, serving a large variety of spaghetti and pizza dishes for 18 kronor ($4.28) per; the more centrally-located **Mamma Mia** at 40 Gamla Brogatan (a sidestreet off Vasagatan), near the central station, where pizzas, spaghettis and risottos are 16 kronor ($3.80), lasagne al forno 18 kronor ($4.28), and eight daily platters 18 kronor ($4.28) apiece; and the one I like best of all, always crowded with Swedes fascinated by the Italian atmosphere and tasty food: **Osteria il Pozzo,** 16 Skeppergatan, near Ostermalmstorg, open daily except Saturdays until 11 p.m., and serving seven daily platters for 17 to 25 kronor ($4.04 to $5.95). The friendly style and service of il Pozzo is not well reflected by the sign over the cash register which says (in Italian): "Credit is given only to clients over 90 accompanied by their parents."

2. Eat in the "bars"

And don't think we're sending you into taverns; the Swedish word "bar," appearing alone or as the suffix of a word, refers to a cafeteria-type establishment, where food is picked up by the diner either from a serving line or at a window opening into the kitchen where meals are prepared. Among the largest "bars" in Stockholm is the exotically-named (for Sweden) **Clock,** 22 Sergelgatan, in the heart of the Hötorget skyscraper development, which serves soup and bread for 7 kronor ($1.66), large hamburger platters for 11 kronor ($2.61), ice cream desserts for 5 kronor. Other "clocks" are at 56 Götagatan, next to the Medborgarpladsen T-bana stop (largest branch of the chain) and at 50 Kungsgatan, the latter again in the Hötorget skyscraper development . . . This time in the Kunstradgarden—the central city park where free concerts are held on summer days—another "bar" is the similarly-priced **7 Sekel Cafeteria** (across the street from the NK Department Store), where you can dine indoors in what looks like a botanical garden, or outdoors at one of the white tables, right in front of a beautiful fountain. Soups from 6 to 8 kronor, daily platters (such as Swedish meatballs with potatoes, beetroot and salad) for 18 kronor, a banana split is 9 and coffee 5 kronor.

Other recommended and popular bars include the **Olo** at 7 Olofsgatan, corner of Tunnelgatan (in the Hötorget area; big hot platters for 16 to 19 kronor ($3.80 to $4.52), including bread, butter and a glass of milk); **Petter** at 81 Folkungagatan, near Slussen (only 16 kronor, $3.80, for a beefsteak with onion sauce or pork chops with boiled potatoes and salad, only 14 kronor ($3.33) for a daily platter of cheaper ingredients); **Palmen** at 93 Birger Jarlsgatan, near Odengatan, 17 kronor for hot platters accompanied by *pudding,* bread, butter and milk. At the latter spot in the fall of 1979, I gorged on three potato dumplings almost the size of tennis balls, stuffed with meat, accompanied by the aforementioned pudding, a cabbage salad, bread, butter, and a big glass of milk. Seventeen kronor ($4.04) remains the price for this repast in 1980, says the Yugoslav owner of the Palmen.

"Bars" are scattered throughout the city—look for the magic three letters.

More "bars" in Hötorget City

A word about the site of the "Clock-bar" mentioned above: **Hötorget City** (also called Hötorgcity) is a project in the center of town that somewhat resembles our Rockefeller Center, except that it's years more modern. You'll spot the five gleaming white skyscrapers of the Hötorget (Haymarket) from almost any point in the city, but the "Star Wars" feeling they cause is most intensely felt on the elevated sidewalk on the plaza in front of the buildings, where several other inexpensive restaurants are located. To reach the plaza, walk up Kungsgatan until you see a big square on your left, where the Concert Hall of Stockholm stands. That's the Hötorget. Turn left, walking in front of the Concert Hall (with its unusual Carl Milles statues), and you'll come to the Sergelgatan, with its new underground passage and shopping center and tall glass obelisk standing in an enormous fountain basin, illuminated at night by multi-colored lights. A meal in one of the many "bars" in this area—like the unusually inexpensive **Hurtig** at 90A Drottninggatan, serving quick lunches for 17 kronor, $4.04—will make you think you're in an ultra-advanced civilization, full of people sprouting antennas from their heads—a literal world of tomorrow.

3. Eat in the department store cafeterias

The cheapest and best of these is the mezzanine restaurant of the **Tempo Department Store** at Kungsgatan 44, just directly opposite the large open-air market ("Haymarket") in front of the Concert Hall that adjoins the skyscrapers of the Hötorget. Here, a complete special lunch is 17 kronor, most other hot plates are 12 to 16 kronor, and—glory be—they're all openly displayed, so that you can merely point to what you want. The Tempo also serves a 8-kronor continental breakfast, which you can embellish with a 2.50 kronor egg. . . . Slightly higher in price is the 2nd floor cafeteria of Stockholm's newest department store, **Ahlens** (corner of Klarabergsgatan and Drottninggatan), near the railroad station, where some main courses are 18 kronor, and the posted menus are translated (thankfully) into English. (Incidentally, the sub-basement of Ahlens is probably the world's largest and most elegant grocery store, and free samples are sometimes offered; it's also open every day including Sundays until 10 p.m. and sells a variety of ready-made picnic items—entrance is from T-Centralen subway station). A final possibility are the restaurants of the various **EPA stores** around town, where the price is 18 kronor for a plate, bread and butter, and milk, but the food items aren't displayed and menus aren't translated. You can skip the restaurant of the famous **P.U.B.** store, which concentrates on cold open sandwiches (8.50 to 10 kronor per sandwich), and do the same at **NK**, except during summer when NK offers its 24 kronor ($5.71) "snabblunch" of bread, butter, a hot dish (from three choices) and coffee. That's in quite an elegant setting of crystal chandeliers, high-backed wooden chairs and turquoise tablecloths.

4. Eat with the students

Stockholm's students eat cheaply, and neither of Stockholm's two major student restaurants requires student identification cards. First in preference is the **Restaurant Lantis,** which not only provides you with a cheap meal but with a chance to view the birth of a university city. Take the subway from the central station to University City at Frescati (fourth stop, 4.50 kronor fare) and walk another five minutes to the Lantis, to the right of the ultramodern university block. Then step up to two enormous, carousel-type, round trays on which are displayed the day's offerings: perhaps roast liver with fried potatoes, roast beef with pickles, cooked fish with spinach, all served with potatoes or another vegetable, and costing from 10 to 15 kronor ($2.38 to $3.57). The restaurant is open from 11 a.m. to 2 p.m. from June 1 to August 31, until 6:30 p.m. the rest of the year, but is closed on Saturdays and Sunday. (And note that the underground line reaching out here was cut through solid rock—an enormous engineering task.)

5. Eat smorgasbord for brunch or lunch

Fill up once a day on an all-you-can-eat feast of Swedish specialties, and you can taper off eating for the rest of the day with minor snacks. If you like your big meal in the morning, get over to the **railroad station restaurant** (called "Centralens Pub") between 6:30 and 9.30 a.m., 8 to 10:30 a.m. on Sundays, where you can dive into a "smorgasbord breakfast": juice, cereal, anchovies, jams, coffee, tea, chocolate milk, buttermilk, bread, rolls, eggs, smoked sausage and cheese—and all the servings you have the nerve to go back for!—at the reasonable $4.52 price of 19 kronor. The entrance to the restaurant is to the left of the main entrance to the railroad station, as you face the station, and they also serve "Today's Lunch" (hot dish and coffee) for 20 kronor ($4.76), including service, from 11 a.m. to 2 p.m., Monday through Friday.

6. The best of the budget restaurants

The popular **Konditori Metro** at 24 Grevturgatan (which runs parallel to the Sturegatan), open weekdays only, from 9 a.m. to 4 p.m., offers 10 different "quick lunches" for 17 kronor ($4.04): you get orange juice first, coffee and dessert at the end, and a main course of such inexpensive items as roast sausages with french fries, or spaghetti, always accomanpied by a salad and bread. Come early or late to find a chair.

Stockholm's vegetarian restaurant—always a good bet for inexpensive eating—is **Grona Linjen,** at 10 Master Samuelsgatan (2nd floor), near the Norrmalmstorg. Here, the brightly-garnished plates are mostly 15 and 20 kronor, soup and dessert are each 8 kronor, and the restaurant itself is a large, bright and airy place that sports a traditional green porcelain stove, of the sort you normally see at folk museums in Sweden. Open weekdays until 4 p.m. . . . To the left of the entrance to the Wasa ship exhibition (see further on), the unusual, self-service **Cafe Bla Porten** at 64 Djurgaresvägen, features salad dishes which you choose and mix yourself, and which range in price from 10 to 19 kronor ($2.38 to $4.52), depending on the items you select. In a setting like that of a modern art gallery, plastered throughout with abstract expressionists, this is a fine place to eat either before or after visiting nearby Skansen or Gröna Lund. Open weekdays until 9 p.m., weekends until 5 p.m. . . . The ground-floor level of the **Restaurant Pilen** at 12A Bryggargatan, two blocks from the railroad station, serves traditionally Swedish dishes in an informal atmosphere. Stop by on weekdays for the "Snabb-Lunch," a hot plate with bread, butter, milk or beer, for 22 kronor ($5.23). . . . If, but only if, you're in the area of the Odenplan, you might also want to try the **Restaurant Wienerwald** (having no connection with the chain of the same name), 99 Luntmakargatan, which serves Austrian/Hungarian food to students and other youngsters who pack it at lunchtime. Servings here are massive and prices reasonable: 8 kronor for a filling goulasch-soppa (goulash soup), 12 kronor for bratwurst and red cabbage, 22 kronor for a huge "Budapestschnitzel".

7. The best of the big splurge restaurants

Timjan is a tiny, one-room restaurant, two blocks off the Stureplan at Riddargatan 8 (look for the vertical green sign above the door). But the food here is exceptionally well-prepared for the price and well-deserving of its popularity. With pine tables, calico shades on the hanging lamps and burlap cafe curtains at the windows, Timjan attracts a young crowd and is filled to overflowing at lunchtime. Lunch is served from 11 a.m. to 4 p.m.; "snabb lunch" from 11 a.m. to 2 p.m. The latter costs only 20 kronor ($4.76), and could typically consist of Swedish meatballs with cranberry sauce, small potatoes, bread and butter, milk or beer. Taken à la carte, a similar meal (say, stewed halibut in melted butter, with horseradish sauce, and steamed potatoes) might run 25 kronor. Then there's the summer bestseller for 22 kronor ($5.23): a delicious salad (tuna or chicken with tomatoes, cucumber and peppers), freshly prepared before your very eyes; the two English-speaking waiters do all this with a touching concern. Timjan, unfortunately, is closed on weekends. . . . The artists' and writers' restaurant of Stockholm is **Prinsen,** Master Samuelsgatan 4 (one block from the Stureplan, in the direction of the Nybroplan), whose walls are covered by the original art with which indigent painters often pay for their meals there. Not entirely cheap, so choose carefully or you'll overspend. Once again, avoid the printed menu and pick from the typewritten menu of daily "specials," on which soup is priced at 15 kronor, lunch dishes (from 11 a.m. to 3 p.m.) from 19 to 29 kronor, and dinner plates (from 6 to 8 p.m.) for the same. Get there before 8 p.m., when the "specials" are taken off—regular dishes start at 26 and more.

8. Some final food tips

The word, "Korv" that you've been seeing on menus and signs all over town, means "sausage"—always a cheap, tasty dish. . . . A late night's snack?

On the Norrmalmstorg side of the City Garden Park (Kungstradgarden), you'll find lines of late-night stands, in summer, serving waffles, fruit, hot sausages. . . . Swedish meatballs? They're called "Kottbullar" here, and are always marvelous. . . . The tastiest Swedish specialties? Try: blood pudding with lingonberries (blodpudding, lingonsylt), stuffed cabbage (kåldomar), delicious thick pea soup (artsoppa), and one dish which sounds like a children's game—pytt-i-panna—but turns out to be a simple but delicious hash. . . . On Thursday, it's traditional to eat pea soup followed by pancakes, washed down with hot punch. "When in Sweden . . . !"

And now, with rooms and meals behind us, we begin our tour of Stockholm.

THINGS TO DO, PLACES TO SEE: For some time now, Stockholm has maintained an entire new complex of offices solely to service visitors who want to know "where to go and what to do." Called **Sverigehuset** (Sweden House), it is staffed by the Tourist Office of Stockholm and houses a **Tourist Center** for questions and aid, a **Student Reception Office** (in summer only) to help international students passing through, and the offices of the **Sweden at Home** program, through which you can meet and visit with a Swedish family in their home. Sweden House is located at Hamngatan 27, opposite the NK Department Store. Stop by at least once to collect their free hand-outs on what's going on in town; to ogle the reception staff of seven, bright, young, multi-lingual ladies wearing blue skirts, yellow blouses, and flags indicating the languages they speak; or to book any of the sightseeing tours offered in Stockholm (which include a full-day, archipelago fishing trip on a professional trawler, weekends only, from May to September).

Tourist Aids

Besides the considerable services offered above, Stockholm makes its English-speaking guests feel welcome in a variety of ways. Every weekday afternoon in summer at 6 p.m., the Stockholm radio station broadcasts an English-language "Calling All Tourists" program, announcing the events and activities scheduled in Stockholm that evening and following day. If you miss it, simply dial 22-18-40 and an English-speaking "Miss Tourist" will give you recorded information on the day's events. Every day, there's an English news round-up in the Swedish papers. And special dances are always announced in both languages in the entertainment sections of the papers. Yet, despite all Sweden's efforts to let us know that we are welcome, there is probably no program that warms a tourist so totally as that which invites you to spend an evening with a Swedish family at home.

Sweden at Home

To apply for the "Sweden at Home" program, you must go in person to the Tourist Center at Sweden House (Hamngatan 27) and fill out a form specifying your age, profession, hobbies and interests. The office will then contact a suitable host family who will invite you for a simple afternoon or evening of conversation. There are no rules as to age or sex on this program, and any interested visitor is welcome to apply. Nor is there any cost, of course, but it is customary to bring a little house gift—flowers, chocolates, a book or an attractive glass of after-dinner mints. Your hosts will speak fluent English and are usually as interested in talking about your country as you are about theirs. The program emphasizes that hosts cannot be expected to provide accommodation. My personal recommendation is to give it a try; Swedes seem somewhat stand-offish and over-polite in public but they relax and warm up quickly in the familiar setting of their own living-rooms.

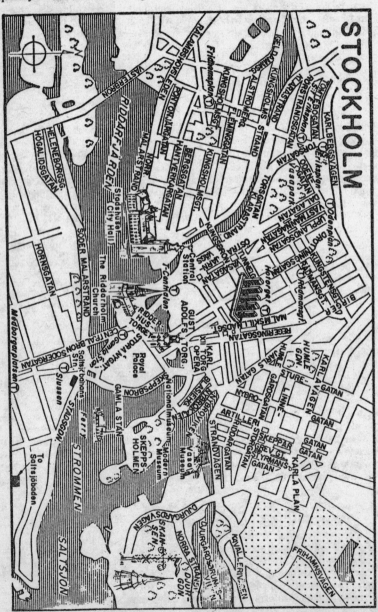

Tours

The cheapest and, in some ways, most useful tour of Stockholm, is the 17 kronor, one-hour, *non-stop* city tour, which leaves from the Karl XII-Torg, near the Opera House (you'll see signs and a ticket booth) at 11 a.m., noon, 2 and 3 p.m., daily from June 1 to August 31. Despite its short duration, it's an amazingly far-ranging jaunt that passes through the most important sections of the town, and includes a short stop at Fjällgatan, where you'll enjoy a panoramic view of Stockholm.

I'd follow the city tour with a one-hour canal tour (it's called the **"Around Djurgarden Tour"**), which leaves every hour in summer from 10 a.m. to 7:30 p.m., from a dock (the "Strömkajen") diagonally in front of the plush Grand Hotel (you ought to take this occasion to wander through the lobby of the Grand, simply to see old-time European elegance). But don't mistake this sightseeing boat for the larger archipelago boats (about which more later) moored directly in front of the Grand. The seagoing tour costs only 17 kronor, heads through the harbor of the city and around the Deer Garden, past the breathtaking "Embassy Row" of Stockholm, and under the bridges that vault over Mälaren Lake. Don't confuse this excursion with the more leisurely and costly (25 kronor) **"Under the Bridges"** canal ride offered by most sightseeing companies, which necessarily overlaps with portions of the shorter tour.

Then, if you wish an intensive escorted tour of the city (my suggestion is that you do it yourself, via 3-kronor subway rides and free or three kronor admission to the city's various museums and sights), you can consider the normal commercial offerings of the various sightseeing companies, whose buses leave from a little ticket booth near the Royal Opera House at the Karl XII Torg. They offer three basic tours:

Grand City Tour No. 1, which costs 45 kronor ($10.71), and leaves daily between April 1 and October 31, at 9:45 a.m., goes to the Royal Palace for a guided inside visit, then to the Riddarholm Church (burial place of the Swedish kings), and finally to the Old City, where you take a walk through.

Grand City Tour No. 2 sets out at 1:45 p.m., also costs a high 45 kronor, visits the Carl Milles Sculpture Garden, the City Hall (an inside visit), passes by the stately embassies of Stockholm, and onto the "Deer Garden" island.

On both these tours, the 45 kronor price includes admission charges to the various parks and exhibits, which lowers the relative cost of the tours somewhat.

A more unique experience is the famous **"Swedish Way of Life Tour,"** or **"Life-Seeing in Stockholm"** tour, which takes you to a children's day-nursery, a kindergarten, to specially-constructed old-age pensioners' apartments, and other sites associated with Sweden's highly-developed welfare system. It departs at 9:45 a.m. from the Karl XII Torg, Monday through Friday only, and only between June 25 and August 31; the cost is again 45 kronor ($10.71).

Finally a trip through the **Archipelago of Stockholm**—the fantastic complex of over 10,000 islands leading out to the Baltic—is an absolute must at some point in your Stockholm stay. All the ships leave from in front of the Grand Hotel, make varying trips, the cheapest of which is a 3-hour round-trip to Vaxholm for 33 kronor. But to do this one right, a 5-hour round-trip—such as the one to Grinda (33 kronor)—is more highly recommended. There's a restaurant on board, and the trip makes a fine outing. Check the schedules carefully.

Skansen

While organized tours are handy if you're cramped for time, as always in this book we'd suggest that you can save more money and see the city more thoroughly by touring on your own, possibly with a three-day tourist pass in hand for unlimited transportation.

To start with the past, schedule one of your early trips to this unique open-air "museum," located on the Djurgarden—which itself is a vast island-park. To **Skansen**, the Swedes have moved more than 150 of the ancient farmhouses, Lapp huts, 16th-century churches and meeting halls that once were scattered all over Sweden. Their purpose was to preserve and maintain these buildings as a heritage for the nation—a re-creation of what Sweden was like hundreds of years ago. You'll want to spend a full afternoon wandering over Skansen's peaceful grounds, riding in the little "children's" electric train (3 kronor) that goes past the chief buildings, gazing into the enclosures-without-bars where polar bears and oxen are kept in the midst of the re-constructed "towns," watching demonstrations of glass-blowing, cheese-making, butter-churning and basketry. It's like no other park or museum in the world, with a wonderful "au naturel" quality about it, and while the admission charge is 7 kronor for adults, 2 krona for children, the attractions are enough to keep you fascinated for hours.

To get to Skansen, take bus #44 to #47 from the Nybroplan, which goes directly there (3 kronor per person), or take the sea-going ferry from the Slussplan or the Nybroplan, which charges 3 kronor for the ride. But don't leave too late in the afternoon, for the buildings at Skansen close at 5 p.m., although the park itself stays open until 11:30 p.m.

When dinnertime approaches, you can have a big-splurge meal without leaving Skansen at the famous, but ultra-expensive, ($20 and up) **Solliden Restaurant,** directly in front of which is a large bandstand where folk dances and even Swedish-language operas, are performed on weekend evenings, free. Or, for a cheaper meal, you can try the **Värdhusen Cafeteria** at the rear side of the Restaurant Solliden building, where daily platters are 20 kronor ($4.76); or the even cheaper selections at the numerous food stands in the old farm-houses (the ones with grass and flowers on their roofs) about a minute's walk from the cafeteria. There, hot pancakes—called "wafflors"—are 5 kronor ($1.19), sausages 4 kronor (95¢) and there are wooden benches and tables for enjoying the meal.

And then, at around 8 p.m., the action will explode at the dance halls on the base of Skansen hill, and in the **Tivoli Gröna Lund,** about 100 yards away—which now brings us to the chief topic of this Stockholm chapter:

Girl-Watching

In the area around Skansen, you'll soon discover why the girls of Sweden are that nation's chief export, best tourist attraction and most highly developed achievement. Imagine, if you will, a number of dance halls where the wallflow-ers look like young versions of Ingrid Bergman, Greta Garbo and Anita Ekberg —this is the spot to witness that phenomenon. They are utterly unbelievable, and there will be times when you'll simply stand with mouth agape, drinking in the view.

The younger dance-seeking crowd goes to an open-air dancing area at the top of Skansen Hill. You enter through the main Skansen gate (fee is 7 kronor), take the escalator and then walk a few minutes until you see the dancing area, near the church on top of the hill. Here, from Wednesday through Sunday evenings, in summer, large groups of young people take part in folk and similar dances. If you're in that age group, you might watch for a while to learn how it's done, then try for yourself; no matter what your age, though, you'll want to see the girls.

Near Skansen, and still on the Djurgarden, is the huge amusement park of Stockholm, called **Gröna Lund,** and sometimes also referred to as the **"Tivo-li."** Open from 2 p.m. Monday to Saturday and noon on Sunday, the admission charge is 7 kronor throughout the day. As you walk in, you'll see another outdoor dance floor, named **Dans Ut,** that caters to staid, older couples and features the traditional Swedish dances. I'd pass that by and keep walking to the indoor establishment called **Dans In** (next to the ferris wheel), where recently, within a period of six minutes, Hope and I spotted four girls who would make Candice Bergen look plain. Entrance fee of 15 kronor, with all drinks priced at 8 kronor thereafter.

The Wasa

The eeriest and most thrilling visit in Stockholm is to the **Wasa Museum** ("Wasavarvet"), on the Djurgarden, which houses the warship "Wasa," resurrected from the bottom of Stockholm's harbor in 1961, after it had lain there for over 300 years! It has now rightfully become the most-visited tourist attraction in all of Scandinavia.

The history of the Wasa is a fascinating one. For years, ocean archaeologists had hoped to recover one of the famous wooden warships of history, whose locations, on the ocean's floor, are generally well-known. One of them—Anders Franzen, of Stockholm—surmised that such ships would still exist only in areas where the salt content of the water was insufficient to permit wood-devouring sea worms to exist. Subsequently, he learned that the harbor of Stockholm was one such place, and after searching through ancient naval archives, he discovered that a Swedish warship—the Wasa—had sunk in the Stockholm harbor, in 1628, just as it was leaving port on its maiden cruise.

Franzen proceeded to spend many summers crisscrossing the harbor of Stockholm in a one-man motorboat, dropping lines to dredge up objects from the deep. In 1956, he pulled up a wedge of centuries-old wood, and divers soon confirmed that he had found the Wasa, buried almost to the top of its hull in the muds below, and perfectly preserved! It took five years to raise the ship, until, on a thrilling day in April of 1961, with an enormous crowd headed by the King of Sweden in attendance, the Wasa broke surface. Fittingly, the first objects to appear were the sculptured figures of two Swedish sailors.

Because the Wasa would crumble if it were ever to dry out, it has been placed in a specially-constructed museum, whose humidity is kept under constant control.

To see this, take bus #47 from Nybroplan, and ask the conductor to stop near the Wasa Museum, which is only a few hundred feet from the Gröna Lund amusement park. Entrance is 6 kronor ($1.42) for adults, 3 kronor for students with student identification, 2 kronor for children, and the building is open from 9:30 a.m. to 6 p.m. throughout the year. There's a Technicolor movie about the raising of the Wasa which they'll show you after you've viewed the ship, and there's a beautiful oakwood cafeteria just a few feet away. Don't miss it!

City Hall

William Butler Yeats said of Stockholm's **City Hall** that "no architectural work comparable to it has been accomplished since the Italian cities felt the excitement of the Renaissance." As you approach this unusual building, particularly as you stand within its inner court, you may agree—its unique style is strikingly Scandinavian and utterly indigenous to its surroundings. You'll first enter into the famous "Blue Hall" which was originally meant to be painted blue, but remained red in motif when the architect decided not to paint over the bricks. From here, at the top of the stairs, is the Golden Hall, where the Nobel Prize Dinners are held each year. At the end of the Golden Hall—the Room of the 3 Crowns; and elsewhere, the impressive legislative chamber, whose ceiling is decorated as in a Viking home. Multi-lingual guided tours of City Hall ("Stadshuset") are operated weekdays at 10 a.m. sharp, Sundays at 10 and noon, costing 3 kronor on weekdays and at noon on Sunday. You can also make a non-guided visit to the Tower daily in summer from 11 a.m. to 3 p.m., 3 kronor. Visitors are not permitted to tour the City Hall without a guide.

The Milles Garden

The great Swedish sculptor, Carl Milles (1875-1955), who created statues throughout the world, came home to Stockholm in 1906 to spend most of the last years of his life designing and building the **Milles Garden,** on a hill on the island of Lidingo, overlooking all of Stockholm. The resulting works, as you'll immediately see, are a sharp departure from every style of sculpture theretofore known, and extremely moving in the fervor of their message. From the grounds of Milles' home, walk down the long flight of stairs into the gravel garden where the most exciting statues are placed. The Garden is open every day from May 1 through October 15 from 11 to 5, in June and July on Tuesday and Friday evenings (7 to 9 p.m.) as well, and admission is 7 kronor ($1.66). To get there, take subway line #14 to Ropsten (cost is 3 kronor from most points in town), then pick up the #203 bus from Ropsten to the gardens (2 kronor). To return to town, walk around the corner from the entrance to the gardens to the modern Foresta Hotel (expensive) where you'll see a stop for the bus to Ropsten. From Ropsten, the Tunnelbana (subway) will bring you back into town—an easy trip.

The Jolly Optimists

For an afternoon of sailing on Lake Mälaren, which cuts into the heart of Stockholm, take the subway ("Tunnelbana") to the Fridhemsplan stop, where you'll be opposite a dock area called the **"Ralambshov"**—the "dock" consisting of a little green park that slopes to the waters. At the shore, entrepreneur Sture Ed rents out a fleet of "Jolly Optimists"—ten tiny little row-boats and multi-colored little sailing boats. The cost is 9 kronor ($2.14) for an hour of rowing or sailing, and you can make it almost all the way to the royal palace, a windy, refreshing afternoon's outing that should cost just a bit more than $6.40 total. Weather permitting, Sture, who looks like a jolly optimist himself, rents his boats from 9 a.m. to 4 p.m. on Saturdays and Sundays and until 8 p.m. the rest of the week. He's usually sitting in one of the two small green huts near the water (where he keeps the oars), and speaks no English other than "boat," "nine kronor," and "o.k."

Streamlined Suburbs

Farsta, Skärholmen and Vallingby are the names of three suburbs of Stockholm constructed entirely within the last twenty-odd years (Vallingby dates back to 1954, Skärholmen was opened in 1968), according to rigid architectural plans laid down by Sweden's top city planners. Although I've overused the words "World of Tomorrow" in this chapter, that is exactly what these suburbs are—entirely modern cities, with buildings that look as though they were lifted from a World's Fair. To visit them, simply take the subway ("Tunnelbana") to the stop of the suburb's name (each one is toward the end of a different line) and wander through each little city at will.

The Steam Baths

Even more so than in Denmark and Norway, the Swedes go in heavily for "sauna"—that combination of steam baths, showers, massages, and frigid immersions that's supposed to add ten years to your life. They claim, in Sweden, that two hours of sauna (here it's sometimes also called "bastü") equal eight hours of sleep—and that is, in fact, how a roistering Swede—who's been up until 4 a.m.—revives himself to begin work the next day. I tried it on our last trip to Stockholm—and everything they say is true!

There's a steam bath in Stockholm for every purse. The most "luxurious" of the lot is the **Sturebadet,** on Sturegatan (#4) right at the Stureplan (the Sture Square), where a payment of 25 kronor will get you everything they have to offer, other than a sun-lamp treatment and a massage (it's 45 kronor for the entire works). Actually, however, you can go in for a quick swim and one steam room for only 12 kronor—even at the Sturebadet. Slightly less expensive (6 to 12 kronor for a moderate treatment) are the **Kampementsbadet,** at Sandhamnsgatan in the Karlaplan area (take bus #41 to Osthammarsgatan), open weekdays from 8 to 7, on Saturday from 8 to noon; and the **Forsgrenska Badet** (closed in July), in the Civic House at Medborgarplatsen (take the T-bana to Medborgarplatsen), only 6 kronor for sauna and pool. Ask for either the "Herrbastu" (steam) or "Herrturk" (dry heat) treatment, at either.

One of the least expensive baths—and the spot where the young set gathers —is the **Vanadisbadet,** near the Domus Hotel at Vanadislunden, where there's also an enormous outdoor swimming pool. Take bus 52 or 515 to Vanadisvägan, and walk another five minutes; the sauna is free after you've paid 6 kronor for admission to the pool. **Erikdalsbadet,** near Skanstull, is even larger (two pools) and charges the same; take bus 48 or 54 to Skanstull.

Museums

Here's a little-known fact about Stockholm: it has more museums than any European city other than London and Paris. Which ones to visit? Top priority goes to the **National Museum of Fine Arts,** the **Museum of Modern Art,** and the **Museum of Antiquities.** If you have time for only one, make it the Museum of Modern Art on the Skeppsholmen, which is open every day from 11 a.m. to 9 p.m., for an admission charge of 5 kronor to the permanent collection. But now, here's Hope to go into more detail on Stockholm's best sights.

HOPE IN STOCKHOLM: "Maybe it's a personal quirk, but whenever I'm in Stockholm I always get a very 'resort town' feeling; and that's all the more astonishing because this is one of the most urbane and sophisticated of cities. Yet in the summer when the sun is shining and people are strolling leisurely on the streets, with water everywhere, the air shimmering blue, so crisp and clear, one's mood so tinglingly alive and healthy, where else could you be but at a spa? You'll catch this feeling at the places previously described by Arthur, but also—and in particular strength—at **Drottningholm Palace, Prins Eugens Waldemarsudde,** and **The Museum of Modern Art:**

Drottningholm

"Much of the excitement at Drottningholm Palace emanates from performances of opera, ballet and chamber music at the rococo **Court Theatre.** Built for Queen Lovisa Ulrika in 1766, this cream and blue auditorium with its painted-like-marble decorations (it's all plaster) is preserved exactly as it was the day it opened. In fact, it is probably the only place in the world where you can see an opera done just as it was in the 18th century: the settings, the stage effects, even most of the musical instruments, are the original ones (or from that time); the musicians and ushers wear powdered wigs; you may even find yourself sitting in the very chair that was once occupied by King Gustav III (Lovisa Ulrika's son), who wrote plays for this theatre and acted on its stage.

"If you're in Stockholm between May and September, make a special effort to see an opera at Drottningholm Palace Court Theatre: performances begin at 8 p.m., tickets cost between 20 and 55 kronor ($4.76 and $13), and there are special Theatre Buses leaving from the Grand Hotel 45 minutes before curtain time (fare: 10 kronor). If you can't get tickets, then—during the day—at least see **The Court Theatre and Museum** (a collection of costumes, illustrations, and objects dealing with the history of European theatre in the 16th, 17th and 18th centuries: all located in the theatre); and also visit the French-inspired **Drottningholm Palace** (with its impressive sculptured gardens) and little **Chinese Pavilion.** Open any day when the king is not in residence, from 11 to 4, Sundays from noon to 4, in the summertime; and also during the months of April, September and October from 1 to 3 p.m. daily. There are guided tours (in English); entrance fee to the Palace is 5 kronor; and the Theatre Museum and Chinese Pavilion are 5 kronor each. The latter is located on the edge of the estate and is about a half mile walk from the Palace. Known as the 'Queen's Play House,' it's a charming little example of 'chinoiserie,' which was so popular during the rococo period; Queen Lovisa Ulrika (for whom it was built between 1763 and 1769) was especially fond of this style.

"Drottningholm (literal translation is "Queen's Island") is 6 miles west of Stockholm on an island in the Mälaren; to get there take the subway (T-bana) to Brommaplan, change to Mälarö-buses (all lines) for Drottningholm; or, in summer, take the direct boat (40 minutes) from near City Hall.

Waldemarsudde

"Prins Eugen's Waldemarsudde, the former home of the 'Painter Prince' on Djurgarden, is in an idyllic setting—on the water, in the center of an enchanting green park, and surrounded by beautiful landscaped gardens (which contain interesting pieces of sculpture). The Prince was a painter of some note (he did the murals in the Prince's Gallery at City Hall, and also the mural "Rimfrost" in the Royal Foyer of the Dramatic Theatre, among others), and also a great collector of art: so he built a gallery, connected to his home by a long underground passage, to house his treasures (and bequeathed the lot to Sweden).

"The physical surroundings at Waldemarsudde are so luscious that you'll feel more as if you are going on a picnic than heading for a gallery. But an excellent selection of Scandinavian artists is displayed here, including works by Carl Milles, Anders Zorn, Ernst Josephson (don't miss his interesting portrait of Dr. Axel Munthe), and Edvard Munch. The 'Palace' itself, though quite modern, is elegantly decorated and, as per the Prince's instructions, it has remained practically untouched since his death. On the grounds, you'll spot an Old Mill which is no longer working but contains industrial exhibitions that can be viewed in summer, and also 'Gamla Huset' (or Old House), which was the first house the prince lived in before his palace was built: on its first floor is a small museum of personal mementos—family photos, letters, early drawings, paint boxes and equipment, military swords, even his bowling ball and pins (the house is open in summer from noon to 5). Fittingly enough, the romantic prince chose to be buried here in a grave of his own design (a simple stone plaque) in front of 'Gamla Huset,' overlooking the water at his beloved Waldemarsudde. To get to the grounds take bus #47, which practically stops at the front gate, or else simply walk (it's a pleasant stroll) from nearby Skansen. Waldemarsudde is open daily except Mondays, from 11 to 5 in summer, until 4 in winter, and may also be visited on Tuesday and Thursday evenings (7 to 9) in summer; admission is free.

Modern Art

"The Museum of Modern Art, on Skeppsholmen, was a major 'happening' several years ago, mainly because of its display of the spectacular (and uniquely Swedish) sculpture-playland named 'She'—the brain-child and joint effort of Niki de Saint Phalle, Jean Tinguely and Per Olof Ultvedt. 'She' was tagged 'the biggest and best woman in the world' (82 feet long, 20 feet high and 30 feet wide), and was the one lady you got to know inside out. You entered the gigantic, colorfully-decorated female (who was supine) through the womb (which caused some comment) and then discovered wit and amusement in every inside corner: a small cinema showing an early Garbo feature, a Coke bar inside one breast, a look-out point atop the navel, a slide, grinding machines, a lover's nest. I use the past tense because 'She,' who should have been a national monument, was later destroyed, and there's now only a book called 'She' to keep the memory green (15 kronor, on sale at the museum's bookshop). I still find it hard to believe that they really let 'She' go, but those swinging Swedes will probably come up with something equally delightful to replace her, I mean 'she'. The permanent exhibit is a good one, with a broad selection of contemporary American artists (Andy Warhol, Roy Lichtenstein), together with dozens of famous cubist and surrealist paintings; and although the entrance charge is 5 kronor (free on Thursdays); special exhibition), it's well worth it. The museum is open from 11 a.m. to 9 p.m. daily throughout the year, and to get there you simply cross the Skeppsholmen Bridge, which is just opposite the National Museum (near the Grand Hotel), then walk past the church and past the Museum of Far Eastern Antiquities until you spot a wild and jolly mobile by Alexander Calder, which stands directly in front of the Museum of Modern Art.

Some Other Sights

"The attractions remaining are of high calibre—any city would be proud to claim them—but for me they lack something of the air of gaiety and excitement so characteristic of the three major institutions described above. Still, if you have time, look in on the **Nationalmuseum,** near the Grand Hotel, which displays interesting decorative art from the Middle Ages to the present (some 25,000 items!), a number of very fine paintings—including a room-full of Rembrandts and Rubens, some impressionists, Swedish art from all periods—and, of course, a well-chosen exhibit of modern Scandinavian design (silver, jewelry, pottery, glass, rugs and furniture). Open daily from 11 to 5, also Tuesday from 11 a.m. to 9 p.m., admission is free on Tuesday, 5 kronor all other days (for special exhibitions you'll pay an extra charge). . . . Also worth seeing is the vast **Nordic Museum** on Djurgarden, down the street from the Wasa Museum, displaying everything from soup to nuts on the development of Swedish culture from the 16th century to today—agriculture, fishing, folk art and handicrafts, textiles, costumes, furniture, even displays of table settings and food and drink. The entrance fee is 3 kronor (1.50 kronor for students); the hours from 10 to 4 weekdays, from noon to 5 Saturdays and Sundays (winters, closed Mondays). Take buses #s 47 or 44. . . . Elsewhere the **Museum of National Antiquities** ("Historiska Museet"), corner of Narvavagen and Linnegatan, is devoted to Sweden's very earliest history, prior to the 16th century (stone monuments from Gotland, a Viking Room and Gold Treasury, medieval displays and Church Reliquaries, a Gothic Hall, a reconstructed Country Church, and the like). This is the principal museum in Sweden for studying the Viking Age. (It also contains the Royal Coin Cabinet and the Mediterranean Museum). Open weekdays from 11 a.m. to 4 p.m., Saturdays and Sundays from noon to 5 p.m.; admission is free. The museum, incidentally, is within easy walking distance of the Karlaplan subway station and also the Nordic Museum: after you cross the bridge, walk straight ahead on Narvavagen for about two blocks, until you come to the entrance at Narvavagen. . . . For readers who feel uneasy unless they cover every Royal Palace, the **Stockholm Slott** (on the Slottsholmen Island in Gamla Stan, you'll see it from the Opera House) offers tours (every half hour), 10 a.m. to 1:30 p.m., Sunday at noon, of the State Apartments, the Guest Suite, and the Bernadotte Apartments, which are moderately interesting. The charge is 5 kronor for adults, 4 kronor for students, two for children, and everything is closed on Mondays. If you're willing to spend another krona, you can walk through the inner courtyard and visit the Hall of State where you'll see the silver throne which has been in use since Queen Christina's coronation in 1650, and the Chapel—that's on weekdays and Sundays from noon to 3. Changing of the Guard takes place in the courtyard, which is open to the public, daily at noon in summer (1 on Sunday), and on Wednesdays, Saturdays and Sundays in winter. . . . A few steps behind the Royal Palace is **Storkyrkan Church** (meaning "The Great Church"). Begun in the 13th century, it's the oldest church in Stockholm, and has provided the setting for royal weddings and coronations (Riddarholm Church is the Swedish Pantheon). There's no charge to enter, and the Church is officially open to tourists from 8 a.m. to 5:30 p.m. . . . Finally, theatre buffs may wish to make a pilgrimage to the last home of the brooding Swedish playwright, August Strindberg. From 1908 until his death in 1912, Strindberg lived on the fourth floor of an apartment building at 85 Drottninggatan which he called The Blue Tower, describing his mood, not the color of the building. His third wife had left him, and Strindberg couldn't bear to have anything around that would remind him of her; so if the apartment seems sparsely furnished, that's the reason. In addition to the few furnishings, there are photos, first editions of his books and plays, personal mementos, and an especially touching series of pictures of Strindberg's funeral procession, surrounded by crowds, reflecting not only his position in the literary world, but also reminding us of his tremendous popularity as a writer of the people. The apartment is open from Tuesday through Saturday, 10 a.m. to 4 p.m., Sunday from noon to 5 p.m. Closed Monday. Admission is 3 kronor (children are free), and there's a friendly curator who will show you around.

NIGHT-TIME ENTERTAINMENT: Sweden, until very recently, suffered under the strictest of liquor controls, with hardly a bar or non-membership club available for the refreshment of visitors. Now things are opening up a bit and this year Stockholm can boast a number of "pubs" and a whole crop of discotheques where there may be an admission fee, but no membership requirement.

Dancing

First choice for dancing in summertime are those spots at Skansen and Gröna Lund, already referred to above under "Girl-Watching." For disc-crawling or dance spots within the city proper, it's best to make your choice by age group. Teeny-boppers and students under 18 go to the **Kurbits,** Träng-sund 10, a small, dark discotheque in the Old City, where there's an entrance fee of 10 kronor Wednesday and Thursday, 15 kronor Friday and Saturday, no fee the rest of the week, and one beer costs 10 kronor. Older and more sophisticated Stockholmers attend the dances at the rather elegant **Restaurant Baldakinen** at Barnhusgatan 12, where admission is 25 kronor, Tuesday through Saturday, and small beer 7, a hard drink 18 kronor. That's rather expensive, but the Baldakinen offers good pickings to the lone American-man-on-the prowl. With Swedish girls, incidentally, seeking out foreign visitors at the dance spots—brunets are especially in demand. Next door, the **Restaurant Aladdin** advertises it is only for women over 25 and men over 30, from whom it also requires jacket and tie. A dark and cozy dance spot, it charges about the same admission fees as the Baldakinen, and requires at least one drink. Both places are closed Monday.

Jazz

The "in" spot of Stockholm—unbelievably popular although open less than three years—is **Stampen** in Old Town at Stora Gramunkegrand 7 (near the Gamla Stan subway stop). Stampen looks much like an Old British pub. It's draped in Union Jacks and hung with an odd collection of baby carriages, stuffed animals and even one antique sleigh. At one end of the warm and over-crowded room, there's a bandstand upon which appear the finest jazz musicians presently in Sweden—many visiting from America and England. The crowd is enthusiastic, dropping the stolid Swedish mien to "go with" the music, and prices are moderate. Only beer is sold (starting at 15 kronor) and entrance fee is 15 kronor Sunday through Thursday, 20 kronor Friday and Saturday. Jazz begins at 9 p.m.

Rock

Engelen Steakhouse and Pub, 59B Kornhamnstorg on Gamla Stan, a multi-roomed house with pop band upstairs, a discotheque downstairs, and two bars, is Stockholm's most popular pub at the moment of this writing. Entrance fee (applicable as a "credit" towards your dinner) of 12 to 20 kronor, depending on what bands are playing; and a line that stretches far from the door on Saturday nights.

Mosebacke, at Mosebacketorg, directly behind the Katarina elevator, is Stockholm's largest dance and rock-music restaurant, seating up to 400 persons, of whom 200 choose the outdoor terrace overlooking the town. Entertainment is provided by traveling rock and folk musicians. While entrance is a high 20 kronor ($4.76), drink and food prices inside are reasonable, and one-plate meals can be had for 20 kronor, beer for 12 kronor ($2.85). Open daily except midnight from 6 p.m. to midnight.

Theater, Music and Movies

The **Royal Dramatic Theatre** of Stockholm is one of the great playhouses of Europe and prices its seats for as little as 10 to 30 kronor ($2.38 to $7.14). But it's closed in the tourist-heavy month of August. . . . The **Opera,** which has produced such stars as Jussi Bjoerling, Birgit Nilsson, Nicolai Gedda and Set Svanholm, vacations during the same months and offers tickets from an astonishing 20 kronor ($4.76) to a top of 50 kronor ($11.90)—a superb bargain. . . . American and English movies in Stockholm aren't dubbed—they're in English, and tickets are priced from 10 kronor. . . . Almost every day in summertime, free concerts or programs are presented in the **Kungstradgarden,** the City Garden Park. And during the daytime there are concerts, recorded and live, with everything from pop music to the Salvation Army on the docket. Musical and variety programs are often presented at night—always on Sunday. The poster at the park or in the nearby tourist office gives the list of events.

STUDENT IN STOCKHOLM: For you, the key name, and the vital address, is the **Stockholm Student Reception Service** at Sweden House (Sverigehuset), 27 Hamngatan, 2nd floor (phone 22-32-80), opposite the NK department store, which foreign students (and, for that matter, all "youth under 30") are asked to make their very first stop for housing assistance, information, tickets to summer events, and the like. The larger all-year information office of the same official Stockholm student organization is in the modern Domus building at #1 Körsbärsvägen (phone 15-50-90), which performs somewhat similar functions and also deals with the problems (housing, jobs) of students planning longer stays in Stockholm. Both offices will book you into the cheapest and best of Stockholm's student lodgings, which is the 200-room **Hotel Frescati** at 13 Professorsslingen (phone 15-79-96), charging 30 kronor ($7.14) per bed in hostel-type double rooms, not dorms, an extra, one-time, 10 kronor payment for linen. For advance reservations prior to May 31, write to SSRS, Box 5903, 11489 Stockholm. . . . So much for rooms and information. The key social center of Stockholm's student organization is the **Mocambo** in the Forum Hall, 2A Körsbärsvägen, which serves as a quiet club and pub (lectures, discussions, long conversations between international students) most weekday nights, between 8 p.m. and midnight, then becomes a roaring discotheque for foreign students (called "The Village") on Fridays and Saturdays, when admission soars to 25 kronor. Sundays and weekdays are the best days to visit. . . . And for your travel arrangements (including those cheap charters) to other European cities, the organization to see is **SFS Resor,** at 89 Drottninggatan (phone 34-01-80).

THE MEAD-DRINKING, UNIVERSITY TOWN OF UPPSALA: "As you may know, several of the old English texts—for example, 'Beowulf' and the Arthurian legends, the Nordic and Icelandic sagas—are full of mention of the drinking of mead in the huge mead-halls of castles and palaces, for ceremonial purposes, welcomes, toasts, victory celebrations, etc. It served a multitude of uses, not least of which was simply getting plastered. Mead may be imbibed, in great style, just outside the famous city of Uppsala, a handy 50-minute train ride from Stockholm. . . . I spent the morning visiting the Uppsala Cathedral (largest in Scandinavia), the Carolina Rediviva (University Library) with its treasured Silver Codex, a Gothic Bible written in 500 A.D., Dag Hammarskjold's grave, and other sites. Then I took Bus #51 (3 kronor) from the train station (to the left of the exit) and in 10 minutes was in Gamla Uppsala, at the end of the line (a big parking lot). There are the Viking burial mounds, 1500 years old, a 12th century church, and an old Uppland village. But behind the church is the Odinborg Restaurant where one can get a steerhorn of mead for 15 kronor ($3.57). Mine was inscribed with the names of three of Sweden's royalty who, in 1866, 1879, and 1919, had drunk from that horn. The drink is excellent and, being made from honey and hops (a 14th century recipe), tastes like a sweet beer. Drinking with both hands from the steerhorn is atmosphere enough, although the restaurant, especially upstairs, supplies more in abundance, with Viking relics, armour, battle weapons and old Swedish furniture. . . . For anyone interested in old Scandinavian or English history, this can be one way to touch an ancient and cherished part of it. Whether the mead is like that which satisfied Arthur's (no pun intended) throat after defending the realm, is a moot point. It's a fine way to round off an afternoon with the Vikings" (David L. Miles, Charlevoix, Michigan).

A STOCKHOLM SMORGASBORD (Miscellany): If you're as curious as we were about the social and political structure of Sweden, then you may wish to read Marquis Childs' "Sweden: The Middle Way" before setting off for Stockholm. So comprehensive is the welfare program of Sweden that a cartoon in Dagens Nyheter, Stockholm's largest newspaper, showed an old man shocking an audience with the statement: "I retired on savings. I worked for years when they didn't take social security, health benefits, pension payments, union dues, and unemployment insurance out of your pay check." . . . As for the social customs of Sweden, I suggest that you watch the action at the various dancehalls described in our "Girl Watching" section, above. . . . To my ear, Swedish sounds more mellifluous than Danish. . . . Best way to say thank you in Swedish is "tack sa mycket" (pronounced tahk-sah-mick-it). . . . The kingdoms of Sweden, Norway and Denmark were once united, under a symbol of three crowns. Sweden kept the symbol (you'll see it atop the City Hall in Stockholm), uses it everywhere—the Swedish hockey team that beat the Russians was called "The Three Crowns." In this money-oriented book, three crowns means three kronor. . . . A walk, along the Kungsgatan at night is a must, as is a stroll on the main street of Gamla Stan ("Old Town")—the Vasterlanggatan—with its two-yard-wide side-street at #81. . . . For late shopping, remember the **Servus Store,** located in the underground passage of the Tunnelbana at the central station, which is open every day until 9 p.m.

READERS' SELECTIONS: "The finest organized tour I took in Europe was the 'life-seeing' tour offered in Stockholm, which leaves on week-days in summer, at 10 a.m., from the Karl XII Torg. This is a three-hour guided tour by bus, which investigates the Swedish social system by visiting diversified social institutions. There is a visit to a factory, a state-controlled hospital, Farsta, the newest Stockholm housing development (where we actually went into the home of a typical family and a pensioner and saw a recreation center), and a school building. The guide is so informative that when the tour is over, one feels one has really taken a close look at Swedish urban life. Such a tour is also offered in Copenhagen, but I found the Stockholm one far more fascinating" (Milton Schulman, Bronx, New York). . . . "Here's how to make your own personal visit to **Drottningholm Castle:** take subway T Centralen to the Brommaplan (fare, 4.50 kronor); walk down to the square and take the blue bus that says Drottningholm Castle on it (fare, 3 krona). Time: about 30 minutes. Castle admission is 5 kronor, Palace Theatre admission is 5 kronor, and the Chinese Pavilion is 5 kronor. Then, take a different and more interesting route back to town by getting on the ferry where the bus stops. Fare is 10 kronor, and you're back in town in 40 minutes" (Edward Pietraszek, Chicago, Illinois). . . . "For a day of complete relaxation, do as the outdoorsy Swedes do and take the 'Tunnel-Bana' (Subway) to the Fredhall stop. A short distance away, on lovely Lake Mälaren, is located the **Tranebergsbadet** where, for one krona, you can commune with Mother Nature to your heart's content. You may swim either in the Lake itself, or the heated pool, and there is space provided for tanning 'au naturel'; although the latter occupation, unlike St. Tropez, is segregated! Sorry 'bout that" (Carma Bamber, San Francisco, California). . . . "A cheap and expedient way of going from Stockholm to Berlin for the more intrepid train traveler is via the city of Trelleborg, a ferry to the city of Sassnitz in E. Germany. From there a train straight to E. Berlin, which then goes to the Zoobahnhof in W. Berlin—total cost, 2nd class, approx. $68 (depending on the rates of exchange), a saving of around $10 over the cost from Stockholm via Copenhagen and Hamburg to W. Berlin. If you can tolerate the military presence of the DDR for 8 hours or so, the trip brings considerable savings of time and money" (R. Golden, New York, N.Y.)

The last, the cheapest, and not the least of our three Scandinavian capitals, is Oslo—whose prices are at least 10% less than those you'll encounter in Stockholm. It's time—in the good-hearted phrase of the Oslo mayor—to "know the Norwegians." Turn the page.

Chapter IX

OSLO

The Fjord in Your Future

WHENEVER I THINK of Norway, I think of movies on the Late Late
Show, featuring British Commandos joining Norwegian fishermen to blow up
"a key installation." The heroism of Norway in World War II is typical of the
sturdy nature of these people, and of the very sights that you will see in Oslo:
the Kon-Tiki Raft of Thor Heyerdahl, the polar ship "Fram" in which the
Norwegian explorer Nansen went to the North Pole.

As these feats indicate, the sea is very much a part of life in Norway. At
noontime even in the capital city of Oslo, citizens stroll to the docks in front
of City Hall and purchase little bags of freshly cooked shrimp ($1.56), which
fishermen have caught in the night. And when you scan the menu of a budget
restaurant here, chances are that fish will rank over meat as the predominant
bill of fare.

Expect to see a city of nature-loving people, whose resources (except for
reserves of North Sea oil) are few and whose prices are still reasonable by
Scandinavian standards, though they have gone up considerably in the past
year. There is a minimum of elegance or sophistication in this relatively small
town (pop: approx. 500,000), and an emphasis instead upon clean, honest
living, tinged with the outdoors. Norway is a paradise for the sportsman and
Oslo is a perfect starting point for the nature viewing aspects of your European

tour—a refreshing, tingling, frontier-type of city that lets you relax without ostentation, at costs that are marginally below the Scandinavian standard.

A BUDGET SURVEY: Although Norway, and Oslo in particular, have felt the impact of a general European inflation in the past year, accommodations can still be had in a moderate range. In Oslo, rooms in a private home now rent for about $8.50 per person, or in a plain (but quite adequate) pension, from $8.50 to $11.50 person. Food will account for your major cash outlay, but if you follow the eating patterns of the country, as described later in this chapter —a large breakfast, sandwich lunch and hot dinner between 4 and 6 p.m.—and eat at the restaurants suggested, you can keep your food costs to a reasonable level. Simply be careful not to wait too late for dinner, as the majority of budget restaurants close about 6 p.m. and the only ones left open thereafter are those geared—and priced—to the (affluent) tourist trade.

ORIENTATION: The city of Oslo occupies a magnificent physical site, with high hills on three sides, and the great Oslo Fjord—sixty miles long—in front. At some point in your stay, you'll want to see the town from one of its hillside vantage points—the tallest being the **Tryvanns Tower,** on Tryvann Hill, from which you can scan the entire Oslo Fjord as it opens out into the sea (details later).

Directly on the Fjord is the **Oslo City Hall,** and it is from the waterfront street in front of this building that the tour buses leave, as well as the sightseeing launches that traverse the Fjord and the ferries that travel across to the peninsula of Bygdøy, where the majority of Oslo's sightseeing attractions are located. It's here, too, that the famous shrimp boats of Oslo unload their wares.

The main street of Oslo is the **Karl Johans Gate,** a few blocks up from the City Hall. This is the congregating and strolling street for Oslo's citizens, and it serves as your major orientation point. At the top of the Karl Johans Gate is the **Royal Palace,** at the other end is the antique-like **East Station**—the main railroad terminal of Oslo, where you'll find the all-important hotel accommodations bureau. Along the Karl Johans Gate, starting at the palace and continuing for a few hundred yards, is a narrow park. As you walk from the palace towards the station, you'll first pass the famous **National Theatre,** with its statues of Ibsen and Bjornson, then the Parliament Building of Oslo, and finally you'll reach the station. Running parallel to the Karl Johans Gate, starting at the Royal Palace and continuing for several blocks, is the **Stortingsgate,** another important street; and now you're oriented in Oslo.

TRANSPORTATION: The airport coach costs 10 kroner ($1.96) and drops you in the center of town, about one block from the City Hall. An alternative and slightly cheaper route from airport to city is via municipal bus #31, which leaves from and arrives at the National Theatre for a one-way fare of 6 kroner ($1.17). Within the city, bus and tram fare is 4 kroner (78¢) per ride, with free transfers within an hour of boarding.

Oslo also operates two "tunnel railways," which are electric lines that travel out to the suburbs, partially without tunnels and partially overground. These are simple to use and provide the quickest, and most direct, method of reaching such spots as the Tryvanns Tower and the Munch Museum. One line leaves from behind the National Theatre, the other from the East Station; fares vary according to destination.

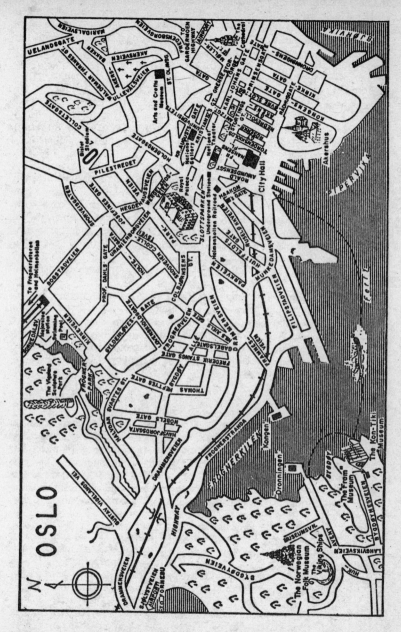

HOTELS: Of all the Scandinavian cities, Oslo has the tightest summer hotel situation—particularly in late June, August and September, when the town is jammed (July, for some unknown reason, isn't half as bad). But Oslo is also the only one of the major Scandinavian capitals whose tourist association will make advance reservations for you, thus sparing you the job of writing to possibly successive hotels. If you'll write a reasonable time in advance to the **Oslo Travel Association,** 19 Radhusgaten, specifying your requirements and the dates of your stay, they'll make all the arrangements. They will even, at your request, book you into a low-cost room in a private home, *whether or not* the hotels are filled. Thus, Oslo is the only one of the Scandinavian capitals to put the interests of its tourists ahead of its major hotels—and I, for one, say three cheers! Accompany your reservation request with a deposit (bank draft only) of $11.76 (60 kroner) *per person.* Of this, $9.80 (50 kroner) will be applied to your rent and $1.96 (10 kroner) deducted as a booking fee. In return, you will receive in the mail your confirmed reservation, plus a small map and tourist guide to Oslo.

But you'll suffer no catastrophe if you arrive without a reservation. For then, you simply go to the **Innkvartering** desk inside the East Station, where attendants are on duty from 8 a.m. to 11 p.m. in summer (but from only 6 p.m. to 11 p.m. in winter) to find you a suitable room in your price range. Here, again, rooms in private homes will be arranged upon request priced at from 60 kroner ($11.76) single, from 90 kroner ($17.64) double—and they are all thoroughly-proper places which have been checked by the travel association. Booking fees at the accommodations desk are 10 kroner ($1.96) for a single room, 15 kroner ($2.94) for a double, 4 kroner (78¢) for each extra person in a room.

A single warning: the young people who staff the "Innkvartering" service often make the typically-Norwegian assumption that you'd prefer the rural outskirts of Oslo to the central, urban section of the city. They may, therefore, book you at a hotel located on a mountainside, two- or three-hundred yards from the last stop of the electric train that took 20 minutes to get you up there. Be sure to inquire about the *precise* location of the hotel they've chosen.

Budget Pensions and Hotels

Apart from rooming in a private home, the best way to stay on a budget in Oslo is to live in a "hospits" or pension, many of which charge $7.50 or less per person. What's the difference between a "hospits" and a pension? No one seems to know. Some Oslo-ites claim that "hospits" is simply an older and now out-of-fashion word for "pension"; others will tell you that the owners of "hospits's" need not be licensed or know several languages, as must the operators of more formal establishments. Physically, the two species have always seemed identical to me—they're almost always a single floor of an office or apartment building, with rooms for overnight guests—although the places with "hospits" in their title seem, often, to charge the lowest prices.

In the following listings, note that prices include service charge, unless otherwise mentioned, but not breakfast. Keep in mind, too, that many Oslo pensions and hotels add a surcharge of 5 kroner (98¢) per person for a mere one-night stay; inquire.

Double Rooms for $11.76 to $17.64

First, a cluster of inexpensive pensions, some of which are ultra basic, some of which are quite charming but open only in summer.

Least expensive of all and suitable *only* for those who are willing to sacrifice amenities for convenience and price, are an assortment of starvation-budget-quality spots in the vicinity of the railroad station. But equally cheap, and far better located *outside* the railroad station area, is the **Ellingsen Pensjonat** at 25 Holtegate (phone 600-359), near the Oranienborg subway stop behind the King's Palace, where twenty-one rooms on three floors rent—to readers of this book only—for only 40 kroner ($7.84) single, 80 kroner ($15.68) double, including free showers. Breakfast, however, is not served. The couple operating this pension are quite friendly and helpful, and will point the way to a nearby cafe where breakfast can be had for 14 kroner. To find their pension, look first for No. 25, then walk through a small garden to the main entrance where the name is posted at the doorbell.

Or try, again outside the railway station area, **Bergsliens Hospits,** 1 Bergsliensgate (phone 60-24-51), which is operated by friendly, English-speaking Lüftü Güven—of Turkish extraction—who has been a seaman and therefore tends to attract a seagoing clientele. Twenty-four rooms, only three with running water, but there is a bathroom and sinks in the hallways for taking water to your room. Though the rooms are simple and the building antiquated, the pension is clean and the owners helpful. Still, the masculine ambiance might be better appreciated by men than girl travelers. Singles cost 45 kroner ($8.82), doubles go for 60 kroner ($11.76). Take tram #1 or 11 from the East Station to Rosenborg, and walk two minutes from there; entrance is on Sporveisgate and the pension itself is on the fourth floor of a walk-up building.

Cochs Pensjonat, 25 Parkveien (phone 60-48-36), is a excellent value: an 72-room pension that keeps about 55 rooms for transients, it is located on the third floor of an elderly building with ornately tiled hallways. The rooms are high-ceilinged, spotless, newly-painted and equipped with the usual narrow Norwegian beds. All rooms have hot-and-cold running water, and there are two bathrooms for the use of transients and no charge for baths. Singles (of which there are very few) cost 64 kroner ($12.54), doubles 90 kroner ($17.64), triples 135 kroner ($26.47), four-bedded rooms 165 Kroner ($32.35). If you are reserving ahead, you'll be requested to mail a 50-kroner per person deposit. Tram #11 or 17 connects you with the center of town.

THE NORWEGIAN CURRENCY: Presently selling at 5.10 kroner to the dollar, each krone has been valued by us at 19½¢ for the conversion of kroner prices into dollars in this chapter.

Double Rooms for $16.86 to $21.56 (some on the outskirts)

Helga and Dag Sylou-Kreutz, a smiling Norwegian couple occupying a home at 100B Pilestrade (phone 69-29-22), rent three double and three triple rooms at a uniform price of 43 kroner ($8.43) per person per night, no breakfast, but free showers, and you're given a key to come and go as you please. Only five minutes from the center; take streetcar 7 to the Adamsvejen stop, and you'll find their house in the garden with the white gate and lonely birch tree.

Somewhat further out, on a hill overlooking the city, the pensione **Be-ti-Fire** in a two-story building with red roof at 10 Bravnfjellvejen (phone 19-37-

34), rents a big 60 beds, some in an annex next door, for 60 kroner ($11.76) single, 110 kroner ($21.56) twin, no breakfast, all in rooms furnished country-style with unpainted wooden beds, wardrobes, chairs and tables; some rooms enjoy a spectacular view of Oslo harbour. Added feature: a beautiful reception-ist named Kirsti Langaard, who could model for a "Visit Oslo" poster. And the name? "Be" stands for Braunfjellvejen, "ti" for the number ten, "fire" (—four) for the annex house number. Easily reached from the center (a ride of less than 10 minutes) by bus no. 24 to the Braunfjellvejen stop.

Finally, if you don't mind staying in the outskirts, a good address is the private home (with a fruit and tobacco shop inside, a nearby gas station which is theirs also) of **Olav Birkheim** at 47 Ringeriksvejen, Sandvik (phone 54-84-39); the Birkheims' son, who runs the shop, understands English, and the visit is an intense "Meet the Norwegians" experience. Sixteen beds in several rooms rent for a most reasonable 50 kroner ($9.80) single, 86 kroner ($16.86) twin, 110 kroner ($21.56) triple, no breakfast. From the center, either take bus 36 or 39 (7 kroner) and pull the string above your seat immediately after the Sandvik stop, or take the train to Sandvik from the West Station, a 25-minute trip.

Double Rooms for $16.66 to $26.47

A really excellent summer guesthouse is the **Sta. Katarinahjemmet Pen-sion,** Majorstuveien 21B, phone 60-13-70 or 60-13-71, which is operated by the sisters of a Dominican convent and takes guests from May until the first of September. The guesthouse (which houses working girls in the winter) is set in the wooded convent grounds; the rooms are neat and modern. In the dining room you breakfast off a three-centuries-old Norwegian table; in the library you can choose from books in several languages; in the chapel with its multi-colored windows you can even attend Mass daily in summer; guests are welcomed but never in any way urged. The guesthouse is non-sectarian—the white-robed nuns efficient but discreet. Highly recommended for both men and women. Singles are priced at 85 kroner ($16.66), doubles at 125 kroner ($24.50). Break-fast is an extra 22 kroner.

Viktoria Hospits, 29 Niels Juelsgate off Frognerveien (phone 44-52-56), is located in one of the most pleasant residential districts in the city. Its 50 large rooms are simple and good, all with hot-and-cold running water, modern furnishings and worthy carpets. Some are quite spacious and freshly painted. Although there is no elevator, there is a TV lounge for guests, and genial Mr. Rolf Schroeder is the host; there's perfect English spoken here. Singles are 65 kroner ($12.74), doubles 85 to 100 kroner ($16.66 to $19.60). Tram #2 stops in front of the door.

St. Hanshaugens Hospits, 31 Geitmyrsveien (phone 46-84-28), is an excel-lent 60-bedded guesthome in a big white house across from a lovely park and with a picturesque mountain backdrop. The rooms are spotless, spare and modern, the house comes equipped with a free, 16-car parking lot, and the proprietors—Mr. and Mrs. Rolf Berge—are English-speaking and friendly. All rooms are equipped with hot-and-cold; the house itself has six showers (free) and two baths. Rates are 80 kroner ($15.68) single, 135 kroner ($26.47) double, 40 kroner for an extra bed in a double room. Take bus #17 to Louisenberg.

On the western outskirts of Oslo (15 minutes from the center by bus or train), is the recently-built **Baptistsamfunnets Skoler** (the educational center of the Baptist Union of Norway), 55 Micheletsvei, Stabekk/Oslo (phone 53-38-53), which converts into a hotel from June 1 through September 1. Here there are 30 rooms with running water, built-in closets, modern furnishings and large windows overlooking the surrounding lawns. Tubs and showers (free of charge) are available in the hallways. This is a superb place for people who are driving (unlimited parking), who have children (the lawns are for playing), or who prefer a rural setting with easy access to town. Singles are priced at 90 kroner ($17.64), doubles at 125 kroner ($24.50), triples at 145 kroner ($28.43), breakfast an extra 20 kroner. From University Square, take bus #32, 36 or 37; get off at Kveldsroveien and walk across the bridge to the school building.

Another top-rated pension is the **Seminarheimen,** 3B Josefinesgate (phone 69-10-06), which has 13 lovely, well-kept guestrooms and a charmingly rusticated sitting room furnished in traditional carved wood pieces, an immense fireplace, a piano and grandfather's clock. Everything is immaculate, the atmosphere is genteel, all rooms have hot-and-cold running water, the bath is free, but the pension, unfortunately, is open only in summer (from June first to August 15). There is ample parking space to the rear of the house or you can take tram #7 to the Bislet stop. Doubles in 1980 will cost 135 kroner ($26.47), triples 170 kroner ($33.33), breakfast 28 kroner ($5.49), the latter including an egg and cheese.

Doubles for $29.41

Now for the costlier pensions and standard hotel rooms. In the very center of town and only three blocks from the East Station, is the **Hotel Fonix,** 19 Dronningensgate (phone 42-59-57), which charges precisely 150 kroner ($29.41) for one of their smaller double rooms (these are actually singles equipped with a supplementary single bed), 180 kroner ($35.29) for a normal double without bath, 95 kroner ($18.62) for a single, service included. Clean, newly-painted throughout, and respectable, and moderately priced for its category.

In the peak summer period between June 20 and August 20, the **Y.W.C.A. Home (K.F.U.K. Hjemmet)** at 3B Neuberggaten (phone 44-17-87), near Frogner Park, houses both men and women in its 13 single and 13 double rooms for 95 kroner ($18.62) single, 150 kroner ($29.41) double, including continental breakfast and use of a pleasant lounge, sitting rooms, laundry room and garden. Unlike many establishments of this sort, there's no evening curfew, and a modern, mature atmosphere.

Hostels and Dorms

Oslo's youth hostel—and an excellent one it is—is the **Haraldsheim,** Haraldsheimveien 4, Grefsen/Oslo (phone 02-218359). Situated in a countrified setting on the eastern outskirts of the city (on Grefsen Hill), it takes only those who have International Hostel cards during the summertime (May through September) but anybody who wishes to come, regardless of age, in winter. The overnight charge for bed-and-breakfast is 45 kroner ($8.82). Add 8 kroner ($1.56) for renting a sheet sleeping bag (which is required). The building is modern and well-maintained; the bedrooms are closed from 10 a.m. to 4 p.m., but the outdoor picnic area, in front, enjoying a beautiful vista of the harbor of Oslo, is available all day, and the restaurant serving hot two-course meals for 20 kroner opens after 4 p.m. Beds are bunks in either six-bedded or eight-bedded rooms, and the hostel has a capacity (often filled in summer) of 260 persons. When it is filled, overflow goes to the modern **Bierke Student Home,** charging similar rates, nearby. At both, curfew is a reasonable 1 a.m., and to reach both, take tram #1 or 7 from the East Station or National Theatre (look for the sign "Sinsen" on the front of the tram) to the last stop. Or take the train (free to Eurailpass holders) from the East Station to Grefsen, from which the Haroldsheim is a 150-yard walk. Late, January, 1980 flash: Haroldsheim will now house non-members of the Youth Hostel association, but at a supplement of 8 kroner ($1.56) per night over the hostel level.

PRIVATE-HOMES-THAT-READERS-HAVE-LIKED: "There is no better accommodation for families than at **Bella Vista Hospits,** at 11B Aarundveien, Arvoll (phone 21-66-78), six kilometers from the East Station in Oslo, where there are English-speaking proprietors (Capt. and Mrs. J. A. Madsen), large rooms, rates of 60 kroner ($11.76) per person, double occupancy, 80 kroner single, with breakfast for 13 kroner and showers for free" (Dr. Anna Tollenaere-Blank, Warmond, Holland; note from AF: to reach the Bella Vista (which is near the airport), take bus No. 31, which runs between airport and town, and ask the driver to stop at the hospits—he knows it).

EATING IN OSLO: On this subject, a preliminary and important note: the mealtime habits of Norwegians are somewhat unique, and you may be puzzled by the resulting restaurant situation, unless you know them. The basic puzzle stems from the fact that very few Norwegians eat lunch—or at least lunch as we know it. How or why the custom began, no one seems to know; but the fact is that most people in Oslo work straight through the day without a lunch hour, and are thus enabled to knock off from work by 3:30 or 4 p.m.

How do they keep going? Around noontime, a Norwegian office worker will usually break out an open sandwich, brought from home, and eat it at his desk—working all the while. When he does leave the office, he then has an immediate big meal—inaccurately called a "middag," which is really a dinner. That means that the evening eating hours are unusually early in Oslo—many of the less expensive restaurants have completed serving their evening meals and are entirely shut down by 6 p.m.

For the same reason, you'll often enter an Oslo restaurant around noontime, only to find sandwiches—and nothing else—being served. If you'll come again at 2 p.m., however, you'll find the staff first starting to prepare the really big meal—the "middag." The lesson to learn from this is to schedule your evening meal for as early as 5 p.m.

But having absorbed this information, you can now proceed to forget most of it, because you won't be having lunch at your desk. I've sought out restaurants that do offer hot meals beginning at about 1 p.m., although again you're warned to return for supper no later than, say, 5:30.

The Kaffistova's

To get your cheapest but most filling meal, go to the **Stortorvet,** a big square with a church on one side, a flower market in the center, and a major department store—the **Christiania** (former name of Oslo) **Glasmagasin**—on the other. Overlooking the Square from a picture window on a second floor location, at #13 Karl Johans Gate, is a member of the **Kaffistova** chain—the plainest, most basic restaurants in Oslo, owned and operated for country folk coming to town by an organization called "The League of Country Youth." The prices here are low, and the meals enormous—don't try them unless you're ravenously hungry. Huge hunks of meat slathered with a thick gravy (the Norwegians go heavy on gravy), with a separate vast dish of potatoes accompanied by another tureen of gravy, and peas and carrots—for two such plates, along with two Cokes, Hope and I paid 40 kroner ($7.84), total. It is entirely possible to order one serving for two people—and even then you may not finish this "nourishing lunch."

There's an even better **Kaffistova** at Rosenkranzgate 8 (second floor), near the expensive Bristol Hotel and near the Karl Johans Gate, where the food seems a little more delicately cooked. But don't confuse this establishment with the not-quite-as-cheap "Grillstova" downstairs at the same location.

All Kaffistovas are self-service, cafeteria-style establishments, and all serve, in addition to their hot plates averaging 19 to 21 kroner, fine shrimp appetizers (9 kroner the serving), a big bowl of soup for 6 kroner, a dessert for 6 kroner, and various open sandwiches starting at 7 kroner. . . . But note with care that all Kaffistovas close at 7 p.m. on weekdays, at 4 p.m. on Saturdays, 6 p.m. Sundays.

Four very special budget restaurants

Norrona Cafeteria, up one flight of stairs at 19 Grensen heart of town, is our very top budget choice: clean, spacious, with moderate prices for top quality food, 300 comfortable chairs, wall-to-wall carpeting, white curtains on windows, a quiet and cultivated atmosphere, and all superbly supervised by Mr. Dugas, who also manages the mission hotel in the same building; he's fluent in English. He also maintains a separate dining room for non-smokers! Most patrons start with soup for 5 kroner (98¢); move on to Norwegian fishburgers for 17 kroner ($3.33), roast sausages with mashed potatoes for 18 kroner ($3.52), more elaborate meat plates with vegetables for 21 kroner ($4.11), or simply two eggs on toast for 9 kroner ($1.76). Desserts are 2.50 kroner (49¢) to 5 kroner (98¢), the latter price for pudding with cranberry sauce; and there's an English-language menu card which you can request. Mornings, the normal continental breakfast for 17 kroner ($3.33) is far exceeded in value by an all-you-can-eat buffet breakfast for 25 kroner ($4.90): as much as you want, filling up for the day, on eggs, sausages, other cold cuts, four kinds of bread, cheeses, marmalades, cornflakes, milk, tea, coffee. Hours are Monday to Friday from 8 a.m. to 5 p.m., Saturday to 3 p.m., Sunday again to 5 p.m.

Venstreshus Kafe, on the second floor of a building called "Venstre Hus" at 16 Möllergatan, a five-minute walk from the Oslo Cathedral, is a conservatively furnished and decorated self-service restaurant heavily-patronized by the employees and sales personnel of the surrounding business and shopping area. It offers as many as ten, filling, main dishes—such as fish cutlets with sauce remoulade and steamed potatoes—for an average of 20 kroner ($3.92) per, which many patrons precede with soup for 6 kroner. Try, especially, the excellent spinach soup.

Frisksportrestauranten, 18 Grensen, is Oslo's major vegetarian restaurant, and offers some of the best values in town—like a three-course meal of spinach soup, followed by soyabean "hamburgers" with roast potatoes, green peas, cabbage, cucumbers, carrots and tomato, then banana in vanilla sauce and whipped cream for dessert, all for 24 kroner ($4.70). A large raw mixed salad is 12 kroner. The 24 tables are usually crowded by noon, so it's best to get there either before 12 or after 2. Open weekdays until 8 p.m., but only until 6 p.m. on Saturdays, and closed Sundays.

Cheaper—in fact, one of the budget standouts in Oslo—and much stricter and more intense in its vegetarian zeal, is the **Kurbad Restaurant** at 74 Akersgatan, five minutes on foot from City Hall, and owned by Seventh Day Adventists who prohibit the use of alcohol or cigarettes on the premises, and dress their employees in neat orange-brown uniforms. A typical, three-course "menu" might consist of carrot soup, lentil beef hash with vegetables, and figs with vanilla sauce for dessert, for only 20 kroner ($3.92). Closed, naturally, on Sundays. Walking here (it's across from St. Olaf's Church), you'll pass a modern, gray post office building with a mural of fishermen with a net: this is a Picasso original.

The other budget restaurants

A slightly less heavy meal than those served at the "Stova's" is available at the very good (but also slightly more expensive) **Promenadekafeteria**, Övre Slottsgate 12 (second floor), in the very heart of town, just off the Karl Johans Gate, near the Parliament Building ("Storting"). Here, you'll first choose your dishes from a glassed-in display counter, then tell a lady-in-a-cage what you want, pay her, go back to the counter, and then take the food to your table. We each had a flavorsome Wienerschnitzel with anchovies baked into the top, for 25 kroner ($4.90) per person. An extremely homey, old-fashioned cafeteria. . . . Closer to the East Station, the well-liked coffee shop of the Viking Hotel, called **"Den Lille Fiol"** (Little Violet), offers a choice of three daily platters for 24.50 kroner ($4.80), and is open seven days a week from 7 a.m. to 11:30 p.m.

At lunchtime, the large and brightly-colored **Expressen Cafeteria** at 11 Fred Olsensgate, in front of the East Station, offers bargain-rate dishes such as fishburger with a generous helping of salads for 20 kroner ($3.92), a vanilla pudding dessert for 6.50 kroner ($1.27), a daily soup (tomato cream, for example) for 6 kroner ($1.17). It's open weekdays from 7 a.m. to 6:45 p.m., Saturdays from 8:30 a.m. to 4:30 p.m., Sundays from noon to 5:30 p.m.

For open-air dining, and a light meal with a good view, the **Cheese Inn,** on the spectacular Vikaterrassen at 3 Ruselokkeveien, is unusual, and moderately priced. Cheese is the feature: quiche lorraine for 13 kroner, Welsh rarebit 15 kroner, a choice of 12 different and unusual cheese sandwiches (averaging 18 kroner), soup for 10 kroner, a small beer for 12 kroner. . . . **Samson,** diagonally across from the Promenadecafeen, at Ö. Slottsgate 21 (corner Karl Johans Gate), is another cafeteria-style restaurant, where you order your food and pay for it at the counter and then a waitress brings it to your table when it is ready. An attractive upstairs room, with large windows overlooking the main street and lots of ornamental black wrought iron to divide the seating areas, it serves mammoth hot plates starting at 22 kroner. Open 8 a.m. to 7 p.m. on weekdays, to 4 p.m. on Saturday, and closed Sunday.

THE SPECIALTIES: In observing your fellow diners, you'll find that smoked salmon with scrambled eggs, bread and butter, is particularly well-liked by Norwegians, but it comes high—about 23 kroner for a serving. Nevertheless, the least expensive dishes in Oslo are generally those involving fish, which is always excellent. If you'd like a very inexpensive meat dish, the two Norwegian staples are "kjottkaker" (meat cakes) and "lapskaus" (hash). The latter dish looks like just-plain-hash, but somehow—in Oslo—it tastes better than our American variety. Always reasonably-priced.

Some Oslo establishments serve "brun lapskaus" (hashed pork and potatoes, 20 kroner), or else such remarkable weirdies as reindeer-hamburgers-with-cream-sauce-and-red-whortle-berries, 20 kroner (and if you think I'm making this up, then ask for "rensdyrkarbonader med fløtesaus og tyttebaer")! Order milk with your meal, not beer. As in all the Scandinavian countries (even more so in Sweden), the cost of beer is increased by heavy, punitive taxes; in most restaurants, a bottle is now 15 kroner ($2.94).

RESTAURANTS—THE BIG SPLURGE: And now, when you're willing to spend upwards of $8 per meal, try the following:

The Theatercafeen: Every day from 3:30 to 6 p.m. and from 7:45 to 11:45 p.m., four musicians—usually a pianist, two violinists and a bass fiddler, all professionals and serious—perform Strauss, Bach, Mozart and a few modern (but not too modern) composers from a balcony overlooking the large, tastefully-furnished dining room of the **Theatercafeen** in the Hotel Continental building at 24 Stortingsgaten—one of the last remaining restaurants in Europe to offer such accompaniment. I'm told that 50 years ago, the restaurants of Vienna were famous for this sort of cultivated atmosphere, which exists today only at the Theatercafeen in Oslo! The menu is classical, too, with its roast leg of mutton with salad (41 kroner, $8.03), wienerschnitzel with vegetables (43 kroner, $8.43), poached flounder (38 kroner, $7.45), and Theatercafeen salad bowl (consisting mainly of cheese, shrimps and chicken (38 kroner, $7.45).

Tostrupkjelleren Restaurant, 25 Karl Johansgate, is both chic and traditional, and perhaps the most expensive of our big splurge choices. A cellar restaurant just opposite the Parliament Building, it is definitely a place where you would dress up a bit to go to dinner. The decor is an elegant combination of contemporary red leather banquettes set in alcoves and crystal chandeliers from an earlier era. Everything is à la carte. You'll find lots of unique Norwegian specialties, but you can well shoot the wad. Among Americans the most popular dish here is the fried trout in sour cream with new potatoes for 52 kroner ($10.19), or the occasionally served reindeer steak with cream sauce for slightly more, but numerous dishes can be had for only 38 to 42 kroner ($7.45 to $8.23), the cheaper price for beef tostrup with potatoes and vegetables.

READERS' RESTAURANT SELECTIONS: "At **Aulakjelleren,** a student cafeteria in the University at 47 Karl Johansgate, opposite the National theater, you may have not only hot dishes, but warm sandwiches—the latter a good substitute for dinner on the starvation budget. While the food isn't always the tastiest, it's cheap, and you will meet Norwegian and foreign students, without being asked for a student card" (Vegard Elvestrand, Oslo, Norway; note from AF: walk into the left side of the huge building with the four tall pillars, then down the steps next to the students' book store).

THINGS TO DO: You ought definitely to start with a trip up Tryvanns' Hill for a view of the Fjords, Norway's crowning glory; then visit the shrimp boats; then have a steam bath—and only then embark on the standard sightseeing.

A Trip Up Tryvanns Hill

It can be a full afternoon/evening's outing, which starts by walking to the electric train behind the National Theater and taking the Holmenkollen line to the Voksenkollen stop (4 kroner one-way). From there, hike up the hill to the **Tryvanns Tower,** a fifteen-minute walk. Then take the elevator to the observation gallery on top (4 kroner for adults, 2 kroner for children), and you will be standing at the highest point is Oslo, commanding—on a clear day—a view of 5,000 square miles, down the Oslo fjord and across to the Swedish border. Hours at the tower are 9:30 a.m. to 10 p.m. daily in June and July, from 10 a.m. to 8 p.m. in May and August and from 10 a.m. to 6 p.m. in March, April and September.

After leaving the tower, walk downhill until you come to the lodge-like **Frognerseteren Hovedrestaurant,** where you might next stop for a snack or a "Big Splurge" meal and to take in the fabulous view. But be sure never to go inside (where meals start at $25), but rather to use the open-air, self-service, terrace cafeteria, commanding the most spectacular view imaginable of Oslo and the Fjord—the photos you take here will be among the most memorable of your trip. Daily platters average 25 kroner ($4.90), sandwiches 12, coffee 8 ($1.56), with beer out of sight—that curiously Puritanical Scandinavian phenomenon. Although daylight lasts until 9 p.m. in summer, it's best to arrive no later than 5 or 6 for the best view and picture-taking possibilities. Independently visited, the Frognerseteren Restaurant is a ten-minute walk from the Frognerseteren electric train stop.

Leaving the restaurant, you can then walk down a marked path to the famous **Holmenkollen Ski Tower,** where annual ski jump contests in March attract champions from all over the world and huge crowds of spectators. You can take the lift to the top of the jump for still more amazing views, then visit the highly-original **Ski Museum** at the foot of the jump. A combined ticket costs 7 kroner for adults, 3 kroner for children. Admission to the ski jump alone is 4 kroner for adults, 2 kroner for children. Hours are 10 a.m. to 10 p.m. daily in summer, but considerably more limited in winter.

From the ski jump, it is just a short downhill walk to the Holmenkollen electric train station, where you can catch a train back to the National Theater, refreshed and ready for city life again after your foray into the Oslo hills!

Shrimp Boats are A'Coming

Throughout the night in the waters outside Oslo, local fishermen gather in vast quantities of tiny shrimp. At least three of these boats then sail to the dock that stands in front of the Oslo City Hall, cooking the shrimp as they go, in vats on the decks of their boats. Starting at around 11 a.m., on every day except Sunday and Monday, the citizens of Oslo wander to the docks, pay 8 kroner ($1.56) for a tin can-full of freshly-cooked shrimp, and chomp them down, sitting on the edge of the quay with their feet dangling over the water, and throwing the husks of the shrimp into the bay (where they're quickly gobbled up by the ever-present sea gulls). It's all great fun, and it costs only $1.56 (which buys more than enough for two people). But warning: the shrimp are so delicious that you're tempted to eat too many of them, thus spoiling your appetite for lunch!

Steam Baths

Yes, Oslo has them too, and the steam bath for budgeteers (men only, unfortunately) is a huge, community-owned proposition called the **Torggata Bad,** on the corner of Torggata and Henrik Ibsens Gate, just a block from the big downtown square where the Folketeatre (housing "Den Norske Opera") is located. In the summer of 1978 after paying 25 kroner for the complete works (several different steam rooms, swimming pool, individual sleep cubicles, everything but a massage), in the ground floor portion of the baths, I walked out refreshed, clean and content, only to be told by some incoming customers that I could have had almost the same items *upstairs* for nearly a third the price. Upon my return visit, in 1979, I checked that out and found that they were absolutely correct! While on the ground floor, you can get the full treatment for 25 kroner, upstairs you can have the steam room, swimming pool and shower—everything but the sleep cubicle—for only 10 kroner. You know which we recommend. The smaller **Bislett Baths** (closed in August) at 60 Pilestredet, is similarly priced, and is open seven days a week, on weekdays and Saturdays until 6 p.m., on Sundays until 11:30 a.m. It's also open in July, when the Torggata Baths are closed. Both men and women, in separate areas, are accepted at the **Toyen Baths,** 90 Helgesensgate, next to the Munch Museum (phone 671-889), at a charge of 7 kroner for both sauna and swimming pool, 2 kroner for children.

For no steam

The outdoor swimming pool of Oslo, whose temperature is maintained at a constant 70°, is the **Frognerbadet** in Frogner Park, near the Vigeland Sculptures (the season is from May 20 to around the 10th of September). Entrance is 6 kroner, and there are cafeterias, sunbathing areas, fine lawns. The beach of Oslo is the much-frequented **Ingierstrand Bad,** on the east side of the fjord, reached by bus no. 73 or 75 from Wessels Square; entrance is free.

SIGHTS TO SEE: The indispensable sights of Oslo are six in number, and they are all quite thrilling—a major highlight of your European tour. We'll first describe the sights themselves, and then discuss the best methods of seeing them.

The Viking Ships

It was as recently as 1904 that excavators found the last of the only three Viking ships to have survived the ten centuries since they were built. All three ships were apparently used as burial chambers for well-to-do Vikings, and all three have been magnificently restored and displayed in the **"Viking Ship Hall"** on the Bygdøy Peninsula, fifteen minutes from the heart of Oslo. You'll see the Oseberg ship (reputedly the burial chamber of a lady of high rank), the Gokstad ship, and the smaller Tune ship, along with the relics that were found in each boat. It's thrilling to contemplate that the courageous Norwegian Vikings may actually have crossed the Atlantic in vessels of this sort. Open from 10 to 6 in summer, from 11 to 3 in winter, admission is 5 kroner, and the address is Huk Aveny 35, Bygdøy. Take bus #30 or, in summer, the ferry from Radhusplassen (City Hall Square), Pier 3.

The Polar Ship "Fram"

This is the famous vessel that took Nansen to the Arctic in 1893 and Roald Amundsen to the South Pole in 1910. The entire ship has been hauled on land, and placed into a unique, pyramid-shaped building—mainly so that you can see the ingeniously-designed round hull that enabled the ship to ride up and over the crushing masses of polar ice. The Norwegians are fiercely proud of their polar explorers, which accounts for their having made this unique building to cover the Fram. Again located on the Bygdøy Peninsula, with hours from 10 a.m. to 6 p.m. in summer, with shorter hours in the fall/winter months and closed entirely from December 1 to April 15. Admission is 4 kroner for adults, 2 kroner for students and children.

The Kon-Tiki Museum

This modern counterpart of the great polar feats of Norwegian sailors is only a few steps from the building housing the Fram. Here you'll see the balsa-wood raft on which Thor Heyerdahl and his companions floated more than 5,000 miles, from Peru to Polynesia, to test the theory that South American Incas may have settled the South Pacific. Since the language of formal communication in the Norwegian navy is English, all the diaries and records are in English, and they're well displayed for your perusal. It's exciting to see this monument to a bit of history that occurred in our times, and it's a reminder that we ought to do the same with Col. John Glenn's "Friendship 7." Available for viewing from 11 to 4, normally; from 10 to 6 in summer; admission of 4 kroner, 1.50 kroner for children. As this edition goes to press, a new wing is being added to the museum to house the papyrus boat, *Ra II,* on which Heyerdahl and eight companions travelled 3,270 miles in 57 days from Morocco to Barbados to test the theory that Mediterranean vessels built before the time of Columbus could have made the trip.

The Vigeland Sculptures

Gustav Vigeland (1869-1943) was a Norwegian sculptor who created the controversial, sometimes depressing, but immensely impressive **Vigeland Sculptures,** which depict the life-cycle of man, from birth to death. The statues are utterly explicit in their nudity and candor, and they are a major achievement which should be seen. Admission is free, and the park is open every day. In the **Vigeland's Museum,** 32 Nobelsgate, just to the left of the Park, you can see how this monumental work was created. Take tram #2 from the National Theatre to the main entrance at Kirkeveien. The museum is open daily except Monday from 1 to 7 p.m.

The City Hall

This lavishly-decorated building, which has become a symbol of Oslo, was completed in 1950. Its central hall contains the largest oil painting ever done, and the other rooms glitter with the best of Norway's crafts and art, including the painting "Life" by Edvard Munch, Norway's most famous artist. Despite the rich use of stone and woods, in intricate designs employing a rainbow of colors, the overall effect is strong and peculiarly Scandinavian, a superb architectural feat. Open in summer from 10 a.m. to 2 p.m. weekdays, from noon to 3 p.m. on Sundays, and also from 6 to 8 p.m. on Mondays and Wednesdays, with no admission charge at any time. Winter hours are 11 to 2 daily, and noon to 3 on Sundays.

The Munch Museum

Last of the six, this is one of the world's greatest museums, containing virtually the entire life work (1,100 paintings, 4,500 sketches) of Edvard Munch, Norway's greatest contemporary artist. He bequeathed them to the city as a testamentary gift; they have now been arranged, chronologically, in a stunning, Scandinavian-style building at Toyengate 5B, and it's fascinating to start with the artist's earliest works and then to watch him developing in power as he progresses to the macabre style for which he's most famous. Admission to the museum (open daily except Monday from 10 a.m. to 8 p.m., Sundays from noon) is free at all times, and you can get there via a 4-kroner-ride on bus no. 29, which leaves from City Hall, or on bus #20 from Majorstua, or on the new subway from the "Centrum" Station to the Tøyen stop—4 kroner also. Don't miss.

Getting to the Sights

To visit five of these sites with a guide, you can take two half-day city tours described in our "tours" section, below. The morning tour covers the City Hall and Vigeland Sculptures; the afternoon trip goes to the Viking Hall, the Fram, the Kon-Tiki raft, and also takes in the interesting open-air Norwegian Folk Museum, which is also on the Bygdøy Peninsula. To get to Bygdøy on your own, simply take the Bygdøy ferry, which leaves every half-hour in summer from Pier 3 in front of the City Hall, takes ten minutes to make the trip, charges 4 kroner per person. To visit the Vigeland Sculptures, your best bet is tram No. 2, which passes directly in front of the main entrance to Frogner Park.

Sightseeing Tours

The buses all leave from in front of the City Hall ("Radhuset"), on a variety of differently-priced trips. One excursion leaves at 10 a.m. (60 kroner, 3 hours), drives through the city, and then stops for visits to the Vigeland Sculptures in Frogner Park, the Holmenkollen ski jump, and City Hall. But the trip I prefer is the afternoon tour (2:30 p.m., 60 kroner for adults, 30 kroner for children, 3 hours) that passes through Oslo and its suburbs, and includes full-fledged stops at the Viking Ships, the Kon-Tiki Raft, the Polar ship "Fram," and the outdoor Norwegian Folk Museum. The tour is marvelously planned, it does not seem overly rushed, and yet it takes in a great deal. . . . There's also a sightseeing launch that leaves every hour in summer from a pier in front of the City Hall, and sails on a 50-minute cruise through the Oslo Fjord. Tickets are 20 kroner for adults, 10 kroner for children. Every hour on the hour (daily from 10 a.m. to 9 p.m., from May 20 to August 27 only), the same sort of launch embarks on a longer two-hour trip through the islands and along the beaches and narrow sounds in the west part of the Fjord. Cost is 40 kroner for adults, 20 kroner for children; go to Pier 2 or 3, again in front of the City Hall. . . . For more ambitious tours of Norway, **Winge Travel Bureau,** at 33 Karl Johans Gate, offers escorted coach journeys that aren't too expensive.

Other Sights

Remember the late Sonja Henie, of the ice-skating movies? She was married to Norwegian shipping tycoon Niels Onstad and together, in the summer of 1968, they donated to Norway the Sonja Henie-Niels Onstad **Art Center** at Hovikodden, Baerum, about 7½ miles from the center of Oslo. The Center is a unique concept, in that it is both a museum, exhibiting the couple's private collection of over 200 works of art (none of which pre-date 1918), and a cultural foundation encouraging experimental work in the live arts of theatre, music, dance, film, literature, architecture and arts and crafts. The building itself is worth the visit; spread fan-like over the plateau of a promontory jutting into the Oslo Fjord, it consists of five "leaves" and a "stem." The "leaves" are the exhibition halls and concert rooms; the "stem" is occupied with administrative offices. The halls are windowless and shut off from the magnificent view, in order to keep the two experiences separate. But between the rooms and leading out from the cafeteria and restaurants are terraces facing toward the fjord. Surrounding the museum is a 35-acre park and a walk through it will bring you to a small harbor and bathing beach. In the park is a sculpture garden and amphitheater. Getting to the Art Center is simple: take bus #32, 36 or 37, all of which leave from the University Square, take 25 minutes and cost 7 kroner. The Center is open from 11 a.m. to 10 p.m. daily; admission 10 kroner for adults, 5 kroner for children. Ask at the Center or the Tourist Office for a copy of "Oslo This Week" and keep your eye open for announcements of special programs to be held at the Center which, if they live up to present plans, promise to be very exciting. . . . Other activities in Oslo? *Oslo's Tourist Information Office* at 15 Munkedamsveien (phone 42–71–70), a five-minute walk from City Hall, behind the West Station, will provide you with maps, brochures, and every sort of advice, service and assistance except the sort relating to hotel bookings, which is the exclusive prerogative of the "Innkvartering" desk at the East Station. . . . And now for some final comments on sightseeing in Oslo, here's Hope.

HOPE IN OSLO: "The Munch Museum, described earlier in this chapter, has rightfully become one of the city's top sights. But for his admirers, there's much more Munch in Oslo to meet the eye, and real aficionados will want to see his paintings at **The University Aula** (noon to 2 in summer, daily except Sundays); or in the canteen at the Freia Chocolate Factory, Johan Throne Holsts Plass 1. (There's also a Munch on the first floor of City Hall.) Most important, however, is the exciting collection of Munch at **The National Gallery**—a must!—where the best paintings are found in the 'Munch salen' (others are in Rooms 9 and 10) on the second floor. Here, the air fairly vibrates with the bold color, direct force, and sheer unmitigated aliveness of this man's creations, and simply to stand in the center of the room is a breath-catching experience, like a punch in the stomach. Take special note of the eerie 'Dance of Life'; the very famous 'Shriek' (1893); 'White Night'; 'Moonlight' (1893); 'Ashes'; and the fantastic self-portraits. The rest of the gallery is also well worth seeing: its emphasis is on 19th and 20th century Norwegian artists, scattered among a quite respectable collection of French Impressionists and Moderns, a few 16th and 17th century masterworks, and sculpture by Renoir, Vigeland, Rodin and Maillol. The museum is centrally located at Universitetsgaten 13 (just behind the University). Admission free, Monday through Friday 10 to 4, Saturday till 3, and Sunday from noon to 3, also Wednesday and Thursday evenings from 6 to 8.

"If you liked the Viking Ships at Bygdøy and want to learn more about the culture that produced them, then pay a visit to the University's 'Collection of Antiquities' at **The Historical Museum,** which houses Norwegian finds from the Stone Age through Medieval Times. Here you'll find Viking household articles, jewelry, art, tools, weapons, etc.; you'll also see 'The Treasure Room' displaying valuables of silver and gold from all ages. In addition to the comprehensive Viking collection, there is also a fine display from the Middle Ages, including very impressive Stave Church facades (note especially the elaborate and intricately carved doors, almost pagan in appearance, with motifs of lions, snakes and dragons), and what is often referred to as Oslo's richest collection of art up to 1530. Open daily except Mondays, in summer from 11 to 3 (winters from noon), admission free, the museum is situated just behind the National Gallery, at Frederiksgate 2.

"Only moderately interesting to visit, but of considerable historical significance, is **Akershus Castle** (for me the old castle has more mystery and atmosphere when its brooding presence is viewed from across the fjord in front of City Hall). Built in 1300 by King Haakon V Magnusson, it proved an impregnable fortress as well as royal residence; but much of what you'll see today was the work of one of our favorite Danes, Christian IV, who transformed the fortress into a Renaissance Palace when he was king of both Denmark and Norway (1588 to 1648), and Oslo was known as 'Christiania.' There's a touching monument on the castle grounds dedicated to Norwegian patriots who lost their lives here during World War II when the Nazis used Akershus as a prison and execution area, and next to the monument is Oslo's new **Resistance Museum (1940 to 1945),** open daily from 10 to 3, Sundays from 11 to 4, for an adult admission charge of 3 kroner. From the castle grounds, there are beautiful views of Oslo and of the Oslo fjord. The castle is open in summer from 11 to

2:45 p.m., Sundays from 12:30 to 2:45 p.m. (spring, fall and winter, open Sundays only), with guided tours at 12:30 and 1:30, for a 2 kroner entrance fee; the best approach is from Radhusgate.

"If you happen to be in the Market Place on Stortorvet (one of Oslo's main shopping streets), you should take a look at the **Dom Church** or Oslo Cathedral, which was consecrated in 1697 but has been restored many times since then, most recently in 1950. Today, the inside of the cathedral is new, bright, clean and cheery, with the most wildly colorful ceiling I've ever seen in a church. Though the style of painting is nouveau-moderne (like Radio City Music Hall in New York), somehow the effect is luminescent and uplifting. The cathedral may be visited weekdays from 9 to 3, Saturdays til noon in midsummer, from 10 to 1 winter weekdays. Services are on Sundays at 11 a.m. and 6 p.m.

"There is, finally, an interesting and well-displayed collection at **The Oslo Museum of Applied Art,** St. Olavs Gate 1, of Norwegian and European decorative art from the Middle Ages to the present day, which includes tapestry, furniture, metalwork, carved woodwork, weapons, glass, ceramics, statuary, costumes, etc. The Norwegian tapestry collection is especially good, and the most prized possession of the museum is the very rare and treasured Baldishol Tapestry, which was made at the end of the 12th century (there are only five tapestries from this period left in the world). Special exhibitions of modern Norwegian design are frequently presented on the ground floor. Admission is free from 11 to 3 (also Tuesday and Thursday evenings in winter from 7 to 9), closed Mondays."

NIGHT-TIME ENTERTAINMENT: There's little organized night life in nature-loving Oslo. Best thing in summer is simply to stroll along the Karl Johans Gate, stopping for beer or hot chocolate at one of the cafes in the "Student Grove" at the head of the street. But if you prefer something livelier, try the following.

Dancing

In central Oslo, the undisputed favorite amoung dancehalls is the **Ridderhallen** (meaning "medieval knights' hall"), at 5 Torgatan, near the Oslo Cathedral, where the motif is swords, suits of armor and heraldry, but most of the waiters hail from Tunisia. They serve up beer (17 kroner, $3.33), three sizes of pizza (small, 22 kroner; medium, 25; large, 30), and more expensive à la carte plates to the more than 600 guests attracted there by modern dance music appealing to all age groups and supplied by high quality bands. Free admission on Mondays and Tuesdays, 10 kroner on Wednesdays and Thursdays, 20 kroner on Fridays, Saturdays and Sundays. If Ridderhallen is sold out (and it often is), you might try a nearby discotheque called **Kroa**, at 22 Storgaten, but its appeal is mainly to the under-25 crowd, and it is closed on Sundays, Mondays and Tuesdays. 10 kroner to enter, and only beer is served thereafter, at 17 kroner per glass.

If you're above the age of 25, you'll enjoy **El Toro** at 7 Kristian IVs Gate in the heart of town (where there's a nightclub show from 9 to 10 p.m., then dancing to a live combo Monday through Saturday; you can dance and see the show from the bar for admission of 25 kroner and a compulsory beer for 18 kroner); or a swinging disco next door, called the **Leopard Club,** which stays open until 3:30 a.m. Admission is 20 kroner, beer 18 kroner before 11:45 p.m., 25 kroner thereafter.

Folklore Evenings at the Folk Museum

Some of the travel agencies in Oslo sell 85 kroner ($16.66) tickets for a Monday, Wednesday and Friday evening summer tour to the restaurant of the Norwegian Folk Museum (on the Bygdøy peninsula) for an exhibition of Norwegian folk dancing and a meal (the meal is $10.78—55 kroner—extra, making a grand total of $27.44 per person for this evening of lore). On the bus going to the museum, the guides wear colorful folk costumes, they play a violin as they lead you up the hill to the restaurant, and the resulting picture is so attractive that tourists unable to get on the bus (space being limited) usually gnash their teeth and wail. Few of them realize that the same tour can be made, sans guide and sans group, for a fraction of the commercial cost. This, indeed, is a rule of budget travel in Europe: whatever a guided tour can do, you can do better.

Here's how it's done. On weekdays in June, July and August, from the City Hall Pier, take the 6:15 or 6:45 p.m. boat to Bygdøy (4 kroner, 78 cents), get off at the first stop, and walk uphill for 15 minutes to the museum, where the entrance charge is 7 kroner ($1.37). Once inside, walk uphill again to the restaurant, where the one-hour folkdancing show starts, weekdays, at 8 p.m. (there is no extra charge). But eat not at the costly, candle-lit restaurant, but at the ground-floor cafeteria serving various hot dishes for 20 to 30 kroner, coffee or tea for 6 kroner. Then take bus No. 30 back to City Hall square for 4 kroner; it leaves every 15 minutes from the right of the museum's entrance. And compare. The people on the sightseeing tour have paid over $27 for this combination of elements; you have paid a total (including round-trip transportation) of about $9, provided you order one of the cheaper meals (which is precisely what the people on the tour are getting).

Theater, Music and Movies

The **National Theatre**, on the Karl Johans Gate, just before the palace, is the very building in which the plays of Henrik Ibsen were first presented to an outraged Oslo populace, who booed them roundly. Let that be a reassuring lesson to all early failures. Cheap ticket prices (15 to 35 kroner), but the plays are in Norwegian. . . . Movies are probably your best bet in Oslo, because they're subtitled, not dubbed, and American films are therefore in English. But the showings begin promptly at 5, 7 and 9 p.m., and no one is seated after that time—a rigid Oslo custom that spares early-arriving spectators from the bother of latecomers. The 5 p.m. movies are the cheapest (12 kroner) and need no reserved seats. . . . Free **Orchestra Concerts** are scheduled every Sunday in summer at 1 p.m. and Wednesday at 7 p.m. at the Vigeland Museum. . . . **Folk dancing** exhibitions are presented every Monday and Thursday evening in July and August by the Young Peasants' Association (that's their name), at the new Oslo Concert Hall, 14 Munkedamsveien. Programs run from 9 to 10 p.m. and admission is 25 kroner. . . . And always watch, as noted before, for the programs at the **Sonja Henie Museum,** which has become a center of living arts in Oslo.

AN EVENING ABOARD THE BARODD: From April to the end of September, daily from 5 p.m. from Pier 1 in front of Town Hall Square (Radhusplassen)—the very same spot where the shrimp boats dock—the 60-ton, 40-year-old motorboat known as the **Barodd** sets out for a 5-hour fishing trip into the Oslo fjord. Its captain is a lawyer named Kristian Frederik Falck, obviously smitten by the sea, who becomes as excited as everybody else when a fish is caught and drawn on board, and even rings the ship's bell if the size is above average: you sense that this is as much a hobby for him as a profit-making venture. After dropping anchor an hour into the fjord, he and his crew pass around fishing tackle (hand rolls) with prepared bait (mussels), and you and your fellow passengers lean hopefully over the dark blue waters for the evening's sport: you'll be amazed at how many cod, mackerel, flounder and other sea creatures two to 25-inches long are caught within the next few hours. You can then either carry the fish home, or fry and eat them in a small cabin on the journey back. Beer, mineral water and coffee are served on board.

The reasonable price is 50 kroner ($9.80) for adults, 25 kroner ($4.90) for children; and bookings are made by phoning 462584 before 10 a.m., or 412853 between 11 a.m. and 4 p.m. I predict that an evening on the Barodd, in the fjord of Oslo, is something you'll remember for a long time.

READERS' SELECTIONS: "Add the Parliament Building (Stortinget) to your tour tips. Free 45-min. tours at 11 a.m., noon, and 1 p.m., from June 15 to September 30(when Parliament does not meet except in emergencies). Rooms are beautifully decorated—guide speaks English, Norwegian, German & perhaps more. He didn't give just a memorized talk, but *knew* much of Norwegian history as well as about the Parliament, and he encouraged questions of all sorts. Even our children said "That was good—we learned something" (Mrs. George Wallach, APO 80, New York). . . . "We spent one afternoon at the beach, at **Ingierstrand,** via motor launch from the city hall piers. It costs 4 kroner going, and 6 kroner returning, for both of us. The 'beach' is mainly rocks, but is an experience not to be missed, for those who haven't been to Scandinavian beaches before" (Mrs. Randell C. Widner, St. Petersburg, Florida). . . ."In the new university campus situated at Blindern, you will find a students' travel bureau where, with a student card, you can buy tickets to London for $62 one-way, or join group train transports in Europe for half the fare. Phone 46-68-80. You can reach the campus by tram no. 7—Ulleval Hageby—to the end of the line (4 kroner) or by taking the subway marked "Sognsvanns-banen" from the National Theatre to Blindernveien for 4 kroner" (Vegard Elvestrand, Oslo, Norway; note by AF: the agency in question is the "Universitetenes Reisebyraa," Universitetssentret, Blindern, Oslo). . . . "There is boat transportation from Oslo to Copenhagen, daily throughout the year, on the M.V. King Olav V and M.V. Prinsesse Margrethe, for which space can be booked from any travel agency in Oslo" (Pauline Rissman, Chicago, Illinois).

THE REACTIONS OF READERS TO NORWAY: "Anyone who gets as far north as Copenhagen or Stockholm, and doesn't go to Norway is silly. And anyone who gets to Oslo and doesn't venture into the Norwegian countryside is mad. This is the most spectacularly beautiful country in all of Europe. The mountains may not be as tall as in Switzerland, but there is a far greater variety of natural sights, and an overwhelming sense of surprise. The cross-country trip from Oslo to Bergen is one of the most exciting in Europe, as the train ascends higher and higher into the mountains. Another special attraction is the train trip from Myrdal to Flaam, which lies at the head of the Sogne Fjord, the longest in Norway. This is a 48-minute spectacular that can't be beat anywhere. A giant waterfall roaring away at your window, steep mountains leading down to peaceful valleys, a river that flows under a mountain and comes out on the other side. A ride that shouldn't be missed. And it can be taken free with a Eurailpass. My paean to Norway is inspired not only by the country, itself, but by the Norwegians, who I found to be the most unforgettable people of my trip. Nowhere have I met persons who gave of themselves so completely and unashamedly. The farthest North I got was Bergen, but I vowed to return to Norway someday and do a lot more exploring" (Milton Schulman, Bronx, New York). . . . "If you take the morning train from Oslo to Bergen, but detour at Myrdal to Flaam, then I recommend staying overnight at the **Heimly Pensjonat,** which is situated right at the head of the Fjord, so that you can see the magnificent fjord as you dine (supper is 40 kroner, but worth it: accommodations about 140 kroner for two persons, with private shower and breakfast). And if, in the morning, you take the ferry through the fjords to Gudvangen, the ascent by bus to Stalheim and Voss is even more spectacular than the descent from Myrdal to Flaam. At Voss you pick up an early afternoon train to Bergen—it's all timed very nicely" (Polly Chill, New York, New York). . . . "If by the time you reach Oslo, you crave an excursus from a steady diet of European cities, a fantastically beautiful and pleasantly informal mountain-fjord tour can be had by merely taking the morning train from Oslo to Bergen, the hydrofoil along the Atlantic coast from Bergen to Stavanger, and the train back again to Oslo. The train rides will bring you through some of the most breathtaking mountain and valley scenery anywhere, including tourist-infested Switzerland, with stops along the log cabins of colorful mountain hamlets. Bergen is a small town where villagers and seamen gather at twilight on the docks to sing hymns. The town and seaport can best be viewed at twilight and sunset from the hill just north of the train station. The train arrives late afternoon and travelers should consult the tourist office three or so blocks east for overnight accommodations. I stayed at the **Bibelskolen** on the docks for less than $8 per night. There are morning and afternoon hydrofoils to Stavanger, more commercial than Bergen but thereby a better place to shop for sweaters, souvenirs and gifts" (Jay Evans, Colorado Springs, Colorado). . . . "Please emphasize the advisability of taking the Myrdal-Flaam train trip, but explain it's on the way to Bergen from Oslo, so people can plan to get off *before* Bergen to take the trip" (Ilse Gleestadt, Belmont, California).

Back, now, to the mainland. We continue with a tour that leads to the south of Europe, beginning with Munich, in the Bavarian Alps.

Chapter X

MUNICH

Beer and Wurst at Bargain Rates

THE NORTH AND CENTRAL parts of Germany are often industrial and grim. Unless you've studied German, or have a profound knowledge of the culture of that nation, you probably won't want to include these areas on a first-time European vacation. The south of Germany is another matter. This is Bavaria, and its capital is Munich—a light-hearted, fun-loving city, whose residents look upon the pursuit of pleasure as nearly a full-time profession. If you want to imbibe something of the atmosphere of nineteenth-century Europe —go to Munich.

Munich has the best beer in Germany and the best food. Its avenues are broad, its theaters and nightspots numerous, and the low rates of its restaurants tend to offset the rising rates of its popular hotels. Can you live in Munich on a budget? Here's how:

A ROOM IN MUNICH: Apart from staying at the large Hotel-Pension Beck (where doubles, including service and tax, rent for only $8.94 per person; see our "super budget" section for details), the cheapest way to live in Munich is to take a room in a private home renting to tourists (see our "super budget" discussion several pages on), or else seek out one of its many pensions—which invariably turn out to be large apartments, occupying one or two floors of an apartment house or large, two-family home. Although many of these lack elevators, they are remarkably comfortable and homey, old-fashioned places,

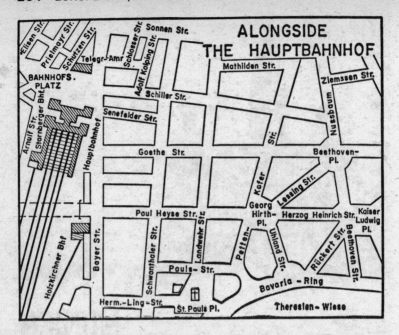

with homey, old-fashioned German "hausfraus" as their proprietresses; and many are quite centrally-located, one block or so from the main shopping streets of Kaufingerstrasse and Neuhauser Strasse.

We'll group the pensions by geographical area, and discuss them in generally ascending order of cost within each area.

Alongside the "Bahnhof" (Railroad Station)

The least expensive of our pensions? One of them is the tiny **Pension am Bahnhofplatz**, at 5 Bahnhofplatz (phone 59-50-45), superbly situated less than one hundred yards from Munich's bustling railroad station, with its swarm of stores, shops, restaurants and wurst stands; leaving the station's main entrance, turn left.

No other pension is so centrally located, and the view from your room window over the Bahnhof area is quite a sight. Frau Feigl rules with a firm but friendly hand, and also charges special rates to readers of this book: 25 marks ($13.15) single, 35 to 40 marks ($18.42 to $21.05) for a small double, 50 marks ($26.31) for a triple room, But breakfast isn't served. Push button no. 4 inside the tiny red elevator that takes you up.

In the station area

Somewhat further from the station, but still within walking range, is an almost comparable low-cost value—the **Pension Hungaria**, 42 Briennerstrasse (phone 52-15-58)—whose owner, the cultivated, English-speaking Dr. Erika Wolff, charges from 20 to 24 marks per person, including breakfast, service and tax, in a double room, 22 to 28 marks in a single, and is happy to take families with children, for whom special rates are often offered. Breakfast, to repeat a point, is included; the beds are modern and comfortable; the rooms attractive—as is Dr. Wolff, a lady in her 40s. To reach the Hungaria (a 10-minute walk from the station), turn left upon leaving the station and follow Dachauerstrasse several blocks to Augustenstrasse, which shoots off to the right. Walk one block up Augustenstrasse to Briennerstrasse, and the pension is on the corner.

Elsewhere in this area, the **Pension Jedermann**, at 95 Bayerstrasse (phone 53-32-67), is quite a delightful and different place whose English-speaking owner, Mr. Werner Jenke, makes a hobby out of decorating his premises: the entrance hall, for instance, is colorfully papered to resemble a rock garden and is filled with plants and bowers of vines. There are 32 rooms, located on four floors reached by an elevator; singles (including breakfast, service and tax) are 26 to 30 marks, most doubles are 42 to 50 marks (again with everything included), triples 56 to 62 marks. And the Jedermann is easily reached from the station: this time, turn right when you exit from the front, and right again at the corner, which is Bayerstrasse; then follow Bayerstrasse for about 5 minutes to No. 95, where you walk through a lighted alleyway into a courtyard and are then directed by signs to the pension. Highly recommended. . . . In the same building at 95 Bayerstrasse (entrance at the end of the courtyard), the **Hotel-Pension Isaria** (phone 53-36-39) is an acceptable alternative at slightly lower rates: 22 to 32 marks ($11.57 to $16.84) for bathless singles, 38 to 55 marks ($20 to $28.94) for doubles, 60 to 65 marks ($31.57 to $34.21) triple, including a continental breakfast enhanced by cheese, sausage and honey, and free showers. Owner, Herr Bullinger, and his wife, both speak English well.

Finally, the **Pension Alba**, located on the first floor of a rather unimpressive elevator-equipped office building at 1 Mittererstrasse (phone 53-14-48), is a somewhat old-fashioned establishment heavily patronized by a family trade. There are 12 rooms and all are doubles: four rooms, the slightly smaller ones, rent at 34 marks ($17.89), eight larger rooms at 36 marks ($18.94), all including service, and 3 marks per person for breakfast. The pleasant Frau Hoos, who operates the pension understands English a good deal better than she can speak it. To reach the Alba, exit from the front of the station, turn right to Bayerstrasse: turn right on Bayerstrasse, proceed about 2 blocks, and then turn left on Mittererstrasse. It's a five-minute walk in all.

Off the "Walking Street," near Town Hall

This has become the most spectacular section of Munich, for the two avenues leading to Town Hall—the Neuhauserstrasse and the Kaufingerstrasse —have recently been made into pedestrian promenades, free of cars, and lined with stone sidewalk benches, outdoor cafes, statuary, flowers, and flag-like streamers. And it is just off this area that the famous Viktualienmarkt—a colorful open-air market square of luscious meats, sauerkraut and pickles, exotic vegetables and other drool-causing items—is found. If you walk from the station to the Karlsplatz (more colloquially known as the "Stachus"), you'll be at the beginning of the Neuhauserstrasse; walk along until you reach Eisenmannstrasse, and turn right for one block to Damenstiftstrasse. The rather plain, but entirely proper, **Hotel Münchner Kindl**, at 16 Damenstiftstrasse (phone 26-43-49), has pleasant, airy accommodations (some with Persian rugs), brightly-lit and wallpapered corridors, and 25 double rooms renting for 53 marks ($27.89), including breakfast, service and tax. But better yet:

One block away, around the corner at 15 Altheimer Eck, the **Pension Diana** (phone 260-3107) is more highly recommended, despite the fact that you must go through an iron gate and climb 3 flights of stairs to reach its newly-decorated, spotless and cheerful rooms. There are modern furnishings, gleaming wooden floors with red carpeting, vines and plants spotted around the exceptionally sunny breakfast room. Singles, including breakfast, service and tax, are 32 marks ($16.84), doubles 50 marks ($26.31) triples 67 marks ($35.26); and although owner Heinrich Sauer speaks very little English, he is delighted when Americans ring the bell.

Near the "Stachus" (Karlsplatz)

A block-and-a-half away from the important traffic circle of downtown Munich, whose formal name is "Karlsplatz," the **Pension Zöllner,** 10 Sonnenstrasse (phone 55-40-35), is undoubtedly the best for the price (20 to 25 marks single, 38 to 45 marks-$20 to $23.68—for double rooms, breakfast, service and tax included) in Munich—a cleanly modernized apartment-type dwelling that would undoubtedly charge far more if it had an elevator; unfortunately, there are four and five very long flights to climb. Frau Kaechelen is fluent in English, and serves a generous breakfast that includes cold cuts and cheese.

THE MARK AND THE DOLLAR: As we write this Munich chapter, the German mark has strengthened to the point where its exchange rate is 1.90 marks to the dollar. Thus, one mark is presently worth 53 U.S. cents, but keep in mind that the figures may change by the time of your own trip to Munich.

In "pre-war" Munich

And now we move to an area largely untouched by World War II bombs and still marked by the stately gray-stucco buildings associated with pre-1940 Germany. To the left of the train station (as you face it) is the important Goethestrasse. Walk down Goethestrasse for five blocks and the area becomes almost entirely pre-war, residential in character and extremely pleasant. At #51 Goethestrasse, above a small Bavarian-style restaurant, in a building with vaulted stone entrance, old tile floor, wrought iron banisters along stairs, the **Pension Tirol** (phone 53-46-90), managed by English-speaking Maria Schmitzberger, is an old-fashioned, quiet apartment featuring feather blankets on comfortable, new beds and rates of 28 marks single, 42 to 45 marks ($22 to $23.68) double, 60 marks triple. The **Hotel-Pension Mariandl** (phone 53-41-08), in the same building, offers more or less the same (28 marks single, 45 marks double, 60 marks triple, 78 marks for a four-bedded room, including breakfast), and owners Hans and Judith Brugger have promised a 10% discount off the above to bearers of this book. (They also operate a flourishing budget restaurant in the same building, mentioned in the restaurant section of this chapter).

In a vaguely-similar area, ten minutes on foot from the colorful "Viktualienmarkt"—Munich's central fruit, meat and vegetable market—an oddity and a bargain is the 50-bed **Gasthof Vietnam** (owned by a refugee Vietnamese professor who also operates a Vietnamese restaurant downstairs at which readers of this book, showing this book, will receive a 20% discount), 14 Utzschneiderstrasse (phone 242-430), where doubles with breakfast are 38 to 44 marks ($20 to $23.15) and showers are sometimes free (from the Hauptbahnhof, take streetcar no. 19 or 20 and get off at Reichenbachplatz). It's really worth staying here simply to view the Viktualienmarkt and especially the sauerkraut stand (in the middle of the market, near the blue and white pole) of sauerkraut king Ludwig Freisinger, whose deftness in scooping the sauerkraut (90 pfennigs per pound) out of large wooden barrels is something to see. Nearly as delicious are his sour cucumbers (40 to 60 pfennigs per), which you munch on the spot, like the dozen-or-so other gourmets around you.

Near the German Museum (on the Isar River)

Pension Dollmann, 49 Thierschstrasse (phone 22-56-61), on the first three floors of a large, stone, but rather shabby-looking, building, in an attractive, quiet residential area, is a real find; it has large, pleasantly furnished rooms, friendly owners, and rates of 35 marks ($18.42) single, 55 marks ($28.94) double, including breakfast, service and tax. The structure housing this pension is located one block from the tram stop at the Max II Monument; it is a fairly dignified place recommended for readers who do not crave to stay in or near the more frenetic nightlife sections.

And finally, the **Mariahilf-Stüberl,** 83 Lilienstrasse (phone 48-48-34), is a small (three-story, 30-bed) typically Bavarian guesthouse two blocks from the Deutsches Museum, near the Mariahilfplatz. Its English-speaking manager, Frau Maria Stössel, charges 32 marks ($16.84) for a single room, 50 marks ($26.31) double, 75 marks ($39.47) triple, 90 marks ($47.36) for her one quadruple room, including breakfast, service and tax; you'll like this friendly place. To reach it from the station, take streetcar No. 7 to Mariahilfplatz, the sixth stop.

Near the Octoberfest meadow (a short walk from the train station)

Pension Westfalia, 23 Mozartstrasse (phone 53-03-77), on the third floor of a handsome, elevator-equipped, four-story house near Goethe Platz, just two blocks from the Octoberfest meadow (take the #17 tram, or U-Bahn 3 or 6 to Goetheplatz), is one of the city's outstanding pensions. The rooms are spotless, all with shiny wooden floors and bright print drapes; and Herr Bertram Hoos, the new owner of this budget house, received his training at the Berlin Hilton! I'm usually chary about using the word "excellent," but this one is. Singles are 28 marks ($14.73), doubles 40 ($21.05), including breakfast, service and tax, and there are rooms with private bath for only slightly more.

In this same broadly-defined area (because the pensions here are quite scattered), you'll find two similarly-priced establishments, of which my own preferred choice would be the **Hotel Uhland,** 1 Uhlandstrasse (phone 53-92-77), on the top four stories of a baroque old building, whose wide and polished stairway is usually lined with pots of flowers, making more enjoyable the climb to the top floor (there is, however, an elevator). Here the inclusive charge (room, breakfast, service, tax) is 38 marks ($20) single, 45 to 60 marks ($23.68 to $31.57) double, 60 to 75 marks ($31.57 to $39.47) triple, but the rooms are exceptionally good and large. From the right side of the Bahnhof (as you leave), walk down either Goethestrasse (to Pettenkoferstrasse, turning then into Georg-Hirth Platz) or down Paul Heyse Strasse directly to Georg-Hirth Platz; or, take the #17 tram from behind the station, two stops to Georg-Hirth Platz; the pension is just off the Platz, on a short, tree-lined, quiet street. If I could take my pick of any pension in the city, I think I would stay at either the Westfalia (see above) or the Uhland, where there are phones and sinks in all rooms, and gleaming wooden floors; at the end of the street is the meadow which hosts the Octoberfest, and on clear nights you can see the Bavaria Statue shining across the field.

In Schwabing

The "Greenwich Village" of Munich, Schwabing is a district of artists and scholars, students and drop-outs, sidewalk cafes and galleries—but of very, very few moderately-priced lodgings for transients. So far, the single low-cost oasis in my wanderings through here has been the **Pension Schwabinus** at 2 Georgenstrasse (phone 395-928), within an easy stroll from Schwabing's youthful nightlife, in a building whose nineteen rooms are named after impressionist painters. Rates, with breakfast, service and tax always included, are 35 marks ($18.42) single, 55 marks ($28.94) double; breakfast and free showers included. The pension is easily reached from the "Giselastrasse" subway stop. Simply walk into Georgenstrasse from Leopoldstrasse, to the second house on your right.

Hotels

The budget hotels of Munich are generally a bit more expensive than the pensions ($11 to $15 per person, when taxes and service charge are included), but most of them have elevators, and nearly all are in relatively-modern buildings, of post-World War II construction (when much of the central area of Munich was devastated by bombs). And where do you find the $11 and $15 hotels? They are located in every section of Munich, both near and far from the railroad station, but my advice is to walk no more than a block or two for yours. That's because Munich is one of the several cities in Europe whose railroad area is no dark and depressing place, but a fairly decent center of town. When you arrive by train in Munich, you can pick up your bags and find several recommended hotels just a short walk away.

Schützenstrasse and Senefelderstrasse

For example, as you step out of the main entrance of the Munich Bahnhof (the railroad station), you'll see, directly ahead, a 100-foot underpass which tunnels below Bahnhof Platz and emerges on a little two-block thoroughfare called Schützen Strasse. Here there stands a perfectly adequate little hotel, the **Hotel Zum Schützen (1)**, Schützen Strasse 3 (phone 59-37-55), an unprepossessing place from the outside (it doesn't look like a hotel from the outside, and its lobby is one flight up), but with every ingredient inside for a thoroughly satisfying hotel experience: polite personnel, continually clean rooms, creamy-white linens with feather blankets—and moderate prices. The Zum Schützen has several single rooms for 33 marks ($17.36) a night, none higher than 40 marks ($21.05), including service charge and tax, and doubles for 27.50 to 30 marks on a per person basis. Even a double room with private shower costs only 75 marks ($39.47), all in, and it's the sort of room that would rent for nearly twice as much in the United States. Breakfast is included.

A relative value, but higher in price than the Zum Schützen, is the **Hotel Europäischer Hof (2)**, 31 Bayer Strasse, corner of Senefelderstrasse (phone 55-46-21), to the right of the railroad station, by a half block, as you leave. By any standard—courtesy, cleanliness, extra services—this is now the top "big splurge" of Munich. The hotel literally shines. It has hospital-clean rooms, an elevator and unusually attractive dining hall, a reasonable price structure for bathless double rooms of 65 to 75 marks ($34.21 to $39.47), including breakfast, service and tax; and there are a great many rooms in the lower range.

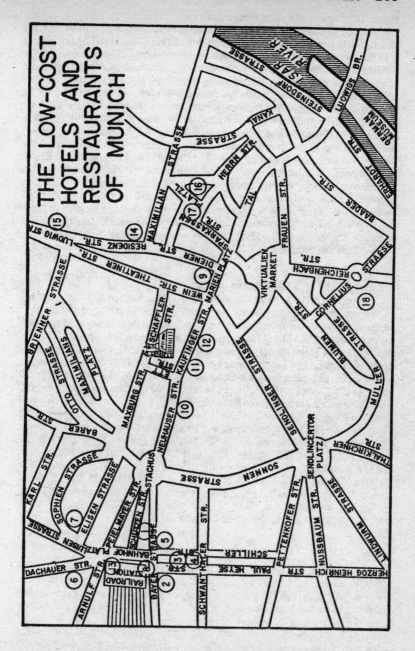

THE LOW-COST HOTELS AND RESTAURANTS OF MUNICH

Singles rent for 35 to 40 marks, again including breakfast, service and tax. What's all the more surprising about the Europäischer Hof is that it's a modernistic, seven-story structure whose appearance would ordinarily lead you to expect far more costly rates than these.

Nearby alternatives to the Europäischer Hof, if it happens to be full, are also in the big splurge range—although one of these, the **Hotel Senefelder,** is a particular value that's just barely beyond our limits. That's found on the convenient Senefelderstrasse, which runs alongside the Europäischer Hof, the exact address being 4 Senefelderstrasse (phone 59-28-27); and the charge is 33.50 marks ($17.63) per person (*including* breakfast, tax and service) for its modern and well-furnished bathless double rooms, 38.50 marks for singles.

Alternatives to the Hotel Senefelder, on the same block: the slightly more basic Hotels **Monachia** and **Salzburg** at #'s 3 and 1 Senefelderstrasse, respectively. Neither of the two compares with the former—but then, both have numerous double rooms that rent for 59 to 63 marks and less per night, singles for 37 marks, including service, tax and a generous breakfast. The Monachia is the better choice, with its spacious and well-furnished rooms. It sports, in addition, an unusually attractive breakfast room, and is owned and operated by the ladylike Frau Irene von Mazzucchelli, who is fluent in English. If there was ever a hotel whose narrow, cramped entrance gave no hint of the quality inside, this is it. Phone 55-52-81 to learn about vacancies at the Monachia, 59-56-27 for the Salzburg.

The less expensive Schillerstrasse hotels

Sadly, however, there will be times (convention weekends—Munich is big on conventions) when the hotels on Senefelderstrasse are filled. When that happens, return to the Bahnhof entrance, look to the right, and you'll spot two alternate choices: the **Hotel Haberstock (3),** Schillerstrasse 4 (phone 55-78-55), and the **Hotel Helvetia (4),** Schillerstrasse 6 (phone 55-47-45). The Haberstock, of course, is by far the superior of the two: typically Bavarian in style, comfortable, and pleasantly old-fashioned. Its rates in 1980 will average 30 marks ($15.78) per person including breakfast, service and tax. The Helvetia, whose entrance is through a courtyard, and which has a colorful Bavarian-style breakfast room upstairs, will charge a lower 27 marks ($14.21) per person for a double room, including breakfast, service and tax. Down the street by about a block, the **Hotel Daheim** at 20 Schillerstrasse (phone 59-39-24), asks 35 marks ($18.42) single, 55 marks ($28.94) double, including breakfast, service and tax; and after that you might try (in order of preference) the less expensive **Pension Wissinger,** 24 Schillerstrasse (phone 59-43-47), only 16 marks per person in double rooms, but not including breakfast; or the **Pension Augsburg,** 18 Schillerstrasse (phone 59-76-73), 22 marks ($11.57) single, 35 marks ($18.42) double, 5 marks per person for breakfast.

And the Ys

The YMCA in Munich is the **"CVJM"** at 13 Landwehrstrasse (phone 555-941), a long block from the train station and a few hundred yards from the Stachus, and although its rooms are rather spartan, it's an always reliable budget lodging for both men and women. 21.50 marks ($11.31) per person triple, 23.50 marks ($12.36) per person double, 27.50 marks ($14.47) single, including breakfast and free showers, with a surcharge of three marks for senior citizens over the age of 27. And there's a modern ground floor cafeteria (50 seats, open Tuesdays through Saturdays from 6 to 10:30 p.m. only) serving one-plate meals for 6.50 marks ($3.42), like grilled cheeseburgers with rice and salad, and offering half a liter of Löwenbräu beer for 1.90 marks ($1)—no other restaurant in Munich sells beer for less. A small, but friendly gesture, is the free cup of tea for all diners.

READER'S HOTEL SELECTIONS: "**Hotel Bayernland** at 73 Bayerstrasse, phone 533-153 or 539-478, just three minutes from the Munich train station by turning right at the Bayerstrasse exit and walking one block, was our best find in three months of travel. This large, modern, elevator-equipped hotel offers spacious rooms, even with 15-foot ceilings, at prices lower than many nearby pensions. Singles are 30 to 50 marks, doubles 48 to 72 marks, including breakfast, and showers are free" (Jim Fuhrman, Beverly Hills, California). . . . "Please include **Hotel Grafinger Hof,** at Zenettistrasse 7; it is a few short blocks from the Oktoberfest park, directly across the street from a laundromat and Catholic church. Gerhard Meyer, the English-speaking proprietor, was more than a host. He even offered to walk several blocks to pick up our rental car. His immaculate, twin-bedded rooms rent for 44 marks ($23.15) nightly, including breakfast. Showers are 2 marks extra. . . . Enough cannot be said for the friendliness, good times, good food and drink in Munich" (Tom and Michelle Flesser, Evergreen Park, Illinois).

READERS' PENSION SELECTIONS: "We heartily second your recommendation of Fremdenheim Weigl, but on our return to Munich it was full. After much searching, we came up with **Hotel-Pension Alpina** at 49 Landwehrstrasse (phone 538-0722), a five-minute walk from the station, exceptionally clean, roomy, warm, and the best bargain we could find at 40 marks ($21.05) double" (Larry Warren, Sioux Falls, South Dakota. . . . "**Pension Süzer** at 3 Mittererstrasse (phone 53-35-21), near the station, is recently opened and operated by the very friendly Errol Süzer. Rooms were well appointed and spotless, and for a change there was toast for breakfast! Fourty marks ($21.05) for a double room, plus three marks each for breakfast" (P. Sheriff, Belmont, New South Wales, Australia; with an additional recommendation from Dr. George Sandusky, Thornville, Ohio; note by AF: owned by an English-speaking Turkish family, the Süzer reduces its rates to 18 marks ($9.47) per person in a triple, 17 marks ($8.94) per person in a 4-bedded room, with breakfast optional at 3 marks. Very clean, and on the third floor of an elevator-equipped apartment building). . . . "A truly budget-priced find: **Hotel-Pension Erika,** 8 Landwehrstrasse (phone 554-327), one very long block from the station, where a large, clean single room in summer was had for 25 marks ($13.15), including a huge breakfast (both black and white bread kept fresh in glass receptacles, butter, jam, coffee and an egg), modern plumbing in each room, a parking lot for guests, an elevator. Frau speaks 'not too good English', but it's not at all needed. Truly, I feel, a buy in this 'not-so-inexpensive-for-singles' Bavarian capital" (Michael J. Romano, Staten Island, New York). . . . "Also thought I'd mention the **Pension Altstadt,** 5 Josefspitalstrasse (phone 242-657). The price for a double with free shower was 46 marks ($24.21) breakfast included, and the proprietor—a young woman from Finland—speaks fluent English" (Steve Holub, Columbus, Ohio). . . . "**Pension Casino,** 13 Marsstrasse (phone 593-407), is operated by Paula Gerstl, who charges only 38 marks ($20) for a double without breakfast. Convenient location, about three blocks from the Hauptbahnhof" (R. N. Sealy, c/o Aramco, Dharan, Saudi Arabia). . . . "**Pension Schmellergarten,** 20 Schmellerstrasse (phone 77-31-57), is only a five minute U-Bahn ride from the Marienplatz to Poccistrasse. Here are spacious rooms renting for only 42 marks ($22.10) double, 28 single, 63 triple, including breakfast, service and tax, which is quite a bargain for Munich. I haven't words enough to praise the proprietors, Herr and Frau Ambie!" (Carolyn Planutis, Chicago, Illinois; note by A.F.: made suspicious by the name, I've checked the Munich phone book, and sure enough, the Schmellergarten exists!). . . . "Frau Gebhardt, owner of the **Pension Gebhardt,** 38 Goethestrasse (phone 539-446), is warm, friendly and outgoing, and speaks enough English to assist non-German-speaking tourists. She also loves children, as our son Kevin can attest. Rates, including breakfast, are 32 marks single, 50 marks double, 65 marks triple, 78 marks for a four-bedded room, children 4 to 12 half price, baths 2.50 marks" (Carol Conklin, Canton, Ohio; and strong recent seconding recommendations from Patricia A. Kennedy, Brooklyn, New York, and others). . . . "Mr. and Mrs. Hinterwimmer, owners of the **Hotel-Pension Altona,** Dachauer Strasse 35 (phone 59 14-80 and 59-37-51), are extremely friendly people, eager to provide information, and helpful in every respect. Their double rooms rent for 48 marks, including breakfast, and they also have three-bedded and four-bedded rooms, in which each bed costs 19 to 20 marks" (Mr. and Mrs. Ernst Wolferstetter, Milwaukee, Wisconsin). . . . "One of the great advantages of the **Pension Rottmuller** at 36 Gollierstrasse, apart from the warmth and kindness of the lady who owns it, is its location in a residential area containing supermarkets, bakeries and numerous other convenient shops. We paid 40 marks for a double room, with breakfast" (Charles Buettner, Lindsay, California). ... "We arrived in Munich during the Octoberfest and also at the time of an International Fashion Show. To make matters worse, we were delayed on our flight from Copenhagen, and the pension where I had reservations, rented our room 20 minutes before we arrived, because they thought we were a "no show." Needless to say, Munich was jammed. The lady at the pension made several phone calls and obtained a room at the **Hotel Pension Terminus,** 44 Bavaria Ring (phone 77-65-85), directly across the street from the Meadow where the fest was being held. This was a find. The owner, Frau Hermann Ernst, was wonderful. For 45 marks ($23.68), we had a beautiful, clean well-lighted room, breakfast for two included, while singles with breakfast are 30 marks. The Terminus is connected to everything in a nice residential area. The tram ride to the Karlsplatz is 10 minutes. Highly recommended" (Harry T. Wilson, Camden, New Jersey). ... **"Pension Tirol,** at 51 Goethestrasse (phone 534690), charged 42 to 45 marks, all included, double with breakfast" (M. A. Carbonell, Montevideo, Uruguay). ... "Two good pensions in Munich charging from 24 to 30 marks ($12.63 to $15.78) single, 44 to 52 marks ($23.15 to $27.36) double, including breakfast, service and tax, are: **Pension Am Sankt Anna Platz,** 8 St. Anna Platz, phone 222-860, located in the Lehel District, which is considered typical 'Old Munich,' and **Pension beim Haus der Kunst,** 4 Bruderstrasse, phone 22-95-48, next door to the Haus der Kunst and near Prinzregentenstrasse" (Nick Lorey, Munich, Germany). ... **"Pension Flora,** located near the train station at 49 Karlstrasse (phone 59-70-67), provides a double room for from 38 to 45 marks, breakfast included" (Pat Clark, Fanwood, New Jersey). ... From A.F.: other scattered recommendations this year for **Pension Theresia,** 51 Luisenstrasse (phone 52-12-50), 38 to 40 marks double, 20 to 25 marks single; **Pension Viola,** 47 Goethestrasse (phone 53-15-89), 42 to 50 marks double, 25 to 30 marks single, and **Pension Wagner,** 77a Bayerstrasse (phone 53-37-74), 32 to 36 marks double. ... "A good find is **Hotel Kreuzbräu,** at Brunnstrasse 3 (phone 24-24-66), with unbelievable rates: single 25 marks ($13.15), double 42 marks ($22.10), triple 54 marks ($28.42), quadruple 62 marks ($32.63), and a room with five beds for 80 marks ($42.10). Breakfast is 4 marks extra (optional), and showers are free. The owner, Herr Ingberg, gave me a 10% discount on these rates when I showed him the book. Kreuzbräu may not be ideal for older tourists, but it certainly was perfect for me. And to top it all off, it is located right in the center of town, between the railway station and the Hofbrauhaus, two minutes from Marienplatz" (Tina Lorey, Pforzheim, Germany). ... "At the **Pension Fraunhofer,** 10 Fraunhoferstrasse, where I'm staying with my wife and 3 children, the owner, Mrs. Herzog, is extremely outgoing, speaks English and is very helpful in solving the tourist problems that arise in a foreign country. Her rooms are warm and extremely clean, all have recently been redecorated, and they're situated near most of Munich's main attractions. As you can imagine, with a family of 5, this saves quite a lot of fares. Rates for 1980 will be 31 marks ($16.31) single, 48 marks ($25.26) double, including free showers and breakfast served to the room" (M.O. McClennan, Seminole, Florida; note from AF: streetcars 7, 19 and 20 go from the station to the Fraunhofer-Müllerstrasse stop). ... "For the longer term visitor to Munich, Herr Rudolph Kreis rents efficiency apartments in his **Pension Welti** at 45 Uhdestrasse (phone 791-15-42) in the quiet residential neighborhood of Solln. Each apartment consists of a bedroom/livingroom, bathroom, fully equipped kitchen, and included are television, telephone, all linens, and daily maid service, all for a 1980 price of 55 marks ($28.94) per apartment per night. Take the U-Bahn to Harras, and then bus 63 or 64 to Bastian-Schmidt-Platz, from which it's only a short walk to Uhdestrasse" (James A. Pope, Greensboro, North Carolina; note by AF: Rudolph Kreis was born in Germany, emigrated to the U.S., served 12 years in the U.S. Army, and then returned to Germany (from New York City) in 1963; motoring tourists can park in his underground garage for an optional charge).

HOTELS AND PENSIONS SEEKING MENTION: "Besteht die Möglichkeit, dass Sie auch meine Pension, die nur 5 minuten vom Hauptbahnhof entfernt liegt, in Ihr Buch eintragen konnten? Wir haben sehr schöne Zimmer mit fl. warm u. kalt Wasser, Lift, und ich spreche Englisch. Der Preis für das Doppelzimmer ist DM 45 zu 48—inclusive Frühst. u. Bedienung, Familien mit Kindern sind bei uns gerne gesehen, da wir auch grosse Mehrbettzimmer haben. Hochachtungsvoll!" (Herr Mosthav, **Pension Marion,** 25 Luisenstrasse, phone 59-25-54). ... "I have 46 rooms with 94 beds. The price for a single, including breakfast, is 32 marks, for a double 50 marks, and I would be willing to give a 10% discount, as well as free showers, to readers of your book. We are located west of the railroad station, going down Bayerstrasse; take trolley 19 or 29 in front of the station to the fourth stop, 'Trappentreustrasse' " (Gerhard F. Hahn, **Hotel Taxer,** 117 Landsbergerstrasse, phone 50-11-58; recent enthusiastic reader's recommendation for the Taxer from Marjorie Monahan, Washington, D.C.).

SUPER BUDGET (BY MUNICH STANDARDS): Single rooms for as little as $9.50? Doubles for $8.42 per person? Hustle over to 36 Thierschstrasse, near the central Isartorplatz, to the 100-year-old apartment house converted into a budget hotel known as **Hotel-Pension Beck** (phone 22-07-08 or 22-57-68). It offers perfectly respectable rooms with modern furniture, wall-to-wall carpets, brightly-colored wallpaper, for 16 to 20 marks ($8.42 to $10.52) per person in three-to-five-bedded dorms, 17 to 21 marks ($8.94 to $11.05) per person in bathless doubles, 18 to 24 marks ($9.47 to $12.63) single, with breakfast optional at 4 marks; free showers. Exact amount you'll pay within each range depends on floor number (there are five of them, and no elevator) and size of room, a determination judiciously made by energetic Frau Beck, who offers a special welcome to families with children, and a fully-equipped kitchen on each floor, for free use by all guests. From the main station, take the S-Bahn (on which you can use your Eurailpass, free) three stops along to Isartorplatz, and walk a hundred yards from there, or take streetcar 1, 20 or 21 from the station to the Max-Monument stop.

A second "super budget" selection? This time head to Schwanthalerstrasse 112, to the **Hotel Maria** (phone 50-30-23). That's a modern, five-story building less than 15 minutes on foot from the railroad station, where bathless singles are 23 to 28 marks, ($12.10 to $14.73), doubles 36 marks ($18.94), triples 48 marks ($25.26), without breakfast, but including service and tax, and everybody speaks English. They're attractively-furnished rooms, too. From the station, walk up the Bayerstrasse, turn left at Martin-Greif-Strasse, and you'll see this wondrous budget lodging at the corner of Martin-Greif and Schwanthalerstrasse, in front of a modernistic apartment block. . . . And if the Maria can't take you, then walk five minutes further down the street and around the corner to the astonishingly low-priced **Fremdenheim Weigl,** 32 Pettenkoferstrasse (second floor, phone 53-24-53), which has 15 to 17 marks single, 24 to 26 marks ($12.63 to $13.68) doubles, and one triple room for 34 marks, including service and tax. Mrs. Maria Dorsch is the fiftyish owner, a kind and attractive lady. The **Pension Spranger,** downstairs in the same building (phone 53-20-46), charges 18 to 22 marks ($9.47 to $11.57) single, 30 to 36 marks double, including service and tax, and its owner speaks fluent English. . . . Super budget pensions, with rooms for $12 to $13 per person? Try phoning the highly recommended **Pension Utzelmann,** 6 Pettenkoferstrasse (phone 59-48-89); singles for 25 marks, doubles for 38 to 50 marks, including breakfast, service and tax.

Private homes—for $6.57 to $12.50 per person

If you'd now prefer a family-type atmosphere, or a closer contact with local residents, you'll want to consider one of the following seven private homes in Munich, all visited as recently as late 1979.

Frau Roswitha Giland, at 42 Blutenburgstrasse, third floor, rear building (phone 184-618), offers a single and a double room, each with hot and cold running water, for 19 marks ($10) per person, not including breakfast (which you can prepare yourself in her kitchen). That's in a fairly central location, near Rotkreuzplatz, reached from the central station by streetcars 4 or 21 to the

Lazarettstrasse stop. Frau Wolfer speaks excellent English, and there's a coffee shop around the corner, for breakfast, at 4 marks.

Herr Friedrich and Frau Theresa Boiger, a friendly, middle-aged couple (whose relatives own a hotel in the Catskills), at Hans-Sachs-Strasse 9 (phone 260-3835), charge 22 marks ($11.57) per bed for their single and two very large double rooms, but add 2 marks a day if your stay is for less than three days. Bath and showers are free, and so is the use of their kitchen, including equipment and refrigerator space; you can also employ said kitchen for ordering an optional, 5 marks breakfast that includes at least three cups of coffee or tea, cheese and cold cuts. You'll like the enormous, yellow bathtub, largest I've ever seen; and you should try to rent room number 5, which comes with five corner windows. Very quiet and yet very central, behind the Viktualienmarkt, a five-minute walk from the Marienplatz, and the sole drawbacks are a 53-step walk to the third floor (there's no elevator here), as well as only a nodding acquaintance with English on the part of Herr and Frau Boiger.

Herr Siegfried Bayer, 17 Adlzreiterstrasse (phone 7-25-13-82 or 7-76-407), resides in a modern apartment house in the quiet Goetheplatz area, where he rents two double rooms at 20 marks ($10.52) per bed. Rooms are clean and attractive, and a single disadvantage is that very little English is spoken. Since Herr Bayer works elsewhere during the day, chances are you'll reach him only after phoning the second of the above phone numbers, which is his sister's. Take the subway to Goetheplatz, then walk about 100 yards into Lindwurmstrasse, turning left into the street with the tongue-twisting name; Herr Bayer's house is on the left.

Frau Theresa Schramm, 25 Residenzstrasse, fourth floor, elevator (phone 220-198), is the unquestioned star of all private-room-renting people in Munich, for three reasons: her rates are economical, the location could not be better, and Frau Schramm offers free use of hotplates, cooking utensils, and even her pressing iron. Each room is large and airy (one has the only balcony on the entire Residenzstrasse), and furnished with taste. Each room also possesses hotplate and sufficient platters, pots and cutlery for preparing an entire meal, and while three of the rooms are without running water and two have cold running water only, use of the bathroom (with tub and shower) is free. As I've said, this amazing landlady will permit you to use her pressing iron, and she will keep your perishable food in the fridge for no extra charge. And how much for all this largesse? 25 marks for each of the five twin or double rooms, or 12.50 marks ($6.57) per bed! This poor man's Shangri-la is located between Marienplatz and Odeonsplatz but nearer to Odeonsplatz. Look for a famous "confiserie"—the "Konditorei und Cafe Hag"—in the same building.

Frau Katharina Mörtlbauer is a friendly, fast-talking lady who speaks some English and lives in a grey apartment block at 14 Passauerstrasse, third floor, 49 steps up (phone 760-7891), where she rents two double rooms—very nicely furnished rooms—at 17.50 marks ($9.21) per bed, with breakfast optional at 4 marks more, and showers for free. Take the U-Bahn to the Harras station (the location is central), and walk about two minutes from there.

Frau Sophie Decker, whose residence at 19 Am Brombeerschlag (phone 714-97-96) is in a quiet residential area where buildings more than two stories high aren't permitted, rents a single room for 27 marks ($14.21), a double for 25 marks ($13.15) per person, including breakfast and free showers. Best for readers with cars, Mrs. Decker's is only 20 minutes by public transportation from the center of Munich, but you have to change twice. A taxi, for your initial trip there, will run about 14 marks.

Herr Matthias Vogel at Lincolnstrasse 41 (phone 690-68-55), near the U.S. Army's McGraw "Caserne" (barracks), gives preference to long-stay guests, for whom the charge is 215 marks ($113) per person per month for a two-bedded room in a garage-type annex with private w.c., but without hot water; nevertheless, you might phone him for a shorter vacancy. The redbearded Mr. Vogel lived for several years in Australia and speaks perfect English. From the station, take streetcar no. 7 to Schwanseeplatz (final stop, 20 minutes away), and walk for 10 minutes from there.

STUDENT ACCOMMODATIONS: The smaller of two local student hotels, situated in the very heart of town and open to both male and female foreign students from August through October and March through April, is the recently-built **Newman-Haus,** 29 Kaulbachstrasse (phone 28-50-91), which charges 17.50 marks for a single, 13.50 marks per student in a double room, 3.50 marks for breakfast. . . . Larger and less than ten years old (as of March 1980), the bright, new 400-bed **International House** ("Haus International") at 87 Elisabeth-strasse (phone 18-50-81), near Schwabing (the city's Greenwich Village), charges 19.50 marks ($10.26) per person in a five-bedded room, 20.50 marks in a quadruple, 22 marks per in a triple, 24.50 marks double, 27 marks single. For young people of both sexes up to 34 years of age, open all year round, and with a free indoor swimming pool. . . . The female-only counterpart of the above establishment, charging 17 marks ($8.94) per person per night in its double and triple rooms, 20 marks in single rooms, always with breakfast included, is the nun-operated **Internationales Jugend Hotel,** at 9 Goethestrasse (phone 55-58-91), just a half-block from the side of the railroad station, which sometimes is known as the **"Jugendwohnheim".** Actual lodgings at 9 Goethestrasse are in a huge, unmarked building with no sign outside; ring the buzzer.

A "sleep-in" for the young

Every summer from June 22 to September 2, the city adds to its student accommodations by erecting a large circus-type tent at a place called "In den Kirschen" (phone 14-14-300) in the Nymphenburg-Botanical Garden area (from the station, take streetcar no. 21 to the Botanical Garden stop—third stop after Nymphenburg Castle—then cross the street and walk into Franz-Schrank-Strasse until you spot the circus-like tent). The resulting **International Youth Camp Kapuzinerhölzl** is then stocked with 400 air mattresses and blankets, for which the charge, to both young men and women, is only 3 marks ($1.65) a night. No curfew; no official age limit; and no alcoholic beverages, either (tea is handed out free).

Youth Hostels and Camp Sites

Munich's largest youth hostel, the **Jugendherberge** at 20 Wendl-Dietrich-strasse (phone 72-36-50), near Rotkreuzplatz, can accommodate up to 500 guests in dorms with double-decker beds, at a charge of 7.10 marks ($3.73) per night for "juniors" (under the age of 26), 9.10 marks ($4.78) for "seniors" (over 26), plus a one-time charge of 1.80 marks (95¢) for sheets. Breakfast is included; hot showers are free; and a "canteen" serves two-course meals for 4.50 marks ($2.36) from 5:45 to 7 p.m. Take streetcar no. 4 from the station to Rotkreuz-platz, then walk into Wendl-Dietrichstrasse. . . . Munich's slightly classier youth hostel, the **Jugendgästehaus** at 4 Miesingerstrasse (phone 723-17-07), near the Hellabrunn Zoo, accommodates up to 344 persons, some in single and twin-bedded rooms, most in dorms with three to six cots, at a charge per person, including breakfast, of 15 marks ($7.89) single, 13 marks ($6.84) twin, 11 marks ($5.78) triple or quad, 9 marks ($4.73) in six-bedded dorms. Showers, meals, and other policies identical to those at the Jugendherberge. Take street-car #29 to Boschetsrieder-Plinganserstrasse, or Bus #31 or 57 to Thalkirc-hnerplatz. Both hostels, unfortunately, require an International Hostel Card.

Munich's largest camping site, the **Campingplatz Thalkirchen,** at 49 Zen-trallandstrasse (phone 723-17-07), open from mid-March through October, is located in picturesque, park-like surroundings along the Isar River, in a setting spacious enough for 2,500 guests and their caravans, cars, bikes and tents, for whom it provides washrooms, kitchens, self-service cafeterias, and even a bank. The per person per night charge is only 3.50 marks ($1.84), plus 4.50 marks per trailer ("caravan", here), 3 marks per tent, 2.50 marks per car, one mark per motorbike. If you're on foot, take the U-Bahn to the Implerstrasse Station and change there to Bus #57, which stops but two minutes' away from the camping site. If you're with car or bike, simply ask for the "Zoo area".

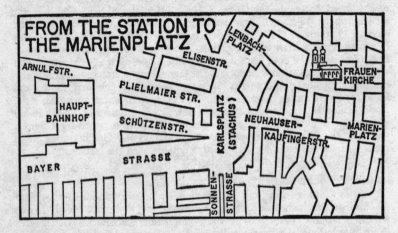

RESTAURANTS: I envy anyone their first trip to Munich. Even now, the memo-ry of Bavarian cooking lingers in both my mind and taste buds. And what a thrill it was to obtain these feasts for a sum that would buy much less at home. Have you got $3.50? With that in your pocket, you'll never go hungry in Munich. For instance:

(a) The Meals for $3.50 and under

Even the department stores serve surprisingly tasty, non-institutional dishes, and for proof of that I recommend, first, the enormously popular, hideously-crowded, stand-up, basement restaurant of the **Kaufhof Department Store** on the "Stachus" (Karlsplatz), 200 yards from the Train Station, where there's always an attractive, copiously-portioned "sonderangebot" (special, daily, one-platter meal) such as stuffed roast veal with dumplings and string-beans for 6.50 marks ($3.42). In the same downstairs area, liver dumpling soup for 2.20 marks ($1.15), supplemented by a roll for 25 pfennigs (13¢), is a meal in itself; and half a roast chicken, particularly tasty, and served with a big mixed salad, costs 6.75 marks ($3.55). . . . Even less expensive, and with chairs, no less, is the second floor restaurant of the smaller **Bilka Department Store** at 15 Kaufingerstrasse (about halfway between Stachus and Marienplatz, on the famous shopping street maintained only for pedestrians), where you'll find an adequate two-course meal for 4.75 marks, a more-than-filling two-course meal for 5.75 and 6.75 marks ($2.50, $3.02 and $3.55). And don't overlook the tempting display of cakes and pastries (1.30 to 1.90 marks) in the center of the room; the "windbeutel" at 1.70 marks, a kind of soufflé filled with whipped cream, is sheer poetry. . . . Incidentally, a general rule for budget living in any German city is to search out the major department store and then head for its **basement** restaurant, which is always half as costly as the already-inexpensive upstairs restaurant that most German department stores maintain. The basement of the **Kaufhof** is a prime example.

A less-than-$3.50 meal outside the department store district can be had at the **Restaurant Mariandl,** 51 Goethestrasse, not far from the train station in the area of the Munich medical school. Here, weekdays only, and from 11:30 a.m. to 2:30 p.m. only, a home-cooked mensa-menu of two courses (example: a creamy cauliflower soup followed by roast leberkäs with mixed salad) is offered in a large, 150-seat dining room for only 5.50 marks ($2.89), service included. While officially for medical students only, the restaurant admits everyone, and the location is quite easily found from the train station, in the upper area of Goethestrasse, near the trees.

(b) The Meals for $4

The cheaper sit-down meals in Munich are to be had at the restaurants of Munich's famous beer companies, which operate these places as much for prestige as for profit. There are eight such restaurants in Munich, huge establishments offering Bavarian specialties at extremely low prices. Two of the best are found on one of Munich's main streets—Neuhauser Strasse, which becomes Kaufingerstrasse just before it approaches the Munich Rathaus. The biggest, best and least expensive of these is the **Augustiner Grossgaststätten (10),** 16 Neuhauser Strasse, which is also the most typically-Bavarian in decor, with tremendous vaulted arches and scrubbed oak tables. Here the price for a ½ liter of Augustiner beer is among the cheapest in town (2 marks), and the prices for solid food (all Bavarian) are correspondingly low: 2.10 marks for Munich's famous "bread soup with brown onions," 6.90 marks for a stew of chicken and giblets ("geflügelreis") and light, fluffy dumplings. Important—order only from the typed menu headed "Tagesspezialitäten" (which lists numerous main plates for less than 7.90 marks ($4.15), numerous wurst dishes for 3.60 and 5.50 marks); and go only into the blue-tableclothed room on the left (it bears the sign "Augustiner Bierhalle"), and not into the better-furnished, white tableclothed area on the right, where the prices rise by 20% and more. . . . A few doors up, the more modern and therefore duller **Pschorrbräu-Bierhallen (11),** 11 Neuhauser Strasse (operated by the company that produces Pschorrbräu beer), is somewhat more expensive unless you know how to order Munich's cheap "wurst" specialties, from the typewritten menu, but I was still recently able to have bouillon with liver dumplings (2.20 marks), a main plate of Bavarian sausage with mixed salad (7.50 marks), and of course a huge glass (½ liter) of Pschorrbraü beer, for less than 13 marks.

When, by the way, you've completed the walk down Neuhauser Strasse, into Kaufinger Strasse, you'll eventually arrive at the Munich Rathaus (City Hall), at which this pedestrains' thoroughfare widens into a small square in front of the city building. The street just before the Rathaus is called Weinstrasse, and at the corner (#1 Weinstrasse) is the famous, old **Donisl Restaurant,** formerly a guard-house, and now the city's oldest restaurant, with a Bavarian-type skylight, held aloft by wooden walls garlanded with green leaves and blue-and-white ribbons. It is, despite these charms, one of the cheaper spots in Munich, serving two-course meals (and large portions of them) for only 8.50

to 10 marks; and it opens as early as 9 a.m., when it specializes in the famous white sausage ("Weisswürste"—4 marks for two of them, accompanied by sweet mustard) of Munich—something you should try. . . . Specializing entirely in sausage dishes (including weisswürste) is the nearby **Bratwurst-Stüberl** at 3 Heiliggeiststrasse, only a few yards from Marienplatz, near the huge Viktualienmarkt. Here, if you arrive as early as 7:30 or 8 a.m., you'll already find tables crowded with Muncheners merrily munching away on weisswürste, which are produced fresh on the premises each day. Average price for a dish of sausages (posted on blackboard menus) is 5 marks ($2.63), and you can choose among eight different brands of beer costing 2.20 marks ($1.15) per half liter. At the Donisl, a great many customers are tourists; at the Bratwurst-Stüberl, you'll be among the very few outsiders. Keep it in mind, too, for luncheon in Munchen (couldn't resist that). Closed Sundays.

In and Near the Railroad Station

In Munich's railroad station (Hauptbahnhof), you'll be happy to learn, there is now a self-service cafeteria ("Gaststätten Selbstbedienung") which stays open, as best I can determine, from dawn till midnight. Its offerings are tasty and inexpensive. I recently had a good Deutsches Beefsteak, mashed potatoes and gravy, vegetables, salad and really excellent coffee (1.30 marks), for a total of 7.50 marks ($3.94). Meat entrees range from 3 to 5 marks and vegetables are 2 marks. The selection is not large (about six entrees a day), but you don't have to wrestle with the language here, and can simply point to what looks good.

Again in the station area, one block up Bayerstrasse, on the corner of Zweigstrasse, is the even more exciting (but slightly more expensive) **Schuler Bufeteria**—to my mind, the city's finest cafeteria—with a larger selection of plates than at the train station and with fewer of the George Grosz-types that sometimes inhabit the station establishment. Light and modern in a Scandinavian manner, the Schuler prices numerous main plates with vegetables at 5.50 marks ($2.89), charges only 1.40 marks for soft drinks, and carries a large selection of light-to-the-stomach items, including the traditional Bavarian mixed-cold-meat salads, covered with onions, lightly doused with oils and spices (3.80 marks). Watch particularly for the "Sonder Angebot", a daily special usually announced on the special counter sign, and selling for only 3 marks—as, for example, a large platter of meat and potatoes.

A less modern and more typically-Bavarian dinery (waitresses in dirndls, yellow-and-brown tablecloths, birch chairs) in the railroad station area is the **Badische Weinstuben,** 3 Lammerstrasse (in the rear of the Hotel Württemberger Hof; from the front entrance of the station, turn left along Dachauerstrasse, then left at Marsstrasse to Lammerstrasse). This is a choice for our more adventurous readers in search of truly typical Bavarian fare (liver dumplings, blood sausages, and all the rest). While everything here is à la carte, dishes are all reasonably priced and marvelously varied: gravy-covered noodles cooked with ham and served with mixed vegetables, for 7 marks ($3.68), grilled heart of beef with dumplings and salad for 9.50 marks ($5). And although the liver dumpling soup at 2.80 marks ($1.47) is priced higher than elsewhere in Munich, it's of top quality. You'll enjoy a good meal at the Badische Weinstuben for $6.50, a feast for $8 (if you include the leber-knödelsuppe—liver dumpling soup—worthy of a Michelin star).

Probably the most popular restaurant in the station area, famous for its large portions, is the **Gaststätte Grüner Hof**, at Bayerstrasse 35, in front of the side entrance to the station, which offers five two-course menus daily ranging in price from 4.80 to 7.50 marks ($2.52 to $3.94); à la carte plates from 3.50 to 10 marks ($1.84 to $3.94). Their schweinebraten with semmelknödel and krautsalat for 7.80 marks $4.10) is unique in Munich for size, price and quality (they have their own butcher shop). Open every day, from 7:30 a.m. until midnight.

Near City Hall

The **Murr Stube**, at the rear of the Vinzenz Murr butcher and delicatessen shop at 7 Rosenstrasse, one block from Marienplatz (and the Town Hall), is a delightful place tucked away at the back of a butcher/grocery shop, and serves a daily self-service "gedeck" (table d'hote meal) for 5.90 marks ($3.10), sometimes for less, that usually consists of something like a meat platter with fried egg, salad, and a fruit salad. Most hot plates range from 1.40 to 6 marks. The Murr also serves marvelous leberkäse (made on the premises and therefore very fresh) for 2 marks the portion, as well as a large variety of sandwiches from 1.40 to 2 marks. The Rosenstrasse, where all this is found, is the street directly opposite the City Hall; go there at 11 a.m. to see the famous bellringing figurines, then head for lunch to Mr. Murr's remarkable butcher shop!

In the very same area, the **Weisses Bräuhaus,** 10 Tal (just off the Marienplatz—walk through the archway near the Beck store), a typical, old, Bavarian restaurant with a fortress-like arched dining room, serves two-course menus for 7.30 marks ($3.84), a mammoth schweineschnitzel with mixed salad at 9 marks that is more than enough for two, and is especially known for its unusual "Weizenbier" or "Weissbier," a bittersweet-tasting white beer brewed with wheat and served in an oversized champagne glass, with a slice of lemon on top: 2.10 marks ($1.10) per half liter. Note how the waitresses, all middle-aged, keep leather money bags under their tiny white aprons.

In Schwabing

In **Schwabing,** the "Greenwich Village" of Munich, budget restaurants are fairly numerous, but certainly one of the most popular is the **Gaststätte Weinbauer** at 5 Fendstrasse, off the Leopoldstrasse, where the "day's menu" ranges from 5.50 to 9 marks, and the servings are huge. Almost painfully plain in appearance, it is jammed with customers who crowd around large tables, and pack most massive plates of meat in gravy, mounds of potatoes and vegetables. Closed Wednesdays.

The broad **Leopoldstrasse,** from which the Weinbauer is just a short walk, is generally considered to constitute the heart of Schwabing (the small streets at the end are actually far less commercial and more truly Bohemian). On the Leopoldstrasse itself, the budget champion is **Gaststätte Leopold** at 50 Leopoldstrasse, which serves a daily two-course menu for as little as 6.80 marks, and numerous especially-cheap vegetable platters ("vegetarische speisen" on the menu) for 5.80 (fried eggs with spinach and mashed potatoes) and 6 marks (vegetable ravioli with mixed salad). In the summer of 1979, my particular 7.50 mark "Gemüseplatte" here—a sectioned-off platter of beets, spinach, potatoes, carrots, cauliflower and fried eggs—was a high-light of the Munich visit!

A final Leopoldstrasse restaurant—the definitive student hang-out in Munich—is the large and usually-jammed **Hahnhof** at 32 Leopoldstrasse, on that stretch of the wide boulevard where sidewalk artists and sellers of handicrafts station themselves in summer. Here, on weekdays only, and in summer only, the typewritten menu lists two-course dinners for 7.50 and 10.50 marks, service and tax included, and the meals are consumed in a vast sidewalk-cafe-area of the restaurant, packed with long-haired types of both sexes. If you can't meet a German girl here, you never will!

Near the Bavaria Ring

At the end of the Schwanthalerstrasse (where some of you may be staying), at no. 85, you next find: the good, grey, and very pre-war **Gasthof zur Fest-wiese**, plain, all of wood, and with no tablecloths, but with hearty two-course meals for 5.50, 6.50 and 7.50 marks (the latter including dessert).

In the University Area

Schellingstrasse, which runs off Ludwig Strasse, just below the Siegestor and the university buildings, is the classic budget restaurant street in the university area. One block down Schelling, at the corner of Amalienstrasse: the very local, Bavarian-style **Gaststätte Atzinger** serves two-course meals for 6 and 7.50 marks, all included; big platters for 5 and 6 marks. Not far from Schellingstrasse, at Türkenstrasse No. 33, **Gaststätte Allotria** is only slightly higher priced, but also offers nightly jazz starting at 9 p.m., for which there is no extra charge.

Elsewhere

And always remember that meals at the **Mathäser Bierstadt**, 5 Bayer-strasse, which you'll be visiting later in this chapter, are highly favored by the Bavarian citizenry, far more so than at the Hofbräuhaus. Sausages and sauer-kraut for 5 marks ($2.63); two eggs with spinach and roast potatoes for 5.50 marks; complete dinners are priced at 11 marks. The "Beer City" has a cheap sausage stand out front and various large rooms; many platters are priced under 5.50 marks, and I find the food pretty good for a mass-produced operation.

The least expensive area of the Mathäser is the corridor-like restaurant through which you'll first pass on entering, on your way to the main rooms. There you'll be given a special small menu (it bears the designation, at the bottom, "Schnellgaststätte") offering unusually good prices for Munich—soup for 1.75 marks, wurst plates for 3 and 4.50 marks, main courses for 3.50 and 5.50 marks—unavailable in the large, non-corridor-like areas. One budget tip here is to order half a roast chicken ("½ Brathuhn"; 6.75 marks) for two persons and share it; it's more than enough. Then, after gorging at unusually low cost, you can head upstairs to the mammoth "Bierhalle" with its brass band and "Zum Prosit" songs, or to any of the several other dining rooms in this veritable "beer city."

Something lighter? Thousands of Munich's working people walk every day through the underground shopping center of Stachus, where many make a short detour to the **Sandwich Buffet** (near the escalators) to munch one of 50 varieties of sandwiches, priced from 1.50 to 2.50 marks, and all named after cities: the "London", consisting of a Zeppelin-shaped roll stuffed with butter, roast-beef, salami, lettuce and cucumbers, and spiced with paprika, is the Bavarian version of our hero sandwich. Half a liter of beer adds 2 marks more, but a glass of milk is only 80 pfennigs.

(c) A budget recap

To single out the top budget values from the foregoing list: they're the **Gaststätte Grüner Hof** alongside the station; the second floor restaurant of the **Bilka Kaufhaus**; the restaurant of the Vinzenz Murr butcher shop (**"Murr**

Stube"), near the Town Hall; the basement of the **Kaufhof Department Store;** the corridor-like "Schnellgaststätte" of the **Mathäser Bier Stadt;** the **Augustiner Bierhalle;** and the **Weinbauer** in Schwabing.

(d) Some final thoughts

An important food tip: never order coffee with your meals in Germany. It has a foul taste, and it's liable to cost as much as 1.50 marks (79¢) a cup. Order beer, Coca-Cola or an Apfelsaft (cider)—uniformly good, and uniformly priced at about 65¢ a glass.

I can't end this section on eating without urging you, strenuously, to taste the "Leberkäs" (literally, "liver-cheese") at the **Imbiss Cafe** in the railroad station—for what may turn out to be the most delicious snack of your life. You'll find this sort of "Leberkäs" only in Munich, and in its best form at the aforementioned spot. Walk along the inner portion of the railroad station (next to where you go out to the trains, in front of track No. 16) until you see a counter surrounded by twelve upturned beer kegs—that's the Imbiss, which is also on the other side of the station's Schäffler-Saal Restaurant (you eat the Leberkäs standing up, at one of the kegs). A portion of Leberkäs, with "eine semmel" (a roll) and a large glass of beer will cost 4.60 marks. Douse it well with your serving of mild mustard, eat it, and you'll not only re-order another portion (2 marks; bread is 25 pfennigs, and the ethereal mustard—"senf"—is free), but you'll dream of it later—as I presently am doing—in other cities, and at other times, when Munich-style Leberkäs isn't attainable at four times the price.

READERS' FOOD COMMENTS: "We'd like to vigorously dispute one point with you: You say never order coffee in Germany—that it's bad tasting and very expensive. Germany is the first place after almost seven weeks of touring where we found honest-to-goodness, good, American-type coffee . . . *everywhere.* And we found it cheaper than beer in many places" (Jess and Alice Brewis, Taylor, Michigan). . . . "I have insufficient words to praise the Munich beer. It was wonderful. The food, too, was excellent, although I found the sausage skins a little too tough for my teeth" (H. R. Baker, Rockhampton, Queensland, Australia). . . . "A night at the Hofbräuhaus or Mathäser Bierstadt is not complete without sampling German white radishes (about the size of a cucumber), served spiraled and salted" (E. M. Swan, Alexandria, Virginia).

READERS' BREAKFAST SELECTIONS: "One can eat breakfast for about a mark if, in the morning, one walks up the Sendlingerstrasse from Marienplatz. On the right side of the street, about two or three blocks from Marienplatz, is a bakery; stop there and grab a few breakfast rolls. Continue in the same direction, and on the left is the **Tschibo Coffee Store,** where a full cup of good coffee is 50 pfennigs" (Lynn A. Davis, Munich, Germany). . . . "A cheap cup of coffee? At the numerous **Tschibo** coffee stores, coffee is sold at 50 pfennigs ($26¢) a cup. You drink it standing up, but it is about as good as anywhere else here. Where to find one? Try **Rosental,** near the Viktualienmarkt (the open-air green-grocery market)—also near the Rathaus" (Dr. L. K. Wynston, Long Beach, California). . . . "For people like me who are still hungry after a continental breakfast, Munich's **Kaufhalle Department Store** on Neuhauser Strasse's mall, offers an inexpensive treat from 9 a.m. to 11 a.m. at its basement snack counter. For DM 1.95 ($1.02) you are served a boiled egg, two rolls, butter, jam and coffee or tea; for DM 2.90 ($1.52), you get the same with coldmeats" (Mary Cummings, Minneapolis, Minnesota).

THE BEER GARDENS: If it's a sunny day between May and October, and you're tired of sights and craving simple relaxation, you head—in Munich—for any of a dozen "biergarten" (beer gardens), which are open-air restaurants under shady trees (usually chestnut), serving beer and a small variety of such cold food items as sausages with black bread, cheese, roast chicken. These are found in every location, but my favorites are the **Augustinerkeller** at 52 Arnulfstrasse (near the Starnberger Bahnhof at the side of the main station); the **Chinesischer Turm** in the Englischer Garten (English Gardens; take the subway to the Giselastrasse stop in Schwabing and walk from there); and the **Aumeister** at #1 Sondermeierstrasse, reached by taking the subway (U-Bahn) to the Studentenstadt stop in Schwabing, and walking for about 15 minutes into the English Gardens. In the beer gardens, price for a "mass" (liter) of beer served either in a large glass (big enough for raising a couple of goldfish) or earthen mug or stein is 4.80 marks, including a tip earned by the middle-aged waitress (some looking like Olympic discus champions) who carries up to 12 steins at a time (the world's record, held by a Munich waitress, naturally, is 20 steins). Buying a "mass" is your admission ticket, and nobody casts a dirty look if you bring along your own food (thereby saving money) and start cutting up bread and meat on the wooden table, like everyone else is doing. Here's a thoroughly "gemütlich" experience.

THE BIG SPLURGE: For this, **Weinhaus Neuner,** located halfway between Karlsplatz (Stachus) and Marienplatz, at Herzogspitalstrasse 8, is the place to go. Housed in a 300-year-old building (once a Jesuit monastery), it consists of two large wood-paneled dining rooms which create a kind of old-Heidelberg atmosphere in which you'll find total gemütlichkeit at extremely reasonable rates: only 6 to 8 marks for a large variety of local dishes; schnitzel with salad at 12.50 marks. And you eat and drink to popular and classical music performed by several accordion and violin players. Open seven days of the week, from 11:30 a.m. to around 1 a.m., Saturday and Sunday from 6 p.m.

An alternate splurge, the **Nürnberger Bratwurstglöckl am Dom,** 9 Frauenplatz, is next to the distinctive two-tower cathedral of Munich, a short walk from the City Hall. An atmospheric old restaurant, with an "Albrecht Dürer" room upstairs, it is so very traditional that it serves in traditional tin dishes! Hot plates average 9 to 13 marks, but you might possibly like to order the cheaper and renowned "Schweinswürstl" specialty—tiny sausages, about as large as your little finger. Four of these served with sauerkraut make a very tasty lunch at 4.70 marks. With soup at 2.20 marks and salad for 2.50, you'll be riotously stuffed for less than 9.50 marks. The normal meals, however, will run around 14 marks ($7.36), and this time are almost as memorable for the setting (Hansel and Gretel-type chairs, old oak tables, etchings and flowers) as for the food. Location, once again, is directly at the back of the Dom (Cathedral).

STARVATION BUDGET MEALS: A word of cheer for young folks: the **University Mensa,** at 13 Leopoldstrasse (subway station is Giselastrasse), officially for students with student cards only, is so busy serving an average of 7,500 meals per day that spot-checks are very rare, and practically any student-age person, whether enrolled at the University or not, can get a two-course, soup-and-main-course plate meal for either 1.80 marks (95¢) ("Stamm") or 2.80 marks ($1.47) ("Auswahlessen"), Monday through Friday from 11 a.m. to 2 p.m. Get there early, buy a yellow chip for Stamm or a blue one for Auswahlessen at one of the ground-floor booths, then walk up to the first-floor dining rooms. The menus (listing, by the way, the number of calories next to each item), are posted on the walls. Similar meals, rates and hours are available at the **Mensa** of the **Technische Universität,** 17 Arcisstrasse, 10 minutes by foot from the railway station. And still another Mensa can be found in the Olympic Village area (now partly used as student quarters and dorms), at Helene-Mayer-Ring 9. This is **Mensa Oberwiesenfeld,** which looks like a cafeteria, but serves lunch only, Monday through Friday, from 11 a.m. to 1:45 p.m. Take the subway to Olympiastadion. . . . On my last trip to Munich in the summer of 1979, I also found that the lunch counters in Munich's dime stores (such as the "Woolworth-Imbiss" at 27 Kaufingerstrasse) still serve a mountainous plate lunch (bratwurst, potatoes and sauerkraut) for exactly 4.50 marks (only $2.36). . . . The town is studded, as well, with the German equivalent of hot dog stands, serving Bavarian sausages-on-a-bun that would please a gourmet at three times the price. At one of these, nearly a half-pound of sausage on a large roll, with mustard, costs 3.50 marks ($1.84), and it's a meal in itself. Apfelsaft (cider) or lemonade costs 1.50 marks. And shaslik (chunks of meat, interspersed with onions, served on a stick) is yours for exactly 3.50 marks ($1.84).

GETTING AROUND TOWN: Subways are the key; Munich's subway system is a marvel. Completed in 1972 for the Olympic Games, it utilizes every sort of up-to-date electronic feature, and whisks you about almost soundlessly at an average fare of 1.12 marks. The main and most frequent service is on the "U-Bahn" (meaning Untergrundbahn) line, but criss-crossing the U-Bahn at Marienplatz are the more extensive S-Bahn (Stadtbahn) services into suburban locations; since the S-Bahn is a state railway, it accepts the Eurailpass! If you aren't equipped with one, purchase a "Mehrfahrtenkarte" (Multiple Journey Ticket) for 4.50 marks at vending machines in the subway stations; these red tickets—do not take the blue and green ones—come in 8 segments worth 56 pfennigs each; you fold up two segments for your average ride and stick them in to be stamped by little blue machines at the entrance to the tracks. You'll soon acquire the hang of it. Under no circumstances should a budget traveller consider taxis in Munich, as they're fiendishly expensive.

ENTERTAINMENT: Munich is a city where you can, and should, indulge in a heavy dose of night-lifing. The cafes, dance halls, and night clubs here are as varied and numerous as in any major capital, but at a price level so low as to make you blink. Germans, you see, rarely entertain at home. Every evening in Munich, vast numbers of the citizenry descend on cafes and dance halls—and they expect to be received in a relaxed, non-gouging manner. The tourist benefits from the fact that night-clubbing in Munich is not a once-a-year activity for most of the populace.

The place where they most frequently go, and the spot that you can't miss, is the boisterous **Hofbräuhaus (16),** at Platzl 9, Germany's largest beer hall, where literally thousands of gallons of the foamy stuff are consumed each night. This is your choice for an inexpensive evening full of Teutonic hanky-panky. On the ground floor, called the "Schwemme", you drink beer costing only 4 marks for a full liter at long benches, and listen to a little brass band. On the second floor, there's a restaurant serving enormous German sausage meals for 4.30 marks (or you can order soup—2.20 marks, followed by wienerwurst mit sauerkraut—4.70 marks). Don't go downstairs unless you're willing to link arms and bellow out a song with your table mates. . . . Across the street from the Hofbräuhaus is the **Platzl (17),** another large beer hall, with a daily 8 p.m. floor show of topical skits on Bavarian life, and performers who yodel and do "schuhplattlen"—the footstomping, thigh-slapping dance of the Alps. Entrance fee here, however, is 7 marks ($3.68), whereas the Hofbräuhaus is free.

The chief competitor of the Hofbräuhaus is the more modern—but equally mammoth—**"Mathäser Bier Stadt"** (Mathaser Beer City), at 5 Bayerstrasse (near the Stachus), which advertises that it has 5,000 seats. A slightly more refined (but equally cheap) version of the Hofbräuhaus, and perhaps patronized by fewer tourists and more local residents, it features a little brass band on its top floor, plus the usual camaraderie and beer guzzling (a full liter for 4.50 marks), plus several different restaurants in the same building (the quieter Kleiner Saal on the ground floor, where you eat; the upstairs Festsaal, where you dance on special holiday occasions; and most exciting of all, the mammoth Bierhalle, half a flight up on the mezzanine, where a center bandstand—like a boxing ring—blares music, and all the patrons drink and sing). While this "beer city" doesn't approach the atmosphere of the Hofbräuhaus, which it is obviously trying to emulate, it does offer far better food, served in far cleaner and tidier surroundings, and at moderate prices; a number of different wurst (sausage) dishes with potatoes for 4.50 marks; sauerbraten with dumplings (knödel) for 10.50 marks; the city's specialty—kassler rippchen (smoked pork chops)—for 10 marks, including sauerkraut and mashed potatoes; leberkäse and potato salad for 5.50 marks ($2.89); a half liter of beer for 2.25 marks. Most Germans make an entire evening out of the dining and the endless quaffing of beer here, surrounded by thousands of their compatriots.

For Dancing

That famous mecca for shy bachelors in Munich—the Ring Cafe—has been torn down, and we'll therefore have to limit our low-cost dancing recommendations to the following two almost-as-good establishments: First, the gigantic cellar-dancehall of the **Hackerkeller**, 4 Theresienhöhe, open seven days a week from 6:30 p.m. to 1 a.m., where a dance band in Bavarian costume alternates between modern and folk music, while up to 250 couples dance. There's no entrance fee, but you're expected at least to drink (beer for 2.50 marks per half liter) or earlier in the evening to eat (various menus from 5.50 to 10 marks, or a 14 mark portion of beef cut before your eyes from a whole steer rotating on a spit). Take streetcar 19 or 20 from the station to the Theresienhohe stop; the Hackerkeller is in the futuristic block of buildings overlooking the Octoberfest meadow. Second, the **Park Cafe**, 7 Sophienstrasse (in the "Alter Botanischer Garten"), recently renovated, which consists of a restaurant section (daily menus from 8 marks up) and a large dance establishment open daily from 4 to 6 p.m. for afternoon waltzes and the like, very conservative, and again from 8 p.m. to 1 a.m., this time with hot music, a large dance floor and good bands playing. There's no entrance fee, but you'll be asked to purchase a 14 mark ($7.36) "gedeck" consisting of a small bottle of champagne and accompanying bottle of beer or orange juice; and all this is but a five-minute walk from the railway station: turn left into Luitpoldstrasse (site of the large Hertie Department Store), cross the Luisenstrasse, and you're at the door.

For a more elegant, but still relatively inexpensive, evening, try **"P1"** (pronounced "pay eintz"), a truly enchanting nightclub with a sloping glass roof, modern art on the walls, and continuous dancing. "P1" is named after its location: Prinzregentenstrasse 1, which is also the site of the Haus der Kunst, Munich's large museum of modern art (the nightclub is partly inside the museum). This is a favorite late-night (9 p.m. to 4 a.m.) hangout of Munich's artists and writers. There's no cover, no entrance fee, no minimum. Because tourists haven't yet discovered "P1," the *non*-alcoholic drinks are relatively inexpensive (3 marks for a Coke) for so sophisiticated a spot (although Scotch is $5), and so is the food ($3 for a club sandwich). Dress up for your visit, though; "P1" is patronized by elegant intellectuals, not beatniks; and keep in mind that the cost of your evening will be a bit higher than at the other dance-providing nightclubs we've mentioned.

For Bohemians

But now for the flower people. The Greenwich Village area of Munich is "Schwabing"—and in some respects, it's zanier and more colorful than anything New York offers.

Schwabing is made up of two distinct sections, however, and only one of the two is really "far out": the northernmost district of Schwabing, at the end of the big Leopoldstrasse, where a number of little streets—**Occam Strasse, Feilitzschstrasse,** and **Ursula Strasse**—are literally jammed with cheap coffee houses and bars that cater to the rather sophisticated university elements of Munich. The most candle-lit, cave-like, dark, and girl-crowded spot is the **Nachteule,** at 7 Occam Strasse, where beer (2.50 marks per half-liter) is all you'll have to buy. That's followed by the **Schwabinger Spritzn** and the **Schwabinger Brettl,** both also on Occam Strasse, at No. 15 and No. 11, respectively. At the Brettl, the attempt is to recapture the atmosphere of Munich in the 1920s. On many nights, customers contribute old German folk songs, poems, or little philosophical talks, as was the custom in Schwabing in former years. Lively and interesting. No admission; the singing starts around 10 p.m.; a half liter of beer costs 3 marks, but the first glass must be accompanied by a shot of schnapps, for a total price of 6 marks.

In Lower Schwabing

A much more normal area, and with much larger dance floors, less "mod" in character than the district described above, is the stretch of Schwabing that proceeds along the wide **Leopoldstrasse,** above the Siegestor; it's flanked, in summer, by sidewalk cafes and artists sketching caricatures, etc. Here you'll find, in quick succession, the famous **Käfig,** 19 Leopoldstrasse, a huge basement nightclub, with no admission and some stag girls—a bottle of wine is 22 marks, the average hard drink 8 marks; the **Ba-Ba-Lu,** 27 Leopoldstrasse, with an admission charge of 2 marks; and the **Flash** at 68 Leopoldstrasse, cheapest of the three, featuring a discotheque, one-armed bandits, and billiards; no admission and beer only 2.50 marks. . . . Catering to a very, very young crowd are two final Leopoldstrasse clubs, both extremely inexpensive, of which the better is the **Rumpelkammer,** at Trautenwolfstrasse 1, corner Leopoldstrasse, where the dancing is to records, there's no entrance fee, and a beer costs 2 marks. The other is the **Piné,** a basement club at 25 Leopoldstrasse, where sometimes the dancing is to records, sometimes to long-haired bands imported from England. This time a 7-mark admission fee, which entitles you to two beers or two cokes.

For Theater

Like London, Munich has a magnificent selection of theaters, with wonderfully cheap entrance prices. Contemporary plays are shown at the **Münchner Schauspielhaus,** Maximilianstrasse 26; at the huge **Deutsches Theater,** Schwanthalerstrasse 13; at the theater **"Die Kleine Freiheit,"** Maximilianstrasse 31; and in at least a dozen lesser playhouses. Seats are available at all the foregoing spots for as little as $4, sometimes less. . . . Operettas (Strauss, Zeller, Offenbach), operas (Mozart, Rossini, Puccini, Händel, and Bizet) and ballets (Delibes, Egk, Henze), are beautifully performed in a gem-like setting

at the **Staatstheater am Gärtnerplatz (18),** 3 Gärtnerplatz, a 9-mark taxi ride
from the Bahnhof. Ticket window is open here from 10 to 1 and from 4 to 6;
you must go in advance for tickets, but you can always buy standing room at
the time of the performance for a little over 5.50 marks ($2.89). Seats range
from 9 marks ($4.73) to a high of 36 ($18.94). Don't miss this place: spectacular
scenery on three revolving stages, a spirited chorus and principals, an adequate
corps de ballet. Their performances of "Die Fledermaus" put our Met to
shame. . . . Opera is presented nightly at the superb **Nationaltheater** (Bayeris-
che Staatsoper), on Max-Joseph-Platz, famed for its progressive versions of the
standard classics. Unfortunately, tickets—while standard in price—are hard to
get: give serious thought to standing room. Somewhat lesser operatic productions, but still of a high order, are done at the **Cuvilliéstheater,** 1 Residenzstrasse. . . . For theatrical classics (Goethe, Schiller), go to the **Bayerisches
Staatsschauspiel,** in the **Residenztheater,** Max-Joseph-Platz 1, where again
you can obtain perfectly adequate seats for 8 marks.

READERS' TIPS: "Tickets for the opera and for operettas are hard to get but can be obtained
best by standing in line at the theatre the night you wish to go. If you are a student, show
the identity card for your university—you'll get a discount. This goes for museums in
Munich, as well" (Peter W. Bailey, Washington, D.C.). . . . "Students with international
identity cards can line up an hour before opera time during the Summer 'Festspiele' (July
15 to Aug. 5) to see the international stars who perform during this time for about 7
marks. Surprisingly, tickets can run as high as 40 marks for the best seats and most operas
are completely sold out months in advance" (Edward H. Pietraszek, Chicago, Illinois).
. . . "Buy a one-day "Turistenkarte," for 5 marks, entitling you to unlimited tram and
U-Bahn trips for 24 hours" (Mrs. Catherine P. Martin, Santa Barbara, California).
. . . "In the **Gaststätte zum Grüner Inn,** 38 Türkenstrasse, there meets every Tuesday
evening a society called the 'Columbus Gesellschaft,' a German-American society, over
beer. No membership is required for Americans in transit, and proceedings are as
informal as they can be. Further information can be obtained from the Amerikahaus,
Munich, or by phoning 59-56-72 on Tuesdays and Thursdays between 11 a.m. and 1 p.m.,
activities include rap-sessions, museum visits, walking tours and films. This Gaststätte
is also one of the cheapest in Munich" (G. O. Piper, A.P.O., New York). . . . "A summer
gathering place for students is the **Internationaler Studentenclub** in the 'International
Foyer', 15 Adelheidstrasse, Schwabing, where there's dancing and socializing on Thursday and Saturday nights from 7:30, discussions, bridge and chess on Wednesday and
Friday evenings, other activities during the day" (Pauline Hadley, New York, New
York). . . . "North of the Löwenbrau Brewery on Nymphenburgerstrasse is the **Dantebad
Swimming Pool,** open until 4 p.m., and charging only 3.50 marks for adults, 2.50 marks
for children" (Jeff and Barbara Wasserman, Oakdale, New York).

THE TOP SIGHTS: After you've sampled the entertainment of Munich, your
remaining schedule should at least include a long visit to the city's top attraction: the great **Deutsches Museum,** on an island in the Isar River (the "Isarin-
sel"; open daily from 9 to 5; admission three marks, students one mark). This
is the largest scientific and technical museum in the world, with displays
brilliantly arranged to show you the inner workings of man's finest machines
and engineering feats. And to give you a theoretical grounding in science, the
Museum maintains a physics department on its first floor, made up of glass
display cases with protruding handles and levers, that you operate, and that
illustrate the basic laws of physics.

It would take days to wander through the entire museum; if you have only
a brief time available, go first to the aviation room on the first floor, where
actual aircraft—dating back to World War I—are preserved for you to clamber
over and into. Then watch for the actual casting of aluminum on the ground
floor at 10:30 a.m. and 2:30 p.m., the processing of plastics on the 21st floor
at 11:30 a.m. and 3:30 p.m., other daily events listed on the wall opposite the

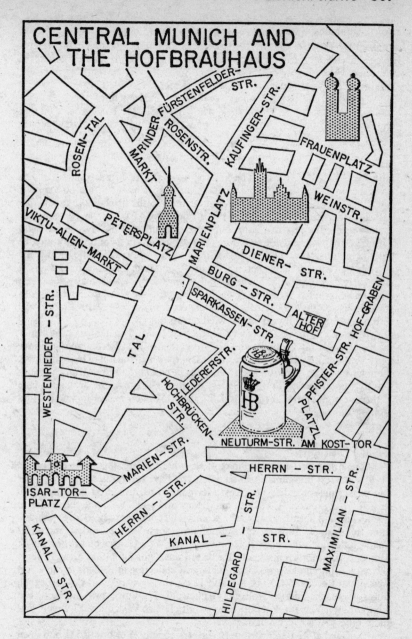

CENTRAL MUNICH AND THE HOFBRAUHAUS

ROSEN-TAL

RRINDER FÜRSTENFELDER- STR.

ROSENSTR.

MARKT

KAUFINGER-STR.

FRAUENPLATZ

VIKTU-ALIEN-MARKT

PETERSPLATZ

MARIENPLATZ

WEINSTR.

DIENER- STR.

BURG – STR.

WESTENRIEDER – STR.

TAL

SPARKASSEN- STR.

ALTER HOF

HOF-GRABEN

LEDERERSTR.

HOCHBRÜCKEN-STR.

HB

PFISTER-STR.

PLATZL

MARIEN-STR.

NEUTURM-STR. AM KOST-TOR

ISAR-TOR-PLATZ

HERRN – STR.

HERRN – STR.

HILDEGARD STR.

STR.

KANAL – STR.

KANAL – STR.

MAXIMILIAN – STR.

information booth at the entrance.

The **Frauenkirche** is the distinctive, two-domed cathedral ("Dom") of Munich, from whose south tower you will have a panoramic view of the city, and—on clear days—of the foothills of the Bavarian Alps, about 40 miles away. The ascent to the tower is by elevator (although you must first climb 80 steps to reach the lift), the elevator fee is 2 marks for adults, one mark for students and children, and the entrance to the tower is alongside the ticket booth at the outside of the cathedral entrance. Repairs to the tower, currently in progress, may prevent use of the elevator for several months in 1980.

There are, of course, numerous museums in Munich, of which the outstanding one is the **Alte Pinakothek**, at 27 Barer Strasse; but for more on that and Munich's other top attractions (including the important Nymphenburg Palace and its associated sights), I give you my wife Hope:

SIGHTSEEING WITH HOPE: "The key to the charm of Munich is that it is a Bavarian city. And the citizens of Bavaria, almost by definition, are simple, warm, friendly (rural, if you like), and devoted to the principle that enjoying oneself is the highest goal in life. (The magnificent Alpine scenery in this part of the world must certainly contribute to the feeling that life is to be savored.) Although the people work as hard as any 'Prussian' (a local term for anyone born in another part of Germany), they retain a characteristic easy-going attitude—as witness their tolerance for the fascinating, infamous King Ludwig II. Bizarre and fanciful as his behaviour always was, nobody really got upset, until he bankrupted the country building his story-book castles and then offered, as his solution to the collapse of the economy, a trade with France—all of Bavaria for a small islet in the Mediterranean!

"Add to this the fact that since World War II, Munich has become a center for the German intellectuals who used to gather only in Berlin, and you have a city with a rich and diversified appeal. Along with all the fun of beer-drinking, shoulder-clapping 'gemütlichkeit,' and a rich peasant culture, Munich enjoys a lively, sophisticated, up-to-the-latest moment climate in the arts, and some of the finest museums in the world. In short, Munich makes for unique and exciting sightseeing.

The Alte Pinakothek

"Head first for the Alte Pinakothek, which in my opinion is one of the world's greatest museums. And go when you have several hours to spend, for this is the longest gallery in West Germany, with over 900 paintings (140 termed "masterpieces"), some so marvelous that you'll welcome the luxury to stop awhile and absorb what you're seeing. The collection ranges over painters from the 14th to 18th centuries, including some of the wildest and most wonderful religious allegorical paintings (in the West Gallery on the first floor); Albrecht Altdorfer's remarkable 'Battle of Issus,' which took the artist 12 years to complete (Room III, upstairs); the largest collection of Rubens in the world (upstairs in Rooms VII, VIII, 8, 9 and 12); and elsewhere, works by Brueghel, Dürer, Cranach, Giotto, Holbein, Grünewald, Da Vinci, Fra Angelico, Fra Filippo Lippi, Van Dyck, Hals, Rembrandt, Titian, Velazquez, El Greco, and many others. It's overwhelming!

"Located at 27 Barer Strasse (streetcars 15 and 25 or bus #53), and open daily except Mondays from 9 to 4:30, also Tuesday and Thursday evenings from 7 to 9. Admission is free on Sundays. At all other times, the Alte Pinakothek will provide you with a lifetime's worth of memories for just 3 marks ($1.57).

The Neue Pinakothek

"Here we'll briefly note the scheduled re-opening of Munich's more famous **Neue Pinakothek** on October 29, 1980, after a generation of reconstruction work following its complete destruction in World War II. Classic paintings of the 18th and 19th century—Delacroix, Gainsborough, Lenbach—will be featured; hours and other policies will parallel those of the Alte Pinakothek; but further description must await next year's edition of this book. Location is right across the lawn from the Alte Pinakothek.

The Haus der Kunst

"A long, five-block walk away (or else via Bus #55 from the Central Station), the enormous, modernistic **Haus der Kunst,** 1 Prinzregentenstrasse (near the Hofgarten), houses two separate galleries: one, on your left, displays 20th century classics (e.g., Kokoschka, Lionel Feininger, Salvador Dali, Andy Warhol, Robert Rauschenberg, Paul Klee, Wassily Kandinsky, De Chirico), while the other wing (entrance opposite, a city block away, on your right) is given over entirely to changing exhibitions, which often consist of the works of exciting new artists, whose canvases are on sale as well as on display. A disadvantage is that you must pay a separate entrance fee for each section of the museum: 2.50 marks ($1.31) to the permanent exhibition, open daily except Monday from 9 a.m. to 4:30 p.m., Thursday evenings from 7 to 9 p.m.; a stiff 4 to 5 marks ($2.10 to $2.64) to the changing exhibitions in the wing on your right, depending on the show (and the latter wing is open seven days a week, until 7 p.m.) Despite the high cost, this is an extremely worthwhile museum experience. Best transport for reaching the Haus der Kunst is tram no. 20 (to Prinzregentenstrasse) or buses 53 or 55 (to Haus der Kunst). East Wing (with changing exhibits) charges a stiff 5 marks admission every day from 9 to 6, while the Neue Pinakothek and Staatsgalerie Moderner Kunst are more popularly priced at 2.50 marks. But this is a worthwhile museum experience and you can enter the West Wing galleries free on Sundays. Open 9 to 4:30, daily except Mondays. On Tuesday and Thursday evenings the museum is open from 7 to 9 p.m.

Nymphenburg

"Now, for a delightful day's outing, make an excursion to Munich's historic **Nymphenburg Palace,** the magnificent Baroque-Rococo (begun in 1664, but not completed till 1823) Wittelsbach summer residence. To get there, take streetcar #21 from Dachauerstrasse, near the front of the Bahnhof, across from the Deutscher Kaiser Hotel, a 1.25-mark, 15-minute ride, going in the direction away from the center of town; get off at Schloss Nymphenburg, look to your left—you can't miss it (from the streetcar stop, it's about a 10-minute walk along a small canal)—and you'll see a semi-circle of buildings around the main Villa, with a jet-water fountain and lovely green lawn in front. The moral of Nymphenburg is Never Judge a Palace By Its Cover. From the front it looks pleasant enough (you could put up with it), but after a closer look at the grounds you'll be enchanted and never want to leave. There's a stunning park (about 500 acres!) sculptured with statues, lakes and waterfalls, and bordering the central formal gardens on both sides are forests of rustic splendor. For 4 marks ($2.10), you can buy an all-inclusive ticket which admits you to the Palace, Marstallmuseum, Amalienburg, Badenburg, Pagodenburg, and Magdalenenklause—there's so much that with time off for dreaming in the forest, you can easily spend an entire day at Nymphenburg, lunching in the exotic atmosphere of the palm house for fairly reasonable prices (bockwurst mit senf und brot, 3.50 marks; bouillon, 1.50 marks; beer, 2 marks; or a Coke for 1.70 marks). In a hurry? Then buy the 3-mark 'Kleine Karte' which admits you simple to the three top sights of Nymphenburg: The Schloss, Amalienburg, and the Marstallmuseum.

"Here's a plan for taking in all the sights: first, visit **Schloss Nymphenburg** itself (which is close to the ticket booth), an elegant French-style 'Villa' and the main abode for the royal summer residents; this was the first completed building and is the very nucleus of the entire Nymphenburg complex. Inside, head in particular for the South Pavilion, also known as Queen Caroline's apartments, which has the bedroom (opposite the entrance, off the main drawing room) where Ludwig II was born on August 25, 1845. In the dining room is King Ludwig I's well-publicized 'Gallery of Beauties'—portraits of some very attractive court ladies, including Crown Princess Marie (Ludwig II's mother), and the fascinating Spanish dancer-courtesan (of Irish descent) Lola Montez, who ruined King Ludwig I's reputation in his declining years, and whose antics, politicking and complete dominance over the infatuated old man so annoyed the people that she became a contributing factor to the Revolution of 1848 and was banished from the country.

"The next stop is the **Marstallmuseum** (turn right as you leave the Palace, last building in the immediate rectangle), which is one of the finest Coach Museums in all of Europe and houses Royal Bavarian carriages, sleighs and harness. And here, don't miss the Sleigh or Coach "innovations" of Ludwig II. In his attempt to bring back the grandeur of former days, he created a Carriage that Cinderella would have blushed in, so heavily laden with gold it looks as if a 20-mule team couldn't pull it; the hub, the spokes of the wheels, every inch of it is sculptured gilt, curlicues, cherubs, lions and roses. And look for the elaborate display (with eight papier mache horses) of Kaiser Karl VII's 'Krönungswagen,' a glass Coronation Coach made in Paris in 1740.

"Now to the park itself—and you'd best consult a plan of the grounds near the entrance so you won't get lost. Since I believe in saving the best for last, and the gem of the park is Amalienburg, I suggest a counter-clockwise tour. To the right of the entrance, and in a somewhat remote spot behind the hot-house and refreshment center, is the **Magdalenenklause,** a sort of religious retreat for royalty, where half the building is a Chapel, with an imitation Grotto. Continue way up the road on the same side of the lagoon to the **Pagodenburg,** built in 1716-19 by Max Emanuel who wanted to create a Chinese Tea House, but couldn't resist decorating the first floor and staircase in Dutch tiles. He was more successful on the upper story, but the place is tiny, somewhat disappointing though richly decorated and a charming play-house in total effect. Directly opposite, but on the other side of the park, across the lagoon (follow the signs), is Max Emanuel's **Badenburg** (or Bath House)—a swimming pool two stories high, the upper half in blue and white Delft tiles.

"Now walk back towards the Palace (passing a small 'village' on the grounds) to the treat of Nymphenburg, the little **Amalienburg**—in the very height of rococo fashion. Built in 1734-39 as a 'Hunting Lodge' for Electress Amalia (note the Diana over the front doorway), the first two rooms carry out the hunting and country theme, and then suddenly the remainder of the house takes on a highly decorative silver rococo style that surpasses anything found in the main palace, including a Hall of Mirrors that is as splendid a room as you're likely to find anywhere. The detailed sculptured silver reflected in the mirrors is breath-taking. And how's that for roughing it in a 'hunting lodge'!

"Finally, on this tour of Nymphenburg, china lovers can also visit the **Royal Porcelain Factory,** which is in a small 'guest house' (#8) in the block of buildings opposite the Marstallmuseum. Entrance is free, but buying prices are high (30 marks for a small white ashtray) though the figurines are wonderfully real and done with some sense of humor. Castle hours are generally from 9 to 5 (winters 10 to 4) daily, except Mondays, with all the park pavilions (except Amalienburg) taking a one-hour lunch break.

Residenzmuseum and Schatzkammer

"Back in town but still in Royal company, the **Residenzmuseum,** which was the official Palace, and the **Schatzkammer,** or Treasure House, are both located at 3 Max Joseph Platz (from the Bahnhof take the S-Bahn to Marienplatz, or take street-car # 1, # 4, or # 21, and get off at the Opera—it's behind the Rathaus, near the theatre) and share the same hours (except that the Residenzmuseum closes for lunch from 12:30 to 1:30 p.m.): Tuesdays through Saturdays from 10 a.m. to 4:30 p.m., Sundays from 10 a.m. to 1 p.m.

"The Schatzkammer has to be seen to be believed: it is an inconceivably splendid collection of jewelry and riches, including diamonds as big as hubcaps, rubies and emeralds in such profusion you'd think they were on sale at Woolworth's, plus silver, gold, ivory and pearls—all reflecting the vast wealth of the Bavarian royalty. There are jewelled crowns and crosses, goblets, medals, scepters, swords, dishware, personal items, and—in the third room—a stunning necklace and a magnificent statue of St. George Slaying the Dragon, made in 1590 and all inlaid with precious stones—a bit 'ostentatious' but quite beautiful. The Residenzmuseum, in the same building, contains court rooms from practically every period (Renaissance, Baroque, Rococo and Classic); it was badly damaged in World War II, but has now been totally restored to its former splendor. Among the many formal rooms, cabinets, audience chambers and bedrooms in the enormous place, I find most interesting the gold and glitter of 'the Ancestors Gallery' with its portraits of all the Bavarian kings and related royalty; the lavishly frescoed 'Antiquarium' (Antiques Hall: entrance off the Grottenhof), one of the earliest museums; and the Elector's bedroom ('Paradeschlafzimmer'), with the traditional railing around the bed in gold and white. It will cost you 1.50 marks to visit the Schatzkammer, the same at the Residenzmuseum.

Städtische Galerie im Lenbachhaus

"Located at 33 Luisenstrasse, just off Königsplatz, and not far from the Alte Pinakothek, the **Municipal Gallery** is devoted to Munich artists, whose work is displayed in an imitation Italian Villa with a small garden in front. Though painters are represented from the 15th through the 20th centuries, the real impact of this gallery is felt from its more recent works. In fact, the main reason for a visit is to see the comprehensive collection of Vassily Kandinsky, whom some people call 'the father of Abstract Art.' The sheer number of Kandinsky's works amounts to an in-depth retrospective (it's the largest collection from his early period anywhere in the world), and it's fascinating to be able to trace the artist's development—from landscape painter to the abstraction of his 'Der Blaue Reiter' stage ('The Blue Rider' is the name of a group that Kandinsky started with Franz Marc). And in 'The Blue Rider' section of the museum, there's also on view works by intimate friends of Kandinsky's devoted mistress Gabriele Münter (including a study of Kandinsky by her); and some very interesting early Paul Klees, among others. The work of 'The Blue Rider' group slowly casts a spell over you, taking you into a world of mutual friends until you feel you know all of them almost as well as you'd know the characters in a good novel. Be sure to view the Kandinsky paintings upstairs at a distance, as well as close up—and you'll see how they change. (Kandinsky and 'friends' are now housed in a new wing, inaugurated in '72—the older part of the Villa contains the home, studio, work and collections of Germany's most famous 19th century portrait painter, Franz Lenbach.) The museum is open daily except Monday from 9 to 4:30, Tuesdays until 8 p.m., for a 1.50-mark entrance fee (students: 50 pfennigs), but is free on Sundays.

The Antikensammlungen and The Glyptothek

"**The Museum of Ancient Arts and Crafts** and **The Glyptothek** are both located directly across the street from The Lenbach Galerie on **Königsplatz**—a vast and startlingly impressive square designed à la Grec, and featuring imitation Greek temples facing each other across acres of white stone. All this was built in the first half of the 19th century by King Ludwig I to house his enormous and precious collection of ancient Greek and Roman works. Ludwig was a great patron of the arts, and a dedicated Munich builder, especially fond of the classical period; you'll spot numerous plazas, squares and buildings sponsored by him. The **Staatliche Antikensammlungen**, open Tuesdays through Sundays from 10 to 4:30 and Wednesday from noon to 8 p.m., focuses on small sculpture (Greek and Etruscan statuettes and bronze tripods); pottery, glassware, and jewelry (intricate gold and silver work, in the basement). But the museum's star attraction is Ludwig's collection of Greek vases (mainly from the 5th and 6th centuries B.C.), all in excellent condition, quite beautifully cleaned and restored: seeing them is like walking through an art gallery in which the 'paintings' are on vases, pitchers and serving dishes.

"**The Glyptothek**, which suffered extensive damage in World War II, is now completely (except for the original neo-classical interior decoration) and most tastefully restored in plain white brick, high ceilinged, 'Roman Bath' style. It's an impressive collection of Greek and Roman statuary, mosaics, busts and grave reliefs (Greek works to the left, Roman to the right), of which the outstanding pieces are the exquisite 'Barberini Faun' (Room II, to your left as you enter the museum), a Greek work from 220 B.C.; and the famous 'Warriors from the Temple of Aphaea at Aegina' (at the back of the museum, Rooms VII-IX), which are ancient sculptures (around 500 B.C.) that once decorated a pediment of the temple, depicting scenes from the Trojan War. You may also be quite smitten with a tiny Peloponnesian Zeus from 520 B.C. (Room I, in a lighted case), and by rooms full of Roman busts placed on almost eye-level stands—they give you the feeling you're walking through the Forum meeting Romans. The Glyptothek keeps the same hours as the Antikensammlungen, except that it stays open half an hour later, and on Thursday evenings from 7 to 9. A two-mark entrance fee (except on Sundays, when admission is free) will admit you to both museums.

The Bayerisches Nationalmuseum

"The **Bavarian National Museum**, at 3 Prinzregentenstrasse (a few steps down the street from the Haus der Kunst and also serviced by bus #53 and #55), has a vast and outstanding collection, emphasizing the historical and cultural development of Europe and Bavaria, from the Middle Ages through the 19th century. Here you'll see French ivories, Limoges enamels, church art, statuary, special craft exhibitions, armor, jewelry and costumes, textiles and tapestries, ceramics, furniture, stained glass, many other items, all gorgeously displayed. Outstanding are the famous Christmas Krippen (Nativity Scenes), and the Folk Art section—both in the basement, the Augsburg Weavers Room with its painted ceiling (room #9), the Passau Room with Gothic furniture (room #10), the recently-opened armory room, and the Late Gothic Church Art Room—a particular joy because the setting provides such a perfect background for what it contains (room #15). Admission to the museum is 2 marks (students and scholars free), free on Sundays and hours are from 9 to 4 (Saturday and Sundays 10 to 4), daily except Monday.

Münchner Stadtmuseum

"The title of the **Munich Municipal Museum,** at #1 St. Jakob's Platz (just two blocks from Marienplatz and the Rathaus; follow Rindermarkt, the street on which St. Peter's Church stands, into Oberanger, then look for an orange corner building with a tower and a red roof), would gull one into believing that here was a collection illustrating the history of Munich. Not altogether so—the Bavarian National Museum is older, larger, more important and more impressive historically—but, while there *are* some historical exhibitions to be found here, the general tone of the establishment is much like that of the Museum of Modern Art in New York: lively and sophisticated, human-sized and fun.

"The Museum is divided into several departments: Munich City Planning (including a recently-added model of Olympic City); a German Beer Brewing Museum; a Photo and Film Museum; Model Rooms and 'The Children's World' (2nd floor, these *are* historical displays—the rooms are designed to show how residents lived in Munich in the 17th, 18th and 19th centuries—and the 'Children's World' is filled with antique cribs, furniture, toys and games which kids love to see); Textiles and Costumes; a Puppet Theatre and Musical Instrument Collection. Outstanding, and not to be missed amongst all this 'fascination,' are the 'Morisco Dancers' and the Puppet Theatre Collection. The famous 'Moriska-Tänzer' (on the ground floor), fashioned in 1480 by Erasmus Grasser for the 'Dance-Hall' of the old Rathaus, are small (about two feet high) statuettes, all caught in motion, dancing, with bizarre, individualistic, unforgettable faces—ten of them, richly decorated in red and gold: they couldn't be more alive. The Puppet Theatre Collection is truly a marvel and the most comprehensive display of everything to do with puppets (not simply the dolls themselves but paper scenery, stages, etc.) that I've ever seen—it traces the history of puppetry from its beginnings and in all countries. And, irresistible—there's a good-sized theatre where you or the kids can try your hand at being puppeteers. Open every day except Monday from 9 to 4:30 for a 1.50-mark entrance fee; free on Sundays.

The Deutsches Museum

"An additional word on the important **Deutsches Museum,** already described by Arthur: it's fascinating and completely absorbing, but overwhelming, with nearly 16 kilometers of corridors, endless demonstrations and shows; you must be selective, gearing your visit to where your own interests lie. Among the major departments are Marine Navigation, Aeronautics, Mining (in which you walk through model mines), Land Transport (every kind of vehicle imaginable, including another one of King Ludwig II's ornate chariots), Chemistry, Physics, Musical Instruments and Salon (where demonstrators play precious key board instruments from the 16th, 17th and 18th centuries), 'Astronautics' (where one can trace the historical development of the rocket, and peruse all manner of space vehicles), and dozens of others. So that you can plan your day, you'll want to know that the major demonstrations are scheduled as follows:

Casting of Metals (ground floor), 10:30 and 2:30; High Voltage Plant (ground floor), 11, 2, and 4; Model Railway (ground floor), every hour on the hour, starting at 10; and Zeiss Planetarium (sixth floor), 10, noon, 2 and 4. Summing up in its own words, the museum seeks 'to present visually the historic development of scientific and technical knowledge . . . by the display of originals and reproductions of historic apparatus and machinery and by means of models and demonstrations.' Here is a highlight of your European museum-going.

And finally

"Want some more? Just off Marienplatz near the Rathaus is **St. Peter's Church** (known to Münchners as 'Alter Peter'), the oldest parish church in Munich, begun in 1050 and finished in 1294. Very few of the original trappings remain in the interior of the church, which is now gleaming white and gilt rococo; but the church possesses a grisly visit-worthy relic that rivals any Alfred Hitchcock creation: a thoroughly gilded and bejewelled whole skeleton of a martyr (Saint Munditia, patron saint of lonely women), with fake eyes stuck into the skull and gems where the teeth should be, and a jeweled coronet on its head of fake hair (in a case on your left, at the back of the church). . . .The **Theatinerkirche**, across the square from the Residence Theater on Odeon Platz, with its great white, ornate interior, is widely regarded as the most beautiful Baroque church in Munich. . . .The Old Residence Theatre, or **Cuvilliés Theatre,** around the corner from the Residence Museum, is named for the architect who was commissioned by Max II Joseph to design it in 1753. Cuvilliés, a dwarf, began his career at court at the age of 11 as a King's jester, then later became one of Munich's foremost architects—another of his rococo masterpieces is the Amalienburg at Nymphenburg Palace. The breathtakingly beautiful and ornate 'candy box' auditorium, done in gilt, white and red, can be seen daily between 2 and 5 (Sundays from 10 to 5) for 1 mark; and perhaps you'll also be one of the lucky few able to purchase a ticket to see an opera here. . . . Munich is a superb art gallery town. If you like this sort of thing, you'll want to proceed to a virtual colony of galleries at 60 Prinzregentenstrasse, where there is not only the city-operated **Museum in the Stuck Villa** (restored home of the painter-teacher Franz von Stuck, now hosting changing exhibitions daily except Monday from 10 to 5), two marks entrance, but also a virtual epidemic of small, private galleries with no entrance fee (they want you to buy their paintings), and showing some very 'now', very exciting work (from 'classic' modern to Pop). Watch particularly for the **Wolfgang Ketterer;** the **Galerie Van De Loo** (they're fond of Warhol and Lichtenstein here); and the **Gallery Christoph Dürr**—all usually open during regular business hours."

TOURS: You needn't, in Munich, take any of the three-hour, expensive variety. A perfectly adequate view of this medium-size city can be had on a 1¼-hour, non-stop city drive, costing 10 marks ($5.26). The city sightseeing buses that make these curtailed trips leave from the foot of Prielmayerstrasse (near the railroad station), right at the Hertie Department Store, at 10 and 2:30 p.m. Look for a parked bus marked "Müncher Fremdenrundfahrten." For more elaborate tours of Munich and vicinity, you'll be happy with the services of a jolly Bavarian named Hugo M. Weichlein—he has a goateed beard and moustache—whose office on the 5th floor of 7 Weinstrasse (phone 29-26-86) has always been especially kind to readers. Among his full-day offerings: a Bavarian Alps Tour (daily at 8:30 a.m.; 25 marks); one of Berchtesgaden (8 a.m.; 28 marks); another to the Bavarian Royal Castles (8:30 a.m.; 25 marks).

THE BLITZ BUS: No one should pass through Munich without using the opportunity to make a fast foray into the incredibly picturesque villages of the Bavarian Alps, which lie about 60 miles south of the city. There are scores of outstanding towns here—Mittenwald, Oberammergau, Oberstdorf, Berchtesgaden—but the city I'd pick for a first visit is Garmisch-Partenkirchen, site of the 1936 Winter Olympics, which lies just below the towering Zugspitz, Germany's highest mountain. As a G.I., I once was stationed for several months just twenty miles from Garmisch, and I can tell you it is magnificent. But another reason for traveling from Munich to Garmisch is the fabulous **"Blitz Bus"** of the Garmisch Casino, which takes you there and back for the extremely low price of 10 marks ($5.26).

The normal round-trip train fare from Munich to Garmisch is 21 marks. To cut this cost, and thereby attract visitors to its roulette wheels, the Garmisch Casino (one of the most sophisticated in Europe) recently decided to operate its own bus, at a reduced fare. The bus departs weekdays at 5:15 p.m., Saturdays and Sundays at 2 p.m., from a point at the right side of the Munich Railroad Station (as you face it), next to the Air Terminal (look for a sign marked "Bahnbuslinien", stop No. 11). Get to the station at around 5 p.m., wear only your best clothes (tie and jacket are required of men), and start looking for a bus marked **"Casino Garmisch"** (which is not to be confused with another bus marked "Casino Express" that drives on weekends to a lesser-known gambling den in the town of Bad Reichenhall.) The bus makes the trip to Garmisch Casino, nonstop, in exactly one hour and 25 minutes. The 10-mark ticket permits you to enter the Casino, right away. You can stroll around Garmisch for a couple of hours, although you must then eventually put in an appearance at the Casino to have your ticket stamped valid for the return trip (no one, however, twists your arm to spend anything at the Casino). The bus then returns to Munich, punctually at 10:55 p.m., and the return ride at night is an even quicker trip, bringing you to the center of Munich at half past midnight.

I think you'll like this fast evening-excursion to Garmisch. For the first hour of the ride, you'll pass through rolling countryside, of great beauty. But then, gradually, the land will become hillier, and suddenly, looming through the mist, you see—an Alp! And then another and another, until you're in one of the most breathtaking mountain areas of Europe.

MUNICH MISCELLANY: One of the key rules of budget travel is to eat what the locals eat. In Munich, it's readily apparent that the cheapest—and, at the same time, most expertly cooked—main courses are the popular local pork dishes—particularly those that come in the form of "wurst" (sausage). There are as many different varieties of sausage in Munich—weisswürste, bratwurst, Pfälzer fleischwurst, Griebenwurst, and so on and on—as there are cheeses or wines in Paris. . . . The student travel bureau of Munich is **Studentenreisen,** 47 Türkenstrasse (at the corner of Schellingstrasse, about 300 yards from the main building of the University), phone 28-77-77, open weekdays from 9 to 5:30, Saturdays from 9:30 to noon; they'll get you cheap intra-Europe flights, trains, buses and ships. . . . The spirit of Munich has been influenced not only by the French, but by that eccentric trio of 19th century Bavarian emperors: Ludwig I (of Lola Montez fame), Maximilian I, and the supposedly "mad" king Ludwig II—who was "mad" enough to have discovered Richard Wagner. At least one of Ludwig II's extravagant castles near Munich—some of them unabashed copies of Versailles (to a smaller scale)—should definitely be seen by you. They include **Schloss Linderhof** near Oberammergau, **Schloss Neuschwanstein** near Füssen, and **Schloss Herrenchiemsee** near Prien, all of which can easily be reached via a simple second-class train ride from Munich, on do-it-yourself excursions whose freedom and privacy make them infinitely preferable, in my view, to escorted group tours. Trains leave from the Starnberger Bahnhof, which is the little station attached to the right hand side of the main station (Hauptbahnhof) as you face it.... Berlin is 675 kilometers from Munich. Three trains leave Munich each day, at 7:44 a.m., 12:26 a.m and 10:28 p.m., arriving in Berlin at 4:49 p.m., 9:25 p.m. and 7:44 a.m., for a cost of 89.40 marks ($47.05), one-way, second class ... Picnic ingredients? What may be the finest delicatessen in all the world is **Alois Dallmayr's** world-renowned shop at 14 Dienerstrasse, near the City Hall. It's not entirely inexpensive, but its offerings are so exotic and attractive that you might wish simply to wander through, even if you don't end up buying a thing. Cheaper picnic ingredients are found in the basement of the **Kaufhof** department store, at the Marienplatz. ... Best beer in Munich is on draft; ask for it, therefore, "vom Fass".... A large, **self-service laundry,** with 10 machines, is open Monday through Saturday at 38 Lindwurmstrasse, next to Goetheplatz. Five marks for seven kilos, 50 pfennigs for drying. ... Rent-a-bike? Try **Fahrradvermietung Buss** at the corner of Königinstrasse and Veterinärstrasse, bordering the Englischer Garten ("English Gardens"). But phone first (470-46-59), as this is not always open when the weather is uncertain. Rental charge is 4 marks ($2.10) the first hour, 2 marks ($1.05) each additional hour, and you can pedal for at least 20 miles up the garten, along the Isar River, passing several of Munich's most popular beer gardens. Nearest subway stop: Universität. ... Arriving in Munich without hotel reservations during the Octoberfest period of 1980 (from September 20 to October 5), don't even attempt to find a bed at the addresses in this chapter. Rather, apply at the Tourist Information Office at Track #11 in the Central Railway Station, and throw yourself upon their mercy; they maintain an emergency room service for the difficult dates. ... More on beer: that cast-iron construction across from the delicatessen on the ground floor of the **Hofbräuhaus** (to your left after entering) is Germany's—and the world's—only beer stein safe—a "Bierkrugsafe". Some 200 Munchners keep their personal steins—the kind with a movable zinc top—locked in separate compartments here, and there is currently a waiting list for at least 50 more! ... In case you've been wondering, the current population of Munich is 1,300,000 persons—and growing fast.

PILGRIMAGE TO DACHAU: "An important side trip from Munich is a trip to the concentration camp and memorial at **Dachau.** Trains leave the Munich Hauptbahnhof approximately every twenty minutes for the town of Dachau, and a bus from the railroad station goes to the camp which is virtually untouched—a shocking reminder of recent history" (Ronald Kluger, Irvington, New Jersey). ... "The pilgrimage to **Dachau Concentration Camp,** about ten miles from Munich, is heartbreaking but a must; trains run every 20 minutes, a round-trip ticket costs only 5.00 marks, and from the Dachau railroad station one can go straight to the camp for 70 pfennigs on the bus marked "Dachau Ost" (Alan Schwartz, Detroit, Michigan). ... "Consider a possible sidetrip to **Dachau,** which you reach from Munich by first taking the train to Dachau (5.00 DM, round-trip) and then the Dachau Ost bus (70 pfennigs) which meets the train. The camp is the next to last stop. This is not a pleasant trip, but worthwhile if it causes the traveler to remember what actually happened in the past and to determine that it shall never happen again" (John M. Littlewood, Champaign, Illinois; note by A.F.: since the completion of the Munich subway, Dachau is most easily reached via S-Bahn (train S-2) to the Dachau station, and on bus L-3 from there to the camp. Do not confine your visit to the main museum building of Dachau, but walk from there to the far end of the grounds and the unspeakable "brausebad" and "krematorium," which should never leave the memories of any of us. The Dachau memorial site is open 9 a.m. to 5 p.m., entrance is free, and the English version of the documentary film ("K2 Dachau", 22 minutes) is shown daily at 11:30 a.m. and 3:30 p.m.).

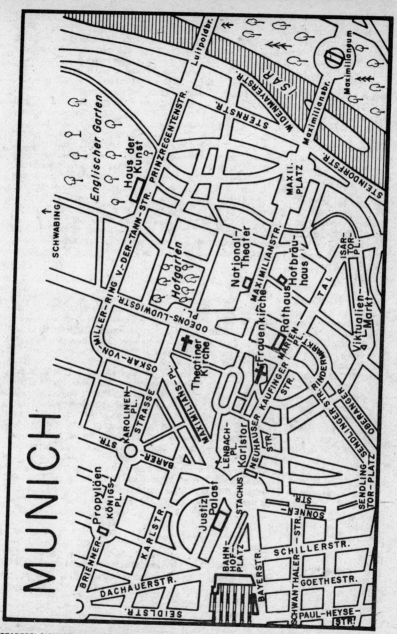

READERS' SIGHTSEEING SELECTIONS: "Please urge your readers to take a day to visit the fantastic, fairy-tale like castle of Neuschwanstein, in the Bavarian Alps near Füssen. It can be seen in a one-day tour from Munich, and it is an unforgettable sight perched on the summit of its own mountain with a mirror-like lake at its foot. Don't miss it" (Ronald A. Audet, Portsmouth, Virginia). . . . "A Saturday afternoon trip out of Munich to Prien by train, then boat to Chiemsee Island to Herrenchiemsee, a tour through the Castle, and then a 40 minute concert by candlelight (May to September only), is a must. Your Eurailpass takes you there and back. Tours by bus also go there. The concerts are at 7:30 and 8:30, Saturday evenings only. Be sure to start early in the afternoon as the last tour through the castle is at 4 p.m." (Lilly G. Doerre, St. Louis, Missouri). . . . "Visitors to Munich should be advised to visit the still-standing **Olympic Village**, which is easily reached by subway. You'll be amazed at the architecture. And remember that a Eurail-pass is good for the S-Bahn trip there" (Dave Shribman, Swampscott, Massachusetts). . . . "Your readers might well look into the schedules and offerings of **Gerhard Bennek,** Reiseburo-Omnibusbetrieb, Frauenstrasse 17 (phone 22-24-51), who operates extremely inexpensive bus trips on a fairly regular schedule to such cities as Salzburg, Innsbruck, Garmisch, etc. We took a round-trip tour to Salzburg on a Sunday in November for the total price of 8 marks per person. We travelled in a comfortable bus with local residents, and had a grand time" (Daniel H. Bonchek, Givataim, Israel). . . . "A fun and inexpensive day in Munich begins by taking Tram #7 to the northern end of the line. Spend the morning exploring the Olympic Village; then at about noon go to the BMW factory, sign up for the free tour (which is given in German, English, French or Italian as needed), and visit the museum until the tour begins. The BMW factory has the best and most thorough industrial tour we've ever seen and should not be missed by anyone who is even the least bit interested in cars, motorcycles and/or industrial tours in general" (Larry and Trudy Phelps, Jacksonville, Florida). . . . "Don't miss swimming in the **Olympic Schwimmhalle** at the Olympic site, open daily from 7 a.m. to 9 p.m. Admission, including free use of a locker, is 4 marks for adults, 2 marks for students" (Barry Bloom, Bronx, New York).

READERS' EXCURSIONS: "A very interesting trip north from Munich is the 53-mark **Europabus** ride over the so-called 'Romantische Strasse,' passing two fantastic towns—Dinkelsbühl and especially Rothenburg—whose beauty is something I still can't get over; eventually, the bus heads for Würzburg and Frankfurt" (John M. Littlewood, Champaign, Illinois; note by A.F.: The Europabus departure, "über die Romantische Strasse" —is at 9 a.m. from the right side of the Munich Railroad Station (as you face it), arriving Frankfurt at 8 p.m.). . . . "Holders of the Eurailpass should know of a way to approach Munich that is really fantastic. Although the fact is not often advertised, the Eurailpass entitles tourists to free tickets on the Europabus 'Romantic Road' route, operated from May through October. I took the trip from Frankfurt to Munich, a twelve-hour jaunt. The bus has an English speaking guide who pointed out all the sights as we passed them, and we were given a lengthy sightseeing stop in Rothenburg-ob-der-Tauber, a perfect gem of a walled medieval town which has not changed in hundreds of years. This trip is a marvelous way to get to see more of Germany than the large towns, and its ready availability to Eurailpass holders makes it a real find" (Ronald A. Audet, Portsmouth, Virginia). . . . "The normal price for a trip up the **Zugspitze,** Germany's highest mountain is 32 marks from Garmisch to the top and back down. The German Railroad offers special fares of 38 marks, however, from Munich to Garmisch, up the Zugspitze, and return to Munich. This makes the Munich-Garmisch trip cost only 6 marks ($3.15)" (Dr. L. K. Wynston, Long Beach, California).

And now it's time for Vienna. The Orient Express leaves Munich at 9:46 a.m., takes five hours and 35 minutes to traverse the breathtaking valleys and mountains of Central Austria, deposits an excited you, as the day begins to wane, in the famous City on the Danube.

Chapter XI

VIENNA

Strauss and Strudel

THIS IS A CITY of ever-present nostalgia. The trappings of the old Austro-Hungarian Empire are faded by now, and the great rococo buildings of Vienna are weatherworn and chipped. The city is no longer the powerhouse of Central Europe—and its charm has increased for that very reason. Having witnessed so much turbulence in their time, the Viennese are willing to chuck the ambition and concentrate on life. The mood all around is like an old Nelson Eddy film, gracious and slow, courtly and polite. It can be the relaxing mid-point of your European tour.

Your accommodations in Vienna can also be the very best of your trip, for the quality is high in the low-cost pensions. But care is still needed, and pitfalls exist. Here's how to live in Vienna on moderate costs:

ROOMS IN PRIVATE HOMES: The cheapest accommodations are the non-commercial ones. Provided only that your stay in Vienna is for three nights or more, you can obtain a room with a private family by simply contacting one of two extremely helpful organizations: either the Information Office of the **Wiener Verkehrsverein** in the "Opernpassage" (the underground passage and shopping center near the renowned State Opera House—the "Staatsoper"), where Frau Gerlinde, who speaks English very well, is the information clerk; or else the privately-owned **Österreichisches Verkehrsbüro** at 3 Opernring, opposite the Staatsoper (ask for Anneli Kienast on the first floor); the former has the advantage of staying open seven days a week from 8 a.m. to 8 p.m., while the Österreichisches Verkehrsbüro maintains normal office hours until 5:30 p.m. and is closed on Saturday afternoons and Sundays. Both organizations have copious listings of families accepting tourists in their homes at rates averaging 150 to 180 schillings ($11.11 to $13.33) for a single room, 190 to 270 schillings ($14.07 to $20) double, plus 35 schillings ($2.59) per person for a non-obligatory breakfast; and both will phone the home and make the booking for a charge of about $1.50. The homes themselves, I must admit, don't always provide an experience in "Meeting the Viennese" in the way that Scandinavian private accommodations often do; the rooms are usually in the apartment of a widow desiring additional income, and you come and go as you please but—ordinarily —with little personal contact. My advice is that you first seek to obtain accommodations in one of the excellent Viennese pensions described below, and only failing that should you pay a visit to the tongue-twisting organizations named above.

There are, however, several exceptions to that advice, and these consist of eight specific private homes ferreted out on my most recent stay in Vienna. On subsequent visits, we'll try to expand the list to at least twenty recommendations, for which these provide a start:

For $8.50 to $11 per person, without breakfast

Frau Renate Gajdos, at 28 Pressgasse (phone 577-416), centrally located near the Karlsplatz, rents five double rooms and one single in her large second-floor apartment for an average of 160 schillings ($11.85) per bed, which includes breakfast served on heavy oak tables with benches; her two daughters, 21 and 22 years old, are fluent in English, and the dog, a lassie named Dania, barks but does not bite. Supplement for a third bed in double rooms: 130 schillings. From the Westbahnhof, take the S-train to Kettenbrückengasse, and walk (three minutes) from there. From the Südbahnhof, take bus 13 or 61, which both stop almost in front of the door.

Herr und Frau Julius and Elisabeth Ziegler, both with an excellent command of English, occupy our most picturesque private home selection at 30 Villenweg (phone 322-361), on top of the Kahlenberg, which is the towering hill overlooking the Vienna Woods and Danube Valley. They rent five rooms in their 100-year-old villa with spectacular cast-iron staircase, for 160 schillings ($11.85) per person including a breakfast that comes with boiled egg and cheese. Rooms are spacious, window views are breathtaking, showers are free, and a single problem is location, an hour from downtown Vienna. Take the S-train to Nussdorferstrasse, then streetcar no. 38 to Grinzing, connecting with bus no. 38S to Kahlenberg, all for a total of 10 schillings. Better if you have a car.

Herr Bruno Elbel, at 62 Seutergasse (phone 826-8272), rents three rooms of his nice little house for 130 schillings ($9.62) per person, double or twin; 175 schillings single; but adds a 20% supplement if your stay is for less than three days. Showers are 15 schillings extra, but the small swimming pool, flanked by an apricot and peach tree, is free to guests. Herr Elbel is a retired police officer, and his hobby is staying in contact with colleagues all over the world; witness his living room wall covered with police emblems and sheriffs' stars from Texas to Australia! Take the S-train to Hütteldorf, and walk from there (you'll pass the Lainzer Tiergarten populated by deer and wild boars—free entrance); or else drive past Schönbrunn Castle to the Elbel home.

Herr Rupert and Frau Elfriede Koch, at 49 Steinböckengasse (phone 948-135), on the outskirts of Vienna near the West exit of the Salzburg Autobahn, are a blessing for travelling families: they rent five rooms, including two children's rooms, and a tiny, Scandinavian-style washroom (where showers are free) in bright colors and so clean you could eat from the floors. The price is

120 schillings ($8.88) per bed, 30 schillings extra for (an optional) breakfast served to your room in a basket, all plus a 20% surcharge if you stay for less than four nights. Quiet location, beautiful garden, inexpensive grocery next door, and Herr Koch is a taxi driver who will grant a 10% reduction if you use his services. His wife speaks English, Italian and Turkish. Take streetcar 52 or 49 to the final stop called Hütteldorf, from which the house is a 20-minute walk.

Herr Rudolf and Frau Valerie Pöchhacker, at 8 Sechskrügelgasse (phone 735-173), offer five unusually large rooms with parquet floors, most facing a quiet garden, for a rather high 140 schillings per person ($10.37), without breakfast, and charge 25 schillings for a bath. The address, however, is quite a central one, 15 minutes on foot from the Stephansplatz. Although very little English is spoken, there's enough to answer your basic questions.

Frau Marie Kossowski, at 6/14 Czerningasse (phone 26-43-94), near the Praterstern, rents a twin-bedded room for 185 schillings ($13.70), a triple for 270 schillings ($20), a 4-bedded room for 330 schillings ($24.44), breakfast extra, in a simple and plain, no frills apartment where only basic English is spoken. From the Südbahnhof take streetcar "O" to the Franzensbrücke stop; from the Westbahnhof, take streetcar "58" to the Ring, and change there to streetcar "BK" or "AK", descending at the Aspernbrücke stop.

Frau Theresia Tichy, at 7 Scheugasse (phone 64-22-02), is a kind, gray-haired lady who lives alone in a small house where she rents three of her rooms (2-5 beds in each) at 110 schillings ($8.26) per person, plus 33 schillings ($2.44) extra for an optional breakfast that includes boiled egg and homemade marmalade. Two of the rooms are communicating and ideal for families or a small group. Scheugasse is near the Südbahnhof; take the U-Bahn to Keplerplatz and walk around 5 minutes from there. As for Frau Theresia, she speaks very little English, but somehow understands you, and you will, with patience, understand her.

Frau Hilde Wolf, at 7 Schleifmühlgasse (phone 574-90-94), is an English-speaking lady who loves books, which are everywhere in sight, even in the rooms she rents: for 200 schillings ($14.81) single, 275 schillings ($20.37) double, a supplement of 80 schillings for a third and fourth bed. The double rooms are particularly spacious and crammed with fin-de-siecle furniture. Breakfast is 35 schillings ($2.59) more, and Frau Wolf assures me that readers of this book can have second (and more) helpings of coffee, bread, butter and marmalade at no additional charge. Schleifmühlgasse is a typical, old-Vienna street, near the central Karlsplatz and the Naschmarkt, the popular market area. From the Westbahnhof, take streetcar E2 or G2 or H2 to Naschmarkt; from the Südbahnhof take the "O" streetcar to Südtirolerplatz and change there to the U-Bahn going to the Taubstummenstrasse stop.

HOTELS AND PENSIONS: Apart from apartments and homes, budget-priced lodgings of a non-private nature are available in substantial quantities here. They are, however, scattered—not clustered—over large areas of the city. In one neighborhood, you may find a rock-bottom hotel standing side-by-side with a moderately-priced one, which is itself across the street from a relatively expensive hotel; it's hard, in other words, to find a single block or area in which the budget establishments are lined in a row.

Therefore, in order to give some geographical unity to our discussion, we've had to mix together establishments of differing cost—dealing, in one area, both with hotels that charge $17 and $19 a night for a bathless double, without breakfast, and with those that charge as much as $27, double, without breakfast, as well. It's important, as a result, not simply to assume that the following establishments are all uniformly-priced, but to examine carefully the specific 1980 rates that I'll quote for each one. We have, however, divided our recommendations to deal separately with pensions and hotels:

The Viennese Pensions

These provide your most consistently-reliable, consistently-inexpensive rooms. In the many years spent researching this book, I have never found a slovenly Viennese pension, or received more than a scattered complaint about any of them.

Off the Graben

The best-located of the Viennese pensions (and with slightly higher quality than our other selections) are the **Pension Nossek,** at Graben 17 (phone 52-45-91), and the **Pension Aclon,** at 6 Dorotheergasse, phone 52-54-73 (just off the Graben), both in that quite lovely area to the side of St. Stephen's Cathedral, in the very center of the inner city. The **Nossek** is the more elegant of the two, yet less expensive: its double rooms, most of which rent for 360 schillings without bath to 575 schillings with bath ($26.66 to $42.59) (breakfast and all service charges and taxes included), are outside our range, but it's an unusually refined establishment that occupies the 2nd, 3rd and 4th floors of an elevator building, and is superbly managed by Hans and Hilde Rakowitz, both of them graduates of the Austrian Hotel College. The **Aclon** is nearly as nice as the Nossek, but charges a uniform 250 schillings ($18.51) for singles, 415 schillings ($30.74) for doubles (with breakfast again included). Location of the latter is only a few feet from the Nossek, on a slightly noisier block; to find it, turn off at Graben 10 into Dorotheergasse, a small alleyway of a street.

A nearly-budget-priced choice in this area, is the **Pension Pertschy,** at 5 Habsburgergasse (phone 52-38-67), just a few steps off the Graben, 4 tiny blocks from the Stephansplatz, and more precisely located on the first, second, and third floors (there is an elevator) of an ancient "palais" built in 1725 and now an official historical landmark. The ceilings are high and vaulted, the floors a rich warm wood, and to get from room to room, you walk along an enclosed catwalk on a balcony that traces around the courtyard; the Pertschys themselves are a nice young couple with two sweet girls (and a boy), who encourage families to come, and understand the problems of traveling parents. Mr. Pertschy lived in Canada for 10 years and all the family speak perfect English. How much for all these features? 380 schillings ($28.14) for a double room, breakfast, service and taxes included, which is almost as low a price as Vienna goes nowadays for such pleasant accommodations; 220 schillings ($16.29) for singles, 430 schillings ($31.85) triples, 540 schillings ($40) for four in a room—again, with breakfast, service and taxes included. All rooms are recently redecorated and 60% of them come with private shower or bath for 420 to 460 schillings double. Central heating in winter; highly recommended.

A capsule summary of the geography of these pensions: walking down the Graben toward St. Stephen's Cathedral, the streets running off the Graben on the right are in this order: Habsburger (Pension Pertschy), Bräunerstrasse, Dorotheergasse (Pension Aclon), Spiegelgasse, Seilergasse, and you are at Stephansplatz. The Pertschy and Aclon are just steps off the Graben, while the Nossek is right on it.

Also in the Inner City

The small, six-room **Stadtpension,** Annagasse 3a (phone 52-49-04), is another one beautifully situated off the Kärntnerstrasse, halfway between the Opera House and St. Stephen's. Here the rooms are large, simple, homey and clean and some are big enough to accommodate three or four beds. Frau Hoffman, a perky woman with a good command of English, keeps the pension running and the attention personal. Singles are 270 to 300 schillings ($20 to $22.22), doubles 370 to 420 schillings ($27.40 to $31.11), triples 530 to 680 schillings ($39.25 to $50.37), breakfast, service and taxes included; and the pension is on the first floor of an elderly apartment building—walk in, walk up the first long flight of stone steps, turn right, and there you are.

In the Alserstrasse area

A street in Vienna that is packed with pensions (but in differing price ranges) is Alserstrasse (8), which passes next to the University of Vienna; the lowest-priced of the establishments here is the **Pension Vera,** Alserstrasse 18 (phone 43-25-95), where you'll be charmed by the warmth of your reception and the old-fashioned rate for your room—190 schillings ($14.07) single, 330 schillings ($24.44) double, breakfast and service included (and though it's a fairly basic, but friendly, place, it's recommended for travellers of all ages). Prices and quality ascend sharply, however, in the other pensions on the street, until they reach a budget limit at the **Pension Zenz,** Alserstrasse 21 (phone 42-52-68), which is a top find—the best, but one of the more expensive, of Vienna's low-cost pensions. During the summer of 1980, a double room at the Zenz, with two breakfasts, a private shower, all taxes and service, will cost 415 Austrian schillings—$30.74. Eliminate the shower, and the price is 380 schillings—$28.14. A single, again with shower, breakfast and taxes, will be 240 schillings ($17.77). The clientele? Well, the medical profession won't appreciate my giving away the name of this one; it's a favored stopping-place for American M.D.'s attending lectures at the famous Vienna University Hospital (where Freud once worked), across the street. They receive wonderfully big and spotless rooms, furnished with heavy wood pieces, well-oiled and cared for. . . . If the Zenz can't take you, try the nearby **Pension Astra** at 32 Alserstrasse (phone 42-43-54), with its cheaper rates of 200 schillings single, 290 schillings double, 30 schillings for an optional breakfast; and don't form the impression, upon entering, that you've wandered into a railroad station or museum hall—this is how some houses in Vienna were designed a hundred or more years ago! Upstairs the rooms are quiet and clean, the proprietress—Frau Maria Palfrader —extremely cordial. Phone first for vacancies.

Just 2½ blocks off Alserstrasse, the **Pension Columbia,** at Kochgasse 9 (phone 42-67-57), is another establishment back in the lower-priced category of the Pension Vera: 160 schillings ($11.85) per person, breakfast, service and taxes included, in triple rooms; 180 schillings ($13.33) per person in a double. Plenty of hot water, and a pleasant, English-speaking host (Mr. Naschenweng) who gets very concerned lest his guests fail to see all that's worth seeing in his beloved Vienna. Possibly more comfortable than the Vera, if not as well located.

And finally, a newcomer to this book is the 84-bed **Hotel Thüringerhof,** 6 Jörgerstrasse (phone 42-81-98), where English-speaking owner Herr Rolf Wilhelm charges 160 to 210 schillings ($11.85 to $15.55) single, 310 schillings ($22.96) double, including free showers and continental breakfast plus an egg or sausage. To find the Thüringerhof, walk to the end of Lazarettstrasse and cross the Währinger Gürtel.

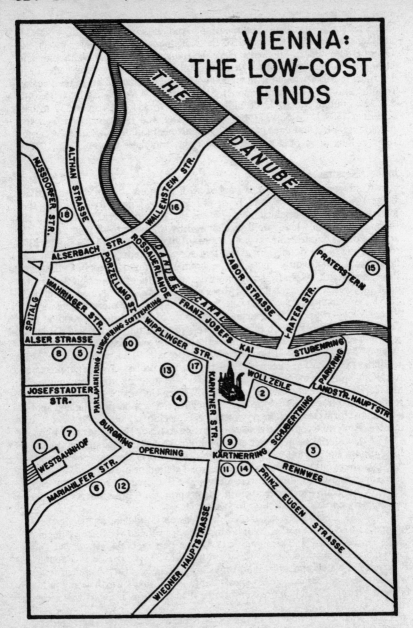

Near the Town Hall and University

Comparatively central (bus #8, tram #43 or #5 from the Westbahnhof), and within walking distance of the Ring and the Rathaus, is the **Pension Edelweiss**, 61 Lange Gasse (phone 42-23-06), whose 13 rooms are all rather spacious, airy, high-ceilinged, and therefore quite pleasant. Rates include breakfast, service and tax, and, for 1980, are 190 to 230 schillings ($14.07 to $17.03) single, 360 to 400 schillings ($26.66 to $29.62) double, 420 to 520 schillings ($31.11 to $38.51) triple. Mrs. Weidmaier, the manageress, speaks excellent English. From the Westbahnhof, take streetcar #5.

Close by at 49 Lange Gasse, the **Pension Zipser** (phone 42-02-28) is a really superb choice, with 52 rooms, many of which overlook lovely gardens and even have balconies for making the most of the view. Large clean rooms, all with double doors for extra quiet, go for 185 to 210 schillings ($13.70 to $15.55) single, 350 to 420 schillings ($25.92 to $31.11) double, and 460 to 540 schillings ($34.07 to $40) triple, with breakfast, service and taxes included.

Alternatively, and on the same block, the newly furnished **Pension Rathaus,** 13 Lange Gasse (phone 43-43-02), offers extra large rooms but splurgy rates: 250 schillings ($18.51) single; 500 schillings ($37.03) double, including breakfast and free showers.

The **Pension Amon,** Daungasse 1 (phone 42-01-94), is also located near the university (take streetcar H2 from the opera) and is a 12-room pension which takes on personality from its English-speaking owner, Mr. Amon, who hunts for a hobby and decorates the hallways and lounge with the trophies. The rooms are comfortable, if old-fashioned, and Mr. Amon is a willing dispenser of tips on where to go and what to see in town. Singles cost 225 schillings ($16.66), doubles are priced at 340 schillings ($25.18), triples at 440 schillings ($32.59), with breakfast, service and taxes included.

On and off the Mariahilferstrasse

Now we're in the area of the Mariahilferstrasse, one of the two main shopping streets of the city (the other being the more elegant Kärntnerstrasse). And here, for parties of three traveling together, or for families (the owners of the pension about to be named act as baby sitters), the **Pension Carina,** at 134 Mariahilferstrasse (phone 82-49-554), is an exciting find, whose location is at the end of Mariahilferstrasse closest to the "Ring"—in other words, in an excellent spot. It charges 220 schillings ($16.29) for a single room, 340 schillings ($25.18) for a double, 465 schillings ($34.44) for a triple room, exactly 530 schillings ($39.25) for a room with four beds, all taxes and service charges included; less off-season. Breakfast is an extra 35 schillings ($2.59). All rooms are furnished in modern style, with plug contacts for electric razors; the street here is quiet; and finally, there's that baby-sitting service, plus all the extra-large rooms; a high recommendation.

Just a short walk away, the tiny 30-bed **Pension Reimer,** 18 Kirchengasse (phone 93-61-62), is a somewhat more basic spot, and its proprietress, Margarete Mattis, speaks only a smattering of English. But her price for a single (service included) is this time only 160 schillings ($11.85), for a double 260 schillings ($19.25), for a triple only 420 schillings ($31.11), and four beds in a room go for 480 schillings ($35.55). Breakfast is an extra 30 schillings. Rooms are large, clean, with modern furniture, neat but sparsely decorated; there's a comfortable television lounge for the use of guests (and the owners' tykes), and the entire establishment is a homey, pleasant place, if a bit plain. Try it.

Near the Südbahnhof

A fine pension (one of our stars, in fact), and within walking distance of the Südbahnhof, the **Pension Esperanto,** 53 Argentinierstrasse (phone 65-13-

04), rents eleven pin-neat rooms with country-style iron bedsteads and gleaming wood floors. Frau Hildegard Hahn, who requires that you stay for a minimum of three days, is the efficient owner; English is well-spoken; and singles are priced at 160 schillings ($11.85), doubles at 260 schillings ($19.25), service and taxes included; while breakfast is an extra 35 schillings ($2.59). Take tram D or 66/67 from the Opera House or tram #18 from the Westbahnhof.

Vienna's Budget Hotels

Now we move to the larger ones. We'll deal first with the "B" class hotels (doubles without breakfast for $27 to $31), then with the "C" class establishments whose charge for a double is usually $17 to $24 and under.

The "B" class (second class) hotels

To start with a big, big splurge, the **Hotel Austria (2)**, in the very center of town at Wolfengasse 3 (phone 52-62-21), near St. Stephen's Cathedral, is among my favorite Viennese hotels, even though its minimum prices for bathless rooms with breakfast, service and taxes included (325 schillings-$24.07-single, 505 schillings-$37.40-double), are considerably higher than I usually like. But for several years now, manager Herr Walter Koschier has offered to grant a 12% discount to anyone producing this book, and so far as I know, he's kept to his pledge (the book, however, *must* be shown on arrival and not suddenly produced upon check-out—that's a tax technicality). You will, I think, be well-pleased with this hotel: the staff spares no effort to be helpful (tickets to the Opera, tours), and there's no hanky-panky with the prices when the final bill is prepared. To reach the hotel from the Westbahnhof, take the "stadtbahn" (subway) to Schwedenplatz or Fleischmarkt; from the Südbahnhof, take tram D to the Ring, then change to tram A or B going to Schwedenplatz. And then walk to Wolfengasse, which is a tiny lane off the "Fleischmarkt"—Vienna's meat market in medieval times. Arriving by cab, your best bet is to ask not for Wolfengasse, but for "Fleischmarkt 20"—that being the corner building from where one turns into the tiny lane. . . . A final word about the discount offered at the Hotel Austria; it's available only to readers who have not booked their rooms through travel agents (including the information people at the railroad stations), to whom the hotel would have to give still a second discount.

In a far cheaper range, the **Hotel Kongress**, at 34B Wiedener Gürtel (phone 65-91-65), directly across from the Südbahnhof (South Railway Station), is rather a plain hotel, with old-fashioned furnishings and non-descript decor, but with elevator, clean linoleum floors, a friendly and English speaking staff, and neat, comfortable rooms. Rates are 215 schillings ($15.92) for bathless singles, 370 schillings ($27.40) for bathless doubles, plus 30 schillings ($2.22) per person for breakfast. And all rooms have hot and cold running water. Recommended.

A special splurge that is far better located, in the heart of the inner city, is the superb **Hotel Graben**, at Dorotheergasse 3 (phone 52-15-31; it is enthusiastically recommended by me), on a narrow little side street only 20 yards from the lovely Graben, which itself runs off from St. Stephen's Cathedral. From 510 to 660 schillings ($37.77 to $48.89), for a bathless double, breakfast, service and taxes included, for which you receive comfortable rooms, attended by people who bow from the waist in old-world Viennese style. Franz Kafka was once a guest of the Graben!

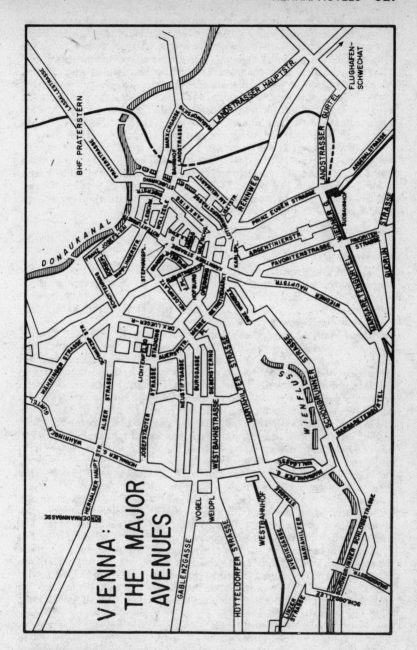

VIENNA: THE MAJOR AVENUES

Near the Westbahnhof

All of the above choices, as you've seen, are scattered around town. About the only "cluster" of budget hotels in Vienna is found in the area of the

Westbahnhof (West Railroad Station), where you may very well arrive. These include, first, the handy and handsome **Hotel Mariahilf (6)**, at Mariahilferstrasse 121B (phone 57-36-05), which is within walking distance of all the downtown activities, and where you won't be disappointed—as many bigsplurge-type readers have confirmed (it's not to be confused with the tiny Pension Mariahilf, at Mariahilferstrasse 49). Price per person for bathless double rooms is exactly 240 schillings ($17.77), breakfast, service and taxes included, 250 schillings for singles, all included. There are 30 such bathless singles, which means good hunting for the lone traveler. . . . But if you'd like to stay even closer to the Westbahnhof, and spend less money as well, then try the newly refurbished **Hotel Westbahn,** 1 Pelzgasse (phone 92-14-80), directly across from the station, where doubles are 450 schillings ($33.33), two generous breakfasts, service and taxes included; or the recently renovated **Hotel Fuchs,** at Mariahilferstrasse 138, phone 83-12-01 (exit from the Westbahnhof down the steps to the right; the hotel is a short walk from the station), where bathless doubles go for 460 schillings ($34.07), including breakfast.

"C" class hotels

Thus far, we've dealt primarily with "B-class" hotels in Vienna—the "B" designation being the Austrian equivalent of the "2nd Class" category used in other countries of Europe. The best of the "C" class hotels—with bathless double rooms averaging $17 and $19 a night (though some run higher, some lower)—are the following:

Hotel Wolf, 10 Strozzigasse (phone 42-23-20), in the Josefstadt district, a charming, quiet area of the city within 10 minutes' walking distance of the Ring. A small hotel, 2 floors only, with no elevator, but where the furnishings are modern, rooms are spotless, floors are linoleum, decorations are neat and simple, and English is perfectly spoken by the friendly, helpful manager who goes out of his way to give budget travelers tips on cheap restaurants nearby. All 53 rooms, single, double and triple, are priced from 135 to 220 ($10 to $16.29) per person (depending on the size and location of the room), breakfast, service, taxes and free use of the showers, included. From the south station, take bus No. 13; from the air terminal tram J; from the west station, take tram No. 8 and change to No. 46 downtown.

The **Goldenes Einhorn,** Am Hundsturm 5 (phone 55-47-55): Another personality place, packed with Old Vienna atmosphere. It's a tiny, two-story, 28-room hotel in a little old-fashioned building with white stucco walls and arched hallways, potted plants in alcoves, and the usual cat-walk-style, enclosed balcony overlooking a courtyard and hung with plants and vines. The Viennese lady who tends the hotel speaks English, and is delightfully cordial and courtly in her manners. Rooms are spotless, pleasantly filled with the usual mixture of modern and antique furnishings, and rates are: 140 to 210 schillings ($10.37 to $15.55) for singles, 235 to 365 for doubles ($17.40 to $27.03), service and taxes included. The top-priced double comes with a bath, the majority are share-bath; the hotel is located in a quiet residential area, about a ten minute tram ride from the Opera House.

Hotel Neubau, 141 Neustiftgasse (phone 93-47-35), not far from the Westbahnhof, also offers good value. A small, 32-room hotel, its hallways are drab and unappealing but rooms are surprisingly well fitted-out, scrubbed up and attractively priced. Singles range from 180 to 200 schillings ($13.33 to $14.81), doubles from 250 to 340 schillings ($18.51 to $25.18), triples from 280 to 410 schillings ($20.74 to $30.37), including service and tax but not breakfast, which costs an extra 40 schillings per person. Rates differ according to size and situation of room; those which cost most are equipped with private showers.

Two "park hotels" charging $14.80 to $18.50 double, including breakfast

Two very special selections offer good value and reasonable rates, but both are located in the outskirts (although within city limits).

Haus Starkfried, at 15 Starkfriedgasse (phone 47-15-28), is a non-profit, 150-bed, student-style hotel, recently built in a beautiful park area containing swimming pool, tennis courts (racket rental: 20 schillings per hour), many rare trees, a chapel and mosque. It rents single rooms for 150 schillings ($11.11), small twins for 200 schillings ($14.81), large doubles for 270 schillings ($20), and triples for 300 schillings ($22.22), with optional breakfast for 28 schillings ($2.07). From central Vienna, take streetcar 41 to Pötzleinsdorf (last stop, a 20-minute trip) and then walk five minutes to this comfortable choice.

Europahaus, at 429 Linzerstrasse (phone 94-32-51), is one of several structures making up the Miller-Aichholz Castle, built in 1750 by the famous architect Fischer von Erlach, whose better-known masterpiece is Schönbrunn Palace. Originally owned by industrialists who supplied Empress Maria Theresia's army with uniforms and such, it changed hands several times, became French occupation army headquarters in 1945, and was then ceded to the Austrian government which used it as a conference center for political studies. Today, it is an all-year-around hotel offering singles for 180 schillings ($13.33), doubles for only 250 schillings ($18.51), breakfast included, and the bonus of a large, modern public swimming pool about 100 yards away. From the Ring, board streetcar 49, and 35 minutes later get off at the last stop called Hütteldorf.

A modern budget hotel

So far, we've quoted rates only for bathless rooms; the city's largest array of moderately-priced rooms *with* private shower is found at the gigantic (900 beds) modern student residence known as **Haus Döbling,** 85 Gymnasiumstrasse (phone 34-45-45), which is operated for tourists of all ages from July 4 to September 27 at a rate of 250 schillings ($18.51) single, 400 schillings ($29.62) double, breakfast included. Döbling is well stocked with English-speaking personnel, operates a budget restaurant where two-course meals cost 80 schillings, and can be reached from the Westbahnhof for 10 schillings by first taking the S-Bahn to Nussdorf and then streetcar no. 38 for two stops.

Summertime splurges

Finally, you'll always find rooms, but fairly extravagant ones, at two other of the city's most modern student residence halls, which are opened to tourists in July, August and September; the **Haus Ober-Österreich,** at Hermanngasse 2a (phone 93-22-85), close to the Westbahnhof (take trams #52 and 58 from the Ring), is the most central. It has 160 rooms, all with identical furnishings: long desks, narrow beds, linoleum floors, wash basins with hot and cold water. Some rooms have small balconies; hallways sport large community shower rooms; each floor has a brightly-accented sitting-room; and the staff is composed of students who operate the hotel with an almost touching earnestness. Rates? Well, of the 160 rooms, a full 104 are singles priced at 200 schillings

($14.81), while doubles are 340 schillings ($25.18), with breakfast, service and taxes included.

Even better in quality, but situated in a city suburb, is the **Haus Dr. Schärf**, 1 Lorenz-Müllergasse (phone 338-171), which has 104 single rooms, 56 double rooms, all ultramodern and equipped with private showers. In 1980, it will accept tourists only from July 1 to September 30. Here, the rooms are as impersonal and efficient as those at any good-class hotel, but prices are a bit lower and a student staff sets the tone for a high-spirited atmosphere. Singles cost 180 schillings ($13.33), doubles are priced at 320 schillings ($23.70), breakfast, service and taxes included. Take the Stadtbahn to Heiligenstadt (fare 10 schillings) or, if you're traveling in a group, take a cab from the city center for 70 to 80 schillings.

ROOMS FOR THE STARVATION BUDGET: Some of the cheapest, but most atmospheric, accommodations in Vienna, are offered at the **Hostel Ruthensteiner,** at 24 Robert-Hamerling-Gasse (phone 83-46-93 or 83-08-265), about a ten minutes' walk from the Westbahnhof; this one is run by a charming young couple, Erin and Walter Ruthensteiner, and since Erin is an American girl from Pittsburgh, you know the management will understand you! There are four dorms (two with four beds and two with 12 beds), in which beds rent for an amazing 70 schillings ($5.18) per night, while accommodations in either single, two-bedded or three-bedded rooms cost 100 schillings ($7.40) per person per night. No age limit, no curfew. To top it all, you can grill your own sausages, steaks or whatever, on a self-service charcoal grill in the courtyard—which, incidentally, is big enough for a garden party of up to 20 people. You can, of course, save money by cooking your own, and the only expense is a five schilling contribution for the charcoal. Latest (early 1980) addition to the remarkable Ruthensteiner is a micro-snackbar next to the ground-floor reception desk, where you are served, through a tiny window not much larger than this book: coffee for 6 schillings (44¢), rolls for 12 cents, and portions of butter and marmalade for 23 cents each. Showers are free.

THE AUSTRIAN SCHILLING: In this chapter on Vienna, we've assumed the exchange rate of the Austrian schilling to be approximately 13.50 to the dollar, thus making each shilling worth approximately 7.4 U.S.¢.

A hostel for Eastern Europeans

Continuing in the more exotic vein, you might next want to consider the 70-schilling-per person ($5.18) beds at the **Pension Maria Wild**, 10 Lange Gasse (phone 43-51-74), on the third and fourth floors of an old apartment building. Herr and Frau Wild are in charge; their daughter speaks English. This is a private, pension-style hostel with about 40 beds, in triple and four-bedded rooms—all very simple and without frills, but clean and with all the necessary amenities, including hot and cold running water in each room, free use of the kitchen and showers. The most interesting thing about the Wild is that it caters to tourists from the Eastern European countries—Hungarians, in particular—which should intrigue our more politically-minded younger readers (and I would recommend the Wild to young, low-budget travelers).

Vienna's youth hostel

The official hostel, open all year, is the **Jugendgästehaus Hütteldorf** at 8 Schlossberggasse (phone 82-15-01), a five-minute walk from the last station of the stadtbahn (subway), called Hütteldorf-Hacking. Its rates are a refreshing 65 schillings ($4.81) the first night, 50 schillings ($3.70) for all subsequent nights, 27 schillings ($2) for an obligatory breakfast, about 40 schillings for lunch and dinner. If you're over the age of 25, you'll be asked to present a youth hostel card.

The low-budget hotels

Extra-cheap hotel rooms? **Zum Auge Gottes,** 75 Nussdorferstrasse (open only from July 1 to September 30), phone 34-25-85, charges 120 schillings ($8.88) per person per night, but without breakfast. And if you're a student, don't forget the astonishing rates of the **Student Home of the University of Vienna** (Studentenheim des Asylvereines der Wiener Universität), open July 1 to September 27 at 30 Porzellangasse (phone 34-72-82); 85 schillings ($6.29) per person per night. It's reached via the "D" tram (Sundays via the #36 tram).

READERS' PENSION SELECTIONS: "Breakfast in bed, free shower, a good clean room, are available at 225 schillings ($16.66) for two, cheaper for three or four, at **Pension Quisisana,** 6 Windmühlgasse, phone 573-341" (Paul Kirios and Nick Pierias, Hamilton, Ontario). . . . "For 320 schillings ($23.70) a day, we stayed at the **Pension Lindenhof,** 4 Lindengasse, tel. 93-73-62, in a huge double room with a good breakfast (served in the room); baths extra. The owner, Mr. Kurt Pavlczynski, speaks English and is always ready to help or provide information on Vienna. His pension occupies the third floor of an old building a block off Mariahilferstrasse" (Valentin Gomez, Buenos Aires, Argentina; note from AF: In 1980, the Lindenhof will rent single rooms for 200 schillings ($14.81), doubles for 320 schillings ($23.70), multibedded rooms (3 to 5 beds) for 160 schillings ($11.85) per person, always with breakfast included; shower or bath 25 schillings extra. Location is behind the large Herzmansky department store at Mariahilferstrasse). . . . "**Pension Haus Vindobona,** at 36 Laudongasse, phone 42-15-16, a block from the Alserstrasse, is a summer-hotel open July to September, which turned out to be one of the best bargains I found. My room included sink, shower and was quite clean; breakfast was served downstairs. Price for the single 175 schillings ($12.96). From the Westbahnhof, take tram No. 5 right to the door. It's a 10-minute ride" (Bennet D. Alsher, Atlanta, Georgia) . . . "**Pension Am Operneck,** 47 Kärntnerstrasse, offers an excellent location diagonally across from the Opera House and on one of Vienna's most popular shopping streets. An immaculate, high-ceilinged, bathless single, with a large double bed, cost about $11.50 a night, breakfast included" (Chris Buba, Secane, Pennsylvania; George Schaefer, Forest Hills, New York; John K. Ries, Brooklyn, New York).

PRIVATE HOMES THAT READERS HAVE LIKED: "As you leave Vienna, driving east, you pass the Prater amusement park, and then cross the Danube on the new bridge ("Reichsbrücke"). The street you are on as you come off the bridge is called the 'Wagramerstrasse,' and at #18, on your right, is a Gasthaus run by **Frau Elisabeth Werner** (tel. 23-57-12), which is so new and comfortable that it is graded Class 'A.' This is a private home with a modern annex built in the back. The rooms are comfortable, and pine-paneled throughout, and there is off-the-street parking, in a locked parking lot. Frau Werner's price is 110 schillings ($8.14) without shower, 150 schillings with shower, per bed per night, for a stay of 3 nights or more. If you stay less than 3 nights, there is an extra charge of 25% per bed per night. It was a very pleasant stay" (Mr. and Mrs. Murray Rubin, APO, N.Y.; strong second from Elizabeth Dickinson, Palm Springs, California, and from Doris R. Lawrenz, Skokie, Illinois). . . . "We found a warm welcome at the home of the **Karl**

Schurz family at Hungereckstrasse 36 (phone 67-13-733), Inzersdorf, Vienna, which is in the suburbs on the highway leading in from Italy, through Tarvisio and Velden. We had *two rooms* for $20 total. Breakfast was 80¢ extra per person for delicious rolls (plenty of them), butter, jam, coffee and milk. Frau Schurz washed our clothes, did our ironing (a small fee), and babysat while we went to the opera (no charge). Fine people. We had privacy, comfortable rooms, and plenty of hot water" (Raymond T. Lahar, Pomona, California; note by AF: Herr Schurz disposes of 2 double rooms (90 schillings ($6.66) per person) and 2 triples (85 schillings per person). . . . "For 150 schillings ($11.11) I had bed and breakfast (enormous) and stayed with the nicest family in the world, **Mr. and Mrs. Walter Lorenz.** They live at Schwarzenbergplatz 10, Wien IV. Telephone 62-12-814. The family has room for about 3 people. I was treated as a member of the family and utterly spoiled" (Joanna Fisher, Khandallah, Wellington, New Zealand). . . . "One of our most pleasant stays while in Austria was that spent in the home of **Herr and Frau Stadler,** Dobrowsky-Gasse 9 (off Triesterstrasse 255, one of the main roads leading into the city once you leave the Autobahn coming from Graz), phone 675-282. This is a quiet suburb and only a short bus ride from the center. Their son, Robert, speaks excellent English and was a big help in acquainting us with the city. The Stadlers offer one single room, 160 schillings ($11.85); five doubles, 260 schillings ($19.25); and one triple, 360 schillings ($26.66); central heating and hot water. Breakfast, included in the price, consists of fresh rolls, butter, jam, coffee, tea, milk, or hot cocoa, and is served in a pleasant room overlooking the garden" (Nicholas Evangelos, North Andover, Massachusetts). . . . "Our best find so far is in Vienna and was obtained because the Karl Schurz family had a full house and referred us to the **Hoffinger family,** located about a mile closer to the city than the Schurz place. The Hoffingers, a very nice young couple who speak good English, have a brand new building with six rooms, located at Dessoffgasse #7, about 8 short blocks west of the Trieste Road and a 10-minute drive from the Opernring. The rooms are quite lovely and very well furnished with plenty of hot water, towels, etc. The room charge is 130 schillings per person and breakfast, if wanted, is 25 schillings per person extra. The breakfast, too, is delicious, as Mrs. Hoffinger provides all kinds of home-made cakes, biscuits, jams, etc., and all served in a very nice little dining room. Their telephone number is 67-31-30 or 67-14-734, and anyone having trouble finding the house can ring them up and they will drive to wherever necessary to collect their guests. They are very kind and helpful people. For example, they provided me with hose, sponges, etc., with which to wash the car. Altogether it was one of the nicest places we have ever found and I can heartily recommend it to everyone. There are shops and a good laundromat nearby" (W. W. Nourse, Milford-on-Sea, Hants, U.K.). . . . "Especially can we recommend **Frau Maria Uhlik,** at 32 Rechtebahngasse (phone 73-20-923), near the Hilton Hotel. Frau Uhlik is a Viennese widow who rents out rooms for as little as 215 schillings ($15.92) double, including free showers and use of her kitchen. Although she does not speak English, there were other people staying with her who spoke no German and did not find this a deterrent. She is so good-natured, generous and accommodating that we felt our stay in Vienna was much heightened just by knowing her" (Mrs. Anne Stern, London, England). . . . "We arrived in the middle of the Festival, and were placed in the apartment of **Frau Balaban** at 1 Jacquingasse, Wien III (tel. 72-30-054 or 73-75-323), where for 200 schillings—$14.81—per couple, my parents, husband, and I had 2 adjoining bedrooms and an adjoining kitchen and bathroom. Baths were extra. Frau Balaban was an exceptionally nice person and most helpful. She advised us of the places we had to see in her beloved city and how to get to them. Our stay coincided with a Middle East crisis, which caused us much worry. Frau Balaban gave us all the news that she had heard on the radio and was herself most concerned about it. I would highly recommend her place to $15-a-Day'ers who are interested in meeting the local residents. Frau Balaban suggests that people write her in advance to assure a vacancy for them" (Mrs. Joan Deifell, Edinburgh, Scotland). . . . "If you want to be mothered, stay with **Maria Kienast,** Alserbachstrasse 4, Stiege 2, first floor, room #19 (phone 348-9953 or 393-9545). She exudes warmth and helpfulness and on our wedding anniversary even served up rosebuds and cake in our elegantly furnished room (235 schillings double). Her apartment is spotless and on the bus line, 15 minutes from the Graben and halfway to Grinzing" (Monica Narodny, Barbados, West Indies). . . . **"Mr. and Mrs. Auguste Kozian** live in the 14th District at Gamandergasse 14, phone 9427533, where they provide fine accommodations (including bathroom facilities near your room) and the best breakfasts we had in Europe for $13 a day per couple. Their home is in a nice quiet section of Vienna, near the Vienna Woods" (Raymond Wilcove, U.S. Dept. of Commerce, Rockville, Maryland; note by AF: the Kozians' 1980 rates: 115 schillings single, 150 to 200 schillings double; not including breakfast). . . . "We have nothing but praise for **Ludwig and Elisabeth Agnezy,** Bobiesgasse 14, 1233 Wien 23, tel. 67-16-59, at the outskirts. They welcomed us into their charming home where, for 275 schillings ($20.37) per couple, we enjoyed a bright, comfortable, spotlessly clean room with a delicious breakfast of rolls, homemade jams and hot chocolate. Their friendliness and help in planning our sightseeing trips made our visit to Vienna a memorable one" (Mr. and Mrs. Roy Higgins, Burlington, Ontario, Canada; seconded by Mr. and Mrs. Wm. Kellar, Millgrove, Ontario, Canada).

READERS-ON-THE-STARVATION-BUDGET (ROOMS): "I am the owner of a boarding house (rooms with breakfast), where numerous young people, other university teachers with family, have enjoyed their stays in Vienna, near the Vienna woods. The cheapest rooms we can offer are double-rooms and cost Austrian Schillings 150 for two persons. Of course we have also better ones, with private bathroom too, which are more expensive. Breakfast costs 27 schillings—per person—and is generally very appreciated by my guests for both quantity and quality" (Adolf Kestler, **Pension A. Kestler,** Rodaun, Ketzergasse 356, phone 884-4385; note by AF: to reach Mr. Kestler's haven, take the Stadtbahn (S-Bahn, or local train) from the Westbahnhof and get off at Hietzing, then board trolley no. 60 and leave at the last stop, Rodaun. Total cost: 10 schillings).

STUDENT IN VIENNA: For you, first stop should be the **Austrian Student Travel Office** at 13 Reichsratstrasse (phone 42-15-61), behind the Rathaus in the University area, which operates a **Student Accommodation Service** throughout the year; staff here will make direct bookings for student visitors in several hotels they control where prices average 150 schillings ($11.11) per person in one-, two-, or three-bedded rooms with running water and the use of community showers, or about 200 schillings ($14.81) in somewhat more sophisticated accommodations. You'll need a student ID card, which you can pick up for 20 schillings at the Office upon showing proper credentials.

Also available at the Student Travel Office are: information on student discounts for sightseeing, plays and concerts; cheap student flights within Europe; and special discounted tours. Throughout the year, for instance, the Office runs weekend tours to Budapest for students only, and these are the cheapest available—800 schillings, including visa. Office hours are 9 a.m. to 4 p.m., weekdays only.

Closer to the center of town, at 10 Führichgasse (near the Opera), the same Student Travel Office operates a small **student "mensa"** (messhall) serving filling weekday lunches for 30 schillings. Officially for students only, it employs no one at all to check student credentials, and thus attracts a broader clientele.

As for lodgings that are just for you, try first the modern student hostel known as the **Heim der Musikhochschule,** at 8 Johannesgasse (phone 52-05-05), quite centrally located, which charges a high 200 schillings ($14.81) per night in a single room, 175 schillings ($12.96) per person double, but only 145 schillings ($10.74) per person triple, 110 schillings ($8.16) per person quadruple, including breakfast; it's open, in 1980, from June 30 through September 30.

STUDENT SELECTIONS: "We had only one day to spend in Vienna, and as pensions are not happy to take guests for one night, we were lucky to discover a student hotel, open from July through September. At **Auersperg,** Auerspergstrasse 9 (phone 432-549), we had a huge, immaculate double with private shower, including a good breakfast, for 380 schillings a night" (Shirley Ziffer, Ramat Aviv, Israel).

RESTAURANTS: Frankly, finding a budget meal in low-cost Vienna is no great accomplishment; but that relatively-simple task will become almost effortless if you keep in mind certain categories of low-cost restaurants.

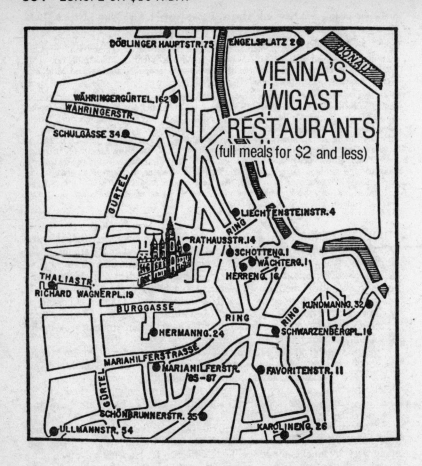

The Wigast's

The best spots for your basic, low-cost meals (the hurried and unextraordinary ones) are a string of restaurants known as "Wigast's"—a contraction of the ominous-sounding words: "Wiener Gaststättenbetriebsgesellschaft." These are city-operated, self-service cafeterias (of the sit-down variety), where beer and drinks are also served, and they are extremely reasonable in price, with some "menüs" (two-course, price-fixed meals) going for as little as 24 schillings ($1.77), others for 29 and 40 schillings—and none higher than that.

The biggest **Wigast,** open daily (including Sunday) for lunch only, is at 85 Mariahilferstrasse (on the shopping avenue that leads to the Westbahnhof), but you won't begin to glimpse how vast it is from the restaurant's simple entrance, which bears only a small neon sign reading "Wigast."

There's a second Wigast at Schottengasse 1 (**10**), corner of Freyung, only two fairly long blocks in from the "Ring" (in the inner city); another at Schwarzenberg Platz 16 (**11**) (both of these are also open daily for lunch but closed on Sundays); and 4 others (whose locations appear on our map above, and whose limited hours are 11 a.m. to 3 p.m., closed Saturdays and Sundays).

Take particular note of the Schwarzenberg Platz Wigast—an oasis of gentle costs in the hideously-expensive Opera area of Vienna (where such establishments as the Promenaden Cafe on Schwarzenberg Platz charge 65 schillings for two hot chocolates, without whipped cream). It (the Schwarzenberg Platz Wigast) was recently (1979) "promoted" into a restaurant called "Naschmarkt," apparently to attract a clientele preferring table service and willing to pay higher prices for a more refined atmosphere and greater variety of choice. Open seven days a week from 7 a.m. to 9 p.m. (and from 9 a.m. on Sundays), the Naschmarkt serves two excellent 3-course menüs for 35 and 45 schillings ($2.70) and ($3.33).

At all other Wigast's, the luncheon menu features two 2-course menus ("Menu A," "Menu B") for either 24 or 29 schillings ($1.77 or $2.14). I last had, for 29 schillings, a bowl of creamy rice soup followed by a plate of liver-cheese dumplings, with a lentil-bean vegetable. Some readers take all their meals at the Wigast's, and then write in about the subtle differences between the $1.77 feasts served at each!

The Billaterias

The chief competitive counterweights to the Wigast's are two cafeterias called **"Billaterias"** (after the German word "billig," meaning cheap), whose dishes are all à la carte, but at prices that almost—but not quite—permit you to put together multicourse meals for as little as you could at a Wigast. For example, during one recent summer, I priced leberkäse with mashed potatoes at 39 schillings ($2.88) at the Billaterias, only 35 schillings ($2.59) at the Wigasts. Still, the Billaterias offer a change of pace and should be visited. Of the two Billaterias, the branch at 5 Babenbergerstrasse, which is just two short blocks from the start of the Mariahilferstrasse, is the most pleasant (soup for 13 schillings, main courses with two vegetables for 16 to 40 schillings), and the cleanest in appearance, but the branch you'll probably be passing with most frequency is the one that's downstairs at 6 Singerstrasse (where it's named the "Stadtkeller"), just a few feet off the Kärntnerstrasse near the Graben, and near St. Stephen's Cathedral, in the center of the inner city. This Billateria opens at 7 a.m., when it serves a continental breakfast for only 25 schillings ($1.85); it then roars on throughout the day, dispensing courses so very low-priced that it's virtually impossible to spend more than $5. One recent dinner, I priced Hungarian goulash, french fries, salad and a glass of beer, at 65 schillings ($4.81).

The Beisels

What's a beisel? It's a small, plain, pub-style place with no identifying characteristics other than the occasional appearance of the words "Gasthaus," "Gaststätte" or "Gastwirtschaft" in its title, and the fact that it's family-operated and modest in price for good, home-style food: 50 to 60 schillings ($3.70 to $4.44) for two-course luncheons, from 50 to 70 schillings for main courses at night. A typical beisel in the inner city is **Gastwirtschaft R. and K. Körber** at 4 Schulerstrasse, corner of Domgasse, directly behind St. Stephen's, where Rudolph and Kornelia Körber specialize in Schweinebraten with cooked rice (50 schillings), in wiener schnitzel (an enormous portion) with salad (57 schillings), and in a usually-accompanying quarter-liter of white wine for 14 schillings. Incidentally, this is a favorite eating place of the *fiakers*, the famous Viennese horse-taxi drivers stationed around the Stephansdom. You're sure to recognize them by their black bowler hats, which they keep on even while eating. Cheaper is the **Stadtbeisl Feuerwehrstuben** at 21 Naglergasse, near the Freyung, which serves an excellent goulash for 50 schillings ($3.70); the beisel known as the **Pantherbräu** at 10 Judenplatz (full-course meals for 42 schillings, wiener schnitzel with mixed salad for 60 schillings); and the **Gasthaus Riedl** at 24 Berggasse, corner of Porzellangasse, in the University area, of which half is pub, half a simple restaurant, serving cold platters for as little as 20 to 30 schillings. The latter is open daily except Saturday, from 9 a.m. to 9 p.m. And then there's the **Gasthaus Mayerhofer,** at 29 Ungargasse, near the Stadtpark, where main dishes are only 20-28 schillings ($1.48-$2.07). A small place, it has the reputation of serving especially good "heuriger" wine (a dry white, made from grapes harvested the year before) for only 14 schillings. Open weekdays only, until 10 p.m. Monday through Thursday, until only 6 p.m. on Friday. A final "beisel": the **Müllerbeisel,** at 15 Seilerstätte, a street running parallel to the Kärntnerstrasse, less than 5 minutes on foot from the Stephansplatz. Here, if you're sick and tired of Wienerschnitzel (which costs 75 schillings at the Müllerbeisel), you can order such exotic (for Vienna) plates as fried squash with sauce tartare or stewed eggplant in meat sauce (50 schillings, $3.70 each), or a "kesselgulasch für 2 personen" for 100 schillings ($7.40). Served to your table in a big copper pot, it's more than enough for two persons (who thus pay $3.70 apiece), and could even suffice for four persons (who would pay only $1.85 apiece)!

The Remarkable Sandwich Bars

Vienna possesses two unusual sandwich shops, famed throughout the city, where a near-banquet of hot and cold items can be put together for a moderate outlay. Where else but at **Pic-Pic,** 4 Bräunerstrasse (a small side-street off the Graben, near the Pestsäule Monument), for instance, could you eat all the following for only 60 schillings ($4.44): a ham-and-egg club sandwich plus a plate of bean soup with a roll plus a glass (krügel) of draft beer plus a delicious apfelstrudel followed by a cup of coffee? Fifty varieties of sandwiches sell at Pic-Pic for either 3.50, 6.50, or 10 schillings; a take-away lunch of three sandwiches and a Coke, all in a yellow plastic bag, are only 40 schillings ($2.96); a tiny, ⅛-liter glass of beer called a "pfiff" (whistle), designed for ladies, is priced at only 3.50 schillings (26¢); and the wine listed at 10 schillings for a quarter liter is the same brand used at the glamorous Hotel Sacher. Closed Saturday afternoons and Sundays; get here before noon or after 2 p.m. to insure a seat. . . . Pic-Pic's competitor is the older **Trzesniewski** at 1 Dorotheergasse (a side-street parallel to the Bräunerstrasse), where exotic open sandwiches are offered for 4.50 schillings (hot ham or anchovies with mushrooms on delicious fresh bread). Beer or apple cider is another 4 schillings, a glass of authentic Polish vodka (ask for a "stamperl") at 10 schillings, and Trzesniewski is highly recommended not merely for its values (see "Readers' Selections" for additional description), but for its typical Viennese atmosphere. Closed Sundays.

The Cellars and the Wine Houses

To find other budget meals, look for the "keller" restaurants; and for even cheaper meals, eat in the wine houses.

The largest "keller" restaurant? That's the **Duran,** 11 Rotenturmstrasse (a block from St. Stephen's Cathedral, toward the Danube), whose five separate downstairs rooms are usually filled with boisterous merrymakers downing platters of Hungarian goulash for 42 schillings, wiener schnitzel with rice and salad for 55 schillings, and various self-service menus for 32 schillings each.

One of the cheapest of the kellers? That's the **Melkerstiftskeller,** at 3 Schotten-gasse, where a full, several-course meal costs 72 schillings (open only from 5 p.m. to midnight, closed Sundays and holidays). The most modern keller? That's easily the **Schottenkeller,** 6 Freyung (across the street from the Wigast Restaurant on Schottengasse), which offers rich peasant soup at 18 schillings and tasty filling plates from 44 schillings (for cevapcici) to 75 schillings (for super-schnitzel with mixed salad and fried potatoes). The most atmospheric keller? The **Zwölf Apostelkeller** at 3 Sonnenfelsgasse, where you descend two flights of stairs to sit in the underground catacombs of Vienna dating back to the 13th century, and snack on a "Liptauerbrot"—a spicy cheese mixture spread on a thick slab of rye bread for 11 schillings, and washed down with a cool "Veltliner," a mug of white wine, for 16. Hot plates range from only 18 to 35 schillings. The most rustic keller? Try the **Alter Rathauskeller,** at 8 Wipplingerstrasse, near the Hoher Markt, a few minutes from Stephansplatz. Generations of Viennese have eaten in this room, where the city of Vienna offers banquets to visiting dignitaries (of a fairly low level). Walls are decorated with old rifles and hunters' trophies, and specialties are all strictly local, such as "beuscherl mit knödel" or "saure niernderl" with roast potatoes, the first being cooked cow's lung, cut into strips, the second roast pigs' kidneys, both cooked and served in and with vinegar sauce (40 schillings—$2.96—each). From personal experience, I can tell you they taste better than they sound. The things I do for readers!

Still another popular keller, small but atmospheric in the evening, is the **Zum Kleinen Rathauskeller,** at 11 Rathausstrasse. During the day it's an ordinary restaurant where goulash costs 42 schillings and a giant wiener schnitzel (larger than the plate it's served on) with salad is 60 schillings. But after 8 p.m., the owner's wife, blonde Frau Gitta Erdmann, sings Viennese songs, accompanied by a small group. Closed Sundays.

The wine houses are, of course, much cheaper. You'll spot them all over town (particularly outside the inner city), and you'll find that virtually all of them have blackboard menus listing the classic Austrian dishes. They are not for our more fastidious or timid readers, and one should not be wearing one's best clothes, but after you've overcome the initial hesitation, you may form such an attachment that you'll eat in one every day. Sample sit-down meal in one of the better neighborhood wine houses: a Bauernschmaus (sausages and sauerkraut), cucumber salad, and beer for me; a beef goulash, and one Coke for Hope; total for both of us: 140 schillings ($10.37).

The Hotel Restaurants

Surprisingly enough, some of these can be inexpensive, even though elegant in decor. The most surprising of all is the "Second Class" dining room of the First Class **Hotel Regina,** 15 Rooseveltplatz (across from the Votivkirche and the University), which offers a daily three-course lunch or dinner for only 75 schillings ($5.55), including service, a more elaborate one for 110 schillings, and individual courses that can range from 50 to 70 schillings. It's easy to spend sparingly in this tall, airy dining area with vaulted ceilings, mammoth brass chandeliers, and colorful Tyrolean paintings of farmers in native costumes—the most unexpected moderately-priced restaurant in all of Europe. Stay away, though, from the First Class dining room, where the brass chandeliers change to crystal ones, and also avoid the left side of the outdoor terrace area; in both these latter spots, prices rise sharply.

Another of these restaurant surprises is provided by the **Hotel Graben,** in the heart of the inner city at 3 Dorotheergasse, which charges 40 schillings

($2.96) for a two-course meal, 75 schillings ($5.55) for a three-course meal, 120 schillings ($8.88) for a gargantuan four courses. On my last visit there, I began with a rich cream of mushroom soup which had fresh sliced mushrooms floating in it; then went on to a tender serving of smoked pork with dumplings and sauerkraut, accompanied by a salad plate of tiny tomatoes, sweet and sour cabbage, lettuce, and potato salad; and then barely managed to finish a dessert of fruit and ice cream—the whole meal for 110 schillings ($8.14).

Other Cheap Restaurants

The **Imbisstube,** at 62 Mariahilfstrasse, is small but popular, serves beef goulash with boiled potatoes for 35 schillings, and a large variety of sandwiches averaging 6 schillings. . . . If you like fish, you will like **Nordsee,** 34 Mariahilfer-strasse, where fishburgers cost 15 schillings, steamed cod filet with vegetables 38, and a Coke 11 schillings. . . . One of the most popular self-service restaurants in town is the **Duran-Superimbiss,** at 14 Alserstrasse, in the University area, where you can choose between at least a dozen plate dinners averaging 30 schillings. There are also at least 25 varieties of open-face sandwiches, from 6 to 8 schillings each. . . . The **Wienerwald** chain operates eleven chicken restaurants in Vienna. The two easiest to find are at 1 Annagasse and 12 Bellariastrasse. Half a roast bird will cost you 50 schillings, but they also serve less expensive dishes, like Hungarian goulash (44 schillings), ham and three eggs (30 schillings), and a remarkable portion of pommes frites (over the counter) for 15 schillings. . . . The self-service snack bar (Imbiss) at the **Steffl** (only large department store on the Kärntnerstrasse), serves a filling 2-course menu, Monday through Saturday, for 33 schillings ($2.44), and many other moderately priced items, including goulash with dumplings ($3.25), a pair of frankfurters for $1.48, bean soup for $1.45, beer for either $1 (medium glass), $.81 (small glass), or $.44 (tiny glass—a so-called "pfiff"). After entering the Steffl, turn left and roll down the escalator to the basement where the Imbiss is found. . . . A final suggestion: just about the best budget find in town is the tiny **Gasthaus Zum Kirchberg,** at Burggasse 4, near the Naturhistorisches Museum: daily menus for 36 schillings ($2.66), large wiener schnitzels, with salad, for 56 schillings ($4.14).

ORDERING IN "AUSTRIAN": Several readers have taken me to task for failing to provide a translation of Austrian menu terms, claiming that our German menu guide, at the back of the book, just isn't sufficient for Vienna. There may be some merit to that claim, and to fill the gap, we'll now set forth a few of the items that recur with particular frequency on an Austrian menu.

Among the soups, you'll most often find *Griessnockerlsuppe* or *Suppe mit Griessnockerl* (which both refer to a clear soup with Semolina dumplings), *Leberknödlsuppe* or *Suppe mit Leberknödeln* (both referring to soup with liver dumplings), *Rindsuppe* (beef broth), and *Gulaschsuppe* (a liquid-y Hungarian goulash).

The fish dishes carry designations almost identical to the ones you'll find in Germany. But among the meat plates, there's *Bauernschmaus* (a combination of many varied sausages and pork items with sauerkraut and dumplings) or *Tafelspitz* (boiled beef with vegetables), or simply *Rindfleisch* or *Beinfleisch* (boiled beef). You'll also encounter *Backhendl* (fried and breaded chicken) with some frequency, as well as the omnipresent *Wiener Schnitzel* (breaded veal cutlet) and *Natur Schnitzel* (plain veal cutlet). And finally there's *Gulasch* (stew), which comes either Hungarian-style *(Ungarisches Gulasch)* or plain.

In the vegetable area, the item to remember is *Nockerln,* which are little dumplings, usually served with a marvelous sauce, and altogether delicious. For dessert, you'll be offered the world's best *Apfelstrudel* (which is apple strudel) or *Palatschinken* (which are light, sugared pancakes), or *Salzburger Nockerln* (a soufflé), or finally, *Kaiserschmarren* (a diced omelette, served with heaps of jam and sprinkled with sugar).

A word, finally, about Viennese coffee. It was brought here 300 years ago by the Turks, who had sought unsuccessfully to conquer Vienna and left this exotic souvenir, much in use by the anti-alcoholic Moslems but unknown until then in central Europe. Like tea to the British, coffee soon became an institution to the Viennese, who proceeded to create more than 20 varieties. You'll need to recognize the *"kleiner schwarzer"* (small cup without milk), the *"kleiner brauner"* (small cup with a little milk), the *"melange"* (large cup with milk), the *"melange mit schlag"* (same as above with whipped cream on top), the *"einspänner"* (glass of coffee topped by whipped cream), the *"Türkischer"* (black coffee boiled in a copper pot and served in tiny cups)—and there are endless others. But puzzlingly enough (to me, at least), the coffee you order is often accompanied by a glass of excellent Viennese water—piped in from the Alps, and perhaps intended as a gesture of courtesy to the customer. Anybody heard another explanation?

THE BALKAN RESTAURANTS (A MINOR SPLURGE): The influence of the Eastern European countries on the Viennese cuisine, and the existence of numerous Balkan-style restaurants, are an important aspect of the restaurant scene of this city. At the large and fairly utilitarian **Servus,** 57 Mariahilferstrasse (next to the Mariahilf Church), a memorable Serbian white bean soup is 22 schillings ($1.62) and you can follow that with grilled cevapcici (highly spiced ground beef rolled into sausage shape) for 54 schillings, including crisp french fries. There's little atmosphere here, but excellent Balkan dishes, moderately priced. Closed Sundays. . . . And for an amazing combination of Greek and Viennese cuisine, the **Restaurant Der Grieche,** 5 Barnabitengasse (off the Mariahilferstrasse, about half-a-block from the Gerngross department store), gets a resounding recommendation. Panos Tsatsaris (he's Greek) is owner-chef, and how he can cook! For two persons who are both very hungry, I'd suggest, first, the Hellas-Platte, which costs 150 schillings for two ($11.11) and includes several cutlets, pork chops, shish-kebab, cevapcici, all on a bed of rice with french-fried potatoes and vegetables, accompanied by a large Greek salad. The lamb chops (lammkotelett) for 80 schillings are as crisp and well-spiced as any I've ever tasted, and for a special treat, you can try either the Tarama Salat (red caviar mixed with goat's cheese, oils and spices) for 20 schillings ($1.48) or a mammoth Griechischer Bauernsalat (green salad with olives, onions, pieces of goat's cheese, and spiced rice in vine leaves) at 45 schillings ($3.33) for two persons. This is a simple and quite unadorned restaurant to which you should go simply for the personal attention and quality of the food. Open seven days a week. . . . Possibly the least expensive of all the centrally-located Balkan restaurants is **Diogenes,** Landesgerichtsstrasse 18, a small, cellar establishment situated a scarce block from the University, two blocks from the Rathaus. Warm and student-filled, it charges from 35 to 55 schillings for large spicy platters, an extra 13 schillings for soup. A wall mural of the Seeker himself, with lantern, seems to stimulate heated philosophical discussions at night. Closed weekends.

THE BIG SPLURGE: For 85 schillings ($6.29) per person, you can eat magnificently in Vienna—as, for example, in the spectacular setting of the **Wiener Rathauskeller,** on Rathausplatz, where it's even possible to keep costs below that figure by ordering simpler dishes. Usually, however, you should plan to spend around 90 to 100 schillings or so for a thoroughly Viennese meal in this stunning vaulted cellar, with colorful ribbons and murals, which should be seen. A four-man band plays Viennese music every night. Closed Sundays.

At a cheaper price and for evening dinner-and-dancing, you'll like the vast **Volksgarten,** which is on the Ring, just opposite the Parliament building. Entrance fee to this football-field-sized garden is 50 schillings ($3.70) per person, of which 25 schillings are applied towards the cost of dinner. There's continuous dancing to sophisticated bands; fairly-inexpensive meals (dinners, with care, for about $5); and lots of singles in attendance. Be sure you locate the right dance area, which is about 100 yards from the Ring. For costlier (though moderate) outdoor dining, the **Restaurant Leopold Hauswirt (12),** Otto Bauergasse 20, has a beautiful dining-garden, replete with striped awning and serves a daily, three-course lunch for exactly 110 schillings ($8.14). Dinner will run close to 160 schillings per person. Closed Sundays.

Try, during your stay, to schedule at least one meal at Vienna's famous 250-year-old, **Wegenstein Zum Weissen Schwan (18),** Nussdorferstrasse 59, where it is possible, by choosing wisely, to stay under 110 schillings ($8.14) per person for a memorable series of dishes. Specialties of the latter establishment are geese (gänse), duck (ente), other poultry and venison, cooked with a flair developed over 250 years. Closed weekends.

And finally, for that really special evening out, you'll want to know about **D'Rauchkuchl,** Schweglerstrasse 37 (phone 92-13-81), where the waiters dress in medieval doublets and the ceiling and furnishings are hand-carved in the tradition of the 17th-century Tyrolean peasant. In winter here, you dine by crackling firelight; in summer, you can sit out in a flower-filled garden. While you *can* spend immense sums at this restaurant, there is no need to—if you simply choose from the many main courses priced from 65 to 110 schillings ($4.81 to $8.14), such as the "Shepherd's Spit" for 100 schillings or the small entrecote for 80. Open Thursdays for dinner, every day but Wednesday for lunch; go only into the less expensive side of this two-part restaurant.

READERS-WHO-HAVE-SPLURGED: . . . "If you really want to splurge, try **Demels,** located at 14 Kohlmarkt (which is between the end of the Graben and Michaelerplatz); it's the most exclusive pastry shop in Vienna. Just to sit in this elegant atmosphere among the Viennese aristocracy sipping coffee is worth it! Pastry and coffee add up to about 55 schillings" (Robert L. Borland, East Rockaway, New York; note by AF: at Demel's nothing has changed since 1884, and you can have the ($3.33) culinary experience of a lifetime by ordering a Sacher Torte with whipped cream on the side, 45 schillings).

MEALS (STUDENT VARIETY): For youthful companionship: the **"Mensa"** of the Technische Hochschule Wien, a cafeteria on the ground floor of the famous school, Karlsplatz 13, which serves a filling two-course lunch on weekdays only for only 32 schillings ($2.37). The school is only a short walk from the Opera; if you're elsewhere in Vienna, take the Stadtbahn to the Karlsplatz station.

READERS' RESTAURANT SELECTIONS: "**Alte Schmiede,** 1010 Wien, Schönlaterngasse 9, is a cultural as well as a gastronomic experience. Traditional Viennese meals are served in a vaulted cellar restaurant (65 schillings will buy a three-course meal), and on the premises you'll find a blacksmith, pottery workshop, a library and literary meeting place where you can attend free readings by well-known writers. Open daily from 10 a.m. to midnight" (Susan Mulhern, Los Angeles, California). . . . "Have your breakfast at a confectionery ('konditorei') shop in Vienna; superb pastry and cocoa for only 35 schillings" (Myles Silberstein, Philadelphia, Pennsylvania). . . . "The basement cafeteria of **Gerngross'** department store at #48 Mariahilferstrasse (5 minutes walk from the Westbahnhof) is a Best Buy for tasty lunches. A generous portion of cevapcici (a Balkan meat specialty) with vegetables cost only 40 schillings; about ($2.96). A giant sausage plate costs even less while chops are priced slightly higher" (T. K. Moy, Woodhaven, New York; note by AF: at Gerngross, the giant sausage is 24 schillings ($1.77), the daily "menu" only 35 schillings, $2.59; although the entire Gerngross store (Vienna's Macy's) burned down in early 1979, and will not be completely rebuilt until 1981, one of the first sections to be rebuilt and reopened in July, 1979, was the basement cafeteria described above! That was to continue servicing readers of this book, of course. . . . "A student-type **Mensa** (card not necessary), serving three-course meals for 22 schillings, is located near the crossroads in Schwarzspanierstrasse. Another mensa charging 22 schillings is in the New University at 7 Universitätsstrasse" (Mary Corcoran, Cologne, Germany; note by AF: the first of these establishments is the **Mensa des Afro-Asiatischen Instituts,** 15 Schwarzspanierstrasse—the building, incidentally, in which Beethoven died—which seats 100, is open only between 11:30 a.m. and 2 p.m. Monday to Friday, and serves typical three-course meals—like bean soup, fried fish fillet with potato salad and sweet pudding—for 22 schillings, about $1.62).

READERS' SNACK SELECTIONS: "Whenever we felt like a cheap, light meal—or even just a snack—in Vienna, we went to **Trzesniewski's Buffet.** It is very centrally situated, in the Dorotheergasse, only two doors up from the Graben (which of course is right by St. Stephen's). Here you get delicious pieces of fresh bread, liberally spread, with various spreads, such as pimento with egg, cucumber, spiced egg, cheese spread, tomato and pepper. The spreads are made, so we were told, from old and closely guarded family recipes. Certainly they are better than anything we had elsewhere. And the price? 4.50 Austrian schillings (33¢) per piece. There is also beer or apple juice for 3.50 schillings. So a light meal, with a drink, can cost you less than 17 schillings. There is only one problem—the place is well-known amongst the Viennese, and is usually packed out. Incidentally, the sandwiches can also be obtained in a box to take away" (Peter and Renata Singer, Oxford, England).

READERS-ON-THE-STARVATION-BUDGET (MEALS): "One afternoon I went to the produce market, where I put together a sausage, bread and raisin lunch for less than $1" (Victor Weisskopf, Frankfurt, Germany). . . . "A delicious moneysaver is to 'do as the Viennese do'—walk along with ½ pound of incomparable Viennese delicatessen ('Aufschnitt') in one hand and crispy Austrian 'Salzstangerl' in the other, happily munching away. The Viennese eat constantly, in all places, at all times" (Lisa Fellner, Wayne, New Jersey).

THE SIGHTS OF VIENNA: And now that you've unpacked in a budget room, and have marked out the nearest "Wigast" for lunch, you'll turn to the visual glories of this magnificent city—once the hub of Europe—whose sights are associated with many of the most colorful, dramatic events of European history. It's thrilling to realize that such personages as Maria Theresa, Franz Josef, Haydn, Beethoven, Metternich, Brahms, Mozart, Liszt, Franz Lehar, Strauss, Madame de Stael, all lived and worked in buildings in Vienna which remain untouched to this day.

As a prelude to all your touring, go to a bookstore (or else to the Wiener Verkehrsverein in the Opernpassage) and pick up a thick 10-schilling brochure called "Introducing Vienna," which was published by the city government, and whose pages are keyed to the unique, numbered plaques that are affixed to the front of every building of historical interest in Vienna. You'll spot these plaques everywhere: they sport four little red-and-white flags in summer and carry a number which corresponds to a similarly-numbered explanation and description, in English, in the "Introducing Vienna" booklet.

You may, of course, want to take an introductory guided tour, and for that, a number of tour operators—a typical one is **Vienna Sightseeing,** 4 Stelzhamergasse, near the Hilton Hotel and Bahnhof Landstrasse, phone 72-

46-83—offers 3½ hour trips through Vienna, which depart in summer at 9:15 a.m., and 2:15 p.m., daily, from in front of the Opera House, cost 190 schillings ($14.07), and are an almost indispensable way to learn the arrangement, and chief sights, of the city. Another popular bus tour (250 schillings—$18.51; 2:15 p.m.), conducted by the same company, among others, goes through the romantic Vienna Forest to **Mayerling,** where Crown Prince Rudolph and Maria Vetsera committed suicide. But don't expect to see the hunting lodge where all this happened; it's been replaced by a chapel, housing an order of nuns.

For a more extended visit to the incomparable **Schönbrunn Palace,** you can take tram #58 from along Mariahilferstrasse to Schönbrunnerstrasse and Grünbergstrasse (a 15-minute ride, 10 schillings per person). That lets you off at a side entrance to the palace grounds, which are open from 8 in the morning until 8 at night. The Palace itself closes at 5. Its former occupants, the Habsburgs, are—by law—prohibited from entering Austria.

If you're a summer traveler, you won't, unfortunately, be able to see the great **Spanish Riding School** ("Spanische Hofreitschule," in the Hofburg), whose performances, in 1980, take place on Sundays at 10:45 a.m. from September 7 to December 14, and from March 2 to June 15 only. During the same period, however, you can watch rehearsals of the school on Tuesdays through

Saturdays from 10 a.m. to noon, and throughout the year you can take tours of the stables (sometimes including the riding arena as well) from 2 to 4 p.m., Monday through Saturday, from 10 a.m. to noon on Sundays. Tickets can be purchased at the main entrance of the Hofburg (Michaelerplatz 1, first door on the left, under the cupola) from 9 a.m. to 3 p.m. Tuesday through Friday, from 9 to noon on Saturday, cost 30 schillings for training sessions and tours, from 40 schillings (standing room) all the way up to 350 schillings for performances—the latter often being booked up as much as a year ahead. . . . The famous **Vienna Boys' Choir** performs during Catholic high mass in the Chapel of the Imperial Palace (Hofburgkapelle) on Sundays at 9:25 a.m., but only from mid-September through June. Tickets can sometimes be purchased at the booking office of the Burgkapelle on Fridays at 5 p.m., but are more safely obtained by writing well in advance to **Verwaltung Hofmusikkapelle,** attention Herr Leopold Rupp, Schweizerhof, Vienna 1; they cost 25 to 60 schillings, but the money need not be enclosed with your reservation requests; rather, you pay upon picking up your tickets at the booking office on Sunday before mass. The Burgkapelle itself is open to visitors on Tuesdays and Thursdays from 2:30 to 3:30 p.m.; entrance fee being 5 schillings (37¢).

MUSEUMS: There are more than 40 important ones. Some you might consider are the enormous **Kunsthistorisches Museum,** on the Maria-Theresien-Platz (paintings, sculpture, antiquities); the **Albertina,** at 1 Augustinerstrasse (world's largest collection of engravings and prints); the **Beethoven Museum,** 8 Moelkerbastei (home of the composer); the **Haydn Museum,** 19 Haydngasse (home of the composer); the **Schubert Museum,** 54 Nussdorferstrasse (birthplace of the composer); the **Schubert-Sterbezimmer,** 6 Kettenbrückengasse (room where he died); the state rooms and private apartments of **Schönbrunn Castle;** the **Hofburg** (apartments of the Emperor Franz Joseph); the **Kapuzinergruft,** 2 Tegetthoffstrasse (crypt of the Habsburgs); the **Schatzkammer,** in the Hofburg (the imperial treasure); the **Mozart Museum,** 5 Domgasse (relics of the composer); the **Academy of Art,** 3 Schillerplatz (classic paintings); the **Museum des 20. Jahrhunderts,** in the Schweizergarten (modern art). And for a report in depth on the outstanding Viennese sights, here's Hope:

HOPE IN VIENNA: "In this remarkable city, everything, from the people themselves to the Sacher torte, seems mature and cultivated. Nowhere else do you feel so deeply the manners and mores of days gone by—all the romance, grace and civilization of Old Europe stick to Vienna through the memories of its residents who have seen better days and understand so well that this is the way of the world. And the cultivated character of the Viennese is illustrated in part by their interest in the arts and in good living. The Royal Palaces are charming, the theatre and opera are old and popular traditions, and fine museums and interesting monuments abound in such profusion that one is faced with an embarrassment of riches. Here are only a few among many interesting things to do and see in Vienna:

The Kunsthistorisches

"Head first for the **Kunsthistorisches Museum** (Museum of Fine Arts), 1 Maria Theresien-Platz (across the street from The Hofburg), which is another of the world's great museums. Go directly to the second floor where the gallery is. The collection, which by anybody's standards is a good one, becomes absolutely fabulous at many points, and is sensibly arranged chronologically and by country. To your right at the top of the staircase, under the dome, are Dutch painters—'Holländer and Flamen'; off the room, #15, is Jan Vermeer's renowned 'Artist in His Studio'. Just off the first Rubens Room are two smaller rooms of Rembrandts, including the wonderful painting of his mother and three self portraits. But the high point of the entire museum is a shattering room-full of Bruegels, including 'The Hunters in the Snow' (you can hardly believe it's not real), 'The Tower of Babel', 'Peasant Dance', and many others of equal renown. In the side rooms are excellent Holbeins and paintings from the 15th and 16th centuries, some very important Dürers, Van Eycks, and Memling's famous 'Adam and Eve'. Then, on the other side of the staircase, are Italian, French and Spanish painters, with important works by Titian, Giorgione, Tintoretto, Caravaggio and Velazquez, among many others. Downstairs (first floor), to the right of the entrance, there's a collection of Egyptian, Greek and Roman antiquities (many uninspired Roman copies of Greek originals, but also a famous assemblage of cameos); and to the left, medieval, renaissance and baroque works, including the world's largest collection of tapestries (nearly 800 pieces)—the most important, must-see piece being Benvenuto Cellini's gold 'Saltcellar for King Francis I', the very height of ornate Mannerism. For 20 schillings ($1.48), you can have this experience of great art every day, except Monday, from 10 to 3, Saturday and Sunday from 9 to 1, as well as Tuesday and Friday evenings from 7 to 9.

Schönbrunn

"To visit Vienna and not to see the lovely 'summer palace,' **Schönbrunn**, is like not visiting Vienna at all. The glorious grounds of Schönbrunn, which were transformed into a formal Baroque garden, have belonged to the Habsburgs since 1569. The present Palace was begun in 1695 by Emperor Leopold I, but it was really Empress Maria Theresa who left the greatest imprint on Schönbrunn: in the course of having 16 children, running the country (with quite an able hand), and fighting a war for her right to sit on the Austrian throne, she still found time to decorate and redesign Schönbrunn (1743 to 1749) and it has remained virtually as she left it. To see the inside of the predominantly white and gilt rococo palace, you must wait for an English guide to take you through from 9 to 12 and 1 to 5 (till 4 in the winter), or during special summer evening guided visits on Wednesdays, Thursdays and Saturdays at 7:30 and 9:15 p.m.; the charge will be 20 schillings (5 schillings if you're a student), but the guide tells you everything about the Palace, and usually throws in some historical commentary, too. Outstanding among many ornate rooms are the exotic 'Chinese Rooms'; the Large and Small Galleries; Napoleon's Room (where he stayed when at Schönbrunn); all the Guest Rooms, but especially the cunning 'Porcelain Room,' all in blue and white with inlaid drawings on the walls; and the stunning 'Millions Room' in the most highly ornate rococo, with its gold-framed mirrors and Indian paintings on rich wood-panelled walls. When you finish with the Palace, you can take a delightful walk around the park where you'll see The Gloriette, an enormous classical stone arch which is direclty opposite the Palace on the highest point in Schönbrunn, with excellent views of the surrounding countryside; the lovely Neptune Fountain; artificial Roman ruins; followed by a Zoo and the largest hothouse in Europe, the 'Palmenhaus'. Close to the main entrance is the lovely rococo **Schönbrunn Theatre**, the oldest in Vienna, but the only way (and the best way) to see the theatre is to attend a summer opera performance here—try to schedule one during your stay. Finally, to the right of the main entrance, closer to the Palace, there's a **Carriage Museum** called the **Wagenburg**, containing imperial stage

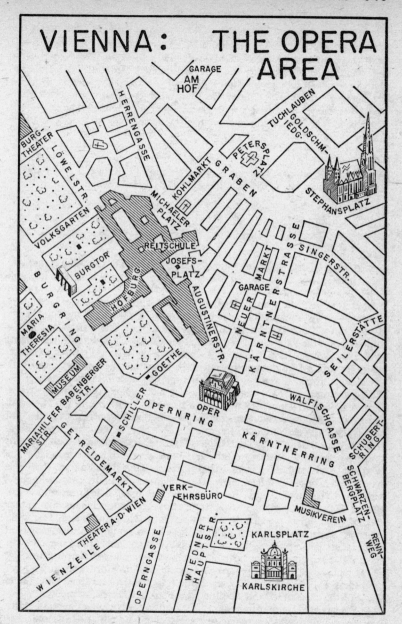

coaches, including a children's phaeton constructed for Napoleon's son, the Duke of Reichstatt.

"To get to Schönbrunn, take street car #58 from anywhere along Maria-hilferstrasse; it'll cost 10 schillings (74¢), and the trip requires about 15 minutes.

St. Stephen's

"Back in the city, every foreign visitor must pay tribute to **St. Stephen's Cathedral,** which is the focal point of Vienna—it has the highest steeple and is at the heart-beat of one of the busiest intersections in town (close to the Graben, the elegant shopping street with the famous baroque 'Plague Column' built by Leopold I to commemorate the end of a terrible epidemic of plague in Vienna in 1679). The church was founded in the 12th century, but what you'll see today is mostly from the 14th century—it's a handsome grey stone Gothic church with some Romanesque elements, and the interior decorations have just enough Baroque gilt to add flavor. The old wood work of the roof went up in flames in the last days of World War II (April 1945) but has now been completely rebuilt in steel. You can visit St. Stephen's daily from 8 to 5. And for 20 schillings you can take an elevator to the north tower for an excellent view, while for 15 schillings ($1.11) you can visit the crypt.

The Hofburg

"**The Hofburg,** which was the official residence of the Habsburgs and was built between the 13th and 20th century in every conceivable architectural style, is an enormous complex of buildings bounded by vast parks and open spaces. It's more like a small city than a palace, and you can easily spend days here getting lost looking for what you came to see (in several trips to Vienna I have not yet managed to see all of The Hofburg!). The Swiss Court is the oldest part of the Palace, and in the oldest building is The Gothic Royal Chapel where the Vienna Boys' Choir sings. Not far away is St. Augustine's Church (best approached from Augustinerstrasse), which has the Loreto Chapel with its famous 'Heart Crypt'—a room containing 54 urns with the hearts of the Habsburgs in them! (This same church also made some pretty good matches: Empress Maria Theresa was married to Franz Stephen here, Marie Louise by proxy to Napoleon, and Emperor Franz Josef to Elisabeth). Close by (off Josefsplatz) is The National Library with its celebrated baroque State Room. Actually located in the Old Castle is **The Schatzkammer,** which contains imperial and religious treasures: the museum is divided into two sections—The Crown Jewels and the Ecclesiastical Treasure Chamber. Among the items you'll find inside are christening robes of the imperial family; swords, imperial crosses; Coronation Robes from the 12th through the 13th centuries; two prized Habsburg heirlooms with strange mystical and religious significance ('The Agate Bowl,' mistakenly thought to be the Holy Grail, and 'The Ainkhurn', associated with Christ and also with sovereignty); the silver-pearl-gilt Empire cradle given to Napoleon (and his Austrian wife Marie Louise) by the city of Paris in honor of the birth of his son, who was immediately dubbed 'The King of Rome'; 'The Insignia and Regalia of The Holy Roman Empire,' including The Sabre of Charlemagne; the Imperial Crown made in 962 (highlight of the collection); and The Imperial Book of Gospels, to mention a few. The Ecclesiastical section contains relics, paintings, statuary, vestments, altars, crosses, prayer books, etc.—and a wooden cupboard with a black and ivory crucifix which holds the keys to the Habsburg coffins. Though not nearly as sumptuous as the Bavarian Treasure House in Munich, this collection should be visited because of its great historical significance. Open Monday, Wednesday and Friday from 10 to 3, Tuesday and Thursday from 1 to 5, and Sunday from 9 to 1, for 10 schillings. Closed Saturdays. . . . Then, to see the **Imperial Rooms** (which, while historically evocative, seem a little plain after the splendor of Schönbrunn), walk through the courtyard to the Reichskanzleitrakt (Chancellery of the Empire Building). You'll pay 10 schillings for a guided tour through the apartments of Franz Josef, Elisabeth, Czar Alexander I of Russia (a prominent guest at The Congress of Vienna), and the last Emperor of the Habsburgs, Charles I. Tours (which are occasionally conducted in German only) leave every 15 minutes from 8:30 to 4:30 weekdays, 8:30 to 1 Sundays. The predominant feeling of the rooms is Victorian for Franz Josef, baroque and rococo for Elisabeth, Alexander I and Charles I. Elisabeth was a beautiful and vain woman—she decreed that she would sit for no more portraits after the age of 30—and here you see her personal gymnasium where she kept in shape. The family portraits are interesting, so is the history: Franz Josef and Elisabeth lived apart because she had a morbid fear that a strain of family insanity would manifest itself in her; later she was assassinated in Geneva. . . . Another wing of the Burg (the one next to the Burgtor) worth a visit is the **Neue Hofburg:** it houses the world's second largest collection of armor (largest is in the Metropolitan Museum of Art in New York), and a unique assortment of ancient musical instruments, including the pianos of Beethoven, Schubert and Gustav Mahler. Open Tuesdays to Fridays 10 a.m. to 3 p.m., Saturdays and Sundays 9 a.m. to 1 p.m.; entrance fee 5 schillings; closed Mondays. . . . Next a walk through the lovely St. Michael's Gate and turn right to get to the **Spanish Riding School and Stallburg (Stable Castle).** In July and August, the famous Lippizaner horses don't perform, but they can be seen (60 of them) in their stables at The Stallburg, which was built in 1565 by Ferdinand I. The Spanish Riding School (so-called because only Spanish stallions were used) is directly across the street. The Lippizaner horses are surely the most famous classical-style equestrian performers in the world (state owned, they've been doing the same act for nearly 400 years), but even without the spectacular show it's worth-while to take a look at the beautiful Baroque Riding Hall which was built in 1735 by Fischer von Erlach for Charles VI, and which was also used as a ballroom during the Congress of Vienna (that epic conference in 1814 at which the wily Metternich was a principal character, as was Talleyrand, and where the great nations tried to reconstitute Europe after Napoleon's defeat). The Spanish Riding School has conducted tours on weekdays in July and August from 2 to 4, Sundays from 10 to noon every half hour, and you'll pay 25 schillings to see the Stables and the School; the Stables alone are 5 schillings.

Belvedere

"If I were in the market for palaces, I'd buy the lovely grey stone **Belvedere Palace,** with its unbelievably gorgeous sculpture garden, rather than Schönbrunn. True, you don't get the space you have at Schönbrunn and some of the rooms are not as lavish, but Belvedere, a light airy Baroque Palace built by Hildebrandt between 1714 and 1723, has a grace and unity about it that I like very much. It was built as a summer residence for Austria's beloved Prince Eugene (from Savoy), who successfully protected his adopted country from a couple of Turkish invasions, and was rewarded for his service and devotion by being made Minister of War, then later Prime Minister, by Emperor Charles VI. The elegant Belvedere is now the home of **The Austrian Gallery** (Österreichische Galerie), which has collections in three parts. Upper Belvedere Palace, the more formal and lavish Palace, was used for state occasions and for guests (it was here in the Great Hall that the 'liberation' or 'Treaty of State' was signed on May 15, 1955, after World War II); it's now a gallery for 19th and 20th century art. The moderns are on the top floors of the museum, and there are interesting paintings by Wilhelm Thöny, Richard Gerstl, Herbert Boeckl and Egon Schiele. But look especially for the pictures of the now famous Oskar Kokoschka, and also for an artist who is new to me, Gustav Klimt (1862-1918), whose Tiffany-like style and use of gold and fancy design is very exciting: be sure to see the room devoted to his work, including 'The Kiss' and 'Judith,' among others. Upper Belvedere is host to changing exhibitions, too, and there are wonderful views of Vienna from the top floor. Across the garden is the Lower Belvedere, the Summer Palace where Prince Eugene actually lived, now the Museum of Austrian Baroque: there are some fine frescoes, an elaborate gold Chinese room with a statue of Prince Eugene. The Museum of Medieval Austrian Art is in the Orangerie and has an interesting collection from The Middle Ages, comprised mostly of Church Art or Biblical subjects—don't miss the Flügelaltar by the Donauschule in the last room. Belvedere is located at Prinz Eugen Strasse 27, and is open Tuesday, Wednesday, Thursday and Saturday from 10 a.m. to 4 p.m.; Friday from 10 a.m. to 1 p.m.; and Sunday from 9 a.m. to noon; the Baroque and Medieval Museums are a good buy for 10 schillings, and the same ticket entitles you to visit the Upper Belvedere Gallery of 19th and 20th Century art (except during special exhibitions when the entrance fee goes up an additional 5 schillings). All three collections are free on Saturdays and Sundays in winter.

Crypts of the Habsburgs

"Most visitors feel themselves duty bound to make an historical pilgrimage to The Kapuziner Church (located close to The Albertina, behind the Opera House, on the little Tegetthoffstrasse 2—a street which becomes Neuer Markt), where the **Kaisergruft** or **Royal Crypts** are located. This has been the burial place of the Habsburgs for the last 300 years, with some very elaborate funeral biers next to relatively simple ones—the coffin of Franz Josef is particularly plain and tasteful (Franz Josef's son Rudolf who died at Mayerling is buried here too): notice the bronze plaques above the lights reading 'Pax.' The crypt is open in summer from 10 to 4 (closed between noon and 1 for lunch) for 10 schillings. Most of the year (October 1 until May 1), open only from 10 a.m. until noon.

Composers' homes

"Music lovers can have a field-day in Vienna, the city which nurtured and inspired some of the greatest European composers. There are monuments to the musical giants everywhere—one of the loveliest is the airy romantic white stone circle of figures with Johann Strauss playing in its center in the Stadtpark (there are monuments to Franz Schubert and Anton Bruckner in the same park). Memorial rooms of Mozart, Beethoven, Schubert and Haydn can also be visited (all open daily, except Monday, from 9 to 4, Sunday till 1, for 5 schillings entrance fee, but free to students), but are recommended only for devotees, because all are plain and unadorned and only for someone who gets a kick out of just knowing that a great musical genius lived and composed in these very rooms (the Schubert Museum is in the actual birthplace of the composer, and the Haydn Museum is located in the house where Haydn died). For instance, at **'Figarohaus'** (Domgasse 5), which was Mozart's home from 1784 to 1787, 'The Marriage of Figaro' was composed in the small baroque room in the back—in the salon he played chamber music concerts with Haydn, and accepted the 17-year-old Beethoven as a pupil. But aside from a scattering of pictures, letters, and scores written in his hand, there is little else to see. The house is located in a quaint old section (from the back of St. Stephen's Cathedral, walk to Domgasse—through the wooden doors and the arcade), which at that time was a wealthy neighborhood (he spent his prosperous days here); but later Mozart lived in poverty and died in poverty—Wolfgang was usually one step ahead of the gang of wolves at his door: a blight on Vienna and on all of us who persistently refuse to recognize and reward great artists while they're alive. . . . The moody and rebellious Beethoven fared much better than Mozart did. Rich men vied to become his patron. But he was such a stormy personality and his habits were so irregular (he sometimes played and composed in the middle of the night), that he was constantly being evicted from apartments all over Vienna. There was one landlord who loved him, however: Mr. Pasqualati, who owned **Pasqualati Haus** at Moelkerbastei 8, and always kept Beethoven's apartment free—no one else was allowed to live in it, even when the restless Beethoven was not there. As a result, Beethoven lived here, on and off for 11 years, from 1804 to 1815, and the 4th and 7th Symphonies as well as his violin concerto and some chamber music were written here. It's a long four flight climb to see such personal effects as Beethoven's sugar box, a few portraits (including one of Beethoven's grandfather), and his scores."

READERS' SIGHTSEEING SUGGESTIONS: "Take the train to Melk from Vienna (free to Eurailpass holders) and visit the famous monastery. Return via the downstream boat on the Danube at 4 p.m. (free for Eurailpass holders). Get off at the Nussdorf stop, have a glass of wine at a Heurige and listen to music. Then take the #6 streetcar back to Vienna" (Mr. & Mrs. David Arnold, Falls Church, Virginia). . . . "Persons sympathetic to music should not leave Vienna without visiting the central cemetery ('Zentralfriedhof,' 234 Simmeringer Hauptstrasse) where, within feet of each other, are the graves of Beethoven, Brahms, Schubert, Johann Strauss, Franz von Suppe, Hugo Wolf and Arnold Schönberg, along with a memorial to Mozart. This section of the cemetery contains some of the most exquisitely beautiful gravestones I have ever seen, many of them true works of art in their simplicity and eloquence. To get to the cemetery, take tram #71 from Schwarzenberg Platz and get off at the next to the last stop" (Milton Schulman, Bronx, New York). . . . "To see the Viennese at leisure, spend Sunday afternoon strolling at Schönbrunn. . . . This is a gorgeous city, the highlight of our trip" (Christie J. Bentham, Scarborough, Ontario, Canada). . . . "By the time we reached Vienna, we were accomplished 'standers' so we suffered no discomfort or inconvenience in buying standing room to the performance of the Spanish Riding School. Standing room can be bought only on the morning of the performance at the box office, which is located in the cupola of the Hofburg. The office opens at 9 a.m., but be there an hour or so early. We bought 30 schilling tickets for the upper balcony, and, as it turned out, the people who had seats up there had to stand anyway so they could see everything" (Margaret Kendrick, Davis, California, and Cheryl Riggins, Woodland, California). . . . "Did you know that for a very small fee one may visit the stables of the famed **Spanish Riding School** and gaze close range at the horses to one's heart's content?" (Mrs. Harcourt M. Stebbins, APO, New York). . . . "If you want to see the Spanish Riding School, I advise you to go during a morning practice session. You can watch from 10 until noon and it only costs 30 schillings. Come early and wait in line. It is worthwhile because by 9:30 the line is 2 blocks long. I was in line at 9 and had an excellent seat and was not in the mob" (Stephen A. Singer, Chicago, Illinois). . . . "Nearly every large city in Europe boasts a church or cathedral which is well-publicized and visited, but in Vienna I would also recommend a visit to the **Synagogue**, at 4 Seitenstettengasse, near Judenstrasse, which opens at 4:40 p.m. on Fridays and Saturdays, 5 p.m. Sunday through Thursday. The area alone takes one back to a period of from fifty to one hundred years ago. The Synagogue, recently rebuilt within the walls of the old building, is a stark contrast between old and new and a beautiful symbol of faith and courage. The members, justly proud of their building, are friendly and interesting (however, only German or Hebrew is spoken). This, to me, will be a long cherished memory" (Mrs. Harcourt M. Stebbins, APO, New York). . . . "No Vienna visitor who is even mildly interested in Austria's past can afford to miss the **Austrian Museum of Military History.** It is, in my opinion, the best thing of its kind in Europe—

surpassing even the Musée de l'Armée in Paris. Among its exhibits is the automobile in which Archduke Francis Ferdinand and his wife were riding when they were assassinated on June 28, 1914—the spark that ignited World War I. Francis Ferdinand's blood-stained uniform is also on display. There are, additionally, countless mementos of Austria's great generals: Prince Eugene, Archduke Charles, Radetzky. This is quite in addition to the usual large collection of guns, uniforms, and sabres, all of which the museum exhibits very skillfully. I sincerely hope you will see fit to mention the museum in next year's edition of your book. The location is the Habsburg arsenal, Objekt 18, reached by taking a tram to the Südbahnhof, then walking a few blocks. You can probably pinpoint it better by consulting a city map" (Bill Murchison, Jr., Corsicana, Texas). . . . "If you would like to visit the **Vienna Woods** on your own, take trolley A or B near the Opera House to Schottenring, where you change for tram 38 (use same ticket) to Grinzing. At Grinzing take the bus via the Vienna Woods to Kahlenberg. The round trip costs 20 schillings and takes an hour each way. Much cheaper than the regular tour, which costs 250 schillings. There is a panoramic view of all Vienna from Kahlenberg" (Morton I. Moskowitz, Brooklyn, New York). . . . "To reach the far more attractive area of the **Vienna Woods,** take the Baden bus from across the street from the Opera House (Opernring and Operngasse)—28 schillings, ½ hour. Once in Baden, walk up through the Kurpark to Rudolfhof, for a beer there. The park melts into the Vienna Woods, and this is the **elegant** Vienna Woods that Strauss' music describes" (Arthur E. Banta, Imperial Beach, California). . . . "In Vienna, the tobacco shops sell booklets of discount tickets for public transport ('vorverkaufte Fahrscheine') at 36 schillings for five tickets, saving you almost three schillings per ticket on all modes of buses, trams, schnellbahns and stadtbahns" (Joseph P. Voith, Washington, D.C.). . . . "While in Vienna, no one should miss a delightful boat ride on the Danube. We took a train to Melk (fare 76 schillings per person), visited the famous Monastery there, and caught the downstream boat back to Vienna at 4 p.m., arriving about 8 p.m. (cost 180 schillings per person). The scenery is breathtaking, the boats are charming and have wonderful food, delicious Rhine wine and good Bavarian beer at very cheap prices. If you prefer, you can take the boat all the way to Linz, stay overnight, and come back the following day, thus enjoying two complete days on the Danube at extremely reasonable fares" (William H. Read, Los Angeles, California). . . . "A 25-schilling ($1.85) tour of the Opera House, including a visit to the Theater Museum, which shouldn't be missed, is conducted at 3 p.m. daily during most of the year, daily at 9, 10, and 11 a.m., at 1, 2 and 3 p.m. in summer" (Jay Wolf, New York City). . . . "The most complete and panoramic view of Vienna is from the **Kahlenberg** hill; buses will take you up there. In the twilight, Vienna surrounded by the Vienna woods, with the blue Danube making a path around the city, is a sight not to be missed" (Grete and Charles Schwarz, New York City).

EVENING ENTERTAINMENT: The primary night-time attraction here is theatre —particularly musical theatre. In summer, the recently-reopened **Theater an der Wien,** 6 Linke Wienzeile, which witnessed the premiere of "Die Fleder-maus," presents that and other Viennese operettas in a jewel-like setting, for which standing room ("stehplatz") is only 10 schillings (74¢)—but try to get a seat (they range from 60 to 380 schillings). In the non-summer months, performances of the renowned **Staatsoper** (Austrian State Opera)—ensconced in the world's most resplendent opera house—are a major experience for which seat prices range as high as $35, but locations several tiers up provide perfectly adequate views and sell for 200 schillings ($14.81). The season lasts from September 1 to the end of June, and the best place to purchase tickets is at the Opera House box office, open weekdays from 9 to 7, and Sundays from 9 to noon. Standing room (which starts at 15 schillings) is superb here, because standees are lined up on a graded floor, behind railings on which they can lean. . . . Again in summer, the jewel-like **Kammeroper** at Schönbrunn Palace, presents operettas and comic operas for $4 to $10 per seat, while much lower prices are charged at the **Burgtheater** (as little as 30 schillings ($2.22); closed July and August), located across from the Rathaus, and showing the classic works (Schiller, Goethe) as well as modern plays; the **Akademie Theater** (contemporary playwrights) at 1 Lisztstrasse (tickets from 50 schillings ($3.70);

and at the **Volksoper** (spectacular operettas), which charges as little as 60 schillings ($4.44) for fairly remote locations.

At least one evening should be spent at the famous amusement park of Vienna, the **Prater (15),** which is best-known for its ferris wheel (the "Riesen-rad," built in 1896), largest in the world, on which a 10-minute ride will cost 20 schillings for adults, 10 for children. But there is no admission charge at all to the grounds; only tiny fees for the various games, sports and other rides; and at least four cheap beer-garden restaurants scattered throughout the park. You'll get quite a charge out of the Viennese touches that are added to the normal carnival attractions.

OTHER $$$-A-DAY BOOKS: Europe on $15 a Day has now been supplemented by six other $$$-a-day guides dealing with individual European countries or areas: **Ireland on $15 a Day, Greece and Yugoslavia on $15 & $20 a Day, Spain and Morocco (plus the Canary Islands) on $10 & $15 a Day, England and Scotland on $20 a Day, Scandinavia on $20 a Day,** and **Turkey on $10 & $15 a Day.** In contrast with the book you are now reading, which deals primarily with 17 major European cities, each of the above guides treats in depth one particular country or area, and sets forth hotel, restaurant and sightseeing suggestions for literally scores of individual cities and tourist destinations in that country or area. The $$$-a-Day Books can be obtained at most bookstores, or by mailing the appropriate amount (see list on last page of this book) for each book to: Frommer/Pasmantier Publishing Corporation, 380 Madison Avenue, New York, New York 10017.

Dancing

For meeting people at night (but only in summer), your very best prospects are at the vast **Volksgarten** (mentioned under "Big Splurge" restaurants), located directly on the Ring, opposite the Parliament Building. For here, in a massive garden-like setting, large numbers of Viennese turn out to dance the warm evenings away—often stag and often in hopes of encountering visitors from other countries. Admission is 50 schillings (of which 25 are credited to your first drink); the bands are live and given more to dance tunes than acid-rock; and the clientele bridges all the generation gaps.

For the very young and student-age, there are the two popular and adjoining discotheques on Annagasse (off Kärntnerstrasse) in the inner city: **Tenne,** at #3; and **Take Five,** at #3A. Tenne charges a 20 schilling entrance fee, Take Five charges none (but a Coke is 50 schillings). Personally, I see little to choose between them—except that Tenne has live, modern groups, while the other sticks to records. For the same age group, the **Atrium,** 10 Schwarzenbergplatz, combines the concepts of wine house and discotheque and charges an entrance fee of 30 schillings; it has the historic honor of having been Vienna's first discotheque.

While the already-described dance spots are excellent for lone visitors who want to make contact with the inhabitants, **Scotch Dancing,** at 10 Parkring, is a good place to go once you have—most of the people there are coupled. One of the nicest dancehalls in the city, Scotch is a discotheque (some rock music, mostly slow and romantic) in a dark, candlelit cellar that's popular with the 23-to-30 crowd. Dancing from 8 p.m. on; there's no admission, but a Coke costs 50 schillings once inside.

Some special spots

The **Alte Backstube,** Lange Gasse 34, is the most unusual cafe in the entire city. Set in a 17th-century house which operated for two centuries as a bakery, it has been restored into a combination cafe and museum, illustrating the history of baking. Walk through the front room, which looks just like any pastry shop, and through the narrow corridors into the back, where you will see the original ovens and old-style implements. Then, in the candle-lit cafe at the rear, you can sit in comfortable chairs and sip coffee for 16 schillings or a glass of wine for 25 schillings.

The **Griechenbeisl,** in the historic center of the city at Fleischmarkt 11, is one of the oldest restaurants and beer parlors in Vienna, dating back to the 15th century. Food here is too expensive for us, but go late at night for a 30-schilling beer (a smaller glass, called a "Seidl," costs only 22 schillings) and to listen to the zither and accordion music. Fantastically picturesque, this seven-room spot is located off an old crooked alley. The walls are yellowed; there are medieval mottoes printed over the mantelpieces and inside the bays of windows; and a "signature room" contains the autographs of Beethoven, Richard Wagner, Count Zeppelin and Mark Twain on wall and ceiling. Simply poke through all the rooms until you find one whose atmosphere suits your mood.

An evening stroll

And one evening, equipped with your "Introducing Vienna" brochure, you ought merely to wander through the Inner City ("Innere Stadt"), into the "Am Hof"—to me, the most picturesque square of Vienna, which houses the oldest and most picturesque cellar of Vienna at the **Urbanikeller,** Am Hof 12, where there's recorded music, vaulted brick ceilings and medieval furniture, a somewhat cool temperature, but also warming glasses of fiery Slivovitz (the almost tasteless Yugoslavian liqueur, that has a faint apple-like aftertaste) for 30 schillings a shot, or a 25-schilling glass of Vienna's best white wine ("ein Viertel Gumpoldskirchner"). Entrance is free.

But don't go home yet. For another Viennese experience, have an 11 p.m. (it closes at 12:30 a.m.) glass of wine at the famous, old **Augustiner Keller,** 1 Augustinerstrasse, in the Albertina Building, behind the Opera, where "ein Viertel" (quarter-liter) of cold, white wine costs 16 to 20 schillings, and where there's much Viennese flavor to the entire establishment. After 6:30 p.m., when a small Schrammelmusik band plays, there's a 5 schilling entertainment charge.

And then, for a budget midnight snack, stop at one of the mobile hot dog stands of Vienna (there's always one next to St. Stephen's Cathedral, another at the corner of Mariahilferstrasse and Neubaugasse) and order not frankfurters (which are just frankfurters), but a "Burenwurst"—a big fat sausage, bursting with flavor, for which the price is 20 schillings, including a big chunk of black bread and mustard.

And after such an evening of strolling and dreaming and drinking, you may burst into song as one American girl we overheard, did, to the tune of the Vienna Waltz: "Oh, we are in Wien, da dum, da dum, Yes we are in Wien, da dum, da dum . . ."

GRINZING: One other night of your stay should be reserved for this attraction— "Grinzing" being the generic term for an entire area of open-air wine houses on the northwestern edge of the city, about 5 miles from the center; it can be reached by direct tram line, #38, from the University for a fare of 10 schillings. You'll quickly find that drinking in Grinzing is a unique Viennese experience and, rather than being a tourist activity, is engaged in mainly by the Viennese themselves; you're bound to end up talking to the locals and getting happily involved in the sentimental music and international gossip that characterizes these be-flowered wine gardens, where everybody drinks and sings. Even during the winter and fall seasons, there's action: accordionists wander through the wine-halls and everyone joins in the soft Viennese airs. None of the establishments charges a minimum or cover; you can buy a ¼-liter mug of wine for 25 schillings ($1.85) and spend as long as you wish over it.

CAFE LIFE: The **Cafe Leopold Hawelka,** 6 Dorotheergasse (right off the Graben), is the one definitive meeting place of Viennese bohemians, attracting a heavily bearded, intense-talking crowd of young (and older) intellectuals and pretty young girls. Crowded tables, a hodge-podge of chairs, assorted caricatures and commentary art upon the walls, English and American newspapers to read; you can sit all night over a 12 schilling cup of coffee (small) or a large one for 18 schillings. Specialty of the house is *buchteln* (sort of a doughnut) baked fresh daily by Mrs. Hawelka and sold for 6 schillings apiece.

READERS' ENTERTAINMENT SUGGESTIONS: "The first stop any visitor to Vienna should make is at the **'Opernpassage'.** Located under the intersection of the Opernring, the Kärntnerring, the Kärntner Strasse, and the Wiedner Hauptstrasse, it houses a small, moderate restaurant and the principal office of the city tourist office. You can buy your 'Introducing Vienna' booklet here, pick up a map of the city, get advice on things to see and how to get there, and check the weekly schedule of theater performances. If anything at the state theaters interests you, ascend to the Staatsoper and proceed to the box-office (on the other side of the Operngasse) where tickets are available to the Staatsoper, the Volksoper, the Burgtheater and the Akademie-Theater. Tickets go on sale four days before the day of performance: I had no trouble getting tickets for a performance at the Volksoper for the night I arrived (Saturday) and a performance at the Staatsoper Sunday. Unlike Italy, where tickets are available for opera almost to curtain time, tickets in Vienna should be obtained in advance, especially for the Staatsoper" (Robert L. Guenther, Mt. Marion, N.Y.). . . . "For about two dollars, you can buy standing room for the **Volksoper.** We tried it both ways—we had $10 tickets one night and we stood the next night—and we could see and hear much better from the standing room section. And anyway, you can sit during the intermission in the empty seats" (Mrs. Jack Gordon, Collingswood, New Jersey). . . . "The **Vienna Symphony** conducts concerts during the summer at least twice a week beginning at 8 p.m. in the city Rathaus (city hall), which is on Dr. Karl Lueger Ring, I believe: You see, the Rathaus is like a hollow square, the symphony playing within the walls and at the same time under the moon and stars. It is a thoroughly enchanting experience. Tickets may be obtained at the Rathaus earlier in the day, and cost 40 Austrian schillings ($2.96)" (Michael D. Colman, Huntington Woods, Mich.). . . . "There is a literally huge weinkeller called the **Twelve Apostles,** at 3 Sonnenfelsgasse, two or three streets beyond St. Stephen's on the right along Kärntner Strasse, walking into the Innenstadt from the Ring. It is about a block off Kärntner Strasse. This place has three or four levels, jammed on Saturday and other nights with students. Our party of three shared a quart of the 'heuriger' wine, and this cost us 60 schillings. The keller also serves light snacks, which we didn't try. I would especially recommend this place

for students" (Victor C. Weisskopf, Frankfurt/Main, Germany). . . . "Tickets for the
evening's performance at the **Staatsoper** are often unobtainable anywhere. Fortunately,
there's nearly always a medical convention in Vienna, and where there are doctors, there
are opera tickets. A well-dressed American can walk up to the registration desk at any
of these conventions, urbanely say 'I did not order my tickets in advance, but do you have
any?' and usually get the finest seats available, in all price ranges. Alternatively, try the
concierge at any splurge-priced hotel" (Pauline Rissman, New York, N.Y.). . . . "It is
almost impossible to get seats for the Opera in season. If you know exactly when you
will be in Vienna, you should write ahead for tickets or deal with a ticket agency and
pay the 20% fee. Otherwise, you will have to line up for standing room. In that case,
go very early, take food along, and follow this procedure: If you are near the head of the
line, get **Parterrestehplatz** (orchestra standing room). If you cannot get this, get **Galerie**
(upper balcony) standing room for 15 schillings. You will then line up on the stairs and
when the signal is given dash upstairs with the mob and run for the Mitte section of the
Galerie. Your 'seat' is reserved by tying a scarf or handkerchief to the rail. (We were
friendly with an English couple—the husband was a basso studying in Vienna on scholarship and knew all the ins and outs of where to sit and stand, as they went every night).
If you can get seats, the best ones are Mitte Balcony. Remember, if you get tickets ahead,
you can always sell them if you can't make the performance, as the Staatsoper is
completely sold out all the time and there are always more people wanting tickets than
there are tickets available, for any and all performances" (Sara and Peter Cleveland,
Sharon, Massachusetts.). . . . "One of the best aspects of Vienna is its music (of course),
and you can hear a free concert every night in the **Stadtpark**—outdoors in good weather,
indoors in bad. For a seat, one must sit at a cafe there, but one drink will last all night,
and it can be a cheap apfelsaft, if you wish" (Charles M. Super, New Haven, Connecticut;
note by AF: this is a romantic (and cheap) evening activity, presented in the park
adjoining the Hübner Kursalon Restaurant at 33 Johannesgasse. There is no admission.
Go only to the inexpensive lower level, where you can sit over a Coke or beer all night.
From April to November, concerts are presented from 8 to 11 p.m. nightly, and Strauss
concerts are given inside the restaurants during tea-time, from 4 to 6 p.m.). . . . "From
May to November, there are free organ recitals every Wednesday night from 7 to 8 on
the new organ in **St. Stephen's Cathedral**, the sound of the instrument played by the
resident organist is a treat which no music lover should miss" (Theodora and John
Austen, Sandringham, Australia).

VIENNA MISCELLANY: For picnic ingredients, snacks and exciting atmosphere,
the open-air meat-and-vegetable market of Vienna ("the Naschmarkt"), located on the Wienzeile, three blocks from the Opera (see our map of the Opera
Area), should definitely be given an hour or two. Here you'll find the Theatre
an der Wien (operettas), and across the marketlined street, one of the cheapest
restaurants in Vienna (probably because it's so close to its food suppliers):
Restaurant Ruzizka, at 7 Rechte Wienzeile, where soup is 12 schillings, and
most main plates range between 28 and 40 schillings. . . . Vienna's only bicycle
rental firm is **Fahrradverleih Mazanek**, 32 Grosse Sperlgasse (phone 338-
3172), which charges 50 schillings a day and requires a returnable 500 schilling
deposit. Take streetcar A or B from the Opera to Schwedenbrücke, then change
to streetcar #26 and get off at the Bayrischer Hof station. . . . Laundromats
in Vienna? There's great news: a new Westinghouse Automatic has opened in
center city at 12 Tuchlauben, about 1½ blocks from the Hotel Wandl, and also
near the Hoher Markt. And there's an equally-good establishment at 59 Josef-
städterstrasse, called Miele Selbstbedienung Münzautomaten. Both charge 45
schillings ($3.33) for a wash of up to 5 kilograms, 15 schillings to dry. . . . Best
way to obtain definite reservations to various spectacles and performances in
Vienna: write first to the **Fremdenverkehrsverband für Wien** (the tourist
office), 5 Kinderspitalgasse, A-1090 Vienna, for a program of what will be
playing during your stay in Vienna, then write directly for seats (enclosing
money) to the following: (for performances of the Spanish Riding School)
Spanische Hofreitschule, Hofburg, Vienna—write at least three months in

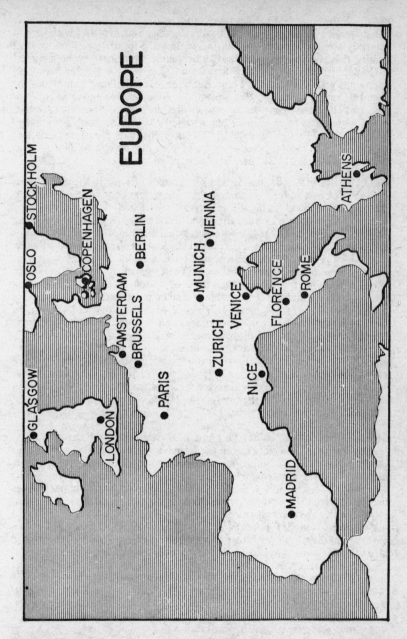

advance; (for the Vienna Boys Choir) **Hofmusikkapelle,** Hofburg, Vienna—at least two months in advance; (for the Opera, Volksoper, Burg- and Akademie Theatre) **Bundestheaterverband,** Goethegasse 1, Vienna 1. As luck would have it, nearly all these are closed throughout July and August. . . . Although there's not much to see beyond various items of furniture and books, his beige velour hat and black walking stick with ivory handle, you may feel a thrill and certainly awe and respect (as I did) in visiting the former study, library and waiting room of **Sigmund Freud,** at 19 Berggasse, which has now been opened to the public, Monday through Friday from 10 a.m. to 1 p.m., and on Saturdays and Sundays from 10 a.m. to 4 p.m. Entrance is 20 schillings, 10 for students. Freud lived and worked in this typical, old, Viennese apartment house from 1891 to 1938, when he moved to London after the Nazi occupation of Austria. . . . For babysitters in Vienna, phone 95-11-35, the offices of **Baby Sitter Zentrale,** whose sitters charge 50 schillings an hour, plus transportation. . . . And for the most delicious pastries of your life, make a definite effort to stop at a Viennese "konditorei" at 4 p.m. of an afternoon.

WEEKEND IN BUDAPEST: It may be a shock, upon arriving in Vienna, to learn that you've come so far East that you're almost next door to Budapest—and that you can go there! All the Viennese travel agencies sell tickets for a weekend bus tour to Budapest, which departs from Vienna early every Saturday morning and returns late Sunday night, with occasional additional departures in summer. But you'll pay less for the tour if you buy a ticket directly from the Vienna branch of the official Hungarian tourist bureau, called **Ibusz,** 26 Kärntnerstrasse (three blocks from the Opera). There, payment of 1,150 schillings ($83.92) in summer, 1,000 schillings ($74) off-season, takes care of everything but your visa (an additional 54 schillings) and booking fee (50 schillings more); transportation both ways, meals, lodgings, a 4-hour city tour of Budapest, an evening of wine-tasting with gypsy music, and enough free time to do some worthwhile poking around on your own.

You'll need to check in at Ibusz at least a few days in advance to reserve a place on this tour, and *must* turn in your passport two days before departure to get your visa (the passport is returned to you just before the bus leaves Vienna). A multilingual guide then accompanies the bus from the Hungarian border to Budapest and on the city tour, and the accommodations are at a good Budapest hotel. Amazing, nicht?

SWIMMING IN THE DANUBE: This is a final, wait-until-I-tell-the-folks-back-home experience. You can dunk in the Danube either informally, and without benefit of bathhouses, at numerous public beaches along its banks; or else more elaborately at the **Gänsehäufel**—a beautifully scenic swimming park—where lockers cost 25 schillings, low-cost restaurants abound, and ping pong tables are strewn about the grounds. To do either, walk to the bottom of Rotenturmstrasse (where the inner city meets the narrow Danube Canal) and then board a #B trolley. It heads for the Danube, 15 minutes away, and ultimately crosses that river at the temporary bridge replacing the old Reichsbrücke, on the other side of which you can descend and head for public beaches. But for Gänsehäufel, change at this point for a #25 or #26 trolley, stay on till the end of the line, then follow the crowd to this Coney Island-type establishment, and buy your locker key. Earlier, as you cross the bridge to Gänsehäufel, you'll enjoy a panoramic view of Vienna's skyline, the United Nation's skyscraper complex, and the Kahlenberg Hill where Prince Eugene of Savoy defeated the Turks in 1683, thus preserving Christian civilization.

———————

By this time, you've had enough of the Germanic countries. The trains for Italy leave from the Südbahnhof.

Chapter XII

VENICE

Don't Go Near the Water

VENICE is a fantastic dream. To feel its full impact, try to arrive at night, when the wonders of the city can steal upon you, piecemeal and slow. At the foot of the Venice railway station, there is a landing from which a city launch embarks for the trip up the Grand Canal. As you chug along, little clusters of candy-striped mooring poles emerge from the dark; a gondola approaches with a lighted lantern hung from its prow; the reflection of a slate-gray church, bathed in a blue spotlight, shimmers in the water as you pass by. This is the sheerest beauty, and it is a moment that no one should miss.

In the daytime, the city becomes a commotion of people and exotic sights. There's no need to buy your entertainment in Venice. You'll want nothing more than to stroll and window shop along its narrow streets; or to listen to a band concert in the Piazza San Marco; or to sail through the canals on a 60¢ vaporetto ride. In considering your basic costs, remember that Venice caters to many more French and German tourists than to Americans, and there are thus numerous moderate hotels and restaurants scattered throughout the city. By living where the Europeans live, you can thrive in Venice on entirely moderate costs. But that requires not only specific lists and data, but also some general knowledge about Italian tourist accommodations:

HOTELS: Italian hotels are classified by the Italian government, and prices within each class are rigidly controlled by law.

The official rates are fairly reasonable. In Venice, for instance, the highest category third class hotels (there are two lower categories—fourth and "locande") can offer singles without bath for prices ranging to a high of 13,000 lire ($15.66), including service charge and taxes, at the very height of the summer season. Doubles without bath cannot go higher than approximately 23,000 lire ($27.71), and that again includes service and tax. For a bed alone, you can therefore figure that your per-person costs (in a double room, without bath) can rise to a high of about $14 a day in the highest-priced of the third class hotels (of which only two or three charge that much). And they can, of course, be kept to a much lower figure in a *fourth* class hotel, in a *pensione*, in a *locanda* (inn), or even in the lower-priced of the third class hotels.

THE ITALIAN LIRA: For the purposes of this chapter, we've converted Italian lire into dollars at the rate of 830 lire per dollar —the approximate "floating" rate of the lira as of the time of writing. Thus, 100 lire have been assumed to equal approximately 12 U.S.¢. Though you can expect further fluctuations by the time of your own stay in Italy, the variance should not be substantial.

But now take note of a gimmick that exists in Venice and a few other seaside towns, but almost nowhere else in Italy. Since these resort areas swarm with tourists in the summer months, the pressure on hotel prices is something fierce. Therefore, to bypass the government-imposed price limitations, the majority of hotels in Venice will absolutely require that you take at least two meals at the hotel (breakfast and one other) as a condition of getting a room. By then charging a high $3 for breakfast and $8 for lunch, the third class hotels are enabled to increase their rates to an average of $25 per person for room without bath and two meals ("demi-pension"). While the hotel meals are admittedly good, that still isn't $15-a-day living.

How do you beat the system? By staying either in hotels that lack facilities for serving meals, or in lower category hotels. We've listed a number of them later on.

Remember, though, that these tactics are practiced only in the summer months. For, while Venice is the most expensive Italian city in summer, it is—paradoxically—the least expensive city in Italy off-season, when the multitudes of hotels here have gaping vacancies. Then, you can write your own ticket—just as American tourists do in Miami Beach, off-season. Walk to the counter, announce with firmness that you're seeking a double room for 18,000 lire ($21.68), and, nine times out of ten, you'll get one.

Ferrovia

If you're unhappy about lugging heavy suitcases into a sea-going streetcar (the vaporetto), then don't budge from the railroad (ferrovia) area. It hardly differs in character from the rest of Venice (there being no heavy industry here, no cars or trolleys), is located on a canal, and has an excellent selection of restaurants nearby.

Lista di Spagna (moderate-to-expensive)

As you leave Venice's modern railway station, look left. The street you see is the **Lista di Spagna,** and on it, within two or three blocks, are seven Second Class hotels, whose rates fall only into our Big Splurge range; six Third Class hotels; and four Fourth Class hotels. Walking down the Lista di Spagna, the Second Class hotels that *do not require the taking of meals* are: the **Terminus (1),** Lista di Spagna 116 (phone 715-045); the **Union (2),** Lista di Spagna 127 (phone 715-055); the **Corso,** Lista di Spagna 119 (phone 716-422); the **Austria (5),** Lista di Spagna 227 (phone 715-300); and the **Universo (6)** Lista di Spagna 123 (phone 715-076). The Third Class hotels dispensing with the meal requirement are the **Zecchini,** Lista di Spagna 152 (phone 715-060), the **Nazionale (7),** Lista di Spagna 158 (phone 716-133); the **Caprera (8),** Lista di Spagna 219 (phone 715-271); and the **Adriatico (9),** Lista di Spagna 224 (phone 715-176). Fourth Class hotels on the same street are: the **Adua (10),** Lista di Spagna 233 (phone 716-184); the **Minerva (11),** Lista di Spagna 230 (phone 715-968), and the **Guerrini,** Lista di Spagna 265 (phone 715-114).

Which to choose? The best *value* in the area is Mario Indri's second class **Hotel Terminus;** that's because Mario Indri has offered a special rate to readers throughout 1980 of 12,000 lire ($14.45) per person, breakfast included, in a bathless double room; considerably less off-season (Nov 1-Mar 31). Runner-up is the third class **Hotel Adriatico** (also 12,000 lire-$14.45-but without breakfast), followed by: the fourth class **Hotel Adua** (10,500 lire-$12.65-per person), **Hotel Minerva** (10,000 lire $12.04-per person) and **Hotel Guerrini** (9,000 lire per person). All remaining non-meal-serving second class hotels on Lista di Spagna—the **Union, Corso, Universo** and **Austria** —charge 18,000 lire ($21.68) per person, double occupancy, without bath and without breakfast; while the remaining third class hotels—the **Nazionale** and **Caprera** —charge 14,500 lire ($17.46) for the very same facilities, but with breakfast.

The very cheapest of the Lista di Spagna establishments—both recommendable—are the **Locanda Carretoni** at No. 130 (phone 716-231), and the **Albergo Moderno** at No. 154B (phone 716-679). The Carretoni, a cross between a pensione and a hotel, charges only 8,000 lire ($9.63) single, 14,000 lire ($16.86) double, for simple but adequate rooms, and the staff here has been exceptionally helpful to $15-a-day readers, occasionally offering special rates to families or students. The Moderno, a tiny, 14-bed lodging reached through a corridor-like entrance, rents its singles for 12,000 lire ($14.45), doubles for 19,000 lire ($22.89), and charges 2,000 lire more for breakfast. Appropriately enough, the rooms are also tiny—but clean.

Lista di Spagna sidestreets (moderate and inexpensive)

To find several other inexpensive hotels in the station area, watch for two narrow sidestreets that appear on your left, as you walk down the Lista di Spagna. The first of these, a few steps from the station, is the hotel-jammed **Calle Priuli,** a favorite of penny-pinching German tourists, for whom the Teutonic-sounding **Hotel-Pension Stella Alpina Edelweiss,** Calle Priuli 99D (phone 715-179), is the big draw in the big splurge range. It offers no meals other than breakfast, charges 26,000 lire ($31.32) for a double with two breakfasts, has a nice garden for sunbathing in back, and moderately-large rooms. . . . Closer to the Lista di Spagna, again on Calle Priuli, is the clean and decent **Alloggi Orsaria,** Calle Priuli 103 (phone 715-254), with much cheaper rates (double room without meals or bath for 12,500 lire ($15.06) total, triples for 16,000 lire; proprietors are two charming little old ladies whose favors to readers—tea on a rainy afternoon, helpful suggestions—go way beyond the normal hotel amenities); and elsewhere on the street is the higher priced **Hotel Dolomiti,** 72 Calle Priuli (phone 715-113), which charges 14,500 lire ($17.46), per person, including breakfast, service and tax. All these latter choices have somewhat forbidding exteriors, but please keep an open mind until you've seen the rooms; and don't be discouraged by the unusual narrowness of the street— as you get to know Venice, you'll discover that most of the streets are that narrow!

The next intersection, a few feet further down the Lista di Spagna, is the more attractive Calle Misericordia, whose particular star is the reliable **Hotel Atlantide,** Calle Misericordia 375a (phone 716-901). It charges 23,000 lire ($27.71) at the height of the season for a double without bath, taxes and service included, 13,000 lire for a single, and does not require that you take meals, although it does offer demi-pension for the good price of 20,000 lire ($24.09) per person; it's located about 50 yards down the street. . . . A fair distance further down the street, with slightly-higher prices (23,500 lire double, service and tax included), is the **Albergo Santa Lucia,** Calle Misericordia 358—recognized by its stone terrace with sun chairs in front—a place for older folks; phone 715-180. . . . And still further along, the **Pensione Villa Rosa** (which doesn't serve meals), Calle Misericordia 389 (phone 716-569), is not quite of the standard of the other Misericordia hotels, but may have vacancies on the day you're there. 22,500 lire ($27.10) for a double, breakfast included. Alternatively, try the **Casa Hilber** at 378 Calle Misericordia, phone 37-737, whose 18 rooms sometimes go as low as 18,500 lire ($22.28) double, 12,500 lire ($15.06) single, including service and tax.

If you arrive in Venice in July or August, you may have to trek to a number of the station-area hotels to find a vacancy, but somehow, you will always find one. Still, check your bags at the station first (300 lire for 24 hours), then find the room, then return for your bags—and in that manner, the whole process can lose its terror.

Piazza San Marco Area (expensive, but with some exceptions)

How about a hotel on the little inner canals of Venice, along alley-like streets that look like a set from Othello? If you don't mind searching and asking for directions, then take the vaporetto to the Piazza San Marco stop, and start looking for the **Albergo Atlantico,** located less than a hundred yards from the Piazza, at 4416 Calle del Rimedio (phone 709-244), on the canal of the Bridge of Sighs; from St. Mark's Square, walk down the Calle Larga San Marco till you pass the little Calle va al Ponte de l'Anzolo, and turn into that tiny street, then turn left just before the Trattoria alla Canonica, and then right on Ramo de l'Anzolo, where you'll find signs pointing to the Atlantico—a huge, labyrinthine building whose large stone rooms are almost entirely bare, without decoration of any sort, and without furniture other than beds, chests of drawers and wardrobes. It's perhaps because of this lack of "overhead" that owner Laura Innocenti can charge the following high season rates: 11,000 lire ($13.25) per person in a double room, breakfast, service and taxes included, 10,000 lire per person in a triple or enormous four-bedded room; probability of a 10% discount to bearers of this book who present a copy on registering.

For our less demanding readers, the Atlantico will provide adequate accommodations in friendly surroundings; half the staff seems composed of stranded young Americans or girls from England who have run out of funds and are working for their keep—and their presence lends an invigorating air!

If the Atlantico is full, try first the nearby **Locanda Riva,** 5310 Ponte dell'Anzolo (phone 27-034), whose kindly owner, Isidoro Salmaso, charges

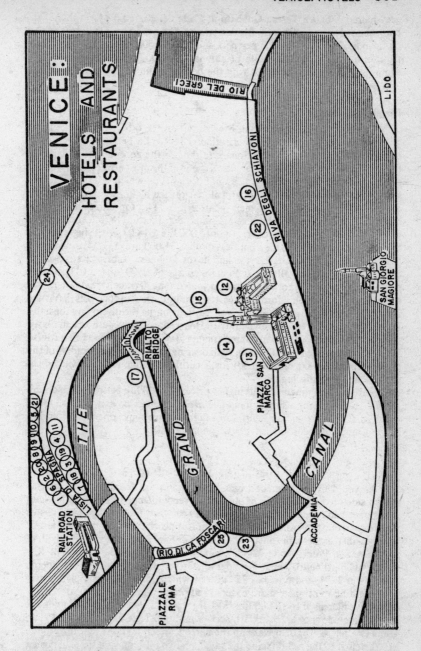

8,500 lire single, 16,000 lire double, 7,500 lire ($9.03) per person for a triple
or four-bedded room, with breakfast included. But if that, too, is full, you can
then seek out the utterly spotless private home accommodations of kindly,

grey-haired **Signora Teresa Gobbato** at Calle del Rimedio 4406 (phone 702-866), about 150 yards from St. Mark's Square. She has 15 beds to rent, and they go for only 7,000 lire ($8.45) per person double, 6,500 lire ($7.83) per person triple or quadruple, with breakfast (optional) at 2,000 lire. Your landlady, once again, is Signora Gobbato, but ring the bell with the name Kantz on it.

For older readers

Not far from the Piazza San Marco, but on the other side (to the left of #13 on our map), is the already-mentioned Teatro La Fenice (Venice's opera house), at the peaceful Fenice Square (although the approach to this area is through narrow streets, the Square itself is one of the most attractive in Venice). And running off this square are pleasant little lanes on which you'll find elegant, small third class hotels, all quiet, and all patronized by knowledgeable middle-aged persons and other extremely genteel folk. The top choice here is the beautifully-furnished **Hotel Ateneo**, Campo San Fantin (1876 Calle Minelli), phone 700-588, whose 1980 charges are 15,000 lire ($18.07) for a single without bath, 22,000 lire ($26.50) for a bathless double, 31,000 lire ($37.34) double with bath, and with breakfast, service and taxes included. Individual room air-conditioners are also available, at an extra charge of 2,500 lire ($3.01) per room per night. Do ask to go out on the former dining terrace (breakfast is now served indoors), which affords a superb panoramic view of the roofs of Venice. And follow the Calle de ca'Giustinian Orsato from the theatre to find the hotel. In the very same area, and owned by the very same people, are the similarly-priced **Hotel Kette**, 2053 San Marco (phone 70-77-66), and **Hotel San Moisé**, 2058 San Marco (phone 70-73-55), both offering a special rate to readers of this book only, of 22,000 lire ($26.50) for a bathless double room—their official price is substantially higher.

Fairly similar amenities but higher prices (14,500 lire per person in double rooms, 16,500 lire in a single, including *breakfast,* service and tax) are found in the smaller **Albergo San Fantin,** one flight up in an apartment-like building at the Campiello della Fenice 1930a (phone 31-401).

Ca' Foscari or San Toma Area

As you'd expect, Venice's best hotel values are found on the non-San Marco side of the Grand Canal, and we've recommended numerous low-cost "pensiones" and locanda there—much cheaper than the establishments listed thus far—in our "starvation budget" section appearing later in this chapter. Of better quality in this same area—Ca'Foscari or San Toma—is the **Albergo Iris,** at 2910A San Polo (phone 22-882), next door to the pleasant, outdoor Ristorante al Giardinetto, which was upgraded from pensione status to the albergo category in 1974, and now has 75 beds, of which 35 are in a completely new wing, with new entrance, marble steps, and brand new furniture. Rates, naturally, have increased to 13,000 lire ($15.66) single, 23,000 lire ($27.71) double, but they include shower, breakfast, service and tax. Take vaporetto #1 to San Toma (station #10), then walk up the narrow street, take the first turn to the 'eft, then first to the right, facing the canal, and you'll soon spot the sign posted Signor Enzo Fullin, who operates both the pensione and the restaurant 're he serves meals to guests taking demi-pension arrangements). Try for v wing.

Riva degli Schiavoni

Back now to the costlier choices. Just beyond the Piazza San Marco on the Grand Canal, you'll see a broad quay called the **Riva degli Schiavoni,** which can be further recognized by the large statue of a man-on-horseback in the center of the quay. In this setting, a few steps away, the **Casa Paganelli,** 4182 Riva Schiavoni (alternate entrance at 4687 S. Zaccaria), phone 24.324, is a surprisingly modern, 38-bed pension charging 27,500 lire ($33.13), breakfast, service and taxes included, for a double room. And for similarly-priced, pleasant and clean rooms nearby, walk from the Riva degli Schiavoni along the Canal, back in the direction of the Piazza San Marco, where soon you'll pass a narrow street, the Calle delle Rasse, which runs between the two buildings of the swank Hotel Royal Danieli. Turn in, and ten yards up, at Calle delle Rasse 4551 (phone 28.814; vaporetto is S. Zaccaria, #16), you'll find the **Hotel Pellegrino e Commercio (29),** which never requires that you take meals, and which charges exactly 32,000 lire ($38.55) for a double *with* bath, breakfast, service and taxes included, 19,500 lire for a single on the same arrangement. . . . Or, walk along the Canal in the other direction from the Riva degli Schiavoni, and you'll soon pass the little Campiello del Vin. Turn in, and in 15 yards, you'll be upon the cute **Pensione Campiello,** 4647 Campiello del Vin (phone 35.643), with extremely pleasant proprietors and far better rooms than the entrance would indicate. Here, the charge is 11,500 lire single, 21,500 lire ($25.90) for a bathless double room with *breakfast,* service and taxes included —an excellent rate for high-priced Venice.

The Rialto Bridge

Two popular Third Class hotels in Venice are handily located just next to the Rialto Bridge—a famous shopping center. These are the **Hotel Marconi (17),** Rialto 729 (one of whose wings was a former Venetian palace), and the **Hotel Rialto,** Rialto 5147. Throughout the year, doubles without bath, but with breakfast included, are 26,000 lire ($31.32) at the Marconi, 24,500 lire ($29.51) at the Rialto, while demi-pension in a bathless double is 22,500 lire ($27.10) per person at the Marconi, 19,500 lire ($23.49) per person at the Rialto. No elevators at either place, but fascinating and utterly authentic Venetian furnishings, and a magnificent location. The Rialto (phone 24.204) is the better of the two; take the vaporetto to "Ponte di Rialto."

(Incidentally, next door to the Hotel Marconi is a small trattoria called **"Sommariva,"** which has ten sidewalk tables facing the Canal Grande. I've often found it relaxing to sit here around 8:30 p.m. and watch the serenading gondolas as they pass on their summer evening parade under the bridge. Naturally you'll have to order something. Hope usually has a "coppa sport" for 1,700 lire—a glass filled with mixed ice creams and whipped cream, with a cherry on top. Unfortunately, the restaurant closes at 10 p.m.)

On the Giudecca Canal

Here you'll find two unique Venice institutions that catered to a highly intellectual sort of British tourist until British currency restrictions diminished the flow of English tourists to Venice. The **Pensione la Calcina,** 780 Zattere (phone 27.045), and the **Pensione Seguso,** 779 Zattere (phone 22.340), are both highly attractive hotels, the latter in marble with Venetian antiques and Murano glass, but neither would normally be thought to be well located—unless you crave an absolutely quiet situation away from commerce, drenched in sunlight and space, and directly facing the broadest segment of the Giudecca Canal.

Charges at the Calcina are 28,000 lire ($33.73) for a double without bath, but with two breakfasts included; at the costlier Seguso, half-pension is required, at a charge of 23,000 lire ($27.71) per person, in bathless rooms. Although the Zattere is serviced by a different vaporetto than the one that makes the trip up the Grand Canal, you can still reach it in the normal manner by going to the Accademia stop, and walking across the narrow neck of land from there. In fact, both the Seguso and the Calcina are only 200 yards from the Accademia Bridge on the Grand Canal; walk over that bridge and in a trice you're at the Piazza San Marco. Try the Calcina first (its middle class English atmosphere, with lace curtains on the windows, may prove a respite from the exotica of Venice).

In the Fondamenta Nuova area

An oddity ends our hotel discussion. Ideal for families, small groups basketball teams and choirs, who will enjoy rooms the size of museum exhibition halls, is the **Hotel Madonna dell' Orto**, at 3499 Cannaregio (phone 700-555), its foundations dating back to the 14th century. Originally the dwelling of a rich Venetian merchant of Marco Polo times, it later housed the Napoleonic embassy, then the governor of the Austro-Hungarian Empire, before its later conversion into a nunnery in 1918, after which it became a hotel. Rooms have terrazzo floors, high stuccoed ceilings, antique furniture, solid walnut doors and balconies, and are so large that your voice will echo if you speak loudly enough. There are, to top things off, so many corridors, halls, cellars and secret doors that a ghost which reputedly wanders through the hotel is undoubtedly a tourist who got lost there years ago! Breakfast is served in a garden (complete with grotto used as a bar) and atop the structure is a spectacular terrace overlooking Venice. The price? 26,000 lire ($31.32) for a bathless twin room, inclusive of breakfast, 10,000 lire ($12.04) for each additional bed with breakfast—and you can add quite a few to the average room. From the station, take the circolare No. 5 motoscafo to the Madonna dell' Orto stop (one leaves every 15 minutes from 6 a.m. to 9 p.m. on the 12-minute trip, 600 lire); from there walk through Ramo Terzo Piave and, passing a drugstore called Despar, to the canal facing the hotel.

READERS' HOTEL SELECTIONS: "We were lucky to find the **Hotel Basilea,** Rio Marin 817, telephone 21-853, rated as a Third Class hotel but with service I have not seen equaled in America; the charge for a double room, including breakfasts, service and taxes, is 25,000 lire ($30.12), 30,600 lire ($36.86) for a double with private bath and breakfast; 14,500 for a single including breakfast and service" (Charles Hooper, Dallas, Texas; note by A.F.: this is a very short walk—two bridges—down the Rio Marin, across the Grand Canal from the railroad station). . . . "We stayed one block from Piazza San Marco at the rather basic but inexpensive **Alloggi Valentino** at 4228 Calle Albanesi (no phone). A nice, clean double room cost us 13,000 lire per night, no breakfast served. And the lady who manages the place speaks English" (Pauline Maud, New York City).

READERS' PENSIONE SELECTIONS (IN ROUGHLY DESCENDING ORDER OF COST): "The **Pensione Ca' d'Oro**, 4391a Strada Nova (phone 34.797), is a classic Venetian pension, with marble floors and Baroque furnishings, and charges 11,000 lire single, 19,500 lire double without bath, 23,000 lire double with bath. Breakfast is 2,000 lire. Take vaporetto #1 from the Piazzale Roma or train station to Ca' D'Oro, walk straight from the stop to the first big street, turn right, and 150 yards along you'll find it next to the Argentine Consulate. The young managing couple are most friendly and helpful, and speak English and German" (Mr. and Mrs. Robert W. Byrne, Jr., Indianapolis, Indiana; seconding recommendations m Dr. William K. Linson, Asbury Park, New Jersey, and George Farwell, Australia). "The **Budapest**, near San Moisé Church, just off St. Mark's Square, is a fine pensione, g 23,000 lire for a double with shower, 2,200 lire extra for breakfast. The Toth family are in charge, and they are nice people" (Harry Ritz, Pittsburgh, Pennsylvania). ... "May I recommend the beautiful **Casa Frollo,** Island of Giudecca No. 50, tel: 22723, just across the Grand Canal from the Piazza S. Marco, and only a few steps from the vaporetto stop 'Le Zitelle' (vaporetto stop #5, second stop from S. Marco). The house is 16th century, with a superb large breakfast room with authentic old furniture, whose windows as well as a number of rooms overlook an incomparable two miles of Venetian scenery, including San Marco and La Salute. The pensione is well run by the very friendly blonde Venetian, Mrs. Flora Soldan, and is a meeting place for quiet people and for artists. I met an American writer (lady) who stayed there for more than one month. Unlike other Italian hotels, it has no televison or radio set in the hall nor in the breakfast room, so that you can stay there reading or talking, as you like. It also has a nice garden, for sunbathing. Have a look at the kitchen: you'll see a fantastic old collection of copper kitchenware. Rates for 1980 are 12,000 lire ($14.45) in bathless singles, 21,000 lire ($25.30) for bathless doubles, breakfast included, and as no other meals are served, there is no need for demi-pension arrangements. The view of Venice's skyline from the seven enormous breakfast-room windows is unique" (Emilio Fumagalli, Milano, Italy; note by A.F.: access to Casa Frollo from the train station is via boat #5, on the "linea circolare"). ... "The pensione of **Maria Bazzano,** two blocks from St. Mark's Square at 456B Corte del Forno (phone 33-113), was a real delight and a true Venetian experience: we had a large, immaculately clean room with three windows on the canal, through which we watched the serenading gondolas drive by. 1980 rates will be 16,000 lire ($22.89) double, 21,000 lire ($25.30) triple, 1,800 lire ($2.16) for breakfast, 750 lire more for unlimited showers" (Andrea and Peggy Di Spigna, Farmingdale, New York). ... "At the **Locanda Sturion,** near the Rialto Bridge at 679 Calle Sturion, Riva del Vin, San Polo (phone 36243), I am in a pleasant and spacious double room which costs 14,500 lire ($17.46) for two people. Breakfast is optional for 2,000 lire and baths cost 750. In addition to several spacious and well-furnished rooms, there is a large day room with tables which offers a magnificent view of the Grand Canal and Rialto Bridge. The Calle Sturion, where this is located, is a short distance from the Rialto Bridge—most easily reached by walking from the Bridge past the Marconi Hotel until you see it on the right. A building bridges the entrance to the street, but the sign for the Locanda Sturion is clearly visible just beyond" (P.R., name withheld on request; seconding recommendation from David H. Hosley, Stanford, California, who writes that the "view of the Grand Canal and Rialto Bridge [from the Sturion] was spectacular, and the sight of the singing gondoliers at night was like a fairy tale"). ... "We stayed at the **Alloggi Vicky,** a 5-minute walk from the Piazza San Marco, on the Calle del Rimedio 4407 (phone 38-880), where for 16,500 lire, we had a nicely-furnished, sunny, clean double room with breakfast included. Owners are a hospitable Venetian couple who greet you with a smile and make you feel very welcome" (Florence Lane, Madrid, Spain). ... "The best of many, many hotels on our trip, was found just a two-minute walk from the railroad station. When you leave the station, turn left and walk on Lista di Spagna until you see on your right the Hotel Continental. Immediately after it, you find a very narrow passage called Calle de Forno; in the house numbered 180 (30 feet in the calle and up about 60 steps), you will find your best buy: **Alloggi Casa Rina Ottolenghi** (phone 28838). There, for a spacious room with twin beds, sink with hot and cold running water, new and nice furniture, a very, very clean bathroom, we paid only 13,000 lire, for both of us, with tax and service already included. That was in the height of the season, and no meals were required. We have asked the owner, who told us that three persons in a room pay only 14,500 lire. There are no rooms for singles" (C. Rapoport, Jerusalem, Israel).

READERS' SELECTIONS FOR READERS IN MESTRE: "Instead of staying in high-priced Venice (the most expensive town in Italy, on-season), our Italian friends in Sorrento advised us to stay in Venice-Mestre, outside of Venice. Therefore, we stayed at the **Hotel Venezia,** Piazza 27 October (phone 972-400), Venice-Mestre. It was only 15 minutes by bus from our hotel entrance to the end of the Venice causeway and the start of the Grand Canal. We had no problem with luggage, garage, etc. And, we had a double room without bath for only 16,800 lire, taxes and service included, breakfast at 2,000 lire per person extra (singles were available for 11,500 lire)" Mark and Ruth Marron, Hayward, California; note by A.F.: we've had numerous other recommendations for the modern, 90-room Venezia, whose rooms with private bath are in the budget range, too; there apparently is a Pam department store directly opposite the Venezia, serving price fixed meals for 5,500 lire—more typical of Italian prices than what you'll encounter in Venice). ... "Anyone coming to Venice by car, train, or plane has to go through Venice Mestre, and it's there that he would do well to sleep, and to take at least some of his meals. For one thing, the grocery stores and bakeries in Mestre are cheaper and better than in Venice, permitting you to take wonderfully inexpensive picnic lunches with you on your daily trips into Venice (less than 8 km. away). My husband and I, and our two children, stayed in Mestre at the **Locanda Montepiana,** 17 Via Monte S. Michele (phone 92-62-42) for 24,500 lire ($29.51) per night, and for this we had two large rooms, tastefully furnished, spotless, and most attentive service. Each double rents for 12,250 lire. The owners recommended the nearby **Trattoria da Bepi** where we had the best Italian food of our entire stay. Each dish was exquisitely prepared and served—truly Lucullan—but at prices you'd pay for ordinary food: about 5,500 lire ($6.62) for a meal to remember. The Montepiana is within 5 minutes walking distance of the station" (Esther Kirschner, Oak Park, Michigan). . . . "We always stay in Mestre instead of Venice. Two years ago we did the same thing and stumbled onto the **Locanda Maria Luisa** on Via Parini 2 (phone 93-1968), off the street where the Ambassador Hotel is. There is a sign on the corner. It is a new hotel, or was four years ago. There are signs posted in four languages, but the owners speak only Italian and German. We stayed there again this year, and had a double room with a bed that could have slept four. Showers and baths are free, as is parking in the lot downstairs. For this we paid 13,000 lire, all included" (James and Alice Walker, Howard Beach, New York). . . . **"Albergo Col di Lana,** Venice-Mestre, at Via Fagare 19, tel: 926-879, was recommended to us by the fully-occupied Pensione Villa Montepiana and just around the corner from it. New and modern, spotlessly clean. A double room with sink and hot water (no meals served here) cost us 14,500 lire per night, all included. There is a bathroom and W.C. to every three rooms. Parking space in their locked lot behind the hotel is free, and it's only a five minute walk to bus, tram, and train stations, and to good restaurants" (Mr. and Mrs. Dennis Orwin, Hollywood, Florida). . . . "My wife and I stayed two nights in mid-October at the **Locanda Corso** in Mestre, on the third floor of a new ten-story building, half-a-block south from the Ambasciatori (Ambassador) Hotel, at 231 Corso del Popolo, phone 93-00-75. Our room had all new furniture, comfortable beds, a balcony, polished marble floors, and a spotless tiled bathroom was next door. The cost for a double room with breakfast, bath, and service charges included (for two) was only 15,600 lire. One of our best finds in Europe" (John J. Chalmers, Alberta, Canada; strong seconding recommendation from Mrs. Frank L. Meyer, Vista, California). . . . "Instead of staying in Venice, try the **Pensione Trento,** 2 Via Fagarè (phone 926-090), in nearby Mestre. It is rated Third Class, but we never could understand why. We had a lovely room with balcony and plenty of heat on chilly nights for 12,000 lire ($14.45) in October" (Frank and Linda Peterson, McLean, Virginia; note by A.F.: doubles at the Trento rent for 14,500 ($17.46) in summer of '80, not including breakfast). . . . "I hit a train strike on the way in from Vienna, so the train stopped in Venezia Mestre and was not allowed into Venice itself. Remembering what several readers had said, I decided to stay in Mestre, and booked into the **Hotel Centrale,** Piazzale Sicilia 15 (telephone 985-522), which proved to be the most modern hotel I stayed in in Europe. The hotel has 105 rooms (230 beds), all modern conveniences, free showers, a staff of bellboys and the like. I got clean towels every day and the maids even folded my dirty wash when I happened to leave it out! The cost? Only 9,500 lire for a single—a price unheard of in Venice proper. Breakfast is 1,800 lire additional, is delicious and is brought to your room on request. Commuting to Venice? Bus no. 2 stops right smack in front of the hotel, takes 15 minutes for the trip to Venice, costs 200 lire, 24¢. Other conveniences of the hotel (small things in America, but greatly appreciated in Europe): phone and hot and cold running water in all rooms; pull cords on the curtains; U.S.-style toilet facilities. And the staff will even mail your postcards and letters for you!" (Mark Estren, Middletown, Connecticut).

READERS' SELECTIONS (MARGHERA): "The closest hotels on the main route from Padua are a cluster in the city of Marghera. A short bus ride takes you direct to Piazzale Roma (in Venice), or if you prefer, you can drive there and park (though the lot may be crowded and a bit expensive). Two of the hotels I liked were the **Lugano** (11 Via Rizzardi, phone 92-0111), and the **Lloyd** (32 Via Rizzardi, phone 930-798). A double room without bath at the Lugano (which was built in 1964) costs 18,000 lire ($21.68), breakfast 2,200 lire extra, and that qualifies it for the budget category. Doubles with bath at the Lloyd are ?2,000 lire, breakfast 2,200 lire more" (G. Shapiro, Berkeley, California). . . . "I must ?l you about the wonderful, friendly establishment where I and my two back-packing ?anions stayed in Marghera (Venezia). The proprietress, Albina Giocutri, was like ?er to us, and meeting her and staying in her pensione for 7,800 lire per person per night in a double proved to be one of the most cherished moments of our trip abroad. That's the **Locanda Rizzardi**, 30175 Marghera (Venezia), Via Rizzardi 67, phone 921203" (Martha McGrath, Granada Hills, California).

READERS' SELECTIONS (LIDO): "The **Pensione Villa Parco**, located in Lido at Via Rodi 1 (telephone: 760-015), is a proof positive that the 'exclusive' Lido section doesn't necessarily have to cost an arm and a leg. This is a charming family pensione which has recently been renovated, and rates are 21,000 lire for a double 10,500 lire for a single, including breakfast. The Parco has a beautiful shaded garden and is located in a very quiet section right near the beach. In case you are arriving by car, they have a parking lot which is absolutely free to all guests" (Berne Thompson, New York, New York; recent seconding recommendations from other readers). . . . "For travelers who would like to combine a visit to Venice with a stay at a beach resort, we heartily recommend the **Hotel Union-Lido** (telephone 968043), located on a peninsula seaward from Venice, near the famous Lido. Part of a giant resort complex near Cavallino, it includes a large sandy, private beach; various outdoor sports facilities; several bars and restaurants; a supermarket; resident physician; and one of Europe's largest and best campgrounds; and charges for a double room during low season (before May 24 and after September 6) are 24,500 lire; during high season (May 25 to September 7) 29,500 lire. Each room includes a private bath with hot shower and is beautifully furnished. The hotel requires that rooms be rented for a minimum of a week from Saturday to Saturday. (Bungalows are also available for those who might have their own bedding, at about half the cost of the hotel rooms.) This is primarily a 'family-type' resort. Minors are admitted only when accompanied by parents. To reach the Union-Lido from Venice, go to the Riva degli Schiavoni near St. Mark's Square and board one of the ferry boats to Punta Sabbioni, which makes a stop at the Lido before reaching Punta Sabbioni. The boats leave daily from 6 a.m. to 10 p.m. at regular intervals, and cost 600 lire (72¢) per person, one way, for the 40-minute ride. On reaching Punta Sabbioni, board the public bus across the street (one always meets each ferry) and tell the driver to let you off at the 'Union-Lido'. Motorists can reach the Union-Lido via Jesolo and the peninsula drive" (Len and Jean Gashel, Malvern, Pennsylvania).

THE LOWER-PRICED ROOMS: As we enter 1980, Venice's most comfortable low-budget value for men is a modernistic, little Hilton-like place called the **Domus Cavanis** (sometimes known as the "Istituto Cavanis"), at #912a Accademia (phone 87.374), diagonally across the narrow street from #989 Accademia (the only street number you'll be able to spot); from the main side of the Grand Canal, walk over the Accademia Bridge to the renowned Accademia museum, then walk up the street alongside the museum to find the Domus, on your right. Operated by a religious organization, equipped with an elevator, with stylish Scandinavian-modern furnishings, and a large breakfastroom lounge, and open to foreigners (males only, but of all ages) only in summer, the Domus has more than 70 rooms, renting for 5,000 lire ($6.02) per person in doubles or triples, not including breakfast. That's for plain rooms, of course, with narrow beds; but some rooms even sport a small balcony! Don't, of course, confuse this recently-built portion of the Domus with its older wing.

If you're a female budgeteer, try the **Domus Ciliota**, next door to 2976 Calle de la Muneghe (phone 704-888), two short blocks from the Campo S. Stefano (nearest vaporetto is stop #13), and therefore only five minutes on foot from the Piazza San Marco, on the main side of the Grand Canal. A large rust-colored building operated as a school in winter (it has the pace and tone of a convent), this one accepts foreigners in July and August, occasionally in other months as well; and specializes in girls and families, although it will sometimes (but not often) take "well-mannered" young men, as two tiny nuns on duty explained to me last summer. About 60 rooms in all, for which the charge is 9,000 lire ($10.84) single, 16,000 lire ($19.27) double, no breakfast; from the huge Campo S. Stefano, walk two short blocks down the Calle de la

Boteghe until you see Calle de la Muneghe on your left—the Ciliota is 30 yards down that street, on your left.

A third and primarily-student hotel, but this time definitely for ladies only, is the **Casa della Studente "Domus Civica"**, at 3082 S. Rocco (phone 24.332), three short blocks from the Campo S. Rocco and its famous Scuola S. Rocco. This establishment, operated by the "Associazione Internazionale al Servizio della Giovane", but accepting women under 25 in summer, is on the quieter, cheaper and non-tourist side of the Grand Canal, and the building is considerably more comfortable than the usual hostel of this sort. You'll pay 5,000 lire ($6.02) per person, in double rooms; and you'll encounter an 11:30 p.m. curfew. Highly recommended. From the Campo S. Rocco, walk down the Calle Tintoretto into the Calle delle Chiovere which leads to the Calle de le Sechere, site of the large "Casa". Nearest vaporetto stop: S. Toma.

Finally, **Casa Duval** at 3198 Calle San Bernardo (phone 31-715), near San Barnaba, normally a student establishment, rents its 20 beds to tourists during the summer months, for 6,000 lire ($7.22) per person in a 10-bed dormitory, for 8,000 lire ($9.63) per in a simple double room. The old palace housing this hostel is positioned to face the Canal Grande, and the view from the huge balcony on the second floor is alone worth the effort to find it: take the vaporetto to Cà Rezzonico, and then ask the way to the narrow, lengthy Calle San Bernardo; but phone first.

The "locandas" of Venice

Beneath the fourth class category of Italian hotels is still a lower subdivision known as "locanda", but if the thought causes you to quake—it shouldn't. I've found, after examining several in Venice, that they scarcely differ from the more simple forms of pensions; and indeed, several of them have actually replaced the "locanda" in their title with the words "pensione" or "casa"—boarding house. Yet because of their category, they charge as little as 14,500 lire ($17.46) for a double room, service included. A typical example is the **Locanda Semenzato**, 4363 Calle Bembo (phone 27.257), just off the S.S. Apostoli, which charges just that for a double room on its third floor, only 24,500 lire ($29.51) for a "family room" housing four. What's more, they're English-speaking at the Semenzato (the wife, Miriam, is from Long Island, New York), and have two modern baths and showers, whose use costs 1,000 lire. Take the vaporetto to the Ca' d'Oro stop (#6), walk up Traghetto Street to "Strada Nuova", follow that to the right until you reach the Campo S.S. Apostoli, and when you're in front of the church that you'll soon see, take the first turn on the left (the square building to your right is one of the few Lutheran-Protestant churches in Italy), pass the coffee shop and the pharmacy, and then turn into the first narrow calle (street) to the left. And add 1,500 lire per person for breakfast. Phone first. . . . Alternatively and around the corner from the Ca' Foscari university building (pass a bridge to reach it), the **Locanda Ca' Foscari**, at 3888 Calle della Frescada (phone 25817), is managed by Signora Meneghetti and her English-speaking son Walter, offers 30 beds in one single, three double, and several triple and four-bedded rooms, at the reasonable rates (for Venice) of only 8,500 lire ($10.24) single, 14,500 lire ($17.46) double, 18,500 lire ($22.28) triple, 24,500 lire ($29.51) quadruple. Breakfast is 2,000 lire extra. Nearest vaporetto stop: San Toma, #10.

It should be stressed again that this area of Ca' Foscari, between the San Toma and Ca' Rezzonico vaporetto stops, on the non-San Marco side of the nd Canal, is considerably less expensive, and less touristic, than across the From the Calle Larga Ca' Foscari, for instance, walk down the Croseria to the Calle S. Pantalon, and on that last named street, you'll find several establishments (such as the one at #3737) selling delicious portions of fried fish (which you eat on the spot) for 1,700 lire per portion. Or, from the Campo (Square) San Barnaba, and the Ca' Rezzonico stop, walk down the Calle Lunga, and you'll pass trattorias selling full meals for 5,500 lire and less. This is where the Venetians go to eat, and cost-conscious travelers will join them.

Back, though, on the main side of the Canal, and only 200 yards from St. Mark's Square, the **Locanda Silva,** 4423 Fondamenta del Rimedio (phone 27.643), offers clean rooms in a surprisingly quiet location, all under the calm management of Signor Ettore and his daughter Sandra (the latter acting as interpreter). Their charge, which *includes* breakfast, is 8,500 lire ($10.24) single, 14,500 lire ($17.46) double, 18,000 lire ($21.68) for a room with three beds. The Silva is just around the corner from the central tourist office of Venice ("E.P.T.", "Ente Provinciale per il Turismo"), and you can find it by following the yellow E.P.T. signs posted at various house corners in the Calle Larga San Marco and on the Piazza San Filippo e Giacomo.

Still another outstanding locanda, that ranks with the Silva, is **Locanda San Stefano,** at 2957 Campo San Stefano (phone 24.460), near the Accademia Bridge on the Piazza San Marco side of the Grand Canal, where a tiny little elevator (which is probably the only elevator in any Venetian locanda) links the 20-or-so tiny, but stylish, rooms. The Campo San Stefano is a big, open square on a direct walking route to San Marco; it possesses a stylish little lobby, of all things; and someone will someday get around to reclassifying it upward into hotel status—until they do, you'll pay only 12,000 lire ($14.45) for a double room, service and taxes included. Don't confuse the San Stefano with the **Casa de Stefani,** another cute and inexpensive little place (doubles 13,000 lire) that's 30 yards from the Ca' Rezzonico vaporetto stop. Again on the Campo San Stefano, if you'll walk past the only newsstand, and turn left at the flower shop, you'll be surprised to find a small elevated square with one side covered by climbing plants—an unusual sight for Venice. The green door there is the entrance to the **Locanda La Fiorita,** 3457a San Stefano (phone 34.754), which has nine rooms, 19 beds, and proprietor Signor Lorenzo Solda, who looks like Ronald Colman. He charges 15,000 lire ($18.07) for doubles, 20,000 lire for triples, *including* breakfast, and charges nothing for cold showers, 900 lire for hot ones.

A last locanda, in the Via Garibaldi area (nearest vaporetto stop, no. 18, is "Giardini"), at 269 Castello (phone 70-42-03), in a new building with modern furniture and spectacular Murano lamps, is the **Santa Anna;** it's operated by a particularly friendly Venetian family named Vianello, and if you'll phone Signor Bruno Vianello from the station, he'll send over either son Walter (16 years old) or daughter Antonella (15) to meet you at the Giardini vaporetto station—both speak English. Singles 8,500 lire ($10.24), doubles 14,500 lire ($17.46), triples 20,000 lire ($24.09), a large, four-bedded room 25,000 lire ($30.12), with showers 1,500 lire extra.

Two religious hostels

Cheaper than the average locanda are two religious hostels, of which one is under Catholic auspices, the other a Protestant house.

Istituto San Giuseppe, at 5042 Castello (phone 25-352), a private Catholic kindergarten operated by nuns, accepts up to 50 tourists, male and female, from July 1 to September 30, in bathless twin rooms renting for 5,500 lire ($6.62) per person per night, without breakfast. This is in a unique central position, and easy to find: walk through the Clock Tower (Torre dell' Orologio) at St.

Mark's Square into the Merceria, then take the second turn right, pass the movie theater and vegetable shop, cross the small square called Campo della Guerra, then walk over the bridge (called Ponte della Guerra): the opaque glass door in the marble arch right after the bridge is the Istituto's entrance. Ring the small brass bell, and a friendly nun will greet you with a smile.

Foresteria della Chiesa Valdese, at 5170 Castello (phone 27-594), consists of two very large, high-ceilinged rooms on the second floor of an old palazzo, one with 12 double-decker beds for men, one with 10 for ladies; before falling asleep, you can admire the paintings on the ceiling. Price is 5,000 lire ($6.02) per person, without breakfast, and without curfew; but Pastore Garufi—the Protestant clergyman in charge—will ask that you be in by 9 p.m. on your first night there. If, after that, he ascertains that you're the proper sort (he won't, for instance, allow "noisy people" to remain), he'll provide you with a house key, and you'll make your own hours. Again, a central location: walk first to the Istituto San Giuseppe (see above), but keep walking straight ahead after the Ponte della Guerra, cross another bridge and the Campo Santa Maria Formosa, then walk into the Calle Lunga, at the end of which is another bridge (Ponte Cavagnis) leading directly to the Foresteria at #5170. Open all year.

READERS' BUDGET SELECTIONS: "The best of many, many hotels on our European trip was the **Locanda Rossi,** a five-minute walk down Lista Di Spagna, then a left to Calle Delle Procuratie 262 (phone 715-164), one block down this street on the left; for a very spacious room with twin beds, sink with hot and cold running water, nice furniture and generally clean accommodations, we paid 7,000 lire, or $8.43 per person. Although the official marked price was slightly higher, the government tourist agency at the railroad station had quoted us 7,000 lire with tax and service included; the owner guaranteed the 7,000 lire price to people bearing a copy of *Europe on $15 a Day,* and no meals are required there even during the height of the season" (Joseph Blum, San Francisco, California; note by A.F.: 1980 rates at the Rossi for readers of this guide only, are 8,500 lire single, 15,000 lire double; you'll be pleasantly surprised by the character of the pastel-colored rooms— some of which directly overlook the park—and by the long-tressed daughter of the owner).

THE YOUTH HOSTEL: Venice's youth hostel, the **Ostello Venezia,** a fortress-like red-brick building at 86 Zitelle, on the Giudecca Island, facing the lagoon next to the Zitelle motoscafo stop (phone 38-211), was completely modernized and expanded in the fall of 1977 to accommodate up to 300 guests in large, airy, 30-bed dorms, girls on the first floor, boys on the second floor, each floor containing eight showers, nine wash basins and eleven toilets. Provided you have a hostel card (which you can purchase on the spot from bearded manager Paolo Berni for 9,000 lire), you will pay only 3,500 lire ($4.21) per night for your bed, breakfast included. Downstairs is, also, the best budget restaurant in Venice, which can be patronized by non-hostel-card-holders as well—even adults, if they wish!—who pay only **2,500** lire for a "menu" consisting of spaghetti or soup, meat dish with vegetable, one item of fruit and a roll. Beer or wine are 500 lire extra, and hours are from 7 to 9 a.m., noon to 2 p.m., and 6 to 8 p.m. To reach the hostel, either from the railroad station or St. Mark's Square, take motoscafo #5 (600 lire) to the Zitelle stop.

READERS-ON-THE-STARVATION BUDGET: "Archie's Backpacker's Home, 979A Fondamenta di Cannaregio (no phone), less than ten minutes (with backpack) from the station, is an ᵃmazing European find at only 4,500 lire ($5.42) per day in a clean room with shower ʾ kitchen facilities, central location. From the station, walk the length of the Lista di ᵃ, pass the Guglie Bridge, turn left, and it's 300 yards ahead. Look for a small arch ᵗ's Arch) with the number 977, and go through it" (Bobby Davenport, Dartmouth ᴴanover, New Hampshire; note from AF: open only from May through October, and admitting newcomers, only on Mondays, Wednesdays and Fridays from 9 to 5, Archie's accepts up to 50 young men and women in four-bedded, dorm-type rooms; the 33-year-old Archie, different in every way from his U.S. television namesake, speaks nine languages, and dreams of a "utopic world community without prejudices between people." When I first visited in October, 1979, a dozen-or-so lodgers were busily preparing a communal meal of octopus stew and wine, at a cost of 2,000 lire ($2.40) per person. There are footlockers and free showers, two kitchens with pots and pans, and the absence of sheets is remedied by linen sleeping bags that can be rented for 750 lire (90¢); 4,500 lire is the 1980 bed rate. Turn immediately left after crossing the Guglie Bridge (the one with the four small obelisks), and walk along the canal to Archie's).

RESTAURANTS: Italian restaurants dish out huge, filling portions of the food they serve. You'll find that one or two courses, chosen from any à la carte menu, are all you'll need or want for at least one of your daily meals in Venice. By limiting that meal to a sensible two courses, you'll also keep eating costs around $3, and still emerge with bulging Bermudas.

Thus, for example, a large plate of spaghetti with meat sauce—a full meal—costs 1,200 lire ($1.44) in most Venetian restaurants. Antipasto, enough for a light lunch, ranges around 1,700 lire. A meat plate with vegetables is rarely more than 2,800 lire ($3.37). If you eat more than this, you'll feel the effects as you stagger out into the broiling midday sun to continue your touring activities.

In the evening, of course, you'll want a full dinner, and for that purpose, the prix fixe meal—several courses for one lump sum—is the item to find. Here, it's called the "pranzo à prezzo fisso," and it's huge: spaghetti or minestrone, followed by meat course and vegetable, followed by salad, with cheese or fruit for dessert, and often with wine or bread included in the price of the meal. In France, as you'll recall, similar meals average slightly under $6.50. In most Italian cities, they're easily found at numerous restaurants for 5,000 lire ($6.02). In tourist-happy Venice, as you'd expect, the normal prezzo fisso dinner is a higher 5,500 lire ($6.62), although we'll find a few restaurants charging considerably less.

Also in Venice, you'll encounter the most frequent new Italian variation on the "prezzo fisso" meal, called the "Menu Turistico." Since a prezzo fisso can vary considerably in the number of items provided on it (either two or three courses, with or without beverage, with or without service charge), the Italian tourist authorities recently came up with a new designation—"Menu Turistico"—which must, by law, refer to a three course meal with beverage, service charge and bread included; when you order a "Menu Turistico," at a certain price, there mustn't be a single penny added to that price on your bill. The official regulations read: "The Tourist Menu consists of a first course, a second course with vegetables, then cheese or fruit or a sweet for dessert, and ¼ liter of wine or a glass of local beer or other aerated beverage, or a half bottle of mineral water. The price includes bread, cover charge, service charge and taxes." For present purposes, keep in mind that a "Menu Turistico" is often different from a "prezzo fisso"—it contains more items and fewer surprises.

The magic words "prezzo fisso" or "menu turistico" can be spotted all over Venice, but they're most easily found in the area of the railroad station: at the Mensa DLF, and along the street called Lista di Spagna.

The Mensa DLF

From the railroad station, walk down the station steps almost to the water, then turn immediately right for 100 yards, and you'll spot a modern building at 19 Fondamente S. Lucia that houses the **Mensa Dopolavoro Ferroviario**

(Mensa DLF for short), which shares honors with the youth hostel restaurant (see above) and the stand-up Rosticceria S. Bartolomeo (see below) as the top budget restaurant of Venice. Here, in a mammoth L-shaped dining room, you select your dishes from a self-service counter, where you'll find soup or pasta for 900 lire, main courses for 2,000 lire, vegetable or salad for 750 lire, a quarter liter of wine for 350 lire—meaning that you can compose a full-course meal similar to a prezzo fisso for 4,000 lire—a full 1,500 lire less than you would pay in the waiter-equipped dining room next door (the cafeteria is open for lunch only, from noon to 2:30 p.m., but seven days a week). Operated by the railway workers union, Mensa DLF caters to just about every secretary, shopgirl and gondolier in the area. Why aren't our railway workers this enlightened?

On the Lista di Spagna

Another major area for budget restaurants serving "Menu Turistico" meals is along the **Lista di Spagna**, the street which runs from the left of the railroad station. The first of these, which can be seen from the station steps, is the **Trattoria Roma (18)**, Lista di Spagna 122Q (not to be confused with the more expensive Ristorante Roma), serving spaghetti or soup, then Veal Cutlet Milanese, salad, cheese or fruit, wine, and large chunks of fresh Italian bread, for exactly 5,500 lire ($6.62). This is almost directly across the street from the more easily found Trattoria Bella Venezia (see below), has no identifying sign out front, and is highly recommended—not only for its food, but for its backroom garden, which faces directly on the Grand Canal. If you plan at the Roma to order à la carte (pasticcio di lasagne 1,700 lire, fritto misto mare—fried fish—3,200 lire), you can save money by sitting at the solid wooden tables without tablecloths where the normal 500 lire cover charge and 12% service charge asked of à la carte diners is not assessed. Closed Fridays. . . . Only slightly more expensive are the meals (on a "Menu Turistico") to be had a few doors up for 6,000 lire ($7.22) at the **Trattoria Bella Venezia (19)**, Lista di Spagna 129. This, by the way, is a beautiful place, with clean table cloths and flowers, and cool air, even in the midday sun. Excellent food and friendly waiters, but not the standout that the Trattoria Roma is, and closed on Thursdays. . . . The **Ristorante Caprera (20)**, at Lista di Spagna 225A, closed on Wednesdays, serves a similar Menu Turistico, for 6,000 lire, the well-recommended **Trattoria Nuova**, 189 Lista di Spagna, closed Fridays, charges 6,000 lire for its M.T., and the **Trattoria Tre Gobbi**, 148 Lista di Spagna, wants 6,000 . . . To lower this cost, keep walking up the Lista di Spagna, and in a couple of blocks you'll reach the little square called Campo San Geremia, on which you'll see the **Ristorante Alloggi "Al Brindisi" (21)**, closed Thursdays, offering three courses plus service for 5,500 lire ($6.62), but without beverage. . . . These, by the way, are the prices charged at the height of the summer season: they're often less in other months.

Beyond the Lista di Spagna

As you walk to the end of the Lista di Spagna (around the Campo San Geremia), this broad (for Venice) street continues as a major thoroughfare under other names, which in turn are grouped under the heading "Strada Nova"—the street continues nearly to the Rialto Bridge, and along its length you'll find other budget restaurants that generally undercut the Lista di Spagna establishments by from 500 to 1,000 lire. Thus, for example, at 2232 Strada Nuova, the **Trattoria Da Luciano** (closed Sundays) serves a three-course prezzo fisso—including everything except beverage—for 5,000 lire; another trattoria at 5619a Campiello Riccardo Selvatico offers the same repast for 5,000 lire (closed Mondays); and for 500 lire more, around the corner from the last-named spot, and on a tiny canal at 5597 Calle Dolfin, you'll find the best of these eateries—the **Trattoria al Vagon**—with a 5,500 lire summer season meal.

Piazza San Marco

More prezzo fisso meals near the Piazza San Marco? There are a number of good ones, but mainly in the $8 price range. At the right of the stunning Ducal Palace, along the Canal, you'll see the very swank Hotel Royal Danieli. It's composed of two buildings. Between those buildings, you'll note a little alleyway called the **Calle delle Rasse (22)**. Walk down this street for fifty yards, and you'll pass no fewer than three prezzo fisso restaurants offering meals for 6,000 lire (the best of them being **Ristorante Nuova Grotta,** at #4538, where you might order the zuppa di pesce—fish soup, or the spaghetti alle vongole—with clam sauce). The price ascends to a high 8,000 lire (including beverage and service—it's a "Menu Turistico"), however, at **Ristorante La Gondola,** 4610 Calle Rasse, which you might try and where the zuppa di verdura is especially good. . . . Nearby, at 4620 Calle delle Rasse, the small, self-service **Rosticceria Scarpa** is an alternative for quicker meals, such as a plate of Pasticcio di Lasagne for 1,000 lire, or delicious hot sandwiches baked in oil ("Mozzarella in Carozza") for only 450 lire. . . . At the end of Calle delle Rasse, you'll be on a square called Campo S. Filippo Giacomo ("Giacomo Square"), where the large **"Conca d'Oro"** serves the city's best pizza—some varieties for only 1,600 lire, others for 2,000—always in sufficient sizes for a light-to-moderate snack. Sidewalk tables here, a big awning, waiters wearing red-striped gondolier's T-shirts, and the city's most unusual 6,000 lire Menu Turistico, considering the choices: first course is either spaghetti, soup or a pizza; second course is meat, frittura mista (fried fish), omelette, or 12 mussels, all with a vegetable or salad; and two rolls are thrown in, as well. Closed Tuesdays. . . . Off the Giacomo Square, you'll then find a tiny alleyway called the Calle degli Albanesi, which runs parallel to Calle delle Rasse and whose only inhabitant seems to be the large and pleasant **Taverna dei Dogi,** 4250 Calle Albanesi, closed Tuesdays, serving a three-course meal, wine and service included, for 6,500 lire; on that meal is an incomparable specialty of Venice—"Fritto Misto dell Adriatico," sometimes known as "Frittura dell Adriatico"—which are tiny, goldfish-sized fish fried in batter, and something you really should try. The picturesque dei Dogi is highly recommended by me.

Alternatively, if you either walk or take the vaporetto one stop beyond the first Riva degli Schiavoni stop, in the direction of the Lido, you'll quickly find the **Calle della Pescaria,** site of the **Trattoria alla Bronza** (serving a true Menu Turistico for 6,500 lire; sidewalk tables), **Trattoria alla Doccia** (sea food specialties; Menu Turistico 6,000 lire); and best of all, the **Ristorante Tcson** (beautifully-cooked 6,500 lire Menu Turistico). The 6,000 lire trattoria here— the Doccia—is undoubtedly one of the cheapest in the San Marco area, but the location is a good five-minute walk from St. Mark's along the canal going towards the Lido (watch the side streets on your left, one of which is the Calle della Pescaria). . . . Nearby, at 3983 Bragora, a small, new fish restaurant called **Friggitoria Caratteristica Veneziana** opened in 1977, and is slightly less expensive than the restaurants on the Calle della Pescaria: menu turistico for 4,500 lire, polenta 600 lire, fried octopus or grilled fresh sardines for 3,000 lire, two glasses of white wine 500 lire. There is no other place in Venice where you can

eat fish specialties for less money. Location: just around the corner from
Trattoria alla Doccia, about 20 yards away.

Finally, a few short blocks from St. Mark's Square, at Calle Fuseri 4359,
the two white-smocked Zorzi brothers (both over 70) still operate the restaurant they opened many years ago, the **Latteria e Cucina Zorzi.** When you ask
a Venetian today where the best whipped cream (panna montata or just panna)
is being served, the reply is sure to be "at Zorzi's." In addition to this specialty
—still prepared the old-fashioned way by hand in large copper bowls—the
restaurant (32 seats on the ground floor, 70 on the first floor, 14 steps up) serves
one of the tastiest vegetable soups I have ever eaten for 900 lire ($1.08), large
plates of spaghetti for 1,000 lire ($1.20), ½ roast chicken for 2,400 lire ($2.89),
beefsteaks for 3,500 lire ($4.21), various fish dishes ranging from 2,500 to 3,000
lire ($3.01 to $3.61); and, of course, an enormous portion of the fabulous panna
(whipped cream crowned with a round biscuit) for 1,000 lire ($1.20), the same
price being charged for a glass of hot chocolate topped with panna. Closed
Sundays.

Friggitoria da Bruno

A budget stand-out on the *other* side of the Grand Canal, the **Friggitoria
da Bruno,** 2754 Calle Lunga, is just a few yards off the Campo S. Barnaba, and
offers a remarkable meal of pasta, followed by meat or seafood with one
vegetable and one roll for only 4,000 lire ($4.81), including beverage and service
charge (a special rate guaranteed to bearers of this book until the end of 1980).
In this white-tiled little eatery with modern art on the walls the selection of
dishes is a surprisingly wide one, the food unusually tasty, and the location—
away from the more heavily-touristed areas of Venice—is probably the explanation for the atypical prices. Operated by a charming Venetian family, Gilber-
to Santini and his wife Edelweiss (he cooks, she serves); closed Sundays.

The Santa Margherita area

Want some more? Less than five minutes by foot from Friggitoria Da
Bruno are a cluster of budget-type trattorias on the Campo Santa Margherita
(which is the largest square or piazza in town, after San Marco and San Polo).
Try: **Sole di Napoli** (house # 3023—look for the yellow phone disc sign above
the door), which offers a quite remarkable prezzo fisso for 4,500 lire ($5.42),
with a broad variety of choices and an attractive waitress; **Due Torri** (house
3408), with no Menu Turistico, but with à la carte three-course selections
totalling less than 5,500 lire ($6.62); **Antico Capon** (house # 3004), where the
three-course Menu Turistico is priced at 5,000 lire; **Vini Piave** (house # 3062,
at Rio Terra Canal), popular for its fried fish (a large portion is 2,600 lire,
spaghetti with tomato sauce is 1,000 lire); and, finally, **Ai Padovani** (house #
2839, near Ponte dei Pugni), now a self-service rosticceria, very popular among
students from the Ca'Foscari University a few hundred yards away, who buy
filling meals there for less than 5,000 lire. (Ai Padovani is next to the canal
where Katharine Hepburn fell into the water in *Summertime*.).

Of all the budget trattorias in the Campo Santa Margherita area, Sole di
Napoli—owned by a couple from Naples, Nina and Carmelo Esposito—is the
budget stand-out (see above for its address and location). For, in addition to
guaranteeing their 4,500 lire prezzo fisso meal until the end of 1980 to bearers
of this book, the Espositos also offer a "menu studenti" (it's available to anyone
of any age, student or not) for only 3,000 lire ($3.62), consisting of spaghetti
or minestrone, followed by any of six second choices (fish filet, pork chops,

calves liver, omelette), to which you can add bread for 200 lire, and wine, beer or mineral water for 500 lire more. Or you can simply request "pizza and spaghetti" for 2,500 lire ($3.01), if you're not to anxious to down a Venetian banquet in the broiling sun. Closed Tuesdays.

How to find Campo Santa Margherita? Coming from San Marco, walk over the Accademia Bridge and then always keep to the right, crossing three other small bridges before you arrive at the Campo. And after you've found the Campo Santa Margherita, look for a big red flagpole with a golden lion on top. If you turn left behind this flagpole, you will have found Sole di Napoli. Congratulazione!

VENICE'S SELF-SERVICE RESTAURANT: Yes, there is one—and to adaptable tourists, it offers fabulous value—but it's unlike any cafeteria you've ever seen: stand-up only (sometimes you eat your meal right on the ten-yard-long display counter), very plain in appearance, but with delicious food. Operated by the three Rizzo brothers—Gianni, Renato and Paolo—its name is **Rosticceria S. Bartolomeo,** and it's at 5423 Calle della Bissa (just off the Campo San Bartolomeo, which is itself just a few steps from the Rialto Bridge; cross the bridge to the San Marco side, walk 30 yards to the Campo San Bartolomeo, and on the Campo (square), take the underpass to the left marked "Sotoportego de la Bissa"). The restaurant opens for dinner at 5 p.m. It offers no fewer than 11 different "risotto" dishes (vast mounds of rice flavored and topped by other ingredients) for only 900 lire ($1.08). Other massive plates of more varieties of pasta than you ever dreamed possible are 800 lire (96¢) per (try pasta e fagioli, a Venetian specialty), sandwiches are 400 lire, a rugged glass of plain white or red wine is 200 lire; meat dishes are comparatively expensive, but still as little as 2,200 lire ($2.65) for much more than you can possibly eat. As in any Italian self-service place, order and eat the pasta (or the risotto or the gnocchi) first, before you select your meat course, as chances are you won't be able to finish the pasta alone! Highly recommended for readers with adventure in their blood. Closed Mondays.

Somewhat smaller, but better located, and operated on the very same principles by the very same family, is a semi-cafeteria called **Rosticceria al Teatro Goldoni,** at 4747 Calle dei Fabbri, next to the Campo San Luca, only 200 yards from St. Mark's Square (on the square, walk over to the famous Café Quadri, where starts the Calle dei Fabbri). The four "pezzi forti" (most popular dishes) here are (a) the "pasticcio di lasagne al forno" and "gnocchi di patate con ragout," two pasta appetizers for only 900 lire ($1.08) apiece; (b) "baccalá con polenta," a filling fish platter with hot ground corn, a specialty of northern Italy, for 1,800 lire ($2.16); (c) "mozzarella in carrozza," a delicious hot sandwich filled with mozzarella cheese, only 400 lire (48¢); and the "piatto del giorno," actually a two-course menu with wine and a roll, all for only 2,900 lire ($3.49). Closed Wednesdays.

A RECAP: To summarize, the city's best food values are: the 2,500 lire meals at the ground floor restaurant of the Venice youth hostel (**Ostello Venezia**), open to all; the stand-up meals at the **Rosticceria al Teatro Goldoni** near St. Mark's Square or at the **Rosticceria S. Bartolomeo,** near the Rialto Bridge; the 4,000-lire meals of the **Friggitoria da Bruno,** off the Campo S. Barnaba, on the **other** side of the Grand Canal; the 4,000-lire meal of the **Mensa DLF** near the train station; the 4,500-lire (and upwards) meals of the trattorias on the **Calle della Pescaria,** a short walk beyond the Riva degli Schiavoni (and the Piazza

San Marco); the 4,500 lire three-courser at **Trattoria Sole di Napoli** on the Campo Santa Margherita.

SOME THOUGHTS ON VENETIAN MEALS: The kitchens of most trattorias and ristorantes close at 10 p.m.; if you need to eat at a later time, go to the Piazzale Roma near the train station—that large and very unpicturesque square of garages—where the **Trattoria al Bolognese** (at #462) serves a 5,500 lire pranzo prezzo fisso (spaghetti alla bolognese, veal cutlet bolognese—veal slathered with melted cheese and ham, swimming in olive oil—and fruit or cheese) until nearly 11 p.m. Closed on Saturdays. . . . Some specialties of Venice, which you shouldn't miss: spaghetti alle vongole (spaghetti with clam sauce, usually 1,200 lire), zuppa di pesce (fish soup, 1,800 lire), and especially "frittura mista" or "frittura di pesce"—tiny fish of the Adriatic, fried in crisp batter, and so delicious (and cheap) that the waiter will nearly bestow congratulations as you order it. . . . Everywhere on menus, you'll see "risotto di pesce," "risotto de fegatini," "risotto de . . . ," all of which refer to a vast mound of rice, covered with sauce, and interspersed with the ingredients (pesce—fish, fegatini—chicken livers) named above.

STARVATION BUDGET MEALS: They're available for only 2,500 lire ($3.01), and consist of three courses and a roll, but with wine or beer extra for 300 lire (36¢), at the 400 seat **Mensa dell' Istituto di Architettura** at 2480 San Polo, Monday through Saturday, noon to 2:30 and 6:30 to 8:30 p.m., from January through the 19th of July, and then from September 16 onwards. While technically for students of Venice's large architectural institute (a high school with university status), nobody will object if you simply quietly join the queue—unless you're carrying a suitcase, that is! Pay first at the cashier's box, then step in line for your tray, and later take a seat at one of the long tables. But first you'll need to find this slightly difficult address: take vaporetto no. one to the San Tomà stop, walk to the Frari church square, then over the bridge with the white marble handrails (Ponte dei Frari), turn left (along the canal), passing over a second, smaller bridge, pass a police station (the yellow building), and the Mensa is in the first street turning right. And if you lose you way, ask for the "Archivio di Stato"; the Mensa is next door.

THE BIG SPLURGE: Take it at the well-known **Ristorante Peoceto Risorto,** Calle della Donzella (phone 25.953), just a few steps before the fish market at the Rialto Bridge, where a Menu Turistico (everything you could possibly eat) is 7,500 lire ($9.03); the chef here is particularly good (he specializes in spaghetti alla Carbonara for 2,200 lire), the setting particularly pleasant (in traditional, re-created Italian inn style), and the meals are usually far more expensive than the special tourist menu would indicate. Closed Mondays.

READERS' RESTAURANT SELECTIONS: "There is a very cheap, simple but clean and efficient **vegetarian restaurant** (the 'Piccola Cucina Serprado') at Lista di Spagna 230a (not far from the railway station). Very good for huge plates of spaghetti, rice, or all types of egg dishes (and one of the few places where you can get boiled eggs)" (Mr. and Mrs. H. B. Valman, London, England).

THE PICNIC CENTER: Do-it-yourself meals? Take the vaporetto to the Ca' D'Oro stop, then take a gondola directly across the canal for 100 lire (you'll see a couple of beatup boats that ply this shuttle route). You'll arrive at the

Rialto Marketplace—a colorful collection of grocery stalls, meat and fish stands, offering exotic and delicious foods. Bread, fruit, cheese, olives and prosciutto, which make a good picnic lunch, cost very little when purchased here. But open only from 7 a.m. to 2 p.m., Monday to Saturday.

THE CHIEF VAPORETTO STOPS

THE VAPORETTO: Transportation within Venice is reasonably-priced—provided you stay away from gondolas. They cost as much as $12 an hour (per person!) in the summer season. Take the vaporettos instead—the large motorboats which criss-cross on a regular schedule through the Grand Canal. These latter vessels charge a top fare of 500 lire (60¢) or 600 lire (72¢) for trips of even a fair distance.

Just like our own buses and subways at home, the Venetian boats are either "locals" or "expresses"! The slowest and cheapest boats, making every stop, are the mis-named "acceleratos", which are Line No. 1, and bear a Number 1 on their sides. These take more than half-an-hour for the ride from the railway station to the Piazza San Marco, charge only 500 lire for that trip up the entire Grand Canal, and are best for camera fans and contemplative sorts. The number 2 line—the "diretto"—is faster and less comprehensive; it cuts through the Rio Nuovo, and therefore misses much of the Grand Canal, but takes half the time. It charges 600 lire for the railway station-San Marco trip. Lines Nos. 3 and 4 (line #4 is the Grand Canal express) are even faster than Line No. 2, but Line No. 3 omits so many stops that it cannot be taken without first seeking advice from the ticket seller on whether it goes to your destination. Line No. 5 is the "Circolare" (circular) line, which passes along the outside of Venice on the Giudecca Canal going to Murano. Its route is more fully described in our touring section, below. And finally, Line No. 6 is the big double-decker boat (the "motonave") that goes to the Lido from the Piazza San Marco. Although the No. 1 and 2 lines also make that trip, Line No. 6 does it non-stop and charges 600 lire for the trip. You pick up the No. 6 from in front of the Royal Danieli Hotel next to the Piazza San Marco, from which it leaves at 5 minutes, 25 minutes and 45 minutes past the hour, but only from 7 a.m. to 8 p.m.

TOURS: The best tour of Venice is the one you can take by yourself. Venice is a relatively small city; it can be covered almost entirely in two days of walking. It's fun simply to wander—through streets so narrow your outstretched hands can touch the buildings along each side—to gaze in stores where eels and octopus are the merchandise. Then take a marathon vaporetto ride: start at the railroad station and glide up the Grand Canal to the Lido at the other end. That takes an hour and costs 500 lire (60¢) on vaporetto #1, or 40 minutes and 600 lire on express vaporetto #4, and provides your best all-around look at the city.

But don't confine your sightseeing to the Grand Canal; you haven't really seen Venice until you've also made the trip around the outside of the city, via the equally important Giudecca Canal. From the San Zaccaria station (#16) near St. Mark's Square (and also near vaporetto stop #15, but not to be confused with it), **Motoscafo Circolare** (Circular Motorlaunch) **No. 5** makes an entirely circular tour of the city—one boat goes clockwise, the other counter-clockwise—and leaves at 15-minute intervals until 11 p.m. From San Zaccaria, No. 5 "Destra" goes first to San Giorgio, then through the Giudecca Canal to the Railway Station and the Ghetto, and then, after stopping at the Fondamente Nuove and passing the cemetery island of San Michele (where Igor Stravinsky is buried), it reaches famous Murano with its glass factories and glass blowers. The trip takes one hour and 10 minutes, and costs 600 lire. Coming back, you can board Motoscafo Number 5 from Murano (the Museo stop), and return directly for another 600 lire to San Zaccaria near St. Mark's Square. Or, you can make the entire circular tour without ever leaving the boat for 1,200 lire—the cheapest 1½-hour sightseeing tour in the world!

Murano, Burano and Torcello

If you're the most avid sort of sea-goer, you might also want to consider an extension trip that you can make from the Fondamente Nuove to the island of San Erasmo for only 500 lire, round-trip, lasting nearly two hours. But you take this one only for the boat-ride and the rest; peaceful vegetable gardens are all that await at San Erasmo. A far more interesting cruise, and an excellent value, is the 6,000-lire tour (escorted) operated by the Bassani and Serenissima Companies to the three major islands of the Venice lagoon: Murano (for its glass factories), Burano (for its lace factories), and Torcello (for its church, oldest in Venice). The boats leave twice a day, at 9:30 a.m. and 2:30 p.m., from a dock almost directly in front of the Bridge of Sighs, near San Marco Square (look for the sign reading "Escursione alle Isole"). You'll return at 1 p.m. or 6 p.m., having visited all three islands at a cost that is less than some tour companies charge for the Murano visit alone.

The Lido

Swimming in the Adriatic, at the beaches along the Lido, is another thrill that cannot be missed. The key to doing it is the "camerini"—little dressing rooms along the shore which you are required to rent in order to use the beach; you cannot simply undress on the sands (as in Coney Island). Various Lido hotels charge varying prices for their "camerini"; the Bucintoro beach (just to the left of the Via Gran Viale on the Lido) charges 3,400 lire a day for two persons, 1,500 for a third person, 1,000 for children under 14; but if you walk a fair distance to the left, to the "Bagni Comunali S. Niccolò," you'll get a "Camerini a Rotazione" for only 1,200 lire per person. That's a camerini in which you undress in a private cabin, but then leave your clothes on a coat hanger guarded by an employee in a large room.

To reach the famous Lido, take boat No. 6 from its dock opposite the Royal Danieli Hotel (near the Piazza San Marco and the Bridge of Sighs); this is a large, double-decker vessel that makes the trip non-stop in about 15 minutes, charges 600 lire, and leaves every 20 minutes. When you land at the Lido, you'll find public bus #4 waiting to take you (for 100 lire) out to the public beach (last stop), which is just to the side of the San Niccolò beach, and which charges no admission at all. Before boarding that bus, you might first want to seek out the Standa Department Store on the Lido's main street—Viale S. M. Elisabetta—where you can buy inexpensive picnic ingredients, even on a Sunday.

Murano alone

Finally, you ought not to leave Venice without first taking a side-excursion to the Island of Murano, whose factories turn out the famous glassware of Venice, spidery, rainbow-hued and sold at mile-high prices throughout the rest of the world. Don't, however, take one of the organized 6,000-lire tours to the Island. Either board vaporetto #5 to Murano from St. Mark's Square (600 lire) or take the same boat from the **Fondamente Nuove (24)**, at a round-trip cost of 1,200 lire. The factories of Murano then admit visitors free for a glass blowing exhibition, hoping they'll stay to buy glassware in factory showrooms. But you needn't delay your purchases of Venetian glass that long: many-many trips there, and the confirming comments of numerous readers, support the conclusion that Murano prices for glass are often higher than in Venice itself (that's how you indirectly pay for the factory visit!) Do, however, pick up a pedestal ashtray for around 5,000 lire. They shimmer in water-like tones of blue and rose, and will forever remind you of the look of Venice.

READERS' SIGHTSEEING SUGGESTIONS: "The **Ancient Ghetto** in Venice is the 'original' ghetto, in that the word itself comes from the Italian for 'foundry,' once nearby. It today possesses five very old, elaborate synagogues which can be visited by applying to the office of the Jewish community at 1188A Ghetto Vecchio, within easy walking distance of the railway station. Services and tours (there's a museum) are scheduled at 9 a.m. and 3 p.m., but it would be wise to check in advance. Extremely interesting" (Ruth Gruber Fredman, Rockville, Maryland).

HOPE'S VENICE: The soul of Venice is, of course, its art and architecture. Hope has briefly itemized, in the report that now follows, the outstanding churches and museums that a first-time visitor will want to see:

"The lush, sumptuous fantasy that is Venice was never meant to be a tourist attraction, nor did the Italian government construct it (as one American lady once suggested) to compete with our Disneyland! To understand the overwhelming richness of the city's external aspect, you must know that in the 15th century, Venice was the capital of one of the world's greatest empires, and the undisputed ruler of the Adriatic, a natural gateway for trade between East and West. What you see today are vestiges of the proud and wealthy "Serene Republic" ("La Serenissima"), and that peculiar (to Venice) merging of the sensual East with the Christian West.

"Some of my happiest hours have been spent wandering simply at random in Venice and I recommend that aimlessness to you because, in a way, the entire city of Venice is a kind of bizarre museum in which deliberate visits to specific museums and sights seem almost superfluous. But believe it or not, the interior of some Venetian 'palazzos' are just as exciting as their exteriors, and therefore well worth a specific trip.

Around the Piazza San Marco

St. Mark's Basilica

"You'll of course want to explore the inside of the voluptuously Byzantine-Romanesque-Gothic Church of San Marco, which stands on the square of the same name, and has always been intimately associated with the history and political life of the town (in the early days it was the 'Doge's Chapel'; meetings were held and proclamations were heard there). Legend has it that in 828, four Venetians (a monk, a priest, and two merchants) conspired to "rescue" the remains of St. Mark from an Alexandrian Church, and smuggled the sacred relics to Venice. Thus it was that St. Mark replaced the Greek St. Theodore as patron of the city, and the citizens vied with each other in donating gifts for the final resting place of the saint (now under the high altar, in front of the gorgeous 'Pala d'Oro').

"On the way in from the square, look up at the four bronze horses galloping on the balcony; not only are they incredibly beautiful and graceful, but historic as well—thought to be Greek works of the third or fourth century B.C., brought to Venice in the 13th century from Constantinople.

"But it is the glittering mosaics of the church, which took 700 years to complete, and which literally cover its interior and explain its nickname 'Church of Gold', that are really the outstanding feature here. (A favorite with the experts, and easily overlooked, is the exotic little mosaic rendering of 'Salome's Dance' in the Baptistry—first door on your right as you enter; look directly above). For a better view of the mosaics, pay an extra 300 lire and go up to the gallery—from this vantage point you can begin to distinguish detail, see the bizarre pattern of the floor, and get a better appreciation of the church as a whole. That 300 lire fee also admits you to the gallery of the bronze horses, where you'll have a nice view of the Piazza below; and to the Museo San Marco (liturgical treasures—tapestries, robes, rugs, the lion of St. Mark).

"Entrance to the church, which is open from 9:30 to 5:30 (Sundays and holidays 2 to 5), is entirely free. But there is a charge of 300 lire for those wishing to see the 'Pala d'Oro', the staggering jewel-encrusted golden altarpiece (with 2,486 jewels!) in the Presbytery; and the Treasury, which was begun in the 13th century with Crusaders' plunder from Constantinople, and contains many sacred relics. I'd see them.

The Palace of the Doges

"The interior of the pink-shimmering, Oriental-looking Palazzo where the Doge lived, and which was also the home of government and the courts, is almost as rich as its exterior (with its cunningly carved columns; famed 15th century 'Porta della Carta'—the main entrance to the Palace where the Doge's proclamations were posted; and the splendid inner courtyard which, because of the double row of Renaissance arches on the Palace, look rather like a sugary stage setting, topped off by the elegant 'Giant's Staircase'). Inside you'll see wood-paneled courts and meeting rooms richly decorated by the cream of Venetian painters (Veronese, Titian, Carpaccio and Tintoretto), an actual chastity belt (complete with spikes, the first I've ever seen!) in the Armory Museum, the cells of prisoners formerly incarcerated here, and the Bridge of Sighs—over which you'll actually walk. Of special interest historically is the Room of the Council of Ten (the dreaded Star chamber of an otherwise admirable and efficient, albeit strictly patrician government) with its adjacent vestibule, the Sala della Bussola, containing the last complete 'lion's mouth'—a container (like a small door in the wall) into which secret denunciations of suspected enemies of the state were placed for quick action by the Council. The most impressive room (among many riches) architecturally is the vast and open Great Council Hall (constructed with no supporting pillars), enhanced by Tintoretto's masterpiece 'Paradise' (above the Doge's chair) and a spectacular 'Glorification of Venice' by Veronese in the oval on the ceiling—the portraits of the Doges all around the top of the room were also done by Tintoretto (whose portrait of Doge Faliero, you'll notice, has been painted out in black: he was a traitor, beheaded in 1355). Open in summer from 9:30 a.m. to 4 p.m. daily, entrance fee of 1,000 lire, 300 lire for students.

The Campanile

"From the top of the straight and simple red brick bell-tower, you'll have a really splendid view of Venice and vicinity. On a clear day you can see the Lido and all the way out to the sea. Open summer from 9:30 a.m. to 10 p.m.; take the elevator to the top for 600 lire.

The Correr Museum

"Also located on St. Mark's Square, directly opposite the Basilica, this rather interesting museum contains a first floor section dealing with Venetian history (costumes, coins, replicas of boats, paintings of sea battles, weapons), and an outstanding second floor art gallery displaying some wonderful primitives (look for Cosmé Tura's 'Pieta', among many others), as well as more sophisticated work by Bellini, Carpaccio (including his famous 'Two Courtesans'), Canova, and Lorenzo Lotto, to mention a few. Entrance fee of 500 lire; viewing hours from 10 to 4; Sunday, mornings only, free. Closed Tuesdays.

And along the Canals

Ca' Rezzonico

"The Ca' Rezzonico (which you reach by taking the vaporetto to stop #11, called Ca' Rezzonico) is an 18th century palazzo, now a museum containing articles relating to 18th century Venetian life—furniture, paintings, various artifacts. The collection itself is fairly good and if you're curious to see what living in an 18th century palazzo was like, this is a pleasant way to do it. You'll definitely want to see the charming mezzanine apartment once occupied by Pope Clemente XIII, and at another time the home of Robert Browning. Entrance fee of 500 lire; hours from 10 to 4; Sunday mornings (9:30 to 12:30) free. Closed Fridays.

Scuola di San Rocco

"This is a vast monument to the work of Tintoretto, the largest collection of his paintings anywhere (and some of the largest canvases I've ever seen)—a must for all art lovers. You'll find, among many impressive works, 'The Slaughter of the Innocents' (on the ground floor, with seven other New Testament scenes), which is so full of dramatic urgency and energy that figures seem almost to tumble out of the frame; and, in the center of the ceiling of the Great Hall upstairs, the mystical and powerful "Miracle of the Bronze Snake" (the paintings on, or near, the staircase are not by Tintoretto). You can reach the Scuola on foot from the Ca' Rezzonico, or else take the vaporetto to stop #10—'S. Toma.' Entrance charge of 900 lire (500 lire on Sunday mornings); hours in summer from 9 to 1 and 3 to 5; Sundays from 9 to 1 only; from November to March 31, open 10 to 1 only.

St. Mary's of the Friar's Church

"A few steps from the Scuola di San Rocco, the Friar's Church is particularly impressive because it houses the melodramatic and grandiose tombs of two famous Venetians—Canova and Titian—and also because there hangs, behind the High Altar, Titian's 'Assumption of the Virgin' and in the left nave his 'Virgin of the Pesaro Family'; you'll also see Bellini's triptych, 'Madonna and Child' (through a door on the right, in the Sacristy), and an almost primitive-looking wood-carving by Donatello of 'John the Baptist'. Entrance is 200 lire; hours are from 9:30 to 12 and 2:30 to 6, winters til 5—but no visiting during services.

Ca' Pesaro (Gallery of Modern Art)

"Further up the Grand Canal, past the Rialto (take the vaporetto to stop #5, called 'S. Stae'), the Ca' Pesaro Gallery has an exciting array of masterworks by Chagall, Klee, Rouault, Rodin, Moore, Kandinsky, Bonnard. And all of this is supplemented by the equally exciting opportunity to see what the inside of one of those Baroque, beside-the-waters palazzos (which this is) looks like. Entrance of 250 lire; hours from 10 to 4; from 9:30 to 12:30 Sundays, free.

Ca' d'Oro

"Close to Ca' Pesaro, but on the opposite side of the Canal, is Ca' d'Oro (or Gallery Franchetti, vaporetto stop is Ca' d'Oro), the best preserved (15th century) and most impressive of the patrician Venetian Palazzos; entrance to the museum is directly opposite the vaporetto stop, and the street number is 3932. You'll first pass through a cool green courtyard and emerge into one of the most glorious rooms I've ever seen, with ornately decorated beamed ceiling, colorful mosaic floor and rose walls. The atmosphere conjures simultaneous visions of Othello, Machiavelli, the Renaissance. A graceful outside stairway takes you to second floor exhibits where you'll see furniture, tapestries, medals, and the art gallery (there's Titian, Tintoretto, Carpaccio, Mantegna's famous 'St. Sebastian', a Van Dyck and works by lesser Flemish and Dutch masters), but the main point of interest is the Palace itself. Admission is 200 lire (Sundays free); the gallery is open from 10 a.m. to 4 p.m., Sundays to 1 p.m. Ca' d'Oro was closed for repairs, at the time of this writing, but will open again sometime in late 1980 or 1981.

Galleria dell' Accademia

"The Academy of Fine Arts (vaporetto stop #12, 'Accademia') is the definitive treasure house of Venetian painting, exhibited chronologically from the 13th to the 18th century. Many Carpaccios (keeping company with Titian, Veronese, Tintoretto, etc.), Giorgione's fascinating 'The Tempest,' and a magnificent collection of scenes by Bellini, Bastiani, and Mansueti in Room XX— my own favorite among the many rooms. You can't make a better 200 lire investment than this gallery, and on Sunday morning you can enter free. Open from 9 to 2, Sunday 9 to 1, closed Monday.

The Guggenheim Collection

"The best for last. The home of the late Peggy Guggenheim (Palazzo Venier dei Leoni, #701 Dorsoduro, a short walk from the Accademia) is open to the public (from around April 1 through October) on Mondays, Wednesdays and Fridays from 3 to 5 p.m.—and if you miss this place, you can kick yourself! The collection inside is best described by Herbert Read in his foreword to a souvenir book available on the premises: 'The collection of 20th Century paintings and sculpture formed by Peggy Guggenheim is the only one in Europe to have a systematical historical basis. It embraces all the major movements which since about 1910 have transformed the very concept of art and which can now for the first time be seen in a unified perspective.' There are works by Picasso, Chagall, Leger, Braque, Dali, Jackson Pollock (almost a dozen of his canvases —in the basement), and many others too numerous to mention, as well as rooms in the basement devoted to young up-and-coming artists. As a sidelight, by the way, you receive from this visit an idea of what a wonderful life hers must have been, surrounded by great art. One exhibition room, a dining room, was obviously used for living purposes as well. The home, once more, is open to the public on three afternoons a week; and I say: 'Hats off to you, Ms. Guggenheim, you were a woman of great soul!' "

MUSIC AND MUSEUMS: To repeat a money-saving point, all but five of the museums in Venice (the Gallery of St. Mark's Church, the Doges' Palace, Scuola San Rocco, San Giorgio Schiavoni, and the Clock Tower) charge no admission on Sundays, and of the five that do, all but the Doges' Palace lower their entrance price to 100 lire. . . . Three times a week, but on varying days (watch the posters), the municipal government offers free band concerts in the Piazza San Marco, at 5 p.m. Sundays and 9 p.m. the other two days. . . . Your theatergoing should be confined to the jewel-like **Teatro della Fenice** (mainly grand opera, occasionally classic dramas), and to the "loggione" seats of that theatre (second gallery, costing 2,200 lire). Weekdays, performances start at 8:30 p.m., Sundays at 3:30, and a few loggione are sometimes available a few minutes before starting time. If they aren't, then standing room is also 2,000 lire, and well worth it. Casts are composed of Italy's finest singers, particularly in the summer months when Milan's La Scala Opera shuts down.

PAINLESS NIGHTSPOTS: There are two, and only two, methods of inexpensive nightclubbing in the Venice area, and the first is to visit **"Discoteca Piper 5"** at 124 Lista di Spagna, in the area of the Venice railroad station.This is the place to meet young, single and unaccompanied Venetian girls, who are attracted to the spot in quantity by the management's policy of charging an entrance fee of only 4,200 lire, which *includes* the right to a beer or "aranciata" (orange soda)—the only drink you need imbibe to spend an entire evening in this haven—and thus, you have a total expense of a little over $5 for dancing, liaisons and drink. Following Italian custom, the second drink costs considerably less (2,500 lire). Open from 9 p.m. to 1 a.m., with two dance floors, psychedelic lights, and live musicians alternating with the discs.

Venice's other budget nightspot, the **"Club 22"**, is on the Lido, at 22 Lungomare Marconi, and is open during the summer months from 4 to 8 p.m. and from 9:30 p.m. to 4 a.m. daily, in all other months on Saturday and Sunday evenings only; it charges 3,500 lire for entrance (which includes the right to one drink), but only 2,000 lire for every successive drink; the action occurs on an elevated platform above the sandy Adriatic beach, where patrons dance. To find the club, walk up the Gran Viale from the boat stop until you reach the sea front, then walk right along the coast line, passing the Grand Hotel des Bains (where much of the motion picture "Death in Venice" was filmed), until you reach Club 22, on your left.

Nightspots to avoid on the Lido: everywhere other than the above establishment, and most particularly, the nightclub at the Municipal Casino on the Lido, and the Casino itself (5,000-lire "membership" fee—of which 2,000 lire is for entrance, and 3,000 for chips—to watch Tulsa oilmen and Cincinnati brokers listlessly lose at roulette).

A VISIT TO THE GONDOLA FACTORY: Several hundred of the unique black gondolas now in service in Venice, including the one owned by Peggy Guggenheim, were built by a 70-year-old master craftsman and greatest living gondola expert, Cavaliere Giovanni Giuponi, who entered the profession 58 years ago as an apprentice to his father. Cavaliere Giuponi's tiny shipyard, one of three in Venice, still manufactures four or five gondolas each year, and the proud cavaliere is happy to show you around. He requires three to four months to construct a gondola, which is made of seven different types of wood, has a life expectancy of 20 to 25 years, and costs approximately eight million lire (about $9,600), of which 10% goes for the *ferro* alone, the famous metallic bow or nose.

Best visiting hours for the "shipyard" are from 9 to noon or 3 to 6, Monday through Friday. To get there, walk over the Accademia Bridge to Zattere, then board a ferry-vaporetto (the stop is in front of the Gesuati church, the boat leaves every ten minutes, and costs 500 lire) for a five-minute ride to Giudecca island. There, turn left and walk along the waterfront, over the little bridge called "Ponte Piccolo," into the first very narrow street turning right called "Calle Stretta Ferrando," pass the club of the Communist Party (you can't miss the red flag), and ring the bell at house number 410A. Either Signor Giuponi or his assistant will let you in to a pocket-sized factory that has accounted for a large percentage of the 500-or-so gondolas gracefully floating on the canals of Venice.

After your visit, I'd suggest you walk back to the Giudecca waterfront, turn right over the large iron bridge called Ponte Longo and over another smaller bridge, passing the Redentore Church to the Zitelle boat stop; from there, take Motoscafo Circolare No. 5 (there's a boat every 15 minutes) back to St. Mark's. This ten-minute, 600-lire trip provides a spectacular panoramic view of the Campanile, St. Mark's Church, and Doge's Palace. And if hunger strikes before or after your excursion to Signor Giuponi, try the **Trattoria Al Vaporetto,** in front of the Giudecca boat station, where an unusually solid meal sells for 5,500 lire or less. The house number is 448.

THE SELF-SERVICE LAUNDRIES OF VENICE: The most easily-found is the "Lavaget," at 1269 Cannaregio ("Al Ponte delle Guglie"—at the Guglie Bridge). From the railroad station, walk down the Lista di Spagna until you come to the bridge at Cannaregio, walk over the bridge and immediately turn 20 yards left. Three and a half kilos of laundry will cost you 2,800 lire at the Lavaget, and that includes detergent and drying. Hours are Monday through Friday, 8:30 to 12:30 and 3 to 7, closed Saturdays and Sundays. . . . Nearer to St. Mark's Square: **Lavanderia a Gettone Gabriella,** at 985 Calle Colonnette, where four and a half kilos of laundry, washed and dried, are 2,800 lire. This time, walk from St. Mark's Square through the clock tower into the Merceria (the main shopping street), then turn left, walk over the bridge into Calle Fiubera, make your first right and first left. And if you get lost, ask for the Hotel Astoria: Gabriella is in the block behind this small hotel. Open Monday through Friday, 8:30 to 12:30 and 3:20 to 7:30, closed Saturdays.

STUDENT IN VENICE: For youth-oriented charter flights, cheap student ship tickets to Yugoslavia, Greece and Israel, cheap student train tickets to northern climes, try **"ESTA"** (the so-called European Student Travel Association) at 3282 Calle del Fabbro, near Ca'Foscari, phone 705-660, open Monday through Friday, 9:30 a.m. to 12:30 p.m. and 3:30 p.m. to 7 p.m., Saturdays 9:30 a.m. to noon.

VENICE MISCELLANY: While the game of trick-the-tourist is a highly developed art in Venice, developed over decades, sometimes tourists overreact and suspect everyone. In fairness to the men who run the vaporettos, let it be known that they *do* have a right to require that you pay 500 lire for every large suitcase you bring aboard. See why it pays to travel light? . . . The same applies to the seemingly-wily behavior of the waiters at the Piazza San Marco, who will sometimes charge 1,300 lire, at other times 2,000 lire, for a cup of espresso. They're not pocketing the difference; the 700 lire is a music tax; to avoid it, order **and** pay for your drinks while the band is **not** playing. . . . That's not to say that the outdoor cafes at the Piazza aren't expensive; they are, and the cheapest thing you can have is a cup of espresso. . . . The stalls at either end of the Rialto Bridge ("Ponte Rialto") offers your best shopping buys; their prices for scarves, ties and women's wool sweaters are easily a third less than elsewhere in the city, and the stall owners will bargain, occasionally knocking 1,000 lire off the price. . . . The greatest free sight in Venice is simply the Piazza San Marco, a world in itself. . . . Parking your car at one of the big garages near the Piazzale Roma costs less than 4,000 lire per day, for all but the very large cars. . . . In Venice, never ask what an item or a service costs: simply hand the man the lowest amount of change your courage will allow, and look confident—it works! Crossing a canal on a shuttle-gondola, I recently gave 200 lire to the gondolier and it was accepted. A Venetian who got on after me handed him only 100 lire for the same ride, apparently the standard charge!

A READER'S TIP: "While Alitalia provides bus service to the airport for 1,800 lire, a city bus marked "AV" makes the same trip for a good deal less (500 lire), leaving from the Piazzale Roma, directly behind the point from which the Alitalia buses depart" (Norman Lowenthal, Kensington, Maryland).

Venice, to be savored, should be sipped in small doses—it can become a little too rich for the blood. Three or four days make a perfect visit; and then it's off to Florence. Prior to departure from the Venice railroad station, you can buy a box lunch for the journey ("Cestino da Viaggio") in the station restaurant. The carton contains a serving of roast veal, French fries, cheese, fruit, bread and a little flask of wine—all for 4,500 lire ($5.42). Almost before the last crumb is brushed away, your train nears Florence.

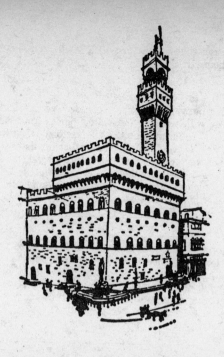

Chapter XIII

FLORENCE

City on the Arno

AFTER THE FRENZY of Venice, this is a city for reflection. The museums of Florence have a near monopoly on the artistic masterpieces of the Renaissance. The treasures here are so thick that Raphael's priceless Madonna of the Chair is casually stuck away in a little nook of the galleries of the Pitti Palace.

This is also a city for buying gifts. You'd do well to hold off on your European shopping until you've seen the leather goods stalls in the Florence straw market or the jewelry shops on the Ponte Vecchio. Items which sell for $20 and more on New York's Fifth Avenue are priced here at less than five bucks. If you've followed the $15-a-day regimen on the earlier part of your trip, you should have enough stashed away by now for a gift-buying splurge. Here's how to continue living on a budget—in Florence.

HOTELS: We'll discuss hotels in ascending order of price, beginning with the very cheapest. For Florence has some of the least costly hotel "finds" in Europe—so many of them, in fact, that it really isn't necessary to move as high as the Second Class category—although there are some pretty superb choices in that classification, too.

You ought to know, preliminarily, that some of our selections are pensions —those tiny European hotels that offer meals along with their rooms (some, however, do not require that you take the meals). In Italy, the normal pension ("pensione") consists of a single floor of an apartment house or office building, almost always upstairs; and you must reserve judgment until you've actually ascended in the elevator and inspected the accommodation. Particularly in Florence—which is an ancient city, historic, and with virtually no modern buildings—the inside appearance of most pensions is far better than their shabby 18th-century exteriors would indicate. Some of them offer amazingly large rooms, with balconies, parlors, all sorts of added features. To prove it, we'll immediately proceed to discuss the areas in which you'll find these choices, and then the choices themselves:

The Via Faenza

The most startling proof that outward appearance can deceive, is found on a street called the Via Faenza, which is only three short blocks from the railroad station. If, from the station, you'll walk up the Via Nazionale for two blocks and turn left on the Via Faenza, you'll soon find a rather nondescript building at 56 Via Faenza that once was a monastery, now houses several stores on its ground floor, and will fill you with apprehension as you near it. Yet upstairs are five pensions whose owners, amenities, atmosphere—and price policies—are among the most charming in all Europe!

THE ITALIAN LIRA: For the purposes of this chapter, we've converted Italian lire into dollars at the rate of 830 lire per dollar —the approximate "floating" rate of the lira as of the time of writing. Thus, 100 lire have been assumed to equal 12 U.S.¢. Though you can expect further fluctuations by the time of your own stay in Italy, the variance should not be substantial.

The stars of 56 Via Faenza (although they have close competitors) are the three lovely Azzi sisters, who operate the **Pensione Azzi** on the second floor (phone 21-38-06), where they dispense a kind of hospitality that is straight from the pages of Louisa May Alcott—this establishment, with its typical Florentine furnishings and cozy rooms, is the Italian equivalent of that mood. The rooms are of course impeccably clean, and—because they are in the back of the building, away from the street—unusually quiet. For such rooms, with breakfast, with all service charges and taxes included, the charge is only 6,500 lire ($7.83) single, 9,000 lire ($10.84) double, 13,000 lire ($15.66) for a group of three.

On the same floor, the **Locanda Armonia** (phone 211-146) has proprietors —Alighiero and Artea Pedani—who have their own qualities to commend them. They hand you a free map of Florence as you register, tell you to regard their establishment as your "second home", and intervene on your behalf to "salvare la situazione" with troublesome railway officials, tour operators, auto mechanics, and other tourist banes; they'll even watch your children when you go out for the evening. For tastefully-furnished rooms, the charge here is exactly 4,800 lire ($5.78) per person in a double room, service and taxes included, 4,250 lire per member of the group for three or more sharing the same room. English is spoken by both hosts.

One flight up, proprietor Bramante Bernardi of the **Locanda Anna** (phone 298-322) does not speak English (although his lovely daughter, Loretta, does), but he refuses to let that be the slightest deterrent to the warmest sort of welcome, in rooms with marble floors and frescoed ceilings, with fresh cut flowers in the lounge, clean towels every other day, and an occasional piece of cold watermelon which he'll sometimes hand you as you return from a hot day in the museums. Here the rate is a uniform 5,500 lire per person (service included) in twin rooms, 4,500 lire per person for groups of three, 1,500 lire extra for an optional breakfast; and again the rooms and bathrooms are scrupulously clean. . . . The other occupants of 56 Via Faenza are the **Pensione Merlini** (phone 212-848), whose furnishings would be the envy of any antique collector (9,500 lire double, and breakfast, 1,500 lire extra, served on a terrace decorated with frescoes by American art students), and the **Pensione Marini** (phone 284-824), which is as friendly as the rest (and also offers similar rates of 9,500 lire double, without breakfast, 4,250 to 4,400 lire per person in triples or large 4-bedded rooms). The Marini has recently inspired a flood of admiring letters from readers.

If these are full, then try the almost equally pleasant **Locanda Marcella,** next door at 58 Via Faenza (phone 21-32-32), some of whose rooms have a beautiful view out over Fiesole, and whose owner, Signor Noto Calogero, is a warm and welcoming gentleman whose rates are 5,500 lire ($6.62) single, 4,500 lire ($5.42) per person in doubles, triples and quadruples, all without breakfast. Due to flood damage, the stairway here is one of the worst (in appearance) you'll ever see; but upstairs you'll emerge into a well-furnished home atmosphere. In the same building, the **Locanda Mia Cara,** 58 Via Faenza (phone 216-053), charges a remarkable 4,000 lire per person in doubles or twins, plus 1,800 lire for breakfast, is one of the cleanest of the cheapest, and has a hardworking manager, Mr. Noto Pietro. . . . Or walk over to Mario Noce's **Locanda Panichi,** one flight up at Via Faenza 89 (phone 212-039), which consists of nine beautifully furnished rooms with shining brown ceramic floors. Although it's by far the most expensive locanda on the street (11,500 lire single, 16,000 lire double or twin, 23,000 lire triple, inclusive of breakfast and free showers), a great many readers seem to regard those rates as justified by the comfort and impeccable cleanliness of the Panichi. . . . Or have a look at the less attractive **Soggiorno Monica,** 66 Via Faenza (phone 28-38-04), whose bathless doubles rent for 8,500 lire, singles 6,800 lire, doubles with private bath for 11,500 lire; at the pleasant and highly popular **Locanda Pina,** 69 Via Faenza (phone 212-231), offering doubles and triples for 4,200 lire per person, no breakfast; at the **Soggiorno d'Errico,** 69 Via Faenza (phone 214-059), 5,500 lire single, 8,500 lire double, 11,000 lire triple; or at **Locanda Nella,** 69 Via Faenza (phone 284-256), 4,200 lire per person in triple or four-bedded rooms, including breakfast brought to your room on a copper trolley.

A final, if somewhat splurgey, standout on the Via Faenza: the 24-room **Hotel Nuova Italia,** at #26 (phone 287-508), with its modern furniture throughout and wall-to-wall carpeting in every room. Singles 12,500 lire ($15.06), doubles 19,500 lire ($23.49), supplementary beds 8,000 lire ($9.63), and non-obligatory breakfasts 2,500 lire ($3.01). Signora Elida Viti, the Italian version of a Jewish mother, watches over all, assisted by her son Luciano and his wife Eileen. And how could the daughter-in-law be named Eileen? Fourteen years ago, she vacationed here with her family from Montreal, staying at a pensione chosen from this book—then called "Europe on $5 a Day" (happy days!) There she met the son of the pensione owners, Luciano Viti, and (you guessed it) they married. And that's why, today, any reader of this book will receive a slight discount off the prices quoted above!

If all the establishments on the Via Faenza are full (which is unlikely), then ask for directions to the Via Fiume, a block away from Faenza, and only one block from the side of the station itself. The **Auberge Petrarca,** at 20 Via Fiume (first floor, phone 260-858), is a cheerful little place in an elevator-equipped building, whose proprietress speaks a bit of "hotel English" and charges 13,500 lire ($16.26) double, including breakfast (6 rolls, 4 pats of butter, 2 dishes of jelly, warm milk and a large pot of coffee, actually witnessed on my last visit), service and tax for two.

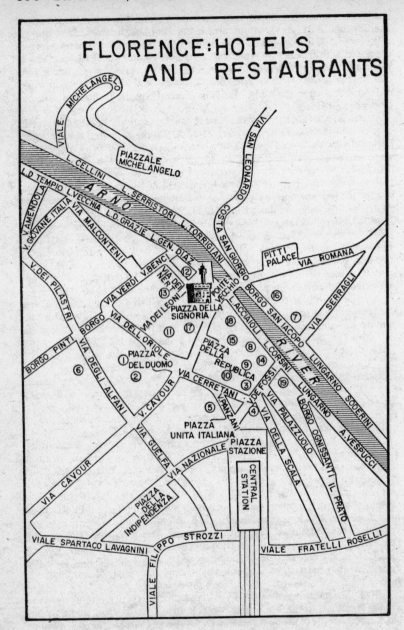

FLORENCE:HOTELS
AND RESTAURANTS

Near the Duomo

This is the next general neighborhood in which I'd continue my search.
The cathedral square of Florence ("Piazza del Duomo") stands almost in the

very center of the city, and the Duomo itself—with its exotic, pink-white-and-green-marble exterior, and its famous Ghiberti doors, which Michelangelo said were "fit to stand at the gates of Paradise"—is an important focal point of your touring activities. For one thing, the Academy Museum ("Accademia"), at the Piazza San Marco, is only a few short blocks away, and it's here you'll find the original David by Michelangelo—which you cannot, under any circumstances, fail to see.

Off this square, on the second floor of 3 Via dei Conti (a side-street off the Via de Cerretani; phone 21-52-16), the highly-recommended but somewhat pricey **Pensione Centrale** rents ten extremely large rooms of the former patrician residence ("Palazzo Malaspina") it occupies. Including breakfast, service and tax, its high-season rates are 14,500 lire ($17.46) single, 23,000 lire ($27.71) double or twin, 9,000 lire ($10.84) for an extra bed in a double room—the rooms being especially suitable for travelling families. There's a friendly and English-speaking staff, and although you'll initially glimpse an enormous marble staircase, there's also an elevator. . . . A less expensive alternative to the Centrale, in a nearby location: **Pensione Sally (1)**, Via dei Servi 3 (phone 284-519), whose managers are the Sergio Avellinos. They charge 8,000 lire ($9.63) per person, breakfast included, in a double room, 10,750 lire ($12.95), breakfast included, for one of their very large singles, and the situation of their "hotel" is magnificent, just a few feet from the Duomo. Stairs only; a fairly forbidding exterior; but large rooms.

Piazza SS. Annunziata

The lodging for worshipers of the Renaissance is the surprisingly-spacious **Hotel Morandi (6)**, at Piazza SS. Annunziata 3, phone 212-687, on a square so picturesque and unchanged that if you were to take away the autos, you'd instantly be in another age. There are loggias on three sides. Directly across from the hotel is the famous foundling hospital of Florence (oldest in Europe and the first Renaissance structure in Florence) with its arches designed by Brunelleschi and with the world-famous "putti"—or swaddling babies—of Della Robbia. In the square stands a statue of Ferdinand de Medici, and two beautiful fountains of Pietro Tacco. The entrance to the Etruscan Museum is also in this square. And, of course, the baroque-style Church of SS. Annunziata is an important Florentine site—a place to which the brides of Florence, by custom, bring their wedding bouquets.

Now the Hotel Morandi itself is in an ancient—and at times, rather formal—building, but it has an elevator, and the rooms inside have character (beamed ceilings, among other things) and are quiet; and finally, the prices are good: room-*and*-breakfast ranges from 9,000 to 11,350 lire ($10.84 to $13.67) per person per day, depending mainly on whether you occupy a double or single room; discounts are granted to groups or families occupying rooms with three and four beds. Highest recommendation.

Piazza di Santa Maria Novella

We move now to two higher-priced and fairly large Third Class hotels, located only two blocks from the railroad station, on or near the famous and often-pictured Piazza di Santa Maria Novella—a huge, quiet square with two giant obelisks in its center, a classic loggia on one side, the Church of Maria Novella on the other—really an awesome sight. Directly on the square, the always serviceable, if unexciting, **Hotel Universo,** Piazza Santa Maria Novella 20 (phone 272-184), is elevator-equipped and charges 12,000 lire single, 17,500 lire ($21.08) double, including service and tax. Dreary entrance and corridors, but quite satisfactory rooms.

In previous editions of this book, I gave a high recommendation to the beautiful **Hotel Croce di Malta,** which is half a block off this square, on the Via Della Scala, and has its own open-air swimming pool. Unfortunately, the Croce di Malta has equipped so many of its rooms with private bath, that it no longer fits within our price range. Therefore, Hope and I just recently walked several feet further away from the square to a building that had often intrigued us, where we now discovered the **Hotel Aprile (4),** at Via Della Scala 6 (phone 21-62-37)—and it's a worthy successor to the Croce di Malta. A low, three-story building, the Aprile turns out to be nothing other than a former palace belonging to the Medicis (and once called the Palazzo del Borgo), completely remodeled, with thirty very fine rooms, plus lounges and a garden. From April through October, the Aprile charges (to readers of this book only) 17,000 lire ($20.48) per person in a bathless room, including breakfast, service and taxes; and although that's above our limits, the hotel and its amenities are really quite outstanding: there are marble tiled corridors with blue-and-yellow gilt doors, etchings on the walls, tastefully decorated rooms. Those with private bath and private facilities are 18,000 lire ($21.68) per person, breakfast and all else thrown in.

Near the Railroad Station

For your most plentiful supply of budget rooms, the street where you'll always find something is the little **Via Panzani (5),** which is located off the Piazza Unità Italiana, almost directly in front of the railroad station. You'll have to carry your luggage less than a hundred yards before you come upon it; and then, stretching before you for a solid two blocks, you'll pass an unbroken line of Third and Fourth Class hotels, all with tiny lobbies, and most with stairs only; but some with surprisingly decent and comfortable rooms (not, however, to be compared with selections in other areas of town).

In the Third Class category, you'll probably find the best rooms at the **Lombardia,** Via Panzani 19 (phone 21-52-76) (doubles for 15,000 lire, not including breakfast); next at the **Romagna,** Via Panzani 4, phone 211-005 (9,000 lire single, 15,000 lire double or twin, service included; don't be put off by the plain lobby); and then, with nothing much to choose between them, the **Gioconda,** Via Panzani 2, phone 21-31-50 (twins with private shower for 24,000 lire, service and taxes included, doubles without shower for 19,500 lire, singles 14,500 lire, breakfast 2,000 lire); and the less expensive—but still Third-class rated—**Polo Nord,** Via Panzani 7 (phone 287-952), charging a special rate to readers of this book of 7,500 lire ($9.03) per person, service, taxes, and free showers included.

Higher-Priced—Along the Arno

This is the river that courses through Florence, and that caused the tragic flood of November 4, 1966. So thoroughly unchanged are the buildings and famous bridges along it, that in winter and spring—when the river is full—the resulting scene looks as though it were lifted unaltered from the famous painting that shows Dante first espying Beatrice, as she walks with companions at the river's edge. Generally, this is also the most expensive area of Florence, but there are some budget exceptions in it.

The best of these is the **Pensione Adria (7)**, Piazza Frescobaldi 4 (phone 21-50-29), which is just across the Ponte San Trinità (one of the world's most beautiful bridges), on the far side of the Arno. The Adria requires that you take "half-pension" (room and two meals), but offers a special rate for same to readers of 17,500 lire ($21.08) per person, service and taxes included; and it serves its meals in an upper-story, glass-enclosed dining loggia and lounge overlooking all of Florence. New owner is a charming blonde, Giuliana Nardi, who makes a point, however, of offering only a brandname Chianti, at 3,000 lire per bottle, with your evening meal; dispense with it.

Then there's the real star of the neighborhood—but a relatively expensive star. For, among the top moderately-priced hotels of Europe—let alone in Florence—is the famous and often crowded **Hotel Berchielli (8)**, Lungarno Acciaioli 14 (phone 21·1-530), whose classification is at the very top of the Second Class category. A lovely, gracious, subdued hotel, it has the best location in Florence, on the Arno, just one block from the famous Vecchio Bridge (Ponte Vecchio), and a few blocks from the central railway station. Some of its rooms are beautifully decorated in Renaissance style, and all are extremely clean. While the prices here soar as high as 16,000 lire ($19.27) for a bathless single (taxes and service included) and to 26,500 lire ($31.92) for a bathless double, without breakfast, they purchase such a pleasant hotel experience that we can endure this departure from our usual standard. Highly recommended. Very little difference in off-season rates.

Not directly facing the Arno, but near it (and near the Berchielli), is one of the best bargains in town: Signora Ada Cestelli's four-room **Soggiorno Cestelli**, 25 Borgo Santi Apostoli (phone 212-413), at which the kindly proprietress offers very special rates to readers of this book only (guaranteed up to the end of 1980): 7,000 lire ($8.43) for a small double; 10,000 lire ($12.04) for each of two enormously large double rooms with mammoth beds à la Medici and antique furniture; 13,000 lire ($15.66) for the only room with bath. Third and fourth beds are available at a supplement of 40% to the twin rate. From the central station, walk up the Via Tornabuoni to Piazza Santa Trinità, and then turn left into the narrow Borgo Santi Apostoli.

Far Side of the Arno

For readers who seek a quiet location, or need parking space for their car, the large **Hotel-Pensione Silla**, Via de Renai 5 (phone 284-810), is an appropriate choice. It's operated by a genial, English-speaking gentleman named A. Silla, and offers a fixed-priced policy to readers of this book: 12,000 lire ($14.45) per person in a double room, with breakfast, taxes, and service charge included. A large and luxurious summer terrace is available for guests; in fact, you'll be flabbergasted, I think, to find such comfort and tasteful decoration behind such battered walls. Best of all, the building occupies a residential location, with virtually unlimited parking space on the street below (a crucial feature for motorists in Florence), yet close to everything important—on our map, it's located diagonally across the river from #12, just above the last "r" in the words: "L. Serristori".

Near the Piazza della Signoria

The best known site of Florence is, of course, the Piazza della Signoria, in front of the Palazzo Signoria, Florence's City Hall, where stands the well-known copy (not the original) of Michelangelo's David. It is here, too, that you'll find the renowned Uffizi Galleries; and all of this is but a block-or-so from the Ponte Vecchio (the famous covered bridge of Florence) and the Arno River.

In the area around the Piazza are found several relatively large, relatively old, Second Class hotels. They strain the budget somewhat, but they are each well-suited for older tourists who'd like a touch of history and 19th century atmosphere in their hotel—but at moderate cost.

Typical among this group, and to be considered only on a Big Splurge basis, is the venerable **Hotel Porta Rossa (9)**, Via Porta Rossa 19 (phone 287-551), at the corner of Via Monalda, one block from the Arno. Built around a medieval tower dating back to the 13th century, the Porta Rossa has been officially listed as a hotel since the year 1386! Now completely modernized, its lounge facilities are spacious, with heavy leather chairs that make you feel cool and relaxed on the hottest day, and the tastefully furnished rooms are unusually large (because it is such a very old hotel). Singles 12,000 lire, including service charges and tax; bathless doubles 17,800 lire, with service and tax. Breakfast: 2,800 lire extra, per person.

In the same area, only one short block from the Piazza della Signoria, is a big (probably largest in its category) and somewhat costlier Third Class hotel that is again one of the oldest in Florence (its dining room was once the Parliament chamber of Florence; the age of the building means that its bed-rooms are, once more, unusually large). That's the **Hotel Columbia-Parlamento,** at 29 Piazza San Firenze (phone 23-400), corner of Via dei Leoni and Borgo dei Greci, with 92 rooms renting for 20,400 lire ($24.57) double, 14,500 lire single, including service and taxes, but not breakfast (3,000 lire extra); there's an elevator, after you walk up the first flight of stairs to the huge dining room, with its frescoed ceilings and portraits of Garibaldi; you may want to sightsee through the dining room, even if you aren't staying at the hotel.

Finally, two blocks from Piazza della Signoria, at Via Dei Pepi 7, next to Piazza Santa Croce and 100 yards from the home of Michelangelo (Casa Buonarroti at Via Ghibellina 70), **Pensione La Locandina** (phone 211-031) offers special rates to bearers of this book: 17,000 lire ($20.48) for a bathless double room, 19,500 lire for a double with bath or shower, including breakfast. Normal rates are 18,000 and 20,000 lire, respectively. Located on the first floor of a 14th century palace, La Locandina has 15 doubles only, no singles, and English-speaking owner Lola Pacchiega is one of the kindest hoteliers of Florence.

The Shopping Area

An alternative choice in the same central area, the **Pensione La Residenza**, Via Tornabuoni 8, phone 284-197, is located on the most fashionable street of Florence, which is lined with elegant stores, good for window-shopping only. But La Residenza itself is fairly moderately-priced, and is again an excellent buy for older tourists. It's on the second, third and attic floors of a 14th Century building, no less; the lounges and rooms are beautifully furnished and upkept by an attentive staff, supervised by the bi-lingual Gianna Vasile; and it offers special prices for readers of this book who display a copy upon entering: 17,000 lire for bathless singles, 25,500 lire ($30.72) for bathless doubles, with breakfast, service and taxes included. The management will normally want you to take half-pension, however, which is priced (again for readers only) at exactly 22,800 lire per person for bathless rooms, at 25,200 lire per person with private bath or shower. Excellent food; discounts for families traveling with children; two large lounges; television; roof garden; elevator; garage service; and bar.

READERS' PENSIONE SELECTIONS: "On one of our recent trips to Florence (my husband being a medical student in Italy), we stayed at **Locanda Orchidea,** 11 Via degli Albizzi (phone 296-646), owned by an Italian family who lived for 30 years in England, and then returned to Italy to "retire" with a pensione. In addition to being totally fluent in English, they're friendly and helpful, their rooms quiet and clean, and their rates in 1980 will be only 7,000 lire ($8.43) single, 10,800 lire ($13.01) double" (Natalie Urban, Bristol, Rhode Island; note from AF: this is an especially good location, only a short distance from the Duomo and Piazza Signoria) . . . "**Soggiorno Adua,** 20 Via Fiume (phone 28-75-06), rents well-furnished rooms for only 10,500 lire ($12.65) double, 7,000 lire ($8.43) single, with breakfast for 1,800 lire ($2.16) extra; the view from the kitchen balcony across the red tile roofs to the Duomo is alone worth the price! But owners Anna and Otello Bartarelli are friendly and helpful, too" (Victor T. Ecklund, Bellevue, Washington). . . . "Signor Antonio Minoia's **Soggiorno Satellite,** top floor of 14 Via Fiume (phone 294-796), just around the corner from the railroad station and off the noisy main streets, offers many extras in the way of old Florence atmosphere: high ceilings in large, spacious rooms, lovely antiques in reception and breakfast area, spotlessly waxed floors and clean beds, an elevator, rooms with French doors leading to balconies with views of distant hills over Florence rooftops, fresh air stirring, birds singing—what a treat after a hot noisy day in the city! Double rooms with breakfast for 14,000 lire ($16.86), singles for 8,000" (Mary L. Radcliffe, Cottonwood, Arizona; similar raves from Stephen Hellman, Department of Political Science, York University, Ontario, Canada, who points out that the Satellite's rooms, "given their internal location, are extremely quiet—something of a rarity in Florence during the summer. Several rooms even offer a marvelous view of an old courtyard framed by the nearby hills of Fiesole"). . . . "**Pensione Apollo,** 77 Via Faenza (phone 284-119), is the best ever! Paintings by Sra. Vezzani's professor-daughter amid art books, flowers and sculpture. We paid 17,500 lire ($21.08) for a large double bedroom with private shower" (Libby and John Morse, Penn Yan, New York). . . . "I certainly hope you'll find room to include Signora **Aldini's Locanda,** 13 Via Calzaioli (phone 214-752), which is just a half block from the famous Duomo, and where a room for three, with breakfast in bed, and a shower in the room, was a mere 21,500 lire ($25.90). Such a pleasant atmosphere surrounded this home it would be a shame to overlook it" (Susan Lynn Boettcher, Lawndale, California, seconded by Monica Lidral, Rhinelander, Wisconsin; all double and triple rooms are with private bath, yet will rent in 1980 for only 16,500 lire double, 23,000 lire triple, 27,500 lire quad, breakfast included). . . . "**Pensione Manuelli,** Via Martelli 6 (phone 270-893), conveniently located near the Duomo and Bapistery, has beautifully-kept rooms with charming touches, for which it charges 14,500 lire ($17.46) for two, per night. On the third floor of an elevator-equipped building; its proprietress is a gentle, gracious lady; and no meals except breakfast are served, thus giving one the opportunity to enjoy the many fine Florentine restaurants" (D. J. Abbate, Wolcott, Connecticut). . . . "**Soggiorno Iris** at Piazza Santa Maria Novella 22 (phone 296-735), less than 300 yards from the train station, was one of our best buys in more than five years of travelling in Europe. Austerely furnished but spotless and spacious, its owners—Antonio and Teresa Campagna—are always happy to practice their Australian-acquired English. 5,750 lire single, 9,900 lire double, 14,000 lire triple, with breakfast included" (David and Brenda Bendler, New York, New York; seconded by Abbie Cobb, West Chester, Pennsylvania, and Colin Carter, Cheyenne, Wyoming, who characterize the Iris as "basic but clean"). . . . "**Pensione Il Magnifico,** 7 Via Ginori (phone 28-48-40), was recently purchased by a good friend of the owner of the Locanda Daniel; at their request, I visited it this morning, inspected it quite thoroughly, and found it to be one of the most elegant low-cost places I have yet discovered. Rooms, among other things, are very spacious and very clean, and the gentleman who runs it is most amiable. He charges 9,000 lire ($10.84) for a single room, 7,500 lire ($9.03) per person for multiple-bedded rooms, 2,000 lire for breakfast. The entrance room is also large and beautiful, being furnished with some pieces that date from the sixteenth century (the building itself dates from the fifteenth century: 'Lorenzo il Magnifico slept here'). There's a good-sized, airy dining room, and a tranquil terrace where one can have a cup of coffee" (Laura Kadwell, Annandale, Virginia; note by A.F.: Pensione il Magnifico, centrally located in Florence, once appeared in this book, was then dropped by me from an earlier edition before it changed ownership; its new owner, Signor Antonio de Rosa, writes that he "is confident that this pensione, in its present condition, can rank with any other pensione or hotel of the same category. The terrace has been transformed into a gracious courtyard furnished with umbrellas and tables and lined with potted plants. The bathrooms have also been completely remodeled. Thus the pensione offers not only the classical charm of an Italian 'Palazzo' but also all the modern conveniences"). . . . "The **Pensione**

Cristallo-Giardino, Via Cavour 29 (phone 287-651), is very centrally located right near the Duomo, but its most important asset is its reasonable prices and good food—7,000 lire for a single; 12,500 lire double, 1,700 lire per person for breakfast" (Paul Lipkin, Brooklyn, New York; recommendations from other readers as well). . . . **"Pensione Desirée** is less than a block away from the station at 20 Via Fiume (phone 262-382). The husband and wife who own it are about the most delightful people I have met in all of Europe; the service is excellent; the rooms are large and airy; the bathrooms are ultra modern; and the food is superb. The charge for room: 8,000 lire for singles, 14,000 lire for doubles without food, service included: Breakfast is 2,000 lire extra" (Sondra Schear, Cincinnati, Ohio). . . . **"Pensione Gioia,** 25 Via Cavour (phone 282-804), is a jewel of a place—a home away from home. Excellent meals, large, beautiful rooms, a warm host and hostess (Mr. and Mrs. Carlo Tatini, son Carlo and daughter Carla) that I shall long remember and hope to see again in the near future. Doubles without bath will be 13,000 lire ($15.66) in 1980. What a family! What a place!" (Elvira C. Weeks, New York City). . . . "An absolute gold mine was the **Pensione Gioia,** Via Cavour 25, where we had an immaculate room, which included two enormous feasts (breakfast and full-course Italian dinner) and hot baths. Cost for both of us: 33,000 lire ($39.75), demi-pension, and including private bath! We were in walking distance of the magnificent Piazza Duomo and the unbelievable shoppers' paradise, the flea market. The family which ran this pension not only took us into their lodgings, but into their lives. They guided us everywhere and even called ahead to Rome when we were ready to leave Florence and booked us hotel reservations for the upcoming holiday weekend. They also had a van which picked up guests arriving on late evening trains into Florence. This is our third trip to Europe and I must say the Pensione Gioia is one of our treasured finds" (Dr. and Mrs. Barry Levy, Pompano Beach, Florida). . . . "For people wanting clean, comfortable and cheap accommodations when visiting Florence: try **Soggiorno Internazionale,** 24n Via Nazionale, approximately 350 yards left of the main entrance of the Railway Station. And if you feel like telephoning the Pensione for information: tel: 496-447, the owner is most friendly and will most likely come to the station himself to pick you up. Rate for rooms: 13,000 lire double per night, including service and tax; showers extra at 1,800 lire. Single rooms 9,500 lire. Hot and cold running water in each room" (Mr. Colin Tang, Wewak, New Guinea). . . . "We drove out to the hill suburb of Fiesole and found the **Hotel 'Villa Bonelli',** Via Francesco Poeti, N. 1 (phone 59-513), one of the finest places, ideal for anyone visiting Florence. Cool and pleasant, new and very modern in every way, it was a choice spot at a little over 11,400 lire ($13.73) per day per person, breakfast included for a double, we found nothing to equal it anywhere in Italy. Bus service to Florence is excellent (about a ten minute trip), making it practically the same as living in the city" (A. E. Roper, Middletown, Ohio; note by A.F.: the famous, cool Fiesole is an Etruscan city built before 500 B.C., several hundred meters above Florence. To get there, take the No. 7 bus from the central railway station square in Florence, 20 minutes away. As for the Villa Bonelli, it was recently purchased by Silvano and Andrea Boninsegni (brothers), who will be charging 14,000 lire single, 22,800 lire double, 26,400 lire for a double with private bath, always including breakfast, in 1980; some readers have already reported in that the Boninsegni brothers seem unusually eager to please their guests. . . . **"Soggiorno Amalfi,** 23 Via Oriuolo (phone 26-06-14), is less than half a block from the Duomo, on the second floor of a typical Florentine building. Signor and Signora Oretti, the young couple who own it, do not speak English, but they seem to understand every language and take care of all their guests' needs. Height of the season prices are 10,000 lire for each of the five double rooms, 6,500 lire for the one single. Breakfast is 1,200 lire, showers and baths 800 lire. These are gracious hosts; there were many days when I returned to the Amalfi, tired from sightseeing, and was met with a piece of melon or a glass of wine" (Judith Kurland, Washington, D.C.). . . . "For the second year in a row I stayed at **Locanda Giovanna,** 69 Via Faenza (phone 261-353), near the railway station; it has a warm and friendly atmosphere, is exceptionally clean, with two bathrooms and facilities for washing clothes, and charges 3,750 lire per person and a smile" (Charles Parisi, Sydney, Australia; note from AF: in 1980, the five-room Locanda Giovanna will offer single rooms for 5,000 lire, doubles for 7,500, triples 10,000, quadruples 14,000, shower 1,000 lire, breakfast unavailable. Signora Giovanna does not speak English, but is very good at guessing what you mean, and uses sign language for communication).

READERS' SELECTIONS FOR READERS WITH CARS: "Arriving by car in the middle of the maddening traffic of the city, I decided to stay outside of the center in a quiet and sane section, characterized by broad boulevards, yet within walking distance of all the attractions. And I found the **Pensione Losanna,** 9 Via Alfieri (phone 587-516), to be spacious, clean, quiet—and with virtually unlimited parking space. The English-speaking proprietor charges 9,000 lire for singles without bath, but including breakfast and service; 14,000 lire ($16.86) for doubles without bath, including breakfast and service; 17,000 lire for doubles with private bath; 13,000 lire per person for room and two meals. I enjoyed my stay here and the reprieve it offers from the Florentine bustle" (Mrs. Herbert Miller, New York City; note by A. F.: several other recommendations for the Losanna, including one from Michael Meade of Hays, Kansas, who writes: "As you know, Florence can be very noisy in the center. Here, all the rooms face on a garden. . . . The Losanna's proprietor and his wife are a charming couple from Calabria who have lived a number of years in Australia and speak English well. I'm sure you'll find Signor Vicenzo Campagna as pleasant and helpful as I did"). . . . "We decided to stay outside the town and were directed to the **Hotel Trieste,** at 16 Via Campo Sportivo (phone 44-33-49) in Sesto Fiorentino. It was a wonderful bargain for a new, well-furnished clean double with bath—all for 15,000 lire. The same room without bath would have been only 12,000 lire ($14.45). There is a direct bus service to Florence every 20 minutes" (Gita Gopalakrishnan, Calcutta, India).

PENSIONES SEEKING MENTION: "Florence so captured my heart that I not only fell in love with its museums, churches, piazzas and streets but also with a handsome young Florentine named Antonio. One month after graduating in Modern Languages and Literature from the University of Toronto, I just simply forgot to go back home to Canada and shortly afterwards married Antonio. Hard work and good fortune combined helped us to acquire a small but very modern and up-to-date locanda which we have named **"Tony's Inn"**; it's at #77 Via Faenza (phone 217-975). Our rooms are large, have hot and cold running water, tasteful furniture, and our prices are reasonable: 9,000 lire ($10.84) single, 16,000 lire ($19.27) double" (Rosemarie Lelli, Florence, Italy).

THE BIG SPLURGE PENSIONS: Two particular pensions deserve special mention and special consideration by readers willing to spend just a bit more for their accommodations.

Directly on the Arno River near the Ponte Vecchio, the **Pensione Quisisana,** 4 Lungarno Archibusieri (phone 216-692 or 215-046), is serviced by a burnished-wood elevator that takes you into a heavily furnished, labyrinthine, 40-room apartment whose interior resembles that of Rembrandt's home in Amsterdam. There's punctilious polite service by a staff of white-jacketed stewards and rates of 25,500 lire (about $30.72) for bathless doubles, breakfast, service and taxes included.

Smaller and more lightly elegant, and again on the Arno, is the **Pensione Bretagna,** 6 Lungarno Corsini (phone 263-618), whose parquet floors, crystal chandeliers, gilt and embroidered furniture, are constantly being polished or swept by a crew of white-aproned, black-uniformed maids; every room, even the bathless ones, has a bidet in it; and there's a lovely balcony off the drawing room that looks out over the Arno. Here the charge for bathless rooms is 12,900 lire ($15.54) single, 21,900 lire ($26.38) double, but that includes continental breakfast, as well as service and taxes.

STARVATION BUDGET: There are important finds for the indigent in Florence, too. First we'll consider the rock-bottom rooms and then the rock-bottom meals.

Cheapest of the cheap, in tutta la città, is the privately-operated 150-bed **Centro Turistico Santa Monaca** at 6 Via Santa Monaca (phone 26-83-38), which charges only 3,000 lire ($3.61) per person per night, plus 500 lire every four days for the rental of a linen sleeping bag, and 800 lire for breakfast. Better than a youth hostel, but not as good as a pensione, it takes both men and women, whom it places in rooms with 6 to 20 beds, imposes a midnight curfew and closes the dorms from 9:30 a.m. to 6 p.m. for cleaning, offers free showers but no meals, and stays open all year around. Europe on $4.50 A Day! That's on the far side of the Arno; from the station walk to the Piazza Santa Maria Novella, then down the Via dei Fossi, cross the Arno bridge (Ponte alla Carraia), walk up the Via dei Serragli, and the third street to the right is Via Santa Monaca. Personally-measured walking time: 12 minutes. . . . Second cheapest in town, but with only 80 beds, is the **Casa di Ospitalità Sette Santi** at 11 Viale dei Mille (phone 576-298), under religious auspices, but managed by a lovely spirit, Father Bottai, a great believer in the brotherhood of man, who makes it a point to shake hands with and talk to the guests of his lodgings, which operated as a convent until only a few years ago. This one is open from July 1 to September 30 only (but will accept a limited number of transients in other months), charges only 2,200 lire per person in dormitories, 3,100 lire in triples, 3,700 lire in doubles, features free showers, a midnight curfew, no meals, and is best reached from the Station by taking bus # 17 to the Sette Santi (7 Saints) Church and walking a minute from there.

If neither the "centro" nor the "casa" can take you, then head for one of those ancient pensions in Florence that cater particularly to foot-loose and "poverty-stricken" Americans. Most popular of these is the **Locanda Daniel**, Via Nazionale 22n (phone 260-267), 4th floor (turn left as you leave the station and walk down the Via Nazionale for about five minutes), managed by a nice husband-and-wife team, who offer very basic but clean rooms to readers of this book for: 2,500 lire single, 5,000 lire double. In seeking the Daniel, be sure to look, on the Via Nazionale, for #22 black ("22n") and not for 22 red ("22r"); Florence has a confusing system of alternate street numbers.

READERS-ON-THE-STARVATION-BUDGET: "A new find in Florence! **Soggiorno Erina**, 17 Via Fiume (phone 284-343), is only three blocks from the station, charges 10,100 lire double, 13,100 lire triple, 16,100 lire for four persons in a room, 19,100 lire for five. Immaculate rooms, in an elevator-equipped building. And any guest can try his hand at chess with Pietro, the owner" (Antonette Mendelsohn, Collegeville, Pennsylvania). . . . "At the **Soggiorno Sampaoli**, 39 Via San Gallo, phone 493-614, the charge is only 7,000 lire for a twin-bedded room for two with hot and cold running water, a large closet, table, chairs, and a large window. Signora Sampaoli is a warm and friendly woman who waited up to see that we returned safely from an evening out. Breakfast included hot bread with butter and jam, and cookies and cappucino—as much as you wanted—for 1,500 lire per person. Definitely a happy lodging" (Angela De Vincenzo, Philadelphia, Pennsylvania). . . . We stayed at the **Locanda Tina**, at Via San Gallo 31 (phone 483-519), where the charge was only 9,500 lire for a double" (James and Alice Walker, Howard Beach, New York; note by A.F.: Singles at the Tina are 7,000 lire, including service and tax). . . . "A Belgian student stopped me at the station and recommended the **Locanda Sofia** (21 Via Cavour, phone 283-930, about two blocks from the Duomo and only about four or five from the station). For a comfortable bed in a five-bedded room, very clean surroundings, and a pleasant proprietor couple, I paid only 5,000 lire a night. One floor lower is the **Locanda Colomba**, phone 263-139, being renovated, but even then it was full up with customers also paying 5,000 lire per person for similar comforts. There is no need to worry about coming in late at the Sofia, as the management gives a key to each guest. Both are very simple places" (Donald F. Dean, Berkeley, California). . . . "The tidy **Locanda Enza**, 47 Via San Zanobi (phone 490-990), within walking distance of the train station, charges 8,000 lire ($9.63) for a double without bath, and although its proprietor speaks only French and Italian (no English), he is extremely cooperative and friendly" (Stephen C. Becker, Asbury Park, New Jersey). . . . "We have discovered a gem: **Locanda Ester**, via Nazionale 6, 2nd floor (there is a lift), phone 21-27-41; directly opposite Via Fiume, two minutes' walk from the railway station. Doubles are 10,000 lire, triples 14,000 lire, all without breakfast. The triple room we had was very large with a balcony where you could hang your washing which the proprietress took in and folded when it started to rain. I felt things were safe at the Ester, as the door was always locked and only guests would be admitted. Showers are 1,000 lire and you get a large bath towel" (Ms. Helen Chadim, Curtin, Australia).

READERS-ON-THE-SUB-STARVATION-BUDGET: "The Youth Hostel called **"Villa Camerata"** is located at 2/4 vl. A. Righi, in a fine park at the last stop of bus # 17 B, and can house as many as 450 persons. Since I live in Florence, I am not allowed to spend my nights there, but many people have told me that this is one of the best in Europe. The fee per night is 2,900 lire (including sheets), and if you do not have a membership card you can buy one there for 9,000 lire (valid all over the world). By the way, and this is something only a few people know, you have free entrance in all Italian State museums (which are almost 95% of the museums, and the most important ones) upon presentation of any national Youth Hostel card, or with an International Student Card" (Giuseppe M. Massaro, Florence, Italy; note by A.F.: the stunningly beautiful youth hostel of Florence, the "Europa Villa Camerata", 2/4 Viale Augusto Righi (phone 601-451), reached by bus no. 17 B from the central train station, is a mammoth villa of the 15th century surrounded by a large park and garden, on the outskirts of Florence; it houses 450 persons in rooms containing from 15 to 20 beds per room, takes both men and women, but requires that you have a youth hostel card, obtainable in the U.S. from American Youth Hostels, Inc., 20 West 17th Street, New York, N.Y. 10011, for $6. Summer rates are 2,900 lire per person, breakfast included, 1,500 lire for a non-obligatory breakfast, evening curfew of 11 p.m. Important warning: if you arrive in summer, always phone first to this immensely popular place before embarking on the long bus ride, and don't appear before 4 p.m.—the time when new arrivals are accepted. And finally, don't be dismayed to discover that from the bus stop (in front of the huge park of the hostel), you'll need to walk about half a mile along a winding alley to reach the hostel).

FLORENCE'S STUDENT HOTELS: Two modern new structures opened in 1974: the 90-bed **Casa dello Studente Salvemini** at 15 Piazza Indipendenza (phone 471-581), reached from the Central Station by simply walking for five minutes along the Via Nazionale; and the 432-bed **P. Calamandrei** at 51 Viale Morgagni (phone 477-831), reached by taking bus # 14 to the stop called "Calamandrei". Both are open to foreign visitors only from the 1st to the 31st of August, both require a student card, and both offer private rooms renting for 5,400 lire single, 7,700 lire double, at the Casa dello Studente Salvemini; for 6,000 lire single, 9,000 lire double, at the Calamandrei.

Other student accommodations? Inquire at the offices of the **C.T.U.** (Centro Turistico Universitario) opposite the Student Mensa building (see below), at Via San Gallo 12 (phone 29-65-86). Its hours, unfortunately, are only from 9 to 12:30 and from 3:30 to 6:30 p.m. weekdays, from 9 to noon Saturdays; closed Sundays.

RESTAURANTS: The budget restaurants of Florence are scattered throughout the city, in every major district. We'll discuss them by area, in roughly ascending order of cost:

Near the Railroad Station

You'll find some real stars here, beginning with the restaurant of the railway workers' union—patronized by many middle class Florentines—on the street that runs along the side of the railroad station. It's called the **"Mensa DLF,"** is located at 6 Via Luigi Alamanni, operates only from noon to 2:30 p.m., and from 7:15 to 9 p.m., and charges 600 lire for soups, 650 to 800 lire for pasta of various sorts, 2,000 to 2,300 lire for most main courses, 450 lire for fruit. Leave the station from the side of the telephone office (look for the sign "Telefoni"), walk down the steps, turn right, pass the ground floor supermarket and the florist, continue walking, always keeping the long gray wall to your right, and after about 300 yards you will have reached the Mensa DLF.

Tinier, but of equal value in the same area, is **Trattoria Guido e Lina** at 4 Via Panicale, heart of the market area near the Via Nazionale and the station.

It serves a three-course menu for 4,000 lire ($4.81), not including wine (500 lire extra), and if that's too much to eat, you can limit your meal to exactly $3 by ordering either the spaghetti alle vongole, the tagliatelle al pomidoro or the risotto al burro (1,300 lire, $1.56, apiece), and dining on that one dish, accompanied by a glass or two of Chianti, bread and service. Everything here is fresh and of the best quality, and you'll have no language problem with owner Guido, who worked as an extra in Rome's Cinecittà during the filming of Burton and Taylor's Cleopatra, many years ago. Closed Mondays.

Three normal commercial restaurants hereabouts: the superb little basement restaurant called the **Trattoria Antichi Cancelli**, at 73r Via Faenza, which charges exactly 6,000 lire ($7.22) for a true "Menu Turistico" (three courses, including bread, wine, cover and service)—it's always crowded, but worth the wait, closed Wednesdays; nearby, at 34r Via Faenza (which is not to be confused with 34n), the **Trattoria Guido**, charging 5,500 lire ($6.62) for a tasty Menu Turistico (but one that does not include wine), served in spotless surroundings, closed Wednesdays; and, further up from the station, the exciting **Taverna Medici**, 61r Via Cavour (corner of Via Guelfa), which is patronized by some of the nicest people in Florence, and operates a self-service section downstairs, where main courses are 1,800 to 2,200 lire, vegetables 600 to 900 lire, pastas 900 to 1,000 lire, cheese and ice cream 800 lire (you'll pay 20% more for the same items on the ground floor). In the station itself, you'll quickly spot a counter restaurant identified as a **Tavola Calda**, which serves a huge bowl of spaghetti for 900 lire, or a sizable hunk of pizza alla napoletana for 1,300, or pizza Margherita for 1,400, any one of which is enough for a full meal. Go first to the "cassa" (cashier), tell her what you want, pay, pick up a ticket, sit down and order.

Behind the Uffizi Galleries

The only cluster of moderately-priced restaurants in Florence is found at the side of and behind the Uffizi Galleries, on two little streets—the **Via dei Neri (12)** and more particularly, on the **Via dei Leoni (13)**. For value received, these can scarcely be equalled throughout the rest of Europe. On Via dei Leoni alone, there are four restaurants serving three-course prezzo fisso meals for 5,000 to 6,000 ($6.02 to $7.22)—and two of them include a quarter of a liter of wine in the basic price. They are: the **Ristorante Montecatini**, Via dei Leoni (5,500 lire, which includes cover charge and tip); the **Buzzino**, Via dei Leoni 8 (5,500 lire, including wine, service charge and cover); the **Trattoria Roberto**, which is on a continuation of Via dei Leoni, called Via dei Castellani, No. 4r, near the river (5,500 lire for soup or pasta, main course with vegetables, fruit or cheese, a quarter of a liter of Chianti, and bread; closed Wednesdays); and the **Trattoria Quo Vadis**, 16 Via Castellani (5,000 lire for three courses without wine—700 lire extra—as well as 24 varieties of pasta and 30 pizza choices, including a gargantuan double pizza called "calzone" for 2,700 lire). Again on the Via dei Leoni, at #14, the **Trattoria Alfredo**, charges 6,000 lire for yet another three-course meal, including service and wine (closed Wednesdays). And even if you order à la carte at these places, you can still get away for very little. At the Buzzino, I recently had spaghetti, roast chicken, cheese, and wine for 5,800 lire ($6.98). Sample à la carte meals at the Ristorante Montecatini: "cotoletta alla Milanese" for 3,000 lire ($3.61); spaghetti for 900 lire ($1.08); minestrone for 800 lire (96¢).

Which of the five seem outstanding? I vacillate between Alfredo's and the Roberto, but usually end up going to Roberto's. If you're approaching this area from the river, try the nearby Roberto, which is where most of the museum guards at the Uffizi eat. If you're walking down the Via dei Leoni from the Piazza della Signoria, try Alfredo's. But if you're feeling flush and willing to blow an extra 500 lire, then try the attractive Montecatini, and order either its "ravioli fatti in casa" (home-made ravioli, a specialty) for 1,700 lire, or its "petti di pollo dorati" (chicken in an egg batter, a Florentine specialty) for 2,800 lire.

Cheapest place to eat à la carte in this area? That's at **Trattoria da Benvenuto,** 16 Via dei Leoni, where the spaghetti is only 800 lire (96¢), fried fish with green sauce 2,200 lire ($2.65), zucchini salad 750 lire (90¢), a quarter liter of red wine 600 lire (72¢), cover charge 500 lire, and service 12%. Finest individual dishes? The *risotto alla Fiorentina,* available at most ristorantes hearabouts—it's a delicious rice-and-tomatoes treat; the chicken cacciatore; the tender gorgonzola cheese called verde dolce.

And where do you go if you simply want a light snack or something less than a full meal? Well, in the same area, a small *rosticceria* at 74r Via dei Neri sells tasty sandwiches for 1,200 lire ($1.44); a *frigittoria* at 8 Via de Neri specializes in pizza for 1,400 lire; and a baby-sized *wineteria* (simply called "vino" and no larger than a telephone booth) at 70r Via dell' Anguillara, a side street off the Via dei Leoni, sells 25 different kinds of local wines at 200 to 350 lire (24¢ to 42¢) per glass, as well as rye bread sandwiches for 400 to 600 lire. This place is crowded if more than one client is inside, and nobody minds if you drink your glass of *orvieto sole* or *chianti controllato* on the sidewalk—you won't be the only one.

In or near the Piazza della Signoria

At least one of your meals—preferably in the evening—should be taken at the **Ristorante Orcagna (17),** the big outdoor establishment on the Piazza della Signoria. Prices here are not the cheapest, but with care a meal can be held below $7. Recommended feast? Start with the luscious tortellini and meat sauce ("tortellini al sugo di carne") 1,500 lire, then order liver à la Venice ("fegato alla Veneziana") 2,500 lire, and have a tomato salad (it's a huge one) on the side, 1,000 lire. Total: 5,000 lire, plus bread and cover charge of 700 lire, plus 12% service, for a grand total of $7.69. And there's also a three-course prezzo fisso here for 5,500 lire ($6.62), wine included. The view is worth the price: This is the square on which the most successful copy of Michelangelo's David stands, along with Cellini's famous Perseus Holding the Medusa's Head and other masterworks of sculpture. . . . Not directly on the Piazza della Signoria, but only a few feet from it, is the **Ristorante Buca Poldo,** 2 Chiasso degli Armagnati, which is both a bit cheaper and better than the fortunate restaurants that find themselves within the square. To find the Buca Poldo, first look for the Via Vaccherecchia, which leads off from the square at the side that is directly opposite from the David; the Chiasso degli Armagnati, housing the Buca Poldo, is a little passageway off that street. The restaurant (which is closed Tuesdays) serves a top-notch, three-course prezzo fisso (including wine and service charge), and charges 5,800 lire for it, service and wine included; ask specifically for the prezzo fisso menu.

Near the Piazza del Duomo

Here's a choice for a popular area, and one in which you'll enjoy a price advantage. At the **Trattoria la Cupola,** 7r Via Folco Portinari, those unfortunate souls who don't use this book pay 6,000 lire ($7.22) for a three-course *prezzo fisso,* including a quarter liter of red or white wine. But! . . . if you, cherished readers, will show this book to Signor Pietro, the manager, you'll pay only 5,000 lire ($6.02) for the same meal. À la carte specialties at the Cupola: *tortellini alla Romagnola* (the green variety of pasta, filled with Ricotta cheese) for 1,800 lire ($2.16); *risotto alla pescatore* (rice with mussels, squid, octopus and garlic) for 1,800 lire ($2.16); marvelous *scaloppini* (tender veal cutlets with a cheese (gruyère) sauce for 3,000 lire ($3.61); and on Fridays only, a Florentine-style bouillabaisse, here called *zuppa di pesce,* a meal in itself, for 3,800 lire ($4.57). As you can see, it is possible to put together a one-pasta-dish-with-wine light meal for 3,600 lire ($4.33) even after you have paid the 500 lire cover charge and 12% service assessed to persons who don't take the prezzo fisso. From the Piazza del Duomo, walk down the Via dell' Oriuolo, and the first side street to the left is the Via Folco Portinari. Closed Mondays.

If you're tired of these heavy meals, then head for the **Due Ponti (18),** a self-styled American cafe on the Lungarno Acciaioli (#34r), between the Hotel Berchielli and the Ponte Vecchio. It offers light lunches (soup and sandwiches) for 1,700 lire ($2.04), ice cream sundaes for 1,300 lire ($1.56). In mid-afternoon, you can sit on the shaded terrace with a cup of espresso and a large hors d'oeuvre (half-a-roll with hard-boiled egg, tomato and sauce) for 1,700 lire ($2.04); and at night, you can stop for a snack at almost any hour; from May to October, the cafe is open until 1 a.m., later than any other I know in Florence.

SELF-SERVICE RESTAURANTS: There are two large ones in Florence, the better of which is called **Self-Service Restaurant,** without more, and is located upstairs at 5 Via Pecori, near the Via Vecchietti, 1½ blocks from the Duomo. From the Baptistery of the Duomo, walk down the Via Pecori; the first side street you'll pass will be the Via dei Brunelleschi, the second is the Via Vecchietti; between these two, on the Via Pecori, look up and you'll spot a self-service sign—entrance is up a plain stairway between a purse store and the subscription offices of the newspaper, "Corriere della Sera." Once upstairs, you'll find crowds of Florentines (mainly at lunch, less so at dinner), who pack away servings of pasta (900 lire), soups (600), main courses with vegetable (most of them 2,000 lire), desserts (700 lire). Some budget rules for cafeteria dining in Italy: make your main course pasta with meat sauce, rather than meat and vegetables—you'll save 500 to 600 lire; choose ordinary wine, not the brand name; choose, pay for, and eat one course at a time—then go back (if you can) for more; the eyes of many tourists are bigger than their stomachs, and funds are wasted on selections that can't be finished. Open 12:15 to 3 and 7 to 10; closed Saturday.

The other major cafeteria? That's the **"Self Service Giannino in San Lorenzo,"** next door to the ristorante of the same name, at 31r Borgo S. Lorenzo—50 yards up from the Via Panzani, and just around the corner from the Medici Chapels and the San Lorenzo Church. Prices somewhat higher (main courses for 2,500 lire, pasta or soup for 900) than at our preferred self-service spot. Closed Tuesdays.

PREZZO FISSO VS. À LA CARTE: Which should you seek? In Italy, the price of a *prezzo fisso* (table d'hote) meal may seem high in comparison with the à la carte cost of individual plates; however, persons dining à la carte must usually pay a cover charge of 500 lire and a service charge of 12%. Since these items are *included* in the price of a prezzo fisso meal, the prezzo fisso can often bring a price advantage to you. On the other hand, the prezzo fisso meal may not include the restaurant's most attractive specialties. So which should you choose? Hmmm. . . .

READERS' RESTAURANT SELECTIONS: "The 4,000-lire price of **La Botteghina Rossa,** Via degli Alfani 24r, five blocks from the Duomo, is immediately justified when a gallon of red/white wine and mineral water are placed on the table. The meal begins with hors d'oeuvres: we had curried rice and ripe olives, mixed bean-onion-tomato salad, sardines, tomatoes, minced carrots, spiced pickles. For pasta we had a superb meat sauce ravioli. Then came the entree—the fish consisted of two entire grilled fish (out of this world), a crayfish (delicate and sweet), and three baby clams (a whole plate appeared when we expressed our delight). The food is of such unbelievable quality and quantity that our bread was left untouched. This place is an absolute must!" (Mr. and Mrs. Rollin K. Daniel, New York, N.Y.; note by A.F.: this remarkable establishment, frequented by artists, students and high and low society—it's a very 'in' place—is managed by an aristocratic lady named Ferdinanda Cristina Martini Monti Vedova Dini Foschi. Her three-course meals, accompanied by red wine and served on Limoges or Rosenthal china, are an astonishing value at the 1980 price of 4,000 lire ($4.82), and will appear in the main text of our 1981 edition. Closed Sundays). . . . "The **Piccadilly Pizza** at 43 Via Por S. Maria, a block from the Ponte Vecchio, serves huge, thick slices of pizza with twelve different choices of topping—ham and artichoke, onions and mushrooms, sausage and peppers, etc.—for 800 lire, with cold drinks for 600 lire. A quick, delicious lunch for under $2" (Prof. S. Friedland, Brooklyn, New York; note by A.F.: In addition to selling unusually-flavored ice cream cones for 500 lire (60¢)—"uva" (grape), "mulatta" (chocolate with almonds)—Piccadilly Pizza offers a specialty known as "mangia e beve" (literally: eat and drink), which consists of fresh lemon juice and vegetable and fruit salad, all served in a large beer mug with spoon and straw, for 1,500 lire ($1.80). Excellente! And open daily except Mondays from 11 a.m. to 10:30 p.m. . . . "A new self-service restaurant, the **Grande Italia,** 25 Piazza della Stazione, has opened just opposite the railroad station, on the corner of the Piazza Stazione and the Via Nazionale. It is clean and roomy, the food is cheap and hot, and there is a wide variety of selections to choose from. I was in Florence in January with two other Brothers, and we ate here all the time (except on Fridays, when the restaurant is closed). A typical à la carte meal price for pasta, chicken with chips, bread and a bottle of wine is 4,500 lire" (Brother Dunstan Henry, Marcellin College, Auckland, New Zealand). . . . "We stumbled by chance upon **Trattoria Filippo,** at Via Palazzuolo 68, which seems to be serving one of the most economical tourist menus in town: 5,000 lire for two courses, including bread and wine. There are just two small rooms, but the food is good. Closed Mondays" (Jill Levey, New York, N.Y.; note by A.F.: from numerous recent comments, Filippo appears to be one of the top values in Florence, and certainly will be on my own viewing list for 1980: spaghetti for only 900 lire, main courses for 2,000 lire, vegetables or salad 500 lire, wine 500 lire). . . . "Although the **Ristorante Il Cupolone** at 66 Via dei Servi, halfway between the Duomo and the Piazza della Annunziata, is open to all, it caters mainly to college-age students, and if you look vaguely under 30, the friendly student at the front desk will hand you a card entitling you to a 10% discount! An average, three-course, self-service meal, should run you about 4,500 lire. The servings are immense!" (Gene Paglis, Calsbad, California). . . . "At the **Trattoria Anita,** corner of Via del Parlascio and Via Vinegia, about three short blocks from the Uffizi, salads and vegetables are 700 lire, pasta 900, delicious ravioli 850, main courses 2,500, wine 600 lire for half a liter. Go early, as the Anita is very popular with Florentines and you may end up sharing your table by the end of dinner. It's off Via de Leoni, and cheaper and better than Trattoria Roberto" (Monica Lindra, Rhinelander, Wisconsin). . . . "We discovered the **Trattoria Palle D'Oro,** Via S. Antonino 45 R, between the market and Via Faenza, where we ate twice: pasta 800 lire, meat dish, 2,300 lire, vegetable 800 lire, and the cover charge with bread was 350 lire. Thus, a very delicious meal comes to 3,630 lire without wine, which is 450 lire for a quarter liter, and service is 10%. The kitchen is open so you can select your meal by pointing if you don't understand the menu" (Victor Honig, San Francisco, California).

READERS' FOOD TIPS: "Do mention the lovely, marble market building diagonally across from the Medici Chapels. Ask for the **Public Market** if you miss it. Open mornings from about six to noon. The place for a portable feast and a glimpse of Italy in action. Marble stalls stacked with rabbits neatly arranged, their pink ears in a pile, fruit sellers with barrels of olives, lovely pears, grapes, whatever is in season, butchers with sausages fat and slim, all nicely spiced, and counters of cheeses—you can buy just one slice, and sample many—a separate section for fish, and much more. A shopping idea: buy a few tubes of anchovy paste, maybe a couple of catsup and mayonnaise. All packaged like toothpaste. Cheap, non-breakable, and they won't leak if you open them" (Dr. and Mrs. Kenneth Korver, Susanville, California; note by A.F.: the advice to consider an occasional picnic lunch in Florence is an excellent one, and if you're not near a large market, simply look for the delicatessens bearing the words "salsamentaria" or "gastronomia" in their titles. At one of the most expensive of these on the Piazza San Marco, Hope and I recently purchased a bottle of Chianti for 1,800 lire, an enormous roll (big enough for two) for 200 lire, a hunk of soft, white cheese, two large slices of lunch meat, and two tomatoes covered with "salsa verde" (green sauce) for an additional 3,800 lire, making a total of 5,800 lire, or about $3.50 apiece, for a refreshing, wine-accompanied lunch that we ate in a nearby cool, green park).

STARVATION BUDGET MEALS: For meals, Florence offers three exceptionally low-cost dining halls, of which the most important is the **Student Mensa** of the University of Florence, at Via San Gallo 25a, about three short blocks from the Piazza Indipendenza. Walk inside, into the courtyard, where you'll see a neon sign reading "Bar"; walk up the 41 steps at that point, and you'll find the huge Mensa, serving equally huge meals (ask for the "Pasto Completo") for 2,500 lire (three courses), including wine—you can't possibly spend more than $3. Hours are noon to 2:15 p.m., and 7 to 9 p.m., Monday through Saturday, and the posted regulations (which are not always observed) require a student card.

Unfortunately, the Mensa closes from August 1 to September 15. When that happens, you'll want to seek another budget haven, but one that has no student affiliation, called the **Casa di San Francesco**, which is maintained by a religious order, at 2 Piazza SS. Annunziata. Pay 2,400 lire at the door, then walk inside to partake of pasta, a main course with salad or vegetable, plus fruit and wine. You'll dine among a wonderful melange of students and old people, priests and workingmen; and you'll simply have to point at what they're eating to order from the waitress—there's no menu. Don't wear your newest and most expensive clothes. Serving times are from noon to 2:30 p.m., for lunch only. Closed Sundays.

Again for lunch only (11:30 a.m. to 2 p.m.), there's also the city-subsidized **Ristorante Economico** at 28 Via Porcellana, which serves a surprisingly decent, two-course, self-service meal for only 1,650 lire ($1.98), 180 lire more for wine, every day of the year except May 1—which tells something about the politics of Florence. A la carte prices are also amazingly low (pasta 400 lire, main courses 1,050 lire), quality excellent, and all told, this is probably the best bargain in all of Florence. From the station, walk first to Piazza Santa Maria Novella, then take the first street to the right, which is Via del Porcellana. Or simply look for the large Hotel Croce di Malta; the Economico is just behind the hotel.

THE BIG, BIG SPLURGE: It costs 10,000 lire ($12.04), but it's a feast you'll long remember, at the **Ristorante Il Latini**, 6r Via Palchetti, where Narcisio Latini and his sons Giovanni and Torello operate one of the busiest trattorias in town: three small rooms with about 100 seats, where you'll be lucky to find a chair between noon and 3 p.m. or from 7 to 10 p.m. (closed Mondays). One way of arriving there: from the Arno, walk up the Via Tornabuoni, turn into the second street to your left (Via della Spada), again the first to your left (Via Federighi), and 50 yards to your left again is The Latini, buzzing with activity: the old man standing behind his counter, watching with an eagle eye, shouting orders, talking to four persons at once, placing telephoned orders to his own farm in the famous Chianti valley about 20 miles from Florence, and never losing control over the wonderful chaos. If you crave atmosphere, this is the place. Some 50 hams (they sell for $60 apiece) hang from the ceiling, walls are covered with colorful pictures, and wine, mineral water, and aromatic white bread can be taken "a volontà," meaning "as much as you like"—they're already included in the $12.04 banquet, which also includes: (1) an aperitivo (local sweet wine); (2) an antipasto (one slice of crude ham, same type as dangles from the ceiling, and two slices of local sausage); (3) homemade noodles, or one of five other first dishes; (4) a plate with four different cooked or roast meats (pork, chicken, veal and rabbit) on it, or one of seven other specialties of the house; (5) fruit **and** ice cream, or "Ricotta Ubriaca" ("intoxicated cheese", an interesting dish of chilled Ricotta cheese mixed with sugar and sprinkled with pulverized coffee and brandy); (6) one cup of espresso; and (7) a small glass of sweet wine served with almond biscuits. You can eat less for about 7,000 lire ($9.03), (for example, a large plate of noodles, roast lamb with salad, and all the wine you can drink), but my guess is you'll enjoy the works.

THE FOOD OF FLORENCE—A RECAP: Summarizing the lengthy and possibly confusing discussion just ended, here's a quick listing of Florence's finest food values: (1) The 2,500 lire ($3.01) menu, wine included, of the **Student Mensa** at 25A Via San Gallo, closed Sundays and from August 1 to September 15; (2) The one-plate pasta-meals-with-wine for 3,600 lire ($4.33) at **Trattoria La Cupola**, 7R Via Folco Portinari, closed Mondays; (3) The self-service meals for 4,000 lire ($4.81) and less at the **DLF Mensa**, 6 Via Luigi Alamanni next to the train station, open daily; (4) The 4,000 lire ($4.81) feast—not a meal, a feast!—with wine, at the unique **Botteghina Rossa**, 24R Via degli Alfani, closed Sundays; (5) The two-course luncheons, with beverage, for 2,400 lire ($2.89) at the **Casa di San Francesco**, 2 Piazza Sant' Annunziata; and (6) The no-frills, last-resort menu (spaghetti or soup, then meat or fish with vegetable and bread) for less than $2, at the **Ristorante Economico**, 28 Via Porcellana, open seven days a week.

MUSEUMS: Florence has over forty museums and art galleries, and none of them asks admission on Sundays. The two giants are, of course, the **Uffizi Galleries** and the **Pitti Palace** (both closed Mondays), both of which charge 250 lire (30¢) on their admission days. They contain priceless collections of the world's greatest art, and require slow, unhurried, reflective visits for maximum enjoyment.

One other Florentine museum—the **Accademia** near the Piazza San Marco (from the Duomo, walk down the Via Ricasoli to reach it)—may alone be worth your entire trip to Europe. For here, in a magnificent setting, stands the original of Michelangelo's David; and when you've seen it, you'll realize how inadequate are the weatherworn copies scattered elsewhere in Florence. Here, too, are several unfinished sculptures of Michelangelo, all the more fascinating because they give you a glimpse into the method of their creation. Admission charge of only 150 lire on weekdays (when the hours are 9 to 2, free admission on Sundays (open 9 to 1). Closed Mondays.

AN IMPORTANT TIP: "In almost any German city, before travelling to Italy, you can purchase, for 2.50 marks, from any of the many branches of the Dresdner Bank a 'tessera' (pass) issued by the Italian Ministero della Pubblica Istruzione entitling the bearer to free entry to all state museums in Italy" (Karl-Heinz Ries, Hanover, Germany). . . . "It is a must to get a museum pass before going to Italy. We got ours from the Royal Automobile Club in London for 50 pence and saved a ton of money" (Diane Currano, Evergreen Park, Illinois; note by A.F.: see our Rome chapter for other sources of the invaluable 'Museum Pass').

READERS' MUSEUM SUGGESTIONS: "The Gallery of Modern Art in the **Pitti Palace** contains a super collection of all-Italian artists representing at least the first 30 years of this century; it may one day be the outstanding Italian collection representative of our times" (Victor Henry Matson III, Torrance, California). . . . **"Casa Buonarroti,** 70 Via Ghibellina, should be on the list of Michelangelo lovers. This house, once occupied by a nephew of the sculptor, is now a museum (closed Tuesdays) charging 500 lire entrance. In addition to three original figures by Michelangelo, there is a large collection of his anatomical and architectural sketches. For those who have already admired his Pietas in the Duomo and the Accademia, the museum has reproductions of the other two which are in Milan and Rome. Wonderful if you like to compare" (Marianne Durand, San Francisco, California). . . . "One note about museums: scout around to the far end of the Pitti and knock (hard) at the door of the carriage museum. We had a most interesting tour by the lady caretaker who somehow managed to make us understand, even with our limited Italian. The carriages are beautifully preserved and very colorful" (Christie J. Bentham, Scarborough, Ontario, Canada). . . . "While wandering around the cathedrals of Florence, we realized that we should take a pair of lightweight binoculars to see the detailed work on the domes. Our enjoyment of such wonderful structures as the Baptistry was immensely enhanced . . . No guide book mentions a visit to the **Jewish Synagogue** on Via L. C. Farini, whose entrance is through a garden. It is an excellent example of moorish architecture, built in 1882, and the woman who opened the door for us modestly stated: 'This is the most beautiful synagogue in all of Europe'. We think she's right! The synagogue is open from 8:30 to 12:30 on Tuesday, Wednesday and Thursday, and admission is free" (Victor Honig, San Francisco, California).

TOURS: C.I.T., at the corner of Piazza della Stazione and Piazza della Unità Italiana, offers two separate half-day motorcoach tours of Florence, including visits to the Medici Chapels, the Uffizi Galleries (except on Mondays), and the breathtaking Piazzale Michelangelo, on a hill overlooking the city. Price for each half-day is 9,500 lire.

The same company operates an 11,000-lire, half-day tour to Pisa—but that's a trip which can be duplicated on your own for less cost and with a much greater range of activities. Simply take a round-trip ride by train from Florence to Pisa (3,300 lire, second class). When you arrive in Pisa, take the bus marked "Duomo" from in front of the railroad station (round-trip bus ride, 200 lire). Then buy a 1,000-lire admission ticket to the Leaning Tower. For about $5.50, you'll have visited the key attraction of the commercial tours, and you'll be able to spend as much time in Pisa as you like.

Incidentally, the round-trip fare to Venice from Florence is 10,300 lire, and a train leaves every 2 hours or so.

READERS-ON-AN-OUTING: "For a wonderful side trip from Florence, spend a day in Siena. For 2,800 lire ($3.37), you can buy a round-trip bus ticket from the SITA company located near the train station on Via S. Caterina di Siena. The trip takes 1½ to 2 hours, but for the shorter journey, make sure you take the bus indicated as "via superstrada". Buses go in both directions several times a day, and the bus leaves you a 10-minute walk from the heart of Siena. The 'musts' to see in Siena are the Palazzo Pubblico (with its towering Campanile—200 lire to climb—which offers a fantastic view of the entire area), the Duomo (which ranks with the finest in all of Italy), and the Museo dell' Opera del Duomo (500 lire), containing magnificent paintings by Duccio" (Lewis and Deanna Rappaport, Brooklyn, New York). . . . "For only 2,400 lire, you can make a round-trip by bus returning the same day, from Florence to **San Gimignano,** the most medieval, fortified town you can imagine on Italian soil. The bus follows part of the same route as the 12 noon Sita bus to Siena, but you continue after a short pause at Poggibonsi in another bus" (Oscar Gilson, Munich, Germany). . . . "Most of the Italian cities have bus lines following a scenic circular route, on which a ride costs as little as 100 lire. From the railway station in Florence, bus lines 13 and 19—Circolare Sinistra and Circolare Destra—cover some of the most admirable sights for only 100 lire" (Karl Heinz Ries, Hannover, Germany). . . . "Walk to the coffee house in the **Boboli Gardens,** where you can sit forever with an 800-lire Coke and look over the whole of Florence and on to the hills beyond Fiesole" (Polly Cobb, Blacksbury, Virginia).

FLORENCE MISCELLANY: Got only a day to spend in Florence? Early in the morning, get set at the **Piazza della Signoria,** dash into the **Palazzo Vecchio,** then the **Uffizi Galleries** next door, cross over the **Ponte Vecchio,** glancing at its shops, examine the **Palazzo Pitti** and the **Boboli Gardens,** have lunch; retrace your steps to the **Baptistery,** go into the **Duomo,** walk up the **Bell Tower,** enter the **Medici Chapels,** and then—as dusk falls—head up to the **Piazzale Michelangelo,** overlooking the city, for a Florentine sunset. . . . Then, after you've decided to spend a week in Florence, be certain to visit the **Church of Santa Croce**—the "Pantheon of Tuscany"—with its memorials to Dante, Galileo, Michelangelo. In 1965, the city celebrated the seventh centenary of Dante (whom it exiled); in his Divine Comedy, Dante glorified Florence, but not the Florentines, for whom he invented exquisite tortures in hell. . . . Pass up, however, the shops and "leather factories" on Santa Croce Square—they're among the most expensive in Florence. . . . And after you've decided to take up permanent residence in Florence, consult the **American Agency,** 33R Via Del Ponte Rosso (phone 475-053), for its apartment listings. . . . Now, here's my wife Hope for a closer look at the glorious art treasures of Florence:

HOPE'S FLORENCE: "Many of us first fully realized what Florence meant to us in those anxious days following the flood of November, 1966. I, for one, was almost physically ill at the thought that anything in Florence might be damaged or lost. And I felt moved beyond measure when hundreds of Europeans and Americans (especially younger ones) converged on the city to save its priceless treasures of literature and art.

"Florence is so very important and dear to us because it is in the very fabric of our civilization; it provides the roots of what we are today. The home of the Renaissance, of Michelangelo, Dante, DaVinci, the Medicis, Donatello, Cellini, even Machiavelli—it is a simply overwhelming city which at times seems almost too much to cope with: walk into even the tiniest church, and you'll find something vital to see. Obviously, on a short stay, you'll want to concentrate on the major areas and sites that Arthur has described; but if you have the extra time, then don't overlook the following:

Around the Duomo

"On the Piazzas del Duomo and S. Giovanni, which is really one large plaza and a focal point of the city, you'll find the **Cathedral of Santa Maria del Fiore** (the duomo); **Giotto's Tower;** and the **Baptistery**—all done in that dramatic multi-colored marble of Tuscan style.

The Baptistery

"A good place to start is at Lorenzo Ghiberti's famous doors (on the side of the **Baptistery** directly opposite the Cathedral), christened for all time by Michelangelo when he first saw them and exclaimed, 'These doors are fit to stand at the Gates of Paradise!' The glittering gilded doors were twenty-seven years in the making and depict scenes from the Old Testament. The second door at the entrance to the Baptistery is by Andrea Pisano, and depicts the life of John the Baptist, the patron saint of Florence (to whom the Baptistery is dedicated). The final door is an earlier work of Ghiberti's illustrating the New Testament.

"Now you must not fail to go inside the Baptistery to see the colorful 13th century mosaics which cover the ceiling (they're by Cimabue, Andrea Tafi, Apollonio Greco, others)—don't miss the Inferno of Hell, above you to the right of the main entrance, with the terrible horned monster gobbling up little people. Among many points of interest is Donatello's exotic wooden statue of Mary Magdalen.

The Cathedral of Santa Maria del Fiore

"The first architect for the Cathedral was Arnolfo di Cambio (whose name has been associated with the Palazzo Vecchio and Santa Croce); but the real masterwork of the Duomo is Brunelleschi's soaring Dome—a daring concept in its time, built with double walls but without any support from the floor below. Under the Dome are stained glass windows made by Ghiberti, Donatello and Uccello; the painting on the Dome itself is 'The Last Judgment' by Vasari and Zuccari. Also inside this rather stark and bare Cathedral are some very nice stained glass windows, many of them by Ghiberti; decorations by Luca della Robbia; and a couple of incongruous and military-looking equestrian frescoes—one by Paolo Uccello, the other by Andrea del Castagne. But most important of all is Michelangelo's other and unfinished 'Pietà,' made when he was more than seventy-five years old; the figure of Nicodemus (or Joseph) is supposed to be a self-portrait of the artist—old, tired and nearly blind. Legend has it that Michelangelo later sought to destroy the work, and it is generally accepted that the figure of the young girl (Mary Magdalen) is a subsequent addition and not the work of the master. You can climb up to the gallery of the Dome for 500 lire, from 8:30 to 12:00 and 2:30 to 6. Recently opened to the public here: the ruins of the pre-existing, 10th century, S. Reparata cathedral once standing on this site, now viewed below the ground floor.

The Campanile

"Giotto spent the last three years of his life working on the Campanile; he died in 1337 before it was completed. Although his work on the Florentine Gothic tower was then carried forward by Andrea Pisano and Francesco Talenti (with contributing work from Luca Della Robbia), the structure is always referred to as **Giotto's Tower.** Note especially the fine bas-reliefs around the tower, attributed to Pisano, Della Robbia, and Arnoldi (all copies: the originals are now in the Museo del Duomo). For 500 lire, between the hours of 8:30 and 12 and 2:30 and 6, you can climb to the top of the Tower for good views of the Cathedral and Florence.

Museo dell' Opera del Duomo

"Directly behind the Cathedral, at Piazza Duomo #9, is the **Museo del Duomo** (or Museo dell' Opera di Santa Maria del Fiore, as it's sometimes called): open daily from 9:30 a.m. to 1 p.m. and from 3 p.m. to 6 p.m., for a 300-lire entrance fee. Easily overlooked by tourists, this quiet, airy, little museum contains all the art works and furnishings that used to be in the Cathedral. Even in the ticket office there's a bust of Brunnelleschi, and over the doors two glazed terracottas by the Della Robbias. In the second inner room (to your left) you'll find the remains of the old facade of the Cathedral (destroyed in 1587), including work by the original architect Arnolfo di Cambio, a weather-worn but noble 'St. John' by Donatello, and Nanni di Banco's intriguing 'San Luca.' Upstairs in the center room are some unusually powerful statues by Donatello and Nanna di Bartolo, and some work which was removed from the Campanile in 1941 (by the aforementioned artists; as well as some attributed to Maso and Giovanni di Giuliano da Poggibonsi); but the special treats are the marble choirs of Luca della Robbia and (opposite) Donatello—Luca's choir has been removed down to eyelevel for better viewing. Della Robbia's singing gallery is based on the 150th Psalm of David ("Praise the Lord in song and gladness . . .") and you'll smile when you see it—for it's filled with realistic bambinos having such a good time making music: the work is infused with joy and mischief. Directly across the way, Donatello's choir is equally delightful and a good contrast to della Robbia—here, the highly stylized little cherubs explode in dance, running wild with exuberance. In the room to the left there has been assembled the cycle of bas-reliefs from the first and second stories of the Campanile (removed in 1965; mostly attributed to della Robbia and Alberto Arnoldi). Another priceless and fascinating masterpiece, in the last room on the second floor, is the Silver Altar Piece with Stories from the Life of St. John The Baptist—a joint effort by Betto di Geri and Leonardo di ser Giovanni, and perhaps Paolo and Michele di Monte (and others), with a wonderful central statuette of John the Baptist by Michelozzo. (I wonder, did Edward Albee get the idea for his play "Tiny Alice" here? All the little figures in the wonderfully alive Altar Piece seem imprisoned, but nevertheless leading independent lives of their own.)

The Medici-Riccardi Palace

"Close to the Duomo (from the main entrance of the Cathedral, face the Baptistery, turn right to Via de Martelli, proceeding one block to a pile of dark stones resembling a squat fortress) is the **Medici-Riccardi Palace** at 1 Via Cavour, commissioned by Cosimo il Vecchio (and built by Michelozzo, Brunelleschi's pupil, between 1444-64); this was home to Cosimo the Elder and Lorenzo the Magnificent. The Medici Museum (to your left as you enter the courtyard) contains paintings, busts, medals and documents pertaining to the history of the Medici (of special interest are little portraits of the family, and a death mask of Lorenzo il Magnifico). Across the courtyard, there's a second-floor Baroque gallery with Giordano's frescoes illustrating the 'Apotheosis of the Medici Dynasty'; and, the best for last: a Chapel with magnificent frescoed walls by Gozzoli (the artist included the Medici and some of the local citizens in the scene). Open daily from 9 to 1 and 3 to 5 (Sundays 9 to 1) for an admission charge of 200 lire, except Sundays when it's free. Closed Wednesdays.

The Medici Chapels

"The **Church of San Lorenzo,** at 9 Piazza San Lorenzo, is across the street from the Medici Palace; upstairs in the Cloister of San Lorenzo is **The Laurenziana Library,** built for the Medici by Michelangelo. All the way around the Church, on Piazza Madonna, is the entrance to the **Medici Chapels** (250 lire admission, open from 9 a.m. to 7 p.m. weekdays, Sundays from 9 to 1); go to the 'New' Sacristy first, which contains Michelangelo's Tomb for Lawrence the Duke of Urbino (with the figures of 'Dawn' and 'Dusk') and his Tomb for Giuliano the Duke of Nemours (with the figures of 'Night' and 'Day'). Chairs are provided for comfortable contemplation, and the longer you look at the works, the greater they'll appear. The other chapels, decorated to their Baroque teeth, are almost jolly in their aspect, with six enormous tombs lining the walls; there are two rooms behind the altar containing treasures and religious relics, very much in the Italian manner (bones of saints entwined with pearls in golden cases, etc.).

The Church of Santa Maria Novella

"Not far from San Lorenzo is the **Church of Santa Maria Novella,** (walk up Via del Giglio or Via Melarancio), on the striking Piazza Santa Maria Novella, with its church cloister that charges 500 lire to enter (9 to 2 weekdays, 8 to 1 on Sundays, when admission is free; closed Fridays); the Florentines are casual in pointing out that the church contains works by Lippi, Ghiberti, Ghirlandaio, Brunelleschi, Giotto and others; the cloister dates from the 14th century, and contains a particularly magnificent room called the 'Spanish Chapel.'

Starting at Piazza della Signoria

"Now head for the Piazza della Signoria, the landmark square of Florence where you are probably already spending a great deal of your time. It hardly seems necessary to advise you to take a good look at the lovely Loggia, a virtual outdoor sculpture gallery; in front of the fountain with the huge white statue of Neptune (by Ammannati) is a small round disc marking the spot where Savonarola was burnt alive in 1498 (ironically, he was executed here, in the same Piazza where he had previously burned such heretical objects as books and pictures); and of course you already know that the great Uffizi Gallery is right next door to the Palazzo.

"Now I suggest you take a quick tour through the **Palazzo della Signoria** (better known as the 'Palazzo Vecchio'; open from 9 a.m. to 7 p.m. weekdays, for 500 lire, and on Sundays from 8 to 1 for free, closed Saturdays), to get some feeling of the place where many of Florence's most historic events occurred, and also to learn how the other half lived (Cosimo I de Medici resided here for ten years). Of special interest is the Hall of the 500 built during Savonarola's term, and there are excellent views of the city from the top floors and tower.

The Uffizi

"The **Uffizi,** or "offices", built in 1560 by Duke Cosimo Medici to house the city administration alongside the Piazza della Signoria, were converted a few years later into a museum that today receives more than 1,000,000 visitors per year, more than to any other museum in Italy except those of the Vatican. And no wonder: here is exhibited some of the finest works of genius that Western civilization has produced: Giotto's Madonna (painted in 1310), Botticelli's Birth of Venus and Allegory of Spring (painted in 1486), Leonardo DaVinci's Adoration of the Magi, Cranach's Adam and Eve, Michelangelo's Holy Family, Titian's Flora, Rosso Fiorentino's charming Cherub Playing a Lute, Tintoretto's Leda and the Swan, Caravaggio's Medusa, Rembrandt's Self Portrait As a Young Man, Canaletto's Ducal Palace in Venice, Raphael's Self Portrait, the enchanting Medici Venus, to name but a few. All these can be seen on the third floor! The Uffizi is open weekdays except Mondays from 9 a.m. to 7 p.m., for an entrance charge of 250 lire, and you might conclude your visit with a stop at the cafeteria, not necessarily to eat anything, but simply to enjoy a breathtaking panoramic view of the Piazza della Signoria, the Ponte Vecchio, Il Duomo, and, on that distant green hill, Fiesole.

The Church of Orsanmichele

"Very close to Piazza della Signoria (exit kitty-corner to the Palazzo Vecchio to Via Calzaioli, one of the main shopping streets of Florence) is the little 14th century **Chiesa Di Orsanmichele,** which was originally built to do double duty as a Church and store-house for grain. Inside, the Church has vaulted Gothic arches, lovely stained glass windows, and frescoed walls and ceiling dating from the 14th and 15th centuries. But the star attraction, which you'll spot immediately if you enter from the Via Calzaioli, is the colorful sumptuous Tabernacle by Andrea Orcagna (14th century)—be sure to ask to see it with lights on, revealing that every inch of it is filigreed and sculpted. In the niches all around the exterior of the Church you have a history of Florentine sculpture from the 14th to the 16th century: each statue was sponsored by one of the medieval guilds (on Via Calzaioli, facing the entrance, to your left, is 'St. John' by Ghiberti and to your right 'St. Thomas' by Verrocchio; the medallions above are by Luca della Robbia). Open weekdays from 9 a.m. to 2 p.m., closed Sundays, entrance is free.

Palazzo Bargello

"Located between the Duomo and the Piazza della Signoria, at 4 Via del Proconsolo, is the **National Museum** (or Bargello Palace: the former home of the 'People's Representative,' then a prison, and finally an office for the 'Bargello,' or Chief of Police), in another romantically medieval building with astonishing treasures: Michelangelo's 'Bacco', his 'Madonna Teaching Jesus and St. Giovanni to Read', 'Brutus', and the unfinished 'Martyrdom of St. Andrew'; as well as Ammannati's famous 'Leda and the Swan', Gimbologna's statue of 'Mercury', Donatello's sculpture of 'St. George', works by Cellini and Giovanni Della Robbia. Open weekdays from 9 a.m. to 2 p.m. (150 lire), Sundays from 9 to 1 (when entrance is free to all), closed Mondays.

Casa Buonarroti

"Now, as you exit from the Bargello, walk up the street and turn right on Via Ghibellina; at #70 you'll find the **Casa Buonarroti,** the graceful house that Michelangelo bought and designed for his nephew, and which his heirs turned into a museum. For admirers of the master, it's worth a short visit, since here one finds 4 large early statues and 2 marble reliefs; drawings; plans; and the largest collection of his small-size models. There's a small gallery of works by other artists assembled by later members of the Buonarroti family. Admission is 500 lire; open weekdays from 9 to 2, Sundays from 9 to 1, closed Tuesdays.

The Church of Santa Croce

"From the Casa Buonarroti, it's only a short walk to the Franciscan **Church of Santa Croce,** the Pantheon of Florence (containing actual tombs or monuments to such as Michelangelo, Dante, Macchiavelli, Galileo, Rossini). But to me the most interesting features of the interior of the church are the restored Giottos, some work of Donatello, and the Pazzi Chapel by Brunelleschi (seriously damaged by the flood, but now completely restored). Previously the entire church was covered with frescoes by Giotto and Cimabue, but when the altars were built these were painted over with whitewash! So what you see now is the restored work of Giotto (in the first two chapels to the right of the main altar); or rather, the artist's designs, like an outline, without his original color. In the first chapel on the right are Scenes in the Life of St. Francis (in the little picture of the death of St. Francis, the guards are anxious to point out the figure of one kneeling friar who took this opportunity to pick up St. Francis's robe and check on his stigmata!); the other chapel contains stories of St. John. On the left, in the Bardi Chapel, is the wooden crucifix by Donatello, and his striking bas-relief of the Annunciation is on the right side of the church, just a few steps from Machiavelli's tomb. The entrance to the Cloisters (which now contain the Church's museum, and a leather factory and showroom) and to the Pazzi Chapel is on your right at the back of the church.

And Elsewhere

The Museum of San Marco

"Often referred to as **The Angelico Museum in The Convent of St. Mark,** because it's a virtual monument to the work of Fra Angelico, the museum is located near the Academy Gallery (from the Piazza Duomo, walk up Via Ricasoli to the Piazza San Marco). The monastery provides a remarkably beautiful and evocative setting for Fra Angelico's works. In the Hospice (first room on your right as you enter) is the largest collection of Angelico's movable paintings in Florence: Old and New Testament scenes, ornate, detailed and yet somehow simple and mystical (note the very explicit and gory tortures of Hell in his 'Last Judgment')—it is said that for Fra Angelico painting was the same as praying. The Chapter contains Angelico's large and impressive fresco of 'the Crucifixion', a very fine and interesting work although somewhat formal and idealized; while on the staircase leading to the upper floor, there's the Refectory of the Guest Room with one of Domenico Ghirlandaio's depictions of 'The Last Supper': this has his usual amount of realistic detail, with Judas seated in the foreground in front of Jesus, and a cat on the floor. At the top of the stairs you'll be stopped in your tracks by one of the most famous and beautiful of Angelico's masterpieces, 'The Annunciation'. The monks' cells in the dormitory on the second floor were either painted by Fra Angelico himself or by his assistants under his direction; and to me the work upstairs is even more exciting than what we've seen before—less ornate, simpler and somehow freer. The final must-see attraction of San Marco is the cell of its former Prior, the fanatic enemy of the flesh, Savonarola. Located at the end of the corridor, the cell contains a stark portrait of Savonarola by his convert Fra Bartolomeo, his sleeping chamber, note-book, rosary, and remnants of the clothing worn by him at his execution. For your 150 lire entrance fee (100 lire for each person in a group, students free, Sundays free), you'll have a memorable experience at San Marco: open daily except Monday from 9 to 2; Sunday from 9 to 1.

The Pitti Palace

"Cross the bustling Ponte Vecchio (the bridge nearest the Piazza della Signoria) and walk straight up Via Guicciardini to the **Palazzo Pitti,** which is not a whit the 'itty-bitty-Pitti' you might have been expecting, but looks more like a great stone penal institution. Begun in 1458 (from plans by Brunelleschi) for the rich banker Luca Pitti (later occupants included the Medici family and the House of Savoy), the Palace now contains a complex of museums: the Palatine Gallery (star attraction); the Monumental or Royal Apartments; the Silver Museum; the Gallery of Modern Art (on the second floor); the Carriage Museum; and the Boboli Gardens (open from sunrise to sunset in the summer). Do not miss the Palatine Gallery (entrance through the main door), despite the fact that the place itself is so ornate and the lighting so poor that it's hard to see the paintings. Everybody knows about the outstanding Raphaels collected here (his most famous round panel 'Madonna of the Chair'; the splendid master portraits of 'Angelo and Maddalena Doni'; and 'Tommaso Inghirami', to mention a few), but there is also a large collection of works by Andrea del Sarto; Fra Bartolomeo's beautiful 'Deposition from The Cross' and 'San Marco'; some superb works by Rubens including 'The Four Philosophers' and his famous 'Isabella Clara Eugenia' (who looks something like Bette Davis dressed up for a role in 'The Bells of St. Mary's') and also his usual large cartoons; Tintoretto; Veronese; some absolutely stunning portraits by Titian—'Pope Julius II', 'The Man with the Grey Eyes', and 'The Music Concert'; a curiously sensual and ascetic portrait of 'Cardinal Bentivoglio' by Van Dyck; and work by the fascinating mystic Dosso Dossi. By the way, this is a wonderful place to look at the backgrounds in the pictures—you'll be stunned to notice in many cases it's the same countryside you see outside Florence today (those rolling hills and gorgeous trees were not a product of fanciful imagination, but were painted from reality!). The Royal Apartments are ornate, gilded and chandeliered—and also contain some interesting portraits of the Medici. Open weekdays, except Mondays, from 9 to 2, for a 200-lire entrance fee; Sundays from 9 to 1, free entrance. The Museo degli Argenti is open daily except Mondays,—the Royal Apartments open Tuesday, Thursday and Saturday."

SIGHTS AND SOUNDS: There's little decent night life in Florence, particularly in summer when residents take off for the cool hills of Montecatini. Best thing to do is simply stroll or relax in the **Piazza della Repubblica,** and listen to the open-air bands. . . . An evening of semi-inexpensive dancing can be had, however, at the enormous (it holds as many as 1,000 persons) "audio-visual, multi-media environment dance hall" of **Space Electronic,** at 37 Via Palazzuolo, which charges a total of 4,500 lire for entrance-and-one-drink, from 1,000 to 2,000 lire for the second drink, and will sometimes lower the admission to 3,500 lire for bearers of this book. A creation of four avant garde architects—Signori Birelli, Caldini, Fiume, and Galli—who have exhibited at the Museum of Modern Art in New York, the Space Electronic is what the name implies; a crazy collage of machines and artifacts, ranging from an open parachute over the dance floor to TV cameras that film you as you dance atop a stainless steel floor. Open daily in spring and summer from 9 p.m. to 1 a.m., open Tuesdays through Sundays only in winter. From the Piazza S. Maria Novella, walk down the Via dei Fossi, and the first street to your right is the Via Palazzuolo. . . . Don't miss the daytime view of the whole of Florence, from the **Piazzale Michelangelo.** Bus #13 goes there. . . . A fairly recent addition to the sights of Florence: the home of Elizabeth Barrett and Robert Browning (**"Casa Guidi"**), 8 Piazza S. Felice (Via Maggio, near the Pitti Palace), which is now being restored to its original state after 100 years of disuse and is open to the public (4 p.m. to 7 p.m., Monday through Friday).

The Red Garter

I hesitate to recommend one final Florentine nightspot (open May through October only) because it is so very American in both form and substance that one wonders why anyone should travel several thousands of miles to visit it. You'll know its character from its name: the **Red Garter,** at 33r Via dei Benci (off the bottom of the Piazza Santa Croce), pursues the roaring twenties theme, with banjos and straw hats, schooners of tap beer, and a wooden-barn, sawdust-covered-floor interior that's an exact replica of hundreds of beer-and-booze hangouts on the campuses of our U.S. colleges. To round out the scene (an Italian sociologist was taking notes during my last visit), at least two-hundred-

or-so U.S. collegians turn up here every night in summer (from 8:30 p.m. on, daily except Mondays) to belt out multiple choruses of "This Land is My Land," just as if they were back at old Iowa U. Why did they ever leave home? 2,000 lire to enter, which includes the first drink.

READERS' ENTERTAINMENT SUGGESTIONS: "Opera in Florence at the **Teatro Comunale,** 16 Corso Italia (box-office phone 216-253), is excellent—our second gallery seats were 1,500 lire—and the opera hall is new and beautiful" (Evin C. Varner, Jr., Clinton, South Carolina). . . . "There are open-air concerts, like those in the Vienna Rathaus, in the courtyard of the **Palazzo Pitti,** two nights a week during the summer. The artists are young Italians, some good, some not so good; still, the atmosphere is quite charming, and some performances are surprisingly worthwhile. Seats cost 2,500, 1,200, or 500 lire (the last are unnumbered and rather far back); students with international identity cards get half price on the first two categories only" (Mark Estren, Middletown, Connecticut). . . . "I would like to suggest the **Piscina Bellariva** (public Olympic swimming pool) in Florence for weary tour-worn travellers who have several days to spend in this lovely city. The pool can be reached by bus #14 from the station or Piazza del Duomo (200 lire), and admission charge is 1,500 lire, which includes a dressing stall in the bath house. Snack bar and juke box are provided, plus beautiful surrounding landscaping with umbrella tables, footbridges, and the like" (Alayne Brown, Arlington, Virginia).

SOME FINAL REMINDERS: Bus #7 goes from the central railway station square to the hill town of Fiesole (with its fantastic view) in about 20 minutes, and leaves every 25-or-so minutes. Fare is 200 lire. Bus #13 goes from the train station (at Piazza Stazione) to the Piazzale Michelangelo, overlooking Florence. . . . Mondays and Tuesdays are the days to be wary of museum visits; half the major museums are closed on one or the other day. . . . A round-up of youthful information: the student restaurant is at 25a Via S. Gallo, the youth hostel at 4 Viale Augusto Righi, the camping area at 80 Viale Michelangelo.

THE LAUNDROMATS OF FLORENCE: I've found four of them—the **Lavaget** at 110r Borgo Ognissanti (2,300 lire for the machine, including detergent, 800 lire every 30 minutes for the dryer; open 8 to 8, Monday to Saturday); an unnamed "washerette" at 1 Via XXVII Aprile, corner of S. Reparata, a block from the Piazza San Marco (same prices; attendants will operate the machine while you dash out to see Michelangelo's "David," in the Accademia, nearby); a **"Lava-matic"** in the area of the Piazza della Signoria at 46r Via dei Neri; and another **Lavaget** at 3 Via Guelfa, near the corner of Via Cavour, where the hard-working owner, Signora Maria Innocenti, promises a 1,000 lire discount off the official rate of 3,500 lire for 5 kilos washed and dried, to anyone who displays this book.

SHOPPING IN FLORENCE: Discussed at length in our shopping chapter, near the back of the book. But while we won't trespass on that shopping information here, we will point out that most interesting market in Florence for sightseeing purposes is the huge **Mercato Centrale,** open from 7 a.m. to 1 p.m., at the Piazza del Mercato Centrale, near the station. The outdoor stands on the Via dell' Ariento (which starts at the Via Nazionale), and the vast indoor market itself, should both be seen.

ADVANCE READING: Irving Stone's best-selling biography of Michelangelo, *The Agony and the Ecstasy* (available in an inexpensive Signet paperback edition), can make all the difference in your stay. For Michelangelo was a Florentine, and many of the major episodes of his life—which the book de-

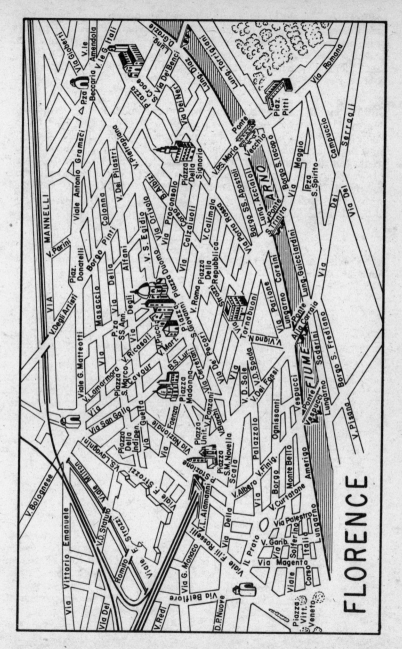

scribes in great detail—took place in the very buildings and square which you will view today.

Nearly half the statues made by Michelangelo now stand in Florence: at the Accademia, in the Medici Chapels, in the Casa Buonarroti (Michelangelo's family name being Buonarroti), in the Duomo, and in the Bargello. A painting of his hangs in the Uffizi Galleries. When you have read the fascinating background of these masterpieces, which is related to the turbulent times of Renaissance Florence, you'll receive an unparalleled thrill from seeing them before your very eyes.

CODA: All the ancient bridges of Florence, other than the Ponte Vecchio, were destroyed by the Germans in their senseless defense of the city in 1944. On the Ponte Vecchio there is now affixed a tiny plaque whose proud inscription gave me a particular thrill, which I would like to share with you. The inscription reads: "On the 11th August 1944, Freedom, the Sole Dispenser of Social Justice, Not Granted but Reconquered, At the Cost of Destruction, Torture and Blood, Thanks to the Rising of the People and to the Victory of the Allied Armies, Has Taken Her Place in this Palace of our Fathers, Amid the Ruins of our Bridges, Forever."

Coming up: another high-point of your tour. It's off to Rome, just four hours away by train.

Chapter XIV

ROME

The Arithmetic of a Roman Holiday

ROME NEEDS NO BUILD-UP in this book. A vast number of Americans saw "La Dolce Vita" and have ached to get here ever since. They won't be disappointed. The excitement of Rome has an almost physical impact as you step from the train. You immediately know that this is a Capital—a pulsating center of creation and activity, whose ideas and tastes are felt round the world.

But keep in mind two very basic facts about Rome. First, this is not a city which can be covered in two or three days of touring. Rome is too large, too varied, too abundant with sights. If you're to realize anything from your stay, you must schedule several more days to it than you devoted to other comparable European towns. Second, this is not an easy city in which to keep costs down—although it doesn't approach Paris in that respect. Nevertheless, you can be clipped unmercifully if you wander by mistake into the wrong hotel or restaurant. If you're to live on $15 a day in Rome, you must set out now to orient yourself in the city. We'll start with the spot where it all begins:

TERMINAL STATION: Your train will arrive in Rome at Terminal Station—a big ultra-modernistic building that's a city in itself. If you've been rumpled by the ride, then all you need do is walk downstairs to the Albergo Diurno ("day hotel"), where you'll find baths and showers (costing $1.80), a barber shop, women's hairdresser, cleaners, many other conveniences. In addition to these facilities, the station has restaurants, money-changers (usual rate is 830 lire to $1), cable offices, even a small department store. . . . The plaza in front of Terminal Station is also a starting point for many of the city's bus and trolley lines: to get to the Vatican area (where we'll recommend several hotels), take bus No. 64, which is also marked "San Pietro." Trip to St. Peter's costs 100 lire, another 100 lire for your larger pieces of luggage. For transportation to American Express, which is just next to the Spanish Steps (a central point), take bus No. 77 or 78 (and get off at Largo Goldoni), again for 100 lire. And for the Colosseum, take bus No. 27 or 792, changing later to bus No. 118 for the Baths of Caracalla. At night, the bus marked "Roma-Tivoli", leaving from a little depot near the station (we'll describe its location further on), goes to the illuminated Fountains of Tivoli and the Ville d'Este—and that means that nearly all the major sights of Rome are serviced by the buses leaving from "Stazione Termini."

HOTELS: For your rooms in Rome, we'll deal first with hotels, then with the far less expensive, usually far more attractive, "pensiones."

Three areas in Rome possess most of the good budget hotels: the streets on both sides of Terminal Station; the section to the south of the Vatican; and the area in front of, and behind, the Spanish Steps (the American Express area). Each of these sections, in turn, possesses several particular Second Class hotels that star: the **Bramante** in the Vatican area: the **Croce di Malta** near American Express; the **Y.M.C.A.** and the **Touring**, next to the station. Most of the latter, of course, are in the Big Splurge category only; from $22 to $24 for a bathless double room without breakfast, by the time all taxes and supplements are totaled up; from $15 and up for a single. But each of them is either surrounded by, or near to, other less expensive Second Class establishments ($18 to $20 for a double, all included), and even less costly, but still satisfactory, Third Class houses ($8.50 per person). Each is also the focal point for a cluster of attractive and less expensive pensions ("pensiones") which we'll describe in a later and separate section of this chapter, and which provide the true budget lodgings in Rome.

The Vatican Area

We'll assume, first, that you crave peace and quiet, even at the cost of being across the river from the downtown theatres and cafes. This area is, of course, the most subdued section of Rome, lovely and restful. Take bus No. 64 from the train station or air terminal, which comes directly here.

You'll alight at the broad boulevard, the Via della Conciliazione, which leads to St. Peter's. Fifty yards away, the **Hotel Bramante** at 24 Vicolo delle Palline (phone 654-04-26), provides the best of moderately-priced lodgings in the Vatican area. The building itself is an historic one, begun in the 14th century; from the backyard garden, where breakfast is served in summer, you can see a medieval escape wall used by popes and other dignitaries to walk unseen from Vatican City to the safety of the fortress-like Castel Sant'Angelo. Today, a proud Roman named Publio Mariani, who was born in this very building, both owns and operates the Bramante and charges a moderate 10,900 lire ($13.13) for bathless singles, 18,250 lire ($21.98) for bathless doubles, with breakfast optional for 2,200 lire ($2.65) more, and showers for free. Two blocks away, at 134 Borgo Pio, the far more modern **Hotel Santa Anna** (phone 654-18-82) takes the overflow for 19,200 lire ($23.13) single, 29,000 lire

($34.93) double, 39,500 lire ($47.59) triple, 46,500 lire ($56.02) quad, this time including breakfast for all, and private showers (but not w.c.'s) in each room.

Five long blocks from the Santa Anna, the **Hotel San Pietro**, at Via Cardinale Cassetta 9 (phone 630-876), is a modern, new budget hotel (15,000 lire $18.07 for a bathless double, service and tax included, around $23 double with private shower), but only for people with cars—they're long blocks. A crisply functional building, very clean, whose owner—Sr. Ernesto Felicetti—is English-speaking and cordial to Americans. Especially good for families. And finally, still in the Vatican area, but a bit more remote from St. Peter's (you'll think yourself in the country, with the singing of birds the only sound you'll hear), is the 350-bed **Casa Tra Noi** (that means "house for us") at 113 Via Monte del Gallo (phone 630-213); from the Piazza Cavour next to Castel S. Angelo, take bus no. 34 to its last stop, and walk 150 yards up the foot path. Primarily a group hotel for religious pilgrims and such, but with frequent vacancies for individuals, the Casa provides balconied rooms with private bath, modern furniture and ceramic floors, elevators and restaurant facilities, adjoining park and beautiful flower beds, yet at remarkably moderate rates that provide good value: 10,000 lire ($12.04) single, 18,000 lire ($21.68) double or twin, 22,000 lire ($26.50) triple.

The American Express Area

Here's where you'll find the Spanish Steps, at the Piazza di Spagna, a block away from the spot where Americans gather once a day for mail. Directly to the side of the steps, at 9 Piazza di Spagna, the **Hotel-Pensione Lago di Alleghe** (phone 679-5174) is a tastefully furnished small hotel managed by Signor Giorgio Valdroni, who has pledged to offer special 1980 rates to readers of this book: 13,500 lire ($16.26) single, 19,000 lire ($22.89) double or twin, an extra 7,000 lire ($8.43) for each supplementary bed in a double room. That latter feature makes this hotel ideal for families or small groups: room no. one has four beds in it, room no. two has six beds, and both rooms face directly onto the magical Piazza–no other hotel in Rome, high-priced or low, can offer you that!

THE ITALIAN LIRA: For the purposes of this chapter, we've converted Italian lire into dollars at the rate of 830 lire per dollar —the approximate "floating" rate of the lira as of the time of writing. Thus, 100 lire have been assumed to equal 12¢ U.S. Though you can expect further fluctuations by the time of your own stay in Italy, the variance should not be substantial.

Directly in front of the steps is the swank Via Condotti, lined with the most elegant shops of Rome. If you'll walk down the Via Condotti and then turn left, you'll be on the Via Mario de Fiori, which is a bustling, narrow and picturesque street only one block from the famous square where you began. Here you'll pass the **Albergo Condotti**, 37 Via Mario de Fiori (phone 679-4769), high Third Class; all-year rates of 19,500 lire ($23.49) for a double room with shower, 12,000 lire for a bathless single, all taxes and service included; a quiet, refined hotel, with elevator, recommended particularly to our older readers; then the **Albergo Piazza di Spagna**, 61 Via Mario de Fiori, phone

679-3061 (a third class hotel that has been considerably improved in recent years, and charges 11,000 lire ($13.25) single, 16,500 lire ($19.87) double, tax and service included); and next the Third Class **Albergo San Carlo,** around the corner at 93 Via delle Carrozze (phone 678-4548). Here, you're only two blocks from American Express, in budget rooms priced at 17,500 lire (including shower, service and tax) for a double, 12,000 lire (including tax and service) for a single, 7,500 lire for a 3rd bed in a double room; but the hotel is an exceedingly plain establishment that is suitable only for the most casual of tourists; nevertheless the rooms upstairs (there's an elevator) are surprisingly better than the dreary entrance would lead you to expect. A last and much better budget hotel nearby is the more modern, third class **Albergo Homs,** 20 feet off the Via Mario de Fiori, on the small Via della Vite (#71; phone 679-2976). 18,000 lire ($21.68), service and tax included, for a double room, 11,500 lire ($13.85) for a bathless single. And how well they maintain these rooms is revealed by the fact that the Homs is a particular favorite among Scandinavian and Swiss tourists! . . . Rated in order of quality, this group of hotels would begin with the Lago di Alleghe, then continue with the Homs, followed by the Condotti, then the San Carlo.

For single persons who'd like a slightly better, $14 single room, the **Hotel Croce di Malta,** Via Borgognona 28 (phone 679-5482), has several of them. That's on the street running parallel to the Via Condotti, nearly within sight of American Express. . . . Two other fairly simple hotels in this area: the **Albergo Frattina,** Via Frattina 107 (phone 679-2071), 13,500 lire single, 18,500 lire double, showers for free; and the nearby **Pensione Sorriso,** second floor of 7 Via Bocca del Leone (corner of Via Frattina), phone 679-86-61, managed by English-speaking Signor Carniero. Nine thousand five hundred lire ($11.44) single, 17,800 lire ($21.44) double, 1,800 lire for breakfast, showers free. . . . The strange thing is that few Americans know of the existence of this hotel area, just two and three blocks below American Express.

Atop the Spanish Steps

Still a second area in the American Express section begins at the very top of the Spanish Steps. Ascend the steps and you'll immediately spot the swank Hotel Villa Hassler, which stands at the beginning of the Via Sistina, a rather elegant shopping street. But walk down the Via Sistina for a few yards, past the first class Hotel de la Ville, and you'll arrive at the glamorously-decorated **Pensione Trinità dei Monti,** Via Sistina 91 (phone 679-7206), which charges 15,000 lire ($18.07) for a single with private shower, 16,500 lire ($19.87) for a bathless double, breakfast and all service charges included—and is quite heavily booked in season; doubles with private shower are 11,800 lire per person ($14.21), once more with breakfast and service included. Next door, the **Pensione Scalinata di Spagna,** 17 Piazza Trinità dei Monti (phone 679-3006), has now added a private shower to every double room, but still charges only 14,000 lire ($16.86) per person for bed and breakfast, service and taxes included; again heavily-booked and reservations are advisable.

Various streets that jut off from the Via Sistina, fifty yards or so from the Spanish Steps, possess other Third Class choices. For example, you can walk from the Via Sistina into the Via Gregoriana which, despite its exterior appearance, is one of the most fashionable streets in Rome. Lodgings at the **Pensione Suisse,** 56 Via Gregoriana (phone 678-3649), cost 10,375 lire ($12.50) per person for bed-and-breakfast, 12,000 lire ($14.45) per person for a twin with private bath, and there's a sunny, beflowered roof garden here for relaxation. Mrs. Jole Ciucci is the English-speaking owner, and the recipient of numerous written commendations from satisfied guests, who usually remark about the particularly friendly and personal atmosphere. At the end of Via Gregoriana (one long block down), you'll then come to the Via Capo le Case, and there, the **Albergo Concordia,** 14 Via Capo le Case (phone 679-5693), is another outstanding 3rd Class choice; 17,000 lire ($20.48) for a bathless double without breakfast, but with service and taxes included, is the normal price, but they'll give an off-season (Nov. 1 to March 30) discount of 10% to readers who mention this book, as well as unlimited free baths or showers, and free use of the washing machine (you pay only 500 lire for soap). There's a roof-top terrace here with a sweeping view of the city; children and pets are welcomed; location is about a block from American Express; and the hotel is highly recommended.

Between Piazza di Spagna and Piazza del Popolo

There's a final gem of a choice available to you nearby, if the ones we've listed in this area seem packed. From the Piazza di Spagna, walk down the Via Babuino halfway to the Piazza del Popolo, then turn left down the tiny Via Laurina. At #34 Via Laurina, smack in the midst of art galleries and studios: the modern-art-filled **Hotel Margutta** (phone 679-8440), with rooms that all come equipped with private bath or shower, and yet at moderate prices that range between the Second and Third Class categories (12,500 lire per person, double occupancy, breakfast, service, bath, and taxes included).

Terminal Station Area

Here, of course, is the most numerous concentration of hotels in Rome. We'll deal, first, with a particularly outstanding choice in the area to the right of the station, and then with an entire cluster of budget finds grouped in the area to the left. The area to the right (as you leave) is, to my mind, far more pleasant and also endowed with better budget values than you'll find on the left side of the station.

To the right of the station (as you leave)

As you leave the main entrance of Terminal Station, turn right onto the street that borders the big plaza in front of the Station, walk straight ahead on that street, along the Plaza, until you come to the first turning, then turn right again for a block, and you'll be on the little Piazza Indipendenza. There, at #23C Piazza Indipendenza (phone 464-921), stands a seven-story building constructed in 1956, which houses the **Y.M.C.A. Hotel**—but it's not a "Y," it's a hotel, open to men, women and families alike, and offering moderately-priced values. For, in addition to its 110 rooms, the hotel operates a large restaurant downstairs (6,000 lire for minestrone, roast veal and spinach, cheese, fruit or ice cream; 2,800 lire for a breakfast of fruit juice, an egg, rolls or toast with butter and coffee), an even cheaper snack bar, a gym, a Sauna department, a TV lounge, a huge lobby with interesting bulletin boards, a billiards room, ping pong room, and a play area for little children!

Rooms without private bath or shower rent at the "Y" for 12,000 lire ($14.45) single, 19,500 lire ($23.49) double, including breakfast, service and tax. For women and families, the hotel rents double rooms with semi-private showers for 24,000 lire ($28.91), again with breakfast and all else included. And for families, the hotel disposes of several "apartments," which consist of two double rooms, an anteroom, a private bath and a toilet, and which rent—total —for 48,000 lire ($57.83) a night. To get any of these accommodations, particularly in summer, write well ahead for reservations, or phone the number given above upon your arrival in Rome; the "Y" hotel is always heavily booked.

If the Y is full, look across the square to the crumbling, unattractive facade of the **Hotel Salus,** 13 Piazza Indipendenza (phone 495-0044); swallow hard as you recall that key rule of budget travel ("disregard the facade of hotels"); walk inside; and voilà! (or ecco!), there's a relatively modern interior with a good lounge (sporting an Italian tv set), and large, clean (if undecorated) rooms renting for 14,000 lire ($16.86) double, 11,500 lire ($13.85) single, not including breakfast, which is 2,200 lire more.

To the left of the station (as you leave)

There are other budget hotels on the other side of the station, although these tend to be more expensive and less desirable than the hotels and pensions we've listed for the above area (see our pension descriptions further on). As you leave the main entrance, this time turn left, and you'll immediately see a number of expensive First Class establishments: the **Hotel Mediterraneo,** the **Massimo D'Azeglio.** But avoid those. Keep walking to the streets behind these edifices, and you'll find whole clusters of Second and Third Class choices.

In this area, the best of the Second Class hotels are the big **Albergo Nord Nuova Roma (4),** Via Giovanni Amendola 3 (phone 465-441), which has 180 rooms, and the magnificently-furnished **Hotel Diana,** Via Principe Amedeo 4 (phone 475-1541), both listed here only for the purpose of warning you that virtually every room in these supposedly-Second Class structures has now been equipped with private bath, and thus soars way outside our price range. (When you glimpse the spectacular interior of the Diana particularly, you'll share my own regret over this bit of progress). Only several doors away from the Diana, however, at 34 Via Principe Amedeo, is a more moderately-priced and yet thoroughly reliable Second Class establishment called the **Albergo Touring** (phone 465-351), whose fairly small and plain lobby is no indication at all of the quite serviceable rooms it offers upstairs. An amiable management, and prices of 21,500 lire ($25.92), taxes and service included, for a twin-bedded room without bath; but better still, the Touring operates a much plainer annex called the **Annex** at Via Principe Amedeo 2 (phone 471-911), which charges only 8,800 lire for a single, 14,000 lire ($16.86) for a bathless double, including service and tax. Both the main building and the annex are recommended by me.

On the Via M. D'Azeglio which runs through the heart of this area, the recommended Second Class hotel is the **San Remo,** Via M. D'Azeglio 36, phone 461-741 (average rates here: 15,500 lire single, 27,500 lire ($33.13) double, including breakfast, tax and service; a nice place). . . . On the Via Cavour, #47, the **Hotel Cavour** (phone 486-620) is a 45-room, recently completely modernized hotel, which charges considerably less (22,000 lire) for a bathless double, all included.

In the less expensive Third Class category, however, a better bet in this area (just a block away from the station), is the **Albergo Capitol,** Via G. Amendola 77, phone 462-617 (one flight up), charging 15,500 lire ($18.67), for a double, 9,500 lire for a single, 7,000 lire for an extra child's bed in a double room, all taxes and service included. While the Capitol is not as highly recommended as our pensions described further below (rooms there are strictly utilitarian), it does provide a good opportunity for finding a vacancy on days when the town is packed. . . . In the same building that houses the Capitol (across the inner courtyard), the **Albergo Termini** (phone 464-302) isn't nearly as good, but charges only 8,500 lire single, 13,000 lire ($15.66) double, 2,000

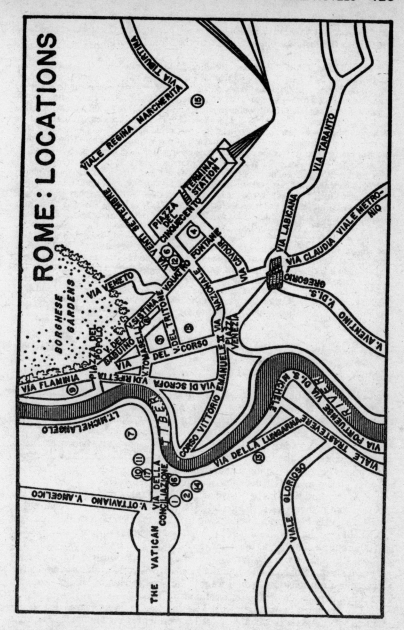

ROME: LOCATIONS

lire for breakfast.

And Elsewhere

Want a room near the Colosseum? Try the Fourth Class **Hotel Perugia,**

Via del Colosseo 7 (phone 679-7200), where the most expensive bathless double room runs about 6,000 lire ($7.22) per person per night, but not with breakfast, and where the distance is quite short to the Roman Forum.

READERS' HOTEL SELECTIONS: "**Pensione Adriatic,** 25 Via G. Vitelleschi (phone 656-9668), can be reached by taking bus No. 64 from the main train station. (When you get off at the end of the line on Borgo Sant'Angelo (right near St. Peter's), you go under a portal, continue on Via Porta Castello until you reach the main intersection with Via G. Vitelleschi and turn left.) Here, double rooms are only 12,000 lire (4,000 more with bath), single rooms without bath 8,000 lire, with service and tax included. And Lanfranco Mencucci, the proprietor, and his wife, take great pride in their hotel and see to it that the rooms and bathrooms are kept clean and attractive. We make frequent trips to Rome, and will continue to stay at the Adriatic because the Mencucci family always makes us feel at home" (Judy Scarpella-Walls, Bowling Green, Kentucky). . . . "One wonderful hotel no one in your book mentioned was the **Memphis,** at 36a Via Avignonesi (phone 485-849), on a narrow street near the Piazza Barberini (we were told about it by a Danish family over lunch one day). We went and looked it over. A double room *with* private shower, breakfast, service and taxes included, is 25,000 lire ($30.12). Clean as a pin, with a small lobby and elevator. She said it would be cheaper out of season and by the week" (Mrs. Howell Evans, Nashville, Tenn., plus recommendations from other readers as well, who point out that all rooms here have private shower and toilet, and rent for 15,000 lire single, 25,000 lire double, breakfast, service and tax included). . . . "I want to recommend highly the **Pensione Cristallo,** Via Montebello 114 (phone 475-9810), where bed alone in a very clean double room was 5,500 lire per person. The Cristallo is in the Station Area. Signora Maria Boccone, the proprietress, treated us like her own children; she helped us plan our sightseeing in Rome, and a trip to Greece. When we decided to hitchhike to Brindisi, she not only planned the best route for us, but held all our extra clothing and luggage free of charge" (Judith De Leo, Brooklyn, New York).

Now we move to a category of generally less expensive accommodations:

PENSIONS: The Roman "pensione" is always on the upper floor of an apartment house or office building, is apt to have surprisingly large and comfortable rooms. For the "king" of pensiones, turn to "The Big Splurge," and read about the **Texas.** For the best of the lower-priced establishments, walk one long avenue block from Terminal Station to the Piazza Esedra (also known as Piazza della Repubblica), the site of a lovely fountain—the Fountains of Esedra— which are beautifully illuminated at night. The business building at 47 Piazza Esedra houses four particularly good pensions.

On the third floor is the **Pensione Esedra (6)** (phone 463-912), best of the four, whose manageress is the genial Mrs. Moretti. She does not require that you take meals. Her prices for 1980 will be 7,500 lire ($9.03) for her only single room, all taxes and service included, 7,500 lire ($9.03) per person for a double, 1,500 lire for a continental breakfast, 800 lire for a bath (much too high, Mrs. Moretti!), 700 lire for a shower. Despite the location of this pension on a busy plaza, it is remarkably quiet—and the rooms are as comfortable as you'd wish. In certain front locations, you'll want to lie abed for hours, simply watching the lights play on the dramatic Fountains of Esedra.

On the same floor as the Pensione Esedra, again at Piazza Esedra 47 (phone 460-334), a young couple named Imperoli have bought the old Pensione Alle Terme Romane, changed its name to the explosive sounding **Pensione Eureka,** refurbished the pension throughout, and come up with an establishment that is not the equal of the Esedra, but a value nevertheless. Its prices are somewhat lower than those of the Esedra (7,000 lire single, 12,000 lire double, 16,000 lire triple, 1,500 extra for breakfast) and its star attraction is the impish

Mrs. Imperoli, who is a dead ringer for Romy Schneider (she also speaks perfect, unaccented English). Unfortunately, the pensione has recently converted several double rooms into four-bedded, share accommodations (at 5,000 lire a head) and couples desiring privacy won't always find it.

Again in the same building as the Pensione Esedra (same address, second floor), the **Pensione Terminus** (phone 461-505), is somewhat more commercial in aspect, and substantially higher in price, but offers especially large rooms and comfortable public facilities. Just before presstime, the management wrote that "in view of [our] preference for American tourists," they would abide by the following reduced prices for anyone flashing them a copy of this book on registering **and** staying for 5 nights or more: double rooms for 8,000 lire per person, including breakfast, service and taxes; triples for 7,500 lire per person; four or five-bedded rooms (there are six of this size) for only 6,000 lire ($7.22) per person, breakfast always included. There's an ornate large dining room in which you'll take the morning meal, and the food is prepared with care. . . . If all three of these pensiones at 47 Piazza Esedra are fully booked, then go upstairs (top floor) to the **Pensione Wetzler** (phone 475-1994), where you'll find proprietress "Mama Clara" and rates of 6,000 lire ($7.22) per person for dorm-type rooms of two to four cots apiece.

At the side of the railroad station

Now, as you leave Terminal Station, turn right and walk three short blocks along the Via Marghera to the Via Varese and the exciting **Hotel Venezia**, 18 Via Varese (phone 495-0036), one of the foremost stars of this book, where Mrs. Diletti (she's Swiss) has five floors and 65 rooms of an elevator building, and offers special rates to $15-a-day'ers only: 9,300 lire ($11.20) per person in a double room (breakfast, service and taxes included), 7,300 lire per person in a triple, 8,200 lire ($9.87) per person—breakfast and service again included—in a four-bedded room. She is a cordial lady; her hotel is kept impeccably clean; and it occupies a nice, quiet area, despite the nearness of the station.

If the Venezia can't take you (and I hope it can; this is a low-budget wonder, with brightly-furnished rooms, outlets for American razors, a fresh and friendly atmosphere), then walk one short block along this excellent hotel street (the Via Varese) to a string of generally higher-priced but relatively moderate hotel-pensions at #s 6, 8 and 10 Via Varese. The **Albergo Montagna**, at 10 Via Varese (phone 495-3329), leads the trio, with its peaceful inner courtyard dotted with chairs and umbrella-topped tables, its carpeting on marble steps, and rates of 24,000 lire ($28.91) for a bathless double, two breakfasts included, which are then discounted by 10% to bearers of this book. The **Hotel Select** (phone 49-11-37), next door at #6 Via Varese (bathless doubles for $22.89 (19,000 lire) with breakfast, service and taxes included), and the **Hotel Astoria Garden** (phone 49-53-653) at #8, charging 13,000 lire single without bath, 24,000 lire double with bath, breakfast and service included, are of the same high quality, peaceful variety (all with inner gardens, polite old porters dozing next to softly-tuned-in-television sets), and all three establishments—the Montagna, Select, and Astoria—are particularly recommended by me to older budget tourists, although readers of any age should first seek space at the Pensione Venezia. Finally, you might like to try the **Pensione Varese** at #26 Via Varese (phone 495-2694), whose 40 rooms are currently owned and managed by the Fanelli brothers, and rent for 18,700 lire double ($15.66), without bath, but with breakfast, service, free showers and tax included—a rate that's specially for readers of this book; or the similarly priced **Pensione Ascot** at 22 Via Montebello (phone 481-675), charging 12,000 lire for a double, including free showers, service and tax, but not breakfast.

Now is as good a time as any to repeat that this area to the right of Terminal Station (as you leave the station) is infinitely to be preferred to the area to the left of the station; it's quieter, less hot and dusty, and more budget-oriented, with several of the cheapest "trattorias" (family-owned restaurants) in town.

Off the Piazza Esedra

Just next to the building that houses the pensiones Esedra, Eureka, and Terminus, you'll find the beginning of the important Via Nazionale, which sweeps downhill for several hundred yards. All along its length, but particularly near the Piazza Esedra, are inexpensive pensions which usually come three or four to a building. In our price range, I particularly like the pensiones at 13 Via Nazionale (the Casa Christina, on the 5th floor, the Scaligera on the 4th, the Enotria on the 3rd, the Millefiore on the 2nd); they're led by the **Casa Christina** (phone 460-014), whose rather flamboyant owner fills her pensione with vast amounts of furniture (and the rooms are fairly small), hangs paintings and numerous decorations on the walls and ceilings, and charges 16,000 lire ($19.27) for a double room, including breakfast and service, 10,500 lire for a single and breakfast. The **Maxim** (phone 486-837) is somewhat more sedate and Italian, has a particularly beautiful dining room, but does not require that you take meals, and posts a higher 9,500 lire ($11.44) per person for bed and breakfast, service and tax included. The **Millefiori,** on the second floor (phone 475-0108), charges 16,000 lire ($19.27) for a bathless double, with breakfast for two included; the building itself is almost next door to "St. Paul's Within the Walls"—Rome's American Episcopal Church.

If these are full, then try the higher-priced **Pensione Giolli,** which occupies the upper four floors (there is an elevator) of 69 Via Nazionale (phone 462-393); its English-speaking owner, Signor Pino Lasalandra, has recently installed new furniture in most of the rooms, and now charges 17,000 lire single, 22,000 lire ($26.50) twin or double, not including breakfast, which is optional at 1,400 lire extra. Showers are free and discounts of 1,000 lire are given to readers in off-season periods. From Termini Station, take double-decker bus #64 for 100 lire and get off at the fifth stop called "Palazzo Esposizioni" directly in front of the Giolli.

Finally, three blocks to the side of Piazza Esedra (take bus #64 from Terminal Station and get off at the third stop), the **Pensione Hannover,** 4 Via XX Settembre (phone 461-162), offers on-season prices to readers of this book only, of exactly 11,000 lire ($13.25) per person for room and breakfast, service and taxes included, and has unusually quiet rooms, some of which overlook the stately Prince Barberini Gardens, and all of which have a far-away view of St. Peter's. Proprietors here speak excellent English, and their sense of the proprieties is such that they kick back to you the commission that hotel owners normally receive for booking tours! You ought to know, too, that the clientele often includes Protestant church groups from the U.S.—which should give you an idea of its character. Well-recommended for older readers.

In the American Express—Spanish Steps Area

Here, the unhesitating choice is the warm and friendly **Pensione Erdarelli,** 28 Via Due Macelli (phone 679-1265), whose five floors have just been freshly redecorated, yet without a significant increase in rates, which are special to readers of this book: 11,500 lire ($13.85) per person, breakfast, service and taxes included, in a double room; 12,500 lire in a single, and no insistence at all on taking meals other than breakfast. The pension is only two short blocks from the Spanish Steps; all rooms are brightly and colorfully furnished, some have balconies, all have telephones, the building is elevator-equipped, and the Italian family who operate the pension (and place fresh flowers everywhere) are a sheer delight. Run, do not walk.

Across the Tiber

On the Vatican side of the Tiber, far from the hustle of downtown, the Third Class **Pensione Fabrello-White** (phone 360-44-46) is a thoroughly refined but struggling-along pension, which stands in a quiet location (7), on the third floor (via elevator) of an old Ducal palace at 11 Via Vittoria Colonna. Its charges—quite moderate for such a cultivated atmosphere, and always including breakfast—are 12,500 lire ($15.06) single, 9,500 lire ($11.44) per person double, 8,500 lire ($10.24) per person triple, only 7,500 lire ($9.03) per person quad. After several years of writing: "Warning—the doors close here at 10 p.m., and you nearly have to sing arias from the street to get in," I am now told that extra keys have been bought, and each guest gets one key. Signor Renato Marchi is the amiable, English-speaking owner; his terrace-breakfast room affords a panoramic view of Rome's skyline, including the Trinitá dei Monti church atop the Spanish Steps.

Via Veneto and elsewhere

A pension on the swank Via Veneto? I've scoured this lush, expensive area of Rome and, much to my own surprise, found two moderately-priced pensions on my last visit. One is at 24 Via Sicilia, a sidestreet just off the activity of the Via Veneto, where the **Pensione Sicilia** (phone 493-841) offers rooms all equipped with private bath or shower, heavily decorated with bric-a-brac and Italian antiques, with plants and pictures everywhere, a gracious English-speaking manageress in charge. The rooms themselves are rather small, but rent for 16,500 lire ($19.87) single, 25,000 lire ($30.12) double, including breakfast, service and tax, which are astonishing prices by the standards of the Via Veneto, just steps away. There's a not terribly attractive entrance to the building, but a good, modern elevator, and older readers should be well pleased with both the location and the amenities. For cheaper digs in the same area, try the 15-bed apartment of the gentle Signora Amelia Pacelli, the **Affitacamere Pacelli**, 20 Via Quintino Sella (phone 462-198), where the charge is only 7,500 lire ($9.03) per person in a double, 9,000 lire single, and the showers are free. Breakfast, served on request, is 1,500 lire, and the current manager is Signor Basilotta, who lived for many years in Australia and speaks excellent (Oxford) English. To find the Pacelli, walk through the main door into the small garden; then take the first door to your right and the elevator to the third floor. Even in these modest accommodations, you'll be near the glamorous people and appurtenances of Rome's most famous avenue, and at night you can join the sidewalk sitters and watch the passing parade of monocles, gigolos—all the exotic, high camp life of Rome's upper-income, international set.

The most numerous collection of pensions? They're on the Via Principe Amedeo, between the Via Gioberti and the Via Cavour—at least thirty of them (eight alone are in the building at 9 Principe Amedeo), the best being the four establishments in 76 Via Principe Amedeo, followed by those at #62, #67 and #79. Try, for instance, Signora Regina Charles' **Pensione Tony**, 79D Via

Principe Amedeo (phone 736-994), charging 9,500 lire single, 12,000 lire double, 800 lire for a shower including towel **and** a bar of soap. Or try the **Pensione Giorgina** next door at 67 Via Principe Amedeo (phone 476-118), 4th floor, where large doubles are 10,500 lire, triples 14,500 lire, 4-bedded rooms 16,500 lire. That's only a block from the railroad station (to the left, as you exit from the main entrance) and you'll have to shop around to find a pension that suits you.

PENSIONES SEEKING MENTION: "The coming season will be my sixteenth as owner-director of **Forti's Guest House**, Via Cosseria 2 (phone 382-431). Already recommended by the American, Belgian, German, Norwegian, Greek and Portuguese automobile clubs, our pensione is regularly used by the South African, Japanese and Pakistan embassies to host newly assigned personnel and their families until they find permanent housing. The American, Australian and Nigerian embassies have also sent official representatives and nationals desiring comfortable, quiet, economical accommodations in clean family atmosphere. Basic prices are: 8,000 lire for a single with continental breakfast, 13,500 for a double with breakfast, 13,500 lire per person for half pensione; 16,500 for full pensione. All prices include service and tax. We also have several triple rooms from 19,000 including breakfast, for 3 persons. Individuals in triples desiring meals get spaghetti or soup, meat, vegetable, and fruit or cheese, for 6,000 lire. We also serve bacon and eggs, hamburgers, hot dogs and other American snacks not generally found on the pensione circuit. There is no charge for showers or baths. Our location is excellent. Via Cosseria is a private street with ample free parking only one block from the Tiber (on the Vatican side) between Viale Giulio Cesare and Viale delle Milizie in Prati. We also have a garage in our building. We are only 20 yards from bus lines leading to Termini (99 and 78), Via del Corso and Caracalla (90) and about 50 yards from the #30 line for St. Peter's and the Vatican Museums. We are in a quiet residential area removed from the noise and the confusion of downtown Rome, yet only minutes from all historic and scenic points of interest" (Charles Cabell, Rome, Italy). . . . "My **Pensione Brotzky** is located at Piazza del Popolo in Via del Corso 509 (phone 678-9062), a very clean and quiet establishment with a lovely sitting area on the roof that overlooks Rome. Rooms are large, with character, and the price is 8,000 lire per person, including service, tax, and free showers" (M. Brotzky, Pensione Brotzky).

A READER'S PENSIONE SELECTION (NEAR PIAZZA BARBERINI): "To make your stay in Rome a pleasant one, make the **Pensione Tofanelli** your home. It is located at 125 Via Sistina (phone 47-45-504), near Piazza Barberini, and three or four doors up from the Theatre Sistina. For a double room and breakfast only, you'll pay a total of 14,000 lire ($16.86), service and tax included. The Tofanellis are very friendly and speak enough English to suffice, and the pensione offers showers or baths with oceans of hot water, television, telephone, hints to tourists regarding the city, and best of all a very friendly, quiet atmosphere" (Don R. Prinzler, Los Angeles, California, plus enthusiastic reports from other readers as well: note from AF: this 30-bed pensione is on the third floor of an elevator building; triples are 17,000 lire, large quadruples 19,500 lire).

READERS' PENSIONE SELECTIONS (NEAR TERMINI STATION): "**Pensione Trusso Egle,** on the third floor of 33 Via Quintino Sella (phone 465-227), offers everything you could want in a low-cost lodging (free showers, free elevator, advice and assistance from Madame Trusso), and rates of only 5,000 lire per person per night in double or triple rooms, plus 1,500 lire for breakfast. Five minutes from the Central Station" (Kaulesh B. Shah, Bombay, India; warmly seconded by Sandra Leana, Freeport, Grand Bahama). . . . "**Locanda Aurora**, 39 Via Magenta (phone 495-7613), two blocks from the railroad station, was the cleanest and most comfortable of our travels, and its proprietors—Mr. and Mrs. Gigliesi—the most cordial. 12,000 lire ($14.45) for a double room and two breakfasts" (Mr. and Mrs. Paul Sieczkowski, Omaha, Nebraska, seconded by Catherine Ronconi, San Lorenzo, California, and by Mr. and Mrs. Gary Goldetsky, Minneapolis, Minnesota). . . . "We're enthusiastic about the home of **Signora Antonelli**, Via Quintino Sella 20, telephone 460-617, where the 1980 charge is only 4,500 lire ($5.42) per person in a double, 4,000 lire ($4.81) per person quad. Look for 'scala A, interno 9.' In Rome, which has become increasingly expensive, we managed to stay under fifteen dollars a day" (John Reynolds, East Orange, New Jersey; note by AF: this is centrally located, in the area between Piazza della Repubblica and Via Veneto). . . . "The owners of the **Hotel**

Pensione Sonya, at Via Viminale 58 (telephone 475-9911), are a wonderful family named Velletrani, who treat you as one of them. Their pension is immaculately clean, well-located (near the station), and close to buses. . . . These people were so terrific, I cried when I had to leave Rome. They didn't tell you where the bus stop was, they *walked* you to it. And one day, when I was going to the beach for the day (Lido, according to your instructions), they packed an unbelievable lunch for me and my Japanese friend! Their token of hospitality! Price was 9,500 lire, single, with everything (breakfast, tax and service) included. Running water and bidet in the room, bathrooms available very close by" (Irma Mitchell, Sherman Oaks, California). . . . "I would strongly recommend the **Pensione Andreotti,** at Via Castelfidardo 55, phone 483-553, just three short blocks to the right of Termini Station, on the first three floors of the building, with 36 rooms, and free showers on every floor. 1980 rates will be: singles 9,500 lire, doubles 13,000 lire, breakfast 1,500 lire. Mr.and Mrs. Andreotti speak English and treat everyone like family" (Jacqelyn J. Vollmer, Jacksonville, Florida). . . . "Mrs. Govoni has been managing the **Pensione Govoni** on the 4th floor of 79A Via Principe Amadeo (phone 73-47-71) for 20 years, and is unusually accommodating to her guests. Singles are 5,000 lire ($6.02), doubles, 8,000 lire ($9.63), but breakfast isn't served. Children staying in their parents' room, I might mention, are charged only 1,000 lire more" (Clara B. Kneip, Chicago, Illinois).

READERS' HOTEL SELECTIONS: "We were advised to try the 4th class **Albergo Trevi** (Vicolo del Babuccio 21, phone 689-563), which was clean, very well located (30 seconds from the Trevi Fountains), and cheap (9,600 lire for a double). Take any bus that goes down Via Corso or to the Piazza San Silvestro and ask directions to the Trevi Fountains. The hotel is in a tiny alley that is a bit hard to find: take the first street diagonally to the left opposite the fountain; go one short block, past a movie theatre, and turn left, and about 4 or 5 doors down is the hotel" (Tom and Gale Lederer, Richmond, California). . . . " **Hotel Pincio,** Via Capo le Case 50, phone 679-1233, located between Via del Tritone and the Spanish Steps, definitely deserves to be recommended. Its owners, Renato Carosi and his wife Olga, have spent quite a few years in England, so there is absolutely no language barrier. Rates, which include breakfast, are single 10,000 lire, double 16,500 lire, breakfast included" (Mrs. Karen L. Prisco, Bogota, New Jersey).

READERS' PENSIONE SELECTIONS (NEAR THE COLOSSEUM): "I located a clean and comfortable room with free use of showers at the **Albergo Valle,** Via Cavour 136 (phone 465-837), a newly-redecorated place located halfway between the railroad station and the Colosseum; the all-inclusive cost of a single was 8,500 lire, doubles are 12,500 lire, and showers are free!" (Henry S. Sloan, New York, New York).

GET THEE TO A NUNNERY: There is yet a third type of accommodation available to you in this city, in the form of convent quarters—and I am utterly serious. Several religious orders in Rome help support themselves by taking paying guests. Several others do so merely to be of service. In both instances, the rooms offered are spotlessly clean and proper, and the prices charged for room and all three meals average $16 per person per day. Families, particularly, should give these a try.

To illustrate: in the area of the Vatican, where numerous such institutions abound, a convent known as the **Casa N.S. di Fatima,** Via Gianicolo 4a (phone 654-3349), charges 15,000 lire a day ($18.07) for room and all three meals, 13,500 lire ($16.26) for room and two meals, but boards women and families only, for whom it has nearly 100 beds. Highly recommended; take bus #64 from the railroad station to Ponte Vittorio (at the side of St. Peter's) and walk from there. . . . Nearer to the Vatican than the above-named, is the convent of the **Graymoor Sisters,** Via Monte del Gallo 105, phone 630-782; 15,500 lire ($18.67) for full pension; 60% reduction for children under 6; and all the Sisters speak English. Single men are not admitted; couples with children are preferred (babysitters are always available); location is to the left of, and behind, St. Peter's on a steep hill—again best for readers with cars, but also reachable by bus no. 34 from Piazza Cavour. . . . Nearby, the **Sisters of the Immaculate**

Conception at 38 Via Monte del Gallo (phone 630-863) charge 12,000 lire ($14.45) per person for room and two meals a day, but do not speak English. They have singles, doubles and triples—a total of 80 beds—but also impose an 11:30 p.m. curfew.... A final and much more expensive convent-run establishment is the well-located **Foyer Unitas Casa** (operated by the Dutch order known as the Ladies of Bethany, particularly for non-Catholic visitors to Rome), which has space for about 25 guests at 12,500 lire ($15.06) per person for bed and breakfast, in the Pamphili Palace (elevator to 4th floor) on the Piazza Navona, entrance at 30 Via di S. Maria dell' Anima, phone 656-5951 or 654-1618. True to their birthplace, the sisters offer large Dutch breakfasts (cheeses, jams, good crusty rolls) and particularly spacious and well-furnished rooms. It's not at all necessary to have a private bath, as all showers and public bathrooms are sparkling clean and always available. Closed during some summer weeks; best write ahead for reservations.

READERS' CONVENT SELECTIONS: "One of the best convents for tourists is the house run by the **Soeurs de Lourdes,** the Religious of N. S. di Lourdes, at Via Sistina 113 (tel: 48-93-24). It's just a quick walk from Piazza Barberini, the Via Veneto, the Largo Tritone, the Central Post Office and ... the Spanish Steps. They have 50 beds (1 or more per room). Full pension is 14,000 lire per person; room and breakfast 6,000 lire, and half-pension is 9,500 lire. The place is very clean, has hot water in all rooms, a shower and bath every three rooms. I think they have a similar place, with similar rates but accommodations for 100 people, at Via Domenico Tardini 40" (Rock Caporale, Purchase, New York; note by AF: this is a 3-story, elevator-equipped building; buses stopping at the Piazza Barberini bring you very near).... "Excellent convent: **Suore Oblate dell' Assunzione** at 42 Via Andrea Doria in the Vatican area. Accommodations are clean and comfortable, courtyard is lovely, showers are *hot,* sisters are friendly. Cost is 6,000 lire per person for bed-and-breakfast in either single or double rooms, and the phone is 359-9540 or 385-337" (Robert Hearn, Auburn, New York).... "The **Instituto Piccole Suore Sacra Famiglia,** 92 Viale Vaticano (phone 319-572), almost opposite the entrance to the Sistine Chapel, is run by nuns and reasonably priced at 4,000 lire ($4.81) per person per night" (Mrs. Willard Rhodes, Highland, New York).

A READER'S SELECTION FOR GROUPS: "I made my 'nth trip to Italy this summer as chaperone to high school students. We stayed at the **Centro Universitario Marianum,** near the Church of St. John Lateran (Via Matteo Boiardo #30, phone 757-4241). Immaculate rooms with toilet facilities, shower, spacious atmosphere, friendly personnel—and the food! Not once were we able to eat all that was offered! And good! All for 12,000 lire ($14.45) per person per day, including all three meals" (Mary Ferro, New Haven, Connecticut; note by AF: Marianum is under religious auspices, but accepts groups of any kind, with no questions as to religion asked).

STUDENT IN ROME: For you, the street to seek out is the Via Palestro, several short blocks to the right of Terminal Station, as you leave it. Traditionally the site of Italy's official student organization (including the new **Relazioni Universitarie** organization at 11 Via Palestro (phone 47-55-265); "R.U." currently performs many of Italy's student travel functions, including the selling of student charter flights, and will assist arriving student travellers to find low-cost rooms, meals and tours in Rome), this fairly quiet thoroughfare has known so many student travellers over the years that pensiones along it (and there are many of them) have specialized in offering rates as low as 3,500 lire ($4.21) per person per night, sometimes by creating multi-bedded rooms. Numerous Via Palestro pensiones will, in fact, charge 3,500 to 4,000 lire and less in 1980: among them, my own preference would be: the utterly unique, outstanding **Pensione Katty,** 35 Via Palestro (phone 475-1385), whose owners—Nelmo and Lucia Casadio—have made dozens of lasting friendships with vacationing American students, despite the fact that they speak scarcely any English! Three thousand five-hundred lire ($4.21) per person for triple or 4-bedded rooms, 4,000 lire per person double, including free hot showers and a map of Rome. In the same building, try the equally cordial and this time English speaking **Pensione Michele,** 35 Via Palestro (phone 474-3383), 3,000 lire per person, and management by a friendly brother-and-sister team; the top-floor apartment at 35 Via Palestro (phone 484-574) of **Giuseppina ("Pina") Polverini** (4,000 lire, plus free ice water from the fridge); the **Locanda Bolognese,** 15 Via Palestro (phone 485-848), doubles for 4,000 lire ($4.81) per person, singles for 6,000 lire; **Locanda Marini,** 35 Via Palestro (phone 482-333), only 4,000 lire per person.

If you'd prefer an actual student hotel, then try phoning the important youth hostel called **Ostello per la Gioventù del Foro Italico,** 61 Viale Olimpiadi (phone 396-4709), on the Lungotevere Maresciallo Cadorna (Piazza Maresciallo Giardino), with its 25 dormitories and 18 bedrooms (men on the ground floor, girls upstairs), where everyone pays 3,500 lire per night (sheets, hot water, showers and breakfast included), 2,500 lire for lunch or dinner. At the Ostello, you'll need an International Youth Hostel Card, but they'll sell you one on the spot for 9,000 lire.

STUDENT RAIL TRAVEL: "Another student travel office, the **CTGS** (Centro Turistico Giovanile Studentesco), at 16 Via Genova, phone 475-5762, is especially good at obtaining discount rates on scheduled trains (e.g., Rome-Vienna $25, Rome-London $54)" (Janice R. Bellace, London, England).

STARVATION BUDGET: You won't be many days in Rome before you hear talk of a 180-room hotel called the **Albergo del Popolo** ("Hotel of the People"), which charges only 5,500 lire a night ($6.62) per person for single—that's right, single—rooms (and it rents only singles). The Popolo happens to be one of those amazing European establishments which is nominally under the auspices of a charitable organization (in this case, the Salvation Army), but is maintained as a normal tourist hotel, with nothing charitable about it—the Mission hotels in Scandinavia are of the same type. Although it is located in a workingmen's quarter of Rome, at 41 Via Apuli (phone 49-19-39), just off the Via Scalo San Lorenzo (behind Terminal Station), the hotel is a modern and quite pleasant building that was erected only a few years ago, and that sports a peaceful garden and bar.

Throughout the year, the del Popolo accepts male tourists only, but recently it opened a small next-door annex at 39 Via Apuli accepting ladies at a charge of only 2,000 lire ($2.40) per night in tiny cubicles containing a cot apiece; a similar annex at 40 Via Apuli accomodates men for only 2,000 lire, but in dorms; both annexes are closed for cleaning from 9 a.m. to 3 p.m. Even in the men-only section, the del Popolo is a thoroughly proper and well-maintained tourist hotel, whose 5,500 lire rates for privacy-affording single rooms make it one of the best starvation budget finds of this book. From Terminal Station, take either a #11 or a #66 bus, and ask the conductor to let you off at the "Quartiere San Lorenzo." You will, I think, find it edifying and exciting to live in a typical quarter of Rome, where tourists rarely go.

Starvation budget pensiones? They're found in the streets to the immediate right and left of Terminal Station, particularly on the Via Palestro (which is lined with them), the Via Montebello, and the Via Principe Amedeo (where there are nearly two dozen). On the latter street, I particularly like the **Pensione Carmelo Cortorillo,** 79/A Via Principe Amedeo (phone 731-6064), where if you're lucky, you can get one of the large single rooms (with a picture window and sink with three faucets—hot, cold and specially chilled) for 5,000 lire, a double for only 4,000 lire per person. Breakfast will be brought to your room by Signora Cortorillo—a warm gracious lady who speaks not a word of English —for another 1,800 lire, and you'll be lucky to finish it. Take the stairs on the right side of the building to the fifth floor. Other pensions in the same building —such as **Aldo Pezzotti's** on the second floor (phone 73-11-561, and take the stairs to your left)—charge as little as 4,500 lire per person in a double room, only 5,000 lire single.

READERS-ON-THE-STARVATION-BUDGET: "For only 3,800 lire ($4.57) per person in a double, 3,000 lire ($3.61) in a four-bedded room, you'll be given spacious, clean accommodations at Signor and Signora Rossi's **Locanda Otello**, 13 Via Marghera (phone 490-383), fourth floor, half-a-block from the side entrance to the central train station" (Hiroko Ishikawa, Tokyo, Japan; with seconding recommendations from Mary Scent, Melbourne Beach, Florida; Fausto Trubano, Natick, Massachusetts; and Ruth Ann Kelleher, Canal Zone, Panama). . . . "We frequently travel to Rome and always stay at the 15-room **Pensione Di Rienzo** for 3,500 lire per person. That's at 79A Via Principe Amadeo (phone 736-956), two blocks from the station; Mr. Di Rienzo speaks some English" (Lorraine Callahan and Carole Ann Murphy, New York City, New York). . . . "I'd like to recommend the **Pensione Vanny**, Via Treviso, 31, apt. 11, phone 859-354, as a place for students who aren't afraid to rough it a little and who are unable to pay the high price of Rome pensions during the summer season. The owners of this little 5th floor place (which bears no sign; look for the doorbell marked Vanny) are very, very nice people. The man is Egyptian and an excellent conversationalist! English is well understood, and American students are his most popular summer clients. The Vanny is not in the center of the city, but it is located in a lovely neighborhood with trolleys and buses easily accessible, leading to all parts of the city. A double room cost us 3,000 lire apiece per night, and singles (4,000 lire) just a bit more. The address is Via Treviso #31, and the pension can be reached by buses 6, 9 and 67 (from the station). It's a short walk from the famous Piazza Salerno" (Linda Millet, Long Island City, New York; plus the following comment on the Vanny from Mrs. Barbara Pepesch, Switzerland: "This was the stellar find of the past six months. It enabled us to live in Rome for what we spent in Izmir . . . and we thought *that* was great! It is one large apartment in a very nice apartment house in a quiet and good residential section, very near all public transportation methods. An Egyptian gentleman and his Italian wife run it, and English is spoken. He does want to get a bigger apartment whenever he can, and so might not be at the same address any longer, but he is worth any means of tracing. His place was a fantastic oasis in the money-grubbing of Rome, at the price of 6,000 lire for a large double room, all included; and he will put up single people either in small individual rooms—4,000 lire—or in 3-bedded or 4-bedded 'dormitories' for 3,500 lire per person. I cannot say enough for this man's attitude toward his guests"). . . . "At **Locanda Anita**, 114 Via Montebello (3rd floor, phone 460-066), near the train station, you can find a comfortable bed in a clean and very cozy atmosphere for only 3,000 lire a day, including one free hot shower per day. The service is excellent, there are no extra charges at all, and if you have to share, it would always be with somebody nice, and usually English-speaking" (George McLaughlin, London, England). . . . "**Centre Pax Christi** at 21 Piazza Adriani (phone 65-68-140), open from 15 July to September 30, offers the cheapest lodgings in town, but is worth a visit even if you don't plan to stay. Write in advance for reservations to M. Luciano Montemauri, 1 Lungo Tevere Vallati, Rome 00186; the house itself is operated by the International Catholic Movement for Peace" (Pauline Hadley Maude, New York, New York). . . . "The **Nuova Foresteria** (also known as the "Casa del Conservatorio"), 62 Via del Conservatorio (phone 659-612), is located near the Tiber, between Ponte Sisto and Ponte Garibaldi; from Terminal Station, take bus #75 to Ponte Garibaldi. Each bed costs 4,000 lire in a triple room, 4,200 lire per person in a double; there are several floors, on two of which families with children can find accommodations! But the clients here are mainly student-age; they like the lounges, and the generally pleasant atmosphere" (James Sullivan, New York City). . . . "I paid only 6,000 lire ($7.22) for a single room at a pensione called **"Student's House"**, which occupies apartments 3 and 5 at no. 12 Via Curtatone (phone 462-358 or 495-5297), near Terminal Station. While this is a basic place, which does not include breakfast in the price (which is set at only 8,000 lire, $9.63, for a double room), the location is central, there's no curfew, and the young owner is a friendly chap who speaks excellent English" (D.J. Ames, Highton, Victoria, Australia).

Next, a touch of elegance in your Roman Tour.

THE BIG SPLURGE: A bright, young Italian named Guido Agnolucci, and an American named Marvin Hare, teamed up some years ago to open a pensione in Rome that would cater to the thoughtful tourist—people anxious to absorb the highest cultural lessons of the city. To give their establishment a name no one would ever forget, they called it the **Pensione Texas (12).** You'll realize how perfectly inappropriate that monicker is when you enter this tastefully-decorated, duplex apartment at Via Firenze 47 (phone 485-627), just two short blocks from the important Via Nazionale. Whenever 6 p.m. approached last summer, Hope and I felt a genuine urge to rush back to the "Texas" to hear the exciting conversation that fills the cocktail-lounge of the pension (our fellow guests, among others: a member of the Minneapolis Symphony, and his wife; a professor from the Nationalist Chinese University on Taiwan). How much for all this culture, comfort and charm? 16,000 lire ($19.27) per person for a bathless room (that's for one of the Texas' several "budget rooms"), *with* breakfast and one other large meal (demi-pension), taxes and service included, at the height of the summer season—an excellent value, justifying this just-once departure from normal budget limits. Recently, the Texas has also taken over the **Pensione 7 Hills** (phone 484-846), downstairs in the same building, where they offer the same demi-pension arrangements (that is, bed and two meals) for 16,000 lire ($19.27) per person in twin-bedded rooms without bath, tax and service included. Guests at the Seven Hills—which is operated with punctilious care, in the manner you'd expect from Messrs. Hare and Agnolucci—are permitted to use the cocktail lounge of the Texas, upstairs. Rooms with bath are also available. Next door to the Texas, by the way, at Via Firenze 38 (phone 460-368), the **Pensione Americana Nardizzi** is less insistent on the demi-pension requirement, asks 14,500 lire double without bath, 16,500 lire with shower, including breakfast, service and tax in each case, all for large and well-furnished rooms enjoying a nice view over Rome. Signor Nardizzi speaks English well, and will treat you like a V.I.P. if you're a user of this book. In the same building (38 Via Firenze), **Pensione Oceania** (phone 475-0696), managed by Armando and Luisa Loreti, a very friendly husband-and-wife team (Armando speaks some English), rents 12 impeccably clean rooms. Singles with shower and W.C. for 9,500 lire ($11.44); doubles without bath, 14,500 lire ($17.46); doubles with shower, 16,700 lire ($20.12); doubles with shower and W.C., 18,000 lire ($21.68); 6,500 lire per bed for third and fourth beds (if you need one of these, ask for the largest room, No. 8); optional breakfast for 2,000 lire ($2.40). And the name "Oceania"? It reflects the sympathies of the Loretis for Australians and New Zealanders, who often find their way here.

A runner-up to the Pensione Texas? There are several possible candidates, and one of them—the **Pensione City,** 200 yards from the bottom of the Spanish Steps, at 97 Via Macelli (phone 678-4037)—is another proof for the rule that you can't judge an Italian hotel from the outside. Up one flight from a not terribly attractive entrance, you'll suddenly enter into a world of silver tea services and parquet floors, soft and courteous attention, sunny, dignified rooms of which the half without bath rent for 21,000 lire ($25.30) double, including breakfast, service and tax, with no requirement that you take additional meals. Umberto Scarfone is the fluent-in-English manager; you'll feel like congratulating him on his pension, which also offers an elevator, once you ascend the first flight.

One of the most modern budget hotels in Rome, **Albergo Villafranca,** 9 Via Villafranca (491-152), enjoys a location close to Terminal Station and the Air Terminal. Leaving the station at the side entrance facing Via Marsala, walk up Via Vicenza: Via Villafranca is the fifth street going left. This huge, six-floor, 140-bed, elevator-equipped establishment is managed by bright, moustached

Gianni Schifano who speaks excellent English, the result of having worked in New York restaurants until 1971. His offerings: single rooms for 9,000 lire ($10.84); doubles or twins 14,400 lire ($17.34); triple rooms 18,000 lire ($21.68); quadruple rooms 21,500 lire ($25.90); breakfast for 2,000 lire; showers free. On clear days, one has a beautiful panoramic view of the Castelli Romani area from the roof garden, where you can sit and relax and drink a Coke or a small bottle of wine (450 lire each).

READER'S PENSION SELECTION: "**Pensione Lidia**, at 42 Via Sistina, near the Spanish Steps (phone 679-3815), is recently redecorated, nicely operated and furnished, and charges only 18,800 lire for a double with private shower, 11,200 lire single, breakfast included" (Libby Lumb, Sydney, Australia).

RESTAURANTS: Rome is a difficult town in which to find budget restaurants. There are only three small areas in this entire large city where you'll discover anything resembling a cluster of good, low-cost eating spots. But there are, in addition, a number of isolated budget restaurants; and there are, finally, the unique stand-up counter establishments called "Rosticcerias-Tavola Calda." We'll start with the cheapest of the cheap, and then gradually ascend in price.

The Subsidized Restaurants

The very least expensive meals in Rome are to be found in the restaurants that operate in Italian government offices as semi-official canteens for civil servants—these, almost without exception, serve the public as well. On the fifth floor of the Ministry of Agriculture building at 7 Giosuè Carducci, near the American Embassy—to cite one example—the 320-seat **Mensa Del Corpo Forestale** serves hot lunchtime meals (two courses, bread, wine an extra 400 lire), Mondays through Saturdays from noon to 3, for 3,000 lire ($3.61). Entrance is next to the plush offices of Saudi Arabian Airlines, and at this fifth-floor restaurant (take the elevator after first walking through the white gate and turning left), you'll even find an outdoor garden terrace on which to enjoy your $3.60 repast.

Restaurants for Occupational Groups

Every union, every military branch, has its own restaurant in Rome—and many of them are open to the public. In the area of Terminal Station, you'll find two particularly good examples—the "**Dopolavoro Ferroviario Mensa Tavola Calda**" (Restaurant of the Railway Workers), the best, is at 88 Piazza dei Cinquecento, on the first floor of the building with a "SNIA" sign on top, to the immediate right of the station as you exit from it. It charges 2,000 lire for main meat courses, 600 lire for vegetables, 700 lire for pasta dishes with sauce, 350 lire for fruit, 400 lire for cover. Order your dishes at the "Cassa" (cashier) first, then consume them at pleasant little tables in a spacious hall. Open noon to 9:30 p.m., seven days a week. . . . Cheaper, but for servicemen only, is the military restaurant operated directly in the station (lower level); enter it from the Via Giovanni Giolitti at the side of the station, at that point where you see a sign reading "**Posto Sosta e Ristoro per Militari**"; it's about 100 yards down the side of this immense building at #44 on the street. While preference here is given to Italian soldiers and airmen, military of other nations are occasionally also served, at prices that average 1,800 lire for main courses, 300 lire for fruit, from 600 to 800 lire for soup and pasta. Closed Fridays.

Restaurants in Trastevere

The most typical part of Rome, so the Romans say, is Trastevere, in the southwest section of the city, on the left bank of the Tiber. For centuries, artists and writers have worked and lived here, inspired by the special atmosphere and excellent cuisine; today, as happens with Greenwich Village-type places, Rome's most elegant restaurants are also to be found in Trastevere. But among them is the miraculously low-priced **Mario's**, at 53 Via del Moro, where à la carte charges (there is no fixed price menu) are so very reasonable—pasta for 500 lire, at least 19 main courses, for 900 to 1,300 lire ($1.08 to $1.56)—that you can easily put together a three-course meal including wine for 3,000 lire or else simply choose the fixed price meal, one of the cheapest and best in the city for only 3,000 lire ($3.61). Or you can eat for considerably less by ordering a large bowl of minestrone (vegetable and noodle soup) for 400 lire, two fried eggs and a "ciriolina" (a large white bread roll, a specialty of Trastevere bakers) for 550 lire, grilled liver with onions for 800 lire. 37-year-old Mario presides over all, aided by Mamma Clelia, wife Vanda, sister Lina, brother Giorgio, and sister-in-law Rosalba. From Terminal Station, take bus #75 to the Ponte Garibaldi, cross the bridge, then turn right and walk towards the Ponte Sisto—half way along, on your left, you'll find Mario's (which also displays a yellow telephone disc over its door). Inside, in true Trastevere spirit, dining room walls carry paintings by promising young Roman artists, including one—by Semjonov—that's of art gallery standards. Closed Sundays.

Rome's New Cafeterias

While Rome has always had a species of self-service restaurants called "rosticcerias" or "tavola caldas" (see our discussion below), the eternal city has sprouted three honest-to-goodness cafeterias in recent years; the largest, brightest and—to a slight extent—most "expensive" of these is the exciting **Piccadilly**, at the bottom of the Via Barberini (#'s 2 to 16), just before the big Piazza Barberini. Costly in comparison with the cafeterias in Paris, with all sorts of complex, multi-ingredient appetizers, it nevertheless serves soups and pasta plates for prices ranging from 700 to 900 lire, meat plates with vegetables for 2,000 to 2,300 lire, tomato salads for 700 lire, cheese for 850, fruit for 500—and it offers up these items in spacious, clean surroundings, calm and cool. We repeat here our budget litany for eating in any Italian cafeteria: order a pasta dish first, pay for it, eat it, and only then go back to the serving line for other courses. You'll be surprised to discover how seldom you're able to eat another thing! And always order pasta with meat ingredients or sauces, in preference to the more costly meat-and-vegetable plates. The Piccadilly's serving counter is in operation from noon to 3 and from 7 to 10:30 p.m., daily except Sunday.

Somewhat cheaper than the Piccadilly is the modern **Self-Service Falcioni**, at 47 Piazza Cinquecento (in front of Terminal Station and directly to the left of it as you exit), which is not to be confused with the expensive Ristorante Falcioni, next door at 45 Piazza Cinquecento (to reach the cafeteria, you go next door, through a small room, and then downstairs). There are attendants here who carry your tray (tip them 50 lire), plenty of free drinking water, wine for 750 lire a flask, and very tasty dishes, priced usually at 700 lire for soup, 2,500 lire for main courses with vegetables, 1,000 lire for pasta. Sample meal possibilities: minestrone soup, roast beef and spinach, baked custard for dessert and red wine: 2,800 lire ($3.37); macaroni, pot roast and peas, and red wine: 4,200 lire ($5.06); a quarter of a roast chicken, a big plate of rice with tomato sauce, and a flask of white wine: 4,500 lire. Closed Sundays.

Rosticcerias

Generally, however, your most effective money-saving method is to eat at cafes and bars in Rome that carry the sign "Tavola Calda" (hot table), sometimes preceded by the word "Rosticceria." Normally, these are stand-up eating spots, although quite a few have tables and chairs in the back. They nearly always feature a glass counter with trays of hot and cold food from which you can choose, and they are perfect for fast-moving tourists. You can have either a large hors d'oeuvre-sandwich, or a bowl of pasta, or a plate of hot meats, with rolls, and you can order the marvelous "cappucino"—the nearest Italian equivalent of our coffee (350 lire)—to top it off. If you do take snacks in a rosticceria, in preference to the normal 2-hour Italian meal, you'll feel light and relaxed for your touring activities, and you'll rarely ever encounter prices that strain a modest budget.

Care to have the addresses of a few typical rosticcerias? Just next door to the Hotel Pincio, at 53 Via Capo le Case (near American Express and the Spanish Steps), you'll find **Fuligni**, a rosticceria "tavola calda" where I often eat—always for less than $5. Just off the Piazza del Popolo, at #11 Via Flaminia, an elaborate "tavola calda" shop is the well-known (and somewhat high-priced) **Ristorante-Rosticceria Catena;** but a cheaper, more typical and suitable rosticceria-tavola calda is the **G. Scialanga,** up a block and across the street at 34 Via Flaminia (soup 750 lire, pasta 1,000, main courses mainly 2,000 to 2,600). And finally, back at the station, there's the stand-up **Rosticceria Mancia** just to the side of the station at 65a Via Giovanni Giolitti: soup for 700 lire, pasta for 1,000, and closed Sundays.

The Budget Areas

Of these there are several—we'll deal with them in roughly ascending order of cost:

To the right of Terminal Station (as you leave)

The largest cluster, and the very cheapest, of Rome's budget restaurants are found in the streets in the area to the immediate right of Terminal Station, as you exit from the station; and the cheapest of all—cheapest, perhaps, of all commercial restaurants in Rome—is the amazing **"Da Peppino"** at 35 Via Castelfidardo, a 10 x 15 snackbar with one long table and one long counter, selling a three-course dinner (spaghetti or soup, then meat or fish with vegetable, and fruit for dessert), including bread, wine or a coke, and service, for exactly 2,700 lire ($3.25)! Owner and cook, Peppino, has been operating this small eatery for more than 50 years! And he'll be happy to replace the three-course feast with a one-plate meal with wine for only 1,500 lire ($1.80; spaghetti) or 1,200 lire ($1.44; cheese omelette). Closed Fridays. But Da Peppino is only one of a number of such "little wonder" places in the nearby complex of streets—the Via Varese, the Via Montebello, the Via Palestro (near student headquarters), the Via Vicenza, Via Volturno, Via Curtatone—they're all in the same basic area. **Hostaria da Marcello,** in the basement at 56A Via Vicenza, for instance, serves a three-course prezzo fisso for 4,000 lire, soup for 750 lire, pasta for 1,000. A similar and rather basic basement eatery, the **Al Varesino,** at 5b Via Varese, charges 4,500 lire for three courses, including service, and such widely renowned specialties as canelloni or spaghetti alla carbonara for 1,800 lire. Closed Fridays. The somewhat larger **Osteria da Salvatore,** at 39C Via Castelfidardo, corner of Via Montebello, charges only 3,000 lire ($3.61) for a full "Menu Turistico" (three courses, including bread, wine and service), specializes in fish dishes. One could also have a filling à la carte meal here—like spaghetti, two fried eggs, wine, bread—for 1,800 lire. Salvatore, Rocco and Carmine, the three brothers who operate the Salvatore, are quite eager to please holders of this book. Closed Tuesdays. The **Trattoria Montebello** and the better **Trattoria Carosi,** directly on the open market street called Via Montebello (at #'s 25 and 28, respectively), charge 4,200 lire ($5.06) for their all-inclusive "Menus Turistico"; and for an inexpensive "rosticceria-tavola calda", where you can see what you're ordering, you'll want to try the **Gelateria,** at 44 Via Volturno (near the Via Gaeta): 1,600 lire for a succulent plate of lasagne. Verily, this area—which you can find on even a condensed city map—is Rome's best for rock-bottom-priced meals, with Osteria da Salvatore leading the list of sit-down restaurants: you can't eat better, for only 3,000 lire, at any other establishment to the left or the right of Terminal Station.

To the left of Terminal Station (as you leave)

Here, the pickings are fewer (in the budget range, that is), but you might nevertheless try the tiny **Trattoria Angelo,** 104 Via Principe Amedeo, two short blocks to the left of the train station as you leave; it's a cool, calm little spot, and Angelo is a friendly little restaurateur who charges 5,500 lire ($6.62) for a "Menu Turistico" consisting of three courses, bread, wine, cover and service charge. Closed Wednesdays. Nearby, the **Trattoria Alfredo** at 126a Via Principe Amedeo, charges a similar 5,000 lire ($6.02) for its own "Menu Turistico," and is open daily except Sunday. Better-located, cheaper, but perhaps not as good, is the **Rosticceria Picca** at 7G Via Principe Amedeo, where the "Menu Turistico" (a three-course, all-inclusive meal) is only 4,200 lire, and Roman gnocchi (1,400 lire) are served on Thursday. À la carte, you'll pay 750 lire for soup, 900 lire for pasta dishes (most Italian meals start with either soup or pasta), 2,000 to 2,800 lire for main dishes with vegetables.

Near American Express and the Spanish Steps

A single phenomenon makes this an area for budget restaurants: the price war presently raging between the **Hostaria il Cantinone,** 21 Via Vittoria (5,000 lire for a three-course meal, including service and wine), the picturesquely-decorated **Hostaria Taverna Etrusca,** 58 Via Vittoria (6,000 lire for a three-course prezzo fisso meal, including wine; only 5,500 lire for a two-course meal with wine, in which the second course is chopped meat or an omelette, with potatoes and salad; closed Wednesdays), and the **Trattoria Porcellino,** across the street at 16a Via Vittoria (which charges 5,000 lire for a somewhat similar meal, either at lunch or dinner); all three restaurants offer refreshingly low prices for à la carte selections as well. How to find them? Well, the Via Vittoria, site of the epic gladiatorial contest, is stuck among the collection of small streets in front of the Spanish Steps, in the direction of the Via del Babuino (that is, on the other side of the steps from American Express). You can reach it by either walking to the end of the Via Bocca di Leone and turning left, or by doing likewise on the Via Mario de Fiori. Or, from the Spanish Steps, walk one block down the Via Babuino and turn left. The Cantinone is by far the preferred choice of the three at present, after which comes the Etrusca, as much for its colorful, Italian inn-type decor, as for its meals; but don't necessarily count out the Porcellino if the Etrusca is packed. All three are open from noon to 3 for lunch, from 7 to 10:30 for dinner, with the Etrusca closing on Wednesday, the Porcellino on Sundays.

Around the Piazza Barberini

In this central area, at the foot of both the Via Barberini and the Via Veneto, there's of course the Piccadilly Self-Service, which we've described above; but just 50 yards further down the hill, off the big Piazza Barberini, is the start of the Via Sistina, where you'll find the **Trattoria Pepi** at 150 Via Sistina. Its front portion resembles a grocery store; in back, however, is a normal dining room where the brothers Anzuini serve a "Menu Turistico"—three courses, plus wine, bread and service—for exactly 5,500 lire ($6.02). A la carte choices are in the same low-cost vein, and "spaghetti al sugo" (spaghetti with sauce) sells for 1,200 lire. Open every day except Sunday.

Near the Piazza Venezia

The main square of Rome is the Piazza Venezia, at the head of which stands the monstrous Victor Emmanuel Monument—Mussolini delivered his major speeches from the balcony you'll see at the side of the Square. If you'll walk from here to the nearby Corso Vittorio Emmanuele, and head down the avenue to the Largo Argentina, another square, you'll soon discover on the Largo, at 67 Corso Vittorio Emmanuele, Rome's largest delicatessen-type restaurant—**Il Delfino**—which has a marvelous array of spit-roasted chickens, hors d'oeuvre counters, pizza ovens. Walk into the big, hot, crowded room to the left (where the prices are the least expensive), sit at one of the bare tables, and order a Pizza Capricciosa (1,800 lire), which is a pizza covered with at least four different ingredients—a big pizza, enough for a full meal. There is soup for 1,000 lire, pasta for 1,300, meat dishes for 2,400 lire, but the Pizza Capricciosa is the standout find. Closed Mondays.

Fountains of Trevi

A second cluster of moderately-priced restaurants is found on the little streets that branch off from the Fountains of Trevi, with its magnificent pool into which you toss a coin, and make a wish, to insure your return to Rome.

I'd head for the **Piazza Fontana di Trevi (5)** for at least one meal in Rome—the surroundings are fabulous, and the fame of the fountains has caused almost a dozen trattorias to spring up. These come in two types: the restaurants on the plaza itself, which charge $9 and up for a prezzo fisso meal (at least three courses); the restaurants on the little streets that branch off from the plaza, which charge $7 and less, for the same three-course prezzo fisso meal.

On the plaza, the **Ristorante Il Fedelinaro,** at No. 95, seems your best bet in this high-priced category; it serves a 7,500 lire ($9.03) prezzo fisso, and fairly high-priced à la carte plates as well, perhaps because of its unique amenities: it has no door, no windows, in fact no front wall. The diners sit in an open three-sided room, which gives them an unobstructed view of the Trevi Fountains, and of all the doings and hangers-on about them. Closed Tuesdays.

These restaurants on the plaza are much too expensive, however. You'll get nearly the same quantity and quality of food on the four narrow streets which branch off from the plaza. These streets are, looking away from the fountains, from left to right: the Via del Lavatore, the Via di S. Vincenzo, the Via delle Muratte, and the Via de Crociferi.

Hope and I particularly like the **Hostaria Trevi** on the Via del Lavatore, No. 42 (just a few feet from the plaza), where for 6,000 lire ($7.22) apiece, we recently ordered and received a well-cooked prezzo fisso meal, including wine and service: two large bowls of minestrone, then veal with vegetables, cheese for dessert. Closed Sundays. But two doors up, at 40 Via del Lavatore, stands the budget standout of the Trevi Fountains section—a more modern eatery called **"Al Picchio"**, which offers four fixed price meals: for 3,500 lire (vegetable soup, veal cutlet with roast potatoes, beverage, bread), for 3,300 lire (spaghetti, roast chicken and potatoes, beverage and bread), for 3,800 lire (spaghetti, beefsteak with potatoes, beverage and bread), and for 4,000 lire (vegetable soup with noodles, pork chop, potatoes, fruit salad, beverage and bread), always with service included. Look for the semi-basement eating room, down three steps. Closed Mondays.

Probably the best moderately-priced restaurant in the area (but $7.22—6,000 lire—for its meals) is the **Trattoria Quirino**, 84 Via delle Muratte, which is slick and clean, and yet not overly commercial. Closed Saturdays. . . . And on the Via de Crociferi, you'll find a number of other recommended spots, including **La Toscana** at No. 13 (about $7 for dinner), closed Mondays.

Near St. Peter's

With but a few exceptions, the meals around here come relatively high; but the variety of choice is great. In the streets to the right of St. Peter's (as you face it) are clustered a whole host of trattorias that cater to the pilgrims and visitors who throng to Vatican City. These include: **Da Romolo alla Mole Adriana (10)**, at Via Fosse di Castello 19, two short blocks to the right of Via della Conciliazione (closed Mondays); and across the street, on Via di Porta Castello 11, the less expensive **Trattoria e Pizzeria "Federico" (1)**, closed Fridays. Typical of both these restaurants are the following values: veal scallops in white wine sauce ("scaloppini al vino bianco") for 3,300 lire ($3.97), soup for 900 lire or pasta with sauce for 1,200 lire; spaghetti for 1,200 lire. In addition, "Federico's" serves a 5,000-lire dinner of spaghetti or soup, followed by meat or fish, bread, fruit and a glass of wine, beer, orange drink or (mirabile dictu) Coca-Cola; and both places serve pizza (1,500 lire for a medium size) after 6:30 p.m. Federico gets the better recommendation, because of the graciousness towards readers of Federico himself.

READERS' RESTAURANT SELECTIONS (TERMINAL STATION): "Along the side of Terminal Station at 209 Via Giolitti, the rather simple **Trattoria La Scaletta** serves spaghetti or soup for 800 lire, chicken or pork with vegetables for 2,000 lire, fruit for 600 lire, wine 500 lire, and a prezzo fisso meal for 5,000 lire" (Jill Levey, New York, N.Y.). . . . "An alternative self-service cafeteria to the Picadilly is the **Tavola Calda** run by the railways. Facing the station, it is to the left of it behind the ancient piece of wall. A square, glass, air-conditioned building seating hundreds, it is slightly more expensive and less geared to the tourist, but has the advantage of being open on a Sunday (few places are) and is lovely and cool" (Leslie S. Woodcock, Bradford, Yorkshire, England).

READER'S RESTAURANT SELECTIONS (PIAZZA BARBERINI AREA): "At **Ristorante Giacinti**, 128 Via Quattro Fontane, a delicious three-course meal is only 5,000 lire, including a choice of five first courses, five main courses with salad and potatoes, and fruit and ice cream for dessert, plus wine and bread" (Diane Martin and Lynda Holden, Minneapolis, Minnesota).

A READER'S BREAKFAST TIP: "In Italy, the usual continental breakfast of two hard rolls with marmalade and a cup of coffee costs $2.50 to $3 in a hotel. Try the Italian method instead: buy your espresso and brioche (much more tasty than hard rolls) at one of the numerous stand-up coffee bars for about a dollar. If you should happen into an establishment that has a place to sit down, that brings the price up about 20%" (Jean Johnston, Poughkeepsie, New York).

A READER'S PICNIC TIP: "For picnic lunches near St. Peter's: the **Borgo Pio**, a street to the right of St. Peter's as you face it, has many food shops along its length that sell all sorts of picnic fare (cheeses, salamis, ham, rolls, olives, pickles, etc.) at low prices. Some stores sell these items prepackaged, thereby eliminating all language problems. It is easy to assemble a lunch for $4.50 or less—a quick procedure, and a good change from the heavy Italian fare" (John E. Westcott, Jr., Bethesda, Maryland).

MEALS—THE BIG SPLURGE: A big splurge in food? Maurice Chevalier once called the **Trattoria Romolo (13)** an "endroit de rêve." This is a garden restaurant, set in the courtyard of an old Renaissance home, near the Aurelian wall, at 8 Via di Porta Settimiana (far side of the Tiber). Launch your meal with spaghetti alla boscaiola (spaghetti with tuna, mushrooms and cheese) for 1,500 lire ($1.80). Go then to abbachio al' cacciatore (4,000 lire), followed by insalata mista (1,000 lire) and top it all off with charlot for 1,000 lire (charlot being a sponge cake covered with whipped cream, chopped-up cherries and grated peanuts). Total cost is 8,500 lire ($10.24), including service, for an unequalled dinner. Closed Mondays.

More easily found, however, are the splurge-type restaurants on the Via della Croce, just off the end of the Piazza di Spagna (and thus near the Spanish Steps), where the choice is between the **Trattoria Otello alla Concordia,** at #81 on the street (a large garden restaurant topped with a vine-covered trellis, homey and middle-class in nature, heavily patronized, with à la carte prices allowing a 7,500 lire ($9.03) meal—order only from the Italian menu; closed Sundays), and the much slicker, tourist-oriented, but fairly moderate (despite the acceptance of credit cards, the photos of movie stars hung about) **Re Degli Amici,** at 33/b Via della Croce, where $8.43 will suffice for a two-course meal with wine and service included. Closed Mondays. . . . Just down the street, at 39 Via della Croce, the **Fiaschetteria Beltramme** is heavily patronized by a local Roman clientele who find that they can construct a tasty, filling meal from the à la carte menu for less than 6,500 lire ($7.83): "spaghetti al sugo di vitella" (spaghetti covered with a delicious white sauce of cream and veal juice) for 1,300 lire, boiled beef tongue or a quarter roast chicken for 2,500 lire, parmesan cheese (the soft type, to be eaten with a piece of white bread) for 1,000 lire, all of it accompanied by an excellent red (rosso Chianti) or white (bianco Castelli) wine for 1,900 lire per liter.

READERS WHO HAVE SPLURGED: "We find there is really only one restaurant which best combines excellent cuisine and the gracious atmosphere of old Rome with the traveller's budget. It is **Le Tavernelle,** 48 Via Panisperna, centrally located near the Via Nazionale and the Piazza Venezia, and closed Mondays. Our meals there are among our fondest memories of Rome and typify the hospitality which distinguishes Rome from other European capitals. The owner, Goffredo, is a true continental host, charming and courteous as only a Latin can be. His three-course prezzo fisso meal (wine and service included) is 8,000 lire ($9.63), but his specialty is cannelloni, which, being our favorite dish, we sampled all over Italy and found to excel at Le Tavernelle—at the price of 1,500 lire ($1.80)" (Betty Woodside, El Paso, Texas, and Mary M. Addison, Klamath Falls, Oregon).

READERS' TIPS: "Do you ever advise your readers of the simplicity of assembling sandwiches on one's own? For instance, on a side street in back of the Due Macelli, which runs into the Via Mercede, many Italians (and at least two Americans I can name) frequently stopped into the bakery for a bun or two which the bakeryman sliced, moved down the block to the small grocery which is almost half butcher shop, very clean and of excellent variety, stated the number of grams of cheese or salami or cooked ham or other cold meat which they wished sliced and placed in the buns, and then moved back to the wine shop in between the two and ordered a glass of cold wine, all of which could be carried out to a pleasant garden area in back or eaten at the counter. This repast can be made into a really sumptuous picnic by the addition of Krik Krok potato chips, olives, pickled onions, peppers and other delicatessen items from the butcher counter, and it

would be difficult to spend more than $3.50 per person" (Dr. and Mrs. A. M. Cooper, Fresno, California). . . . "I do not think you emphasize strongly enough how important it is to barter in not only Rome but all of Italy. It is not unusual or hard to get a quarter or even a third off the asking price in some cases. Furthermore, this does not refer only to a few products but rather most. I found even the ice cream men would barter!" (Dale Watts, Dearborn, Michigan). . . . Some food notes from AF: first, you should know that a "trattoria" is usually simply a small restaurant, smaller and less pretentious than a "ristorante", although that isn't always the case. Inside, food items are normally grouped under the titles "antipasti" (appetizers), "zuppe" (soups), "asciutte" (pasta dishes such as spaghetti), "carne" (meat). Hardly any budget-minded Italian begins, though, with "antipasto"; but instead with soup or pasta, and so should you. The typical Italian meal consists of either soup or pasta, then a main course, then fruit for dessert. But you're under no obligation to order all three courses, and you might definitely consider skipping the first one, especially on hot days; a simple dish of fresh melon with thinly-sliced prosciutto ham ("prosciutto melone") accompanied by a small bottle of mineral water, can often provide the most refreshing sort of lunch, particularly if you plan to stroll the Palatine Hill in the broiling sun afterwards.

PORCHETTA ROMANA: Ever try a Porchetta Romana (spiced roast pig) sandwich? It's as typical of Rome as pizza is of Naples, and will cost you only 600 lire, plus 250 lire for a quarter liter of wine, if you buy it at a tiny shop about the size of a train compartment, called **Vino e Porchetta Romana,** and located at 2F Via del Viminale (between Via Giovanni Amendola and Via Principe Amedeo, near the big square in front of Terminal Station). Owner, Signor Franco Fioravanti, is busy all day selling his tasty and filling sandwiches, as well as separate orders of porchetta alone (1,300 lire for 100 grams) and his excellent wine in one liter bottles (1,500 lire). I'm told the turnover is one roast pig per day. Closed Sundays.

THE ORGANIZED TOURS: So vast is Rome, and so infinite its sights, that the basic city tours are cut into four parts, each lasting half-a-day, and each costing from 9,500 to 11,000 lire ($11.44 to $13.25). Tours 1 and 2 generally split up the town between them (9,500 lire each); tour 3 takes in the Vatican Museum, Sistine Chapel, and Pincio Gardens (11,000 lire); tour 4 goes to the outlying sections, including the Old Appian Way, the Catacombs, the Quo Vadis Chapel, and so on (10,000 lire). Among the companies offering these escorted rides, I like **Carrani Travel Service,** an Italian outfit with intelligent, multi-lingual guides, whose offices are at 95 Via Vittorio Emmanuele Orlando (phone 460-510 or 482-501), opposite the plush Grand Hotel. They offer a discount of 10% off any tour purchased by a reader of this book (flash them a copy), a discount of 20% for taking two tours, and also operate all the standard one-day and two-day excursions to Capri, Sorrento, and other near-Naples sites, as well as to Florence. Tours start at 9 a.m. and 2:30 p.m.; ladies planning to visit churches and cathedrals should wear long-sleeved dresses.

A FREE TOUR: Europe's most amazing tours are operated in Rome, every month except August, by a small group of multi-lingual Dutch nuns, wearing ordinary street clothes, who constitute the **"Foyer Unitas"** and operate out of the beautiful Pamphili Palace, which faces the Piazza Navona (the exact entrance being at 30 Via di S. Maria dell' Anima, Rome, phone 656-5951 or 654-1618). The tours, to begin with, are absolutely free. And they are offered primarily to *non*-Catholic visitors—not for proselytizing reasons, but simply on the grounds that there are plenty of Catholic organizations in Rome that will take care of Catholic tourists. The tours operate daily except Thursdays, at 9:30 a.m. The procedure for you is simply to stop by at the above address and express your interest—the sisters will then tell you what's scheduled, or even inquire as to what you'd like to see.

What's the catch? Well, these are not ordinary tours. They are for a "special" kind of tourist, who has a serious and intense interest in the history or culture of Rome—and is willing to examine particular sites *in depth*. The sisters may spend an entire morning, for instance, showing you one building, or one particular area, of the Vatican. They'll spend hours discoursing about the history and background of one of the Roman catacombs, another morning taking you through the Vatican Museums. They will not rush from place to place, and they will make no concessions to the tourist who simply wants a fast tv-type briefing on the art of a particular century.

Obviously, I hesitated long and hard about disclosing the existence of these tours—despite their "budget" aspect. Please, please stop by *only* if you are quite certain that you are willing to give the kind of serious attention that these fine ladies deserve. If you do, you'll receive a profoundly educational experience that costs not one lira—except for a tiny contribution (100 lire) towards the guide's expenses. For the work of these sisters—communicating the glories of Rome—is their vocation and the reason for their organization.

LOW-COST SIGHTS: The Colosseum, of course, which charges no admission for entrance to its ground floor, and no admission at all to visit any part of the ruins on Sundays (from 9 to noon only). . . . Following that, drive out as far as you have time to go along the ancient **Appian Way** ("Via Appia Antica," not to be confused with the modern "Via Appia Nuova"). . . . It's here that you'll pass the several largest Christian catacombs. Most interesting and significant of these are the **Catacombs of Saint Sebastiano** (once the burial place of both St. Peter and St. Paul), which are the second catacombs you'll pass as you proceed along the Appian route. The monks charge only 500 lire (60¢) for a multi-lingual guided tour, and operate them every day of the year except on Thursdays and on Christmas, New Year's Day and Easter Sunday. If you haven't a car, take bus #118 from the Colosseum to reach the catacombs.

The **Vatican Museums,** with the **Sistine Chapel** and **Raphael Rooms** (admission fee of 1,500 lire for all three, except on the last Sunday of each month, when admission is free; closed the first three Sundays each month, and holidays), are also musts. Remember that they are at the rear of the Vatican, a long walk from the front of St. Peter's, and that they close for the day at 4 p.m. (although St. Peter's itself stays open until 5). . . . Downstairs in St. Peter's a number of glass-sided coffins containing bodies of the Popes, are on view. . . . The figures inlaid on the floor of St. Peter's show the length of other famous cathedrals, thus giving you an indication of the enormous size of **St. Peter's.**

In the Villa Borghese Gardens, you won't want to miss the fabulous **Museo Borghese** (sometimes called the "Galleria Borghese"), admission 200 lire, with its treasures of paintings, sculpture and furnishings. On the first floor, there are works by the great sculptor Bernini (his famous Rape of Persephone is here); on the second floor is Raphael's "Descent from the Cross," together with several Titian's and a whole array of paintings by my own favorite, the master Caravaggio. And, of course, Canova's erotic sculpture of Paolina Borghese on the ground floor. Open daily except Mondays from 9 to 2, Sundays until 1.

Finally, the grandest sight in Rome, to my mind, is the **"Campidoglio"** (Capitoline Hill), the sight of which has caused many a tourist actually to weep over its sheer beauty. The steps and approaches were designed by Michelangelo; the plaza holds one of the few classic bronze statues in existence—the

Emperor Marcus Aurelius on horseback—which was discovered several centuries ago on the bottom of the Tiber, where it had been thrown by Roman-hating barbarians. When Michelangelo was asked to design a pedestal for the statue, he answered, "I am not worthy." If the horse itself seems somewhat oddly-proportioned, it is because (some experts think) the statue was made to stand at a great height, which would have corrected the perspective view.

Try, if you can, to visit the Campidoglio at night, when the sounds of the city are stilled, and the bronze of the statue takes on a dull glow. Then go to the back of the hill, which overlooks the Roman Forum from the very best vantage point in town, and offers a quiet, half-illuminated view of the Roman Forum that will cause you to reflect upon the rise and decline of great civilizations. . . . Wandering through the Roman Forum, in the daytime, costs 200 lire.

TIP: "Visit the small **A.T.A.C.** office amid the 'bus lanes' outside the central station where, for 3,500 lire, you may buy a pass entitling you to travel on nearly all routes for a week. A bus map (Rete dei trasporti Atac Stefer) costs 500 lire. The savings are considerable, not only in money, but in energy, shoe leather and time. The trip to the Catacombs can then be done for only 300 lire, which is admission and guide fee. The men in the office speak some English and are very helpful about many matters" (Leslie S. Woodcock, Bradford, Yorkshire, England).

CHECK LIST: Because there is so much to see and do in Rome, it occurred to me that it might prove helpful to end this chapter with a fast summary of the indispensable sights for a first-time visitor. If there were only ten visits for which I had time in Rome, I'd make them: **(1)** St. Peter's and the Vatican Museum (including the Sistine Chapel and the Raphael Rooms); **(2)** the Colosseum; **(3)** the Roman Forum (preferably at night); **(4)** the Campidoglio Hill (Capitoline Square), again at night; **(5)** the Via Veneto, in Spring, Summer or Fall; **(6)** the Villa d'Este, in Tivoli, on the outskirts of Rome (best at night); **(7)** the Appian Way and the Catacombs; **(8)** the Baths of Caracalla; **(9)** the Pantheon; and finally, **(10)** the Piazza Navona, with its three Bernini fountains. And as my final send-off to Rome, I'd go to the **Restaurant Tre Scalini** on the Piazza Navona and I'd have its specialty—a "Tartufo" (ice cream covered with whipped cream, cherries and bitter chocolate chips), which costs 2,000 lire if you sit at the outside tables, but only 1,500 lire if you have the same Tartufo inside. Closed Wednesdays.

HOPE'S ROME (A POSTSCRIPT): Aghast and appalled, however, that I could pare down the sights of Rome to 10 (which is a pretty monstrous thing), Hope has asked for equal time to discuss a few others, all in aid of readers who may have more than the normal five-or-so days to spend here. This is her report:

"Rome defies organization. It's a city layered with history, like the skins of an onion—you peel off the top layer and immediately find another, ad infinitum. It seems to me that the most exciting approach to Rome is through the spectrum of history, visiting the sights chronologically as much as possible.

The Etruscan Museum

"You can make a good start with the Etruscans, at **The National Museum of Villa Giulia** ('The Etruscan Museum'), just at the other end of the park from the Galleria Borghese, 9 Piazzale Villa Giulia (open daily except Mondays from 9 to 2, Sundays from 9 to 1, entrance of 100 lire, free on Sunday), which displays the world's finest collection of Etruscan sculpture, jewelry, pottery and household goods.

"Who were the Etruscans? That's the $64 question! Nobody really knows where they came from or even exactly when or where they landed in Italy (at some point, they settled in Tuscany, bringing with them a highly-developed culture). According to legend, they were one of the three tribes (the Latins, Sabines and Etruscans) living on the hills of Rome, who ultimately banded together for protection. And Etruscan kings are actually thought to have ruled Rome for at least a century, about 100 years after the legendary founding of the city by Romulus and Remus (753 B.C.). Whatever their origins, it is clear that they beautified and improved wherever they went, and what is known today about their civilization is based on what has been found of their art, which is astonishingly advanced and "modern" (I saw one vase that I'd swear was a Picasso). Most artists, anthropologists, and archaeologists would never pass through Rome without making a pilgrimage to the Etruscan Museum; don't miss Room VII, which houses what experts consider to be the most important find of the museum (The 'Apollon'); and don't miss the famous 'Sarcophagus of Caere' on the first floor.

Historical station break

"With the expulsion from Rome of the last ancient king, in 509 B.C., the era of the Roman Republic was launched. It lasted for nearly 500 years—through the vicissitudes of the invasions of the Gauls and the sacking of Rome by them in 390 B.C.; the two Punic Wars; and the attack by Hannibal—until Julius Caesar became dictator, and the colorful era of the Roman Emperors (Julius Caesar, Augustus Caesar, Tiberius, Caligula, Claudius and Nero) began. To have a marvelous glimpse into those times, try the:

Palatine Hill

"The **Roman Forum** and **The Palatine** form the very heart-line of ancient Rome, and are also the very best buys in town—a 200 lire ticket admits you to both sites, daily except Tuesday, from 9 a.m. until one hour before sunset (Sunday admission is 100 lire); enter from the Forum on Via dei Fori Imperiali (and head for the Arch of Titus to find the right path up the hill). The Palatine is one of the most stirring spots in all of Rome for appreciative eyes (there are scholars who spend months here). For this is where the Roman Empire had its beginnings—on this hill Romulus ploughed the acres that became the first city; later the Emperors erected their palaces here, in the choicest locations, overlooking the Forum. And the ruins, which indicate buildings of staggering proportions, sumptuousness, culture, comfort and beauty, give you an insight into 'La Dolce Vita' of the average Roman Emperor and upper-class citizen. You'll see the Baths of Septimius Severus; the Stadium of Domitian; the Domus Augustana (official palace built for the Imperial family); the Flavian Palace; the Temple of Cybele; the Palace of Tiberius. But whatever you see, don't miss the House of Livia (which was really the House of Augustus), with frescoes inside that are 2,000 years old and absolutely thrilling (if necessary, ask the guard to open the doors for you)! For maximum enjoyment I suggest you buy a map to guide yourself through.

National Roman Museum

"The local citizens know this as the **Museo delle Terme;** it's located on the Piazza Esedra (Piazza della Repubblica), directly across from Terminal Station, in the Baths of Diocletian. Entrance is a very-well-spent 200 lire (free on Sundays), and hours are daily except Mondays from 9 to 2, on Sundays from

9 to 1. Don't miss such famous pieces of Roman sculpture and art as 'The Pugilist' (a copy from the Greek original) in Room III (which earns its title of 'The Room of Masterpieces'), the 'Head of a Young Girl' in Room IV, the 'Marble Altar of Ostia' in Room VII, and the 'Fragments of the Secular Games' held under Augustus Caesar and Septimius Severus; and don't fail to allow plenty of time to explore all the treasures of Roman statuary and mosaics.

Basilica of Santa Maria degli Angeli (the Baths of Diocletian)

"Just next door to the Terme Museum (walk down the street to your right as you exit from the Terme) is the best-preserved hall of the **Baths of Diocletian,** which were converted by Michelangelo into the "Church of Santa Maria degli Angeli". Constructed in the fourth century A.D., this was one of the largest baths of its kind, with staggering proportions that make our modern-day saunas seem puny indeed (of course, the Roman baths were social gathering spots as well, where concerts and lectures were often held). Entrance is free; the hours vary, so check them in 'This Week in Rome'.

The Capitoline Museum

"Arthur has already referred to the great Campidoglio, on one side of which is the **Capitoline Museum,** with the **Conservatori** on the other. You'll want to spend most of your time at the Capitoline (daily except Mondays from 9 to 2, on Tuesdays and Thursdays from 5 to 8 p.m., and on Saturday evenings from 8:30 p.m. to 11 p.m.; free on Sundays, 400 lire otherwise, 500 lire on Saturday evenings), which will provide you with a rare and wonderful opportunity to put faces on the ancient Romans. There are several rooms devoted to busts of "just plain folks" from the Imperial era, and other rooms containing the better-known heads of Roman Emperors and other celebrities of the time. And don't miss the mosaics from Hadrian's Villa, the famous statue of The Dying Gaul, and the equally renowned 'Boy Extracting a Thorn from His Foot' (the latter two being copies from the Greek). All of these—except 'the Boy'— are in the Capitoline; he's in the Conservatori.

The Pantheon

"**The Pantheon,** at Piazza della Rotonda (take buses 26, 87 or 94), is the only complete major building of ancient Rome left standing—and it's one of the greatest free sights in the world. From it, you'll get a good idea of how to fill in the details of other Roman buildings that have only a column or two remaining. Built by Agrippa in the time of Augustus Caesar (around 27 B.C.) as a temple to the gods Venus and Mars, it was originally a rectangular structure. Later, all but the front columns and portico were destroyed by fire, and when it was rebuilt under the Emperor Hadrian (130 A.D.), it was constructed as the inspiring round architectural wonder that you see today. The painter Raphael is buried here (among many other dignitaries). Since the sole source of interior light is from a hole in the impressive dome, the Pantheon stays open only from 9 to 5, and is closed from 1 to 2 p.m.

Take an Imperial Walk

"Start at **The Colosseum,** where it's worth your while to take some time to contemplate the size and grandeur of this magnificent structure—imagine it covered with marble and filled with thousands of ancient Romans shouting thumbs up or thumbs down! Look below into the pits where lions, Christians, and general provisions were kept. Across the street is the **Arch of Constantine,** and the **Roman Forum;** to your left is **The Palatine.** Continue your walk up the Via dei Fori Imperiali (heading in the direction of the Victor Emanuele Monument), and when you are nearly past the Roman Forum, across the street, to your right, you'll see **Augustus' Forum;** further along and to your left is **Caesar's Forum;** and further still is **Trajan's Forum,** with its magnificent **Trajan's Column,** covered with winding bas-reliefs depicting Trajan's victory over the Daci. Across the street is **Trajan's Market** (entrance at 94, Via IV Novembre), which you can visit for 200 lire every day except Monday, from 9 to 1 and 3 to 6, winters, 10 to 4 (Sunday from 9 to 1, free admission); it will give you a good idea of how vast and impressive the ancient Roman markets were.

The Church of St. Clement

"And finally we come to the Christian era. If you'd like to experience in a most direct way what it must have felt like to be an early Christian in Rome, make a visit to the lower depths of the **Church of St. Clement,** on the Via S. Giovanni in Laterano, a street at the side of the Colosseum. Even if you later visit the massive Catacombs outside the city, you'll have a more intense experience here, because you are allowed to wander through the maze of underground rooms (which include several 1st century houses and a 4th century church) by yourself, without benefit of a guide. It's sinister and dark, with the spooky sound of rushing waters beneath the ground in this early meeting place of Christians and worshippers of Mithra (a vigorous, masculine cult who venerated the God of Light—or the Sun). The Church itself, medieval and made of stone in that distinctive yellow-orange earth color that you see only in Rome, has a mosaic in the Apse which dates from the 12th century, and is run by Irish Dominican Fathers, whose charge of admission to the excavations is 300 lire, and hours of entrance are from 9 (Sundays from 10) to noon and 3:30 to 6. Take the subway ("Metropolitana") to the Colosseum, walk to your left around the Colosseum to Via S. Giovanni in Laterano (the second street on your left), and then walk down the street for two blocks.

Churches in Rome

"This is like talking about coals in Newcastle, and I certainly won't attempt to provide a complete listing of all the major churches in Rome, but merely point out the most important or interesting ones to see. Generally the churches open around 7 a.m., close from noon to 3:30 or 4, and open again until sunset. The very most important sightseeing attractions, like St. Peter's and the other main Cathedrals, are an exception and remain open all day long.

The Big Four

"The four main Cathedral Churches of Rome, after **St. Peter's,** are the **Church of St. John Lateran, Santa Maria Maggiore,** the **Church of St. Paul,** and **San Lorenzo Outside The Walls.** The limited scope of this book does not permit a detailed description of **St. Peter's,** but the Church of the Vatican State stands on one of the most beautiful and harmonious squares in the world (by Bernini), and the interior, created by such as Michelangelo, Raphael, Bernini, Bramante and others, deserves careful scrutiny. Immediately to your right as you enter is Michelangelo's spell-binding 'Pietà'; it breathes! The Dome was also done by Michelangelo; the Papal Altar and Canopy, and the exuberant 'Gloria' Apse, are by Bernini. . . . Next in importance is **S. Giovanni in**

Laterano (located very near St. Clement; just continue to the end of Via S. Giovanni in Laterano), the oldest church in Rome (built on Pagan ruins, and incorporating many styles), and given to the Popes by the Emperor Constantine —it's often referred to as **the** Cathedral of the world. Among the treasures of the Church are a piece of the table of The Last Supper (facing the Apse door); a part of the original altar on which St. Peter said mass; and a great bronze door (now in the middle of the main entrance) from the Senate House of the Roman Forum. . . . Across the Square are the **Scala Santa** or **Holy Stairs** (located in a building which used to serve as residence and private chapel of the Popes), which consist of twenty-eight steps from Pontius Pilate's Villa brought to Rome by St. Helen (Constantine's mother); it is supposed to be the stairway that Christ ascended when he was condemned to death. Pilgrims from all over the world come here to do penance by climbing up the steps on their knees, receiving years of absolution for their efforts. . . . Interesting for a short visit is the **Church of St. Maria Maggiore** (located a few blocks from the Railway Station, off the Via Cavour). Built on the site of the so-called 'Miracle of Pope Liberio' (snow fell here in August), it has The Holy Crib, and a beautiful ceiling made of the gold that Columbus brought back from the New World. . . . Unless you're on a Pilgrimage, you may not wish to see **San Lorenzo Fuori le Mura** (St. Lawrence Outside the Walls, located alongside Rome's Monumental Cemetery; take bus #66 from the Via Nazionale), which does not offer as much of interest as other major basilicas. . . . But **San Paolo Fuori le Mura** (St. Paul's Outside the Walls) is outstanding: a 20 minute ride from central Rome on bus #55 (catch it along Via Nazionale, or take the Metropolitana), and remarkable for its sheer size—second only to St. Peter's in Rome. This great cathedral, with the remains of the Apostle under the Confessional Altar, was almost completely destroyed by fire in 1823. What remains of historical importance are a 5th century mosaic on the Arch of Triumph, a Tabernacle by Arnolfo di Cambio over the Main Altar, and to the right of the Main Altar, a superbly sculptured Pascal Candelabrum dating from 1170 (also, take a look at the lovely 13th century Cloisters here). What's 'new' in the Basilica and of special interest are the unique alabaster windows which suffuse the Church with soft and romantic lighting; and the 275 mosaic portraits (all around the upper wall) of all the Popes since St. Peter. If the main door of the Church is closed, enter around the side. . . . And finally, between St. Maria Maggiore and the Colosseum, or at the bottom of Via Cavour (go up a long stairway), on the Piazza St. Pietro, there's **St. Pietro in Vincoli** (St. Peter in Chains), which does have St. Peter's chains, but is notable chiefly because it houses the unfinished tomb of Pope Julius II by Michelangelo, with his magnificent 'Moses.'

Just for fun

"And now, if you're feeling in a prankish mood, you might next head for the **Coemeterium Capuccinorum** (Capuchin Church) at the bottom of the Via Veneto (#27) near the Piazza Barberini, where the monks have made decorations out of the skeletons of their dead brothers. Walk through the Church, and behind the Altar on your right you'll find a stairway to the bone cellar where every inch of the ceiling is decorated with bones. Even the lamps are made of bones and skulls. It's like a Hitchcock nightmare, with mummified monks bowing graciously amid the rubble of pelvi and tibia. Open from 9:30 to 12 and from 3 to 6, and entirely free, except for a small donation which you'll want to make.

Some final data

"While the **Vatican Museums** charge a high 1,500 lire entrance fee (and are free only on the last Sunday of each month!), there is more here than one can possibly see on a single visit. I suggest you take the elevator to the top floor and work your way down. In addition to the Sistine Chapel and the Raphael Rooms, there is also the Pio-Clementino Museum (ancient Greek and Roman sculpture) adjacent to the Belvedere Courtyard (with four corners of masterpieces, including the 'Apollo' and the famous 'Laocoon and His Sons'), and the stunning ancient Greek fragment 'The Torso of Belvedere'; the Egyptian Museum; the Etruscan Museum; the Borgia Apartments; the Pinacoteca, a picture gallery with a fine collection; a missionary museum; and much more. Keep in mind that the museum is closed the first three Sundays of each month, and holidays (otherwise, open 9 to 4). . . . Close to St. Peter's and the Vatican and dominating the skyline, is the imposing **Castle Sant' Angelo,** charging an entrance fee of 200 lire on weekdays, 100 lire on Sundays and holidays; open daily except Mondays, from 9 to 2, on Sundays until 1. The Castle is a large, dreary, maze-like building, full of history, but you'll have to climb a very long ramp and interminable stairs before you get to where the action is. Built originally in 139 by the Emperor Hadrian as his mausoleum, it has through the ages served many and varied purposes—as a fort, a Papal refuge (there's a tunnel connecting the Castle to the Vatican), and a prison (among its inmates were Cellini and the notorious Cenci family). There are numerous points of interest in the Castle (weapon and uniform exhibits, etc.), but don't miss, in particular, the ornately decorated Pauline Hall, Perseus Room, or the Library on the third tier. There are also excellent views of Rome from the high terraces of the Castle, and a place for light refreshment at the top. . . . If you have spare time in Rome, spend it in the enchanted **Piazza della Bocca della Verità** (on the Tiber opposite the Ponte Palatino, within hiking distance of the Campidoglio Hill, the Palatine, and Circo Massimo). Nearby are the arches underneath which the Cloaca Maxima once dumped its sewage into the Tiber, and on the Piazza itself are two ancient buildings: the **Temple of Fortuna Virilis,** a small square Temple with Ionic columns built at the end of the second century B.C.—it is the oldest, 'still in one piece' (miraculously) building of its kind in Rome—and the younger (100 B.C.), round, and graceful **Temple of Vesta.** These two structures, seen together, are majestic spellbinders. As for the Piazza itself, it's named after the 'Mouth of Truth', a stone mask which supposedly has the power to bite off the hand of a liar. If you're anxious to test your integrity in this way, you'll find the mask on the porch of **The Church of Santa Maria in Cosmedin** (8th century, built on pagan ruins, with ancient columns inside; it, too, is worth a short visit). . . . From the **Pincio,** at the edge of one side of the Borghese Park, you'll have a beautiful view of Rome. Directly below, on the **Piazza del Popolo,** the **Church of St. Maria del Popolo** (completed in the 15th century) has many treasures, including the Chigi Chapel designed by Raphael, and two enthralling paintings by Caravaggio (to the left of the Main Altar).

A Short Trip to Tivoli

"Tivoli, where you can visit the **Villa d'Este** and **Hadrian's Villa** (in Italian, 'Villa Adriana'), is about forty-five minutes outside Rome—from Via Gaeta, a little street off the Piazza della Repubblica, near Terminal Station, take the coach marked 'Autobus Per Tivoli' for a round-trip fare of 1,400 lire. Buses run nearly every half hour, but check the timetable coming back or you'll wind up spending the night in Tivoli. The most efficient way to make the tour is to take the bus all the way into Tivoli and see the Villa d'Este first, then take Bus '2' or '4' from town to Hadrian's Villa (Bus '2' deposits you closer to the entrance).

"The **Villa d'Este,** built by Cardinal d'Este in the 16th century on the site of what is virtually an oasis in dry territory, is the grandest happy play-ground of water you'll ever see. The tiered garden of trees and near-tropical vegetation, interspersed with every conceivable size and type of water fountain, has a most delightful and intriguing effect. It also happens to be a great engineering feat, for the 500 varied fountains are run strictly through the aid of nature. No gadgets or pumps whatsoever were used. (Like the saying, there's water everywhere, but only one fountain is safe to drink from, so be careful). Hours are from 9 to an hour before sunset every day, for a 200 lire entrance fee (Sundays free).

"The **Villa Adriana** is open every day except Monday from 9 til about an hour before sunset (summers as late as 8 p.m.; admittance up to 1 hour before the Villa closes), for a 150 lire entrance (Sunday free, and if you're going by car, you can drive in part of the way for an additional 100 lire, well worth it in shoe leather, and the parking lot inside is free). The mis-named Villa, which was Hadrian's Hideaway, turns out actually to be a small-sized town where the Emperor tried to recreate architecturally all the beautiful places in the world he'd seen. Work was begun in 118 A.D., and it is thought that the Emperor himself closely supervised the designs. Among many other ruins, you'll see the Circular Portico or Maritime Theatre, a small circular apartment completely surrounded by water (it's thought that Hadrian came here for quiet contemplation), which is in sufficiently restored condition to allow you easily to fill in the gaps; and the marvelous Canopus, an artificial valley with a gorgeous pond decorated with statues, surrounded by small apartments close to the Bath, and bounded on one side by the small museum at the side of the pond, which houses statues that once stood on the Canopus (many archaeologically interesting pieces found on this site have been moved elsewhere—lots are in Roman museums). In its time, the Villa Adriana must have afforded its residents a kind of luxury undreamt of today. It's still an enchanted place."

READERS' SIGHTSEEING SUGGESTIONS: "No one should leave Rome without visiting **New Rome.** This is the section called EUR, and is reachable by taking the Metropolitana (subway) to the Esposizione (West or East) stop. There is a splendid view, with the wonderful sports stadium at the top of the hill, a magnificent sculpture garden, and lakes and play areas all around it. On the other side is a modern rendition of the Colosseum which is used as a state office building, a magnificent new cathedral, and dozens of beautifully landscaped private homes. New Rome was started by Mussolini as a showplace of Fascism, and completed by the Republic as a showplace of Italian architecture and design, and it is every bit as charming as Old Rome. For the young, sturdy readers, there are small paddle boats for rent at the modest charge of 1,200 lire an hour on the artificial lake in front of the Stadium. An hour's paddle will give you a cool, enjoyable, everchanging view of some of the most beautiful scenery south of Tivoli" (Burt Wolfson, New York, New York). . . . "The best museum for students of Latin and Ancient History is the **Museo di Civiltà Romana,** in the new section of E.U.R., easily accessible by subway. There are separate rooms devoted to Caesar, Cicero and Virgil" (Mrs. Doris M. Bacon, East Aurora, N.Y.; note by AF: hours are 9 a.m. to 2 p.m., daily except Monday, admission 200 lire). . . . "Add to your visit to **St. Peter's** the 800-lire elevator ride to the roof, to view those splendid statues that edge the roof. Then continue your ascent of the dome itself by a winding stair for a magnificent view of Rome and the Vatican gardens. You can also get onto a lofty balcony overlooking the interior of St. Peter's" (Thomas S. Mortimer, Silver Spring, Maryland). . . . "Please stress **Trajan's Market** a bit more—it's the only one place in Rome where, thanks to reconstruction, a visitor can have a sense of what it was like to walk down a Roman street in a market district. It's also very quiet and has few visitors, and is a good place to escape the bustle and noise, or eat a picnic lunch" (John Goldrosen, Chapel Hill, North Carolina). . . . "A tip for tourists who go to the **Sistine Chapel:** bring along small opera glasses, as the ceiling is very high. These would also be useful on the tours of the gorgeous palaces all over Europe to study more closely the ceiling paintings" (Mrs. Paul Lauzon, Pittsfield, Mass.). . . . "Anyone who has read Kenneth Clark's 'Civilization' will want to see Bernini's 'St. Teresa in Ecstasy' which many pinpoint as the embodiment of high Baroque. The sculpture is to the left of the main altar in the Church of Santa Maria della Vittoria on the Piazza San Bernardo (across the street from Saint Susanna's)" (Janice R. Bellace, London, England). . . . "The Metro Underground, main entrance in the Termini, costs 250 lire, stops at the Colosseum and the Basilica of St. Paul. Literature buffs may wish to get off at the Piramide stop to visit the **Protestant cemetery** for the grave of John Keats, without his name but with the epitaph he wished: "Here lies one whose name was writ in water' " (James L. Rohrbaugh, Seattle, Washington). . . . "The graves of Keats, Shelley, and John Addington Symonds, in the Protestant cemetery, deserve a visit by those interested in the 'English Rome' " (Lawrence Poston, Lincoln, Nebraska). . . . "Most visitors to **Piazza Venezia** in Rome look up at the famous balcony where Mussolini made the world tremble with his terrifying threats, but very few know it is possible to enter for a few lire through a side entrance on the left into a quiet, beautiful courtyard, up steps trod by numerous heads of state and finally into a huge palace salon which Mussolini used as his office. It gives you an eerie, spooky feeling" (Professor Carlo Vacca, Framingham, Massachusetts). . . . "If you are going to **Tivoli** from Rome on any conveyance other than a tour bus, try and stop at one of the travertine quarries along the road. They have been worked for two thousand years and the whole bit is free. The one where we stopped was quarrying 25-ton chunks for a new opera building. The foreman's English and my Italian were both nonexistent, but we got along fine and he was most friendly and happy to explain as best he could, and show us where to stand for the best view" (Daniel M. Kappel, Poughkeepsie, New York). . . . "A 'do-it-yourself' walking tour: from **Terminal Station,** walk first to the **Colosseum,** then to the **Roman Forum,** then up the **Spanish Steps** to the **Villa Borghese.** After visiting the museum there, take a #30 bus from in back of the zoo to **St. Peter's.** From there, a #64 bus back to **Terminal Station.** Warning: this is only for the hardy" (Roselyn Yung Yap, Cambridge, Mass.). . . . "All the ruins are best seen at night, when fantasizing is possible" (Mark Estren, Middletown, Connecticut).

READER'S SIGHTSEEING TIP: "The real money-saving idea for those who can prove they are teachers, professors or students—immediately upon arrival in Rome, drop everything and rush to the 'Ministero della Pubblica Istruzione (Direzione Generale Antichità e Belle Arti), at 18 Piazza del Popolo. Here, for 500 lire (60¢) they will issue a pass which will give free admission to national galleries, etc., all over Italy! Then you will save the 500 lire at the first place you visit, be it the Roman Forum, Tivoli Gardens, or whatever. At each place you visit, you merely sign the guest register and are given a free admission ticket. Otherwise, you pay and pay and pay" (Harry Sortais, Monterey, California; note by AF: business hours at the Ministry (at least for securing 'gratuito' cards) are limited to 10 a.m. to 1 p.m., Monday through Saturday, but the card is invaluable and will be issued not only to you, but to your non-teaching or non-student wives, brothers, sisters and children. The same museum pass can usually be purchased by anyone, teacher or no, at any U.S. office of Alitalia (the one for mail order purchases being Alitalia, 666 Fifth Avenue, New York, N.Y. 10019) or the Italian Line, and the $1 payment brings spectacular savings, even though it's valid only at national museums and excavations, and not at municipal or civic museums (such as most of those in Venice). Once at the Capitoline in Rome, which doesn't accept the pass, I received a discount upon shyly presenting it at the ticket window! Still another museum pass for readers not in the academic profession can be had through membership in **Italia Nostra,** 287 Corso Vittorio Emanuele II, whose 3,000 lire yearly fee will also bring you free entrance (via a membership card) to most of the museums of Italy). . . . "Here in Germany I got my museum card (it's called a 'Kulturausweis' or 'Museumkarte') for less than a dollar from the Dresdner Bank, together with a booklet of some 250 names of Italian art collections, giving the handy information of what they exhibit, where they are and when they are open" (Sabino A. Vengco, Jr., Trier, Germany). . . . "I obtained my museum card in Vienna at the Osterreichische Landerbank at 4-6 Kärntnerstrasse, a couple of doors from the ENIT office, at a cost of 21 schillings (about $1.60 at the time)" (Lynn Petersen, Hollywood, California). . . . Final note from AF: students possessing an International Student

Identification Card need buy none of these museum tickets, as their student card will itself be accepted as a pass to most Italian museums.

READERS ON SCOOTERS: "We rented a scooter from **Scoot-A-Long** at Via Cavour 302, near the Coliseum, for the low cost of 16,000 lire ($19.27) a day, plus gas. Then we went to Naples for the day, leaving in the morning and returning at night after a wonderful day of sightseeing" (Janice Wakelin, Rome, Italy). . . . "A fine place for renting licensed motor scooters is the **Scoot-A-Long Agency,** Via Cavour 302, tel. 678-0206, for approximately $19.27 a day, less on a weekly basis. This is more expensive than a car for the daily rate, *but* there is no kilometer charge and that is where you save money. It's also a heck of a lot more fun and convenient for parking in overcrowded Rome. We used both car and then scooter and much preferred the latter" (Dana A. Regillo, Lexington, Mass.). . . . "My wife and I rented a Vespa for one month for 160,000 lire ($193) from the **Scoot-A-Long** office, and traveled on it through Italy, Southern France, Spain, Morocco, Algeria and Tunis. That's quite an inexpensive way to travel, and we had little difficulty with the scooter" (William D. Jeffrey, Chicago, Illinois; note by AF: Scoot-A-Long has been known to reduce the price to 13,000 lire per day on rentals in excess of 7 days).

TERME DI CARACALLA: Open-air opera at the Baths of Caracalla (bus #93 takes you there) is one of the great summer events of Europe. The opera stage is set amid the gigantic ruins of the former Roman bath house, and the setting is spectacular—for certain productions, the ruins are actually employed as part of the scenery. Performances are scheduled almost nightly from July 4 to August 15, with tickets ranging downward from a high of 6,000 and 4,000 lire, to 3,000 lire, the 3,000 lire seats being perfectly satisfactory; they can be purchased in advance at the Rome Opera House (off the Via Firenze) from 10 to 1 and from 4 to 6:30. Try, of course, to get to any of the performances, but if a production of "Aida" is scheduled, then rise from a sick bed to be in attendance, because you'll see a spectacle that's equaled by no other opera company. A near-army of extras fills the stage during the triumphal march of the second act, and an elephant or else a brace of horses comes charging in at the climax. With all this, the voices may seem overlooked, but the overall effect is stupefying.

For summer concerts in Rome, again from July 1 to August 15, you'll want to be at the periodic recitals of the renowned Santa Cecilia Orchestra, performed at the **Basilica of Massenzio** (entrance on the Via dei Fori Imperiali, with the background setting being the Roman Forum). But take nothing better than the 3,000 lire ($3.61) seats—only the crowd from the Hotel Excelsior goes for the higher-priced variety.

EVENING ENTERTAINMENT: The discotheques and nightclubs are atrociously expensive, and many visitors simply devote the evening hours to a leisurely, late meal. Apart from that, the most popular form of evening entertainment in Rome is to sit at a sidewalk cafe on the Via Veneto, and watch the passing parade—a wonderfully varied procession of chic women, tailored men, types and characters of every sort. The cafes charge no more than 1,200 lire for a coffee, and a coffee will last you an hour or even two. An interesting sidelight: each year on the Via Veneto, one or two particular cafes become mystically selected as the places to sit. Their sidewalk tables are then fully packed, while the cafe next door—same prices, same decor—is empty and forlorn. The next year, an Italian movie star may take a liking to the sidewalk tables of the formerly-forlorn cafe, and the situation is instantly reversed. I sometimes wonder how Via Veneto cafe owners sleep at night; in 1979, Doney's and Rosati's were the favored spots, but who knows what next year will bring? In any event, be sure to spend a few evening hours simply sitting there over a $1.45 (1,200 lire) coffee; you'll be glad you did.

One other suggestion for evening activities: go to a museum. There is at least one major museum open every weekday night in Rome, between the hours of 8:30 and 11 p.m. That permits you to keep up with your sightseeing schedule in Rome, and to do it at the best time of day. While these late-hour evenings vary—and must always be currently checked—the **Capitoline Museum and Conservatori** atop the Campidoglio Hill (one of which is devoted to paintings, the other to sculpture, with one 300-lire ticket admitting you to both), most definitely stay open late on Saturday evenings, from 8:30 to 11 p.m. and daily except Mondays and Saturdays from 5 to 8 p.m.

OUTING: The subway in Rome (the "Metropolitana") has only one line—from the front of Terminal Station to the port of Ostia, on the Mediterranean—but what a line that is! If you buy a 500-lire ticket (1,000 lire round-trip) and stay on the train until two stops beyond Ostia, you'll be at the sea, within a few blocks of several public beaches. But if you get off at "Ostia Antica," two stops before Ostia, you'll find excavations that rival Pompeii. Ostia was a well-developed port in the days of ancient Rome during the reign of the Emperor Claudius, particularly—and archaeologists are currently digging in a huge area of the imperial city. Entrance to the grounds (which are closed on Mondays) is only 150 lire, and you can eat a picnic lunch while sitting on the ruins.

READERS ON AN EXCURSION: "From Rome, it is simple for readers to make their own trip to Pompeii, Sorrento and Capri. Take the early train to Naples (4,650 lire; round-trip fare between Rome and Naples is 9,300 lire) and in Naples walk two blocks to the Circumvesuvio station. Here, obtain a ticket to Pompeii and stop off at Pompeii for at least 1½ hours to visit the museum and the ruins; then take the Circumvesuvio train to Sorrento, and use Sorrento as your overnight base in preference to going to the much higher priced island of Capri. After breakfast, take the ferry from the harbour to the Blue Grotto and Capri. In Capri ride the funicular to the top level and make good use of the buses which take you, inter alia, to Marina Piccola (where you can swim—don't forget to go inside the Canzone del Mare where there is a lovely swimming pool); and to Anacapri, where you can take a cable car to the top of the mountain and enjoy a panoramic view of the island. To return to Naples, you can take a boat from Sorrento (1 hour)" (Lenard G. Lever and Ben-Zion Surdut, Cape Town, South Africa). . . . "
Rome-Naples-Sorrento-Capri: This 4-day trip was one of the high points of our travels this year. From Rome to Naples, take the train from Terminal Station at 8 a.m.—9,300 lire, round-trip, second class—2½ hours to Naples. There, about 100 yards in front of the station, is a Garibaldi statue and the street car lines in front run on Corso Garibaldi. Take bus #49 to the National Museum to see the wonderful friezes, statues, bronzes and mosaics from Herculaneum and Pompeii—the best works from both places are here. Now take bus #54—on the left one block as you leave the museum, to Portici, then bus #225, from the same stop at Portici to Herculaneum (Ercolano in Italian). Here, don't hire a guide but wander and let the custodian for each section tell you about their sections—in broken English but very understandable. Plan on about 2 hours, for the things they can show you are very interesting. Then take the #225 bus to the R.R. Station, at Naples. Spend the night at Hotel Mignon—7 Corso Novara—two blocks on the right as you leave the station. (This hotel compares with the Pensione Texas in Rome). They charge 19,000 lire for an excellent double without bath, but with breakfast and all else included, 12,000 lire single.

"In the morning, take the Circumvesuviana R.R. from the station at 339 Corso Garibaldi—same place where you take the bus to the museum—buy a ticket to Sorrento (600 lire) and get off at Pompeii. Again make friends with the custodians in each block and they will show you unusual sights for a small tip. Then get back on the train and continue to Sorrento.

"At Sorrento, you can buy a round-trip ticket to Capri for 3,000 lire which includes the boat direct to the Blue Grotto. The boat waits while you transfer to a rowboat for 1,500 lire and your pass (without the pass it's an additional 1,000 lire). See the grotto, and then the boat will take you to Marina Grande, the big port. See the island, then in the afternoon the same boat takes you back to Sorrento. To get back to Rome on any day but Sunday, take the bus from the main square near the Campidoglio. On Sundays you'll have to take the Circumvesuviana to Naples and the train from Naples to Rome" (Mrs. E. R. Toporeck, Santa Barbara, California).

FLEA MARKET: Though nearly every major European capital has a Sunday "flea market," I like the one in Rome best. It's cheaper than its Paris equivalent, provides better bargaining opportunities (offer only 50% of the asking prices, and stick to your guns), and has a far wider selection of articles—everything from seventeenth-century candelabra to second-hand toothbrushes!

For those unfamiliar with the term, "flea market" refers to a big open field in Rome on which merchants, every Sunday, set up make-shift booths, or spread a blanket on the ground, for the sale of every conceivable secondhand article—clothes, old gramophones, wooden Sicilian statues, old busts and medals of Mussolini, fraying-at-the-edges etchings and posters, antique door-knobs. If you bargain properly, you can stock up on amazing values, limited only by your estimate of what you'll be able to stuff in your suitcase. Naturally, you'll be heartbroken over having to pass up the bulkier items that are too heavy to lug across Europe. Hope still dreams of the two 6-foot-long torches-on-a-pole (painted pale blue and yellow, the kind that lean out from a wall, at an angle), which we couldn't carry away from our last trip to the Rome flea market. They were priced at $30 apiece; they would've gone for $150 or more at the furniture auctions in New York.

The flea market in Rome is located at the Porta di Portese (bus #57 from Terminal Station goes within 3 blocks of it; get off at the stop called "Ponte Sublicio"), in the Trastevere section—ask anyone to point the way—and operates only once a week, on Sunday, from 6 a.m. to 1 p.m., when it closes punctually. It's such an exciting, colorful sight that I've placed it here, rather than in the shopping chapter of the book, because you'll want to see it, even if you don't plan to buy a thing.

The daily market

The huge and bustling **Piazza Vittorio Emanuele** (to the side and behind the railway station, within walking distance of it) is the daily grocery-and-clothes market of Rome, an open-air fiesta of such exotica as you'll never find at the A&P: live chickens, pigeons and rabbits, tripe, octopus, mortadella (a kind of pork sausage), all sorts of other cheeses, live fish, ten types of olives, canaries, kidneys, cheap shoes, pants and ladies blouses (on the far side), an area inside for eating the picnic meals you'll pick up here (try 300 lire of sour olives, then cheese and bread), and a children's playground to boot. Don't miss.

HOURS: Rome closes down tight from noon to four p.m., when people return home for their biggest meal of the day and a snooze. They go back to work at 4, stay hard at it until 8 p.m. . . . This will significantly affect your eating hours, for no restaurant really begins serving meals until 1 p.m. (for lunch) and 7 p.m. (for dinner). Don't show up before those times, or you may have to wait unattended in an empty restaurant. . . . You'll find, by the way, that the habit of a noon-day siesta in sunny Rome is a marvelous way to stay refreshed during the remaining, cooler periods of the day. And since all stores and museums close down for those four hours, it's fruitless to spend the time on your normal sightseeing rounds.

ODDS AND ENDS: No Italian restaurant serves spaghetti with meat balls, and no one here has heard of biscuit tortoni. . . . The pasta dishes are eaten by discerning Italians only at lunch-time; the evening meal is a lighter one, and begins with soup, not pasta. . . . The funniest travel story I know, is a true one, and concerns an American couple who asked the owner of a pensione in Rome to recommend a tourist attraction which they might visit. He advised them to see the Roman Forum. They returned two hours later, white with anger, grim and trembling. "I had no idea you Italians were so nationalistic," said the wife. "Our first day in Rome, and you send us to see what the American bombs did." . . . Read *I, Claudius,* by Robert Graves, and you'll be able to create a wonderful fantasy-world about the ruins and sights in Rome. Or, for a more contemporary view, read H. V. Morton's magnificent *A Traveler in Rome.* The city requires advance preparation and study for its maximum enjoyment. . . . One of the time-honored methods of touring the city for a pittance is to take a bus ride on the "Circolare Sinistra" bus that starts at Terminal Station and makes a loop through the city, ending at Terminal Station, for 100 lire. The CS bus has now been redesignated as Bus #30; walk 50-or-so yards to the front of the station, turn left, and you'll see its pick-up point. . . . Alternatively, you can bear in mind that bus #64 (which is often a double-decker) starts at Terminal Station, goes down the important Via Nazionale into the Piazza Venezia, turns over to the Largo Argentina, and then crosses the Tiber to St. Peter's, a trip with a goal. But remember that the museum areas of the Vatican are closed after 4 p.m. . . . And look for that little bus station at the corner of Via Gaeta and Largo Giovanni Montemartini, behind the Museo alle Terme (near the Piazza Esedra). It's from here that a bus leaves every half-hour for Tivoli, for a one-way fare of only 700 lire. Once at Tivoli, it'll cost you 200 lire to enter the gardens. . . . A gentle warning: Rome's 100 lire bus fare is, at the moment, the biggest bargain in town, but not if your pocket is picked on the bus; keep your wallet where you can feel it. . . . Though every concierge, information office, and taxi driver will deny it, there is a cheap (300 lire) city bus to the secondary airport of Rome, Ciampino, from which charter flights leave. It's the A3, which stops—among other places—at Via Giolitti, near the air terminal at Termini Station. . . . The international hospital of Rome, with many English-speaking doctors, is **Salvator Mundi,** 67 Viale Mura Gianicolensi (phone 586-041). Ask for the Directress, who is especially helpful. . . . **"Baby Parking,"** a day-night nursery at 16 Via Santa Prisca (phone 577-8638), near the Piazza Venezia, will take care of your toddlers up to the age of ten, for 5,000 lire per hour. . . . In months when the Pope is in Rome (usually every month other than July and August), Papal audiences are held on Wednesdays at 11 a.m., at a new audience hall near St. Peter's. You can obtain a ticket to attend either at the Bishop's Office for United States Visitors to the Vatican, at 30 Via dell' Umiltà (phone 672-2256), one block from the Trevi Fountains (the office preferring that you write ahead, adding the zip code 00187 to their Rome address), or at the easily-found headquarters of the English-speaking Paulist Fathers, in the **Church of Santa Susanna,** at 14 Via XX Settembre on the Piazza S. Bernardo (near the Piazza della Repubblica); their hours are daily from 9 to 12 and 4 to 7; go there to reserve a ticket; pick up the ticket between 4 and 6 on Tuesday. If you can't attend a Wednesday audience, you can see the Pope—but from a much further distance—at noon on most Sundays, when he appears promptly at the strike of the hour upon a high balcony overlooking the square of St. Peter's Basilica, to deliver a short sermon to an applauding crowd below. That's almost every Sunday, in fact.

A LAUNDROMAT IN ROME? I've found two standouts, of which the most handy is the **Lavanderia Automatica**, at 11 Via Montebello, just off the Via Volturno, which is to the right of Terminal Station as you leave it; 3,800 lire for 5 kilos of wash, including drying. While your laundry dries, you can eat across the street at the **Trattoria Carosi,** 28 Via Montebello, which serves three courses, wine, bread and service included, for 4,000 lire ($4.81), or take a haircut at the genuine Italian hairdresser located at 15 Via Montebello. In the area of the Vatican, the **Lavanderia Automatica** at 189 Borgo Pio charges 2,500 lire for 3 kilograms, 750 lire for each additional kilo.

AMERICAN G.I.'s: Numerous facilities are available to American military on leave in Rome at the **USO (17),** 2 Via della Conciliazione. The center is open daily from 9 a.m. to 7 p.m., runs low-priced tours of the city, helps arrange Papal audiences, offers information, aid and advice, and throws in nursery, kitchen and shower facilities. Phone 656-4272 for further details.

TRANSPORTATION TIP: Taxicabs in Rome are painted either yellow or green with black trimming. They have meters, and they're moderate in price—around 4,000 lire for the trip from the railroad station to St. Peter's. Steer clear of the little men who operate cars painted in different colors, who will tell you they're taxi drivers. They're not, and the prices they charge are three times what a regular cab would cost.

A READER'S COMMENT: "There is a suggestion I would like to see printed somewhere, for women traveling alone, or in the company of other women, or with their young children, as I was doing in Latin countries. That is, not to be insulted by, or to ignore, the open admiration that the Latins have for the female. They admire beauty in everything, be it a woman, a tree, a ripe fruit or vegetable. When they speak to a stranger at the Piazza della Repubblica or Via Veneto or Piazza San Marco, they are not being fresh. Hopeful perhaps, but they never intend to be rude. They are curious, intrigued and sincere in their admiration. Time and again, throughout Italy and France, I saw American women asserting their virtue by repulsing the Latin, when all he wished was a little warmth of conversation. The woman is not respected for her behavior; she is considered cold, unpleasant and unfeminine, and conclusions are drawn that we American women are all this way. I believe it would be safe to say that should the woman prove to be simpatica, the Latin would not object if events developed beyond the conversation, and in fact would bring all his charm into play to bring this about. If, however, this is not agreeable to the woman, she may politely refuse (this may be necessary several times, a bit firmer each time) and that will be that. The pride of the Latin seems stronger than the desire. If the woman refuses smilingly, she wins his respect and a true admirer who leaves with a pleasant memory of an enjoyable interlude and with his dreams intact" (Mrs. Harlan Hall, Baton Rouge, Louisiana).

————————

By now you'll be weary of this constant touring. It's time to stretch out on a warm, sunny beach, with the blue Mediterranean lapping at your feet. The French Riviera is next—on $15 a day.

Chapter XV

NICE

Bikini Land without the Bite

THE FRENCH RIVIERA is a never-never land for many American tourists. Tales of outrageous prices, of extortion-type menus and hijacking hotel bills, have all combined to scare the more cautious traveler away. Any substance to these fears?

In resort towns like Juan-les-Pins or St. Jean-Cap-Ferrat, yes. These are the haunts of international high society—the Jackie Onassis set—and prices are wondrous to behold. But Nice is different. Endowed with all the beauty of the Riviera—the palm trees, the Mediterranean, the sun—Nice is nevertheless a city, and not simply a cluster of elegant hotels, snuggled around a small bay. If you'll take time to learn the lay-out of that city, you can live moderately in Nice, just as do many middle-class French citizens, who flock here for their summer vacations and live on costs that approximate $15—and less—per day.

HOTELS: To understand the hotel situation in Nice, look at our map, and imagine that you are walking from the railroad station to the sea. As you near the water, hotel prices increase; arriving at the waterside, hotel prices become astronomic; if you stay near the railroad station, hotel costs are entirely moderate. While there are one or two outstanding exceptions to this rule, the bulk of our hotel selections will be found in the station district.

Don't assume, though, that staying in a hotel near the top of the map will keep you from the all-important bathing and sunning facilities of the town. Nice is packed into a relatively small area, and the railroad station is only a short walk from the beach. Furthermore, the station section is as quiet and clean as any other in the city.

The street which runs in front of the railroad station is the Avenue Thiers, and running perpendicular to it are a series of little side-streets—the treasured locales of my favorite budget hotels in Nice. The hotel to which I head happens to be one of the plainest and most basic in the area—don't stop here if you require creature comforts. But the **Hotel Darcy (1)**, 28 Rue d'Angleterre (phone 88-67-06), not only has rock-bottom, third-class prices (38 francs—$8.75—single; 56 francs—$12.88—double; 70 francs triple; 85 francs quadruple; with breakfast, service and taxes included), but has for years served as a virtual "clubhouse" for its $15-a-day guests, for whom its proprietors—currently M. and Mme. Servole—act as translators, information center, ticket bureau and confidantes. Whenever Hope and I look in on the Darcy, we are invariably besieged by young couples and students, all begging us to sing the praises of the hotel. We fully agree.

THE FRENCH FRANC: Presently exchanged at the rate of 4.30 francs to one dollar, the French franc is therefore worth slightly under 23¢.

There are immediate, nearby alternatives to the Darcy, if the Darcy is packed: first, the 29-room **Hotel Novelty** at 26 Rue d'Angleterre (phone 87-51-73), with nearly identical rates for clean, sunny and typically-French rooms, well-maintained by English-speaking owners, the Truchets; and then, the much better, impressive former mansion that's now the **Hotel Belle Meuière**, at 21 Avenue Durante (phone 88-66-15), two short blocks from the Darcy, and with a gravel courtyard in front for parking. At the latter, bathless doubles can run as high as 58 francs ($13.34), again with breakfast, service and tax included.

Up in quality

Back in the more familiar area of second-class accommodations, the older tourists will find an exceptional value in the sunny, pleasant, and elevator-equipped **Hotel D'Orsay (2)**, at 20 Rue Alsace-Lorraine (phone 88-45-02), just two short blocks down from the station, and slightly to the east of it. 49 francs for a bathless single with breakfast, 63 francs ($14.50) for a double, in a clean and quiet building. The D'Orsay merged, several years ago, with the Hotel Azurea, next door, and now offers plentiful rooms, as well as full-board arrangements in winter to retired Americans. But if the D'Orsay is full, the **Hotel Normandie,** around the corner at 18 Rue Paganini (phone 88-48-83), can take the overflow (but for $2.50 per person more, as virtually all rooms here are with private shower); while the newly-redecorated, elevator-equipped **Hotel Trocadero,** 7 Rue de Belgique (phone 88-24-31), will put you up for 75 francs ($17.25) for a double without bath, but with private w.c., breakfast, taxes and service included; and with discounts for families or groups of three persons sharing a two-person room. To give you an idea of the respectability of this budget establishment, the Trocadero's management makes a point of personally informing guests about the Sunday-morning services at "The Church of the Holy Spirit," 21 Boulevard Victor Hugo, a short walk away. Highly recommended.

For readers who can't take another step, the 61-room **Hotel des Nations (3)**, 25 Avenue Durante (phone 88-30-58), is located directly in front of the railroad station (but faces a large garden on the other side), and has always found favor with $15-a-day'ers. Average rates of 48 francs ($11.04) for a single with breakfast, but without private bath; 60 to 65 francs, depending on size of the room, for a double with two breakfasts, and with service and taxes included. While the superficial impression of the hotel, from the railroad station, is not a good one, once inside you'll not only look out upon the aforementioned garden, but find a quiet reading room, surprisingly quiet bedrooms, parking space for your car, and rates of less than 42 francs ($9.66) a night for double rooms on the 5th floor. A good budget choice.

Along the Avenue Thiers, which runs in front of the station, there's a great variety of budget establishments, some with rock-bottom prices, but none as well recommended as those listed above. The **Hotel Lyon-Milan (4)**, at 5 Avenue Thiers (phone 88-22-87), typical of the station hotels, charges 44 francs ($10.12) for one person, 55 francs ($12.65) for two, 72 francs ($16.56) for a three-person room, 95 francs ($21.85) for four, including service and taxes. The hotel is clean and well-maintained by an owner who has traveled in the United States. . . . Up the street, the **Hotel Choiseul (5)**, 29 Avenue Thiers (phone 88-96-81), is another budget-priced hotel, which possesses an elevator and places a telephone in each room. Rates: 77 francs ($17.71) for a double room and two breakfasts, 46 for a single. . . . The **Hotel Rochambeau**, 27 Avenue Thiers (phone 88-96-18), charges 68 francs for their bathless doubles (with breakfast); and at the other end of the street, the **Hotel de Berne (6)**, 1 Avenue Thiers, will quote only slightly higher rates: 75 francs double, including breakfast (in any month other than August).

Near the sea

Now we'll take up those rare exceptions to the rule that moderately-priced hotels are to be found only in the station area. One block from the sea, directly behind the swank hotels of the "Promenade des Anglais" ("Europe on $50 a Day"), the little Avenue de Suède houses two exciting finds: the **Hotel Meurice (7)**, 14 Avenue de Suède (phone 87-74-93), which charges 79 francs ($18.17) for a bathless double room, breakfast, service and taxes included; and the recently-upgraded **Hotel Harvey**, 18 Rue de Suède (phone 87-78-00) which asks a splurgly 135 francs ($31.05) for its double rooms *with* private bath (and that includes breakfast, service and tax). Lobby of the Meurice is on the second floor of its building (take the elevator); and rooms are cool and almost antiseptically clean. The Harvey was thoroughly re-done in recent years by its new and charming owners, the English-speaking Passeris, who installed air conditioning and an elevator. If both hotels are filled, then try the cute, little **Hotel Paris-Nice**, again only a block from the beach (but at 58 Rue de France, phone 88-38-61), with rates of 86 francs ($19.78) single, 130 francs ($29.90) for a good double with private bath, with new carpeting, breakfast, service and taxes included. That's just behind the deluxe Hotel Negresco. If the Paris-Nice can't take you, walk over to **La Gavotte**, 7 Rue Halevy (second floor), phone 87-13-87, only half a block from the sea, where Monsieur D. Yon charges 60 francs ($13.80) double (French beds only), breakfast and all else included. Formerly a pension, the Gavotte is now a hotel serving no meals other than breakfast; but the kind proprietor will help you select cheap restaurants in this costly sea-side area.

Two areas for older readers

The Rue Paul Déroulède, just off the Avenue Jean-Médecin (Nice's main boulevard), and only a few short blocks from the beach, is an oasis of quiet and calm, with fewer humans and activity than you might find elsewhere, and two top budget hotels: the **Hotel d'Italie**, 9 Rue Paul Déroulède, phone 88-35-90 (as pleasant as they come, and highly recommended; 72 francs ($16.56) for bathless doubles, 10 francs extra for a shower, but breakfast and all else included), and the older and even slightly elegant (it has a drawing room lifted straight from the time of Napoleon and Josephine) **Hotel Athena**, 11 Rue Paul Déroulède (phone 88-03-19), where all rooms have private bath and rent for 60 francs ($13.80) per person in double rooms, breakfast, service and tax included. Both hotels are virtually in sight of the sea, and perfect for our quiet-living readers; they are, indeed, perhaps the best of Nice's moderately-priced hotels, in this middle range.

Two other relatively-inexpensive hotels are found about halfway between the station and the sea—both near the intersection of the Boulevard Victor Hugo and the Rue Grimaldi. These are: the **Nouvel Hotel**, 19 bis Boulevard Victor Hugo (phone 87-73-60) and the **Hotel King-George**, 15 Rue Grimaldi (phone 87-73-61). Because of their location, both charge highest second class prices: 78 francs for a bathless double at the Nouvel, 120 francs for a double with private bath or shower at the King-George. The Nouvel should be your first choice.

OTHER $$$-A-DAY BOOKS: Europe on $15 a Day, has now been supplemented by six other $$$-a-Day guides dealing with individual European countries or areas: **Ireland on $15 a Day, Greece and Yugoslavia on $15 & $20 a Day, Spain and Morocco (plus the Canary Islands) on $10 & $15 a Day, England and Scotland on $20 a Day, Scandinavia on $20 a Day,** and **Turkey on $10 & $15 a Day.** In contrast with the book you are now reading, which deals primarily with 17 major European cities, each of the above guides treats in depth one particular country or area, and sets forth hotel, restaurant and sightseeing suggestions for literally scores of individual cities and tourist destinations in that country or area. The $$$-a-Day Books can be obtained at most bookstores, or by mailing the appropriate amount (refer to the last page in this guide) for each book to: Frommer/Pasmantier Publishing Corporation, 380 Madison Avenue, New York, New York 10017.

On the sea

If you insist on a room that is actually on the sea, about the best you can do is at the small white villa with adjoining garden that constitutes the **Hotel Eden**, 99 bis Promenade des Anglais (phone 86-53-70), five blocks along the sea from the world-famed Hotel Negresco. Proprietors M. and Mme. Prone like having U.S. guests (and that's a fact) and charge only 55 francs ($12.65) for bathless singles, 95 francs ($21.85) double or twin, 132 francs ($30.36) triple, 150 francs ($34.50) for a four-bedded room, inclusive of breakfast. Four-course meals are also served, in a charming, ground floor dining room, for 35 francs ($8.05). If you're traveling alone, try to rent the single room near the reception desk, from which the Mediterranean is in plain view. . . . Cheaper than, but almost as suitable as, the above, but fifty yards away from the sea, is the larger and therefore more easily-booked **Hotel Magnan,** on Square Général-Ferrié (phone 86-76-00), a modern, elevator-equipped, six-story building in which most rooms have balconies looking onto the Mediterranean, and nevertheless rent for 95 francs ($21.85) a night, double, private shower included. Each floor also possesses a 155 franc-a-night suite easily capable of sleeping four. At the Magnan, you can put on bathing suits in your room, then—in beach robes— walk the fifty yards to the Promenade des Anglais and the sea. A high recommendation.

A final, unique, near-the-sea selection is the apartment of **Mrs. Sophie Koelichen** at 20 Rue de France (phone 88-26-70), to which I've been tipped by several readers' letters. Because their description is so complete (see "Readers' Selections," below), I'll simply add that to find Madame Sophie's apartment, you walk through the large street door, then turn left into the first corridor with the doctor's name plate. This is apparently a top find, with a pleasing rate of 70 francs ($16.10) per double room.

Several scattered choices

Hotel Les Charmettes, 105 Promenade des Anglais (phone 86-66-35), is a small villa of 15 rooms situated 50 yards from the sea, on a wide palm-lined drive; some rooms have a view of the sea. Rooms—each a housekeeping-type accommodation—are small and incredibly crowded with beds, sink, hot plate, cupboard, etc.; but they are light and cheery in spite of the crowded conditions, and come with floor-to-ceiling French windows. 43 francs ($9.89) single, 77 francs ($17.71) double with shower, 95 francs ($21.85) triple—*plus* the cost of electricity (each room has its own meter). Here's a way to be near the beach at budget rates.

Hotel Canada, 8 Rue Halevy (phone 87-98-94), has 14 rooms, a block from the sea, all small and pullman-style, but clean and attractive. Doubles 65 francs, with shower 85 francs, including breakfast. A good buy for the location, and well-managed by a couple named Bouchardy (she speaks English).

Hotel de la Victoire, 43 Avenue Jean Médecin (phone 88-02-05), is a small (only 14 rooms) but very friendly place, which charges 38 francs ($8.74) single, 60 francs ($13.80) double, breakfast included.

Hotel-Meublé Wilson, 39 Rue de L'Hotel-des-Postes (phone 85-47-79), is plain but clean, and in a superb location within short walking distance from the central Place Massena. Seventeen rooms on the 3rd floor of an elevator-lacking apartment building in which doubles rent for only 50 francs ($11.50), singles for only 32 francs ($7.36), no breakfast, with additional beds at 15 francs and showers for 4 francs. Proprietress Madame Zerbib speaks just enough English for basic communication.

If most other hotels are full, then consider the large, Swiss-run **Hotel Interlaken,** 26 Avenue Durante, phone 88-30-15 (directly in front of the station, yet with chintz curtains and other genteel touches): 70 francs ($16.10) for a double—including breakfast and service—and highly recommended.

Private rooms with kitchenettes

Finally, for readers travelling with children, or planning a lengthy stay in Nice, an important address is 7 Rue de France, center of town, where you board a midget-sized elevator holding one person per trip (you'll feel like Santa Claus in a chimney) going to a third floor office of the **Meublé Reverso** (phone 87-11-77) to meet Mr. and Mrs. Reverso (they speak French and Italian, no English, but can phone English-speaking friends who act as interpreters). The

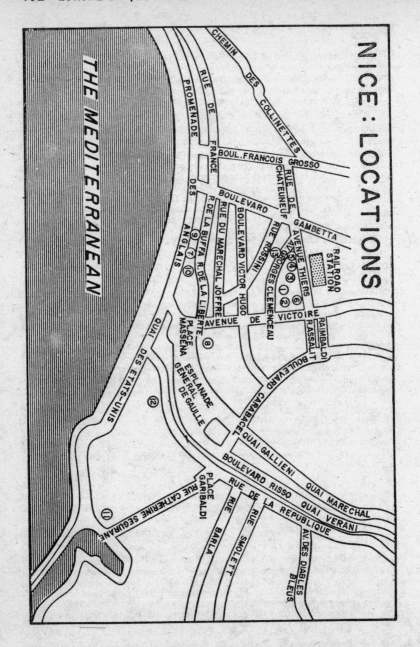

NICE : LOCATIONS

THE MEDITERRANEAN

CHEMIN DES COLLINETTES

PROMENADE DES ANGLAIS

RUE DE FRANCE

BOUL. FRANCOIS GROSSO

RUE DE CHATEUNEUF

BOULEVARD GAMBETTA

BOULEVARD

BOULEVARD VICTOR HUGO

R.DE LA BUFFA   R.DE LA LIBERTE

RUE DU MARECHAL JOFFRE

RUE ROSSINI

RUE GEORGES CLEMENCEAU

AVENUE THIERS

RAILROAD STATION

⑨   ⑦   ⑩

⑤ ④ ③   ① ②   ⑥

AVENUE   DE   VICTOIRE

RAIMBALDI

R.ASSALIT

BOULEVARD

PLACE MASSENA

⑧

ESPLANADE GENERAL DE GAULLE

CARABACEL

QUAI DES ETATS-UNIS

QUAI GALLIENI

QUAI MARECHAL

BOULEVARD RISSO   QUAI VERANI

QUAI DE LA REPUBLIQUE

⑫

⑪

RUE CATHERINE SEGURANE

PLACE GARIBALDI

RUE BARLA

RUE SMOLETT

AV. DES DIABLES BLEUS

object is to rent one of the Reversos' 15 small apartments, each two to three rooms in size, with kitchenette, and each capable of housing from two to seven persons at a price of 42 francs ($9.66) per adult. Try especially to rent one of the top floor rooms which come with verandahs enjoying a panoramic view of NIce.

READERS' HOTEL SELECTIONS: "We loved the **Hotel Meublé "Les Orangers Fleuris,"** 10 bis Avenue Durante (phone 87-51-41). It's just two blocks from the train station, and for 35 francs apiece a friend and I shared a large room with a double bed, single bed, bathroom with shower, and fully equipped kitchen" (Christine Miller, Amityville, New York). . . . "For those anxious to escape the downtown din, I recommend the **Hotel Helios,** 54 Boulevard de Cimiez (phone 53-04-55). A single room was 52 francs; continental breakfast 10 additional francs, a shower 7 francs. The hotel is situated on a hill above Nice, with a bus route providing frequent and quick transportation" (Dale C. Dalton, Sunnyvale, California). . . . "The **Central Hotel,** 10 Rue de Suisse (phone 88-85-08), offers charmingly furnished rooms at low prices—60 francs double, including breakfast. And location is quite near the railroad station" (Vincent and Nancy Traina, Studio City, California; Harriet Baumgarten-Schultz, Portland, Maine). . . . "The **Hotel Drouot,** 24 Rue d'Angleterre (phone 88-02-03), has 22 newly renovated rooms, all but three equipped with kitchenettes. Prices range from 35 to 50 francs" (Mara Borkan, Portland, Oregon). . . . "At the **Hotel "Le Clemenceau,"** 3 Avenue G. Clemenceau (phone 88-61-19), we enjoyed a spotless double room with comfortable beds, and the freshest continental breakfast we had in months, all for 52 francs ($11.96). This is near the station·and the beach and is managed by the former director of another of your recommendations, who still has the 'touch' " (Dr. and Mrs. Robert Gillen, San Marino, California; note by A.F.: In 1980, 'Le Clemenceau' will charge 40 francs single, 52 francs double, 62 francs triple, 75 francs for four persons, all rates including breakfast, and all for large, cheerful rooms with high ceilings and terra cotta floors). . . . "**Hotel Le Petit Monarque,** at 31 Rue Lepante (85-09-61), offers charming, comfortable rooms at 50 francs ($11.50) double, 60 francs in August. Location is near the train station, and proprietor is extremely likable" (Gary Gottesfeld, Denver, Colorado). . . . "Many of our American guests are surprised not to find our hotel in your guidebook, as we charge only 60 francs for a double room, 75 for a triple, service, breakfast and tax included. We are located in the same building as the Restaurant Maire" (**Central Hotel,** 10 Rue de Suisse, phone 88-85-08; note: numerous readers have written enthusiastic seconding recommendations for the Central Hotel and its helpful English-speaking proprietor, M. Amiel— among them, David and Maureen Latanick of Saint Paul, Minnesota; Edward Erwin of Coral Gables, Florida; and Mr. and Mrs. Robert Blomstrom of Madison, Nebraska). . . . "We must recommend the **Hotel Prior,** 5 Rue d'Alsace-Lorraine (phone 88-20-24), right off the Avenue Jean Médecin, where the two of us had a huge room with two double beds, breakfast included, for $6.30 per person. The concierge and his wife are unusually friendly and charming people and acted as our personal travel agents and information bureau in Nice. They were a pleasure to come home to" (Marilyn Silver, New Hyde Park, New York; strong seconding recommendation from Judith Weiner, New York, N.Y., who points out that 1980 prices with breakfast will be only 55 francs double (there are no singles), 70 francs triple, 90 francs quadruple. This would appear to be an almost ideal budget establishment, with a pleasant terrace for breakfast or lounging). . . . "Pension-style accommodations are available in the private apartment of **Mrs. Sophie Koelichen,** 20 Rue de France (phone 88-26-70), whose flat is located on the main floor of the famous, historical Palais Marie-Christine, in the very heart of the city and a block away from the Promenade des Anglais. While the exterior is sumptuous, with a little palm-tree square in front, the interior has been converted into apartments with modest appointments, but including everything that is necessary for a pleasant stay. Upon our arrival, we found a large double bedroom with twin beds, a table, a vanity, night-tables, armchairs and chairs. There were flowers on the table and a platter of oranges to welcome us. Mrs. Koelichen (or Madame Sophie as everyone calls her) is an unusually warm and hospitable person, who does her utmost to help and make one's stay pleasant and home-like. She allows young people to use her kitchen, thus enabling them to save on food, and repeatedly invited us to tea. She has stacks of letters from grateful tourists and students from all over the world, many of them from the U.S. and Canada, where she is called "our dear French Mother", "our good angel", "our loved Friend". She charges 70 francs for two and while breakfast is not included, she will serve one upon request. We strongly feel that she deserves to be included in your book" (Prof. Monique Wagner, Wayne State University, Detroit, Michigan, seconded by Mrs. T. Rubnikowicz of London, who describes Madame Sophie as "an ex Polish aristocrat, who formerly owned the Palace in which she now has a large flat. She is always gay, and speaks so many languages I have lost count. She helps young people with their shopping to save costs, and they can get breakfast there, prepared by her, or they can cook something for themselves. The location is superb, parallel with the Promenade des Anglais"; note by A.F.: in 1980, rates here will be 55 francs ($12.65) single, 70 francs ($16.10) double; use of showers is free; and up to 7 persons can be accommodated).

APARTMENTS AND FURNISHED ROOMS: "The **Meublé du Port** (Jacques Baixas), 28 Rue Segurane (phone 55-11-36), second floor, has equipped each of its rooms with a little kitchen, including an electric stove and refrigerator. Yet double rooms, so equipped, cost only 45 francs ($10.35) a day, including free showers. Immaculate. Larger doubles cost 55 francs. Five minutes walk to the beach. A charming young concierge who does all to be helpful." (Elaine Grossman, Brooklyn, New York, with recent seconding recommendations from other readers). . . . "The **Liberty Hotel,** 5 bis Rue Berlioz (right near the Promenade des Anglais, phone 88-59-23), is run by an extremely friendly and helpful manager who lets large, comfortable doubles for just 45 francs ($10.35). Each room has a delightful feature: a kitchenette complete with electric stove and sink and all the pots, pans, crockery and cutlery you would want. This can cut living costs wonderfully" (Mr. and Mrs. P. Hirst, Chatswood, N.S.W., Australia; note by AF: scores of young Americans, in particular, stay each year at the Hotel Liberty, and fill its guest book with enthusiastic appreciations. On a recent summer day, Hope and I met five football-types from San Jose State College who were all living in one double room at the Liberty, for a total of 59 francs (less than 12 francs per person) per night—and cooking their own meals!). . . . "As it is situated on the inner court of a pedestrian mall, the **Hotel Rex,** 3 Rue Massena (phone 87-87-38), is extremely quiet. And since it is only three short blocks from the sea, you save money on bus fares—everything is convenient (the old town, bus station, Prisunic and markets). All rooms are with private showers, some with kitchenettes, some with balconies, and rates vary according to length of stay and season: singles in 1980 will be 55 to 62 francs ($12.65 to $14.26), doubles 66 to 84 francs ($15.18 to $19.32), with kitchenettes an extra 10 francs ($2.30) per day; proprietress is the charming, vivacious Mme Claude Verna" (Aaron B. Everett, St. Peter, Minnesota). . . . "Try 'housekeeping' to beat the August prices for rooms in Nice. At the **'Primavera,'** 3 Avenue Auber (phone 88-44-23), just half a block north of Blvd. Victor Hugo on the west side of the street, one can obtain bathless rooms, double, for low cost, depending upon how well you negotiate with the proprietors. We paid $12.60 double, with the proviso that we wouldn't cook *too much* (though we could heat morning water for shaving and coffee). Pots and pans are provided for breakfast and snacks" (John and Florence Lane, Salt Lake City, Utah; note by A.F.: in 1980, double rooms will be 55 francs in July and August, 40 francs the rest of the year; single rooms will be 40 francs in July and August, 35 francs the rest of the year; other "meublés" in Nice, offering kitchen facilities, and some superior to the Primavera, are the **Hotel-Meublé Flor-Amy,** at 13 Rue d'Italie, phone 88-56-92;(35 to 40 fr.); the **Meublé Nancy,** at 21 Rue d'Angleterre; **"La Villa",** at 11 Rue d'Angleterre; **"Le Déroulède"** at 19 Rue Paul-Déroulède (phone 87-23-55), 45 francs per room, only 35 francs off-season). . . . "The newly established **Le Panorama** of Madame Sornas, at 38 Rue Segurane (second floor, phone 55-29-36), one block from the port and near the beach, provides clean, bright and newly decorated rooms with sink, stove, and a complete array of pots and pans. There is lots of free hot water and central heating, and a community refrigerator with 23 individual compartments. Prices range, per room, from 50 to 80 francs ($11.50 to $18.40)" (Kathleen H. Morgan, Illinois).

A GEOGRAPHICAL NOTE: The main street of Nice, formerly the Avenue de la Victoire, was re-named the Avenue Jean Médecin in recent times, after the gentleman who was mayor of Nice from 1928 to 1965. The name remains "Avenue de la Victoire" on our map of Nice (we'll change it next year) and may occasionally be referred to as such by the citizens of Nice.

We turn to food:

RESTAURANTS: Loosen your belt, take a deep breath, and pitch in: Nice is a gourmet's paradise, at low (for France) prices. This is mainly because the fixed price ("prix fixe") meal in Nice is no rarity, but the general rule. In a city with over one hundred and fifty restaurants, there are less than ten which offer only à la carte selections. And, while a Parisian restaurant normally serves three courses on its "prix fixe," the restaurants in Nice throw in four or five. This, remember, is the city where the Frenchman comes to relax: the meals are huge and delicious.

Moreover, the **most** you need pay for one of these four-course feasts (except in the first class or de luxe restaurants) is 27 francs ($6.21)—and there are spots in town that charge 20 to 22 francs ($4.60 to $5.06) for almost the same meal! Hope and I have had at least one course at each, and can advise that there's only the subtlest of difference between the highest and lowest-priced (although there's often a course-or-two lacking in the 20-franc places). We'll discuss them in descending order of price, and suggest that you carefully note whether the charge includes service and/or wine.

For 27 francs ($6.21)

Costliest of our choices, but well worth the splurge, are three widely scattered restaurants: first, the tiny **Restaurant Le Prony,** near the railroad station at 3 Rue Alsace-Lorraine. Open seven days a week from noon to 2 and from 7 to 9, it charges precisely 27 francs for *four* gigantic courses, all in heaping portions, from hors d'ouevres to desserts . . . **L'Etoile d'Or** is a larger establishment that overlooks the famous flower market of Nice (don't miss it) from the second floor of 26 Cours Saleya. Popular for its wide variety of menu choices, it, too, charges 27 francs for no fewer than four courses, wine included . . . In "Old Nice", which you also should see, **La Taverne du Chateau** is an historic old place serving a carefully-prepared, three-course, 27-franc menu, but without wine (4.50 francs extra). That's at 42 Rue Droite, and it is closed on Mondays.

For 24.50 to 26 francs ($5.63 to $5.98)

The restaurant of the **Hotel Interlaken,** 26 Avenue Durance, almost directly in front of the train station, is a large and attractive establishment with plenty of seating both inside and outdoors (on a large garden terrace). Here, 26 francs will bring you a phenomenal four-course meal, including wine, and 35 francs will result in *six* courses (easily enough for two people). . . . **Restaurant Arc-au-Ciel** ("rainbow"), at 6 Place Wilson, is a rather distinguished restaurant patronized by upper-middle-class residents, yet it charges only 25 francs, all in, for three courses, 27.50 francs for four courses, but with wine extra. Walk up the Rue des Postes behind the Galeries Lafayette department store; Place Wilson is the square with enormous trees, a small park complete with fountain and children's playground equipment. . . . At the **Restaurant Dauphinois,** corner of Rue Pertinax and Rue Miron, you can either select the hearty, four-course meal for only 24.50 francs, or simply content yourself with a giant "plat du jour" for just 18 francs. The latter is actually a meal in itself, as the "platter" includes soup first, then perhaps a grilled fish fillet with potatoes and salad. But wine is an additional 4 francs, and the restaurant is closed Sundays. . . . In the old city ("Vieux Nice"), a superb value is had at the **Restaurant la Brigue,** 14 Rue de l'Abbaye, and don't be confused by the initial appearance, which resembles a simple bar: if you'll walk through the first room, with its eight tables, you'll emerge into a 100-seat dining room of canny Frenchpersons savouring three-course meals for only 24.50 francs, *including* wine. Example: an interesting sardine-and-anchovies appetizer, followed by stuffed meat rolls with tiny green peas and luscious French fries covered by a Béarnaise-type sauce, with oozing camembert cheese and tiny crackers for dessert; all accompanied by a flagon of red wine, and all costing only 24.50 francs! Open weekdays from 6 to 11 p.m., closed Sundays; manager is a M. Anclen, whose sister lives in Chicago.

For 22 to 24 francs ($5.06 to $5.52)

At the clean, airy, popular and always crowded **Restaurant Maire,** upstairs at 10 Rue Suisse, in the very heart on Nice, monsieur the owner sits behind the cash register surveying all, and the three, good-looking blonde waitresses with napkins over their left shoulders, are his daughters and daughter-in-law. They dispense three course meals for just 22 francs, and you can choose from five different first courses (which usually include the classic Quiche Lorraine appetizer), 15 main courses, and five types of dessert! Open from 11:30 to 2, from 6 to 9, and closed Saturdays. . . . **Restaurant Pallanca,** 56 Rue Gounod, next to the post office in front of the station, belies its mirror-lined appearance with a 22-franc price for three courses, with wine extra at 3 francs. . . . Nearby, at 12 Rue Belgique (a few yards from the Pallanca), **Restaurant aux Voyageurs** provides four courses for 23 francs, wine extra at 3 francs, and offers a choice of five items on each course. The friendly Rouchy family operate aux Voyageurs, and they'll provide, on request, a typewritten English-language translation of the hard-to-decipher, handwritten French menu. Closed Saturdays. . . . **Restaurant le Tropical** is a tiny place at 23 Rue de France near the Massena Museum, catering primarily to people working in the area; 24 francs for three-courses, and closed Sundays. . . . **Brasserie le Gioffredo,** at 56 Rue Gioffredo, near the central Place Massena, offers the same sort of three-course, 23 franc menu, but also serves onion soup (a specialty), à la carte, for 12 francs, and various superb omelettes for 9.50 francs. . . . Nearby, the tiny **Restaurant Le Poelon,** at 2 Passage Malaussena, near the large Hotel Monsigny, offers a four-course meal for 24 francs, an evening "plat du jour" with dessert for 16 francs, but adds 4 francs per person for wine. . . . Perhaps the most conveniently located and most easily found, in this price category, is the **Restaurant Renady,** in the "Galerie (Arcade) de la Victoire" at 58 Avenue Jean Médecin, the main street of Nice. It serves a 24 franc meal that begins with a large tureen of soup which is then followed by no fewer than three additional, tasty courses. An excellent flask of red wine is 3 francs. Open daily except Monday from 11 to 2 and from 7 to 9 p.m.

For 20 francs ($4.60)

Evenings only (from 6 to 10 p.m.), the long reliable **Restaurant au Soleil,** in business for many years at 7 Rue d'Italie, corner of Rue de Russie, in the very center of Nice, charges only 20 francs for a special "petit repas" (small meal), including wine, service and cover. Daytimes, the charge increases to 26 francs, wine included, for a toothsome three-course menu, but you'll pay one franc less by showing this book to your waiter; the same discount is not available at night.

Four courses for 20 francs? At 26 Rue Lamartine, corner of Rue Tiranty (Rue Lamartine runs parallel to Avenue Jean Médecin), the 20-table **Restaurant Chez Marius** serves four full courses for 20 francs, an incredible five-course banquet for 25 francs; they also serve, à la carte, the renowned bouillabaisse of the Riviera for 32 francs plus 12½% service, which compares with the rock-bottom minimum of 50 francs that you'd pay for the same savory seafood stew in most of the sea-side restaurants of Nice. By the way, please note that when you order a fixed price meal in Nice or other French cities, you do not pay the 12½% service charge appended to à la carte plates.

À la carte ordering for 20 francs—and less? For that, you join a galloping herd of impecunious French, German, Italian, Spanish and Belgian tourists who, at mealtimes, come converging from all over the city to the rock-bottom **Self Service Saint Michel**, at 15 Avenue Georges-Clemenceau (just off the Rue d'Angleterre, in the same building that houses the huge Hotel Escurial), the world's plainest self-service restaurant, where the servings on each plate are gargantuan enough to feed three people. I mean that literally. You'll see families at the Saint Michel sharing a single course, which is precisely what Hope and I do.

You line up in front of a hot, steamy zinc counter, and receive your food directly from the stoves on which it's cooked. The appetizers cost 5 francs (like an enormous plate of sliced tomatoes and onions) and contain enough "appetizer" for two people. The main courses (like boeuf bourguignon and carrots) cost 14 francs and contain what seems like a skillet-full of meat, a pot-full of carrots. Hope and I took two empty dishes, and then ordered one appetizer, one main course, a side dish of tomatoes provencale, one Coca-Cola and one bottle of mineral water, and one orange, and then divvied up the servings between us. Our total cost for the meal: 34 francs, or $3.95 apiece.

Be prepared: this is an extremely basic place, serving hundreds of people each meal; but it does so with élan and dedication. You can, on good days, take the food to a little covered garden ouside the restaurant. Don't confuse the St. Michel with another restaurant called St. Michel, on the corner of Rue d'Angleterre; entrance to the cheap, self-service one is next to the entrance of the Hotel Escurial. Open 11:45 to 2:15 for lunch, from 6:45 to 9:15 p.m. for dinner; closed Sundays.

For 13 to 17 francs ($2.99 to $3.91)

Since lunch is the big meal in France, many other restaurants also reverse the American trend and charge less for dinner than for lunch. For example, the **Restaurant Frites Parisiennes**, 16 Rue Paganini (a few hundred yards from the station) charges 23 francs for lunch, but only 17 francs for a *petit menu du soir* that might consist of tomato soup, an omelette with vegetables, and cheese or fruit.

Evenings only, the **Arc-au-Ciel Restaurant** at 6 Place Wilson, described above in our 24.50-to-26-franc section, also follows the Nice custom of serving a small but refreshing combination of one hors d'oeuvre, a cooked vegetable and a dessert, for 16 francs, service included. That's from 6:45 p.m. to 9:15 p.m.

A thirteen-franc meal at lunch? **Snack La Frite**, at 11 Rue Halevy, a short block from the sea, charges 13 francs ($2.99) for an almost-raw "steak-haché frites" (hamburger steak with french fries; if you don't like it in the French manner, ask that it be well done); 13.50 francs for one quarter of a chicken and french fries ("poulet frites"); 4 francs for a small pitcher of wine.

In the old city

Finally, we can't resist adding an à la carte restaurant that dishes up the city's most authentic Niçois cooking at meal prices ranging from $6 to $6.50. To find it, walk along the Avenue Jean Jaures (12) until you come to an archway topped with a sign reading "Basilique Cathedrale." The natives calls this "La Porte Fausse." Through the archway are steps leading down to a medieval world—the old section of Nice ("Vieux Nice")—and also at the bottom of the steps is this most perfect restaurant find: **Casa Julio,** 1 Rue Francis-Gallo, a stucco-walled room with beamed ceilings, whose kitchen is filled with jolly, plump ladies preparing fabulous dishes, scarcely any of which cost over 20 francs. Order, first, the Potage au Pistou (11 francs), a bean soup whose main ingredient is basilic, laced with garlic and cheese. Next, a serving of "Ratatouille Niçoise"—eggplant and vegetables with tomato sauce (10 francs); and accompany that interesting dish with a meat plate. On Friday, you'll get a fish dish instead, but ask that it be served with the weekly batch of "aioli," a renowned and purely-local sort of mayonnaise, flavored with garlic—and mixed with olive oil. Alexandre Dumas, on a trip to Nice, said that ordinary mayonnaise tastes like marmalade, after you've tasted "aioli." . . . With all this, you'll be doing well if you can push the bill at Casa Julio to even near $7. Open from noon to 2, and from 7 to 10:30, closed Thursday.

An alternative to Casa Julio? It's **Chez Palmyre,** at 5 Rue Droite (again in the old city), with only eight tables, all covered in red and white checked oilcloth. The food is so good that you'll have to wait unless you come early. Three courses (five or six choices of appetizer and entree, plus fruit, cheese, or yogurt) cost 24 francs ($5.52); wine is 3 francs extra. Lunch begins at noon, dinner at 7, and the restaurant is open seven days a week.

The cheaper meals

Funds depleted? Then turn to our "Starvation Budget" section, or else head—but only in the direst of emergencies—for the **Restaurant Municipal,** at 1 Rue Guigonis, in the old city, near the Place St. Francois. This is Nice's city-owned people's restaurant, officially open only to local residents, but they may be willing to serve you lunch (not dinner), from 11:45 a.m. to 1 p.m., and the price for a two-course menu, with no choices about it, is 4 francs (92¢). And after that, head for the nearest telegraph for funds to return home (or to the **Accueil de Nuit,** 14 Rue Jules-Gilly, also in Old Nice, where you can stay for free, demi-pension!).

PICNICS AND PAN BAGNAT: As we've pointed out before, the mid-day meal in the restaurants of Nice is the "expensive" one; the evening meal always plummets in price. To beat the relatively high cost of lunch, and to eat sensibly at the same time, you'll occasionally want to consider a do-it-yourself picnic. And the place for those picnic ingredients is the unusually inexpensive grocery section (look for the sign "Libre Service Alimentation") of the **Prisunic Department Store** on the Avenue Jean Médecin, corner of Avenue Marechal Foch, where huge chunks of cheese are 4 to 5 francs, a container of milk is 2.40 francs, enough lunch meat for three large sandwiches is 8 francs, and cucumber or carrot salad or tomatoes provençales sell for 10 francs the kilo (2.2 lbs.)! In a restaurant, you'd pay 6 francs for a large bottle of brand-name mineral water; here the same bottle sells for 1.80 francs. A huge quart-and-a-quarter of good red wine is 3.80 francs; even a full quart bottle of Coca Cola is only 2.20 francs. And, of course, vast loaves of French bread sell for 2 and 2.50 francs—and under.

The Prisunic is also where you may be introduced to Nice's famous fill-you-up-for-hours sandwich, a picnic lunch in itself called the "Pan Bagnat". Best described as a salade niçoise inserted into a 6-inch-diameter roll, a Pan Bagnat (enough, believe me, for lunch) sells for only 5.50 francs ($1.26) at a ground-floor counter found just as you walk through the corner entrance of the Prisunic. That may be the city's cheapest price for pan bagnats, which are found in snack bars, bakeries and charcuteries (delicatessens) all over town. A pan bagnat near the sea? Try the **Station Uvale**, a snack stand selling them for 6.50 francs, on the Rue Halevy, 20 feet from the Promenade des Anglais.

READERS' RESTAURANT SELECTIONS: "**Self-Service Cafe de Paris**, 42 Rue Pastorelli, has excellent cold hors d'oeuvres, several of which, along with cheese, bread and wine cost 10 to 13 francs. Hot dishes are also good quality and reasonably priced, and the sidewalk cafe atmosphere is unique for this kind of establishment" (G. Wehrenberg, Kent, Washington). . . . "Another self-service cafeteria in Nice is the **Café de Paris** at 42 Rue Pastorelli, just off the Avenue Jean-Médecin, where hors d'oeuvres start at 3 francs, meat plates at six francs, desserts at 3.50 francs, drinks at 3.50 francs, although most items sell for more than those minimums. This is quite similar to the cafeterias in Paris" (Pauline Rissman, New York, N.Y. . . . "The **Restaurant d'Angleterre**, at 25 Rue d'Angleterre, serves soup, a main plate (perhaps a meat course with vegetables) and a dessert for 19 francs. Wine is 3 francs more. They also offer a daily platter for 15 francs" (Susan Pollak, Brunswick, Maine). . . . "You must include **Restaurant Chez Davie** at 13 Rue Grimaldi, only three blocks from the ocean, where we had the best three-course meal of our European trip for only 26 francs—$5.98—apiece" (A. Guilbaut, Vancouver, Canada).

TRANSPORTATION: No need to rent a car; try a motorized bicycle ("un Moped Ciao") instead. These can be had at **"Motorent"**, 3 rue Barrális (phone 87-48-78) (reached by walking up Rue de France to No. 30, and turning the corner). There's a completely refundable deposit on the bike, and a rental charge that comes to exactly 30 francs per day.

SIDE-TRIPS: Nice should be made your headquarters for forays along the Riviera. That way, you'll be able to dart to high-priced Monaco or Cannes in the day, but return to a budget-priced pad in low-cost Nice at night. The train takes exactly 22 minutes to make the trip to Monaco, costs 6.20 francs one-way, leaves about once per hour. But caution: the last train leaves Monaco for Nice at 12:47 a.m. The trip to Cannes takes 34 minutes, costs 10.20 francs one-way, and leaves at half-hour intervals. . . . You'll want to make at least one run to Monaco by bus, along the incredibly beautiful Moyenne Corniche. Buses depart from the Gare d'Autobus, approximately every hour from 7 a.m. to 7:30 p.m. Monaco features: the Casino at Monte Carlo (entrance fee of 12 francs, but no admission charge to the room of "one-armed bandits"; passport essential; sober dress—tie and jacket—usually required), the palace of our own Princess Grace, a yacht basin often filled with the pleasure craft of Greek millionaires, and the famous "Musée Oceanographique," world's largest marine museum (entrance 16 francs). You may have no present liking for the subject of sealife, but you'll soon pick it up at this place; a fascinating, weird series of exhibits. . . . Whatever you do, don't stay overnight in Cannes, the most expensive city on the Riviera, totally lacking the hordes of prix fixe restaurants and budget hotels found in Nice. . . . On a day excursion to Cannes, however, try to get to the island of Ste. Marguerite, a mile away, to view the fort built by Richelieu, where you can still see the cell where the Man in the Iron Mask was held prisoner for 11 years by Louis XIV. . . . And if you have a car, drive eight kilometers beyond Cannes on the sea road to the village of La Napoule and its **Henry Clews Museum**. Both Hope and I look upon our accidental visit to this museum (the former villa of the underrated American sculptor) as one of the high points of our trips to Europe. Admission is 4 francs (2 francs for students and children) to view the lifework of an amazing, off-beat mind. Open daily except Sunday from 3 to 6 p.m.

On our most recent trip to Nice, Hope and I spent an afternoon in **Vallauris**, the village in which Picasso developed his own unique style of ceramic designs. The entire town has now turned to pottery-making, and offers mountains of cheap pottery to visiting tourists, but the chief attraction of Vallauris is the **National Picasso Museum** (open daily from 10 to noon and from 2 to 5), which has a stunning impact, and the pottery store of **Madoura,** which is the only shop in town that is licensed to sell copies of Picasso's own pottery designs (some plates go for as little as 180 francs). The trip is made via train from Nice to Golfe Juan (30 minutes, 7.80 francs per person) and by then taking a 2 franc bus from Golfe Juan to Vallauris. I mention it here only as an example of the many interesting, one-day excursions you can make from Nice—to Cannes, to Juan Les Pins, or to the fabulous St. Tropez, for example —all of which will cost you nothing if you have a Eurailpass, and very little even if you don't.

READERS ON AN OUTING: "We rented two motorized bikes for 3 days and with these we surveyed all of Nice, traveled to Cannes, Vallauris, Monte Carlo, Monaco, and all the villages along the coast. We strapped food packs to our bikes and had all the freedom of time and place which public transportation doesn't allow. And for the leery—it is easier than pedaling a bike!" (Gordon and Lori Burghardt, Chicago, Illinois). . . . "From Nice, I took a bus to the Italian border, then traveled by S.A.T.I. bus to Rapallo on the Italian Riviera—a journey I recommend most wholeheartedly. Total cost for the Nice-Rapallo bus trip (two tickets) is about 60 francs, one way. It was comfortable, the driver was an expert at his job, and the couriers most efficient. No resort, however small, was omitted, so it was in effect a grand tour of the Cote d'Azur and the northern Italian coast" (Edward A. Creed, Salisbury, Rhodesia). . . . "Please mention another worthy side trip out of Nice, to the strikingly small chapel at Vence, executed by Henri Matisse" (Marianne Durand, San Francisco, California). . . . "Buy a Niçoise sandwich—a "pan bagnat"—and a bottle of wine at a side street delicatessen, and take the bus to Monaco for the changing of the guard at 11:45 a.m. Then have lunch on a bench overlooking the sea" (Arthur F. Damon, Roseville, Minnesota).

A NICE MISCELLANY: Nice has several coin-operated laundromats! **Taxi-Lav,** at 22 Rue Pertinax, is just a block-and-half from the Avenue Jean-Médecin, near the railroad track end; 7 francs for 4 kilos; open from 7 a.m. to 8 p.m., Monday through Sunday. The **Washeteria** at 4 Rue Spitalieri, is similarly priced, as is the **Laverie Libre Service** 29 Boulevard Raimbaldi, and **Le Lavoir,** at 10 Rue d'Angleterre. In the Old City ("Vieux Nice"), the same facilities and prices are available at the **Lavazur,** 2 Rue Rossetti, just off the small church square of this colorful quarter, and at the **Lavomatique,** 11 Rue du Pont Vieux. . . . For organized sight-seeing tours your best bet is the large, bustling office of **Santa Azur,** at 2 Place Massena (phone 85-46-81), which owns its own buses, and passes on no middleman's fees to you. Their basic tour of Nice daparts at 9:30 a.m., costs 28 francs, while other tours go daily to Monte Carlo (2 p.m., 40 francs), to the perfume factories at Grasse (2 p.m., 40 francs), and to other key locations along the Riviera, including the fabled St. Tropez (70 francs). . . . On your visit to Monaco, try to catch the noontime changing of the guard at Prince Rainier's palace. Like a fairy tale.

EVENING ENTERTAINMENT: There is, of course, no really inexpensive way to while-away the evening in a Riviera gaming hall. But the casinos at Nice offer perhaps the least pressured forms of gambling of all the European rooms of this type. Certainly, you'll spend less here, and you'll do it more enjoyably, than in the fabled, but disappointing, Casino at Monte Carlo, where the crowds are monstrous and the croupiers grim. At the **Ruhl Casino** on the Promenade des

Anglais in Nice, entrance fee is only 20 francs, and chips are as little as 20 francs apiece at most of the roulette tables. Play it cool, study the game well before you plunge, and tip the croupiers if you win a pile of chips: if you do, they'll call it your way on the disputed plays. . . . Keep in mind that you'll be made to present your passport on entering; don't leave it at the hotel. . . . Care to know a time-honored (if somewhat boring) method for winning (I don't guarantee it) at roulette? Write down the numbers 1, 2, 3, 4, 5 in a column, then bet the total of the top and bottom number (1 and 5 = 6 chips) on a 2-1 chance (odd or even, red or black). If you win, cross out the top and bottom numbers (1 and 5). If you lose, place the number of the chips you lost at the bottom of the column, and again bet the total of the uncrossed-out top and bottom numbers (this time, 1 and 6), crossing out those numbers each time you win. Unless your luck is unusually bad, and you lose several bets in a row (thus pushing this progression to unacceptable limits), you'll eventually cross out all the numbers and retire a winner, having depleted the French economy by about $4.

STARVATION BUDGET: The long-time, rock-bottom champion of Nice is the **Hotel Petit Parc** in a (you guessed it) tiny, quiet park at 6 Allée Thiole (phone 80-45-33), the very center of Nice opposite the Gare du Sud. Thirty-five francs ($8.05) for doubles, 22 francs ($5.06) single, no breakfast, for very, repeat, very simple rooms on three floors of a non-elevator-served building. Manager Monsieur Maurice, who speaks English well, once advised me to warn that unlike most other hotels which provide electric sockets with 220 voltage, the Petit Parc supplies only 110. . . . A bit further off the beaten path (but not much) is the tiny **Hotel Soleil d'Or**, 16 Avenue des Orangers (phone 88-91-68), charging 35 francs ($8.05) double, 30 francs single.

Restaurant Universitaire

For your most decent low-cost meal, you'll need to walk about half an hour from the center of Nice, but you'll save at least 10 francs per meal by dining at the **Restaurant Universitaire**, 5 Avenue Robert Schuman, during the 10 months (September through June) when it's in operation. Head down the Rue de France, turn right into the Boulevard Francois Grosse, cross under the highway bridge, then left into the winding road that's the Avenue Robert Schuman, passing palm trees, a small restaurant, a yellow wall bearing student inscriptions ("liberez Corsica"), and then, on your left, the Restaurant Universitaire. Step inside to the "caisse" (cashier), request a "tarif passager" meal ticket for 12 francs ($2.76—no student card required), and you'll receive a three-course meal, plus an orange, in the cavernous, 600-seat basement dining hall. Watch the hours, which are from 11:30 to 1:30 for lunch, 6:30 to 8 for dinner, Monday through Saturday only.

SUB-STARVATION BUDGET: Europe on $2 a day? In Nice, it's possible, but only suggested if you're really down and out. The **Restaurant Municipal**, 1 Rue Guigonis (in the old city), is a city-owned people's restaurant. If you go to the *Bureau d'Aide Sociale de la Ville de Nice* (that's welfare), at 4 Place Pierre-Gautier (ground floor left, no questions are asked), you can purchase a 4 franc meal ticket good for a two-course menu at the above, served from 11:45 a.m. to 1 p.m.

If a turnout of pockets doesn't produce even 4 francs, despair not. Just head for the spartan but clean dining room at the **Fourneau Economique**, 1 Rue du Choeur (also in the old city), where Catholic nuns dish out hot soup Monday through Saturday from 11:30 a.m. to 1 p.m.

And while you're thinking of ways to earn some cash, or waiting for a check from home, you can get a bed and half-board (just enough to survive) at the **Accueil de Nuit,** 14 Rue Jules Gilly (old city). The first five nights are free; after that you can stay for eight more nights paying 4 francs (92¢) per night. Accommodations are dormitory style; men and women are accepted; apply between 6 and 7 p.m.

LA MER: Unlike the beach at the Lido in Venice, long segments of the beach at Nice are admission-free—as, for example, nearly the entire stretch of beach to the east of the Ruhl Plage (in front of the former Ruhl Hotel). Where a hotel controls a particular stretch, the price of admission is 12 to 15 francs, including a cabin, showers, etc. . . . It costs 2 francs to sit in a beach chair on the Promenade des Anglais.

MUSEUMS OF THE RIVIERA: There's more, however, to Nice and vicinity than sunning and swimming. Hope has contributed the following report on the culture of the Côte d'Azur:

"Rainy days on the Riviera can be richly rewarding if you spend them visiting some of the fast-growing number of museums that dot the area. With Nice as your base, you can take a train or bus to nearly every point of interest; the train for coastal locations, the bus for the inland hills.

"The train station in Nice you already know; the bus depot called "Gare Routière" is behind the Place Massena, between Ave. Felix Faure and Ave. Jean Jaures, and has large blue and white signs clearly indicating different destinations; buses leave with some frequency, and you can pay on board. In addition to the spots already mentioned by Arthur, and whatever the weather, you should bend every effort to get to the following:

In the Area Near Nice

Foundation Maeght—Saint-Paul

"The **Marguerite and Aimé Maeght Foundation,** built by the well-known gallery owner and art lover on his estate just outside Saint-Paul (a quaint looking, but really swinging, old walled city which you should take time to explore), is part of an eventual art center, and is undoubtedly the most revolutionary advance in museum design since the construction of the Guggenheim Museum in New York. I urge you to see it—the site is like a happening in Total Beauty. Every element of it is placed organically—the breathtaking natural setting is used as a background for sculpture, and in turn, the trees, plants, and flowers take on the aspects of works of art; the two white concrete arcs (that look like the tops of nuns' hats) on the roof of the building are incorporated into the symbol which guides you to the museum; the front 'lawn' is scattered with delightful modern sculpture that seems as though it had grown in the garden—gigantic bronze, steel and lead flowers sharing space with the trees. And the interior is no disappointment either (the setting is blunt stone walls and terra cotta floors), with many of the 'old' masters represented—Giacometti (the largest collection I've ever seen, and most impressive), Braque, Matisse, Chagall, Bonnard, Leger, Miró, Calder; and perhaps equally important, a really superb presentation of what's fun and 'now' in modern art—Adami, Bury, Chillida, Rebeyrolle, Riopelle, Tapies. Plus a fascinating library of originals, all for sale, including Chagall, Steinberg, Miró, and more: it's a small gallery

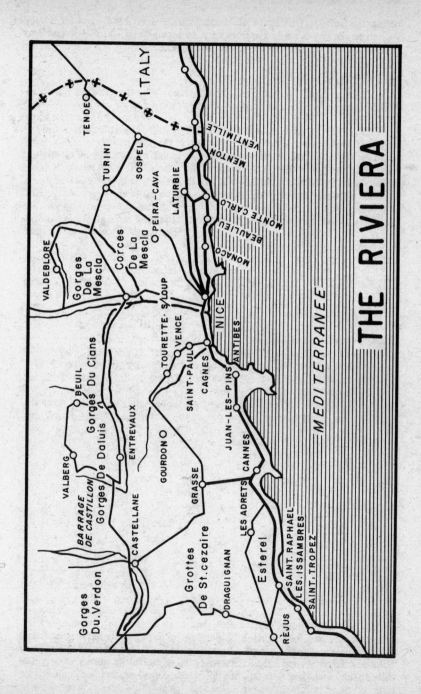

within the gallery. This Be-In of Modern Art is available to you for a very well-spent ten francs (only five francs for students), from 10 to 12:30 and 3 to· 7 in summer, from 2:30 to 6 p.m. all other times.

Musée Picasso—in Antibes

"Another 'must' on your list should certainly be the **Chateau d'Antibes Musée Picasso,** on the ramparts of Antibes (10 minutes from Nice on a fast train; from the station walk to the port, turn right, and signs will point the way); open daily from 10 to noon and 3 to 7 (winters till 5, closed Tuesdays and the month of November), and charging 5 francs. This ancient, white-washed Castle (built on the ruins of a Roman camp) formerly known as 'Chateau Grimaldi', was Picasso's home for several months in 1946-47. It now houses a large collection of the Master's pottery and paintings (some exhibited tastefully next to ancient pillars and fragments) that you have probably never seen before (including some works of wry humour: fawns, sprites, centaurs), and you are not likely to see anywhere but here. Although the museum sometimes exhibits the works of other artists, it is truly a celebration of Picasso—and a rare experience I hope you won't miss. (You might also enjoy a stroll around the quaint old part of the town near the ramparts; and archaeology buffs *only* may want to look in at the **Bastion St. Andre's Archaeological Museum**—open 9 to 12 and 12 to 6 (closed Tuesdays and the month of November), for 4 francs—whose collections are billed as '4,000 years of history': i.e., what's been dredged up from the sea in and around Antibes.)

Musée Fernand Leger—in Biot

"The **Musée National Fernand Leger,** located in the small town of Biot (near Antibes), and open daily except Tuesdays from 10 to noon and 2:30 to 6:30 (winters, 2 to 5) for a 6-franc entrance fee (3 francs for students), is difficult (but not impossible) to reach without a car—the train deposits you a good distance from the country-like hill on which the museum stands. It's a healthy hike; catch a bus or ask some local people to point you in the right direction. But when you arrive you'll be delighted, for you'll find a rich, white-carpeted, marble and stone, spankingly modern museum which offers a thorough retrospective showing of this important modern (including some striking ceramics, mosaics and tapestries), who specializes in large, 20th century, machine-like paintings. Here you can trace Leger's work at various stages in his development, noting with particular interest in some rare compositions the influence of African art on the artist—I get the distinct impression that Leger's intention was to be a 'modern primitive,' to paint with new eyes (breaking with old forms) the latest totems of his society: the machines. The final room you'll visit (on the second floor) is almost entirely devoted to canvases of modern man and industry, the only exception being the artist's occasional reversion to circus themes, with his special fondness for acrobats and musicians. It's an impressive collection, starting outside the building, where an enormous mosaic mural by Leger covers the facade.

Le Trophée des Alpes—at La Turbie

"The **Trophy of the Alps** is a spectacular and partially reconstructed Roman ruin (and the only surviving monument of its kind), built in 6 B.C. to commemorate the conquest of the Alps by the Emperor Augustus (thus Rome joined Gaul and Germania to Italy, guaranteed her security, and opened the historic route from the Mediterranean Coast, spreading Roman civilization to the ancient world). At the highest point of the Roman artery, La Turbie, the Trophy was erected; on its face is an inscription honoring Augustus and listing the 45 conquered hostile tribes—this has been called 'the first page of French history'—and on either side are reconstructed bas reliefs. It's presumed there were originally statues between the pillars on the upper level, and a statue of Augustus or a decorative trophy at the very top of the monument; as you look, try to imagine them. Behind the monument is a small museum displaying pillars and fragments found at the site, a model showing how the original Trophée looked (it must have been gorgeous), and exhibits illustrating the process of restoration. Behind that, the terrace affords panoramic views of Monaco and the entire coast. The Trophée, open from 9 to 12:30 and 2 to 7:30 p.m. (winters from 9 to 12 and 2 to 5) for a 4-franc entrance fee (half price to children and students), is located directly above Monaco, but can be reached by bus from Nice (a 45-minute trip, cost is 7.50 francs: but service is limited—there are buses leaving at 7 a.m. and 11:15 a.m., last bus back to Nice from La Turbie is at 6:10 p.m.—to be sure, best pick up a schedule at the bus station); the ride along the Grande Corniche is breathtaking, and, as you approach La Turbie, the view of the Trophée is one you will long remember and treasure.

In Nice

"You can sun on the beach with a clear conscience, rather than spend any time at the **Musée des Beaux Arts,** at 33 Avenue des Baumettes (dedicated to Jules Chéret, a rather interesting, vivacious painter with a distinctly '20's' style), because there is not much here, in my opinion, that is really first rate. The following are of more interest.

Villa des Arènes—Cimiez

"Way up in the hills of Nice (take city bus #15 or 17 from the side of the now defunct Municipal Casino, just across the street from the Galeries Lafayette, or from 'Magenta', a 3.50 franc ride—but cheaper if you buy a 11.50 franc carnet of bus tickets, good for 4 normal city rides), you'll find the **Villa des Arènes,** which houses both the **Matisse Museum** and the **Museum of Archaeology** (open in summer from 10 to 12 and 2 to 7, closed Sunday mornings and all day Mondays; in winter open from 2 to 5, closed Mondays and the entire month of November; admission is 4 francs, half price for students and free entrance on Saturdays). The first, of course, houses an interesting collection of Matisse's paintings, drawings, studies, models (including those for his Chapel in Vence), and some of the famous 'cut-outs.' It's a profound sensory pleasure to view this artist's work in the setting in which he actually painted because, as you enter the museum still tingling with the unique Riviera atmosphere in your mind's eye, you'll realize you are seeing nature as he saw it—and suddenly you'll appreciate why he chose to paint in the vivid colors of his most familiar works. And in a small room of Matisse's furniture, it's fun to recognize actual items you've seen portrayed so often in his paintings. The Archaeology Museum on the first floor (no extra charge) displays a nice little collection of artifacts found at or near the site—ceramics, coins, sculpture, tools and jewelry. Outdoors, all around, are the ruins of Cimiez (founded by the Romans under Augustus in the 1st century B.C., the town later became the Roman capital of the Maritime Alps), which, like a park, stay open most of the day—and the 1st century Amphitheatre is used for public performances for a month during the summer Cimiez Art Festival. But you must pay an additional franc to wander the 'streets' of the archaeological site, and inspect the Roman Baths (all 1st-3rd centuries).

Musée Chagall

"Above Nice on the way to Villa des Arènes (you can make a day of it in the hills; again take bus #15 or 15-A, a 2.50 franc, 10 minute ride; ask the driver for 'Chagall' or look for the 'Dr. Moriez' stop, walk uphill in the same direction the bus is going, and around the first bend you'll see a sign pointing the way) is the brand new **Musée National Marc Chagall** (open daily, except Tuesdays, from October 1 to June 30 from 10 a.m. to 12:30 p.m. and from 2 to 5:30 p.m., from July 1 to September 30 from 10 a.m. to 7 p.m., for a 5-franc entrance fee, half price on Sundays). The museum itself, a squat white stone modern building in a park-like setting, is pleasantly light and airy inside, and all the works exhibited (which were donated to France by the Chagalls) deal with Biblical subjects—but, because it's Chagall, that's a much livelier experience than one might anticipate. Note, particularly, the three large stained glass windows, the several rooms of large grand-scale canvases (e.g., 'Moses and The Burning Bush'), 'The Sacrifice of Isaac', and a room of stunning paintings illustrating 'The Song of Songs'—all in lush tones of purples and reds, both hot and cool.

Musée Masséna

"The Musée Masséna, which fronts on the Promenade des Anglais just across the street from the Hotel Negresco (although the entrance is around the block at 65 Rue de France), open every day except Monday from 10 to 12 and 2 to 5 for a 4 franc entrance fee, is devoted mainly to regional art and objects pertaining to the history of Nice. This elegant Villa, built in 1900, was the former home of Victor Masséna (a grandson of Napoleon's Marshal), and was donated to the city by the Masséna family in 1919, on the condition that it be maintained as a museum of local history. Its first floor consists of the original Empire furnishings (tastefully done in muted brown, red and green, with gilt accessories), and some sculpture and paintings of Napoleon's family—an amusing classic statue of Napoleon as a Roman emperor, a portrait of Josephine, and a copy of Canova's bust of Pauline Borghese, Napoleon's sister—the Massénas were apparently very proud of their Napoleonic connection. But head immediately upstairs to the second floor for the star attraction of the museum: two rooms full of light-hearted Dufys, which alone make the visit here worthwhile. A third room contains pictures of other painters who lived around Nice, including Monet and Renoir, some primitive Niçois paintings and sculpture from the 15th century, and objects relating to the Masséna family, Napoleon and Nice. The third floor has more on the history of Nice (including a room devoted to Garibaldi, who was born in Nice, in 1807, and an exhibition of applied arts—jewelry, furniture, Church reliquaries, swords, armor, guns, and the like.

La Tour Bellanda

"Located at the end of the Promenade des Anglais (or the Quai des Etats Unis; walking east from the center of town) is **La Tour Bellanda,** a popular tourist attraction because it offers not only a lovely winding park (with a Chateau, ruins of the ancient Fort-Palace, later Cathedral, on top—this is where the town of Nice began) and a small **Naval Museum,** but also, because it is actually a small mountain, with a marvelous view of Nice. I suggest you take the elevator up (1.40 to ride up; another 1.40 francs to ride down; or 2 francs for the round-trip) and walk down, stopping on your way to see the Naval Museum (open every day except Tuesday from 10 to 12:30 and 2:30 to 6:30, for a 3 franc entrance fee; the park is open summers til 8 p.m., but the elevator closes at 7). The little Museum has all kinds of maritime memorabilia reflecting the naval history of Nice, but the most fun is a high-powered telescope which you can train on the city to check the local action."

READERS' SIGHTSEEING SUGGESTIONS: "Please do not neglect to mention Nice's other fine museums: the **Musée des Beaux Arts,** also known as the Jules Cheret, 33 Avenue des Baumettes, with a roomful of Nice carnival posters, sculpture by and a fine portrait of Rodin (by Carrière), a bust and a portrait of Somerset Maugham (the latter by MacAvoy), ceramics by Picasso, paintings by Renoir, Monet, Degas, Dufy; countless other works of interest; the **Musee Barla** (natural history), 60 bis Blvd. Risso, unique for its collection of artificial mushrooms [Note by HA: closed in August; and Tuesdays— open 9 to 12 and 2 to 6; 3 franc entrance fee, and located across the street from the Flea Market]; and the **Musée du Vieux Logis** at 59 Avenue St. Barthelemy. The modern **Church of Ste. Jeanne d'Arc** is on the Avenue Borriglione and has interesting frescos by Klementief. The **Russian Orthodox Cathedral,** famous for its iconostasis (an ornamented screen bearing sacred images), is on Blvd. du Tzarewitch. There are small galleries and many other corners of interest, as well" (Dr. and Mrs. A. M. Cooper, Fresno, California). . . . "Recently restored and re-opened in 1969, you might like to take a look at the **Palais Lascaris** at 15 Rue Droite in the Old City of Nice, open from 9:30 to 12 and 2:30 to 6:30 (winters till 5:30 on Wednesday, Thursday, Saturday and Sunday); for 5 francs you can visit with a guide, 4 francs solo. Lascaris, built in 1648 and restored in 1706, is now a fading Baroque patrician mansion with mostly Provence-style furniture (all of which had to be replaced, since everything disappeared during the French Revolution). The ceilings are attributed to the 17th century Carlone; and on the ground floor there's an antique pharmacy which was founded in 1738. It was an amusing experience to me because some of the decorations here are so garish they were almost like 'Pop Art'. Lascaris is also the headquarters for 'Visites Commentées du Vieux-Nice', several tours of old Nice, which are usually scheduled daily at 10, 3 and 5, and cost around 4 francs per tour" (Pauline Hadley, New York, New York). . . . "To combine a pleasant outing with a cultural feast, take a one-day joint excursion to Beaulieu-Sur-Mer and Saint-Jean-Cap-Ferrat. At Beaulieu you'll find a lovely beach, and the **Foundation Theodore Reinach's Villa 'Kerylos'** (open daily, except Monday, from 3 to 7 in the summer, for a 7 franc admission price), a remarkable reproduction of a Greek Villa of the 4th and 5th centuries B.C.—around the Age of Pericles. Reinach, an archaeologist, scholar and numismatist, built and lived in the house for 18 years—and all the furniture (except a few Roman and Egyptian chairs) and decorative elements are as exact a duplication of a wealthy ancient household as Reinach's scholarship, with the help of imported craftsmen, could accomplish: the construction of the building alone cost 8 or 9 million *gold* francs. I never dreamed anything like this existed—from the tranquil inner courtyard, mosaic floors and precious marbles, the painted walls and beamed ceilings, the dining room with a reclining chaise for the master of the house, to the shower, and the sunken marble bath—all conspire to make one feel like a privileged visitor to the Villa of an ancient, aristocratic Greek. Reinach chose this gorgeous spot by the water because it reminded him of Greece ('Kerylos' means 'Bird of the Sea'); it's just opposite Cap Ferrat, and from here you can see the **Villa-Musée Ile-de-France** (you can probably catch a bus, or even hike to Saint-Jean-Cap Ferrat), the former home of Madame Ephrussi de Rothschild. It's filled with Madame Rothschild's vast collections—precious tapestries (Aubusson, Gobelin); Regency, Louis XV and Louis XVI furniture (including pieces that belonged to Marie Antoinette); a priceless porcelain collection; objets d'art from the Far East; Fragonard, Boucher, and some impressionist paintings. To give you some idea of the sumptuousness of this Villa, just imagine using a Gothic confessional to cover a service entrance (as Madame did)! And the surrounding gardens are magnificent. Open from 3 to 7 in the summer (winters, and that's through June 30, from 2 to 6; but the Gardens are open mornings from 9 to 12); the admission is 10 francs for the museum and the gardens, 5 francs for the gardens only. Note: both the above museums are closed Monday, and have annual closings during the month of November. And to wander around Cap Ferrat, with its beautiful port, elegant mansions, and lovely little beaches is a sheer delight" (Pauline Rissman, Miami, Florida). . . . "The lofty old 'top of the mountain' walled (formerly part of the fortress) village of **Roquebrune** (above Cap Martin), with the remains of an 11th century Carolingian Castle (open from 9 to 12 and 2 to 8 for a 2 franc admission: just the prison and a few sparsely furnished chambers are all that's left now, but there's a nice view from the top), is a charming medieval town with narrow, up-and-down, completely covered streets. The ancient character of the village is so intact, it's a heady experience to walk through it (seems to be a gathering of artists and craftsmen here too, taking inspiration from the spot); but it's quite difficult to reach without a car" (Angela Marto, New York, New York). . . . "If you find yourself in Monaco (and who won't?), you might like to visit the **Exotic Garden**, which is cut out of the side of the mountain above the Palace (but not reached from the Palace), and has the largest (and probably the tallest) assortment of cacti one is ever likely to see—I began to feel I was walking through Rousseau's painting 'The Dream.' Open from 9 to 7 in summer, 9 to noon and 2 to 6 the remainder of the year, for a 6 franc entrance fee (3 francs for children), this may be one of the last sightseeing bargains left in Monaco (which has become such a tourist trap). For the same admission you can also see **The Grotte** (underground caves which were a prehistoric dwelling place, with stalactites and stalagmites—you must wait for a guide to take you through, though), and **The Anthropology Museum** (with finds from the Grotte and the nearby area—tools, bones, etc.; an interesting exhibit on prehistoric art; a Roman collection; and skeletons known as Grimaldi negroids and Cro-Magnon men). Oh, and there's a beautiful view of Monaco and its port from the Terrace. You can catch a bus directly back to Nice from the Jardin; across the street from the tobacco shop is the 'Nice Arret', but the last bus for Nice from here is at 7 p.m." (Adam Slote, New York, New York). . . . "The Riviera trains are very cheap and run fairly frequently all along the coast. But for a ride on the breath-taking Moyenne Corniche (middle road) or Grande Corniche (high road), take the bus, and do stop at **Eze**, a medieval village perched 1200 feet over the water just off the Moyenne Corniche. Charming, no carts, all footpaths only, and a spectacular view" (Phil and Maryjane Bradley, Watertown, Massachusetts). . . . "The **Nice Tourist Office**, on the Avenue Thiers (in the small building to your left as you leave the station), is staffed with friendly, young, English-speaking French girls who, aside from answering all your questions about Nice and surroundings, will give you a free map of Nice, a list of museums and other informative brochures. Open Monday to Friday, 8:30 to 12 and 2 to 6:30." (Michael Mendelsohn, New York, N.Y.)

SALADE NICOISE: Some final names and addresses include the **Galeries Lafayette**, local branch of the huge Parisian department store, which is open daily except Sunday, from 9 a.m. to 7:15 p.m. The ground floor is where you'll pick up beach wear at excellent prices. That's at the near-the-sea end of the Avenue Jean-Médecin. . . . The largest, most exciting charcuterie (delicatessen) of Nice—where you can pick up unbelievably attractive ingredients for a picnic lunch (and you should)—is **Germanetto**, at 13 Rue Masséna, which is closed on Mondays and afternoon on Sundays; this is, of course, more expensive than the Prisunic earlier described, but more elaborate and exotic in its offerings. . . . If your stay in Nice is for three nights or more, it will pay you to purchase a 40-franc **Carte Touristique**, available at the Nice Tourist office booth at the railroad station, and entitling you to a free admission to nearly all museums, free use of city buses for up to a week, free maps and brochures, and to discounts at shops. . . . For reputable babysitters, phone 63-87-31. . . . And don't conclude your stay without visiting Nice's **flower market**, near the Opera House. While the market building may look like a bus terminal, inside is an overwhelmingly beautiful display of flowers and plants—the perfect background, also, for color photographs. That's open daily except Monday from 6 to 11 a.m.

No trip to Europe is complete without a stay in Switzerland. For a first visit to that nation, try the city of Zurich.

Chapter XVI

ZURICH

Accounting in the Alps

IMAGINE A BOULEVARD lined at one end with banks and squat department stores, which suddenly opens into a lake of the brightest blue, covered with sailboats and swans. Consider a city of enormous commercial fame, where stock markets and brokers' houses stand a five-minute walk from brooding forests and mountain chateaus. Think of efficient business activity carried on amid sidewalk cafes and tearoom conversations.

Zurich, the locale of these contrasts, is the city I'd choose for a first introduction to the land of contrasts, Switzerland. It is, to begin with, a functioning Swiss city, and not a single-minded resort center like Lucerne or St. Moritz. And yet it enjoys all the better attributes of a Swiss tourist attraction: heartstopping scenery; the restful calm that comes from an atmosphere of cleanliness and honest dealing; the variety and interest to be found in the multi-lingual, multi-national character of the country; and finally, costs that, if not low, are at least moderate enough to remove the fear of over-expense from your vacation thoughts.

TIP: If your trip to Europe is a summer one, try to schedule your Zurich stay for August 1, the national independence day of the country, when bonfires are burned on the mountain tops, bands play on every city square, and cafes stay open all night. The holiday is lovingly celebrated by the Swiss; every home in Zurich puts out a Swiss flag, and the banners of the twenty-three Swiss cantons are displayed round the lake. During this period, the hotel situation in Zurich becomes very tight (although not desperate), and you'd do well to stop in at the "Verkehrs Bureau" (city tourist office) in the railroad station building, to the right as you leave the main entrance, and request their aid in finding a room (booking fees of 2 francs for one person, 3 francs for two, 4 francs for three).

At all other times in Zurich, you can do it without official aid by simply consulting the recommendations that follow below.

HOTELS: There is no such thing as a bad Swiss hotel. This is the "nation of hotelkeepers," the training ground for aspiring hotel managers of every land. The standards taught at the famous Swiss hotel schools are so very impeccable as to be downright ridiculous. I visited a class in Lausanne where aspiring "hôteliers" were being taught which of six glasses to use for serving Bordeaux wine.

The difference, therefore, between a low-cost and a deluxe Swiss hotel is in decoration, not in comfort, and not in service. The budget hotels could not possibly be any cleaner than they already are; and the service could not be more polite. Because of that, and to be perfectly frank, you need have no qualms about staying at virtually any budget hotel in Zurich. But we'll set forth the chief qualities of a few outstanding choices. Unless otherwise stated, all the following hotels have elevators, and most of them provide a free breakfast for the price of a room (all also include service and taxes in their rates, which means that their prices aren't quite as high as might first appear). Those in our first category are listed in ascending order of preference, beginning with five rather basic spots, then moving on to two normal budget hotels—the Bristol and the Limmathof—and then continuing with the type of Swiss hostelry about which we can wax rhapsodic.

Zurich's least expensive hotels

Hotel Schäfli, 6 Badergasse (phone 32-41-44), one of the cheapest we've found, is—as we've warned—a rather basic hotel in Swiss terms, with no showers or bathrooms, but with running hot water in each room that lasts until at least 10 a.m. each morning; it's also located over a busy little restaurant where a Swiss "oompah" band sometimes rocks the ceiling. But if you can tolerate those slight deficiencies (and on a short stay in Zurich, they won't bother you), you'll enjoy rates that are among the lowest in the city: in 1980, these will be 24 francs single, 38 francs ($22.35), double, but without breakfast (an extra 4 francs); with a couple of extra large doubles with private bath going for 50 francs. Manager of the Schäfli, Mr. Marth, speaks English well, and is most helpful about giving directions to various points in town. The hotel is located near #13 on our map, on a tiny alleyway off the Limmatquai, two blocks from the Rudolf-Brun Bridge; it is, again, only for the *least* demanding of our readers.

Rössli Hotel, at Rössligasse 7 (phone 32-71-66), a tiny street just off the Limmatquai, near Schiffländeplatz, is perched over a moderately-priced restaurant, and the modest establishment upstairs rents single rooms at 19 to 25 francs ($11.17 to $14.70), doubles at 38 to 50 francs ($22.35 to $29.41), triples at 60 to 75 francs ($35.29 to $44.11). The restaurant, under the same management as the hotel, is open daily except Sunday for lunch and dinner, offering two two-course meals for 7 francs ($4.11) and 8 francs ($4.70), respectively. The Rössli's owner, Herr Treichler, has assured me he will give the best possible service to readers of this book.

Hotel Italia, Zeughausstrasse 61 (phone 241-4339), is managed by the hard-working Papagni family, who offer simple but thoroughly clean accommodations. Rates are 30 francs ($17.46) single, 45 francs ($26.47) double, 60 francs ($35.29) triple, breakfast included. From the main railway station, walk up to Löwenstrasse, turn left at Löwenplatz, cross the bridge over the Sihl-

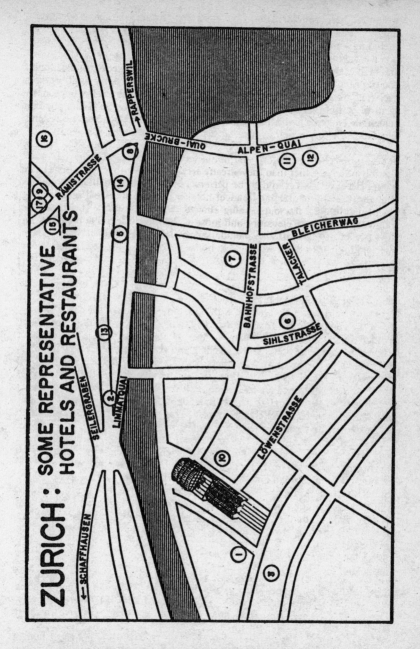

River, walk into Militärstrasse, and turn left into Kanonengasse.

Pension Dula, 50 Clausiusstrasse (phone 322-422), near the University, occupies three floors of an old but well-preserved and well-kept building in which 20 guest rooms are simply but adequately furnished; there is no elevator. Single rooms are 25 francs ($14.70), but doubles only 35 francs ($20.58), including continental breakfast served in a tiny kitchen on the third floor where you can help yourself to as much coffee, milk and bread as you wish. Proprietress Hilde Dula, who speaks perfect English, also rents three tiny single rooms, the size of a railway compartment, for only 15 francs ($8.82), a light breakfast included, but these are usually in permanent use by Swiss students. From the Central Station, take streetcars 10 or 6, and get off at the ETH Station, from which the Dula is a five-minute walk. ETH stands for "Eidgenössische Technische Hochschule", which in turn means "Federal Technical University."

THE SWISS FRANC: For the purposes of this chapter, we've assumed that the worth of the Swiss franc is about 59 U.S. ¢, reflecting a current exchange rate of approximately 1.70 francs to the dollar. Prices set forth in Swiss francs, in this chapter, are correct for 1980; however, their dollar equivalents may vary slightly from what we've calculated.

Hotel Bristol, 34 Stampfenbachstrasse (phone 47-07-00), is one of the largest of Zurich's budget hotels, with 60 rooms, and one of the best located—from the Hauptbahnhof (main railroad station) walk over the Bahnhof Bridge (which doesn't appear on our map) to Stampfenbachstrasse, turn left for about 100 yards, and there you'll find it. A plain and simple four-story grey building, very much in the Swiss style, it rents bathless doubles for between 45 to 60 francs (from $26.47 to $35.29), breakfast and service charges included; singles for 35 francs (and there are lots of singles); triples and four-bedded rooms for much less per person; caters mainly to students, but accepts guests of all ages, and families to whom it offers family-plan arrangements permitting children to sleep free in the room of their parents, sharing a parent's bed.

Hotel Limmathof (2), 142 Limmatquai (phone 47-42-20), always one of our best-recommended budget hotels in Zurich, has been working through a long-term renovation project and has surfaced as an attractive, well-kept and beautifully-located small hotel (55 rooms) that is excellent value for the money. Situated on the Limmat River, directly across the Bahnhof Bridge from the railroad station, the Limmathof has retained its charming turn-of-the-century façade while up-dating its interior. All the rooms have shiny parquet floors, most have modern suites of furniture and bright Persian throw rugs. The breakfast room, with its Swiss chairs and open balcony, is charming. And on the ground floor, there's a rustic "Weinstube" that provides a meeting-place for locals and guests. All in all, a good buy at the uniform charge of 26 francs ($15.29) per person in bathless rooms, double, breakfast and service charge included, 22 francs per person in triples, 30 francs single.

Pension Fontana, 57 Gloriastrasse (phone 323-453), in the University area, has been in business for more than 100 years, enjoys 40 beds, four floors, no elevator, and charges 25 francs ($14.70) single, 40 ($23.52) double, 52 francs ($30.58) triple, for nicely furnished rooms inclusive of breakfast. Its present owner, the energetic and charming Frau Rosa Evelyn Bircher, keeps the establishment clean and shining with the aid of numerous Spanish and Italian chambermaids and charwomen whom you will constantly see washing up and waxing floors, dusting and polishing. From the Central Station, take streetcar 6 and get off at the Voltastrasse stop, which is directly in front of the Fontana.

The alcohol-free **Burma Hotel**, a 5-minute tramride (#11 or #14) from the station, at Schindlerstrasse 26 (corner of Stampfenbach), has singles at 32 francs and doubles for 50 francs ($29.41), including breakfast, service and taxes. Friendly and cheerful, although somewhat less personal than others we've named, it is a fine budget establishment, with a sober-style restaurant downstairs where substantial hot plates start at a low 5 francs. Phone: 26-10-08.

Hotel Seefeld Garni, at Seehofstrasse 11 (phone 34-95-70), near the Opera House and the lake, is heavily patronized by Swiss businessmen who praise its quiet and central location. Manager Herr Platten charges 28 to 30 francs ($16.47 to $17.64) for a single, 44 to 50 francs ($25.88 to $29.41) for a double, breakfast included. To find the hotel, walk to the lakeside end of Bahnhofstrasse, cross the Quai-Bridge, and turn into Uto-Quai (the street facing the lake); Seehofstrasse is the third street turning left.

Pension Titlis, named after a mountain peak near Lucerne, is in the central but quiet section of town called "Hottingen," at 44 Rütistrasse (phone 34-73-59), and can be reached by streetcar #3 from the station (get off at Römerhof). Multilingual Frau Hulda Züsli-Minder keeps everything spotless and pleasant, at reasonable rates: 20 to 25 francs single, 40-45 francs double, breakfast included.

Zurich's moderately-priced hotels

Hotel Limmathaus (3), 118 Limmatstrasse (phone 42-52-40), less than 10 minutes on foot from the station, is a big and highly recommended tourist class establishment, and probably the most recently-built (but the highest-priced) of all the hotels in this chapter. The 100-bed building looks as if it had been designed by Walter Gropius; the rooms are furnished in Scandinavian-style, with all-new furniture; there's an exceedingly helpful and friendly staff; and prices are 36 francs single, 75 francs ($44.11) for a double, with breakfast, showers, service and taxes always included. A top find. Take tram #4 or 13 to Limmatplatz—a four minute ride from the station (second stop).

Hotel Rothus (5), Marktgasse 17 (phone 34-15-30), another big hotel, is located in the most interesting area of Zurich—the "Niederdorf," just a block or two from the river, in the center of the city, but in a quaint unchanged, medieval section of the town, filled with narrow streets for walkers only, statues and fountains at every small plaza, and packed also with the cafes and nightspots of Zurich—the Rothus (whose lobby is one flight up) is above a nightclub, whose activity and noise may disturb, but may delight, you. It is, as I have said, a large place, with 100 beds, neat and proper in the clean, woodsy, old-fashioned Swiss-style (there are big feather blankets on each bed), and the prices are fairly good for high-priced Zurich: 32 francs for a single with breakfast, 56 francs for a double with two breakfasts, 70 triple, 92 quadruple, with service charge included. Don't be deterred by the astonishingly ugly downstairs exterior; upstairs is a large and attractive lobby, and excellent budget rooms. In the vicinity of the Rothus, and with similar prices: **Hotel Splendid** at Rosengasse 5 (phone 34-58-50), recently modernized and redecorated by four new young owners—singles for 30 francs, doubles for 50 francs, including service and taxes; and the highly-recommended **Hotel Biber**, Niederdorfstrasse 7 (this one charging 36 to 40 francs per person in a double room, 48 francs single, breakfast, shower, private w.c. and service included), phone 34-22-20. Generally speaking, the latter two establishments (particularly the Biber) are a bit more conservative than is the Rothus and therefore might be preferred by readers wary of the sometimes boisterous life that can erupt after 10 p.m. on the Niederdorfstrasse. Indeed, the reserved owner of the Biber, Herr Erwin Asch- inger-Schmidt, likes to say that his hotel is "am Hirschenplatz"—and not on the Niederdorfstrasse. His rates are particularly good for groups of four persons —as little as 27 francs ($15.88) per person for bed and breakfast, service included, in a multi-bedded room.

A newcomer to this book is **Hotel Regina**, Hohlstrasse 16 (near Helvetia- platz), where rates are 30 francs ($17.64) single, 46 francs ($27.05) twin, only 42 francs ($24.70) double, 55 to 60 francs for a triple—all including breakfast, but with an extra 3 franc charge per room for baths. The owner's wife, Frau Gmür, supervises the **Falstaff**, a ground-floor restaurant offering a choice of 15 two-course menus ranging in price from 6 to 10 francs. From the central railway station, Regina can be reached by a 15-minute walk or a five-minute bus ride (#31); get off at Kanonengasse, the second stop. . . . Not far away, at 121 Langstrasse, **Hotel Rothaus** (phone 241-24-51) is an unusually well run (even by Swiss standards), newly re-decorated hotel. The Fumasoli family, who run it, have managed hotels for many years, speak English fluently, try hard to please their customers, take pains in maintaining virtually soundproof condi- tions (through double-glazed windows), and charge only 32 francs ($18.83) single, 50 francs ($29.41) double, always including breakfast. A restaurant on the ground floor serves various daily menus ranging from 6.50 to 12 francs. From the central station, take bus 31 and get off at the fourth stop, called Militär-Langstrasse.

Hotel Sternen Oerlikon, Schaffhauserstrasse 335 (phone 46-77-77), is less central than any we've named (only ten minutes, however, by a #7 or #14 tram from the train station; the stop is "Sternen"), but good value for moderate prices; a large, but restful and quiet, old-fashioned hotel, with a particularly distinguished restaurant and wine cellar. It charges 36 francs per person for a single room with breakfast, 62 francs ($36.47) double with breakfasts—includ- ing the service charge.

Those are the best individual budget hotels. The best **area** for moderately- priced (not cheap) rooms is along the side of the lake, next to the Stadttheater of Zurich, where there's a lovely little section, jammed with small hotels and pensions that normally cater to somewhat older and more relaxed tourists (the area is located precisely where the word "Rapperswil" appears on our map of Zurich). To reach it, simply take your luggage and you on board a streetcar to the Kreuzstrasse, whose lakeside location you should love. There, just be- hind the nearby Stadttheater, you'll find the modest **Pension Beau-Site**, 40 Dufourstrasse (phone 32-11-47), a converted townhouse whose appearance is like that of a 19th century Victorian home: it's only 25 francs ($14.70) for bed-breakfast-and-service in a single room, 48 francs ($28.23) for a double; reservations are probably needed in high season, since the capacity is only 24 beds, but you can try phoning. . . . For much cheaper rooms than any we've named, see "Starvation Budget" later in this chapter.

The Resort Hotels

For a change of scene, the influential, long-established Women's Temper- ance Union of Zurich operates two moderately-priced resort hotels on the outskirts of the city, and they are spectacular in terms of both rates and setting. Imagine checking into a beautiful mountainside resort in Sun Valley, Idaho, in high season—and paying only $19 per person for room, breakfast and service! These two hotels—the **Zurichberg** and the **Rigiblick**—fit that descrip- tion: they are located on the hills that surround Zurich, and from their flowered terraces you have a panoramic view of the town, the lake and the mountains. Both charge 38 francs ($22.35) for a single, 32 francs ($18.82) per person double, for room and breakfast, with no service charge added and no tipping allowed. The 100-bed Zurichberg is located at Orellistrasse 21 (phone 343848), a four-minute walk from the Allmend Fluntern streetcar terminus, from which there is frequent trolley service into town. To reach Allmend Fluntern, take tram #6 from the railroad station to the end of the line, and switch there to tram #5, which goes to the Allmend Fluntern terminus, high overlooking Zurich. The 30-bed Rigiblick, whose situation is more remote, is at Germaniastrasse 99 (phone 264214), but easily and quickly reached by Tram No. 10 and the Rigiviertel Cable Railway. Both resorts are superb for families with children; they proudly proclaim that "no alcoholic beverages may be brought into the hotel, even on a physician's prescription." There are also good roads that reach both resorts, and adequate free parking areas. Make reservations well in advance in the summertime.

Into the suburbs

If everything we've listed is full, there's still no reason to despair; head instead for the Zurich Railway Station and look for an automatic hotel telephone booking service near the escalators leading downstairs to the underground shopping center; then, push the button marked "Thalwilerhof", lift the receiver, wait a few seconds, and soon you'll be talking without charge to a Heidi-type hostelry that can put you up in summer for as little as 20 francs ($11.80) per person, including breakfast.

Herr Roduner's **Hotel Thalwilerhof** (phone 720-0603), subject of these complex instructions, is located directly in front of the train station (but in a Swiss-pretty lakeside setting) of Zurich-Thalwil, six miles southeast of town, near the lake shore. No fewer than 80 trains a day make the 15-minute trip from 5 a.m. to midnight from the Zurich train station, 80 other trains return from Thalwil to Zurich, and round-trip fare is 4.40 francs—the same ticket being valid in summer for a lake steamer which cruises every hour between Zurich and Thalwil. What makes the Hotel Thalwilerhof such a find are not its normal double rooms renting for 42 to 50 francs, including breakfast, but its "notzimmer" or emergency rooms on the ground floor, which Herr Roduner offers as 3-4 bed dorms in summer, and prices at 20 francs ($11.80) per person, including breakfast. Add to that your daily 4.40-franc transportation cost for commuting into Zurich proper, and the result is still so easy on the pocket that you won't mind the single major drawback of the Thalwilerhof's conference room "dorms": since they have no running water in them, you're instructed to take the elevator upstairs to use wash-up facilities. Another plus for the Thalwilerhof is a restaurant with a beautiful terrace overlooking the lake, where you can dine while watching the sailing boats and steamers along the Zürchersee. Filling plate dinners, like meat balls with vegetable and roast potatoes, are priced at 7.50 francs ($4.41).

An alternate to the Thalwilerhof, especially in September when fairs, exhibitions and conferences can cause a severe bed-shortage in Zurich itself, is the suburban **Hotel Bahnhof** at 1 Neue Dorfstrasse (phone 713-31-31), in Langnau am Albis, again about six miles outside Zurich. At this small and intimate hotel, managed by Frau Barmittler, singles are only 18 francs ($10.58), doubles 35 francs ($20.58), triples 52 francs ($30.58), always including a hearty breakfast. From Zurich's Selnau Station, trains to Langnau run hourly, take 20 minutes, cost 2.40 francs one-way, and the hotel is directly across the street from Langnau station.

READERS' PENSION SELECTIONS: "We rank the **Pension Riby,** Volkmar Strasse 5 (phone 26-91-30), as among the best we found in Europe, because of the very nice accommodations and the charm of the manageress, Frau Riby. She greeted us with a wonderful, though baffling: "Goodbye, goodbye, I do not speak too good English." But her English is quite adequate, and her friendliness is contagious! Rooms rent for 50 francs ($29.41) for two persons, singles are 25 francs ($14.70), all including breakfasts" (Dr. and Mrs. Ben Burnett, Whittier College, Whittier, California; note by AF: Frau Riby is a heavy-set, jovial lady, and very sweet; her pension occupies the top floor of an elevator-lacking three-story house whose sitting-room is a hodge-podge of elderly lady's belongings, including huge pink lampshades. The guestrooms themselves are unusually comfortable, with big sitting chairs and full carpets. One ceiling is painted with pastel murals. Singles 25 francs, doubles 50 francs, including breakfast, service and tax; take tram #7 from the station). . . . "**Hotel Poly,** 63 Universitätstrasse (phone 28-94-40), operates an **Annex** where I recently obtained a bathless single room for only 32 francs ($18.82), including breakfast in the main house" (D.I. Wardle, Riverdale, New York; note by AF: doubles here are 50 francs). . . . "**Justinus Heim** at 146 Freudenbergstrasse (20 minutes from the station; take tram #10 and the Seilbahn) is usually the residence of students from four and five continents. I paid $14 for a spacious single room with breakfast, and free use of the showers downstairs" (Joseph Kaposi, Willowdale, Ontario, Canada; note by AF: this is a modern, non-profit hotel, which specializes in accommodating students from developing countries, but accepts everyone, provided space is available. It's well managed by Herr Max Giger, an idealist in the best sense of the term, and will charge, in 1980, 24 francs ($14.10) for a single, 40 francs ($23.53) double, 60 francs ($35.30) triple, including breakfast. No curfew; free showers; 5 floors of rooms serviced by a lift; and free use of a large kitchen with 12 hot plates (automatically switched off after 15 minutes, a clever energy-saving device). When I last visited (in mid-1979), students from 32 nations (and 9 religions) were in attendance, including representatives from Peru, Uganda, Cyprus, Poland, Chile and Macáo, most of them studying at the Technical University. Phone 361-38-06). . . . "At the **Pension Peyer,** 39 Feldeggstrasse, on a quiet street near the lake, our double room for 50 francs ($29.41), including breakfast, was large and sunny, well furnished, had a tv set and elegant balcony with turn-of-the-century, art nouveau, stained-glass windows. And guests could use the refrigerator and washing facilities" (Charles Dicken, San Diego, California).

READERS' HOTEL SELECTIONS: "**Hotel Otter,** in the old district of Munster, Oberdorfstrasse 7 (phone 32-22-07), has outstandingly clean double rooms for 50 francs a night. The hotel is quiet, but in the center of everything" (CDR J.B. Farrell, Ewa Beach, Hawaii). . . . "The **OASE** at Freiestrasse 38, 8032 Zurich, offers clean, modern rooms in addition to excellent facilities—laundry, TV and living rooms, music room, gymnasium, etc. Singles are 30 francs, doubles 22 francs per person (less for longer stays), those rates including breakfast and use of a small kitchen. A family-style lunch is 6.50 francs, supper 6 francs. Take Tram #3 from the Central Station (Hauptbahnhof) to Steinwiesplatz" (Beth Kelsey, Fedora, North Dakota). . . . "**Hotel Rütli** at 43 Zähringerstrasse (phone 32-54-26), not far from the station, is a brand new little hotel of the women's temperance organization ('Frauenverein'), located over their restaurant of the same name. Price is 25 francs per person in double rooms, singles 28 francs, not including breakfast, and showers on each floor are free. A particularly good choice for single girls" (Ingeborg Söderlund, Stockholm, Sweden). . . . "**Hotel Hinterer Sternen** (phone 32-32-68), over the restaurant at 7 Freieckgasse (a tiny street off Theater Strasse and across from the Bellevueplatz tram stop and the lake), charged only 41 francs for a double without bath and without breakfast. Clean and convenient" (E. W. Gilbertson, Brooklyn, New York).

FOR GIRLS, FAMILIES AND COUPLES ONLY: Zurich's accommodations for

female and family travelers are among the best in Europe: they include, first, the big and recently-built **Foyer Hottingen,** 31 Hottingerstrasse (phone 47-93-15), whose most attractive feature—apart from its phenomenal (for Switzerland) prices of between 11 and 20 francs per person, including breakfast—is the exceptional warmth, charm and efficiency of a dedicated staff, headed by a remarkable Mother Superior, Joseph-Marie. Open the entire year, and operated by a Catholic organization, the receptionist here is a nun, and the only inconvenience is a strict midnight curfew, after which the front door is locked. The

Foyer will take not only young women, but older ones, as well as families with children and mature couples. Take tram #3 from the main station to Hottingerplatz. . . . Even more modern than the Foyer, but for women and married couples only, is Zurich's Y.W.C.A., located in a spectacular new building called the "**Martahaus,**" at 36 Zähringerstrasse (phone 32-45-50), directly across the river from the main railroad station (near #2 on our map; walk across the bridge in front of the station, not shown on our map). Both the building and its interior furnishings could win an architectural award, and the prices win our $15-a-day award: exactly 22 Swiss francs ($12.94) per person for bed and breakfast in double rooms with private bath, only 17 francs ($10, including breakfast and free showers) in the dormitory. Write well in advance for summer reservations, and address your letters to the "Martahaus". . . . A close runner-up to the superb Martahaus is the smaller (80 beds) **Pension Josefsheim** at 64 Hirschengraben (phone 322-757), five minutes on foot from the station. A modern, Catholic institution managed by an English-speaking nun, Sister Michel, it prices singles at 28 francs, doubles at 21 francs per person, triples and four-bedded rooms at 19 francs per bed per night, including breakfast and free showers. While there's a 12:30 a.m. curfew here, that regulation isn't strictly observed during the three summer months, provided you inform Sister Michel in advance of your late homecoming. Atmosphere is pleasant, location ideal, and the Josefsheim even provides supper for 8 francs.

FOR MEN ONLY: The center-city **Y.M.C.A.** (Sihlstrasse 33, phone 221-3673), rents a few rooms (but very few) to transients, in its large and rather modern building, at the price of 15 to 18 francs ($8.82 to $10.58) per person, service included. Low-cost food is available in the first-floor cafeteria and guests are invited to join in "Y" activities.

FOR THE RELIGIOUS-MINDED: A tastefully-modern structure called the **Hotel-Methodist Center Zelthof,** 18 Zeltweg (phone 47-80-66), is exactly what its name describes, but I've never heard of them putting religious questions to prospective guests. The charge is from 24 to 29 Swiss francs ($14.11 to $17.05) per person for room and breakfast (double occupancy), with no service charge, no tipping, and no alcohol allowed; it's 26 to 34 francs for a single room and breakfast. The location is on a residential street near the Kunsthaus (Zurich's major art gallery), between #'s 9 and 16 on our map; and the friendly manageress is Anne-Marie Lang-Noetzli.

CAFES: The cafes of Zurich are in a class by themselves. They're meeting halls, trysting spots, employment centers—and each of them caters to a specialized conversational group. The citizens of Zurich relax in cafes for hours on end. The waiters would no sooner ask you to move on than they would criticize the Sacred Swiss Army.

The venerable **Odeon Cafe (8),** on the corner of Limmatquai and Torgasse, where Lenin sat out the First World War, is the most famous and sophisticated of the Zurich cafes. (It charges 1.80 francs for a cup of coffee). The much more slickly-modern **Select Cafe,** at Limmatquai 16, corner of Schifflände Platz, is populated largely by aging artists, and it's a pleasant though no longer very European spot. Alcohol is not served, but coffee is—the best coffee in Zurich—and you can sit here all day and evening on a single cup (1.80 francs).

MEALS: "Fondue"—melted cheese with wine and Kirsch, lapped up with chunks of bread—is the food specialty of Switzerland, and you ought to head immediately for a place that serves it. Try, for instance, the well-managed **Restaurant Walliser Kanne (10)**, a block from the railroad station at Lintheschergasse 21, corner of Schützengasse. This is a relatively high-priced steakhouse, but it dishes up a huge portion of fondue Valaisienne for 10.50 Swiss francs ($6.17). The more moderately priced **"Blockhaus,"** on Schifflände 4, serves a similar fondue, and this time for only 7.50 francs (Fondue Neuchâteloise), with other inexpensive items to round off the meal. Order, however, only one serving of fondue for two persons—it comes in quantities much too massive for a single $15-a-day'er—but don't specifically advise the restaurant of your intention. Let one of you order the fondue, the other a cheaper item; it is served in such a way (small squares of bread, a metal bowl of melted cheese) as to make it easy for both of you to dip away together. . . . "Rösti"—a specially-made, Swiss type of fried potatoes—is another dish found only in this country. It's usually served with sausages and salad, costs about 4.50 francs ($2.64) in that plate combination. If ordered separately, order again only one portion for two persons; the plate of rösti I had last summer in Zurich was as big as a pizza pie. Where to find it? Try the **Olivenbaum**, at 10 Stadelhoferstrasse, where various plates are priced at 5.80 to 6.80 francs and are served all day. Open daily, from 6:30 a.m. till 8:30 p.m. on weekdays, to 7:30 p.m. weekends.

And a bit about "raclette"

The **Restaurant Raclette-Stube**, at 16 Zähringerstrasse, is the only full-time "raclette stube" in Zurich. And raclette consists of a large platter of melted cheese accompanied by a boiled potato, pickled onion, and pickle: you spice the cheese with paprika, salt and pepper, then eat it with the chunks of potato and pickle (one uses forks and knives for this, unlike fondue). Each platter costs only 3.70 francs and the idea is to eat one platter, then request another and go on like that until you are full. In some parts of Switzerland, they even have raclette-eating-contests to see who can get down the most platters (on a very hungry evening, I only managed to polish off three). Closed Wednesdays.

The Frauenverein Restaurants

The most phenomenal budget eating spots in Zurich are a somber chain of restaurants operated by the city's Women's Temperance Union ("Zürcher Frauenverein für Alkoholfreie Wirtschaften"), which are generally known either as "Frauenverein" restaurants or simply "Alkoholfreie" restaurants, and where the strongest drink served is cider; they're often filled with hard-eyed, pinch-mouthed people who look eternally suspicious that somebody, somewhere, is enjoying himself. I'd go there for most of my meals, nevertheless, because they're moderately-priced and typically Swiss.

There are nine such places in Zurich, each bearing a separate name. Hope and I last ate at the **Restaurant "Rütli,"** at 43 Zähringerstrasse, a clean, woodsy-looking and austerely joyless place (like all the Alkoholfreie restaurants), where Hope had, for 8.50 ($5) francs, a big bowl of mushroom soup and black bread, followed by a huge plate of Hungarian goulash and rice, and salad. For the same 8.50 francs, I had soup, a small mixed grill, cauliflower and potatoes. Not only was there no service charge, but better yet, tipping is absolutely prohibited throughout the Frauenverein chain.

A larger Frauenverein restaurant, and one I'd more strongly recommend, is the previously mentioned **Olivenbaum,** 10 Stadelhoferstrasse, in the building next to the Zurich-Stadelhofen Railroad Station, in the area of the Stadttheater, near the Lake. It's open every day of the week, and if you'll order from the German-language menu—never the English one—you'll find two-course meals priced at not more than 6.80 francs, plus two francs for dessert, with the service charge always included in the price. Simply look for a sign reading "Alkohol-freies Restaurant," which designates the Olivenbaum. Prices here are slightly higher on Sundays.

A smaller and again earlier-mentioned "Frauenverein" restaurant called the **"Rütli"** is found at Zähringerstrasse 43, directly across the river from the railroad station; the largest of the Frauenvereins is the **Volkshaus** (also called the "Kafi"), a monumental-style structure with unique saddle-roof, at Helvetia-platz, near St. Jacobs Church, with prices identical to those of the Olivenbaum; and there's still another important member of the chain (the **"Restaurant Seidenhof"**) in the same building that houses the popular Seidenhof Hotel (which is also owned by the ubiquitous Frauenverein) at 7 Sihlstrasse, just a block from the Jelmoli Department Store, off the Bahnhofstrasse.

The fabulous Restaurant Urania Löwenbräu

The largest budget restaurant in Zurich, and the most consistently satisfy-ing (although a bit higher in price than the Frauenvereins), is the **Urania Löwenbräu** at 9 Uraniastrasse (one block off Bahnhofstrasse)—which you reach from the station by walking down Bahnhofstrasse and turning left at the second traffic light. Actually, there are several Urania Restaurants in the same building. The one you're looking for is the "Laube"—a 200-person room, light, bright, and without tablecloths, but with plate meals (to be ordered only from the daily, typed "tageskarte") averaging 8 and 9 francs, some of which are preceded by soup. Every day after 3 p.m., Laube serves its famous "Wädli" for 4.50 francs: salted and cooked pork pieces—rib, leg, and tongue—which pro-vide reason enough for paying it a visit. Evenings a 4-piece band plays music for dancing—at a small extra charge to you.

The Tea Rooms of Zurich

Another category of budget eateries in Zurich, where you won't be allowed to "miss the Swiss," are generally known as "tea rooms": they're charming, typical, hearty places that serve monstrously big meals, for the most part, and allow you to linger as long as you like over a cup of tea or coffee. The Swiss go here to read the newspapers (supplied by the tea rooms) and may sometimes join you at a table and converse, if you seem friendly. These, obviously, are quite a bit livelier than the members of the "Frauenverein" chain, and the majority of them serve meals, as well as pastries and beverages—the meals being invariably cheaper than at regular restaurants.

The most attractive of Zurich's tea rooms, in my opinion, is the **Troika,** at Werdmühleplatz 3 (if you walk three blocks from the Bahnhof, down Bahn-hofstrasse, and turn left, you will enter Werdmühleplatz); this is a large tea room with an outdoor cafe in warm weather. It is richly decorated with heavy, grained, wooden tables, large carved wooden chairs with maroon leather seats, a ceiling hand-painted in colorful folk designs. During the day and evening, a piano player reels off renditions of "Exodus" and other pieces of portent. White-jacketed waiters wander around with trays of impossibly rich pastries and dainty tea sandwiches. Yet the charge for lunch and dinner (the menus are the same) is 7.20 to 8.20 francs for at least three fixed-price meals of soup, main dish and salad. (Service is included.) This tea room is so popular with the Zurich gentry that they almost invariably take out-of-town guests to dinner there at least once (or so I'm told). Closed Sundays, and at 9 p.m.

There are tea rooms all over the city. In the area of the Bahnhof, for instance, try the **Cafe Littéraire** (sans alcohol), one block from the station at the corner of Schützengasse and Lintheschergasse. Good food. Popular with a talky and attractive crowd of Swiss. Two-course menus from 7 to 10 francs. I once had a delicious filet of flounder with pepperoni, curry, fruit and creole rice for 7.50 including soup. Near the Limmat River and not far from the lake, at 66 Limmatquai, the popular, **Gran Cafe** offers light snacks only. But close by, at 30 Stadelhofer Strasse, you'll find **Go-In**, a new cafeteria where most one-course meals cost 5.50 francs: you might have, for that price, a salad bowl, ham and eggs or hamburger with pepper sauce, and potato salad.

The Silberkugels

A Chock Full O'Nuts in **Zurich**? This may come as a great surprise to visiting New Yorkers, but the **Silberkugels** are almost an exact copy (Swiss translation) of that venerable budget institution. There are nine such restaurants in the city and they all feature the familiar quick counter service, a limited, low-cost menu, and "Absolutely No Tipping Allowed." All are new, bright, modern and friendly and well-frequented by Swiss lunchers-in-a-hurry. Even the bill of fare is Americanized. Here you can get a "Beefy" hamburger for from 1.80 to 4.30 francs. But you'll eat more cheaply by choosing one of the two daily hot plates, priced from 3 francs up, and augmenting that with a delicious bowl of yogurt mixed with fresh fruits for 1.50 francs. The most convenient Silberkugel to the main railway station is at Bahnhofplatz 14— across from the front entrance and to the right. The other branches are located in the subway passage under the Bahnhofplatz (this one stays open late), at Badenerstrasse 120, Löwenstrasse 7, Limmatstrasse 46, Bleicherweg 33, Franklinstrasse 11, Altstetterstrasse 124, and Stampfenbachstrasse 48. All nine also have "Take Out" sections.

Others

A good, typical, moderately-priced restaurant? Across the Limmat River from the railroad station side, walk up Kirchgasse until you pass Oberdorfstrasse. Turn right and walk to #20 Oberdorfstrasse. You'll come upon the **Restaurant Weisser Wind (13)**, a large, but quaint, and absolutely authentic Swiss restaurant, where for 8 francs ($4.70), you can have "Kässchnitte mit Ei und Schinken"—melted cheese on bread, with a fried egg on top, and cooked ham on the side. There are one or two cheaper plates than this, and two-course meals for as little as 7 francs ($4.11). Closed Sundays.

Another highly atmospheric restaurant, well worth a stop-in for lunch or a Swiss specialty, is the relatively new **Zur Kantorei** on the ground floor of a picturesque 18th-century building in the tiny square of Neumarkt. Up above the restaurant is a long-established and well-known school for voice students, and therefore it's become a gathering place for singers and other people in the performing arts. The interior, with its hanging lamps of green glass, soaring windows and leather-covered seats, is an imaginative and comfortable setting for dining and conversation. Lunchtime is the best time to go, as set three-course lunches are priced from 6.50 to 7.50 francs. Throughout the day you can order cheese fondue for 9.50 francs. There are some costly items on the menu, but the majority are reasonably-priced and the quality high.

A Snack of St. Galler Bratwursts

Snack stands all over Zurich sell these famous white wursts, which are made from veal, not pork, but I'd buy mine at the renowned **Bell's,** 102 Bahnhofstrasse (one block from the station), which is undoubtedly the world's most beautiful butcher shop—even the lowly hamburger here has tastefully-arrayed cloves stuck in it. Hot grilled bratwursts sell at Bell's for 2 francs without bread, for 2.30 francs with, and there are attractive open sandwiches en gelee for 1.40 francs, as well as other picnic ingredients and salads.

Dining with the Swiss Army

A short walk from Zurich's central railway station at 3 Militärstrasse, the Swiss Army serves civilians and soldiers alike at its **Militär-Kantine,** open Monday through Saturday from 11 to noon, Monday through Friday from 5:30 p.m. to 8 p.m. And while the civilian price for a two-course meal of 8 francs ($4.70) isn't exactly cheap (an example is a piquant vegetable soup, followed by a large and crisp cordon bleu with cauliflower and fried potatoes), the portions are huge and quality as good as in any far-more-expensive Swiss restaurant. Interesting as an oddity, and for top quality at moderate cost; naturally, the military pay considerably less than you for the same meal.

Jelmoli

Finally, go for at least one breakfast or lunch in Zurich to the stunningly-modern third floor restaurant of the **Jelmoli Department Store** (pronounced yell-moe-lee) on the Bahnhofstrasse, where you can fill up for the day on the special Buffet Breakfast consisting of your choice of 20 kinds of Swiss bread, butter, eggs, six kinds of meat, cereal, fresh fruits and juices—all you can eat—for 8 francs ($4.70). Two-course luncheons (plus salad) start at 6.20 and go up to 10.20 francs. And if you're really starved, you can go down to the basement, which houses one of the world's most beautiful supermarkets, and pick up the free food samples (cheese or paté on bread) to eat as your appetizer course.

READERS' RESTAURANT SELECTIONS: "The **Rheinfelder Bierhalle,** Niederdorf Str. #76, was our discovery. We ate there several times: the food is good and plentiful and very inexpensive. We had vegetable soup, beef goulash, boiled potatoes, lettuce and radish salad, all for 7 francs," (William A. Hagemann, Forest Hills, New York; note by AF: somewhat cheaper is the **Rheinfelder Bierhaus** at 19 Marktgasse, where the average price for a two-course "menu"—say, soup, wiener schnitzel with pommes frites and salad, is 6.60 francs. The food is fine, but the atmosphere a bit dark and dreary). . . . "Our **Hürlimann Braustube,** directly opposite the Central Station at Bahnhofplatz #9, offers a self-service cafeteria on the ground floor where complete meals may be had for from 6.60 to 10 francs" (Dominik Betschart, Manager, Hürlimann Braustube). . . . "The **Kosher Restaurant Schalom** in the Jewish Center Building at 33 Lavaterstrasse, near the Rietberg Museum and Enge Train Station, serves a filling daily menu for 11.50 francs (example: soup, beef rolls filled with sour cucumbers, stewed tomatoes and mashed potatoes). It's open Sunday through Friday from 11:30 a.m. to 2:30 p.m., and 6 to 10 p.m.; Saturday from 11:30 a.m. to 3 p.m." (Pauline Rissman, Chicago, Illinois).

STARVATION BUDGET: For lower-priced rooms and meals, you'll find that Zurich offers several unusual rock-bottom facilities: a pair of Salvation Army hostels for normal tourists, and a series of "City Kitchens."

Salvation Army ("Heilsarmee") Hostels

Right off, be reassured that Zurich's Salvation Army Hostels—one for men, one for women—aren't maintained for down-and-out'ers, but for normally-employed, if somewhat low income, single men and women; they also are entirely accustomed to accepting starvation-budget-style tourists. In fact, the male hostel—the 90-bed **Männerheim der Heilsarmee**, at 76 Dienerstrasse (phone 242-48-11)—sets aside its entire third-floor dorm for male travellers, for whom the charge is an unbelievable 6 francs ($3.52) per night; Herr Edwin Güt is the friendly, English speaking manager. The smaller female hostel, the **Frauenheim der Heilsarmee** at 6 Molkenstrasse (phone 242-48-00), supervised by Frau Dössegger, also English speaking, accommodates lady tourists in very simple, very clean, one-to-three-bedded rooms for 6.50 francs ($3.82) per person in doubles or twins, 15 francs ($8.82) single. Both hostels are centrally located in the Helvetiaplatz area; both are rigidly segregated by sex and impose a 10 p.m. curfew; but both men and women can use the mensa-type restaurant at the Männerheim, where a three-course hot meal for 5 francs ($2.94) is served from noon to one, and from 6 to 7 p.m., seven days a week.

City Kitchens

The next low-cost boon: at various residential locations throughout this city, the Zurich government maintains **"Stadtküche Zürich"** (Kitchens of the City of Zurich), a subsidized chain of cheery, little flower-bedecked restaurants, open only on weekdays, that serve full meals for less than 6 francs. These are not charitable establishments, for the reason that no one in Switzerland is really poor; they are simply municipal restaurants, and tourists whose funds have faded should keep them in mind.

There are Stadtküche at 27 Luggwegstrasse (the **"Altstetten"**); at 332 Rohr Sihlquai (the **"Rohr"**); at 16 Schipfe (the **"Schipfe"**); at 34 Zentralstrasse (the **"Zentral"**); and elsewhere in town. The most centrally-located of these is the Schipfe branch, housed in a long low building on the Limmat River, on the railroad station side, between the Rudolph Brun and the Rathaus Bridges, directly across the river from a large shoe store. Cross the Rathaus Bridge, then turn immediately right along the river and walk through a tunnel marked "Zum Bahnhof"—this will lead you to the proper riverside stretch of Schipfe, which is not to be confused with another segment of the Schipfe that goes uphill. The building housing the Schipfe "Stadtküche" is variously marked "Limmat-Club Zurich" and "Möbel-Wittwer," and is situated directly on the water. Hope and I recently ate at one of these "Stadtküche," which turned out to be a wooden, chalet-like building, in a rustic setting, replete with oilcloth-covered tables and little vases of flowers, and a self-service counter. For 2.80 francs ($1.64) apiece, we each had a huge plateful of bratwurst and "rösti" (roast potatoes) and a lettuce salad; and for 80 centimes more, we had tea. There were more costly three-course meals available for 4 francs.

Migros

Something less expensive? In one of my worst penny-pinching periods, I was often able to keep lunch costs in Zurich to about $1.50. How is it done? At least 45 A&P-type supermarkets called **"Migros"** are spotted throughout Zurich—two of them in each district. The counters at Migros offer up the following items, among others: a cellophane-wrapped package of sharp cheddar cheese; a package of cellophane-wrapped rolls; and a banana. Take them to the check-out counter, and you'll be charged 2.30 Swiss francs ($1.35) for the lot.

With your paper bag of groceries, you can then amble over to the banks of the Limmat, and munch away while the river flows by. Oh, happy days!

More recently, as an added bonus, 15 of the Migros Markets have installed self-service, sit-down "Imbiss" sections which may be the cheapest places to eat in all Zurich: breakfast for 2 francs, hot and cold platters for between 3.50 and 7.50 francs, a "Day's Menu" for only 4 francs. There are more Migros Markets in the residential districts than in the heart of the city, but you'll find one located about four blocks from the Bahnhof at Löwenplatz; another conveniently placed on Limmatplatz near the Limmathaus Hotel; and a brand-new one in the center of Altstetten (the old town).

Picnics at the Taverna Catalana

Another picnic-type place: the **Taverna Catalana**, at 8 Glockengasse, near the Bahnhofstrasse (from which you walk down Augustinergasse to find this on the first corner). With its distinguished waiters, polished oak tables and parquet floors, you'll swear you stumbled by mistake into a big, big splurge; yet this is about the only middle-class restaurant in Zurich that serves no hot meals, but rather encourages patrons to bring their own food, provided they order a drink, such as a large bottle of beer for 2.60 francs. With half a chicken bought at Jelmoli's or Bell's for 3.50 francs, you'll dine in splendor among a crowd of Zürchers that includes not a single other tourist. Open daily except Sundays and Mondays from 11 a.m. to 11:30 p.m.

The spectacular, new University "Mensa" (Restaurant)

A remarkable futuristic structure seating 1,000 persons, with terrace view overlooking all of Zurich, the three-year-old **University Mensa** at 33 Leonhardstrasse serves anybody at all, student or not, at rates that start as low as 4.80 francs ($2.82) for, say, hamburger steak with sauce, noodles or salad, and ascend to 6.50 francs ($3.82) for fried filet of sole with boiled potatoes, mayonnaise and salad; actual students eat for about 20% less. Open Monday through Friday from 11:15 a.m. to 1:30 p.m., and from 5:30 to 7:15 p.m., the Mensa (whose actual affiliation is with the Swiss Federal Institute of Technology; Albert Einstein once taught there) is most easily reached by taking the Seilbahn cable car (Polybahn)—40 centimes up, 40 down—from Centralplatz, then turning right at the top, across the large panoramic terrace into the underground mensa. Atop the terrace, students operate an auxiliary, weekday cafeteria selling open sandwiches and a glass of süssmost (sweet apple cider) for as little as 3.90 francs ($2.29).

READERS-ON-THE-STARVATION-BUDGET (BY ZURICH STANDARDS): "Another cheap place to eat is at the cafeteria of the **Y.M.C.A.**, Sihlstrasse 33, *upstairs,* where two-course meals are 5 to 5.80 francs. There is a sign outside saying "Cafe I. Stock." This is *not* to be confused with the main floor restaurant of the Glockenhof Hotel next door. Clean, cheap and no tips. I always go here because it's *quiet.* Between 2 and 5 p.m. it is so peaceful, you can write letters there" (Mrs. S. C. Juillerat, Jura Bernois, Switzerland). . . . . "A perfect picnic: Start with a loaf of French bread (one over a yard long costs 1 franc). Then buy a *whole* roast chicken. You can 'splurge' for this item at Bell's, where such a chicken costs 6 francs ($3.52), but numerous nearby snack stores charge only 5.50 francs ($3.23) for a chicken, and you can buy one in the delicatessen of the Globus Department Store for only 5 francs ($2.94). Buy a bottle of mineral water, in any store, for about 1.50 francs (88¢), and you have easily enough for two meals for a couple or four meals for one person—for $4.41. Top that!" (Mark Estren, Middletown, Connecticut).

SUB-STARVATION BUDGET: The ultra-modern, stunningly-designed **Youth Hostel** ("Jugendherberge") of Zurich, 114 Mutschellenstrasse (phone 45-35-44), a 20-minute ride from the main station aboard tram No. 7 to Morgental, charges only 7 francs ($4.11) per person in 8-bedded rooms, 13 francs in double and triple rooms, but requires membership in the international youth hostel association, which they'll sell on the spot for 25 francs; if you plan to hostel elsewhere, or to stay for a relatively long time in Zurich, it might pay to join up.

STUDENT IN ZURICH: Since there are no student hotels in the technical sense, in Zurich (there are Ys, hostels and the like), students arriving in Zurich should first obtain their own accommodations at one of the recommendations appearing earlier in this chapter. But then they should quickly head to the **SSR** (Schweizerischer Studentenreisedienst), the Swiss Student Travel Office, at 10 Leonhardstrasse (phone 242-30-00), which offers several important services and products: among them, student charter flights, student train tickets at reductions up to 40% off standard fares, student hotels in resort cities other than Zurich: in Klosters, Davos, St. Moritz, Lucerne, Leysin, and Andermatt, for instance (**SSR** also maintains offices in Geneva at 3 Rue Vignier, phone 299-733; in Basel at 14 Friedensgasse, phone 259-820; and in Lausanne at 8 Rue de la Barre, phone 203-975). To get there speedily, simply walk out the front exit of the main station, turn left, cross the bridge, then walk diagonally across the central square and take the tiny **Polybahn** cable car to the top of the hill (40 centimes going up, 40 coming down). Turn left when you leave the cable car and walk about three blocks to the address. . . . Summer hours for **SSR** are: 9 a.m. to 5 p.m. on weekdays, from 10 a.m. to noon on Saturday. . . . During winter, the office will again give you what aid you need (from 10 a.m. to 5 p.m. on weekdays, 9 to noon on Saturdays), and also in winter, they'll admit you to the **SSR's** Thursday night **Travel Club** ("Reise Club"), at 8:30 p.m. No entrance fee; the purpose is to meet and discuss places recently visited. . . . Incidentally, the city of Zurich gives considerable discounts to holders of student I.D. cards: 40% off on theater tickets, a lesser reduction on other scattered facilities. And you can take city sightseeing tour "A," which operates throughout the year, for half-price or six francs. . . . Finally, international students (show your cards) are welcomed as guests at the members-only **International Students' Club**, Augustinerhof 1, where there are dances on Wednesday, Friday and Saturday nights, discussions and musical programs throughout the week.

TRANSPORTATION: To get around the city cheaply and best, learn to use the local buses and trams. From the airport, for instance, you can either take the regular airport bus, which brings you into the Swissair Terminus at the side of the Bahnhof, for a fare of 5 francs, or hop local bus #68, which also ends up at the main railway station, for a fare of 2 francs. On the city buses and trams, the fare is 80 centimes for up to five stops, 1.20 francs for from six stops to the city limits. If you plan to do a good bit of traveling, buy a "day ticket" for 3.50 francs, which is good for unlimited rides around the clock and valid for one 24-hour period. And if you're spending some time in Zurich, it might pay to purchase one of two different discount booklets of tickets, available at major newsstands, the first for 11 short rides at 6 francs, the other for 14 long rides, at 12 francs. The Tourist Office in the Bahnhof will give you a free transportation map.

One quirk of Zurich trolleys about which you should be informed: tickets for single rides can only be purchased from dispensing machines located at trolley stops, and must be punched in another machine at the same stop, before you climb aboard!

MUSINGS: Thoughts that assail one upon arriving in Zurich at the end of a European tour: how strange to be in a country where (a) everything works, (b) everyone seems to be well-off, (c) all appliances, machinery, telephones and gadgets are more modern than ours. . . . Notice, too, how everyone in Zurich says "merci" instead of "Danke schön." Strange. . . . Most beautiful sight: the swans on the Limmat; handiest store for discount toiletries and odds and ends: the EPA at Sihlporte. . . . The best thing about Zurich is that it's a base, so very well-located that nothing worthwhile in Switzerland is more than an hour or two away.

MUSEUMS AND TOURS: Hope has done the survey of Zurich's museums and sights in her section, "Hope in Zurich," appearing later in this chapter. But I'd merely add a suggestion that you do visit, while here, an especially beautiful museum of art, with a stunning collection of 19th and 20th-century moderns. That's the **Kunsthaus (15)**, on Heimplatz, just a block away from the Schauspielhaus. There's a Shavian drama behind the construction of this architectural masterpiece. An unsuccessful art student named Bührle went into the munitions-making business in Zurich, made a fortune, and then gave over the whole of his ill-gotten gains to build a new wing of this museum, which was finished just after his death in 1958. Entrance is 2 francs ($1.17), except during special exhibition periods, when the charge is from 3 to 5 francs. Open Tuesday through Friday from 10 a.m. to 9 p.m., Saturday and Sunday 10 a.m. to 5 p.m., Monday from 2 to 5 p.m. . . . Tours of Zurich cost 12 francs ($7.05), last 1½ hours, and leave at 10:30 a.m. and 2 p.m. throughout the year and at 9 a.m., noon and 3:30 p.m. in the summertime only, from in front of the railroad station. . . . Excursions outside of Zurich, however, leave not from the railroad station, but from the Opera House ("Stadttheater"), and the best of these is a 5½-hour trip to Lucerne and alongside the Lake of Lucerne that leaves daily at 2 p.m., costs 30 francs, returns at 7:30 p.m., and takes you into the "William Tell country" on the fringe of the Alps. Other full-day bus tours—primarily to Alpine villages and other woodsy mountain attractions—leave from the same spot at 8 and 9 a.m., via a cluster of buses that advertise their destinations and prices on sidewalk signs at the side of the Opera House. . . . Nor should you forget the magnificent Swiss Railways, whose frequent and on-the-minute departures from the Main Railroad Station offer countless opportunities for cheap, do-it-yourself excursions. It's often fun, and instructive, simply to take a train to a nearby Swiss location, and then to roam through the towns or countryside, independent and relaxed. There are specific train excursions that go to the high-altitude Jungfraujoch peak in the Alps and to the Bernese Oberland, to Lugano and Locarno (and then through the Gotthard tunnel into Italian Switzerland), to Montreux and the Castle of Chillon, to Lausanne and Geneva. . . . For general sightseeing in Zurich, concentrate along the banks of the Limmat, where everything is older and more interesting; that's also where most of the specific sightseeing attractions are located.

DAY IN THE COUNTRY: Carved into a hillside overlooking the city, the **Dolder Schwimmbad (16)** (swimming pool) offers a full day of bathing, lolling in the grass, and blonde beauty-gazing for an admission fee of 5 francs. It's a remarkable pool: for ten minutes each hour, electric motors create artificial waves—huge, high breakers simulating the roughest surf. The summer days in Zurich are apt to be surprisingly warm and a day at the Dolder, in a spectacular outdoor setting, is a treat that rivals the Riviera. You can merely observe (with no swimming) for an admission price of only 2.50 francs (which entitles you to a free soft drink or coffee), and you can either bring food along or eat at the poolside cafe for about $2.50.

To get to the Dolder, take a #6 trolley from the railroad station to the end of the line, then change at that point to a #5 trolley and go to the end of that line (which is the high-altitude "Allmend Fluntern" station). It's only a short walk from here (about 10 minutes) to the Dolder, on a trail that leads through one of the loveliest forests of Europe. And by the way, the trolley ride up here is in itself one of the highlights of your stay in Zurich, revealing the entire city below.

OTHER SWIMMING OPPORTUNITIES: Why it is, I can't explain, but swimming always seems to me an especially pleasant and appropriate activity in Zurich, whatever season I'm there. In addition to the spectacular outdoor pool at the Dolder Grand, there's a swimming area—**"Badeanstalt Utoquai"**—directly in the Lake of Zurich at the Utoquai, where you can swim among the swans every day of the week from 8 in the morning until 7 p.m., for 1.50 francs. Bathing suits are available for rental. And for indoor swimming throughout the year, you ought not to miss the vast **Hallenbad City,** a huge, glass-sided building just off the Sihlstrasse (between the Sihl Square and the Sihl River), which houses one of the most imposing swimming pools—more than 50 yards in length—that I for one have ever seen. You can rent a suit at a little shop opposite the ticket window, and your entire afternoon, including swimming suit, should cost no more than 3.80 to 4.50 francs, only 2 francs if you bring your own suit. Closed the first Monday of every month; Thursdays from 4 to 7 p.m. are for women only. At the time of writing (December, 1979), the Hallenbad is closed for renovations, but should re-open at some later time in 1980; check before going there.

THEATRE: The **Zurich Schauspielhaus (17),** Rämistrasse 34, is a highly-regarded European theater, whose repertory ranges from classic to modern, from old Greek tragedy and comedy to contemporary playwrights of all countries. In June, prominent troupes are invited to participate in a festival in English, French and Italian, while the Schauspielhaus presents its own productions in German. Ticket prices from 6 to 25 francs ($3.52 to $14.70). Regrettably, the Schauspielhaus remains closed from July to early September. . . . You won't understand the farce comedies presented at some of the more local theatres, particularly those in which the star hams it up in "Schwyzerdütsch" while the rest of the company speaks German. Schwyzerdütsch is the local lingo that's been called "not a language, but a throat disease". . . . Tickets for the opera, at the **Opernhaus,** start as low as 6 francs, which may be the world's lowest price for such; again, closed July and August. . . . Movies are a particularly good bet for Americans in Zurich, because they're subtitled in the multiple languages of Switzerland, rather than being dubbed with new voices, as in Italy and France. Several of Zurich's motion picture houses specialize in the American and English classics: "Rebecca," "Odd Man Out," "Brief Encounter."

DISCOS, JAZZ AND DANCING: We'll deal with these in ascending order of age groups. The younger teen-agers hang out at **Piccadilly Circus,** a Dixieland jazz house at 35 Zähringerstrasse, where entrance is free, but there's a minimum required drink of 4.50 francs. Closed Sundays. . . . University-age people go, first, to the **International Student Club,** at 1 Augustinerhof, near Paradeplatz, where the admission is only one to two francs, the dances take place on Wednesday, Friday and Saturday nights, and you'll have the best chance of meeting other singles and stags, but where you **must** have your international student card to enter; or, alternatively, to the larger and relatively expensive **Mascotte Discotheque,** 10 Theaterstrasse, which offers the city's best dance floor and dance-band for an entrance fee of from 5 to 10 francs, depending on the night of the week (ladies are admitted free Sunday to Tuesday), with drink prices pegged at a minimum 10 francs. A sophisticated young crowd (mainly in their 20s, some in their early 30s) attend. And then, at 13 Stadthausquai, near the Fraumünster Cathedral, there's **La Ferme,** a popular discotheque for the 21-to-30 age group, decorated like a rustic farm scene, with leaf-sprouting trees, wooden fences, a large mill wheel against one wall. There's also a large dance floor and the usual American-British discotheque music, for which you pay 5.50 francs to enter on Monday (folklore night), 3.30 francs Tuesday to Thursday, 6.60 francs on Friday, 6.60 on Saturday, free entrance on Sunday afternoon, 3.30 francs on Sunday night. Americans are made to feel very welcome; there are lots of stags; and you are not required to wear a tie (men) or a skirt (ladies). . . . A slightly older group patronizes the **Redhouse** at 27 Marktgasse, open daily except Sundays from 9 p.m. to 2 a.m., to view both a floorshow and a striptease at an admission price of 8.80 francs, which includes the first drink. Interesting, Las Vegas-type attractions, including, on my 1979 visit, a magician who walked through a solid glass window, changed a dog into a canary, and conjured up 12-or-so lighted candles from the nose of a guest. . . . Tourists and residents of all ages go, finally, to the somewhat more expensive **Hazyland,** in the "Kongresshaus" near the lake, where entrance is 6 francs Sunday to Thursday, 8 francs Friday and Saturday, free for women Sunday to Tuesday, drinks average 9 (beer) and 10 (whiskey), and the meeting possibilities—in the 25-to-40-year range—are good.

SWISS-STYLE GEMÜTLICHKEIT: The **Schäfli Restaurant,** at 6 Badergasse, just off the Limmatquai, next to the Rudolf-Brun Bridge, offers country shows to complement its two-course menus priced at only 6.80, 7.80, and 8.80 francs. Every day in summer, from 8 p.m. to midnight, five musicians (accordion, trumpet, horn, clarinet and guitar) play Swiss, German, Austrian and Jugoslav folk music; but every day also, there's a "daily attraction" which, when I was last there, was a Japanese yodler, whose skilled voice, combined with the frenetic applause from the enthusiastic audience, caused windows, glasses (and my eardrums) to vibrate close to the breaking point. There is no entrance fee, but the price of drinks contains a special music supplement, which brings beer to 3.50 francs, local wine to 5 francs. The restaurant is in the same building as the Hotel Schäfli, mentioned above, under "Zurich's least expensive hotels" . . . During the afternoon and at night, you can stop into the very central **Bierhalle Wolf** at Limmatquai 132, a few doors down from the Seilbahn cable car, where a hearty Swiss "oompah" band in native costume performs at frequent intervals. This is an Alpine-inn sort of a place, very relaxed and friendly, where the band jokes with each other and the audience, and where you're likely to catch some genuine Swiss folk songs and a bit of that famous Swiss yodelling. There's no admission in the afternoon, a charge of only 2.20

francs in the evening, and beer is priced as low as 2.70 francs, soft drinks at 3.30. Here, the food is moderately-priced and you can have a three-course meal for about 7 francs. . . . Elsewhere on the cowbell scene, the recently-opened **Châlet** at 14 Marktgasse claims that it provides "real" Swiss folklore (a colorful floorshow with yodelers, flag swingers, alphorn blowers), and also promises not to charge an entrance fee to bearers of this book. Here's a chance, in pleasant fashion, to learn about old Swiss traditions, surrounded as you'll be by farm house tools, harnesses and pitchforks, all the while imbibing soft drinks for just 5 francs, the hard stuff for 7.50 francs.

BOATING: On sunny days, the green waters of the Lake of Zurich ("Zürchersee") are the place to be, either for a tour of the lakeside towns, or for an hour of boating, among the swans (250 of them) and the many little ships that dot the lake. For either activity, go to the end of the Bahnhofstrasse, where you'll find a pier from which the lake ferries depart at nearly half-hour intervals. To the right of the main pier, as you face the lake, you'll then find a smaller pier at which boats are rented.

From the big pier, a boat departs at frequent intervals on a "Grand Tour" of the Lake taking you to Rapperswil at the far end, near the foothills of the Alps. The trip lasts 2½ hours in either direction, and costs 13.80 Swiss francs, second class.

From the smaller pier, however, a 1½-hour tour of the lake costs only 5.60 francs, or in substitution for that, you can rent a row-boat for two persons (6 francs an hour), or a pedal boat for two to three persons (3.50 francs *per person* per hour). You might also rent a sailboat (15 francs per hour for two persons, one franc extra for each additional person, up to a maximum of five; 50 francs deposit). The same rates are available at the "Bootsvermietung" (Boat Rental) pier located just off the Bellevue Platz, at the Limmat River.

THE BIG SPLURGE: For the sake of your travel memories, shoot the wad at least once for a dinner consisting of "Fondue Bourguignon," that renowned Swiss specialty which is more a method of serving, than a specific food item. What happens is that flaming braziers topped with bowls of boiling oil are placed on your table, along with trays of raw steak, cut into 1-inch squares. You stick long toothpicks into the squares, dip them each into the bowls of oil until they're cooked as you desire, then immerse the chunks in any of nine superb sauces placed on your table. If the chunks of meat are good, red beef, and if the sauces are well-concocted (they usually are), then you'll have a memorable feast, and you'll run right out to Jelmoli's Department Store the next day to buy a brazier for serving Fondue Bourguignon to your astonished guests at home.

At several of the restaurants of Zurich, you'll be able to get a Fondue Bourguignon dinner for from 25 to 30 francs ($14.71 to $17.65), but that's too much, even for a splurge. There's a 20-francs per person Fondue Bourguignon ($11.76) at the "Walliser Keller" of the **Hotel Zürcherhof**, 21 Zähringerstrasse (a well-known restaurant to Zurich's gourmets, but with a surprisingly low-priced all-beef fondue, which must be purchased by at least two persons; closed Sundays); while at the **Restaurant Schützengarten**, 15 Bahnhofquai, you may order a single portion for only 18.50 francs ($10.88); the fondue is always available, even though it may not be listed on the colored menu card. And if the waitress should tell you that single portions of fondue bourguignon are not served, then simply ask for the young, English-speaking manager, Herr Schumacher—he'll overrule. Open seven days a week, from 9 a.m. to midnight, the location is easily found: leaving the main entrance of the central railroad station, turn left, and look for the "Bank of Tokyo", "Bosch", and "Qantas Airways" signs on the building. I like the fact that Schützengarten will supply you the ingredients for mixing your own sauces: curry powder, slivered almonds, tartare sauce, paprika, small dill pickles, small pickled onions, a heavy French dressing, homemade mayonnaise.

ZURICH MISCELLANY: Laundromats abound. Ask your hotel for a nearby address, or try **"Sofort Reinigung Terlinden,"** at 148 Stampfenbachstrasse, charging 12 francs for 5 kilos, including drying. Cheaper is **Reinigung und Waschsalon J. und F. Schatt,** 11 Mühlegasse, a few minutes from the railway station (simply walk over the Brun-Bridge), which is non-automatic but still will wash and dry your laundry in 3 hours. Nine francs for 4½ kilos; closed weekends. In the same building is a Post Office which accepts overseas parcels. . . . A popular shopping center for people in a hurry is **Shopville,** located in the under-passage leading from the central railroad station to the Bahnhofstrasse. You can find practically everything there for your daily needs, and to help you in locating the various shops, there's an electronic shop finder near the bank. If you're hungry, stop in at the **Milchbar** for inexpensive milk shakes, ham and cheese sandwiches, and at the **Gourmetbar,** for weiners, soups, minipizzas, all inexpensive. . . . Star-gazing in Zurich is the latest game in town, with budget-minded astronomers flocking to the **Urania Observatory Tower** at 9 Uraniastrasse, in the same building as the popular Restaurant Urania-Löwenbräu, where they can gaze through a Zeiss telescope with a 30 centimeter lens (largest in Switzerland) at the moon, Saturn (see its engirdling rings) and other celestial bodies, provided weather conditions permit. Hours are 8:30 to 11 p.m. from April through September, 8 to 10 p.m. at all other times, and charge is 3 francs for adults, one franc for children. . . . For English-speaking babysitters in Zurich: phone 23-37-87 . . . A pharmacy (chemist) open 24 hours a day: at no. 14 Theaterstrasse, near Bellevueplatz. . . . And a cozy reading room with English newspapers and magazines, all for free, can be found in the Pestalozzihaus, No. 17 Zähringerstrasee. . . . Restroom, shower, or toilet? You'll find all three in the underground shopping center known as "Shopville", in front of the central railway station. . . . Best, and highest, daytime view of Zurich (and the nearby Alps) is from the tower atop the **Uetliberg Hill;** trains costing 6 francs roundtrip go there from the Selnau Station. Best medium-altitude view of Zurich is from the plaza at 33 Leonhardstrasse, in front of the main university building. Walk up Rämistrasse to Künstlergasse, turn left on Künstlergasse for one short block. Or take the tiny Limmatquai cable car called the "Polybahn" (which you should learn to use), from the side of the Limmathof Hotel, which brings you up here for 40 centimes. And for an evening view, wander to the St. Peterhofstatt, with its illuminated clock tower of St. Peter's—Europe's largest clock face. This is the Europe of a century ago, and you can stand in the square and dream.

Here, now, is Hope:

HOPE IN ZURICH: "A trip to Zurich is like going home to Mother—to that secure haven where everything works properly, where you are cared for fondly in impeccably clean surroundings, and where your schedule—in keeping with the atmosphere—is orderly and moderate. Add to this the natural beauty of the city, and you'll realize that the best way to spend your time in Zurich is unwinding from the tumult of your earlier European stops. And the best places to unravel in Zurich (if weather permits) are on the lake, on excursions to nearby natural wonders, in window shopping on the remarkably-attractive Bahnhofstrasse, or on strolls through the picturesque streets that jut off from Niederdorfstrasse (on one side of the Limmat) and from the Schipfe (on the other).

"And you can lounge about without a guilty conscience, because there are, in my opinion, only four 'must see' sights in Zurich. The rest, which we have also described, are strictly elective.

The Big Four

"**The Landesmuseum** or **Swiss National Museum,** located directly behind the Main Railway Station on Museum Strasse, charges no admission, is open every day except Monday morning from 10 to noon and 2 to 5, and is one of the most interesting museums I've ever seen. Housed in a grey stone Victorian building that looks like Ronald Searle's St. Trinians, the museum is gigantic in both size and intention. To quote The Swiss National Museum's booklet (which you can buy for one Swiss franc, to guide yourself through the exhibitions): 'The Museum collects Swiss antiquities of considerable historic, industrial or artistic importance, from primitive times until 1920. Its aim is to provide a systematic survey of our past, embracing all aspects of life, cultural epochs and regions of the country.' Here you have a kaleidoscope of Swiss life through the ages, from many aspects, all arranged neatly in chronological order. The story is told through church art (a fine collection); through magnificent model rooms from various periods, including the cloisters from The Blackfriars Monastery, several rooms from the Fraumünster Abbey, and representations of wealthy homes (all the furniture is authentic); through costumes; silverware; furniture; weapons; military uniforms; musical instruments and, of course, through an exhibition tracing Swiss clockmaking from the 16th to the 18th century. Viewing the exhibit is like standing on a Swiss mountain top—you get a panoramic view, with reflections of other European nations. Don't miss the historical handicraft shops (corn mill, shoemaker, cartwright, winepress, all from the 19th century) in Rooms 11 to 13; the magnificent furniture, including a coal stove dating back to 1620, in Room 29; The Mint, Room 75; or the Helmet and Sword of Zwingli (more about him later) in Room 50, the Weapons Hall. Free guided tours in English are offered in summer, usually at 10 a.m. and 11 a.m. For information, ask at the entrance desk, or phone 221-10-10.

"**The Kunsthaus,** previously mentioned by Arthur, and located on Heimplatz, directly across from the Schauspielhaus, is open Tuesday through Friday from 10 a.m. to 9 p.m., Saturday and Sunday from 10 a.m. to 5 p.m., Monday from 2 to 5 p.m., and is a superbly-designed art gallery, with near-perfect lighting: daylight is used whenever possible, but even artificial lighting is employed without glare (at last!). The Museum has a vast collection, but is well planned and pleasant to wander through, with two sculpture gardens in the center (which you'll see from outside). One wing accommodates changing exhibitions (usually very exciting fare); the older part of the museum has the permanent collection, which includes Swiss painting, but can also boast of ancient art; early Church art; paintings by Rubens, Hals and Rembrandt; French impressionists; and a broad collection of modern sculpture and painting, including works by Picasso, Rodin, Arp, Lipschitz, Giacometti (100 works by Giacometti), Marini, Maillol, Munch, Kandinsky, Mondrian, Chagall, Miro, Rauschenberg, Bonnard, Segal, and others too numerous to mention.

Entrance fee is 2 Swiss francs, but goes up to 3 to 5 francs when a special exhibition is in progress.

"The **Rietberg Museum,** entrance free, open Tuesday through Sunday from 10 to 5 p.m. (closed Monday), additionally on Wednesday evenings from 8 to 10 p.m., and located in the Rieterpark (a green, pine-treed place with a lovely view of the lake and the town) at Gablerstrasse 15, is about a 10-minute ride from the center of Zurich; take the #7 streetcar to the Rietberg museum stop. The loosest definition best describes the famous collection of Baron von der Heydt which is housed here: it is an art gallery of non-European art. There's a bit of everything, including ancient art; works of the Indians from North, Central, and South America; Indian and South East Asian art; a Chinese and Japanese collection including sculpture, painting, ceramics and works in bronze; and so-called 'primitive' African art. But always the emphasis is on Art, for the Rietberg Museum is an art gallery, not an anthropological or ethnological collection. There are many beautiful things to see here, all delightfully displayed, but particularly fascinating are the most famous Indian treasure of the museum, 'The Dancing Shiva,' upstairs in Room 12; the enormous votive stelae from the archaic Buddhist period of the Wei dynasty, in Room 9; the beautiful Chinese and Japanese paintings in Rooms 13 to 15; and the highly interesting African section, with its outstanding collection of African masks in Rooms 17, 18 and 19 (look for the wooden 'puffy-cheeks', my favorite).

"The **Grossmünster Church,** located a block or two from the City Hall just above the Limmatquai (you can't miss it—it dominates the area), may be visited from 9 to 6 (winters til 4; afternoons only on Sunday), and is an enormous Romanesque Church whose present structure was begun in 1100 over the ruins of two former buildings: an earlier church and a convent. The oldest parts of the existing church are the crypt and the choir; the murals in the choir date from the 14th and 15th centuries. In the crypt is a large, primitive looking statue of Charlemagne (built between 1450 and 1475), who is said to have founded the church when his horse bowed down here, on the very spot where the Zurich martyrs were buried; there is a stone relief inside the church on the north wall celebrating the event. Grossmünster is The Church of Zurich, and the home of the Swiss Reformation, for this was Huldrych Zwingli's pulpit from 1519 until his death in 1531. Here he preached zealously for the Gospel against the sale of Church dispensations; rebelled against the Church hierarchy and some of its mysticism; urged priests and nuns to marry openly (as he himself had done); persuaded the Swiss that it was a sin to hire themselves out as mercenaries; and took up the sword against those Swiss cantons that disagreed with him. He was killed in the battle of Kappel and his body was torn apart and set on fire. Grossmünster bears the mark of these troubled times: it was stripped of all religious ornamentation, and to this day looks bare and austere. But perhaps it's the presence of so much light in the Swiss Church (especially after the semi-dark, romantic, mysterious cathedrals of France and Italy) that makes it look so stark. It's as though church officials decided that The Reformation was a matter of letting in more light.

The Six Electives

"The **Wasserkirche** or Waterside Church, on Limmatquai (with a statue of Zwingli on the square in back), was built between 1479 and 1488, supposedly on the spot where the three Zurich martyrs were beheaded. The Church is pure Gothic but so spare and simple it looks almost modern.

"The **Helmhaus,** at the same location as The Wasserkirche, 31 Limmatquai, second and third floors, is a city-run gallery which hosts changing art

exhibits (usually pretty good fare), for which there is no admission charge. Open every day, except Monday, from 10 a.m. to 6 p.m., Thursday evenings from 8 to 10 p.m.

"Diagonally across the bridge from The Wasserkirche is The 'Meise' Guild House, one of six exquisite Guild Halls in Zurich. Most of the lovely old Guild Houses have today been converted into private clubs or public restaurants; but this one, built in 1757 and formerly The Wine Merchants Guild, contains the permanent exhibition of the Swiss National Museum's 18th century porcelain and furniture. It provides a good way to see the inside of a Guild House for free (and without having to take a meal). Open every day, except Monday, from 10 to 12 and 2 to 5 (winters till 4).

"Located directly opposite The Wasserkirche (but the entrance is all the way around on the other side) is the Fraumünster Cathedral, which was founded in 853 and used to be The Fraumünster Abbey, some of whose rooms you've already seen at The Landesmuseum. The present edifice was begun in 1170 and is a grey stone Gothic Church with impressive stained glass windows (including six new ones by Chagall and one by Giacometti), an impressive organ, and some remains of frescoes in the late Romanesque choir which date back to the 13th century; the cloisters have modern murals depicting Zurich's religious history. You may visit the Church daily, except Sunday mornings, from 9 a.m. to 6 p.m.; winters, from 10 a.m. to 4 p.m.

"St. Peter's Church is the oldest Parish Church in Zurich, and stands in the heart of the oldest section of town. Its tower can be seen from The Fraumünster (and from practically anywhere else in Zurich), but the best way to get here is to cross the bridge opposite the Rathaus and then walk up the street off the right of the bridge, Weggen-Gasse (this avoids a long flight of stairs leading to the back door, which is locked anyway). It's a handsome church in modified Baroque style done in dark woods against decorated white walls. One of the Church's pastors was Goethe's friend, John Kasper Lavater. The clock in the tower has the largest face in Europe (its minute hand is 4 yards long), but this is no surprise—we're in Switzerland, after all.

"The Rathaus, on Limmatquai, built between 1694 and 1698 in late Renaissance style with touches of Baroque, is a handsome grey stone City Hall with dark wood interiors and antique porcelain heating stoves. The large meeting hall upstairs has a tapestry which shows the heraldry of all the villages of Kanton Zurich, and glass-paintings showing the heraldry of all the Swiss Kantons. It's about as interesting as any City Hall could be, but it's free (just tip the concierge who shows you around) and open to the public Tuesdays, Thursdays and Fridays from 10 to 11:30 a.m."

READERS' SUGGESTIONS: "Contact the Zurich Tourist Office, and they will put you in touch with a Swiss family of equal age, occupation and family background so that you 'Don't Miss the Swiss.' We got to know a charming family who met us with their car, drove us out to their home, and showed us all over their house and garden, talking about Canada and Switzerland generally. They then gave us coffee, Kirsch, and homemade cream cakes. If they ever come to Canada, we will reciprocate, as it was a most enjoyable evening after our hotel life" (Mrs. G. Bird, Montreal, Canada; note by AF: tourists can apply for the "Don't Miss the Swiss" program at the tourist office in the Main Station, Bahnhofplatz 15, phone 211-40-00, on weekdays from 8 a.m. to 2 p.m.). . . . "The extraordinary E. G. Bührle Collection of French impressionists, 172 Zollikerstrasse (open Tuesday and Friday afternoons from 2 to 5 p.m. for an admission charge of 4.40 francs, 2.20 francs for students), while not as large as the one at the Jeu de Paume in Paris, is every bit as breathtaking and probably more unusual. In addition to the numerous Manets, Monets, Renoirs, and Degas, there are some brilliant Rembrandts, Rubens, Fragonards, Hals, and others—and sections, although rather small, on medieval religious statuary and early 20th-century expressionist art. This is by far the most stunning private collection we have ever had the pleasure of viewing" (Mr. and Mrs. Vladimir Padunov, Long Island City, New York). . . . "Please call the attention of your readers to a 2-½ hour walking tour of the old town of Zurich, offered at 9:30 a.m. and 3 p.m. from June to September on Tuesdays, Thursdays and Saturdays. The meeting point is the Tourist Office, Bahnhofplatz 15. We found it to be enjoyable and informative" (Samuel Katz, Philadelphia, Pennsylvania).

READERS-ON-AN-OUTING: "Take an express train to Lucerne, and you'll get there from Zurich in 50 minutes. Avoid the locals, which go by an entirely different route and take, believe it or not, a full hour and fifty minutes for the trip. At the Lucerne railroad station, get bus #1, marked Kriens, give the ticket-dispenser one franc, and ask to be let out at the stop nearest the Pilatus Railway. Walk up the hill at which you get out, and you'll find the station from which cable cars leave for the trip up Mount Pilatus. Sad to say, the trip to the top is far too expensive for the likes of us—28 francs, or $16.47 per person, round trip—but you can afford a round-trip ticket for the first station on the way up, called Krienseregg. That costs 8.40 francs ($4.94) per person, and allows you to spend as long as you like wandering around the mountain before taking your cable-car back down. The air is brisk and bracing, the ride itself thrilling and a little overwhelming, and the whole outing an experience not to be missed" (Mark Estren, Middletown, Connecticut). . . . "From Zurich, take the very beautiful excursion to **Rheinfall**—the waterfall of the River Rhein—which is the greatest waterfall in Europe. You can go to Rheinfall by train from the Central Railroad Station in Zurich to the Neuhausen and Rheinfall stop. The round-trip ticket for 2nd class seats costs 13 francs ($7.64) per person. It is about 50 minutes from Zurich to Neuhausen by train and from the Station in Neuhausen to the waterfall about 15 minutes by foot. The boat fare under the waterfall is approximately two francs" (Dr. Z. and M. Palikan, Brno, Czechoslovakia). . . . "Make a side-trip form Zurich to Interlaken, and then up to Grindelwald. It is along the same run as the train to Jungfrau, but is one of the earlier stops. Jungfrau is hardly in the price range of most budget tourists since it costs about $50 per person to make it all the way up. But Grindelwald is quite pretty, gives a great view of some very high peaks (the Eiger and Fiescherhörner), and is more affordable (about $5). And mention that the steamer-ride on the Zurchersee is free to those with Eurailpasses. It is also possible to ride on the boat one-way and hop on the train for a quick ride back to Zurich" (Lorna M. Rosenblith, Little Neck, New York).

———

With this tour of Zurich, we've now canvassed the fourteen most accessible major cities of Europe—the key targets for a first-time trip abroad. With some effort, but without overcrowding your tour, you can also extend your itinerary to include one or two further-removed cities: Madrid, Athens or Berlin. The first two are particular "budget paradises," but even the last-named can be done cheaply and well, as you'll begin to see in our chapter on Berlin, coming up next.

Chapter XVII

BERLIN

Threepenny Opera

THE "BELEAGUERED ISLAND," the "enclave" behind the Iron Curtain, the "bastion of democracy"—those are the terms that have frightened some Americans from attempting a trip to Berlin. The result is that many prices in touristless Berlin are considerably below those in West Germany. But that isn't the only reason for going to Berlin.

Berlin possesses a kind of sophistication that will not be found in the rest of Europe. The city lives on the brink of danger; its citizens live from day to day. And yet, this insecurity has resulted in alertness rather than resignation. There's a lively, electric feel to the city; a drink-and-be-merry-for-tomorrow-we-die mood; an urge to experience the new and the different. To some extent, these attitudes account for the highly esoteric and intense nightlife of the city—for clubs like **Cheetah,** largest discotheque in Germany, where six different dance floors create a futuristic wonderland, or the **Riverboat,** which features the most frenetic jazz this side of Birdland.

To witness all this on a visit to Berlin is a strange, and exciting, experience. It's also exciting, but depressing as well, to see the hideous wall that separates West Berlin from the unhappy Eastern sector of the city. You can feel the monotony of an authoritarian state by simply staring across the street into the Soviet zone near high vantage points at Potsdamer Platz or the Brandenburg Gate. The contrast between the relative bleakness of that area, and the life of West Berlin, is startling.

But that's the only depressing feature of a trip to Berlin. The rest couldn't be more contrasting, for Berlin has an amazing variety of entertainment attractions, sights to look at, places to tour, theatre to watch. Many persons regard Berlin as the most advanced cultural center in the world. Whether you come for that reason, however, or simply to see history-in-the-making, you'll be thrilled to your marrow by even a short visit to this key European city.

Hopeful signals and proof of the city's will to survive and prosper: the recent (1979) opening of the "ICC," world's largest congress center, near the Funkturm, already completely booked with international fairs and exhibitions through 1983; and the simultaneous construction of four giant new hotels. Berlin lives!

TRANSPORTATION: Arriving at Tegel Central Airport, you will be landing in the very center of the city. There is no airport limousine. Simply hop the city bus marked "9" (one mark thirty pfennigs), which runs from Tegel down the length of the Kurfürstendamm, Berlin's two-mile-long main street.

THE GERMAN MARK: At the time this chapter on Berlin was prepared, the German mark was worth almost exactly 53 U.S.¢ ($1=DM 1.90), and we've converted local prices into dollars at that approximate exchange. Rates set forth in marks should remain at the figures we've used, but their dollar equivalents may vary by the time of your own stay in Berlin.

Berlin also has a subway system called the U-Bahn, on which single fares cost 1.30 marks, and you can transfer between bus and underground by purchasing a "Sammelkarte" costing 5.50 marks for 5 rides. If you plan to do considerable traveling around the city, you'll save by picking up a **Touristenkarte** at the BVG kiosk in front of the central Zoo railroad station; it costs 17 marks ($8.94) and is good for four days of unlimited travel on city buses and the U-Bahn.

There is another transportation system in Berlin, called the S-Bahn—a surface railroad system owned and operated by East Berlin, but which runs throughout the entire city. This is the cheapest system—only 1 mark per ride—and takes you out to the lakes on the outskirts of the city; it also provides the easiest method of getting to East Berlin (where there's a checkpoint for foreigners in the Friedrichstrasse station). But it is owned by East Berlin; every bit of western currency paid into it disappears behind the Iron Curtain; and for that reason West Berliners boycott it unless its use is absolutely necessary. Needless to say, your Touristenkarte is not good on the S-Bahn.

ACCOMMODATIONS: For the budgeteer, they're in the heart of the city. The main street of Berlin—the **Kurfürstendamm**, which the Berliners call "Ku-Damm"—and the small side-streets heading off it, are literally crammed with small pensions and hotels. There is thus no need to leave the center of all activity in Berlin to find budget-priced rooms. We'll deal, first, with the least costly ones, then with the moderately-priced variety.

Doubles for 35 to 43 marks ($18.42 to $22.63), plus breakfast

Among the cheapest of our choices is the pleasant, fourteen-room **Pension Alter Westen**, Genthiner Strasse 30k (phone 261-29-95), which occupies the second floor of a pre-war building on the eastern side of West Berlin, quite close to Checkpoint Charlie (take bus "No. 9" from Tegel or the U-Bahn to Kurfürstenstrasse). Rooms all have hot and cold running water and are spotlessly

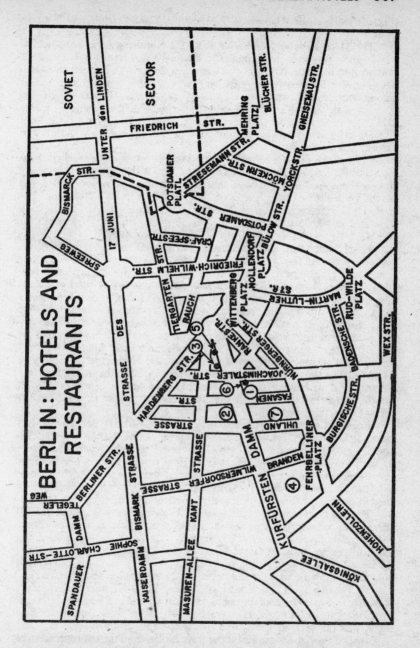

clean, if proportioned on the small side, and the proprietress, Frau Gertrud von Piechowski, speaks adequate English. Her pension is plain, but comfortable and homey, and 1980 prices, which in this establishment *include* breakfast, are a gentle 26 marks single, 43 marks ($22.63) double, 57 marks triple, and 72 marks quad.

The **Hotel-Pension Nürnberger Eck**, 24a Nürnbergerstrasse (phone 24-53-71), has—like so many buildings in Berlin—a deceptively ugly facade of grayish stucco; inside, however, you'll find a restored town house with rococo paneling, wood-carved newel posts, and large baroque doors! Rooms in this second-floor pension, which are clean and airy, rent for 23 marks single (the 23-mark variety being so spacious they're virtually doubles), only 40 marks ($21.05) double, inclusive of breakfast. English is spoken by proprietor Kurt Lippert (who also works as a stunt man in German movies), and Persian carpets line the floors.

In an elevator-equipped building at 1 Meierottostrasse, the excellent **Pension Berlin** (phone 881-9442) is owned by a Mr. Wohlauer, who is intensely serious about his duties as a host, collects information for visitors to use, and makes a practice of taking guests on tours of Berlin in his Volkswagen. His rooms are all large, clean, simply but attractively furnished, and rent for 25 to 30 marks single, 35 to 42 marks double, 56 marks triple, plus 5 marks for breakfast. No charge for a hot shower. Highly recommended.

Hotel Stadt Tilsit, at 9 Stuttgarter Platz (phone 324-52-61), is actually a pension occupying the first and second floors of an old apartment house furnished with pre-war beds, chairs and other pieces—they're adequate and comfortable. Frau Dams, the Tilsit's current owner, charges 24 marks ($12.63) single, 36 marks ($18.94) double, 15 marks ($7.89) for additional beds, and 5 marks ($2.63) for optional breakfasts, served in an unusually large breakfast room. From Tegel Airport, take bus #9 to the Kaiser-Friedrichstrasse stop. Far more centrally located, in an area rougly between the Kadewe Department Store at Wittenbergplatz and the Kurfürstendamm subway stop, but similarly priced, is the small (20 beds) **Pension Fischer** at 24a Nürnbergerstrasse (phone 24-68-08). Here you'll like the high-ceilinged rooms, all on the second floor; the English-speaking manageress, Frau Weschke; and rates of 35 marks ($18.42) double, 22 marks ($11.57) single (but there are only two of them), 13 marks ($6.84) for a third bed in the room.

Pension Centrum at 31 Kantstrasse (phone 31-61-53), is a tiny, 10-bed boarding house in the convenient Savignyplatz area (take bus no. 9 to Leibnizstrasse), managed by a friendly couple, Herr and Frau Schmücker, who charge 27 marks ($14.21) single, 38 marks ($20) for a twin or double, plus 5 marks ($2.63) more for an egg-with-sausage breakfast served in a cozy dining room. While the Schmückers don't speak English, their daughters living elsewhere in the city are happy to act as interpreters over the phone.

Pension Hagera, on the third floor of 3 Giesebrechtstrasse (phone 883-58-06), a sidestreet off Kurfürstendamm near Adenauerplatz, is in an old house with large rooms and heavy, stolid, Teutonic-type furniture. Mr. Kreutz, the English-speaking owner, charges 30 marks ($15.78) single, 43 marks ($22.63) double, 62 marks ($32.63) triple, plus 5 for an optional breakfast of cheese, cold cuts and rolls, with virtually unlimited—well, two cups at least—coffee.

At **Pension Viola**, 146 Kantstrasse (phone 31-64-57), near Bahnhof Zoo, single rooms are larger than the doubles in most other Berlin pensions, and rent for 27 marks ($14.21) single, 42 marks ($22.10) double. This is a quiet establishment, well run by Herr Carls, who speaks some English.

Just off the Ku-Damm and about three blocks from the Bahnhof Zoo, the 53-room **Hotel Viking**, Carmerstrasse 17 (phone 312-1060), is a large, elderly apartment house that has been completely converted by its English-speaking owner, Frau Cebulla, into a clean and comfortable, genuine budget-style hotel. Rooms here are high-ceilinged and newly-painted, with hot-and-cold running water in each; many are furnished in the Scandinavian style, with two narrow single beds running along one wall, topped by freshly-covered eiderdowns; downstairs, there's a large breakfast room, a small souvenir shop, and cold-drink machines, with outdoor tables for sipping drinks in summertime; and there's even an elevator, plus all the personal attention Frau Cebulla can bestow. 1980 rates, including service (breakfast is 5 marks extra), are 28 marks ($14.73) single, 40 marks ($21.05) double, 54 triple, and 2.50 marks for bath or shower. To reach the Viking take the No. 9 bus down the Ku-Damm to Uhlandstrasse, walk under the S-Bahn, two blocks to Steinplatz, turn left, and left again into Carmerstrasse.

And still another suitable accommodation in this price range is the **Pension Cortina,** 140 Kantstrasse (phone 313-9059), whose Italian owner and blonde German wife charge only 42 marks double, 54 triple, 64 quadruple, and 5 marks for breakfast. You'll have to walk up 30 steps before reaching the elevator landing (I did), but once upstairs, you'll be well-pleased with an efficient, pleasant operation. Take bus No. 9 from Tegel Airport to Bahnhof Zoo, and get off at the Bleibtreustrasse stop.

Doubles for 44 to 60 marks ($23.15 to $31.57), plus breakfast

Pension Lenz, at 8 Xantener Strasse (phone 881-51-58), is a choice selection for traveling families. That's because four of its 16 rooms are large "family" rooms—each spacious enough to sleep a family of four. Frau Karla Born is a friendly hostess, who speaks English well and takes great pride in making guests feel at home. (If you want to strike up a conversation quickly, just admire her beagle, "Whiskey"—her pride and joy.) All rooms have both hot-and-cold running water and telephones and are furnished in overstuffed German fashion, with big chairs and couches and heavy dressers. Prices are specially slanted toward budget-minded Americans (mention this book when you check in), with singles at 35 to 45 marks ($18.42 to $23.68), doubles from 60 to 70 marks ($31.75 to $36.84), triples at 70 marks ($36.84), plus 5 marks for breakfast, all including service. To get to the Lenz from Tegel airport, take the No. 9 bus down Kurfürstendamm.

Pension Nickel, at 1 Meierottostrasse (corner of Fasanenplatz, phone 881-8756), a five-minute walk from the "Ku-Damm," is one of the oldest and plainest pensions in Berlin. Yet, to me at least (and to many readers who write in its praises), it is a charming place managed by just about the most talkative little lady in the city, the charming 86-year-old Mrs. Nickel, who has regaled hundreds of tourists with stories relating to the history of Berlin, Germany, and of her own life. Mrs. Nickel rents seven rooms, all but one with running hot-and-cold water and the other with a marvelous big marble washstand right out of a Gary Cooper movie. In the lounge, she has a concert piano and invites guests who can play to use it; her kitchen is always available for fixing snacks; and since Mrs. Nickel never leaves the house at night, parents with children can leave them in her care—at no extra charge. Her rates are only 24 to 28 marks ($12.63 to $14.73) per person, plus 5 marks for an optional breakfast, which includes an egg and various meats and cheeses.

Pension Wittelsbach, 22 Wittelsbacherstrasse (four blocks from the Ku-Damm via Konstanzerstrasse, near the intersection of Brandenburgische and Konstanzer, phone 87-63-45), is a somewhat plain and old-fashioned establishment but with large and comfortable rooms and beds; it was owned until recently by an elderly and friendly German couple who get along acceptably (not fluently) in English and French. Their homey, antique breakfast room is so typically Old Germany that I could barely suppress a grin when I last saw it. Just before press-time, a younger couple, Mr. and Mrs. Arzt (he speaks perfect English), took over, and much modernization is now in progress—but with not much increase in minimum rates, thankfully. In 1980: 23 to 50 marks (depending on size) single, 44 to 75 marks double, 18 marks for a third or fourth bed, 6.50 marks for a superb breakfast (whose ingredients change daily), 9 to 12 marks for supper, 3 marks for a bath, showers for free.

Readers have also been pleased with the **Pension Alster** at 10 Eisenacher- strasse (phone 246-952), managed by Frau Ingeborg Viebahn, who has a big shepherd dog that barks but does not bite. Singles there are 29 marks, doubles 56 marks, breakfast included, and Frau Viebahn provides showers (with a large towel) for 3 marks extra.

For "big splurgers" desiring a top-quality pension—and willing to pay the price—there's the exceptionally attractive **Hotel-Pension Pariser Eck**, Pariser Strasse 19 (phone 881-21-45), with 13 rooms, all huge and lovely, and with sitting areas in each. Frau Otto, a gracious hostess, makes a point of keeping the surroundings "quiet and comfortable." The walls are painted white, the baths tiled, and every room has its own sink and telephone. Rates in 1980 are 32 marks ($16.84) single, 52 marks ($27.63) double, with service and tax included. A large breakfast, with egg, costs 6 marks; an extra bed costs 22 marks. Take the No. 9 bus to the corner of Kurfürstendamm and Bleibtreu- strasse and walk two blocks down Bleibtreustrasse and Sächsische Strasse to the pension on the corner of Pariser Strasse.

At 7 Motzstrasse, a serviceable 130-bed businessmen's-type-hotel called the **Sachsenhof** (phone 216-2074), charges 28 marks for a bathless single, 55 marks double, 87 marks for a 4-bedded room, plus 5 marks per person for breakfast. Owner Klaus Manzke operates a restaurant in the same building, where you can have a good two-course meal for 10 marks.

And now we arrive at the marvelously-located **Hotel-Pension Fasanen- haus(1)**, which is a half-block off Kurfürstendamm at Fasanenstrasse 73 (the famous, deluxe Hotel Kempinski is located diagonally across the street), phone 881-6713. White singles here are as high as 30 marks ($15.78), doubles rent for as little as 48 marks ($25.26) and never for more than 60 ($31.57), triples 70, quadruples for 82, breakfast is 5 marks extra, and service is included. The Fasanenhaus is run by an "old Berliner," Frau Groth, and her English-speak- ing student son, who know their beloved city well, are generous with informa- tion, and maintain a marvelous "at home" atmosphere in their pension. Take the bus to the "Uhlandstrasse" stop. . . . Not far away, the **Hotel-Pension Dittberner**, 26 Wielandstrasse (phone 881-64-85), with its wall-to-wall carpet- ing in guest rooms, its lounge decorated with Japanese prints, an elevator, offers unusual comfort at a relatively moderate price: 56 marks ($29.47) for double rooms, 5.50 marks per person for breakfast. Location is on a sidestreet just off the Ku-Damm, reached by taking bus no. 19 to the Leibnizstrasse stop.

An alternative to the Dittberner, located virtually next door to the famous Kempinski, is the pleasant and highly recommended **Pension d'Este**, 29 Kur- fürstendamm (phone 881-49-47), where the rates are 33 marks ($17.36) per person, including breakfast, service, free showers and baths. Here the owners are Herr and Frau Rosenkranz, whose daughter graduated from a U.S. college. Both speak English, the gentleman quite fluently, and their rooms (which are vast) contain big beds and spotless eiderdowns. The setting, in the very center of town, is a pre-war building surrounding a courtyard, with massive carved wooden doors opening into the tiny lobby.

Another excellent value, in this price category, is the recently-redecorated **Pension Finck** at 54 Güntzelstrasse (phone 861-2940), 10 minutes on foot from Bahnhof Zoo, where pleasant Frau Finck charges 32 marks for a single, 62 marks double, 20 marks for a third or fourth bed, always including breakfast, and throws in hot baths for free. That's on the third floor of an elevator building.

Pension Astrid, Bleibtreustrasse 20 (phone 881-5959), offers quiet, centrally located lodgings, and the warm hospitality of owner, Frau Ruth Sterl. Singles for 34 marks ($17.89), doubles, 61 marks ($32.10), and those rates include a huge breakfast.

If the Astrid is full, try the nearby **Pension Royal,** Bleibtreustrasse 34 (phone 883-1800), charging 31 marks ($16.31) single, 56 marks ($29.47) double, 6 marks additional for breakfast. Owner Renate Otto speaks English.

The tiny **Pension Brinn,** Schillerstrasse 19 (phone 312-1605), just a five-minute walk from the Zoo station, is popular with actors from the nearby Schiller Theater. Well-furnished and well-cared-for rooms rent for 32 marks ($16.84) single, 53 marks ($27.89) double, plus 5 marks ($2.63) for breakfast.

And finally, **Hotel-Pension De Luxe,** Lietzenburgerstrasse 76 (phone 881-4717), is the domain of U.S. citizen Ernest Kingsley (from Commack, Long Island), who rents singles for 42 marks ($22.10), doubles for 61 marks ($32.10)—breakfast and chats about "back home" included.

Doubles from 60 marks ($31.57) to 65 marks ($34.21), plus breakfast

Directly on the Kurfürstendamm, at #62, you'll now find a single, substantial building housing three "hotel-pensions" that fit into this slightly higher price range. The least expensive is the 20-room **Hotel-Pension Leibniz-Eck** (phone 883-5055 or 883-1550), whose heavy oak furniture and old-fashioned decor is the kind you might have found in a pre-World War II, middle-class German home. The proprietor is the genial Rudi Jacubke, who very literally treats his clients as if they were guests in his own home. Special rates to readers of this book are 42 marks ($22.10) for a single, but only 65 makrs ($34.21) double, including service and tax. Upstairs in the same building, the **Hotel-Pension Luxor** (phone 883-5025) is a slightly more elegant apartment, with crystal chandeliers, large rooms, and lots of carpets. Here, some of the double rooms without bath rent for 65 marks, but others ascend to 82 marks, including service and tax; inquire carefully before deciding to stay. And make the same inquiries at the equally elegant **Hotel-Pension Bärbel,** again at 62 Kurfürstendamm (on the same floor as the Leibniz-Eck), phone 883-6161, whose rates are 35 to 50 marks single, 65 to 80 marks double.

If all the foregoing hotels haven't any vacancies (unlikely), then you're sure to find rooms at the big, 76-room **Hotel Frühling Am Zoo (3)** at 17 Kurfürstendamm (phone 881-8083), corner of Joachimstaler Strasse, one block from the Zoo railroad station. While this is a top-rated hotel, its rates for bathless rooms are quite low—priced this year at 49 marks single, 80 marks ($42.10) double, 26 marks for an extra bed, all including breakfast, service and tax. That, again, is for rooms without bath, but all ornate and chandeliered, in a perfect location, in the very center of the city, only yards away from the most important sections of the Kurfürstendamm. If it had an elevator, the Frühling Am Zoo would undoubtedly be rated a First Class hotel; and even now, it has the top quality of all the hotels we've listed.

In a slightly less expensive category, the big **Hotel Europa,** about 2 blocks south of the Kurfürstendamm at Konstanzerstrasse 60 (phone 882-1091), is a modern, elevator-equipped building whose office is on the first floor. 1980 rates here, for modern but bathless rooms, are 42 marks single, 70 marks ($36.84) double, 31 marks per person in triples (with breakfast, service and tax included). Best bet for budget travelers are the rooms on the 5th floor—all of which come with small dormer windows and bright red eiderdown covers. Several of these are triples and quite charming indeed for three girls or a family. . . . Alternatively, try the pleasant, small **Hotel les Nations** at 6 Zinzendorfstrasse (phone 391-9026), whose English-speaking proprietress, Frau Meier, charges 39 marks single, 66 marks twin, 84 marks triple, for clean rooms with totally new furniture, and all in a quiet location 20 minutes on foot from the Kurfürstendamm. Take bus no. 23 from Bahnhof Zoo, or else go by subway (U-Bahn) to the Turmstrasse stop.

A top-quality pension is the **Hotel-Pension Funk,** Fasanenstrasse 69 (phone 881-51-52 or 881-5573), with its sweeping white marble staircase in the entranceway and huge double-bedded rooms done in French provincial furnishings. Herr Groth, the proprietor, speaks English, and will fill you in on what's happening at the theater, opera and nightspots, in addition to providing hints for shopping and sightseeing. Rates are 61 marks ($32.10) double, 39 marks single, 75 marks triple and 88 marks for four beds. Breakfast (which includes an egg, cheese and cold cuts) is 6 marks and baths are free. Take the No. 9 bus down the Ku-Damm to the corner of Fasanenstrasse.

Not far away, the 30-bed **Pension Modena** at 26 Wielandstrasse (phone 881-5294), kept spotlessly clean by manager Frau Brigitte Toboll, charges 40 marks ($21.05) single, 68 marks ($35.78) double, including a hearty breakfast. . . . Similarly-priced, and only a few minutes' walking distance from Bahnhof Zoo, is the tiny, 16-bed **Pension Chilcott,** 16 Meinekestrasse (phone 881-1297), charging 34 marks single, 58 marks double, 4.50 marks for breakfast. Frau Feig is the lady to see.

And finally, the **Hotel Burckschat** in the center of the inexpensive shopping street, Wilmersdorfer Strasse, at # 67 (phone 323-4245), is for those who prefer modern but strictly impersonal surroundings, and who mainly want a private shower at a reasonable price. The large, straight-walled Burckschat has 130 rooms, all with private shower (but not toilet)—the majority of the rooms singles. Rooms are identically furnished in spare contemporary style. Singles in 1980 will be priced at 34.50 marks ($18.15); doubles at 60 marks ($31.57).

READERS' PENSION SELECTIONS "Pension Bamberg, 58 Bambergerstrasse (phone 211-78-77), charges just 28 marks for a single 37 marks for a double, not including breakfast. These lodgings are clean and quiet, yet less than six minutes from the Kurfürstendamm" (Marty Hallinan, New York, New York). . . . "Last month, I spent three weeks in a splendid pension in Berlin, one certainly deserving of mention in the book. It is the **Pension Molthan,** Lietzenburger Strasse 76 (phone 881-7973), located one block from the Ku-Damm; it has immaculate, palatial rooms, and the proprietor, Frau Molthan, simply couldn't be more considerate. Rates are about average (30 DM for a single), but the rooms and service are the best I've seen" (Leon Platinga, New Haven, Connecticut; note by AF: recent rates here were 30 marks single, 45 to 50 marks double, including service, but plus 5.50 marks for breakfast, including a boiled egg. There's an elevator and a pleasant breakfast room). . . . **"Pension Atlas,** 172 Uhlandstrasse (phone 883-7919), is just off the Ku-Damm a couple of blocks from the Zoo, an almost perfect situation. The lady in charge speaks no English, but merely thinks that a delightful challenge, and has little trouble communicating. The place is clean and as inexpensive as anything can be in this city where accommodations come high" (G. Berkowitz, DeKalb, Illinois; note by AF: Atlas rates in 1980 are 30 marks single, 45 double, 62 triple, 5 breakfast, 2.50 showers).

READER'S PRIVATE ROOM RECOMMENDATION: "I found a real gem of a private room in the apartment of **Frau I. Zimmerman** at 69 Bergstrasse (phone 796-13-12), who has a special fondness for Americans—offering hospitality and friendship that make you feel a guest, not a customer. Our double room costing only 40 marks ($21) a night was wonderfully comfortable, clean, spacious, the bathroom modern, with free baths and oceans of hot water, and included in the rate was breakfast with meat, cheese, bread, egg, coffee or tea.

From the Zoo, take the U-Bahn, line # 9, in the direction of Steglitz, get off at Walter-Schreiber-Platz, and from there take bus # 2 or # 81 to Bergstrasse (4 stops); she lives right at that corner" (Thomas T. Tenenhaus, Binghamton, New York; note from AF: having zipped past briefly in the fall of 1979, I can report only that Mrs. Zimmerman's apartment is in a small, red-brick house facing a cemetary, in ultra-quiet surroundings).

READERS' HOTEL SELECTIONS (BIG SPLURGE VARIETY): "Just around the corner from your recommended Hotel-Pension Fasanenhaus, at Kurfürstendamm 217 (phone 881-6400), we found the **Hotel-Pension Adler,** which has most luxurious double rooms, spacious as in a palace, at 75 marks per day for two people, without bath. Breakfast is extra, served by polite and helpful maids (one of them accompanied us to the Dahlem Museum, just to show us the way)" (Robert S. Milne, Yonkers, New York; note by AF: 1980 rates are 50 marks single, 81 marks, double ($42.63), plus 5 marks for breakfast). . . . "The **Hotel Juwel,** at 26 Meinekestrasse, just off the Ku-Damm (phone 882-7141), is a little steep for the $15 a day budget, but really is excellent. We paid 60 D.M. ($31.57) for a beautiful clean double room with a balcony. The price included a delicious breakfast (with a soft-boiled egg) served by the delightful lady owner, taxes, service and all the baths we wanted to take. The location can't be beat" (Sandra and James Risser, Des Moines, Iowa; note by AF: at the Juwel, normal singles will rent in 1980 for 36 marks, doubles for 55 marks, service but not breakfast included).

STARVATION BUDGET: The youth hostels of West Berlin are open throughout the year, charge an all-inclusive rate (bed and all three meals) of only 19.10 marks ($10.05) per night; 22 marks ($11.57) for those over 25. There's also a bed-and-breakfast rate of 10.50 marks ($5.52; 12.50 marks ($6.57) for over 25's. Those rather amazing prices are available, for instance, at **Jugendherberge "Ernst Reuter,"** Hermsdorfer Damm 48 (phone 404-16-10), in Berlin Hermsdorf (a huge, interesting hostel), or at **Jugendherberge Bayernallee,** 36 Bayernallee (phone 305-3055), in Berlin-Charlottenburg. Newest and most comfortable of the youth hostels, but also more expensive, is the **Jugendgästehaus Berlin** at 3 Kluckstrasse (phone 261-1097), whose 435 beds rent for 22 marks ($11.57) with all three meals. This one's in the center of town, near the Kurfürstenstrasse U-Bahn station, and while it lacks the grounds and hearty outdoor flavor of the Bayernallee and Ernst Reuter hostels, it's probably better suited to sight-seeing young tourists, interested in the downtown life of West Berlin. There's a midnight curfew at all three hostels, as well as a requirement that you hold a Youth Hostel Card, which, however, can be purchased on-the-spot for 20 marks ($10.52).

READERS-ON-THE-STARVATION-BUDGET (ROOMS): "A very good pension is the **Ansbach Pension,** at 11 Ansbacher Strasse (phone 24-63-35). Here we had a large twin-bedded room for just 22 marks a night. It's well-located and the memorial church is only a 5-minute walk away" (Dale Watts, Dearborn, Michigan; note by AF: 1980 rates are 20 marks single, 28 to 35 double. Cold running water only).

READERS-ON-THE-SUB-STARVATION-BUDGET: "For rock-rock bottom accommodations you don't even have to leave the station. There's a **Mission Dormitory** right inside the Zoo terminal. It charges $4.50 a night for hostel-type cubicles—with hot water and lockers, but not showers" (Nat Freedland, New York, N.Y.). . . . "At my price level (the lowest) I recommend the **Bahnhof Mission**—they have an office in the Bahnhof and the Mission is right downstairs. It's a spotless, dormitory-style place, and costs 8.50 marks" (Pete Wilford, Morris Plains, N.J.;- note by AF: the central train station in West Berlin is known as "Bahnhof Zoo," and is located across from the large Berlin Zoo; entrance to the Bahnhof Mission—which has a midnight curfew, and literally kicks you out of bed at 7 a.m.—is in the ticket-selling portion of the station next to the post office; you'll see signs. An even larger **Mission Dormitory** for both men and women, of which the railroad station is an annex, is found at 27 Franklinstrasse in the Tiergarten district, near the Ernst-Reuter-Platz U-Bahn stop. 8.50 marks per person is the price, including a spartan breakfast of coffee, bread and marmalade, and 11 p.m. curfew. Both missions are closed 10 a.m. to 3:30 p.m. to be cleaned).

MEALS: Have your very first meal in Berlin at the domed third-floor restaurant of the **Bilka Department Store** (Germany's answer to Macy's) at Joachim-stalerstrasse 5, near the Zoo station in the heart of town. The single most popular budget eatery in Berlin, the Bilka restaurant is a vast, glassed-in room housed in a futuristic world's fair type building. You can have an excellent three-course meal here for only 7 marks ($3.68), including tax and service, from 11:30 a.m. to 6 p.m. weekdays and till 2 p.m. Saturdays. Another bargain at Bilka: an American breakfast served from 9 to 11:30 a.m., consisting of coffee, juice, two eggs, rolls or toast, butter and marmalade for only 3.50 marks ($1.84)—a special rate for readers of this book!

Another excellent choice—possibly for your second meal in Berlin—is the tiny, family-operated **Theaterrestaurant** at Uhlandstrasse 28, a few steps off the Kudamm, where the walls are plastered with autographed pictures of artists and actors who frequent the place. A choice of three, three-course menus priced at 6.80, 7.50 and 9 marks ($3.57, $3.94 and $4.73) is offered daily except Saturdays and Sundays from 11:30 a.m. to 7 p.m., and à la carte dishes are also reasonably priced. For example, a large wiener schnitzel with french fries and salad is 9 marks. Apart from other readers of this guide, you're likely to be the only tourist here.

Yet a third worthy budget establishment, **Postklause Bei Robby**, Leibniz-strasse 70, off the Kudamm, is heavily frequented by students attracted by 12 varietes of hot stew. They cost about 5 marks ($2.63) per plate, and come in combinations like sauerkraut stew with sausage, lentils with pork, and vegetables with meat. Open Monday to Thursday from 4 p.m. to 2 a.m.; Friday and Saturday from noon to 2 a.m.; closed Sundays.

And finally, don't miss **Tegernseer Tönnchen,** at 34 Mommsenstrasse (from the Kurfürstendamm, turn right on Wilmersdorferstrasse, then left on Mommsenstrasse), where the decor and atmosphere is pure Bavarian beer hall. Open daily until midnight, it offers hearty one-plate meals from 7 to 12 marks ($3.68 to $6.31). Whatever you order, wash it down with some imported Tegernseer beer (3 marks for half a liter).

The budget-minded Balkans

If at this point your system has been saturated with the flavors and fats of the classic German cuisine, you might like to search out the increasingly popular Balkan restaurants of West Berlin, whose lighter and spicier cuisine can sometimes provide a welcome change. We recommend three, in particular: the **Paprika Grill,** 73 Fasanenstrasse (near the Kudamm), where a large plate of stuffed peppers and potatoes costs 8.50 marks ($4.47); the **Belgrad-Grill,** 67 Uhlandstrasse near the Ku-damm, serving "schaschlik" for 5 marks ($2.63), a "puszta-platte" (pork cutlets on curried rice, with salad) for 8.50 marks ($4.47), all of it accompanied by excellent Yugoslav red wine at 4.50 marks ($2.36) per quarter liter; and **Athener Grill,** Kurfürstendamm 156, corner Albrecht-Achilles-strasse, open from noon to 4 a.m., serving lamb cutlets with french fries or salad for 4.90 marks ($2.68), Greek salad for 3.80 marks ($2), and a large selection of Balkan-style pizzas for 4 marks ($2.10). At some of the above, waiters and waitresses are colorfully attired in Yugoslav. Hungarian, or Greek costumes, and in the evenings musicians usually play and sing Balkan folk songs.

The Italian "spaghetterias"

Six marks ($3.15)—that's the cost of a huge platter of spaghetti and appropriate accompaniments, at three Kurfürstendamm cookeries, of which the easiest-to-find is **Italsnack** at 246 Kurfürstendamm, between the Marmormoviehouse and the futuristic Wertheim department store. Small and barely-furnished, but incredibly busy, it serves mammoth pizzas, salad bowls and spaghetti platters for an average of 6 marks ($3.15), sometimes less. Nearby, at 12 and 13 Savignyplatz, in the Technical University area, the **San Marco** and the **Pizza** offer and charge the same, and also serve a "student meal" consisting of spaghetti or pizza, plus beer or a Coke, for 6 marks—but nobody checks whether you really are a student. My personal favorite, however, is the **Ristorante Pizza** at 69 Kurfürstendamm, corner of Kudamm and Wilmersdorferstrasse, near Adenauerplatz, because the servings are especially large, the quality first class, and meals are served until 4 a.m. Twenty different varieties of pizza sell for an average of 5 marks ($2.63), ten different spaghetti combinations for 6 marks ($3.15), ice cream for 2. And there are outdoor tables.

The $4 to $6 restaurants

Along the Kurfürstendamm, and on the side streets directly off it, are a host of other places where one can dine well for a higher $3.50 to $5. These include the long-established, well-known budget restaurant called **Hardtke's,** at 26 Meinekestrasse, just off Kurfürstendamm, in a building heavily damaged during the war, but now restored to its traditional Germanic state, with beamed ceilings, wood paneling and brick, scrubbed pine tables, and chairs made of rush. Every day from 11:30 a.m. to four, it offers at least one two-course "gedeck" (meal) for 11 marks ($5.75), but day and evening there are à la carte plates of Hardtke's famous "wurst" (sausage) specialties for either 5.50 marks (bockwurst und kartoffelsalat) or 5.50 marks (schinkenknacker und kartoffelsalat), which can always be supplemented by a 2.20 mark bowl of soup and a 1.90 mark quarter liter of beer, for an around $5.30 meal; order from the typewritten "tagesgerichte" menu.

To vary the surroundings, you can alternate meals at Hardtke's with the equally-fine German specialties available for the same price at the **Restaurant Schultheiss,** at 237 Kurfürstendamm (which has the advantage of being almost directly across from the bombed-out "Kaiser-Wilhelm-Gedächtnis-Kirche," the aesthetic-even-though-ruined cathedral in the center of the city: a spectacular sight). Look this time for the "Mittagsgedecke," usually one two-course menu for 10 to 12 marks, and two three-course menus for 13 and 16 marks respectively, served from 11:30 a.m. to 5 p.m. Practically next door to Schultheiss, the **Self-Service Restaurant** of the modernistic new Wertheim Department Store offers a large variety of typical dishes and has, since its opening, become quite popular among Berliners; an entire roast chicken costs 7.90 marks ($4.15), half a chicken 3.95 marks, and a bowl of chicken soup, 1.65 marks. You could make a meal out of two rolls (20 pfenning each) and a bowl of thick pea soup with slices of weiner sausage swimming in it, 3.50 marks ($1.84). The restaurant, in the basement of the department store, next to the food department, shares store hours: Monday to Friday from 10:30 a.m. to 6:30 p.m., Saturday until 2 p.m. . . . There are, as you'll notice, a whole string of similar-looking restaurants along the Ku-Damm, but none of them offers the same fixed-price values as are available at Hardtke's, and at several different Ku-Damm branches of the Schultheiss. If you can't make out the German menus at these places, simply order the fixed price meals—you'll find that they're well-planned, and contain no weird surprises.

And finally, you might want to visit one of the several restaurants at the big **KaDeWe Department Store,** Tauentzienstrasse, corner of Wittenbergplatz. These include the self-service **Zille-Stube** on the third floor (daily platters from 6 to 7.80 marks—$3.15 to $4.10), and adjoining, sit-down **"Restaurant"** with waitress service and three-course table d'hotes for 9 to 11 marks—$4.73 to $5.78. In the same "KaDeWe" (standing for "Kaufhaus des Westens"—it's the largest department store in Germany), top (sixth) floor, is a gigantic food department containing, among other features, a dozen stands selling wieners, sandwiches, roast chicken, wine, sweets, soups and fishburgers. All these are open Monday to Friday, from 10 a.m. to 6:30 p.m., Saturdays until 2 p.m.

On Wilmersdorferstrasse

The cheap shopping street of Berlin is not the elegant Kurfürstendamm, but the pedestrians only Wilmersdorferstrasse, where a stroll provides insight into the life of the average-income Berliner. Most of them are drawn to the bustling department stores here, including a low cost **Herties** (known for particular values in low-cost shoes), whose unusually cheap cafeteria serves fixed-price, three-course meals for 7.50 and 10 marks. Across the street, the cafeteria of the **Quelle Department Store** offers lighter two-course menus, for 6 and 7 marks, while the fourth-floor restaurant of the **Karstadt** store goes down to 5.75 marks ($3.02) for two courses. A constant price war. And there are countless small, inexpensive restaurants crammed between the shops. Try, for instance, at 105 Wilmersdorferstrasse, the simple—but popular—**Köpke,** featuring various forms of "eintopfgerichte" (literally: one-pot-meals), such as a meat-and-potatoes stew, or a bowl of pea-soup with sausage bits, all filling and all priced under 3.50 marks. Across the street: the fish-featuring **Fischgaststätte Bunte Kuh,** at 95 Wilmersdorferstrasse, where 7.95 marks results in a large fish filet and a mountain of incomparable German potato salad. Down the street, at 117 Wilmersdorferstrasse, **Joseph Langer** sells a pair of wieners with a bowl of pea soup for 1.50 marks (79¢), while **Pufferpfanne,** at the corner of Kantstrasse, specializes in a filling potato omelette served with apple sauce and known as "kartoffelpuffer"—only 2 marks ($1.05). Guten Appetit; and keep the Alka Seltzer handy.

In the Europa Center

The recently-completed "Europa Center"—a 22-story skyscraper topped by a twirling Mercedes star, on Tauentzienstrasse (across the street from the bombed church)—houses 10 restaurants, which go under the overall title of "Haus der Nationen" (each represents a different nationality). One of them—the **Bierstube Alt-Berlin,** on the second floor of the adjoining shopping compound—offers fixed price meals (at lunch only) for under 9 marks, and remains fairly cheap at night, too. There is a Bavarian band in attendance on Friday and Saturday evenings (yet there is no admission or minimum).

Loretta's Garden

Is a place to eat outdoor picnic meals, without anyone requiring that you buy a thing. Walk up the Kurfürstendamm from the Europa Center side, turn left into Knesebeckstrasse, walk on for a block, and there you'll see: Loretta's Garden, with 100 tables, open to the public, weather permitting, from noon on. If you haven't brought the fixins, you can obtain all you'll need from nearly a dozen shops in the area selling beer, soft drinks, sausages and the like (an average of 2.50 marks—$1.31—per). You can go there at night, too, when amateur bands play.

THE WIENERWALDS: There is also in Berlin a chain of restaurants serving spit-roasted chicken—the **Wienerwald Brathendlstationen**—which you ought to try at least once: they are one of the great success stories of postwar Germany. Their originator, a restaurant waiter, once visited the Oktoberfest in Munich, where he saw Germans by the thousands wolfing down huge quantities of roast chicken—then a relatively-expensive luxury in Germany. Determined to make roast chicken a mass-market commodity, he traveled to the United States, studied our chicken-roasting methods, and then—on the merest of shoestrings—opened a restaurant that would serve only a single item, roast chicken, for $2.25. He decorated the place in crowd-pleasing cornball Vienna Woods fashion, called it the "Wienerwald," and expanded so quickly that he was soon operating scores of Wienerwalds, of which 21 are in West Berlin.

The Wienerwalds now serve half a roast chicken, plus salad, for 8.55 marks ($4.50). They also serve thick chicken soup (with noodles and several chunks of chicken) for 2.90 marks, and a small beer for 1.20 marks. The one we last visited was at Tauentzien Strasse 16 (near the pedestrian bridge connecting with the Europacenter, corner of Marburger Strasse), but there are other members of the chain at Schwedenstrasse 19, Neue Kantstrasse 17, Turmstrasse 26, Kurt-Schumacher-Platz, Tegel Schloss Strasse 1, Bayerischer Platz 2, and at fifteen other locations throughout the city. It's a filling meal, and the mass production of the roast chickens should amuse you.

READERS' RESTAURANT SELECTIONS: "At **Novo Skopje**, 38 Kurfürstendamm, you can get terrific "pola pola"—pork sausage, beef, vegetables and a delicious sauce—plus a beer, for 10 marks" (Peter Hrycenko, Fleetwood, Pennsylvania). . . . "We went to the **Town Hall**, located in what is the John F. Kennedy Square. Up on the third floor, there is a large room full of big wooden tables and chairs. There is nothing fancy about it, but they serve very good, cheap meals. This is where most of the city council members eat, sometimes even the Mayor. We had a bowl of home-made soup (2.40 marks), a dish of apple sauce (80 pfennigs), a plate of bread and butter (80 pfennigs), total: just under 4 marks. Platters are priced from 3 to 6 marks" (Karen Worden, Plymouth, Wisconsin; note by AF: the **Mensa** of the Town Hall (Schöneberger Rathaus) is open to the public from 8 a.m. to 4 p.m., serves six different three-course menus for prices ranging from an incredibly low 2.75 marks to 7 marks). . . . "Our least expensive and most nutritious meals were had at the mensa of the **Technical University**, two blocks from Amerika Haus, at 34 Hardenbergstrasse, where one has a choice of three dinners, all including large portions of meat, potatoes and vegetables, with dessert, for under $2. You line up and buy a ticket, then go upstairs where, upon surrendering the ticket, you receive a tray" (Carol Fleischer, Baguio City, Philippines). . . . "The **Verena Vegetarian Restaurant**, located just off the Kurfürstendamm on Clausewitzstrasse, and open daily except Fridays, and except Saturday and Sunday evenings, is not only inexpensive, but quiet, dignified, clean and attractive, with an extensive menu of tastefully prepared food—vegetable soup, 2.50 marks; cinnamon rice with cooked apples, 4.50 marks; yogurt, 1.50 marks—which non-vegetarians like ourselves found an enjoyable change of pace" (Barbara S. Lesko, Oakland, California; note by AF: open daily from noon to 9, exact address is 67 Kurfürstendamm, and two-course menus are priced from 7.50 to 9.50 marks, but some content themselves with simply the cooked rice with stewed fruit for 5 marks).

READERS' FOOD-AND-DRINK TIPS: "The finest and cheapest cup of coffee in Berlin (and in many other large German cities) is served not in restaurants or lunch rooms, but in specialty stores selling coffee in packages or cans. The theory is that a possible customer looking for a package of coffee to take home, should be given a sample cup, fresh-made, at 50 pfennigs (about 26¢) a cup. In actual practice, the stores are crowded most of the day by people who only want a cup of coffee. I have seen a line of 20 or 30 persons being served at the rate of 12 to 15 per minute. Each is quickly given a cup of boiling hot coffee, a little cream, and two or three lumps of sugar. He drinks it at a stand-up table where there is a pitcher of lukewarm water to stretch or weaken the coffee if he wishes. Two of these places are located on the same street, Kurfürstendamm, each within a hundred feet of the famous ruined church which stands almost in the center of the main business section. One of them is on the same side of the street as the church and a few doors from American Express. You can't miss it, the shop is filled with customers drinking coffee. A sign on the shop window reads 'Tchibo.' Directly across the Kurfürstendamm is another shop advertising 'Eduscho Kaffe.' These little shops are not old fashioned second-rate places, but bright and shining and as up-to-the-minute as the best places of business in the city" (Albert Gerlach, Miami, Florida).

STARVATION BUDGET MEALS: Because they're such exciting secrets, I almost hate to divulge that Berlin possesses two mensa-type restaurants (army-style "messhalls"), totally proper and attractive, yet practically unknown even to the average Berliner, where filling, two-course meals can be had at lunchtime for less than $2!

The immense, 600-seat **Mensa der Technischen Universität** at 34 Hardenbergstrasse, easily found less than 250 yards from Bahnhof Zoo (it's the modern, low construction with red windows), is theoretically maintained for students. But if you'll walk through the student area, and then up the stairs, you'll find a public, non-student dining room where waitresses serve three daily dishes for only 2.25 marks ($1.18), like vegetable stew with sausage; or two-course luncheons for only 3.50 or 4 marks ($1.84 and $2.10), like fish filet with salad and dessert, or goulasch with noodles, plus fruit. There are à la carte delights for 4.90 marks ($2.68; chicken stew with vegetables) and 7.50 marks ($3.94; sauerbraten with red cabbage and potatoes); coffee for 80 pfennings (42¢); cokes for 90 pfennings (47¢); beer for 1 mark (52¢). And hours are from Monday through Friday, 11:30 a.m. to 2:30 p.m. only.

Then there's the **Kasino im Haus des Senators für Wirtschaft,** on the fifth floor (via elevator) of 105 Martin Luther Strasse, facing the Schöneberger Rathaus (take the subway to this stop). There, soup is 90 pfennigs (47¢), two-course meals are 3.80 and 4.20 marks ($2 and $2.21), à la carte offerings range from 4 marks (grilled sausage with red cabbage) to 7.50 marks (rumpsteak), and hours are again on weekdays only, from 11:30 a.m. to 1 p.m. . . . Meals for $1.95? **Burger-King,** corner of Ku-damm and Meinekestrasse, and open daily from 9 a.m. to midnight, charges 1.70 marks (89¢) for a hamburger, 95 pfennigs (50¢) for french fries, a mark for a Coke.

ENTERTAINMENT: Now for the action. You ought not to miss the **Cafe Keese,** 108 Bismarckstrasse (a 10-minute walk from the Ku-Damm), a large, cheerful dance hall populated by singles and couples in the 25-to-40 age range, where the gimmick is the "Ball Paradox"—a system by which the woman asks the man to dance and it is against the house rules for the man to refuse! Only on the hourly "Men's Choice," can the man issue the invitation (those males wanting to sit it out retire to the bar; the rest are fair game). Cafe Keese claims 41,000 couples to date who have met and married under the auspices of three German branches. Clientele is well-dressed and comparatively attractive; there's no admission charge and reasonable drink prices (6 marks a beer, including tax and service); orchestra is live and the dances tend to be slow—with very little in the "rock" line.

People of all ages might enjoy the lively dancing and beer-swigging at the **Munich Hofbräuhaus,** across from the bombed church on Hardenbergstrasse. Admission to the atmospheric upstairs room as 1 mark on weekdays, 2 marks on Friday and Saturday. The band is brassy; the crowd happy and noisy. A half-liter of beer costs 5 marks, a full liter, 8.50.

For much younger readers, the major teen-age spot in Berlin is the **Big Apple,** on Bundesalle, where all the latest dance steps are frenetically practiced, against an ear-shattering din of noise. Entrance fee (which is all you need spend) is 2 marks from Monday through Thursday, 3 marks on weekends, a mark less for girls, and payment of entrance is considered to be a "Verzehrbon," exchangeable for one free drink inside.

Crowds are always waiting to get into the **Big Eden** at 202 Kurfürstendamm—a monstrous discotheque that holds up to 2,000 people and is bugged from one end to the other with zany electronic gimmicks. Lights flash, sounds swell, the record player is a masterpiece of electronic workmanship. Every sort and species of young Berlin swinger turns up at the Big Eden—most in costume —as well as all young internationals who hone in on the "sound." The Big Eden is specifically geared to the thin pocketbook. During the week, you need purchase only a 5 mark "Verzehrbon" at the door; on Friday, Saturday and Sunday there's an additional 1.50-mark entrance fee. Every drink is priced at 3.50 marks, including tax, and if you sit in the booths along the wall where there is a sign reading "Selbstbedienung" (self service), you won't be bothered by waitresses and can go up to the self-service counter and buy drinks as you please, without further service charge. At one circular counter, there's pizza for sale at 1.50 marks per serving, spaghetti at two marks, and a steak platter for 8 marks. And all around there are lone, young Berliners ready and willing to strike up conversation with lone, young tourists. Open until 3 a.m. weekdays, until 5 a.m. weekends. (By the way, unescorted girls are never charged an admission here, nor is anyone—male or female—who shows this book or chapter at the door.)

The futuristically decorated **Cheetah** at 31 Hasenheide, looking for all the world like something out of "A Clockwork Orange," is another big hangout for the under-25 set. Here you'll find 2,000 people on six dance floors, with top bands and show orchestras—among the best Berlin can offer—featured as entertainment. There's a 3 mark entrance fee only on Saturdays; beer is 3 marks; a small whiskey is 5 marks; and bottles of wine start at 17 marks. Open Friday, Saturday and Sunday only, from 8 p.m.; take the subway to the Hermannplatz station.

Two other popular clubs on the Kurfürstendamm—the **Alt-Berliner Bier-Salon** at No. 225, and the **Tanz-Palast Berlin,** at No. 24—cater to all age groups. The Alt-Berliner Bier-Salon does not charge an entrance fee, offers dancing daily to standard dance bands, and charges 3.50 marks for a beer and 8 to 10 marks for a two-course meal. The Tanzpalast Berlin, located right across the street, is more sophisticated, with two dance bands playing, one beginning at 3 p.m., the other joining in at 8 p.m. Again, no entrance fee, but slightly higher prices than the Alt-Berliner: 3.80 marks for a beer, 25 marks ($13.15) for a bottle of Rhine or Mosel wine.

We've saved one of the most exciting spots for the last. Berlin—true to its wild, woolly, avant-garde tradition—has another of these weird, labyrinthine nightspots (patronized mainly by people under 30), in the 1,300-seat **Riverboat** (at 174 Hohenzollerndamm; take the subway to Fehrbelliner Platz), whose motif is that of a Mississippi riverboat, and whose layout is like the maze of a fun-house: there are seemingly endless galleyways with booths on either side, portholes, photostat blowups of famous riverboats, from four to seven bands all playing at once (they're all doing "acid rock"), and such stellar aggregations of entertainers as the "Gloomy Moon Singers." Entrance is 4 marks on weekends, 2 marks on weekdays; a glass of beer is 3.80 marks; stags of both sexes are much in evidence; and the Riverboat is closed Mondays.

READERS' ENTERTAINMENT SUGGESTIONS: "Deutsche Oper begins its season towards the end of August and runs until mid-July. You can get a pretty good seat for 8 marks, but in order to be sure of obtaining a ticket, it's better to make an advance reservation at the opera house (take U-bahn to Deutsche Oper). The box office is open between 10 a.m. and 2 p.m. and again one hour before the performance. You can also make reservations at any ticket agency" (Vera Wongcruawal, Bangkok, Thailand).

READERS' DAYTIME SELECTIONS "No one visiting Berlin should fail to see the **Schöneberg Rathaus,** where the Freedom Bell is, and where President Kennedy made his famous 'Ich bin ein Berliner' speech. There is free admission to the public on Wednesdays, Saturdays and Sundays from 10 a.m. to 2 p.m." (I. Skolnik, Bronx, New York). . . . "Berlin can be very warm during the summer, and so visitors will find that the cafes on Kurfürsten-damm are deserted and the sidewalks are lifeless. Where is everybody? You'll find hordes of Berliners at the outdoor swimming pools and lake areas, which in addition to being good places to cool off, are also the best spots for viewing the Berlin babes with all the latest bathing outfits. The best ones are **Olympia Stadium** (take U-bahn to Olympia Stadium), **Sommerbad Wilmersdorf** (take S-bahn to Hohenzollerndamm, pool is in front of the station, across the street), and **Wannsee Strandbad** (take S-bahn to Nikolassee). Admission to these pools is 1.50 marks. If you prefer lakes and woods, head for **Krumme Lanke** (take U-bahn to Krumme Lanke, and turn right in front of the station along Fischerhüttenstrasse)" (Richard Strasslein, Wilmington, Delaware).

TOURS: Three companies, all of whose buses leave from the Kurfürstendamm-Uhlandstrasse corner, operate escorted tours of Berlin. Oldest and largest is **Severin und Kühn,** 216 Kurfürstendamm (opposite the Kempinski Hotel), whose most popular tour goes into both West and East Berlin, lasts 4¼ hours, costs 30 marks, plus 12 marks for the East Berlin guide, leaves daily at 10 a.m., is perfectly safe, and shouldn't be missed; a condensed version of the same thing, confined almost entirely to East Berlin, leaves at 10 a.m. and 2 p.m., lasts only 3¾ hours, and costs 19 marks, plus the 12 mark East German fee and an additional mark for an optional visit to the Pergamon Museum. If you merely wish to tour West Berlin, you can take a 3-hour tour at 10 a.m. or 2:30 p.m. for 20 marks, or a 2-hour tour at 11 a.m., 2 p.m. and 4 p.m. for 16 marks. Definitely take the one that goes into both halves of the city—and then read about do-it-yourself tours of East Berlin, below. Finally, you might want to consider an excursion to historic Potsdam, which includes a visit to Sanssouci Castle and New Castle (the former Cecilienhof Palace, where the Potsdam Agreement was signed in 1945). Departures are every Tuesday, Thursday and Saturday at 9:30 a.m. for this eight-hour trip, which costs 75 marks, and includes lunch in a Potsdam restaurant. Severin und Kühn also sells theater tickets and acts as a general tourist information office.

A DO-IT-YOURSELF TOUR OF EAST BERLIN: The commercial tours of East Berlin are good for orientation purposes, but they are limited, for the most part, to lifeless statues and memorials—such as the Soviet War Cemetery—and fail to give you a real picture of life in East Berlin.

Despite the Wall, anyone other than a West Berliner is permitted to enter East Berlin on their own, at designated crossing points. To do so is precisely like crossing a border, except that the process is dragged out to a half-hour of passport-checking and questionnaire-filling, which is particularly infuriating when you realize the illegality of the entire procedure. But if you will tolerate that 30 minutes of red-tape, and refrain from making comments about it to the East German Volks-Polizei, the whole business becomes routine.

Once again, it is—at least at the time of writing—entirely safe to enter East Berlin on your own. If you have any qualms about it, then register your name with the American MP's at Checkpoint Charlie, tell them the time at which you plan to return, and if you're not there at that time, they'll take action. But no normal tourist is detained. On our most recent trip to Berlin, Hope and I met dozens of American G.I.'s who had made so many weekend jaunts into East Berlin that they were walking encyclopedias of the sights to be found across the Wall.

To get to Checkpoint Charlie—which is your best crossing point—take the U-Bahn from the Zoological Garden Station (near the Kurfürstendamm) to the Hallesches Tor station, and change there for the train that goes to **Kochstrasse,** just a couple of stops further on. The Kochstrasse exit is a block from the wall-crossing point. Before actually entering, you'll need to change 6.50 marks into 6.50 East-marks—this is required—and then pay over 5 marks to the Volkspolizei for your visa (valid 24 hours).

Once in East Berlin, you can take a cab to the places you'd like to see, or better yet, you can simply wander on foot, which is the preferred way to absorb the atmosphere of this unusual city. After visiting East Berlin's incomparable Pergamon Museum, Hope and I recently walked to the Friedrichstrasse Station, entered a huge market-place where we ate what seemed like sawdust-filled sausages for a snack, then took a long, long walk along Unter den Linden, and finally headed over to the showplace street of East Berlin (past the new Palast der Republik), once the famous "Stalinallee," but now renamed "Karl-Marx-Allee."

There are three restaurants on the Karl-Marx-Allee—the relatively expensive **"Moskau,"** which features Russian specialties such as chicken à la Tabaka (4.75 East German marks, filet steak Minsk 7.50 marks); and the less costly **"Budapest"** (where roast duck with pineapple slices and french fries costs 6.60 marks) and the **"Warschau"**—both on opposite corners of the intersection made by Fruchtstrasse. We had coffee at the Warschau, but could have had a meal for 7 East German marks (which are now the exact equivalent of 7 West German marks).

Several establishments serving lighter—and therefore lower-priced—meals are located nearby. At **Ermeler-Haus,** 10 Märkisches Ufer, you can sit in either the basement or garden, and have beefsteak with mushrooms for 5.50 marks, or a large beer for 1.36 marks. At **Gastmahl Des Meeres,** on the corner of Spandauer-Liebknechtstrasse, you eat fish, in a large (East Berlin's largest) and reasonably-priced fish house (fish stew is 3 marks; most expensive item on menu is filet of sole with vegetables and french fries for 5.30 marks). At the **Crusta-Stube,** 78 Warschauerstrasse, the specialty is grilled toast (six varieties) selling for 1.85 marks (with scrambled eggs) to 3.90 (with beef tartare). And finally, in the impressive, new government building called **Palast der Republik,** at Marx-Engels-Platz, three restaurants (the "Spree," "Linden" and "Palast") list a long assortment of traditional dishes, including franks with potato salad (1.80 marks), veal cutlet with mushrooms (3.50 marks). And then, having had enough, you can take a cab back to the crossing point, recross, and ride the U-Bahn to the Kurfürstendamm, where you'll emerge to the neon-lit, bustling life of free West Berlin. It is only, I think at the moment that you return to the "Ku-Damm" that the contrast between it and the dull existence of East Berlin really begins to sink in.

It might, of course, be well to precede your own tour of East Berlin with one of the commercial, guided variety. But don't miss a tour on your own—it's your chance to see current history, currently lived about you.

READERS' SELECTIONS (EAST BERLIN): "The opera is good in East Berlin and is worth seeing. Another experience we would recommend is to attend church services some Sunday morning in East Berlin. For Protestants, we recommend the Marienkirche. You'll have to ask directions, but it is within walking distance of Checkpoint Charlie" (Alan and Marti Lata, Gersweiler/Saar, West Germany. . . . "I suggest that budget travelers try the **Automat** on the Alexanderplatz, near the Centrum Warenhaus, for it has good hot meals for 2 marks, delicious coffee, and a lively crowd" (Tom Craig, Moore, South Carolina; note by AF: to visit the "Centrum"—East Berlin's largest department store—take the underground from the Pergamon Museum (which should be the first stop on your East Berlin tour) to Alexanderplatz. After touring the store (which is quite an experience), take the underground to Schillingstrasse, where you can then walk down to the Karl Marx Allee). . . . "After an interesting all-morning tour of the **Museum für Deutsche Geschichte,** I got tipped off by a friendly museum guard that a good place to eat (the cafeteria or mensa in the building is not recommendable, I was told) is at the **Zentrales Haus der Deutschsowjetischen Freundschaft,** Am Festungsgraben 1, just behind the Monument to the Unknown Soldier beside the museum. It was worthwhile information. Go right up the carpeted stairway to the second floor and proceed to your right. For a little over 4 marks one can have a choice of Russian and German dishes. Do not be intimidated by the name or purpose of the house. Many West German tourists take advantage too of its inexpensive and relatively good restaurant" (Sabino Vengco, Jr., Bulacan, Philippines). . . . "We lunched at the Ratskeller underneath their Rathaus where the atmosphere is really elegant (stained glass windows, etc.) and service is excellent, but the food is very inexpensive" (Celia and Jim Miner, Watertown, So. Dakota). . . . "I had a cheap and relatively good meal in a place called **"Haus Berlin"** on Strausberger Platz, which is a square about half way down Karl Marx Allee" (Ulf Ziecker, Hanover, Germany). . . . "Since the erection of the Wall, West Berliners seldom travel to East Berlin, and as they were in part the patrons of East Berlin theatres, there are usually tickets available. However, allow time for border crossing, as the guards sometimes get nasty about it, especially if you appear obviously in a hurry. Unlike Vienna, where tie and jacket are required, the Socialist paradise makes no such imposition on its theatre goers" (Burt Wolfson, New York; note by AF: a theater service for international tourists is operated by **Reisebüro der Deutschen Demokratischen Republik** at 5 Alexanderplatz (phone 215-44-02), which also arranges tours and the like. The week's schedule of theater performances and concerts is posted all over East Berlin. Tickets are not expensive (from 6 to 14 marks for the Berliner Ensemble, for instance) and seats are usually available). . . . "When visiting West Berlin, you can rent a car and go to East Berlin without any extra formalities, except that you have to write the registration number on the usual "money-declaration-card." The 24-hour cost for a Volkswagen is 34.75 marks, plus 32 pf/km, plus petrol" (Lennart Weibull, Lerum, Sweden).

STUDENT IN BERLIN: Student headquarters in Berlin is the **ARTU** at 9 Hardenbergstrasse (near Amerika Haus and the Tourist Information Office), open weekdays only from 9:30 a.m. to 6 p.m., Wednesdays from 10:30 a.m. to 6 p.m. (phone 31-07-71), and providing information on student charter flights, student discounts, and the like. For student meals, you head directly across the street to the **Student Mensa,** at 34 Hardenbergstrasse, where the lunchtime menu features soup at a mark; and main plates with vegetables from 1.60 to 2 marks. I.D. card needed. Both these outfits are located a short three blocks from the main Zoo railroad station . . . High quality student lodgings are provided by the centrally-located **Studentenhotel Berlin** at Meininger Strasse 10 (phone 784-67-20), near the Rathaus Schöeberg (City Hall) on John F. Kennedy Platz. Rates there for accommodations in a four-bedded room are 20 marks per person, 22 marks in a two-bedded room. Breakfast is included at no extra charge, a student bar operates every evening, a self-service restaurant runs throughout the day, and a complete Finnish sauna—on the premises—takes care of the resulting weight problems. Take Bus 4, 85 or 73; the U-Bahn station is Rathaus Schöneberg.

BERLIN MISCELLANY: You'll quickly discover that Berliners are an atypical breed of Germans—witty, sophisticated, and totally irreverent. For instance, they've named the new chapel and bell-tower, adjacent to the ruined Kaiser-Wilhelm-Gedächtniskirche on Kurfürstendamm, "the lipstick case and the powder box." Take one look and you'll see why. And what do they call the magnificent new Congress Hall? The "pregnant oyster" . . . What makes for this great humor? The Berliners attribute it to the city's dry, stimulating air—"Berliner Luft." It supposedly renders one tolerant and open-hearted, energetic and creative. . . . Don't be confused by Kurfürstendamm addresses; the numbers on one side of the street bear no relation to those on the other. . . . For theatre enthusiasts, the point to remember is that the theatres in West Berlin are surprisingly tiny. Therefore, always get the cheapest seats—you'll see fine. And don't walk away if the theatre is sold out. Nearly always, a few extra seats come available several minutes before curtain time. West Berlin's most famous theatre, and one you should see, is the **Schiller** (tickets start at 5 marks). . . . Berlin's flea market, **Die Nolle,** open daily except Tuesdays from 11 a.m. to 7:30 p.m., is located in 16 old subway trains at Nollendorfplatz, a 10-minute walk from Wittenbergplatz, which is the square near the large KaDeWe department store. Even if you don't plan to buy an old sewing machine, pictures, furniture, coins or antique dolls, you might want to relax after-browsing at the small flea market restaurant, ordering a Berliner boulette (a hamburger without the bun) for 2 marks. . . . For students of the new math (readers under 12), that mysterious grouping of lights atop a steel pole at the corner of Kudamm and Uhlandstrasse is neither a traffic indicator nor a radar trap, but rather the world's largest (and only) clock based on the theory of sets. Top two rectangular rows show the hours, with lights in the uppermost row standing for 5 hours, those in the lower row for one hour (you add them together). The two orange rows mark the minutes: lights in the upper row each indicate five minutes, those below are one minute (and again you add them together). What's the reason for it? To slow traffic, as motorists laboriously figure the time? To confuse the Russians? To prove that even clocks can be avant garde? Only in Berlin. . . . King of the Berlin laundromats is **LAR,** 137 Kantstrasse, corner of Schlüterstrasse. Open from 8 a.m. to 8 p.m. weekdays, 8 a.m. to 2 p.m. Saturdays, this large, brightly-lit "washeteria" provides do-it-yourself washing machines (6 marks for 5 kilos), automatic dry-cleaning machines (50 pfennigs for 5 kilos), and an ironing board and iron with which you can smooth out the wrinkles for one mark extra. **LAR** has branches elsewhere, also, as at 63 Uhlandstrasse and 23 Steglitzer Damm. . . . Best way to orient yourself in Berlin—and best over-all view of the city—is from the top of **I-Punkt Berlin,** the 22-story skyscraper in the Europa Center. You'll pay 1.50 marks to go up to the viewing terrace, called **Zur Fernrohrstrasse,** or literally translated, "Viewing Street," and there you can use the telescopes for free. Walk all the way around the terrace to your right and look through the furthest telescope and you can see across the Wall into East Berlin and focus on the Brandenburg Gate and Alexanderplatz. . . . The fact that Berliners are a different breed of Germans has already been mentioned, but notice how that holds true right down to the women, who have lost the hefty wenching-girl appeal of the beer-drinking Bavarian, and are instead tall, slim, chic and incredibly well-dressed. They are referred to in awe by visiting West German tourists as **"Berlinerwunderfräulein".** . . . Two handy English-language booklets, available at the Tourist Office or your hotel: **"Places of Interest"** and **"Berlin Programm."** Both provide theater and concert schedules; while in "Places of Interest" you get a handy map of the U-Bahn. . . . The famous colored sculpture of the Egyptian Queen Nefertiti, created some 3,300 years ago, is displayed at the **Museum of Egyptian Art** at 70 Schloss Strasse, opposite Charlottenburg Palace. . . . The leading art gallery of West Berlin, and one you should visit, is the **Dahlem Museum,** Armin-Allee 24, open every day except Monday, charging no admission, and containing the world's largest collection of Rembrandts—24 paintings in all. But for more on that institution, and for a description of (a) East Berlin's sights, and (b) the sights of the immense Charlottenburg Palace, I give you to Hope:

HOPE'S BERLIN: "Berlin is as exciting as a frontier town. But it has its disappointments—it won't be anything like you expect it to be. For instance, there's not a shred of Old Berlin left: that was totally reduced to ashes in the last days of street fighting at the end of World War II. Unter den Linden will never be the same; Christopher Isherwood's Berlin no longer exists. And there is not even very much left to remind one of Hitler, or that World War II took place—only the Reichstag (near the border of the two Berlins), an empty hulk by the end of the war, but now reconstructed; the famous Brandenburg Gate where the Russians placed a Flag of Victory and which was once a local viewing point into East Berlin; Goering's Headquarters; the Plötzensee Memorial, in a steely gray courtyard of a government building, where a plaque commemorates the German patriots who sought to assassinate Hitler and were hanged here; and the bunker where Hitler and Eva Braun committed suicide. But perhaps the most sensible monument to World War II is the **Kaiser Wilhelm Memorial Church,** left standing in ruins in the center of West Berlin (at the bottom of the Kurfürstendamm) as a permanent reminder to the German people, and all peoples, of the horrors of war.

"The next thing one looks for in Berlin is evidence of the Cold War, the Air Lift, and of the heroes of the beginning of that period (like Ernst Reuter, the first mayor of free West Berlin). Of course in Berlin the Cold War is all around you in the shape of the hideous Wall, but don't expect to see any spies (if you spot one, he's not a very good spy), and the feeling of intrigue in the city has considerably diminished with time. Even the Eastern Sector has been built up and today looks fairly presentable. There is a monument to the Air Lift at the former Tempelhof Air Terminal, a modern piece of sculpture by Ludwig. And you may also visit the **Schöneberg City Hall** (Rathaus), on John F. Kennedy Platz, where the late president delivered his famous 'Ich bin ein Berliner' speech, and whose tower contains an American gift: the Freedom Bell, along with a document signed by 17 million American citizens in support of West Berlin (the tower is open to visitors on weekdays, but it's advisable to phone 78-33-318 first). At Checkpoint Charlie, which is the route through which most tourists pass into East Berlin, there is the not-to-be-missed **Museum of the Wall,** which includes documented history of all the grisly events that have taken place around the Berlin Wall. Upstairs there's a closed circuit television set trained on a central spot in East Berlin.

"When all the reconstruction is finally completed, West Berlin may emerge looking like The City of The Future. In many ways it already does, with its handsome new 'Europa Center', the new Philharmonic Hall, and the American-built architectural wonder, **The Kongresshalle** (an exceptionally dull tour of the Congress Hall is available for one mark, half price for students, from 10 to 5). Then there is the unique **Hansa Quarter** (near the Victory Column, off the Street of the 17th of June), which was built in 1957 as part of an architectural exhibit—all totally new (rather sterile in toto), with each building having been created by an architect from a different nation. **Corbusier House** was designed for the Hansa exhibition but was too gigantic to fit in the Quarter and

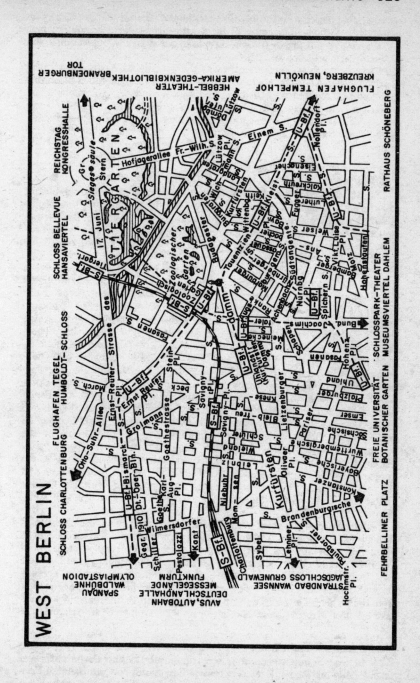

was therefore placed near the Olympic Stadium: it's Berlin's largest apartment house, with 530 dwellings, most of them with multi-colored balconies which create an interesting facade (the effect is old to our eyes now, but was undoubtedly another Corbusier breakthrough).

"More than thirty years after the war, the city still has the dispersed feeling of a displaced person. The situation in West Berlin is, after all, rather like trying to re-build Manhattan in the Bronx. And for your museum going, you'll find yourself traveling fairly far to see the best. (In all fairness to the exuberant and energetic Berliners, I must mention that an entire complex of modern new museums is being built around St. Matthew's Church near Philharmonic Hall to house their vast collections, but until these are completed. . . .)

The Dahlem

"Your first trip should be to **Dahlem**, a fantastic, exciting complex of galleries and museums: it's downright cultural gluttony—at closing time people have to be thrown out bodily. Dahlem's vast collections include **The Picture Gallery; The Department of Sculpture; The Department of Prints and Drawings; The Ethnographical Museum** and **The Museums of Far Eastern, Islamic and Indian Art** (recently opened).

"See the Gallery first (enter at 23/27 Arnimallee, then proceed to your right on the first and second floors), which is a vast and rich treasure house of paintings—600 in all—from the 13th to the 18th centuries. Since nearly everything shown is outstanding, I'll confine myself to what is merely fantastic. In the first rooms you'll encounter the marvelous early panel paintings, which should not be missed—notice especially Multscher's 'Wurzacher Altar'. There are a number of Dürers (also Giottos, Fra Angelicos, Ghirlandaios), and Titian's famous 'Venus with the Organ Player'. On a rather crowded wall you'll bump into some exquisite Botticellis, including the celebrated 'Venus'; while another room contains the equally renowned 'Merchant George Gisze', a portrait by Hans Holbein, the Younger. In other rooms, the Flemish and Dutch masters are well represented with works by the prolific Rubens; Van Dyck; Frans Hals; Jan Steen and Vermeer. But the top attraction of the Dutch section is the world's largest collection of Rembrandts, 24 paintings in all, on the second floor. Rembrandt's overflowing humanity makes me weep in public places: there's a sweet portrait of Saskia, a sexy one of Hendrickje Stoffels, the gorgeous 'Der Mennonitenprediger Anslo und seine Frau'. And the gem, and the most famous, of this collection is the stunning 'Man With The Golden Helmet,' which is so three dimensional and so alive I refuse to believe it's only paint.

"Every one of the other numerous departments in this museum complex displays its own fabulous treasures (and will show more of their rich collections when they move to new quarters). Would you believe that what has been described is only a bare fragment of what's available to delight you at Dahlem?

"Admission to all of this is free; and the collections are open Tuesday through Sunday from 9 to 5. To get to Dahlem take bus 1, 10 or 68; or walk from the Dahlem-Dorf subway stop (right as you exit to Brummerstrasse, then take a left on Fabeckstrasse, and left again when you come to Arnimallee).

The Museums of East Berlin

"In order of importance, your next trip must be to **East Berlin's Museum Island.** Museum Island, located in central East Berlin between Bahnhof Friedrichstrasse and Bahnhof Marx-Engels Platz (which is also a healthy but interesting walk from Checkpoint Charlie—head for Unter den Linden, then go past the Historical Museum and across a small bridge to your left), includes **The Pergamon Museum, The National Gallery, The Bode Museum, The Altes Museum,** and **The Neues Museum.** The entire trip is worthwhile (including any fuss at the border) just to see The Pergamon Altar. The entire museum was built around it, and it's a spectacular sight: picture an enormous white marble Hellenistic temple with about 30 steps, and virtually intact—not even in Greece itself does one get a more solid idea of the glory of Greek civilization. In addition to The Pergamon Altar, there are intricate and gorgeous mosaics, smaller temples, a stunning Roman Market (Attilos), Roman and Greek statues, the fabulous Triumphant Way of Nebuchadnezzar, the Islamic Museum, and fantastic collections from Egypt and Mesopotamia. The **Bode Museum** (named after the imaginative and energetic curator of The Prussian Cultural Foundation who was responsible for most of what is seen today in both East and West Berlin) is noteworthy for its Egyptian Museum and its early Christian and Byzantine art—there are also paintings and sculptures from Medieval times to the 18th century. **The National Gallery** shows, primarily, recent German artists, romanticists, impressionists, expressionists, abstract art, and such special exhibits as 'Proletarian and Socialist-Realist Art'. There is also a unique collection of 30,000 drawings from the 19th and 20th centuries. You might then like to pay a visit to the aforementioned, and heavily political, **Museum of German History,** at Unter den Linden 2, which has permanent exhibits of Germany from 1789 to 1949. It's quite a fascinating place for many reasons, not the least of which is a heavy dose of propaganda, described as follows in the official booklet: 'The Museum approaches the arrangement of its exhibits in a new way. It demonstrates the laws by which German history has progressed, putting the spotlight on the masses, the people, as the creators of history. Many original objects and books, pictures and documents of the given periods, most of which are now accessible to the public for the first time, show which forces brought war and misery to the German nation and who represented the German nation's genuine peaceful and democratic interests.'

"On Museum Island the museums are open from 9 to 6, daily except on Mondays and Tuesdays for the Bode Museum and National Gallery, every day of the week at the Pergamon. The Museum of German History is open daily from 8 a.m. to 7 p.m. and Sundays from 10 to 4. You may find it ironic that while most of Capitalistic West Berlin's museums are free, the People's Museums of East Germany charge admission: it'll cost you 1.05 marks for the museums on Museum Island (half price to students), and 50 pfennigs for The Museum of German History (30 pfennigs for students).

Charlottenburg Palace

"Back in West Berlin, you'll want to spend another day at **Charlottenburg Palace,** which in addition to being a lovely Garden Palace which you can visit, is now also the home of **The Museum of Pre- and Early History; The Museum of Arts and Crafts;** and across the street in new headquarters **The Department of Greek and Roman Antiquities,** and nearby, at 70 Schlosstrasse, the **Department of Egyptian Antiquities,** where you'll see the single most famous object of art that Berlin possesses: the painted limestone bust of Queen Nefertiti, which was created over 3,300 years ago. The beautiful Nefertiti is an ageless, serene beauty (who, in profile, does somewhat resemble Barbra Streisand!), perfect down to the shadows on her throat. She casts a spell of timelessness which makes one feel quite peaceful.

"Now you'll want to explore the museum of the Palace itself. Even after suffering considerable damage during the war. **The Museum of Pre-and Early History** displays a fine collection of objects illustrating the life of pre-historic man in Europe and the Near East, starting with the Early Stone Age (a great drawback is the frustration one feels trying to follow the written commentaries handicapped by the language barrier). Take special note of Schliemann's Trojan finds and the curious face urns from North-East Germany and Poland (6th and 7th Century B.C.). . . . Directly across the street from the main courtyard is **The Antiken Museum, or Department of Greek and Roman Antiquities,** which contains half the treasures from the old Antiquarium (the rest are shown at The Pergamon Museum) including Greek vases, small statues and urns from Greek and Mediterranean cultures, a display of ancient glass and jewelry, and some outstanding Egyptian mummy portraits. To me, however, the most interesting of this second 'complex of culture' is **The Museum of Arts and Crafts,** devoted to a survey collection of European applied arts from the Middle Ages to the 18th century. The organization of the exhibits allows you to compare kindred pieces of work from different countries, displayed in the same time slot. Among the items you'll see are such classics of medieval ecclesiastical art as the Guelph Treasure (don't miss 'Das Kuppelreliquiar aus Köln' from 1175); plus highly decorated Scandinavian ivory horns; an Austrian reliquary of St. George; Gothic tapestry; as well as watches, games, drafting instruments, pottery, and silver and gold ware. There are also exhibits of porcelain, including Meissen, Bing and Grondahl and Nymphenburg china (and more in Charlottenburg Park at **The Belvedere,** which houses the Museum of historical Berlin porcelain), and some wonderful Tiffany vases (this is the first place I've ever enjoyed looking at china), and a showing of exotic jewelry on the second floor (from the 1900's). . . . You can take a tour of **The Historical Rooms of Charlottenburg Palace** Tuesday through Sunday from 9 to 5, for 1 mark, but the guide speaks only German. . . . And you can see **The Gallery of Frederick The Great** (it's his great grandfather, the Great Elector, depicted in the equestrian statue by Schlüter, who stands in the courtyard in front of the Palace) during the same hours as the historical rooms, but for free. Downstairs there is Empire furniture and paintings, upstairs it's baroque; probably the only painting you'll recognize is J. L. David's portrait of Napoleon, which graces the Courvoisier Cognac bottle. . . . Back of the rambling Palace are lovely grounds with a lake. If you're strolling around behind The Museum of Pre-and Early History you'll find the **Charlottenburg Mausoleum** (open every day except Monday from 10 to 6, 20 pfennigs to enter) which has the tombs of King Friedrich Wilhelm III and Queen Luise by Ch. D. Rauch. . . . All the museums are closed on Tuesdays (except the Palace rooms, which close on Monday) and weekdays they are open from 9 to 5, on Sundays beginning at 10; the one exception is The Department of Greek and Roman Antiquities which has special hours on Wednesday from 2 p.m. to 9 p.m. All the museums are free (except the Palace and Mausoleum, whose prices have already been listed). To get to Charlottenburg you may take buses 21, 54, 55, 62 or 74; or walk about three blocks from the Sophie-Charlotte-Platz subway stop (go up Otto-Suhr-Allee to Spandauer Damm).

And Elsewhere

"Berlin's newest and most heavily frequented museum (opened in 1968), is the **New National Gallery** at Potsdamer Strasse 50, an immense and starkly modern building set into a vast square and surrounded by a sculpture garden. To my mind, and on first impression, the building is all lines and angles; but exciting exhibitions of modern art are changed with some frequency, and the collection is quite a comprehensive one, spanning the 19th and 20th centuries, and such artists as Manet, Renoir, Monet, Courbet and Pissarro, as well as Munch, Klee, Kokoschka, Picasso, and several of the newer German, European and American painters. Admission is free and the gallery is open on Monday from noon to 8 p.m., Tuesday through Thursday, Saturday and Sunday from 9 a.m. to 5 p.m., closed Friday. Take bus # 24, 29, 75, 48 or 83.

"For the most far-out modern art, you may finally want to visit the **Akademie der Künste (Academy of Art)** at 10 Hanseatenweg, in the Hansa Quarter. Housed in a handsome new building that rather reminds one of a ski-lodge, the museum hosts exhibitions from all over the world of the very latest in art. Summers they're usually open every day from 10 to 7, and sometimes have two exhibits going at the same time—downstairs is free, while upstairs in the larger exhibition quarters you'll pay 2.20 marks to have a look at what's new. (You may find lectures, performances of experimental music and theatre in the studio of the Akademie in the evenings.)"

READERS-ON-EXCURSIONS: "For the somewhat more adventurous tourist who is considering visits to Berlin, Munich and/or Vienna, there is an interesting side excursion that can be made to the city of **Krakow** in southern Poland, with its medieval charm. By train from the East Berlin bahnhof, the transit time is about 12 hours (overnight). The East German transit visa is 5 DM; a Polish visa is 28.50 DM ($15); and a one-way second class ticket to Krakow costs exactly 52.40 DM ($27.57). . . . From the 14th to the 16th centuries, Krakow was the capital of Poland. Of note in Krakow are the Jagellonian University (Collegium Maius), founded in 1364; the Royal Wavel Castle, home of Polish kings (there is a mimeographed guide book available in English; ask for it); St. Mary's Church, with the ornate 15th century Wit Stwoiz Altar; the Market Square and Cloth Hill; the Barbican and St. Florian's Gate; and numerous museums. In appearance, Krakow is perhaps the closest thing to Russian architectural style, within reasonable travel distance of West European cities. For accommodations, try the **Dom Turysty,** Westerplatte 15, the most moderately-priced of the hotels available in Krakow. A single there cost around $6 when I was there, and accommodations were very comfortable and immaculate. . . . From Krakow, one can easily get to Prague, Czechoslovakia. The train leaves at about 1 a.m. from Kantowice, a 50-minute, $1 train ride from Krakow. Travel time is about seven hours. Not having the time to get a Czech visa in Berlin, I was easily able to obtain one on the train at the frontier. . . . As you emerge from the main railway station in Prague, across the street is a park. Cut across the park in a direction perpendicular to the street in front of the rail station. Having traversed the park, continue in this same perpendicular direction for two long blocks. The street you come upon is Na Prikope, and **Cedok** is located at Na Prikope 18. Cedok, the Czech Travel Bureau, will be able to book you into moderately-priced hotels. The single I had cost $12, including breakfast. . . . Prague offers a full complement of tourist attractions, and from May 15 to September 15, offers conducted tours. The neon lights of the three or four downtown airline offices and the hustle and bustle of Prague offer a pronounced contrast to the subdued and medieval-like flavor of Krakow. From Prague, the train leaves in mid-morning for Nuremberg, Frankfurt, and for cities connecting with Munich. A one-way, second-class fare from Prague to the German border is 18.90 marks ($9.94). From there, Eurailpass, if you have it. . . . In both Poland and Czechoslovakia, German is virtually a second language, but even if you do not speak German, there is still no great problem" (Matthew J. Klempa, Los Angeles, California; note by AF: At the moment, Czech visas can be obtained only at Czech embassies or consulates; visas are not supplied at border crossings. Cedok now books only with half-board, and the price of a single in 1980 will be about $25. Several readers have claimed that rail fares within the Eastern European countries are cheaper if purchased in East Berlin than in West Berlin).

READERS' SUGGESTIONS: "The easiest way to get to Berlin from West Germany (we went from Hannover) is by train. You can even get a visa on board" (Patricia Zavoina, Lakeland, Florida. . . . "A very cheap method of traveling to Berlin, and one that we highly advise to every American (one-way; both ways may be a bit too much) is from Copenhagen by East German train to East Berlin, and then over to West Berlin by the

S-Bahn. This approach furnishes a fantastic contrast between the two German areas that we all should have" (Dr. and Mrs. Ben G. Burnett, Dept. of Political Science, Whittier College, Whittier, California). . . . "My suggestion may help some travellers going from Copenhagen to Berlin. Take a train to Gedser (from where the train crosses to Grossenbrode Kai and thence into West Germany) and get off. Walk over to the East German boat pier and take an East German boat to Warnemunde. Visas can be purchased on the boat. My brother and I went on a Sunday morning, and in addition to us, there were only seven passengers on a two-hundred-and-fifty passenger vessel. In Warnemunde you can get your money exchanged into East German marks, catch lunch, and then board a train for East Berlin via Rostock and Neu Brandenburg, no changes. Get off the train at the main building which is a checkpoint between East and West Berlin, then back upstairs to the S-Bahn and into West Berlin. We left Gedser at ten in the morning, got to Warnemunde at twelve, boarded the train at two, and were in East Berlin by six-thirty that evening. The tickets from Gedser to East Berlin can be purchased at the Copenhagen train station for about $33 per person" (Philip Perkins, Washington, D.C.). . . . "My wife and I drove to Berlin on the Autobahn Helmstedt-Marienborn. The cost of our visas, obtained at the East German Control Point, was 10 marks per person ($5.26). The charge for use of the Autobahn was 5 marks ($2.63) one way, and 5 marks return. It took us 40 minutes to check in, obtain the necessary documents, and so forth. Total elapsed time from border to the center of Berlin was 2 hours 40 minutes, but this was under unusually good conditions with little traffic" (Henry Gassmann, Fresno, California). . . . "It's no longer necessary to fly to Berlin. Last summer, I went there by bus from Hanover, and could have gone by train. The trip is a bit of a nuisance because of the Latin-American style ruckus at the border. But the bus carries an interpreter to help foreigners through. I was the only American on the bus; they weren't getting many that way. Did I check with the American consul? No. I just went" (Thomas Morley, Botany Department, University of Minnesota, Minneapolis, Minnesota).

If you're really ambitious, you'll now venture a trip to faraway Athens. The quality of this experience is something special—exotic, eastern and ancient. And it can be enjoyed at rock-bottom costs, because Greece ranks with Spain as the least expensive of all the European nations.

Chapter XVIII

ATHENS

Doping the Drachmas

TO RIDE FROM THE AIRPORT to Athens in a glass-topped bus, and suddenly to see the stately Parthenon, on the Acropolis, high overlooking the city, is literally a thrill that comes once in a lifetime. Dazed by the sight, and deep in thought, you then plunge into the maws of Athens, a raucous and exotic town, and quickly you realize that this will be an experience wholly unlike the great part of your European tour.

Athens is a hybrid. The birthplace of Western civilization, with reminders everywhere of the great classic age, it is today the least Western of all European cities. In one moment, you'll tread where Demosthenes orated and Socrates taught, but in another, you'll pass pungent-smelling coffee houses where men alone—scores of them—sit chattering about the daily news—just as they do in Cairo or Teheran.

There's nothing chic about Athens. It's a raw and a blunt place, with an unusually low price structure, and a hearty attitude towards life. If you'll enter into that mood, enjoying the low costs on which your stay there is possible, then you won't miss the minor comforts of other European capitals that are sometimes lacking in Athens. Instead you'll be able to focus clearly on the real aim of your trip: the first-hand experiencing of the great classic Greek civilization, which shaped our own.

First, we'll take care of the mechanical details:

HOTELS: Most readers are aware of the demarcation that exists in cities such as Hong Kong or Algiers between the so-called European section of the town, and the native quarters. Something of the same sort exists, amazingly enough, in Athens. The tourists, for the most part, stay in a single, confined area around Constitution Square ("Plateia Syntagmatos"), which has tall buildings, and is modern and unexciting. The Greeks live elsewhere. A meeting of the two worlds occurs in the area around Omonia Square, which combines a little of both.

If you're adventurous enough to plunge into the very heart of things, away from the tourists, in a noisy neighborhood filled with bazaars and crowds, then you'll stay at the recently-built (1966) and really quite spectacular, 10-story **Hotel Alkistis,** on the Place du Théâtre (18 Plateia Theatrou), phone 3219-811, where nearly every room has a view on the Acropolis and a pleasant little balcony, and all rooms have private bath or shower. Singles with breakfast run to a maximum of 520 drachmas ($14.44), everything included, doubles with two breakfasts are fixed at a top of 700 drachmas ($19.44), and those prices, once again, are for rooms with private facilities. All this makes for an extremely comfortable stay, and one that is highly recommended, provided you're game for perfectly-safe, but Eastern-style, surroundings.

If you'd rather stay in the more sedate Constitution Square section, then about the best you can do is at the smaller, 45-bed, and much less pretentious, **Hotel Imperial,** at 46 Mitropoleos Street (phone 322-7617), which is only two short blocks from the downhill end of "Syntagma" (Constitution Square), almost directly opposite the Athens Cathedral. Here, the lobby is upstairs, but the manager (Mr. Klissouris) is English-speaking and extremely helpful, the rooms all come equipped with private shower, and the rates, with breakfast, service and tax included, are 585 drachmas ($16.25) single, 770 drachmas ($21.38) double. Alternatively, if you crave a higher-category hotel, and are willing to pay up to 1,150 drachmas for a double room with private bath, again with breakfast for two, service and taxes included, you can try to get into the superb **Hotel Plaka,** six short blocks from the bottom end of Constitution Square, at 7 Kapnikareas & Deka Streets (phone 322-2096). This modern, seven-story building, which has a marble-lined lobby, a snack bar decorated as an old Athens tavern, and a roof garden restaurant with a magnificent view of the Acropolis, is undoubtedly among the best of the moderately-priced hotels in Athens in terms of comfort and service, but certainly not the best bargain; in addition, demi-pension arrangements are sometimes required. Much cheaper in the same area is the tiny, 22-room **Hotel Cryst,** atop a grocery store at 14 Apollonos Street, only three blocks from Syntagma Square, where singles are 320 drachmas ($8.88), doubles or twins 500 drachmas ($13.88), with shower 600, triples 650 drachmas, rooms with four beds 750 drachmas, an optional breakfast 50 drachmas per person. Phone 323-4581.

It's simply foolish, though, in a town as inexpensive as Athens, to pay as much as the Plaka asks, merely because of the sedate character of its street. Just a few blocks away, in the semi-tourist, semi-Greek area of Omonia Square, new hotels approaching the quality of the Plaka are springing up at the rate of two and three a year, offering clean, modern rooms with private bath or shower for only $13 to $17 double—all because they lack the favored Constitution Square location. Indeed, as you begin to walk from Constitution to Omonia Square, and even before you reach the latter, you'll encounter lower prices in a whole host of modern, good hotels.

On and Near Omonia Square

Best of these, to my mind, is the cordial **Carolina Hotel,** 55 Kolokotroni Street (corner of Kalamiotou, phone 322-0837), which is owned by two brothers from South Carolina, of all places—and how they got here, no one seems to know. They're constantly cheerful, constantly helpful beyond call, and while their 35-room hotel is not the most comfortable in this area (although it's fairly

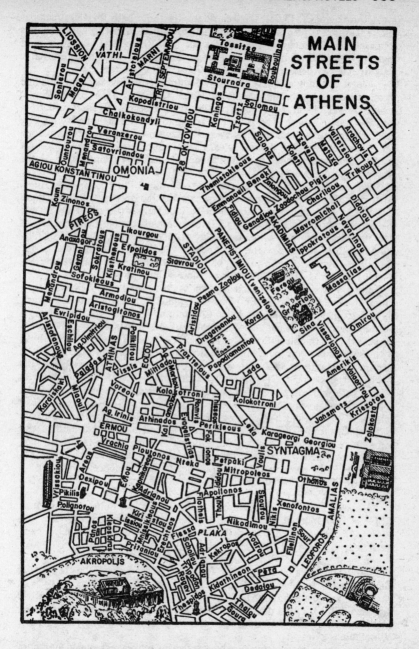

**MAIN
STREETS
OF
ATHENS**

new), it has all the amenities you'll need (elevator, lounge, snack bar, etc.) and fabulous rates. There are 17 double rooms with private bath that rent for a total of 580 drachmas ($16.11), service and taxes included; five singles without bath for 470 drachmas ($13.05); thirteen doubles without bath for 480 drachmas ($13.33); three triples with bath for 580 drachmas ($16.11); and breakfast (optional) is 50 drachmas ($1.38). Europe on $10 a day! Location is on a segment of Kolokotroni Street (a bustling thoroughfare of retail stores) that is roughly halfway between Omonia and Constitution Squares.

Closer to Omonia Square, yet more comfortable and perhaps better suited to older tourists, is the splurge-priced **Hotel Acadimos,** 58 Acadimias Street (phone 362-92-21), near the National Library of Greece and a short walk from Omonia Square, whose slick, balconied appearance is like that of a Hilton. The hotel has two elevators, a large lobby with restaurant and bar, and eight floors; yet it charges only 850 drachmas ($23.61), including service and tax, for a double room with private bath, telephone, and balcony facing either on the Acropolis or on Lycabettus Hill.

One tiny block off Omonia Square, the 64-room, third class **Hotel Alma,** fairly recently built at 5 Dorou Street (phone 522-2833), charges 650 drachmas ($18.05) for a double room with private bath or shower (breakfast and service included); only 480 drachmas ($13.33) for a bathless double and breakfast, as does its nearby sister hotel, the **Amaryllis,** at 45 Veranzerou (phone 523-8738). Singles with breakfast are 360 drachmas at the Alma, 560 drachmas at the Amaryllis—the latter with private bath. Neither, however, is as well-recommended by me as the Acadimos or the hotels that follow.

Even cheaper—but still modern—hotels are found on the Agiou Constantinou, an avenue which runs into Omonia Square. Fifty yards from the square, the 105-room **Hotel Ilion,** at 7 Agiou Constantinou (phone 523-7411), charges only 600 drachmas ($16.66), service included, for a bathless double, 900 drachmas ($25) for a double with shower and service (that's a modern 8-story hotel with elevator and four lounges); while two blocks further down the avenue, at 32 Ag. Constantinou, the even more modern but big-splurge-priced **Hotel Achillion** (phone 523-0971) charges 1,100 drachmas ($30.55) for a double with private bath, including breakfast and service. This latter establishment is deservedly popular with tourists, as is the **Hotel Nestor,** 58 Agiou Constantinou (phone 523-5576), which offers a well-furnished double room with private bath and breakfast for 690 drachmas ($19.16), service and tax included, a single with same for 520 drachmas. Danish and Swedish tourists stay in this latter spot, in great numbers; American tourists haven't yet; to build up the hotel's American clientele, the owners of the Nestor, Messrs. D. Tsemberas and E. Apostolou, have offered a small discount to guests who show a copy of this book upon registering.

Elsewhere, in the same area, the recently-built and quite modern **Hotel El Greco,** one block to the south of the Square, at Athinas Street 65 (phone 324-4554), charges 825 drachmas ($22.91) for a double with private shower and breakfast, including the 15% service charge (singles are too high for this book). It's an 8-story building with two elevators, three lounges, a bar and balconies—and altogether quite plush. . . . And to the left of the Square, the cheaper but almost equally suitable **Hotel Arcadia,** 46 Marni Street (phone 522-6571), charges only 500 drachmas ($13.88) for a bathless double, service included, 690 drachmas ($19.16) for a double with private shower; 340 drachmas for singles without showers, 500 drachmas for a single with private shower. Breakfast is 60 drachmas extra.

All of these hotels are superbly situated for touring. The main station of the subway that runs between Athens and Piraeus (where "Never On Sunday" was filmed) sits smack in the center of Omonia Square; while the bus to the Archaeological Museum stops only one short block from the Alma Hotel.

THE MODERN SIGNIFICANCE OF ATHENS: Out of a total Greek population of 9.5 million persons, 3.6 million—or 38%—live in Athens. Compared with that, only 5% of all Italians live in Rome, 15% of the British in London, 20% of the French in Paris.

The Less Costly Guest Houses and Pensions

This alternate sort of accommodation in Athens is apt to be a bit more personal and intimate than the typical, large Athenian hotel. And the best known of these establishments, smack in the heart of Plaka, is the renowned "Cleo's Guesthouse", consisting of **Cleo's "Hotel"**, at 3 Patrouu Street (phone 32-29-053) and **Cleo's Guesthouse,** at 18 Apollonos Street (phone 32-35-640), both in the same building. At the former (which is operated by Cleo's partner, Vassilis (whom everyone calls Bill), all 19 rooms have private bath, yet rent for only 500 drachmas ($13.88) double, 600 drachmas ($16.66) triple, provided your stay is for more than two nights; there are no singles. At the latter, which is smaller, and personally overseen by Cleo, rooms are extremely simple, and without running water, but the charges are as low as 220 drachmas ($6.11) single, 360 drachmas ($10) for twins or doubles, 440 drachmas triple. As thousands of travellers have learned, Cleo will let you use her kitchen to make coffee, and she will lend you an iron for 20 drachmas per hour; but above all, she has an open ear and mind for such problems as you may want to bring to her attention. To reach Cleo's from Constitution Square, walk down Mitropoleos to Patrouu Street and turn left on Patrouu.

A few blocks away, two flights upstairs at 18 Eolou Street (phone 32-22-997), **Giorgio's Pension** takes the overflow from Cleo's—up to 50 guests—in two-to-five-bedded dorm-like rooms renting for an average of 120 drachmas ($3.33) per bed, plus 35 drachmas (97¢) for breakfast. Because Giorgio's has undergone successive changes of ownership, enhancing its reputation all the while, its present manager is a non-Giorgio named Fanis Michaloakis, who's assisted by a charming French wife, Michelle. Both speak English. An alternative in the same area, but not nearly as attractive, is the guesthouse called **Elena's** at 14 Apolonos Street (no phone), corner of Niki Street, managed by a kind, young Tunisian named Soki who will store your luggage free of charge if you shoot off to the Islands. Triple-decker bunks here are 90 drachmas ($2.50) per person, twin-bedded rooms 120 drachmas ($3.33) per person. Much more desirable is **Diogenes House** at 12 Herefondos Street (phone 32-24-560), in a quiet neighborhood near Hadrian's Arch, named after the famous Seeker because he (allegedly) lived in his tub in this very area about 2,300 years ago. Here, a variety of rooms are available at good, low costs, and with free showers thrown in: 130 drachmas ($3.61) in five-bedded rooms, 150 drachmas ($4.16) per person in quads, 175 drachmas ($4.86) per person in doubles, 250 drachmas ($6.94) single, only 80 drachmas ($2.22) in cots on the covered rooftop. Bearded Paleologos Alexandros, who is perfect in English, is the owner.

Two alternate possibilities in the Plaka Area: **Guest House Kouros,** 11 Kodrou Street (phone: 322-7431), whose owner, Mr. Nicolas Kiskirdis, offers singles for 250 drachmas ($6.94), doubles for 370 drachmas ($10.27), triples for 390 drachmas ($10.83), rooms with four beds for 480 drachmas ($13.33), and showers for free. And finally, at the very foot of the Acropolis, and only a few minutes' walk from the scene of "Sound and Light," **Laki's House,** 11 Parthenonos Street (phone 92-26-440), sells singles for 280 drachmas ($7.77), doubles for 400 ($11.11), four- and five-bedded rooms for 130 drachmas per person. Breakfast isn't served in this little, 34-bed inn, but showers are free and there's a spectacular roof garden on which you can sip cokes for 12 drachmas per bottle.

READERS' HOTEL SELECTIONS (OMONIA SQUARE): "New Athenian hotels as a method of attracting business, offer unusually good rates during their first several years of operation. One of the newest—it opened in late 1971—is the C-category **Hotel Keramikos** at 30 Keramikos Street (phone 524-7631), near Omonia Square, where every room has private bath, yet will rent (in 1980) for only 350 drachmas ($9.72) per person in doubles, 280 drachmas in triples, 225 drachmas per person in 4-bedded rooms, not including breakfast, which is 48 drachmas per person" (Pauline Rissman, New York, New York). . . . "At the **Hotel Epidauros,** 14 Koumoundourou Street (phone 523-0421), near Omonia Square, we paid 650 drachmas ($18.05) for a double room, breakfast, service and tax included, and received free use of showers, lots of hot water and fresh linen, the cleanest room we had in Greece" (Mrs. Charles Szumski, Arbuckle, California). . . . "We highly recommended the **Hotel Pythagorion** at 28 Agiou Constantinou Street (phone 524-2811) near Omonia Square. For 680 drachmas ($18.88), my husband and I had an attractive, spacious room with a modern desk, a huge clothing closet, a balcony, and a private bath with all facilities, with breakfast (which included croissants, a kaiser roll and fruitcake) included in the price of the room" (Mrs. Michael Popkin, New York, New York; seconding recommendations from Ruth Sussles, Alhambra, California, and Sharon Todd, Norfolk, Virginia).

READERS' HOTEL SELECTIONS (CONSTITUTION SQUARE): "My wife and I stayed at the **Hermes Hotel,** 19 Apollonos Street, phone 3235-514, just three short blocks from Constitution Square. The charge was 600 drachmas plus 58 drachmas each for breakfast, a total of 658 drachmas ($18.27) for a double room with shower and phone. Our first room there had a view of the Acropolis, and when we returned after a cruise of the Greek Islands our room had a balcony 6 x 10 feet—just perfect for drying clothes" (John W. Hart, Pittsburgh, Pennsylvania; note by AF: Hermes is a modern hotel completed in 1968; Apollonos is a narrow, ethnic, and extremely interesting street near Constitution Square). . . . "**George's Guest House** at 32 Nikis Street (3d floor), phone 322-2697, asks only 150 drachmas a day per person, plus 40 drachmas for breakfast, possesses multilingual proprietors, clean rooms, location near Syntagma Square" (Shelley Mills, Thetis Island, British Columbia, Canada; note by AF: George's Guesthouse, viewed too late in 1979 for inclusion as one of our own recommendations, charges its 150 drachmas ($4.16) rate per person for rooms with two to five beds, rented on a first-come first-get basis. George's guestbook is filled with drawings and odes in all languages to owner George Charalambidis, who speaks English with an Oxfordian accent and personally serves drinks—including a 'Watergate special' for 18 drachmas (it's only ouzo)—from the small bar on the roof garden).

READERS' HOTEL SELECTIONS (PLAKA): "My wife and I now live in Athens, but before we were able to find an apartment we had to live in a hotel for two weeks. By chance we were directed to **Clare's House,** a charming place at 16A Frynichou Street, phone 3229-284, right in Plaka and within easy walking distance of the Acropolis, Syntagma, Zappion, and most other attractions. Lissikratous runs off Amalias at Hadrian's Arch. Clare's House is run by Clare, an Englishwoman, and Manos, her Greek husband. Their hospitality, helpfulness (Manos, being Greek, is of course a wealth of suggestions and information and speaks perfect English), and warmth make any stay there a pleasant experience. The rooms are clean, comfortable, and attractively furnished. Doubles are 540 drachmas ($15) with free hot showers included; breakfast is 50 drs. ($1.38) and consists of all the coffee, tea, hot bread, butter, and home-made jam you care for. The dining area is used as a lounge for reading or cards or letter writing when meals aren't being served. Clare is also an excellent cook and prepares dinner several times a week for guests who are tired of restaurant fare. This is our second trip to Europe and we have stayed in many hotels. Few can compare to Clare's House for location, friendliness, price, and comfort" (Michael L. Chernoff, Athens). . . . "Hotel Tempi, 29 Aeolou Street (phone 321-31-75), is a small and cozy, clean, and wonderful, D-class hotel in the Plaka area operated by Mr. Kostas, a warm, friendly and English-speaking gentleman who offers an outdoor, rooftop lounge, a little coffee bar on the first floor, and a lending library of used books. The price is right—300 drachmas ($8.33) for bathless singles, 400 drachmas ($11.11) for bathless doubles, 50 drachmas ($1.38) for breakfast—the atmosphere terrific" (Judy Kinis, Hollywood, Florida). . . . "At the **Adonis Hotel,** 3 Koudrou, in Plaka (phone 324-9737), where we had a double room with private shower and huge balcony for 710 drachmas ($19.72), the best feature is the roof garden containing both a bar and dining area. Breakfast (coffee and rolls) is served there and is eaten as you view the Acropolis and Lycabettus Hill. A real find!" (Michael and Juliette Hedger, Cremorne, Australia; note from AF: singles with private shower and breakfast, in 1980, are 540 drachmas ($15), doubles the same as above). . . . "We like to stay in the Plaka, near all the tavernas, where there's a new hotel on a fairly quiet street—the **Hotel Karyatis,** corner of Nikodimou and Thoukudidou Streets (phone 32-25-098), not far from the Monastiraki subway. The rooms are very large with wood floors and a double with breakfast is 720 drachmas ($20), with triples renting for 900 drachmas ($25), quadruples for 1,100 drachmas ($30.55). Showers are free" (Mr. and Mrs. T. W. Pew, Jr., Houston, Texas).

HOTELS SEEKING INCLUSION: "**Koyros Pension,** Pittakou 6, Plaka (tel: 324-8165), has lovely rooms overlooking a garden. Rates are 310 drachmas single, 370 drachmas double; and free showers are available" (P. Katsimbras, Manager). . . . Our **Pension Pagration** at 75 Damareos Street (phone 751-9530), in one of the best neighborhoods of the city, is a Residence for Young People, and has two, three and four-bedded rooms, as well as ironing and laundry facilities, cooking equipment, TV room, and a small cafeteria. The charge is only 110 drachmas ($3.05) per night, and we'll put up people (who have their own sleeping bags) on our roof terrace in summer for only 70 drachmas per night. We also provide free luggage storage for clients who wish to go away for a few days (for example, to visit the islands), and finally, we'll charge only 2,500 drachmas (in a room) for a one-month stay" (John Triandaphyllou, Residence Pagration).

STUDENTS IN ATHENS: For student visitors to Athens, there's actually no need to search for hotels. Because Athens is headquarters of an utterly unique, budget-oriented, student-oriented travel agency called **Viking's Travel Bureau,** which is headed by a trio of young English-speaking Greeks—the Cocconi brothers. Their office is at 3 Filellinon Street (phone 3229-383), just off Constitution Square, and you ought to put in an appearance there immediately upon your arrival, because they can get your housing far more easily—and perhaps far more inexpensively—than you could do it yourself.

For starvation budgeteers, Viking's will find accommodations in extremely simple hotels whose charge will be either 150 drachmas ($4.16) or 190 drachmas ($5.27) a night; for luxury-loving readers, they'll obtain hotel rooms *with* private bath or shower, costing around 600 drachmas ($16.66) a night.

They provide other student services as well, including arrangements for student charter flights to various European and Middle East locations (similar flights to London and Israel, among other destinations, are handled in Athens by **Student Travel Service, Ltd.,** 1 Filellinon Street, phone 3227-993, and by **Lotus Travel Office,** 7 Filellinon Street, phone 322-1680, the latter a member of the International Student Travel Conference, and heavily involved in exciting travel programs and student charter flights). And for students and non-students alike, Viking's operates the fabulous program of "Do-As-You-Like Tours" of Greece, which you'll read about in a later section of this chapter.

Don't neglect—if you're a student—to visit this unique institution, the moment you set foot in Athens.

RESTAURANTS: The best street for budget restaurants serving palatable food is Jan Smuts Street (also known as Voukourestiou Street), which juts off Venizelou Street, only a few steps from the top of Constitution Square. There are, of course, many much-cheaper restaurants than these in Athens, most of them, however, serving dishes that simply aren't acceptable to Western tastes. Because there's a vast difference between the meals a Greek workingman eats (heavily oiled, often sour) and those we're accustomed to, Athens is the only city in Europe in which I've specifically sought out the *tourist* restaurants. But don't expect corned-beef-and-cabbage; these are moderately-priced tourist restaurants, and therefore the food is still Greek, although a few concessions are made.

Most popular of all is the **Restaurant Vassilis,** 14a Jan Smuts Street (and also 14a Voukourestiou Street), two minutes from Constitution (Syntagma) Square, which is open every day of the year from noon to 4 p.m. and from 7 p.m. to 11:30 p.m. Because of its immense popularity among foreign tourists visiting Athens, and the quality of its Greek and foreign dishes, Vassilis is no longer a strictly budget restaurant—by Greek standards; nearly every large plate with vegetables (beef with onions, curry chicken with rice, for instance) is priced at 110 or 140 drachmas (from $3.05 to $3.88, including service charge), even the usually-inexpensive (in Greece) lamb dishes. Still, the various soups are only 35 drachmas, desserts, cheeses and salads range about 40 and 60 drachmas, and you can eat well here for $5.50, or for about $4.50-or-so if you have eggplant moussaka (95 drachmas) or meat-stuffed vine leaves (65 drachmas) as your main course. Flocks of customers are evidence of the tastiness of Vassilis' food. But to compare these rates with the more normal prices of Athenian restaurants, stroll over to the popular **Taverna Platanos,** on a quiet, shady square at the foot of the Akropolis hill, 4 Diogenes Street, where moussaka is only 60 drachmas ($1.66), maccaroni 27 drachmas (75¢), roast veal with french fries 75 drachmas ($2.08), feta cheese 15 drachmas (41¢), half a liter of retsina wine 38 drachmas ($1.05). In business since 1932, the Platanos is only 200 yards from the Cathedral (Mitropolis Church), between Adrianou and Mnissikleons streets in the heart of Plaka and is open daily except Sundays from noon to 3:45 p.m., and from 8:15 p.m. to midnight; its rates are Greek, and not tourist-oriented. . . . Or try the **Restaurant Kentrikon,** 3 Kolokotroni Street, on the way to Omonia Square (you'll see the same Greeks and foreigners eating there over and over again), where the spicy lentil soup (35 drachmas—97¢) is almost a meal in itself, where the stuffed peppers plate is 90 drachmas, and the cream custard (35 drachmas) is like the finest Mexican flan. Most chicken specialties here are 85 drachmas, roast lamb with cheese-flavored macaroni is 130 drachmas, and the highest item on the menu is a plate of wine-soaked shish kebab—and that comes to 180 drachmas ($5), including service charge.

But you'll still want to try the now "high-priced" Vassilis at least once. And if it's overly crowded on the occasion of your visit, you can simply walk two short blocks over to 6 Kriezotou Street, where you'll find the **Restaurant Corfu** (next door to the King's Palace Hotel), a much slicker and more modern restaurant than Vassilis, but with fairly similar prices: 60 drachmas for a tomato salad, 130-or-so drachmas for a plate of moussaka (a ground-meat-and-potatoes casserole). The Corfu is usually uncrowded, which Vassilis isn't.

Rather than go to the Corfu, however, I'd take a longer walk to Omonia Square, where the **Restaurant Nea Olympia** (at 3 Emmanuel Benaki, just off Stadiou Street, two short blocks from the square) is to that area what Vassilis is to Constitution Square: It's larger than Vassilis, almost equally known, and actually less expensive than either Vassilis or the Corfu: 50 drachmas for tomato salads, 85 drachmas for moussaka, 175 drachmas for roast lamb. Hope and I, on our last visit, had two tomato and cucumber salads, two moussakas, 1 glass of beer, one orangeade—and the total bill came to 320 drachmas, about $8.88 including tip. The Nea Olympia, by the way, sometimes lists the Athenian specialty—"dolmothakia"—a concoction of rice and meat served in vine leaves, for 42 drachmas ($1.16), which you ought to try.

Other tourist restaurants? Near **Constitution (Syntagma) Square**, the really superb and quite cheap **Syntrivani**, an open-air garden restaurant at 5 Filellinon Street (a few steps from the square) has an English-speaking owner— the white-haired, eager-to-please Kiriakos Nistos, an English menu, prices somewhat lower than those at our foregoing selections and is open seven days a week, from noon to midnight. Simply to obtain a price comparison with the other restaurants we've named, I had my standard Athenian meal in this quite comfortable place—cucumber salad, moussaka (can't get enough of that stuff), a small beer, and a large slice of watermelon—for a total charge, including service, of 170 drachmas. Remember this street: **Filellinon**. It is directly off Constitution Square, and crams budget restaurants such as the Syntrivani and budget travel agencies—Viking's and Lotus—along its length. Just off Filellinon, the rather new **Restaurant Meteora,** at 10 Xenophontos Street, serves good, home-cooking-type food at budget rates: 35 drachmas for a filling platter of bean soup, 65 drachmas for a large spaghetti dish, 80 drachmas for a quarter roast chicken lavishly garnished.

Near Monastiraki (much cheaper)

In the area of the flea market (in front of the church), at 2 Platia Monastiraki, the **Restaurant Sigalas** is one of those typical Greek eateries where you walk into the kitchen, peek at bubbling pots and pans, and then point to what you wish to have. At this popular restaurant with its straw padded chairs, à la carte prices are so reasonable that you can feast for less than 110 drachmas ($3.05): moussaka is 55 drachmas ($1.52), Greek salad 35 drachmas (97¢), stuffed tomatoes 35 drachmas (97¢), a garlic soup called "Patsas" 38 drachmas ($1.05), "Psarri"—stewed fish with tomatoes, a house specialty 60 drachmas ($1.66). And an excellent retsina wine, stored in five large barrels in the back, is 55 drachmas ($1.52), all items including service charge (although it's customary to tip the young waiters 10 drachmas). Everything can be bought to take out for picnic purposes for 10% less. Open daily except Sundays, from 8 a.m. to 11:30 p.m., and supervised by jolly Apostolos Karabassos in tall white hat, bearing a striking resemblance to the Swedish chef of the "Muppets' Show."

In Plaka

Two final selections, for the Plaka area, always popular for its cheap (but tasty) food and cool local wines, begin with the **Taverna Byron,** at 1 Vakhou Street, in the very center of Plaka, where you'll be sitting among many more Greeks than tourists. Stuffed vine leaves for 50 drachmas, french fries 18, Greek salad 65, Souvlaki 65, and half a liter of open white, red or rosé wine, served in colored aluminum pitchers, for 60 drachmas. Look for a green glass roof in front, and try for a seat on the roof garden, from which the Acropolis is in full view. . . . Or seek out my own Plaka favorite: the big **Taverna Poulakis** at 6 Panos Street, next to the Roman Agora, peaceful and relaxing. Costliest dish there is lamb chops with fried potatoes for 100 drachmas, but almost everything else is cheaper: moussaka for only 55 drachmas, a large stuffed tomato for 50 drachmas ($1.38), french fries for 12, a liter of retsina wine for 30, black olives 10, feta cheese 15, and so on. From Monastiraki Square, walk up Areos Street, turn into the first street that goes left (the one with the basket shops), pass the stone wall, and the second street turning right (you cannot turn left) is the short Panos Street, lined on both sides with the 100 tables and the 350 chairs of the Taverna Poulakis.

READER'S RESTAURANT SELECTIONS: "The **16th Century Restaurant,** Kydathineon 5, Plaka, offers a choice of five tourist menus, the cheapest of which is only 85 drachmas ($2.36) and includes spaghetti, tomato and cucumber salad, cheese, bread, and fruit, as well as service and taxes. The above meal with moussaka instead of spaghetti is just 75 drachmas ($2.08). The finest value I've found in Athens, its breakfast costing 68 drachmas ($1.88) includes two eggs any style and is so popular you are lucky to get a seat. It's the only restaurant I know in Athens where you sit in easychairs, and it is open seven days a week" (R. H. Alexander, Middlesex, England). . . . "I usually ate at the cheap and friendly **Taverna Psarra** (meaning 'fish') at 16 Erechteos Street in the Plaka, filled with Greeks all eating together like one big family; usually someone has a guitar, and then everyone sings, and some even leap onto a table for a Zorba-like dance. A big salad is 27 drachmas, cheese 24 drachmas, moussaka or fish 60 drachmas, a half liter of retsina wine only 18 drachmas" (Sigrun Oladottir, Rejkjavik, Iceland; note from AF: in Plaka, look for the large signs pointing to the Taverna Attalos, walk 22 steps up, and you'll find Taverna Psarra in the corner with the three trees). . . . "My wife and I recommend **Gianakis,** Agiou Konstantinou 15, just two blocks from Omonia Square. The atmosphere is friendly and the surroundings clean. Chicken with rice, potatoes, macaroni, pumpkin or okra is 55 drachmas, a side order of tomato or cucumber salad, 35 drachmas, feta cheese, 17 drachmas, coffee, 18 drachmas, and a dessert of crême caramel, 18 drachmas—all of which adds up to quite a large meal for just a little over $3, service included" (Don & Shirley Ward, Unionville, Ontario, Canada). . . . "Consider the **Ideal Restaurant,** 46 Panepistimiou St. It's a clean, inexpensive place near Omonia Square. Dinners are delicious, the menu is varied, and selections can be made from samples in the front window. A full meal can be had for 130 drachmas, and vegetarians can feast for about 85. It's right next to the Ideal Cinema" (James L. Damewood, Dayton, Ohio).

READER'S BIG SPLURGE SELECTION: "**Seven Boats,** at 371 Sygrou Avenue, serves fresh seafood that you select yourself from a large tank, and provides excellent service as well as moderate prices averaging about $7.50 per meal" (Jo Anne Lavely, Fremont, California).

CURRENCY: In this chapter, the drachma has been converted into dollars at the rate of 36 drachmas per dollar, which makes each drachma worth about 2.77 U.S. cents. That rate, of course, fluctuates, but should not swing too far from the 36:1 ratio by the time of your own trip to Athens.

FOOD AND DRINK: As earlier noted, virtually all the Athenian restaurants we've discussed are tourist restaurants, equipped with menus printed in English or French. Because of that, and because few of our readers (including your author) can read Greek, we have not included a translation of Greek menu terms in our menu chapter, appearing further on in this book. But we do have some menu comments:

When in doubt, ask your waiter for "moussaka"—a staple dish served in many of the Athenian restaurants and in all of the "tavernas" (smaller and totally unpretentious restaurants). Moussaka consists of baked, ground meat, covered with vegetables and spices, and sometimes topped with a layer of dough or mashed potatoes. Its quality varies from place to place, but if you're lucky you'll make a wonderfully tasty meal of it. And it's filling: you'll be more than stuffed if you have, for dinner, a plate of moussaka, a tomato salad, bread and wine. Eaten in the normal taverna, that combination should rarely cost more than 110 drachmas ($3.05).

We've already mentioned "dolmothakia" (rice and meat in vine leaves). For a lighter snack, ask for "souvlakia," which are roasted and spitted chunks of lamb, flavored with oregano.

The Greek table wine is "retsina"—a red wine flavored with resin (pine sap)—and it's death to American tastes. To get it without the resin, specify that you want your wine "aresinato."

The Greek aperitif—a before-meal drink—is "ouzo," which is terribly cheap (about 70¢ a shot), and is taken either straight or in water (which it turns cloudy white). A Seven-Up type drink, which Hope very much likes, is "gazoza" (or at least that's how it's pronounced!).

READERS' SELF-SERVICE SELECTIONS: "In Athens, the food problem is a lot nearer solution with the brand-new **Floca Self-Service** at 16 Emanuel Benaki, about 4 blocks from Omonia Square. It's the first U.S.-type cafeteria in Greece. I ate there at least once a day and ordinarily spent just about 160 drachmas, usually for something like a macaroni moussaka, spinach-cheese pie, beer, ice cream and coffee. The big wall menu is in English, and most of the counter girls are English-speaking coeds at the University and very helpful. I understand the management is planning more cafeterias directly on Omonia and Constitution Squares" (Nat Friedland, New York, N.Y.). . . . "At the **Restaurant Chez-Nous** at 53 Patission Street, across the way from the National Archaeological Museum, most of the food is displayed in a glass case, so one can order by simply pointing to what's desired. Soups are only 20 drachmas, ground meat dishes 65 drachmas, veal, lamb and chicken in stews 100 drachmas, alone 80 drachmas, and there are at least a dozen different types of salad, including the typical Greek country salad of cucumbers, tomatoes and goat's cheese served with oil, vinegar and spinach, 50 drachmas. Small, but clean and pleasant, with good food and friendly people" (Merrill Mead, West Hartford, Connecticut). . . . "The extremely inexpensive **Rodeo Self Service** at 17 Satobriandou, half a block from the back corner of the Omonia Hotel on Omonia Square, serves a large plate of delicious Greek-style lima beans for 30 drachmas, a plate of french fries for 20 drachmas, macaroni in sauce 16 drachmas, tomato salad 18 drachmas, moussaka 38 drachmas, fried eggs for 12 drachmas each. Particularly good when you are in a hurry, as there is no waiting" (John Bennett, Houston, Texas; note from AF: at the Rodeo, there are seats upstairs, and waiter service, without service charge. Closed Sundays).

PLAKA: This is the most ancient residential section of Athens, on a hillside directly below the Acropolis, best-known today for its outdoor taverns, which feature guitar music and folk-singing. Nearly a score of such places are crammed into the area, all varying widely in price, but none of them expensive —particularly if you stick to a single plate (with wine) as your late night snack. The best of the streets in Plaka, with the most action, is **Mnisikleos** (and that's not a typographical error), where you might look in on a rather expensive taverna called **"Mostros"** (22 Mnisikleos), which sometimes has a tiny floor show to supplement the usual trio of guitar players. But there are many less costly places on the side streets intersecting the Mnisikleos (such as the marvelously cheap **Taverna Attalos,** at 16 Erechteos, where prices for typical Greek dishes range from 200 to 300 drachmas), or the **Taverna Seven Brothers** at 39 Iperidou Street, which features an orchestra and six dancers whom you can watch while devouring a 400-drachma fixed price meal consisting of appetizer (stuffed vine leaves, fish-egg-salad, "satziki"—made of yogurt, garlic and cucumbers), a main dish such as Souvlaki or Shish Kebab with Greek salad, accompanied by half a bottle of white domestic wine (alternatively, you can limit your order to half a bottle of white or Cambas wine for 240 drachmas, which is served with fresh fruit at no extra cost—lowering the tab to about $6.50 for a pretty remarkable folkloric evening). . . . And there are other such buys all up and down the Plaka. Wander first, then choose.

DINING IN DROSIA—A DAY IN THE SUBURBS: On hot summer days, in-the-know Athenians take to the northern suburbs, where the air is cooler and open-air restaurants serve good food at reasonable prices. Such a one is the **Taverna Mitsos** in Drosia (about 20 miles north—take bus #'s 134, 135, 136 or 137 from Kaningos Square), where you can dine al fresco under tall pines. (Menu in Greek only, but waiters will take you to the kitchen and let you point, if need be). Large steak with french fries, 104 drachmas ($2.88); meatballs with vegetables and french fries, 55 drachmas ($1.52); Greek salad, 28 drachmas (77¢); penerli—the local answer to pizza—73 drachmas ($2.02). A liter of retsina accompanying the meal, 40 drachmas ($1.11), is a must.

DAYTIME: There's so much to know and learn about Athens that it's best to take, first, a guided half-day tour, and then retrace your steps with lesser speed and greater deliberation. Best bet for this is the "Condensed" 4-hour tour (9 a.m. to 1 p.m.), which all the tour companies (the best one is **CHAT**, 4 Stadiou Street, phone 3222-886) offer for 450 drachmas ($12.50), and which is much to be preferred to the exhausting day-long variety 700 drachmas ($19.44), or the insufficient (it omits the Archaeological Museum) afternoon, 3-hour tour (360 drachmas—$10). By the end of 4 hours, you'll be aching to be let out to examine these thrilling spots at your own pace. All the tour companies of Athens run the same three standardized city tours, and all charge similar rates.

The tours devote a big thirty minutes to the exciting **Archaeological Museum,** 44 Patission Street (admission: 50 drachmas), which, in its own way, is as absorbing as the Acropolis. The Golden Mask of Agamemnon is here, as well as the statue of the Child Jockey, the Thundering Zeus, and all the other works of classic sculpture at which we used to gaze, as kids, in The National Geographic. Here, too, are the recently added frescoes from the island of Santorini—alone justifying a visit. Schedule a full morning for this (and remember that the museum is closed Mondays, while there's free admission on Sundays). The **Benaki Museum** at 1 Koumbari (50 drachmas; closed Tuesday), deals with a more recent Greek age, is interesting only for its basement of Greek costumes and clothing on life-sized models.

The **Acropolis** (50 drachmas) charges no admission on Sundays, and here, of course, you'll want to wander for hours. Remember that this site, on the dramatic hill overlooking Athens, is revered by all Greeks. There's a guard present to prevent you from forming human pyramids, standing on your head, etc., for picture-taking purposes, just as we'd prevent tourists from sitting on the lap of Lincoln, at the Memorial in Washington, D.C. As we've noted, fifty drachmas admission is charged on admission days, twenty-five drachmas for students.

Two other visits should be coupled with your trip to the Acropolis. Behind the hills is the magnificently-reconstructed **Stoa of Attalos** in the ancient Agora, the main market place and gathering spot of ancient Athens (admission: 25 drachmas). Again no charge on Sundays. . . . And carved into the side of the Acropolis is the **Theater of Dionysus** (free admission on Sundays, 25 drachmas all other days), which stands today almost exactly as it stood twenty centuries ago, when the comedies of Aristophanes were performed on this very stage and to these very same stone seats; a profound experience, especially for those knowledgeable in the theatre, who will know the names, as I'm proud to say Hope does, of the various portions of the stage and anterior stage.

EVENING: The "Sound and Light" presentation in Athens is a wonder, and shouldn't be missed. It's shown every night of the spring, summer and early fall months from a location on the "Pynx," a little hill that stands in front of the Acropolis (taxi from Constitution Square shouldn't cost more than 60 drachmas—$1.66), starting at 9 p.m. for English-language "performance." I won't describe any part of the show, except to say that it's done in sound and light, and that the ruins of ancient Athens are the performers. Take nothing better than the 75-drachma seats (which sell for 50 drachmas to students); the spectacle lasts only 50 minutes.

And after Sound and Light? Head then for either the Plaka (see above) or visit the nearby Greek-folk-dances (nightly at 10:15 p.m., Wednesdays and Sundays at 8 p.m. and 10:15 p.m., from May to September) in an open air theatre at the foot of Philopappos hill. Ninety drachmas for backless chairs, 130 and 160 drachmas for the more supportive ones. And keep in mind that on nights when Sound and Light isn't showing—because of the full moon—the Acropolis is available to visitors in all its glory—and until late in the evening. Go for one of the great sights of our world.

STARVATION BUDGET: The YWCA in Athens (its Greek initials are "XEN") is housed in a big, modern, clean and beautifully-located building at 11 Amerikis Street (phone 362-4291). Its very highest-priced rooms with bath go for 220 drachmas ($6.11) in summer; descend to 183 drachmas without bath, descend as low as 148 drachmas (including breakfast), if you'll stay in the dorm. No young lady should pass it up. . . . But the YWCA takes on more importance, to my mind, for its cafeteria, which is open to both sexes and all ages. Meal times are daily except Sundays from 7 to 9:30 a.m. for breakfast; from 12:30 to 2:30 p.m. for lunch; from 7 to 9 p.m. for dinner; and from 8 a.m. to 2 p.m. and 6 p.m. to 9 p.m. on Sundays. The cafeteria is in the large basement of the building; and there's a one drachma per person entrance charge. After that, prices are pleasantly low (soup 20 drachmas, salads 20 drachmas, meat plates 65 drachmas) for basic, but well-prepared, food. I had a tomato salad, baked lamb and mashed potatoes, watermelon, bread and beer; Hope had lamb croquettes and mashed potatoes, and iced tea. The total cost for both of us was 120 drachmas ($3.33), and our fellow-eaters were a number of interesting young people from all over the world.

A "Y" for men? The YMCA of Athens (whose initials here are XAN) is at 28 Omirou (phone 362-6970) corner of Acadimias, three-or-so short blocks from Constitution Square, in a relatively modern but utterly bare stone building. Beds in the dormitory-type rooms, which house from 4 to 9 persons, cost 110 drachmas ($3.05), and at that price it's hard to complain; there's also a games room, reading lounge, and photography dark room one flight up.

Athens also possesses three different Youth Hostels, all charging a uniform 80 drachmas ($2.22) per person per night for dormitory accommodations, and all bearing rather logical, unemotional and un-Greek titles using numerals: **Athens Youth Hostel No. 1** (57 Kypselis Street, phone 822-5860, take yellow bus no. 2 from Syntagma or Omonia to the Zakinthou stop); **Athens Hostel No. 2** (87 Alexandras Avenue, phone 646-3669, bus 10 or 16 from Syntagma, bus 170 from Omonia); and **Athens Youth Hostel No. 4**—No. 3 has just closed—(3 Hamilton Street, phone 822-0328, take yellow bus no. 12, 3 or 5 from one of the two main squares to the stop called OTE). Numbers 1 and 4 are official members of the International Youth Hostel Association, and therefore require a youth hostel membership card of their guests (which they will sell on the spot, however, for $10; it's good all over the world). Numbers 1 and 4 also operate cheap cafeterias selling breakfast for 40 drachmas, lunch or supper for 60 drachmas. Number 2 is managed by a Mr. Babis Maurogiannis and stays open 24 hours a day. No hostel card is needed for stays here. Flipping a coin is perhaps the best way to choose among them.

A new and big find: only two blocks from Syntagma (Constitution) Square, at 30 Mitropoleos, phone 324-3048, bearded John Armacolas and wife Josephine operate the hostel-type guest house called **"The Funny Trumpets"**, where dorms with 5 to 12 double-decker beds rent for only 80 to 150 drachmas ($2.22 to $4.16) per person per night, plus 40 drachmas per person for a hearty breakfast of coffee, two fried eggs and sliced bread. Showers are free, hot water is on 24 hours a day, and in Mr. Armacola's tiny office, you can borrow paperback, English-language books for free; buy cokes (12 drachmas) or Amstel beer (28 drachmas); or book a seat on Mr. Armacola's daily coach service to various European cities at amazing rates: to London, $50 (and 60 hours), to Amsterdam $45 (45 hours), to Istanbul, $30 (24 hours), in vehicles whose two drivers alternate on virtually (except for rest stops) non-stop trips.

Finally, for sub-starvation budget travellers, there's always the **Peta Inn** at 10 Peta Street in Plaka (no phone yet), which charges only 60 drachmas ($1.66) for one of 25 roof-top mattresses, 100 drachmas ($2.77) per person in four- and five-bedded dorms, nothing for showers and nothing for use of the kitchen facilities. There's also no curfew. Manager of this recently-opened haven is English-speaking Giorgio Kokotakis, and the location is quite easy to find: from Syntagma (Constitution) Square, walk up Fillelinon Street, pass the church with the three palm trees, turn right after the church with the single palm tree, and there's tiny Peta Street.

Roof space for your sleeping bags? **Pension "Diana the Huntress"** at 3 Kotsika Street (near 70 Patission), advertises an offer of 65 drachmas ($1.80) a night for a roof slot, including free hot shower next morning. Phone 822-3179 first, then take trolley 5, 12, 2 or 3 from Syntagma or Omonia Squares and ask the driver to let you off at **"O.T.E."** (pronounced "Oh-Teh"—the Athens Telephone Building). Around the corner is Diana the Huntress, where normal rates for regular rooms will, in 1980, be 200 drachmas ($5.55) single, 185 drachmas per person ($5.13) double; 170 drachmas per person ($4.72) in a triple or four-bedded room. Breakfast is 30 drachmas extra. This is a very, very plain place, but with a way-out atmosphere, and an American manager.

READERS' SELECTIONS (STARVATION BUDGET): "The **Student Inn** is located in the heart of the Plaka, only a short distance from the Acropolis at 16 Kidathineon Street (phone 32-44-808). Rooms are clean, and a three-bedded room was just 150 drachmas ($4.16) per person. Hot showers are free 24 hours a day, and you may also use the washing machine at no charge. Owner Spiro is extremely friendly and helpful, and speaks fluent American: he lived 25 years in Manhattan before returning to Athens" (Craig Gross, Yale, South Dakota). . . . At **Fantis House**, 39a Nikis Street (phone 3232-592), which is quite worthy of mention, we paid 175 drachmas ($4.86) apiece for a double room, but could have had a 4-bedded room for only 130 drachmas per or a 6-bedded dormitory for 110 drachmas apiece. Although the hotel is close to Syntagma (Constitution Square), it is on a back street, so there was none of the noise from trams and other vehicles. There was also a communal kitchen with a refrigerator, which proved a godsend in the heat, for we were able to buy watermelons and keep them there, running downstairs every so often to munch on a cool and thirst-quenching slice. There is also accommodation on the roof-top (only 90 drachmas per night) for those who come with sleeping bags" (Frances Bluh, Flushing, New York; similar recommendation from Anthony Williams of Seattle, Washington, who characterizes Fantis House as a "student hotel . . . which offers dormitory accommodation for 110 drachmas, and which is well located about three blocks from Syntagma Square"). . . . **Hotel Kimon** (phone 323-5223), located at #27 Apollonos Street, just around the corner from Cleo's Guest House (which is often full), is a nice hotel with extremely friendly owners who charge 270 drachmas single ($7.50) and 340 drachmas double ($9.44) per night, not including showers: if there are three of you, ask for the room on the roof, which is quite roomy, and comes with its own shower and view" (Susan Feringer, Mercer Island, Washington). . . . "The **Student House of Athens** (student card required) at 279 Patission, with 280 single rooms, but only 7 doubles, is in a nice residential neighborhood far away from the tourist-choked area. For 300 drachmas a night, you can get a single room with free shower and ice water down the hall, and with breakfast included. Sparkling clean, modern, and very friendly personnel. There is a snack bar, TV lounge and even an indoor swimming pool downstairs. Across the street is an open air cinema and up one block on Patission is a cheap self service cafeteria. The management usually requests that you stay at least two nights. Still a bargain. Take the #3 trolley from Syntagma or Omonia. The #3 trolley in the other direction takes you to the American Embassy on Vassilias Sofias, which is a long walk from Syntagma" (Blake Redding, Houston, Texas; note by AF: another and even larger students' home, is found at 8 Issou Street (phone 743-279), in the university district, but both student homes (open from July 1 to September 28) are primarily intended for groups of students or students studying in Athens. On the off-chance of an occasional vacancy for individual visitors, phone or visit the **National Foundation "King Paul,"** 9 Filellinon Street (phone 3220-193), which operates both homes). . . . **"Pericles' Student Hotel**, 39 Kapnikareas Street (phone 32-48-805), near the Plaka, a 36-bed hotel, is operated by an extremely kind Greek named Georgi, assisted by a Greek girl who serves breakfast. Rate is only 150 drachmas ($4.16) per person per night" (Eduardo Blanchet, Buenos Aires, Argentina).

ATHENS MISCELLANY: The twenty-minute subway ride from Omonia Square to Piraeus costs 8 drachmas (22¢). . . . Ask for Constitution Square as "Syntagma Square" and the local residents will understand you. . . . From Constitution Square, catch bus #16 to the Acropolis and the Stoa of Attalos; bus #12 or the yellow trolley #12 (going in the opposite direction) brings you to the Archaeological Museum. . . . While most museums are open and free on Sundays, their Sunday hours are only from 10 to 2—beware. . . . Monastiraki, site of the daily flea market in Athens, is the first subway stop after Omonia Square. . . . Next to the last stop is Phaleron, where there are swimming beaches and seaside resorts. . . . It's probably best, however, not to swim at Phaleron, where there have been reports of serious pollution. In fact, it's best not to swim at any point closer to the city than Asteria Beach; and of course, after Asteria, you'll reach the ethereal, magnificent beach of Vouliagmeni. . . . There are virtually no drunks in Greece, and no drug problem. That's because, says a Greek friend, the Greeks have too much energy to be in need of such pick-me-ups. . . . A shoeshine in Athens costs 20 drachmas; so does a charcoal-roasted ear of corn, sold by various sidewalk vendors. A portion of that delicious skewered meat ("souvlaki") which you'll see at numerous open bar-b-que-type places around Omonia Square, costs only 25 drachmas, and wrapped in a doughy piece of bread, with relish upon it, it makes a perfect snack. . . . Most centrally-located of the self-service laundromats is at 24 Kidathineon Street (phone 322-16-88), in Plaka, which is the third street turning right from Fillelinon Street, coming from Syntagma (Constitution) Square; there is no sign at all, but look for the words "Magic Bus" above the door, indicating a travel agency on the second floor that sells motorcoach transportation to London for 4,200 drachmas, to Sydney, Australia, for 17,800 drachmas, among other places. The energetic lady who manages the laundromat speaks some English, and charges 80 drachmas ($2.22) for 4 kilos washed and dried. Hours are from 7:30 a.m. to 4:30 p.m., Monday to Saturday; closed Sundays. Try, alternately, the **Maytag** self-service laundry at 46 Didotou Street near Omonia Square, whose charges are about the same. . . . Care to ship a parcel home? The **Parcel Post Office** is at 29 Odos Koumondourou Street, near Omonia Square, and is open weekdays only, from 7:30 a.m. to 7:30 p.m. At #31 on the same street, a small shop specializes in packing parcels, and will also sell all sizes of cardboard and wooden boxes. . . . Whether or not you plan to stay at the Hotel Alkistis, schedule a visit to the wholesale market place behind the hotel, where you'll see mountains of olives, oceans of olive oil, and hills of coffee. . . . If you're in Athens in August, don't fail to get tickets (some cost as little as 50 drachmas) to the **Athens Festival,** in the Herod Atticus Theatre that's carved into the side of the Acropolis. The setting alone is a memorable experience, and if The National Theatre of Greece is doing a classic (a comedy by Aristophanes, a drama by Euripides), you'll have an evening of theatre that you will never forget. And take standing room (which means that you'll sit on mountainside rocks, above the last row of seats) if all seats have been sold.

IT'S GREEK TO ME: The fact that few tourists learn to speak a single word of Greek is really shameful. The words for "please" and "thank you" should at least be tried. "Please" is pronounced "pah-rah-kah-loh." "Thank you" is: "eff-hah-ree-stow." For both words the emphasis is on the last syllable. You'll get a big reaction when you mispronounce these words, as you always will; most Greeks fail to suppress a broad smile, when I do.

Some other useful Greek words: "nero" (accent on the second syllable)—water; "kalimera"—how do you do, or good day.

OTHER TIPS: If you want American coffee in a Greek restaurant, ask for "Nescafe" (this is not a commercial). If you ask for "coffee," they'll bring you Greek coffee, which could power an automobile. Ask for Nescafe, and they'll bring you instant Nescafe, which, by some feat of salesmanship, seems to be the only American coffee stocked by the budget restaurants. . . . Scarcely any theatre in Athens charges more than 100 drachmas, and you might take a look. . . . The "Flea Market" in Athens operates every day in the Monastiraki area. . . . Motion picture houses in Athens show a great many American and British films in English, with subtitles. Often, the Greeks attend a showing from 10 p.m. to 12, and then go out for dancing and music—a custom that will explain the deserted appearance of most "tavernas" in the pre-midnight hours. . . . Virtually all the museums, exhibits and monuments of Athens charge no admission on Thursdays, and some are free on Sundays as well. . . . How to Ingratiate Yourself Among the Greeks: complain vehemently about the British refusal to return the "Elgin Marbles" to Athens. Those are the magnificent bas-relief sculptures that once adorned the front of the Parthenon. In 1800, the British ambassador, Lord Elgin, shipped the "marbles" to the British Museum in London, purportedly to protect them from Turkish vandalism. The Greeks want them back, and they should be back (advt)!

BEACHES: Most beautiful of all is at Sounion, which is, however, a two-hour ride by public bus from Athens. Sounion is a peninsula on the southeast tip of Attica (the province in which Athens is located). The beach is set next to the quite stunning Ruins of Poseidon, and the swimming is excellent.

Much closer to town are four other renowned beach areas, of which **Varkiza** beach (entrance fee of 35 drachmas) is probably the best; it features modern bathing facilities set amidst palm trees, flower beds, and soft sands cleaned each day by special machines; very spiffy. Runner-up: the often crowded **Vouliagmeni** beach, where 20 drachmas—a great bargain price—brings you private locker, beach chair, umbrella and showers (and nearby is a natural open-air swimming pool in an extinct volcano crater which obtains its sweet water supply from (reputedly curative) underground warm springs; known as "Limni Lake", it's open from 8 a.m. to 5 p.m., for an entrance fee of only 20 drachmas (55¢). And then there's the much less crowded Asteria Beach at **Glyfada** (next to the airport) charging a surprisingly-high, for Athens, 60 drachmas ($1.66) to enter. All three beaches can be reached by bus No. 90 (11 drachmas) from outside the Zappion in downtown Athens.

A READER'S SUGGESTION: "We hope that anyone who is in Greece from July to September will go to the town of Daphne, just outside of Athens, to the huge wine festival, which lasts for three summer months. Buses to Daphne leave Athens from all over the town at frequent intervals; stations can be located by the crowds of flagon-bearing Greeks who disembark from the buses, singing and laughing. The festival is held in a pine grove, enclosed and surrounded by oleander bushes. There is an open-air restaurant, folk-dancing displays, a dance floor where anyone can dance, a cafeteria, and 52 different wines in booths attended by girls in regional dress. The entrance fee is 60 drachmas and after that, all the wine you can drink is on the house—and you can drink all 52! The grove is open until about 1 a.m. every night, children are entirely welcome, and the atmosphere is gay and friendly" (David and Elizabeth Garin, Bloomington, Ind.). . . . "On the return trip from Piraeus to Athens, take green bus no. 165 (for 10 drachmas) instead of the subway, and you'll be able to see, on the half-hour ride, several residential, commercial, industrial areas of Athens-Piraeus, thus glimpsing how the Greeks live and work, away from the tourists. It's better than any guided tour" (Joel E. Abramson, Washington, D.C.).

HOPE IN ATHENS: And now, for a more intensive look at the sights of Athens, I give you Hope, who has had, on each one of our trips, a more rapturous reaction to the city than before. Here's her report:

"There's a message whistling round the ancient stones of Greece—prepare for it, listen for it. It's like the song of the Lorelei: once you hear it, you are changed forever. And in days to come, whenever petty, temporal irritations enter your life, you need only think of the stones of Greece to dispel them forthwith.

The Parthenon

"This jewel of 'The Golden Age of Pericles' (built in honor of Athena, patroness of Athens) should be the focus of your stay: it's considered by experts to be the most perfect building ever created by man. And it's deceptive: although, at first glance, a normal, rectangular, Doric structure, every one of its lines is subtly tapered to optically correct a straight line (which would otherwise recede or advance in viewing) into a graceful and slender perspective. There are "curves" everywhere. Take, for example, the columns, which are not straight, as they appear to be, but gently tapered, and convex in their middle portions, thus making the top part appear more slender. For proof that the curves do exist, try this simple experiment: stoop down to the eye-level of one of the steps at the side of the Parthenon. You will immediately see a 'bulge' in the center of the step! . . . And this mathematical and aesthetic masterpiece becomes an even greater testament to the builders' art when one remembers that no mortar or cement of any kind was used in its construction; rather, each piece was carefully ground, chiseled and polished to make a perfect fit with the preceding piece. It staggers the imagination!

Temple of Athena Nike and the Erechtheum

"While you're atop the Acropolis (to which the entrance fee is 50 drachmas, with free entrance on Thursdays and Sundays), look carefully for the delicate, little Ionic **Temple of Athena Nike** (to your right as you approach the main entrance to the Acropolis, located almost over the stairs), which still has some of its original friezes depicting battles with the Persians and the Gods of Olympus; the temple is dedicated to the "Wingless Victory"—wingless, else victory can fly away. . . . Then, walk to the **Erechtheum,** a larger Ionic temple perched on the original site of the even older Temple of Athena, which is supposed to have stood on the plot of land where Athena and Poseidon battled it out for God-supremacy of Athens. Athena brought forth an olive tree (there is still a little tree in front of the temple!) and Poseidon smote the earth and brought forth sea water. You'll probably remember the Temple best for its Caryatides (or Maidens), six of them easily and gracefully supporting a heavy porch ceiling on their heads.

The Acropolis Museum

"And for heaven's sake, don't miss the tucked-away, easy-to-overlook **Acropolis Museum** (behind, to the right, and a bit downhill from the Parthenon; for which there's an additional entrance charge of 50 drachmas), which contains some of the relics and pieces of statuary found on the Acropolis. You'll find some violent sculptures here (lions and lionesses tearing bulls and calves to pieces), the wonderful, Egyptian-looking Korai, parts of friezes that adorned the Acropolis temples (look for the ones that decorated the balustrade of the Athena Nike Temple), and the breathtaking, famous bas-relief of "Athena Nike Adjusting Her Sandal"—a show stopper! The Museum is open daily except Tuesdays from 9 to 3:30 (summers from 8 til 7), Sundays from 10 to 6:30. The Acropolis itself is open every day: summers from 8 to 7, winters from 9 to 5.

Elsewhere on and near the Acropolis

"No scholar would leave this area without also exploring the **Hills of the Pnyx and the Aeropagus** (both former assembly meeting places) and the **Hill of Philopappus,** with its monument of the same name at the top, built in the second century A.D. by the Roman consul, Philopappus, in honor of his two sons. It has an excellent view. And to be thorough you'll also want to clamber along the side of the Acropolis (on Dionysiou Aeropagitou Street) to see the **Theatre of Herod Atticus** (built in the second century A.D.), the **Temple of Asclepius** (he was the God of Medicine; his daughter was Hygeia), the **Stoa of Eumenes,** and the grand, oldest theatre in Greece, the **Theatre of Dionysus,** described earlier in this chapter.

The Agora and the Stoa of Attalos

"Just a word about these other two Acropolis sights, referred to earlier by Arthur. As you walk through the ruins of the **Agora** (market place), keep in mind that this was the magnificent city-center of Athens, where Socrates and his disciples came daily for discourse. One of the first buildings you'll see is the **Temple of Hephaistos (the "Theseion")**, named after the god who shared with Athena the honor of being a patron deity of the arts and crafts. The temple was built between 450 and 440 B.C., and is the best preserved of all the Greek temples. Between the Theseum and the Stoa of Attalos, you'll simply have to imagine that you are walking between other now-demolished temples, government buildings, a gymnasium and stoas (colonnades). On the way, you'll note a fragment of a colossal statue of the Emperor Hadrian (benevolent Roman ruler of Athens from 117 to 138 A.D.); sculptured on the torso is a small Romulus and Remus suckling at the Wolf of Rome. The **Stoa of Attalos,** your eventual destination, is a marvelous re-creation of the original, done by the American School of Classical Studies, and now a fascinating museum (open daily except Tuesdays from 8 a.m. to 7 p.m., Sundays from 10 to 6:30) housing all the other relics of the Agora.

The National Archaeological Museum

"With what you've now seen, you'll be ready to take on the National Archaeological Museum—the second (after the Acropolis) indispensable visit of your Athens stay (open from 7:30 a.m. to 7:30 p.m., Sundays 10 to 6, closed Mondays). And then, you'll want to wander further afield to the astonishing

Cemetery of Keramikos

"Located in the Monastiraki section (entrance at 148 Ermou Street), a 15-minute walk from Constitution Square, this is an ancient burial ground (sometimes also called the Dipylon Cemetery), some of whose relics date back as far as the Mycenaean era. It's an exciting place to visit because the excavations bring you the same sense of discovery that an archaeologist has—although there's a small museum on the site (with interesting grave findings), and a pamphlet-guide available, nothing outside is tagged, and you can simply walk around, finding things! You'll see the most unusual (and most ancient) gravestones in Greece, including a reproduction of the renowned monument that bears a bas-relief of a woman whose maid is bringing her her jewels to gaze upon for one last time before death—a scene that has been an inspiration to so many poets (the original is at the Archaeological Museum). Excavations have recently unearthed an aqueduct here, as well, which is, in its own way, equally as remarkable as the statuary and fine arts. And the digging continues. Who knows what may be found next year? Admission of 25 drachmas (Sundays are free); open Wednesday through Monday from 7:30 a.m. to sunset—usually 7:30 p.m.; Sunday from 10 a.m. to 6 p.m. Closed Tuesdays.

The Temple of Olympian Zeus and Hadrian's Arch

"Before you part from the ancient sights of Athens, see the **Temple of Olympian Zeus** (admission of 25 drachmas, free on Sundays), begun in the 6th century B.C., but not completed until Hadrian came to Athens. People of that time described it as the most splendid building they had ever seen; only 16 Corinthian columns now remain. Hadrian not only finished the building, but also built the **Arch of Hadrian** next to it, which served as the marker between two cities; on one side, the Arch carries the inscription: 'This is Athens, the Ancient City of Theseus'; on the other, 'This is the City of Hadrian, and not of Theseus.'

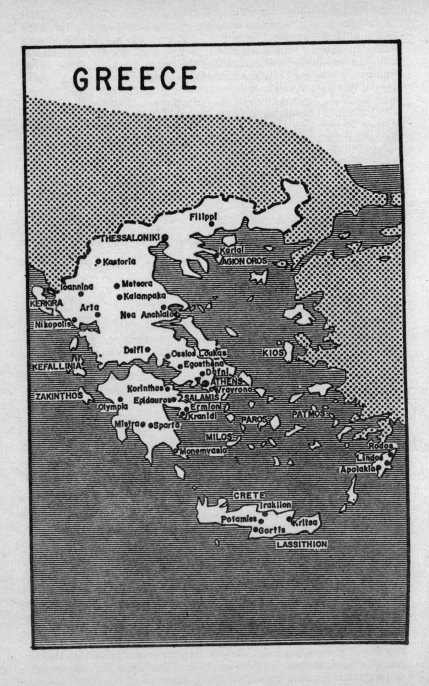

The Byzantine Museum

"For a direct contact with Byzantine art, the Greek-Orthodox art of the Middle Ages, you might also want to visit the **Byzantine Museum** (22 Vassilissis Sophias Avenue), which contains a world-famous collection of Byzantine artifacts; free entrance on Sundays, 50 drachmas at all other times; hours are 7:30 a.m. to 7:30 p.m. Sundays from 10 to 4, closed Mondays.

A Byzantine Church

"Then take in the 7th century Greek Orthodox church of **St. Eleftherios,** next door to the Mitropoleos Church (or Cathedral of Athens).

"And on all your tours in Athens, wear rubber-soled shoes with low heels—particularly for the climb on the Acropolis!"

ANTI-CLIMAX: By the following comment, I certainly don't mean to downgrade Athens. This city is part of everyone's heritage, and should be seen. But in three days, you can see about everything you'll want to see in Athens, whose sights are magnificent but few. Utilize your remaining time to travel in the outlying islands and provinces of Greece, which are spectacularly beautiful and astonishingly cheap.

Rock-bottom Tours

The very least costly way to do this is by using the facilities of **Viking's Travel Bureau,** 3 Filellinon Street (phone 322-9383), off Constitution Square, whose student services have already been described in an earlier portion of this chapter. Viking's deals with tourists of all ages, not merely with students, and their most popular program is a series of wonderfully-planned "Do-As-You-Like" tours, for which they furnish the transportation, guides, and fairly basic lodgings, but you find your own meals (advised by the guide) in the towns where you stay overnight. I've known readers who have kept their food costs to under $2 a day on these tours, by eating the typical Greek shepherd's meal—ingredients are available at local markets for a few pennies—of olives, goat cheese ("feta"), bread, the Greek country wine ("retsina") and yoghurt.

The five-day "Do-As-You-Like" tour to Thebes, Delphi, Olympia (the most superb site in Greece), Tripolis, Argos, Epidauris, Mycenae, Corinth and Eleusis costs $155 for students and teachers, $175 for all others, leaves every Thursday throughout the year, as well as on Saturdays and Tuesdays from April to October. That price works out to not much more than you'd pay for a simple bus fare to these spots, and yet you receive, for no extra price, the services of a trained guide who comments on the sights, as well as your accommodations. It's an unparalleled value, the likes of which is offered in no other European country.

In 1979, Viking's also ran a 6-hour tour, on Tuesdays, Thursdays and Saturdays, to the Temple of Poseidon (70 kilometers from Athens) at Cape Sounion for only $10; they will repeat this trip in 1980. The tour leaves at 3 p.m., begins with a drive along the seaside road that some people call the "Riviera Attica," visits the Temple of Poseidon, permits you to take a fast swim in the Aegean, gives you a glimpse of the sunset at Cape Sounion, then drives back along the Saronic Gulf. The $10 charge (which is the student and teacher's price; others pay $12) covers everything.

Other "Do-As-You-Like" tours that Viking's will operate in 1980: a unique, new one-day tour to Delphi leaving every Thursday from April through October for $25, including transportation and guides; an 8-day, 7-night motorcoach tour of **"Golden Greece and Turkey,"** including visits to Thermopylae, where Leonidas and his 300 Spartans fought the Persians in 480 B.C., to the hanging monasteries of Meteora (Greece's Tibet), to recent archaeological excavations near Saloniki, and to Istanbul for a three-night stay and an excursion over the new Bosporus Bridge into Asia, preceded by lunch in a seafood restaurant at the Bosporus, the entire journey departing from Athens on Tuesdays from April to October in 1980 at a charge (including air-conditioned bus, bed and breakfast in tourist class hotels with private shower, English-speaking guide) of $325 per person, only $295 for students and teachers; and finally, a splurgey 7-day cruise by private yacht to the Cyclades, Mykonos, Corfu, the Ionian and Aegean Islands, and Turkey, priced too high for recommendation in these pages; several other tours (to **Rhodes,** to **Santorini,** to **Crete** (remember "Zorba the Greek"?), to **Skaithos,** and to **Kos**—home of Hippocrates) as well. Lest there be any misunderstanding, let us repeat again that these are not limited to students or student-age people, but only to the "young in spirit," which can include oldsters (who receive student reductions if they're over the age of 65!) and youngsters alike.

The Normal Tours

Readers who aren't up to the "Do-As-You-Like Tour" of the classic sites outside of Athens, can obtain a less strenuous, but still inexpensive, alternative by visiting any travel agency other than Viking. All the companies in Athens offer the very same tour for the very same price: $195 for four days and three nights, on an itinerary that includes Delphi, Olympia, Epidauris, Mycenae and Corinth. That includes room, board, guide and bus; and many of the guides are remarkably well-informed on the vast sweep of ancient Greek history.

The Greek Islands? To make a fairly full circuit of both the Cyclades and the Dodecanese groups, your least expensive bet will be the four-day cruises of the M/S *Oceanos* of the Epirotiki Lines, which embarks from Piraeus (the port of Athens) at noon every Monday from April to October in 1980, goes to Mykonos, then to Kusadasi in Turkey, from where Ephesus and Patmos are visited, then to Rhodes, then on to Herakleion on Crete and to the volcanic island of Santorini, and back to Piraeus, with fairly lengthy daytime stops at each island. Charge per berth in a three- or four-person cabin is $385, including transportation, three meals a day and a midnight buffet over the four-day period. The ship returns to Piraeus on Friday morning at 7 a.m.

Believe me, though, an almost equally good glimpse of what the islands are like can be had by taking the simple trip on the afternoon steamer from Piraeus (check the days) to the wonderful island of Mykonos, seven hours away; followed by a couple of days in Mykonos. For hotel recommendations in Mykonos, see our "Tale of Many Cities" chapter. And to get the ferry to Mykonos, simply take the subway to Piraeus, then walk two short blocks to the dock.

READERS IN THE ISLANDS: "If you have only a short time to spend in Greece, and want to see a Greek island, you can take a boat from Piraeus (one block from the subway) to nearby **Hydra.** Deck class costs about 150 drachmas one way, takes about four hours. Go for the day or stay overnight (we did for about $5 per person). The harbor and town are beautifully picturesque, although the beaches are very small" (Elaine Mura, Clifton, New Jersey). . . . "Please advise readers that boats to Mykonos do not sail daily, and not to visit the closer islands—Aegina, Poros, Hydra—on weekends, when they are more crowded than Constitution Square" (L. Bernstein, Haifa, Israel). . . . "Having only a short time in Athens and wanting to take a look at a Greek island, we asked at the port of Piraeus if there was any boat which would take us for a quick trip to an island. We were directed to a ferry which, for 25 drachmas, took us on a beautiful 35-minute trip to the island of **Salamis** (12 miles from Piraeus). Upon debarking, we discovered a typical 'Zorba-type' island where they seldom see a tourist. They have a Tourist Directory, though, in which was listed a museum, monastery, and beach. We wandered around and it was just like a Greek movie" (Mrs. H. Brautman, North Miami Beach, Florida). . . . "If you haven't time to go to the famous Greek Islands, taste the real ethnicity of Greece by going from Athens to the nearby island of **Selinia**. Take the Metro to Piraeus and from Piraeus pay 20 drachmas to travel thirty minutes to Selinia. Sunning on the cliffs to the background music of a Greek inn will prove to be most exciting. Buy your lunch or dinner at the local grocery store where not a word of English is spoken but where a woman is more than glad to assist you with what you may want. Our one and only side trip from Athens, Salinia offered us the true Greek ethnicity that was lacking in Athens" (Rosalyn A. Paul, Chicago, Illinois). . . . "A lengthy but worthwhile one-day excursion from Athens is a public bus trip to **Cape Sounion** and the **Temple of Poseidon**. If you go early in the day you can even take a swim in the Aegean. The people at most travel agencies will tell you where to catch the public bus" (Deirdre Henderson and M. Koplik, New Haven, Connecticut).

ADVANCE READING: At least one of three unforgettable books, *The Colossus of Maroussi* by Henry Miller, *The Bull of Minos* by Leonard Cottrell, and *The King Must Die* by Mary Renault, should be read either before or during your trip. All three are in paperback, they weigh very little, and they'll add immeasurably to the fun of your stay in Greece.

READERS' TRANSPORTATION SUGGESTIONS: "A cheap way to get to Greece (there are several alternate methods) is to take the train to Brindisi from Paris, Bologna or Rome and then take the 18-hour overnight ferry to Patras; the fare is $51 (but students get a 30% discount), meals extra. From Patras, drive or take the bus to Athens for an additional $6.50." (Alexander Sterne, New York, New York; note by AF: from Rome to Brindisi is 7 to 10 hours by train, and costs $18 (second class); from Brindisi to Patras by ferry is a 20-hour trip, costing $51 (minimum); apart from flying there, this is the quickest way to get to Athens from Western Europe). . . . "Although it takes 24 hours, the cheapest and easiest way to go to Greece from Europe, or vice-versa, is to take the ferry between Brindisi, Italy and Patras, Greece. It's a beautiful ferry, equipped with an outdoor swimming pool, bar, lounge and restaurant; the price of $51 makes it very popular with Europeans. Food is expensive aboard, so buy your own before leaving. Of the two ships, the Appia is newer and prettier than her sister ship, the Egnatia; contact the Hellenic-Mediterranean Line if interested" (Linda Blum, Buffalo, New York). . . . "A word of warning! Get to Brindisi at least three hours before the boat leaves if you can, they have no idea what 'organization' is there. If you are a Eurailpasser, don't let them try to tell you there is no place for you—they have only arbitrary law there. And be prepared to shell out a 3,600 lire debarkation tax. However, no problems at Patras in Greece, going in the other direction. They have figured it all out, like clockwork. You walk down the street to the left from the station (you'll see boats docked there), stop in the Hellenic Mediterranean office on the way, get your ticket, pay your tax, go thru customs on the dock, and jump on the boat. I would recommend you stock up on food and drink before getting on—the bar and meals on board are rather steep" (Danielle Rappaport, A.P.O., New York). . . . "We returned via a Yugoslavian cruise ship for under $90 each. It left from Piraeus, went to Venice, and also afforded us the opportunity to see different parts of Yugoslavia, as well as Delphi. This was one of the highlights of our trip, a very clean boat, good service, good food, a good rest, and the price was only slightly more than the cost of the train to Brindisi from Rome and then the boat to Piraeus from Brindisi" (Mr. and Mrs. Victor A. Lobree, San Lorenzo, California). . . . "One day I went from Athens to **Porto Rafti** by bus, for 20 drachmas (55¢) each way. Porto Rafti is on the other side of the Greek peninsula which Athens is on. It has a little harbor on the Aegean Sea, and is just a little fishing village where Greeks go to bathe and spend the day on picnics. Tourists never seem to go there. But the ride up over the mountains and through the groves of olives, vineyards and fig orchards was lovely, and so very interesting. It took a little more than an hour each way. The buses run every hour and leave from just past the Polytechnic Institute on a square (many of the out-of-town buses start from this special square). Pack your lunch and make a day of it at this little village so quiet and beautiful. There are many small sandy beaches, and one rather large one" (Madelin L. Lawler, Mt. Prospect, Illinois). . . . "Try the Greek buses. From Athens, one may take a bus to Corinth. From Corinth, a bus to Mycenae. From there a bus to Argos and Tripolis (of little interest), but from there a 4½ hour ride to Olympia. From Olympia, ride the bus to Pyrgos, Patras and Aeghion. Take the ferry to Itea, and Delphi is a short ride away. Then a bus back to Athens. This do-it-yourself tour lasted five days (with overnight stays in Mycenae, Olympia, Patras and Delphi), cost less than $50 for transportation" (Raymond Ginn, Hermosa Beach, California).

SOUTH FROM GREECE: "For your readers who get as far as Athens, it is just a short flight to Cairo, the capital of the Arab world. The cost is $180 round-trip fare, $125 for students. Cairo, on both banks of the immortal Nile, is quite fascinating with its mosques, bazaars, modern section along the Nile, the panorama from the Cairo tower, and of course the Egyptian Museum housing a collection of treasures that is worthy of several visits. The people are extremely friendly and most do speak English well.

"Just outside of Cairo are Sakkara with its tombs and step Pyramid of King Zoser, Memphis with the colossal statue of Ramses II, and of course the pyramids and sphinx of Giza—don't miss the Son et Lumiere!

"For those with more time—and by all means find it—trains and inexpensive flights whisk you down to Luxor, ancient Thebes, with relics that will make the trip up the Nile one you'll never forget. The temples of Luxor, Karnak and the tombs on the west bank, the feluccas sailing by on the Nile, all contribute to a scene as tranquil as one could imagine. South of Luxor is Aswan, famous for its new high dam. The Nile is quite lovely here with monuments, Nubian villages and botanic islands. Hydrofoils leave Aswan for the temples of Abu Simbel which have miraculously been saved by engineers who lifted them from the reach of the rising Lake Nasser.

"With the tourist rate of 75 piastres per dollar, Egypt is inexpensive and the Oriental souvenirs (jewelry, camel saddles, hassocks, wall hangings, alabaster, etc.) are irresistible" (Lloyd H. Orloff, Brooklyn, New York).

We'll move next to the country whose accommodations are even less expensive than those of Greece. At some point in your trip, you'll want to be in the price paradise of all—Spain.

Chapter XIX

MADRID

Bullfights and Bargains

A TRIP TO SPAIN is like an intense session of daydreaming—except that it's real. Those three medieval horsemen who ride across the bullring at the start of a *corrida* in Madrid, aren't putting on a show for tourists—they're for real, and no one smiles. The farmers tossing grain into the air to rid it of chaff; the women drawing water from a village well—these are scenes that can be found ten minutes from Madrid, and they are as real as if the Twentieth Century had never occurred. In no other land will you feel, so much, that you have stepped through a time-machine into the past. There are plains in Spain where you needn't even shut your eyes to imagine that Don Quixote and Sancho Panza are riding on the scrubby, bare land that stretches into the distance, unmarred by billboards or smokestacks.

Against such a background, your visit to Spain will be a joy, because the Spanish people are honest, dignified, friendly and helpful. Since it's so easy to live among them on the lowest of costs, we'll engage in only the briefest survey of accommodations in Madrid. Remember that if you avoid only the obviously de luxe establishments, you'll automatically be on a budget standard; and if you then choose well, you'll find surprisingly pleasant rooms for those low rates.

HOTELS: For one startling example of the price levels of Spain, we'll begin with an establishment—the Francisco I—that is located in the very center of the city.

Whenever I argue with an anti-$15-a-day'er, I use the **Hotel Francisco I** as a case in point—not because it's a low-cost hotel (it's not), but because it reveals how sharply the cost of hotels descends when one ventures to the lesser-known establishments, and how moderate is the price level of even quality hotels in Spain. For this tastefully-furnished hotel, done in classic Spanish style, and situated at 15 Arenal (phone 248-02-04), just off the Puerta del Sol—the central-most square of Madrid—charges only 2,100 pesetas ($31.81) for an immaculate double room with private bath and breakfast for two, 1,530 pesetas ($23.18) single. Just a few hundred yards away, at the Plaza de España, the four-star-and-famous **Hotel Plaza** charges nearly twice as much. I defy anyone to shuttle back and forth between the two hotels, and then assert that the Plaza is *that* much better.

In the Center of Town

Nor is this an isolated example. In the very center of Madrid are numerous almost-elegant hotels offering double rooms with private bath for $34, $32, $27, $21, even $19 and under. We'll begin with the highest priced of the lot, and then descend to the more simple—but still attractive—establishments that either charge $12 and less for a bathless double, or else charge $12 per person for room and all three meals.

Doubles with private bath for $21 to $34 a night

The best-located (because it's central, yet in a quiet area) of the moderately-priced hotels is the **Hotel Carlos V,** 5 Maestro Vitoria (phone 231-41-00), a block from the Puerta del Sol (center of the city), where the highest-priced double room with private bath costs 2,300 pesetas ($34.85), breakfast and service included. That outlay brings you a well-appointed bed chamber with crystal chandeliers, in a hotel that the Spanish government ranks as "Three Stars," and in a seven-story, air-conditioned, 70-room building filled with marble and brass that is constantly being polished by an army of maids. Such are the values of Spain.

Even better finds are located on the Avenida José Antonio, which is the main street of Madrid, and one of the best of these (although it won't initially seem that way from the appearance of its downstairs lobby) is the **Hotel Lope de Vega,** 59 José Antonio (247-70-00), with an unprepossessing entrance, but a stunning interior of paneled lounges and red velvet chairs, and large, tastefully-decorated bedrooms. Singles with private bath are 1,100 pesetas ($16.66), doubles 1,800 pesetas ($27.27), all with breakfast, service and tax included. And all 50 rooms are on the ninth floor of a 12-story building, with superb views over Madrid. . . . Nearby, on a side street off José Antonio, at 29-31 Calle San Bernardo, the modern **Hotel-Residencia Alexandra** (phone 242-04-00) charges a fairly similar 1,150 pesetas ($17.42) for a single, 2,150 pesetas ($32.57) for a twin or double room, again with bath and breakfast. . . . If all three of these initial choices are packed, then try the **Hotel Lacorzán,** 31 Avenida José Antonio (phone 222-83-60), where singles with private bath and breakfast are 1,000 pesetas ($15.15), without 720 pesetas ($10.90), and all double rooms—each of which is with private bath—go for 1,800 pesetas ($27.27). . . . And then walk over to the **Hotel Europa,** 4 Calle de Carmen (phone 221-29-00), just off the Puerta del Sol (by 20 feet), in the very heart of Madrid, where doubles with private bath are 1,700 pesetas ($25.75), singles with bath 1,000 pesetas. All rates include breakfast. The staff at this remarkably low-priced, well-located, 60-room hotel is a particularly courteous one, by any standard, although the Europa isn't nearly of the same quality as the Lope de Vega or Carlos V, our two top choices.

Two other hotels with private-bath-doubles for $21 to $32 a night are located near the important Atocha Railroad Station (where the trains from Barcelona arrive) in Madrid. Cheaper of the two is the fairly modern **Hotel Mediodia,** 8 Plaza Emperador Carlos V (phone 227-30-60), directly across from the Atocha station, charging 648 pesetas single without bath, 865 pesetas with bath; 940 pesetas double without bath, 1,350 pesetas ($20.45) with bath, including breakfast. A few steps away, the spanking-new and much better **Hotel Mercator,** 123 Atocha (phone 239-26-00), has now equipped each of its

90 rooms with private bath, yet charges only 2,100 pesetas ($31.81) double, 1,350 pesetas ($20.45) single, for a room so equipped. While the avenue on which it stands is not a terribly interesting one, it is quite close to the Prado and might be considered by tourists planning extensive and frequent visits to that renowned museum.

Finally, a number of $27 a night doubles (with private bath) are to be found on the street that runs alongside American Express, in the well-located, pleasant area of Madrid near the important Cortes (parliament) building. In the corner structure at 3 Plaza de las Cortes, are several of these, of which by far the best is the strikingly lovely **Residencia Trianon** (phone 231-3605), which takes up the building's third floor (there's an elevator), and also offers bathless doubles, without breakfast, at 1,100 pesetas ($16.66). Next door, somewhat simpler, but English-speaking, is the **Hostal Florida** (phone 232-7920), in the building at 25 Marques de Cubas, across from the side entrance to American Express, where doubles with private bath but without breakfast are 1,750 pesetas ($26.51). Phone first to each of these popular pensions.

THE SPANISH PESETA: Just so you'll know, we've converted pesetas into dollars at the rate of 66 pesetas to the dollar, which should be the amount you'll receive in mid-1980.

Doubles for $19 to $30 a night

Back in the center of town, a romantic-sounding street called the "Mesonero Romanos," which is right off the important Avenida de José Antonio, is the site of the huge, 10-story **Hotel Regente**, Mesonero Romanos 9 (phone 221-29-41), which charges 1,180 pesetas ($17.87) for a single with shower, 2,000 pesetas ($30.30) for a double with shower; has plenty of these rooms available; and keeps them spare but well-maintained: most budgeteers seem to like the Regente less for its hotel aspects than for its nearby flamenco nightclub, the "Torre Bermejas," to which guests of the hotel are admitted at a 10% discount. But it's a thoroughly proper, desirable hotel, that has facilities for families and some English-speaking personnel well-supervised by an energetic, new owner-manager, Señor Luciano Sanchez. You may want to comparison shop between the Regente and the more intimate **Hotel Negresco,** Mesonero Romanos 12 (phone 222-65-30), which offers air-conditioned doubles with bath and breakfast for 1,980 pesetas ($30), and is a top-rated budget choice, although its rooms are fairly compact in size. Or try, again in the very heart of Madrid, the small **Hostal Maria Christina** on the second floor of 20 Fuencarral (phone 231-63-00), where doubles with bath and w.c. are 1,250 pesetas ($18.93), singles 690 pesetas ($10.45), breakfast extra.

Doubles for $11 to $21 a night

Much cheaper than these, but also in a central location, is the fine **Hotel Continental,** at 44 Avenida José Antonio, phone 221-46-40 (the street which is known as the "gran via"). Singles here rent for a reasonable 700 pesetas ($10.60) including breakfast, doubles with private shower and breakfast for

1,300 pesetas ($19.69), doubles with bath and breakfast for 1,450 pesetas, ($21.96). There's an unusually friendly management, and a kitchen and cook so good that I would enthusiastically recommend you take demi-pension terms (room without bath, breakfast and one other meal, if they're offered to guests at the time of your stay). Highly recommended.

In the same building that houses the Continental (44 José Antonio) are no fewer than five other budget hotels—one per floor—of which my own preference would be for the cozy, 7-room **Hostal de Alibel** on the 8th floor (phone 232-15-78), whose middle-aged proprietors speak little English but charge only 1,120 pesetas ($16.96) for a double without bath, including breakfast taken at a corner cafe downstairs; it's here also that you'll find the Restaurant Valencia, recommended in our "big splurge" restaurant section, directly below. If the building is full at the time of your visit, then walk over to a somewhat higher-priced, hotel-filled structure at #34-#38 Avenida José Antonio, housing the **Hotel California** (phone 222-47-03), a 25-room pension with a friendly atmosphere, whose proprietors—a charming family—will offer the following in 1980: singles with shower, no w.c., 1,050 pesetas with breakfast, doubles with shower, no w.c., 1,700 pesetas with breakfast.

A final and much cheaper selection in this low-priced category is found in the old section of Madrid, directly opposite the colorful cafe "Las Cuevas de Luis Candelas" (whose doorman is dressed as an 18th century Spanish bandit). That's the **Hostal La Macarena,** Cava de San Miguel 8 (2nd floor), phone 265-9221, a friendly and fairly spacious, two-floor pension whose new owners, Mr. Antonio and Mrs. Julia, charge a low 500 pesetas ($7.57) for a single with breakfast, 725 pesetas ($10.98) for a bathless double with two breakfasts. From the train station, ask a cab driver to take you to the "Plaza Mayor—frente Cuchilleros" (it'll cost 200 pesetas, if you have suitcases with you), and then point to the above address, which is best recommended for our younger readers, for its colorful location, its largely student clientele, and the large number of rooms of which it disposes. To the many readers who have asked, "Macarena" refers to the "Holy Virgin of Sevilla," and triple rooms here are 950 pesetas ($14.39), including breakfast with an egg! If, improbably, La Macarena is full, then try the "costlier" **Hostal Roma,** nearby in a quieter location at #1 Travesia de Trujillos (phone 231-19-06), and occupying an entire old apartment building with enormous staircase. In 1980, the Roma will be charging 750 pesetas ($11.36) for singles with breakfast and free showers, 1,350 pesetas ($20.45) for doubles on the same basis, all for simply-furnished, but large and clean, rooms with parquet floors.

Additional clusters of $11-a-night doubles? See our "Starvation Budget" section, below, for a dozen or so selections; and see "Readers' Selections," below, for additional doubles charging less than $15 a night.

READERS' HOTEL SELECTIONS: "Plaudits to **Hostal-Residencia Fénix** at 6 Calle Concepción Arenal (phone 232-0112), 1½ blocks from the Avenida José Antonio, and with prices well within your range, large, airy, and spotlessly clean rooms, free baths, accommodating personnel" (Sandra Azus, Skokie, Illinois). . . . "**Hostal Lisboa,** 17 Ventura de la Vega (phone 222-83-45), is nothing on the outside, but elegant inside; located just a few blocks from American Express and within easy walking distance of virtually everything worth seeing in the downtown area; spotlessly clean; and offers double rooms for 900 to 1,100 pesetas, the higher-priced rooms with showers or baths. Breakfast is 100 pesetas extra, but they'll bring it to your room, if you wish" (John Wilcock, New York City). . . . "At the **Hostal Residencia Rifer,** #5 Mayor (phone 232-3197), two of us stayed five nights in a spotless, well furnished double with shower for only 850 pesetas ($12.87) for both of us. Location is only half a block from the Púerta del Sol" (Cecilia Brenner, Lakewood, New Jersey). . . . "We spent six nights in the pension **Hostal Amaya,** José Antonio 12 (phone 222-2151), on one of the main streets. Our large spacious room had two beds, a double and a twin, as well as a bath with bidet, but with toilet in the hall. We paid 900 pesetas (with breakfast for two included). Doubles with shower were only 1,000 pesetas, breakfast included. Singles with breakfast are 550 pesetas. Although the family spoke very little English, they were more than accommodating and invited us to join them in the living room and watch TV" (Frank and Debby Buffum, China Lake, Calif.; enthusiastic seconding recommendation from Mrs. George Yamaoka of New York City, who speaks of the Amaya's "typically Spanish atmosphere" and its "charming, intelligent owner, Doña Encarnita"). . . . "**Hostal Santa Cruz,** at 6 Plaza Santa Cruz (2nd and 3rd floors), phone 222-2441, is a fairly typical Spanish pension, but there is a difference. It is bigger, and is run somewhat half way between the style of a hotel and a pension. The prices (single with breakfast 740 pesetas, double with breakfast 1,240 pesetas) are those of a pension, while the service is that of a hotel, preserving, nevertheless, the friendly home-like quality of a pension. The Plaza Santa Cruz is a square of historical interest, very much in the center of the most interesting part of Madrid, 50 yards from the Plaza Mayor" (Rev. C. David Burt, Waltham, Massachusetts; strong second from Dominick Cinciripini of Pittsburgh, Pennsylvania, who calls the Santa Cruz "the absolute best in service, cost, management, aesthetics and location of any lodgings I have experienced"). . . . "**Hostal Cosme,** on the third floor of 1 Principe (two blocks from the Puerta del Sol), phone 232-3305, is a brand-new hostal run by a charming (but non-English-speaking) woman and her young son. We had the cleanest room we'd ever seen, including a sink and brand new shower unit, for 900 pesetas a night. There is a telephone and a television set for guests, and the entire establishment is like a large, extremely well-kept home, carpets and all" (Mrs. Ray Fisher, New York, New York; hearty second endorsement from Mr. and Mrs. Peter Young, West Hempstead, New York). . . . "**Hostal Matute,** 11 Plaza Matute (phone 228-6904), was excellent—double room with private bath and shower for only 1,300 pesetas ($19.69), with breakfast. Owner speaks English very well—has spent some time in the U.S.A." (R. J. Scheurenberg, London, England, and also endorsed by Luis Sanchez, Hialeah, Florida, and John G. Sindorf, Palmer, Alaska). . . . "My hotel find was the **Hostal Barajas** at 17 Augusto Figueroa (phone 232-4078), where a single with private shower cost only 650 pesetas." (T. K. Moy, Woodhaven, New York). . . . "Discovered an excellent pension, the **Mondragon,** at Carrera San Jeronimo 32, phone 222-57-57, located midway between Puerta del Sol and the Plaza de las Cortes. There's an elevator to your lodgings, four floors up, and our 780 pesetas ($11.81) room had beds for three, a sink, a small foot tub, a small terrace, and was clean and quiet" (John and Jean Dabel, Dover, Delaware). . . . "**Hostal Don Juan,** 18 Calle Recoletos (phone 275-00-64), located just a short block from El Retiro park, and accessible to the park via an underpass that tunnels below the street, is especially suitable for families traveling with small children. The obliging young couple who run the Don Juan obtained a crib for our daughter, and charged only 600 pesetas per person for adults, 450 pesetas for children" (Robert George Schuur, New York, New York). . . . "My daughter and I can't say enough about the hospitality and kindness we received from the hard-working couple - Mr. and Mrs. Yanez - who operate the **Hostal Ginebra** at 17 Fuencarral. Although their English is limited, their French is fluent, and they assist in any way, even lending irons and dryers. Their location also can't be beaten, half a block from the José Antonio metro stop. 600 pesetas ($9.09) single, 1,000 pesetas ($15.15) double, breakfast included, and the latter with bath" (Julia Alvarez, New York City). . . . "At the **Hostal-Residencia Deljina** on the 4th floor (elevator) of 12 Avenida José Antonio (phone 222-64-23), we had an immaculately clean double room, well furnished, with highly shined floor, private bathroom and shower, but without breakfast, for 1,000 pesetas ($15.15) per night. No English spoken, but the proprietor manages well in German. Highly recommendable" (Mr. and Mrs. Tom Curry, Decatur, Illinois).

ROOMS—THE STARVATION BUDGET: The "first class" pensions (as rated by the Spanish government) of Madrid charge about $5.50 per person for double rooms, and two of the best-located of these, both on the broad Paseo del Prado, a few steps from the Prado and a short walk from the Atocha Station, are the well-furnished and quite lovely **Hostal Residencia Sud America,** 12 Paseo del Prado (phone 239-1634), 700 pesetas for a bathless double; and, in the same building, the simpler, second class **Hostal Residencia Coruña,** 12 Paseo del Prado (phone 239-1434), charging 680 pesetas for a bathless double, 420 pesetas single; owner of the Coruña, Señor Luis Justo, possesses an excellent com-

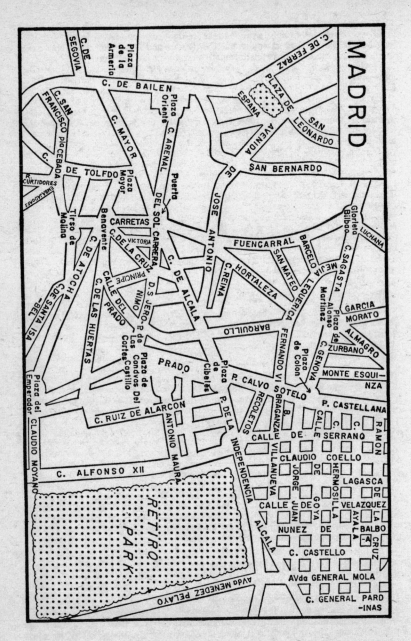

mand of English. He also offers several multi-bedded rooms (4 beds and up), for which the price is only 200 pesetas ($3.06) per person per night! Another building housing three such pensions, on a small sidestreet just off the mid-point of the important Avenida José Antonio, is #6 Calle Concepcion Arenal, where you'll find the **Hostal Concepcion Arenal** (phone 222-6883), the slightly higher-priced (by pennies) **Pension Fenix** (phone 231-4120), and the cheaper **Hostal Regional** (phone 222-6127), at the last-named of which there are free hot showers, as well as the right (gratis) to use the owner's ironing board and iron. Double rooms without bath cost 680 pesetas at the Concepcion, 780 pesetas at the Fenix, 700 pesetas at the Hostal Regional.

Scattered choices, but quite well and centrally located, include the **Hostal-Residencia Monte Jardin,** 10 Calle Jardines (phone 221-2537), small but popular, especially frequented by artists (including a merry group of British pop-singers when last I visited in 1979), and managed by Señor Aurelio Burmudaz, who charges 600 pesetas for a single, 950 pesetas double, nothing for showers. That's almost mid-way between the Puerta del Sol and the Avenida José Antonio; and try, too, **Hostal Residencia Piquio,** 21 Calle San Mateo (phone 445-21-16), a 30-bed pension, impeccably clean, in which all rooms are equipped with shower. 415 pesetas single, 700 pesetas double, and the friendly dueña is Señora Paquita Barba Rodriguez.

The best streets for finding starvation-budget hotels in Madrid (rooms for $5.90 and less, per person) are the **Calle del Principe** (which runs off the Plaza de Canalejas) and the **Calle de Echegaray,** one block away, where you'll discover several such places. Try the Calle del Principe first, and don't be deterred by the entrance appearance of the hotels; such choices as the excellent **Hostal Regional,** 18 Calle del Principe, phone 222-3373 (500 pesetas single, 780 pesetas double) may have an utterly plain stairway "lobby," but many of their rooms face onto the pleasant Plaza St. Ana, around the corner, and although fairly spartan, they're clean and attended by a friendly staff and management.

Student hotels? The most plentiful of the student accommodations are out at University City (Ciudad Universidad), which played such an important role in the Spanish Civil War; take the subway to the Moncloa stop. That's where you'll find the **Colegio Mayor José Antonio** (a well-appointed, 204-bed facility taking both men and women), in a mammoth park, 10 minutes on foot down the Avenida Seneca, from the Moncloa station. Full board ranges from 900 pesetas in a single to 750 pesetas per person in a double. Often full, and you ought first to phone 243-2600. Next door, housing the overflow, is the **Colegio Mayor Hispano Americano Nuestra Señora de Guadalupe,** another modern university residence (built, like the José Antonio residence, in 1954). Phone 243-5200. Since both "Colegios" give preference to long-stay guests, the advice to phone first is more urgent and emphatic than is normally the case.

The official student travel agency in Madrid is **Tive,** at 88 Calle Fernando el Catolico (phone 449-6800), directly opposite the main entrance to the University, and only one block from the Moncloa subway station (buses #'s 61 and 16 also stop just outside). It's open weekdays from 9 to 1:30 and from 4:30 to 6:30, Saturdays from 9 to noon, for information on student charter flights and the like. It also issues the International Student Identity Card, whose cost you'll recoup on your first visit to the Prado—to which I.D. holders are admitted free!

READERS-ON-THE-STARVATION-BUDGET: "I am writing with particular enthusiasm about the **Hostal Residencia Valencia,** 2 Plaza de Oriente (phone 248-7558; subway: Opera), in an unbelievably good location, directly across from the Royal Palace, next to the Opera, and within walking distance of almost everything of interest. The price is 450 pesetas ($6.81) per person (although there are no single rooms) for thoroughly attractive, comfortable and clean accommodations. Very little English is spoken (except by the son of the family), but the proprietors are delightful and helpful, and refer to everyone staying there as their international 'family' " (Prudence Woodford, Chicago, Illinois). . . . "A fabulous little third-floor pension is the **Hostal Sabina,** 2 Calle Duque de Rivas (phone 265-30-84), where my girlfriend and I had a large, clean room for 650 pesetas per night, plus 60 pesetas for a shower. There was hot running water in the rooms, and small balconies that overlooked our street. Manager Mrs. Sanchez spoke only Spanish and French, but we never seemed to have trouble communicating. Location is within walking distance of the Puerta del Sol" (Lorrie R. Williams, Burnaby, British Columbia, Canada). . . . "A pension for women called the **Residencia Femenina Marian,** is ideally located at 13 Calle de Prim (phone 231-5053), just around the corner from the Gijon Restaurant, 1½ blocks from the post office and therefore only a short distance from the Prado. Price per person is 350 pesetas a night. Because of the ideal location and Marian's hospitality, I wouldn't think of staying elsewhere in Madrid. I might add that it's not just a place for students, but that any young woman should find the Residencia more than satisfactory" (Kay E. Weston, Durham, North Carolina). . . . "My real find was a pension for girls in Madrid, the **'Residencia Femenina,'** Fuencarral 107 (phone 445-2107), whose busiest season is in the winter when it is used as a dormitory by girls from all over Spain and from South America who come to Madrid to study. In the summer, it's empty. Price per person is 270 pesetas in a double, 210 in a four-bedded room. A capsule vocabulary knowledge of Spanish is necessary, but there will often be someone there who speaks English and can translate your basic needs" (Leonora Kandiner, University of Pennsylvania, Phila-delphia, Pennsylvania; numerous seconding recommendations from other young ladies; take subway line #1 to Bilbao, three short stops from the Puerta del Sol). . . . "For the three of us—myself, my wife, and our 2½-year-old-son—we paid only 820 pesetas ($12.42) a night at the **Hostal Residencia Carreras,** 18 Calle del Principe (phone 222-0036), in a large room, with unlimited hot showers free" (Tom Webber, Newport Beach, California). . . . "**Hostal Vazquez de Mella,** 1 Plaza Vazquez de Mella (phone 222-3214), is situated in the very center of town, two short blocks from the Gran Via, and charges only 420 pesetas ($6.36) per person per night, plus 70 pesetas for a hot shower" (S.Z., Honolulu, Hawaii). . . . "My starvation budget find in Madrid is the **Hostal Pascual** (phone 228-6375), Calle de las Huertas 20, in a good location, close to the Prado, Puerta del Sol, and American Express. Here I pay 550 pesetas ($8.33) a night for a really clean and bright room with a balcony overlooking the tiny Plaza de Matute. The Señora speaks no English, but is very friendly and helpful, and there is a little T.V. room down the hall. Doubles are also available at 850 pesetas ($12.87). Breakfast is 60 pesetas extra, but no other meals are served. . . . Please mention the night watchmen or "Serenos" of Madrid. There's one of these for each block, and if you arrive home after 10:30 you just clap your hands and he comes and opens the door. A tip of 5 pesetas is customary" (Mark Evrett, Vancouver, B.C., Canada). . . . "By far the best accommodation we encountered through-out Europe was the **Hostal Buelta,** 4 Dr. Drumen (phone 239-98-07); tariff was an unbelievable 830 pesetas for a double room, and location was across the Plaza del Emperador from Atocha railway station, convenient for visits to El Retiro park (directly opposite) and the Prado. The genial manager is keen to show rooms to prospective guests before bookings are confirmed" (George Wilson, Box Hill, Australia; note from AF: Hostal Buelta is ideal for single travellers: of its 112 rooms (on six floors; there's an elevator), 60 are singles selling, in 1980, for 520 pesetas ($7.87); that's without breakfast, but at least your coffee shops around the corner fill the gap).

READERS-ON-THE-SUB-STARVATION-BUDGET: At the **Pension Fé** (phone 226-43-76), you can find a double room for 450 pesetas ($6.81); it's located just two or three blocks off the Alcalá (a principal route in Madrid) on Claudio Coello, on the second floor of a large apartment building—better ask directions. It's very modern and clean and I highly recommend it" (Elaine Mura, Clifton, New Jersey). . . . "An extraordinarily cheap and clean pension lies within 5 minutes of American Express. It's **Huespedes Fucar,** Calle Fucar 6 (phone 230-3418). Friendly owner, shower, immaculate rooms, all for only 300 pesetas ($4.54) per night per person" (Herb Kestenbaum, Maplewood, New Jersey). . . . "I shared a double for only 250 pesetas ($3.78) a night at the **Hostal-Residencia Benamar,** in the heart of the city at 20 Calle de San Mateo (phone 419-0222), and could have had a single for 330 pesetas. A shower or bath located down the hall is free of charge. Large and comfortable, with a pleasant sitting room where you get acquainted with other guests" (Glenn Moses, Georgetown University, Washington, D.C.; strong second from Paul Forchione, Northlake, Illinois, who adds that "the Tribunal station of the metro is just one block from the Benamar, and the important Avenida de José Antonio is within easy walking distance. The extremely friendly and helpful English-speaking proprietor, Mr. Benjamin Viñuela, makes this a pleasurable and convenient place to stay").

RESTAURANTS: Madrid is where you'll discover miracles in the pricing of meals, ranging downwards to a restaurant charging 100 pesetas ($1.51) for a three-course dinner, including service—we've described it further on in this chapter. You'll also encounter a regulation requiring that every restaurant in Madrid offer a fixed price. "Tourist Menu" (also known as the "Menu del Dia") consisting of three courses, bread, wine and service—all at a sum appropriate to the official classification of the restaurant. And for each course served on that meal, there must be at least three available choices (i.e., at least three different appetizers, three different main courses, and so on) carrying no supplement to the fixed price, although other choices can be priced a few pesetas higher.

Such is the proud independence of many Spanish restaurateurs, however, and their dislike of the Menu del Dia rule, that numerous restaurants in Madrid offer an even **lower**-priced meal—called a "cubierto" or a "cubierto de la casa"—which again consists of several courses, but offers no choice within each course. These "cubiertos" are what the budget tourist will seek out. They're found in restaurants that cluster in four particular areas, as follows:

On the Calle del Barco

Currently the best street for budget restaurants in Madrid, the Calle del Barco is found behind the Sepu Department Store, which is on the Avenida José Antonio; from the store, walk down the Calle Gonzalo Jiminez de Quesada, which leads directly to the del Barco. And there you'll find, in quick order, four pleasant and quiet restaurants—the **Restaurant Pagasarri**, at 7 Calle del Barco; the **Restaurant Nuevo Barco**, at 6 Calle del Barco; the **Restaurante Archanda**, at Calle del Barco 8; and the **Restaurant Copatisan** at No. 18—all serving either "cubiertos" or Menus del Dia for 250 to 300 pesetas (that's as little as $3.93 to $4.54 for three courses, beverage and service, remember), and offering à la carte selections for much less. The Pagasarri, for instance, serves a one-egg Tortilla Española (an omelette mixed with potatoes, a Spanish mainstay, but a dish that many Americans don't like) for 70 pesetas ($1.06), a two-egg Tortilla Española for 90 pesetas. The Nuevo Barco serves the thrilling gazpacho (the cold, summer fruit-and-vegetable soup, flavored with garlic, a Spanish classic that you must try at least once) for 80 pesetas on Thursdays and Sundays. All the restaurants also serve "platos combinados"—combined plates, increasingly popular in Madrid, and consisting of large, single-dish meals, with several different items on them for only 70 to 100 pesetas, a high of $1.51. Last summer at the Restaurante Archanda, I had gazpacho (which was thick, creamy and bland, not thin, oily and tart as sometimes is the case in U.S. Spanish-style restaurants), followed by a two-egg tortilla española, with flan for dessert, bread and beer on the side, and my total check, including service, came to 300 pesetas ($4.54).

Across from the Atocha Station

Directly across the wide boulevard from the front of Atocha Station, the **Restaurant La Viña de Atocha**, at 11 Plaza del Emperador Carlos V, charges 300 pesetas for its Tourist Menu, but only 280 pesetas for its "cubierto"—the "cubierto" consisting of soup, roast veal with vegetables, bread, wine, dessert and service charge. Fairly regional in character, and less tourist-oriented than our Calle del Barco choices, this will repay the intrepid tourist who steps inside with a meal entirely typical of Spain. Closed Thursdays. Along the right side of Atocha Station (as you face the front of the station), the **Restaurante El 5 del Paso**, 5 Paseo de las Delicias, is a smaller and more simple place serving a Menu del Dia (three courses) for 300 pesetas ($4.54), while a few steps from the Viña de Atocha, the **Restaurante Estoril**, 9 Glorieta del Emperador Carlos V, offers à la carte dining at prices that total well under 300 pesetas for a full meal. Note how the former establishment—the "5 del Paso"—maintains a "Libro de Reclamaciones" (a complaint book) for recording clients' criticisms, surely a mark of the management's confidence. Closed Wednesdays.

On the Ventura de la Vega

Now you're in the area of American Express. As you walk past AmEx, uphill on San Jeronimo, you'll see a statue of Cervantes in a small square. Behind the statue there begins a street called Calle del Prado. Walk up this street until you pass a sidestreet called "Ventura de la Vega" on your right; here you'll find the largest number of budget restaurants in Madrid, with rates entirely similar to those on the Calle del Barco.

You'll want to stroll along the Ventura de la Vega, comparing menus and interiors. The **Restaurante Bilbaino** at #11 on the street, charges 330 pesetas for its three-course-with-wine Menu del Dia, as does the **Restaurante El Santuario** at #11. And both restaurants offer "platos del dia" (daily specials) at remarkable prices; Spanish omelettes ("tortilla española") for 75 pesetas ($1.13); fish soup for 65 pesetas; string beans with ham (judias verdes) for 70 pesetas; the famous flan dessert for 35 pesetas (53¢). Cheaper still is the **Restaurante Ballestreros** at 6 Ventura de la Vega, whose tourist menu is only 280 pesetas, and which frequently puts on a special "cubierto"—again three courses in size—for only 200 pesetas—a starvation budget wonder! There are at least three other budget finds on the street, including the well-recommended **Restaurante Hylogui** at #3 Ventura de la Vega, the **Restaurante Toscana**, and at #s 12 and 13 the **Casa Ramon** (closed July) and **El Churro**.

For variety, you might also like the **Restaurante La Choza** at 11 Calle Echegaray, one block from the Ventura de la Vega and parallel to it, where a three-course cubierto (but without wine) is 330 pesetas, and a half-bottle of wine sells for exactly 70 pesetas ($1.06). Don't be distressed by the outward appearance of this self-styled "restaurante economico"; push aside the curtains at the door, walk inside, and you'll find a pleasant interior, with a motherly, white-haired cashier at the desk. Sundays for lunch (La Choza is closed on Sunday evenings), you'll receive paella as the main course on the 260-peseta "cubierto". Slightly less expensive, at 3 Calle Echegaray, **La Casono** serves a three-course menu, wine included, for 280 pesetas ($4.24), a daily-changing "plato del dia"—such as fried "calamares" (superb, crispy squid) for 180 pesetas ($2.72).

Behind the Edificio España

Finally, a last major cluster of these "one fork", 280-peseta-charging restaurants is located, rather surprisingly, behind the plush Hotel Plaza and the Plaza de España, at one end of the José Antonio, on the little Calle San Leonardo and the intersecting Calle de San Bernardino. One such is the **Restaurant Veracruz** at 5 Calle San Leonardo, a long, narrow, trattoria-like place that prices its tourist menu at 280 pesetas ($4.24). And there are higher category, but still refreshingly moderate, meals a short block away. If you'll walk that far up the Calle San Leonardo, you'll cross the Calle de San Bernardino; look left (uphill) and you'll see the remarkable **Restaurante Lo-Ma** at 13 Calle de San Bernardino (one of Madrid's very best in the low-cost field); look right (downhill) and you'll spy the **Restaurante Comicay**, at 1 Calle de San Bernardino. At the antiseptically-clean, light and bright Lo-Ma, where waiters out-number guests, a three-course "Menu del Dia" (including wine, bread and service) is 300 pesetas ($4.54), fish soup ("sopa de pescado") is 60 pesetas, and some young things, weak from the heat, have been known to make a meal out of the tomatoes, lettuce and onion salad (60 pesetas). The Moorish-looking Comicay is slightly cheaper, and offers a three-course "menu del dia" for 250 pesetas, all included, a one-egg omelette for 55 pesetas. That's less than 20 yards from an exit of the Plaza de España subway station. At 6 Calle San Bernardino, opposite the Comicay, **Restaurante Aranjuez** serves a good 330-peseta menu, wine included; and, a few yards further down the street, at 5 Calle de los Reyes, you'll pass the simple-but-popular **Taberna Restaurante Reyes**, where you can have a daily menu (three courses, including wine) for a 300-peseta price. Main reason for the popularity of the Reyes is that it offers a large variety of good local wines, 60 pesetas (90¢) for half-a-jug.

SELF-SERVICE MEALS: You may prefer a more quickly-served meal (a rarity in this slow-living town, where residents order several successive courses and spend hours consuming them). Throughout Madrid are restaurants calling themselves "cafeterias"; but they're not—at least in our sense of the word. A "cafeteria" in Spain is more akin to a counter-style snack-bar, and in Madrid some of them seem to combine, in my experience, the worst aspects of American and Spanish "snacks". They're also not particularly inexpensive, and I'd pass them up. Among the few true self-service cafeterias in Madrid, a major establishment which you should visit, is the **Tobogán**, at 1 Calle Mayor, just off the big Puerta del Sol, which many consider to be the center of Madrid. Its sign is almost indistinguishable and it's confusingly situated next door to the Nebraska Cafeteria (i.e., a Spanish non-cafeteria), but it's a phenomenal place inside—clean, air-conditioned, fairly cheap—and fast. Offerings range from cubiertos at 210 pesetas (here taking the form of a single tray on which are three courses and a flask of the Tobogán's own brand of wine) to individual meat-and-vegetable plates at 125 pesetas. Sunday is paella day, when a little iron skillet of the fabulous stuff goes for 120 pesetas. Open from 12:30 to 4 and from 7:30 to 11:30 p.m.; take care lest you choose more plates than you can finish.

THE CHEAPEST RESTAURANT IN THE WORLD: Two short blocks to the side of the Avenida José Antonio (at the end near to the big Plaza Cibeles) is a restaurant-and-bar street called the Calle Barbieri, off which runs the Calle de San Marco. I walked down these streets one year, passed a restaurant sign offering a three-course meal for 100 pesetas ($1.51), walked on a few steps, froze, and suddenly wondered if the work of doing this book had permanently addled my senses. But the **Restaurant El Criollo**, at 21 Calle Barbieri, actually does serve a three-course, meat-for-the-main-course meal for only 100 pesetas ($1.51). Its owner, a determined gentleman named Alejandre Yubero, candidly admits that "mi familia no queria que me dedicase a negocios"—and how right they were! "Cual es el secreto?" (How do you do it?), I asked Sr. Yubero. "Uno sencillo," he answered firmly. "Aprovechar todo" (Very simple, I waste noth-ing). Open daily, except Sunday evening, from 1:30 to 4:30 p.m. for lunch, from 8:15 p.m. to 11 p.m. for dinner.

THE BIG SPLURGE: A restaurant in Madrid where budget-living French tou-rists go, is the **Valencia**, at 44 Avenida José Antonio (one flight up), in the heart of the city. And that's a far better recommendation than mine for the quality of the Spanish food served there. Several different three-course prix fixe menus are offered; I'd take the 400 pesetas ($6.06) "cubierto," although it is possible to eat cheaper, if you are less than ravenously hungry. And for your beverage, I'd pass up the wine in favor of a big pitcher of "sangria"—a milder, iced wine-and-fruit drink—which comes with the cubierto. Lunch is the most carefully-prepared meal of the day; "pechuga valenciana" (a baked chicken dish) is the specialty of the house. Closed Mondays.

A super splurge: for outdoor dining in the summertime, **Restaurante "El Pulpito"** at 9 Plaza Mayor, affords an exciting view of the majestic Plaza Mayor with its 17th century façades, and serves the most typical of Spanish food items, well prepared and flavored, but not in the more expensive fashion of Madrid's best restaurants. Although this is a "Four Fork" restaurant with high à la carte prices, it serves a three-course-and-wine "Menu del Dia" every day (top of the menu) for exactly 700 pesetas ($10.60), service and tax included, and if you'll stay with the set meal—choosing "pechugas en bechamel" (breast of chicken with sauce bechamel) as your main course—you'll be delighted with both the culinary and financial results.

And lastly, in the American Express area, the most popular tourist restaurant of them all—the **Edelweiss** (corner of Calle de Jovellanos and Calle de Zorilla, directly behind the Cortes building) charges 700 pesetas ($10.60) for a three-course meal, wine and service included, consisting mainly of German specialties, but also serves a truncated "tourist menu" of soup, a main dish, bread and a glass of wine for 300 pesetas ($4.54)—you'll want to steer a course between the two price levels. Turn right at the corner as you leave American Express, walk in one block, then up. Best thing about the Edelweiss? It opens for dinner at 7 p.m., much earlier than most other restaurants in Madrid, but is closed Sunday evenings.

(Which reminds me to mention that dining hours in Spain are unusually late: some restaurants in Madrid aren't open until 1:30 or 2 p.m. for lunch, until 8 p.m. or even 8:30 p.m. for dinner.)

READERS' RESTAURANT SELECTIONS: "In my opinion, the restaurant in Madrid that offers the most good food for the least money is the **Restaurante las Arenas,** at Calle de Embajadores at the corner of the Calle de Fray Ceferino Gonzalez (right around the corner from the 'Jumble Market'). For 350 pesetas ($5.30), I received a half-bottle of wine, bread, a small dish of the best paella I've ever had, a main course of steak and french fries, and my choice of any dessert on the regular menu (e.g., an ice cream sundae worth about 45 pesetas). For an extra 40 pesetas, one can have an enormous green salad. In addition, each table has a large pitcher of ice water—a welcome 'extra' on hot Spanish afternoons" (J. David Murphy, Barrie, Ontario, Canada; note from AF: Restaurante las Arenas is open daily except Sunday evenings, from 1 to 4 and 9 to midnight, and several other readers have rhapsodized about owner Elias Ferrero's gazpacho soup for 40 pesetas). . . . "Our find for food is on the Calle Principe #33, and known as the **Restaurante Sevillano.** For a cubierto of 300 pesetas ($4.54), which includes a small bottle of wine, one can have a three-course meal that is tasty substantial and has many choices. First course is one of five kinds of soups, all delicious and thick, second course is either ¼ chicken and salad or fish or meat or paella or a few other things I couldn't translate, and a roll, and for dessert either fresh fruit, a fruit compote, or flan (pudding). The place appears fairly high class, is clean and well-lighted, has nice waitresses, and good paintings on the wall, as well as photographs of bullfighters and Spanish dancers who must be part of somebody's family, and even possesses a television set!" (Duke Shepherd, Santa Ynez, California). . . . "**Terra a Nosa,** at Cava San Miguel 3, is just behind Plaza Mayor, across from the big Mercado. A 330-peseta fixed price dinner is available, but if one watches what the locals eat, a better choice for less can be made from the à la carte menu. The atmosphere is typical and friendly, and the food is delicious. Closed Wednesdays. We came back three times to be able to sample different items from the menu" (Malcolm and Karla Lansky, Los Angeles, California).

CITY TRANSPORTATION: Just as in Rome, you'll have to learn to distinguish a cheap taxi from a costly one: the official, metered cabs have a red band around them, and are surprisingly cheap—30 pesetas (45¢) at the drop of the flag, 20 pesetas for each additional kilometer (⅝ of a mile), 15 pesetas per suitcase, 25 pesetas for entering or leaving a railway station; the entire trip from the Camartin Station to the Plaza Mayor, with a suitcase, and with the one-time railway station charge, will set you back less than 160 pesetas ($2.42). And the trip from Barajas Airport to town, in a real cab, will amount to about 500 pesetas ($7.57).

But—there's another type of cab, without the red band and without meters. If, at the airport, they wave you into one of these (and sometimes, at the airport, you'll have no choice), the charge will run to nearly twice as much, with the same disparity occurring in trips within town as well. Avoid them. At the airport, if there's no red-banded taxi in sight, simply wait for the "Ciudad-Aeropuerto" bus, which costs all of 50 pesetas (75¢) for the trip to the well-located city airlines terminal.

Best of all, learn how to use the easy-to-use subway ("metropolitano") system of Madrid, whose three major lines all converge and cross at the Puerta del Sol. The charge is only 10 pesetas (15¢) one way, 15 pesetas round trip anywhere in town, except on Sundays, when the fee goes up to 15 pesetas (28¢) for a one-way ticket, and there are no reductions on the round-trip fares.

THE TRAIN STATIONS: There are three of them, and it's important you know which cities they service. Largest and most important is **Atocha Station,** which serves key suburban points (Toledo, Aranjuez, Guadalajara), as well as the south (Granada, Valencia, Málaga, Algeciras, Córdoba, Sevilla); it's from here that you take the night express to Portugal, or go onwards to Morocco (via maritime connections). In the northern part of Madrid is the modern **Chamartin Station,** from which trains go to Barcelona and to France (by way of Irún), but also to Bilbao and San Sebastián, and via day express to Portugal, surprisingly enough. From the **Príncipe Pío Station** in the western part of Madrid, trains leave for León, Galicia, Asturias, Santander and Salamanca. . . . Best of the Spanish trains are those called "TALGOS" or "TERS", which follow electrified lines and attain speeds of up to 140 kilometers per hour.

To purchase a ticket on the Spanish Railways, one can go either to the train stations or into the office of any travel agent. For Pullman reservations, go to Wagon-Lits Cook at 23 Alcala. And always obtain advance reservations for all long-distance Spanish trains, even if you possess a Eurailpass and do not need to buy a ticket—on some Spanish trains, persons not possessing a reservation will not be allowed on if there are no seats.

DAYTIME SIGHTSEEING: Toledo and Aranjuez, El Escorial and the Valley of the Fallen, Segovia and La Granja—these cities and sites, all an hour-or-so from Madrid, are what's important in this area of Spain, and each of them can best be reached on do-it-yourself excursions by bus or train, or by renting a car for the day if you're three or more. There's scarcely a valid sightseeing attraction in the world that's limited only to persons on a commercial tour, or that can't be reached simply by means of public transportation—as all of the above can. As one reader recently commented: "Take the public bus from Madrid to Toledo; it's not only money you save, it's the fun and depth of the experience you have. Get a taxi in Toledo to take you to the lookout at the other side of the river and then to drop you off at one of the city gates. Then get lost on your own and you won't soon forget Toledo. The State Tourist brochure is all you need to guide you around the city; the patter of a commercial guide is silly."

Best of the bus stations for Toledo is the **Estacion Sur de Autobuses** at 17 Calle Canarias (subway station is "Palos de Moguer"), from which coaches leave at frequent intervals on the one-hour trip to Toledo, charging 156 pesetas, one-way. Or you can take (for 165 pesetas) the "Ferrobus"—a self-propelled, four-coach electric train—from tracks ("vias") 7, 8, 9, 10 or 11 of the Atocha railroad station, as early as 7:10 or 8:40 a.m.

If you're determined, nevertheless, to take a commercial tour, keep in mind that most of the above attractions are visited both on half-day and full-day excursions, and that often the major difference between the cheaper half-day tour and the costlier full-day tour is that you don't waste endless time, on the former, waiting for lunch in the tourist restaurant (they invariably serve boiled pork on a 95° day) to which the full-day tour takes you; the half-day tour also leaves an hour earlier in the morning, and often covers almost the very same ground as the latter. And finally, if you must take a tour, try **Viajes Marthe** at 9 Calle San Bernardo (corner Avenida José Antonio, same block as Hotel Emperador, phone 248-34-99)—they at least use cheaper, more typical restaurants on their full-day tour, and save you money; they also promise a 10% discount to bearers of this book, including a reduction in that amount on "toros con panoramica," the popular Sunday tour that combines city sightseeing with the late afternoon bull-fight. Viajes Marthe is open weekdays from 9 to 1:30 and 4:30 to 7, Saturdays from 9 to 1:30.

In town, the major sights are of course the **Prado Museum** (see below), the **Royal Palace** (on the Plaza de Oriente, nearest subway stop is Plaza de España), a **bullfight** on late Sunday afternoons (subway is Ventas); and then, secondly, **El Retiro Park**, the **Museum Lazaro Galdiano**, the **Royal Tapestry Factory**, the tiny **Panteon de Goya**, all with normal viewing hours and either free or nominal admission, except for the Royal Palace, which charges 120 pesetas. Most of the above are closed on Sunday afternoons, when it's time to buy that paperback edition of "Death in the Afternoon" and prepare for the bullfight.

THE PRADO: Surely, this is the greatest museum in the world. It is smaller and better arranged than the Louvre; it is far more selective and would never think of accepting the trivia (murals by David) with which the Louvre fills its halls; and it has a greater concentration of masterpieces than even the Uffizi in Florence—works by El Greco, Goya, Velasquez, Titian, Tintoretto, Rubens, Van Dyck, Murillo, Ribera, Breughel—you will reel from the impact of this great art collected in one spot. The Prado is open daily from 10 to 6, Sundays from 10 to 2 only, and charges admission of 50 pesetas. . . . High spot of the museum, in my poor opinion, is the room of sketches by Goya on the first floor, in Room No. LIII, which make fierce, passionate commentaries on the themes of war, death, poverty, tyranny. The Velasquez room (room No. XII) is another indispensable stop. . . . For lunch-time visitors, the Prado maintains a courtyard buffet restaurant (open every day except Sunday) next to its room of Breughels, with sandwiches for 90 pesetas, and a particularly-popular 250-peseta meal: soup, a beefsteak with fried egg and mushrooms, and dessert. Closed at this moment for repairs, the Prado restaurant plans to re-open in mid-1980. . . . Schedule the Prado for the beginning of your Madrid stay; you'll want to shoot yourself if you find only a few hours available for this profound experience at the end of your visit.

BULLFIGHTS: They're presented in the famous **Plaza de Toros** of Madrid every Sunday and on holidays from Easter Sunday till the end of October, beginning late in the afternoon—often as late as 6 p.m. Tickets can be obtained either through your hotel (usually) or by going directly to the mid-town ticket center for the bullfights, at 3 Calle de la Victoria (just off the Puerta del Sol; walk one short block up the Carrera de San Jeronimo, and then turn right on Victoria), which is open on Saturdays from 10 to 1 and from 5 to 9, and on Sundays (the day of the fights) from 10 to 5. Tickets for normal fights—that is, those not involving the most celebrated matadors—start as low as 180 pesetas for the worst "sol" (in the sunlight) seats, ascend to a high of 900 pesetas for the best "sombra" (in the shadow) locations, and it's my recommendation that you buy the 350-peseta variety ("tendidos bajos, filas 1-14, sombra") which are perfectly adequate, and will cost you 400 pesetas when the ticket broker's 15% fee is added on. The subway station for the Plaza de Toros is Ventas, seven stops from the Puerta del Sol.

When you arrive at the ring, be sure to rent a leather cushion (only 10 pesetas) from the vendors under the stands—that's to place on the concrete seats. If you don't you'll wish you had! And to get back to town after the "fights" are over (when every cab is taken), simply walk into the subway on the corner of the Plaza de Toros, and take the first train that comes along to the Puerta del Sol stop; you're thus back in the center of everything.

If there isn't a bullfight during the days of your stay in Madrid, then at least visit the bullfight museum ("Museo Taurino") next to the rear entrance of the Plaza de Toros arena. Here, memorabilia of the great bullfighter, Manolete, are revered like religious relics. And by looking down from the inside windows on the second floor, you can see the open-air stables where black bulls stand or lie on sawdust and straw, stoically awaiting their performance and last glorious moments. Open Monday through Saturday from 10 a.m. to 1 p.m. and from 3:30 to 6 p.m., for a 10-peseta admission fee.

For non-violent sightseeing, here, now, is Hope:

HOPE IN MADRID: "The spirit of Madrid is elusive. And filled with contradictions. And not what one expects. Perhaps because our heads are filled with dreams of castles in Spain, we come to Madrid expecting an immediate impact transporting us into passionate, mantillas-to-the-wind, roses-between-the-teeth, sunny Iberia! Instead, on a first glimpse of Madrid, one is disappointed to find a bustling, 'moderne' city—a lingering flavor of the 20's and 30's in decay—with broad boulevards, chunky stone monuments, and tall buildings.

"Ernest Hemingway rushed to the defense of Madrid in his classic work on bullfighting, 'Death in the Afternoon' (as he also did during the Spanish Civil War). He acknowledges that Madrid has been accused of being the 'least Spanish' of all the cities of Spain. But he proclaims that since Madrid is a large melting pot for all of Spain, and offers the visitor a variety of life-styles to observe and enjoy, it is actually the **most** Spanish of cities.

"I can only recommend that you relax and let the Spain in Madrid unfold itself to you bit by bit.

Sightseeing in Madrid

"Go to **The Prado** first. It's the most important gallery in Madrid, the city's 'number one' sightseeing attraction. If you can spend a couple of days there, you're to be envied.

"The second most interesting 'sight,' in my view, is the **Plaza Mayor**, a large formal 17th century square built by Philip III, whose cobblestones have seen bullfights, tournaments, and the most severe punishments of the Spanish Inquisition. Today, you'll find shops, markets, restaurants, outdoor musicales on summer evenings, and the most intriguing surrounding neighborhood in all of Madrid for wandering and explorations.

The Outskirts

"Before probing Madrid in any greater depth, take the more important excursions outside the city (by bus or train). An hour out of Madrid, and a real must, is El Greco's town—Toledo—looking exactly as he painted it. Once there, try to see the **Cathedral; El Greco's House and Museum;** the **Tránsito Synagogue;** the **Church of Santo Tomé; Museum of Santa Cruz;** the **Alcázar;** and more (hours mostly from 10 to 2 and 3:30 to 7, admission of 45 pesetas per visit, except at Santa Cruz where it's 50 pesetas). . . . And then, you won't want to miss **El Escorial**, Philip II's 16th century monastic retreat—an enormous, square, granite pile of stones, quite accurately described by all who see it as 'the penal institution.' Nonetheless, there's a famous library here, as well as important collections of paintings and tapestries; the Royal Pantheon; the King's Apartments; the Church; the Prince's Cottage; and again much more—depending on your time and durability. An all-inclusive ticket costs 125 pesetas, and the hours are from 10 to 1 and 3:30 to 6:30. . . . Further from Madrid (and well worth the trip) is the typically Castilian town of **Segovia**. There, among many treasures, the outstanding sights are the splendid, eerie, almost perfectly preserved **Roman Aqueduct** (which is still in use!), and the **Alcázar,** a pink-shimmering, real fairyland castle in the clouds. Begun in the 11th century and added to by each succeeding generation, this has, among several layers of history, the Throne Room where Isabella was proclaimed Queen of Castile, a chapel, and adjacent 'retablo' with 15th century decorations. Open daily from 10:30 until sun-down for a 25-peseta entrance fee. . . . But as far as I'm concerned, and unless you've a taste for the macabre, you can skip that 'eighth wonder of the world,' the **Valle de los Caídos** (Valley of the Fallen), a monument to the dead of the Spanish Civil War, and burial place of Spain's long-time dictator, Generalissimo Franco, as well as of José Antonio, father of the Falangist Party. Essentially, this is a huge cathedral carved into the center of a mountain, and a monumental bore.

Back in Town—El Retiro

"If you're spending a great deal of time at The Prado, you may feel the need for an occasional respite from paintings, and you can easily take a welcome breather at **El Retiro**, Madrid's beautiful green-tree park (entrance on Calle de Alfonso XII, two blocks, uphill, directly behind the Prado). During spring and summer, you can boat for 50 pesetas an hour on the little lake, perhaps catch an open-air concert, or visit the Rose Garden. Entrance to the park is free and it's open from 7 a.m. to 7 p.m., summers til 9, with one section remaining open til 2 a.m.

The Royal Palace

"The **Palacio Real** (built on the site of the old Alcázar Real; sometimes referred to as the 'Palacio de Oriente' and located on Plaza de Oriente, nearest subway stop is Plaza de España), begun around two hundred years ago, but completed only a hundred years ago, is no less lavish because of its relative youth. Conceived on a grand scale, it has some 2,800 rooms! But you will probably walk through only 50 of them if you take the combination Palace and Private Apartments Tour for 120 pesetas (a 155-peseta entrance fee includes a visit to the adjoining gallery of Gothic tapestries—a rich collection from the 15th and 16th centuries). The Private Apartments here are every bit as ornate as the Palace proper. In the private Royal Chapel, a focal point is a glass case displaying what appears to be a strange over-sized doll. Actually, it's bones of a Roman Christian Martyr (St. Felix), wrapped in wax and silk and made to look like a small person (a gift to Queen Isabella II from the Pope).

"If you're so inclined, you can also tour the antique **Royal Library,** with over 300,000 books (impressive-looking in mahogany, with priceless early 15th century books, rich book bindings; engravings; Queen Isabella's prayer book; rare manuscripts); **The Museum of Coins and Musical Instruments**—including five violins by Stradivarius made for the Spanish Court (admission is 50 pesetas); the **Royal Pharmacy** (with 18th century documents and pieces on display; this pharmacy serviced the royal family: admission, 25 pesetas); the **Royal Armory** (an interesting collection which ranges from the 15th to the 18th century, all pieces belonging to Spanish monarchs; Charles V's armor, ornate saddles, bows, guns, etc., children's armor—to get the little tykes accustomed to the weight of war: admission 25 pesetas); and finally, through a lovely, cool, green garden, in Campo del Moro (directly behind the Palace), **The Carriage Museum** (antique carriages and harness: entrance, 50 pesetas). The Royal Palace is open from 10 to 1:30 and 4 to 6:15, Sundays from 10 to 1:30; a 255-peseta ticket admits you to everything, but that's quite a lot to see.

Lázaro Galdiano Museum

"Very much out of the way (at Calle de Serrano 122—from Puerta del Sol take bus #51), but a perfect little gem of a museum, is the **Museo Lázaro Galdiano,** open daily from 9:15 to 1:45; admission is 10 pesetas, Sundays 5 pesetas. Housed in a small mansion, its four floors and 30 odd rooms are chock full of treasure—objets d'art, furniture, paintings, all vying for your attention. For instance, on the first floor there are small art objects and ecclesiastical art from all over the world (Spanish altar pieces, Maltese crosses), gold, silver and glassware; cases of charming antique jewelry (medieval, Renaissance and baroque); Celtic and Iberian pre-historic bronze pieces, as well as Roman and medieval bronzes. And to top off the ground floor, there is, tucked casually in a corner (on your right at the end of the floor, off a room with mini-copies of Roman statuary) in a green velvet niche, a portrait by Leonardo da Vinci of a winsomely sad young lady—the Gioconda in reverse. I now suggest you take the elevator to the top floor (4th, that is) and work your way down. Along the route you'll see famed tapestries and textiles (some pieces from the 15th and 16th centuries), embroidered ecclesiastical robes, a display of fans, collections of weapons and armor, pottery, clocks, ornate and interesting furniture, paintings by Bosch, Dürer, Memling, Rembrandt, Van der Meer, Breughel, Van Dyck, El Greco, Velásquez, Lucas Cranach, and a room-full of Goyas. And my listing of what's to be seen here is by no means complete!

The Royal Tapestry Factory

"The **Real Fábrica de Tapices,** at Fuenterrabía 2 (in the neighborhood of the Atocha Railway Station) is a fully operational tapestry-making plant (of the highest order), which still uses antique hand looms from the mid-eighteenth century. You'll tour the factory and be given a complete demonstration of how tapestries are made; the employees are quite accustomed to being interrupted by rubber-neckers and seem to take great pride in showing off various stitches, and happily gossiping about the wealthy buyers of their current work. It is, in sum, a jolly tour (more so if you speak Spanish), and available to you weekdays only from 9:30 to 12:30 for an admission fee of only 15 pesetas. But closed on Sundays and the entire month of August.

The Army Museum

"Just a few blocks from The Prado, at Méndez Núñez 1, is the **Museo Del Ejercito,** which is open from 10 to 2 every day except Monday for a too high 50-peseta entrance fee; children under 14 are admitted free of charge. Located in a former royal palace (built during King Felipe IV's reign—the frescoed ceilings inside were designed by Velásquez), this long red-brick building is immediately recognizable as an Army Museum—the porch is littered with dozens of cannons. At the door, there's a model of the Alcázar of Toledo showing the damage it sustained during the Spanish Civil War. Inside, the museum contains well-displayed exhibits of uniforms, armor, flags, medals, coins, guns, swords (including those of Boabdil, the last Moorish king of Granada; El Cid Campeador; and one attributed to Cervantes), etc.; a vast collection of historical objects from all eras, up to the Civil War. Of special interest to me is the room dedicated to historical mementos of the age of Spanish Colonization (including Pizarro's flag), a Moorish-style campaign tent of Carlos V, and a letter signed by Admiral Nelson; the tiny uniforms for royal infants; the model of Madrid under seige during the Civil War; and (downstairs) a room devoted to military medicine, and another to the Civil Guard, with a gruesome album of pictures supposedly honoring the National Guard.

The Pantheon of Goya

"In an isolated, somewhat difficult to find spot (beyond the North Station on Paseo de la Florida) is the **Panteón de Goya** in the **Ermita San Antonio de la Florida,** a tiny church which is the burial place of the artist and contains a famous and very fine ceiling fresco by him, painted on the dome of the church. It's worth a visit if you have the time, but don't be confused by the identical church across the street which is used for services. The church you're looking for is on your right, and is exclusively a memorial to Goya. Open daily except Wednesdays from 11 to 1:30 and 3 to 6, Sundays 11 to 1:30 (winters from 10), and the entrance fee is 25 pesetas.

The Convent of Las Descalzas Reales

"Would a 'Royal Nunnery' interest you? Then go to the **Museum of the Convento-Monasterio de las Descalzas Reales,** located on the Plaza de las Descalzas (off the Avenida José Antonio's Plaza de Callao—take the small street called Postigo de San Martin; the Convent's to your left), open daily from 10:30 to 1:30, and Monday through Thursday afternoons from 4 to 6, for a 50-peseta entrance fee. This medieval (15th century) mansion which was turned into a convent by Princess Juana of Austria in the 16th century, was always closely associated with the Palace (as a royal retreat), and aristocratic ladies who were so inclined, took the veil here. Since it is still a working convent (of the very strict Franciscan Clarissas Order), you must wait for a guide to take you through. The old building itself is interesting, with a magnificent frescoed hall and staircase (the beginning of the ancient palace). Inside you'll see priceless antique tapestries (two rooms contain 'El Triunfo de la Eucaristía,' made from cartoons by Rubens), priests' robes and vestments gorgeously embroidered with gold thread and jewels (like matadors' capes), a small art gallery which includes Flemish primitives, a Breughel, a Titian, and a Caravaggio, as well as 15th and 16th century sacred and religious relics.

The Cerralbo Museum

"This is not an 'important' museum, but it possesses a certain charm and gives you a peep into the inner sanctum of the Spanish nobility in days of yore. The mansion, located at 17 Ventura Rodriguez (behind the Plaza de España), was built during the last half of the 19th century, and the house with its collections was donated to the state by the last childless Marquis of Cerralbo. The collection includes some good paintings and drawings: an El Greco (in the home's private chapel), other works by Ribera, Zurbarán, Veronese, Titian, Tintoretto, Tiepolo, Van Dyck (one or two works from each); an upstairs gallery of the family's armor; and porcelain and china. But the real interest remains the house itself; though somewhat faded now, it's still like a miniature, but very homey, palace. These nobles provided themselves with a billiards room, a beautiful library, and their own little ballroom, with a special balcony for the orchestra and a gilded ceiling decorated with cupids. You'll find murals and ceiling frescoes in many of the larger, more public salons, but even in the cozier family-only rooms the decor is rich and elaborate running to garish (note, for the latter quality, the Venetian chandelier in the music room downstairs). Open daily, except Tuesday, from 9 to 2, for an entrance fee of 50 pesetas. Closed during the month of August.

Recent Additions

"Recently re-opened after extensive renovations, the **Museo Nacional de Artes Decorativas** at Montalbán 12, off the Plaza de las Cibeles (walk past the Post Office, then left), offers a rich collection of ceramics, furniture, and other decorative art objects from all the regions of Spain, displayed in 62 rooms ranging over 5 floors; exhibits are organized chronologically (as far as possible), so that each floor (starting with the second) represents a different century—one can practically trace the history of furniture in Spain. Among many riches (including examples of pre-Christian glass) on the ground floor, Room 8, a chapel with leather tapestries and an elaborately worked leather altar, is a knock-out; on the next floor, in Rooms 12, 13, and 14, ceilings and arches are Gothic with a distinctly Moorish influence, and there are large tapestries, delicately carved statutes, beautifully worked chests. Upstairs again, one finds **the** most Baroque bed, two types of 17th century kitchens, an 18th century collection of dolls and dolls' houses, a room-full of fans, opera glasses and walking sticks, and much more to intrigue and delight you. Leave enough time to enjoy it. Open daily except Monday, Thursday and Friday from 10 to 2, for a 50-peseta entrance fee. . . . A few years back, Madrid opened its new **Zoo** at Casa de Campo, and it's a beauty, one of the most modern, well organized, attractive Zoos I've seen. It's divided by continents, and currently on display is wildlife (2,500 animals) from Africa, Europe, and China (including two pandas presented to Spain upon the occasion of the King's visit to Peking in 1978). Most animals are in the open (without cages), separated from the public by moats, and children are permitted to pet the accessible ones (like the little beavers romping on the grass). To get to the Zoo, take the Metro to the Batan Station, and exit at the right side for the Parque, then bear left for the healthy walk to the Zoo; or take the bus (Linea 33, cost 16 pesetas), which you can pick up at Plaza de España directly to the Zoo. Hours are from 10 to sunset, and admission is 150 pesetas, 75 pesetas for children up to 8 years, free for those under 3. . . . Madrid's newest attraction is the Museo de Cera Colón (The Wax Museum), on an underground floor of the new modern sky-scraper ('Centro Colón') on Plaza Colón, open daily from 10:30 to 1:30 and 4 to 8:30. While admission charges, at 200 pesetas for adults and 100 pesetas for children, are overly high, the museum is tremendous fun. There are interesting historical tableaux (some with films); wax representations of distinguished people in the arts (Cervantes is the feature of a wonderful panorama of scenes from Don Quixote, accompanied by music from 'La Mancha'), sciences, sports (bull-fighters receive special treatment with a slide-show and a grisly representation of the hospital room in which Manolete died); a collection of the famous and the infamous. Some of the living come off not so well (Taylor and Burton look terrible, as do Churchill and Kennedy), but there are so many good tricks—a room of mirrors, magic and monsters; Anthony Quinn 'breathing' (look for him on a bed, covered with a Mexican blanket, right behind Golda Meir!); Rasputin pushing open a door; and a wax guard planted next to one of the exhibits (I won't tell where), who looks so alive you feel he's about to tell you not to touch.

Miscellany

"All galleries pale in the aura of The Prado. But, if you're in Madrid for some time, you might want to look in on the **Museo Real Academia de Bellas Artes de San Fernando.** Located at 13 Alcalá (the broad boulevard between Puerta del Sol and the Plaza de las Cibeles), this rather badly-lit museum contains Spanish painters from every era (some non-Spaniards as well: Van Dyck, Correggio, Bellini, Rubens' 'Susannah and The Elders'), including Ve-lázquez, Murillo, Sorollo, Vincente Lopez, Ribera and Zurbarán, and is, for the most part, not really a first rate collection. One star attraction, however, is a fine room full of Goyas (the first room you'll see), including his famous festival scene 'El Entierro de la Sardina.' The museum is ordinarily open daily except Sundays, from 10 to 2, for an entrance fee of 25 pesetas (Sundays, 7 pesetas, and free on Saturday afternoons). . . . A once-important "complex of museums' at 20 Paseo de Calvo Sotelo (right off Plaza de Colón) has now been dispersed: 19th century art is currently displayed at **Cason del Buen Retiro** (located near the Prado, open from 10 to 2 and 5 to 8, weekdays, until 8 Saturdays, Sundays 10 to 2, for a 25-peseta entrance fee—but not a very interesting collection). The **Spanish Museum of Contemporary Art** (open weekdays except Mondays, from 10 to 6 and 10 to 2 on weekends, for an entrance fee of 50 pesetas) is currently housed in a modern glass and steel building at Ciudad Universitario (look for the black tower) displaying paintings, sculptures, designs and other works of contemporary Spanish artists. The **Museo de America,** also on the university campus, deals with the civilizations of the people of the Americas, including the Philippines, who were touched by Spanish colonization; open daily except Mondays from 10 to 2, for a 50 peseta entrance fee—but not really worth the excursion at present, unless you'd like to see University City; nearest Metro is Moncloa. The museum at 20 Paseo de Calvo Sotelo is open now only for special exhibitions (usually quite good), from 10 to 2 and 5 to 9, Sundays til 2, for a 25 peseta entrance fee, but on the other side of the building is the **Archaeological Museum** (at Serrano 13, open from 9:30 to 1:30, and charging 50 pesetas), which has been redecorated and where the exhibits are now so attractively displayed, that a visit becomes not only intellectually stimulating, but a real treat. The collection ranges over pre-historic and ancient to medieval times: Greek and Roman displays, ancient Iberian sculptures, 10th century bronze pieces; a 12th century choir stall; tapestries, furniture and church trappings from the 15th and 16th centuries; Visigothic jewelry, including a gorgeous crown from the 7th century; and a small masterpiece sculptured in ivory, the Fernando Crucifix (Isidoro de Leon, 1063). If you can't get to Altamira, you can see a reproduction here of the important 15,000-year-old Altamira cave paintings (viewed via an entrance in the garden to the left of the main gate). Your 50-peseta ticket will also admit you to the Altamira Pinturas, provided you use it immediately; otherwise you'll pay an additional 10 peseta entrance fee. Tip: once inside the cave, sit down—you'll see better.

"Don't, by the way, waste any time at the **Romantic Museum,** in Madrid, an impressive building, filled only with Victorian knickknacks and furniture à la Español."

READERS' DAYTIME SUGGESTIONS: "On an August day, nothing beats a trip to the pool. A fantastically large, inexpensive one (85 pesetas per person) is found at the **Parque Sindical.** Take the metro to Moncloa, where tickets are sold for the bus trip to the park, which also features other sports facilities and serves inexpensive refreshments" (Jill and Randy Freese, Erie, Pennsylvania). . . . "On my last trip, I found an inexpensive way to go to **El Escorial.** First, take the Madrid subway (10 pesetas) to the Atocha Station. Trains leave for El Escorial nearly every hour and the travel time is one hour. All trains carry uniformly priced coaches, and the fare roundtrip is 196 pesetas. At the station one can take a bus for 16 pesetas or walk to Escorial and see Phillip II's cottage en route. An entrance ticket for all the places of interest may be purchased for 40 pesetas. A side trip by local bus to The Valley of the Fallen can then easily be arranged in El Escorial, but leave Madrid early to do all of this in a day" (Edward J. Walsh, Riverdale, New York). . . . "We spent a couple of pleasant days in Madrid cooling off at the **Casa de Campo** municipal swimming pool, which costs 100 pesetas for the whole day and is a great way to meet young Spaniards. Just take the Metro to the El Lago stop" (Muriel Feiner, Brooklyn, N.Y.). . . . "Don't miss the **Archaeological Museum.** Its Roman mosaics, prehistoric cave paintings and Visigoth crowns are among the finest in the world" (Dr. James Gould, Tampa, Florida). . . . "So pleased were we with the directions for going to El Escorial via public transportation that we found our way to **Toledo** the same way! As we do not speak Spanish, we had someone write down our destination and off we went to the railway station with paper in hand, bought our tickets and took the train. After a day in Toledo we found there is a bus that runs back to Madrid every hour, and with great ease we took the public bus back. We had a grand day travelling with Spanish families and we were amazed that it was so very much cheaper than taking a "tourist tour" for the day . . . and I might add, more enjoyable" (Anne Brown, Port Washington, New York). . . . "Here is an easy and economical way to get to Toledo from Madrid. Just take the Southbound No. 3 "Metro" Subway to the Palos de Moguer stop (third stop beyond Puerta del Sol), where you'll find an exit going directly into the bus station. Step to Window 24 where for 312 pesetas you can buy a round-trip bus ticket to Toledo. Summertime, there is a 12 noon bus leaving Madrid for the one-hour ride, giving you five full hours in Toledo before catching the bus which leaves Toledo at 6 p.m. for Madrid" (Raymond Holbrook, Dallas, Texas). . . . "When I visited Toledo, I looked at the train schedule. One train left for Madrid at 6:45 p.m., the last departed at 8:20 and was marked "Fiesta". This meant that the train travelled at this time only on Sundays and holidays. Because of this quixotic labeling, I missed my train to Madrid. The day that this mishap occurred was August 14, the event of the Assumption, which is Toledo's special holiday. As the hotels were filled, I wandered about all night long, and I left at 6:35 a.m. On one of the pages of your book, a reader says, '. . . Then get lost on your own and you soon won't forget Toledo.' I did just that, perhaps more so than this reader had intended" (Charles W. McDonald, Memphis, Tennessee). . . . "A one-day trip to Toledo has to be planned very carefully from the time standpoint. The 9 a.m. bus arrives at 10:30 a.m., and you must then immediately proceed to the cathedral, for it closes at 1 p.m. and does not re-open till 4 p.m. The last bus to Madrid leaves at 7 p.m. From the bus station near the Atocha Railroad Station, the buses leave at 9 a.m., 12, 3:30, 6, 7, and 8 p.m. going. Apply at ticket window Number 12; there are dozens of windows with no labels, and if you wait in line at the wrong window you will miss the 9 a.m. bus. . . . In Toledo don't get off at the bottom of the hill where the walls are. Stay on to the last stop at the Alcazar. . . . Spend the morning at the Cathedral—one of the great treasure houses of Christianity. It will take all your time until 1 p.m. Then, after lunch, get down to the Church of Santo Tome, where El Greco's greatest painting. "The Burial of the Count of Orgaz," is on view (a terrific experience). Do not go to El Greco's so-called house, for it is a terrible disappointment. Head along the street by San Tome below near the river to the Synagogue of El Transito, which has been beautifully restored. Next, rush to the Museum of Santa Cruz, which is across from the Alcazar, before it closes. Then go to the bus station by the Alcazar to catch the 7 p.m. bus" (Lester B. Bridaham, Denver, Colorado).

THE NIGHTLIFE OF MADRID: Flamenco dancing—that and bullfighting are the two major art forms of Spain, as far as I'm concerned, and the "tablaos" of Madrid (the flamenco nightclubs) can keep me rooted to the spot for hours. To attend a "tablao" requires only the purchase of a single drink, which you can nurse all evening, but the drink, quite naturally, comes high; 700 pesetas ($10.60) at the **Torre Bermejas** on the Mesonero Romanos (just off the Avenida José Antonio); 600 pesetas at the **Villa Rosa**, 15 Plaza Santa Ana, or at the **Arco de Cuchilleros**, 7 Cuchilleros, at the bottom of the steps leading to the Plaza Mayor, and directly across the street from our recommended budget lodging at the Hostal La Macarena. At all of these, the show is a near-continuous one (from 10:30 p.m. to 3 a.m.), and you ought not to feel distressed if a singer is performing at the moment of your entrance—the foot-stomping dancers will come on soon.

If the flamenco clubs are still too costly for your budget, you might be able to see a bit of flamenco at one of the two major music halls of Madrid (usually, but not always, presenting an evening of variety acts—be sure to check). These are the **Teatro de la Zarzuela**, at 2 Jovellanos, a block behind American Express (where most seats range from 100 to 300 pesetas, with only a few choice orchestra locations costing 300, 480 and more), and the **Teatro Calderon** at 18 Atocha (where most seats are 200 to 300 pesetas). At both, shows go on twice nightly, at 7 and 10:30 p.m.

And if it's Saturday night when you're in Madrid, inquire about the possible scheduling of a special Saturday evening (11 p.m.) bullfight (by apprentice matadors) at the Plaza de Toros. That's become an important new evening activity in Madrid, although some Madrileños are so repelled by the awkwardness of most apprentice bullfighters that they do all possible to prevent publicity about these fights. The seats, in any event, are cheaper than for Sunday afternoon corridas, and kids under 14 years of age are permitted to attend—the only time when they can.

MADRID'S TIVOLI: Just recently, Madrid opened its answer to Copenhagen's Tivoli and Los Angeles' Disneyland, and—can you believe it?—they've come up with an entertainment that quite respectably compares. The **Parque de Atraciones**, in the Casa de Campo, is a combination carnival-park, pleasure-garden, World's Fair and restaurant-dancehall complex, that has quickly become a nighttime must on a visit to Madrid. A 25-peseta entrance fee (15 pesetas for children), admits you to the festival grounds laced with Venetian-type canals—a park area where it's cool on even the hottest of nights—and 25 pesetas is the charge for most of the rides, which are creative and unique. From the Plaza de España, take the suburban subway to Batan, and from there it's but a short stroll to the Parque.

DISCOS AND TASCAS: Yes, traditional Madrid has the more modern form of nighttime entertainment, too. Sophisticated discotheques for Madrileños in their early 20s: the **Victor III Club** on the 3rd floor of the Hotel Sanvy (first drink charge to men is 180 pesetas weekdays, 300 to 350 pesetas weekends; women pay half); the ultra-slick **Piko's** at 43 Avenida José Antonio, which charges 375 pesetas per drink on most weekday evenings but only 170 or 190 at "matinees"; **J.J.** (pronounced Hota-Hota), a noisy stroboscopic, Electric Circus type place, whose entrance is alongside the movie theatre at 44 Avenida José Antonio, opposite the Galerias Preciados department store. . . . Early evening (7 to 10 p.m.) entertainment in Madrid is primarily devoted to "tasca-hopping"—making the rounds of one bar (tasca) after another to sample "tapas" (tid-bits and hors d'oeuvres), washed down by "chatos" (small glasses) of wine (12 pesetas per glass). The Plaza St. Ana is one area for tascas, as is the Calle Echegaray and the Calle Barbieri, the latter the location of the largest and best tasca I've found: **Valderas** (1 Calle Barbieri, corner of Calle de las Infantas), which has a 10-yard-long bar lined with exotic tapas. Unless you choose the varieties involving fresh shrimp, most tapas should cost you no more than a few pesetas.

MORE NIGHTLIFE IN MADRID: We should expand a bit on **Teatro Calderon,** 18 Atocha, which charges as little as 200 (and up to 400) pesetas for seats; it's the variety music hall of the working folk of Madrid, with pop singers, acrobats, spicy skits that are not for children. **La Latina,** at 2 Plaza de la Cebada, is somewhat similar, and charges 150 to 350 pesetas for seats. . . . Most of the film theatres of Madrid are dreary places showing hackneyed, Latin-American comedies, but one—the **Cine Bellas Artes,** next door to the Teatro Bellas Artes on the Calle del Marques del Marques de Casa Riera, which is just off the downhill end of the Avenida José Antonio—shines forth like a diamond among the dross, showing films by Losey, Kurosawa, Truffaut, Schlesinger, and attracting Madrid's brightest set, who line up as early as 3:30 p.m. to see the day's feature that begins at 4 p.m. Seats ("butacas") are 150 pesetas, and just as on New York's Third Avenue, the lines are almost as interesting as the films.

MADRID MISCELLANY: Recommended parking place for your car: the underground "Estacionamiento de Coches" at **Plaza de las Descalzas,** which charges 250 pesetas ($3.78) for 24 hours, 40 pesetas for one hour; a similar establishment in **Plaza Santo Domingo** (look for a large "P" on a blue-background sign) charges about the same. . . . The real Madrid, where streets look like Spanish streets are supposed to look, is located behind the Plaza Mayor, and a daytime stroll there can be fascinating. From one corner of the Plaza Mayor, walk down the steps into Cuchilleros (tourist Madrid), walk to the end of Cuchilleros into the ancient street called Cava Baja, then walk to the end of the Cava Baja and you'll find the Mercado (Market) de la Cebada (fresh fish, rabbits, much exotica) and next to it, the Piscina de la Latina, a 75 peseta swimming pool. If this ten-minute stroll is too much of a chore, then at least walk from another end of the Plaza Mayor along the Cava de San Miguel, which at night resembles a set from Carmen. . . . When in doubt, order "pechuga", the famous breaded breast of chicken dish of Madrid, always tasty, or "merluza" (hake), the always fresh, always inexpensive and popular fish specialty of Spain. . . . Open seven days a week until midnight, the **OK Drugstore** at 25 Avenida José Antonio, corner of the Calle de la Montera, carries everything a tourist needs (newspapers, books, toothpaste, aspirins, batteries). . . . Across the street, at 3 Calle Fuencarral (look for the tall building with the clock and antennas), the **International Telephone Office,** open daily from 9 a.m. to 2 p.m. and from 4 to 10 p.m., charges 1,200 pesetas ($18.18) for a three-minute call to New York. . . . A cheap and almost-constantly-open laundromat: the **Lavomatique** at 19 Calle Manuela Malasana, off the Calle Fuencarral. It operates seven days a week from 8 a.m. to 10 p.m., and charges only 95 pesetas for 4-½ kilos washed and dried. . . . A life-saving tip: don't assume that Madrid's taxi drivers will stop for traffic lights. Look, and await an absence of traffic, before you cross the street. . . . The indispensable Sunday morning visit (9 a.m. to 2 p.m.): to the famous flea market of Madrid (**"El Rastro"**). Take the subway to Tirso de Molina, then walk to Plaza de Cascorro. . . . As earlier noted, **Tive,** 88 Calle de Fernando El Catolico, one short block from the Moncloa subway stop, and open from 9 to 1:30 and 4:30 to 6:30 only, is the official student travel agency of Madrid. It concentrates on student charter flights and trains, but occasionally assists with accommodations and sells city sightseeing tours at a discount. . . . Madrid's newspaper of entertainment activities and attractions is a tiny little weekly called **Guia del Ocio,** (20 pesetas), but I prefer to use one of the two major daily newspapers: **Ya,** or better yet **ABC,** whose listings are extensive and designate the non-dubbed films with the initials "V.O." . . . Swimming pools throughout Madrid charge as little as 50 to 100 pesetas, but an outlay of 650 pesetas ($9.86) will entitle you not simply to admission, but also to unlimited buffet snacks and unlimited wine, at the swank roof-top pool (open June to September, daily from 11 a.m. to 7:30 p.m.) of the **Hotel Emperador** in the heart of the city at 53 Avenida José Antonio (take the self-service elevator to "Piscina"). A fine pool, which provides an added sociological insight into how Madrid's upper crust spend their day; how you'll react is up to you.

Where to from Madrid? There are at least one hundred other good towns from which to make your choice—all briefly described in the next chapter.

A REMINDER: Several thousands of the readers of this book are now members of a unique travel "co-operative," the **$15-a-Day Travel Club.** Because other readers have said they missed seeing the description of the club appearing in Chapter II, we've decided to repeat the description here, just ahead of our "Tale of Many Cities" chapter that virtually all readers consult. **$15-a-Day Travel Club,** which has gone into its 16th successful year.

The Club was formed at the urging of numerous readers of the $$$-a-Day and Dollarwise Guides, who felt that such an organization could provide continuing travel information and a sense of community to budget-minded travelers in all parts of the world. And so it does!

In keeping with the budget concept, the membership fee is low and is immediately exceeded by the value of your benefits. Upon receipt of $10 (U.S. residents), $12 (Canadian and Mexican residents), or $14 (other foreign residents) in U.S. currency, to cover one year's membership, we shall send all new members, by return mail (book rate), the following items:

(1) The latest edition of *any two* of the following books (please designate in your letter which two you wish to receive):

Europe on $15 a Day
Australia on $20 a Day
England and Scotland on $20 a Day
Greece and Yugoslavia on $15 & $20 a Day
Hawaii on $25 a Day
Ireland on $15 a Day
Israel on $15 & $20 a Day
Mexico and Guatemala on $10 & $15 a Day
New Zealand on $15 & $20 a Day
Scandinavia on $20 a Day
South America on $15 a Day
Spain and Morocco (plus the Canary Is.) on $10 & $15 a Day
Turkey on $10 & $15 a Day
Washington, D.C. on $25 a Day

Dollarwise Guide to the Caribbean (including Bermuda and the Bahamas)
Dollarwise Guide to Canada
Dollarwise Guide to Egypt
Dollarwise Guide to England and Scotland
Dollarwise Guide to France
Dollarwise Guide to Germany
Dollarwise Guide to Italy
Dollarwise Guide to Portugal (plus Madeira and the Azores)
Dollarwise Guide to California and Las Vegas
Dollarwise Guide to New England
Dollarwise Guide to the Southeast and New Orleans
(Dollarwise Guides discuss accommodations and facilities in all price
ranges, with emphasis on the medium-priced.)

The Caribbean Bargain Book
(A one-of-a-kind guide to the "off-season" Caribbean—mid-April to mid-
December—and the fabulous resorts that slash their rates from 20% to
60%; includes almost every island group in the Caribbean, and covers the
Bahamas too.)

Where to Stay USA
(By the Council on International Educational Exchange, this extraordinary guide is the first to list accommodations in all 50 states that cost
anywhere from $3 to $20 per night.)

(2) A copy of **Arthur Frommer's Guide to New York,** a newly revised
pocket-size guide to hotels, restaurants, night spots, and sightseeing attractions
in all price ranges throughout the New York area.

(3) A one-year subscription to the quarterly Club newsletter—**The Wonderful World of Budget Travel** (about which more below)—which keeps members up-to-date on fast-breaking developments in low-cost travel to all areas of
the world.

(4) A voucher entitling you to a $5 discount on any Arthur Frommer
International, Inc. tour booked by you through travel agents in the United
States and Canada.

(5) Your personal membership card, which, once received, entitles you to
purchase through the Club all Arthur Frommer Publication's for a third to a
half off their regular retail prices during the term of your membership.

Those are the immediate and definite benefits which we can assure to members of the Club at this time. Further benefits, which it has been our continuing aim to achieve for members, are announced to members in *The Wonderful World of Budget Travel (WWBT)*. An eight-page, full-size newspaper, *WWBT* carries such continuing features as "The Traveler's Directory" (a list of members all over the world who are willing to provide hospitality to other members as they pass through their home cities) and "Share-a-Trip" (offers and requests from members for travel companions who can share costs); worldwide travel news and feature stories by our acclaimed expert travel writers; plus tips and articles on specific plans and methods for travel savings.

If you would like to join this hardy band of international budgeteers and participate in its exchange of travel information and hospitality, simply send your name and address, together with your membership fee of $10 (U.S. residents), $12 (Canadian and Mexican residents), or $14 (other foreign residents) in U.S. currency to: $15-a-Day Travel Club, Inc., 380 Madison Avenue, New York, NY 10017. And please remember to specify which *two* of the books in section (1) above you wish to receive in your initial package of members' benefits. Or, if you prefer, use the last page of this book, simply checking off the two books you select and enclosing $10, $12, or $14 in U.S. currency.

Chapter XX

A TALE OF MANY CITIES

Low-Cost Living in
One Hundred Towns

EVENTUALLY, *Europe on $15 a Day* hopes to give the full budget treatment to at least forty major European cities—a chapter on each. But that takes time—and a lot of shoe leather.

In the interval, our notebooks are continually growing with observations on cities only briefly viewed. And, in addition, each day's mail brings tips from readers on hotels and restaurants they've liked in dozens of other European cities.

These finds are too good to waste. As an interim step towards an encyclopedic *Europe on $15 a Day*, this chapter of lists and quick observations has been temporarily inserted into this book. Where a statement is in quotation marks, followed by a name, it represents only the opinion of the reader who mailed it in. I stand by every other statement made. The information is set forth by city, alphabetically, as follows:

AACHEN, GERMANY

"Aachen, both an historic lode of medieval treasures and a modern, cosmopolitan city of beautiful parks, theaters and art galleries, deserves its own separate listing. The **Hotel Frankfurter Hof** in Aachen, 30-32 Bahnhofstrasse (tel. 3-48-62), offers 28 neat and clean rooms at 40 marks single, 65 marks double, with elevator, separate baths, garage, telephone in rooms, central heating, and continental breakfast, and an easy walk from the railroad station. The proprietress, Anni Piper, is friendly and accommodating. My single bathless room, with breakfast included, cost 40 DM, tax and service included. Treasures of the cathedral and of Charlemagne are well displayed in the Rathaus (townhall). Also see the Dom's stained glass windows, octagonal chapel and mosaics" (Mrs. George J. Flynn, Washington, D.C.). . . . "By far our cheapest hotel in Germany was the **Hotel Marx** at 33 Hubertusstrasse, tel. 39-883. It's immaculately clean, and huge Dutch-type breakfasts are included in the price of 28 marks single, 45 marks double! But leave your bags in a locker at the station and just take the essentials for your stay in the hotel, because it is a 20 minute walk up-hill" (Michael and Juliette Hedger, Cremorne, Australia).

ABERYSTWYTH, WALES

"Our best find in England was the **Glan-Y-Mor Guesthouse** at 69 Marine Terrace, Aberystwyth, Dyfed, Wales, tel. 615-312, operated by Mr. and Mrs. George, who are friendly people. Most rooms overlook the water, the whole house has tasteful wallpaper and old furniture, and the meals there are the best I have ever eaten. Price per person, single, double or twin: £5.10. Dinner: £2.25 extra, and is excellent. I'd like other readers to share my good luck finding it" (J. Myers, London, England).

AMALFI, ITALY

"Touring the Sorrento area, the best find of our entire trip was in Amalfi, where we spent a week-end in a lovely pension called **Pensione Sole** (phone 871-147), a few feet from the beach. In season, a bathless double room is 9,800 lire, not including breakfast" (Jacques and Magdeleine Tremblay, Quebec City, Canada; seconding recommendation from Maria Zilzer, New York City). . . . "**Hotel D'Italie et Suisse** (phone 871-444), just beside the sea, is cheap and good. They have a few single rooms for 8,500 lire, during high season and with private shower" (Agneta Palme, Stockholm, Sweden).

AMIENS, FRANCE

"We were directed to the **Hotel Spatial,** near Monument General LeClerq, which turned out to be our best hotel in Europe. Address: 15 Rue Alexandre-Fatton (phone 91-53-23), a block or two from the railroad station. It charges only 45 francs for a bathless double, or 64 francs for a double with bath, taxes and service included. No charge for parking car in rear. Frequented by French travelers. Very comfortable" (Evelyn Lakott, Cambridge, Massachusetts). . . . "To see the cathedral, the most grand, high-flown and triumphant of them all, is to understand how hard men can try (and succeed). Amiens *is* Gothic" (Mrs. Peter Diller, Los Angeles, California).

ANDORRA

"We would recommend a side trip to Andorra for anyone near the Pyrenees. It is a really beautiful country and a shopper's paradise. However, to get there one must ascend very steep mountains via winding roads. Once you reach Andorra la Viella (the Capital) the **Hotel Montserrat** (phone 20083) is an excellent place to stay (its double rooms with shower will rent for 1,200 pesetas ($18.18) in 1980). We had a large, lovely double room with double bed, a balcony, and our own bathroom—with shower, toilet, and sink at a very reasonable price. The management was lovely and very helpful. There are also two self-service restaurants on the street (the town has one main street)" (Mr. and Mrs. Edward Opper, Martinsville, Indiana).

ANKARA, TURKEY

"Prices in the Middle East are really a joy. A fine example is the **Hotel Baykal,** 26 Hukumet Caddesi (phone 117-249), in Ankara, where a brand-new single comparing well with the very best German second-class room, goes for 280 T.L. a night, complete with private balcony. In Turkey, it is impossible to spend more than $4 for a meal, unless one is really stupid; and the food is wonderful" (David D. Morrison, Cambridge, Massachusetts). . . . "In Ankara, the **Cihan Palas,** at 5 Sanayii Caddesi (phone 10-50-60), is the largest hotel in town, yet reasonable in price (120 Turkish pounds for a single sans bath, 220 with bath, 250 double without bath, 290 with bath). The **Piknik** (80 T.L. for the average meal) was our choice for lunch" (Ted & Lynn Kotzin, Los Angeles, Calif.).

ANTWERP, BELGIUM

"For a real treat, go to the center of town, just beside the skyscraper with the Krediet Bank sign on its tower in lights. There, in a building housing a three-story parking garage, is a cafeteria called **Sarma,** parking on one side, eating center at the other end. For about $5.50, you can have a tomato salad appetizer, followed by a delicious steak with mushrooms and wine sauce. The quality and taste are absolutely outstanding. Beer is the big drink in Antwerp, and whoever comes here must try the mussels casseroles, eel in herb sauce, and just about any kind of seafood you can name" (H. P. Koenig, New York, N.Y.). . . . "Antwerp happens to be one of the real undiscovered finds on the international travel beat. Great food, friendly people, just about everyone speaks English. A whole string of restaurants along Suikerrui, running right to the river, only a block from Fabiola, feature such specials as all the mussels and French fried potatoes you can eat for about $4.50. And you can get a steak platter for $5" (Ellen Kaye, New York, N.Y.). ... "This city's **Royal Museum of Art** deserves prominent mention somewhere in your book as possessing one of the best collections of Flemish art in Europe, from the 14th to the 20th centuries. Closed Mondays" (Michael R. Stein, Wauwatosa, Wisconsin).

A NOTE ABOUT READERS' SELECTIONS: Sharp-eyed readers of earlier editions of this book may notice that some readers' selections, appearing in the "Tale of Many Cities" chapter of those earlier editions, are repeated in this edition—but often with minor changes in the prices or other details appearing in them. Because some readers' selections seem too good to be dropped from a new edition, we mail a questionnaire—in November of every year—to every particularly intriguing hotel or restaurant listed in this chapter, requesting that these establishments confirm in writing the prices they intend to charge, and the policies they plan to follow, for the *next year*—in this case, 1980. If they fail to answer, we drop the reader's selection. If they do answer, and their answers show them to be a budget establishment, we re-write the reader's selection to make it accurate and up-to-date for the coming year (or maintain it unchanged if the response shows it should not be changed). Thus, a reader who has earlier written in that he "spent $14 for a double room" at a particular hotel, may find his reader's selection stating, this year, that he "spent $16 for a double room" at that hotel. He may even find a phone number added to the address of his find, or some other bit of technical information that we have gleaned from the hotel's response to our questionnaire.

We hope our readers will forgive this slight tampering with their letters, because its purpose is to insure that every detail, every price, every item of information in this book shall be absolutely accurate and up-to-date for the year in which the book is published. The furnishing of responsible, useful information is the primary aim of this book, requiring a massive amount of research and inspection each year, and warranting—we hope you'll agree— these minor liberties with your letters (which, by the way, we treasure and read with the greatest care and attention).

ARLES, FRANCE

"The modern **Hotel Voltaire**, right off the main square (Place Voltaire, phone 961-358) is spotlessly clean and with a little balcony from which to watch the general proceedings from the cafe tables in the square. Twin-bedded room and breakfast for two, less than $15" (Rochelle B. Seiden, Brooklyn, New York). ... "The **Hotel Terminus & Van Gogh,** Place Lamartine (phone 12-32), combines modern comfort with a 19th century Van Gogh atmosphere. Run by a gray-haired French couple, the hotel offers double rooms for 62 francs, singles for 42 francs, with service charge (but not breakfast— an extra 8 francs) included. Our room had Van-Gogh-style wooden chairs with reed seats, flaming red curtains and sunflower-yellow shutters. The dining room is 19th century in design and Van Gogh prints decorate the lobby. Other pluses: new plumbing, thin gray carpeting, good heating, even a sewing kit in the closet. The Terminus & Van Gogh is three minutes from the train station" (Randy Mink, Elgin, Illinois). ... "This surprising town, where Van Gogh worked for two years, was also an ancient Roman city, built by Caesar some years BC. Many beautiful Roman buildings and ruins remain, including an Arena (where bullfights sometimes take place), an Amphitheatre and many very interesting museums and mosaics. A week here is not really enough to take in all the many sights, including the biggest market we've ever seen selling everything from magician's kits to antiques to live animals! HOTEL: the **Moderne** (phone 960-821), on the Place du Forum, is friendly, clean, and charges between 42 and 58 francs for single and double rooms, with and without bath. RESTAURANT: The **L'Arlaten,** Rue de la Cavalerie, offers gargantuan and delicious three-course meals for 30, 40 or 50 francs ($6.97, $9.30 and $11.62) on its fixed-price menu. It was the biggest and the best-cooked and served meal we've had. SIDETRIPS: Stay in Arles and take a trip to **Nimes** (½-hour away), a city with fantastic Roman monuments including a colosseum almost as big as the one in Rome and perfectly preserved; and some amazing gardens and fountains, with sunken pools and swans. **Les Baux,** a tiny village perched in the mountains, with its fantastic Dead City of the Caves, is half-an-hour from Arles, reachable only by taxi or car, but worth renting either to get to see this unforgettable place" (Mr. and Mrs. Harold Carlton, London, England). . . . "I had a delicious provençal meal at **Le Criquet Restaurant,** Rue Port de Havre; its prix fix menu (the only menu) offers four filling courses, including bread and wine, for 30 francs, not including service—that's left to the customer's discretion. The cheapest restaurant in town" (Lyle Brown, Victoria, B.C., Canada). . . . "It's easy to assume, incorrectly, that the town and its hotels are located just off the area of the RR station. That is only the edge of the city. Proceeding beyond the station, you can go over the hill to many other fine places for rooms and food. . . . By appropriately juggling buses and trains, we managed to see some of Arles, all of Nimes, the Pont du Gard, and return to Arles, all in one day" (Helene Kansas, Satellite Beach, Florida).

ARRAN (ISLE OF), SCOTLAND

"Please find space for inclusion of the **Allandale Guest House,** Brodick Pier, Isle of Arran (telephone Brodick 2278). Mr. and Mrs. Small took a personal interest in all the guests who stayed there, and during the summer months, took them tramping. For £8.50 one got dinner, bed and breakfast, with your own bathroom, shower, tv and toilet. Tea, coffee, sugar and milk were at your disposal day and night (hot-water-machine stood in the hallway), and one helped oneself to coffee, etc. . . . The evening meal is a 3-courser, with coffee taken in the lounge, while for breakfast we had fruit juice, hot cereal, bacon and eggs, loads of toast, and the choice of tea or coffee" (Lecia Katherine Boyd and Robert Terrell Price, Waikeria, Teawamutu, New Zealand; note from AF: Arran is for active and adventurous sorts, who don't mind walking up and down for miles).

ASSISI, ITALY

"I should very much like to recommend the **Convent des Clarisses Colettines Françaises,** 3 Via Borgo S. Pietro, Assisi (takes men and women), phone 812-345, where I had an extremely comfortable room (with wash basin) and breakfast for 12,500 lire ($15.06). The French nuns, although they speak only a little English, are expert at making themselves understood, and understanding all nationalities, and hot water is available. You are given a latch-key on arrival. Incidentally, the station at Assisi is some distance from the town, and a taxi costs at least 5,000 lire. The bus, though only moderately frequent (½ to 1 hourly according to time of day, perhaps more in season), is only 200 lire—quite a worthwhile saving" (Mollie Boyle, Bramcote, Warwickshire, Wales). . . . "A great many tourists come to this beautiful, peaceful town, the birthplace of St. Francis and of St. Claire. The hotels are always full and we stumbled upon a medieval villa, now a Guest House, which turned out to be another Graymoor Sisters', like the one in Rome. It is known in town as the 'American Sisters,' technically **St. Anthony's Guest House,** Via Galeazzo Alessi 10. Telephone 812-542. Full pension is 16,000 lire ($19.27) a day per person. The food is excellent; the service is perfect. Meals are served in a lovely garden overlooking the town and the Umbrian Hills, and all the sisters are most accommodating and speak English. The place is so serene and restful that we stayed four days instead of only two" (Mr. and Mrs. Stanley P. Cooper, Temple City, California). . . . "The **Hotel Windsor-Savoia** (phone 812-210), charges 24,000 lire ($28.91) for a double with shower, breakfast included. Near St. Francis Church, with a beautiful view, and the cleanest hotel we have ever stayed in. 33 rooms" (Dr. Miriam Hubbell, Sylmar, California). . . . "The **Hostel of the Swedish Sisters of St. Birgitta** in Assisi (Suore svedesi di S. Brigida, Via Moiano 1, tel. (075) 812693) is situated on a hillside approximately four minutes' walk from the upper town and overlooking the lower city. The Sisters in attendance at the inn were most pleasant and cordial. Suggest you look this one over as we thought it to be one of the best (including first class hotels) we found in all our travels. The rooms were immaculate, though simply furnished, and the food superb (Italian cuisine, of course). Room and meals (continental breakfast, noon meal and dinner) all inclusive for 17,500 lire ($21.08) per day per person" (Bernard R. Higgins, Cleveland, Ohio). . . . "An excellent pizzeria in Assisi is the **Pizzeria dal Carro.** My wife and I had two soups and two pizzas for 4,000 lire in 1979. I hope this helps" (R. P. Bielawski, N. Oshawa, Ontario, Canada). . . . "Besides the Basilica of Saint Francis with its grotto frescoes, also worth visiting is the crypt, as well as the legendary crucifix that spoke to St. Francis. See, too, the Basilica of Santa Maria degli Angeli in the valley near the station: the Portiuncula is inside, as well as the spot where Francis died, and the rooms where he and his first followers lived and worked" (Danielle Jehanne Rappaport, APO New York).

AUGSBURG, GERMANY

"We spent an exceptionally comfortable night at the **Gasthof Zum Stockhaus,** a building we were told is about 500 years old (though the facilities are 495 years newer). Situated right on the picturesque main street (Maximilianstrasse #73/75), this mansion of some venerable Renaissance burgher boarded the two of us for DM 22. Dinner—excellent boiled ham, sauerkraut, potatoes, beer—ran 9 DM a person. English spoken. Phone 518195. A visitor to Augsburg ought not miss seeing the still-inhabited 'Fuggerei,' founded in 1519 by the fabulously rich Jakob Fugger, banker and financier to the Habsburgs. What is the 'Fuggerei'? A section of homes for the town's poor people. That's 1519, not 1919" (David and Francie Robertson, Los Angeles, California).

AVIGNON, FRANCE

"Avignon, an hour from Marseilles, one of the great art cities of France, was the home of the Popes in the 14th century, and is rich in relics and monuments. Exceptional museum there is the **Calvet Musée,** with an extraordinary collection of art, sculpture and besides this, a charming garden where visitors may wander too" (Loretta Spanover, Fresh Meadows, New York; note from AF: see also the **Musée du Petit Palais,** exhibiting over 400 painting and pieces of sculpture from the Middle Ages).... "At the **Auberge de France,** 28 Place de l'Horloge, formerly Place Clemenceau (phone 82-58-86), the three of us had a wonderful room with bath for 100 francs" (Mrs. Vreni Naess, Chicago, Illinois).... "**Hotel St.-Paul** (phone 81-29-70), two blocks off the main street at 10 Rue Dorée, charges 46 francs single, 50 to 65 francs double, including breakfast. Hot and cold water in room. This hotel is a real find in Avignon. Others were unreasonably high or else a good deal less clean" (Dr. Melbin Palmer, Westminster, Maryland).... "A superb find was the **Hotel du Parc,** 18 Rue Agricol Perdiguier, about 4 blocks from the station, where we had a spotless, spacious double for 50 francs ($11.62), breakfast in bed included. The exceedingly helpful proprietress told us of an inexpensive restaurant—La Marmite—around the corner, where for 30 francs ($6.97) we had the 'menu conseillé,' with choice of hors d'oeuvre, entree and dessert" (Ida Tirone, West Seneca, New York).

BARCELONA, SPAIN

SPLURGE-PRICED HOTELS AND PENSIONS: "I write with particular excitement about the **Hotel Rialto,** at Fernando 40 & 42 (tel: 318-52-12), in Barcelona. This is a charming little hotel with its own superb dining room, operated as a family enterprise. The prices are astoundingly low (1,600 pesetas—$24.24—for a double room with a complete private bathroom, breakfast included) and the staff is warm and friendly. There is one young woman who speaks and understands English very well, and she is assisted by a young man whose English is adequate and improving. Yet another attraction is its location, in the heart of the old city, around the corner from the Plaza St. Jaime, where the citizens dance on Sunday evenings, and a mere two blocks from the Cathedral. Even if you don't stay there, you should try its dining room for a superb example of Spanish cooking, well served and, of course, reasonably priced" (Ann Harvey, Exeter, Devon, England, and Mr. and Mrs. Philip Kraysler, Frankfurt, Germany).... "At the beautiful modern **Hotel Gaudi,** Conde del Asalto 12, tel: 317-90-32, we paid 1,850 pesetas for twin bed room #520 with bath and balcony, tax and service included. Lift, English spoken" (Mr. and Mrs. Anthony Yourevich, San Francisco, California).

BUDGET HOTELS AND PENSIONS: "I would like to tell readers about the **Hostal Residencia La Hipica,** General Castaños 2 (phone 319-4500), just a ten-minute walk from the Ramblas. The management is friendly, the location central and your room, with tub and shower, will be clean. The rates: just 650 pesetas a day for a double room" (Stephen Kraus, New York, New York).... "We found a pleasant room at the **Hostel Tobogan,** #10 Plaza Real (phone 318-7970) for 1,100 pesetas ($16.66—double room with shower and step-down mini-tub). The Plaza Real is very central and we took the subways without any problem" (Mrs. Lee Weisman, Los Angeles, California)....
"**Hostal del Mar,** Plaza del Palacio just off Paseo de Isabel II near the post office (phone 319-3302), charges 340 pesetas single, 620 pesetas double. Hot and cold water with a shower in the room. Rooms were large, exceedingly clean, even a bit antiseptic from my

view. Nice for those bothered by Barcelona's pollution". . . . "We went to the desk of the **Hotel Internacional,** 78 Ramblas (on the corner of Boqueria and the Ramblas, phone 302-2566) and found that we could have a double with complete bathroom with balcony overlooking the Ramblas for 1,500 pesetas. Location was perfect, only several blocks from the Plaza de Cataluna, with the bustling Ramblas to walk up and down just outside our hotel door" (Raoul and Linda Weinstein, St. Thomas, Virgin Islands).

STARVATION BUDGET PENSIONS: "While working in Barcelona this past year, I've been living at **Hostal Residencia Lesseps,** Calle Mayor de Gracia 239 (tel: 218-4434). Recently opened, it charges 310 pesetas ($4.69) per person in a double room, 380 pesetas ($5.75) for a single. The rooms are well-lighted, modernly furnished, and quite comfortable. Breakfast is the only meal given, costing 60 pesetas (coffee and croissant); cold baths and showers are free, but hot ones will cost another 75 pesetas. Only Spanish is spoken, but the management is a pleasure to deal with, in any case. Mayor de Gracia is quite centrally located, as it is merely a continuation of Paseo de Gracia on the other side of Avenida Generalissimo", (Roberta Carr, Barcelona, Spain; note by A.F.: numerous other letters from readers, all enthusiastic; some claim English *is* spoken). . . . "**Pension Lepanto** (302-0081), 10 Raurich off Calle Fernando (near the Ramblas), charges only 310 pts. for a single with a double bed, 480 pts. for a double room with a single and a double bed. Cold water sink. Exceedingly comfortable, a great place to congratulate yourself on living so cheaply after Copenhagen. Breakfast is 80 pts., and a bath is 75 pts. extra" (Alan C. Feuer, Oak Park, Michigan). . . . "At the **Hostal Venezuela,** Calle Ataulfo 45 (near Plaza San Jaime), tel. 318-6987, I had a single with a big bed, a sink with hot and cold water, and even a balcony, all for only 430 pesetas ($6.51). Right next door is a budget restaurant with a 280 pesetas ($4.24) menu, and one of the choices offered is paella" (Diane MacDicken, Vancouver, B. C., Canada).

RESTAURANTS: "Our prize find of our whole trip was a tiny, knotty-pine-paneled restaurant in the old quarter of Barcelona. They have—believe it or not—a 100 peseta ($1.51) menu, an alternate 150 pesetas ($2.27) feast. Our meal (very well prepared): vegetable soup, then a tremendous platter of vermicelli (thread-like noodles) and spaghetti in a delicious meat and tomato sauce, then breaded veal cutlet and green beans, a green tossed salad, bread, and a banana for dessert. We forked over a total of 250 pesetas, or $1.89 each, plus service. Where is this find? It's the **Restaurant Casa José,** 10 Plaza San José Oriol, which is 2-3 blocks off the Ramblas, and hidden just behind a large Cathedral which dominates the Plaza. Closed Saturdays" (Jess and Alice Brewis, Taylor, Michigan; note from AF: Casa José is highly recommendable. Its owner, Señor Jesus Ruiz, does everything imaginable to please readers of this book. Ask for the typewritten, English-language menu). . . . "We visited the new **Picasso Museum** (open 9:30 to 1:30 and 4:30 to 8:30) which is on Calle Montcada 15, off Calle de Fernando (which is one block north of the Plaza Real). Continuing along de Fernando which runs into Jaime I Square and is then called Princesa, we ran into a real bargain in a typical Spanish restaurant catering to working and business people in the area. For 275 pesetas we had the cubierto consisting of mixed salad, sopa de pescado, chuleta de lumo (veal chop) with patatas fritas, vino, pan and fresh fruit. The waiter left us a large bottle of wine telling us to have as much as we wanted. All the food was excellent, the service quick, and for less than $4.25 each, we had one of the tastiest meals in Spain. It's called **El Rincon de la Mancha,** 50 Princesa, and is on a corner—you can't miss it. Also, being fairly close to the Picasso Museum which closes at 1:30 p.m., it's a great place to stop for lunch" (Mrs. Lee Weisman, Los Angeles, California).

SIGHTSEEING, NIGHTSPOTS AND TRIPS: "The '**Pueblo Español**' was built in Barcelona as part of an international exposition in the twenties, and is a fascinating Spanish 'village' where every house is in the style of a different region of the country. Craftsmen make and sell all sorts of articles in the houses, and the prices are quite reasonable. We even got a copy of a medieval saint's statue for $3.25 after having seen the same thing in town for $6" (Mrs. Thomas E. Carnell, Trotwood, Ohio). . . . "Fifty cents will buy you a view of the most fantastic architectural sight in all Europe: the Cathedral of the Sacred Family, the masterpiece of the Barcelona architect Gaudi, not to be missed" (Mr. & Mrs. Loring Eutemey, New York, New York). . . . "Head for **Montjuich Park,** for the best of Barcelona. To get there, take bus #8 from the Plaza de España. The fare is 12 pesetas, or 19¢. First, there is Pueblo Español (Spanish Village) from 9 a.m. on, where you see typical Spanish towns. The price is 50¢ for admission. But the very best of all—and it is free—is a fabulous water play and illumination display of the famous fountains of Montjuich Park on Saturday and Sunday evenings from 10 p.m. to 12 p.m. This is not to be missed" (C. Fieldman, Bronx, New York). . . . "Take the electric Catalan r.r. to **Montserrat,** that spectacular sawtoothed mountain an hour and a half by train from Barcelona. The 350-peseta round trip includes thrilling four-minute aerial tram rides to and from the monastery built upon the high sides of this mountain. Plan to go there in time for the 1:00 p.m. music by the Montserrat Escolania boys choir. Food may be purchased at the self-service restaurant, and splurgers may wish to stay overnight at the Hostal Abat Cisneros (2 persons, max. price 2,100 pesetas for overnight. Breakfast 210 pesetas). There are funicular rides and posted walking trips providing panoramic view. The r.r. trip costs a fraction of the conducted tour price" (Faith C. Callihan, Caldwell, Idaho). . . . "Even if Barcelona were covered only as a jumping-off point to Mallorca, it would be deserved. Boats leave every night but Sunday at 10 p.m. for the eight-hour trip. The cost 3rd class (four to a cabin) is approximately 680 pesetas each way, 2nd class is 1,050 pesetas" (Bill Slagle, Montlake Terrace, Washington). . . . "To get to Palma by boat, turn left out of Francia Station, walk down ½ mile to Via Leyatana, and a boat company is just down on the right. During summer months, get there early to insure a seat on the deck. During nice weather, most everyone travels deck class" (Barry Glen, Cedarhurst, New York).

BARI, ITALY

"We arrived here on the boat from Yugoslavia and found it a fun city to shop in (the prices aren't inflated by tourists) and explore. A good little neighborhood restaurant is **La Rosetta** on Via Cardassi. The waiter took us into the kitchen to show us what they had cooking for lunch. We pointed to what looked appealing, and for 6,000 lire each ($7.22), had a four-course meal including wine, bread, dessert and service" (Carl and Maxine Beckwith, Suffield, Connecticut).

BASEL, SWITZERLAND

"Hotel Helvetia, Küchengasse 13 (phone 23-06-88), was on a small street across from the main train station. 40 to 50 Swiss francs for two, breakfast and service charges included. Very clean and comfortable" (Dr. and Mrs. Ben Burnett, Whittier, California). . . . "We think the best bargain hotel in all of Basel is the **Hotel-Hospiz Engelhof** at 1 Stiftsgasse (corner of Nadelberg), phone 25-22-44 (50 to 62 francs for a double room, breakfast included); if it happens to be full, try the **Hotel Rochat** (same rates), half a block away at 23 Petersgraben (phone 25-8140). Both are Christian hospices" (Mr. and Mrs. James Hester, Binningen, Switzerland). . . . "The totally modern **Pension Steinenschanze**, 69 Steinengraben (phone 23-53-53), is the local Y.W.C.A., takes women and men, too, and charges 52 francs ($30.58), breakfast included, for a double room, 32 francs in a single" (Jeanne Pasmantier, West Orange, New Jersey; note from AF: readers possessing a valid student card will be charged only 20 francs ($11.76) per person, single or double, breakfast included, at the Steinenschanze). . . . "Anyone can stay in university housing in Basel for 15-20 francs, with private bath, and bedding all furnished. However, only July through September" (Walter and Josephine Magnolia, Lynhook, New York). . . . "An important lodging place for students is the 50-bed **Hotel-Restaurant zum Spalenbrunnen**, 2 Schützenmattstrasse (phone 25-82-33), which charges only 25 francs ($14.70) single, 40 francs ($23.52) double, breakfast included; and offers platters in its restaurant ranging from 3.80 francs ($2.23) for mixed salad bowl or meat salad with bread, to 8 francs ($4.70) for soup, veal goulasch with potatoes or steak with french fries and salad. From the central station, take streetcar no. 1 to Schützenhaus (2nd stop), then change to bus no. 3 to the Spalentor stop. Or take a cab for only 3 francs" (Eileen Zarick, New York City). . . . "Cheapest in town is the **Youth Hostel** at 51 Elisabethenstrasse (phone 230-572), with 180 beds priced at 5 francs ($2.94) in an 8-bedded dorm, 10 francs ($5.88) in 2- or 4-bedded rooms; you'll need a hostel card, but you can purchase one on the spot for about $15, less if you are 20 years or younger. This is very conveniently located less than five minutes from the Central Station: walk along the subway passage and follow the "city" signs. When you reach a small park, Elisabethenstrasse is to your left, and the hostal approximately 50 yards down the street to your right" (Adam Slote, New York City). . . . "Our find in restaurants is the **Schuhmacherzunft** on Hutgasse, a small street between the Blaser and EPA stores on the Marktplatz. In this delightful hangout for the Swiss, we've had enormous meals at moderate cost. The food is excellent, the atmosphere unmatched in warmth and hospitality in Basel, and the portions of food unbelievable. There's a menu card in English. Be prepared to share your table with delightful people, from flower peddlers to old gentlemen playing chess. . . . For those people who are taking a quick tour of the city and want a good, cheap, fast, filling meal, one of the two large department stores (the **Rheinbrücke**) would be a good choice. Avoid the restaurant area and head for the grocery section to get a variety of meals at a stand-up counter: one can then be content until time for a late European dinner. . . . One should also make it a point to see the Zoo. Admission 6 SF (children pay 2.50 SF). You can spend hours wandering around. I am quite sure I got closer to some animals than any African hunter. They attempt to put all the animals they can in open spaces surrounded by deep moats. Terrific afternoon for less than $3.50. . . . The **Museum of Fine Arts** (Kunstmuseum) in Basel, closed Mondays, has the best Holbein collection in Europe, plus a very good modern art section and free entrance on Wednesday afternoons from 2 to 5 and weekends" (Mr. & Mrs. James Hester, Binningen, Switzerland). . . . "We ate in a charming little restaurant located near the historic center: **Die Brasserie mit Pfiff**, 35 Falknerstrasse. Reasonable native dinners for 9.50 francs ($5.58), and reduced prices on regular meals after 9 p.m. Daily specials are offered. Strictly local atmosphere and typical Swiss decor. Large portions of tasty and attractively prepared food. A winner!" (Jeff Karp and H. Levinson, Montreal, Quebec, Canada).

BATH, ENGLAND

"We stayed at the **Dorset Villa**, whose proprietress is Mrs. Ivor Ham, 14 Newbridge Road, telephone 25975. We paid £10 for two ($22). To quote my wife, 'the room was a dream, the china and silverware exquisite.' We were served tea and biscuits in bed in the morning, the breakfast was delicious, and we were again served tea and biscuits in our room last thing at night" (H. T. Lewis, Toronto, Canada). . . . "Right beside the highway between Bath and Bristol (the postal address is Bristol, *but* the village is called Saltford), we stopped at **The Old Ship** run by Charles and Mary Windmill, at 548 Bath Road (phone Saltford 2292). Twenty-five years ago they purchased and restored this old building, an inn in the 1670s. Bed and a whopping breakfast of grapefruit, bacon and eggs, grilled kidney, tomato, buttered toast and honey, and tea, totaled £10 ($22) for the two of us. Our room overlooked the flower garden out back. Parking space was provided" (The Otto Steeles, Adel, Iowa). . . . "During our numerous visits to Great Britain, **Portland Villa**, 8 Newbridge Road, Bath, has been the best B & B house my wife and I have ever availed ourselves of, and Mrs. Goodchild the kindest hostess we ever met. We had the choice between two bright, quiet and large rooms with extremely comfortable beds and armchairs, etc. The charge was £4.50 ($9.90) each; the breakfast was prepared with great care and competence. If humane virtues are of any relevance in this context (as I believe) I have to add that when, on the second day of our stay in Bath, we happened to catch a bad cold, Mrs. Goodchild allowed us to keep indoors and gave us meals and medical assistance. Her hot drinks worked miracles" (Dr. Ottavio Di Fidio, Galway, Eire). . . . "We ate at the **Edwardian** at Westgate Street, very close to the Roman Baths (for economy eat downstairs). Informal atmosphere, but a wide selection of excellent food at reasonable prices. I had beef bourguignonne with wine sauce and mushrooms, a large portion of broccoli, carrots and baked potatoes, all well seasoned, and half a pint of beer, for £3 ($6.60), VAT and service included" (Stephen Lepore, Venice, California). . . . "The **Huntsman**, #1 Terrace Wall, North Parade, serves delicious food from one kitchen to a tearoom, pub and dining room. You choose the location according to style and price. We ate several meals there and it is the one place I would go back to after eight weeks of 'eating out' " (Mrs. Kenneth V. Crow, Tracyton, Washington).

BAYEUX, FRANCE

"Visiting the impressive and touching Normandy Beaches, a starting point six miles away is Bayeux, France, where you might like to try the **Hotel Du Luxembourg**, 25 Rue des Bouchers. It's clean and worthwhile; a bathless double in 1980 will be 66 francs, service included; also eat in their restaurant" (Marilyn and Mitchell Shapiro, New Orleans, Louisiana). . . . "We found the **Hotel du Luxembourg** recommended by one of your readers quite comfortable. We paid 128 francs ($29.76) for a triple room with bath and breakfast. . . . The famed Bayeux Tapestry—an 11th century embroidery recounting Duke William's conquest of Britain in 1066—is as impressive as it is made out to be. Entrance is 7 F. Frs. per person, 4 francs for students, with children under 10 admitted free, and we recommend that visitors invest an additional Franc in the 'teleguide' or recorded commentary which points out many an interesting detail one might otherwise overlook. Visitors to the Normandy Beaches would do well to stop for an hour at Arromanches (6 miles from Bayeux) to see ruins of the 'Mulberry' floating harbours designed by Winston Churchill for the Allied landings in 1944. The D-Day

Museum at Port Winston (Arromanches) has an interesting film of D-Day operations as well as touching mementos" (Mr. and Mrs. P. K. Pal, Calcutta, India).

BERCHTESGADEN, GERMANY

"It was late at night and we were in need of somewhere to stay, when we came across the **Hobelbank Gasthaus,** managed by Werner Brunner. There we enjoyed a magnificent meal with some of the best onion soup I've ever had, and the house specialty, toast dishes. We also stayed at the Gasthaus and paid 54 marks ($28.42) for two double rooms without breakfast. The rooms and bathroom were so clean it was a delight to use them" (R. F. Cameron, Vaucluse, Australia). . . . "My best European bargain is, admittedly, in a very touristy area: Berchtesgaden, site of Hitler's home, 20 miles from Salzburg, with its nearby salt mines and skiing. **Haus Platner,** at Königseerstrasse 27 (phone 2204), one block from the train station, is where I've stayed on three occasions. Cross the street from the train station, walk to the traffic light 100 yards away (you can only see this light - no others), turn the corner, go across the bridge, walk one block, it's left up the steps. The cost is only 12 marks ($6.31), including breakfast! Can't believe it isn't yet in your book" (John Holland, APO New York).

BERGEN, NORWAY

"If, by the time you reach Oslo, you crave a respite from a steady diet of European cities, a fantastically beautiful and pleasantly informal mountain-fjord tour can be had by merely taking the morning train from Oslo to Bergen, the hydrofoil along the Atlantic Coast from Bergen to Stavanger, and the train back again to Oslo. The train rides will bring you through some of the most breathtaking mountain and valley scenery anywhere, including tourist-infested Switzerland, with stops along the log cabins of colorful mountain hamlets. **Bergen** is a city where townsfolk and seamen gather at twilight on the docks to sing hymns. The town and seaport can best be viewed at twilight and sunset from the hill just north of the train station. The train arrives late afternoon and travelers should consult the tourist office three or so blocks east for overnight accommodations. I stayed at the **Bibelskolens Sommerhotel** (22 C. Sundtsgate, phone 212-531) on the docks, in a ten-bedded dormitory, for 30 kroner per night. There are morning and afternoon hydrofoils to Stavanger, more commercial than Bergen but thereby a better place to shop for sweaters, souvenirs, and gifts" (Jay Evans, Colorado Springs, Colorado; note by A.F.: Bibelskolen will be open only from May 20 to August 20 in 1980). . . . "We were relieved to find the **Central Pension,** Kong Oscarsgate 34, phone 311-502, about five minutes' walk to the right of the station, at 115 kroner for a double room. The scenery around the fjords and Bergen was magnificent, and the train trip from Oslo to Bergen should not be missed" (Lorraine and Bryan Stone, Victoria, Australia). . . . "**Marie and Sigurd Ringstad,** Nordahl Rolfsensvei 14 (tel. 28 02 76), welcome guests to stay in their pretty modern home. The house is set in a lovely flower-garden. There are nice spacious double and single rooms (60 kroner single, 90 kroner double, breakfast 20 kroner extra) with hot and cold running water, bathroom, comfortable beds, and otherwise pleasantly furnished. Use of telephone. Breakfast if desired. Host and hostess speak English, and you will enjoy good service. No. 2 Bus from the Central Post Office will bring you to your destination after a 12-minute ride through the most beautiful part of Bergen" (Emelie Lang, Berwyn, Illinois, with seconding recommendation from John Gatfield of Napa, California, who recommends that you write ahead for summer reservations if you plan to stay with the Ringstads in summer). . . . "My brother and I found fine accommodations this past August (1979) at the home of **Mr. and Mrs. Christensen.** They have one double room for 70 kroner ($13.72) per night, including private bathroom. Address: Sölvberget 18, phone 257-786, reached by taking train No. 8 and getting off at the Skytterveien stop" (Stephen and George Cronvich, Harahan Louisiana). . . . "We recommend a brief excursion (sans guide, of course) from Bergen to Oslo, which will incorporate a representative selection of scenic grandeur, and yet take only an extra day out of a busy tourist's schedule. Take the 8 a.m. train out of Bergen to Voss. At Voss, a bus will be waiting for the train, which arrives about 10 a.m. The bus proceeds through scenic mountainous countryside to Vangsnes, a hamlet-sized ferry stop. The bus' arrival is timed to meet the ferry which crosses the Sognefjord at that point in 35 minutes. Get off at the next port-of-call, which is a small village called Balestrand, where you overnight. Before leaving in the morning, a walk to a 900-year-old Stave church provides a good diversion from the natural beauties which abound. At 10 a.m., a boat leaves from the dock in front of the hotel for a 4-hour cruise on the Sognefjord to Flam. This is probably the most magnificent cruise in the world, passing through high-walled and majestic fjord after fjord. The mail boat's last stop (cost: 24 kroner per person) was Flåm, the terminal stop of the Flåm-Myrdal spur line. The electric railway winds its way through and up the mountainside past hundreds of waterfalls of all sizes, lazy valleys and jagged peaks. At Myrdal, the electric train arrives just in time to meet the express to Oslo" (Mr. and Mrs. Richard D. Greenfield, Lynbrook, New York).

BERNE, SWITZERLAND

"Hotel Volkshaus, Zeughausgasse 9 (phone 22-29-76), in the very heart of the city, gave us a double room, beautifully furnished, with gleaming floors and lots of Oriental rugs, for 56 francs, including service and a delicious breakfast. This hotel has a very large restaurant where food is truly wonderful and quite moderate. There is an elevator, too" (Dr. J. F. Schleicher, Ottawa, Canada). . . . "I would like to recommend the Hotel Kreuz, 41 Zeughausgasse (phone 22-11-62), which is about two hundred feet up the street from the Volkshaus (the recommendation of another reader). The price structure (32 francs per person, single or double, including breakfast, service and taxes) and the accommodations are comparable to those of the Volkshaus, and the people on the staff are most helpful and friendly. It is an excellent alternative to the Volkshaus and, as you have noted in so many other cities, it is a part of the cluster of good reasonable hotels usually found in a central area" (George W. Crowley, Beverly, Massachusetts; note by AF: major per person reductions are available here for persons occupying triple or 4-bedded rooms). . . . "Berne is charming. A Valium for the soul! Kind people, clean and sunny rooms at the Hotel Zum Goldenen Schlüssel, Rathausgasse 72, telephone 220-216, near the railroad station and close to the center of town. Manageress is Claudia Moser. Double room with breakfast for 50 francs. Good rate for Berne" (Shirley Karpf, Durdas, Ontario, Canada). . . . "I discovered, right in the center of town, an admirable and very cheap restaurant called Gfeller am Bärenplatz; right at 21 Bärenplatz (as its name implies—don't confuse it with the Bärengraben) and only about two minutes from the station. On the ground floor, lunch and dinner are listed at 7.50 and 8.50 francs each—three courses, service included; that's $4.41 or $5. But I preferred to eat upstairs, where from 11 to 3 and from 6 to 8 (including Sundays) there is a self-service, offering a wide choice, and with the great advantage (especially for foreigners) that you can see exactly what you are getting. Roomy, comfortable, spotlessly clean, good food. . . . There is another place in Berne for quick stand-up lunches: upstairs in the Neue Warenhaus A.G., Marktgasse 24. This place is a department store, and so, of course, open only during shopping hours. The Bernese flock into it to get meals at a self-service counter; there are a few tables and chairs, but most of the customers eat standing up, with their plates resting on shelves" (Charles Wrong, Providence, Rhode Island).

BINGEN, GERMANY

"Most castle hotels do not fall into the budget category, but Burg Reichenstein, located along the Rhine River about three miles north of Bingen, will thrill anyone willing to splurge a little. Dating back to the tenth century, this hotel offers a most unique atmosphere: my single room had a stone balcony overlooking the Rhine, yet I paid only 30 marks. Bathless doubles begin at 55 marks. The address is Burg Reichenstein, 6531 Trechtingshausen Am Rhein, West Germany" (Shelby M. Harer, Williamsport, Pennsylvania). . . . "An absolutely delightful pension in Bingen, which is located on the Rhine, just shortly after the steamer leaves Koblenz on the way to Mainz: Hotel Goldener Kochlöffel, phone 13944. The double we had was quiet and comfortable, with W. C. in it; the bath was across the hall. We paid $12, inclusive a lovely continental breakfast with boiled egg. The hotel has a history going back to 1450 when it was a cloister for nuns, and the name Goldener Kochlöffel means the 'golden cooking spoon,' which was derived from the tasty food the nuns prepared and fed the poor who came knocking on their doors" (Mr. and Mrs. Robert K. McKnight, Hayward, California).

BLACKPOOL, ENGLAND

"My wife and I stayed at the Beckley Private Hotel, 520 Queens Promenade (phone 0253-853138), at £5.50 ($12.10) per person per night for bed and breakfast. TV lounge, coffee served on arrival and again in the evening. Highly recommendable. A very charming proprietress. Right on the beachfront" (G. G. Boyce, Cape Town, South Africa).

BLOIS, FRANCE

"A good, centrally located town, from which it is easy to tour the châteaux of the Loire. We stayed at the **Hotel Anne de Bretagne** (31 Ave. Victor Hugo). Parking in front. Cost was 48 francs single, 62 francs double (breakfast 11 francs), and the nice proprietress offered to baby sit for us free of charge after the children were asleep" (Dr. Melvin Palmer, Westminster, Maryland).

BOLOGNA, ITALY

"This city deserves some mention. Its City Museum, art gallery (Pinacotheca) and churches are well worth seeing. As an advance over the better-known Pisa, it has *two* leaning towers. A good place to stay is the **Albergo Rondine** at Via Galliera 93 (phone 267-581), within walking distance of the railroad station, where a double room is priced at 15,000 lire, a single for 10,000 lire (only one single is available). In a nearby tavola calda on Via Righi, inexpensive meals can be eaten or carried out" (Trevor and Laura Robinson, Amherst, Massachusetts; note from AF: Signor Antonino dalli Cardillo, owner and manager of the Rondine, has promised to treat $15-a-day readers with special care). . . . "The conveniently-located **Pensione Miranda**, at 6 Via San Felice, charges 9,000 lire ($10.84) for a clean and spacious double room. Being a major university town, the atmosphere is great and the girls beautiful" (Michel Neroy, Montreal, Canada). . . . "We merely stopped overnight, but thought it a very pleasant, quiet and clean city. The **Hotel Nettuno**, 65 Via Galleria, is not budget at $32 for double with shower, no breakfast, but is an excellent hotel" (Dr. Charles R. Fitz, Toronto, Ontario, Canada).

BORDEAUX, FRANCE

"Try the **Hotel des Pyrenees**, 12 Rue Saint-Remi (phone 48-66-58), which is a five-minute ride on Bus #1 from the Bordeaux rail station. The hotel is spotless, with large rooms, and run by the most courteous French couple I've met. Their son speaks English and is most helpful. The cost of a bathless double room is about 53 francs ($12.32) in this hotel recommended by a number of Touring Associations, and is well worth the money. Right down the street at 64 rue Saint-Remi, the **Restaurant Riche** had excellent food, wine and service in a bright atmosphere, devoid of tourists. I highly recommend this hotel and restaurant" (Harvey G. Lockhart, Brooklyn, New York). . . . "**Hotel du Printemps**, 69 Rue Eugene-le-Roy (phone 91-67-66), is directly across from the central train station (it's really on a side street but its sign is visible across the intersection if you look closely). Cost is 48 francs for a single, warm and clean, and the management so friendly; 56 francs double; 64 francs twin; all rates including breakfast. They even stored my luggage free on a day months later when I happened into Bordeaux during the time of a train strike and wanted to sightsee. Madame Hubert speaks French, Italian and Spanish, not so much English, but she promises special treatment for readers of your book. Tres bon!" (Dr. & Mrs. Kenneth Korven, Susanville, California; note from AF: Madame Jeannette Hubert, proprietress of the du Printemps, has been known to lavish "V.I.P." treatment on readers of this book).

BREGENZ, AUSTRIA

"**Frau Anni Findler** at Kaiserstrasse 31 (phone 238-503), opposite the Central Hotel, and only three minutes from the train station, rents spotlessly clean double rooms for 200 schillings per night, and, if requested, will serve a continental breakfast for 25 schillings. She is a charming person who speaks English and does everything to make her guests comfortable. Fresh flowers in our room the two weeks we stayed with her made us feel very welcome. Anyone who has stayed with Frau Findler wants to return" (Frances H. Sterns, Willimantic, Connecticut).

BREMEN, GERMANY

"Bremen is a good stopover en route by car from Copenhagen to Amsterdam. **Pension Tietjen**, near the station at 22 Slevogtstrasse (phone 341-559), offers large clean doubles at 40 marks, with breakfast 5.50 marks per person. . . . You'll also enjoy a lunch in the town **Ratskeller**, picturesque and low-priced" (Evelyn Lakott, Cambridge, Massachusetts). . . . "**Hotel Buthmann**, Löningstrasse 29, telephone 326-397, is only three blocks from the station, and on a quiet street. Rooms range from 57 to 60 marks for a double, breakfast included. We paid a total of 125 marks for a triple and a double. Operated by Herr Werner Timner, it is very clean, with excellent breakfast, no restaurant, pleasant personnel" (Virginia Gillette, Roxbury, Connecticut). . . . "Grouped around the Marktplatz are most of the worthwhile old buildings in Bremen. The **Cathedral** (currently closed for repairs) is a harmonious mixture of Romanesque and Gothic styles, built in the 11th, 13th, and 16th centuries. A crypt in the Cathedral has the curious property of preserving bodies placed in it; they dry to a black parchment stretched over the bones. For one mark you can see for yourself. The **Rathaus** is well-worth a visit, as you would expect from old whalebones and what-not collected from all over the globe. As the building is still in official use, it can be seen only by guided tour, which takes place Mondays to Fridays at 10 a.m., 11 a.m. and at noon, on Saturdays and Sundays at 11 a.m. and noon. The lore is in German, however. Star exhibit is an eight-foot 1500 lb. model of a warship hung from the ceiling. It used to hang in the Guildhall, on pulleys. When the merchants were good and tanked at one of their feasts, they would lower it to the floor, load its cannons, about 40¼-inch bore cannons, hoist the ship to their ceiling again, and fire away. They shot out most of the windows in the place every time they did it, quite aside from disturbing the neighbors. The **Ratskeller,** in the cellar of the Rathaus, is an excellent restaurant and stocks 600 different German wines. Also on the Marktplatz is the **Guildhall,** the meeting place of the powerful Merchants' Guild, and well worth a visit. Except for the very modern parliament building, the rest of the Marktplatz is bounded by fine old patrician houses. The most charming part of Bremen is the **Schnoor Quarter,** not far from the Marktplatz, a medieval district of narrow streets and tiny houses, dating back as far as the 14th century. The city has turned these houses over to artists, rent-free, on condition that they restore and preserve them. Besides living quarters and studios for the artists, the district is filled with interesting little shops: art galleries, antique shops, etc.; everything from hand-painted fabrics to organ grinders. I did not visit the museums, but the city art museum is said to have particularly good and important collections of Dutch paintings and of modern German Realists. The best thing about sightseeing in Bremen is that practically all the sights are concentrated in the old part of Bremen, within easy walking distance of each other. This is just as well as parking is practically impossible in the center. There is plenty to do at night in Bremen. The theater is considered one of the most progressive in Germany. Tickets, between DM 10 and DM 30, are easy to get, and the best tickets still available on the night of the performance can be had for 5 marks by those who can show student identification. **Die Lila Eule** (the violet owl) in Stielwall Strasse (corner of Bernhardstrasse) is a very lively jazz club which puts on evenings of folk song, beat music, poetry, old movies, and discussion as well. The best jazz in Germany appears there, and the house band is quite good. The prices are unbelievably low, even by German cafe standards: a half-liter of beer for 3.80 marks, wine for 4.50 marks—just a little more than in the average German inn. The management occasionally charges a 3 to 5 mark admission fee, which also buys the first drink. Opens at 8 p.m.; closed Mondays" (Rufus Wanning, Saugerties, New York).

BRIGHTON, ENGLAND

"We've lived in Brighton for 5 months and find it a most delightful town, worthy of space in your book. It's only an hour from London by train, but it's off the beaten path for American tourists, and offers many insights into British social customs, since it was one of the very first seaside resorts. We can recommend **Le Flemings Hotel,** 15 Regency Square, phone Brighton 27-539, £5 per person, a block from the seafront, and close to the central entertainment area. Brighton is also a treat for architecture hounds— the Regency squares and crescents are famous throughout England, and the Royal Pavilion is something out of the 'Arabian Nights' by the Nash Brothers—a pseudo-Indian exterior and a romantic Chinese interior" (Diane Stanfield, Brighton, England). . . . "A charming bed/breakfast hotel, located at 7 Charles Street, is one minute from the sea and two minutes from the Palace Pier, yet on a quiet, well-lighted, picturesque street. The proprietors are **Mr. and Mrs. Moore,** their son Roger, and their friendly cat 'Fluffy.' Terms are £4.25 per person—according to season. Hot and cold water in rooms, also heaters. Telephone: Brighton 65-848" (Rex Coffin, New York, New York). . . . "The **Golden Fry Fish,** at 51 St. James Place, closed Sundays, offers enormous fish-and-chips meals with your choice of four varieties of fish for £1 ($2.20), as well as other types of seafood. This meal was wrapped in the traditional newspaper and was a high point of my trip!" (Nancy Conrady, Amherst, Ohio).

BRISTOL, ENGLAND

"We have a small family guest house pleasantly situated in Bristol, near the Avon Gorge, which provides a lovely view and is a local beauty spot. Contact **Bedford House,** 21 Beaconsfield Road, Clifton, Bristol, telephone 38-273; we have central heating, cold and hot water, TV, and charge single £4, double £6 per night" (Mr. L. W. G. Pedler, Bristol).

BRUGES, BELGIUM

"We stayed at the very picturesque **Hotel Rembrandt-Rubens,** 38 Walplaats (phone 336439), for 750 Belgian francs ($25), including breakfast and service for two. Right on the recommended tourist route" (Evelyn Lakott, Cambridge, Massachusetts). . . . "**Hotel Cosmopolite,** 18 Kuipersstraat (phone 33-20-96), was full of gracious hospitality and friendliness. The rooms are clean and large, and the dining room attractive. Rates are 380 Belgian francs single, 740 francs double, including breakfast" (R. Dahlquist, Michigan City, Indiana). . . . "The **Studentencentrum,** Hauwerstraat 27 (phone 050/336226), offered the best accommodations and finest breakfast I had in three months in Europe. Open to tourists in July and August only, these modern rooms go for 320 Belgian francs ($10.66) single and 540 francs ($18) double. An all-you-can-eat breakfast is included (bread, jam, cheese and a special gingery cake-like bread). And it's only ten minutes from the train station" (Randy Mink, Elgin, Illinois). . . . "In Brugge (which, by the way, is the city in Belgium most worthy of visiting), we happened upon the **Hotel St. Christophe** (Nieuwe Gentweg 76, phone 331176), which is a bit pricey (700 francs for two, including breakfast) but *great!* It has a garden out back where you can have breakfast. In addition to the nice hotel, there are rooms out back, beyond the garden, which are . . . well, just fun to stay in. The service is good, as was the breakfast. We highly recommend both the Hotel St. Christophe and the city of Brugge!" (Richard and Eleanor Leary, Springfield, Illinois).

BUDAPEST, HUNGARY

"In this most beautiful of Eastern European cities, one can easily avoid the high-priced hotels assigned by the state travel agency, for if requested, the **Budapest Tourist Agency** at #5 Roosevelt Square, will provide accommodations in private homes at around $5 per night. This offers a unique opportunity to 'live' in a Communist city" (Mrs. Lorraine DeR. Hedlund, Ardmore, Oklahoma). . . . "While in Vienna, my husband, my son and I decided to go to Budapest. Ibusz, the Hungarian Tourist Office, got us our visas. When I remarked, tongue in cheek, it was too bad that we could not use our Eurailpass on this phase of our wanderings, we were told that the pass was good as far as the Hungarian border, and we would just have to pay from there to Budapest. We took advantage of that both coming and going. As we had been warned, all Budapest hotels were sold out due to an international soccer game, but the Hungarian Travel Office got us a private room for the night in a "government approved" apartment of a widow who must have known much better days, for much of her furniture was magnificent. The owner spoke adequate English. The charge was the equivalent of $9 for the three of us" (Mrs. Elmer S. Zweig, Fort Wayne, Indiana). . . . "A must for all travellers is a step back into the past, with a visit to the **Turkish Bath,** situated near the Erzsebet Bridge, on Szt. Gellert Rakpart. For 50 U.S. cents, you can enjoy a 16th century atmosphere, including two steam rooms, ice-water pool, and a dimly-lit central pool with surrounding smaller pools of varying temperatures. On completion of one's bathing you can relax on a comfortable bed until you are ready to face the outside 20th century world again" (Michael Lemits, Sydney, Australia).

CALAIS, FRANCE

"While passing through Calais, we stayed at the **Hotel Littoral,** 71 rue Aristide Briand—from the station, turn right and then second street on right (phone is 34-47-28). They charged 65 francs ($15.11) for a double room, including breakfast and service. Our windows overlooked the Park Saint Pierre, where a World War II museum is housed in a German bunker used for communications. The bunker was so well camouflaged it was never bombed. . . . With its beaches, Calais is a relaxing place" (Graeme Williams, Dee Why, Australia).

CAMBRIDGE, ENGLAND

"The absolutely spotless **Ellensleigh Guest House** of Mrs. Carol Wilson, 37 Tenison Road (phone 64888), is located near the train station, about a fifteen minute walk from the center of town. They are delightful proprietors and charge only £4.50 ($9.90) per person, including a fantastic, huge breakfast" (Fred Baskind, New York, New York).

CANNES, FRANCE

"We give a high recommendation to the **Hotel de France**, 85 Rue d'Antibes (phone 39-23-34), located two blocks from the public beach, and a really charming splurge-hotel; singles with shower and breakfast are 140 francs ($32.55), doubles with shower-bath and breakfast 180 francs ($41.86). The rooms are large, clean, and very inviting, and the management is exceedingly friendly" (Marilyn and Mitchell Shapiro, New Orleans, Louisiana; strong second from Caron Smith, San Francisco, California). . . . "After much searching, we located the **Hotel Pullman**, at 9 Rue Jean Daumas. While the proprietress there speaks no English, she is quite charming and makes sure guests do not forget their keys. Rooms are large and immaculate. Located 2 blocks from a public beach. 79 francs tout compris for a bathless double" (Pauline Hadley Maud, New York, New York).

CANTERBURY, ENGLAND

"Excellent accommodations are available at the **Pilgrims Guest House**, 18 The Friars (phone 64531), around the corner from the Cathedral and the river Stour; this guest house offers very light, spotlessly-clean rooms with hot and cold water, efficient heat, and electric outlets specially designed for shavers on 220 volt current. The conscientious hosts, Gilbert and Mary Jones; their price for bed and breakfast is from £6.50 per person" (Howard Kissel, Milwaukee, Wisconsin, as well as Robert B. Lawrence, Schenectady, New York). . . . "At **York House**, 22 Old Dover Road (phone 6574.503), the charge is £5.50 per person, and Mrs. Thomas' breakfast of mushrooms and bacon cannot be beaten. A house full of works of art, and clean in every way" (Lester B. Bridaham, Denver, Colorado).

CAPRI, ITALY

"The charming **Pensione Villa Bianca**, Via Belvedere Cesina #9 (phone 837-8016), is only five minutes' walk from the central piazza in the town of Capri. We had a large room with tub, large tiled balcony, and breakfast for two, for 12,000 lire ($14.45) each. This makes Capri on only slightly more than than $10 a day a delightful possibility. Our balcony contained 18 pots of flowers and, besides, was dripping with bougainvillea, which even peeped into the arched bathroom window. We had a sweeping view of the town and the bay. The new owner, Mr. Augusto Ferraro (who is English-speaking), has just taken over the pensione due to death in the family. He had been working as a wine steward in deluxe hotels in Germany and his concept of service continues at the deluxe level. We hope you will have the opportunity of recommending this immaculate and beautiful place" (Dr. and Mrs. Edward Tocas, Gaithersburg, Maryland). . . . "Try the **Hotel Maresca**, on the Marina Grande (phone 837-0442). One can't miss it. It's the only good-looking hotel in the port area. Unbelievable how clean it is. The owner speaks English, German and French. We had a good-sized double with terrace. Even from the bed, you could see the Bay of Naples (Naples, the Vesuvio, Sorrento). Free swimming possibilities. We paid 14,500 lire ($17.46) per person, but breakfast and dinner were included. One of the best buys in Europe" (Dr. George Ballun, Woodside, New York, with numerous seconding recommendations from other readers as well). . . . "I found, in the upper town of Capri ('Anacapri'), a modestly-priced pension called **Albergo Loreley**, tel: 837-1440. On Capri, which is to my mind the most beautiful island in the world (I've made 10 trips to Europe and 4 trips around the world), hotels can be quite expensive. This is a fairly new place (7 years old), small and intimate, very clean. The owner, Sr. D'Angiola, and his family, are extremely courteous and genuinely friendly and helpful. One feels as if in a friendly home. Rates are very reasonable; single rooms with breakfast are 13,000 lire ($15.66), and doubles with two meals are from 14,500 lire ($17.46) per person" (Jerome Siegel, Bronx, New York). . . . "Most of the restaurants in Capri are rather expensive. We stood outside one such costly place and were almost tempted to splurge. Fortunately, my wife smelled a roasting chicken across the street in a modest delicatessen with a few tables. We ordered two platters of fish/vegetables or chicken/pasta, including fresh olives and bread, full meals for some ridiculous price like $3 each. The food couldn't have been better at any price. Our find was **Scialapopolo,** at 31 Via le Botteghe. It's opposite Cappannino, a tourist-type restaurant. To find it, take the funicular to the top, to the main piazza, turn left, and enter the archway just to the side of the Vuotto store" (George Velsey, Port Washington, New York). . . . "For an excursion to Capri, it is far cheaper and certainly more enjoyable to do it on your own, rather than on an organized tour" (Paul Rorovsky, Johannesburg, South Africa).

CARDIFF, WALES

"Although you do not include Cardiff, Wales, in your book, it is a beautiful, fascinating city with very friendly people and certainly deserving of mention. We stayed in the **Coleshill Hotel** (Bed & Breakfast), 142 Newport Road, phone Cardiff 491-798. Our host was absolutely delightful, serving us a delicious breakfast and giving us the nicest and definitely the cleanest double room that we had in three months of travel in Europe. The bus from the train station stops right at the front door (I don't remember the number), and the cost was only £4.50 per person. There was parking, too, and do be sure to recommend a visit to the unique Cardiff Castle. It is like no other in Europe and well worth visiting" (Mr. and Mrs. Mark C. Lee, Modesto, California). . . . "At **Mrs. Ostanek's Guest House,** 1 Dispenser Gardens (phone 33-400), I had a spacious single room with breakfast, bath, service, VAT, all inclusive, for £5. It's right next to the Dispenser Gardens and eight minutes walk from the RR station" (Lecia Katherine Boyd, Waikeria, Teawamutu, New Zealand).

CHAMONIX, FRANCE

"At the **Chalet Ski Station,** Chamonix Mont Blanc 74400, phone (50) 53-20-25, Chamonix, a dormitory-like establishment with separate rooms for men and women, the charge is only 19 francs per bed" (Lori Clark, San Rafael, California). . . . "In expensive Chamonix, we found a pension, the **Hotel du Grépon** (phone 53-13-03), owned by A. Bossonney, a Chamonix guide, serving a 35-franc meal which outclassed anything we found in some of the more expensive restaurants in the main part of the village. The hotel (which charges 40 to 55 francs per person for overnight lodgings) is located on the Impasse du Rhodendrons, and a menu is placed at the intersection of this street and the main street" (Ronald Korman, Los Angeles, California).

CHARTRES, FRANCE

"After leaving the chateaux of the Loire River, we decided to spend the night in Chartres to visit the city's famous and beautiful cathedral; we stayed at the **Hotel Jehan-de-Beauce,** 19 Avenue Jehan-de-Beauce (phone 21-01-41), very close to the train station. For 148 francs we had a large, clean, warm room with showers and toilet, and with three single beds, breakfast and all taxes and services included; normal doubles with private bath are 135 francs, breakfast and all else included. This was our best find in three months of European travel" (Mrs. Sandra Hunt, Poughkeepsie, New York). . . . "Most hotels in Chartres have put up their prices, but at the **Hotel de la Poste** (to the left of the post office), we paid only 65 francs ($15.11) for a clean room and shower for two adults and a child" (Mr. and Mrs. P. K. Pal, Calcutta, India). . . . "There is a youth hostel here with beds for 15 francs ($3.48) a night, and from its windows you see the Cathedral sitting on the hill. To get there, walk to the Cathedral and behind it down to the river, then look for signs that say **"Auberge de Jeunesse".** . . . I suggest instead of enduring the high prices of Paris, to commute from Chartres, it's only an hour by train. And there are enchanting, free organ concerts every Sunday evening at 5 p.m." (Danielle Jehanne Rappaport, APO New York).

CHATEAUDUN, FRANCE

"If you leave Paris, mid-morning, stop and tour Versailles, have lunch, stop and tour Chartres, and continue south on Route 10, you'll arrive in Chateaudun about 5 p.m. We stayed at the **Hotel de Beauce,** #50 Rue de Jallans (phone 45-14-75), which is a short street to the left as you enter town if you are driving south. It was modern, very clean, good restaurant, owner spoke excellent English. Double with private bath was 135 francs, including breakfast" (Dorman and Evie Combest, West Hollywood, California).

CHERBOURG, FRANCE

"I had a single room for 45 francs a night at the **Hotel de la Gare,** 10 Place Jean Jaurés. This is right across the street from the Cherbourg Gare—not the Cherbourg Maritime Gare which lets you out by the ship. A few people sometimes like to arrive at a port a day before leaving, so this little hotel (where doubles are only 55 francs) can be very convenient. Just make sure the train stops at Cherbourg Gare, and not Cherbourg Maritime" (Adrian Allen, Miami Beach, Florida).

CHESTER, ENGLAND

"A city that should be included in your "Tale of Many Cities" is Chester, an historic site with the complete circuit of medieval walls still preserved. (Behind the medieval fronts of the old buildings are modern shopping centers and convenient parking garages.) One of the nicest places to stay here is with Mrs. N. Cowie, who calls her place **Elgin;** it's located at 2 Princes Avenue off Queens Road (which is off City Road, just a block from the R.R. station). Mrs. Cowie will charge from £4 in 1980, plus 30 pence for a bath, no service charge or value added tax. This will include a very satisfactory English breakfast and space to park your car. The city center and main attractions are easily reached by walking and Mrs. Cowie will do all she can to make you feel at home. Telephone number is 23372. Chester is a good touring center for Cheshire, the moors of Derbyshire, and 'Wales" (James and Yvonne Bunting, Woonsocket, Rhode Island). . . . "Chester is one of the most delightful towns anywhere in the world and you should hasten to add the **Hamilton Guest House,** whose 1980 charge is £6.50 per person. Located at 5-7 Hamilton Street in the Hoole area of town, it is neat and outstandingly warm. The hosts make you feel comfortable and 'at home' " (The Stratings, Colorado Springs, Colorado).

COLOGNE, GERMANY

"We were quite satisfied with the **Hotel Heinzelmännchen,** 5-7 Hohe Pforte (phone 21-12-17), which charged 55 marks ($28.94) for a double without bath, breakfast and service included" (William Lydecker, St. Peter, Minnesota). . . . "At least 95 points must go to the spic and span, brightly wall-papered **Hotel Brandenburger Hof.** Only about five minutes from the 'Bahnhof' and near the massively impressive Dom Cathedral, the Brandenburger's rates are 28 to 30 marks single, 38 to 43 marks ($20 to $22.63) double, which includes service and breakfast. The people are just lovely too. Address is Brandenburger Strasse 2-4, and the telephone number is 12-28-89" (Carma Bamber, San Francisco, California). . . . "Readers should make an effort to travel the short distance from Cologne to the former capital of the Holy Roman Empire, Aachen. The cathedral, part of which dates from before Charlemagne, is the most unusual I have seen, and contains the actual throne of Charlemagne. In addition, the area surrounding the cathedral is a delightful maze of twisting, medieval streets with sidewalk markets, and ancient homes. The trip from Cologne and back can easily be made in a day, or even less" (Ronald A. Audet, Portsmouth, Virginia). . . . "From mid-April to mid-October, the Rhine steamer leaves Cologne at 7 a.m. daily and arrives at Mainz at 9 p.m., 14 hours later and a long ride. The fare is 91 DM ($47.89). From Mainz it leaves at 8:45 a.m. and arrives Cologne at 6 p.m., less than 10 hours. I took the 14-hour ride but to anyone considering this interesting trip to old castles, may I suggest either getting on at Rüdesheim or Koblenz and traveling the distance between those two cities, because it's between those cities that the most spectacular scenery and castles are to be found; and both cities are served by connecting trains taking you either to Cologne or Frankfurt, depending upon which direction you happen to be traveling. The food on the steamer is excellent and not really too expensive and the service is incomparable" (Edward H. Pietraszek, Cicero, Illinois). . . . "The **Opera** in Cologne is housed in a very beautiful, modern building which is itself one of the chief tourist sights of the city. What many tourists do not realize is that the performances there are excellent and the price absurdly low, from 7 to 35 marks. For 15 DM I had an excellent seat for a beautifully sung performance of Verdi's 'Don Carlo.' The auditorium is so well designed that there are no really bad seats; you can, therefore, buy the cheapest tickets. . . . Perhaps the most beautiful view in Europe is of Cologne with its cathedral and medieval houses bathed in floodlights as seen from across the Rhine. The best way is to walk across the Deutzer Bridge, just behind the cathedral" (Ronald A. Audet, Portsmouth, Virginia).

CORFU, GREECE

"If you should ultimately find space to include the increasingly popular Island of Corfu in your book, you can recommend the **Hotel Avra** (phone 29-269) in Benitsa (a fishing village nine miles outside the town of Corfu) for persons seeking a comfortable, clean country inn completely unspoiled by commercial greed. Run by the truly hospitable Spinoula family, who treat clients as if they were guests in their own home, it offers a simple but clean room with private shower and full pension of three big, good meals for 740 drachmas per day single, only 1,400 drachmas double; at least demi-pension is obligatory, at a cost of 850 drachmas for a single room, 1,250 for a double. It also has its own private beach and is in a beautiful situation, 30 minutes by bus from town. A favorite with discriminating British travelers, many of whom return annually to the Avra for their holidays" (Bernard K. Schram, Ste. Genevieve, Missouri). . . . "We stayed at **Hotel Cavalieri,** on the city square. Not a budget hotel ($35 for a double, but with half pension) but very pleasant, with food service and fairly good food" (Dr. Charles R. Fitz, Toronto, Ontario). . . . "In Corfu, we recommend **Hotel Bretagne,** 27 National Stadium Street, tel. 30724, where a double with shower and breakfast was only 700 drachmas ($19.44). The owner of the hotel will pick you up from the ferry wharf and return you there on your departure. This is away from the center of town, but delightfully located near the beachfront" (Michael and Juliette Hudger, Cremorne, Australia).

CORK, IRELAND

"The **Killarney Guesthouse** (phone 510491), right across the road from the railway station, charges £5 per person per night for bed and breakfast. A very lovely woman runs the hotel" (J. M. Wilson, Lae, New Guinea). . . . "**Mrs. Ethel Morrissy,** 7 King's Terrace, Lower Glanmire Road, phone 53650, has large, clean rooms, plus the usual large breakfast. Close to train, bus, and downtown. Mrs. Morrissy bent over backward to please her guests. I met several very interesting Irish people here who helped make my stay very pleasant. Charge for a single, bed and breakfast, was £4.25 (doubles £6.25) and Mrs. Morrissy says she won't raise it until costs force her to. There are five other B & B hotels immediately adjacent. On a main road, but not noisy. This is a real bargain" (Floyd M. DeLuey, Pacific Grove, Calif.). . . . "May I suggest to your readers the Ring of Kerry tour. This is a one-day excursion leaving at 10 a.m. and returning at 10 p.m. You see some of the most marvelous scenery, including the Lakes of Killarney and Dingle Bay. There are two stops along the way for meals and several photo stops. You are never rushed, but can eat a leisurely meal. Definitely not to be missed" (Erika J. Papp, Jackson Heights, New York).

CORNWALL, ENGLAND

"Owners Margaret and Cliff Jackson are really working hard restoring the **Globe Posting House Hotel** (phone Fowey 3322) in Fowey, Cornwall, to its original state. It's located in the center of this charming town, across from the old movie theater. For £8.50 ($18.70) we got a double room and breakfast, not to mention free entertainment—their parrot, Ringo sings 'It's Impossible.' This young couple is working very hard to make a success of the place" (Mr. & Mrs. Ray Figelski, Studio City, California).

COSTA BRAVA, SPAIN
(not a city, but the stretch of seashore along the Mediterranean, where Spain joins France)

"We'd like to recommend the **Hotel Diana** (phone 34-03-04) in Tossa de Mar (the most beautiful town on the Costa Brava in Spain). This is a renovated villa right on the beach; we paid 1,400 pesetas ($21.21) apiece for all three meals, and a beautiful double room with private modern bath and balcony" (Arnold Friedman, Flushing, New York; seconding recommendation from Rochelle Seiden, Brooklyn, New York). . . . "I realize that there are many real bargains along this beautiful stretch, but I hardly think the **Cap d'Or** (phone 340081), at 14 Apartado in Tossa de Mar, can be surpassed. Family-run, good food, directly on the Mediterranean, all for 1,450 pesetas single, 1,400 pesetas per person double (full pension). Clientele mostly British and French" (Dr. James T. Vail, Jr., A.P.O., New York). . . . "We scouted three villages, and decided that Tossa de Mar, with its quaint town, its ruined castle, its picturesque cove, was the loveliest spot for a short stay. (If we were settling down for a long stay, we might prefer San Feliu.) At Tossa we stayed at the huge, modern **Hotel Rovira,** Paseo del Mar, on the beach, and had room, with bath, for about 650 pesetas ($9.84) a day apiece. If you are willing to go back a minute or two from the beach, you might try the **Hotel L'Hostalet** (phone 34-00-88), which fronts on the little square where the 'big' church is located and where a room with private bath and breakfast is 700 pesetas per day" (Robert E. Firth, Berkeley, Calif.). . . . "We spent three weeks at the **Hotel Casa Delgado,** 7 Pola (phone 34-02-91), Tossa de Mar/Gerona, Spain, and we recommend it highly. A single with shower is 390 pesetas; double with shower 800 pesetas per person; double with bath 850 pesetas per person, all including breakfast. It's just a few steps from the door to a beautiful beach, and that is free" (Muriel Pierce, St. Petersburg, Florida, with recent seconding recommendations from other readers as well).

CRETE, GREECE

"I recently spent 2 weeks at the **Oceanis,** Florins Street 52, Poros, tel. 284-628, owned and run by George Vlataki and his family—they speak English. The rooms and facilities are adequate and clean and a double costs 280 drachmas per person ($7.77), a triple 210 drachmas ($5.83) per person. The Vlatakis are also very helpful and warm. The pension is a ten-minute walk from the ferry port to Athens, five minutes walk from the beach, and a ten-minute bus ride to the center of Iraklion and the central Cretan bus terminus" (Alvin I. Sher, University of London, England). . . . "I would like to highly recommend the **Vines Pension** in Iraklion, run by the Katsirdakis family. The address is Korytsas 13 (phone 28-57-51), and is actually in Poros, a suburb of Iraklion, but it is only a short walk from where the boats from Piraeus dock. We had a double room, without bath, for 350 drachmas ($9.72). Rooms are large, airy and very clean, and a full bath is just a few steps down the hall" (Ed and Betty Quinn, Skokie, Illinois).

DELPHI, GREECE

"We recommend both the **Hotel Hermes** (phone 82-318), and **E. Zinelis House** (otherwise known as the **Hotel Athina,** phone 82-239). Both were very attractive, had views beyond description, and most pleasant management. We planned to stay a day and we remained a week. At E. Zinelis House, doubles were 470 drachmas, triples 570 drachmas, singles 365 drachmas. We ate and visited at the Hotel Hermes (500 drachmas for a single with private bath, 580 drachmas double with bath, plus breakfast at 70 drachmas per person, and service), which was full the day we arrived" (Frank L. Esterquest, Oxford, Ohio).

DIJON, FRANCE

"During our auto trip from Paris to Lausanne, we stopped at Dijon overnight and discovered by sheer chance a delightful inn called **Hotel du Sauvage,** 64 Rue Monge, tel. 41-31-21. Its motto: 'le Confort Moderne dans un cadre ancien'. A double room with hot and cold running water, breakfast and service included, will cost 54 francs ($12.55) in 1980. It has also a good dining room with moderate prices and good home cooking. Picturesque terrace area outside" (Dana A. Regillo, Lexington, Massachusetts). . . . "At **Hotel Jacquemart,** 32 Rue Verrerie, phone 32-44-96, price for two persons was 75 francs ($17.44), breakfast 8 francs. Located in a beautiful 'old city' area, with museums within easy walking distance" (Lois and Art Leb, Canton, Ohio).

DOVER, ENGLAND

"As many people come from the continent to Dover in the late afternoon and wish to remain there overnight, we think that the address of **Linden Guest House**—Bed and Breakfast, Mr. and Mrs. D. Bowles, 231 Folkestone Road, Dover, Kent, tel: Dover 205-449, would be helpful. Mr. and Mrs. Bowles are charming and kind. Their home is spotlessly clean, with running hot water and heat in each room. Excellent breakfast. No trouble parking car. Bus stops at the corner. Price £6 per person. One should not pass through Dover without visiting the great Norman castle" (Mr. and Mrs. Wm. T. Halstead, Los Gatos, California). . . . "I recommend the **Josefi Guest House,** 169 Folkestone Road (phone 203737), Dover, for £4.75 a night. I had an excellent bed and room (bigger than one I visited in London's plush Europa Hotel) and the best breakfast I've had in years. The place is beautifully decorated—and for winter travelers—warm! Mrs. McMillan runs it" (Luis Muñiz, Santurce, Puerto Rico).

DUBLIN, IRELAND

"I have just returned from a trip to the British Isles and spent several very pleasant days at **Gresmarlin**, 52 St. Lawrence Road, Clontarf, Dublin. This is a delightful guest house operated by Mrs. Bateman, telephone 339-582. I had a very nice room overlooking the rose garden for £5 per night including a sumptuous Irish breakfast" (Reginald V. Lytle, Naples, Florida). . . . "For 5 pounds per day (including a most generous and delicious breakfast, too!), I stayed with a Mrs. C. Drain of 265 Clontarf Road, in a home rightly called **"Bayview"**, as it looks directly across the bay of the Irish Sea. Great view, very nice people—a real "buy" for the money. Mrs. Drain's establishment is but five minutes' bus ride from the center of Dublin. The phone number is 339-870. Whereas your book doesn't have much in it regarding Dublin, I certainly hope that your next edition includes this lovely little place called Bayview—your readers simply can't go wrong" (Robert M. Sullivan, Chicago, Illinois). . . . "We highly recommend a bed-and-breakfast place called **"San Vista"**, at 237 Clontarf Road, phone 339-582. Mrs. O'Connell, the proprietress, was lovely to us. Breakfasts were excellent and served at a time to fit *our* schedule. Her rates for 1980 will be £6 ($13.20) inclusive (no extra charge for tax, baths, etc.), and her home, reached by bus #30, is located right on the main bus line to downtown; just cross the road for the bus! Mrs. O'Connell has taken in guests for 14 years and the comments in her guest book attest to the fact that our wonderful stay was similar to the satisfaction of previous guests" (Marcia Stimatz and Kathleen Gallagher, Butte, Montana). . . . "Dublin is the town of *Ulysses,* and some visitors will want to view the various major sections of Dublin that are referred to in Joyce's epic novel. It takes a day to walk the path of Leopold Bloom's 24 hour journey, but the experience is unrivalled, even though one must depend on his imagination and memory of the book to supplement the direct visual appreciation, due to the changes that have taken place since 1904" (Tom Burnett, Washington, D.C.). . . . "The half-hour visit to the **Guinness Brewery,** St. James Gate, is free, and is followed by an opportunity to sample the product at no cost. This trip should be a must for people staying in Dublin, but, in addition, it is a delightful way to pass the time for anyone with a few hours between planes at Dublin Airport. The route is below; take the airport bus to Dublin bus station (cost 80p—$1.76), walk across the River Liffey to Fleet Street, and take a No. 78 bus to the Guinness Brewery (cost 12p—26¢), take in the half-hour visit and film show, one or two glasses of free Guinness, and then board any bus to O'Connell Street. Walk from there, five to ten minutes, to the bus station and return to the airport via the airport bus, total cost, $4. Time required is about four hours. I landed at 9:20 a.m., visited the brewery, returned to the airport, had lunch, and went out at 2:05 p.m." (F. J. Spencer, Richmond, Virginia). . . . "In Dublin, I found that you could rent a bicycle for a day for about $7.50, by far the cheapest means of sightseeing transportation. The name of the big shop was **Fagans,** and it is located on Capel Street" (Matthew S. Watson, London, England). . . . "Let me offer the following cultural footnote to Dublin for the benefit of tourists interested in literature. Any admirer of James Joyce must not fail to see his museum at the **Martello Tower** in Sandycove. It houses photographs, manuscripts, and memorabilia, and there's a great view from the top. Take the #8 bus from Eden Quay in Dublin to Sandycove Harbour in Dun Laoghaire. It's about a thirty-minute ride; fare each way is 32p. When you arrive, a short walk to the left of the bus stop will bring you to the tower. It's open for summer tourists from 10 a.m. to 1 p.m., from 2 to 5:15 p.m., Sundays only from 2:30 to 6 p.m. Admission 20 pence, students 15 pence and children 10 pence" (James R. Paris, Weehawken, New Jersey). . . . "Take a bus trip (either public service or tour) to **Glendaloch** and its ruins. Another interesting trip is to *Wexford,* especially the free walking tour of the city conducted by Mr. Paddy Doran, a member of the local historical society" (Vincent Garvy, Annapolis, Maryland).

DUBROVNIK, YUGOSLAVIA

"For the tourist who wants to swim and wants to be assured of sun; for the tourist who likes a warm sea; for the tourist who wants to pass his evenings at first-rate concerts and plays—I'd like to recommend Dubrovnik, on the Dalmatian Coast. . . . One can get a charming room with bath in a private home for as little as $7 and can eat in town quite easily for $3.50. . . . Every night in July and August, when the Summer Festival is on, there are several events to choose from. These include operas, a fantastic production of

Hamlet performed in the courtyard and on the battlements of 13th-century Fort Lovrjenac, concerts by visiting soloists and Yugoslavians, folk dancing, etc. The most expensive ticket to *Hamlet* costs $8 and scales down; the best tickets to hear Anton Dermota in a magnificent lieder concert in the Rector's Palace, cost $6.50" (Jay Wolf, New York City). . . . "Dubrovnik, a beautiful city on the Dalmatian Coast of Yugoslavia, is the capital of the ancient Republic of Ragusa, with a wonderful summer festival. When the periodic ships arrive in Dubrovnik, local women descend on them like vultures to offer rooms in their homes to tourists. We took a chance and went with a young girl who spoke some English. The home turned out to be on the top of a very high hill, a literally breathtaking walk, but a magnificent view of the harbor. The family was friendly, and we had a comfortable accommodation for two for $7 a night. Not everyone on the boat made such a good connection, but it's worth a try. If you don't like the first room you choose, there are dozens of women in the streets ready to offer you something else. The lingua franca between room-renters and tourists seems to be German, so the women will follow you asking 'Zimmer'. We had to summon all our broken German and their broken English to say that we already had a room. This gets to be a drag, unfortunately" (Phyllis and Steve Wilson, Chicago, Illinois). . . . "I have seen the coastline of Mexico, both east and west, the coastline all down the western side of South America, and of many parts of the Mediterranean, but I think I shall never see islands and coastline more beautiful and beckoning than those of the Dalmatian coastline. Such terraced fields and vineyards with ramparts of ancient rock, like multifortresses of a disappearing rural existence! The little coves and inlets sheltering pink-roofed fishing villages have a dreamy verdancy, and the rocky shoreline deceptively gives the appearance of roughly packed ancient yellow sand drying in the sun and gently bleaching over the centuries. A coast of history, of fortresses and centuries of battle—right and wrong. The mountains are spaced to blend from a deep blue-green thru the spectrum to a misty blue-grey lost in the horizon. Particularly pleasing to the eye in beauty and strangeness was the island of **Korcula.** If I have lots of money some day and six months I don't know what to do with, I would go to this land and soak up the mystery and beauty of it. It is Yugoslavia" (Madelin L. Lawler, Mt. Prospect, Illinois). . . . "We have an absolutely great suggestion for readers looking for a room in a private home within the walls of the old city. **Mr. and Mrs. Mihocevic** and their two English-speaking sons have two bright, cheerful double-bedded and one twin-bedded rooms to let for stays of several days (Strosmajerova 1, Dubrovnik; telephone 26-172). The house is in a three-floor walk-up in an ancient, but spotless building on a narrow quiet street only one block from the morning open market (great for quick snacks) and a short walk from access to the seaward sunbathing rocks beyond the city walls. Rates are 180 dinar for a double in July and August, 150 the rest of the year, and include touches like Turkish coffee in the morning, slippers at the doorstep of each room, free showers, and an occasional nightcap with the family. The magnificent bathroom right down the hall (with a picture-window overlooking the ancient city, no less) is fully-equipped and has plenty of hot water (30 dinar each bath or shower)" (David C. Brezic, New York, New York).

EDINBURGH, SCOTLAND

This is the capital of Scotland, the home of Robert Burns and Robert Louis Stevenson, and one of the most beautiful cities on earth, boasting a breathtaking boulevard—Princes Street, with its famous Princes Gardens. Prices increase during the first two weeks of the Edinburgh Music and Drama Festival—in 1980 from late August to mid-September—but are quite reasonable at all other times. Even during the Festival period, however, girls arriving in Edinburgh may find accommodations by going to the office of the Edinburgh Central Council of the YWCA, 7 Randolph Place (phone 225-4379), where there's a booking desk and an inexpensive coffee house, open weekdays, 9:30 a.m. to 5, on Saturdays until 1 p.m. I have the assurance of Katherine Steele, YWCA Sec'y, that if she can't put you up at one of the Edinburgh residences of the YWCA, she'll try to find a room in a private home at a special festival charge of approximately $16 for bed and breakfast.

Young men and women arriving in Edinburgh at other times will receive better rates at the **YMCA Residential Club,** 12 Rothesay Place (phone 225-2134; that's at the west end of Princes Street, take bus 3, 31 or 33 to Manor Place), where bed-and-breakfast ranges from £3 in dorm-style rooms, £4.50 in a twin-bedded room, and £5.50 in a single; or at the **Central Hostel,** 14 South St. Andrew Street (556-4303), only a hundred yards from the rail and bus stations, where accommodation is only £3. The latter establishment is open Easter to the end of September only, often takes women as well.

Older readers and couples will want to try the normal bed-and-breakfast houses, whose reader recommendations now follow: "We have been meaning to strongly recommend the **Clifton Hotel,** at 18 Hopetoun Crescent (off MacDonald Road), which has a charming owner, an amusing Victorian decor, and charges £4.75 per person for bed and breakfast. Telephone number 556-1180" (Lynn & Sandy Comesky, Palo Alto, California; numerous recommendations for the Clifton from other readers as well). . . . "We loved the **Lairg Private Hotel,** 11 Coates Gardens (phone 337-1050), whose bed-and-breakfast rate was £5.75 ($12.65) per person, double room. Immaculate, quiet rooms, each with a radio. Other similarly-priced hotels are located on the same block" (Ellen Liman, New York City). . . . "We stayed at **St. Valery Guest House,** 36 Coates Gardens (phone 337-1893), operated by Mr. and Mrs. R. Shannon. They are just charming, and truthfully, we have never seen a more spotless home—it just shines! Here, for a lovely room overlooking several pretty backyards, plus a huge and beautifully served breakfast, we paid just £5 per person per night. We give this the highest recommendation" (Mrs. Robert Wade Hughey, Lafayette, California). . . . "For single girls, let me recommend **Miss Brett's,** upstairs at 44 Haymarket Terrace (phone 337-5916), only a short walk from Princes Street, where we stayed for £3.75 each, bed and breakfast. Each night when we returned, we found a thermos of hot tea waiting, along with a plate of cakes or cookies. This was the nicest place of all" (Marcia Hanf, Urbana, Illinois). . . . "My find in Europe was the **Rosehall Hotel,** 101 Dalkeith Road in the Newington section of Edinburgh (phone 667-5952). Spotlessly clean, convenient and inexpensive for Edinburgh (£7 per person in either single or twin bedded rooms, breakfast and service included); the biggest surprise of all was the breakfast, one of the best I have ever had in my whole life; it must be seen to be believed. Claire Levey is the cordial and helpful hostess" (Michael Hirsch, Albany, New York; note by A.F.: numerous seconding recommendations for the Rosehall Hotel from other readers). . . . "I highly recommend **Mrs. Murray's** boarding house, 116 Mayfield Road, Edinburgh (tel: 667-6433), where I stayed in a most comfortable and clean room for only £4 ($8.80). Included in this price is a serving of tea and cakes before retiring and in the morning a mammoth breakfast consisting of juice, cereal, eggs, ham *and* bacon, toast and tea" (Judy Greene, Sacramento, California). . . . "My husband and I would like to recommend the **Kiloran Guest House,** 17 Leamington Terrace, phone 229-1789, run by Mrs. Lamond in Edinburgh. This delightful woman went out of her way to make us feel at home. She gave us tea after we came from the show and a delicious breakfast in the morning. I'll sum up our stay at Kiloran Guest House by using Mrs. Lamond's own words: 'Even though you are staying for one night, that doesn't mean that I have to treat you like strangers.' Bed and breakfast for one was only £4.25" (Mr. and Mrs. W. F. Payne, CFPO, C.A.F.E.). . . . "The **Gunn Guest House,** 74 Dublin St. (phone 031-556-5032), stands out in my mind. Proprietor Mrs. M. E. Bates is from Canada and told me Americans are among her favorite guests. She and her husband call you by your name and together serve a giant breakfast. Prices are from £10 double, no singles. Dublin Street is really a continuation of South St. Andrew Street, which lies to the right of the railroad station. I found NUS' Edinburgh branch more efficient and less hectic than the London main office" (Randy Mink, Elgin, Illinois). . . . "We found the **Newington Guest House** (18 Newington Road, Edinburgh 9, tel. 031-667-3356) to be just right for us, as it was a bed and breakfast in a spacious old house within walking distance (15 minutes) of the main downtown area. At £6 each, per person, we felt we had done quite well. We noticed that other streets nearby also had bed and breakfast places, though we did not look into any of them. We suspect prices were comparable" (E. Brown, Belmont, Massachusetts). . . . "For a comfortable stay in Edinburgh, I'd recommend Mrs. Milne's guest house, **Arlington,** 11 Eyre Place. For £4.50 per person we had an excellent twin bed room with hot and cold water and a breakfast you should see to believe. Juice or grapefruit segments, cereals or two eggs and bacon or sausage, milk, coffee, butter, jam, etc., served on tables laid with pure linen and china. Flowers on every table. The lady is most helpful and the service impeccable. A good find" (Efi Vicka, Athens, Greece). . . . "We stayed in the bed-and-breakfast house of **Mr. and Mrs. Thomson,** 119 Mayfield Road, phone 031-667-3908, where it was £3.50 per person for a twin-bedded room. The room, breakfast, and Mrs. Thomson were so lovely that we stayed three days longer than we had expected. To get there, take bus #42 from the Royal Scottish Academy on Princes Street to Mayfield Road. If the Thomsons have no room, there are lots of other bed-and-breakfast houses on Mayfield Road. To miss Scotland on a European vacation is very foolish" (Fran Knopf and Marion Buchbinder, Long Island City, New York). . . . "Please be sure to include the friendly, comfortable guest house of **Mr. and Mrs. B. Latimer** at 17 Queen's Crescent, tel. 667-3932. The Latimers are a beautiful young couple who seem to thoroughly enjoy their guests, who, in turn, thoroughly enjoy being there. The house is conveniently located on a quiet street between Dalkeith Road and Mayfield Gardens and, for £4.50 per night per person, one receives a lovely large breakfast along with a night's lodging in an immaculate room, kitchen facilities and a lounge with a color TV. An added plus is that there is no extra charge for showers or heat. We feel we owe our enchantment with Edinburgh to the Latimers" (David and Elizabeth DeLong, Chapel Hill, North Carolina). . . . "I am the proprietor of a small guesthouse situated in a quiet district near the center of Edinburgh; called **Villa Nina**, it consists of six comfortable bedrooms with hot and cold running water, and there are ample facilities for showers and bath, as well as a lounge with color TV available at any time. Our tariff is £4.50 daily, bed and breakfast, low season; £5 in high season. The address: 39 Leamington Terrace, Edinburgh 10, phone 229-26-44" (Mr. B. Cecco) . . . "I would be much obliged if you would list my **Gifford Guest House**, at 103 Dalkeith Road (phone 667-4688). The price is £4.50 per person per night, including breakfast" (H. M. Bride, Edinburgh).

FRANKFURT, GERMANY

"**Pension Lohmann**, Stuttgarter Strasse 31 (phone 232-534), charged us 23 marks ($12.10) per person for a double overnight and breakfast the following morning. Singles with breakfast are 27 marks ($14.21)" (Mrs. Gilbert S. Brown, Dallas, Texas). . . . "**Hotel Wiesbaden**, Baseler Strasse 52 (phone 23-23-47), is just off the Bahnhof Platz, a few hundred yards from where the airport trains arrive and depart. A double without bath, breakfast not included nor required, cost 42 marks, including service and tax. Extremely friendly staff" (William Lydecker, St. Peter, Minnesota). . . . "My husband and I stayed in a large, clean, very reasonable pension only two blocks from the main train station. The owner, Doris Hohmann, was extremely helpful. Cost: 37 marks for a double, with breakfast an additional 4 marks per person. Address: **Pension Hohmann**, Mainzer Landstrasse 105, tel. 23-30-98" (Layle Reiber, Salt Lake City, Utah). . . . "Don't miss the opera in Frankfurt. The opera house is less than 13 years old, every seat is a good one, and the productions are top quality. . . . For other evening enjoyment, head for **Sachsenhausen**, just across the Main River. This is the old section of the city, and the streets are lined with gasthouses where you can sing, link arms and drink apple wine (the 'national drink' of Frankfurt), all very inexpensively. A large glass of apple wine costs 2 marks ($1.05), and at that price, you'll be unconscious before too long" (Bill Buck, APO 57, New York, New York). . . . "You can't visit Frankfurt without seeing **Sachsenhausen**, the area of town reached by crossing the Main on the Alte Brücke (Old Bridge). First you will see the modern, 120 meter silo-tower of **Henninger Brewery**, with the two revolving restaurants on top; the area all around contains outdoor applewine inns, and, as in Vienna's Grinzing district, one can spot these places by the lanterns bedecked with green boughs. The people are warm and friendly and invite you to link arms and sing, whether you know the songs or not" (Marcia Hanf, Urbana, Illinois).

FREIBURG IM BREISGAU, GERMANY

"An outstanding "Gasthaus" in Freiburg was the **"Goldener Sternen"**, at Emmendinger Strasse 1 (phone 278-373); when we called them, they sent a taxi to pick us up and were most helpful. Tariff was 45 marks for 2 persons, including breakfast; and the proprietress speaks good English" (Mr. F. Wherritt, Marlin Waters, Queensland, Australia).

GARMISCH, GERMANY

"The **Pension Haus Mirabell**, Hindenburgstrasse 20 (phone 4826), had a spotlessly clean double room for us for about 24 marks ($12.63) per person including breakfast" (Paul Simon, Troy, Ill.). . . . "We found the **Gästehaus Kornmüller**, Höllentalstr. 36, to be superb, and extended our stay there because of the excellent arrangements. Frau Kornmüller could not have been pleasanter or more helpful in responding to our needs. We paid 16 marks per person, including breakfast served in the garden; and were advised by her to dine at the Restaurant Frauendorfer in Partenkirchen (corner Ludwig-Mittenwaldstrasse), where the food was reasonable, excellent, with a Bavarian band playing—it is well worth a visit" (Virginia Gillette, Roxbury, Connecticut). . . . "I heartily recommend the '**Gästehaus Kornmüller**', Höllentalstrasse 36, phone 3557. Excellent rooms in a typically Bavarian home, range from 15 to 20 marks ($7.89 to $10.52) per person, including breakfast" (Edwin C. Carlson, D.D.S., St. Petersburg, Florida). . . . "The 'find' of our summer trip was the **Zur Schönen Aussicht Hotel,** Gsteigstrasse 36, phone 2474. This is a beautiful, and fairly new, hotel above Garmisch-Partenkirchen, out of town, with a spectacular view of the mountains and the Olympic Ski area from most bedrooms, and a terrace restaurant. Right across the road are the start of several mountain paths. Having a car would help, but it can be reached by bus and a short walk from the busline. Prices: single room, 22 DM; double, 40 DM; double with bath and balcony, 50 DM; and breakfast is included in all rates. We hope to return here for a longer stay sometime" (Duane Sandgren, Salinas, California). . . . "At the **Gästehaus Jocher,** St-Martin-Strasse 19 (phone 3642), we were well received, had a room with balcony for 16 marks ($8.42) per person, including a good breakfast in our room or on the balcony, and the entire house was well painted, clean and well landscaped" (Name withheld, Costa Mesa, California).

GENEVA, SWITZERLAND

"**Hotel Tor,** 3 Rue Levrier (phone 32-39-95), a short walk from the main railway station, has a new entrance and new elevator, and the accommodations, two floors up, are very comfortable. Double room and breakfast costs 43 Swiss francs ($25.29), including service, and breakfast is brought to the bedroom" (G. H. Jenkins, Queensland, Australia). . . . "At a pension, the **Cornavin,** 14 Place Cornavin (phone 325-948), directly across the street from the train station, we three shared a room (full-length mirror, *hot* and cold water, *and* a radio) for only 41 Swiss francs, plus 3 francs apiece for a hearty, delicious breakfast! Similarly-styled double rooms are 35 francs. The owner, a Swiss woman with two grown-up children, is just wonderful—permits guests to share her living room and television, etc." (Debby Kaufman, Paterson, New Jersey, Ellen Jacobsen, Narberth, Penna., Fran Fishback, Versailles, Kentucky). . . . "The **Hotel Belmont,** owned and managed by a most charming and congenial young couple, is at 26 Route de Chêne, tel. 35-78-11, perhaps 10 minutes by tram from downtown, in the exclusive, private-school end of town. It has a garden, a fine place for parking one's car, and is quiet. The rooms are spotlessly clean and luxuriously comfortable, and Mme. Smith-Carbonnier provided extra comforters at night. The polished hard wood floors shine splendidly and provide a perfect background for the oriental rugs. The bathrooms are gleaming white and chrome and the hot water most plentiful. For this very first-class accommodation in beautiful, expensive Geneva, the Belmont will charge, in 1980, 36 francs ($21.17) for singles, 50 francs ($29.41) for doubles. Breakfast is included, and they now provide a 24-hour laundry service at low prices in their own laundromat" (Estelle O. Webb, Costa Mesa, California). . . . "Next door to the mammoth Hotel du Rhone where the Rhone becomes Lake Geneva is the **Hotel des Tourelles,** 2 Bd. James-Fazy (phone 32-44-23), only ten minutes by foot from the train station. My husband, son and I spent six days there, with breakfasts, for 324 francs ($190.58). We had just as clean, comfortable and uncrowded a view of Geneva as the diplomats did next door where they were paying $60 a day" (Mrs. Merle Haskins, Sundland, California; note by A.F.: singles at des Tourelles are 26 to 28 francs, doubles 38 to 42 francs). . . . "At Cité 27 in the Old Town is the delightful **Cafe de la Cité,** where for 7.50 francs I had an enormous pot roast, potatoes and creamed spinach and dessert. Wine was a mere 1.70 for a bottle. This is an inexpensive, family-operated establishment with a homey atmosphere" (Doris Weedon, Dix Hills, New York). . . . "Students visiting Geneva can stay at the **Cité Universitaire** at 26 Avenue de Miremont (phone 462-355), in the older section of the city. The accommodations are dorms, in which you pay 8 Swiss Francs for a bed; the building is new, clean; showers are free with hot and cold water; and you can have breakfast upstairs in a nice cafeteria for 3 Swiss Francs. Unfortunately, you get locked in at 10:30 p.m., though it is possible to enter after that if you knock hard enough on the doors. One must also be out in the morning at 10:30 a.m., and the dorm is closed till 4 p.m. Considering I met girls who were paying 45 Swiss Francs for a double room, the dorms are much to be preferred. Take Bus #33 outside the train station to a stop two blocks away" (Mona Sajous, New York, New York). . . . "Don't fail to mention the '**Centre Universitaire Zofingien,**' 6 rue des Voisins (phone 242-546). Bus #11 from the Cornavin train station stops close to it at the Boulevard du Pont d'Arve. The hotel is situated on a relatively quiet side street five minutes walking distance from the old town in the very neighborhood of the University. During the year the house serves as a student residence, but in summer it is a regular hotel (July-November). Each room has its own bath (shower) and a complete kitchenette. There is also a living-room with TV as well as a studying-room. Prices are 32 Fr. ($18.82) for one person per night; double is 50 Fr. ($29.41). Students pay 20 Fr. ($11.76). Special rates are given to people who stay for a longer time. Included is a good breakfast with croissants at the restaurant downstairs, where a French cook prepares delicious meals for about $4 to $4.50. At eating times (noon and evening) it is usually crowded with students, because of its good reputation" (C. Frey, Flurlingen, Switzerland). . . . "A pleasant, and inexpensive, place to lunch or dine after exploring the Vieille Ville is the **Taverne de la Madeleine,** nestled against the old city wall below the Cathedral of Saint Pierre. It is located just across the street from the Eglise de la Madeleine which is at the corner of the rue Fontaine and rue de Purgatoire, one block up toward the Old City from the rue de Rive, the main shopping street. Or you can walk down one 'block' from the Place de Bourg-de-Four in the old city. The Tavern is one of several 'restaurants sans alcool' in Geneva and serves dinners from 6 to 8 francs (the restaurant is closed Sundays). And you can get beer with no alcohol! Eat inside with a newspaper or on the terrace" (H. D. Heath, Hayward, California). . . . "I'd like to suggest the **Restaurant Sans Alcool,** 17 Place Montbrillant, where the food is substantial and a three-course meal is 6.50 to 7.50 francs; to reach the restaurant, face the railroad station, walk to your left to the rear of the station, look directly across the street from the Swissair garage" (W. Foster, Geneva, Switzerland). . . . "Here's a tip that will help any frugal visitor to Geneva. The canton of Geneva helps finance the **Restaurant Universitaire,** 2 Avenue du Mail, just off the Place du Cirque. This modern, clean restaurant, open from 11:30 to 1:30 and 6:30 to 8:30, sells full-course dinners for 4.50 and 8 francs ($2.64 and $4.70). And the food is really good. It's frequented mostly by students, but I saw plenty of smart people there who were old enough to be my grandfather. Unfortunately, the restaurant closes down for inter-session for three weeks in the month of July or August" (Allen Young, New York City). . . . "Readers of Voltaire may want to visit the **Voltaire Museum** (10 minutes' walk from the railroad station) at 25 Rue des Delices, telephone 447-133, open Monday through Friday, 2-5 p.m., free admission, while readers of Rousseau may want to visit the **Jean-Jacques Rousseau Museum** (25 minutes' walk from the station) in the University Library, Promenade des Bastions, telephone 20-82-66, open Monday to Friday 9-12 a.m. to 2-6 p.m. and Saturday 9-12 noon, free. For me this was the highpoint of my visit to Geneva" (Professor Carlo Vacca, Framingham, Massachusetts). . . . "A boat trip on **Lake Leman** is delightful. We took the boat to Lausanne and back, but the trip all the way to Montreux may be more spectacular and should be worth a day's time. Fare to Lausanne and return is 38 francs first class or 25 francs second. First class is up top. Round-trip fare to Montreux is 58 francs first class, 38.60 francs second class" (Rev. B. Gurley, Washington, D.C.). . . . "A magnificent view of Geneva on one side and the French Alps and Mt. Blanc on the other, can be had from Salève, France. An inexpensive way is to take the #8 bus from Course de Rive station in downtown Geneva. Buy a round trip ticket which includes the cable car ride to the top for 12 francs. Note: you must take along your passport for the short walk across the Swiss-French border to Salève from the end of the bus line" (David Goldenberg, New York, New York). . . . "There is an automatic laundry on Rue de Monthoux (#29) just off the Rue Lausanne, which is open daily from 7 a.m. to 10 p.m., charging 6.80 francs for 5 kg. washed and dried" (Edward H. Pietraszek, Cicero, Illinois); note from AF: And there's a similarly-priced laundromat at 61 Boulevard St. George, just off the Place du Cirque).

GENEVA AT NIGHT: "**The Folk Club** takes place every Tuesday (not July/Aug.) at the Brasserie International, Place du Cirque (bus #1 or #11, tram #4 or #44), 15 minutes walk from the Youth Hostel. Amateur folk singers from Europe and the States entertain a young public from 9 p.m. until 1 a.m. It's a meeting place for youth from all over the world, living in or just visiting Geneva. Admission 2 francs, drinks around 2 francs each.

"**The Wednesday Club** at the Café du Grand Pré, 15 Rue Hoffman (bus no. 3 from Cornavin to Grand Pré), organizes a gathering every Wednesday, where visiting youths will have the occasion to meet with local students and young employees/workers, most of them English-speaking. No entry is charged, a soft drink or a beer costs 2 francs. The W.-Club also organizes skiing weekends (Sat/Sun) from Jan. to April at approximately 60 francs, including bus transportation from Geneva to a mountain resort, one night hotel, a four-course meal and dancing on Saturday night. For bookings, just contact Hans Hoffmann during the meetings.

"**The Pickwick Club** at rue de Lausanne 80 (bus 5 to Butini) is the meeting point for the large English-speaking community of Geneva, mostly employees of the U.N. and other international organizations. A darts board, English beer and a lively crowd assure a good atmosphere every evening. Drinks start at 2.50 francs.

"**Open-Air-Concerts** are organized by the City of Geneva during the months June/July/August. Generally, no admission is charged. At the Quai de Mont-Blanc and/or the Jardin Anglais (nr. the Flower Watch, bus 1, 11, 5, 6, 22). U.S. University Bands, Pop-Groups, Jazz and Classical Concerts are presented.

"**Pop Corn Jazz Club,** 13 rue de la Fontaine, in the Old Town (bus 1, 11, 5 and tram 12, trolley 2 and 22). No admission. First drink 15 francs, then 5 to 10 francs. Meals from 9-25 francs. Pub-style restaurant/night club starring famous European trios with such American jazz musicians as Eddie Davis, Slide Hampton, Teddy Wilson, Milt Buckner, etc.

"**Maison des Jeunes,** rue du Temple 5 (bus 1, 11, 7). Meeting place for local and visiting students. Has a limited number of sleeping accommodations available. Rock, Folk and Jazz Concerts, Cinema, modern theatre and conferences take place nearly every evening. Admission between 3 and 8 francs. Also includes a self-service restaurant, meals from 5 to 6 francs.

"**Radio Studio,** Boulevard Carl-Vogt (bus 4, 44) nr. the Youth Hostel. Classical Concerts nearly every Wednesday. Entry approx. Fr. 3. Try to see the Orchestre de la Suisse Romande (OSR)" (Richard R. Heimann, Geneva, Switzerland).

GENOA, ITALY

"I was booked at the **Hotel Pension Lausanne,** 33a via Balbi (phone 261-634), just to the left of Columbus' statue off Piazza Stazione. I paid 7,500 lire for a single for one night, plus 1,800 lire for breakfast. Doubles are 12,000 lire" (J. Raymond Reid, Soest, Germany). . . . "I was quite lucky to find a comfortable, nicely furnished, quiet room with running hot and cold water at the **Pensione Della Posta,** Via Balbi 15, tel: 280-103, on the top floor of an elevator building, about 500 yards from the railway station and 200 from American Express. The English-speaking owner himself will serve your breakfast in your room, for which he charges 8,500 lire ($10.24) single" (Peter N. Abbot, New York, New York). . . . "We highly recommend the **Pensione Olympia,** where we had a spacious, comfortable double room without bath but with plenty of instantly hot water for only 12,000 lire. It was immaculately clean and the management so friendly that every time we went out the manager would precede us to push the elevator button. It has an excellent location at 21 Via XX Settembre, only a few blocks from the Station Brignole, not to be confused with the Centrale Station. English is spoken, there is a parking lot for cars, and right around the corner in the Standa store is a supermarket. Telephone for Pensione Olympia is 59.25.38" (Neva and Don Kaiser, Miami, Florida). . . . "The **Locanda Silvana,** Via Andrea Doria 4 (phone 255-287), to the right of the Piazza Stazione, charges 11,500 lire for a double and 7,500 for a single overnight, plus 2,000 lire for breakfast. Very clean, and with hot and cold running water. The gentleman who runs it speaks English. Conveniently, a pretty good Tavola Calda is just a few meters down the road" (Sabino A. Vengco, Jr., Trier, Germany). . . . "**Pensione Bel Soggiorno,** Via XX Settembre 19 (phone 581-418), in the center of town, is operated by a lovely couple, Ingrid and Sergio Possio. She is German, he Italian. Both speak excellent English. A bathless single was 8,800 lire" (Helen Hasler, Kent, England).

GHENT, BELGIUM

"For those of student age, the best bargain in Europe is **The Home A. Vermeylen,** Stalhofstraat 6 (phone 22-09-11), which gives you a private room with sink, bedside light controls, your choice of four radio stations on the intercom, all in a very modern and clean building, and all (including continental breakfast) for under $10. Lunch, if you want it, is an extra 70 francs, dinner 70 francs. In addition there's a library, modern *hot* showers, and a bar and lounge where you can meet the other student inhabitants. The Vermeylen home is open only from July 15 to the end of September" (Pauline Hadley, New York City). . . . "Please encourage your readers not to pass through Belgium without stopping to see Van Eyck's painting, 'The Mystic Lamb,' in Saint Bavon's church in Ghent. (You can take one of the railroad's 'Beau Jour' excursions from Brussels to Bruges, with a stop at Ghent to see the painting.) The admission is a paltry 20 francs to see this magnificent work in its authentic setting. One of the panels has been stolen, but a copy has replaced it, so you still get the full effect. If you ask him, the guard will shut the painting so that the outside of the altar panels can also be studied" (Luella Boddewyn, New York, New York).

GLASGOW, SCOTLAND

"At **Mrs. Auld's Guesthouse,** 8 Belgrave Terrace (phone 339-8668), the rate is very reasonable—about £5 per person, for clean and comfortable rooms, and Mrs. Auld does a wonderful job of making everyone feel at home. She served a good breakfast and every evening had a big pot of tea and refreshments set out" (R.N. Palmer, Vancouver, British Columbia). . . . "Glasgow is probably the most overlooked and underrated tourist center in Britain. It may not be the most beautiful city in the world, but it has many outstanding attractions, including the Kelvingrove Art Gallery, the Pollock House, and the Museum of Transport. Nearly all the city's museums offer free admission—not the least of Glasgow's attractions for the budget traveller" (John Warrick, Dardanelle, Arkansas).

GRANADA, SPAIN

"**Hotel Victoria,** Puerta Real 3 (phone 257-700 or 04), is a three-star hotel which may be considered expensive at 1,700 pesetas ($24.29) for a double room with breakfast, bath and shower, but it is extremely comfortable and has the cleanest dining room in town" (L. L. Farkas, Tucson, Arizona). . . . "At the **Hostal California,** Cuesta de Gomerey 37 (phone 22-40-56), I had a beautifully clean and spacious double room with bath for only 600 pesetas. Meals are also very cheap and very fine food, and, oh, so filling! The owner, Sr. Miguel Quijada, is a wonderful host. I do hope you will include this amazing hotel in your book, so that others can enjoy a very warm and pleasant few days at what must be the very best value in town" (Philip Wolanski, Sydney, Australia). . . . "The **Landazuri Hotel,** Cuesta Gomerez 24, telephone 221-406, is 100 meters from the Alhambra, very clean, with home-like atmosphere and little traffic noise. A room with a double bed and private bath is 1,200 pesetas, with continental breakfast included" (Bill Dozier, Stockton, California).

HAARLEM, NETHERLANDS

"Haarlem is a beautiful Dutch city only 15 minutes by train from Amsterdam; in the spring, its fields are covered with tulips, daffodils and hyacinths. We stayed there with **Mrs. M. Ferwerda Terol,** 33 Kleine Houtweg, telephone 023-323661, an exceptionally warm and friendly lady. We had big breakfasts (they were so huge we packed our lunches from them), free showers, and paid about $7.50 each. Be sure to autograph her tablecloth. She will later embroider your signature to keep as a memory of your visit. A great example of Dutch hospitality" (Mary Pommert, Amelia, Ohio).

THE HAGUE, NETHERLANDS

"For travelers on a rigid budget, let me suggest a student guest house called the **Haus Grüno,** at Sweelinckstraat 49 (phone 63-22-77). We arrived late on an afternoon and were shown an attic room, small yet comfortable, with a gabled window and cots and a sink. The proprietor seemed so elderly that I feared he'd never make it to the top of the stairs and I wouldn't let him tote our bags. But he was a nice, old gentleman, and he included a breakfast in the 17.50 guilders each he charged us—the lowest rate we paid in Holland. By the bye, The Hague has *two* great collections: don't go only to the **Mauritshuis** in the center of town with its Rembrandts and Vermeers, but be sure to see the **Haags Gemeentemuseum** on the outskirts, with *inter alia,* the greatest Mondrian collection in the world, tracing the development from his post-Impressionist period up to his characteristic later geometric-abstract style" (Richard M. Koffler, Philadelphia, Pennsylvania). . . . "We stayed at **Pension Mem,** 8 Anna Paulowna, telephone 637571. For 22.50 guilders per person, including breakfast and free access to showers, you are only a couple of blocks from the Peace Palace and the trolley going directly to the beach. Excellent English spoken. Probably best for people with cars (free parking in tree-lined car park)" (J. R. Burge, APO New York).

HAMBURG, GERMANY

"Go to the **Hotel-Pension Adina,** at 63 Johnsallee (phone 44-29-59), near the University. 30 marks ($15.78) for a single room big enough for a football game, 55 marks double, including breakfast" (Joel Kerbel, Toronto, Ontario, Canada). . . . "The 100-bed **Hotel Schmelzer,** Moorweidenstrasse 34 (one block from the University), tel: 44-35-33, proved to have one of the nicest rooms of our trip. A large pleasant double room with balcony overlooking a garden came to 58 DM (taxes, breakfast and service included). There were a number of other pensions in this building so that it probably would be a good place to go to be assured of obtaining a room" (Robert S. Kaplan, Ithaca, New York). . . . "Last month we stayed at the **Paulinenhof**, at 12 Paulinenstrasse (phone 430-0223), whose owner and manager is friendly Herr Hahn. The bar never closes and it is two minutes from the famous Reeperbahn. For 23 marks ($12.10) per person, we had a double room with some sort of gas contraption furnishing instant *very* hot water. This included breakfast with an egg" (Mrs. Edward Kendrex, APO, New York). . . . "Hotel-Pension Gertrud Meyn, Hansaplatz 2, phone 24-53-09; we obtained this room (a large double with inexhaustible hot water) located on the second floor (as are very many of the pensions of this variety) of a building about two blocks from the main rail station. The room, breakfast included, cost DM 50" (Charles T. Morello, Jr., Norwood, New Jersey). . . . "The delightful pension called **Elite**, 24 Binderstrasse, phone 45-46-27, is operated by Frau Carla Feld, a charming hostess who went to no end of trouble to make us feel at home during our 10-day stay. Situated near the university, in walking distance from the Dammtor Bahnhof, spotlessly clean rooms, excellent breakfast, very reasonable prices" (Elizabeth and Sid Aron, Victoria, Australia). . . . "At the **Pension Alte Flöte**, Koppel 6 (phone 24-53-65), a 5-minute walk from the central station, the charge is 32 marks ($16.84) for a double without breakfast. Its manager also runs the Alte Flöte Restaurant just below, so one has to enter the restaurant first to speak to him. While in Hamburg, be sure to visit the Planten und Blomen Park. It has beautiful flowers, open-air concerts, and other amusements, such as unusual fountains and watergames" (Lorna M. Rosenblith, Little Neck, New York). . . . "**Restaurant Intermezzo**, Steindamm 1, close to the main railroad station, a quick cafeteria-type eatery, has many low-priced, simple plates. I had two hamburger meatballs with mashed potatoes and spinach for 5.70 marks ($3). Other restaurants are all more expensive, in the 12-15 marks range, in that neighborhood" (Thomas A. Endrey, Lakehurst, New York). . . . "Along the Reeperbahn, the night-life section, there are many low-cost eating places, as well as cabarets and strip shows where one can nurse a 7 DM beer for an hour or so. The more expensive **Tabu Club**, on a street called Grosse Freiheit (#16) at the end of the Reeperbahn, has quite a good show and a decent atmosphere; some of the other places are clipjoints. I also went 'beyond the wall' to the Herbertstrasse (the red light district), which is partitioned off to keep out juveniles, but found the atmosphere low and degenerate and quite a contrast to Amsterdam. Otherwise, Hamburg is a beautiful city and a sightseeing tour is worthwhile" (Henry S. Sloat, New York, New York).

HANOVER, GERMANY

"**Pension Indra**, Am Schiffgraben 46, phone 81-01-09: For DM 48($25.26), we had an unbelievably large double with a table and chairs and a refrigerator. The pension is located about four blocks from the main rail station and is operated by a very friendly woman, Frau Dralle. We were startled by our breakfast the next morning (included in the price), as Frau Dralle brought it to our room, where we ate in private: egg, breads, honey and strong coffee" (Charles T. Morello, Jr., Norwood, New Jersey, with enthusiastic recent seconding letter from Lorna Rosenblith, Little Neck, New York: "breakfast [at the Indra] was immense, and could have fed five people (we were two)"). . . . "For an inexpensive meal and a real taste experience, try the **Reformgaststätte** at Karmarschstrasse No. 16 (about four blocks from the train station): you take the elevator up to a beautiful dining room on the third or fourth floor. The restaurant is strictly vegetarian, but we had one of the best meals of our trip there: for 8.50 marks ($4.47) we received a huge eggs-potatoes-mushrooms omelet and a wonderful salad of sweet red pepper, sweet cabbage, onion and oranges (!) in a delicious sauce. Less expensive 'menus' are 7.50 marks. Hours are 11 a.m. to 3:30 p.m. weekdays, 11 a.m. to 3 p.m. Saturday, closed Sundays. Excellent, hospitable service" (Anne and George Fattman, Johnstown, Pennsylvania).

HARZ MOUNTAINS, GERMANY

"Untouched by war and nestled in the Harz Mountains (of birdseed fame) is **Bad Harzburg**, about 40 miles southeast of Hanover. **Goslar** is another 'jewel' town on the way there, where the finest singing canaries have been raised for over 700 years. The freshness and beauty of these places can hardly be described. In a fairy tale setting—so perfectly undisturbed that you arrive by chugging steam-engine-pulled train—is a town but a few minutes from East Germany. There are mountain rails through forests that have a perfect Hansel and Gretel atmosphere" (Mrs. Peter Diller, Los Angeles, California).

HEIDELBERG, GERMANY

"We found a delightful place to eat called **Das Goldene Schaf.** It's near the Club 1900, which is at 117 Hauptstrasse. A large plate of sausage, kraut and potatoes, with beer was both excellent and cheap—under $3!" (Tali & Lynn Petersons, Hollis, New York). . . . "The **Gasthaus zur Backmulde,** Schiffgasse 11 (phone 22-551), is beside the old University. One enters a courtyard from Schiffgasse, a narrow street leading up from the river. The window where rooms are booked overlooks the courtyard from the kitchen of the restaurant which is also part of the establishment. Double rooms are 42 to 55 marks a night, including breakfast and service charge, singles are 27 marks, and there's an inexpensive 6-mark restaurant in the basement. The building has been newly furnished and decorated and is extremely clean and attractive. Bathrooms may be used for only a slight extra charge and with the use of large and abundant towels. Beside our twin beds were a couple of delicious chocolates and a card wishing us a good night. On the table were fresh flowers. Outside was an ancient tower which housed many doves, and below was a part of the Heidelberg University. Delightful" (Mrs. J. Paul Boushelle, Las Cruces, New Mexico). . . . "**Pension am Neckar,** 18 Neckarstaden (phone 22-123), charges 42 marks for a double including breakfast in room, service, and tax. Some rooms overlook the beautiful Neckar River. The owners are friendly and got us up at 5 a.m. with breakfast waiting, for our early departure. Convenient location" (Tom and Val Wolf, Cortland, New York). . . . "**Hotel Goldener Falke,** on Haupt Strasse, 204 (phone 26474), is in the old city, near the University. A room with bathtub and sink (no toilet) is 42 DM ($22.10) for two, but no breakfast. Floors tilt slightly, but room was very clean. Another hotel we inspected (and it was a toss-up where we stayed) was **Hotel Zum Pfalzgrafen,** Kettengasse 21 (phone 20489), charging 44 DM double, 26 DM single, breakfast included, with toilet and bath, 1 DM extra, on the same floor" (Nat and Inge Frankel, Oakland, California). . . . "At the **Hotel Goldener Adler,** Rathausstrasse 8, telephone 30-982, the charges are: DM 24 for a single w/o bath, and DM 45 for a double w/o bath. (There is even one room with a bedding capacity of 6 to 7, but not that many people are going to be travelling en masse). Food is served, and is good (I gained lots of weight here) and reasonable. Run by Herr und Frau Rodemer, who speak English, it is located in the part of town called Rohrbach, near the headquarters of U.S. Army Europe. Strassenbahn is right near hotel, 20 seconds walking time, and you are in downtown Heidelberg in minutes" (Eileen O'Brien, New York). . . . "We liked the **Hotel Central,** Kaiserstrasse 75 (phone 20-672), at 56 marks for a twin bedroom without bath, but with breakfast. Very clean and comfortable, within walking distance of the Hauptbahnhof. We did not need a taxi" (Agnes and Jim Neufeld, Lethbridge, Alberta, Canada). . . . "The charming old home of **Erika Jeske** has been converted into a seven-room guesthouse, at 2 Mittelbadgasse, half a block off the market square, a few minutes from the university. For only 24 marks ($12.63) per day for two, we had a cozy third-floor room with window-boxes of geraniums, and overlooking the quiet street. Frau Jeske speaks fluent English and is most helpful. We recommend her to you" (Mr. and Mrs. John B. Stokes, Jr., Moorestown, New Jersey). . . . "In four months of travel in Europe, we found no hotel more gracious than **Hotel-Pension Elite,** 15 Bunsenstrasse (phone 25-734). 10 minutes from the Hauptbahnhof, quiet, beautifully-furnished, spotless clean, charming proprietor—Herr Helmut Knorzer—who speaks English fluently. Then, of course, there are the extra touches, like fresh flowers on the breakfast table, exquisite china cups and a beautiful little patio garden. A real find in Heidelberg! (Lorna and Aubrey McTaggart, San Diego, California; note from AF: 1980 rates here are 30 marks ($15.79) single, 47 marks ($24.74) double, breakfast included). . . . "A must if you're in Heidelberg is the Student Prison (Karzer) in the old university. You have to ring a bell marked 'Karzer,' hidden to the left of the tall doors which front the building (one block off University Square), then you wander alone up a flight of stairs, but at that point a clerk greets you and collects a tiny fee (50 pfennigs each). The five rooms were used for well over a century (until the early 1900's), are decorated from floor to, and including, ceiling with whimsical drawings and writings (done entirely by means such as charcoal and candlewax) on the minds of the students who were detained there for such things as drinking or rowdy behavior. Closed Sundays" (Jess and Alice Brewis, Taylor, Michigan). . . . "Heidelberg is the students' paradise and you can eat a very filling meal for 8 marks ($4.21) if you choose your spot. There are several places in the University area where you select your food at long counters, eat it standing up if you are in a hurry, or carry it to wooden tables in the back. Try, in particular, the **Zum Roten Ochsen** or **Zum Seppl**" (Renee Calipert, Montreal, Canada).

HELSINKI, FINLAND

"We moved to a 'summer hotel' (open only May 20 to September 10) which we recommend very highly. It is the **Satakuntatalo**, Lapinrinne 1 (phone 90-694-0311), where lovely double rooms are 90 to 100 Finnish marks, 30 more for an extra bed, service included, private lavatory adjoining. Showers were down the hall and a sauna was available for about $1! This summer hotel was run by very gracious and helpful students" (Haskell and Margaret Rothstein, East Detroit, Michigan). . . . "In Finland, no one should miss a sauna bath. I had one every day, and I never felt so clean in my life! The energetic old lady scrubs you, rubs you, pummels you, beats you, boils you, rinses you you and splashes you. It's like going through an automatic washer but more pleasant. In the luxury hotel **Vaakuna**, next to the station (which I don't think is so magnificent!), you may use the sauna, and receive a diploma for going through the ordeal! . . . A good way to see Finland, I think, is by ship from Stockholm. It's an overnight trip and the Smörgasbord on board is fabulous. My round-trip ticket cost $50, and I sailed from Stockholm to Helsinki; went by train to Turku; and sailed back to Stockholm. If I'd had time, I'd have gone up into the Finnish lake district. Perhaps next year" (J. R. Reid, New York). . . . "We stayed at a student hotel called **Otahalli**, phone 46-05-44, in a university village named Otahiemi, all in a beautiful wooded area near Helsinki. One can take Bus 102 or 192 to go there. Compared with hotel prices in Helsinki, it was a bargain: 80 markka ($21.27) per night for a double room. Three hundred meters away is a swimming pool and sauna, uimahalli in Finnish. You can rent a bathing suit if you have none along" (John and Jean Lellebid, Colman, South Dakota).

IBIZA, BALEARIC ISLANDS, SPAIN

"My choice is the **Hostal Mar Blau**, Apartado 127, Los Molinos (phone 301284), where my single room and three meals came to 1,200 pesetas ($18.18) per day; it is perched atop a hill overlooking the sea, is very clean, features good food served by the friendly owners, and is located so that one can swim off the nearby rocks" (Marilyn Ramey, London, England). . . . "I took the boat from the port (11 pesetas) to Talamanca Beach, where I stayed in the **Hotel Talamanca** (phone 30-20-93). For a beautiful double with private bath and 3 enormous meals a day, we paid 1,700 pesetas ($25.75) a day for two people. The hotel was beautiful, on the beach. In the evening, a fire was lit in the fireplace in the bar. After traveling as a student in Europe, I felt like a person again" (Barry Glen, Cedarhurst, New York). . . . "This is paradise—a lovely, pine-wooded island edged with beaches, where a double room with a view of the Mediterranean and a private swimming pool lined with flowering oleander trees cost me only $10 a day. When you finally climb out of the pool, just clap your hands and a waiter will appear with a small bottle of iced champagne. This will cost you the staggering sum of $3. There is absolutely nothing to do in this tiny fishing village except swim, fish, relax, read, write, and eat the best seafood east of Maine. Warning to all dieters: don't come here; we all put on so much weight that we can't get into our clothes and have to run around in muumuus" (Ruth Ivor, Siena, Italy). . . . "From Valencia I took a night boat to Ibiza. My ticket cost 410 pesetas ($6.21) third class. I strongly recommend that whenever anyone takes a boat to one of the Balearic Islands during the summer months, they buy only a third class ticket. There is first and second as well as third class, but they are all unbearably hot and stuffy and by morning everyone has thrown pretense overboard and is asleep on the decks. And sleeping under the warm Mediterranean skies is an experience that shouldn't be missed! In Ibiza I have stayed at a new hotel **'Hotel Internacional,'** Apartado 351, Jesus, Ibiza (phone 30-24-92), in a double room (with bath and breakfast) for 1,350 pesetas ($20.45) a night. The very helpful owners are Mr. and Mrs. Green" (Gloria A. Boyd, Brookline, Massachusetts; note from AF: the night boat from Valencia to Ibiza leaves Mondays and Fridays at midnight, arrives Ibiza at 8 a.m., tickets range from 410 to 1,070 pesetas, depending on class of accommadation).

INNSBRUCK, AUSTRIA

"We stayed at the house of a kindly old lady, **Frau Schellhorn**, Gumppstrasse 34 (phone 427-665), who gave us a clean comfortable room for 85 schillings a day ($6.29), including a superb breakfast; she even speaks a bit of English" (David M. Shribman, Swampscott, Massachusetts). . . . "We found a lovely place overlooking the city, a Tyrolean chalet, where each double room has a flower-decked balcony, for 240 schillings ($17.77) per night, breakfast included. It stands not more than a few minutes' drive from the center of the city. The name: **Pension Paula**, Weiherburggasse 15 (phone 37-795). By the way, all prices quoted are for 2 persons, all taxes and services included" (Jacques and Magdeleine Tremblay, Quebec City, Canada, with seconding recommendation from J. M. Ganster, Birmingham, Alabama). . . . "The **International Studentenhaus**, Innrain 64 (phone 27885), spotlessly clean and well run (open in summer only, from July 1 to September 30) charges 150 schillings ($11.11) for a single room, including breakfast, 300 schillings double. Take Tram C from the front of the railway station going left" (Mrs. Lillian Harrington, St. Petersburg, Florida). . . . "We found one very nice hotel in Innsbruck, and a real bargain, the **Gasthof Innbrücke** at Innstrasse 1 (phone 81-934), located right across the river from the center of town. The cost was only 100 schillings per night for a single, 200 schillings for a double, both without bath of course. We didn't mind that breakfast was not included, because the best way to get a wonderful Austrian breakfast is to wander into one of the many pastry shops in Innsbruck and order some delicious pastry and hot chocolate. Incidentally, the Gasthof does serve excellent lunches and dinners, all very reasonably priced. The hotel is run by a very nice Austrian family and the children, who were educated in England, speak perfect English. One suggestion, however: better plan on arriving at the hotel by 10:00 or 11:00 in the morning if you do not have a reservation . . . the place fills up very quickly" (Neil Sheridan, Hartsdale, New York). . . . "The home of **Mrs. E. Prantl**, Hoermannstrasse 7, Pradl, tel: 419195, within walking distance of the train station, was one of the most pleasant surprises of our trip. We were traveling by train from Salzburg to Venice, via Innsbruck, and had no intention of stopping in Innsbruck except to change trains. Mrs. Prantl (who speaks excellent English) met us as we got off the train, and because she was so nice, we decided to accept her offer of hospitality. For 190 schillings ($14.07) per day (excluding breakfast), we had an extremely clean room in her home which afforded us an excellent view of Hafelekar. She has been renting rooms in her home since 1958, and has guest books signed by people from all over the world. We saw a signature in her book of someone I had gone to high school with and had not seen in eight years" (Ronald M. Greenberg, Los Angeles, California). . . . "In Innsbruck—a fascinating city—I was referred to **Frau Anny Gastl**, 81 Prinz Eugen Strasse (phone 44-79-62). She runs a very clean apartment where she rents rooms for 100 schillings ($7.40) daily for a single, 90 ($6.66) each person for a large room with three beds. It's on the first floor. Continental breakfast is included. Baths are extra. I found this to be one of the best of my trip. The location is near St. Paul's Church on Reichenau Strasse. Can be reached with Bus 'R' from the station" (Rose Black, Tucson, Arizona). . . . "For two nights we stayed with a wonderful lady named **Doris Jungwirth**, who was a perfect example of Austrian 'Gemütlichkeit'. The address: 42 Leopoldstrasse, II. Innrain 109. I, the phone number: 26-66-83. You honestly could not find a sweeter, friendlier lady anywhere in Europe! She charges 80 schillings ($5.92) per night per person, 75 if you stay two or more nights. A shower is 10, a breakfast (served in bed) 16 schillings" (Lisa McCabe, Mark Van Krieken, Altadena, California). . . . "In Innsbruck lives a former Northwestern University professor for whom I used to work. He recommends to his ex-colleagues the **Pension Elisabeth**, Elisabethstrasse 2 (tel: 27877). This was once a villa, and so, as we were served continental breakfast in our spacious immaculate bedroom, we looked out on a pretty rose garden and a structure resembling a miniature castle. Located in the direction of the Hungerburg funicular, it must be reached by taxi or Bus C from Bozner Platz, but it is worth the few extra minutes' ride. The complete cost (without private bath) was 285 schillings (Austrian) or about ($21.11) per night for two, including tax, service and breakfast. Singles are 165 schillings" (Queta and Ray Fouke, Lake Bluff, Illinois). . . . "Nowhere were we luckier than in Innsbruck, Austria, when we arrived late in the cold of a November evening with two sick children, at **Gasthof Oberrauch**, Leopoldstrasse 35, tel: 25180. Herr and Frau Konig provided a clean warm room and a lot of service for all of us for 260 schillings ($19.25) per double room per day, including breakfast. Singles are 160 schillings per day. We hope others will enjoy the friendliness and view of the Alps this gasthof provides" (Mr. and Mrs. Daniel Corsello, Whippany, New Jersey). . . . "**Frau Trudi Pichl**, of Mutters near Innsbruck, telephone 21075, after receiving our phone call from the station, picked us up in 15 minutes and drove us up to her charming village. For a large double room we paid 260 Sch., breakfast included—and the cafe adjoining the establishment served the finest wiener schnitzel we have tasted on two world tours" (Mrs. P. W. Pulsford, East Gosford, N.S.W., Australia). . . . "**Pension Kaltenberger**, (phone 272-504), at Mutters, a restful little village just above Innsbruck, was excellent and cost our family (5) 120 Sch. per person, breakfast included. Mutters is delightful for strolling, or take a short walk up the mountain to the cable car going up the Nockspitze" (Ann E. Healy, Milwaukee, Wisconsin). . . . "When I got off the train with a Canadian I had met, we were stopped by a little old lady who asked us in broken English if we needed a place to stay for 70 schillings per night. We said yes, and she first took us to the bank to change money, then to a newsstand for an English paper, and finally she got us on the bus for free and took us to her apartment where she has a couple of rooms for tourists, whom she calls "my tourists". She was very nice and extremely helpful. Her name is **Maria Rauschgatt,** and she lives at Karwendelstrasse 6, 6020 Innsbruck, phone 232-834, about 5 minutes from the station by bus C, or 20 minutes by walking" (Alan Reisner, Jamaica, New York). . . . "One lady in Innsbruck, with whom we spent some time, is really delightful, her heart is as big as the mountains, speaks good English, and loves having Americans and Australians in her home. She is **Maria Wegleitner**, Egger-Lienz-Strasse 32, phone 212-184" (Valerie Colless, Maroochydore, Queensland, Australia; seconding recommendation from Rosemarie Tommaso, Hollywood, Florida, who paid 190 schillings ($14.07) for a double with breakfast). . . . "Just a 30-second walk from the Gasthof Innbrücke mentioned by you, is the **Fremdenzimmer Seep**, over the Cafe Seep. Singles range from 85 to 120 schillings ($6.30 to $8.89), with breakfast in the cozy cafe below. Doubles are 200 schilling ($14.81). I should mention that one can get a room overlooking the Inn-river, but the street that parallels the river seems to be busy with traffic the whole night long. Looking at the brighter side of things, the noise might keep you awake to see the beautiful sunrise over the magnificent Austrian alps" (Karl Bottjer, Craryville, New York). . . . "Tyrolean hospitality is unmatched anywhere in Europe. And in Innsbruck you'll find a warm welcome at **Hotel Leopoldina,** Burgerstrasse 10, phone 29-027. It's a student house for the local university, except from July 1 to August 31 when the house is open to visitors. From the railroad station, go outside to Salurner Strasse, follow it till you pass the 'Triumphal Arch', where the street becomes Maximilianstrasse. Second street beyond the Arch is Burgerstrasse, turn right. Lodgings are one floor up. Prices, including breakfast, are: single 150 schillings, double 270, triple 360. There are facilities for cooking, and showers are free. Innsbruck was the friendliest town I visited during my entire trip. I spent five fabulous days." (Linda Busek, Collins, Ohio). . . . "Take a cable car to the top of **Hafelekar.** This is the highest ski mountain of all the peaks surrounding the city. We enjoyed the view and ate a picnic lunch in the open. (Some of the lunch had to be shared with some sociable mountain goats and a blackbird or two!) If you're very spirited and want to find a bit of privacy from the other picnickers in the chalet, put on your hiking shoes and scramble up one of the peaks close by. Did you ever sit in solitude on the very top of a mountain? Incredible!" (Ann Fomin, Dearborn Heights, Michigan). . . . "I cannot recommend the following course of action too highly. When you reach the Innsbruck train station, phone 24088 and English-speaking **Frau Katie Wolf** will come pick you up and take you to the lovely mountain village of Mutters, overlooking Innsbruck. So pleasant is her hospitality and bubbling personality that people of any age would love this place—to ski or just to retreat. The air in Mutters is bracingly clean, the village charming, and the view—especially at night with Innsbruck twinkling in the valley below you—is wonderful. Katie Wolf's guest house rates are *very* reasonable (90 schillings per person per day including breakfast) and she has a large kitchen. There is a lovely restaurant, grocery store, church and even a bowling alley ('kegelbahn') in Mutters, and a little train runs between the town and Innsbruck below. Write: Katie Wolf, 6162 Mutters/Tirol, Austria, and/or call 24088 when you arrive at the Innsbruck train station" (Joe Cunniff, Jr., Chicago, Illinois). . . . "Our favorite 'big splurge' was the **Pension Lärchenhof** at Axams, approximately 6 miles out of Innsbruck, Austria, telephone 05227/8152; the ski-bus from Innsbruck to the Olympic ski-run at Lizum passes the door. Its proprietor, Josef Sarg, speaks excellent English and his charming wife speaks a little. The pension is the best value we found anywhere in Europe. They charge 350 Austrian Schillings for full pension and the meals are excellent (demi-pension AS 320). Rooms are modern, clean and well heated and there is T.V., sauna, and a swimming pool" (Mr. and Mrs. K. G. Lee, Sydney, Australia).

INTERLAKEN, SWITZERLAND

"Outside of expensive Interlaken, on the road from Brienz, numerous 'Zimmer frei' signs announce spacious single rooms without breakfast for $10 and doubles for $16 in private homes" (Joseph Gibson, Lupkin, Texas). . . . "When we first arrived in Interlaken, we could not find a room for less than $12 a person. Finally, we discovered a wonderful student hostel—a chalet—called **Balmers-Herberge in Matten,** phone 22-19-61. Doubles there are 36 francs ($21.17) per night, but for $8.50 per person, we slept in one of the four-person dorms, a huge double-decker bed, and received a continental breakfast. This clean, but unluxurious, place has a recreation room with a jukebox, where students of different nations congregate; and there are no curfew hours and no requirements of a youth hostel card. About three blocks away from the hostel is the meadow where Schiller's Pastoral Play, 'William Tell,' is presented in a natural setting (they actually use real houses, horses, etc.). The play is in German, but there is also an English 'libretto.' It's worth seeing for the setting, and seats can be obtained for 9 francs" (Susan Miller, Flushing, New York; note from AF: the 80-bed Balmer's Herberge, operated by the jolly Herr Eric Balmer, is a ten-minute walk from the station, permits use of the washing machine for 2 francs, offers space in a 10-bedded dorm for only 10 francs ($5.88) per night, and provides as many cups of hot chocolate as you wish in its continental breakfast). . . . "I returned to Interlaken West and the **Helvetia Hotel** (at 6 Bahnhofstrasse, phone 228-383) this year and it's just as delightful as it was last year. It is located 1½ blocks from the R.R. station and charges 20 Swiss Francs single, breakfast and service included. The bath is on the first floor of the hotel. The coffee is delicious, the hotel immaculate, the view of the Alps from the bedroom is fabulous and the price is only 20 francs per night single, 37.50 francs double, including breakfast. Let's hope you pass this information on to your 1980/81 readers" (Mrs. Leatrice Reid, Ottawa, Ontario). . . . "Four easy blocks from the West Station on a quiet, residential street is the clean and delightful **Hotel Beyeler Garni** run by the Beyeler family at Bernastrasse 37 (phone 22-90-30). All rooms large and airy with hot and cold water and wall-to-wall carpeting. Doubles without bath 18 S.F. per person, doubles with shower 19 S.F. per person, and with complete bath 25 S.F. in winter, with summer rates 3 S.F. more. Breakfast, service and taxes included and English spoken. Open all year. You may even watch Swiss color T.V. in the breakfast room" (Mr. and Mrs. D. C. Gillette, Lake Placid, Florida). . . . "**Hotel Bahnhof,** 37 Bahnhofstrasse, right opposite the railway station at Interlaken West (phone 227-041), offers a comfortable front double room for 48 to 56 Swiss francs (depending on the season), including breakfast and service" (G. H. Jenkins, Queensland, Australia). . . . "A true find, stumbled upon during a Christmas visit to Interlaken, is the charming **Hotel Iris** (tel 22-36-26), which is a refurbished Victorian house on General-Guisan-Strasse, a 5-minute walk from the West Station. For 20 francs ($11.76), I had a beautiful room with antique furniture, lace curtains and a featherbed. Breakfast, which is included, is served by the proprietor, Herr Adolf Jahn, and features homemade bread, if you can believe it. He speaks fluent English" (J. W. Shank, Denver, Colorado). . . . "We had a beautiful room in the home of **Frau Kammer Sonnhalde,** 30 Brienzstrasse (phone 72-67-67), with full use of a kitchen and a free shower, for the equivalent of $5 a day per person. Even when the stores were closed (we arrived on New Year's Day), the landlady gave us food. The house has an incredible view of the Jungfrau and is an easy five minutes' walk from town. On leaving, we were asked to please recommend her house to your book. We do so gladly!" (Lee Steppacher, Canton, New York). . . . "While at Interlaken, we stumbled across a genuine family hotel, five minutes' walk from the train station: **Hotel Lötschberg,** General Guisan Strasse (phone 22-25-45), owned and operated by the Hutmacher family. First class comfort in immaculate surroundings, a good breakfast, friendly, pleasant service, all for 48 francs ($28.23) for a double room" (L. N. Chanaryk, Manitoba, Canada). . . . "The **Raclette Tavern** at the Hotel Metropole in Interlaken offered delightful atmosphere and a new eating experience for only 4 francs" (Patricia Wilson and Diane Larson, Los Angeles, California). . . . "Readers travelling in the Jungfrau region of the Swiss Alps should stay with the warm, friendly Knöpfli family—**Jack and Christine Knöpfli,** Bella Vista, 3855 Brienz, telephone 036-512213— who live in the beautiful lakeside village of Brienz, across the lake from Interlaken. Our happy stay was inexpensive, only 30 francs per night for a double which included baths and an excellent continental breakfast on their patio overlooking the Brienzersee. And our Eurail ticket held valid also for the ferry service to the Interlaken East Station from which leave the private railways for Murren and the Jungfraujoch" (Keith and Jess Parker, Capetown, South Africa).

INVERNESS, SCOTLAND

"I have **Mrs. Campbell,** 13 Denny Street (phone 31726), to thank for a wonderful stay in Inverness. For £9 we had a cosy room—the two beds equipped with electric blankets for warmth—and an excellent and well-served breakfast. What counted most, however, is the friendly atmosphere of the Campbell home. We were made to feel part of the household, sharing their living room at night, before a real fire, over a cup of tea with lots of home made cakes graciously offered by the landlady. Just to tell you what I mean, before we parted, the Campbells bought a bottle of Scotch which we drank together singing 'Auld Lang Syne.' An experience I would not have missed for anything in the world" (Efi Vicka, Athens, Greece). . . . "If you're in the mood to do a bit of exhilarating hiking and enjoy some of Scotland's most spectacular scenery, then take a bus from Inverness to Fort Augustus and Loch Ness (yes, home of the fabled 'beastie'). From there you can 'head for the hills.' Good hiking paths" (Carma Bamber, San Francisco, California). . . . "An unbelievable guesthouse is **Leinster Lodge** at 27 Southside Road (phone 33311), where the rooms are large and beautiful, the proprietress (Mrs. Sime) friendly and helpful, and the charge (including the usual delicious breakfast) is £4 per person" (Fred Baskind, New York, New York). . . . "My recommendation is **MacDonald House Hotel** (phone Inverness 32878), at 1 Ardoss Terrace, on the West bank of the River Ness across the way from the castle. For £5 per person, the proprietress, Mrs. J.K. Allan, provides clean, spacious rooms, (most of them with individual color tv sets), plenty of hot water (a rarity in budget Britain), and a cosy television lounge in which tea and biscuits are served before bed time, and a hearty breakfast (bacon, sausage and eggs, etc.) in the morning. The house is fully carpeted with tartan runners and is quite charming" (Norman Rosenthal, Johannesburg, South Africa). . . . "One of the most beautiful homes at which I stayed was **Duneve**, 28 Old Edinburgh Road, Inverness, tel. 33-297. Mr. and Mrs. Grant, who live there, are a most charming couple, who opened their doors at 7 a.m. to a very tired, middle-aged American tourist who had just arrived on the night train from Glasgow. Their home is 150 years old, filled with gorgeous things, fireplaces in every room and heating blankets on the beds. What a lovely place. They charged £4.50 per night. . . . Inverness is not to be missed, as it is near Loch Ness and has a fantastic Scottish review six nights a week called 'The Kilt is Our Delight', complete with pipes, dancers and all the trimmings" (Connie Nelsen, Tacoma, Washington).

ISCHIA, ITALY

"After Paris we made our way to Ischia, a small island off the coast of Italy, and there we ran into a gold-mine of a hotel—the **Pensione Villa Panoramica** (tel. 991-414)— where a double room with two meals (breakfast and one other) ran us 17,000 lire per person. The rooms are immaculate and the service out of this world, i.e., a maid takes dirty laundry, cleans and irons it, then lays it out for us. The villa is a stone's throw from a beach—sand, not gravel—and a leisurely after-dinner walk brings you to the main shopping centers on the island. One of the rooms we had, had a breathtaking view of the ocean, distant islands, and an island fortress" (Howard Passe, Richard Kelsey, Bob Beccarelli, Charlie Czeupak, Union, New Jersey).

ISTANBUL, TURKEY

Note from AF: As a preface to what follows, bear in mind that the current exchange rate (as of January, 1980) of the Turkish currency is 42 Turkish lira to one U.S. dollar: "I've been staying at the **Hotel Güngör**, 44 Divanyolu Cad., Sultanahmet (phone 26-23-19), a student-type hotel only five blocks from the enormous covered bazaar, near the beautiful Blue Mosque, the famed Topkapi Palace, and St. Sophia. There are dormitory and double rooms. For the dormitory, the charge is 60 lira, for double rooms it's 200 lira, 240 lira for triples. Everyone there is quite friendly" (Tricia Bobnar, Madison, Pennsylvania; plus numerous other endorsements). . . . "Better than the Güngör, in my view, is the **Hotel Pirlanta**, Divanyolu Cad., Sultanahmet (phone 277-085), about 70 yards from the Güngör and equally popular with students. Dorm without shower 30 lira, with shower 70 lira; bathless single 140 lira, bathless double 175 lira" (Christina Lorey, Cologne, Germany). . . . "The **Yücel Tourist Hostel**, Caferiye Sokak No. 6 (phone 22-47-90), was a good home for the week I spent in Istanbul. We had a simple, but clean, triple room with balcony for only 110 lira apiece. A dormitory bed is 70 lira. Hot showers and an outdoor cafeteria downstairs. The desk personnel speak English. Catering mostly to students, the Yücel stands minutes away from such grand sights as the Hagia Sophia, Blue Mosque and Topkapi Palace" (Randy Mink, Elgin, Illinois). . . . "In the center of the city, just off Taksim Square, is the old-fashioned and mysterious **Murad Oteli** (tel. 450-553), where a large double room will run 220 lira although the manager will probably accept less if business is slow. Ask for a room on the upper floors, where there are magnificent views of the Bosporus and the mosques" (Mr. and Mrs. Richard D. Greenfield, Hartsdale, New York). . . . "The **Hotel Kapitol,** at Asmali Mescit Caddesi 54 (phone 44-45-72), is the place to stay. For 125 lira per person, you get a very clean room with sink and just down the hall is a shower and rest room. It is located one block from the American Embassy and within five blocks of Taksim Square, along the Istiklal Caddesi" (Bruce A. Winters, Fresno, California). . . . "**Pera Palace Hotel,** truly a palace, at budget rates! $14 a day with breakfast, for a single room. Highly recommended. It's within walking distance of Taksim-Square, 3 minutes to the Tunel, the world's smallest subway, which takes you down to Galata Bridge. Friendly, helpful staff, and good food, too" (Evelyn Nicholas, Los Angeles, California). . . . "A must trip for anyone in or near Istanbul is a ferry boat ride up the Bosporus; they run frequently. We left at 10:25 a.m., on the trip to Saniyer, taking one and a half hours from pier no. 3, with the boat criss-crossing from Europe to Asia; it touches six Asian ports and one in Europe. Upon arrival in Saniyer at 12 noon, you will have plenty of time to stroll through the town and return to a picturesque restaurant at the pier for lunch before catching the return boat to Istanbul, which leaves at 1:30 p.m. and arrives back in Istanbul at 3:30 p.m. Believe it or not, the cost is 72¢ American for the round trip, so be sure to buy a round trip before leaving. This three-and-a-half hour ride is the longest we have ever had for the money. Avoid the advertised tours of the Bosporus, but be sure to take the above ferry used by the local residents" (William H. Read, Hollywood, California). . . . "A two-and-a-half hour ferry trip from pier no. 5 at the foot of the **Galata Bridge** (old Istanbul side) through the Prince's Islands to Pendik in Asia Minor costs 60¢ second class (the sun deck is open to both first and second class). A fantastic ride back to Kadikoy in a Dolmus (Turkish combination of a taxi and a bus at fixed fare and no tip) cost 72¢, and a ferry back across the Bosporus to Istanbul was 30¢. Round trip cost was $1.62 per person for relaxation, outstanding scenery on an 'island cruise,' and a lesson in the Turkish language and hospitality from scores of curious, friendly commuters. Here is a place where an American is really helped to feel at home" (Lt. and Mrs. William E. Peterson, Portland, Oregon). . . . "Bus #84, #86 or #34 from Yeni Camii (old city end of Galata) goes to the **Archaeological Museum,** Topkapi Saray (the best sight in Turkey—perfect gem of the decadent grandeur that was the Ottoman Empire—admission 25 lire), **Aya Sofia** and the **Blue Mosques.** . . . Don't miss the Karye Museum, the most beautiful Byzantine mosaics we've seen. It's hard to find, though. Take the Edirne Kapa bus to the end of the line, and then ask. . . . Covered bazaar prices are lower in the morning, because the guided tours come by in the afternoon" (Mrs. Barbara Papesch, Switzerland). . . . "For the student traveler to Istanbul, **VIP Youth Travel** at Cumhuriet Cad. 12, Elmadag-Istanbul (phone 462-073), is a must. It is staffed by students on a voluntary basis and directs its work in the area of youth and student tourism, but in addition provides services for adults and other education personnel. In a country where French and German are practically useless, a traveler needs advice because of language and cultural difficulties, and I found these university students particularly adept at conveying the flavor of the New Turkey both in politics, art and interpretation of values. They will suggest restaurants like the **Sofra** (a particularly good Turkish Kebab), and the **Cinar,** where a reasonable meal can be had for less than $3.50. They will also suggest good restaurants that supply Turkish and European food in all price ranges. I found Istanbul a beautiful city, perhaps the most colorful in Europe. The Blue Mosque, Topkapi Palace, St. Sophia, a cruise in the Bosporus, Turkish folk dancing with the Eastern overtones not found elsewhere in Europe, and a lovely climate (70 degrees F); the six days I spent there were a completely enjoyable time" (Jeremid Slattery, New York, New York). . . . "Train fare, 2nd class, round trip from Ankara to Istanbul, is approximately 210 TL (only 85 TL for students). A train leaves each city for the other around 8 to 9 p.m. each day. The compartments are quite comfortable, as are the beds. On arriving in Istanbul, do not let a porter take your bag. They meet you at the train and then carry it onto the ferry that goes from the railway station across the Bosporus and stops just under the Ataturk Bridge. They take the ferry with you and then charge 30TL when you disembark! The ferry is the greatest bargain in Eurasia: 5TL for the entire trip!" (James E. Kennington, Jr., APO, New York). . . . "Be sure to visit **Dolmabahce Palace** in Istanbul. The memory of the excerpt from 'Thousand Nights and a Night' will last longer than any of the photographs I took" (James E. Kennington, Jr., APO, New York). . . . "There are three ways to travel in Istanbul and Ankara—by taxi, bus, and dolmuc (pronounced dole-moosh). Taxi drivers should be questioned about their price to a certain point and always prior to entering the vehicle. Never accept the originally quoted price; arguing for 30 seconds will lower it to what it should be—1/2 to 2/3rds of the original. Dolmuces charge a set fee, an average of 2TL for travelling along a set, major route; they are usually a large automobile or a microbus. Bus prices in Istanbul usually run about 2 to 3TL. To distinguish between taxis and dolmuces is sometimes difficult. In Ankara, dolmuces have a solid yellow line around the car body and usually have a plaque on top, listing the sections of the city that are travelled. The word 'Dolmuc' is lettered on the trunk or rear window. Taxis have a black and yellow checkered border around them. In Istanbul, the story is different. There is no obvious difference between taxis and dolmuces; all of them have a solid yellow line around the body. To catch a dolmuc, stand on a major intersection, or the corner of a street, and when a cab stops, say, 'Dolmuc—(then give the area you are trying to reach)—?' " (James E. Kennington, Jr., APO, New York). . . . "All European marketplaces, bargaining, and goods pale before Istanbul's 'Grand Bazaar,' a labyrinth of tunnels, arcades, and courtyards which could take a most demanding shopper days to go through. Luckily there are some good, cheap and rather clean restaurants in the Bazaar. Suede coats, made to measure, for $40 to $75 . . . quite matchless gold and silver jewelry at all prices . . . $4 could buy a brilliantly colored woven cloth, dinnertable size . . . antique finds of every type . . . sigh" (Mrs. Barbara Papesch, Switzerland). . . . "Anyone can enter the famous mosques, free, but there is a fee for the museums, ranging from 50¢ to $1. The boat trips up the Bosporus and to the Princes' Islands are also inexpensive and highly worthwhile" (Ted & Lynn Kotzin, Los Angeles, Calif.). . . . "The fare from Istanbul to Haifa with **Turkish Maritime Lines** is about $81 (payable in U.S. currency), third class, off-season, ships leave once every two weeks, on alternating Wednesdays, and the trip takes four to five days, including a one-day stop at Izmir. Although third class dormitory conditions are a bit cramped, the food is quite good and plentiful, and all passengers are free to use the decks and lounges" (Henry S. Sloan, New York, New York).

KILLARNEY, IRELAND

"One mile out of Killarney, on the Cork Road, **Mr. and Mrs. Denis O'Donahue** (pronounced O'Dunahoo) operate an immaculately clean B and B. They call their home **Cum A Ciste,** which means Valley of the Treasure. It has eight neat rooms, each with two double beds and a sink as well as other furniture, of course. For 7 pounds we had a good night's rest and a very filling breakfast of our choice, which included porridge, toast, eggs, bacon and coffee. Don't stay anywhere else in Killarney!" (Tom and Michelle Flessor, Evergreen Park, Illinois). . . . "The most delightful stay I had in any pension or hotel in Europe was at **Aisling House** on Countess Road, which runs parallel to the train station, but can only be reached by leaving the station and turning right. Take the first left onto the large road. Pass the cinema and take another left, passing a church. Walk for about 3-5 minutes more. Proprietors are extremely nice and the price was terrific—£3.10 ($6.82) for bed and breakfast" (Sue Ulloa, Bainbridge Island, Washington). . . . "I kept asking what was the attraction of Killarney that caused it to expand in population so greatly during July and August? Some of the reasons are: 1. An easy town to walk in, with shops and accommodations centrally located; 2. Friendly people, the Irish; 3. Abundant restaurants, pubs and entertainment spots; 4. Many excellent tourist accommodations to satisfy every taste; 5. The picturesque scenery surrounding Killarney, the primary reason why so many visit this area of the Emerald Isle" (Al Uher, Delmar, California).

KOBLENZ, GERMANY

"If you are considering a trip on the Rhine by boat, it's especially right to start at Koblenz, ending your trip at Bingen. You will see the greatest number of castles and the most beautiful scenery that way, and the trip is still short enough not to be boring. Eurailpasses are valid for your trip" (J. Thomas Renfrow, Tulsa, Oklahoma). . . . " **Gasthaus Christ,** Schürtzenstrasse 32 (phone 37702), has a very friendly proprietor who charges 20 marks single, 35 marks double, for a clean room with hot and cold running water, breakfast included. There is also a small restaurant there which is quite inexpensive and a good place to meet the local people. We now correspond with a couple we met there" (Ronald M. Greenberg, Los Angeles, California). . . . "**Pension Daheim,** at 26 Schenkendorfstrasse (phone 37842), provided good accommodation for three—a single and a double room—for 58 marks ($30.52). That included everything, and the breakfasts were just fine" (A. A. Walters, Nokomis, Florida).

LAKE COMO, ITALY

"Four kilometers west of Lago Como, in the town of Cernobbio, we found high up on the hill (a car is needed here) the **Hotel Asnigo** (phone 510062), with a superb view of the lake. We stayed here two days, paying 17,000 lire per person per day for half-pension, with well-cooked meals. I cannot recommend this place enough to your readers" (Jacques and Magdeleine Tremblay, Quebec City, Canada). . ... "Our 'find' of this trip was the **Hotel Internazionale**, Via Volta 83, tel: 26-81-06, at Lake Como, Italy, where the price for very large, clean, comfortable rooms was 19,500 lire ($23.49) nightly for a double, plus 22,000 lire ($26.50) for a triple for our children. This place has beautiful old baroque doors, frescoed ceilings. It was obviously once a grand hotel. Parking in an enclosed garden off the street—no extra charge" (Mrs. R. D. Tausch, Mannheim, Germany).

LAKE GARDA, ITALY

"We were just going to stop by, but stayed four days in Sirmione, directly on Lake Garda. There are ruins of the vacation homes of various Caesars, a castle, open-air market, grotto, walks, shops—all fantastic! A great place to flake out and rest. Boy, did we! We had a lovely room at the **Garden-Lido Hotel** (phone 916-102), good breakfast, balcony, lovely lakefront garden, all for 18,000 lire ($21.68), just 300 meters from the heart of downtown. There are hundreds of rooms for far less further out, but still in town, for as low as 12,500 lire double. Lovely boat rides, and close to a nice side-trip—Verona. For a minor splurge, Sirmione is the greatest. I love tortellini (had it 3 nights in a row) in cream sauce, a huge plate was 1,700 lire ($2.04)" (Victor Beard, San Francisco, California).

LAKE MAGGIORE, ITALY

"Touring the Italian lakes, we stopped overnight at Stresa, on Lake Maggiore, where we found the **Hotel "Italie and Suisse"** right on the lake, for only 17,000 lire, double, without bath" (Jacques and Magdeleine Tremblay, Quebec City, Canada).

LAUSANNE, SWITZERLAND

"We stayed at the **Hotel Transit**, 14 Avenue du Simplon (phone 279-252), located on the same block as the railroad station. Our small, but clean and airy, double room cost 44 francs ($25.88) including taxes but not breakfast. The hotel had several dining rooms serving different-priced meals. We ate in the moderately-priced room for about 9 francs ($5.29) each" (Mrs. Bernard Greenberg, Brooklyn, New York). . . . "The **Hotel Pension Georgette**, at 3 Avenue de Georgette (telephone 22-84-28), is within walking distance of the train station (about four blocks). Directrice Mademoiselle A. Buhrer is a charming person who speaks English fluently, and was most helpful in directing me to places of interest and in reading train schedules. She was also of great help in securing emergency dental help for me. A single room was 30 francs ($17.64), which included breakfast" (Tom Kiddon, Miami Beach, Florida). . . . "Go down the stairs at the extreme left of the station (as you face the tracks), then proceed under the tracks to the other side of the station, and you will come to the Avenue du Simplon. Turn left and at #7 is the **Hotel Les Trois Rois** (phone 26-38-22), where a comfortable double room with breakfast may be had for 50 Swiss francs" (James and Yvonne Bunting, Woonsocket, Rhode Island). . . . "**Les Pavillons Près-de-Vidy**, 1007 Lausanne, Chemin du Bois de Vaux (phone 24-24-79), is really a *great* place, with free showers, and is brand new, with a good breakfast, for 16 Sw. francs per person all together; twin-bedded rooms but so many of them that I had mine as a single the whole time. Just a four-minute walk from Lac Leman and it's beautiful and clean. Take Bus #1 at the train station, ask for street address. This place is really fantastic" (Margaret Bratsenis, Branford, Connecticut). . . . "For less than $12 a night, per person, we had a triple room in a charming pension, located 6 minutes' walking distance from the railway station. The address is 11 rue de la Gare, and the name of the establishment is **"The Old Inn"** (Pension des Etudiants). Our room was absolutely huge and lavishly furnished, the proprietress charming and most helpfull" (Diane Neaven, Montreal, Canada; note from AF: 1980 rates at the Old Inn, for rooms with private shower, are 25 francs ($14.70) single, 40 francs ($23.52) double, 60 francs ($35.29) triple, including breakfast). . . . "In Lausanne, Eurailpasses can be used on the metro" (Diane Larson, Los Angeles, California).

LEEDS, ENGLAND

"My wife and I stayed at the **Cardigan Guest House**, 36 Cardigan Road, Headingley, Leeds, at £5.25 per night per person for bed and breakfast. TV lounge, tea and biscuits served in the evening. A friendly proprietress, Mrs. Thompson. Highly recommendable" (G. G. Boyce, Thornton, Cape Town, South Africa).

LE HAVRE, FRANCE

"For inexpensive accommodations in Le Havre, I shared a large double room with a fellow passenger at the newly-decorated **Hotel d'Yport,** 27 Cours de la Republique (phone 25-21-08), near the railway station, paying 33 francs ($7.67) each, plus 8.50 francs apiece for breakfast; this was for a double with running water. Doubles with w.c. are 44 francs; singles with w.c. are 48, with running water 42 francs. I discovered that the **YMCA** at 153 Boulevard Strasbourg (phone 42-47-86) has a few single rooms for men at only 23 francs per night. The Y also issues temporary passes that allow travelers to use their cafeteria, and adequate full-course meals can be had there for 15 francs" (Henry S. Sloan, New York, New York). . . . "Try the **Hotel Suisse** at 3 Rue Racine on Place Gambetta (phone 42-37-05), for a lovely, newly-decorated room for two for 64 francs ($14.88). The management is delightful and most accommodating. Breakfast is 10 francs extra" (Rochelle B. Seiden, Brooklyn, New York).

LEYSIN, SWITZERLAND

"Nestled high in the Alps in Leysin, near Lake Geneva, is the **Club Vagabond** (phone 34-31-21). As the name implies, it's a haven for vagabonds and vagabonds-at-heart. The chalet is more of a friendly club than a hotel, and the proprietors, Allan and Carol Rankin and Dave and Johanne Smith (of Canada), take great pains to keep it that way. Atmosphere and attire are refreshingly informal, and accommodations are mostly in rooms bunking two to four persons. The rooms are basic, but spotless, and most have balconies overlooking the grandeur of the Alps. Their rates are fantastic: a double room with breakfast is 18 francs ($10.58) per person; three and four-bedded rooms 15 francs ($8.82) per person. Winter is the ski season, so prices go up then to 23 francs per person for a double room, 19 francs per person in the three- and four-bedded rooms. Here's a real swingin' place with a young international atmosphere" (Jules Klar, New York City; note by A.F.: the Club Vagabond is a five-minute walk from the Leysin-Feyday railway station, highest in the village).

LIECHTENSTEIN

"**Hotel Meierhof** (tel. 075-21836) is in Triesen, near Vaduz on the road to Malbun, fairly new, clean, and offers a marvelous view. Double room with bath costs approximately 50 francs" (Eugene S. Quillen, Anacortes, Washington).

LIMERICK, IRELAND

"My **St. Rita's Guest House** is on the main road from Limerick to Shannon Airport and also on the road from Galway to Killarney that passes Limerick City. The exact address is St. Rita's, Ennis Road, Limerick (tel: Limerick 55809). The house is Regency architecture and has eight bedrooms, all large and spacious and with hot and cold running water in each. I have a large lounge and dining room so it is quite a home away from home. My terms for Bed and Breakfast usually run around £5 each person or roughly $11. I have adequate toilet and bathroom requirements" (Mrs. Bernadette Clancy, Limerick, Ireland). . . . "**Mrs. Evelyn Murphy,** at 8 Davis Street (phone 47227), is straight down from the train station, very handy to town, buses and train. Good bed and breakfast—single £4.50, double £4 each per night. Very nice lady" (Woodrow and Letress Berryhill, Phoenix, Arizona).

LISBON, PORTUGAL

HOTELS: "Though its name sounds expensive, the one-star **Hotel Americano,** 73 Rua 1 de Dezembro (phone 32-11-89), charges only 500 escudos ($11.60) for a clean, remodeled single. Baths are 30 escudos and there is plenty of hot water from the tap. The Americano's location is perfect, right next to the Rossio train station, in the center of

Lisbon's shopping and business district. And there's a modern supermarket flanking both sides of the hotel's entrance. I stayed here a week" (Randy Mink, Elgin, Illinois). . . . "The **Hotel Portugal,** right off the Praca da Figueira in Lisbon (phone 86-60-29), is a bargain even for that city. Centrally located (near the Rossio), clean, spacious, and with extremely friendly and courteous personnel, the Portugal charges only 220 escudos for a single room (including tax). No meals are included in that price, but in Lisbon, where so many of the attractions are located outside of town—usually requiring day trips—it isn't particularly advisable to stay in a pension requiring meals. And there are so many fine and inexpensive restaurants in Lisbon that I wouldn't recommend taking any meals in a hotel" (Clark R. Norton, Charlotte, North Carolina). . . . "We stayed at the **Hotel Lis,** Avenida da Liberdade 180 (phone 56-34-34). This is a beautiful, wide boulevard in the center of town, with a flower mall running down its center. The hotel was unbelievably immaculate, and charged only 1,100 escudos for a bathless double room and three sumptuous meals, beautifully served (a scrumptious hors d'oeuvres cart is rolled to table before lunch). Imagine all this for approximately $11 per person!" (B. Schwartzman, Brooklyn, New York; seconded by Lucia de Haas, Vancouver, Canada).

PENSIONS: "I've got lots of finds that should go into 'Fifteen A Day,' but one of the best is a small, clean, inexpensive pension which has rooms with private showers (hot) for 390 escudos ($7.80) for two people in a double bed: **Pensao Santa Cruz,** 11 Avenida Da Liberdade. Right on the main street, yet rooms at the back can be had which are unaffected by street noise. . . . Tell your readers to be sure and go up the hill (Bus 37, Trolley 28) to the 'Alfama,' the very old section in and around the Castello Sao Jorge. You can wander through the terraced parks, down twisting winding streets, and generally amuse yourself for hours" (Mr. and Mrs. W. H. Polk, Seattle, Washington). . . . "We were really delighted with the **Pensao Residencial Parisiense,** Praca D. Joao de Câmara 4, third floor (phone 37-08-27), which has a 1A category rating and is spotlessly clean. Our first night there we had a lovely double room with shower and telephone for 665 escudos. The next night we moved to a less expensive room, just as nice but without shower and telephone, for 500 escudos. Other rooms were 580. There was plenty of hot water and the pension was right off the Rossio. To find it, walk up the Rossio heading away from the port and turn left on the street at the end of the square. It is in the building with the huge neon 'Shell' sign on top" (Neva and Don Kaiser, Miami, Florida). . . . "The best find of our holiday was the **Residencia Roma** at Travessa Da Gloria 22A, telephone 360-557/8/9, where the charge for a double room with breakfast is from 850 escudos, including service and tax. Each room has recently been done over and looks clean and modern, with toilet and shower in each" (N. H. Cumming, Umtali, Rhodesia).

SIGHTSEEING AND OTHER: "We enjoyed the bullfights in the Campo Pequeno where, in the Portuguese style, the bulls were wrestled bare-handed. It was daring and suspense-filled every moment" (Manny Mevorah, Brooklyn, New York). . . . "For a lively variety show, visit any one of the several vaudeville theaters located in the **Parque Mayor;** bleacher-type seats can be had for as little as 100 escudos" (Henry S. Sloan, New York, New York). . . . "Use the electric train between Lisbon and Estoril; the 20-mile trip costs about 70 escudos" (H. L. Newton, Monte Estoril, Portugal). . . . "At Estoril, near the Casino, the beach and the former playgrounds of European royalty, try the **Pensao Continental,** 2 Rua Joaquim dos Santos (phone 268-00-50), Estoril, at about $19 per day for room and all three meals. The English-speaking proprietors serve plentiful and tasty food" (H. L. Newton, Monte Estoril, Portugal). . . . "To go to **Belem,** take the number 16 streetcar from Praca do Comercio (right at the water front). The fare is only 10 escudos, and it carries you to the entrance of the Jeronimos Monastery. There are many different places of interest to visit in this area, including museums" (Adrian and Suzanne Allen, Miami Beach, Florida). . . . "Lisbon has a modern airport but it is the only city I know where there is no regular airport bus. To beat the taxi game, walk outside, turn right, and you'll see a bus stop sign in about 30 feet. Bus 1A goes into town. Five escudos" (Dr. & Mrs. Kenneth Korven, Susanville, California).

LIVERPOOL, ENGLAND

"I note that the city of Liverpool is not mentioned. Liverpool is visited by many thousands of overseas tourists each year, including large numbers from the United States. The city's reasonably priced accomodations allow visitors the opportunity to enjoy the area's many attractions, including a wide range of shops, two Cathedrals and other fine buildings, and a variety of excellent facilities in leisure and the arts. Liverpool is also an ideal base for wider travel to places such as Chester, North Wales, or the Lancashire Coast" (Peter Heaton, Publicity and Information Officer, City of Liverpool; note from

AF: Readers visiting Liverpool in 1980 are kindly requested to mail in comments on hotels, restaurants, noteworthy personal experiences).

LOURDES, FRANCE

"The **Estival Hotel** (Rue Alsace Lorraine, phone 94-05-86), a three-minute walk from the Grotto, is a wonderful big splurge selection for a visit to Lourdes. The nice room and three complete meals cost 98 francs per day per person. Demi-pension is 74 francs" (Al Silva, Tulare, California). . . . "We stayed at the very inexpensive **Bearn Hotel**, 13 Avenue de la Gare (phone 94-25-40), where the rooms go for 35 to 55 francs, pension from 60 to 65 francs" (Pauline H. Maude, New York, New York).

LUCERNE, SWITZERLAND

"A tremendous hotel find which should certainly be in your book is the **Hotel Kolping**, located at 8 Friedenstrasse (phone 222901). Here we got a bed in a six-bed dormitory with breakfast, hot water and free hot showers for only 15 Swiss francs ($8.82), which is quite low in this city. It was spotlessly clean and well-located" (Dale Watts, Dearborn, Michigan; note by A.F.: the Kolping has relatively expensive hotel rooms, very inexpensive dorm rooms; therefore, specify that you want the dorms). . . . "I stayed in the **Hotel Kolping** on Friedenstrasse. It is a regular hotel that has a dormitory section costing just 15 Swiss francs a night, including breakfast. And that is not all: it is wonderfully clean and has a super-hot shower at no extra cost. The shower facilities alone are worth the money. To get there, take the bus from the railroad station to Löwenplatz. It's not too far. At the platz you will see the Hotel Union and the Hotel Kolping is just around the corner" (Stephen D. Robb, Flagler, Colorado). . . . "The **Hotel Gambrinus**, at 12 Mühlenplatz (phone 22-17-91), is painted in old Swiss style and offers a single room for 27 Swiss francs ($15.88), including breakfast. The management speaks several different languages and will offer you all the help you want. The beds are the turn-down variety and are so comfortable that you don't want to get up in the morning. Meals may be eaten at this hotel for the moderate sum of 8 francs ($4.70), and they are excellent" (Tom Graviss, Louisville, Kentucky; a similar recommendation for the Gambrinus from Frank L. Esterquest, Oxford, Ohio). . . . "A true Godsend to us in Lucerne was the self-service restaurant in the **Hotel Krone**, on the Weinmarkt Platz. It is unmarked, and is located on the ground floor, to the left of the entrance. Be careful not to go upstairs to the more traditional restaurant. Soup was only 1 franc, a full dinner, complete with soup and salad, was only 6 Swiss francs ($3.52). A must for all $15-a-Day'ers!" (Nikko and Ron Parry, Inglewood, California). . . . "We stayed in a triple and a double room at **Hotel Winkelried**, Winkelriedstrasse 26, tel 23-03-73, 5 min. from the station, for a total of only 104 francs per day. Run by Herr Stockreiter (very pleasant). Rooms are very clean, and eiderdowns are provided. The restaurant is quite reasonable, too" (Virginia Gillette, Roxbury, Connecticut). . . . "A fellow passenger gave us the name of **Pension Panorama** at Kapuzinerweg 9 (phone 36-67-01 or 36-22-98), a quiet street on a hill about 10 walking minutes from the Lion monument. It is operated by the delightful Theresa von Euw, a friendly, English speaking (and singing) lady. We paid 16 francs ($9.41) per person for a gorgeous double overlooking Lucerne and the lake. Mrs. von Euw is a superb and funny lady, and her pension definitely deserves to be listed" (Glenn and Deborah Rifkin, Watertown, Massachusetts). . . . "A necessary trip from Lucerne is to the summit of **Mt. Pilatus**, which can be reached by steamer (free to Eurailpass users) to Alpnachstad, from where you use a *train* to get to the top. The train both ways is 26 SF or you can take the circular tour (down the other side of the mountain) via exciting cable cars to Kriens for 3 additional Swiss Francs, if you present your first train tickets. From Kriens there is a trolley-bus (90 centimes, a 15-minute ride) back to Lucerne. Don't miss it! The total cost came to under $13 with lunch at a self-service restaurant on the summit, as opposed to the $19 commercial tour. Readers can save money by going down by train, which is exciting in itself: the steepest gradient in the world—it seemed nearly vertical" (Wendy E. Peppin and Helen Davis, Elmhurst, New York).

LUGANO, SWITZERLAND

"Lugano is a place where very few Americans seem to go. It is a lovely city and its location on Lago Lugano makes it an ideal vacation spot. We stayed at the **Hotel Ticino** (phone 227-772), which is right next to the end of the funicular run from the railroad station. For 32 francs ($18.82) per person per night, we had a lovely room and breakfast. The service, as it is all over Switzerland, was impeccable" (Francie Diwald, Milwaukee, Wisconsin). . . . "Only three blocks from the Pestalozzi alcohol-free restaurant, at 13 Corso Pestalozzi (phone 23-43-43), we found the **Albergo Hotel Garni Zurigo**—a very real find in high-priced Lugano. For 26 Swiss francs per person we had a large double room with a balcony, breakfast, service and taxes included. The owner said she had other, smaller doubles renting for 22 francs per person. There is also ample parking space behind the building, and the lake is only a short walk away. The clientele seem to be Europeans who return every year; the landlady rarely has Americans staying there" (Luella Boddewyn, New York, New York; also Mrs. Philip Kraysler, East Orange, New Jersey). . . . "The one reasonably-priced eating place is the **Pestalozzi House** restaurant on Pestalozzi Street, close to the lake. Price for a complete meal amounts to 6 to 8 Swiss francs, which comes to $3.52 to $4.70. Two seating rooms are available, one with tablecloths" (Hans Hagen, Sunnyvale, California). . . . "A restaurant worthy of mention is one situated in a department store called **Epa-Unip** on Via Nassa, three minutes from the main square (Piazza della Reforma). Between 11 and 2 o'clock you can have a fixed price meal (pasta, meat, salad) for 4.50 to 6 francs. Or one can choose several fine specialties for well under 7 francs. The restaurant is operated cafeteria style; the chef speaks English well. The other waitresses are most friendly" (Ronald Murdock, Nova Scotia, Canada).

LUXEMBOURG, LUXEMBOURG

"I'd recommend the **Hotel de L'Avenue,** 43 Ave. de la Liberté, 350 francs for a single room, 280 francs per person for a double, and very clean, modern furnishings, airy. It is on the left of the two big avenues coming out from the railroad station" (Thomas Endry, Elmhurst, New York). . . . "For travelers on a tight budget who want to enjoy large, clean, rooms, comfortable beds and fascinating conversation (the latter only if they speak French or German), **Hotel Brezel**, 30 Rue du Fort Neipperge (phone 48-72-55), is ideal. Five minutes by foot from the railway station, a double cost 367 Belgian francs ($12.23), 20 BFR (66¢) for an excellent hot shower. The owner, Madame Brezel, was one of the kindest souls I met during four months in Europe. She speaks a little English. Breakfast is not included, but many quaint boulangerie/patisserie salons are on Avenue de la Gare, a block away" (Nancy Judge, Watertown, Connecticut). . . . "We stayed at the **City Hotel**, 1 Rue de Strasbourg, tel. 484-608, two blocks from the station, in a triple and a double for a total of 1,900 Belgian francs. Clean, comfortable rooms. Has elevator. Restaurant City Cave, below hotel lobby, served best food of entire trip. Menus very reasonable" (Virginia Gillette, Roxbury, Connecticut). . . . "Since many budget readers fly Icelandic Airlines to Luxembourg, they may be interested in how to get from downtown to the airport. Bus number 9 leaves frequently from just outside the train station and costs 12 francs instead of 50 francs for the regular airline buses. Do not confuse Bus 9 with Bus 9A. From the airport to town, walk south out to a parking lot. Look for a bus stop marked Arret Ligne 9" (David W. Smith, Carbondale, Illinois).

LYON, FRANCE

"**Hotel de Geneve**, 10 Quai de Perrache, tel. Lyon 371-159, was very clean, has pleasant owners. My room was in fact a double, normally costing 55 francs for two, petit dejeuner 7 fr. It is only five minutes from the station. Turn right, go down steps to Rue Belier, which then turns left to the Quai. Then turn right and hotel is 100 yards away to your right" (Angela Wear, England). . . . "**Hotel Le Baudelaire** is but a 5-minute walk from the ultramodern transport complex of the Lyon-Perrache railway station, at 6 rue d'Auvergne, a street that runs parallel to the modern pedestrian shopping mall, rue Victor Hugo. Its proprietors don't speak English but are so kind and patient that communication is no problem. We paid 55 francs ($12.79) for a double room, basin and bidet, and an extra 10 francs for breakfast. From the station, follow the path to the left corner of the park (Place Carnot) as you leave the escalator. Cross the rue de Condé and walk up rue Henri IV, which becomes rue d'Auvergne after a couple of blocks. Hotel Le Baudelaire will be on your left. Don't be misled by the drab exterior of the building. Telephone is 378-534" (Melanie Pearce and Kaz Bluhm, Yinnar, Victoria, Australia). . . . "**Liberty Hotel**, 3 Rue Jean-Larrivé, tel. 60-02-65, is in an excellent location, on a quiet street one block from the Rhone. The proprietress is friendly, charming and helpful. We had a small, clean room and bath (modern-style overhead shower), with telephone, radio and TV, for 55 francs ($12.79) for 2 of us. We are Americans resident in France, travel when necessary, but rarely as 'tourists' " (C. Gross, Yvoire, France).

MADEIRA (ISLAND OF)

"Please find space for the Island of Madeira, an autonomous region of Portugal. Many of your readers will be able to stop there free of charge. It beats any Mediterranean island for beauty, and because of a surplus of hotel accommodations, rooms are incredibly low, particularly outside of Funchal, the only large town on the island. In the village of Machico, the **Dom Pedro Hotel** (4-star rating) charges 250 escudos ($5) per person double including breakfast, 300 escudos ($6) single. There are facilities for tennis and water sports. I bet you cannot get better value than this anywhere else in Europe" (José Alves, Port Elizabeth, South Africa).

MÁLAGA, SPAIN

"Málaga is a pleasant city (pop. 300,000) with an atmosphere of quiet gaiety, on the South Coast. Although it is quite a tourist attraction, it is not dominated nor ruined by the tourist, as I understand nearby Torremolinos has been. I stayed in the **Hostal Andalucia,** Alarcón Luján 8 (phone 211-960), just a few steps from the Plaza Queipo de Llano, the main Plaza, and I recommend it highly. Singles are 480 pesetas, double 900" (Robert M. Stanton, Madison, Wisconsin). . . . "It's with much enthusiasm that I recommend the brand-new, spotlessly clean **Hostal Carlos V,** Calle Cister 6, near the cathedral in Málaga (phone 215-120), where—for a single room with hot and cold water—I paid 600 pesetas ($9.09) a day. The manager speaks some English, and everyone is very friendly. No meals are served" (Richard J. Walther, Elizabeth, New Jersey).

MALLORCA (Balearic Islands), SPAIN

"If one wants sheer pleasure rather than just another inexpensive place to stay, try the **Juan Bernadell Duch** (Calle San Elias No. 11, 20, Palma, tel: 215867). A private house, not a hotel, this place has wonderful food, good rooms with large sunny balconies and views, and very personable, friendly owners. Juan, who speaks English very well, offers rapid Spanish courses, and his wife serves the best food in Mallorca. Rooms at $10 a day, rooms and full board $17.50" (D. E. Koné, Oakland, California). . . . "Getting off the boat in Mallorca, one should cross the bridge in front of the building, and take the bus to **Plaza Gomilla,** where any hotel should not cost more than $12 a day per person. There are tourists galore there, but never mind. I took the bus to Illetas Beach, which wasn't crowded at all, and in a nice cove" (Barry Glen, Cedarhurst, New York). . . . "**Hostal Versalles,** 27 Rafaletas, Porto-Pi, Mallorca (phone 230-741), was the delight of our three-week stay in Mallorca. Away from the busy Palma, but near the beaches and town activities, we enjoyed the best of both worlds. A 'football' game on television, a drink at the bar, or a swim in the pool, could occupy a cloudy day. For a double room with bath (in October) and full pension we paid only 1,700 pesetas. The personnel were friendly and many spoke English" (L. Kern, Kingston, Ont., Canada). . . . "We have just returned from Spain and were delighted with the **Hotel Zaida** in Palma (phone 232-547). There are no other hotels on the Paseo Maritimo, at this low price, between the Fenix and Bellevue hotels. Our twin-bedded room had a balcony overlooking the water, and came with three meals a day for 1,200 pesetas ($18.18) per person. Meals and service were superb" (Ben and Esther Horowitz, Miami Beach, Florida). . . . "Palma Nova, a beautiful beach, can be reached by taking a #25 bus for 20 pesetas; it's too far to walk. Rent a Vespa for $7 to see the island; I rented one and drove to Playa Formentor, a lovely beach about an hour and a half from Palma and worth the trip, especially since you see quite a bit along the way. Stay on the left side of the island, which is prettier, and wander over to the Victoria Hotel after 10 any night if you're looking for company" (Elaine Mura, Clifton, New Jersey).

MALMÖ, SWEDEN

"The **Hotel Hembygden** is a small and centrally situated hotel where you pay 60 kronor ($14.28) for a single room. It is old but clean. Address: Isak Slaktaregatan 7 (phone 36428), just off Stortorget" (Agenta Palme, Stockholm, Sweden).

MARSEILLE, FRANCE

"We found a lovely, clean, quiet hotel, only a short block from the Boulevard d'Athenes, the **Saint-Dominique**, 11 Rue St. Dominique. A room with bidet and sink for my wife and myself cost only 55 francs ($12.79); breakfast, with crispy french bread and lots of hot coffee was an additional 11 francs; bath 8 francs extra, respectively. The many sidewalk sandwich emporiums in the area will keep the wolf from the door with no great damage to the wallet" (Robert Schwab, Hydra, Algeria). . . . "Here is one that no economy traveler can afford to miss. Right across from the St. Charles railway station (as you exit from the right), you will see a whole block of hotels, among them the **Hotel de France** at 1 Bd. Maurice Bourdet (phone 39-18-82). This charming and tiny hotel will give you a double room, without bath but with plenty of hot water and a breakfast of hot chocolate (or coffee) and croissants, all for 55 francs ($12.79)! The rooms are tiny, but spotlessly clean, and we liked it so well we stayed there on two occasions. There is one man who speaks English, but if you will try out whatever meager French you possess (and mine was really meager!) you will be given a send-off like a family member when you do decide to leave" (Neva and Don Kaiser, Miami, Florida). . . . "As two students traveling on the common limited budget, we were pleased to find the recently established **Hôtel Pilote**, 9 Rue du Théâtre Française (phone 48-73-74), in central Marseille, where we had a room for two (costing 65 francs), shower or bath (8 francs), continental breakfast (11 francs). We found the proprietor to be a pleasant young man speaking, besides French, English, German and Spanish. He has created a charming and very up-to-date atmosphere with a certain 'freshness' that other hotels in the same price category definitely lack. One who is aware of the cost to stay at this hotel will be pleasantly surprised upon entering" (Leone Crackorowski, Montclair, New Jersey, and Barbara Neisman, Philadelphia, Pennsylvania; note by A.F.: owner of the Pilote has offered a 10% reduction to readers of this book).

MILAN, ITALY

"At Via Paganini #6 are three 4th class pensions, of which we can recommend the **Paganini**, where a double room costs 16,500 lire. A pizzeria close by on the Viale Abruzzi has some of the best pizza we had in Italy at rock-bottom prices. Connoisseurs of flea markets should not miss the one in Milan. It takes place on Saturdays on Via Calatafimi" (Trevor and Laura Robinson, Amherst, Massachusetts). . . . "The **Hotel-Pension Londra**, Piazza Argentina 4 (phone 228-400), is quite close to the station, charges 16,500 lire ($19.87) for a double (including service and taxes). Clean and well-furnished" (Henry B. Coons, A.P.O., New York; note from AF: owner Gianfranco Volante has promised a 10% discount to readers, on these rates, in 1980). . . . "We lived for six weeks at the **Pensione Parva Domus** on Piazza Argentina 4 (downstairs from the Pension Londra), phone 273-915. Its owner, Mr. Rodolfo, speaks English and was helpful to us. The price of a clean, spacious room for two (without bath) was 20,000 lire per night" (Dr. Paul W. Mosler, Seattle, Washington; note by A.F.: numerous other enthusiastic recommendations for the Parva Domus, and for its friendly, helpful Mr. Rodolfo, who is apparently happy to answer telephoned inquiries for assistance and will grant a 10% discount to readers of this book; but try for a room facing away from the street—according to reader Carlo Gurunlian, Montreal, "it sounds like the Indianapolis 500 for 24 hours a day"). . . . "**Motta** is a large and famous quick-service food bar as well as a sit-down restaurant complete with a section that sells speciality foods of the region. It is directly across from the tourist office and to the right as you leave the Duomo. For about $3 you can have a cold meat variety plate, vegetable plate, or your choice of a large salad—a filling meal" (Linda Lusardi, West Covina, California). . . . "To see a performance at **La Scala** for 5,000 lire, including tax, get standing room. We did this, and found the usher motioning us to front row balcony seats as soon as the lights went down. We saw perfectly. The cheapest seats, incidentally, go for 8,000 lire, including tax" (Frank and Linda Peterson, McLean, Virginia). . . . "Scala: When no concierge or 'private contact' could get me a ticket because it was SOLD OUT, I walked to Scala and got one at the box office" (Lida Von Zahn, Johannesburg, South Africa). . . . "The roof of the Duomo is fascinating. You can clamber all over it for a couple of hundred lire (more if you use the elevator) amid a forest of saints and gargoyles, and look over the city through the telescopes. . . . I found the shops in the **Vittorio Emanuele Gallery** a refuge from the rain, and I loved just to sit out at a table in front of the Biffi at the intersection of the walkways with a Cinzano and soda (that's the way everybody drinks it now) and just watch the people go by. Frankly, I enjoyed that more than the Via Veneto in Rome, because there were more people going by in the Galleria in Milan" (J. Raymond Reid, Soest, Germany). . . . "Strong recommendation for Milano. It's part of the new emerging Italy, and it's a city which runs for the Italian, not for the tourist. Be sure to visit the **Sforza Castle** and the **Museum of Science & Technology**, which contains models of Leonardo da Vinci's scientific inventions. They are free throughout the week, but closed on Mondays" (Bette & Paul Wood, Cambridge, Massachusetts). . . . "In addition to the Duomo, visit the Church of Santa Maria delle Grazie, where, on a wall in a room off the church, is painted Leonardo da Vinci's 'The Last Supper.' Closed Mondays" (Danielle Jehanne Rappaport, Munich, Germany).

MONACO

"The **Hotel Cosmopolite,** 4 Rue de la Turbie (phone 301-695), was a real find during our last visit to Monaco. All 31 rooms of this family-run establishment have sink and bidet with hot and cold running water. A double is 60 francs ($13.95), breakfast an additional 13 francs, and fluent English is spoken." (Captain William W. Sullivan, McLean, Virginia). . . . "For those readers who think Monaco is for the very wealthy— nothing could be further from the truth. One can easily spend a day there at moderate cost. HOW? For about $2, one can spend all day at one of the world's largest swimming pools built for the people of Monaco by their prince. A visit to the grounds of the Royal Palace is a necessity and should not be missed. At night a visit to Monte Carlo or a walk through the old streets of the town is a delight. Our hotel, across the street from the railroad station (we lost the name), was $16 for the night, and down the street was a delicious bistro where the food was fit for royalty at prices tailored for the less affluent. All in all, we enjoyed our day in this charming and beautiful principality on the Riviera" (Mr. & Mrs. R. S. Zimmerman, New York, N.Y.). . . . "I discovered the **Hotel de la Poste,** 5 Rue des Oliviers (phone 30-70-56), only two blocks from all the action and the Hotel de Paris, and convenient to the Old Beach Club and other beaches. At the height of the season M. and Mme. Ernest, the proprietors, gave me a single room with a view of the sea, breakfast included, for 55 francs a day (doubles are 65 francs, all included). M. Ernest runs a great little restaurant, **Chez Ernest,** in the Hotel de la Poste, too—one of the best I found in Europe. I noticed that all the musicians from the Sporting Club ate there" (Barron Polan, New York, New York; note by A.F.: demi-pension arrangements, usually required here, are 30 francs extra per person). . . . "I can suggest the **Hotel Helvetia,** at 1 bis Rue Grimaldi (phone 30-21-71), at the head of Rue Princesse Caroline, and only one block from the railroad station, maybe one and one-half blocks. In late July we walked in there at 9 p.m., with no reservations, and found a room for three, with a private bath (and bath tub) and balcony for 164 francs ($38.13), including three breakfasts. There is an elevator, and breakfast is served in a large, pleasant room overlooking Rue de Princesse Caroline and the sea at the foot of the hill. This is a good thing, especially in the heavy season of an expensive area" (Zollene Bennett, La Jolla, California). . . . "The **Hotel du Siècle,** 10 Avenue Prince Pierre (phone 30-25-56), with a restaurant, faces the Monaco railway station and charges 125 francs for a double with bath, 110 francs for a single with shower" (Armand J. Boulay, Berkeley, California). . . . "**Hotel de France,** near the Station at 6 Rue de la Turbie (phone 30-24-64), charges only 65 francs for bathless doubles, 55 francs for singles, and makes special arrangements for students" (Kathy Pasmantier, West Orange, New Jersey). . . . "If you find yourself in Monaco at lunch time, and can't find a budget restaurant, may I suggest that you go to the market, which is inside a large hall at the bottom of the road that goes up to the Palace and expensive Oceanographic Museum. Here you can buy milk, wine, fruits, vegetables, bread, meat, pizza, cheese, etc., which you can then take up the hill, and sit on one of the benches in the little parks on the cliffs (on each side of the museum) and have lunch while looking down at the Mediterranean" (David McCaughna, Northants, England). . . . "There's actually a moderately-priced place to eat in Monaco! From the Place d'Armes (just down from the train station), bear to the left down Rue de Millo. At 18 Rue de Millo, **Le Cigale** has a 28-franc 'Tourist Menu' that is quite tasty and one of the best values around, especially in comparison to the expensive little cafes along the waterfront. (A young American I ran into who was living in Monaco told me over dinner that Le Cigale was the only reasonably priced restaurant in the Principality.) And when you're finished at Le Cigale, head up to the casino, not to gamble away the family fortune, but to the Cinema d'Eté just below it, where for ten francs you get a spectacular view of the harbor and castle by night and a first run movie that is usually in English. It starts at 10 p.m." (Daniel P. O'Connell, Princeton, New Jersey).

MONTREUX, SWITZERLAND

"The charming pension named below is situated on a hill, with a view of the Swiss mountains. The rooms are comfortable, and there is excellent cuisine at very moderate rates: approximately Sw Fr. 27 per person, which includes room and two meals per day. I can recommend the **Hotel-Pension Wilhelm** (tel: 61-26-22), Rue du Marché 13, Montreux, very highly. Also, it is located a short walk from the railroad station, which is convenient" (Rose J. Glukes, Los Angeles, California). . . . "**Villa Tilda au Lac,** Quai Vernex, tel. 613-814, is a small house right on the side of Lake Geneva, as good as all the big, expensive hotels next door. Pleasant lady runs this. Rooms a little old-fashioned, but may appeal especially to American readers. Very comfortable and clean, breakfast served in cheerful dining room. Single room costs 30 fr., free showers and breakfast of course. About 10 minutes from station" (Angela Wear, England).

MONT ST. MICHEL, FRANCE

"Visits Not to be Missed in France: Mont St. Michel (about a three-hour ride from Paris), considered by some to be the Eighth Wonder of the world. This is a small island in the English Channel on which an exceptional architectural phenomenon has grown over the centuries" (Loretta Spanover, Fresh Meadows, New York). . . . "To avoid high hotel prices in Mont St. Michel, stay at the **Hotel de France,** 2 Rue de Rennes, Pontorson. The telephone is 60-10-50. Rates are about 48 francs for two people, plus 13 francs each for breakfast. The hotel itself is old and has only twelve rooms, with no shower or bathing facilities, though sinks are in every room. Rooms are neat and clean and furnished in early antique. There is also a 32 franc menu not to be underestimated because of the price. (This town, however, calls for a gourmet splurge at the **Hotel Montgomery,** serving internationally famous food. Don't miss the feast.) The proprietress of the France speaks no English but is most friendly and outgoing, worth getting to know if you speak the language. Buses or hitchhiking are the best way to arrive at what you came to see, Mont St. Michel" (Christine Aiken, Carmel, California). . . . "Contrary to the warning of high prices in Mont St. Michel, we stayed cheaply at **Hotel La Vieille Auberge,** in a beautiful double room with bidet and lavatory for 58 francs ($13.48), without breakfast" (Dr. Howard A. Hanke, Wilmore, Kentucky).

MOROCCO

"Considering the current popularity of travel in Spain, you should tell your readers to take a side trip into Morocco. Tangier is only a half-hour by jet from Málaga, or a delightful 2½-hour steamer crossing from Gibraltar or Algeciras. We found this trip to be one of the most exciting aspects of our journey, what with all the veiled women, robed Bedouins, camels, mosques, Arab tea houses, snake charmers, etc. Morocco might be on the African continent but you *ought* to give it a mention. It's out of this world" (Mrs. L. Lauler, Los Altos, California; for specific recommendations, see under "Tangier," below).

NAPLES, ITALY

"The really excellent **Pensione Virgilius** at Corso Vittorio Emanuele 737, first floor (phone 680-207), is managed by Signora Tatiana Schmutz and has 15 rooms, all with hot and cold water. Prices are 8,000 lire for a single, 13,000 lire for a twin or double room; breakfast is 1,800 lire extra; and the Virgilius is located right opposite the Mergellina Railway Station" (Adam Slote, New York, New York). . . . "I have been commuting to Naples for two years on a regular basis of three to four times a month. I feel the **Pensione Suisse** is still the best buy in Naples. It is centrally located, yet situated in the better part of Naples in the Santa Lucia cinema building. Several years ago, Tino Hausner and his wife took over the pensione and moved it from the fourth to the second floor. The move was most beneficial to the customer, as the rooms are larger, in excellent condition, and with convenient bathrooms. The price is 15,000 lire ($18.07), per day for two persons, including shower. And that's at Via Raffaele de Cesare 7, phone 425-162" (LCDR R. W. Martowski, U.S.N., FPO, New York; note from A.F.: Of all the pensions in Naples described on this page, Pensione Suisse is the one to which I would give preference—mainly because Tino Hausner and his Italian wife try really hard to make your stay a pleasant one, and their standards of cleanliness and sanitation are above the local level). . . . "The **Hotel Rex,** Via Palepoli 12 (phone 41-61-02), not far from the American

Express office, charged 31,000 lire for a family of five adults. Perhaps we got a special price for an immense family room, but the rates were certainly under those of other hotels we considered. A very satisfactory stop" (Frank L. Esterquest, Oxford, Ohio). . . . "The **Hotel Rex** is rated third class but has clean, good, large, second class rooms, renting—for a bathless double—at 18,000 lire, including tax and service (11,000 lire single). The address is Via Palepoli #12, two blocks from the American Express office in the popular tourists' Santa Lucia area. Take bus #106 or 150 from the train station" (L. F. Ivanhoe, Rome, Italy). . . . "It was late in the evening when we arrived, and so we took the first room we could find near the station. This was the fourth grade **Albergo D'Anna,** 199 Corso Arnaldo Lucci (phone 268-952), which is about 100 yards to the left when leaving the station. Cost was 12,000 lire for a double room without bath but everything else included. This is not the best place in which we stayed in Europe, but it was good enough for the three days we spent in Naples. The hotel clerk was most helpful and took bookings for bus-tours to Pompeii, Amalfi, etc." (Paul Horovsky, Johannesburg, South Africa; note from A.F.: The hotel clerk referred to by reader Horovsky is actually the hotel's owner, Signor Antonio d'Anna, who speaks English well and whose family has owned this hotel since 1900. He offers 60 rooms on three floors. 1980 rate for single rooms is 7,500 lire ($9.03), breakfast 1,800 lire ($2.16) extra). . . . "An excellent pensione which I discovered by accident is the **Albergo Castello,** Via Santa Lucia 90 (telephone 407-786). This is about ten minutes' walk from the Piazza Municipio, and can be reached by taking bus No. 106 from near the station. The manager, Signor Gennaro, spoke more English than most people I met in Rome or Florence, and a single room costs 5,300 lire ($6.38). Doubles are 9,500 lire; all the rooms have hot and cold water, and are kept very clean" (Keith Fountain, Beaconsfield, England; note from A.F.: The starvation-budget-category Castello, on the top floor of a typical Neapolitan apartment building (100 steps), is very, repeat very, simple, and only readers fully aware of that fact should consider it; still, it has an appealing atmosphere and offers good value to unpretentious travellers). . . . "Being Canadians, we were attracted by the sign of the **Pensione Canada,** 43 Via Mergellina (phone 680-952), which is located just across the street from the sea, and looks out to marvelous views. The charge is 14,500 lire ($17.46) for a double room with all-new furniture, and with a balcony facing onto the water" (Mrs. Lina Foy, Montreal, Canada). . . . "For a visit to the **Herculaneum** ruins, take local trolley bus #254 (100 lire—½ hour) to Ercolano. See the ruins (1,000 lire entrance) until 3 p.m., then walk 500 meters uphill to the Pugliano railroad station from which the last SFSM (blue) bus leaves for Vesuvius at 4 p.m. (600 lire round trip). A very interesting ½ hour ride up the side of Vesuvius through farms, grapes, villas, etc., to the foot of the Vesuvius cinder cone. Then by breathtaking chair lift at 1,000 lire round trip to the top of the cinder cone, plus a 'required' guide service of 1,500 lire each to get from the chair lift house to the rim of the crater. (After the money is collected, the guides leave the tourists alone.) The last bus down the mountain to Pugliano station leaves from 'Seggiovia' (chair lift station) at 7 p.m.—reaching the Pugliano station in time to take the 7:35 p.m. train back to Naples. The entire day's sightseeing, including fares and entrance fees, runs to about $5—quite a bargain to see both the view from Vesuvius and the Herculaneum excavations" (L. F. Ivanhoe, Rome, Italy). . . . "Don't let your readers buy a tour to **Capri** . . . it's a simple matter to take the steamer from the main docks, for 2,600 lire round trip. A beautifully-engineered funicular then brings you to the main tourist area, and if you wish you may make bus excursions from there up to Anacapri. The whole island is a bit commercial, but too beautiful to miss. Many tempting boutique shops for the ladies. Hotels looked quite inviting too, if you were planning to stay. The trip to the Blue Grotto costs 1,000 lire by motor launch, *but* you must pay an additional 1,500 lire when you get there to transfer into a rowboat and be towed around inside the Grotto. It would be nice to know this in advance, instead of feeling you've been 'had' " (Mr. and Mrs. Randell C. Widner, St. Petersburg, Florida). . . . "No visitor to Naples should miss a bus ride on the fantastic Amalfi-Sorrento road" (Dr. Jindrich Fantl, Prague, Czechoslovakia).

OBERAMMERGAU, GERMANY

"We stayed with a friendly German family, who rent out four upstairs rooms in their home. The two of us had a double bed and sink, in a clean and nice room, with a beautiful view of the Alps from our window. The charge is 13 marks ($6.84) per person per night, including breakfast, and the address is: **Karl Bierling,** St. Gregor 5, tel. 08822/4579. That's about a block from the start of the cable car, and a ten-minute walk from the center of town" (Mr. and Mrs. Tom Curry, St. Peter, Illinois). . . . "We stayed in over 30 different places during our three months in Europe, but nowhere was our reception better than at the **Pension Wiedemann** (phone 4680). We arrived at their home after dark one snowy evening, without having called first, and Herr Wiedemann simply opened the door and said 'Herein!' His price? 25 marks for a double! We felt, and still feel, that we experienced with the Wiedemanns the *spirit* of hospitality itself" (James Hoggard, Wichita Falls, Texas).

OLYMPIA, GREECE

"The 'D' class **Hotel Pelops** is an exceptional bargain (309 drachmas single, 371 drachmas double), but more than that, I wish to commend the gracious owners of the hotel. In two and a-half months of travel, we found the Hotel Pelops (phone 22-543) the one to which we would most like to return because of the warmth, the hospitality, and the consideration shown us. We went to Olympia for two days but stayed a week, and in our proposed trip this summer, we must return to Olympia—not so much for the ruins—but for Hotel Pelops. For example, when we erroneously thought we could not have our car washed in Olympia, the owners unhesitatingly let us use their hose and water; when we had used all of the hotel's supply of ice for our drinks, the owner wordlessly drove away and obtained additional ice" (Mildred Liles, Houston, Texas). . . . "At the 60-bed **Youth Hostel** in the center of town (18 Praxitelis Kondilis, phone 22580), rates are as little as 100 drachmas per person, and youth hostel membership is not required" (Nickolaus Lorey, Velden, Austria). . . . "Museums in Olympia close on Tuesdays" (Elsie McGillicuddy, Pasadena, California).

OXFORD, ENGLAND

"**Dilkhush Guest House**, 8 Abbey Road, telephone 41-923, is a small private house, containing about 15-20 beds in double rooms, situated approximately 8 minutes from the railroad station by foot. We were very lucky to find rooms in this model clean house. Madame proprietor was very accommodating. There is a big map of the world on the wall there, containing the small flags of towns of visitors who have slept in the house, and many flags are from the USA and Canada, too. The price for a double room, bed and breakfast, is £10 ($22)" (Dr. Z. and M. Pelikan, Brno, Czechoslovakia). . . . "On St. John Street, I rang the bell at #58 (phone 55454), and stayed at the guest home of **Mrs. R. M. Old.** For £4.50 ($9.90), I had one of the largest rooms and breakfasts of my journey. The cozy on my morning teapot will illustrate the type of comfort strived for" (Carma Bamber, San Francisco, California). . . . "At the **Victoria Guest House**, 180 Abingdon Road, rooms were well-kept and breakfast delicious. Though it is a short walk from the center of town, it is well worth it. There is plenty of parking, and the hosts, Mr. and Mrs. Parojcic, will make sure you have a pleasant stay" (Julia Roth, Washington D.C.). . . . "I beg to inform you that I stayed for two weeks at **Mrs. Passmore's Guest House**, 5 Pusey Street, where, for £4.50 a night, I had a big, well furnished room, and excellent English breakfast, which I could not consume at all. The location is central and easily reached on foot from anywhere in town. Telephone Oxford 54605" (Dr. Waguih Tawfik, Assiut, Egypt). . . . "Don't miss dinner at a pub called **Dudley's Lamb and Flag**, about eleven miles out of Oxford on the road to Kingston Bagpuize (but check these directions with an Oxonian!). It's worth the trip, even if you are only spending one night in Oxford. The place is beloved by the natives of the area. They say there is no pub in England quite like it, and I can believe it. The proprietor is straight out of Dickens. When I asked him if he had grouse, he replied, 'If I did serve it, I'd have to charge 30 bob a plate, and that's a little above my station in life, sir—though I'm sure it's not above yours.' We settled for an excellent roast duck, and the bill—which the *diner himself* computes at Dudley's—came to an admittedly steepish £5.50 ($12.10) for the two of us. But this included an after-dinner nectar called 'Monk's Coffee,' which is made with B&B. It was easily worth twice the price" (James Heffernan, Charlottesville, Va.). . . . "Don't miss a walk through Christ Church (College) Meadows to River to watch student crews work out and see their unique boating clubhouses. Herds of cattle—cows, sheep— throughout the meadows. Trees, flowers—all very beautiful against a backdrop of college buildings and spires in the background" (Rex Coffin, New York, N.Y.). . . . "Don't miss a performance at the **Oxford Playhouse**, also known as the University Theatre, where I saw an excellent production of Shakespeare's 'The Winter's Tale' for £3 ($6.60). And it's such fun to sit amongst the students, of all races, and listen to their animated conversations" (Carma Bamber, San Francisco, California).

PADUA, ITALY

"Padua is indispensable for the student and art lover. The Michelin guide gives it one star ('interesting' but not 'worth a visit' or 'worth a detour'), yet it is a fascinating city in its own right and contains invaluable treasures in the Giotto Frescoes of the Capella degli Scrovegni (also called Arena Chapel, for its proximity to the ruins of the Roman amphitheater), and in the Basilica del Santo, with altarpiece and statue by Donatello" (Robert M. Torrance, London, England). . . . **Albergo Igea**, Via Ospedale Civile 37 (phone 36814), not far from the Piazza del Santo, is a new hotel where we had a double room with private toilet and sink (not bath) for 18,000 lire" (Mrs. Andrew Yeoman, Calgary, Alberta, Canada). . . . "A fine place to stay is the **Albergo Riviera**, Via Rudena 12 (phone 665-413), near the Basilica of St. Antonio (double room for 14,500 lire). In the same vicinity are three or four similarly-priced small hotels" (Trevor and Laura Robinson, Amherst, Massachusetts). . . . "The **Mensa Universitaria** self-service university restaurant is open to anyone who looks like a student. It charges 1,800 lire ($2.16) for a really abundant and good three-course meal. Courses can also be purchased separately: 600 lire for pasta or rice with meat sauce, or soup; 1,200 lire for a meat and vegetable course; 250 lire for wine, or Coke, or beer. Address: Via San Francesco 38 (seven minutes' walk from the Basilica), closed on Saturday and Sunday. . . . **The Mensa C.G.I.L.** (working men's restaurant), open to all, is also of excellent value. Anyone looking like a student pays 1,800 lire for a three-course meal. Others pay 2,800 lire. Address: Riviera Tito Livio, next to the student theatre 'Teatro Ruzzante' " (L. Cheles, Letchworth, Hertfordshire, England).

PALERMO, ITALY

"**The Hotel Sausele**, Via V. Errante 12 (phone 230-308), is near the station. It is Swiss owned and operated, with typical Swiss standards of impeccable cleanliness, honesty and efficency. We had a delightful double room without bath but with breakfast included for 19,000 lire ($22.89)" (Dr. Augustus H. Fenn, Portsmouth, New Hampshire).

PALMA, MALLORCA

See "Mallorca."

PENZANCE, ENGLAND

"At the **Commoran**, at 3 Leskinnick Terrace, the rate was inexpensive, and Mrs. Penrose (the proprietress) provided orthopedic mattresses on the beds, and tropical fish to watch while you enjoy your breakfast" (Bill and Betty Blankenship, La Jolla, California).

PERUGIA, ITALY

"The **Pensione Adriana**, 4 Piazza Italia (phone 63-823), provided a room for the three of us that was spacious, spotlessly clean, with large comfortable beds, hot and cold running water, and overlooking the piazza, for only 15,000 lire, service and tax included (doubles are 11,500 lire, singles, 9,000). A shower cost 1,100 lire, a bath 1,700 lire. The pensione is located on the third and fourth floors, and when we were there we had to climb stairs, but an elevator was being installed at that time" (Capt. and Mrs. W. Y. Howell, USN, New York, N.Y.). . . . "The **Mensa Popolare** (patronized by students and workers alike) is off the famous Via Maestra della Volte (ask the traffic controller near the Duomo) and serves only the noonday meal (three courses) for 1,500 lire. The precise address is 16 Via Antonio Fratti. A snack can be had in a little pizzeria on Via di Priori (off Corso Vanucci), where a pizza costs 1,300 lire a portion. If one gets tired of talking to oneself in Perugia, he need only go to the Università per Stranieri, where he will find many Anglo-Saxons in the bar" (C. K. Hunter, Munich, Germany). . . . "Our best find in Italy was the clean, comfortable and friendly **Hotel Minerva**, at Via Cesare Caporali 9 (phone 61128). We were made to feel at home by the helpful Castellani family, especially the young English speaking wife. For a spacious, quiet double with bathroom, we paid 15,500 lire, full pension (superb cuisine) 20,500 lire per person" (S. and J. Misrachi, Sydney, Australia).

PISA, ITALY

"Just one block from the leaning tower was the **Albergo Gronchi,** 1 Piazza Arcives-covado (phone 23-626), with a large room for the two of us for just 14,500 lire ($17.46), not including breakfast. The ceiling was decoratively hand-painted and when we left the next morning, the proprietor came running after us with our little traveling clock which we had left behind" (Paul Simon, Troy, Illinois). . . . "**Hotel Di Stefano,** 35 Via S. Apollonia (phone 26359), was our cleanest and most comfortable hotel in Italy, and charged only 14,500 lire ($17.46) for a double room without bath, with breakfast an extra 2,000 lire per person" (Robin Harper, Augsburg, Germany). . . . "The railway workers' restaurant, **DLF Tavola Calda,** to the left as you leave the station, is also open to the public, at prices about 20% higher. Still, with pasta for 800 lire, meat dishes for 1,900, a quarter liter of wine for 350, and 500 lire for bread and cover, a meal can be put together for about 3,550 lire ($4.27)" (Norriss, Edith and Elizabeth Hetherington, Berkeley, California).

RAPALLO, ITALY

"Try the **Pensione Elvezia,** 16 Via Ferraretto (phone 50564), where the friendly English-speaking proprietress charges 14,000 lire ($16.86) per person in high season for room and full pension (huge, well-cooked meals)" (Gerald J. Veverka, Westchester, Illinois).

RAVENNA, ITALY

"**Albergo Stazione,** at the railway station on Viale Maroncelli 1 (phone 24-486), has small rooms for 11,000 lire single, 16,000 lire double, not including breakfast" (C. K. Hunter, Munich, Germany). . . . "One of our great finds was **Hotel Touring,** 10 Via XIII Giugno. Clean, rather larger-than-average double, for 9,000 lire ($10.84), triples 12,500 lire ($15.06)" (Craig and Carol Kallendorf, Cincinnati, Ohio). . . . "Anyone interested in mosaic-making would be fascinated by a free visit to the mosaic school to watch the artisans at work; the school is located in a courtyard at the corner of Via A. De Gasperi and Via Chartres. Mosaics may be purchased at the school, although even there they are quite expensive" (Mr. and Mrs. Harold Beral, Santa Ana, California).

REIMS, FRANCE

"Reims, whose history dates back to the baptism of Clovis in 496 A.D., is famous for its beautiful cathedral, begun in 1211, the coronation site of French kings, as well as for the numerous underground caverns which house storage facilities for the world-renowned products of the surrounding province, Champagne. Reims is also the place where the Germans surrendered to the Allies in 1945. For $15, the three of us (dad, mom, 15-year-old son) stayed in the attractive and clean **Hotel des Arcades,** at 31 Rue de L'Étape (phone 47-42-39). Our room was bathless, but had a sink and bidet. Breakfast was an additional $6 for the 3 of us. Although restaurants were often higher than our $15 a day budget would allow, we had a good dinner at the **Self-Service Talleyrand,** which is part of a department store of the same name, on the corner of Rue de Talleyrand and Rue de Vesle, the main shopping street. Steak and pommes frites were $2.60, sausage and pommes frites $1.95" (Mr. and Mrs. Victor Malzahn, Colfax, California).

RHODES, GREECE

"This is a greatly favored summer location for Europeans, with wonderful Crusader walls, beautiful scenery, fine trips. Hotels apt to be expensive, but in the center of the town, there is the less expensive **Hotel Spartalis,** Rue Nic. Plastiras (phone 24371), which made a very good impression. Someone staying there liked it very much, and we had lunch and dinner there several times. The charges: 926 drachmas ($25.72) for double with bath" (Mrs. Walter Stuber, Great Barrington, Massachusetts). . . . "This is fast becoming the Miami of the Mediterranean, and it's so full of Swedes that in August, one cannot believe there could be anyone left in Stockholm" (Hanns Ebenstein, London, England). . . . "**Hotel d'Or,** 81 Apolloniou Rodiou & Orfanidou Street (phone 22911), is a family-run hotel, clean, friendly, one block from the beach, with a view of ocean from some rooms. It is as well located as any other hotel (in fact, some of the most expensive hotels of Rhodes are nearby), yet charges only 620 drachmas ($17.22) for a double, including breakfast, service and tax" (Mrs. Charles Szumski, Arbuckle, California).

RIMINI, ITALY

"A real find was the **Ciotti Hotel,** 98 Viale Regina Elena (phone 80055, in Rimini). This Adriatic beach resort is a great favorite of the Swiss, Germans and Austrians, so everyone speaks German and some English. The hotel cost 16,000 lire (in May-June and September), 22,000 lire (in July and August), for full pension per person, and the three meals per day were equal to five elsewhere, and were the best in Italy that we came across. Before May 1st and after September 30th, it is only 11,000 lire. All this for a very clean modern hotel (showers in all the rooms) facing a lovely beach. This would be an excellent break in the travel routine between Rome or Florence and Venice. Rimini is also the place to stop and visit San Marino, which is only a couple of miles away" (Dr. Alex Weiskopf, San Mateo, California). . . . "A city official found us a room at the **Pensione Villa Erika,** 11 Viale Marino (phone 81522), for 16,800 lire per person full pension, 9,500 for our three-year-old son. The pension is ultra-modern, ultra-clean, right on the beach, and would be first class in the U.S. Let me stress that the Erika is the *rule,* not the exception" (Frank and Sara Sharp, Fayetteville, Arkansas). . . . "Going on to Ravenna or Venice? Don't take the train (which has to go through Bologna), but ride in style— *go by ship!* The tourist office will book you on the ship which leaves every Friday at 8:30 a.m. and arrives in Venice at 2:30 p.m., at a cost of 11,500 lire. Don't get the ticket through a travel agent, as they will try to sell you an expensive package deal—i.e., pick you up by bus, serve breakfast and lunch on the ship" (Frank and Sara Sharp, Fayetteville, Arkansas).

ROTHENBURG, GERMANY

"While visiting Rothenburg, my wife and I and our 10-year-old son spent a night at the home of **Mr. & Mrs. Barbl Pfliegl,** Eichenweg 4 (phone 09861-4185). I can wholeheartedly recommend them to your readers. Price for a single room is 15 marks ($7.89), a double is 28 marks ($14.73), and there's a 2 mark discount for those staying more than one night. Included in the price is a delicious breakfast" (Peter Admiraal, Marion, New York). . . . "We stayed at the **Rothenburger Hof** (phone 2270), across from the bahnhof in Rothenburg for 45 DM ($23.68) for the two of us in a lovely clean room, breakfast and service included. In all of Germany we enjoyed Rothenburg the best. Don't miss this walled town. It is on the Romantic Road" (Lily G. Doerre, St. Louis, Missouri). . . . "For the unsuspecting traveller visiting Rothenburg, it smacks of Alice's apocalyptic journey into Wonderland; it truly defies description. Once you've adjusted, however, take at least one of your repasts at the enchanting, ivy-covered **Baumeisterhaus,** located at Obere Schmiedgasse 3. Built in 1596, it offers mouth-watering menus and excellent 'rotwein'—excellent white wine, too" (Pauline Hadley, New York City). . . . "We visited many cities and stayed at many places, and none was nicer or more reasonable in prices of their food or rooms than the **Gasthof Zur Schranne** located at Schrannenplatz 6 (phone 09861/2258). Although the owner could speak no English, she could understand some, and was more than helpful. Our large, newly-furnished, bright, airy room for two cost us 38 marks a day including tax, service and breakfast. Some rooms have showers for 6 marks more per day" (Art Rastetter, Massillon, Ohio). . . . "I was lucky enough to stumble upon the residence of **Georg and Frida Ohr,** 6 Untere Schmiedgasse, phone 4966, where a single room with shower and breakfast cost only 18 marks ($9.47), doubles 30 marks ($15.78). A wonderful couple, they did everything possible to make my stay a pleasant one. They live just down the street from the market square above a beauty parlor. The Herr speaks English. Also, a few steps away is the Criminal Museum which contains a wide variety of torture chamber devices and legal documents of the middle ages. The town itself was perhaps the most photographic of any in Germany" (Robert Ryan, Oak Harbor, Washington). . . . "**Frau Erna Sommer,** 2 Freudengässchen, phone 4498, rents rooms for 32 marks ($16.84), double, including breakfast with an egg and that delicious filtered German coffee poured for us from an attractive pot. Our room was on the ground floor, shining and spotless, with bright modern wallpaper, new furnishings and drapes, and the most comfortable feather beds of our trip. Take the time for a stay in Rothenburg. It's full of medieval half-timbered houses, narrow twisty cobbled streets, fountains and old washing troughs, wrought iron signs, and an absolute explosion of flowers in window boxes. Plumbing, services and prices, however, are modern!" (Mr. and Mrs. F. W. Penberthy, Perth, Western Australia). . . . "A narrow street directly across from the town hall leads into the Kapellenplatz where stands the **Gasthaus Butz** (phone

2201). A room (clean and spacious and cozy) for two costs DM 38, breakfast included. Dinner runs DM 6 and offers good bratwurst, potatoes, salad and beer. The building is fairly new (post W.W. II, we believe) but built with all the 16th-century charm that pervades this fairy-tale town. We cannot imagine a traveller who seeks to discover the soul and spirit of pre-industrial Germany not spending hours exploring and photographing Rothenburg. English spoken at the Gasthaus Butz" (David and Francie Robertson, Los Angeles, California). . . . "**Gasthof Zum Ochsen**, Galgengasse 26, tel. 760, right in the center of this medieval town, has parking area for 8-10 cars! Restaurant was very reasonable as well, especially the menus. Doubles are 32 marks, double with shower 38, triple (no bath) 43 marks. Operated by Frau Emmy Wittemann" (Virginia Gillette, Roxbury, Connecticut). . . . "Found a lovely Fremdenzimmer owned by **Frau Pöschel**, at 22 Wenggasse. For 32 marks ($16.84) had a clean, comfortable double room, including breakfast" (Mr. and Mrs. Randall C. Williams, Tempe, Arizona). . . . "Near the Markusturmtower, you'll find the "**Main-Kauf**" a supermarket with a nice upstairs restaurant, where a rumpsteak with salad and fried potatoes cost 7.50 marks, and a set 3-course menu 6 marks. Surely worthwhile" (Edward Shipton, no address).

SALZBURG, AUSTRIA

"At the **Gasthof Trumer Stüberl**, 6 Bergstrasse (phone 74-776), our room was large and comfortable, the beds were the best we had slept in for months, and the charge for a double was 250 schillings ($18.51). Take any bus from the station to Mirabell-Platz, then walk two blocks down Bergstrasse" (Olivia Stansell, Jonesboro, Arkansas). . . . "At the German-Austrian border on the Autobahn we were 'hijacked.' An attractive young woman accosted us, telling us that rooms were scarce because of the music festival, and that we had better come with her. Or rather, she rode with us, as she directed us to Salzburg-Kasern, to **Frühstück-Pension Christl**, the home of Dr. Kranebitter, 5028 Salzburg-Kasern, Berg Nr. 57, tel. 06222/551187. This is in a rural area, on a hill with a view of Salzburg and the Alps. The pension is one kilometer from the Autobahn exit, 'Salzburg-Nord.' Hot water is plentiful, in rooms and in the baths, there is a 'sun terrace and lawn,' and it is quiet, beautiful and congenial. There is also a farmhouse nearby where overflow guests sleep. Dinner is available for a small additional charge. Singles cost 150 schillings, 250 schillings double, breakfast included. Beer or coffee is served in the evening (optional for nominal fee) after dinner. We became acquainted with guests from other countries, who also were pleasantly surprised by the 'hijacking' (two or three young women 'hijack' at the Border crossing)" (Clifton F. Bennett, Bratislava, Czechoslovakia). . . . "An excellent place to stay while in Salzburg is with the **Schmiedhuber** family, whose large house is located on Scheibenweg 8. It's a 10-minute walk from the railroad station, and if you call (the number is 351-042 or 351-034), Mr. Schmiedhuber will meet you there and carry your luggage for you. The family is warm, friendly and very accommodating. They serve big breakfasts, and will supply you with maps, directions and sightseeing suggestions. When it rains, they will loan you an umbrella, and when the weather is good, you are invited to sit with them in their backyard. The charge for all this was only 130 schillings ($9.62) per person—a real bargain" (Mr. and Mrs. L. Eisenberg, Forest Hills, New York). . . . "On a winter vacation trip through Austria, we found the friendliest establishment and best buy we ever saw in Europe, the **Pension Mayburgerkai**, Mayburgerkai 48 (phone 76579). It was hard to believe that for 160 schillings ($11.85) apiece per night we could get a new, beautifully furnished, and spotless room overlooking the river, and breakfast as well. But the most amazing thing was the warmth with which we were treated by the management, Herr and Frau Pfaffenbichler, who not only lent us ski boots, but sneaked into our room and shined our shoes and laundered our clothes. To top it all off, when we left, they drove us the four short blocks to the railroad station. For location, price and service, this is *the* place in Salzburg" (Thomas Koppel and Howard Handelman, New York, New York, with a recent seconding recommendation from Linda and Howard Huempfner, Fresh Meadows, New York, and from V. E. Sauer, Zanesville, Ohio). . . . "We're living in delightful accommodations in Salzburg, at 200 schillings ($14.81) per day for two people, in the apartment of **Mr. and Mrs. Albert Vogl**, Hans Prodigerstrasse 13 (phone 759-895), Apartment 12. The building is brand new, with elevator, the plumbing is excellent and we have a bathroom to ourselves. It's two minutes by bus from the Salzburg railway station, and the Vogls are most friendly and helpful" (R. S. Milne, Yonkers, New York). . . . "Five minutes from the station, we stayed at the clean and comfortable **Gasthof Zum Jahn**, 31 Elisabethstrasse (telephone 71-405), for 160 schillings ($11.85) double, 30 schillings ($2.22) each for breakfast. When you want a change from cathedrals and castles, visit the beautiful Schloss Leopoldskron, location for the filming of 'Sound of Music'. Close-by are a modern swimming-pool, a minigolf course, and acres of parkland" (Margaret and John Pugh, Rossmoyne, Western Australia). . . . "My wife and I recently spent a night at the home of **J. U. K. Aubock,** 3 Schikanedergasse 3, phone 41-94-90. This fine gentleman and his lovely wife charged us 100 schillings ($7.40) per person for an immaculate room with a great mountain view, plus an excellent breakfast. They maintain a book in which guests register their opinions on this house. All were most complimentary" (John R. Crosby, Fort Wayne, Indiana). . . . "We were extremely fortunate with our accommodation at the home of **Mr. and Mrs. R. Simmerle,** 13 Wachtelgasse, phone 35-67-95. Located a little away from noise and bustle, their garden-encircled home is still within pleasant walking distance from the city center. And the charge is moderate, 120 schillings ($8.88) per person, with breakfast that included fruit juice, sliced meats and cheese, and home-baked dessert cakes" (Herbert Koppel, Melbourne, Australia). . . . "Our highest recommendation for the home of **Frau Rosemarie Steiner,** 156C Moosstrasse, phone 42-83-63. My wife was ill for three days at her pension, where her niece took care of her. She wanted no extra payment for her kind attention, insisting that this was her job. She is indeed a most unusual person in this mixed-up world of ours. She has an extremely clean house with eight rooms, 15 minutes from the Bahnhof, renting for $8 per person per day, including a nice breakfast. We met many interesting people in her home, from Ireland, Switzerland, and the U.S., for example; she had a small group of teenage boys staying with her, from different countries, attending summer school. She was actually a housemother to them while they were away from home" (Arnold F. Perlin, Woodland Hills, California). . . . "**Pension Adlerhof,** 25 Elisabethstrasse (phone 75-2-36), on a street running parallel to the railway station, is clean, comfortable, quiet, and its proprietors—a man and his wife and daughter—make every effort to be accommodating. Rates in 1980 will be 160 schillings ($11.85) for a single, double this price for a twin room, breakfast included" (J. K. Munford, Corvallis, Oregon). . . . "In Salzburg, it's the **Pension Helmhof,** Kirchengasse 29, Lieferinger Hauptstrasse, phone 33079 or 34449. A double room without bath but with breakfast is 280 schillings ($20.74); rooms in the annex, all with bath, w.c., and phone, cost 400 schillings, breakfast included. This may require a taxi from the train station, but it's worth it. The hotel is brand new and clean beyond words" (H.A. Kohfeld, Torremolinos, Spain). . . . "We stayed at the modern, clean and friendly home of **Franz and Maria Raderbauer,** Schiesstattstrasse 65, phone 33-80-07, who have twin and triple bedrooms, with private bathroom facilities, and hot and cold running water, which they rent for 130 schillings per person, with breakfast included. They provide a good breakfast of rolls, jam, butter, and with steaming pots of delicious tea or coffee as you may prefer. Mrs. Raderbauer speaks perfect English and their home is a short bus ride (E bus) from downtown" (W. Yeats, Toronto, Ontario, Canada). . . . "As we were standing at the train station debating the alternatives for lodgings, we were approached by a charming woman who had just seen two people off on the train. Her name was **Hilde Radisch** and she explained that she had rooms available in her home and that she and her husband had a car outside (it was raining) and that we could go to their home and if the accommodations were unsuitable, they would bring us back. We found their home charming, within walking distance from the city center, in a quiet residential area. She rents a single and a double room and an apartment for 4 persons (suitable for a family with children, consisting of two separate bedrooms and one living room). Price: schillings 100 to 120 per person per day, including breakfast. The address: Scheibenweg 5, tel. 32-99-32" (Mr. H. V. Plimpton, Mill Valley, California). . . . "**Frau Maria Gassner,** when rung (428-339), came and picked us up and drove us to her lovely new home, so beautifully furnished. We breakfasted on her terrace and watched the cable cars climb up the snow-clad peak of the Untersberg—glorious scenery. The bus stops almost outside the door and it is a pleasant 10 minutes down into the old city. Frau Gassner knows enough English to be helpful in advising guests where to go and what to see. Her address is Moosstrasse 126. She charges a moderate 120 schillings per person, breakfast included" (Mrs. P. W. Pulsford, East Gosford, N.S.W., Australia). . . . "We stayed at the private home of **Math and Rosa Strobl,** Pfaffingerweg 3, tel 238-242, about 10 minutes from the old city center. Atmosphere was warm and friendly, and the Strobls join you for breakfast, which is included in the room charge of $8.50 per person. Their house is in a very quiet neighborhood and you get a fantastic view of the mountains in the area. Showers available" (Dean Brown, APO New York). . . . "Well worth a visit is the **Mozarteum,** which combines a library and museum of Mozart's scores and letters and an international music academy. A tour, including library, cottage that inspired 'The Magic Flute,' a giant linden tree planted by Lilli Lehmann, concludes with a noontime organ concert of Mozart's music in an elegant concert hall, all for 20 AS ($1.48). Salzburg's Cathedral has a gleaming white interior with lovely dome and paintings all in blue and terra cotta" (Mrs. George J. Flynn, Washington, D.C.). . . . "My nomination for the most beautiful sight in Europe is the view of the colorful little town of Salzburg from the Hohensalzburg Castle. A little railway takes you to the top for $1. Try it at sunset! To offset the Austrian cuisine and the hours of sitting at Festival performances, we took an hour's walk along the outskirts of the city, which brought us to a wooded mountain called the Gaisberg. A chair lift took us up the Gaisberg for a marvelous panorama of Salzburg's mountainous surroundings" (Joan Abel, New York, N.Y.). . . . "Don't miss the **Salzburg Marionette Theater,** at 24 Schwarzstrasse, next to the Mozarteum and the Mirabellgarden. You see amazingly life-like puppets in operas. The setting, costumes, and skill of the operations are excellent. Prices start at 110 schillings, with 150 schillings buying you a more than adequate seat" (Julia and Bill Biggs, Alexandria, Virginia). . . . "Please include mention of the unique and exciting salt mine tour, which I'm afraid many Americans are missing because in August, there were no English-speaking guides—but the tour was so fascinating that it didn't matter. Eight miles south of Salzburg at Hallein is the salt mine, which is busy from morning 'til night, conducting tourists in miner togs up the mountains by a lengthy chair-lift ride, then through an elaborate system of underground tunnels, including seven slides which the group straddles behind the guides. A boat ride on a beautifully-lit underground salt lake is an added highlight, as the group makes a final exit riding on the miners' cars. All this and new friendships for only 80 schillings ($5.92), and the photograph taken as you exit from the mountain is a lasting memory" (Marcia Hanf, Urbana, Illinois).

SEVILLE, SPAIN

"Biggest budget find for me was the **Pension Santa Cruz,** Calle Lope de Rueda 14 (phone 225-030), Seville: 1,100 pesetas ($16.66) for full pension, service included. Located in the labyrinth of the Santa Cruz quarter, this one is a little hard to find; but the location is beautiful and the family wonderful" (Robert M. Torrance, London, England; also Margaret East, Mile End, Australia). . . . "Please tell your readers that anyone who misses Spain, misses Europe. And anyone who misses Seville, misses Spain. While Madrid is big and bustling, it does not hold the country's top attractions as do Paris in France and Rome in Italy. After the Prado in Madrid, turn South. The traveller must visit Andalusia for the real Spain. Seville is the 'Florence of Spain,' having a wealth of the nation's finest art and architecture. The Sevillians are dignified as are all Spaniards, but they seem to have even a further refinement, as do the Florentines over their countrymen" (Ray F. Allen, Upper Nyack, New York). . . . "Fantastic, fantastic find for true Spanish flavor, yet modern conveniences: **Hotel Murillo,** Calle Lope de Rueda (phone 21-60-95), 1,800 pesetas ($27.27) for a double with private bath. Breakfast is included; it's served in the hotel lobby which is filled with old Spanish relics and is charming and lovely. This hotel is in the Santa Cruz district of old, narrow streets. A perfect place to imbibe the spirit of old and glorious Spain" (Judy Ellison, Syracuse, New York, and Jane Glaubinger, Mt. Vernon, New York). . . . "The **Hotel Lyon,** on Vidrio #17, charges 1,100 pesetas single, 1,700 pesetas double, including breakfast and one other meal. I had a charming room, with beautiful massive furniture and private bath. Walking distance to the center of Seville, i.e., the Alcazar, Giralda, etc." (Teresa de la Barrera, La Jolla, California). . . . "**Hostal Residencia Jentoft,** Benedorm 2 (phone 22-09-81), charged us the unbelievable price of 800 pesetas ($12.12) for a clean room with a single bed and a folding bed, plus shower and sink. Location is about two blocks from the Plaza de Armas railroad station. Take the street that angles off from the right side of the station, turn right into the narrow street just past the large Michelin sign. The hostel is indicated by 'Residencia 2 H.' Walk upstairs to the first door on the right" (L. L. Farkas, Tucson, Arizona). . . . "In Spain, the **Hostal Atenas** in Seville (Calle Caballerizas 1; telephone 21-80-48 or 47) was our greatest find, even though to get there we did exactly what we were told *not* to do—we listened to a wizened little man who accosted us at the railroad station. The rate for two persons, breakfast included, but for a bathless room, was 1200 pesetas ($18.18). The atmosphere was great—tiles, interior patio and greenery, and 'family' more than 'staff.' The food was excellent, and we were given numerous choices. English is understood but little; however, we observed one visitor being led smilingly to the kitchen to point to what he wanted, and he returned a witness to a clean kitchen. . . . Seville is a delight, with its horsedrawn carriages; its ancient Santa Cruz district; its beautiful María Luisa Park; the Alcázar; the ornate cathedral, third largest in the world and containing the supposed tomb of Columbus; the adjacent Giralda tower, built by the Moors in the 12th century, and from which one can inspect at close view the gargoyles and flying buttresses of the cathedral. For nine cents each, we took a city bus westward to the end of the line at Santiponce (*not* Aljarafe, as claimed by the Ministerio de Información y Turismo folder on Seville), and walked about a block to the ruins of the Roman city of Itálica, birthplace of the emperors Hadrian and Trajan. Its amphitheater and mosaics are impressive" (Prof. Robert R. Morrison, Collegedale, Tennessee).

SIENA, ITALY

"The **Villa Terraia,** 3 km. from Siena at 13 Via del Ascarello (phone 28-03-61), charged 21,000 lire ($25.30) for a bathless double room. This was the villa where Garibaldi lived and one can see the 9 huge California redwoods he brought around the Horn as seedlings and planted here. After capital-hopping, a few days in a villa in Tuscany are a delight. The villa is clean and filled with art treasures and has a superb view of Siena" (Virginia Ryder, Sausalito, California). . . . "The **Albergo La Toscana,** Via Angiolieri 12 (phone 46-097), is two minutes from the shell-shaped Campo and the Palazzo Pubblico (straight up the road) near the Piazza Tolomei. Albergo Toscana is a 13th century palazzo, now converted into a comfortable modern albergo, plain but very clean and good. With elevator (right up to their own tower!), marble floors, running hot and cold water in the rooms, telephone at bedside, and large cool rooms (the yard-thick stone walls act like air conditioning), it's a bargain: singles for 11,000 lire, and the beds are excellent! Singles with private shower for 14,500 lire ($17.46). The proprietor speaks some English, and he as well as the whole staff are very helpful and nice" (Ruth Ivor, New York City).

SORRENTO, ITALY

"In Sorrento, our best hotel find of all: the **Albergo Midtown Meublé,** Corso Italia 221 (phone 878-5045), on the main street, before the square as you enter the town. Exquisitely-decorated rooms, each with a private bath (including tiled shower), for a lowly 12,000 lire per person. The Italian government deems this a third class hotel; we found it a luxury hotel. The staff speaks English and the service was ideal" (Ardeel Lewis, New York City, New York). . . . "We stayed at the **Hotel Apollo Meublé,** Via Luigi de Maio #13 (phone 878-3701), which is new, modern, clean and centrally located on a street between the two main squares of town. It is convenient to buses, tourist offices, railway station and the port. Our neatly furnished room had a large balcony overlooking the street, was equipped with heating facilities, and can be air conditioned for 1,000 lire a day. The proprietors are very friendly and understand English. Single with bath, 13,000 lire; double with bath, 20,000 lire; breakfast is 3,000 lire per person." (Margie Greenberg, Brooklyn, New York). . . . "Stayed at the **Hotel Schweizerhof,** where I had a single with private shower for 9,000 lire ($10.84). From the Circumvesuviana station, head down a block, turn left, and walk to the main square. Then ask the travel agency there where it is—it's just a stone's throw away" (Danielle Jehanne Rappaport, Munich, Germany).

SOUTHAMPTON, ENGLAND

"For anyone using Southampton as a port-point, we feel that **Beacon Guest House,** 49 Archers Road (phone 25910), is the find of the year. Only ten minutes by taxi from the docks, in a semi-suburban area, this comfortable, clean home is entirely focused on its guests' convenience by the Scottish and Irish ladies who run it. Not a sideline with them, these two people devote their energies to any needs of the traveler. For £4.50—they supply room with hot and cold water, breakfast (copious), evening tea. Dinner was also superbly cooked and cost only £2.75" (Mrs. Theodora Wilbur, Haverford, Pennsylvania). . . . "We found fine accommodations in this major transatlantic English seaport city at the **Polygon Guest House,** 40 Polygon, phone Southampton 28162. Bed and a huge breakfast with tea in your room before breakfast costs £4.50 per person. When we left our friendly and helpful hostess, she called a taxi to take us and our luggage to the docks to catch our ship" (Donald G. Gilbert, Frederic, Michigan). . . . "While in Southampton, we took quite a few little trips to surrounding areas which were very interesting. We spent one day at Bournemouth—a lively resort which was only an 84-mile round trip by bus. One day we took the bus to a town called Beaulieu to see Lord Montagu's castle and his vintage car display. Another day we took the ferry to the Isle of Wight (one hour each way) and the local bus tour on this isle lasted from 1 p.m. to 6 p.m.—very enjoyable. We were quite surprised to find so many interesting places nearby, as we'd been told there was nothing to do there" (Mr. and Mrs. Orbin H. Giles, Cathedral City, California).

SPLIT, YUGOSLAVIA

"The best guesthouse we found was the one run by **Mr. & Mrs. Katica Sanic,** Koncareva 351, 58000 Split. It's on the main road as you enter the outskirts from the south, and public transportation is available to the city center. Their service and hospitality were unsurpassed, and furnishings and baths were all immaculate. A double room cost $15 a night, including a large breakfast with eggs and fresh fruit from their trees" (Christine & Carl Haas, San Jose, California).

STRASBOURG, FRANCE

"**Grand Hotel de Paris,** 13 Rue de la Mesange, tel. 321-550, two blocks from the station, was a "grand hotel" once, is now considerably less then grand, but still very adequate. Rooms were clean and comfortable; Strasbourg Cathedral a short walk away and most interesting to visit. For two doubles and one single we paid 295 French francs, which included 9 francs per person for breakfast" (Virginia Gillette, Roxbury, Connecticut). . . . "**Hotel des Princes,** 33 Rue Geiler, tel. 615519, a two-star hotel, is without question the best hotel value we have found in five months to date of European travel; rooms are large, clean and fresh, service excellent, and location in a quiet neighborhood, a 15-minute walk from the Cathedral and center of town. 1980 rates will be: double with shower 80 francs, with bath 92 francs, continental breakfast an additional 10 francs per person, served in the breakfast room or in bed" (Carl and Jean Auer, Hillsborough, California).

STRATFORD-ON-AVON, ENGLAND

"Alcester Road, about a mile from the center of Stratford, is lined with bed-and-breakfast guesthouses, each charging about £4 per person" (Ellen Liman, New York City). . . . "Shipston Road (coming from Oxford) is [also] lined with bed-and-breakfast places, most of which have hot and cold water in the rooms. We stayed at **Craig House** (Sheila and Bill Giles, proprietors), #69 Shipston Road (phone 29-74-73). Very clean, and costing £4.50 per person" (Mr. and Mrs. Stephen Zeluck, Bayside, New York). . . . "Stratford-on-Avon is on Everyone's itinerary, and therefore often overcrowded and impersonal. But there we found the friendliest welcome of our whole trip (and also the cheapest bed-and-breakfast) at the charming home of **Mrs. Green** at 217 Evesham Road, phone 0789/3794. The Greens have just three rooms, each modern and well furnished, and they offer them with a generous breakfast for just £5 per person. That may be the cheapest room rate in Stratford, but the charm and friendliness of the Hopkins' home would make it a bargain at twice the price. They seem especially to like students and foreign tourists, and Mrs. Green is the sort of person who says a sincere goodbye at the door and then stands waving at the window. It took away all the commercialism which we had been told to excuse in that tourist-filled town" (Mr. and Mrs. Loren L. Wyss, Portland, Oregon). . . . "**Salamander Guesthouse,** 40 Grove Road, phone 57-28, proprietress Mrs. J. Copestick, in a very nice row home, three-story, just 2 blocks from the center, charges £4.75 ($10.45) for room, 25 p. for bath or shower. We recommend it" (Patricia C. Moretti, Norristown, Pennsylvania). . . . "Be sure to check and see if the Royal Shakespeare Company's Stratford Theatre is continuing its policy of holding rear seats and standing room locations open until the day of the performance. They were doing this during my stay, and the result was that I got tickets on the day of the performance to plays which had been sold out for weeks. These seats cost £3.70 ($8.14), 90 pence ($1.98) to stand, and they were excellent values. . . . The theatre-goer trying to pass the day waiting for the evening performance would be well advised to take the Midland Red Bus to **Coventry** for the day to see the glorious new cathedral that has risen out of the ashes of the ancient one which was destroyed during the war. The new cathedral is an architectural masterpiece; and the ruins of the old are still standing. Its cross is made of the shattered beams of the original building, and it will bring tears to the eyes of all but the most iron-hearted. Inscribed in the remnants of what was once the support for beautiful stained glass windows is the prayer, 'Father Forgive,' roughly carved out with the bayonet of a captured German prisoner" (Burt Wolfson, New York, New York).

STUTTGART, GERMANY

"I stayed at **Hotel Köhler,** 209 Neckarstrasse, phone 43-20-04, a very pleasant lodging, especially in the rooms at the back, since the tramways make the street a bit noisy. Singles 31 marks ($16.31), doubles 52 marks ($27.36), breakfast included. On the first floor is a good restaurant, operated by the same owners, a couple who are fluent in English. . . . By all means have a look at the Staatsgalerie on Konrad-Adenauerstrasse, just off the Bahnhof. There are lots—I mean lots—of Renoirs, Picassos, Modiglianis and some of the most magnificent Corots I have ever seen" (Louis Metcalf, Rio de Janeiro).

TANGIER, MOROCCO

"Anyone visiting the Iberian peninsula should make it a point to cross over to Tangier, so close to Europe, and yet an entirely different world. Tangier is 2½ hours from Algeciras, Spain, via boat. Tourist class fares are 850 pesetas one way, 1,300 pesetas first class. Fares to the Spanish port of Ceuta, on the coast of Morocco, are only 480 pesetas tourist class, 700 pesetas first class. . . . I had a clean and comfortable room with private shower at the **Mamora Hotel,** 19 Rue des Postes (phone 341-05), located just inside the old section of town; a double with bath was 52 dirhams. We had dinner at the posh **Marhaba Palace** restaurant, Porte de la Casbah, where a native orchestra and dancers entertained us throughout a five-course dinner that featured couscous and included wine. But several other spots around here are genuine clip joints, with very sexy but also very thirsty B-girls. Tangier is teeming with all manner of con men, money changers, pimps, junk peddlers, etc.; especially to be avoided are the ones who call themselves 'Charlie' " (Henry S. Sloan, New York, New York; note: current exchange rate is 3.8 dirhams to the dollar). . . . "You can go from Algeciras to Tangier via **Cia Transmediterranea** (office about one block from the dock) for about 650 pesetas each way. Don't miss seeing **The Casbah,** but several friends living in Tangier tell me you can really get better buys in the European quarters of the city; they added that if you really feel obliged to buy in the Casbah, ask for recommendations. And by all means try mint tea in a native restaurant. In the evening, go to the Petit Socco and sit at a cafe; it's in the Casbah, but perfectly safe and reeks of atmosphere" (Elaine Mura, Clifton, New Jersey). . . . "Tangier remains the biggest bargain resort in the Mediterranean, especially for those who want to give the appearance of living in luxury on very limited means. There are dozens and dozens of low-priced hotels in the Medina, and even in the town itself, but my recommendation is the **Hotel Mamora,** 19 Rue des Postes (phone 341-05). In 1980, the daily charge for a room with a big double bed is 52 dirhams ($13.68), a single 38 dirhams ($10.33). The place is perfectly clean, decent and respectable" (Hanns Ebensten, London, England). . . . "For travelers going to Tangier, we suggest leaving from Algeciras, just across the bay from Gibraltar. The price is almost half of that from the British port. Tangier is another world, completely different from Europe, and anyone who gets this far south should not miss it. Moroccan leather is unbeatable and dirt cheap, although it takes an expert bargainer to get the good buys. By this time, we qualified, and we filled our suitcases with leather goods" (Barry Saunders, Victoria, Canada). . . . "The best budget hotel in Tangier is the **Hotel Continental,** 36 Dar Baroud (phone 31024), which at one time was the best hotel in the city. The price for two in a room with bath, breakfast and all taxes included, was approximately 45 dirhams. Clean and with all the facilities of a big hotel; and just five minutes from the ferry" (Bob Press, Forest Hills, New York; enthusiastic seconding letter from Celia and Jim Miner, Watertown, So. Dakota). . . . "The **Hotel Continental** in Tangier stands out as the Queen of hotels not only because of its stately structure, extreme cleanliness, its fine, inexpensive food in the hotel restaurant (served by fez-topped waiters), its 1980 rates of 22 dirham single, 27 dirham double, its picturesque location near the Casbah, but most of all because of the extreme helpfulness and interest displayed to each and every guest in this 40 room establishment" (Ann Conley, Belleville, New Jersey). . . . "I ended up at a pleasant little hotel, also close to the dock: **Pension Tantan** (33 Rue de Poste—Petit Socco—tel. 326-41), where I had a very pleasant room under the roof with a nice view of the harbour and lots of sun for about $5. There were a great many young people there as well. It is run by a very pleasant young man, who doesn't speak English (only French and Arabic) but his friendliness makes up for it" (Charles Reynolds, London, England). . . . "At the **Restaurant Economique,** 122 Rue de la Place, the management was very friendly, spoke English, and offered such typical Maroccan dishes as cous-cous, but also steak and chicken. I had a delicious meal of beefsteak, french fries, salad and dessert for 17 dirhams (about $3.94).

This clean establishment is within walking distance of the Casbah" (Rebecca Carter, Columbus, Georgia).

TAORMINA, SICILY

"Taormina, in Sicily, is one of Europe's most famous resorts (Churchill wintered here), high on the slopes of Mt. Tauro, with Mt. Etna (a still active volcano) rising majestically in the distance. The climate is incredible and is comparable only to that of Waikiki Beach in Hawaii. Just as in Waikiki, it almost never rains here, and when it does it is a sprinkling, a 'blessing.' I had planned to spend only two days, but have been so impressed with the beautiful weather that I am extending my stay to a week. Taormina seems to be a favorite with the English, Germans, *and* Italians from other areas of Italy, and there are accommodations to suit everyone. Your budgeteers would have no difficulty finding a room at reasonable rates. Being captivated by the beauty of the city I wanted a room with a view. I found one with private bath in the moderately expensive (16,500 lire single, 27,500 lire double) **Hotel Belvedere**, on the Via Bagnoli Croce (phone 23791), which has been owned and run by the same family since it was built 'by grandfather' in 1906. I open two huge door-windows, step onto the balcony, and there before me is a spectacular view. I am about 300 feet above sea level, at my feet are terraces and patios, rich with palms and other tropical plants and flowers, gleaming in the sunlight. Directly ahead is the blue Mediterranean and just off to the right is the gently curving shoreline of the bay. The water is calm and the only ripples visible are those made by slowly moving sailboats. In the distance at the right is the huge cone of Mt. Etna, with periodic bursts of smoke puffing at the peak" (John W. Scheifele, Bronx, New York). . . . "I shared a room with a friend at the **Pensione Svizzera** on the Via Luigi Pirandello, no. 26, phone 23790. The price for our room—a large room with a private bath—was 26,000 lire a day for two, breakfast and dinner included. A large window in our room overlooked the sea and Isola Bella—a spectacular view. The pension is owned and operated by a young Italian and his German wife and their staff; English, Italian and German are spoken. The funicular that goes down to the beach at Mazzarro is just a few steps from the pension. The congenial atmosphere of the pension, plus the Sicilian sun, made for a marvelous stay in Taormina" (Todd W. Lehman, New York, New York).

TOLEDO, SPAIN

"**Hotel La Almazara:** We cannot say enough about this charming inn in Toledo, and we unfortunately were booked for but one night. Lovely, rustic Spanish decor. Our own balcony overlooked the El Greco city. Ample parking (one needs an automobile here). This will not be a bargain for long, it's much too good. 1,350 pesetas ($20.45) double with bath, 120 pesetas ($1.81) breakfast" (Mrs. E. T. Francis, Livingston, New Jersey).

TOULOUSE, FRANCE

"**Hotel Astrid,** 12 Rue Denfert-Rochereau, tel. 623-871, is small and friendly, and less then 10 minutes' walk from the station (I should add it is at the 'better end', as the part near the station is a bit 'shady'—ladies in doorways!) From the station, cross the canal, turn left and take the first turning right. Go straight on through a small square with a car park, and Hotel Astrid is on the left, before Boulevard Strasbourg. A single costs 45 francs, petit dejeuner 9 francs, which was served in my room at no extra cost" (Angela Wear, England). . . . "Quite excellent is the **Hotel de Bordeaux,** 4 Boulevard Bon Repos (phone 62-41-09). Although the owner does not speak English, she is kind and helpful, which is a big plus. Had a single room for 42 francs ($9.76), an extra 8 francs for breakfast" (Steve Hill, Bedfordshire, England).

TOURS, FRANCE

"We discovered the most charming little hotel in Tours, operated by the Dubernard family—**Hotel Le Belvédère**, 31 Rue Origet, 37000 Tours (phone 64-45-54). The rooms are immaculate and nicely decorated, and the family is warm and helpful. Rates for bathless rooms are 24 francs for a single, 32 francs for a double, 40 francs for a twin" (Cheri Senft & Lisa Specter, Sherman Oaks, California). . . . "The **Hotel des Capucines,** 6 Rue Blaise-Pascal (phone 05-20-41), is my recommendation for Tours, which I am sure most tourists visit at some time, on their way to chateaus. It is a good place for older people, for there are rooms on the ground floor, without any stairs. A small, new hotel just a 'stone's throw' from the buses that take you to the chateaux, every room has a shower, and yet the charge is only 33 to 52.50 francs for ground floor rooms without bath, 40 to 71 francs for rooms with bath on the upper floors—18 rooms in all. Breakfast is 7 francs. Mr. Lawrence, the owner-manager, does not speak English, but he is a helpful, kindly man. On leaving the depot turn left, walk past a dead end street about a block to Blaise-Pascal, turn left to number 6. It is that easy!" (Nellie Hull, Chicago, Illinois; strong seconding recommendation from Elsie Lee, New York, New York). . . . "A good choice is the **Hotel du Cygne:** 65 francs ($15.11) for a double room without bath, breakfast for 11 francs ($2.55) per person more. That's at 6 Rue du Cygne, phone 66-66-41" (Kay C. Roberts, Dayton, Ohio). . . . "**Hotel Français,** at 11 Rue de Nantes (phone 05-59-12), across from the train station's left side, was no Ritz, but it was decent, homey and very clean. The 36 francs we paid for a double room included hot water in the room, though no shower. This is still a fantastic deal in expensive and often-booked-up Tours" (Bram Fine, Oak Park, Illinois).

TRIER, GERMANY

"The **Haus Runne** (Engelstrass 35, phone 0651-79822) is a hotel as well as a restaurant serving very inexpensive meals. Our room was 20 marks ($10.52) per person (I believe singles are the same price)—very clean, with a shower/bath down the hall. A continental breakfast is included in the rates" (Zosia & Gerald Boicourt, West Germany). . . . "Your book omits mention of the city of Trier in Germany, a 50-minute train ride from Luxembourg (for **Icelandic** passengers headed for Germany). It's a place well worth visiting for a variety of reasons. The oldest city in Germany, it has absolutely everything for historians, fascinating Roman ruins (the most spectacular, the Porta Negra, a 10 minute walk from the train station). It has Roman artifacts and excavations in a marvelous collection, the oldest (Romanesque) cathedral in Germany, of aesthetic as well as historic interest, a lovely medieval collection, and, for historians more interested in modern times, the (well-restored) house in which Karl Marx was born. Walking down from the train station, I found the **Hotel Kurfürst Balduin,** about one or two blocks along, in the Theodor Heuss Allee 22 (phone [0651] 48610). It turned out to be a real find. For 29 DM ($15.26), I had a very comfortable, quiet, clean room, and a generous breakfast measured against the usual inclusive continental breakfast, i.e. a fresh egg as well as fresh rolls and coffee. Had I been willing to spend 32 DM for the night (no longer considered more than very modest), I could have had a quite large beautiful double room, with lounge, private bath and WC. The hotel was a bit old-fashioned (no elevator), but very charmingly appointed, good-sized rooms, a lounge-coffee-room with TV for the guests, and a very amiable proprietress who speaks excellent English, and keeps a schedule of train connections to Luxembourg" (Lore J. Wagner, Geneva, New York). . . . "Coming back into Germany we wanted to visit the sights of Trier. But accommodations there were scarce and expensive, so we back-tracked a little to the suburb of Igel, between Trier and the Luxembourg border. Here, the **Gasthaus Zum Löwen** cost us 30 marks ($15.78) a night for two with 2 breakfasts. The kind proprietor knew that our children were with us and agreed to let them sleep in our room. Please remind anyone staying in Igel to view the ancient Roman column there, just a half block up on the left from the Gasthaus Zum Löwen" (Priscilla G. Bornmann, APO New York).

VALENCIA, SPAIN

"There is an entire long block of hotels and hostals on Avd. Neptuno, right on the sea, a 20 pts. bus ride or 100 pts. cab ride from the main train station. We splurged for the last days of our vacation, and stayed at the two-star **Hotel La Marcelina** (phone 371-32-90). Our room, facing the sea, with private shower, was 1,000 pts. (double). The hotel was spotlessly clean, and the hosts delightful, a family one of whom spoke excellent English. We looked at a room at the **Hostal La Barraca** at Avd. Neptuno 36 (phone 371-61-11); it was also nice, though smaller, and went for about 900 pesetas with shower and breakfast for two people. At least four or five other hostals were in the same block, along with over a dozen restaurants" (Joseph F. O'Donnell, Portsmouth, Virginia).

VERONA, ITALY

"Verona is well worth a stop, both for itself, and on a side trip to Lake Garda. From the railway station in the new part of the town, bus #2 goes to the Piazza Erbe (buy bus tickets at the booth in front of the R/R station, 150 lire, and insert in the machine on the bus to validate them). This piazza, and the Piazza dei Signori just behind it, are gorgeous, especially at night, with buildings dating back to the 12th century. Notice the outside staircases. There aren't however, pensions in the piazza area. We finally found the **Pensione Marina**, 5 Via Ponte Nuovo, charging 6,500 lire ($7.83) single, 12,000 lire ($14.45) double, 14,500 lire ($17.46) triple, no water in the rooms but free hot showers and bath. Not the best nor the cheapest pension we had in Italy, but its location a bit behind the Piazza dei Signori is good. To get to it, walk down Via Cairoli from the east end of the Piazza Erbe. There is a large supermarket across the street and a few steps towards the river. . . . The **Simco-Rosticceria** at 29B Corso Di Porta Borsari (walking back toward the train station from Piazza Erbe) has a large selection of salads, pasta and meat to take out. . . . The Italia Nostra pass is good for free admission to the Roman arena and theater, Juliet's tomb, the tomb of the Scaligeras, and the Castel Vecchio. And don't miss the 12th century church of San Zeno Maggiore; a look at its brass doors helps one appreciate Ghiberti's masterpiece in Florence. . . . For Lake Garda, take the 8:10 a.m. train towards Milano, get off at Desenzano (1,400 lire roundtrip), and walk down to the lake. In spring and summer, a steamer leaving at 9:20 a.m. runs all the way up the lake (4-1/2 hours, 2,500 lire each way), but if you stay on all the way to Riva, there won't be much time to find food ashore, so take plenty with you" (Norriss, Edith and Elizabeth Hetherington, Berkeley, California). . . . "People in love will freak out at the sight of Juliet's house and balcony—she and Romeo were real people!" (Danielle Jehanne Rappaport, Munich, Germany).

VICENZA, ITALY

"My daughter is stationed at the American Army hospital in Vicenza, about an hour by train to the west of Venice, near Padova and Verona. She reserved a room for the the weekend for the three of us at the **Albergo Due Mori**, on Via Due Ruote 26, phone 21-886. This is right in the heart of the city: take bus #1 from the railway station, down Viale Roma. Outside, the hotel looks ancient, but inside all is modern, spotless, and beautifully furnished, and for 3 of us, the cost was only 14,000 lire ($16.86) for the room with shower and toilet. Everyone was helpful, kind and sympathetic, I almost felt like one of the family. This is the loveliest hotel of our travels" (Edith M. Gauthier, Buffalo, New York).

WIESBADEN, GERMANY

"We found a most attractive hotel, **Hotel Nassau**, Rheingaustrasse 148, Biebrich (a suburb of Wiesbaden), tel. 66007. Take Bus No. 4 from the Wiesbaden Railway Station to the Biebrich Terminus (about 10 minutes) and the Hotel is situated on the opposite side of the road, and to the left. This point is the Boat Terminus for Rhine River Steamers, and is extremely useful for Eurailpass holders, who can travel 'free' on the Europabus between Munich and Wiesbaden along the 'Romantic Road,' and wish to connect with a Rhine River Steamer for the Wiesbaden-Köln trip, which is also 'free' on Eurail. The rooms of the hotel are very attractive and comfortable and the manageress charming. Double rooms are 46 DM, singles 28 DM, including breakfast. We felt this was very good value as we were advised we would have to pay far more at the Railway Station tourist office" (Roslyn and Cynthia Arnold, Woollahra, N.S.W., Australia).

WINCHESTER, ENGLAND

"A fine bed-and-breakfast home in Winchester, which was once the capital of England, is at **23 Chesil Street**, 15 minutes' walk from the railroad station. Another is **Mrs. Petty's** home at 3A Magdalen Hill, (phone 63-802), two minutes from Chesil Street—also very good. Price for room and breakfast at 23 Chesil St. is £5, at Mrs. Petty's £5.50" (Caroline Strachan, Monterey Park, California).

YORK, ENGLAND

"Mr. and Mrs. Constable are proprietors of **Green View**, 5 Clifton Green, telephone York 21-964, which has accommodation for nine guests, and one could not wish for better or more comfortable rooms at the current rate of £5 per person per night, which includes a most generous full English breakfast" (Con and Jack Richards, Victoria,

Australia). . . . "I have a family guest house in York and throughout the last year have had countless Americans stay with me. I rent single, double and family rooms, at these rates per person per day, inclusive breakfast: one day £4.50, 2 days £9, 3 days £12, 7 days £27, thereafter £3 a day. Evening dinner, served on request, is £2.50. The name is **Rosa Alba Guest House,** the address 79 Bishopthorpe Road, the phone 53-731. We are 10 minutes' walk from the railway station and 5 minutes from the city center. There is hot and cold water in all rooms, and the guest's lounge has a color TV" (Mrs. Sylvia Graham, Proprietress).

ZERMATT, SWITZERLAND

"A must for readers going to Zermatt is the **Hotel Alphubel** (phone 67-30-03). It's a five-minute walk from the train station, right off the main street. A double room with knotty pine paneling, a balcony and a beautiful view of Zermatt's mountains costs from 48 francs ($29.09) up, including breakfast" (Barbara Pilarcyzk and J.R. Ford, Laguna Beach, California). . . . "Right across from the railway station is the **Hotel Bahnhof** (appropriately named) with large dorms (not overcrowded even when full) for 14 francs ($7.36) per person. It's the cheapest you'll find in Zermatt and you get full use of a large kitchen with all the pots, dishes and utensils you'll need. Buy your food at the Coop a block away. Plentiful hot showers are provided at no extra charge" (No name, Los Angeles, California; note: phone 67-24-06 for the remarkable Bahnhof Hotel). . . . "For anyone who loves the outdoors, this has to be as close to heaven as one can find on earth. It is reached only by train and therefore there are no cars in the town. Horse-and-buggies meet tourists at the station. There must be at least twenty different cable cars, cog trains, chair lifts, etc., that can be taken *up* from Zermatt which is already very high—and literally hundreds of trails in the area. It is from this town and its trails that the Matterhorn can be seen. We took cable cars up to where they were skiing" (Norbert H. Roihl, M.D., Fort Lauderdale, Florida). . . . "If any of your readers should consider a trip to Zermatt (a gorgeous village high in the Swiss Alps)—it is not on the Eurailpass but definitely worth going to—you can hitch a ride from Brig or Visp to Tasch and then walk from there to Zermatt. Otherwise the cost is 26 Swiss Francs from Visp, which is still on the Eurailpass. Even paying this amount is worth it, for Zermatt is fantastic. You can go hiking, summer skiing or climb the Matterhorn. And you can eat at the self-service restaurant located on the basement floor of the Migros supermarket. At the self-service, half a chicken, vegetables and mashed potatoes are 6 SF. Other meals are about the same" (Mona Sajous, New York, New York). . . . "We happened upon the lovely **Hotel Mischabel** (phone 67-11-31), where we had a double with breakfast for 52 SF. The people on the staff were among the nicest we met anywhere in Europe. Our room was done entirely in knotty pine and French doors led onto a balcony with a breath-taking view of the Matterhorn. Highly recommended" (Gail Redmond, Jersey City, New Jersey). . . . "Noting that Zermatt was quite expensive, we made use of a hotel in Thaesch: **Hotel Tascherhof,** phone 028/77-402. This was by far the best we have encountered so far in Europe. They charged us 93 francs ($48.94) for a double plus a triple room for my family of five, breakfast included. From Thaesch, you can take the first train to Zermatt, a 10-minute trip. The hotel is opposite the station" (Dr. L. A. Oelofse, Capetown, South Africa).

Throughout your stay in the cities just described, you'll need a mass of technical information: menu translations, vocabulary guides, money rates. You'll also want details on the train situation in Europe. It's all here, in the next four chapters.

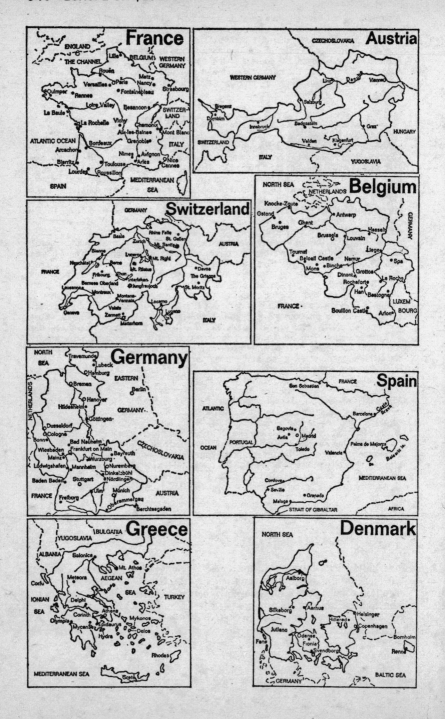

Chapter XXI

CAPSULE VOCABULARIES

For the Essentials of Life

THE MOST FAMOUS last words of the American tourist are: "They speak English everywhere."

Well, they don't. You can, with luck, be stranded in a European town among people who will simply shrug their shoulders to an English-uttered request.

But necessity is not the only reason for studying a foreign tongue—half of the fun of a European vacation comes from trying out the local language! It brings amazing dividends in better service and treatment, too. Europeans, like most persons, are sensitive and proud. They react best to tourists who show some regard for the language and culture of their host country.

To do that, you needn't become a full-time scholar. In any language, a very small group of words and phrases can be shifted and rearranged to fulfill almost any need. If you can learn the foreign equivalents of such terms as "where is," "do you have," "how much is this"—then you can travel comfortably in Europe and make your wants known. Half an hour of study, packed in as your train or plane approaches a particular country, ought to do the job.

What follows below are seven capsule vocabularies—for French, German, Italian, Spanish, Dutch, Danish and Swedish—containing those absolutely essential phrases which you'll use time and again in your tour of Europe. The column at the right-hand side of each page provides phonetic pronunciations of these terms as they'd sound in English. Pronounce the phonetic syllable "ay" as in "play" or "day," never as in "aye, aye, sir."

FRENCH

		Pronounced
Hello	**Bonjour**	bohn-zhoor
How are you?	**Comment allez-vous?**	koh-mawh-tah-lay-voo
Very well	**Très bien**	tray-byanh
Thank you	**Merci**	mayr-see
Goodbye	**Au revoir**	aw-ruh-vwahr
Please	**S'il vous plaît**	sill-voo-play
Yes	**Oui**	wee
No	**Non**	nawh
Excuse me	**Pardon**	par-dawh
Give me	**Donnez-moi**	duh-nay-mwah
Where is?	**Où est?**	oo ay
the station	**la gare**	lah-gar
a hotel	**un hôtel**	uh-no-tel
a restaurant	**un restaurant**	uh-res-tow-rawh
the toilet	**le lavabo**	luh-lah-vah-bo
To the right	**A droite**	ah-drwaht
To the left	**A gauche**	ah-gohsh
Straight ahead	**Tout droit**	too-drwah
I would like	**Je voudrais**	zhuh-voo-dray
to eat	**manger**	mawh-zhay
a room	**une chambre**	ewn-shawm-bruh
for one night	**pour une nuit**	poor-ewn-nwee
How much is it?	**Combien ça coute?**	kawm-byanh-sah-koot
The check, please	**L'addition, s.v.p.**	lah-dee-syohnh
When?	**Quand?**	kawnh
Yesterday	**Hier**	yayr
Today	**Aujourd'hui**	oh-zhoor-dwee
Tomorrow	**Demain**	duh-manh
Breakfast	**Le petit déjeuner**	luh puh-tee day-zhuh-nay
Lunch	**Déjeuner**	day-zhuh-nay
Dinner	**Dîner**	dee-nay

1 **un** (uhnh)	10 **dix** (deess)	19 **dix-neuf** (deez-nuff)
2 **deux** (duh)	11 **onze** (ohnze)	20 **vingt** (vanh)
3 **trois** (trwa)	12 **douze** (dooze)	30 **trente** (trawnt)
4 **quatre** (kahtr)	13 **treize** (trezz)	40 **quarante** (ka-rawnt)
5 **cinq** (sank)	14 **quatorze** (ka-torze)	50 **cinquante** (san-kawnt)
6 **six** (seess)	15 **quinze** (kanze)	100 **cent** (sawnh)
7 **sept** (set)	16 **seize** (sezz)	200 **deux cent** (duh-sawn)
8 **huit** (weet)	17 **dix-sept** (dee-set)	1000 **mille** (meel)
9 **neuf** (nuff)	18 **dix-huit** (deez-weet)	

GERMAN

		Pronounced
Hello	**Guten Tag**	goo-ten-tahk
How are you?	**Wie geht es Ihnen?**	vee gayt ess ee-nen
Very well	**Sehr gut**	zayr goot
Thank you	**Danke schön**	dahn-keh-shern
Goodbye	**Auf Wiedersehen**	owf vee dayr-zayn
Please	**Bitte**	bit-tuh
Yes	**Ja**	yah
No	**Nein**	nine
Excuse me	**Entschuldigen Sie**	en-shool-di-gen zee
Give me	**Geben Sie mir**	gay-ben zee meer
Where is?	**Wo ist?**	voh eest
the station	**der Bahnhof**	dayr bahn-hohf
a hotel	**ein Hotel**	ain hotel
a restaurant	**ein Restaurant**	ain res-tow-rahng
the toilet	**die Toilette**	dee twah-let-tuh
To the right	**Nach rechts**	nakh reshts
To the left	**Nach links**	nakh leenks
Straight ahead	**Geradeaus**	geh-rah-deh-ows
I would like	**Ich möchte**	ikh mersh-ta
to eat	**essen**	ess-en
a room	**ein Zimmer**	ain tzim-mer
for one night	**für eine Nacht**	feer ai-neh nakht
How much is it?	**Wieviel kostet?**	vee-feel kaw-stet
The check, please	**Zahlen, bitte**	tzah-len bit-tuh
When?	**Wann?**	vahn
Yesterday	**Gestern**	geh-stern
Today	**Heute**	hoy-tuh
Tomorrow	**Morgen**	more-gen
Breakfast	**Frühstück**	free-shtick
Lunch	**Mittagessen**	mi-tahg-gess-en
Dinner	**Abendessen**	ah-bend-ess-en

1 **eins** (aintz)
2 **zwei** (tzvai)
3 **drei** (dry)
4 **vier** (feer)
5 **fünf** (fewnf)
6 **sechs** (zex)
7 **sieben** (zee-ben)
8 **acht** (ahkht)
9 **neun** (noyn)
10 **zehn** (tzayn)

11 **elf** (ellf)
12 **zwölf** (tzvuhlf)
13 **dreizehn** (dry-tzayn)
14 **vierzehn** (feer-tzayn)
15 **fünfzehn** (fewnf-tzayn)
16 **sechzehn** (zex-tzayn)
17 **siebzehn** (zeeb-tzayn)
18 **achtzehn** (akh-tzayn)
19 **neunzehn** (noyn-tzayn)

20 **zwanzig** (tzvahn-tzig)
30 **dreissig** (dry-tzik)
40 **vierzig** (feer-tzik)
50 **fünfzig** (fewnf-tzik)
60 **sechzig** (zex-tzik)
70 **siebzig** (zeeb-tzik)
80 **achtzig** (akht-tzik)
90 **neunzig** (noyn-tzik)
100 **hundert** (hoon-dert)

ITALIAN

		Pronounced
Hello	**Buon giorno**	bwohn djor-noh
How are you?	**Come sta?**	koh-may stah
Very well	**Molto bene**	mohl-toh bay-nay
Thank you	**Grazie**	grah-tzyeh
Goodbye	**A rivederla**	ah ree-vay-dehr lah
Please	**Per favore**	payr fah-voy-ray
Yes	**Si**	see
No	**No**	noh
Excuse me	**Scusi**	skoo-zee
Give me	**Mi dia**	mee dee-ah
Where is?	**Dov'é**	doh-vay
the station	**la stazione**	la stah-tzyonay
a hotel	**un albergo**	oon ahl-bayr-goh
a restaurant	**un ristorante**	oon rees-to-rahn-tay
the toilet	**il gabinetto**	eel ga-bee-naytoh
To the right	**A destra**	ah dess-trah
To the left	**A sinistra**	ah see-nee-strah
Straight ahead	**Avanti**	ah-vahn-tee
I would like	**Vorrei**	vohr-ray
to eat	**mangiare**	mahn-djah-ray
a room	**una camera**	oona kah-may-rah
for one night	**per una notte**	payr oona noh-tay
How much is it?	**Quanto costa?**	kwan-toh kaw-stah
The check, please	**Il conto, per favore**	eel kohn-toh
When?	**Quando?**	kwahn-doh
Yesterday	**Ieri**	ee-yay-ree
Today	**Oggi**	aw-djee
Tomorrow	**Domani**	doh-mah-nee
Breakfast	**Colazione**	koh-lah-tzyoh-nay
Lunch	**Pranzo**	prahn-tzoh
Dinner	**Cena**	chay-nah

1 **uno** (oo-noh)
2 **due** (doo-ay)
3 **tre** (tray)
4 **quattro** (kwah-troh)
5 **cinque** (cheen-kway)
6 **sei** (say)
7 **sette** (set-tay)
8 **otto** (aw-toh)
9 **nove** (noh-vay)
10 **dieci** (dee-ah-chee)

11 **undici** (oon-dee-chee)
12 **dodici** (doh-dee-chee)
13 **tredici** (tray-dee-chee)
14 **quattordici** (kawh-tohr-dee-chee)
15 **quindici** (kween-dee-chee)
16 **sedici** (say-dee-chee)
17 **diciasette** (dee-chay-se-tay)

18 **diciotto** (dee-chah-toh)
19 **dicianove** (dee-chay-novay)
20 **venti** (vayn-tee)
30 **trenta** (trayn-tah)
40 **quaranta** (kwah-rahn-tah)
100 **cento** (chayn-toh)
1000 **mille** (mee-lay)

SPANISH

		Pronounced
Hello	**Buenos dias**	bway-noss dee-ahss
How are you?	**Cómo está usted?**	koh-moh ess-tah oo-steth
Very well	**Muy bien**	mwee byen
Thank you	**Gracias**	grah-thee-ahss
Goodbye	**Adios**	ah-dyohss
Please	**Por favor**	pohr fah-bohr
Yes	**Si**	see
No	**No**	noh
Excuse me	**Perdóneme**	pehr-doh-nehmay
Give me	**Déme**	day-may
Where is?	**Dónde esta?**	dohn-day ess-tah
the station	**la estación**	la ess-tah-thyohn
a hotel	**un hotel**	oon-oh-tel
a restaurant	**un restaurante**	oon res-tow-rahn-tay
the toilet	**el retrete**	el ray-tray-tay
To the right	**A la derecha**	ah lay day-ray-chuh
To the left	**A la izquierda**	ah lah eeth-kyayr-duh
Straight ahead	**Adelante**	ah-day-lahn-tay
I would like	**Quiero**	kyehr-oh
to eat	**comer**	koh-mayr
a room	**una habitacion**	oo-nah ah-bee-tah-thyon
How much is it?	**Cuánto?**	kwahn-toh
The check, please	**La cuenta**	lah kwen-tah
When?	**Cuándo?**	kwan-doh?
Yesterday	**Ayer**	ah-yayr
Today	**Hoy**	oy
Tomorrow	**Mañana**	mahn-yah-nah
Breakfast	**Desayuno**	deh-sai-yoo-noh
Lunch	**Almuerzo**	ahl-mwayr-thoh
Dinner	**Cena**	thay-nah

1 **uno** (oo-noh)	13 **trece** (tray-thay)	30 **treinta** (trayn-tah)
2 **dos** (dose)	14 **catorce** (kah-tor-thay)	40 **cuarenta** (kwah-ren-tah)
3 **tres** (trayss)	15 **quince** (keen-thay)	50 **cincuenta** (theen-kwen-tah)
4 **cuatro** (kwah-troh)	16 **dieciséis** (dyeth-ee-sayss)	60 **sesenta** (say-sen-tah)
5 **cinco** (theen-koh)	17 **diecisieto** (dyeth-ee-sye-tay)	70 **setenta** (say-ten-tah)
6 **seis** (sayss)	18 **dieciocho** (dyeth-ee-oh-choh)	80 **ochenta** (oh-chen-tah)
7 **siete** (syeh-tay)	19 **diecinueve** (dyeth-ee-nwaybay)	90 **noventa** (noh-ben-tah)
8 **ocho** (oh-choh)	20 **veinte** (bayn-tay)	100 **cien** (thyen)
9 **nueve** (nway-bay)		
10 **diez** (dyeth)		
11 **once** (ohn-thay)		
12 **doce** (doh-thay)		

DUTCH

		Pronounced
Hello	**Hallo**	ha-loh
How are you?	**Hoe gaat het met U?**	hoo-haht-ut met-oo
Very well	**Uitstekend**	out-stayk-end
Thank you	**Dank U**	dahnk-ew
Goodbye	**Goeden dag**	hoo-dun dahk
Please	**Alstublieft**	ah-stoo-bleeft
Yes	**Ja**	yah
No	**Neen**	nay
Excuse me	**Pardon**	par-dawn
Give me	**Geeft U mij**	hayft oo may
Where is?	**Waar is?**	vahr iz
the station	**het station**	het stah-ssyonh
a hotel	**een hotel**	uhn ho-tel
a restaurant	**een restaurant**	uhn res-to-rahng
the toilet	**het toilet**	het twah-let
To the right	**Rechts**	rekhts
To the left	**Links**	links
Straight ahead	**Rechtdoor**	rekht-dour
I would like	**Ik zou graag**	ik zow hrah
to eat	**eten**	ay-ten
a room	**een kamer**	uhn kah-mer
for one night	**voor een nacht**	voor ayn nakht
How much is it?	**Hoe veel kost het?**	hoo fayl kawst het
The check, please	**De rekening**	duh ray-ken-ing
When?	**Wanneer?**	vah-neer
Yesterday	**Gisteren**	his-ter-en
Today	**Vandaag**	van-dahkh
Tomorrow	**Morgen**	mor-hen
Breakfast	**Ontbijt**	ohnt-bayt
Lunch	**Lunch**	lunch
Dinner	**Diner**	dee-nay

1 **een** (ayn)	12 **twaalf** (tvahlf)	30 **dertig** (dayr-tukh)
2 **twee** (tway)	13 **dertien** (dayr-teen)	40 **veertig** (vayr-tukh)
3 **drie** (dree)	14 **veertien** (vayr-teen)	50 **vijftig** (vahf-tukh)
4 **vier** (veer)	15 **vijftien** (vayf-teen)	60 **zestig** (zes-tukh)
5 **vijf** (vayf)	16 **zestien** (zes-teen)	70 **zeventig** (zay-vun-tukh)
6 **zes** (zes)	17 **zeventien** (zay-vun-teen)	80 **tachtig** (takh-tukh)
7 **zeven** (zay-vun)	18 **achtien** (akh-teen)	90 **negentig** (nay-hen-tukh)
8 **acht** (akht)	19 **negentien** (nay-hen-teen)	100 **honderd** (hohn-dayrt)
9 **negen** (nay-hen)	20 **twintig** (twin-tukh)	
10 **tien** (teen)		
11 **elf** (elf)		

DANISH

English	Danish	Pronounced
Hello	**God Dag**	go da
How are you?	**Hvordan har De det?**	vohr-dan hahr dee day
Very well	**Tak, godt**	tak gaht
Thank you	**Tak**	tak
Goodbye	**Farvel**	fahr-vel
Please	**Vaer saa venlig**	vayr saw venlee
Yes	**Ja**	ya
No	**Nej**	nai
Excuse me	**Undskyld**	own-skeel
I don't understand	**Jeg forstaar ikke**	yai fawr-star ik-uh
Give me	**Giv mig**	gee-mai
Where is?	**Hvor er der?**	vohr ayr der
the station	**jernbanestationen**	yayrn-ban-uh-sta-sh--onun
a hotel	**et hotel**	it ho-tel
a restaurant	**en restaurant**	in rest-oh-rahng
the toilet	**toilettet**	twah-let-tud
To the right	**Til hojre**	til hoi-ruh
To the left	**Til venstre**	till ven-struh
I would like	**Jeg vilde gerne have**	yai-vil-luh gayr-nuh ha
to eat	**noget at spise**	noh-ud ah spee-suh
a room	**et Vaerelse**	it vay-rul-suh
How much is it?	**Hvor meget?**	vohr ma-yud
When?	**Hvornaar?**	vohr-nawr
Yesterday	**i Gaar**	ee gawr
Today	**i Dag**	ee da
Tomorrow	**i Morgen**	ee mawrn
Write it out	**Skriv det**	skreev day

1 **en** (ayn)
2 **to** (toh)
3 **tre** (tray)
4 **fire** (fee-rah)
5 **fem** (fem)
6 **seks** (sex)
7 **syv** (syee)
8 **otte** (oh-tuh)
9 **ni** (nee)
10 **ti** (tee)

11 **elve** (el-vuh)
12 **tolv** (tahll)
13 **tretten** (tret-un)
14 **fjorten** (fyawr-tun)
15 **femten** (fem-tun)
16 **seksten** (saiss-tun)
17 **sytten** (ser-tun)
18 **atten** (a-tun)
19 **nitten** (nitun)
20 **tyve** (tee-vuh)

30 **tredive** (tred-vuh)
40 **fyrre** (fer-raw)
50 **halvtreds** (hal-tress)
60 **tres** (tress)
70 **halvfjerds** (half-yayrss)
80 **firs** (feerss)
90 **halvfems** (hal-femss)
100 **hundrede** (hoon-rud-uh)

SWEDISH

		Pronounced
Hello	**God dag**	goo dah
How are you?	**Hur står det till?**	hoor store det till
Very well	**Tack, bra**	tahk brah
Thank you	**Tack**	tahk
Goodbye	**Adjö**	ah-yer
Please	**Var snäll och**	vahr snell oh
Yes	**Ja**	yah
No	**Nej**	nay
Excuse me	**Ursäkta**	oor-sek-tah
I don't understand	**Jag förstår inte**	yah fur-tore in tuh
Give me	**Ge mig**	yay may
Where is?	**Var finns det?**	vahr finss det
the station	stationen	stah-shoo-nen
a hotel	ett hotell	et ho-tel
a restaurant	en restaurang	en rest-oh-rahng
the toilet	toaletten	twah-let-ten
To the right	**At höger**	oht her-ger
To the left	**At vänster**	oht yen-ster
Straight ahead	**Rakt fram**	rahkt-frahm
I would like	**Jag vill ha**	ya vill hah
to eat	mat	maht
a room	ett rum	et ruhm
How much is it?	**Vad kostar det?**	vahd kaw-stahr dayt
That's too expensive	**Det är för mycket**	dayt ayr fer mik-ket
Something cheaper	**Inte så mycket**	in-tuh so mik-ket
When?	**När?**	nayr
Yesterday	**I går**	ee gore
Today	**I dag**	ee dah
Tomorrow	**I morgon**	ee mawr-rawn

1 ett (et)	**11** elva (el-vah)	**21** tjugoett (chew-goo-et)
2 tva (tvoh)	**12** tolv (tawlv)	**22** tjugotvå (chew-goo-tvo)
3 tre (tray)	**13** tretton (tret-tawn)	
4 fyra (fee-rah)	**14** fjorton (fyoor-tawn)	**30** trettio (tret-tee)
5 fem (fem)	**15** femton (fem-tawn)	**40** fyrtio (fur-tee)
6 sex (sex)	**16** sexton (sex-tawn)	**50** femtio (fem-tee)
7 sju (shew)	**17** sjutton (shuht-tawn)	**60** sextio (sex-tee)
8 åtta (awt-tah)	**18** aderton (ahr-tawn)	**70** sjuttio (shut-tee)
9 nio (nee-joh)	**19** nitton (nit-tawn)	**100** hundra (huhn-drah)
10 tio (tee-yoo)	**20** tjugo (chew-goo)	

Chapter XXII

MENU TRANSLATIONS

In Seven Languages

SOMEHOW, there are few words to describe the sinking feeling in the pit of your stomach caused by a Barcelona menu that lists "alcachofas, angulas y lletados con acelgas" as the choice you face for supper. Absent a translation of these exotic phrases, dinner becomes The Big Surprise. You stab blindly at the bill of fare, hope for the best, and usually end up with "octopus soup" or some similar delicacy.

Obviously, you'll need translations of European menus. They follow below, arranged for seven European languages in the same groupings that you'll find on a menu: soups, meats, vegetables, desserts, and so forth. Pronunciations are omitted; in this area, it usually pays simply to point to what you want.

A preliminary warning: in using these lists, don't be intimidated by the seemingly large number of menu terms that you won't find listed in them. Your bewilderment results from the common practice in European restaurants of adorning menus with fanciful, but totally meaningless, adjectives. Thus, a simple "wienerschnitzel" (breaded veal cutlet) is rarely described as such in a Munich restaurant: it's called a "wienerschnitzel Münchner Art" (breaded veal cutlet Munich style), but at heart, it's a simple breaded veal cutlet. The same literary touches are often indulged in by American restaurants, whose menus offer "Shenandoah County Tomato Juice" or "Special Prime-Tested Kansas

City Steaks." Just look for the basic root of the menu terms, which is all you're getting, in any event. Bon Appetit!

FRENCH MENU TERMS

SOUPS

bouillabaisse	fish soup	potage au vermicelle	noodle soup
consommé	clear soup		
potage (or) soupe	soup	potage aux lentilles	lentil soup
potage à la reine	cream of chicken	potage portugais	tomato soup
		potage Saint-Germain	pea soup
soupe à l'oignon	onion soup	potage de volaille	chicken broth

MEATS

agneau	lamb	gigot ragout de mouton	leg of mutton stew
ailerons	chicken wings		
aloyan	sirloin	grenouille	frog
bifteck	steak	jambon	ham
boeuf	beef	lapin	rabbit
canard	duck	mouton	mutton
caneton	duckling	oie	goose
cerf	venison	pot au feu	beef stew
cervelles	brains	poulet	chicken
charcuterie	cold cuts	poussin	squab chicken
chateaubriand	filet steak	ris de veau	sweetbreads
coq au vin	chicken in wine sauce	rognons	kidneys
		rôti de	roast
côtelette d'agneau	lamb chop	saucisse grillé	fried sausage
dandonneau farci	stuffed turkey	tournedos	small filet steaks
dinde	turkey	veau	veal
foie	liver	volaille	poultry
foie gras	goose liver		

FISH

aigrefin	haddock	huîtres	oysters
anguille	eel	maquereau	mackerel
brochet	pike	moule	mussel
crevette	shrimp	poissons	fish
escargots	snails	saumon fumé	smoked salmon
hareng	herring	thon	tuna
homard	lobster	truite	trout

EGGS

oeufs brouillés	scrambled eggs	oeufs frits	fried eggs
oeufs à la coque	soft boiled eggs	oeufs frits au jambon	ham and eggs
oeufs durs	hard boiled eggs	oeufs pochés	poached eggs

SALADS

crudités	vegetable salad	salade de laitue	lettuce salad
salade de concombres		salade niçoise	tuna salad
	cucumber salad	salade variée	mixed salad

VEGETABLES

asperge	asparagus	navets	turnips
aubergines	eggplant	petits pois	green peas
choucroute	sauerkraut	pommes frites	French fried potatoes
choux	cabbage		
cornichon	pickle	purée de pommes	mashed potatoes
épinards	spinach		
haricots verts	green beans	radis	radish
légumes	vegetables	riz	rice

BEVERAGES, CONDIMENTS, AND OTHERS

beurre	butter	moutarde	mustard
bière	beer	patisserie	pastry
café	coffee	petit pain	a roll
citron	lemon	poivre	pepper
cognac	brandy	sel	salt
crème	cream	sucre	sugar
croissants	breakfast rolls	thé	tea
de l'eau	water	vin	wine
jus d'orange	orance juice	vin blanc	white wine
jus de tomates	tomato juice	vin rouge	red wine
lait	milk	vinaigre	vinegar

DESSERTS

ananas	pineapple	fromage	cheese
compotes de fruits	stewed fruits	fromage à la crème	cream cheese
confitures	jam omelette	fruits frais	fresh fruit
crème à la vanille	vanilla custard	gateau	cake
fraises	strawberries	glace à la vanille	vanilla ice cream
framboises	raspberries		

macedoine de fruits	fruit salad	pamplemousse	grapefruit
omelette	soufflé	petits fours	tea cakes
oranges	oranges	raisins	grapes
		tartes	pastries

COOKING TERMS

à point	medium	meunière (or) au beurre	
bien cuit	well done		buttered
farci	stuffed	rôti	roast
frit	fried	saignant	rare

GERMAN MENU TERMS

SOUPS

Erbsensuppe	pea soup	Linsensuppe	lentil soup
Gemüsesuppe	vegetable soup	Nudelsuppe	noodle soup
Hühnerbrühe	chicken soup	Ochsenschwanzsuppe	oxtail soup
Kartoffelsuppe	potato soup		
Königinsuppe	cream of chicken	Schildkrötensuppe	turtle soup
Kraftbrühe	consomme		

MEATS

Aufschnitt	cold cuts	Kassler Rippchen	pork chops
Brathuhn	roast chicken	Lamm	lamb
Bratwurst	grilled sausage	Leber	liver
Deutsches Beefsteak	hamburger steak	Nieren	kidneys
		Ragout	stew
Eisbein	pig's knuckles	Rinderbraten	roast beef
Ente	duck	Rindfleisch	beef
Gans	goose	Sauerbraten	sauerbraten
Gefüllte Kalbsbrust	stuffed breast of veal	Schinken	ham
		Schweinebraten	roast pork
Hammel	mutton	Taube	pigeon
Hirn	brains	Truthahn	turkey
Kalb	veal	Wiener Schnitzel	veal cutlet
Kaltes Geflügel	cold poultry	Wurst	sausage

FISH

Aal	eel	Karpfen	carp
Forelle	trout	Krebs	crawfish
Hecht	pike	Lachs	salmon

Makrele	mackerel	**Schellfisch**	haddock
Rheinsalm	Rhine salmon	**Seezunge**	sole

EGGS

Eier in Schale	boiled eggs	**mit Speck**	with bacon
Rühreier	scrambled eggs	**Verlorene Eier**	poached eggs
Spiegeleier	fried eggs		

SANDWICHES

Käsebrot	cheese sandwich	**Schwarzbrot mit Butter**	
Schinkenbrot	ham sandwich		rye bread and butter
		Wurstbrot	sausage sandwich

SALADS

Gemischter Salat	mixed salad	**Kopfsalat**	lettuce salad
Gurkensalat	cucumber salad	**Rohkostplatte**	vegetable salad

VEGETABLES

Artischocken	artichokes	**Reis**	rice
Blumenkohl	cauliflower	**Rote Rüben**	beets
Bohnen	beans	**Rotkraut**	red cabbage
Bratkartoffeln	fried potatoes	**Salat**	lettuce
Erbsen	peas	**Salzkartoffeln**	boiled potatoes
Grüne Bohnen	string beans	**Sauerkraut**	sauerkraut
Gurken	cucumbers	**Spargel**	asparagus
Karotten	carrots	**Spinat**	spinach
Kartoffelbrei	mashed potatoes	**Steinpilze**	mushrooms
Kartoffelsalat	potato salad	**Tomaten**	tomatoes
Knödel	dumplings	**Vorspeisen**	hors d'oeuvres
Kohl	cabbage	**Weisse Rüben**	turnips

DESSERTS

Blätterteiggebäck	puff pastry	**Obstsalat**	fruit salad
Bratapfel	baked apple	**Pfannkuchen**	sugared pancakes
Käse	cheese	**Pflaumenkompott**	stewed plums
Klösse	dumpling	**Teegebäck**	tea cakes
Kompott	stewed fruit	**Torten**	pastries
Obstkuchen	fruit tart		

FRUITS

Ananas	pineapples	Kirschen	cherries
Apfel	apples	Pfirsiche	peaches
Apfelsinen	oranges	Weintrauben	grapes
Bananen	bananas	Zitronen	lemons
Birnen	pears		

BEVERAGES

Bier	beer	Eine Tasse Kaffee	a cup of coffee
Ein Dunkles	a dark beer		
Ein Helles	a light beer	Eine Tasse Tee	a cup of tea
Milch	milk	Tomatensaft	tomato juice
Rotwein	red wine	Wasser	water
Sahne	cream	Weinbrand	brandy
Schokolade	chocolate		

CONDIMENTS AND OTHERS

Brot	bread	Pfeffer	pepper
Brötchen	rolls	Salz	salt
Butter	butter	Senf	mustard
Eis	ice	Zitrone	lemon
Essig	vinegar	Zucker	sugar

COOKING TERMS

gebacken	baked	geröstet	broiled
gebraten	fried	gutdurchgebraten	well done
gefüllt	stuffed	nichtdurchgebraten	rare
gekocht	boiled	paniert	breaded

SPANISH MENU TERMS

SOUPS

caldo de gallina	chicken soup	sopa espesa	thick soup
gazpacho	cold soup	sopa de fideos	noodle soup
sopa	soup	sopa de guisantes	pea soup
sopa de cebolla	onion soup	sopa de lentejas	lentil soup
sopa clara	consomme	sopa de tortuga	turtle soup

MEATS

albóndigas	meat balls	**higado**	liver
aves	poultry	**jamón**	ham
cabeza de ternera	calf's head	**lengua**	tongue
carne	meat	**paloma**	pigeon
carne fría	cold cuts	**pato**	duck
cerdo	pork	**pavo**	turkey
chuleta	chop	**perdiz**	partridge
chuleta de carnero	mutton chop	**pollo**	chicken
ciervo	venison	**ragout**	ragout
conejo	rabbit	**riñones**	kidneys
cordero	lamb	**salchicha**	sausage
faisan	pheasant	**ternera**	veal
filete de ternera	filet of veal	**tocino**	bacon
ganso	goose	**vaca**	beef

FISH

almejas	clams	**ostras**	oysters
anchoas	anchovies	**paella**	assorted sea food and rice
arenque	herring		
bonito	tunny	**pescado**	fish
callos	tripe	**salmon**	salmon
caracoles	snails	**salmón ahumado**	smoked salmon
caviare	caviar		
gambas	shrimp	**sardinas**	sardines
langosta	lobster	**sollo**	pike
lenguado	sole	**trucha**	trout

VEGETABLES

aceitunas	olives	**judias verdes**	string beans
arroz	rice	**lechuga**	lettuce
berenjena	eggplant	**legumbres**	vegetables
cebolla	onion	**pasta italiana**	spaghetti
col	cabbage	**patatas**	potatoes
col fermentada	sauerkraut	**pepino**	cucumber
coliflor	cauliflower	**rábanos**	radishes
entremeses	hors d'oeuvres	**remolachas**	beets
esparragos	asparagus	**setas**	mushrooms
espinaca	spinach	**tomate**	tomato
guisantes	peas	**zanahorias**	carrots

SALADS

ensalada de apio	celery salad	**ensalada varias**	mixed salad
ensalada de pepinos	cucumber salad	**lechuga**	lettuce salad

EGGS

huevos	eggs	**huevos fritos**	fried eggs
huevos duros	hard-boiled eggs	**huevos pasados**	boiled eggs
huevos escalfados	poached eggs	**huevos y tochino**	bacon and eggs

FRUITS

albaricoques	apricots	**manzanas**	apples
cerezas	cherries	**melocoton**	peach
ciruelas	plums	**naranjas**	oranges
ciruelas con nata	with cream	**pera**	pear
frambuesas	raspberries	**piña**	pineapple
fruta	fruit	**plátanos**	bananas
fresas	strawberries	**uvas**	grapes
limon	lemon		

DESSERTS

buñuelos	doughnuts	**helado**	ice cream
bruñelos de fruta	fruit tart	**macedonia**	fruit salad
compota	stewed fruit	**el postre**	dessert
flan	caramel custard	**queso**	cheese
galletas	tea cakes	**torta**	cake

BEVERAGES

agua	water	**jugo de tomate**	tomato juice
aguardiente	brandy	**leche**	milk
café	coffee	**licor**	liqueur
cerveza	beer	**sidra**	cider
ginebra	gin	**sifon**	soda
jerez	sherry	**té**	tea
jugo de naranjas	orange juice	**vino**	wine

CONDIMENTS AND OTHERS

aceite	oil	pan	bread
ajo	garlic	panecillo	roll
azúcar	sugar	pimienta	pepper
hielo	ice	sal	salt
manteca	butter	tostada	toast
mostaza	mustard	vinagre	vinegar

COOKING TERMS

asado	roast	frito	fried
cocido	broiled	muy hecho	well done
empanado	breaded	poco hecho	rare

RECURRING ITEMS: Among the classic dishes of Spain, which you'll find on nearly every menu, are **arroz con pollo** (chicken and rice), **paella** (sea food and rice), and **guisado** or **caldo gallego**, which both refer to various types of meat stews. The word **chuletas** refers to cutlets (like **chuletas de ternera**—veal cutlets), **costillas** are chops ("costillas de . . ."), and **relleno** is chopped meat. In addition to wine, a favorite summertime beverage is **sangria**, a punch drink made of fruit juices and vermouth, nearly always served in a big iced pitcher, and quite mild.

ITALIAN MENU TERMS

SOUPS

brodo	consomme	riso in brodo	rice soup
minestra	soup	zuppa alla Pavese	egg soup
minestrone	vegetable soup	zuppa di fagioli	bean soup
pastina in brodo	noodle soup	zuppa di pesce	fish soup

FISH

acciughe	anchovies	merluzzo	cod
aragosta	lobster	ostriche	oysters
aringhe	herrings	pesce	fish
filetto di sogliola	filet of sole	sardine	sardine
scampi fritti	fried shrimps	scampi fritti	fried shrimps
fritto di pesce	assorted fried fish	sgombro	mackerel
		sogliola	sole
frutta di mare	assorted sea foods	tonno	tuna fish
		trota	trout
gamberi	shrimps		

MEATS

abbachio	baby lamb	lingua	tongue
agnello	lamb	maiale	pork
anitra	duck	manzo lesso	boiled beef
bistecca	steak	pancetta	bacon
carne	meat	pollo	chicken
carne fredda assortita	cold cuts	pollo alla diavolo	deviled chicken
cervello	brains	prosciutto	ham
cotoletta alla Bolognese	veal cutlet with melted cheese	reni	kidney
		rosbif	roast beef
cotoletta alla Milanese	breaded veal cutlet	salsicce	sausages
		saltimbocca	veal and ham
fagiano	pheasant	tacchino	turkey
fegatini	chicken livers	tournedo	beef
fegato	liver	vitello	veal
lepre	rabbit		

EGGS

omelette or frittata	omelette	strapazzate al pomodoro	tomato omelette
omelette alla parmigiana	cheese omelette	uova	eggs
omelette di fegatini	omelette w/chicken livers	uova affogate	poached eggs
		uova a la coque	boiled eggs
omelette di funghi	mushroom omelette	uova fritte	fried eggs
		uova strapazzate	scrambled eggs
pandorato	French fried toast		

VEGETABLES

antipasto	hors d'oeuvres	olive	olives
asparagi	asparagus	patate	potatoes
cannelloni	pasta with meat filling	peperoni	green peppers
		piselli	peas
carciofi	artichokes	pizza	you know this one
carrote	carrots	pomodori	tomatoes
cavolfiore	cauliflower	ravioli alla Fiorentina	cheese ravioli
cavolo	cabbage		
cetrioli	cucumbers	ravioli alla vegetariana	ravioli with tomato sauce
cipolle	onions		
fagiolini	string beans	riso	rice
fettuccine	noodles	risotto	rice dish
funghi	mushrooms	sedano	celery
insalata mista	mixed salad	spinaci	spinach
insalata verde	lettuce salad	verdura	vegetables
lattuga	lettuce	zucchini	squash
melanzana	eggplant		

FRUITS

ananasso	pineapple	frutta cotta	stewed fruit
aranci	oranges	limoni	lemons
banane	bananas	mele	apples
ciliegie	cherries	pere	pears
frutta	fruit	uva	grape

BEVERAGES

acqua	water	caffè	coffee
acqua minerale	mineral water	latte	milk
aranciata	orangeade	limonata	lemonade
bibite	beverages	the	tea
birra	beer	vino	wine

DESSERTS

budino	pudding	macedonia di frutta	fruit salad
cassata	ice cream with fruit	pasticceria	pastry
dolci	dessert	pesca alla Melba	peach melba
formaggio	cheese	torta	cake
gelato	ice cream		

CONDIMENTS AND OTHERS

aceto	vinegar	olio	oil
biscotti	crackers	pane	bread
burro	butter	pepe	pepper
ghiaccio	ice	sale	salt
marmellata	jam	sott'aceti	pickles
mostarda	mustard	zucchero	sugar

COOKING TERMS

al sangue	rare	ben cotto	well done
arrosto	roast	lesso (or) bollito	broiled

ITALIAN STAPLES: You'll invariably find, at the start of the menu, a collection of soups including **pastina in brodo** or **tortellini in brodo** or some other "in brodo" combination, which merely refer to various types of pasta served in a soup broth. Into it you sprinkle grated cheese, and the resulting combination makes an always satisfying first course. The spaghetti dishes come next, either **al pomodoro** (with tomato sauce) or **alla Bolognese** or **con carne** (meat sauce) or **alle vongole** (with clam sauce) or, best yet, **alla carbonara** (cooked in egg, with bits of bacon—delicious). Among the main courses, the term **scallopine,**

followed by various words, always refers to slices of veal, cooked in various ways; while **cotolette** is almost always a breaded veal cutlet. **Saltimbocca** is the famous veal-and-ham dish; **bistecca** is beefsteak; **maiale** indicates a pork dish; **manzo** a beef plate; **pollo** is chicken; **ossobuco** is shank of veal; **fegato** is liver. Among the other items, **risotto** indicates a rice dish, served alone or with various sauces; and **cassata** is the name for ice-cream-and-fruit. Among the adjectival food terms, **filetto** means filet (like **filetto di sogliole**—filet of sole); **involtini** indicates something that is rolled (like **involtini di manzo**—rolled beef); and **salsa** or **sugo** means sauce. Thus, **spaghetti al sugo di carne** is spaghetti with meat sauce.

Some recurring main courses include:

Bracciola alla Milanese (fried veal chop)

Manzo bollito (boiled beef)

Pollo alla cacciatora (stewed chicken)

Spezzatino di manzo (beef stew)

Vitello al forno (roast veal)

SWEDISH MENU TERMS

ärtsoppa	pea soup	**kålsoppa**	cabbage soup
buljong	broth	**soppa**	soup

MEATS

anka	duck	**korv**	sausage
biffstek	steak	**kyckling**	chicken
fårkött	mutton	**lamm**	lamb
fläsk	pork	**lever**	liver
gås	goose	**oxe**	beef
kalv	veal	**rostbiff**	roast beef
kalv	calf	**skinka**	ham

VEGETABLES

ärta	pea	**lök**	onion
ärtskocka	artichoke	**makaroner**	macaroni
blomkål	cauliflower	**morot**	carrot
bruna bönor	kidney beans	**potatis**	potatoes
gurka	cucumber	**rödbeta**	beet
kål	cabbage	**sparris**	asparagus

FISH

anjovis	anchovies	torsk	cod
fisk	fish	makrill	mackerel
hummer	lobster	ostron	oyster
karp	carp	sill	herring
kaviar	caviar	stör	sturgeon
kolja	haddock		

DESSERTS

sockerkaka	cake	ost	cheese
kakor	pastry	russinkaka	plumcake

FRUITS

apelsiner	oranges	persika	peach
körsbär	cherry	plommon	plum
leagertrad	avocado	vindruva	grape
paron	pear		

BEVERAGES

kaffe	coffee	öl or pilsner	beer
karnmjölk	buttermilk	te	tea
mjölk	milk	vatten	water
öl	ale		

CONDIMENTS AND OTHERS

ägg	egg	salt	salt
attika	vinegar	senap	mustard
bröd	bread	smör	butter
peppar	pepper	socker	sugar
pepparrot	horseradish	vitlök	garlic

DUTCH MENU TERMS

SOUPS

aardappelsoep	potato soup	kippensoep	chicken soup
bonensoep	bean soup	soep	soup
erwtensoep	pea soup	tomatensoep	tomato soup
groentesoep	vegetable soup	uiensoep	onion soup

MEATS

bief	beef	**koude schotel**	cold cuts
biefstuk	steak	**lamscotelet**	lamb chops
chateaubriand	filet steak	**lamsvlees**	lamb
eend	duck	**lever**	liver
gans	goose	**niertjes**	kidneys
gebraden worst	fried sausage	**ragout**	beef stew
gevogelte	poultry	**spek**	bacon
kalkoen	turkey	**varkensvlees**	pork
kip	chicken	**worstjes**	sausages
konijn	rabbit		

FISH

forel	trout	**makreel**	mackerel
garnalen	shrimp	**mosselen**	mussels
gerookte zalm	smoked salmon	**oesters**	oysters
haring	herring	**sardientjes**	sardines
kabeljauw	haddock	**vis**	fish
kreeft	lobster	**zalm**	salmon

EGGS

eieren	eggs	**spiegeleieren**	fried eggs
hardgekookte eieren	hard-boiled eggs	**zachtgekookte eieren**	boiled eggs
roereieren	scrambled eggs		

VEGETABLES

aardappelen	potatoes	**prinsesseboontjes**	green beans
asperges	asparagus	**purée**	mashed potatoes
augurkjes	pickles	**radijsjes**	radishes
bonen	beans	**rapen**	turnips
bieten	beets	**rijst**	rice
erwtjes	peas	**sla**	lettuce
groente	vegetables	**spinazie**	spinach
kool	cabbage	**tomaten**	tomatoes
patates frites	French fried potatoes	**worteltjes**	carrots
		zuurkool	sauerkraut

SALADS

sla	salad	**komkommersla**	cucumber salad

FRUITS

appelen	apples	**fruit**	fruit
bananen	bananas	**kersen**	cherries
citroenen	lemons	**sinaasappelen**	oranges
druiven	grapes	**pruimen**	plums

DESSERTS

ananas	pineapple	**kaas**	cheese
cake	cake	**nagerecht**	dessert
frambozen	raspberries	**omelette**	omelette
ijs	ice cream	**compôte**	stewed fruits
jam	jam	**zwatre bessen**	blackberries

BEVERAGES, CONDIMENTS, AND OTHERS

azijn	vinegar	**peper**	pepper
bier	beer	**rode wijn**	red wine
boter	butter	**suiker**	sugar
broodje	a roll	**thee**	tea
cognac	brandy	**tomaten sap**	tomato juice
croissants	breakfast rolls	**water**	water
gebak	pastry	**wijn**	wine
koffie	coffee	**witte wijn**	white wine
melk	milk	**zout**	salt
mosterd	mustard		

COOKING TERMS

gebakken	fried	**niet doorgebakken**	rare
gekookt	boiled	**onder de vlam geroosterd**	
goed doorgebakken	well done		broiled

DANISH MENU TERMS

SOUPS AND APPETIZERS

aspargesuppe	asparagus soup	koldt bord	hors d'oeuvres
blomkaalsuppe	cauliflower soup	smorrebrod	open sandwiches
gule aerter	pea soup		

FISH

al	eel	musslinger	mussels
fiskefrikadeller	fish cakes	orred	trout
helleflynder	halibut	pighvarre	turbot
hummer	lobster	rejer	shrimps
krabber	crabs	rodspaette	plaice
krebs	crayfish	sild	herring
laks	salmon	torsk	cod
makrel	mackerel		

MEATS AND EGGS

aeggekage	omelette	kalvesteg	roast veal
agerhons	partridge	kylling	chicken
and	duck	lam	lamb
andesteg	roast duck	lammesteg	roast lamb
blødkogt aeg	soft-boiled egg	lever	liver
bof	steak	leverpostej	liver paté
boller	meat balls	okse	beef
due	pigeon	oksesteg	roast beef
dyr	venison	polser	sausages
fasan	pheasant	roraeg	scrambled eggs
flaeskesteg	roast pork	skinke	ham
gaas	goose	spegepolse	salami
hakkebof	hamburger	spejlaeg	fried egg
hardkogt aeg	hard-boiled egg	svin	pork
kalkun	turkey	tunge	tongue
kalve	veal	vildand	wild duck

VEGETABLES

aerter	peas	kartofler	potatoes
agurk	cucumber	log	onions
asparges	asparagus	ris	rice
blomkaal	cauliflower	rodkal	red cabbage
bonner	string beans	rosenkaal	brussels sprouts
gulerodder	carrots	tomater	tomatoes
hvidkal	cabbage		

FRUITS

aebler	apples	ferskner	peaches
ananas	pineapple	hindbaer	raspberries
appelsiner	oranges	jordbaer	strawberries
blommer	plums	paerer	pears

DESSERTS

budding	pudding	kompot	stewed fruit
hindbaer med flode	raspberries with cream	kager	pastry
		ost	cheese
is	ice cream		

BEVERAGES, CONDIMENTS, AND OTHERS

aeblemost	apple juice	salt	salt
brod	bread	smor	butter
flode	cream	te	tea
kaffe	coffee	vand	water
maelk	milk	vin	wine
ol	beer	Wienerbrod	Danish Pastry
ristet brod	toast		

COOKING TERMS

grilleret	grilled	ristet	fried
farseret	stuffed	stegt	roast
kogt	broiled		

FRANCE

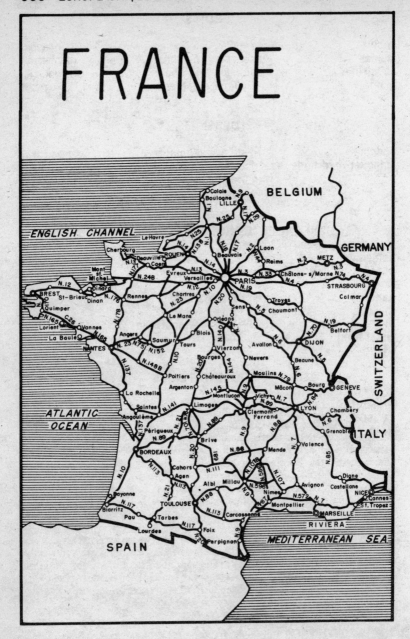

Chapter XXIII

EUROPEAN TRAINS

With Important Class Distinctions

THE LIFE OF EUROPE is mirrored in its trains. You haven't really savored the essence of the Continent until you've chugged along in a second-class compartment and shared the sausage-and-Chianti of an Italian family, or carried on a bouncing conversation in broken French, or simply leaned back and observed the European in his holiday-traveling mood. On most other occasions in Europe, the tourist is likely to be a frenzied animal, divorced from a truly human contact with the population. In a train, this remoteness falls away. A moment occurs when the sights and sounds of Europe become intimate and related to people—and that, to me, is a thrill which no monument or museum can ever provide.

Now, assuredly, the joys of a tiring train trip will not enthrall all the readers of this book. But there will be times and occasions when you can't or won't want to fly from city to city in Europe. You have to consider the science of European train transportation—which is just that, a science. It even has a key formula which, for the budget tourist, goes something like this: *Always travel second class in a major European express.* Here's why:

THE BIG DIFFERENCE: European trains tend to bunch themselves into two categories: magnificent and awful. There is no middle variety. In the first group, you'll find a type of European train which provides superb, lightning-like service. Only around forty of these trains exist, and they can be recognized by the fact that they carry names as well as numbers: the **Simplon-Orient Express,**

the **Treno del Sole,** the **Golden Arrow,** for instance. No one could want better train service than these provide. They normally run overnight, stop only in the largest cities, and cut hours from your travel time. Thus, the Intercity Express makes the trip from Munich to Frankfurt in 3 hours and 45 minutes. Train E3004, traveling exactly the same route, takes 5 hours and 32 minutes. In other words, your choice in Europe is between decent train transportation—and Toonerville Trolleys. Schedule your trips and your connections for the named, international trains, and traveling can be a cinch.

THE MONEY QUESTION: Riding on the great international expresses can have an important effect upon your costs, too, enabling you to buy an inexpensive railroad ticket at no sacrifice to physical comfort. Here's why. You will quickly learn that European trains carry both First and Second Class accommodations. A First Class ticket costs 33%-50% more than a Second Class fare. But while a Second Class ticket on a major international express will purchase a perfectly comfortable, well-padded seat, a Second Class ticket on the wrong type of European train can often lead to disaster. There are short distance trains in France and Austria which provide wooden benches in their Second Class compartments. By traveling on the international expresses, you can purchase money-saving Second Class tickets, and protect your sacroiliac at the same time.

As for traveling First Class in Europe, well, that's very unwise. The difference in quality between First and Second Class seats in a major international express is infinitesimal—a matter of one or two inches of extra padding, at most. The people who travel First Class are also much less interesting types—but we won't go into that. The major gain to be realized from traveling Second Class is a financial one; it can reduce your transportation costs within Europe to a most reasonable expense. For European trains are moderate in price—and less expensive than those in the United States. You may change your notions about the cost of a European vacation when you learn that the long train trip down the boot of Italy from Florence to Rome costs only $10.70 (Second Class). In early 1980, a one-way, Second Class ticket for trips between the major cities of Europe totalled up as follows:

AMSTERDAM to: Paris, $38.20; Copenhagen, $67.10; London, $53.30; Vienna, $89.40; Brussels, $18.40; Frankfurt, $39.10; Rome, $109.40; Venice (via Basel), $97.40.

LONDON to: Brussels, $43.40; Edinburgh, $56.40; Glasgow, $52.90; Dublin, $61.20; Paris, $54.50; Amsterdam, $53.30.

PARIS to: Brussels, $19.90; Amsterdam, $38.20; Madrid, $83.30; Copenhagen, $95; Frankfurt, $42.60; Munich, $63.20; Zurich, $41.90; Rome, $66.50; Cannes, $64; Lourdes, $52.20; Marseille, $52.70; Nice, $65.90; Strasbourg, $31.10.

ROME to: Florence, $10.70; Naples, $7.20; Genoa, $16.70; Venice, $19.10; Milan, $21; Amsterdam, $109.40; Barcelona, $69.70; Brussels, $84.50; Frankfurt, $73.30; Geneva, $44.20; London, $121; Madrid, $107.90; Munich, $40.20; Nice, $24.10; Paris, $66.50; Vienna, $47.50; Trieste, $23.90; Zurich, $45.40.

MADRID to: Barcelona, $38.10; Toledo, $5.10; Valencia, $21.50; Lisbon, $29.30; Paris, $83.30; Rome, $107.90; Seville, $30.40.

BARCELONA to: Marseille, $33.20; Nice, $46.10; Paris, $67.70; Rome, $69.70; Lourdes, $36.10.

FRANKFURT to: Amsterdam, $39.10; Brussels, $33; Copenhagen, $66.30; Innsbruck, $47.20; Milan, $52.90; Naples, $86.28; Paris, $42.60; Rome, $73.70; Venice, $61.70, Vienna, $51.40.

MUNICH to: Amsterdam, $67.90; Brussels, $63; Copenhagen, $87.70; Innsbruck, $14.10; Milan, $28.50; Naples, $47.40; Paris, $63.20; Rome, $40.20; Salzburg, $11.90; Venice, $27.40; Vienna, $30.30; Zurich, $32.50.

PRICE CUTS: In addition to their initially low costs, nearly all the European railways offer money-saving plans of one sort or another. While some of these are fairly worthless come-ons, it may be that a particular plan will fit your travel needs. Here's a fast rundown:

Netherlands Railways, to begin the survey, offers a ticket good for eight consecutive days of unlimited travel throughout the Netherlands, for 110 guilders ($55) in first class, 75 guilders ($37.50) in second class. Write to Netherlands Railways, 576 Fifth Avenue, New York, N. Y. 10017.

BritRail Travel International promotes a scheme of "BritRail Passes" entitling the bearer to unlimited rail travel throughout England, Scotland and Wales, provided that the pass is purchased prior to departure, in North America (through either a travel agent or Brit-Rail Travel International, 630 Third Avenue, New York, N. Y. 10017). You can buy a BritRail Pass either for First Class travel ($120 for 7 days, $180 for 14 days, $225 for 21 days, $260 for one month) or for Second Class travel ($85 for 7 days, $130 for 14 days, $165 for 21 days, $195 for one month), and there's also a second class Youth Pass (for those aged 14 to 25) costing $75 for 7 days, $115 for 14 days, $145 for 21 days, $170 for one month.

French National Railways introduced an unlimited mileage scheme called "France Vacances" in 1979, and what a scheme! In addition to offering endless rail transportation within France for either 7 days ($95), fifteen days ($135), or 30 days ($200), it also throws in, for no extra charge, a one-day car rental, a 4-day Parisian métro (subway) pass, round-trip transportation between airport (in Paris) and air terminal, and a species of museum pass. For francophiles planning a continuous stay in France, this is a good, good value. . . . French National Railways also grants a 75% reduction on the third ticket to a family of three traveling together, provided that they make a round-trip or circular trip within France. . . . Parties of ten or more traveling ensemble get an across-the-board cut of 30%. . . . A special $9 ticket called the "Carte Vermeil" entitles women over 60 and men over 65 to a 30% fare reduction.

Swiss Federal Railways, slickest train company in Europe, offers the choice of either an unlimited mileage pass, or else a voucher entitling you to a 50% price reduction whenever you do buy a railroad ticket in Switzerland. The former is called a "Swiss Holiday Travel Card," can only be purchased in your own home country before you leave, and is available for either 8 days ($75), 15 days ($97), or one month ($134) of second class travel. The latter can be bought either pre-departure (from any Swiss National Tourist Office) or at major railroad stations in Switzerland, and is valid for either 15 days ($28.50) or one month ($37.50), during which time you can buy as many tickets as you want, at half price. Finally, women over the age of 62, and men over 65, can purchase a Swiss half-fare pass valid for an entire year, for only $50. Write to the Swiss National Tourist Office, 608 Fifth Avenue, New York City 10020.

Spanish Railways offers a form of discount coupon for its passengers from abroad. You purchase 12,750 pesetas' ($193.18) worth of coupons, which are valid for 15,000 pesetas' ($227.27) worth of rail travel—approximately a 15% reduction. The coupons are accepted as currency in every sort of train operated in Spain. Consult the Spanish National Tourist Office, 665 Fifth Avenue, New York City (phone 212-759-8822). . . . Actually, it sometimes pays to travel by plane in Spain, whose excellent Iberia Áirlines charges only $46.30 for the long trip from Madrid to Seville.

Italian Railways are so cheap to begin with, that they offer few discount plans; but one that you might want to consider is an unlimited rail pass within Italy (the "Biglietto Turistico di Libera Circolazione") costing $84 for 15 days, $97 for 21 days, $121 for 30 days, second class. Write to Italian State Railways, 500 Fifth Avenue, New York City.

Austrian Railways: Sells an "Austria Ticket" valid for either nine or sixteen days of unlimited, second class rail transportation in Austria, at a cost of either 1,280 schillings ($94.81) for nine days, or 1,760 schillings ($130.37) for sixteen days, with young people under 23 charged half price. Also offers discounts of approximately 25% for groups of ten or more, traveling together; while senior citizens (women over 60, men over 65) regardless of nationality, travel at half-fare by buying a special identification card for 120 schillings, or $8.88, at train stations in Austria.

Finally, there's a particular cost-saving device that virtually all the European railways offer, and you'll want to consider it:

EURAILPASS: This valuable, simple-to-use railroad pass is one of the most ingenious travel ideas in years. All the European railways, other than the British, have together created a single ticket—the **"Eurailpass"**—good for *unlimited* First Class rail travel throughout all of Europe (other than the British Isles) for a specified period of time. A 15-day Eurailpass costs $210; a 21-day Eurailpass costs $260; a one-month Eurailpass costs $320; a two-month Eurailpass costs $430; and a three-month Eurailpass costs $530. Children under 12 go at half fare and children under 4 travel free. Anyone under the age of 26 can purchase a **"Eurail Youthpass"**, entitling them to unlimited *second class* transportation for *two* months—for only $290.

Assume that you've planned a two-month trip through Europe, and that you hope to do a great deal of traveling during that time. Purchase a Eurailpass or Eurail Youthpass *before* you leave for Europe—they are sold all over the world, except in Europe. With one, you can board any train you wish, as often as you wish, flash the pass at the conductor, and take any seat in any First Class compartment on the train. You needn't buy a single other ticket, or pay any supplemental or reservation charges. Theoretically, a man-with-a-Eurailpass could spend 60 straight days on a train—all for $430. A student can do the same, second class, for only $290.

The extent of your savings, with a Eurailpass, will depend upon the length of your expected itinerary. I doubt that a one-month tourist (especially one willing to dispense with first class seats) would normally do enough traveling to make the purchase worthwhile. But the two-month tourist—and particularly the tourist who's over for a longer Grand Tour—will give this gimmick a great deal of thought.

Where do you get them? Write or visit the nearest European railway office in any major city in the U.S., or see a travel agent. If you haven't an address handy, then write to either **French National Railroads**, 610 Fifth Avenue, New York City 10020; 360 Post Street, San Francisco, California 94100; 11 East Adams Street, Chicago, Illinois 60603; or 9465 Wilshire Boulevard, Los Angeles, California 90212; the **Swiss Federal Railways**, 608 Fifth Avenue, New York City 10020; the **German Federal Railroad**, 630 Fifth Avenue, New York City 10020, or 104 South Michigan Avenue, Chicago, Illinois 60603; or the **Italian State Railways,** 500 Fifth Avenue, New York City 10036.

TRAIN HINTS: Finally, a few general railroad rules: First, never discard your train ticket after it has been marked or punched by the conductor. Many European railroad stations require that you later present your ticket in order to leave the station platform at your destination. . . . On an overnight trip, you'd do well to inquire concerning the availability of Second Class "couchettes." These are compartments equipped with six lightly padded ledges along the wall, on which you can stretch out full-length to sleep. They would horrify Mr. Pullman, but they're dirt cheap and a God-send to persons who can't sleep sitting up. . . . To vary the routine of a long Second Class trip, simply walk into the dining car and order a beer. You'll be able to sit there, in a cushioned chair, for hours; for in Europe, no one would dream of asking you to move on. . . . On an overnight trip, be sure to purchase a bottle of mineral water or soda before boarding the train. Rarely does a European train carry a drinking water fountain or spout, and the dining car may be closed. As you'll soon discover, the experienced European traveler comes loaded with hampers of food and drink, and munches away throughout the trip. . . . In nearly every major European city, an English-speaking railway information office can provide you with additional data on schedules, prices and policies. Phone numbers are as follows, in: London (834-2345); Paris (261-5050); Brussels (523-8134); Amsterdam (255-5151); Copenhagen (1417-01); Stockholm (225-060); Oslo (421-919); Munich (412-04-05); Vienna (1734) (Westbahnhof); Vienna (1735) (Südbahnhof); Rome (463-941); Nice (616-165); Zurich (211-5010); Madrid (733-3000); Athens (821-3882).

READERS' TRAIN SUGGESTIONS: "The most direct crossing from England to the continent is via BritRail. Harwich to Hook of Holland takes 6 to 8 hours, and there are two crossings daily. Cost from London: $52.45, first class, $40.02 second class, while overnight berths are $7.40 to $42.10 (de-luxe cabin)" (John O. Wall, Palo Alto, California). . . . "Here's a scenic and inexpensive way for Eurailpass holders to leave Vienna. They are entitled to a free steamer ride from Vienna to Passau, and can stay on the boat overnight for as little as 364 schillings. The boat departs at 8 a.m. and arrives in Passau 1:15 p.m. the following day." (Mr. & Mrs. Robert Clever, Chambersburg, Pennsylvania). . . . "A hint for rail travelers is to travel by night to save a night's lodging and arrive early enough to find plenty of vacant rooms upon your arrival (especially in Scandinavia)" (Robert Hults, New York, New York). . . . "Readers should be aware that it is possible to reserve seats on second class trains. The cost is less than $1 and buys some important advantages. First, of course, is the fact that one can arrive at the station at the last minute and have a definite place to seat himself—the alternative being to arrive an hour (sometimes) ahead of time and search for a seat. Secondly, from what I have observed, there is no guarantee that you'll have a seat if you haven't reserved one. Anyone who has spent the night in the corridor of one of these trains will certainly appreciate what it means to have a seat. The seating situation is most acute during July and August and on weekend travel" (Leonard I. Krauss, Union, New Jersey).

SCHEDULES: In order to plan your European trip, you'll now need a timetable of the major European expresses. That data follows on the next several pages. It requires some explanation.

The schedules are broken down to show the trains which depart from major European cities on your tour. With very few exceptions, only the major international expresses are listed—the fast, crack trains. But not every international express is here, because many of these famous trains have only First Class accommodations. You can be sure that if a train is mentioned in *Europe on $15 a Day*, it has Second Class seats.

The schedules given are those that will be in effect for the period between June 1 and September 27, 1980. But don't hesitate to use this book even at a later date. The departure and arrival times of the major international expresses rarely change—and if they do, they change by only a few minutes. Only the possible introduction of summer daylight savings time in Germany, Austria or Switzerland—a matter that will actually be voted on in Switzerland, in February of 1980—could change certain of these arrival or departure times, in those countries, by exactly one hour! Check.

Unless otherwise stated, these trains make their runs every day of the week and in every season. The abbreviation "lv" means "leaves"; the abbreviation "ar" indicates a train's arrival time. Usually, we'll give the train's departure time from all of the cities in the country from which it sets out, and provide its arrival time in the various cities of the countries to which it goes. Thus, the schedule of the Orient Express—"lv Paris 11:35 p.m.; lv Strasbourg 5:30 a.m.; ar Stuttgart 6:51 a.m.; ar Munich 9:33 a.m.; ar Salzburg 11:27 a.m.; ar Vienna 3:25 p.m."—indicates that the Orient Express leaves Paris at 11:35 p.m. daily, goes to Strasbourg, from which it then departs at 5:30 a.m.; arrives in Stuttgart at 6:51 a.m., in Munich at 9:33 a.m., in Salzburg at 11:27 a.m., and finally pulls into Vienna at 3:25 p.m.

We start with the trains leaving from London.

TRAINS LEAVING LONDON

SIMPLON-ORIENT EXPRESS: London-Paris-Lausanne-Milan-Venice-Belgrade
Lv London (Victoria Station): 10:30 a.m.; ar Paris 6:27 p.m.; lv Lausanne 0:47 a.m.; ar Milan 5:34 a.m.; ar Venice 8:40 a.m.; ar Trieste 11:04 a.m.; ar Belgrade 10:00 p.m. Note: only passengers for Milan and beyond are permitted on this train.

AUSTRIA EXPRESS: London-Brussels-Munich-Salzburg-Belgrade
Lv London (Victoria Station) at 10:44 a.m.; lv Ostend 7:50 p.m.; lv Brussels 9:10 p.m.; ar Cologne 11:05 p.m.; lv Cologne 11:23 p.m.; ar Munich 7:28 a.m.; lv Munich 8:20 a.m.; lv Salzburg 10:09 a.m.; ar Ljubljana 3:10 p.m.; ar Zagreb 5:36 p.m.; ar Belgrade 10:54 p.m.

London-Paris: Trains from Victoria Station. Lv London 10:30 a.m.; ar Paris 6:27 p.m.; lv London 11 a.m.; ar Paris 7:14 p.m.; lv London 2 p.m.; ar Paris 10:30 p.m. Throughout the year, an additional train (for which reservations are required) leaves Victoria Station in London at 9:25 p.m., arrives Paris at 8:42 a.m.

London-Amsterdam: Your best train for this trip leaves London (Liverpool Street Station) at 7:40 p.m.; arrives Amsterdam at 10 a.m. A second train departs the same station at 8:32 a.m., arrives Amsterdam at 8 p.m. (June 22-August 26 only).

London-Brussels: Train leaves London (Victoria Station) at 10:44 a.m., arrives Brussels (Midi Station) at 7:52 p.m. Summer of 1979: two additional trains will leave Victoria Station at 8:32 a.m. and 11 p.m., arriving Brussels at 11:25 p.m. and 11:10 a.m., respectively.

London-Copenhagen: Lv London (Liverpool Street Station), summers only, daily at 3:32 p.m.; lv Harwich 5:30 p.m.; ar Esbjerg at 12:30 p.m. the next day; ar Copenhagen 6:17 p.m.

London-Cologne-Munich: Lv London (Victoria Station) 10:44 a.m., ar Cologne 11:05 p.m.; ar Munich 7:14 a.m.

London-Edinburgh: Lv London (King's Cross Station) daily except Sundays at 8:00 a.m., ar Edinburgh 12:56 p.m.; lv London at noon, ar Edinburgh 4:44 p.m.; lv London 11:15 p.m., ar Edinburgh 6:41 a.m.

TRAINS LEAVING PARIS

SIMPLON EXPRESS: Paris-Lausanne-Milan-Venice-Trieste
Lv Paris (Gare de Lyon) 8:03 p.m.; ar Lausanne 12:44 a.m.; ar Milan 5:34 a.m.; ar Venice 8:38 a.m.; ar Trieste 11:04 a.m. Takes passengers only for stations beyond Milan.

ORIENT EXPRESS: Paris-Munich-Vienna
Lv Paris (Gare de l'Est) 11:35 p.m.; lv Strasbourg 5:30 a.m.; ar Stuttgart 6:51 a.m.; ar Munich 9:33 a.m.; ar Salzburg 11:27 a.m.; ar Vienna 3:25 p.m.

NAPOLI EXPRESS: Paris-Torino-Genoa-Pisa-Rome-Naples
Lv Paris (Gare de Lyon), 8:39 p.m.; lv Aix-les-Bains 2:03 a.m.; ar Modane 3:46 a.m.; ar Torino 5:37 a.m.; ar Genoa 7:48 a.m.; ar Pisa 10:14 a.m.; ar Rome 1:40 p.m.; ar Naples 4:05 p.m.

THE NORD EXPRESS: Paris-Hamburg-Copenhagen
Lv Paris (Gare du Nord) 6:10 p.m.; lv Liège 9:56 p.m.; ar Cologne 10:22 p.m.; ar Hamburg 3:09 a.m.; ar Puttgarden 5:08 a.m.; ar Copenhagen 8:59 a.m.

THE COPENHAGEN EXPRESS: Paris-Cologne-Hamburg-Copenhagen
Lv Paris (Gare du Nord) 10:37 p.m.; ar Cologne 3:15 a.m.; ar Bremen 7:03 a.m.; ar Hamburg 8:21 a.m.; ar Puttgarden 10:22 a.m.; ar Copenhagen 2:09 p.m.

Paris-Frankfurt: Trains depart from the Gare de l'Est: Lv Paris 8 a.m., ar Frankfurt 1:31 p.m.; lv Paris 2:03 p.m., ar Frankfurt 8:22 p.m.; lv Paris 11:20 p.m., ar Frankfurt 7:42 a.m.; lv Paris (summers only) 11:43 p.m., ar Frankfurt 8:31 a.m.

Paris-Brussels-Amsterdam: All trains leave from the Gare du Nord. Lv Paris 7:50 a.m.; ar Brussels 10:50 a.m.; ar Antwerp 11:44 a.m.; ar Rotterdam 1:02 p.m.; ar The Hague 1:22 p.m.; ar Amsterdam 2:14 p.m.
Lv Paris 10:30 a.m.; ar Brussels 1.14 p.m.; ar Antwerp 2:06 p.m.; ar Rotterdam 3:19 p.m.; ar The Hague 3:39 p.m.; ar Amsterdam 4:30 p.m.
Lv Paris 3:19 p.m.; ar Brussels 6:17 p.m.; ar Antwerp 7:09 p.m.; ar Rotterdam 8:23 p.m.; ar The Hague 8:45 p.m.; ar Amsterdam 9:30 p.m.

Paris-London: The following trains leave from the Gare du Nord: Lv Paris 8:08 a.m.; lv Calais 11:50 a.m.; ar London 2:48 p.m. Lv Paris 10:24 a.m.; lv Boulogne 1:50 p.m.; ar Folkestone 2:40 p.m.; ar London 4:42 p.m. Lv Paris 1:30 p.m.; ar London 7:48 p.m.
Lv Paris 9:25 p.m.; lv Dunkerque 2:00 a.m.; ar Dover 3:20 a.m.; ar London 7:45 a.m.

Paris-Barcelona: Trains leave Austerlitz Station. Lv Paris 9:06 p.m.; lv Toulouse 4:54 a.m.; ar Port-Bou 9:15 a.m.; ar Barcelona 11:56 p.m. Lv Paris 9:38 a.m.; lv Toulouse 5:17 p.m.; ar Port-Bou 8:58 p.m.; ar Barcelona 11:58 p.m.

Paris-Madrid: Lv Paris (Austerlitz Station) 6:02 p.m.; lv Bordeaux 10:18 p.m.; lv Irun 1:48 a.m.; ar San Sebastian 2:04 a.m.; ar Burgos 5:24 a.m.; ar Madrid 9 a.m. Alternatively, lv Paris (Austerlitz Station) 10:49 p.m.; lv Bordeaux 4:24 a.m.; lv Biarritz 7:13 a.m.; lv Irun 9:15 a.m.; ar San Sebastian 9:32 a.m.; ar Burgos 2:02 p.m.; ar Madrid 6:15 p.m.

Paris-Luxembourg: Trains leave from the Gare de l'Est: Lv Paris at 8:00 a.m., 10:45 a.m. and 6:49 p.m., arrive Luxembourg at 12:56 a.m., 2:31 p.m., and 10:44 p.m. respectively.

Paris-Rome: Trains leave from the Gare de Lyon. Lv Paris 8:32 a.m.; ar Lausanne 12:49 p.m.; ar Montreux 1:11 p.m.; ar Brig 2:29 p.m.; ar Milan 6:10 p.m.; change in Milan for train departing 7:40 p.m.; ar Florence 11:50 p.m.; ar Rome 3:08 a.m.
   Lv Paris 7:22 p.m.; ar Lausanne 11:57 p.m.; ar Brig 1:31 a.m.; ar Milan 4:53 a.m.; change in Milan, lv Milan 8:25 a.m.; ar Florence 11:50 a.m.; ar Rome 3:10 p.m.
   Lv Paris 10:00 p.m.; ar Lausanne 2:47 a.m.; ar Brig 4:16 a.m.; ar Milan 8:15 a.m.; ar Bologna 10:26 a.m.; ar Florence 11:50 p.m.; ar Rome 3:10 p.m.
   Lv Paris 11:53 p.m.; ar Lausanne 7:00 a.m.; ar Milan 12:50 p.m.; ar Bologna 3:55 p.m.; ar Florence 5:20 p.m.; ar Rome 8:52 p.m.

Paris-Nice: The famous "Train Bleu" (first class sleepers only) lvs Paris (Gare de Lyon) 8:45 p.m.; lv Cannes 7:46 a.m.; lv Nice 8:37 a.m.; ar Monaco 8:54 a.m.
   The normal Paris-Nice train (both 1st and 2nd class coaches) lvs Paris 9:55 a.m.; lv Lyon 2:08 p.m.; lv Marseille 5:14 p.m.; lv Cannes 7:30 p.m.; ar Nice 8:13 p.m. Still another train leaves Paris at 7:45 a.m.; arrives Nice around 6:25 p.m. A final train leaves from the Gare du Nord at 10:57 p.m., arrives Nice 10:43 a.m.

Paris-Geneva: Lv Paris (Gare de Lyon) 11:05 p.m.; lv Dijon 2:19 a.m.; ar Geneva 6:10 a.m. Lv Paris (summer only) 8:23 a.m.; ar Geneva 2:07 p.m.

Paris-Zurich: Lv Paris (Gare de l'Est) 11:10 p.m.; ar Basel 6:18 a.m.; ar Zurich 7:30 a.m.
   Lv Paris (Gare de l'Est) 12:22 p.m.; ar Basel 4:10 p.m.; change in Basel for train leaving at 6 p.m.; ar Zurich 7:14 p.m. Another train leaves Paris at 9:07 a.m., arrives Zurich 3:10 p.m.

TRAINS LEAVING BRUSSELS

OSTEND-VIENNA EXPRESS: Brussels-Cologne-Frankfurt-Vienna
   Lv Brussels (Nord Station) 7:35 p.m.; lv Liège 8:45 p.m.; lv Aachen 8:44 p.m.; ar Cologne 9:24 p.m.; ar Bonn 9:57 p.m.; ar Frankfurt 11:58 a.m.; ar Passau 5:48 a.m.; ar Vienna 9:45 a.m.

Brussels-London: Trains leave from the Midi Station. Lv Brussels 8 a.m.; ar London 3:35 p.m.; lv Brussels 1 p.m.; ar London 8:17 p.m.; lv Brussels (summer only) 12:07 a.m.; ar London 7:55 a.m.

Brussels-Rotterdam-Amsterdam: Trains leave from Nord Station. Lv Brussels 11:13 a.m.; lv Antwerp 11:46 a.m.; ar Rotterdam 1:02 p.m.; ar The Hague 1:22 p.m.; ar Amsterdam 2:12 p.m.
   Lv Brussels 1:09 p.m.; lv Antwerp 1:51 p.m.; ar Roosendaal 2:20 p.m.; ar Rotterdam 3:01 p.m.; ar The Hague 3:19 p.m.; ar Amsterdam 4:05 p.m.
   Lv Brussels 5:02 p.m. (weekdays only); lv Antwerp 5:52 p.m.; ar Roosendaal 6:20 p.m.; ar Rotterdam 7:01 p.m.; ar The Hague 7:19 p.m.; ar Amsterdam 8:05 p.m.

Brussels-Paris: Trains leave from the Midi Station. Lv Brussels 8:15 a.m.; ar Paris 11:17 a.m.; lv Brussels 11:03 a.m.; ar Paris 1:51 p.m.; lv Brussels 2:07 p.m.; ar Paris 4:58 p.m.; lv Brussels 7:07 p.m.; ar Paris 10 p.m.

Brussels-Luxembourg: Lv Brussels (Gare du Nord) 7:28 a.m.; ar Luxembourg 10:02 a.m.; lv Brussels 10:50 a.m.; ar Luxembourg 1:52 p.m.; lv Brussels 1:50 p.m.; ar Luxembourg 5:01 p.m.; lv Brussels (weekdays only) 4:26 p.m.; ar Luxembourg 7:03 p.m.; lv Brussels 7:30 p.m.; ar Luxembourg 10:02 p.m.

TRAINS LEAVING AMSTERDAM

HOLLAND-ITALY EXPRESS: Amsterdam-Milan-Florence-Rome
   Lv Amsterdam 9:25 p.m.; lv Utrecht 9:58 p.m.; ar Cologne 12:06 a.m.; ar Basel 5:55

a.m.; ar Lucerne 7:51 a.m.; ar Milan 1:10 p.m.; ar Florence 5:20 p.m.; ar Rome 8:43 p.m.

THE LORELEY EXPRESS: Amsterdam-Cologne-Basel
Lv Amsterdam 9:18 a.m.; ar Cologne 11:30 a.m.; ar Mainz 1:41 p.m.; ar Basel 5:05 p.m.

HOLLAND-SCANDINAVIA EXPRESS: Amsterdam-Copenhagen-Stockholm
Lv Amsterdam 9:01 a.m.; ar Hamburg 2:07 p.m.; ar Puttgarden 4:04 p.m.; ar Copenhagen 8:02 p.m.; ar Stockholm 7:44 a.m.

NORTH-WEST EXPRESS: Amsterdam-Hamburg-Copenhagen-Stockholm
Lv Amsterdam 9:01 p.m.; ar Hamburg 2:14 a.m.; ar Puttgarden 4:24 a.m.; ar Copenhagen 8:12 a.m.; ar Helsingborg 10:35 a.m.; ar Stockholm 5:44 p.m.

HOLLAND-VIENNA EXPRESS: Amsterdam-Cologne-Frankfurt-Nuremberg-Vienna
Lv Amsterdam 3:51 p.m.; ar Cologne 6:17 p.m.; ar Frankfurt 8:48 p.m.; ar Nuremberg 11:46 p.m.; ar. Vienna 5:40 a.m.

Amsterdam-Munich: Lv Amsterdam 9:18 a.m.; ar Cologne 11:30 a.m.; ar Ulm 4:54 p.m.; ar Munich 6:10 p.m.

Amsterdam-London: Lv Amsterdam 10:30 a.m.; ar London 7:48 p.m.; lv Amsterdam 9:16 p.m.; ar London 9:14 a.m.

Amsterdam-Brussels-Paris: Lv Amsterdam 7:50 a.m.; ar Antwerp 10:11 a.m.; ar Brussels 10:44 a.m.; ar Paris 1:51 p.m.
Lv Amsterdam 10:55 a.m.; ar Antwerp 1:15 p.m.; ar Brussels 1:48 p.m.; ar Paris 4:58 p.m.
Lv Amsterdam 3:55 p.m.; ar Antwerp 6:15 p.m.; ar Brussels 6:48 p.m.; ar Paris 10 p.m.

TRAINS LEAVING COPENHAGEN

ALPEN-EXPRESS: Copenhagen-Munich-Florence-Rome
Lv Copenhagen 3:55 p.m.; lv Puttgarden 7:55 p.m.; ar Hamburg 9:36 p.m.; lv Hanover 12:14 a.m.; ar Munich 7:20 a.m.; ar Innsbruck 9:31 a.m.; ar Verona 2:49 p.m.; ar Bologna 4:24 p.m.; ar Florence 5:45 p.m.; ar Rome 9:05 p.m.

SCANDINAVIA-PARIS EXPRESS: Copenhagen-Hamburg-Cologne-Paris
Lv Copenhagen 9:10 p.m.; ar Hamburg 3 a.m.; ar Cologne 8:16 a.m.; ar Aachen 9:02 a.m.; ar Liège 11:09 a.m.; ar Paris 3:42 p.m.

THE NORTH EXPRESS: Copenhagen-Hamburg-Cologne-Paris
Lv Copenhagen 4:55 p.m.; ar Hamburg 10:24 p.m.; ar Cologne 3:17 a.m.; ar Paris 9:42 a.m.

NORTH-WEST EXPRESS: Copenhagen-Hamburg-Amsterdam-London
Lv Copenhagen 10:15 p.m.; lv Puttgarden 2:05 a.m.; ar Hamburg 3:50 a.m.; ar Amersfoort 10:03 a.m.; ar Rotterdam 11:18 a.m.; ar Hook of Holland 11:37 a.m.; ar London 8:07 p.m.

SCANDINAVIA-HOLLAND EXPRESS: Copenhagen-Hamburg-Bremen-Amsterdam
Lv Copenhagen 9:25 a.m.; lv Puttgarden 1:12 p.m.; ar Hamburg 2:59 p.m.; lv Bremen 4:26 p.m.; ar Amsterdam 10:10 p.m.

Copenhagen-Stockholm: Lv Copenhagen 7:34 a.m.; ar Stockholm 3:44 p.m.

Copenhagen-Vienna: Lv Copenhagen 1:20 p.m.; ar Hamburg 6:26 p.m.; ar Passau 5:19 a.m.; ar Vienna 9:10 a.m. Lv Copenhagen 11:15 p.m.; lv Puttgarden 3:30 a.m.; ar Wurzburg 11:48 a.m.; ar Passau 3:23 p.m.; ar Vienna 7:10 p.m.

TRAINS LEAVING STOCKHOLM

Stockholm-Oslo: Lv Stockholm daily except Sunday at 8:08 a.m.; ar Oslo 2:35 p.m.; lv Stockholm daily except Saturday at 4 p.m.; ar Oslo 9:57 p.m.; lv Stockholm daily throughout the year at 11:05 p.m.; ar Oslo 8:05 a.m.

Stockholm-Copenhagen: Lv Stockholm (weekdays only) 6:22 a.m.; ar Copenhagen 2:36 p.m.; lv Stockholm 12:22 p.m. (except June, July and August when departure is at 1:22 p.m.); ar Copenhagen 8:36 p.m. (9:51 p.m. in June, July, August); lv Stockholm 9:13 p.m.; ar Copenhagen 6:36 a.m.; lv Stockholm 11:00 p.m. (summer only); ar Copenhagen 8:21 a.m.

TRAINS LEAVING OSLO

Oslo-Copenhagen: Lv Oslo 8 a.m.; ar Copenhagen 5:36 p.m.; lv Oslo (summer only) 6:00 p.m.; ar Copenhagen 6:36 a.m.; lv Oslo 11 p.m.; ar Copenhagen 8:53 a.m. In winter each of these trains departs approximately an hour earlier, arrives in Copenhagen at the same time listed above.

Oslo-Stockholm: Lv Oslo (weekdays only) 9:10 a.m.; ar Stockholm 3:50 p.m.; lv Oslo 4 p.m.; ar Stockholm 10:50 p.m.; lv Oslo 11:05 p.m.; ar Stockholm 7:35 a.m. Winter departures are an hour or so earlier than those stated above.

TRAINS LEAVING MUNICH

THE ISAR-RHONE EXPRESS: Munich-Zurich-Berne-Geneva
Lv Munich 8 a.m.; lv Lindau 10:51 a.m.; ar St. Margarethen 11:18 a.m.; ar Zurich 12:58 p.m.; ar Berne 2:33 p.m.; ar Lausanne 3:43 p.m.; ar Geneva 4:18 p.m.

THE ALPEN EXPRESS (Southbound): Munich-Florence-Rome
Lv Munich 7:40 a.m.; lv Innsbruck 9:37 a.m.; ar Bologna 4:24 p.m.; ar Florence 5:45 p.m.; ar Rome 9:05 p.m.

THE ITALICUS: Munich-Innsbruck-Verona-Florence-Rome
Lv Munich 6:50 p.m.; lv Innsbruck 9:20 p.m.; ar Verona 2:56 a.m.; ar Florence 6:23 a.m.; ar Rome 10:22 a.m.

THE BRENNER EXPRESS: Munich-Florence-Rome
Lv Munich 11:15 p.m.; ar Bolzano 5:02 a.m.; ar Verona 6:54 a.m.; ar Bologna 8:40 a.m.; ar Florence 10:15 a.m.; ar Rome 1:45 p.m. At Verona, you can change to trains departing within the hour for Venice or for Nice.

THE ALPEN EXPRESS (Northbound): Munich-Nuremberg-Wurzburg-Copenhagen
Lv Munich 10:35 p.m.; lv Nuremberg 1 a.m.; lv Wurzburg 2:08 a.m.; ar Hamburg 8:09 a.m.; ar Puttgarden 10:13 a.m.; ar Copenhagen 2:09 p.m.

GERMANY-SWITZERLAND: Munich-Zurich-Berne-Geneva
Lv Munich 1:50 p.m.; lv Lindau 4:46 p.m.; ar St. Margarethen 5:13 p.m.; ar Zurich 7:04 p.m.; ar Berne 8:33 p.m.; ar Lausanne 9:43 p.m.; ar Geneva 10:25 p.m.

THE RHEIN EXPRESS: Munich-Stuttgart-Cologne-Rotterdam-London
Lv Munich 11:25 a.m.; lv Stuttgart 2:12 p.m.; lv Heidelberg 3:32 p.m.; lv Bonn 6:06 p.m.; lv Cologne 6:42 p.m.; ar Rotterdam 11:04 p.m.; ar London 9:14 a.m.

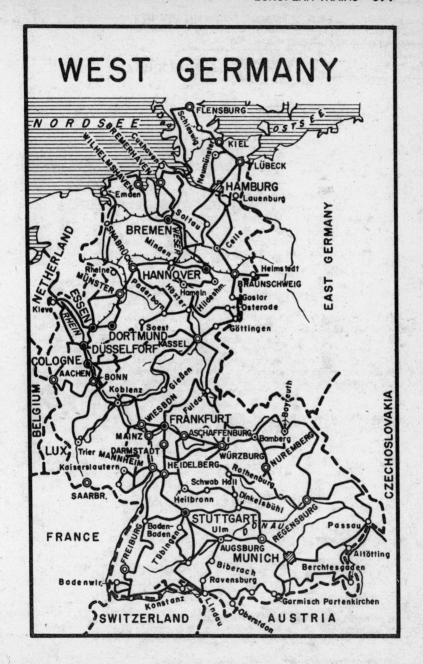

WEST GERMANY

TRAINS LEAVING VIENNA

VIENNA-OSTEND EXPRESS: Vienna-Frankfurt-Brussels-London
Lv Vienna (Westbahnhof) 8:45 p.m.; ar Passau 12:43 a.m.; ar Frankfurt 6:31 a.m.; ar Cologne 9:22 a.m.; ar Aachen 10:23 a.m.; ar Liège 12:15 a.m.; ar Brussels 1:22 p.m.; ar Ostend 2:55 p.m.; ar London 8:17 p.m.

THE ORIENT EXPRESS: Vienna-Munich-Paris
Lv Vienna (Westbahnhof) 3 p.m.; lv Salzburg 6:52 p.m.; ar Munich 8:35 p.m.; ar Strasbourg 2:50 a.m.; ar Paris 7:35 a.m.

DONAU-KURIER EXPRESS: Vienna-Nuremberg-Hamburg-Copenhagen
Lv Vienna (Westbahnhof) 9:05 a.m.; lv Passau 12:58 p.m.; lv Nuremberg 3:14 p.m.; ar Hamburg 10:17 p.m.; ar Copenhagen 6:45 a.m.

ARLBERG EXPRESS: Vienna-Innsbruck-Zurich-Paris
Lv Vienna 9:45 a.m.; lv Salzburg 1:35 p.m.; lv Innsbruck 5:39 p.m.; lv Zurich 10:05 p.m.; ar Basel 11:15 p.m.; ar Paris 8:22 a.m.

Vienna-Paris: Though the Orient and Arlberg Expresses offer your best bet for this trip, there are several other trains making the same journey at different times. They all depart from the Westbahnhof. For instance, lv Vienna 8:20 a.m.; lv Salzburg 12:04 p.m.; ar Munich 1:40 p.m.; lv Munich 1:58 p.m.; ar Paris 11:55 p.m.
Lv Vienna 8:10 p.m.; lv Salzburg 11:45 p.m.; lv Innsbruck 3:38 a.m.; ar Zurich 8:34 a.m.; ar Paris 4:30 p.m. (except Saturdays).

Vienna-Venice: The Adria Express (departing at 8:35 p.m., arriving in Venice at 8:10 a.m.) is your best train for this trip, but there are three other trains which leave Vienna daily for Venice. All depart from the Südbahnhof. For instance, lv Vienna at 8 a.m.; ar Udine 4:07 p.m.; ar Venice 5:57 p.m. As a further alternative, you can, if you want, backtrack to Innsbruck (an exciting ride through the breathtaking scenery of the Austrian Alps), and then take any number of trains which make the trip from Innsbruck to Venice. Trains for Innsbruck leave the Westbahnhof.

Vienna-Copenhagen: Lv Vienna (Westbahnhof), summers only, 9:20 p.m.; lv Passau 1:05 a.m.; ar Puttgarden 1:11 p.m.; ar Copenhagen 4:29 p.m.; or, lv Vienna 9:05 a.m.; ar Hamburg 10:17 p.m.; ar Copenhagen 6:45 a.m.

Vienna-Belgrade: Lv Vienna (Südbahnhof) at 8:05 a.m.; lv Graz 10:58 a.m.; change in Zidani; ar Zagreb 5:36 p.m.; ar Belgrade 10:54 p.m.; lv Vienna 10:50 p.m.; ar Zagreb 7:00 a.m.; ar Belgrade 1:55 p.m.

TRAINS LEAVING ROME

THE PALATINE EXPRESS: Rome-Torino-Paris
Lv Rome 6:35 p.m.; lv Pisa 9:47 p.m.; lv Torino 1:37 a.m.; ar Paris 10:06 a.m.

ITALY-HOLLAND EXPRESS: Rome-Cologne-Amsterdam
Lv Rome 10:20 a.m.; lv Florence 2:09 p.m.; lv Milan 6:45 p.m.; lv Lucerne 10:26 p.m.; ar Basel 11:34 p.m.; ar Cologne 5:50 a.m.; ar Utrecht 10:04 a.m.; ar Amsterdam 10:36 a.m.

THE BRENNER EXPRESS: Rome-Florence-Innsbruck-Munich
Lv Rome 6:00 p.m.; lv Florence 9:06 p.m.; lv Bologna 11:02 p.m.; lv Verona 12:26 a.m.; ar Innsbruck 4:26 a.m.; ar Kufstein 5:21 a.m.; ar Munich 6:50 a.m.

THE SIMPLON EXPRESS: Rome-Florence-Venice-Trieste-Belgrade
Lv Rome 12:40 a.m.; lv Florence 4:07 a.m.; lv Venice 9 a.m.; lv Trieste 11:22 a.m.; ar Ljubljana 1:52 p.m.; ar Zagreb 4:25 p.m.; ar Belgrade 10 p.m.

THE ALPEN EXPRESS: Rome-Florence-Munich-Hamburg-Copenhagen
Lv Rome 9:40 a.m.; lv Florence 1:28 p.m.; lv Bologna 2:54 p.m.; lv Verona 4:14 p.m.;
lv Innsbruck 7:56 p.m.; ar Munich 10:05 p.m.; lv Hanover 6:14 a.m.; ar Hamburg 8:09
a.m.; ar Copenhagen 2:09 p.m.

LORELEY EXPRESS: Rome-Florence-Milan-Lucerne-Basel-Cologne-Rotterdam-Amsterdam
Lv Rome 10:18 p.m.; lv Florence 2:08 a.m.; lv Milan 7:05 a.m.; lv Lucerne 11:04
a.m.; lv Basel 1 p.m.; ar Cologne 6:36 p.m.; ar Rotterdam 11:21 p.m.; ar Amsterdam
11:03 p.m.

Rome-Florence: The following is only a partial listing of the many departures available to
you: lv Rome 9:40 a.m., ar Florence 1:18 a.m.; lv Rome 10:20 a.m.; ar Florence 2:26 p.m.;
lv Rome 2:10 p.m., ar Florence 5:09 p.m.; lv Rome 4:03 p.m., ar Florence 7:10 p.m.; lv
Rome (first class only) 5:30 p.m., ar Florence 8:13 p.m.

Rome-Nice: Lv Rome 10:45 a.m.; lv Genoa 5:48 p.m.; lv Ventimiglia 9 p.m.; lv Monaco
9:23 p.m.; ar Nice 9:36 p.m. Lv Rome 10:58 p.m.; lv Genoa 6 a.m.; lv Monaco 9:42 a.m.;
ar Nice 9:57 a.m. At other times, take any train that goes to Ventimiglia or San Remo,
where you can make connections for Nice.

Rome-Switzerland: Lv Rome 10:18 p.m.; lv Florence 2:08 a.m.; lv Milan 6:54 a.m.; ar Brig
8:35 a.m.; ar Montreux 10:10 a.m.; ar Lausanne 10:31 a.m.; ar Geneva 11:10 a.m.
Lv Rome 6:25 a.m.; lv Florence 10:22 a.m.; lv Milan 4:10 p.m.; ar Brig 5:51 p.m.;
ar Montreux 7:23 p.m.; ar Lausanne 7:46 p.m.; ar Geneva 8:29 p.m. On this trip, a change
of trains must be made in Milan.

TRAINS LEAVING NICE

PARIS-COTE D'AZUR EXPRESS: Nice-Paris-Brussels-Amsterdam
Lv Nice 8:55 p.m.; lv Cannes 9:33 p.m.; ar Paris (Gare de Lyon) 8:27 a.m.; lv Paris
(Gare du Nord) 10:30 a.m.; ar Brussels 1:14 p.m.; ar Rotterdam 3:19 p.m.; ar The Hague
3:39 p.m.; ar Amsterdam 4:30 p.m.

Nice-Rome: Lv Nice 8:19 a.m.; ar Ventimiglia 8:55 a.m.; ar Genoa 12:32 p.m.; ar Pisa 3:39
p.m.; ar Rome 7:50 p.m.
Lv Nice 8:28 p.m.; lv Monaco 8:45 p.m.; ar Ventimiglia 9:05 p.m.; ar Genoa 12:05
a.m.; ar Pisa 3:15 a.m.; ar Rome 7:32 a.m.

Nice-Zurich: Lv Nice 8:26 p.m.; lv Cannes 9:09 p.m.; lv Marseilles 11:59 p.m.; lv Avignon
1:24 a.m.; ar Geneva 6:50 a.m.; ar Lausanne 8:20 a.m.; ar Berne 9:29 a.m.; ar Zurich 10:55
a.m.

TRAINS LEAVING ZURICH

ARLBERG EXPRESS: Zurich-Innsbruck-Salzburg-Vienna
Lv Zurich 7:30 a.m.; lv Buchs 9:10 a.m.; ar Innsbruck 12:05 p.m.; ar Salzburg 4 p.m.;
ar Vienna 7:45 p.m.

KOMET EXPRESS: Zurich-Basel-Hanover-Copenhagen
Lv Zurich 9:13 p.m.; lv Basel 10:54 p.m.; lv Hanover 6:10 a.m.; ar Puttgarden 10:13
a.m.; ar Copenhagen 2:09 p.m.

BAVARIA EXPRESS: Zurich-Munich
Lv Zurich 7:02 a.m.; ar St. Margarethen 8:27 a.m.; ar Lindau 8:52 a.m.; ar Munich
11:26 a.m.

Zurich-Rome: Lv Zurich 11:18 a.m.; lv Lugano 2:20 p.m.; ar Milan 5:02 p.m.; ar Florence
9:40 p.m.; ar Rome 1:04 p.m.
Lv Zurich 4:14 p.m.; ar Milan 9:50 p.m.; ar Florence 2:36 a.m.; ar Rome 6:14 a.m.

Zurich-Paris: Lv Zurich 8:34 a.m.; ar Basel 9:42 a.m.; ar Paris 4:30 p.m. Lv Zurich 10:05 p.m.; ar Basel 11:15 p.m.; ar Paris 8:22 a.m.

Zurich-Nice: Lv Zurich 6:10 p.m.; lv Berne 7:36 p.m.; lv Geneva 9:40 p.m.; ar Grenoble 1:35 a.m.; ar Avignon 4:35 a.m.; ar Marseille 5:54 a.m.; ar Cannes 8:33 a.m.; ar Nice 9:09 a.m.

TRAINS LEAVING MADRID

IBERIA EXPRESS: Madrid-Biarritz-Bordeaux-Paris
Lv Madrid (Chamartin) 12:40 p.m.; lv Burgos 4:37 p.m.; lv San Sebastian 8:57 p.m.; lv Hendaye 11:02 p.m.; ar Biarritz 11:31 p.m.; ar Bordeaux 1:42 a.m.; ar Paris (Austerlitz Station) 7:52 a.m.; an alternate train leaves Madrid (Chamartin) at 10:05 p.m., arrives Paris 4:19 p.m.

HISPANIA EXPRESS: Madrid-Barcelona-Lyon-Geneva-Berne-Zurich
Lv Madrid (Chamartin Station) 10:25 a.m.; ar Barcelona 7:30 p.m.; lv Barcelona 8 p.m.; lv Cerbere 11:08 p.m.; ar Lyon 5:56 a.m.; ar Geneva 7:30 a.m.; ar Lausanne 8:20 a.m.; ar Berne 9:29 a.m.; ar Zurich 10:55 a.m.

LUSITANIA EXPRESS: Madrid-Lisbon
Lv Madrid (Atocha) 11:15 p.m.; lv Valencia de Alc. 6:26 a.m.; lv Marvao 5:56 a.m.; ar Entroncamento 8:14 p.m.; ar Lisbon 9:45 a.m.; alternatively leave Madrid (Chamartin 9:35 a.m.; arrive Lisbon 6:50 p.m.

TRAINS LEAVING ATHENS

HELLAS EXPRESS: Athens-Belgrade-Salzburg-Munich
Lv Athens 8:30 p.m.; lv Thessaloniki 5:50 a.m.; ar Gevgelija 6:00 a.m.; ar Belgrade 5:00 p.m.; lv Zagreb 10:58 p.m.; ar Ljubljana 1:13 a.m.; ar Salzburg 7:57 a.m.; ar Munich 10:35 a.m.

ATHENS EXPRESS: Athens-Belgrade-Trieste-Venice-Milan
Lv Athens 10:50 p.m.; lv Thessaloniki 8 a.m.; ar Belgrade 7:40 p.m.; lv Ljubljana 3:54 a.m.; ar Trieste 8:55 a.m.; ar Venice 11:48 a.m.; ar Milan 6:35 p.m.

Next, the topic with which this book is mainly concerned: the dollars (and their foreign equivalents) from which you'll dole out fifteen dollars a day.

Chapter XXIV

MONEY RATES

The Cost of $15

THE SUBJECT of European currency was once enshrouded in a haze of black markets and mathematical formulas. By skillfully changing your dollars into foreign money at the right time, and in the right place, you could once increase your funds by as much as 30%.

In those days, every smart tourist carried hand-me-down lists of money-changers who performed this feat: a celebrated bartender in Paris, who gave you many more francs to the dollar; a bookseller in Barcelona, who offered half-again as many pesetas as you could obtain at a Spanish bank.

Those days, and those gentlemen, have—sad to relate—vanished with the increasing prosperity of Europe. Today, virtually every European currency is solid and stable—and it's the dollar that's in trouble! Excepting only the currencies of Turkey and Yugoslavia, there no longer exists any significant difference between the unofficial rates of exchange for all European currencies. You'll receive, for instance, almost as many francs for your dollar in Paris, as you will in New York or Switzerland. While, at certain periods of the year, a variance of 1% or so may creep into those rates, the difference just isn't worth the effort to obtain it.

We'll therefore eliminate any general discussion of money-changing from this chapter, and concentrate on bare essentials: the rates of exchange for the currencies of Western Europe, set forth in condensed, easy-to-use style:

AUSTRIA

The unit of Austrian currency is the Schilling, divided into 100 Groschen. Currently, one receives approximately 13.50 schillings for one dollar, and equivalencies are as follows:

Schillings	U.S. $	Schillings	U.S. $
1	.08	20	1.48
2	.15	25	1.85
5	.37	50	3.70
10	.74	100	7.40

BELGIUM

Basic unit is the Franc, of which you get nearly 30 for a dollar; the franc is further divided into 100 centimes.

Francs	U.S. $	Francs	U.S. $
1	.03	25	0.83
5	.17	50	1.67
10	.33	100	3.30

DENMARK

Kroner and ore are the units used. You'll receive approximately 5.25 kroner to the dollar, and 100 ore for each krone.

Ore	U.S. $	Kroner	U.S. $
1	.0019	1	.19
5	.0095	2	.38
10	.019	5	.95
25	.05	10	1.90
		50	9.52

FRANCE

Francs and Centimes are the units used; there are 100 centimes to a franc. Current rate is approximately 4.30 francs for one dollar, making each franc worth about 23¢.

Centimes	U.S. $	Francs	U.S. $
5	.01	1	.23
10	.02	2	.46
20	.05	5	1.16
80	.18	10	2.32
		40	9.30

GERMANY

The basic monetary unit in Germany is the Mark, which is further subdivided into 100 pfennigs. Current rate of exchange is approximately 1.90 marks to the dollar, which results in the following:

Pfennigs	U.S. $	Marks	U.S. $
1	.005	1	.53
5	.03	5	2.63
10	.05	10	5.26
50	.26	20	10.52

GREECE

Drachmas and leptas (but you'll rarely see a lepta). Approximately 36 drachmas to the dollar, and 100 leptas to each drachma.

Drachmas	U.S. $	Drachmas	U.S. $
1	.028	15	.42
5	.14	20	.56
10	.28	30	.83
		100	2.77

HOLLAND

Monetary unit is the Guilder, sometimes known as the florin or the Gulden. Each guilder is divided into 100 "cents." As of the time we wrote this year's chapter on Amsterdam, the guilder was exchanged at a rate of 2 to the dollar, which made each guilder worth approximately 50 U.S. cents.

Dutch Cents	U.S. $	Guilders	U.S. $
1	.005	1	.50
5	.02	5	2.50
10	.05	10	5.00
25	.12	20	10.00

ITALY

The unit of Italian currency is the Lira, spelled in the plural: lire. The exchange rate is 830 lire to the dollar, which makes each lira worth 0.12 U.S. cents.

Lire	U.S. $	Lire	U.S. $
50	.06	1000	1.20
100	.12	5000	6.02
500	.60	10000	12.04

NORWAY

Norway, like Denmark, uses Kroner and ore. You'll receive approximately 5.10 kroner for a dollar, and 100 ore for each krone.

Ore	U.S. $	Kroner	U.S. $
10	.019	1	.19
25	.049	5	.98
50	.098	10	1.96
		25	4.90
		50	9.80

PORTUGAL

The unit of currency is the Escudo; approximately 50 to a dollar.

Escudos	U.S. $	Escudos	U.S. $
1	.02	20	.40
5	.1	50	1.00
10	.20	100	2.00

SPAIN

Spain uses Pesetas and Centimos (100 centimos to a peseta). At a bank or other exchange point, you'll usually receive 66 pesetas for one U.S. dollar.

Pesetas	U.S. $	Pesetas	U.S. $
1	.015	20	.30
5	.075	50	.75
10	.15	100	1.51

SWEDEN

Sweden's basic money unit is the Krona, spelled Kronor in the plural. There are 100 ore per krona. You'll get 4.20 to a dollar.

Ore	U.S. $	Kronor	U.S. $
5	.012	1	.24
10	.024	2	.48
25	.06	5	1.19
50	.12	10	2.38

SWITZERLAND

The Swiss currency, strongest in the world, uses Francs and Centimes. Following successive devaluations of the U.S. dollar, travelers now receive only 1.70 francs to the dollar; and at that current rate of exchange, it's convenient to use 59¢ as the value of the franc.

Centimes	U.S. $	Francs	U.S. $
5	.03	1	.59
10	.06	5	2.94
20	.12	20	11.76
50	.29	50	29.41

UNITED KINGDOM
(England, Scotland, Wales and Northern Ireland)

Basic unit is the Pound, divided into 100 New Pence. The pound is now worth about $2.20.

Pence	U.S. $	Pounds	U.S. $
1	.022	1	2.20
5	.11	2	4.40
25	.55	5	11.00
50	1.10	10	22.00

AND FINALLY

To round off the list: Yugoslavia, having devalued its currency considerably, now gives 18 dinars for one U.S. dollar. Finland exchanges approximately 3.81 Finnish marks ("markka") for one dollar. In Turkey, the official rate is 24 pounds ("lira") to a dollar, but you can occasionally buy the same pounds for less in New York or Switzerland.

Chapter XXV

PACKING TO SAVE MONEY

By Hope Arthur*

SO FAR, the pages of *Europe on $15 a Day* have all been devoted to the inside Europe portion of your trip. I've now been asked to deal with the "home front"—the packing and preparations before you leave. And that's no minor topic. It may be hard to believe that the contents of a suitcase can affect your travel costs, but they do, vitally. The tourist who carries heavy luggage and a complete wardrobe to Europe spends a great deal of money unnecessarily. Here's why:

THE BURDENS OF BAGGAGE: A light suitcase means freedom. To emerge from a train or plane in Europe with bundles and boxes in every hand, means porters, means taxicabs, means that the first hotel you pass must be the hotel in which you'll stay. To jaunt along with a light suitcase is to avoid all these costs, to use buses instead of cabs, to make your hotel choice slowly, carefully, and without desperation. With all the increase in mobility and decrease in fatigue which a light load entails, you can simply walk out when the clerk at the hotel counter quotes too high a price—and seek another hotel.

Don't sneer at this freedom. The traveler whose arms are bursting from their sockets with weight is a prisoner. It costs her or him dollars simply to get from train to hotel; it costs him or her tiring effort simply *to move,* and shopping around for a suitable hotel is out of the question.

A light suitcase means spiritual freedom, too, and an ability to concentrate on Europe in preference to mundane, daily needs. With too many clothes, and too many parcels, you'll spend hours unpacking and arranging your apparel when you check into a hotel. You'll spend hours packing them away again as you prepare to leave. You'll awake on the morning of departure, spend frantic and precious time in packing and wrapping, and finally collapse in sweat on your outgoing plane or train. Moreover, you'll have a disorderly, bursting

*Mrs. Arthur Frommer

suitcase—cluttered with dirty and unwashed clothes—in which to search for items on the trip itself.

Remember, too, that these problems increase as your European trip continues. However heavy your suitcase may have been as you left the U.S., it'll be twice as heavy as you go along. At every stop of your trip, you'll pick up mementos, gifts, books, papers, maps, souvenirs. Unless you've had a one-third-empty suitcase to begin with, you'll be festooned with extra parcels and packages near the end. You'll loop them over your shoulder, you'll squeeze them under your arm, you'll carry some with your little finger—and you'll approach each new city and each new hotel search in a mood of desperation. The first hotel you examine will have you at its mercy.

Make the choice. Decide to live and experience Europe, or choose instead to have an outfit available for every conceivable and far-fetched occasion. Decide to be a frenzied, harried clothes-horse, or a carefree, unburdened world traveler.

If you make the right decision, you'll do the following when it comes time to pack. You'll first buy the lightest suitcase available. You'll then fill it with the skimpiest set of clothing your courage will allow. Having done that, you'll then remove half these clothes from the suitcase, and depart on your European trip. You won't for instance, take eight complete changes of underwear. You'll realize that four are enough; that there are few less-than-a-week laundries in Europe, and that you'll have to wash out those T-shirts yourself, in any event. You'll recognize how depressing it is to cart a suitcase of dirty clothes over half the continent of Europe.

If you've made too many eliminations of clothes before you start, you can always remedy the over-zealousness in a European store. But don't worry. Whatever you take will be much too much.

FOR WOMEN: After many summers of disregarding my own advice, I've finally settled on the wardrobe listed below as perfectly sufficient for a lady traveler going to Europe for four to six weeks. (Only going for a week or two? Eliminate "L," some of the "R's" and "U."):

A. 4 pairs of nylon panties; 2 pairs with pantyhose (you can rinse these out as you travel)

B. 4 pairs of pantyhose or knee-hi's (try to get mesh "can't runs"—and if you don't wear stockings in summer, more power to you; but take at least 1 pair for surprise special occasions or sudden unexpected changes in the weather)

C. 2 panty girdles in quick-drying synthetic fabric (to hold up pantyhose): optional

D. 2 slips of any quick-drying synthetic material (only 1 for a short stay)

E. 2 bras of nylon or other quick-drying synthetic material

F. 1 cardigan sweater (which can double as a "knock-about" sweater or a wrap for cool evenings)

G. 1 pair of jeans, slacks or shorts

H. 1 pair of sandals (for walking, beachwear and bedroom slippers)

I. 1 pair of good, sturdy walking shoes (sensible heels a must!)

J. 1 pair of evening shoes

K. 1 bathing suit and bathing cap

L. 1 daytime dress, wash 'n wear-drip dry; in other words, made of any of the synthetic wonder fabrics

M. 1 traveling suit, pants or skirt (again, synthetic fabric)

N. 2 blouses (drip-dry) or 2 synthetic knit shirts
O. 1 all-purpose outfit (wonder fabric) which can double for afternoon and evening: possibly a decolleté dress with a jacket, or a long skirt which can double with sporty shirt or evening top
P. 1 pair of nylon or dacron pajamas (or nightgown)
Q. 1 nylon or dacron robe (or use your raincoat)
R. Jewelry, scarves and accessories, so you won't go mad wearing the same 3 basic outfits in different combinations day in and day out
S. Cosmetics and toiletries
T. 1 all-purpose rain-proof travel coat, which you can carry onto your plane or ship
U. Your "traveling to" Europe outfit—you can afford to be wistful about this. Just wear something you like. I'd wear the drip-dry traveling suit. But whatever you decide, make sure it's something comfortable because you may find yourself wrapped up in it for several hours, if you're "plane-ing" the Atlantic.

Note for the young, or the young at heart: Please know how gratifying it is to me to have watched the style of traveling change. Today I see hordes of kids—ranging in age from teens to 40's—backpacking, whether they're actually youth-hosteling or not! Most of the young American gals that I see in Europe dress in jeans or a long skirt; these two items in combination with a couple of well-chosen tops complete the *entire wardrobe,* which is carried easily in a backpack. And for my money (and time) that, friends, is the way to travel!

As you can see the above list relies heavily on drip-dries, quick-dries, or other hearty, heavy-wearing clothing. And what is "drip/quick dry"? A catch-all phrase for any number of the new "wonder fabrics," which require no ironing: look for labels reading nylon, dacron, orlon, polyester, Arnel, Banlon, Lycra, Spandex, Qiana, or my own favorite, Trevira (slightly more expensive, but sensuously silky, and wears like iron). Concentrate on clothing made of crease-resistant materials, and in simple, easy-to-care-for designs. Avoid pleats and ruffles (unless they are the permanent kind, with no ironing), and leave at home those lovely light, wispy dresses that need constant care and attention to look fresh.

There's been a slight shift of emphasis on my part from lightweight, cotton-like drip-dries (which are still highly recommended, especially for hot, humid climates) to synthetic knits or silky nylon jerseys (i.e., Banlon or Trevira, both so like matte jersey), which I've found to be marvelous for travel. They pack beautifully. No matter how you roll or bunch them up, they scarcely ever seem to wrinkle, and if they do, you need only hang them up for an hour or so to regain the original shape. (More difficult cases will sometimes come around if you'll take them to the bath down the hall, and steam them there while you shower or bathe.) And, they simply never seem to get soiled or dirty-looking, especially if you choose dresses in dark shades.

At first glance, you might think that synthetic or wool knits (which I like) are too heavy to be comfortable or packable (winter travelers excepted, of course). But even in this respect, they have proved quite adaptable. I traveled extensively with a bare-backed sleeveless black synthetic knit dress, with a jacket that had three-quarter-length sleeves. Without the jacket, the dress was quite comfortable, even in the hottest climates. With the jacket, the outfit was heaven-sent for the chilly weather that you'll sometimes experience in Europe, even in summer.

Fashion here and there: Pants suits are as acceptable in European cities as they are here. Follow this rule of thumb: if it's an outfit you'd wear in your own nearest large city, feel free to wear it in a large European city (rural districts sometimes require more propriety in dress). One vital exception: churches (particularly in Italy and Spain) will not admit women wearing shorts or short-short skirts, frown on "overly casual" attire as being disrespectful, and may require that heads and/or shoulders be covered as well.

About your purse: I used to recommend that women traveling by air take a giant-sized purse into which they might cram all heavy articles that would otherwise exceed the old 44-lb.-per-passenger weight limit. But the International Air Transport Association recently revised the rules regarding baggage and weight allowance (please see the following section, "The Suitcase Itself," for details). But I remain loyal to the "superbag." Obviously, you won't want to carry such a purse on your strolls and tours—it will weigh you down and wear you out. Take a second, smaller purse for everyday use; and take only the tiniest purse for evening wear (if you *must* have an evening bag at all).

A final hint: Plan your wardrobe so that the clothes you take can be mixed and matched into a number of different combinations. Usually, I look for a dress with two possible matching jackets—a long and a short one. Without the jackets, the dress is suitable for evening theatre wear, dancing, other dressy occasions. With the short jacket, it becomes a cocktail dress; and with the long one, a daytime dress for walking and touring. By adding scarves and jewelry, again in different combinations, the possibilities can be further multiplied. (I used to dream about designing the perfect travel outfit, one that would zipper or tie to create 6 or more different combinations—but I think a lady from California has beaten me to it; hers, however, is expensive.)

FOR MEN: The packing list can be even more severe, and still be perfectly sufficient. If you seek comfort and economy on a summer trip, then this is all you need take (in addition to the normal-weight suit worn on the plane) for a 6 to 8 week trip. (Shorter visits, of 1 or 2 weeks? Eliminate "L," "M," and "O."):

A.   3 pairs of shorts (dacron or nylon)
B.   3 T-shirts
C.   3 pairs of socks (all of quick-drying materials)
D.   1 handkerchief (if you're a sport)
E.   1 sweater
F.   2 drip-dry sport shirts (or synthetic knits, or nylon jerseys)
G.   1 drip-dry white dress shirt (the cotton look, or nylon tricot)
H.   1 pair of dress shoes
I.   1 pair of rubber-soled walking shoes, or comfortable all-weather boots or shoes
J.   1 light bathrobe (or wear your raincoat)
K.   1 pair of nylon or dacron pajamas
L.   1 sport jacket
M.   1 pair of durable, but smart-looking, slacks
N.   1 pair of jeans or chinos
O.   1 summer suit
P.   1 raincoat
Q.   2 neckties
R.   1 bathing suit
S.   Toilet and shaving articles (adapted for European use, if electric).

(Note: For information on quick/drip-dry fabrics, please see "For Women," above.)

Don't take another thing! We've based these lists on long, disastrous experience—on days without number when the weight of our suitcases caused a weight in our hearts. Believe me, you won't mind repeating a travel outfit when the returns in lightness and freedom are as great as this.

Our suggested summer wardrobes (which include articles you'll wear on the trip) will add up to much less than the current baggage allotment on an economy flight to Europe. (For new baggage regulations, please see "The Suitcase Itself," below.) They'll leave plenty of room in your suitcase for all the gifts and articles you'll pick up in Europe; and they'll permit you to carry exactly one light suitcase and no other parcels of any kind, on your European trip.

A WOMAN'S WINTER WARDROBE: Winter, of course, means special packing problems. It can be quite cold in Europe, even in Spain and Italy, and you must be prepared with heavy, sturdy, woolen clothing. And that means that you must be even more stern with yourself. Because your bulky winter clothes will weigh far more, you must take far less. You simply cannot afford to fill your suitcase with any non-essential item. Trudging through snow with a heavy suitcase is even worse than trudging in the hot sun. Here are my suggestions for a woman's winter wardrobe for a 4 to 6 week stay (for short trips, eliminate "H," "N" and "W"; combine "J" and "K"):

A. 4 pairs of nylon panties (2 pairs, if you're taking panty hose)
B. 4 pairs of warm woolen or heavier nylon pantyhose (again, a good buy are mesh "can't runs"), or knee-hi stockings (take at least 1 heavy warm pair)
C. 2 panty girdles (optional)
D. 2 slips (nylon or dacron—quick-drying); eliminate 1 for short stay
E. 2 bras (also quick-drying)
F. 1 pair of black warm woolen panty hose
G. 1 heavy woolen cardigan sweater
H. 1 long-sleeved pull-over sweater, preferably something you can combine with the cardigan, if need be
I. 1 pair of heavy corduroy or woolen slacks
J. 1 pair of all-purpose nasty-weather snow boots
K. 1 pair of good sturdy walking shoes
L. 1 pair of evening shoes
M. 1 pair of warm bedroom slippers
N. 1 woolen or wool-knit daytime dress, or skirt and top
O. 1 heavy woolen traveling suit
P. 1 jersey or synthetic-knit blouse or shirt
Q. 1 wool-knit or silk-jersey dress which can double for afternoon and evening wear
R. 1 pair of heavy warm flannel pajamas
S. 1 very warm robe
T. Jewelry, scarves and accessories
U. 1 super-warm coat, rain-proofed, and preferably with a detachable lining
V. Cosmetics and toiletries
W. Your "traveling to" Europe outfit

A MAN'S WINTER WARDROBE: The following should be adequate for a 4 to 6 week visit (for a shorter stay, combine "K" and "L," and eliminate "M")

A. 3 pairs of shorts
B. 3 T-shirts
C. 3 pairs of socks (of which two should be heavy woolen ones)
D. 2 handkerchiefs (1 for short stays)
E. 1 heavy sweater
F. 2 sport shirts (1 in wool or flannel)
G. 1 drip-dry white dress shirt
H. 1 woolen bathrobe
I. 1 pair of heavy warm flannel pajamas
J. 1 pair of dress shoes
K. 1 pair of heavy walking shoes
L. 1 pair of galoshes
M. 1 sports jacket
N. 1 pair of heavy, warm, woolen slacks
O. 1 winter suit
P. 1 heavy coat, water-repellent
Q. 2 neckties
R. Toilet and shaving articles

Spring or fall wardrobe? Strike a happy medium between our summer and winter suggestions, and also take into account the area in which you'll be traveling. Climatic patterns around the world have been changing drastically, but generally, if you'll take the kind of clothes that would be suitable in New York or Chicago during these seasons, you'll be covered for most areas in Europe.

THE SUITCASE ITSELF: For carrying these clothes, you'll want to buy the lightest suitcase available: either a plastic suitcase, or, even better, one made of fabric. Cloth luggage is fairly durable, comes in handsome designs of varying sizes, and is feather light (women particularly, take note). Equally important, they're the cheapest on the market and yet offer the greatest amount of space. You'll value the expandable nature of a fabric suitcase when you start to cram in all the little "odds and ends" you just couldn't resist picking up along the way! (On my last trip I used a cloth case without *any* frame, and was amazed and delighted at how fresh and wrinkle-free my clothes remained. But beware "the hook" at some European baggage claim areas!)

Now, the latest news on baggage allowance for air travelers. Starting in 1979, your luggage will be "weighed in" at airports not by weight at all but by the amount of space it occupies. (This new ruling is in effect for all European destinations, except Spain.) Each economy flight passenger may check aboard two pieces of luggage free of charge, but with space restrictions as follows. Total dimensions of baggage, which you calculate by totaling length, width and depth, must not exceed 106 inches; and each individual suitcase may not exceed 62 inches. In addition to the two cases you may check through to your destination, you are also allowed to board the plane with a "carry on" bag, not to exceed 45 inches. The space allowance is certainly generous. I just measured, and our largest suitcase (a three-suiter) is only 52 inches total—even our "carry on" totals only 42 inches, three less than the legal allotment. (Wouldn't it be grand if airlines offered reduced rates to people taking less luggage?) But take care, excess baggage rates, now computed per bag instead of by weight (and depending upon destination) can still run high if you over-pack by one little suitcase.

Regardless of new airline regulations, strictly for your own comfort, do try to be a one-suitcase traveler. If you're a couple and feel that one suitcase per person just will not do, then, instead of getting another valise, buy a "valpac" (a fold-over, portable wardrobe) as your third piece of luggage. With a valpac, you simply hang up your clothes inside, lock the clothes rack, zip it up, fold the case and—presto—you have a suitcase with a convenient carrying handle. Most valpacs also contain extra inner pockets for shoes, underwear, or other soft goods, and they have loads of useful extra space on the bottom and along the sides. All in all, these foldable bags are the best gadgets I know for keeping wrinkles and creases out of traveling clothes.

Consider seriously the new "carry on" type luggage: a smallish case with handy outerzippered compartments, which slips under an airplane seat. If you can cram all your things into this small case, you'll save lots of time upon arrival, especially if you happen to be flying a stretch-jet or 747!

For women, by the way, most luggage stores sell small wheels that can be affixed with straps to the bottom of your suitcase, making it mobile. And there are now suitcases available with permanent ball bearings on the bottom, and a snap-on guiding strap at one side; they're supposed to "glide."

The latest, most chic case on the market is our old friend the backpack: a bag made with shoulder straps (some also have waist ties; others convert from one to two shoulder use)—and thus the Establishment has finally caught on to the luxury of traveling light and free.

HOW TO PACK: Whenever possible, carry all liquids in flexible lightweight plastic bottles. Then place all "spillables" in a zippered or well-sealed plastic bag to avoid accidents in case of leakage. If you must take along a glass container, such as a perfume bottle, avoid spillage by sealing the cap of the bottle with a layer of candle wax (but consider switching to solid-state cologne or perfume, which is light and practical, with some very nice fragrances now available).

Roll into scroll-like shapes whatever is rollable: underwear, slips, bras, and so forth—all things that don't have to be wrinkle-free. In that manner, these items can be placed along the sides of your suitcase easily, or into the most unusual cracks and crevices (you'll discover plenty of them while packing). For items that do wrinkle, a layer of tissue paper or, more durable, a sheet of plastic (the kind that comes from the cleaners) placed above and below the garment (and one in the folded crease) will prove to be a surprising wrinkle-preventer. Place garments into your suitcase in the shape they should be in, with buttons loosely buttoned, top and bottom (except for men's jackets); and alternate piling, with the top of one piece of clothing placed over the bottom of another.

I must mention here that Arthur uses neither tissue paper nor plastic sheets. He packs all his clothing "raw," and they always travel well. He does know a secret kind of male way to flip a coat or jacket inside out so that it always emerges from a suitcase fresh as a daisy. Something like this: fold back, shoulder to shoulder, then flip. Try as I may, I cannot master it. Good luck to you—I'm stuck with tissue paper.

Finally, conserve space. Don't let anything go to waste. A handbag should be jammed with small articles, shoes jammed with socks, and so on.

One packing method which I've never found satisfactory is the use of plastic bags to compartmentalize the contents of your suitcase—but some lady travelers swear by this system. The theory goes that you should have a different plastic bag for each category of clothing—i.e., that you place all lingerie in one bag, all nightwear in another, and so forth, thus enabling you to extract each item as needed, without disarranging the remaining contents of your suitcase. When I tried the plastic bags, it seemed to me they filled with air and thus added unnecessary bulk to the case. I also found it a patience-tryer and a time-waster to be constantly sorting things out.

What to do instead? I like the layered principle of packing, which simply enables you to flip along the edge of your case to get what you need!

ODDS AND ENDS: Since you will probably be doing your own laundry, however, you must take at least one plastic bag, with a zipper, for carrying wet clothes or wash cloths from town to town. Also recommended is Woolite, the cold water soap. Take as many packets as you think you'll need—one packet will do for a full washbowl of laundry. . . . Since most European budget hotels do not provide soap, you will also need a plastic soap dish with a lid, and, of course, soap. Towels are provided everywhere, so you needn't worry on that score. . . . If you like sleek, well-polished looking shoes, try convenient (in traveling packets) Mr. Shine, available at drugstores or notion sections of large department stores, 26 for $1.50. . . . To repeat a point that cannot be overstressed, invest heavily in drip-dry shirts and underwear—the type that can be washed in lukewarm water, and hung up overnight to dry. Eliminate the clothes that require a fancy cleaning-and-pressing job. Unless you do, you'll spend enormous sums for cleaning and laundry, you'll be continually inconvenienced, and you'll end up—in our worst nightmare—lugging a suitcase full of useless, dirty clothes. . . . To drip-dry your clothes in a hotel room that lacks a private bath, or in a hotel that has no laundry room, start by blotting up the excess moisture with a towel ("towel-drying"), and/or spread newspapers or plastic "sheets" below to catch the dripping.

What do you do when the hotel will not allow laundry to be washed in your room? First, understand their point of view: some hotels recommended in this book have precious antique wooden floors which would be ruined by water spots; others have proprietors so super neat and clean that the very idea of washing clothes in the *hand* basin is an affront to their sensibilities! Second, inquire politely of the management if there is a facility in the hotel for doing your laundry, i.e. a real laundry room, a private W.C. of the management's, a basement. Third, have you considered the "midnight dip"? And if all else fails, pack it up and head for the nearest cheapest laundromat.

On the art of drip-drying: I write this only because so many readers have complained that drip-dry clothing doesn't really work. It does, with the proper care. Here's how. You'll get the best results with clothes that are really dripping wet—the theory being that the weight of the water "irons" the clothes. But even if you can't enjoy the luxury of heavily sodden dripping, you can still do well if you'll remember (1) to separate the material so that the back does not cling to the front and (2) "hand iron" the material—smooth the garment out (or puff it out from underneath) in those areas where it might wrinkle or bunch up. Always button the top buttons, and put collars down and cuffs in shape. Take a few extra seconds to perform these simple tasks, and you'll nearly always enjoy better than decent results.

How about taking pharmaceuticals, water-purifying pills, and the like? Don't. You'll soon discover that Europe is civilized, that there are pharmacies everywhere, and that all these items can be picked up on the spot—when and if needed (except personal prescription medicines, of course). Furthermore, the water, milk and food in all major European cities is today as safe as anywhere you can name.

FOR WOMEN ONLY: Handy neat little luxuries are those small, compact packets, filled with washcloth, shower-cap, little capsules of cold-water detergent, and a portable rubber clothes line (complete with tiny clothespins) capable of being tied and hung up anywhere. These packets are practically weightless, and they can be purchased in any drug or department store. . . . Purse-sized "Wash 'n Dri" towelettes for quick semi-dry washing, can be a lifesaver in any number of travel emergencies (I always carry a cleansing cream as well). . . . Glamour gals will take Andrea nail polish remover pads (14 individually wrapped pads for $1.35); and the overly fastidious may even carry individualized packets of spot remover. . . . A pocket-sized plastic case, containing a tiny toothbrush and a small tube of toothpaste, is also a great comfort on long plane or train trips. These are available at most drugstores. . . . For the young or vain: hotel rooms usually have sinks which are adequate for washing hair. If you must shampoo often and need to carry a hairdryer, don't forget to include an electric converter. A simpler solution? Try a neighborhood beauty parlor, or do as I do: look in the local telephone directory for the nearest "Beauty School" (always the cheapest place in town for a wash and set).

READERS' SUGGESTIONS: "I recently returned from four exciting months in Europe. The trip was marvelous because I was totally free. Before I left I bought a nylon back pack; frame, padding and all for only $19. In it, I had one long skirt for dress and for romping around, a white blouse, sweater, toothbrush, wash cloth, and a pair of sandals. I also had my jeans, T-shirt and hiking boots, which I wore most of the time. Whenever I got tired of these things, I'd buy something else, wear it once or twice and send it home. I really didn't need anything else. Believe me, it's the only way to travel" (A student, San Francisco, California.). . . . "From observations in expensive restaurants, hotels and La Scala Opera, I noticed many European men wearing gray (medium to darkish) suits. Therefore, one well-tailored medium-gray suit should take a man anywhere. And I would not recommend sport shirts at all—any man over 25 looks like a hick in one in public, and the European caricatures of an American man show him with a sport shirt hanging out. Neckties, and shirt inside of pants while in cities, please" (Stephen Beattie, West Orange, New Jersey). . . . "We travel light since porters are expensive and often non-existent. A B-4 bag (softside with outside pockets) plus an oversized plastic flight bag with shoulder strap. That's it for *two*. And invariably we find we have toted things we didn't need. My wife carries our documents and heaven knows what else in a large shoulder-strap handbag. Our motto: Don't travel with more than you can carry" (Norvelle H. Sannebeck, Michoacan, Mexico). . . . "The most useful luggage is 'Dubbel Duffel' (Bancroft Industries, P.O. Box 670, Cabot, Ark. 72023), which is lightweight and expands to twice its size—comes in handy towards the end of a trip! The one pack turns into a backpack" (Carla Miller, Jacksonville, Florida). . . . "After having used your books for 4 years, I want to advise your readers on what I feel is the perfect luggage for a summer in Europe: a flight bag measuring approximately 15″ x 10″ x 5″! All my travel needs can be placed in it: 1 extra outfit, 1 pair of shorts, sweater, sweatshirt, windbreaker, raincoat, swim-suit, toilet articles, etc., towel, and a cut-down copy of 'Europe' on top. When the plane lands in Europe I grab my bag and arrive at my hotel before most of the passengers have located all their luggage!" (William D. Poriz, Norman, Oklahoma). . . . "Instead of one large suitcase, it's much easier to take two very small ones. Often you can leave one somewhere and just take half your clothes with you when off on a shorter excursion. Wheels on suitcases are a must if you travel alone" (Nancy Wasserman, Cambridge, Massachusetts; note from HA: several readers have been enthusiastic about the advantages of carrying two small bags. But to keep my traveling life simple, and packing chores minimal, I'll stick to one case. My oversize handbag will do nicely for shorter jaunts. Men who don't carry purses, might like to try duffle or airline bags). . . . "After several trips abroad, I've finally solved the disorganized 'everything-in-my-purse' routine. Since I just had a baby, I acquired a diaper bag, and on a recent trip used the black patent version as my 'purse'. Its advantages are numerous. It's large and roomy, durable, plastic-lined, has all sorts of compartments (for diapers, formula) that I used for passports, tickets, maps, etc., fits easily on planes, is not weighed as a carry-on because it's my purse, opens easily and you can get to everything. The bag is designed for busy mothers, and on a trip travelers are busy. Everything fits into some compartment; I never lost a thing, organized the entire trip. The bags run about $11, not a huge investment, so if you wear it out in a few trips it doesn't hurt. It's a shame I had to have a baby before I found out the advantages of the bag for my travels" (Patricia Cline, Roselle, Illinois). . . . "For a Carry-On Bag I use a picnic-type insulated bag, which was great for carrying food on trains, ideal for picnics, and also for food kept in our room. I'd also like to recommend packing a folding umbrella, the kind that fits into a large handbag" (Dorothy R. Astman, Levittown, New York). . . . "I do very much disagree with your suggestions of attachable wheels for girls' or anybody's suitcase. All you encounter is stairs, stairs, stairs, and with the additional weight of heavy wheels plus straps" (Ms. Sandra Tanner, Madison, Wisconsin). . . . "If you'll be traveling in the fall, winter or spring, when rain can frequently be expected, take along a pair of Ripple Sole shoes. One walks over the puddles, not through them, and the weight and bother of overshoes are avoided. Usually the uppers of these shoes, not made for 'elegant' wear, are sturdy enough, and lend themselves to waterproofing" (Stephen H. Frishauf, New York, N.Y.). . . . "The best shoes to take are Famolare 'Get-Theres', the ones with the wavy bottoms. They held up under the worst walking conditions, were comfortable, and looked good with dresses, pants and bathing suits. Could be the only shoes you need take on a trip" (Carla Miller, Jacksonville, Florida). . . . "Pack articles which might break, small ones that is, in the toes of that extra pair of shoes every traveller should carry" (Mary Jenkins, Wilmette, Illinois). . . . "I'd like to suggest putting liquids in plastic bottles filled nearly ¾ full. Then squeeze the bottle gently—putting the top on tighter so there's still a 'dent' in the bottle as you let go. This prevents spilling nearly 100%. I am a stewardess and can vouch for many miles in pressurized airplanes which usually invite leaks! We learned this in stewardess training and it's invaluable" (Joellen Ayers, Redondo Beach, Calif.). . . . "Aluminum film containers, available at photo supply shops for around 5¢ each, are the cheapest and best non-breakable receptacles for odds and ends like pills, small amounts of lotion and loose seashells. Get the plastic snap-on lid, the metal screw-on lid will rust" (Lauren Friedman, Bronx, N.Y.). . . . "I use the very light 4¼″ x 1⅝″ containers which hold the Vitamin E I use. When empty, I fill several with the French version of Tide (*very effective*), and use it for washing. These containers are extremely light and easy to carry on trips" (Andrew J. O'Laughlin, Nice, France). . . . "I would certainly recommend the small compressed wash cloths that look like tiny bars of soap and expand when put in water. In addition, I always carry fold-up slippers in my purse, so that I can slip them on while riding on a plane or on long bus or train trips" (Ms. Billie Brooks, Inglewood, California). . . . "On a guided tour when I had a room without bath for a week, I took along a sponge in a plastic bag and in the evening I soaped it well, washed from head to feet, standing on a newspaper or paper bag, rinsed off, and that was that!" (Andrew J. O'Laughlin, Nice, France). . . . "Suggest to your readers that they pack opera glasses: these are wonderfully handy if you are theatre lovers, as we are, and must sit with the gods" (Christie J. Bentham, Scarborough, Ont., Canada). . . . "First, it's a must for people traveling through the hotter countries to take a plastic snap-on cover for soda bottles. We found them indispensable, especially throughout Italy; they're also helpful on those long train trips, and good for wine bottles, too. Another item we brought from home was one of those multi-use pocket knives—the kind with blades, openers, scissors and even spoon and fork. It's small, and oh, so handy for the many times we bought our lunch ingredients at a delicatessen and then needed something with which to cut cheese or meat" (Gloria Ruggiero, Astoria, N.Y.). . . . "We found a small travel kit of a mug and an immersion heater invaluable for that odd cup of coffee or tea. We would heat the water in the mug, brew the tea or coffee, pour it into a yogurt container, then boil more water for the second cup" (Bella and Fritz Goldschmidt, Welkom, Orange Free State, South Africa: note from H.A.: immersion heaters have been around for a long time. Although they're small and compact and I used one when we were traveling with our infant daughter, I haven't felt the need to take one with me since. However, for people like my mother, who cannot open her eyes in the morning until after she has that first cup of coffee, I guess they're a must. And with the price of a cup of coffee going up, up, up (!) the immersion heater could be a real $-saver, and very handy for those "picnic" lunches and suppers. If you take one, be sure it's adaptable for European use). . . . "This is for those of you who are traveling light and must do a little washing every night. Throw your laundry in the bath tub and let it soak right along with you, while you are bathing. Then all it takes is a quick sudsing in the lavatory, as the pre-soaking has hastened the job along" (Mrs. John Frerichs, Girard, Kansas). . . . "Club soda is good for removing stains on clothes; Scotch Tape is great for removing lint, and also for taking up a fallen hem line. In an emergency, toilet paper rolls make excellent hair rollers, and Scotch Tape can be used in place of bobbie pins. These card-board rollers may also be used as funnels when oil or water must be put into a rented car. A nylon slip over your pillow-case will preserve a hair setting, and a lamp shade or hair-spray can can hold that wig" (Mrs. M. Del Pizzo, Miami, Fla.). . . . "Perhaps the most versatile item I took to Europe was a raincoat with a zip-out lining. In a pension, it doubled as a bathrobe for those walks down to the shower. On an all-night train, I used the lining as a pillow and the coat itself for a cover. On picnics, it served as our tablecloth. At the bull fights it served as a cushion; very necessary on those rock or concrete seats. At the beach, you can change your clothing underneath one. Finally, it kind of came in handy when it rained!" (Mark G. Simkin, New City, New York). . . . "Being in the Army, my husband and I have had ample opportunity to travel in Europe and Scandinavia, and we have yet to find a use for our bathrobes and slippers. When one needs to go out into the hall for any reason, we find our coats and shoes just as easy to use over our nightclothes and sometimes preferable. Robes and slippers simply take up valuable space, and add more weight to the suitcase. In lieu of slippers we both carry heavy woolen socks which can, and often need, be worn in bed, as Europeans tend to conserve on heat" (Mrs. Mark Stetson, Orleans, France).

READERS' PRODUCT SUGGESTIONS: "Please, please, let the world in on the glories of Baggies —both sizes. For about 69¢ one has disposable cosmetic cases, wet clothing carriers, sweater-etc.-bags, jewelry cases, soap dishes, make-up savers, food containers for picnics (or whatever), beer tops (saves the carbonation), and a great item in which to wrap odds and ends which are to be mailed home. Take the cardboard roll out of the Baggies, compress them, and bingo—instant traveling. The one (and only) item which we couldn't locate in Europe was cheap, good quality plastic, and when the toothbrush container broke, the soap dish got lost, and the hose snagged if thrown in the suitcase, Baggies saved everything. I'm taking both large (sweater and shoe bags) and small Baggies this time" (Leoni Zverow, Chicago, Illinois). . . . "Glad Bags, which now come in two sizes, have been indispensable to us shutter bugs in protecting cameras, lenses, etc., from water and dust in inclement weather. Only Glad Bags have fold over closure" (Mary Jenkins, Wilmette, Illinois; note from H.A.: Glad Bags also sell for 69¢, $1.09 for the medium size). . . . "On my last two trips I discovered the wonder of Handi-wipes. One Handi-wipe, cut in two pieces, makes a wonderful throw-away wash rag. Obtainable at any supermarket, for about 79¢ here in Dallas" (Mrs. Jas. C. McQueen, Dallas, Tex.). . . . "We found most helpful ear plugs and eye shades, since we are light sleepers. The best of the former we have found are the plastic 'Mack's Pillow Soft Earplugs' that fit over but not into the ear canal. They cost just $2 for 4 plugs from McKeon Products Inc., 121 Elm Park, Pleasant Ridge, Michigan 48069—if not available at your local pharmacy. The same concern has eyeshades or sleepshades for $3.00. Under conditions of noise and bright light, these two items are life savers" (J. Calvin Keene, Canton, New York; note from HA: McKeon informs us their ear plugs are useful for protection while swimming, too). . . . "If your feet have a tendency to ache, Dr. Scholl's arch supports are wonderful. I wear them all the time when walking" (Nell J. Masters, Atlanta, Georgia). . . . "Be sure to take the little toe rubbers that you can slip over any type heel. They were very difficult to find, but certainly well worth the effort" (Billie Brooks, Camarillo, California). . . . "Listerine mouth wash can also be used on cuts and insect bites" (Mrs. M. Del Pizzo, Miami, Fla.). . . . "If you want to drip dry clothing in a hotel room that lacks a private bath, without soaking the floor, pack in your suitcase a square of sturdy plastic. Mine was about 54 inches square, and folded flat to almost nothing. (It was sold in a dime store for a tablecloth, I think.) I spread it underneath my clotheslines, folded the sides over to form a sort of pool, and found that no water could escape. I also took along a sponge to mop up the first deluge. (I loved my braided rubber clothesline, which eliminated the need for clothespins)" (Phyllis Brush, Ipswich, Massachusetts). . . . "In a room with only a washbowl I wash out clothes, squeeze them as dry as possible and hang them on hangers in the closet, with a newspaper below to absorb the water" (Andrew J. O'Laughlin, Nice, France). . . . "Here's a drip-dry tip that proved invaluable to me (after I had stained a floor with wet newspapers). I cut a piece of medium weight plastic (18″ x 36″) from an old shower curtain, and use it with 4 paper clips. I cup the corners of the plastic and secure each one with a paper clip: it makes a perfect pan to catch the drips. Usually I lay a used towel in it—no noise, and just wring out the towel later and use it to wipe out the pan" (Ms. Harriett Ross, Bredeston, Fla.). . . . "I found that a wrap-around dress worked equally well as a daytime casual dress and as a robe for trips down the hall to the W.C. I would suggest that 2 extra plastic hangers are essential for washing out items, but finding a place to hang them is sometimes difficult. We took a large plastic garbage bag, and used it for the dirty clothes on our way home" (Marion J. Durham, Flagstaff, Arizona). . . . "1) Very useful items which take no space in your suitcase are safety pins, rubber bands, and paper clips. 2) Take a small cup, preferably a folding cup, and a bottle opener for those mineral water bottles on train trips" (Roberta and Jack Sarfatt, La Jolla, California). . . . "My best hint for this section is the purchase before leaving of a crazy little device for hanging wet garments—better than all the clotheslines and pins. It is a hanger with one head and about ten arms that fold in or out like an umbrella, with a little clip on the end of each arm. That way, you can hang about ten items from one spot and they all dry overnight. It is compact and folds easily into a corner of the suitcase, and was my life-saver in small rooms. Costs about $1.50" (Mrs. Gene A. Rudolph, Los Angeles, California). . . . "A drip-dry shirt or dress dries much faster and with fewer wrinkles if it is hung from an inflatable plastic travel hanger. We were given one 5 years ago, and I use it now even at home. When not in use, the air is released and the hanger is folded into a small pocket" (Shirley Stein, Downers Grove, Illinois). . . . "I found Travelers Friend Hangers very handy during my travels this past summer. They're light-weight polyethylene hangers that hold garments open in a 3-dimensional form, and clothing dries faster and wrinkle free. Available from Miles Kimball, 41 West 8th Ave., Oshkosh, Wis. 54901" (May-Britt Richardson, Seattle, Washington). . . . "Want that nice touch of fabric-softened clothing without toting a gallon jug of softener on your travels? 'Bounce' (a product of Procter & Gamble) is ultra-lightweight 9 x 11" sheets of non-woven rayon impregnated with fabric softener. Altho specifically designed to be added in an automatic dryer (each sheet does a full washload), it can also be added to the final rinse water of drip-dry items. Each sheet is already partially scored into seven strips and can be divided for 'just this much' in a hand basin. I found it particularly good on Qiana, Arnel, and other 'man-mades' that tended to wrinkle and create static electricity. A small strip of Bounce took care of both of these problems. The product seems expensive ($2.20 for 40 sheets), but considering the mileage one gets out of just one sheet, the cost is negligible. An extra bonus: when packing, if you layer the sheets among your clothing, it will give you fresh scented clothes, because 'Bounce' contains a light fragrance that even men wouldn't object to. Great!" (Carole Sebastian, St. Louis, Missouri). . . . "For a recent trip to the Orient, I purchased a 'Monaco' windup razor made in Monaco, of all places. It shaves adequately and the advantages are obvious. I bought mine for $35, plus $2.50 for postage" (Norvelle H. Sannebeck, Michoacan, Mexico; note from H.A.: this gadget is available from Winston's Sales & Service Co., 143 E. 60 St., New York, New York, 10022. Winston highly recommends the eltron Mobile battery shaver, made by Braun, at the same price of $35 plus $1.50 for 2 C batteries; for mail orders add $2.50). . . . "A hint I have to pass on to you and your readers concerns soap. It was always a fussy bore to wrap up a sticky piece of soap that inevitably dripped and got even more gooey. Then I discovered "Badedas", a liquid soap that comes in tubes and, more recently, small plastic bottles. It can be used for showers, baths and as a shampoo. They also make a lighter solution for young children. At any rate, if Badedas is not available, try to purchase any liquid soap in plastic bottles. Such a blessing!" (Denyse Tessensohn, Singapore; note from HA: in the U.S., "Badedas" is "Vitabath"). . . . "Rather than carry bar soap and a plastic dish on trips, I find it much more convenient to carry just a tube of shaving creme, which I find covers all my needs. Perhaps some of your readers will be as delighted as I was to find that shaving creme works just as well as soap, and by providing for my bathing as well as shaving needs, this one tube eliminates the need to carry soap, soap-dish and the bulky aerosol shave cream can" (John J. Bartko, Ph.D., Bethesda, Maryland). . . . "Handy items I am packing: a wash-and-wear light weight wig (saves time in hairdressers), and a tube of shaving cream for hair washing—no spillage, light weight and doubles as toilet soap and toothpaste!" (Ms. Yvonne Foster, Claremont, Perth, W. Australia). . . . "Clairol makes rollers to take on trips, 'Set to Go' (5 rollers). Check the bottom of the rollers to make sure they work on 115 *and* 220, some of them do not. When you get to Europe, all you have to do is snap on an adapter plug (either a 3 prong for England or the round 2 plug for the Continent). You do not need an adapter for the current. American hairdriers blew out every adapter we had—we finally just bought a British one" (Carla Miller, Jacksonville, Florida). . . . "I spray my outer clothes, coats, hats, scarves and dresses with Scotchgard Fabric Protector to make them water repellent. It works very well on everything but knit fabrics. Scotchgard is manufactured by the 3M Company of St. Paul, Minn., and can be purchased in our supermarkets and hardware stores (about $3.95). Woven woolens, cottons and synthetic fabrics take kindly to Scotchgard and I'm enthusiastic about using it. It seems to make dresses more crease resistant as well as water repellent" (Ruth Graham, Gr. Barrington, Massachusetts). . . . "New Dupont 'Dacron-Tricot' wash and wear shirts can be wrung out, look great, and dry in a couple of hours. These differ from ordinary drip 'n dry shirts in that they needn't be hung up dripping wet, but can be squeezed out in the sink without creating wrinkles" (Charles N. Hardin, Munich, Germany). . . . "An item that's worth the price, about $7, is an expandable 'carry on' bag. There's a zipper around the bottom, and when it's opened the bag becomes about 1/3 as large as in its closed condition. It's great for those extras you'll be coming home with" (Phyllis Eisenberg, Brooklyn, New York). . . . "In preparing for a vacation, I came across a nylon tote bag called Purse-Pal (with flat bottom and flap-snap closing, style #41). Folded up, its weight is almost nonexistent, and at a pliable 3 x 4″ it will fit anywhere. Opened, it measures a roomy 15 x 19″. And it's guaranteed to hold up to 60 pounds! The traveler can dispense with clumsy totes or airline bags going to Europe, yet come home with all her weighty possessions tucked neatly under her seat. And Purse-Pal is waterproof too! I bought mine in a department store for $3. It's made by Fremont Bag Co., Box 74, Brighton, Mass., 02135" (Eileen Shapiro, Brooklyn, New York; note by HA: The Fremont Co. has two other bags which are of interest to travellers: (1) a "Steel Strain" nylon taffeta bag (#1) similar to the Purse-Pal except that it is a 3 x 3″ fold-up (price $3.25), and (2) #57 DeLuxe, a slightly larger (folds flat to 4 x 4½″, opens to 20 x 25) "laundry bag" with 2 drawstrings and an inside hang-up loop ($3.10)—free delivery on all items. . . . Another note by HA: The Kart-a-Bag, a luggage-carrying cane with wheels at the bottom, was recommended by a reader in an earlier edition. I received a later comment about it, and decided I'd best try it myself before re-mentioning it. I found it quite handy and serviceable for the right sized luggage. A thick elastic cord holds the bags in place—important: your luggage must be balanced well. The $18.95 model, which can be purchased from Remin's Inc., 510 Manhattan Rd., Joliet, Illinois, 60433, has a telescoping handle, and the entire gadget, weighing little over a pound, has its own neat carrying case which can be slipped over the arm after checking your bags. Sturdier, more durable models are available, but they're more expensive).

STARVATION BUDGET: "All year long I shop for very, very cheap undergarments in discount stores. I take 1 bra and slip for every 3 days: panties for every other day. After wearing them for the allotted time, I simply discard them. No more washing, hoping it will dry before leaving the next morning. I wear a black dress and take a black cardigan sweater (wear also), and a black skirt—I take no other clothes (the skirt and sweater would serve as an outfit if something drastic happened to my one dress). I take 1 nightgown, 2 bright scarves, wear a dark one around my neck to keep my dress clean; and take a dress-up set of jewelry, wearing a day set. I wear dress-shields, take a bath every night, and thus am as clean and dainty as women who drip-dry and worry about excess baggage. No one has ever noticed what I was doing. As for my make-up, I take small jars, small bars of soap, old washcloth, etc., with just enough to last through the trip and discard before returning home (I also take folding rain boots, raincoat and umbrella). All the above fits into a large tote with zipper, which I carry on board the airplane with me (my large handbag holds maps, tickets, etc.). This system has adequately supplied me for as long as 3 weeks without any problems. Basically, it is a disposal trip. Naturally, my return flight finds me with the lightest luggage of all!" (Ms. Sandra Pearce, Morristown, New Jersey).

"*Every* travel book advises us to take too much to Europe. For a 2 or 3 month summer trip, I do not take a suitcase at all. I take only the give-away airplane bag and my purse.

"I wear a dark, flared, lined rayon suit, long-sleeved, with a dark lace shell. This becomes an evening gown, train travel dress, restaurant costume, or sightseeing outfit, as the occasion demands. *I do not take another outfit.* (If I were the active sports type, I would take a cheap nylon shift, which would double as a night gown.) I do not take a change of underwear—just what I have on. I wash it every night and blot it dry with a hotel towel. I wear very comfortable, dark, pump-type shoes for dress-up. My travel outfit is completed with a package veil-and-ribbon hat, dark gloves that live quite a bit of the time in my pocket, and a coat that serves as raincoat and robe. My shoes are rubber soled for damp sidewalks and a purse-size plastic scarf keeps my head dry.

"In the flight bag I pack (everything in plastic bags) a pair of dark, comfortable, rubber-soled walking shoes; tiny knit bedroom slippers; plenty of medium-sheer hose of the same color; a skimpy nightgown; soap, toothpaste, toothbrush, dusting powder and cold cream (the cosmetics in small amounts and in plastic containers); a fancy dark sweater for an evening wrap, variety in daytime wear, or simply warmth; a needle, thread, small pair of scissors; a moderate supply of the vitamins and medicines that I use; and last but not least, a current copy of Frommer's *Europe on $15 a Day.*

"I keep most of my travelers' checks, my return passage, my health card and my passport in a fool-proof money belt that I made myself. Of course, if I know that I will need any of these things during the day, I put them into my purse before leaving the hotel.

"My purse is a sturdy shoulder bag with a good catch. I never lay it down anywhere. In it I keep a compact, comb, lipstick, Chapstick, pens, Kleenexes, a little notebook, a money changer, and coin purse. I carry bills and travelers' checks in zippered compartments.

"I used to toil under the 'white man's burden', but no more. People who take a lot of stuff do not use it, anyway" (Name withheld, Hollywood, California).

I hope you will send me more of your own packing discoveries (to Arthur Frommer, Inc., 380 Madison Avenue, New York, New York 10017), so that we may further test and amplify the "easy travel" tricks advanced in this chapter. Pending those letters, I'll stick to my theme song: take only one suitcase, and keep it light!

—Hope Arthur

Chapter XXVI

INEXPENSIVE AUTO RENTALS

For Do-It-Yourself Travel

IF THIS IS your first trip to Europe, and you're anxious to cram in a great many different cities and countries, then car travel is not the mode for you—it will necessarily limit the number and variety of your stops in Europe. For, while distances on a European map may seem short, they are deceptively short. Excepting only a few major highways in France and Germany, the normal European road will not permit you to travel as fast as you might in the United States. And if you're to cross mountains on your ride, you'll crawl. The route from Munich to Venice may seem like a short one—but it's over the Alps!

But having painted the foregoing gloomy picture, and having conceded all the drawbacks, I can now with good conscience assert the following stubborn proposition: no one has seen Europe who has not traveled in it by car. The life of the continent from an auto window is a closely-felt, personal experience. It should be tried: not, perhaps, on a first trip to Europe, when you'll want to see a great many cities, in a number of countries—but ultimately, when you're content to examine at leisure a particular country or area through which you've earlier passed.

How can that be done at the least cost? There are a number of alternatives. We'll first discuss the general principles, and then go on to provide specific names and addresses for specific planning.

OUTRIGHT PURCHASE: A most obvious step, but a serious one. Still, if you've already been planning the purchase of a European car, merely put off the purchase until you arrive in Europe. The normal European small car costs at least $200 less overseas than here. The cost of then shipping the car back to the United States (New York) is (for the smaller cars) about $400. Even when U.S. import duty and excise tax are added, you may end up saving some money on the purchase price; but your greatest saving stems from the fact that you will have paid nothing for the use of the car in Europe—a saving of $500 and more.

MONTHLY LEASES: If you plan to stay in Europe at least a month, and expect to do a substantial amount of driving during that month, then your next best course is to lease (rather than rent) for a flat monthly charge that includes unlimited mileage privileges. Such a one-month arrangement presently costs around $610 for a Renault "5," $683 for a Simca 1100 and $813 for a comfortable Volkswagen Rabbit with automatic transmission. Firms usually include full insurance coverage with this arrangement at no extra charge. The only disadvantage in leasing is that delivery and return arrangements tend to be less flexible than with car rental.

SHORT TERM RENTALS: For periods of less than a month, of course, you'll have to rent a car at a daily or weekly rate. That amounts, for autos of the Volkswagen-Rabbit or Renault 5 class, to around $151 per week, if you want unlimited mileage privileges; from $14 per day, plus 14¢ per kilometer (there are about 1.6 kilometers to a mile). Either way, you'll pay about $25 per day for your car (not including gas or added value tax). Most expensive country for auto rentals? Switzerland. Least expensive? Denmark, Spain, Portugal, England, and Luxembourg. By picking up your car in Madrid or Copenhagen, you can save up to $60 (on a 30-day rental) over what you would have spent by renting the car in most other European cities.

Prices vary considerably not only from country to country, but from firm to firm. Various plans, too, are offered by car rental companies, so do check carefully to find an offer that suits your particular budget and transportation needs.

WHEN AND WHERE: In months other than May through September, you can safely wait until you arrive in Europe to make your car arrangements. The local auto firms will greet you with open arms—off-season. In the summer months, the situation can get tight in certain cities and at varying times; although even then, it's often possible to find an available car, simply by appearing on the spot. Moreover, you'll find that the rates you'll obtain from the local and lesser-known agencies in Europe are sometimes cheaper than those offered by U.S.-based firms.

Nevertheless, readers who want absolute certainty in their travel arrangements, would do well to contact any one of a number of American agencies that deal in European car hire. And, of course, if you plan the more serious step of purchasing a car overseas (either with or without guaranteed repurchase plan), then you should definitely make all the arrangements, at least a month in advance, in the United States.

The "ShipSide Showroom"

But you needn't even bother making such long-in-advance arrangements for the purchase of a car—if you fly to Amsterdam. For there, on the grounds of Amsterdam Airport, you'll find a showroom of all the best-known European cars, attended by salesmen who will sell you one on the spot! This quite unique operation is known as the **"ShipSide Showroom"** (although it's at an airport, not at a dock), and its U.S. representatives are **ShipSide Car Delivery, Inc.,**

609 Fifth Avenue, New York, N.Y. 10017, whose brochure about on-the-spot purchase of a European car is quite fascinating (write, and they'll send it to you).

You can pay ShipSide with travelers' checks, certified check, or even personal check (although you'll have to wait for the bank's clearance on the latter form of payment); once payment is made, you can pick up the car immediately—and drive away. ShipSide has been known to complete all the arrangements within an hour after the customer's plane has touched down on the field! Of course, they're also able to have special-make cars available for you, if you can give them advance notice.

As we pointed out before, the purchase of a tax-free European car, in Europe, may involve an initial saving. That, coupled with the absence of car taxes, and supplemented by other reductions brought to you by ShipSide, can result in your paying a little less for a European car purchased in Europe, than for one purchased in the United States or Canada, even when you include the cost of shipping it back home and paying duty on it. And, of course, you have increased that saving by having the car for all your transportation needs in Europe. That latter benefit can amount in value to $500 and more.

Where and from whom to rent

On the straight rental of a car, keep in mind that rental prices vary according to the European city in which you pick up the auto. Currently, the lowest car-rental rates in Europe are offered in Copenhagen, Madrid, Lisbon, London, and Luxembourg.

All the major car rental agencies are of course represented in the major European cities, and several of them—Hertz, Avis, National, Automaggiore, Kemwel, others—maintain rental desks in the Arrival Halls of Europe's major airports, where they can often provide you with cars even if you haven't reserved ahead. For names and addresses of U.S.-based firms where you can rent cars for use in Europe, see our section below called "U.S. firms offering car rentals."

The amazing Mr. Hildebrandt

Now let's talk about the rental of a car that comes equipped with tent, sleeping bags, gas stoves, cooking utensils—and all the other paraphernalia you'll need to join the growing number of persons who are using the vast network of campsites in Europe for their overnight accommodations. Here you'll want to turn to an "underground hero" of budget travel in Europe, a Copenhagen tailor named **Hendrik Hildebrandt** who, from his tailor-shop at 61 Studiestraede in Copenhagen (phone 120-643), began renting a spare car or two a few years ago, and progressed to the point where he now controls a large fleet of autos (equipped with tents and/or trailers) which he continues to rent from the same tailor shop! He has no overhead to speak of, offers the continent's lowest prices for cars-with-camping-equipment, and may even sell you a suit while he's at it.

Hildebrandt will make delivery of a new 1980 car, thus equipped, directly to you at depots in Amsterdam, Brussels, Frankfurt, Luxembourg, Oslo or Copenhagen, at a delivery charge of only $40 in Amsterdam, Paris, Brussels, Frankfurt, Luxembourg and Oslo (none in Copenhagen), and with no later collection fee for picking up the car in those same cities. He achieves this feat by using Danish university students to deliver and collect the car, who thus obtain free transportation on their own vacation travels to those cities. Normal-

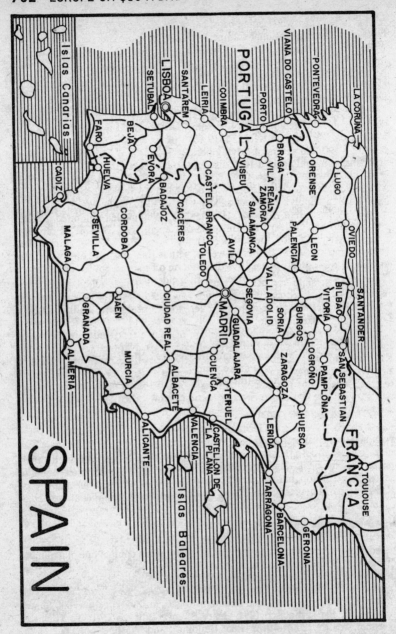

ly, his charge for the rental to 2 persons of a 1980 Fiat 127 (including the delivery charge for Amsterdam, Brussels, Frankfurt, Luxembourg or Oslo, plus unlimited mileage, complete insurance, two-person tent that is physically attached to the car, two sleeping bags, car atlas, camping guidebook, and membership in the International Camper's Union) is approximately $392 for two weeks, $571 for three weeks, $733 for four weeks, and $23 per day for each day in excess of the first four weeks; the charge is only slightly more when 3 or 4 persons use the car (additional tents and sleeping bags are then provided). But beyond that, Hildebrandt will give a 10% discount off these prices to anyone who writes him mentioning this book.

For readers desirous of renting a 1972/76 model Volkswagen "camperbus" (capable of sleeping up to 4 persons), Hildebrandt has that, too, at prices of around $546 for two weeks, $819 for three weeks, $1092 for four weeks, including 100 kilometers of driving per day (and 25¢ per extra km), delivery and collection, and again a 10% discount to readers of this book. For readers who have heard of the new Opel Kadett "Campette" (with seats that unfold within seconds into a double bed with polyfoam mattress and curtains), Hildebrandt has a supply. And for readers who would simply like to rent a car without trailer or tent from Mr. H. (Fiat 127, 1980 model, unlimited mileage, and pick-up and delivery in Amsterdam, Copenhagen, Brussels, Frankfurt, Luxembourg and Oslo), the cost is $318 for two weeks, $458 for three weeks, $588 for four weeks, $725 for five weeks, with a 10% discount off those prices to readers, and an additional 10% discount on off-season rentals ending before May 1 or starting after September 24. If, incidentally, you'd prefer to collect or drop off the car in London or Rome, the supplemental charge is $125 for a tent- or trailer-equipped car, $95 for a car alone. And if you'd like a daily rental only, the Fiat 127 is available from Hildebrandt for only $8.90 a day plus 8.9¢ per kilometer, with 10% off to readers of this book. Rates can change if changes occur in the future value (post March, 1980) of the U.S. dollar vis-à-vis the Danish kroner. For further information on the availability of upgraded cars, or for a brochure, or to make your booking, write Hendrik Hildebrandt, Share-a-Car, Inc., 61 Studiestraede, Copenhagen 1554, Denmark.

A discounted German rental

Readers travelling to Germany may want to know, instead, that the country's largest privately-owned auto rental firm, **Auto Sixt,** 9 Seitzstrasse, Munich (phone 22-33-33), has offered a 10% discount off their normal rates to bearers of this book. Sixt has offices in the ten largest German cities, and at several airports, too, but you'd best phone or write for the discount to the Chief Reservations Manager, Herr Unold, at the Munich headquarters.

U.S. firms offering car rentals

If, in preference to all these alternatives, you'd like to deal with a U.S.-based firm for your European car rental, then you can contact one of a number of major U.S. companies that now do nothing but the rental of cars (or sale of cars) to U.S. tourists vacationing in Europe. Among the largest of these companies are: **Europe by Car, Inc.,** 630 Fifth Avenue, New York, N.Y. 10020 (phone LT 1-3040), which also maintains offices in Los Angeles (9000 Sunset Boulevard), San Francisco (291 Geary Street), Chicago (520 N. Michigan Avenue), Seattle (200—4th & Pike Building), and Washington, D.C. (1506 Wisconsin Ave., N.W.); and **Auto-Europe, Inc.,** 21 East 40th Street, New York City (phone 578-4444). And for the purchase of specific makes of cars, you might want to deal directly with: **Renault USA, Inc.,** 100 Sylvan Ave., Englewood Cliffs, New Jersey 07632 (phone 201-461-6000); **Volkswagen Bristol Motors, Inc.,** 506 E. 76th Street, New York City (phone 249-7200); **Nemet**

Auto International, 153-12 Hillside Avenue, Jamaica, New York 11432 (phone 523-5858), handling all makes of cars but specializing in Triumphs, Jaguars and other British cars; **Mercedes-Benz of North America, Inc.,** 1 Mercedes Drive, Montvale, New Jersey (phone 201-573-0600); **Citroen Cars Coy.,** 31 Garland Way, Lyndhurst, New Jersey 07071 (phone 201-438-9300), with offices in Carson, California (1020 East 230th Street (phone 213-549-9880), which offers an interesting purchase/repurchase plan; or **The Kemwel Group** (all makes of cars), 247 West 12th Street, New York, N.Y. 10014 (phone 675-9000 or 800-221-3276). Brochures available.

CAR STORAGE IN NEW YORK: A thought, now, for readers who plan to drive their own cars to New York and pick up a Europe-bound plane or ship from there: the cheapest storage garage in the U.S. is **"Auto Baby Sitters",** located in a large grey building at 827 Sterling Place, Brooklyn, New York 11216 (phone 493-9800), which charges $27 a week, $54 a month, only $90 for two months, $123 for three months, for keeping your car in a dry, clean, inside storage place, and will pick up the car from you at a pier or airport for only $6 (and thereafter deliver it to you at that airport or pier for $7). They'll pick up the car from your hotel, free. Mr. Norman, manager of Auto Baby Sitters, will also give $1 off the storage price to readers of this book.

Chapter XXVII

BARGAIN SHOPPING TIPS

From $1.50 Ladies' Fans to $6 Gloves

AS YOU PASS THROUGH U.S. CUSTOMS at the end of your trip, you'll be permitted to bring in purchases totalling up to $300 per person without paying duty on the items you've bought. Congress has persistently refused to raise the duty exemption beyond the $300 level.

It's a joy, however, to report that this news should have almost no impact upon the readers of this book—for we've never advocated spending anything like $300 on European shopping. When Hope and I return from a trip, our haul normally consists of a stack of Florentine wallets ($3.50 apiece) for gifts; of seven or eight posters and reproductions (average: $3 per) to place upon our walls; along with two-or-so pairs of chic Italian gloves for Hope ($6.50 the pair); Danish teakwood candlesticks for my mother-in-law (only $7 apiece—she'll flip when she learns); perhaps a new Swiss watch ($35); a few bottles of French perfume; a few books; and our quota of European liquors and brandies. Those items are more than enough to keep us well-pleased for a year, and they cost nowhere near the present duty limits. Three hundred dollars for European shopping? When that becomes your goal, then shopping grows into a feverish, full-time occupation, rather than the fun-filled diversion it should be.

Well, what was once a mere personal inclination, has now become a patriotic duty. We'll continue to concentrate on gifts costing $8 and less, with only an occasional excursion into the $20 and $30 areas. Here's where you'll get them:

AMSTERDAM

The **Tax-free Shopping Center** at Amsterdam International Airport—biggest and best in Europe—is the chief shopping draw of this surprising city. A survey conducted several years ago by *Life Magazine* confined that "Amsterdam Airport is possibly the best in Europe for a variety of dutiable items at the lowest prices. Dutch gin and Bols Geneva are available for $3.80 a bottle, Dutch Schimmelpenninck cigars for $5 per 25, less than half the price of the cheapest Havanas. Perfume prices are as good as those in Paris, in some cases a few cents less. Precision goods are among the cheapest in Europe."

Liquor, particularly, is a stunning value at Amsterdam Airport—priced last year at only $6.50 a quart for such brand-name Scotch as Johnny Walker Red Label, Vat 69, Haig & Haig, Grant's, White Horse, others. That compared with the $8 you'd pay for the same bottle in Copenhagen, the $8.50 to $10 you paid in London, Brussels or Frankfurt, and the $10-and-up charged in New York.

In the city itself, low-cost diamonds and prints are the top buys. Obviously, we'll pursue the latter item only. A wide variety of really superb reproductions and posters are sold at a store called **Kunsthandel Verkerke,** on the important avenue, Leidsestraat, No. 12, just two blocks from the Leidseplein square. A particular rack of prints sell here for 12 guilders ($6) apiece; another 6 to 22.50 guilders; and there are small reproductions for 5 and 6 guilders ($2.50 and $3) on the walls. A similar collection, with some different items (Marc Chagalls, especially), is available in the $5 range at the second-floor shop in the **Stedelijk Museum,** the magnificent modern art gallery at Paulus Potterstraat 13. Rembrandts, on foot-square slabs of beaver-board, average 8 guilders at the **Rijksmuseum,** Stadhouderskade 42. These lay easily in your suitcase; the others must be rolled into a long cardboard tube.... Elsewhere in town, there are establishments which sell Dutch wooden shoes not as souvenirs, but for actual use by Dutchmen! My favorite is **A.W.G. Otten,** 102 Albert Cuypstraat (between Bol Straat and le van der Helstraat), which stands right in the heart of the colorful Albert Cuypstraat street market. Here, large, adult-sized wooden shoes cost only 20 guilders ($10) a pair, smaller ones only 13 guilders ($6.50), and there are also sold the rubber or leather inners that real people, wearing wooden shoes, use. I doubt that you can find better, or cheaper, wooden shoes anywhere else in town.... For hand-painted Dutch tiles, try the shop of an old gentleman named **Kramer,** at 64 Nieuwe Spiegelstraat (between Prinsengracht and Kerkstraat), where authentic, non-imitation, 18th and 19th century blue tiles sell for 25 to 50 guilders apiece; this is the best selection of tiles I've found in town. More centrally located, perhaps, is **Kunsthandel Rembrandt,** 61 Rokin, where a selection of contemporary tiles from the province of Friesland are always available for only 9.50 guilders per tile. That's only 100 yards away from the V.V.V. office on the Rokin.... Don't, by the way, fail to visit the Amsterdam "flea market." In most other cities, the "flea market"—an assemblage of pushcart vendors selling second-hand goods of every type—takes place but one day a week. In contrast, Amsterdam's flea market, on the nondescript **Waterlooplein,** operates every day of the week except Sunday; its offerings include old clothes, books, records and paintings, all kinds of food, furniture and antiques. See it even if you're not planning to buy a thing.... Elsewhere, on the **Albert Cuypstraat,** starting at the corner of Ferdinand Bolstraat, two blocks from the Heineken's Brewery, a several-square-block-long street market also takes place daily but Sunday, and is one of the city's top sightseeing attractions. The goods here are merely cheap, not second hand, but they're just as varied as those offered on the Waterlooplein: ties, socks, vegetables, herrings, clothes, corsets, flowers, fish, hardware. Don't miss it. The pushcarts are colorful, the shoppers even more colorful and volatile, and the entire setting is a picture straight from Breughel!

COPENHAGEN

This is another of the shopper's paradises of Europe. The designs of nearly every Danish article are fully ten years in advance of their American imitations, and prices are fully 20% less. Materials, looking as if they'd come from the hand-loom of Pablo Picasso, cost $4 and $5 a yard here, would cost $7 and $8 a yard in New York. Ceramic ashtrays, teakwood salad bowls and ice-buckets, also go for a fraction of what they'd bring in the States. . . . To view the very best (mainly for comparison purposes, not for actual shopping), head for **Den Permanente,** on the Vesterbrogade near the railroad station, which is a permanent exhibit of the best Danish crafts, limited solely to works that have passed a rigorous jury test. The low-cost items are in the front section (near the windows) of the second floor; most popular of all: the teakwood pillboxes with silver inlay for only 45 kroner ($8.57); three-piece cutlery, in three different colors, Jensen-designed, for 50 kroner ($9.52) per set. And then there are teakwood candlesticks for under $11, worthy of a museum showing; wooden wastepaper baskets ($10), almost too lovely to use; ceramics and items of stainless steel; and, of course, the low-cost ice-buckets and salad bowls that are normally too expensive to purchase in the U.S. Every item is in perfect taste, because everything in Den Permanente has been judged to be the best of its type. For a relatively minor charge, Den Permanente then ships your purchases to the U.S., and takes care of all crating and customs details—but keep in mind that items which you ship home, as opposed to those you carry with you onto the plane, do not qualify for duty exemption under U.S. customs regulations. . . . After viewing the goods at Den Permanente, you can then head for the major department stores at Copenhagen (**Anva's,** for example, diagonally across from the railroad station and air terminal) for occasionally cheaper and almost-as-good equivalents. . . . Elsewhere in Copenhagen, **Illums Bolighus** displays a larger selection of items, somewhat less costly than Den Permanente's, not uniformly consistent in quality. Still, you'll want to look over the latter before making your final choice. . . . Finally, posters and reproductions are a good bet in this city. You'll pay 40 kroner ($7.61) or less, per painting in any number of stores around Town Hall Square.

READERS' SELECTIONS: "Collectors of Royal Copenhagen china and porcelain who normally purchase from the Royal Copenhagen shop on the Stroget, should avoid the ground floor showroom and take the elevator to the 2nd floor, where the second and third 'sortings' (flawed goods) are displayed. Prices are 15% and 40% lower for minor differences in color and shading. And all such pieces are perfect, without chips or cracks. Stocks are changed daily" (F. H. Lambert, Worthing, England). . . . "**Chris Mollers Efte,** across the street from the Danish Resistance Museum at Amaliengade 49, has the most exciting variety of things to buy. For example, there are specially-made lamb skin slippers (only available at this store) for $12 a pair; there are marvelous sheep skin rugs selling for $40 (I saw the same one that we bought for much more in New York); there are heavy Scandinavian sweaters and all kinds of other equipment for sports fans or just plain fans of fine quality goods. And the people who run this store are typical of all Copenhagen— warm, friendly and wonderful" (Mr. & Mrs. R. S. Zimmerman, New York, N.Y.). . . . "Besides the famous 'Walk Street' called 'Stroget' (a little expensive for $15-a-Day'ers), there are two other sections good for shopping. One is **Christianshavn** on the other side of the harbor. Take Tram # 2 from Radhuspladsen heading toward Tivoli, Christianborg, the harbor. After crossing the bridge you're in Christianshavn. Get off at the 1st or 2nd stop after the bridge and you'll be right in the middle of a shopping area (**Torvegade**) where the *Danes* shop. To buy leather goods—purses, jackets, etc.—go to *Handi Sport,* 36 Torvegade, cheaper because it is a factory outlet store. For stainless steel trays, flatware, wood trays, etc., go to **G. Lorich,** Amagerbrogade 55. . . . The other section for shopping is on a street called **Norrebrogade,** reached by taking Tram # 16 from the rr. station to the stop beyond the Lakes. . . . Back in the center of town—a shop for gloves called **Gazelle,** Vesterbrogade 35. . . . "For those delightful and comfortable wooden shoes, go to **Valeur Fodtoj,** where the cost is less than $15 for a large-sized man's shoe. . . . For men's clothing it is **Troelstrup,** Vester Voldgade 5. . . . And, of course, **Anva,** Vesterbrogade, and **Magasin du Nord,** Kongens Nytorv, the two big department stores" (John W. Abrams, Reading, Pa.; note by AF: the very cheapest of the city's department stores—akin, let's say, to Alexander's in New York or Filene's basement in Boston—is **Daell's Varehus;** you'll enjoy a visit to it. The largest department store in Copenhagen—even the Queen shops there—is Magasin du Nord).

LONDON

The major attraction here, of course, is men's clothing—for this country is one of the few in the world where men are generally better-dressed than women! If you have at least two weeks in London, then you should quickly choose a reputable-looking tailor and have him custom-make a suit; it will wear for life, and it will cost half the price of a similar job in the United States. If you don't have that time available, then your best bet for an inexpensive, but well-designed, ready-made suit or jacket is one of the large men's chains, of which a typical one is Montague Burton, Ltd.

You'll see stores with the sign **"Burton's Tailoring"** at over six locations in London, the most central of which is the Burton's at 114 Regent Street, just a block off Piccadilly, where the second floor is packed with racks selling tween sports jackets for 35 pounds ($77), ready-made suits for 50 to 55 pounds ($110 to $121). I picked up a heavy, woolen sports jacket for exactly 45 pounds ($99) that would easily have cost $120 in the U.S. While this may have been a particular bargain, the normal prices at Burton's should not vary upwards by any great amount.

Women's woolen sweaters are a second good buy in London—particularly the ones on sale at **Marks & Spencer Department Store** ("Marks & Sparks," the British call it) on Oxford Street. Hope and I recently found Shetland wool cardigans selling there for $18 (less than 10 pounds), that would have cost at least $25 in the States. We found heavy button-down sweaters selling for thirteen pounds ($28.60), that would certainly cost at least twice as much over here.

Finally, another of the bargains of London are books—purchased at the famous **Foyle's** (world's largest bookstore) on Charing Cross Road (#119), where the hard-cover prices are generally half those of the United States. In fact, some books are priced so low that even the cost of shipping them home will not appreciably affect your saving. And it's wonderful fun to browse through the store.

READERS' SELECTIONS: "Hints for weary and wary travelers: Carry an umbrella wherever you go in London. I found it convenient to buy one of the foldup kind in a slip case (and I could pack it in my suitcase easily, too); as a man, I hooked it into my trouser belt at the side. They cost about 5 pounds in the stores, but the street vendors sold exactly the same umbrella for either 3 or 4 pounds" (Professor Arthur M. Sanderson, Tampa, Florida). . . . "Now that the 'Romantic Look' is highly fashionable again, a must-see for every woman or girl going to London is the moderately priced **Laura Ashley** shop at 71/73 Lower Sloane St., London SW 3, telephone, 730-1771, (it's located near Harrod's, in Knightsbridge). If you hanker for 'English Ethnic', or have always secretly yearned to look just like one of Kate Greenway's illustrations, this is the place for you! Always crowded, this is a 'no-frills,' all clothes hanging, open-to-view, on pipe-racks (on two sizeable floors) establishment. Not much elegant service or individualized attention, but at these prices ($20 to around $38 for long cotton gowns; frilly 'gypsy' skirts $15 and up) who cares? Many good sales here, too" (Arthur Landow, Brooklyn, New York). . . . **"Reject China Shop** at 33 Beauchamp Place, just off Brompton Road near Harrods, carries second and third sortings (rejects) of fine English China, and the selections change daily. Prices range from 50 pence for a small China animal, to 700 pounds for a dinner service" (Dr. and Mrs. Albert O. Girz, Ann Arbor, Michigan). . . . **"Hamleys** on Regent

Street, is a fascinating, twelve-stories-high toy store, and has an excellent selection of dolls for collectors" (Carole Carter, Universal City, California). . . . "Pipe smokers should not fail to pick up some of the pipe bargains offered at **Selfridge's Smoke Shop** during the summer. English-made briar pipes from about £5.25 (about $11.50)" (T. K. Moy, Hempstead, New York). . . . "Shopping area: anywhere in England, but especially in London, a marvelous purchase is the famous lemon soap, **Bronnley Lemons.** Available in boxes or individually, in three sizes, they are found in most department stores and drug stores (chemists). They cost pennies over there (65 pence for a bar of toilet soap, 90 pence for bath soap), and a fortune here in specialty gift shops. A highly recommended purchase" (Dr. & Mrs. Kenneth Korven, Susanville, California).

PARIS

The first floor of the Louvre, off the main entrance, houses a museum store which sells reproductions that (1) aren't usually bought in the United States: and (2) sell for several times the price, when they are. We bought an unsigned Bernard Buffet lithograph of the Ile de la Cité for $15. We saw the very same lithograph, bearing the penciled signature of Buffet, selling for $165 in a gallery on Madison Avenue in New York. We bought a blue-and-white reproduction of a recent Matisse study (now on the foyer wall of our apartment) for $10. It isn't sold in the U.S., and it would cost $25 if it were. . . . In buying perfume in Paris, your aim is to find a "parfumerie" offering the greatest discount off already-low list prices. Contrary to all the touts in the American Express area, these places are not found on the second floor of abandoned warehouses in Montparnasse. Some of the most elegant stores offer the greatest discounts. Try **Paul's** on the chic Rue de Rivoli, No. 210 (take the metro to the Tuileries stop). You'll get the maximum legal reduction, and you'll be treated with honesty and with respect. . . . For cheap articles of French-styled clothing (jazzy sports shirts, scarves) go to the **"Prisunic,"** which is a giant dime-store on the right-hand side of the Champs Elysées as you walk toward the Arc de Triomphe (corner of Rue la Boetie). Shirts for $10, scarves for $5, bikinis for $11. . . . Elsewhere, the **Museum of Modern Art** in Paris (recently moved to the new Georges Pompidou Center of Art and Culture, near the old Les Halles) has good, very modern reproductions (Klee, Leger) for 40 francs ($9.30).

The chief shopping attraction of Paris is, of course, women's dresses, but those are stratospherically-priced in the custom-made shops. I think you'll find something quite comparable, but vastly less expensive, on the third floor of the **Galeries Lafayette,** which Hope and I think is the best department store in the world. On its third floor, Galeries Lafayette sells copies of all the renowned designs, and prices them so well that, during one sale, Hope picked up a Saint-Laurent-type trench coat for 200 francs ($46.51). There are numerous racks of ladies' suits selling for 240 francs, and there are coats that shriek with chic at prices that are substantially lower than American ladies usually pay for comparable items. Everything in the store is the highest fashion, including even the cheapest items, such as the hats and bathing suits that sell on its ground floor; and to relieve the fatigue, there's an open-air cafe on the roof ("Super Terrasse") with gaily-colored awnings and garden-type tables, and moderate prices for lady-like snacks.

READERS' SELECTIONS: "I should like to suggest that you include in your sources for inexpensive goods the **Laboratoire de la Chalcographie du Louvre.** It is located on the third floor of the stairway on the riverside entrance to the Louvre, just a few yards from the main selling room. It is open also on Saturday. The Laboratoire makes reprints from old engraving plates, and sells some for as little as 40 francs (less than $10). They also have a catalogue listing all the 16,000 plates from which they make engravings. The subjects comprise maps; etchings from reproductions of paintings of the 17th and 18th centuries; scenes of Paris, Versailles, etc.; buildings, architectural details, etc., etc. What is particularly interesting is that at such low prices you get an authentic actual print, of which only the paper is modern. Some of these prints are on sale at much higher prices in bookstores, antique shops, etc. Once framed, they cannot be distinguished from the real thing. They make inexpensive, beautiful gifts, which take little or no place in one's baggage and can be sent by mail" (G. A. Loewenthal, SHAPE, APO 55, New York, New York). . . . "While in Paris we felt we must buy some Paris fashions but were on a Chicago budget. We had given up, until we found a small odd-lot clearance shop, **Unishop Shopping,** 50 Rue de la Verrerie, Paris 4, tel. 277-54-42, that had only fine quality women's fashions, many originals included. My wife's black lace formal, an original, was among those on the 60 Franc rack. You take it from there" (Capt. Dean A. Hansen, West Germany).

ROME

The "flea market," focal point for the best low-cost shopping in Rome, open on Sundays only, is described at length in our Rome chapter. . . . On the weekdays, go instead to the Spanish Steps, where you'll find the Via Condotti, then walk down the Via Condotti until you come to the little open square that is the **Piazza di Fontanella Borghese.** Nearly every booth and pushcart in this open-air market is devoted to the low-cost sale of old books, etchings, posters and reproductions. You must bargain, sticking to 50% of the offering price. . . . Rome's most exciting leather goods shop, and one that is nevertheless moderately-priced, is **Elegant Belmonte,** at 32 Via Emilia (the street that runs parallel to, and one short block from, the Via Veneto). Here you'll find a wide selection of leather goods: handbags (15,000 lire and up), colorful umbrellas (7,500 lire), men's wallets (6,000 to 9,000 lire), multicolored coin purses (2,000 lire), etc. . . . And for extremely cheap men's or women's clothing, sold on outdoor stands, head for the mammoth open market at **Piazza Vittorio Emanuele,** described more fully in our Rome chapter.

FLORENCE

The not-to-be-violated rule for a lady shopper in Europe is to resist all temptations until she arrives in Florence. Whatever other women's items you may see in Europe, or in Italy, Florence has them better. Beautiful ladies' gloves, shoes, handbags—elegantly styled but cheap. Throughout the city, you'll find ladies' glove stores, among others, selling gloves for $6 per pair that would be the desperate envy of any far-higher priced American women's store.

As for leather goods—whether men's or women's, household or personal —again, wait until you get to Florence. Magnificent Florentine men's leather wallets are available for $3.50, leather cigarette cases for $4; leather change purses and glass cases with intricately-worked designs, for $3.50 apiece. Ashtrays covered with leather, and with modern, ceramic mosaics inside, can be had for $5; leather notebooks for $2.50. Where to find them? The **Straw Market** in Florence (selling leather, as well as straw products, and open daily from 9 to 7) should be visited for the experience of its bustling, bargaining atmosphere. But the same items sell for much less in the open-air market of pushcarts and stalls along the streets surrounding the **Mercato Centrale,** near the railroad station, which happens to be the place where Florentines themselves—and very few tourists—shop. Walk, for example, along the **Via dell Ariento,** which begins at the Via Nazionale near the station: you'll find ladies' gloves for 5,000 lire (less than $6.50), black leather briefcases for 3,500 lire ($4.21), stylish black leather suitcases for 9,000 lire, ladies' blouses for 7,000 lire, and—best bargain of all—mohair sweaters offered at varying prices (often, only $10), but always unusually cheap. Another way to approach this market area is via the **Piazza San Lorenzo,** behind the San Lorenzo Church, which itself is near the Duomo. Here, too, are dozens of stalls with many of the items

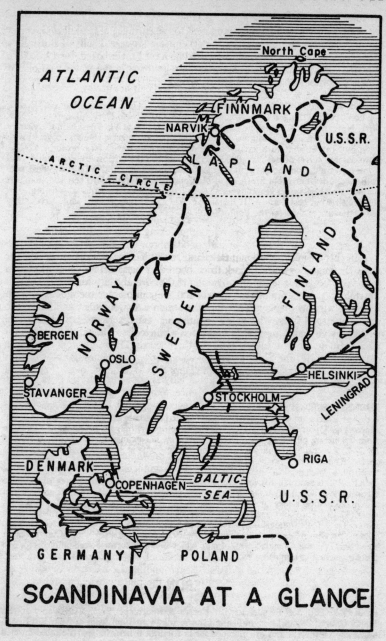

SCANDINAVIA AT A GLANCE

that sell for more at the Straw Market or in the subsidiary tourist market in the courtyard of the Uffizi Galleries. And when you buy here, bargain! You ought never to purchase anything in Florence except at a 20% (or greater) discount off the first price quoted to you.

Finally, the reproduction stand next to the entrance of the Uffizi Galleries has excellent art bargains, including several foot-square details of Botticelli's "Rites of Spring" and "Venus," mounted on hard beaver board, for 12,000 lire ($14.45). These can be laminated when you get back to the States, and placed on the bathroom or kitchen walls of your home.

READERS' SELECTIONS: "If you like **Pucci** go to his shop which is in his Palazzo. Even if you don't buy anything, it's something to see. Elegant!" (Irwin Katz, Mamaroneck, New York; Note from H.A.: Marquis Emilio Pucci's Palazzo is at Via Pucci 6, in the vicinity of the Duomo. In his second floor boutique (walk up the marble staircase covered with a soft blue carpet, then turn left), you'll find occasional bargains (scarves for 4,000 lire, multi-colored velvet purses for 6,000 lire) mixed among the expensive merchandise. And if you turn right, you can peep into the famous showroom). . . . "We went to dozens of leather factories, but **Fibbi Brothers**, at 21r Corso dei Tintori, had the best selection, best qualities and best values. Employees all speak English, and are unusually helpful. For gold jewelry, our best find was **Il Regalo** 32b Via San Giuseppe, near Santa Croce; they had better prices than on the Ponte Vecchio" (Eileen Zarick, New York City).

MADRID

In this cheapest-of-all capital cities, you'll find the world's cheapest shoe store, the huge **Los Guerrilleros,** directly on the Puerta del Sol (# 5). The area to the left (as you face the store) contains the $9 and $12 varieties, the one to the right goes higher in price. You take down the number of the shoes you want from the window display, write the number on a slip of paper, and hand it to one of the sales girls, who will eventually fit you. There are both men's and women's styles, and the pair of well-worn white loafers I bought a year ago for $9 are still on my feet, intact, as I type these words. Directly across the Puerta del Sol, at # 12, the **Casa de Diego** sells nothing but ladies' fans—some for as little as 100 pesetas ($1.51). Bullfighters hats? Authentic ones? Try any of the hat shops on the Plaza Mayor.

READERS' SELECTIONS: "A good starting place for shopping is the large department store, **Galerias Preciados,** where you can establish a price base for comparison with small shops. The **Oportunidades,** just across the street, is the bargain basement of this large store, where we picked up such buys as men's leather-palmed knit-back driving gloves for $2.25 a pair, good quality leather pumps for my wife at $7.50, and leather children's shoes at comparable prices" (W. W. Woodmansee, Santa Monica, California). . . . "Saffron, a spice used in Spanish cooking, can be purchased in cartons of 10 packages each for 140 pesetas ($2.12), and the equivalent would cost $15 in the States for the same quantity. Wonderful buy to bring back to friends who use this spice in cooking. . . . Spain also manufactures a very famous toilet soap called **Maja Jabon,** which sells for 75 pesetas a bar ($1.13). Three of these bars sell for about $4.50 in the States in better department stores. They make wonderful gifts for women back home" (Edward Pietraszek, Chicago Illinois; note by AF: a convenient shop for purchasing Maja soap is **Los Claveles** at 11 Fuencarral, off the Avenida Jose Antonio, which also sells tortoise-shell pillboxes for 325 pesetas, including initial).

LISBON

READERS' SELECTIONS: "Be sure to visit **Correa & Rodrigues,** Praca de S. Paulo 10 (St. Paul's Church Square), for authentic fishermen's sweaters of wool at from $10 to $15 apiece, and although they are intended for Portuguese fishermen, sports-clothes-minded men and women visitors like to wear them. The store expects you to try on sweaters and be entirely satisfied before you buy. They are down near the waterfront where you will wander anyway to see the constantly changing scene of the huge market, with women carrying baskets of fish on their heads, and people hurrying for the ferry which takes you across the River Tagus for a few centavos to **Cachilhas,** an up-and-coming little town.

Cachilhas is worth a ride more than once to see a blend of the old and the new apartment dwellings and to eat the excellent seafood. Many people from Lisbon ride over there for lunch and there is ample time. . . . **Mr. Cork's Shop,** Casa das Corticas, on Rue de Escola Politenica 4-10, is a world-famous store for novelties and useful articles made of cork. Mr. Cork is a genial man who speaks English and will offer you a glass of wine as you enter, and no one bothers you while you browse. We bought only one cork item, a unique landscape of intricately carved, tiny cork pieces, framed, but there are many other items at reasonable prices. . . . The **Thieves' Market** in the Alfama (Old City) is a fascinating place on a Saturday, with its open-air stalls. I understand there are antique treasures if one has the patience and interest to hunt, but it is fun just to browse around looking at the bewildering array of 'stuff.' I bought a new black hat with dashing wide brim, worn by the campions (ranchers), of fine felt, for less than $6. Take a taxi, as this is a steep spot to reach. . . . Finally, for original oil landscapes of typical Portuguese scenes, we recommend a very complete bookshop which sells a few oils, lots of delicate watercolors, and etchings. It is **Livraria Ferin, Lda.,** 70 Rue Nova do Almada. They painstakingly removed our two water-colors from the stretch frames and rolled them for easy packing. Total cost of two paintings was about $29" (Marjorie de Costa, Washington, D.C.).

BARCELONA

READER'S SELECTION: "My wife is a real guitar fan and found a small 'Fabrica de Guitarras' called **Los Flamencos** at San Pablo 28 (just off the Ramblas), half a block from Plaza San Agustin, where she had all manner of beautifully hand-made guitars to choose from. She got one of the lighter models for 2,800 pesetas ($42.42)" (Steven Otto, Apapa, Nigeria).

ISTANBUL

READERS' SELECTION: "Muzaffer Vyanik, who calls himself 'Muzo,' has a shop in the covered bazaar which sells suede and leather coats and jackets at rock-bottom prices. The workmanship is of the highest quality and 'John' has a great deal of pride in his tailors. We bought a full-length green suede lady's coat from him; the identical coat was more than twice as much at the leather shop in one of the leading hotels. This is in the covered bazaar at Stalls #s 21, 23 and 25, under the name **Stil Suet Export**" (Mr. and Mrs. Richard D. Greenfield, Hartsdale, New York).

OSLO

READERS' SELECTION: "We found a fantastic deal on hand-knitted Norwegian wool sweaters at the shop of **Lulle Otterstad,** Solligaten 2 (phone 56 27 00) (near the American Embassy). Ours were $54 each, while downtown the same thing was at least $65. She will ship sweaters home and will fill mail orders" (Mr. and Mrs. Thomas G. Stoebe, London, England). . . . "A visit to **Stallen,** at 8 Grensen, will provide a wide selection of inexpensive, better-than-average household articles. They feature, of course, goods manufactured in Norway, but other Scandinavian countries are represented as well. It is located near the Glass Department Store which, by the way, has an enormous selection of glass, china and stainless steel at 2/3 U.S. prices" (Jay R. Conley, Pittsburgh, Pennsylvania).

VIENNA

READER'S SELECTION: "I'm sure there are many stores in Vienna, but this one captured our attention and enabled us to buy gifts for discriminating friends who never guessed our small capital outlay: **Ernest Sramek,** Mariahilferstrasse 66. It is a small jewelry store, at which we bought the tiny petit point brooches for about 65 schillings ($4.81) each, and the authentic rosebuds and leaves dipped in gold for only 85 schillings ($6.29) each. We ordered more after coming home and received prompt and accurate attention" (Reba June Green, Bristol, Virginia).

LUCERNE

You can't leave Europe without seizing the opportunity to buy a Swiss watch. But the most exciting store for a budget-priced watch is not in Zurich, but in Lucerne, 30 miles away. Take the train to Lucerne (45 minutes) and go to **Birnbaum's,** Pilatusstrasse 34, where every member of the staff is a gracious human being, anxious to help you. Keep asking for the cheaper varieties, until they haul out the $25 and $30 trays. These are superb examples of the Swiss art. They would cost $40 to $50 in the U.S. My own favorites are the brands which have black faces, and severely modern, stripped-of-icing designs. Although many other watch shops in Lucerne offer similar values, Birnbaum's is included here because of their exceptional kindness to readers: they will act as a mail-drop for you, provide information on hotels and restaurants, even make occasional reservations for you!

ATHENS

READER'S SELECTION: "The antique shop of **Dionisios Panu,** which is located at Ifestou 24, near the flea market, offers the greatest selection of antiques at prices so low that my friend and I nearly purchased the entire shop. Cost for a wine set, tray, and six handmade brass cups, was $15 to $20. Other items were even lower" (Allan A. Armour, Brooklyn, New York; note by AF: Ifestou Street is, in reality, the heart of the Athens flea market, although the shops along it stay open throughout the week, and not merely on the flea market's one day [Sunday] of operation. I like the **Curiosity Shop** at # 17, which seems to me to carry the most tasteful collection of ikons, samovars, cow bells, wood paintings —the items featured by the Ifestou Street stores. The subway station here is Monastiraki, one stop from Omonia Square on the way to Piraeus; don't miss the Sunday flea market, in any event).

NICE

READER'S SELECTION: "In France one naturally thinks of perfume, and one of the best perfume shops in the country is **F. Poilpot, Aux Perfumes de Grasse,** Rue Saint Gaetan 10 (aptly near the famous flower market). Over 60 different scents are sold here at 10 francs per glass flask; they're prettily displayed like fruits and vegetables in containers and boxes in front of the shop. Upon request, the owner will help you combine various brands to create a fragrance just for your personality or mood. Open Tuesday through Saturday from 9:30 to noon and 3 and 6" (Yetta Reich, New York, New York).

In the last analysis, the best shopping buys (as well as the best hotel and restaurant finds) are the ones you'll discover yourself. We'll be happy to pass on these finds to other deserving American tourists, if you'll send them in as a "Reader's Selection."

Chapter XXVIII

EUROPE ON $20 A DAY

For Higher-Spending Readers

FOR READERS WILLING to spend more than the sums we advocate, we've compiled, in this final chapter, a brief list of outstanding, but still moderately-priced, hotels in 19 major cities—establishments whose rates require a daily budget of approximately $20 per person for room and three meals. Our list doesn't pretend to be a comprehensive one; it will be expanded, in future editions, to cover each of the cities discussed in the main body of the text, and to contain more selections per city. And it concentrates particularly, in this edition, on those European cities in which $20-a-day recommendations may perhaps be needed most: the relatively-expensive Scandinavian cities and, to a lesser extent, the German-speaking cities—Munich, Vienna, Berlin. Here, of course, our selections are generally of a different sort of establishment than those found in our $15-a-day chapters: in most cases, less intimate, less traditional and more modern, and sometimes more particularly designed to handle heavy summer traffic from overseas, rather than the tourism of fellow-countrymen or other Europeans. For those occasions when you may desire that sort of lodging, these recommendations constitute an initial, and still very sketchy, attempt to be of aid.

Here, now are $20-a-day hotels (and a few $20-a-day-type restaurants) in 19 cities:

COPENHAGEN

One of the finest establishments in its moderate price range, **Hotel Copenhagen** at Vesterbrogade 41 (phone 311-533) offers spacious and impeccably clean, bathless rooms (15 singles, 29 doubles); free showers off the hallway; a location ten minutes from the station; intelligent, friendly management; singles for only 95 to 110 kroner ($19.04 to $20.95); doubles and twins for 170 to 190 kroner ($32.38 to $36.19).

Restaurant Kulkaelderen, Kultorvet 14, has the look of a classical art gallery, with antique furnishings and oil paintings on exposed brick walls. But luxurious surroundings notwithstanding, its copious roast beef meals, followed by Danish blue cheese with bread and butter, and all washed down with Tuborg Pils, will cost you just 51 kroner ($9.71). . . . But if it's only a snack you want, **Husmann's Vinstue,** Larsbjoernstraede 2, serves up the best marinated herring in town, for 12 kroner. Or you can try a special Danish cheese with horse radish and egg yolk (14.50 kroner), accompanied by fiery aquavit (17 kroner). Open daily, except Sunday, from 9 a.m. to midnight.

OSLO

Oslo's vast **Panorama Hotel,** operated by the local university student organization, is set in quiet, landscaped grounds on the outskirts of Oslo, at 218 Sognsveien (phone 23-05-86), and is open to adult tourists from June 1 to September 1. The high-rise hotel, dramatically set on broad lawns, offers 900 tourist beds in a variety of compactly-designed rooms outfitted with modern Scandinavian furniture. Students provide the service, and do it so well that this has become just about the most popular hostelry in Oslo, a welcome respite from city hotels, and only 15 minutes by local train from downtown Oslo (take the Sognsvann line to Krigsja Station). 1980 rates, all of which include continental breakfast (with egg) and service charges, are 155 kroner ($30.39) for a single with hot and cold running water; 195 kroner ($38.23) for a single with toilet and shower; 210 kroner ($41.17) for twin rooms without bath; 275 kroner ($53.92) for twins with toilet and private bath; 58 kroner ($11.37) for an extra bed. And there's a restaurant, bar, bank, souvenir shops, free parking, and all other large-hotel services.

Gamle Christiania, at 1 Grensen, near the Cathedral, is a solid Oslo restaurant—the kind in which the same waiters stay on for years and years, a quiet place with calm, comfortable surroundings, a relaxing mood, and tasty, although non-sophisticated, food: various omelets for 30 kroner, soup (10 kroner), steamed fillet of sole with sauce remoulade and boiled potatoes (36 kroner), fresh-fried salmon with small steamed potatoes and melted butter (48 kroner), T-bone steak with sauce bearnaise (42 kroner), and various other fish and meat dishes ranging from 30 to 55 kroner. Two minor suggestions: try for one of the tables next to the cozy, white-curtained windows, and end the meal with warm apple pie topped with vanilla ice (15 kroner).

MUNICH

Hotel Stachus, 7 Bayerstrasse (phone 59-28-81), a largish (75 rooms) hotel on a shopping street, close to the station, places telephones and radios in each room, as well as comfortable modern furnishings. 55 of the rooms have either private shower (without private toilet), or private bath (with private toilet). Singles with shower are 48 marks ($25.26), singles with bath 58 marks ($30.52); doubles with shower are 79 marks ($41.57), doubles with bath 89 marks ($46.84); all rates including continental breakfast, service and tax. That's good value for the money.

Also close to the station is the 95-bed **Hotel Schweizerhof,** at Goethestrasse 26 (phone 53-96-31), managed by friendly and helpful Herr Kurt

Schlarb; if you'll show him a copy of this book, he'll not only give you a free city map, but also answer any questions about your stay in Munich—whether or not you book a room in his hotel! Herr Schlarb offers special rates to readers of 65 marks ($34.21) single, 85 marks ($44.73) double, all with bath or shower, private w.c., and big, English style breakfast (juice, ham and eggs, etc.). The one exception: during the Oktoberfest period (in 1980, from September 7 to October 10), when prices are higher, as they are in almost all Munich hotels.

Two famous Munich restaurants, both recently completely renovated, are recommended if you can afford to spend a minimum of 13 to a maximum of 22 marks for a meal to remember: one is the **Ratskeller** at Marienplatz 8; the other the **Spatenhaus Bräustuben**, at Residenzstrasse 12.

The Ratskeller, whose entrance is near the fountain in front of the Rathaus, is a spacious and unusually picturesque establishment in the basement of the City Hall, with a long tradition for serving local Bavarian specialties. You'll want to try the spanferkel mit kartoffelknödel and speckkrautsalat (roast baby pig with potato dumplings and kraut salad with special dressing) for 15.30 marks; sauerbraten mit knödeln (10.80 marks); Münchner Wurstplatte (four different sausages, with mashed potatoes and sauerkraut) for 11 marks; turkey steak with mushrooms and rice 13.50 marks; the large variety of wines, costing 2.50 to 5 marks per ¼ liter; and, last but not least, superb Bavarian beer: half a liter is 2.80 marks.

The Spatenhaus Bräustuben (located in front of the State Opera House, less than a five-minute walk from Marienplatz), is a bit more sophisticated, although it also sports a popular salad bowl counter as you enter; for 12 marks you can have as much salad as you can heap on your plate and make it a vegetable day. Tastier are such classics as schweinebraten mit salad (13.50 marks), hasenpfeffer mit spatzle (a kind of hare goulash with noodles) for 13.50 marks, and the renowned Pils Barrel Beer, served in a tulip-shaped glass.

BERLIN

Hotel Alsterhof, 1 Würzburger Strasse (phone 213-7001), three blocks from the very center of West Berlin's downtown area, is another relatively-new hotel with moderate prices, this time with 81 rooms, all with private bath or shower. These have no frills, but are modern, handsome pine bedroom suites with floor-to-ceiling drapes, very much like any first class American hotel. Singles with shower and breakfast are a high 79 marks ($41.57), but doubles (one large bed) with bath a more moderate 99 to 104 marks ($52.10 to $54.73), including breakfast, service and tax.

On numerous picture postcards of Berlin, you'll find the Funkturm, the radio and TV tower that looks like a pocket edition of the Eiffel Tower. Half-way up this landmark is the popular **Funkturm Restaurant,** which offers both meal and view. Eisbein with sauerkraut and mashed green peas, 11 marks; chicken fricassee with asparagus, mushrooms and crayfish, 14.50 marks; roast turkey, 18 marks; original Russian vodka, 3 marks; ice cream topped with whipped cream, 4 marks; and a bottle of light beer, 3.20 marks. Take the S-Bahn to Westkreuz, and then take the elevator (one mark) to reach the restaurant in the sky.

VIENNA

Hotel Academia Wien, at 3a Pfeilgasse (phone 43-16-61), is another brand-new student hotel made available to tourists of all ages in summer (July to the end of September). It is ten stories high, straight-walled, and extremely modern (much like the Scandinavian student hotels), and has 360 rooms, each of which is equipped with radio, phone, bathtub, toilet and sink; many of the rooms also sport private balconies. I should stress, of course, that the rooms are compact: the couch turns into a bed, the desk opens to disclose a little dressing-table mirror, the closet is built in to the entrance hall, and there's another closet at the head of each bed—every inch of space has been used. And the plain, linoleum-tiled hallways, with their identical pine doors, tend to the institutional. But there are offsetting touches—in particular, a sun terrace with lounge chairs on the tenth floor, offering a beautiful panoramic view of Vienna; a full kitchen in the basement. And the location is an excellent one, within walking distance of the University, only 5 minutes by tram 46 or J from the Opera. Rates are: 385 schillings ($28.51) single, but only 520 schillings ($38.51) double, including breakfast, service, taxes, and private bath.

Pension Geissler 14 Postgasse (phone 63-28-03), is a central, very modern pension in a newly built apartment house on a quiet street in the inner city. While the rooms are modest in size (because modern), they havè neat blonde-wood furnishings accented with colorful throw rugs, telephones in all rooms, and 22 rooms come with private bath or shower. These rent, at the peak of the season, for 480 to 630 schillings ($35.55 to $46.66) double, including breakfast for two, service and tax—a high rate, but perhaps warranted by location and bright attractiveness.

Zum Weissen Rauchfangkehrer (The White Chimneysweeper), at 4 Weih-burggasse, near St. Stephen's Cathedral, serves all the Austrian specialties at a moderate price, and offers them up in a wood-panelled dining room that branches out into a number of separate niches with intimate tables, affording privacy and gemütlichkeit at the same time. You'll find all the local dishes, from leberknödelsuppe (15 schillings) to garnierter tafelspitz or wiener schnit-zel (the latter two each 105 schillings) to delicious pastries, like the tongue-breaking brandteigschokoladencremekrapfen (try it and find out what it is), priced at 37 schillings. And although most main dishes range from 70 to 90 schillings ($5.18 to $6.66), you can also order more reasonable plates, like sausages with potatoes or sauerkraut, for 57 schillings.

ROME

Well located at 89 Via Boncompagni, a 5-minute walk from the elegant Via Veneto, the 50-room **Hotel Oxford** (phone 475-1393) is both owned and managed by an energetic gentleman named Ugo Quarta, assisted by a staff whose every member is fluent in English. Signor Quarta has this year (1980) agreed to offer special reduced rates to bearers of this book: 18,000 lire ($21.68) single, 28,000 lire ($33.73) double, always for rooms with private bath, air-conditioning, radio and telephone. Dinner, served in the room-with-a-small-fountain located behind the large, modern lobby, is 8,000 lire ($9.63) for three courses, and nightcaps are available in the bar for 800 lire (campari soda, 96¢) 2,000 lire (whiskey, $2.40), or 2,500 lire (for an expertly mixed, double dry martini, $3.01).

Hotel-Pensione St. Elisabetta 146 Via Veneto (phone 480-318), the most elegant small pension in Rome, with a stunning pink-and-white decor and silk-upholstered furniture, should be your next stop if the Oxford is full—it's only a short block from the latter. The charming, blond-haired Margherita Adnan-Schafer (fluent in English) is in charge; her rates in 1980, special to readers of this book, are 13,000 lire ($15.66) for bathless singles, 22,000 lire ($26.50) for bathless doubles, 28,000 lire ($33.73) for doubles with private bath, breakfast and all else included.

At some point in your stay, you'll want to eat in the picturesque section of Trastevere, but restaurants there are generally more expensive than in the central part of Rome. An exception, and one of my favorites, is **Trattoria da Carlo all' Alberata,** 16 Via Cardinal Merry del Val, which specializes in typical Roman and fish dishes and where one can eat for less than 9,000 lire ($10.84) amidst a crowd of lively, happy Romans, including many celebrities (Peter Ustinov, on my last visit). Try risotto alla marinara (2,200 lire) to start, coda alla vaccinara (cooked ox-tail, 3,500 lire) for your main course, vegetables and dessert (for example, home-made ice cream), 1,200 lire each, half a liter of wine (800 lire), and you'll also pay a 700 lire cover charge and a 15% service (for that, 8,280 lire total—you can spend less). And to reach the restaurant, take bus #75 or 55 from Terminal Station to the Piazza Mastai stop (just after the Garibaldi Bridge), from which Da Carlo is to the right. Open seven days a week from July through September, but closed on Mondays in other months.

VENICE

Pensione Accademia, Dorsoduro, Ponte Maravegie (near the Accademia Bridge), phone 37-846, a little country estate all its own, yet smack in the heart of Venice on the Grand Canal, is the pension that was used as Katherine Hepburn's fictional residence in her film with Rossano Brazzi, "Summertime." That should give you a hint of the picturesque quality of this typical Venetian building surrounded by two gardens, and with its own landing stage for boats. Lavishly furnished, but in non-ostentatious and older style, with beamed ceilings, glass Murano chandeliers, and well-worn, comfortable furniture, the Accademia charges 36,000 lire ($43.37) for a double with bath, 29,000 for a double without bath, including breakfast. Don't expect modernity or excitement; the patrons here "wind down" amidst the bustle of Venice.

In a more central position near St. Mark's Square, the **Hotel Bel Sito,** 2157 San Marco (phone 710-760 or 22-293), offers, to readers of this book only, specially reduced rates considerably below those officially allowed to it: 29,000 lire ($34.93), breakfast included, for a bathless double, 13,500 lire ($16.26) for additional beds in the room. That's for three floors, no elevator, but comfortable, airy rooms with new furniture; and the location is nearly perfect: leaving the hotel, you turn into the first street on your left, keep walking the only possible way, and after two bridges and 300 yards, the unique, visual splendor of St. Mark's Square emerges before you. To reach the hotel from the station, take vaporetto #1, and after traveling almost the entire distance of the Canale Grande, on a memorable sightseeing cruise, get off at the Santa Maria del Giglio stop (one stop before St. Mark's), then follow the narrow street to Giglio Square, site of the hotel.

Near the Rialto Bridge, at Calle della Madonna, **Trattoria Madonna** has been a favorite of middle-class Venetians for many generations. While everything here is à la carte and there is no Menu Turistico, still if you choose carefully, a good meal should cost you less than 9,000 lire ($10.84). Thus, you might have spaghetti or gnocchi or pasticcio di lasagne (each 1,000 lire) to begin, then a veal cutlet with cooked vegetables or roast chicken with mixed salad (3,500 lire each), topped off by fruit, cake, cheese or ice cream 1,000 lire each). Add half a liter of excellent white (Soave) or red (Valpolicella) wine (1,100 lire), plus a 500-lire cover charge, an 11% service charge, and a 200-lire tip, for a grand total of 8,100 lire ($9.75). Closed Wednesdays.

FRANKFURT

Hotel Europa, 17 Baseler Strasse (phone 238-562), conveniently located within a three-minute walk of the central railway station, is a recently-built, five-story structure in which all rooms are with private bath or shower, yet rent for only 50 marks ($26.31) single, 70 marks ($36.84) double, 80 marks ($42.10) twin, with breakfast included. **Hotel Tourist,** next door at 23 Baseler Strasse, takes the overflow at rates about 10% less. Since Frankfurt is often jammed with conventions, you'll want the name of **Dema Travel Office,** 18 Karlsruher Strasse (phone 23-13-22), next to the station, to whom you can write or phone in emergency situations; its owner, bearded Herr Gonzalez (that's his name), has offered special attention to readers, and a 10% reduction on all sightseeing tours and excursions.

NICE

Hotel Saint-Georges, 7 Avenue Georges Clemenceau (phone 88-79-21), only five short blocks from the sea and one block from the Avenue Jean-Médecin, Nice's main street, is easily the best two-star-A hotel in Nice, a stunning white structure with red awnings, with an Empire-style restaurant that looks onto a garden courtyard, a superb and sophisticated staff, rooms tastefully furnished, and rates of about $29 double, for rooms with private bath; $19 double, for bathless rooms—breakfast included.

Just 100 yards from the sea, the casinos, and shopping, the **Hotel Alfa,** 30 Rue Massena (878-863), rents 39 pleasant, modern rooms with air conditioning, bath or shower, w.c. and phone, for 95 francs ($22.09) single, 140 francs ($32.55) double or twin. Manager Monsieur Jesus is especially friendly and helpful to our readers.

MADRID

The **Hotel Emperador,** 53 Avenida de José Antonio (phone 247-28-00), has, as its major attraction, a terraced roof garden with a large swimming pool, and a magnificent location on Madrid's main street; but also 250 well furnished rooms with private bath, for which the charge is 3,500 pesetas ($54.45) for a large double with bath. Downstairs, there's a circular rotunda with impressive marble walls and pillars that leads to a formal dining room, where guests are served by waiters in traditional black ties and tails.

Hotel Arosa, at 21 Salud (a small side street off the Avenida José Antonio (phone 232-1600), is a fully air-conditioned "Four Star" hotel in which two elevators lead to a lobby of opera-red carpets, modern paintings and a "striped pants" management. The spacious and tastefully-decorated rooms rent for 2,700 pesetas ($40.90) single, 3,800 pesetas ($57.57) double, which includes obligatory continental breakfast.

Under the management of the same family for generations, the **Taberna Meson Las Descalzas,** at 3 Postigo San Martin, near Plaza del Callao, boasts an historic dining room (a second one is in the cellar), excellent cuisine, and a manager who looks like a foreign minister, at least. Although you could have the daily, 550-peseta menu, you might want to splurge a bit on such à la carte choices as Castillian soup, followed by paella valenciana, and topped off by a dessert of fresh melon, plus local cheeses. Along with half-a-bottle of wine (you can choose from 30 different brands), the banquet just described will cost 850 pesetas ($12.87).

AMSTERDAM

Near the perfectly central Leidseplein, one block from the Centraal Hotel, is a quiet residential street called the Roemer Visscherstraat, where several beautifully decorated four-story houses have been turned into good, Second Class hotels. Try, first, the **Hotel Sipermann**, 35 Roemer Visscherstraat (tel: 16-18-66), whose manager, Mr. Brouwer, is a former airlines purser who thereby picked up all the finest habits of punctilious attention to your comforts and desires; he has also traveled extensively. His rates include service charge, tax and a Dutch breakfast with at least one egg, which make them not as high as they might first appear for this category: 90 guilders ($45) for a twin-bedded room with private shower and toilet. Well-furnished, large rooms. A few doors down the street, the attractive **Hotel Engeland** (in the former building of the British consulate), 30 Roemer Visscherstraat (tel: 18-08-62); the **Hotel Parkzicht,** 33 Roemer Visscherstraat (tel. 18-08-97); and the **Hotel Roemer Visscher,** 10 Roemer Visscherstraat (tel: 12-55-11), are equally fine establishments, with rates for double rooms that range from a low of 78 guilders ($39) for a bathless double at the Parkzicht, to 92 guilders ($46) for a double with private bath at the Engeland (and there are some bathless doubles here for 68 guilders ($34), to from 85 and 89 guilders for a double with bath at the Roemer Visscher; other hotels on the street charge between 65 and 75 guilders ($32.50 and $37.50) for a double, breakfast for two included. Most rooms in these buildings have no private bath or shower (except at the Roemer Visscher, where virtually all rooms possess private shower), and there are, of course, no elevators in these residential hotels.

Open from 10 a.m. to 10 p.m., weekdays only, the merrily-decorated **Eethuis de Nissen** at 95 Rokin, halfway between the Dam and Mint Squares, was originally a large wine-storage room (nissen means "niches", or small caves, used for the storage of bottles; you still see them) in the cellar of a patrician home. Today it serves rather plain and unadorned dishes, but beautifully cooked and flavored, and at moderate rates: 11 guilders ($5.50) for Dutch steak with french fries, and mixed salad; 8.50 guilders ($4.25) for omelette with veal ragout and fried banana; 9 guilders for beef stew with rice and green peas; only 4.50 guilders ($2.25) for spaghetti Bolognaise (with meat sauce).

A final Amsterdam note: I doubt that I'd be human if I were to resist pointing out that I myself have a hotel here that you might consider for $20-a-day-living in the *off-season* (November 1 through March 14). The **Hotel Arthur Frommer,** 46 Noorderstraat (phone 22-03-28), which, hopefully, will be one of a chain of modern, centrally located, but moderately priced hotels, is an entirely new hotel constructed from the ground up, but designed to re-create the 17th-century building that once occupied the site, both inside and out. The interior resembles that of the Rembrandt House, the staff is clothed in 17th-century dress modeled after a Vermeer painting, and although the plumbing is modern (every room has a private shower and toilet), the bathroom walls are covered in Delft tiles. Since this is a new hotel, with private facilities, and one that was rather expensive to build, high season rates are, unfortunately, not in the budget range. Off-season, however, we'll be renting twin-bedded rooms (to readers only) for a total of 89 guilders (approximately $44.50), including full Dutch breakfast for two, service charges and added value tax, and at that rate, $20-a-day tourists may enjoy this thoroughly Dutch hotel, into which we've tried to infuse a very special atmosphere and character. Location is in the very heart of Amsterdam, just off the Vijzelstraat, about equidistant from the Rembrandtsplein, the Rijksmuseum and Leidseplein.

LONDON

The **Mount Pleasant Hotel,** Calthorpe Street, W.C. 1 (phone 837-9781), is the haven for single travellers to London: it has 280 single rooms as compared with only 113 doubles, all in a relatively modern (for London) building, but in a somewhat nondescript area (although with good subway connections). Still, you'll pay only £8 ($17.60) for one of those bathless singles (all of which have radio, telephone, hot and cold running water), including service charge, added value tax, and a traditional English breakfast; and the hotel also enjoys a large patio where you can drink and read under colorful umbrellas; a coffee bar for light luncheons; a larger dining room.

Simpson's-in-the-Strand (11), 100 The Strand, is a world-famous, and yet relatively inexpensive, restaurant, which concentrates on the food specialties that the English do well. This is a large and gleaming place, terribly correct and British, and staffed by a corps of walrus-mustached C. Aubrey Smiths who seem to be living out their life cycle at Simpson's. They wheel the cuts of beef to your table on silver "dinner wagons," and carve with great ceremony. Don't ask whether the meat is English or foreign, or you'll cause a riot. How much does it cost? Well, I recently had a roast sirloin of beef with Yorkshire pudding and vegetables for £4.65 ($10.23). I could have had roast saddle of mutton with red currant jelly and vegetables for £4.65 ($10.23), or a tasty steak, kidney and mushroom pie for only £3.50 ($7.70); on Wednesdays at Simpson's, I order Boiled Silverside of Salt Beef with carrots and dumplings (the traditional Wednesday special) for £3.80 ($8.36). There's a cover charge per person of 75 pence; a large pot of coffee or tea is 50 pence; and there's a 10% tip which you also should leave—bringing your total cost per person to around $15. This, I repeat, is a required stop for at least one lunch or dinner, your trip to London will be incomplete without it. Closed Sundays.

The second of these establishments, the less expensive **Cheshire Cheese (12),** 145 Fleet Street (phone 353-6170), can be visited—for all practical purposes—only off-season; in summer, the crush of would-be diners is so great that often there's a 30-minute wait for seats. That's because it reeks with even more history and tradition than Simpson's, if that can be imagined, and it has equally good, full-bodied English food at inexpensive prices. Over 300 years old, it was a favorite alehouse of Samuel Johnson and Boswell, whose table on the first floor is still preserved. The restaurant has dark mahogany walls and sawdust on the floor, somewhat reminiscent of Mory's at Yale, except for the prices; £3.20 ($7.04) for the famous Steak, Kidney and Mushroom pie; £3.20 for Roast Beef and Yorkshire pudding; the same for a magnificent mutton chop; 75 pence ($1.65) for a heavy, filling bowl of onion soup, served on Wedgwood china, and pewter candlesticks adorning your table. Add the cost of vegetables and coffee, plus a 15% tip, and your bill will mount to around $13. Best time to eat at the Cheshire Cheese is on the day of your visit to St. Paul's Cathedral, which is just a short walk up Fleet Street from the restaurant. Closed Sundays.

NAPLES

Dozens of modestly-priced hotels are found in the area of the central railway station, yet one of the few that can be recommended without hesitation is the **Hotel Guiren,** 114 Via Bologna (phone 336-030), about 250 yards from the station exit, at Piazza Garibaldi (turn right upon leaving); its 23 bathless rooms will rent in 1980 for 15,000 lire ($18.07) single, 19,000 lire ($22.89) double or twin, and breakfast for 2,500 lire ($3.01) will be served in your room at no extra charge. Owner Guido or Renato (the hotel's title is a combination of their names) is always behind the reception desk in the stainless steel lobby, and will instantly extend a 10% discount if you show them this book! . . . Three classes up in quality and price is **Hotel Britannique** at 133 Corso Vittorio Emanuele (phone 660-933), on a hill in the Mergellina Station area, charging 16,100 to 22,500 lire ($19.39 to $27.10) for singles, from 27,000 to 38,500 lire ($32.53 to $46.38) for doubles, all with large private bathrooms; the higher-priced rooms face the stunning gulf of Naples, with Vesuvius and Capri in full panoramic view, weather permitting. Breakfast is 3,000 lire ($3.61) more. I have a promise from Dottor Ambrosio, owner of the Britannique, that bearers of this book will pay 10% less. Taxi fare is about 3,000 lire ($3.61) from the main station, 1,800 lire ($2.16) from Mergellina station. . . . Superb home-cooked meals and tasty, traditional pizza: at **Ristorante Port' Alba**, 13 Port' Alba (near Piazza Dante), where a huge pizza and beer are 2,800 lire ($3.37), service included. The other specialty is seafood of all sorts: fish, mussels, octopus, tuna, swordfish and sea-urchins. A three-course menu, with seafood as the second dish, and with wine included, is a moderate 7,000 lire ($8.43). . . . For sightseeing around town, you might favor **Cima Travel Office**, 114 Piazza Garibaldi (phone 220-646), a hundred yards from the central station. Owner Dottor Maddaloni, his son, and friendly English-speaking staff, have shown themselves well-disposed through the years towards readers of this guide.

ZURICH

Hotel Goldenes Schwert is ideally located in the heart of the old town, at 14 Marktgasse (phone 34-59-40), a short distance from the station, lake, and museums. The four-story, two-elevator building can accommodate 65 guests, and charges 44 Swiss francs ($25.88) single, 72 for a double, 86 for a triple room, all with bath (but no showers), and including breakfast.

Probably the most popular medium-priced restaurant in Zurich is **Mövenpick Claridenhof**, at 21 Dreikönigstrasse, corner of Beethovenstrasse, a few minutes from Paradeplatz. Here, as at the eleven other Mövenpick Restaurants in Zurich and other European cities, the food is imaginative and the establishment extremely well run. Some samples: smoked trout with horseradish at 10.50 francs; Mövenpick toast (a hot cheese-and-ham sandwich topped with a fried egg), 5.90 francs; boiled chicken Mexicaine, 10.40 francs; boiled shrimps with curry and rice, 19.80 francs. A specialty is the filet de boeuf Claridenhof, a tender filet with green pepper sauce, mushrooms and pommes sautées, 26.50 francs ($15.58) for two of you. You'll like the food, the atmosphere, and the good Swiss wines—about 4 francs per glass.

ATHENS

Two hotels in the center of town, a few yards from Syntagma Square—the **Elektra**, at 5 Ermou Street (phone 32-23-223) and the **Attika Palace**, at 6 Karageorgi Servias Street (phone 32-23-006)—are both in the first-class category (Greek rating), and offer comfortable accommodations for tourists. Both are also seven-story buildings in which marble is lavishly used, each has two elevators, and yet 1980 rates are only 930 drachmas ($25.83) single, 1,450 drachmas ($40.27) double, including bath and private w.c., and breakfast. In winter and off-season, rates descend by 30% to 40%.

The **Delfi**, 13 Niki Street, next to Syntagma Square, can be recommended for quick service, tasty food, excellent wines, air conditioning, English-speaking waiters, an English-language menu, and a stern but well-meaning manager, sitting in the middle at the cash register, who overlooks the scene. Try the fish soup appetizer for 25 drachmas, half-a-bottle of retsina wine, 30 drachmas, the lamb fricassee for 170 drachmas. The Delfi is open every day, from 11:30 a.m. to 12:30 a.m.

STOCKHOLM

The 94-room **Alexandra Hotel**, 42 Magnus Ladulasgatan (phone 84-03-20), is popular with *Swedish* tourists, decorated with modern furnishings, and located in quiet surroundings near Slussen (the subway stop is Medborgarplatsen). Singles with shower are 140 kronor ($33.33); twins with bath, 230 kronor ($54.76); and 63 kronor extra are charged for a third person in the room, breakfast included. The sauna is free.

In Old Town, Gamla Stan, **Restaurant Latona**, 79 Vasterlanggatan (phone 08-11-3260), is fine for either a splurge or an economical meal, because in addition to its costlier plates—reindeer steak with crisp potato croquettes for 50 kronor—it also offers, from 11:30 a.m. to 3 p.m., a filling one-plate meal, averaging 16 kronor (beef with potatoes, for example is 16 kronor). Try, too, the hot herring snacks, like grilled, salted or smoked herring with boiled potatoes, for a fixed price of 13 kronor, including toast, or the Latona's supreme specialty: blueberry ice cream with toasted almonds, 11 kronor.

MILAN

Hotel Virgilio, 30 Via Pier Luigi da Palestrina (phone 270-088), near the monumental railway station of Milan (turn left on leaving the main station exit), is third class in category but utterly pleasant and respectable, charges 14,000 lire ($16.86) for bathless singles, 24,000 lire ($28.91) for bathless doubles, and 20,400 lire ($24.57) and 31,100 lire ($37.46), respectively, for singles and doubles with private bath. And Signor Genchi, the owner, will deduct another 10% for readers of this book. . . . The modern and efficient **Hotel Rubens**, 21 Via Rubens (phone 40-50-51), is less centrally located and far more expensive (second class), but will be handy on "tutto esaurito" days in Milan, when international fairs and congresses have filled all hotels in the center. Owner, Signor Remigio Eder, offers the following, very special and substantially reduced prices to readers of this book: 25,000 lire ($30.12) for singles with private bath and breakfast, 38,000 lire ($45.78) for doubles with private bath and breakfast; there are no rooms of the bathless variety. From the station, take the subway ("metropolitana") to the Gambara Station and walk (five minutes) from there, or else take a cab for 5,000 lire ($6.02). . . . **Trattoria da Angela**, 3 Via Padova, near the Piazza Loreto in the central station area, is a good value at 5,500 lire ($6.62) for its three-course menu, without wine but with an espresso at the conclusion of the meal. Closed Sundays. . . . For train tickets, La Scala, and sightseeing, I like the English-speaking Signora Amedea at **Rinaldi Tourist Office**, 6 Piazza Duomo (the cathedral square, phone 80-25-45). She's patient and industrious, and never fails to provide her clients with excellent free maps of Milan.

FLORENCE

Pension Monna Lisa (and that's no mis-spelling), 27 Via Borgo Pinti (phone 296-213 or 24041), comes first: if the Hotel Berchielli is one of Europe's best budget hotels, this is one of Europe's best pensions. Located on one of the narrowest and least prepossessing streets you'll ever see, its interior causes a gasp as you walk inside and suddenly discover what it's like to live in a palazzo filled with magnificent furnishings and original oils and sculpture, a winding stone staircase, a huge dining room fronting onto a landscaped courtyard (which can also hold your car), with multiple lounges, a courteous staff of long-in-service retainers, and all flawlessly supervised by the chic Mrs. Oslavia Ciardi-Dupré. Most rooms are with bath and rent for 17,500 lire ($21.08) per person breakfast included. Location is central but a bit hard to find at first; from the Duomo, walk down the Via dell Oriolo to the Borgo Pinti, and turn left for about 100 yards. But phone or write first.

Now an alternate choice. Signor Bertolini and Signor Lodovichi, both eager to please readers of this guide, own the large, 400-bed **Hotel Nuovo Atlantico** facing the Florence railroad station at 10 Via Nazionale (phone 216-622). They therefore offer the following: a 10% discount to readers off the official rates for their rooms, which are 16,400 lire ($19.75) for bathless singles, 27,300 lire ($32.89) for bathless doubles, including breakfast and free showers, service and tax (some rooms here have marble floors); a 30% discount off the same rates in off-season (November 5 to March 15); a 15% discount off à la carte purchases in their large, ground floor restaurant; but no discount off an excellent, three-course-with-wine "menu turistico" selling for 5,000 lire ($6.02). You needn't be a hotel guest to eat here, and if you want the reduction off an à la carte meal (which will run to about 6,000 lire ($7.22), flash a copy of this book.

PARIS

The 90-bed **Plaza Hotel**, 177 Blvd. Haussmann (phone 563-93-83), several minutes from the Arc de Triomphe, offers reasonable (in Paris) rates for a superb location and rooms with wall-to-wall carpeting and modern furniture: 135 francs ($31.39) for doubles with private bath and wc, 125 francs ($29.06) for singles with private bath and wc, and only 85 francs ($19.76) single and 110 francs ($25.58) double for 12 bathless rooms on the hotel's 5th and 6th floors, serviced by a tiny elevator which goes to the 5th floor (you walk from there). Helpful, friendly, efficient, and English-speaking staff; nearest metro: George V.

Restaurant Le Poivre Vert, 5 rue du 29 Juillet, near the Tuileries and the Louvre, is equally suitable for lunch and supper, at each of which it serves a four-course, fixed price meal (hors d'oeuvres, soup, main course, cheese), with wine, for 38 francs ($8.83); and if you don't want that much, you can request simply the plat du jour with wine for 28 francs. The white jacketed owner, Monsieur Alain, will help you translate the menu; since this place receives (until now) almost no tourists, every word is in French. . . . In the very same area, the **Restaurant Medova,** 3 rue de l' Echelle, is a larger, 120-seat establishment serving a *prix fixe* for 41 francs ($9.53), but with wine extra at 3.50 francs; this one does cater to a number of tourists. Friday evening, the specialty is a gargantuan Fondue Bourguignonne, served with mixed salad (45 francs, $10.46), that will keep you going for half a week.

And there you have it—*Europe on $15 a Day,* supplemented by a few grudging recommendations for life on $20 a day.

And now, my thanks, my offer to be of aid to those of you who have travel questions, and my very best wishes for a wonderful European trip!

ABOUT THE AUTHORS

Arthur Frommer is a graduate of the Yale University Law School, where he was an editor of the Yale Law Journal, and he is a member of the New York Bar. After service in Europe with U.S. Army Intelligence, he practiced law in New York until a growing involvement with this and other books required full-time attention to activities in the travel industry. He is the founder of Arthur Frommer, Inc., a travel publishing company; of Arthur Frommer Hotels, Inc., which operates moderately-priced hotels on the island of Curaçao, in Copenhagen and in Amsterdam; of the $10-a-Day Travel Club, Inc.; of Arthur Frommer Charters, Inc.; and of Arthur Frommer International, Inc., a wholesale tour operator. In addition to writing *Europe on $15 a Day*, he is the author of *A Dollarwise Guide to New York, Surprising Amsterdam*, and two books dealing with political and legal topics.

Hope Arthur (Mrs. Arthur Frommer) is a graduate of Northwestern University and of The Royal Academy of Dramatic Art in London. She has appeared on Broadway (as Maria in "The Best House in Naples") and in numerous Off-Broadway productions, and has directed plays for the Circle and Cherry Lane Theatres and for the National Academy of T.V. Arts & Sciences. Currently she is on the faculty of the Lee Strasberg Institute. In addition to her theatrical activities, she has written for national magazines.